Mystery Fanfare

Mystery Fanfare

A Composite Annotated Index
to Mystery and Related Fanzines 1963-1981

Michael L. Cook

Library of Congress Catalogue Card No.: 82-73848

ISBN: 0-87972-229-0 Clothbound
       0-87972-230-4 Paperback

Contents

Acknowledgements   3

Introduction   5

Use of the Index   7

Alphabetical List of Code Designations   8

Subject List of Magazines Indexed   9

Guide and Chronology of Magazines Indexed   11

Composite Index to the Magazines   31

Bibliography of Book Reviews   337

ACKNOWLEDGMENTS

The compiler of this work is most grateful to a number of persons who have been helpful and generous in providing information on certain journals, and particular mention should be made of the following:

Philip T. Asdell, Frederick, Maryland

Robert E. Briney, Salem, Massachusetts

Wooda (Nick) Carr, Mesa, Arizona

Julius R. (Bob) Chenu, Merrick, New York

J. Randolph Cox, Northfield, Minnesota

Robert Easton, Santa Barbara, California

Mark J. Golden, Falls Church, Virginia

Douglas G. Greene, Norfolk, Virginia

Nils Hardin, Summerland, California

Lynn A. Hickman, Wauseon, Ohio

Ed Hirshberg, Tampa, Florida

Jim Huang, Englewood Cliffs, New Jersey

Andy Jaysnovitch, Parlin, New Jersey

Dr. Bill Laidlaw, San Luis Obispo, California

Charlotte Laughlin, Brownwood, Texas

Steve Lewis, Newington, Connecticut

Ethel Lindsay, Carnoustie, Angus, Scotland

John J. McAleer, Lexington, Massachusetts

Don Miller, Wheaton, Maryland

Will Murray, North Quincy, Massachusetts

Francis M. Nevins, Jr., University City, Missouri

Timothy J. Rutt, Boulder, Colorado

Arthur C. Scott, Cupertino, California

Steve Stilwell, Minneapolis, Minnesota

James Tinsman, Tipton, Pennsylvania

University of California Los Angeles Library

Robert Weinberg, Oak Forest, Illinois

INTRODUCTION

Fanzines are a particular, little-known, kind of publication, the name being derived from the word "fan" (an admirer, or devotee), and from the last syllable of "magazine." As such, the word is a descriptive term, a magazine by and for fans of a particular subject. And although the term is somewhat disliked by many, it has become a recognized term for amateur magazines devoted to a particular subject.

While fan magazines seem to have started and proliferated in the fantasy and science-fiction field, it was not until more than thirty years later that they appeared in the mystery field and the number of mystery fan magazines has remained relatively small in comparison. A recent check of *The Whole Fanzine Catalogue* (a monthly review of fantasy and science-fiction fan literature) shows that there are more than 125 fantasy and science-fiction fanzines currently being published and hundreds of others have fallen by the wayside; the mystery field has spawned less than thirty if one does not count those pertaining to Sherlock Holmes.

Fanzines are generally considered to be non-commercial, non-professional, small-circulation magazines produced, published and edited by one or a few persons. This definition would certainly be correct for the earlier fan magazines and would still apply to many, but, particularly in the mystery field, some have evolved into professional or near-professional appearance and content.

The earliest amateur fan magazine, *The Comet*, a magazine of "little articles on science," appeared in 1930 and this was followed by many others in rapid succession. The creators of Superman, Jerome Siegel and Joe Schuster, published an early amateur magazine in 1932, *Science Fiction*.

Here, in amateur magazines, one will find both professional amateurs and amateur professionals and it is the fan magazine that serves the valuable need of providing communication and contact between the amateur and professional fields. Writers in the fan magazines are surprisingly outspoken and critical, yet their views are presented in a logical fashion and can be accepted or rejected with the reader wiser for the experience. This is particularly true in the book reviews, and as such, these magazines have become a force to be considered by the author and publisher alike. Perhaps one of the outstanding facets of the contents of these magazines is that they are not controlled or censored by the editor. Writers have a free hand and editors are very conscious of this essential quality. This often serves to put into proper perspective a discussion of a book or an author, his or her methods and intent, and purpose. Many fan magazine writers become professionals and their apprenticeship in the fan press is a most valuable background.

Within the mystery and detective amateur magazines will be found articles and comments by many of the established writers also, plus a host of amateur authors who have a very knowledgeable grasp of their topics and impart valuable information. Research by these is intense and thorough, and as a result, many of the old records of long-gone publishers have been opened and the information presented.

The contents of a mystery fan magazine are of wide variety. Interviews with well-known authors abound, as well as articles and comments and even rebuttals by these professionals. Surveys of the works of an author, including "unknown" writers, and checklists with full bibliographical data provide the scholar and collector with information as well as the reader. Articles are usually well researched and are serious attempts to present facts and conclusions. Mystery and detective fiction is examined from every possible angle. Lists of new publications, and reviews of both old and new books provide readers with long want lists for their reading pleasure. Letters of comment from the readers are amazingly erudite and informative although not always laudatory. The appearance of quizzes, acrostics and crossword puzzles is frequent, and advertisements, limited to the mystery and related fields, are always interesting. Occasional fiction, particularly rare reprints, appears but usually is excluded and reserved for those magazines that feature such.

While many of the early fanzines were crude in appearance, this, too, has changed, and with the availability of low cost offset printing the magazines now are often masterpieces of design and illustration. Distribution has improved, too, in that there are better means of communication and the birth of a new magazine is often heralded in many other publications. Circulation is still small in comparison with professional magazines, but the average circulation in the mystery magazine field has improved greatly in the past ten years and an editor now has the possibility of at least not operating at a loss if he is prudent.

Most fan magazine publishers are such because they want to be, not from an expectation of profit. Indeed, many lose money but realize that their publishing is an avocation, not a business. Several publishers have combined their bookselling activities with their publication in an effort to at least break even. And although there are exceptions, material written is without compensation other than perhaps a few copies of the magazine or free advertising space.

Fanzines, in general, have been overlooked. Academic and general readers do not always know of them; the same is true of most libraries, and the Library of Congress subject listings have no category for fanzines at all. Perhaps as a whole, fan magazines are unconventional. This cannot be said for those in the mystery and detective field, however, as these meet or approach academic standards in most cases and many have attained sizable circulation. Most publishers of these have a lengthy list of library and university subscribers. It can even be said that mystery and detective fanzines have made a significant place for such in the study and development of the fiction, and will continue to do so.

This work is a composite index of the complete runs of all mystery and detective fan magazines that have been published, through 1981. Added to it are indexes of many magazines of related nature. This includes magazines that are primarily oriented to boys' book collecting, the paperbacks, and the pulp magazine hero characters, since these all have a place in the mystery and detective genre. Many of the boy's series books had detectives as their principal character (the Hardy Boys is a prime example); most of the pulp magazine hero characters were the central figures in a detective tale (The Shadow, The Spider, Doc Savage, as examples). And, of course, paperback books have become a vital media in mystery book publishing, with the older examples having attained considerable value.

Michael L. Cook
October 1, 1982

Use of the Index

Since this is a composite index covering fifty-two different magazines, it is necessary to identify magazines by an index code. The list of magazines in alphabetical code order immediately follows this explanation. As example, "TAD" identifies an entry as reference to *THE ARMCHAIR DETECTIVE*.

Reference is also given as to volume and issue number, and page number on which the article or item commences. In cases where the publisher has not indicated a volume number, the identification is by issue and page number.

EXAMPLES:

     (1)   2-3 MF 17   (Vol.2, Issue No.3, of *THE MYSTERY FANCIER*, page 17)

     (2)   20 JD 11   (Issue No.20 of *JDM BIBLIOPHILE*, page 11)

Brief annotations have been added where the title of the article does not adequately describe its contents.

The mystery sub-categories should be understood to refer to either mystery or detective fiction, there being no distinction made for the purpose of this Index. The bibliographical material is primarily collected and listed under the category "Checklists," although some references may be found also under the heading of "Bibliography" and "Index" as well as cross-references.

Reviews of films, stage productions, and television programs have been included in the special Reviews Appendix with identification appropriately shown. Articles and columns of short reviews and commentary on books have been listed in the Index, but books here specifically mentioned are not necessarily listed in the Reviews Appendix. Criteria for listing as a review has at times had to be a matter of judgment and based primarily on whether the mention is that of a bonafide review or just a discussion in an informational column. Books mentioned in articles on authors works and commentary have likewise not been listed in the Reviews Appendix.

The use of the full name of a person has been used rather than nicknames, shortened names, or initials, when known, despite the treatment in the original article.

Occasional early issues of several magazines have not shown pagination. In such cases, pages have been assigned a consecutive number by the compiler and such numbers used in this Index.

As a rule, subject matter of Letters from the readers have not been indexed; the exceptions to this are when the Letter contains such as checklists or an addition to a checklist. It should be noted, however, that there is much valuable information and commentary in the Letters. The names of those persons submitting the published letters are indexed.

Editorial comments, advertisements, and offers to buy, sell or trade have not been indexed. With reference to *THE ARMCHAIR DETECTIVE* it should be noted that issues Vol.4, No.2 through Vol.9, No.2 included as an appendix a portion of Allen J. Hubin's monumental *BIBLIOGRAPHY OF CRIME FICTION*. This, separately paged, has not been included in the Index.

This Index does not incorporate the various volume indexes appearing in various of the journals treated, nor Steve Stilwell's Index to the first 10 volumes of *THE ARMCHAIR DETECTIVE*. No one ever does an index quite the same, and therefore this Index is compiled completely without reference to any existing indexes. Choice of cross references has been that of the compiler.

Alphabetical List of Code Designations

AD	THE AUGUST DERLETH SOCIETY NEWSLETTER		MT	MYSTERIOUS TIMES
BB	THE BOYS' BOOK BUFF		NC	NOTES FOR THE CURIOUS
BC	THE BOYS' BOOK COLLECTOR		P	PULP
BS	BRONZE SHADOWS		PD	THE PONTINE DOSSIER
BY	THE BONY BULLETIN		PE	THE NOT SO PRIVATE EYE
C	CLUES		PP	THE POISONED PEN
CD	CASTLE DRACULA QUARTERLY		PQ	THE PAPERBACK QUARTERLY
CL	CLOAK AND DAGGER		PU	THE PULP ERA
CP	COLLECTING PAPERBACKS?		PW	PULPWOODY
D	DUENDE		QC	THE QUEEN CANON BIBLIOPHILE
DQ	DOC SAVAGE QUARTERLY		R	THE ROHMER REVIEW
DR	DOC SAVAGE READER		SF	SCIENCE FICTION COLLECTOR/ MEGAVORE
DS	DOC SAVAGE CLUB READER		TAD	THE ARMCHAIR DETECTIVE
DSA	DOC SAVAGE AND ASSOCIATES		TB	THE TUTTER BUGLE - OLD SERIES
FC	THE FAUST COLLECTOR		TBN	THE TUTTER BUGLE - NEW SERIES
FM	FANTASY MONGERS		TF	THE THORNDYKE FILE
G	THE GAZETTE - THE JOURNAL OF THE WOLFE PACK		U	THE AGE OF THE UNICORN
HP	THE H.P.LOVECRAFT SOCIETY JOURNAL		WA	THE WOLD ATLAS
JM	JDM BIBLIOPHILE		WT	THE WEIRD TALES COLLECTOR
LR	THE LOCKED ROOM		X	XENOPHILE
LW	THE LONE WOLFE		YB	YELLOWBACK LIBRARY
M	MYSTERY			
MA	THE MYSTERY & ADVENTURE SERIES REVIEW			
MB	THE MAN OF BRONZE			
MF	THE MYSTERY FANCIER			
MM	THE MYSTERY MONITOR			
MN	THE MYSTERY NOOK			
MR	THE MYSTERY LOVERS/READERS NEWSLETTER			

Subject List of Magazines Indexed

MYSTERY AND DETECTIVE

Armchair Detective, The (TAD)

August Derleth Society Newsletter,
  The (AD)

Bony Bulletin, The (BY)

Castle Dracula Quarterly (CD)

Cloak and Dagger (CL)

Clues (C)

Ellery Queen Review, The (QC)

Faust Collector, The (FC)

Gazette, The: The Journal of the
  Wolfe Pack (G)

JDM Bibliophile (JD)

Journal of the H. P. Lovecraft
  Society (HP)

Locked Room, The (LR)

Lone Wolfe, The (LW)

Mystery (M)

Mystery Fancier, The (MF)

Mystery*File (MY)

Mystery Lovers Newsletter, The (MR)

Mystery Monitor, The (MM)

Mystery Nook, The (MN)

Mystery Readers Newsletter, The (MR)

Mysterious Times (MT)

Not So Private Eye, The (PE)

Notes for the Curious (NC)

Poisoned Pen, The (PP)

Pontine Dossier, The (PD)

Queen Canon Bibliophile, The (QC)

Rohmer Review, The (R)

Thorndyke File, The (TF)

BOY'S BOOK COLLECTING

Boys' Book Buff, The (BB)

Boy's Book Collector, The (BC)

Mystery & Adventure Series Review,
  The (MA)

Tutter Bugle, The, Old Series (TB)

Tutter Bugle, The, New Series (TBN)

Yellowback Library, The (YB)

PAPERBACK COLLECTING

Collecting Paperbacks? (CP)

Paperback Quarterly, The (PQ)

PULP MAGAZINES

Age of the Unicorn, The (U)

Bronze Shadows (BS)

Doc Savage and Associates (DSA)

Doc Savage Club Reader (DS)

Doc Savage Quarterly (DQ)

Doc Savage Reader (DR)

Duende (D)

Fantasy Mongers (FM)

Man of Bronze, The (MB)

Megavore (SF)

Pulp (P)

Pulp Era, The (PU)

Pulpwoody (PW)

Science-Fiction Collector, The (SF)

Weird Tales Collector, The (WT)

Wold Atlas, The (WA)

Xenophile (X)

GUIDE AND CHRONOLOGY OF MAGAZINES INDEXED

AGE OF THE UNICORN, THE   Index Code: "U"

Although designed as an advertising journal to fill the need caused by the irregular publication of Xenophile, the articles, checklists, commentary, reviews and letters comprise the majority of this journal devoted to mystery, detective, fantasy, the weird, and science-fiction. There is much of interest to the mystery fan. The journal was published by a firm which was a specialty book publisher in the field of history and genealogy, and the increased time needed for those fields necessitated the discontinuance of the Unicorn. After Issue No.8, however, it was merged with Science-Fiction Collector/Megavore which continued its tradition. At the time of discontinuance the editor had a good backlog of material and a special large issue was published as the last issue (No.8).

                Publication history of issues indexed:
                        No.1   April 1979
                        No.2   June 1979
                        No.3   August 1979
                        No.4   October 1979
                        No.5   December 1979
                        No.6   February 1980
                        No.7   April 1980
                        No.8   June 1980 (Special Issue)

        Size: 8½x11; 50-76 pages (Special Issue 146 pages)
        Current Status: discontinued
        Editor: Michael L. Cook
        Publisher: Cook-McDowell Publications, Inc., 3318 Wimberg Avenue,
                Evansville, Indiana 47712
        Frequency of Publication: Semi-Monthly

ARMCHAIR DETECTIVE, THE   Index Code: "TAD"

Featuring articles, commentary, checklists, bibliographical material, reviews of both old and new books, including paperbacks, mystery films, stage, television, interviews, letters, and advertisements, this was the earliest published periodical devoted to the mystery fan, and remains the dean of such. Special features include the Rex Stout Newsletter by author John McAleer, and Checklists of mystery, detective and suspense books published in the U.S. each quarter. It was published by the founder, Allen J. Hubin, 3656 Midland Avenue, White Bear Lake, Minnesota 55110 for thefirst 34 issues (through Vol.9, No.2). The next 10 issues were by Publishers, Inc., 243 Twelfth Street, Del Mar, California 92014, (through Vol.11, No.4), and subsequent issues were published by the present publisher, The Mysterious Press of Otto Penzler.

Publication history of issues indexed:

Vol.	No.	Date	Vol.	No.	Date
Vol.1,	No.1	October 1967	Vol.5,	No.1	October 1971
1	2	January 1968	5	2	January 1972
1	3	April 1968	5	3	April 1972
1	4	July 1968	5	4	July 1972
2	1	October 1968	6	1	October 1972
2	2	January 1969	6	2	February 1973
2	3	April 1969	6	3	May 1973
2	4	July 1969	6	4	August 1973
3	1	October 1969	7	1	November 1973
3	2	January 1970	7	2	February 1974
3	3	April 1970	7	3	May 1974
3	4	July 1970	7	4	August 1974
4	1	October 1970	8	1	November 1974
4	2	January 1971	8	2	February 1975
4	3	April 1971	8	3	May 1975
4	4	July 1971	8	4	August 1975*

```
Vol. 9, No.1   November 1975      Vol. 12, No.1   Winter 1979
      9     2   February 1976          12     2    Spring 1979
      9     3   June 1976              12     3    Summer 1979
      9     4   October 1976          12     4    Fall 1979
     10     1   January 1977          13     1    Winter 1980
     10     2   April 1977            13     2    Spring 1980
     10     3   July 1977             13     3    Summer 1980
     10     4   October 1977          13     4    Fall 1980
     11     1   January 1978          14     1    Winter 1981
     11     2   April 1978            14     2    Spring 1981
     11     3   July 1978**           14     3    Summer 1981
     11     4   October 1978          14     4    December 1981**
```

*Contents page dated August 1974
**Undated

Size: 8½x11; single-stapled sheets through Vol.9, No.2; saddle-stapled
    subsequent issues; 86-104 pages
Editor: Allen J. Hubin (through Vol.13); Michael Seidman
Current Status: Active
Publisher: (Current) The Mysterious Press, 129 West 56th Street, New York,
    New York 10019
Frequency: Quarterly
Subscription: $16.00 per year; $20.00 outside U.S.

AUGUST DERLETH SOCIETY NEWSLETTER   Index Code "AD"

The official publication of the August Derleth Society, published for the study and
publication of material pertaining to August Derleth, his works, and Arkham House
Publishers. Includes many reminiscences by prominent authors, and unpublished material
by Derleth, as well as news and reviews of pertinent books and items.

```
Publication history of issues indexed:
Vol.1, No.1   (1977)            Vol.3, No.2   (1980)
    1     2   (February 1978)       3     3    (March 1980)
    1     3   (May 1978)            3     4    (June 1980)
    1     4   (1978)                4     1    (September 1980)
    2     1   (--)                  4     2    (December 1980)
    2     2   (--)                  4     3    (March 1981)
    2    3/4  (1979)                4     4    June 1981
    3     1   (October 1979)        5     1    October 1981
```

Issues are undated until Vol.4, No.4

Size: 8½x11; 10-14 pages
Editor: Richard H. Fawcett
Current Status: active
Publisher: August Derleth Society, c/o Richard H. Fawcett, 61 Teecomwas
    Drive, Uncasville, Connecticut 06382
Frequency: Quarterly intended
Subscription: $5.00 per year (to George Marx, 20 E. Delaware Street,
    Chicago, Illinois 60611)

BONY BULLETIN, THE   Index Code: "BY"

Dedicated to the crime stories of Arthur W. Upfield and particularly to those involving
Inspector Bonaparte.

        Publication history of issues indexed:
                    No.1   November 1981

Size: 8½x11; 6 pages
Editor: Philip T. Asdell
Current Status: Active
Publisher: Philip T. Asdell, 5719 Jefferson Boulevard, Frederick,
    Maryland 21701
Frequency: irregular
Subscription: $3.00 for three issues; $3.30 outside U.S.

BOY'S BOOK BUFF, THE   Index Code "BB"

One of the admirable boys' books magazines, suspended after seven issues. Whether one collects boys' books or not, most have read these in the good old days our our youth and the magazine itself is a healthy dose of nostalgia. Of interest to mystery fans since many of the boys' books were mysteries.

        Publication history of issues indexed:
                        No.1   (1977)*
                        2   May 1977
                        3   (1977)*
                        4   (1977)*
                        5   February 1978
                        6   (1978)*
                        7   (1978)*

        * Undated

        Size: 8½x11; 44 pages
        Editor: Robert Jennings
        Current Status: suspended
        Publisher: Robert Jennings, R.F.D.2, Whiting Road, Dudley, Mass. 01570
        Frequency: Quarterly
        Subscription: $9.00 per year

BOYS' BOOK COLLECTOR, THE   Index Code "BC"

A periodical devoted to boys' books, particularly series books, and their authors. This included articles, commentary, reminiscences, checklists, bibliographies, How-to articles, letters, and advertisements. Illustrated.

        Publication history of issues indexed:
        Vol.1, No.1   Fall 1969   Vol.2, No.4   Summer 1971
        1   2   Winter 1970   3   1   Fall 1971/Winter 1972
        1   3   Spring 1970   3   2   Spring 1972
        1   4   Summer 1970   3   3   (1973)*
        2   1   Fall 1970   3   4   (1973)*
        2   2   Winter 1971   4   1   (1973)*
        2   3   Spring 1971

        * Undated

        Size: 5½x8½; 32 pages
        Editor: Alan S. Dikty
        Current Status: Suspended
        Publisher: T.E.Dikty, 1105 Edgewater Drive, Naperville, Ill. 60540
        Frequency: Quarterly

BRONZE SHADOWS   Index Code "BS"

With emphasis on Doc Savage and other pulp heroes, this publication featured articles, commemtary, reminiscences, checklists and bibliographic material. Illustrated.

        Publication history of issues indexed:
        No.1   (October 1965)*   No. 9   March 1967
        2   December 1965   10   June 1967
        3   February 1966   11   August 1967
        4   May 1966   12   October 1967
        5   July 1966   13   January 1968
        6   September 1966   14   March 1968
        7   November 1966   15   November 1968
        8   January 1967

        * Undated

```
Size: 8½x11; 6-24 pages
Editor: Fred Cook
Current Status: Suspended
Publisher: Fred Cook, 501 Farr Avenue, Wadsworth, Ohio 44881
Frequency: Bimonthly
```

CASTLE DRACULA QUARTERLY   Index Code "CD"

A journal devoted to Count Dracula, particularly the movie versions and Bela Lugosi.
Well illustrated, quality fan magazine, but ceased publication after one issue.

```
Publication history of issues indexed:
                Vol.1, No.1   1978


Size: 5½x8½; 44 pages
Editor: Gordon R. Guy
Current Status: Suspended
Publisher: Gordon R. Guy, Box 423, Glastonbury, Conn. 06033
Frequency of Publication: irregular
```

CLOAK AND DAGGER, A MYSTERY FANZINE   Index Code "CL"

A magazine of commentary featuring articles, commentary, reviews, some fiction, letters,
and bibliographic information, devoted to the "cloak and dagger" school of mystery
fiction.

```
Publication history of issues indexed:
  No.1                              No.9    July 14, 1978
  No.2   July 15, 1977             No.10   September 29, 1978
  No.3                             No.11   November 24, 1978
  No.4                             No.12   January 12, 1979
  No.5   November 25, 1977         No.13/14  July 1979
  No.6   February 17, 1978         No.15   August 10, 1980
  No.7   April 7, 1978             No.16   September 30, 1980
  No.8   May 26, 1978

Size: first five issues 8½x11; then subsequent issues 5½x8½; first five
      issues were 1 sheet printed both sides; subsequent 10-16 pages
Editor: Jim Huang
Current Status: Suspended temporarily
Publisher: Jim Huang, 66 N. Virginia Court, Englewood Cliffs, N.J. 07632
Frequency: irregular
Subscription: 5 issues for $2.00
```

CLUES: A JOURNAL OF DETECTION   Index Code "C"

A scholarly journal of the mystery and detective genre with many outstanding academic
style articles. The first issue was predominantly on facets of John D. MacDonald and
his works; the fourth issue outstanding for its coverage of the mystery pulp field.

```
Publication history of issues indexed:
          Vol.1, No.1   Spring 1980
            1     2     Fall/Winter 1980
            2     1     Spring/Summer 1981
            2     2     Fall/Winter 1981

Size: 6x9; squareback binding; 134-136 pages
Editor: Pat Browne
Current Status: active
Publisher: Bowling Green University Popular Press, Bowling Green, Ohio 43403
Frequency: Semi-annual
Subscription: $10.00 per year
```

COLLECTING PAPERBACKS?   Index Code "CP"

A periodical dedicated to paperback book collectors, featuring regular columnists, commentary, articles, questions and answers, checklists and bibliographic material, letters, reviews, and advertisements.

Publication history of issues indexed:

Vol.1, No.1	March 1979	Vol. 2, No.4	(September 1980)*
1	2	(May 1979)*	2	5	(November 1980)*
1	3	(July 1979)*	2	6	(January 1981)* **
1	4	(September 1979)*	3	1	(March 1981)*
1	5	(November 1979)*	3	2	(May 1981)*
1	6	(January 1980)*	3	3	(July 1981)*
2	1	(March 1980)*	3	4	(September 1981)*
2	2	(May 1980)*	3	5	(November 1981)*
2	3	(July 1980)*			

* Undated
** "Farce" issue, not indexed

Size: 8½x11; 23-55 pages
Editor: Lance Casebeer
Current Status: active
Publisher: Lance Casebeer, 934 S.E.15th St., Portland, Oregon 97214
Frequency: Semi-monthly
Subscription: $12.00 per year

DOC SAVAGE AND ASSOCIATES   Index Code "DSA"

Devoted to Doc Savage and association material, with articles, commentary and reviews

Publication history of issues indexed:
No.1 February 1975(?)*

* No year date given

Size: 8½x11; 30 pages
Editor: Mark Stulce and George Rock
Current Status: Suspended
Publisher: Mark Stulce and George Rock (no address given)
Frequency: One issue published

DOC SAVAGE CLUB READER   Index Code "DS"

Although primarily a journal devoted to Doc Savage, this publication frequently included material on other pulp heroes and their creators - The Shadow, The Spider, The Avenger, G-8 and His Battle Aces, Operator 5, Conan, Sinbad, Sherlock Holmes, Tarzan, James Bond, and other popular literature characters. The journal was well illustrated and included material by many well known authors. Commenced in 1977 and published on an irregular basis for twelve issues; announcement was made of a change in name to Nemesis, Inc. for the next issue in order to better reflect all of the pulp heroes included in the contents, but to date this has not appeared.

Publication history of issues indexed:

No.1	(1977)*	No.7	(June 1979)*
No.2	(January 1978)*	No.8	(1979)*
No.3	(July 1978)*	No.9	(May 1980)*
No.4	(--)*	No.10	(1980)*
No.5	(December 1978)*	No.11	(August 1980)*
No.6	(Spring 1979)*	No.12	(February 1981)*

* Undated

Size: 8½x11; 20-32 pages
Editor: Frank Lewandowski
Current Status: Suspended temporarily
Publisher: Frank Lewandowski, 2438 S. Highland Avenue, Berwyn,
    Illinois 60402
Frequency: approximately every four months

DOC SAVAGE QUARTERLY   Index Code "DQ"

With emphasis on Doc Savage material and association items, this publication features
articles, commentary, book reviews, bibliographical material, letters, and some non-
fictional items of associated interest. Illustrated.

        Publication history of issues indexed:
                    No.1   (April 1980)*
                    No.2   (July 1980)*
                    No.3   (October 1980)*
                    No.4   (January 1981)*
                    No.5   (April 1981)*
                    No.6   July 1981
                    No.7   October 1981

    * Undated

Size: 8½x11; 14-24 pages
Editor: Dr. Bill Laidlaw
Current Status: active
Publisher: Dr. Bill Laidlaw, Box 301, San Luis Obispo, Calif. 93406
Frequency: Quarterly
Subscription: $6.00 per year

DOC SAVAGE READER   Index Code "DR"

Articles, commentary, reviews, and bibliographical material on Doc Savage and related
interest. Discontinued after three issues.

        Publication history of issues indexed:
                    No.1   January 1973
                    No.2/3 Spring 1973
                    No.4   October 1973

Size: 8½x11; 12-24 pages
Editor: First issue, John Cosgriff and Mark J. Golden; subsequent issues,
    Mark J. Golden
Current Status: Suspended
Publisher: Mark J. Golden, 2791 N. Quebec Street, Arlington, Va. 22207
Frequency: irregular

DUENDE   Index Code "D"

An irregularly published journal, but eagerly sought by those interested in the pulp
heroes. Includes reviews, articles, checklists, and valuable commentary and letters.
Illustrated; stiff covers.

        Publication history of issues indexed:
                    No.1 April 1975
                    No.2 Winter 1976-77

Size: 8½x11; 32-48 pages
Editor: Will Murray
Current Status: active
Publisher: Odyssey Publications, c/o Will Murray, 334 E. Squantum Street,
    No. Quincy, Mass. 02171
Frequency: irregular
Subscription: $2.00 per issue

FANTASY MONGERS

Index Code "FM"

Although classified as an advertising magazine, the journal contents included various articles and reviews in the mystery, detective, fantasy, and science-fiction field. The publisher is perhaps best known for his weird fiction magazine, Weirdbook, and various other publications of like genre. Fantasy Mongers was conceived to fill the vacuum left when Xenophile became irregularly published, and at the same time as another journal (Age of the Unicorn) with which it was merged after two issues.

Publication history of issues indexed:
                No.1 1979
                No.2 1979

Size: 8½x11; 32-40 pages
Editor: W. Paul Ganley
Current Status: Suspended; possibly revived
Publisher: Weirdbook Press, Box 35, Amherst Branch, Buffalo, N.Y. 14226
Frequency: Semi-monthly

FAUST COLLECTOR, THE

Index Code "FC"

A publication devoted to the works of Frederick S. Faust, noted for mystery and western fiction, the latter written primarily under the pseudonym Max Brand. Featured articles, commentary, reviews, letters, bibliographical material, and reprinted much fiction and poetry by Faust, particularly of his younger days. Ceased publication with the decease of the publisher.

Publication history of issues indexed:

Vol.1,	No.1	February 1969	Vol. 2,	No.1	February 1970
1	2	May 1969	2	2	May 1970
1	3	August 1969	2	3	August 1970
1	3A	(Supplement)	2	4	November 1970
1	4	November 1969	3	1	February 1971
			3	2	January 1973

Size: (1st issue) 5½x8½); subsequent issues 8½x11; 8-12 pages
Editor: William J. Clark
Current Status: Discontinued
Publisher: William J. Clark, 11744½ Gateway Boulevard, Los Angeles, California 90064
Frequency: Quarterly

GAZETTE, THE (THE JOURNAL OF THE WOLFE PACK)

Index Code "G"

An outstanding journal devoted to Nero Wolfe and his creator, Rex Stout, with well researched and conceived articles, commentary, lists, quizzes, and letters. Although far behind in their schedule, memberships continue. Two issues published to date.

Publication history of issues indexed:
                Vol.1, No.1 Winter 1979
                       1   2 Spring 1979

Size: 6x9; 70-78 pages
Editor: Lawrence F. Brooks and Ellen E. Krieger
Current Status: Active
Publisher: The Wolfe Pack, P.O.Box 822, Ansonia Station, New York, N.Y. 10023
Frequency: Stated to be quarterly
Subscription: (membership), $12.50 per year

JDM BIBLIOPHILE   Index Code "JD"

A fan magazine devoted to the works of mystery-writer John D. MacDonald and his
prominent character, Travis McGee. The journal was founded and the first twenty-two
issues published by Len and June Moffatt; with issue No.23 it was assumed by Ed
Hirshberg who enlarged the journal and added stiff covers. An important magazine for
the genre.

        Publication history of issues indexed:
        No.1   March 1965   No. 15   March 1971
          2   May 1966   16   August 1971
          3   August 1966   17   March 1972
          4   November 1966   18   April 1973
          5   February 1967   19   September 1974
          6   May 1967   20   March 1975
          7   August 1967   21   February 1976
          8   December 1967   22   August 1977
          9   March 1968   23   January 1979
          10   June 1968   24   July 1979
          11   April 1969   25   January 1980
          12   August 1969   26   July 1980
          13   January 1970   27   January 1981
          14   August 1970   28   July 1981

     Size: 8½x11; 22-52 pages
     Editor: (through No.22) Len and June Moffatt; subsequent issues, Ed
          Hirshberg with Len & June Moffatt the West Coast Editors
     Current Status: active
     Publisher: Ed Hirshberg, Department of English, University of South
          Florida, Tampa, Florida 33620
     Frequency: Bi-annual
     Subscription: $5.00 per year

JOURNAL OF THE H. P. LOVECRAFT SOCIETY   Index Code "HP"

A journal of critical, biographical and bibliographical material on Howard Phillips
Lovecraft. The Society was formed in 1974 by Raymond H. Ramsey of Berkeley, California,
and the Journal launched in 1976. For various reasons he was unable to publish a second
issue, and the Society came under the control of Scott Connors who published the second
issue. Part of the difficulty for continuance has been the editor's studies in Austria,
and the small membership (less than 50). No further issues have appeared to date.

        Publication history of issues indexed:
                No.1 October 1976
                No.2 October 1979

     Size: 5½x8½; 36 pages
     Editor: (first issue), Raymond H. Ramsey); (second issue) Scott Connors
     Current Status: Inactive
     Publisher: Scott Connors, P. O. Box 354, South Heights, Penna. 15081
     Frequency: irregular

LOCKED ROOM, THE   Index Code "LR"

This mystery and detective fan magazine commenced as a publication under DAPA-EM and
the first four issues were available only to members of that group. With Issue No.5
the magazine became semi-public, being sent to a number of others known to be interested
and was changed from a "personal comment" scope to one of commentary and reviews of
general interest. No issues have been seen after No.10.

        Publication history of issues indexed: *(Issues Nos. 1-4 not indexed)*
                No.5   September 1979
                6/7   March 1980
                8   July 1980
                9   December 1980*
                10   March 1981

        * Undated

Size: 8½x11; 14-50 pages
Editor: Richard Moskowitz
Current Status: possibly inactive
Publisher: Richard Moskowitz, 110 Dunrovin Lane, Rochester, N.Y. 14618
Frequency: irregular

LONE WOLFE / NERO WOLFE AND ARCHIE GOODWIN FANS NEWSLETTER   Index Code "LW"

This short-lived but well-intended fan magazine was devoted to the stories of Nero Wolfe as written by Rex Stout, and included comments, reviews, checklists, and quizzes. The first three issues were titled Nero Wolfe and Archie Goodwin Fans Newsletter.

Publication history of issues indexed:
Vol.1, No.1   January 1975
    1   2   March 1975
    1   3   June 1975
    1   4   September 1975
    1   5   November 1975
    1   6   January 1976

Size: 8½x11; 1-7 pages
Editor: Lee Poleske
Current Status: Suspended
Frequency: bi-monthly

MAN OF BRONZE, THE   Index Code "MB"

There was but one issue of this magazine published, pertaining to Doc Savage and related material with articles, commentary, and reviews.

Publication history of issues indexed:
No.1   1975 (?)

Size: 9½x11; 28 pages
Editor: John Boehm and Mark Justice
Current Status: Suspended
Publisher: Savage Productions, c/o John Boehm, 107 Stoneybrooke Drive,
    Ashland, Kentucky, or Mark Justice, 1708 Callihan Street,
    Flatwoods, Kentucky 41139
Frequency: One issue

MYSTERY   Index Code "M"

A professionally edited and published magazine devoted to "mystery, suspense, thrillers and adventure" with coverage in all media. With Vol.2, No.1, the "National Premiere Issue," the magazine commenced newstand distribution. Full-cover covers, many interior illustrations. Some fiction.

Publication history of issues indexed:
Vol.1, No.1   November/December 1979
    1   2   March/April 1980
    1   3   June/July 1980
    2   1   January 1981
    2   2   March 1981
    2   3   May 1981
    3   1   July 1981
    3   2   September 1981

Size: 8½x11; 48-64 pages
Editor: Stephen L. Smoke (1st 4 issues); subsequent, Thomas Godfrey
Current Status: Active
Publisher: Stephen L. Smoke, Mystery Magazine, Inc., 411 N. Central,
    Suite 203, Glendale, California 91203
Frequency: bi-monthly/irregular
Subscription: $10.00 per year

MYSTERY & ADVENTURE SERIES REVIEW, THE   Index Code "MA"

A fan magazine devoted to boys' series books, particularly such as Rick Brant, Tom Quest, Ken Holt, The Hardy Boys, The Lone Ranger, Bomba the Jungle Boys, and others. Of interest to mystery fans since many of these were juvenile mystery series.

                    Publication history of issues indexed:
                              No.1   Summer 1980
                                 2   Fall 1980
                                 3   Winter 1980
                                 4   Spring 1981
                                 5   Summer 1981
                                 6   Fall 1981
                                 7   Winter 1981

          Size: 5½x8½; 30-34 pages
          Editor: Fred Woodworth
          Current Status: Active
          Publisher: Fred Woodworth, P.O.Box 3488, Tuscon, Arizona 85705
          Frequency: Quarterly
          Subscription: $5.00 per year

MYSTERY FANCIER, THE   Index Code "MF"

Commencing with a 62-page Preview issue which was distributed gratis as an introduction, this mystery fan magazine has maintained a high level of interest with the many fine articles, checklists, reviews, and letters. There is much of bibliographic value to be found here, and the many letters published add both interest and information. Regular review departments provide information on both new and old books. The publisher's own THE NERO WOLFE SAGA was published in a number of installments prior to its appearance in book form.

          Publication history of issues indexed:
          Vol.1, No.1A November 1976*   Vol.3, No.4 July/August 1979
               1   1   January 1977   3   5   Sept/Oct 1979**
               1   2   March 1977   3   6   Nov/Dec 1979
               1   3   May 1977   4   1   Jan/Feb 1980
               1   4   July 1977   4   2   March/April 1980
               1   5   September 1977   4   3   May/June 1980
               1   6   November 1977   4   4   July/August 1980
               2   1   January 1978   4   5   Sept/Oct 1980
               2   2   March 1978   4   6   Nov/Dec 1980
               2   3   May 1978   5   1   Jan/Feb 1981
               2   4   July 1978   5   2   March/April 1981
               2   5   Sept/Oct 1978   5   3   May/June 1981
               2   6   Nov/Dec 1978   5   4   July/August 1981
               3   1   Jan/Feb 1979*   5   5   Sept/Oct 1981
               3   2   March/April 1979   5   6   Nov/Dec 1981
               3   3   May/June 1979

           * mis-labeled March/April 1979
          ** mis-labeled Vol.3, No.4

          Size: (preview issue and first three issues) 8½x11; subsequent issues
               5½x8½; 48-64 pages
          Editor: Guy M. Townsend
          Current Status: Active
          Publisher: Guy M. Townsend, 1711 Clifty Drive, Madison, Indiana 47250
          Frequency: Bi-monthly
          Subscription: $12.00 per year

MYSTERY*FILE   Index Code "MY"

A combined adveertising and commentary periodical of mystery and detective fiction, including book reviews, articles, and bibliographical data.

        Publication history of issues indexed:
                No.1   1974
                2   July 1974
                3   August 1974
                4   October 1974
                5   December 1974
                5A   February 1975
                6   March 1975
                7   May 1975

        Size: 5½x8½; 12-24 pages
        Editor: Steve Lewis
        Current Status: Suspended
        Publisher: Steve Lewis, 62 Chestnut Road, Newington, Conn. 06111
        Frequency: Bi-monthly

MYSTERY MONITOR, THE   Index Code "MM"

Featured news, information and announcements, reviews, and mini-reviews, with comments on forthcoming books and review extracts of mystery and detective fiction.

        Publication history of issues indexed:
        Vol.1, No.1 February 7, 1976   Vol.1, No.9   October 10, 1976
        1   2   March 7, 1976   1   10   November 16, 1976
        1   3   April 10, 1976   1   11   December 25, 1976
        1   4   May 15, 1976   2   1   January 25, 1977
        1   5   June 18, 1976   2   2   February 27, 1977
        1   6   July 3, 1976   2   3   March 27, 1977
        1   7   August 24, 1976   2   4   July 10, 1977
        1   8   September 15, 1976   2   5   April 28, 1978

        Size: 8½x11; 10-22 pages
        Editor: Don Miller
        Current Status: Suspended
        Publisher: M Press, c/o Don Miller, 12315 Judson Rd., Wheaton, Md. 20906
        Frequency: Monthly

MYSTERY NOOK, THE   Index Code "MN"

A well-conceived and edited mystery fan magazine which incorporated Mystery*File, with many valuable articles, checklists and reviews published during its span of publication. The publisher also published The Mystery Monitor, The GMS Review, The GMS Informant, The GMS Newsletter, Sagebrush, Saddles and Six-Shooters, and other similar periodicals.

        Publication history of issues indexed:
        No.1   July 1975   No. 10   May 1977
        2   August 1975   11   June 1977
        3/4   September 1975   12   June 1979
        5/6   October 1975   13   July 1981
        7   October 15, 1975   13A   (Supplement)
        8   December 1975   13B   (Supplement)
        9   August 1976   13C   (Supplement)

        Size: 8½x11; 10-129 pages
        Editor: Don Miller
        Current Status: Active
        Publisher: M Press, c/o Don Miller, 12315 Judson Rd., Wheaton, Md. 20906
        Frequency: Irregular

MYSTERY LOVERS/READERS NEWSLETTER, THE   Index Code "MR"

Commencing with a Prospectus Issue in August 1967, this special issue pre-dated even
The Armchair Detective as the first mystery fan-oriented magazine; the first twelve
regular issues were published as The Mystery Lovers Newsletter, changing with the
October 1969 issue to The Mystery Readers Newsletter. The magazine covered with a wide
range the entire field of mystery and detective fiction with articles, commentaries,
information on authors, new books, old books, checklists and bibliographical data,
and letters, and offered a book-search service for its readers during its early periods.
It was discontinued in November 1973.

Publication history of issues indexed:

Vol.1,	No. 1A	August 1967	Vol. 3,	No.5	June 1970
1	1	October 1967	3	6	August 1970
1	2	December 1967	4	1	October 1970
1	3	February 1968	4	2	January 1971
1	4	April 1968	4	3	March 1971
1	5	June 1968	4	4	May 1971
1	6	August 1968	4	5	July/August 1971
2	1	October 1968	4	6	Sept/Oct 1971
2	2	December 1968	5	1	Nov/Dec 1971
2	3	February 1969	5	2	Jan/Mar 1972
2	4	April 1969	5	3	April/May 1972
2	5	June 1969	5	4	(1972)*
2	6	August 1969	5	5	(1972)*
3	1	October 1969	5	6	(March 1973)*
3	2	December 1969	6	1	July 1973**
3	3	February 1970	6	2	November 1973***
3	4	April 1970			

    * Undated
  ** Cover reads "Summer"
*** Cover reads "Autumn"

Size: 8½x11; 12-50 pages
Editor: Mrs. Lianne Carlin
Current Status: Suspended
Publisher: Mrs. Lianne Carlin, P.O.Box 113, Melrose, Mass. 02176
Frequency: Bi-monthly

MYSTERIOUS TIMES   Index Code "MT"

At the time Mysterious Times was commenced the editor was 15 years old, and as he
stated, "He will be the first to admit that when he started MT, he didn't know what he
was getting into." However, the journal, devoted to the mystery and detective genre, had
an impressive beginning and continued so during the four issues published.

Publication history of issues indexed:
                No.1   April/May 1977
                  2   June/July 1977
                  3   January 1978
                  4   March 1978

Size: (first issue) 8½x11, subsequent issues 5½x8½; 30-48 pages
Editor: William A. Karpowicz, Jr.
Current Status: Suspended
Publisher: William A. Karpowicz, Jr., 1013 Short N.E., Grand Rapids,
    Michigan 49503
Frequency: irregular

NOT SO PRIVATE EYE, THE   Index Code "PE"

A mystery fan magazine emphasizing the private investigators in the mystery and the
detective field, although not restricted entirely to that facet. This magazine has
been an impressive contribution to the genre. It was discontinued in 1980, but
revived in 1982.

Publication history of issues indexed:

No.1	August/September 1978
2	October/November 1978
3	December/January 1979
4	February/March 1979
5	April/May/June 1979
6	October 1979
7	April 1980
8	(1980)*

* Undated

Size: (first two issues) 7x8½; subsequent issues 8½x11; 10-48 pages
Editor: Andy Jaysnovitch
Current Status: Discontinued in 1980, but revived in January 1982 with
    Issue No.9, and No.10 published April 1982, both in digest size
Publisher: Andy Jaysnovitch, 6 Dana Estates Drive, Parlin, N.J. 08859
Frequency: Quarterly
Subscription: (Current) $8.00 per year

NOTES FOR THE CURIOUS   Index Code "NC"

A periodical devoted to the works of John Dickson Carr, but unfortunately limited to
but one issue due to the death of the editor/publisher in an auto accident.

Publication history of issues indexed:
                No.1   1978

Size: 5½x8½; 32 pages
Editor: Larry L. French
Current Status: Discontinued
Publisher: Carrian Press (no address given)
Frequency: stated to be irregular

PAPERBACK QUARTERLY   Index Code "PQ"

Subtitled "Journal of Mass Market Paperback History," this journal emphasizes all
facets of the paperback book, with special attention to bibliographic material and
the publishers. While it is not limited to the mystery field, mystery does comprise
a major portion.

Publication history of issues indexed:

Vol.1, No.1	Spring 1978	Vol.2, No. 4	Winter 1979
1 2	Summer 1978	3 1	Spring 1980
1 3	Fall 1978	3 2	Summer 1980
1 4	Winter 1978	3 3	Fall 1980
2 1	Spring 1979	3 4	Winter 1980
2 2	Summer 1979	4 1	Spring 1981
2 3	Fall 1979	4 2	Summer 1981

Size: 5½x8½, 48-64 pages
Editor: Billy C. Lee and Charlotte Laughlin
Current Status: Active
Publisher: The Pecan Valley Press, 1710 Vincent St., Brownswood,
    Texas 76801
Frequency: Quarterly
Subscription: $10.00 per year; $12.00 outside U.S.

POISONED PEN, THE   Index Code "PP"

One of the most regularly published mystery fan magazines, with a plethora of articles, checklists, interviews, reviews, and letter columns. Much valuable information can be found in the letters and comments from the readers, as well as the other contents, and this entire journal can be considered of value to bibliographers and researchers as well as mystery readers.

Publication history of issues indexed:

Vol.1,	No.1	January 1978	Vol. 3,	No.1	Jan/Feb 1980
1	2	March 1978	3	2	Mar/Apr 1980
1	3	May 1978	3	3	May/June 1980
1	4	July 1978	3	4	July/August 1980
1	5	September 1978	3	5	October 1980
1	6	November 1978	3	6	December 1980
2	1	Jan/Feb 1979	4	1	February 1981
2	2	Mar/Apr 1979	4	2	April 1981
2	3	May/June 1979	4	3	June 1981
2	4	July/August 1979	4	4	August 1981
2	5	Sept/Oct 1979	4	5/6	December 1981
2	6	Nov/Dec 1979			

Size: 8½x11;28-52 pages (double-issue 100 pages)
Editor: Jeffrey Meyerson
Current Status: Active
Publisher: Jeffrey Meyerson, 50 First Place, Brooklyn, N.Y. 11231
Frequency: Semi-monthly
Subscription: $10.00 per year

PONTINE DOSSIER, THE   Index Code "PD"

The journal for members (and others) of The Praed Street Irregulars (featuring Solar Pons, an almost mirror-image of Sherlock Holmes), created by August Derleth), with articles, poems, illustrations, and commentary. A quality journal, professionally accomplished.

Publication history of issues indexed:

Old Series

Vol.1,	No.1	February 1967	Vol.2,	No.2	April 1969
1	2	December 1967	2	3	August 1969
1	3	March 1968	2	4	November 1969
1	4	September 1968	2	5	March 1970
2	1	December 1968			

New Series *(IDENTIFIED IN INDEX BY LETTER "A" SUFFIXED)*

Vol.1,	No.1	Annual 1970	Vol.2,	No.2	Annual 1974
1	2	Annual 1971	3	1	Annual 1975-76
2	1	Annual 1973	3	2	Annual 1977

Size: 5½x8½; Series I (Old), 2-8 pages; Series II (New), 40 page annuals
Editor: Luther Norris
Current Status: Discontinued (editor deceased)
Publisher: The Pontine Press, P.O.Box 261, Culver City, Calif. 90230
Frequency: Old Series: irregular; New Series: annual, except for 1972
     and 1975

PULP   Index Code "P"

A journal devoted to the pulp magazine, particularly the pulp hero characters, and the authors, stories, and bibliography. Some reprint of rare fiction. Well edited and produced, maintaining a high quality and a good dose of nostalgia.

Publication history of issues indexed:

No.1	Fall 1970	No.6	Summer 1974
2	Spring 1971	7	Spring 1975
3	Summer 1971	8	Spring 1976
4	Spring 1972	9	Summer 1976
5	Winter 1973	10	Winter 1978
5A	Special 1973 Pulpcon Issue	11	Fall 1978
		12	Summer 1980

Size: (Nos. 1 to 5A), 8½x11; subsequent issues 5½x8½; avg. 32 pages
Editor: Robert Weinberg
Current Status: Active
Publisher: Robert Weinberg, 15145 Oxford Drive, Oak Forest, Illinois 60452
Frequency: irregular
Subscription: $2.00 per issue

PULP ERA, THE   Index Code "PU"

One of the outstanding periodicals devoted to the pulp magazines, this was published for sixteen issues commencing with one titled "JD-Argassy (The Pulp Era)" #60. The editor and publisher had previously published fifty-nine issues of a "fannish" type magazine under several titles, the last of which was JD-Argassy. The last under that title carried the sub-title "The Pulp Era" and announcement was made that "if you are a faaaanish fan and not interested in science fiction and the old pulp magazines, The Pulp Era will not be the zine for you....The Pulp Era will be a serious fanzine devoted to the old pulp magazines and the new books of fiction and fantasy." Despite this rather specific pronouncement, a majority of the material that appeared in the forthcoming sixteen issues pertained to the mystery pulp magazines and the detective and hero characters.

Publication history of issues indexed

No.60	Winter 1963	No.68	November/December 1967
61	July 1964	69	January/February 1968
62	November/December 1965	70	January/February 1969
63	May/June 1966	71	March/April 1969
64	July/August 1966	72	September 1969
65	September/October 1966	73	December 1969
66	March/April 1967	74	Spring 1970
67	May/June 1967	75	Spring 1971

Size: 8½x11; 22-130 pages
Editor: Lynn Hickman
Current Status: Suspended
Publisher: Lynn Hickman, 413 Ottokee Street, Wauseon, Ohio 43567
Frequency: irregular

PULPWOODY   Index Code "PW"

A newsletter of news and reviews on pulp fandom, featuring regular columnists, mini-reviews, mini-articles, and letters. Two issues published.

Publication history of issues indexed
        No.1   January 1981
          2   February 1981

Size: 8½x11; 4 pages
Editor: Link Hullar
Current Status: Suspended
Publisher: Balderdash, 10942 N. Freeway, Suite 203, Houston, Texas 77037
Frequency: Monthly

QUEEN CANON BIBLIOPHILE, THE / THE ELLERY QUEEN REVIEW   Index Code "QC"

One of the earlier mystery fan magazines, this one dedicated "to the critical appreciation of Ellery Queen...as novelist...editor...scholar." Included in several parts is the first draft of Francis M. Nevin's book ROYAL BLOODLINE, as well as checklists, commentary, articles, letters, and reviews. A worthy landmark to mystery fiction. Title changed to The Ellery Queen Review with the last issue published.

          Publication history of issues indexed:
          Vol.1, No.1 November 1968   Vol.2, No.1 February 1970
            1   2 January 1969   2   2 July 1970
            1   3 March 1969   3   1 April 1971
            1   4 August 1969   3   2 October 1971

          Size: 8½x11; 16-27 pages
          Editor: Rev. Robert E. Washer
          Current Status: Suspended
          Publisher: Rev. Robert E. Washer, 82 East 8th Street, Oneida Castle,
              New York 13421
          Frequency: irregular

ROHMER REVIEW, THE   Index Code "R"

Devoted to the works and life of Sax Rohmer (Arthur Sarsfield Ward), with emphasis on his principal character, Dr. Fu Manchu. Articles, commentary, reminiscences, reviews, and letters, professionally prepared and presented.

          Publication history of issues indexed:
          No.1   July 1968   No. 10 March 1973
            2   January 1969   11 December 1973
            3   August 1969   12 September 1974
            4   March 1970   13 August 1975
            5   August 1970   14 July 1976
            6   February 1971   15 September 1976
            7   August 1971   16 July 1977
            8   March 1972   17 August 1977
            9   August 1972   18 September 1981

          Size: 5½x8½; 26-32 pages
          Editor: Robert E. Briney
          Current Status: Active
          Publisher: Robert E. Briney, 4 Forest Ave., Salem, Mass. 01970
          Frequency: irregular
          Subscription: Inquire

SCIENCE-FICTION COLLECTOR / MEGAVORE   Index Code "SF"

A well produced magazine covering all phases of popular fiction, including mystery and detective, and pulp heroes and magazines. The first nine issues were titled The Science-Fiction Collector; with Issue No.9, Age of the Unicorn was incorporated into the magazine and the scope changed to emphasize mystery, detective and pulp material. With Issue No.10, the title was changed to Megavore, but with Issue No.14, again to The Science-Fiction Collector. Featured much bibliographical material as well as many articles on collecting, and reviews. With Issue No.15, change announced to tabloid size. It was discontinued after Issue No.15½, an issue which was entirely devoted to advertising.

          Publication history of issues indexed:
          No.1   (1976)*   No.9   June 1980
            2   (1976)*   10   August 1980
            3   (1977)*   11   October 1980
            4   July 1977   12   December 1980
            5   September 1977   13   March 1981
            6   May 1978   14   May 1981
            7   July 1979   15   July 1981**
            8   October 1979   15½ September 1981***

* Undated
** Tabloid newspaper format
*** All advertising issue, not indexed

Size: (Nos. 1-14) 8½x11; (No.15) tabloid newspaper 11¼x17; (no.15½)
    tabloid newspaper but all advertising; 48 pages plus advt.section
Editor: J. Grant Thiessen
Current Status: Suspended
Publisher: Pandora's Books Ltd., Box 86, Neche, N.D. 58265; Canadian
    address: Box 1298, Altona, Manitoba, ROG OBO, Canada
Frequency: irregular

THORNDYKE FILE, THE   Index Code "TF"

This journal, devoted to Dr. Thorndyke, the literary detective creation of R. Austin
Freeman, was commenced in 1976 by Philip T. Asdell. In the introduction of the first
issue, Mr. Asdell states that "the orderly and analytical approach to the solution of
the crimes was much to my taste" and knowing of the interest of others who enjoyed the
stories, decided to publish a journal to include articles about Freeman, the methods
and devices used by Thorndyke in the soltuion of the cases, and other related material.
From the first issue, the journal was impressive and continued under Asdell's direction
for ten semi-annual issues. Publication was then assumed by Professor John McAleer.

Publication history of issues indexed:
No.1	Spring 1976	No. 7	Spring 1979
2	Fall 1976	8	Fall 1979
3	Spring 1977	9	Spring 1980
4	Fall 1977	10	Fall 1980
5	Spring 1978	11	Spring 1981
6	Fall 1978	12	Fall 1981

Size: 5½x8½; 36-52 pages
Editor: (Nos.1-10), Philip T. Asdell; subsequent issues, John McAleer
Current Status: Active
Publisher: John J. McAleer, 121 Follen Road, Lexington, Mass. 02173
Frequency: Semi-annual
Subscription: $5.00 per year; $6.50 outside U.S.

TUTTER BUGLE, THE   Index Code "TB" (Old)
                                                          "TBN" (New)
Devoted to the books and stories of Leo Edwards (Edward S. Ellis), and his boys'
stories and books of Jerry Todd (detective), Andy Blake, Trigger Berg, Poppy Ott,
and Tuffy Bean. Featured articles, commentary, reminiscences, bibliographical data,
letters, and advertisements. Note irregular volume numbering.

Publication history of issues indexed:
Old Series
Vol.1,	No.1	Dec. 1, 1967	Vol.2,	No.5	November 1969
1	2	Mar.1, 1968	3	1	April 1970
1	3	June 1, 1968	3	2	June 1970
1	4	(Sept.1, 1968)*	3	3	August/September 1970
2	1	Dec.1, 1968	3	4	October/November 1970
2	2	May 1, 1969	3	5	December 1970
2	3	June 1, 1969	4	1	February 1971
2	4	Sept.5, 1969	4	2	December 1971

New Series
Vol.1,	No.1	April 1, 1973	Vol.2,	No.2	June 1, 1974
1	2	July 1, 1973	2	3	August 1, 1974
1	3	October 1, 1973	2	4	October 1, 1974
1	4	January 1, 1974	2	5	December 1, 1974
2	1	April 1, 1974	2	6	February 1, 1975

* Undated

```
        Size: various sizes, from 4 3/4 x 9, to 8½x14; 4-18 pages
        Editor: Robert L. Johnson and Julius R. Chenu
        Current Status: Suspended
        Publisher: The Tutter Bugle and the Leo Edwards Juvenile Jupiter
            Detective Association; later issues, Jack Tornquist
        Frequency: irregular
```

WEIRD TALES COLLECTOR, THE   Index Code "WT"

A journal devoted to all facets of Weird Tales magazine, its authors and stories.
The periodical has maintained a very high level of quality with the many articles,
reminiscences, and other material and has included a complete index to Weird Tales
as well as other bibliographical material.

```
        Publication history of issues indexed:
                        No.1    1977
                           2    1977
                           3    1978
                           4    1978
                           5    1979
                           6    1980

        Size: 5½x8½; 32 pages
        Editor: Robert Weinberg
        Current Status: Active
        Publisher: Robert Weinberg, 15145 Oxford Drive, Oak Forest, Ill. 60452
        Frequency: irregular
        Subscription: $2.00 per issue
```

WOLD ATLAS, THE   Index Code "WA"

Billed as "a journal of speculation," this magazine consisted primarily of pastiche
material involving the pulp and detective heroes, including Doc Savage, The Shadow,
and Sherlock Holmes. It was discontinued after five issues.

```
        Publication history of issues indexed:
                    Vol.1, No.1  January 1977
                        1    2   Spring 1977
                        1    3   Fall 1977
                        1    4   Winter 1978
                        2    1   Fall 1978

        Size: 8½x11; 16-32 pages
        Editor: Timothy J. Rutt
        Current Status: Suspended
        Publisher: Timothy J. Rutt, 1600 Linden, Boulder, Colorado 80302
        Frequency: irregular
```

XENOPHILE   Index Code "X"

Although commenced as an advertising magazine, most issues included a large selection
of articles, commentary, reminiscences, checklists and bibliographical material, letters,
and reviews, as well as advertisements. Illustrated. Treated complete fields of detective,
fantasy, science-fiction, and the weird in popular literature and its material, on the
whole, is outstanding.

```
        Publication history of issues indexed:
        No.1  1974                      No.10   January 1975
           2  April 1974                 10½    February 1975
           3  May 1974                    11     March 1975
           4  June 1974                   12    Not Issued
           5  July 1974                   13     May 1975
           6  Aug/Sept 1974               14     June 1975
           7  October 1974                15     July 1975
           8  November 1974               16     August 1975
           9  December 1974               17     September 1975
```

No. 18 October 1975	No. 32 May/June 1977
19 December 1975	33 July 1977
20 January 1976	34 August/September 1977
21 February 1976	35 October 1977
22 March/April 1976	36 November 1977
23 May 1976	37 February 1978
24 July 1976	38 March/April 1978
25 August 1976	39 June 1978
26 September 1976	40 July 1978
27 October 1976	41 January 1979
28 Nov/Dec 1976	42 Sept/Oct 1979
29 January 1977	43 January 1980
30 March 1977	44 March 1980
31 April 1977	

Size: (1st 10 issues) 5½x8½; subsequent issues 8½x11; 26-152 pages
Editor: Nils Hardin
Current Status: Suspended
Publisher: Nils Hardin, P.O.Box 429, Summerland, Calif. 93067
Frequency: Monthly, then irregular

YELLOWBACK LIBRARY   Index Code "YB"

One of the best produced magazines devoted to boys' book collecting and includes the field of dime novels. Well edited, good columnists, and valuable bibliographical material.

Publication history of issues indexed:

Vol.1, No.1	January/February 1981
1 2	March/April 1981
1 3	May/June 1981
1 4	July/August 1981
1 5	September/October 1981
1 6	November/December 1981

Size: 5½x8½; 28 pages
Editor: Gil O'Gara
Current Status: Active
Publisher: Gil O'Gara, 2019 S.E.8th Street, Des Moines, Iowa 50315
Frequency: Quarterly
Subscription: $8.00 per year

*****

NOTE: All magazines indexed are indexed for their

complete run, through the end of 1981. The

foregoing publication history represents all

issues published

A Basic Reference Library, (in science-
   fiction), by J. Grant Thiessen,
   14 SF 39
A Beastly Case of Murder, (mysteries
   involving beasts, with checklist),
   by Mary Ann Grochowski, 1-6 PP 3
A Bibliography of Avram Davidson, by
   Richard Grant, 9 SF 4
A Bibliography of Secondary Sources,
   (mystery and related), by Walter
   Albert, for:
   1972, 7-1 TAD 46
   1973, 7-4 TAD 266
   1974, 8-4 TAD 290
   1975, 9-4 TAD 316
   1976, 11-2 TAD 196
   1977, 12-2 TAD 125
   1978, 13-1 TAD 43
   1979, 13-4 TAD 313
   1980, 14-4 TAD 346
A Bibliography of the Works of Anthony
   Berkeley Cox (Francis Iles), by
   Paul R. Moy, 14-3 TAD 236
A Bit of a Twist: The Writings of John
   Lutz, by Mary Ann Grochowski,
   1-2 PP 5
A Bit of Inspiration from Denmark,
   (verse), by Bjorne Nielsen,
   14-1 TAD 30
A Boucher Portrait: Anthony Boucher as
   Seen By His Friends and Colleagues,
   by Lenore Glen Offord, 2-2 TAD 69
A Bow to Cartographers, (biography,
   article, on Richard Sharpe Shaver),
   by Dave and Su Bates, 1-6 CP 24
A Brief Bibliographic Essay on Doc
   Savage, by Link Hullar, 6 U 22
A Brief Encounter with Leslie Ford and
   David Frome, by Bill Lyles, 2-4 PP 15
A Cambridge Mystery, (1931), by Neville
   Wood, 1-2 PP 3; 1-3 PP 3; 1-4 PP 3;
   1-5 PP 3
A Case of Double Identity, (Dannay and
   Lee as Ellery Queen discussion),
   3-2 QC 11
A Case of Identity: Being a Trifling
   Monograph Upon the Similarities
   Between Sir Denis Nayland Smith
   and Sherlock Holmes, by Andrew Jay
   Peck, 2 R 9
A CATALOGUE OF CRIME, Supplements by
   authors (Jacques Barzun and Wendell
   Hertig Taylor, 9-2 TAD 93; 9-3 TAD 209;
   9-4 TAD 271; 10-2 TAD 126; 10-3 TAD 224;
   11-1 TAD 92; 11-2 TAD 203; 11-3 TAD 281;
   11-4 TAD 394; 12-1 TAD 32; 12-3 TAD 262;
   13-3 TAD 208; 13-4 TAD 308; 14-1 TAD 88;
   14-2 TAD 142; 14-3 TAD 228; 14-4 TAD 328
A Chaucerian Fragment, (re: Charlie Chan),
   by Veronica M.S.Kennedy, 5-1 TAD 23

A Checklist of the Short Stories of
   John Luz, by Francis M. Nevins, Jr.,
   1-3 PP 13
A Chinese Detective in San Francisco,
   Chan To(w), by E.F.Bleiler,
   5-3 MF 2
A Chronological Bibliography of the
   Books of Arthur B. Reeve, by J.
   Randolph Cox, 11-1 TAD 29
A Chronology of Crimes, (Nero Wolfe),
   by Stephen F. Schultheis and
   Patricia A. Dreyfus, 1-1 G 41
A Classic Forgery; from THE EXPLOITS
   OF FIDELITY DOVE by Roy Vickers,
   (fiction), 11-4 TAD 357
A Clergyman's Irregular Crime File,
   (book reviews, notes), by Robert
   B. Washer, 17 X 60; 21 X 54
A Coffin for the Avenger, (fiction),
   by Kenneth Robeson, 9 P 13
A Collector Reminisces, (collecting
   mystery fiction), by Neville Wood,
   3-2 PP 7
A Collector's Observations, (mystery
   book collecting), by Steven Miller,
   3-5 PP 13
A Comment from Nick Carr's Typewriter,
   (on Star Wars and the pulps), by
   Nick Carr, 1 PW 2
A Conversation with Joan Kahn, (mystery
   editor), by Robert Randisi, 3-1 M 16
A Conversation with Judson Philips,
   by Bernard A. Drew, 13-4 TAD 325
A Conversation with Nicholas Blake,
   by Jan Broberg, 2-3 MR 3
A Conversation with the deCamps,
   (L. Sprague de Camp and Catherine
   Crook de Camp), by Charlotte
   Laughlin, 1-1 PQ 16
A Cook's Tour of the Pulps, (literary
   reminiscences), by Fred Cook,
   67 PU 43
A Crime Club Selection, (in paperbacks),
   by M.C. Hill, 2-5 CP 14
A Critical Analysis of the Doc Savage
   Novels, (in-depth critical study of
   individual novels as published in
   DOC SAVAGE magazine), by Herman S.
   McGregor,
   Vol.1, #1,2,3,   2 BS 10; 2/3 DR 13
   Vol.1, #4,5,6,   3 BS 8
   Vol.2, #1,2,3,4,   4 BS 8
   Vol.2, #5,6, Vol.3, #1,   5 BS 6
   Vol.3, #2,3,4,   6 BS 15
   Vol.3, #5,6, Vol.4, #1,   7 BS 13
   Vol.4, #2,3,4,   8 BS 11
   Vol.4, #5,6, Vol.5, #1,   9 BS 8
   Vol.5, #2,3,4,   10 BS 9
   Vol.6, #2,3,4,   11 BS 14
   Vol.5, #5,6, Vol.6, #1,   12 BS 11

A Critical Analysis of the Doc Savage
   Novels, (continued)
   Vol.6, #5,6, Vol.7, #1, 13 BS 13
   Vol.7, #2,3,4, 14 BS 5
   Vol.7, #5,6, Vol.8, #1, 15 BS 9
A Critical "Savage" Artist, (Doc Savage
   cover art), by Albert Manachino,
   4 DR 2
A Critical Vocabulary for Crime Fiction,
   by Jacques Barzun, 4-2 TAD 75
A Curious Interview, by James Wade,
   13 R 8
A Day in the Life of a Real Private
   Investigator, by Douglas Christensen
   and Karen Bornstein, 1-3 M 52
A Day in the Life of the Wife of an
   Amachoor Skoller, (regarding John
   D. MacDonald), by June M. Moffatt,
   6 JD 13
A Dead Ringer, by Dana Martin Batory,
   5 U 25
A Decade Later August, (verse), by
   Raymond Roseliep, 4-3 AD 8
A Defense for Crime Fiction, (literary
   quality), by Hilmar Baunsgaard,
   10-4 TAD 358
A Derleth Tribute, (August Derleth),
   by Mary Elizabeth Counselman,
   1-4 AD 1
A Detective Searches for a Clue to THE
   HEART OF THE MATTER, (by Graham
   Greene, 1948), by J.R. Christopher,
   4-1 TAD 32
A Detective Story Reference Library,
   by Adrian Goldstone, 3-1 MR 17
A Different Kind of Murder, (review of
   MURDER WITH A DIFFERENCE, ed. by
   Christopher Morley), by William
   White, 3-5 MR 7
A Discovery in Capek, (re: Karel Capek),
   by Josef Skvorecky, 8-3 TAD 180
A Diversey Checklist, (paperbacks),
   by Lance Casebeer, 3-3 CP 10
A Doc Savage Adventure Rediscovered,
   (on "Who Goes There" by Don A.
   Stuart), by Albert Tonik, 4 DS 10
A Double Memorial, (to August Derleth),
   by (1) A.E. Van Vogt, and (2) Colin
   Wilson, 2-1 PDA 3
A Dream of Reason: The Great Detective
   as True Believer, (classic detectives
   and logical reasoning), by Cathryn
   Lanham, 2-2 C 23
A Failed Experiment: The Laser Books,
   History and Checklist, (analysis
   and bibliography of short-lived
   science-fiction paperback line), by
   Keith L. Justice, 15 SF 4
A Farewell to Max Brand, (literary
   reminiscences on Frederick Faust),
   by Steve Fisher, 1-3 FC 4
A Fatal Attraction, (on the fiction of
   Carroll John Daly), by G.A. Finch,
   13-2 TAD 112

A Few Non-Medical Thoughts, by
   Dr. Bill Laidlaw, D.N., 1 DQ 5
A Few Shadow Offities, (on The
   Shadow), by Frank Eisgruber, Jr.,
   10 P 35
A Fight to the Death, (fiction;
   Tarzan), by Robert Buhr, 4 SF 25
A Flat in Paddington, (verse; Solar
   Pons and Praed Street), by Steve
   Eng, 3-3 AD 3
A Footnote for Shadow Collectors,
   (duplication of titles for
   different stories of The Shadow,
   and other bibliographical notes),
   by Robert Sampson, 4-2 MR 9
A Frivolity (I Would Like to....),
   by Estelle Fox, 5-1 TAD 10
A Frivolity (I Would Like to....),
   by John Harwood, 6-2 TAD 103
A Full Length "Shadow" Novel as Told
   to... (Shadow stories written by
   Theodore Tinsley and Bruce Elliott),
   by Fred S. Cook, 3 BS 12
A Ghost Story, (verse), by Stuart
   Silverman, 3-3 AD 6
A Glance at Paperback History, by
   Mark Schaffer, 2-2 PQ 31
A Glass of Wine Within the Meaning of
   the Act, (use of wine in the
   Dr. Thorndyke stories by Freeman),
   by Oliver Mayo, 7 TF 30
A Great Contemporary: Jose Giovanni,
   (French author's mystery films),
   by Jack Edmund Nolan, 4-4 MR 19
A Guide to Thorndykean Pilopathology,
   (medico-legal importance of the
   skin and hair in the Thorndyke
   stories by Freeman), by Howard
   Brody, 11 TF 3
A Hazardous Occupation, (fiction), by
   Mary Ann Grochowski, 4 MT 1
A Hitherto Undiscovered Reminiscence
   of Dr. John H. Watson, M.D. (of
   Sherlockian interest), by Julian
   Gill, 2-1 PDA 33
A John Creasey Bibliography, (with
   pen names and summary of series)
   by R.E. Briney and John Creasey,
   2-1 TAD 5
A John Dickson Carr Checklist, by
   Rick Sneary, 3-4 MR 13
A John Wyndham Checklist, (with
   bibliographic data), by Philip
   Stephenson-Payne, 8 SF 31
(A JUDGEMENT IN STONE: Ruth Rendell),
   Humor, Horror and Intellect: Giles
   Mont in Ruth Rendell's A JUDGEMENT
   IN STONE, by Jane S. Bakerman,
   5-4 MF 5
A Judy Bolton Mystery - "Blacklisted
   Classics", (girls' series mysteries)
   by Luana Russell, 2-1 C 35

A Justly Celebrated, Elusive American,
(Quentin Locke, detective, on screen),
by Stanley A. Carlin, 3-2 MR 31
A KAHNfidential Interview, (interview
with Joan Kahn, mystery editor), by
Jane Merrill Filstrup, 2-2 C 15
(A KILLING IN XANADU: Bill Pronzini),
Pronzini, Nameless, and a Limited
Edition, (comments on book and
detective character), by Doug Greene,
4-2 PP 11
A Latter Holmes, (on Solar Pons), by
Bruce Kennedy, 1-3 PD 1
A Laughing Ghost, (article review of
GHOST OF THE HARDY BOYS by Leslie
McFarlane), by Kent Winslow, 4 MA 15
A Leo Edwards Imitation, (the Fun
Loving Gang by Harold M. Sherman,
similar to Leo Edwards stories),
by Rick Crandall, 1-3 YB 7
A Lesser Chesterton Detective: Mr. Pond,
by R.W. Hays, 9-2 TAD 125
A Letter from John D. MacDonald, (on
public acceptance of violence),
17 JD 9
A List of August Derleth's Works in
Print, 1-1 AD 2
A Literary Exile Comes Home, (interview
with W.R. Burnett), by David Wilson,
3-2 M 26
A Look at Dell Shannon, by Barbara Buhrer,
3/4 MN 3
A Look at Dupin, (C. Auguste Dupin,
detective), by Steve Miller, 2 MT 20
A Look at Some Books, (reviews), by
Michael L. Cook, 5 U 31
A Look at the Lone Ranger Books, by
Fred Woodworth, 1 MA 11
A Look at the Novels of Ruth Rendell,
by Don Miller, 10 MN A7
A Look at the Short Stories of Ruth
Rendell, by Don Miller, 10 MN A19
(A MAN LAY DEAD: Ngaio Marsh), The
First Appearance: Roderick Alleyn,
by Maryell Cleary, 2-6 PP 12
A Matter of Relative Importance, (fiction),
by Martha Axelrod, 1-2 M 43
(A. MERRITT'S FANTASY), Index (to
pulp magazine run), by Herman S.
McGregor, 74 PU 15
A Mirror to Our Crimes, (true crimes
as mystery fiction), by Edward D.
Hoch, 12-3 TAD 280
A Modesty Blaise Appreciation, by R. Jeff
Banks, 8 MN 3
A Museum of Thorndykean Pathology,
(medical oddities in the Dr.
Thorndyke stories of Freeman),
by John H. Dirckx, 5 TF 2
A Mysterious Quiz, (quiz), by R.E. Briney,
7-1 AD 24
A Name is a Name, (on pseudonyms), by
Richard Gehman, 1-4 MR 16

A New Category of the Mystery Story,
(plots with two possible solutions,
mundane or supernatural), by Frank
D. McSherry, Jr., 2-1 TAD 23
A Night's Work, (fiction), by Paul
Harwitz, 1-3 M 46
A Non-definitive Price Guide to Out-
of-Print Arkham House Titles, by
W.K. Schoonmaker, 18 X 21
A Note About Lewis Carroll, (mystery
elements in his works), by R.W.Hays,
7-2 TAD 95
A Note from Francis Parkman, by R.W.
Hays, 5-4 TAD 193
A Note from John D. MacDonald, 25 JD 15
A Note on Dovelands Cottage, by J.L.
Biggers, 14 R 23
A Note on Harry Stephen Keeler as
Filmed, by Francis M. Nevins, Jr.,
3-3 TAD 165
A Note on Medieval Detection, (fore-
runners: modern detectives), by
R.W. Hays, 5-2 TAD 88
A Note on Rufus King's Series Short
Stories, (with checklist), by J.M.
Purcell, 12-4 TAD 380
A Note on the Chronology of the "Dr.
Thorndyke" Novels, (by R. Austin
Freeman), by Michael G. Heenan,
9-1 TAD 52
A Pair of Aces, (letter from Donald A.
Wollheim on Ace Double Mysteries,
paperbacks), 7 MY 5
A Partial Checklist of Reviews of Books
by Ruth Rendell, (bibliography of
reviews), by Don Miller, 10 MN A23
A Partial History of Pulp Prices
1946-1973, 24 X 40
A Partial Index of Reviews of the Books
of Georgette Heyer, (bibliography of
reviews), by Don Miller, 13 MN 27
A Partial Index to Reviews of Crossen
Books (bibliography of reviews of
books by Kendell F. Crossen, with
abstracts), by Don Miller, 12 MN A5
A Partial List of Paperback Covers
Painted by Norman Saunders, 1-3 PQ
41
A Partial List of Reviews of Books by
Rex Stout, (bibliography of reviews),
by Don Miller, 9 MN A45
A Pile of Pointy Polka Dots, (parody of
Travis McGee), by Bailey Phelps,
26 JD 35
A Portrait of Poe and His Tales, by
Frederick J. Jaeger, 4-6 MR 20
A Possible Source for the Opening of
"Sleuth", (play by Anthony Shaffer),
by Veronica M.S. Kennedy, 7-3 TAD
175
A Preliminary Chronology of the Docu-
mented Cases of Napoleon Bonaparte,
(detective), by William Antony S.
Sarjeant, 12-4 TAD 358

A Preliminary Inquiry Into Initial Costs
Associated With Establishing a Secret
Crime-Fighting Identity, (do you want
to be a masked crime fighter, a la
pulps?), by Robert Sampson, 4-4 MR 28

A Preliminary Study in the Literature of
Nero Wolfe, by Father Francis Hertzberg,
2-4 MR 11

A Profile of Henry Gamadge and an Elizabeth Daly Checklist,(Henry Gamage,
detective creation of Daly), by
Estelle Fox, 4-4 MR 27

A Pulp Cover Gallery, (pulp magazine
covers by Walter Baumhofer), 42 X 23

A Queen Quandary Quickly Quavered in
Quondam Quixotic Quotations, (Ellery
Queen), by Michael Murphy, 14 X 2

(A QUESTION OF PROOF: Nicholas Blake),
The First Appearance: Nigel Strangeways, by Maryell Cleary, 2-5 PP 25

A Question of Time, by Cay Van Ash,
17 R 7

A Quick Look at THE YOUTH'S COMPANION,
(boys' story paper), by Walter H.
McIntosh, 4-1 BC 394

A Readers Supplement to QUEEN'S QUORUM,
(basic mysteries), by Douglas G.
Greene, 12-3 TAD 228

A Reading of Reeve: Some Thoughts on the
Creator of Craig Kennedy, (Arthur
B. Reeve), by J. Randolph Cox,
11-1 TAD 28

A Reading of Rex Stout, (verse), by
Mona Van Duyn, 1-2 G 32

A Recurring Little Villain (Cadwiller
Olden in Doc Savage and The Avenger
stories), by Bill Laidlaw, 5 DQ 9

A Reel Mystery, (film reviews), by
Andy Jaysnovitch, 13/14 CL 13

A Remembrance of Early Pulp Collecting
and Fandom 1938-1943, by Virginia
Combs ("Nanek") Anderson with
William Papalia, 40 X 3

A Remembrance of FN, (notes on FANTASTIC
NOVELS magazine), by James Ellis,
20 X 37

A Rendell Dozen Plus One: An Annotated
Checklist of the Rendell Novels
Through 1974, (Ruth Rendell), by
Jo Ann Genaro Vicarel, 9-3 TAD 198

A Reply to Hal Charles, (on mystery
writing practices), by Gary Warren
Niebuhr, 4-2 PP 12

A Report on Bouchercon I, by Pat Erhardt,
3-6 MR 25

A Report on Bouchercon I, by Leo Rand,
14 JD 7

A Report on Bouchercon II, by Leo Rand,
17 JD 15

A Report on Bouchercon V, by Leo Rand,
20 JD 17

A Report on Bouchercon VII, by Art Scott,
1A MF 18

A Representative Collection, (boys'
books), by Jack R. Schorr,
3-1 BC 287

A Review from the Microcosm, (re:
price guide, Resnicks), by
Marvin Morrison, 28 X 7

A Rick Brant Reminiscence, (boys'
series mystery books), by John
Blaine, 3 MA 3

A Rohmer Miscellany, by R.E. Briney,
11 R 8

A Second John D.?, (comparison of
authors John D. MacDonald and
Charles Williams), by J.M. Carter,
18 JD 15

A Second Round for Doc, (background
of paperback book publication of
Doc Savage novels), by Paul H.
Bonner, Jr., 9 BS 4

A Selection from the Pontine Weapon
Gallery, (re: Solar Pons), by
Roger Johnson, 2-1 PDA 15

A Selection of Reviews of Crossen
Books, (Kendell F. Crossen),
12 MN A11

A Selective Critical Bibliography of
the Genre in the Sixties, (mystery
fiction), by Rev. Robert E.
Washer, 2-1 MR 18; 2-2 MR 3

A Sense of the Under Toad: Play in
Mystery Fiction, by Joan B. Fiscella,
1-2 C 1

A Settling on Accounts, (on "Dallas"
television series), by Emma Lathen,
9 LR 25

A Sherlocko-Pontine Addendum, by J.R.
Christopher, 2-1 PD 3

A Short Report on Bouchercon VI, by
George Fergus, 2 MN 3

A Simon Ark Bibliography (Simon Ark
stories by Edward D. Hoch), by
Edward D. Hoch), 3-4 TAD 248

A Sixth Sense, (on Sax Rohmer), by
Elizabeth Sax Rohmer, 9 R 25

A Song for the Unsung, (Harry Horne,
detective creation of John Gonzales)
by Joseph J. Coffey, 13-1 TAD 67

A Special Report on Shad Roe, (Nero
Wolfe association article), by
Marjorie Mortensen, 1-2 G 51

A Stern Look at McGee, (Travis McGee,
fictional character created by John
D. MacDonald), by Elijah Stern,
15 JD 5

A Stranger Visits "The Land of Leo
Edwards", (comments on Leo Edwards
boys' series books), by Ed Mulford,
2-6 TBN 5

A Study in Black, (supernatural themes
in mysteries), by Frank D. McSherry,
Jr., 5-5 MR 23; 5-6 MR 3; 6-1 MR 29;
6-2 MR 39

A Supplement to THIRTY YEARS OF ARKHAM
HOUSE, (titles published from 1970
to June 1981), by Gunter E. Swain,
5-1 AD 9

A Tale of "Secret Egypt", by Sax Rohmer,
(with commentary by Robert E. Briney
7 R 12), 7 R 11

A Talk with Harry Castlemon, (boys'
books author), by Carabel Lewis Munger,
2-4 BC 250

A Tan and Sandy Thirteenth, (commentary
on A TAN AND SANDY SILENCE by John D.
MacDonald), by Dean A. Grennell, 17 JD 11

A Teacher Meets Agatha Christie, by Gordon
C. Ramsey, 1-1 TAD 13

A Thorndyke Examination, (quiz), by Philip
T. Asdell, 1 TF 32

A Thunder Jim Checklist, (in THRILLING
ADVENTURES), by Will Murray, 1 D 22

(A TOUCH OF DANGER: James Jones), Karma and
Spiritual Responsibility in, by Steven
R. Carter, 13-3 TAD 230

A Tribute to JDM, (re: John D. MacDonald),
by John R. Feegel, M.D., 24 JD 22

A Tribute to Mike Avallone, 1-1 MF 5

A Tribute to the Crowned Queen of
Misdirection: Dame Agatha Christie,
(with paperback checklist), by Richard
P. Hall, 3-3 CP 26

A Tribute to Vincent Starrett, by Michael
Murphy, 2-2 PDA 70

A Very Sad Book Story, (on boys' book
collecting), by Les Beitz, 1-1 BC 26

A View from Wall Street: Social Criticism
in the Mystery Novels of Emma Lathen,
by Jane S. Bakerman, 9-3 TAD 213

A Visit to Baker Street, (Sherlockiana), by
W.O.G. Lofts, 6-1 TAD 15

A Visit to Hi-Lee, (home of Leo Edwards,
boys' books author), by Forrest Campbell,
2-1 TB 3

A Visit to No Man's Land, (pulp magazine
war series stories), by Nick Carr,
10 DS 11

A Visit to Two Museums, (Ackerman's science-
fiction collection, and San Francisco
Academy of Comic Art), by Albert Tonik
10 SF 34

A Visit with August Derleth, by John
Davenport Dixon, 4-1 AD 1

A Visit with Dame Ngaio Marsh, by John
Ball, 3-1 M 23

A Visit with Margaret Brundage, (WEIRD
TALES cover artist), by Forrest J.
Ackerman, 3 WT 17

A Visit with "Mrs. Doc Savage", (Mrs.
Lester Dent), by Bill Smith, 6 BS 3

A Visit with Walter Gibson, by Bernard A.
Drew, 7 U 23

A Walk in the Pulpwoods: Random Recollect-
ions, (pulp magazine reminiscences),
by William F. Nolan, 2-2 C 38

A Walking Tour of Sax Rohmer's London,
(descriptive essay), by Julian L.
Biggers, 18 R 13

A Welcome to the Wolfe Pack, (organization in tribute of Nero Wolfe),
by John McAleer, 1-1 G 15

A Wolfean Double-Cross Tick, (Nero
Wolfe acrostic puzzle), by Tenby
Storm, 1-2 G 34

A Wolfean Quiz, (Nero Wolfe oriented
quiz), by Kevin Barbero, 1-1 G 31

A Woman's Intuition: Wives and Lovers
in British Golden Age Detective
Novels, by Helaine Ross, 2-1 C 17

A Woolrich Preview, (on uncompleted
works of Cornell Woolrich), by
Francis M. Nevins, Jr., 4-3 TAD
145

A Word for John Creasey: J.J. Marric's
GIDEON'S RISK, (critical discussion)
by John Boyles, 11-3 TAD 282

A Word with Dick Francis, (interview),
by Deryck Harvey, 6-3 TAD 151

A. Boucher Bibliography, (Anthony
Boucher), by J.R.Christopher with
D.W.Dickensheet and R.E.Briney,
2-2 TAD 77; 2-3 TAD 143; 2-4 TAD
263

A.D. (essay on August Derleth), by
Fredrick Shroyer, 3-3 AD 1;
2-1 PDA 7

A, Merritt's Mysteries, (fantasy and
fantastic mystery author), by Walter
J. Wentz, 5-4 TAD 204

(Aarons, Edward S.: Sam Durrell series)
Spy Series Characters in Hardback,
Part IX, by Barry Van Tilburg,
5-5 MF 15

(Abbott, Anthony), About the Murders
of Anthony Abbott, by Jon L. Breen,
3-1 TAD 1

(Abbott, Anthony), About the Output of
Anthony Abbott, by Francis M. Nevins,
Jr., 2-1 MR 12

(Abbott, Anthony: Thatcher Colt, det.)
The Thatcher Colt Novels of Anthony
Abbott: A Bibliography, by Jon L.
Breen, 3-1 TAD 5

Abe, Masaki: letter of comment,
2-1 AD 8; 24 X 45; 33 X 115

Abeln, Dennis: letter of comment, 36 X 72

About the Murders of Anthony Abbott,
(author), by Jon L. Breen, 3-1 TAD 1

About the Output of Anthony Abbott,
(author), by Francis M. Nevins, Jr.,
2-1 MR 12

About Critical Essays on Books by JDM,
(discusses reviews of author John
D. MacDonald), by Lawrence Fleming,
16 JD 11

About Dashiell Hammett, by William White,
3-3 TAD 171

About "The Smugglers of Chestnut", by
   Maurice Owen, 1-1 BC 17
Abraham, Terry: Nom De Loup, (on the
   names used in the Nero Wolfe novels
   by Rex Stout), 3 LW 5
Abrahams, Etta C.: Cops and Detectives,
   1-1 C 96
Abrahams, Etta C.: Where Have All the
   Values Gone? The Private Eye's Vision
   of America in the Novels of Raymond
   Chandler and Ross Macdonald, 9-2 TAD
   128
Academic Respectability of Detective
   Fiction, The; An Editor's Intro-
   duction to Thesis Best-Selling
   American Detective Fiction by Joan
   M. Mooney, by Allen J. Hubin,
   3-2 TAD 97
(Ace Books), in Denholms Law #3, (Ace
   Books and Standard Book Numbers),
   by Bill Denholm, 1-4 CP 17
Ace Books, (paperbacks, checklist by
   author), by J. Grant Thiessen,
   1 SF 21
Ace Books, (paperbacks, numerical
   checklist), by J. Grant Thiessen,
   1 SF 3
Ace Carpenter, Detective, (fiction),
   by Hamilton T. Caine, 1-1 M 33;
   1-2 M 47; 1-3 M 54
Ace Checklist, (Ace Books), Additions
   and Errata, by J. Grant Thiessen,
   2 SF 35
(Ace Double Mysteries), A Pair of
   Aces - Letter from Donald A. Wolheim
   on Ace Double Mysteries, (as editor),
   7 MY 5
Ace Double Mysteries, (discussion with
   checklist), by Steve Lewis, 6 MY 3
(ACE G-MAN), checklist of issues, pulp
   magazine, by Lynn Hickman, 75 PU 6
(ACE HIGH DETECTIVE), checklist of
   issues, pulp magazine, by Lynn
   Hickman, 75 PU 7
ACE-HIGH MAGAZINE, (discussion on pulp
   magazine), by Lynn Hickman, 66 PU 3
(ACE-HIGH MAGAZINE), checklist of issues,
   pulp magazine, by Lynn Hickman,
   75 PU 9
(ACE-HIGH WESTERN), checklist of issues,
   pulp magazine, by Lynn Hickman,
   75 PU 8
(Ace Magazines), From Blue Swastika to
   the Ace of Spades, (history of the
   Ace pulp magazines), by Donald A.
   Wolheim, 68 PU 5
Ace Science Fiction Doubles, (on the
   double paperbacks of series), by
   Bill Crider, 3-4 PQ 25
Ace Science Fiction Specials, (on the
   science fiction series, paperbacks)
   by J. Grant Thiessen, 5 SF 21

Ace Science Fiction Specials, a
   Checklist, (paperback book
   series), by William Trojan,
   5 SF 21
Acker, Frank C.: Gilbert Patte,
   The Man and the Magic, (dime
   novels, books, by Patten aka
   Burt L. Standish), 2-2 BC 162
Ackerman, Forrest J.: A Visit with
   Margaret Brundage, (WEIRD TALES
   cover artist), 3 WT 17
Ackerman, Forrest J.: Edmond Hamilton,
   Eulogy, 30 X 13
Ackerman, Forrest J.: letter of
   comment, 24 X 44
Ackerman, Forrest J.: Why I Collect
   Science Fiction, 20 X 5
(Ackerman, Forrest J.) A Visit to
   Two Museums, (Ackerman's science
   fiction collection, and San Fran-
   cisco Academy of Comic Art), by
   Albert Tonik, 10 SF 34
(Acre, Ethridge), Boys' Series Biblio-
   graphies, by Harry K. Hudson,
   1-4 YB 24
Ackroyd, Roger: letter of comment,
   9-4 TAD 296
Acrostic, (acrostic crossword puzzle),
   2-2 M 42
(Adams, Cleve F.), Checklist of works,
   by Francis M. Nevins, Jr. and
   William J. Clark, 8-3 TAD 200
(Adams, Cleve F.), The World of Cleve
   F. Adams, (mystery author), by
   Francis M. Nevins, Jr., 8-3 TAD 195
Adams, Gail: Double Jeopardy, Husband
   and Wife Teams in Detective Fiction,
   8-4 TAD 251
Adams, John: Mr. R. Austin Freeman, A
   Review of His Early Fiction, (1913),
   6 TF 34
Adams, William T.: see Oliver Optic
Addenda to "Chess in the Detective
   Story", by R.W.Hays, 7-3 TAD 203
Additions to a Bibliography of G.A.
   Henty and Hentyana, by Jared C.
   Lobdell, 1-4 BC 125
Addlestone, Alan: letter of comment,
   4-1 TAD 64
Adey, Robert C.S.: Checklist, The
   Modern Publishing Company publi-
   cations, 4-1 PP 4
Adey, Robert C.S.: Codes and Ciphers,
   (discussion), 2-6 MR 11
Adey, Robert C.S.: In Search of the
   "Con Man", (confidence men in
   mystery fiction), 2-4 TAD 259
Adey, Robert C.S.: letter of comment,
   1-3 MF 51; 2-3 MF 73; 2-4 MF 57;
   3-1 MF 49; 3-3 MF 60; 3-5 MF 45;
   4-3 MF 48; 5-1 MF 31; 5-4 MF 44;
   5-5 MF 47; 5-6 MF 53; 4-4 MR 14;

Adey, Robert C.S.: letter of comment,
(continued), 1-2 PP 29; 2-1 PP 31;
2-3 PP 40; 2-5 PP 42; 2-6 PP 42;
3-1 PP 47; 3-2 PP 33; 3-3 PP 37;
4-1 PP 48; 4-3 PP 35; 4-4 PP 39;
4-5/6 PP 97; 2-3 TAD 205; 2-4 TAD 279;
4-2 TAD 124; 5-3 TAD 167; 6-1 TAD 45;
6-1 TAD 48; 6-4 TAD 278; 7-4 TAD 300;
8-3 TAD 238; 10-2 TAD 161; 11-3 TAD 213;
11-2 TAD 186; 13-2 TAD 161; 13-3 TAD
239

Adey, Robert C.S.: The Modern Publishing
Company, (mystery publisher data),
4-1 PP 3

Adey, Robert C.S.: My Favorite Detectives,
(literary discussion),
Sir Henry Merrivale, (by John Dickson
Carr), with checklist, 3-2 MR 11
Mr. Verily, (by Peter Anthony),
4-3 MR 21
Sergeant Beef, (by Leo Bruce),
5-3 MR 20

Adey, Robert C.S.: Partial Checklist,
"miraculous crime" novels and short
stories, 5-3 TAD 168

Adey, Robert C.S.: Peter Godfrey - a
Reprise, 3-5 PP 9

Adey, Robert C.S.: Symbolic Motifs,
(mystery-identifying logos of
publishers, with illustrated
checklist), 3-4 MR 27

Adey, Robert C.S.: Two from the Telly,
(British television detective
series: Sapphire Steel, and The
Professionals), 5-6 MF 19

Adey, Robert C.S.: Unknown Authors,
Theodore George, 4-3 PP 19

Adey, Robert C.S.: West End Notes, (mystery
stage productions in London), 4-2 TAD
114

(Adey, Robert C.S.), Meet the Author,
Robert C.S.Adey, by Allen J. Hubin,
2-4 TAD 261

Adieu to the Avenger, (pulp hero character)
by Nick Carr, 11 X 123

Adkins, Mrs. Cynthia: letter of comment,
9-2 TAD 161

Adley, Derek J.: letter of comment,
5-5 MR 16

Adley, Derek J.: The Paul Temple Saga,
(Temple series by Francis Durbridge
on British radio), 9-4 TAD 267

Adley, Derek J. and W.O.G.Lofts: Was
"Jack Wylde" Really R. Austin
Freeman?, 7-4 TAD 247

Adolf Hitler and John Dickson Carr's
Least-Known Locked Room, by Douglas
G. Greene, 14-4 TAD 295

(Adrian, Chief-Inspector Christopher,
detective: Marguerite Silverman),
Pen Profile No.4, by Barry Pike,
2-4 PP 20

Adrian, Kelly: Dan J. Marlowe, Who
Said He Would and He Did, (on
Marlowe and his works), with
checklist, 3-3 MR 25

Adrian, Kelly: Mike Avallone, a Partial
Checklist, 1-5 MR 5

Adrian, Kelly: Mike Avallone, One of
the Un-Angry Young Men, (sketch and
comments), 1-5 MR 3

(ADVENTURE), The People Were Real
Then, (on fictional characters in
the pulp magazine), by John
Phillifent, 67 PU 25

Adventure of the Elusive Vanardy, The,
(Sherlockian fiction), by Mary Ann
Grochowski, 1-1 PP 7

(ADVENTURE OF THE HOLMES-DRACULA FILE:
Fred Saberhagen), Mystery Plus,
(discussion), by R. Jeff Banks,
2-4 PP 16

Adventure of the House With the Baboons,
The, (fiction, Classic Corner, rare
tales), by Bertram Atkey, 13-2 TAD
125

Adventure of the Pastiche Craftsman, The,
(August Derleth and his Solar Pons
pastiches of Sherlock Holmes), by
A.E.Van Vogt, 2-1 PD 1

Adventure of the Purloined Red Herring,
The, (on THE PROFESSOR KNITS A
SHROUD, by Martha Wirt Davis), by
Edward Lauterbach, 3-5 PP 3

Adventures in Noonland, (verse), (re:
Mike Avallone's Ed Noon), 2-2 MR
14

Adventures in the Mail, (boys' book
collecting experiences), by Jack R.
Schorr, 2-2 BC 192

Adventures: of Arthur Conan Doyle, The,
by Felix Arnstein, 3-3 TAD 166

Adventures of Chubblock Homes, The,
(comic strip parodies of Sherlock
Holmes), by W.O.G.Lofts, 8-3 TAD 193

Adventures of Nick Carter, The,
(review of television show), by
J. Randolph Cox, 5-2 MR 35

Advice Unheeded: Shakespeare in Some
Modern Mystery Novels, (Shakespeare
associations in mystery novels), by
Jane S. Bakerman, 14-2 TAD 134

Affair of the Purloined Plot, The, in
Rare Books are Getting Scarce, by
Bruce Taylor, 1-3 CP 18

Agatha Christie, (verse), by Jean
Balderston, 12-3 TAD 210

Agatha Christie in the Dell Mapbacks,
(Dell Publishing Company's map-
back series; Christie mystery
novels; paperbacks), by Bill Lyles,
3-3 PQ 26

Agatha Christie is Still Alive and Well,
(comments), by Amnon Kabatchnik,
2-6 MF 9

Agatha Christie;s Alter Ego: Ariadne
Oliver, by Sylvia W. Patterson,
14-3 TAD 222

Agatha Christie's Other Detectives,
Parker Pyne and Harley Quin, by
Earl F. Bargainnier, 11-2 TAD 110

Agatha Christie's Portrait of the Artist,
(self-revelation), by Margaret Boe
Birns, 1-2 C 31

(AGE OF THE UNICORN), First Annual
Index, by Dana Martin Batory,
7 U 32

(Agent G-X, pulp character), The Phantom
Fed, by Tom Johnson, 10 P 5

Agent Nine: A "G" Man Series, (boys'
books series), by Robert L. George,
1-3 YB 3

(Agent "X"), The Leopard Lady, (pulp
magazine villain in stories of
G.T.Fleming-Roberts), by Tom
Johnson, 8 DS 16

"Aging" of Travis McGee, The, (comments
on character created by John D.
MacDonald), by John D. MacDonald,
20 JD 3

(Aiken, Joan), Checklist, by Audrey I.
Pacheco, 5-4 MR 25

(aircraft), "The Blue Max", (observations
on the World War I aircraft used in
the film), by Dave Prosser, 66 PU 5

Aird, Catherine: Checklist, Josephine
Tey works, 2-3 TAD 157

Aird, Catherine: Josephine Tey, (biog.
and literary sketch), 2-3 TAD 156

Aird, Catherine: letter of comment,
3-2 TAD 134

(Aird, Catherine), An Interview with
Catherine Aird), by Lianne Carlin,
4-2 MR 29

(Aird, Catherine), Checklist of works,
by Jim McCahery, 1-2 PP 22

(Aird, Catherine), Meet the Author:
Catherine Aird, by Allen J. Hubin,
2-3 TAD 157

Alan, G.: Notes of a Pulp Collector,
(Gracie Culver detective stories
in THE SHADOW magazine), 15 BS 14

Alan, G.: The Pulp Hero Quiz, (quiz),
11 BS 13

Alan, G.: Pulp Quiz, (quiz), 14 BS 12;
15 BS 18

(Alaska - regional mysteries), The
American Regional Mystery, Pt. XI,
by Marvin Lachman, 9-1 TAD 11

Albert, John: letter of comment,
4 DS 4; 13 X 60

Albert, Walter: A Bibliography of
Secondary Sources, (mystery and
related reference), for:
1972, 7-1 TAD 46

Albert, Walter: A Bibliography of
Secondary Sources, (continued)
1973, 7-4 TAD 266
1974, 8-4 TAD 290
1975, 9-4 TAD 316
1976, 11-2 TAD 196
1977, 12-2 TAD 125
1978, 13-1 TAD 43
1979, 13-4 TAD 313
1980, 14-4 TAD 346

Albert, Walter: letter of comment,
6/7 LR 26; 7 MA 23; 1-1 MF 42;
2-2 MF 54; 2-3 MF 64; 4-1 MF 40;
5-4 MF 43; 6-1 MR 22; 2-4 PP 42;
3-1 PP 43; 4-1 PP 51; 4-5/6 PP 82;
5-4 TAD 239; 6-2 TAD 131; 7-1 TAD
73; 10-4 TAD 386; 13-1 TAD 76;
15 X 13; 24 X 45

Albert, Walter: The Line-Up, (listing
of mystery fan magazines), 4-5 MF 9

Albert, Walter: Murder by Mail, A
Dealer Checklist, (mystery book
dealers), 3-5 MF 7

Albert, Walter: The Skene Melvin
Bibliography of Critical Writing,
(article review of David and Ann
Skene Melvin's CRIME, DETECTIVE,
ESPIONAGE, MYSTERY AND THRILLER
FICTION AND FILM), 5-3 MF 5

Albright, Donn: letter of comment,
5 MA 27

Albright, Donn: Ray Bradbury, An
Index, 13 X 9; 36 X R2

Albright, Donn: The Trip, (Ray Bradbury and William F. Nolan),
36 X R13

Albright, Donn: Why I Collect Science
Fiction, 20 X 6

Aldag, Kurt: letter of comment, 25 JD
37

Aldrich, Pearl G.: Nigel Morland,
Fifty Years of Crime Writing,
13-3 TAD 194

(Aldridge, Howard F.), Department of
Unknown Mystery Writers, (biog.
sketch), by Marvin Lachman,
1-4 PP 15

(Alexander, David), Checklist of works,
by Jim McCahery, 1-6 PP 23

Alexander, Jerry: An Index to COMET
MAGAZINE, 8 U 139

Alexander, Jerry: letter of comment,
13 X 60; 22 X 49; 36 X 73; 43 X 6

(Alexander, Karl: TIME AFTER TIME),
Mystery Plus: A Contemporary Science
Fiction Pair, by R. Jeff Banks,
3-1 PP 16

Alexandersson, Jan, and Iwan Hedman:
Leslie Charteris and The Saint, Five
Decades of Partnership, 4-4 MF 21

Alfred Hitchcock: Dell Paperbacks, by
Billy C. Lee and Charlotte Laughlin,
3-1 PQ 23

Alfred Hitchcock on Television, (survey study), by David Steier, 2-3 M 30

Alfred Hitchcock Theater at Universal Studios, The, 2-3 M 38

(ALFRED HITCHCOCK'S MYSTERY MAGAZINE), Profile: Alfred Hitchcock's Mystery Magazine, by Paul Taublieb, 2-3 M 34

Alfred Hitchcock's TV Shows: A Footnote on Scripters and Literary Sources, by Jack Edmund Nolan, 3-4 MR 17

(Alger, Horatio, Jr.), Digging for Gold, Call About Alger, (crossword puzzle) by Herb L. Risteen, 2-3 BC 222

(Alger, Horatio, Jr.), Favorite Juvenile Authors: What Publishers Said About Their Old Stand-bys, by Gil O'Gara, 1-2 YB 19

(Alger, Horatio, Jr.), Horatio Alger, or, The Man Behind the Great American Dream, by Jack Bales, 2-4 BC 226

(Alger, Horatio, Jr.), The Horatio Alger Paperback First Editions, by Frank Gruber, 2-4 BC 242

(Alger, Horatio, Jr.), Horatio Alger,Jr. and the Horatio Alger Society, by Jack Bales, 1-3 TBN 6

Alias Big Bad John, (Doc Savage association article), by Dafyd Neal Dyar, 6 U 13

Alibis, (verse), by Louis Phillips, 12-1 TAD 63

Alistair MacLean, A Bibliography and a Biography, by Iwan Hedman, 4-5 MR 29

Alive and Doing Well in New York City, (fiction, Doc Savage theme), by John Cosgriff, 1 DR 5

(ALL-ACES), Checklist, pulp magazine, by Lynn Hickman, 75 PU 7

All About Henty, (crossword puzzle), by Herb L. Risteen, 3-1 BC 277

(ALL DETECTIVE MAGAZINE), The Birth of (Dr.) Death, (villain analysis), by Dick Myers, 6 BS 5

All Good Mysteries Are Short Stories: A Polemic, (advantages of short story form), by James Mark Purcell, 4-6 MR 23

All in One World, (legendary facts), by Bill Laidlaw, 7 DQ 9

All the Short Cases of Inspector Maigret, (stories by Georges Simenon), by Gary L. Gannett, 10-4 TAD 347

All Too True, (books suggested by true crimes), by Mary Groff, 1-1 PP 3; 1-2 PP 15; 1-3 PP 16; 1-4 PP 17; 1-5 PP 13; 1-6 PP 14; 2-1 PP 23; 2-2 PP 20; 2-3 PP 15; 2-4 PP 21; 2-5 PP 19; 2-6 PP 19; 3-1 PP 29; 3-2 PP 19; 3-3 PP 22; 3-4 PP 25; 3-5 PP 21; 3-6 PP 21; 4-1 PP 24; 4-2 PP 15; 4-3 PP 15; 4-4 PP 21; (films based on true crimes), 4-5/6 PP 59

All You Need is a Comfortable Chair, or Did You Hear the One About the Two Tadpoles? (results of "TAD" polls for "best" in several mystery categories), by Jon L. Breen, 6-2 TAD 78

(Allen, Grant: AN AFRICAN MILLIONAIRE), Rogues for the New Century, by Fred Dueren, 5-3 MF 11

Allen, Joseph: Behind the Eight Ball, (fiction), 1-1 M 40

Allen, Joseph: Inside Gumshoe Haven, A Look at LA's Bradbury Building, 1-2 M 27

Allen, Paul C.: FORGOTTEN FANTASY magazine, with checklist and index, 5 SF 23

Allen, Paul C.: letter of comment, 1-4 AD 8; 6 BB 30; 1-3 PQ 6; 4 SF 46

(Alleyn, Roderick, detective series: Ngaio Marsh), The First Appearance, Roderick Alleyn (A MAN LAY DEAD), by Maryell Cleary, 2-6 PP 12

(Alleyn, Roderick, detective series: Ngaio Marsh), Roderick Alleyn, Ngaio Marsh's Oxonian Superintendent, by Earl F. Bargainnier, 11-1 TAD 63

(Allingham, Margery), Bibliography of works, by Barry A. Pike, 6-3 TAD 198

(Allingham, Margery), Checklist of works, by Mrs. Kathy Hoble, 1-3 MR 13

(Allingham, Margery), Checklist addns., 1-4 MR 10

(Allingham, Margery), Margery Allingham's Albert Campion: A Chronological Examination of the Novels in Which He Appears, by B.A. Pike, 9-1 TAD 1; 9-2 TAD 95; 10-1 TAD 25; 10-2 TAD 117; 10-3 TAD 245; 10-4 TAD 324; 11-1 TAD 34; 11-2 TAD 177; 11-3 TAD 279; 11-4 TAD 372; 12-1 TAD 34; 12-2 TAD 168; 12-4 TAD 348

Allison, Bob: Letters to McGee, (Travis McGee, character created by John D. MacDonald), 25 JD 5

(Allison, Hughes), Department of Unknown Mystery Writers, by Marvin Lachman, 1-4 PP 15

(Allison, Hughes), Hughes Allison Revisited, by Marvin Lachman, 4-1 PP 18

(Almquist, C.J.L.), Innocence and Arsenic: The Literary and Criminal Careers of C.J.L.Almquist, by Albert I. Borowitz, 9-1 TAD 17

Almuric, or "Edgar Rice Burroughs Visits the Hyborian Age", (on Robert E. Howards works), by Michael T. Smith, 1-2 PQ 48

Altus, Sidney: letter of comment, 26 X 77

(Alverson, Charles: Joe Goodey series),
The Trenchcoat Files: Meet Joe
Goodey/San Francisco Will Never Be
the Same, by Paul Bishop, 6 PE 31

"Amanda Cross" Case, The: Sociologizing
the U.S.Academic Mystery, by J.M.
Purcell, 13-1 TAD 36

Amateurs' Hour, The, (amateur detectives
in mystery fiction), by Frank D.
McSherry, Jr., 3-1 TAD 14

Amateur Press, The, (mystery publications),
by Don Miller, 1 MN 2; 4/6 MN 9;
8 MN 43

(AMAZING WEB, THE: Harry Stephen Keeler),
The Worst Legal Mystery in the World,
by Francis M. Nevins, Jr., 1-3 TAD 82

(Ambler, Eric), The Films and TV Work of
Eric Ambler, by Jack Edmund Nolan,
3-1 MR 13

(Ambler, Eric), The Works of Eric Ambler,
by George J. Rausch, 2-4 TAD 260

Ambulating Lady, The, (how to write for
the pulp magazines), by Carroll John
Daly, 2-2 C 113

Amelia Reynolds Long, (WEIRD TALES author),
by Chet Williamson, 2 WT 7

America, Ou est-vous? Speculations on
Exbrayat, (Charles Hubert Exbrayat-
Durivaux, by Margery Evernden,
11-3 TAD 254

"American Boy" Reviews, (boys' books book
reviews), by C. L. Messecar, 3-2 BC 318;
3-3 BC 351; 3-4 BC 371

(American current crime), Current Crime -
The American Crime Scene, by Rona
Randall, 5-2 MR 33

American Detective series, The, (early
paperback mystery novels), by Howard
Waterhouse, 2-3 PQ 32

American Paperback Cover Art Exhibition,
3-3 PQ 53

American Regional Mystery, The, (survey
and discussion of mystery fiction in
specific locales), by Marvin Lachman,
Pt.1, New England, 3-3 MR 13, with
addenda, 3-4 MR 22
Pt.2, New York City, 3-2 MR 23
Pt.3, New York City, 4-1 MR 8
Pt.4, New York State, 4-3 MR 3
Pt.5, New Jersey and Pennsylvania,
4-5 MR 2
Pt.6, Washington, D.C. and Maryland,
5-1 MR 3
Pt.7, The South, 5-3 MR 1
Pt.8, Florida, 5-5 MR 1
Pt.9, The Middle West, 6-1 MR 1
Pt.10,The Southwest, 6-2 MR 23
Pt.11,The Mountain States, Pacific
Northwest, and Alaska, 9-1 TAD 11
Pt.12,Hawaii and Northern California,
9-4 TAD 260
Pt.13,Southern California, 10-4 TAD 294

American Sherlock Holmes, The: A
Study in Scarlet Impersonation,
(Holmes & Watson protesting
Craig Kennedy and Walter Jameson's
reputation as the "American
Sherlock Holmes", by Marvin
Lachman, 3-2 MR 2

Among the Book Stalls, (boys' book
collecting), by Jack R. Schorr,
3-3 BC 330

(Among the Sioux), Boy's Series
Bibliographies, by Harry K. Hudson,
1-3 YB 8

Amoury, Gloria: Robert Fish, In Memorium,
(memorial tribute), 14-2 TAD 119

(Amoury, Gloria), The Double Life of
Gloria Amoury, (interview), by Pat
Erhardt, 3-5 MR 3

(AN AFRICAN MILLIONAIRE: Grant Allen),
Rogues for the New Century, by
Fred Dueren, 5-3 MF 11

An Aid to Historical Fiction - Boys'
Books, by Walter H. McIntosh,
3-3 BC 326

An Alphabetical Checklist of the
Science-Fiction Stories of John
D. MacDonald, by Jean and Walter
Shine, 28 JD 25

An Appreciation of Archie Goodwin,
(character creation of Rex Stout),
by Arden Knight, 12-4 TAD 328

An Editor's Outline, (re: Ellery
Queen), by Robert E. Washer,
1-3 QC 23

An Eleventh-Hour Reassessment of
THE ELEVENTH JUROR: Revealing the
Germination of a Successful Mystery
Tale, by Vincent Starrett,
2-2 PDA 48

An Evening With John D. MacDonald, by
George R. Berryman, 22 JD 4

An Exhumation of THE TOMB OF TS'IN
(written by Edgar Wallace), by John
A. Hogan, 6-3 TAD 167

An Explanation of Sorts, or Why Your
Universe Really Will Not Come to
An End (re: Price Guides), by Mike
Resnick, 26 X 14

An Index to OTHER TIMES magazine,
(science fiction), by Darrell
Schweitzer, 8 U 146

An Index to PLANET STORIES magazine,
(science fiction), by Robert
O'Malley, 20 X 42; 21 X 55; 22 X 48

An Informal Survey of the Works of
Sax Rohmer, by Robert E. Briney,
1 R 3

An Inquiry Into Circular Heels, (such
footprints in the Dr.Thorndyke
story of R. Austin Freeman), by
Howard Brody, 12 TF 8

An Inside Look at Captain Future, (pulp hero character), by Edmond Hamilton, 3 P 3

An Interesting Book, This Lavender Look, (review in verse of John D. MacDonald's THE LONG LAVENDER LOOK), by Dave Stewart 15 JD 17

An Interview With a Black Sheep of Amsterdam: Janwillem van de Wetering, by Chris & Janie Filstrup, 13-2 TAD 98

An Interview With A.E.Van Vogt, by J. Grant Thiessen, 8 SF 4

An Interview with Abe Goodman, (Red Circle Magazines, pulps, publisher), by Robert Weinberg, 10 P 2

An Interview with Bill Pronzini, by Robert J. Randisi, 11-1 TAD 46

An Interview with Catherine Aird, by Lianne Carlin, 4-2 MR 29

An Interview with E. Richard Johnson, 2-6 MR 12

An Interview with Elizabeth Linington, by Margaret J. King, 13-4 TAD 299

An Interview with Gregory Mcdonald, by Robert Randisi, 12-2 TAD 134

An Interview with Howard Haycraft, 5-1 MR 11

An Interview with Jay Bennett, by Paul B. Janeczko, 10-4 TAD 342

An Interview with John Lutz, by Mary Ann Grochowski, 12-3 TAD 276

An Interview with Leslie Ford, by Ann Waldron, 4-1 TAD 33

An Interview with Marc Olden, by Robert J. Randisi, 12-4 TAD 324

An Interview with Mary Elizabeth Counselman, by Stephen Gresham, 6 WT 11

An Interview with Max Collins, by Robert J. Randisi, 11-3 TAD 300

An Interview with Peter Lovesey, by Diana Cooper-Clark, 14-3 TAD 210

An Interview with Philip Jose Farmer, by Philip A. Shreffler, 42 X 7

An Interview with Richard Lockridge, by Chris & Janie Filstrup, 11-4 TAD 382

An Interview with Robert Bloch, by Darrell Schweitzer, 1 FM 9

An Interview with Robert Ludlum, by Stephen L. Smoke, 1-3 M 8

An Interview with Stephen J. Cannell, by Hamilton T. Caine, 2-1 M 6

An Interview with Stephen King, by Joyce Lynch Dewes, 2-2 M 6

An Interview with Stuart Kaminsky, by Robert J. Randisi, 13-4 TAD 338

An Interview with Ursula Curtiss, by Ann Waldron, 4-3 TAD 140

An Irregular History, (on the Baker Street Irregulars; Sherlockiana), by Sean M. Wright, 2-2 M 24

An Old Friend - The Detective Book Club, (history of club), by Michael L. Cook, 8-2 TAD 77

(AN OLD FRIEND OF THE FAMILY: Fred Saberhagen), Mystery Plus: Old Friends Break New Ground, by R. Jeff Banks, 3-6 PP 15

An Open-Ended Search for Dead Ends, (Inspector Rason and the Department of Dead Ends stories by Roy Vickers), by Howard Waterhouse, 1-3 PP 7

An Overlooked Boys Series Best Seller, (books by Zane Grey), by Rick Crandall, 1-2 YB 14

An Unknown Mystery Writer Revisited: Mildred Davis, by Marvin Lachman, 3-5 PP 12

An Unpublished Ernest Bramah Letter on Max Carrados, by William White, 3-2 TAD 92

An Unsolved Mystery, (on CLUTCH OF CONSTABLES by Ngaio Marsh), by J.R.Christopher, 3-2 TAD 93

Anaclete, Sister M.: The Derleth/ Sister Anaclete Letters, (correspondence with August Derleth), 2-2 AD 5; 2-3/4 AD 3

Anaclete, Sister M.: Let There Be Music, (verse), 2-2 AD 7

Anaclete, Sister M.: letter of comment, 2-1 AD 9

Anagallery, (verse), by Walter Shedlofsky, 6 WT 22

Anatomy of a Spy Novel, The: Gerard de Villiers and the Modern French *Roman D'Espionnage*, (on spy fiction of deVilliers), by Lance K. Donaldson-Evans, 2-2 C 28

Anatomy of "Romance", The, (as an ingredient in the fiction of John D. MacDonald), by Stan Woolston, 18 JD 13

(Anchor Books), Mass Market Murmurings, (paperbacks), by Barry Bernard, 1-3 CP 5

And a New Land Shall Emerge, (verse), by Wayne Thornton, 8 U 140

...And Great Virtue in a Really Good Feed, (hospitality for Thorndyke in the R. Austin Freeman stories), by Michael G. Heenan, 10 TF 9

Anderson, David R.: "As Far as I'm Concerned, You're Out of It": Wolfe and Archie Apart, (Nero Wolfe commentary), 1-2 G 28

Anderson, David R.: Creative Order in Rex Stout, 9 MN A1

Anderson, David R.: Crime and Character: Notes on Rex Stout's Early Fiction, 13-2 TAD 169

(Anderson, J.R.L.: Peter Blair series), Checklist, by Barry Van Tilburg, 4-2 MF 11

Anderson, Karen: letter of comment, 10 JD 8

Anderson, Poul: letter of comment,
7 JD 3; 14 JD 21; 16 JD 16

(Anderson, Poul), Ten Books, Poul
Anderson and the Best, (comments
on "Best" anthologies), by George
Kelley, 1-3 PQ 33

Anderson, Virginia Combs ("Nanek"):
Dwellers in the Mirage, (verse),
40 X 121

Anderson, Virginia Combs, with William
Papalia: A Remembrance of Early
Pulp Collecting and Fandom 1938-43,
40 X 3

(Anderson, Virginia Combs), Nanek
Today, 40 X 118

(Anderson, Virginia Combs), various
letters to and from pulp authors
and publishers, see 40 X (var.pages)

Andre, Richard: letter of comment,
24 JD 40

Andrews, Al: letter of comment, 65 PU 22

Andrews, Peter: The Subject Is: Detective
Stories, 6/7 LR 29

Andrews, Andrew: letter of comment,
3 U 49

Andrews, Angela: Modern Age Books and
the John Esteven Mystery (identity
of Esteven), 4-2 PQ 29

Andriacco, Dan: Series Synopses, the
Father Dowling series by Ralph
McInery, 12-2 TAD 133

Andy Blake First Leo Edwards Book,
(boys' book series), by Julius R.
Chenu, 1-1 TB 1

Angela, A Chat with Angela Lansbury,
Star of Stage, Screen and Television,
by Pete Christian, 3-1 M 32

(Annesley, Michael: Lawrie Fenton
series), Spy Series Characters
in Hardback, Pt. IX, by Barry Van
Tilburg, 5-5 MF 15

Annotating the Holmes Saga, (Sherlockiana)
by Edward Lauterbach, 7-2 TAD 119

Annual MWA "Edgars" Awarded, (Mystery
Writers of America, Award Dinner,
report), 10-3 TAD 240

(anonyma: EXPERIENCES OF A LADY
DETECTIVE), Female Detectives, Ghost
Books and the Relative Importance of
it All, by E.F.Bleiler, 8-3 TAD 202

(anon.) Ask Mr. Mystery: Writing for
ELLERY QUEEN'S MYSTERY MAGAZINE,
27 JD 12

(anon.: THE SMILING CORPSE), The Smiling
Corpse Revisited, by J. Randolph Cox,
3-3 TAD 170

Another Chapter from DEATH OF A .300
HITTER, by Mike Avallone, 1-1 MF 3;
1-2 MF 11

Another Peacock Cry: Heraldic Birds in
Five Lew Archer Novels (by Ross
Macdonald), by Charles Fishman,
2-1 C 106

Another Side of Harry Stephen Keeler,
(with letters from Keeler), by
Jack Cuthbert, 7-2 TAD 101

Another Watson: Captain Hastings
(Capt. Arthur Hastings, character
created by Agatha Christie), by
Earl F. Bargainnier, 13-4 TAD 354

Ante-Bellem Days: or, "My Roscoe
Sneezed Ka-chee!" (influence of
Robert Leslie Bellem on detective
pulp fiction), by Bill Pronzini,
2-2 C 41

Anthology Index, (index to var. mystery
anthologies), by Don Miller,
2-4 MM Q1

Anthony Boucher, (biog. sketch and
checklist), by Francis M. Nevins,
Jr., 3-2 M 18

Antonelli, George A., and Rob Whaley:
Healing Under the Bare Bulb, The
Detective as Therapist, (methodology
in modus operandi), 2-2 C 1

(Antony, Peter: Mr. Verily, detective)
My Favorite Detectives, by Robert
C.S. Adey, 4-3 MR 21

Apartheid in the Novels of James McClure,
by Donald C. Wall, 10-4 TAD 348

Aphrodisia, Here is Your Hat, (sex in
paperback art), by Tamsen Stocking,
3-4 PQ 28

Apocryphalization of Holmes, The,
(article review of SHERLOCK HOLMES:
THE PUBLISHED APOCRYPHA, ed. by Jack
Tracy), by E.F.Bleiler, 4-5 MF 3

Apostle Apostle, (verse), by Helen
Halbach, 7 X 68

Apostolou, John L.: Japanese Mystery
Fiction in English Translation, with
checklist, 13-4 TAD 310

Apostolou, John L.: letter of comment,
12-1 TAD 92; 14-4 TAD 383

Appelbaum, Alan: letter of comment,
6 JD 12; 7 JD 4

(Appleton, Victor), "Bless You, Tom
Swift", (Tom Swift boys' series
books), by Andrew E. Svenson,
2-1 BC 130

(Appleton, Victor), Boys' Book Oddities,
No.1, Tom Swift, by Harry K. Hudson,
1-2 BC 43

(Appleton, Victor), Checklist, The Don
Sturdy Series, (boys' books), by
Robert Jennings, 1 BB 11

(Appleton, Victor), Checklist, Tom Swift
Series, (boys' books), by John Dizer,
Jr., 2-1 TBN 5

(Appleton, Victor), Don Sturdy and the
Great Search for Adventure, (discusses
Don Sturdy series boys' books), by
Robert Jennings, 1 BB 5

(Appleton, Victor), Shopton, Home of the
Swifts, (locale of the Tom Swift
series), by John T. Dizer, Jr.,
1-3 TBN 11; 1-4 TBN 8

(Appleton, Victor), Tom Loved Mary...
Remember That?, (Tom Swift boys'
series books), by Robert Louis,
4-1 BC 402

(Appleton, Victor), Tom Swift and the
Great Nostalgia, by Col. Paul Deems,
4-1 BC 386

(Aquin, Hubert), BLACKOUT: Hubert
Aquin's Surreal Mystery, by Russell
M. Brown, 13-1 TAD 58

Arabian Nights and Art Nouveau,
(discussion of Edmund Dulac, author)
by Rebecca Bruns, 6 YB 23

Archambault, Jim: letter of comment,
15 X 14

Archer in Hollywood: The "Barbarous
Coast" of Ross Macdonald, (Lew
Archer and locale), by David J.
Geherin, 9-1 TAD 55

(Archer, Lew, detective: Ross Macdonald)
Another Peacock Cry: Heraldic Birds
in Five Lew Archer Novels, by Charles
Fishman, 2-1 C 106

(Archer, Lew, detective: Ross Macdonald)
Archer in Hollywood: The "Barbarous
Coast" of Ross Macdonald, by David
J. Geherin, 9-1 TAD 55

(Archer, Lew, detective: Ross Macdonald)
The Detective as Both Tortoise and
Achilles: Archer Gets the Feel of the
Case in THE CHILL, by William W.
Combs, 2-1 C 98

(Archer, Lew, detective: Ross Macdonald)
Lew Archer's "Moral Landscape" by
Elmer R. Pry, Jr., 8-1 TAD 104

Archer, Marlowe: Eye Appeal, (reviews),
4 PE 24; 5 PE 16

Archibald, Joe: Meet the Author, (by
Joe Archibald), 10 P 10

"Archie O'Neill" - Jim Henaghan, The
Jeff Pride Series, by Bill Crider,
4 PE 15

(Ard, William Thomas), Tracking Tom
Buchanan, by Bernard A. Drew, 8 U 135

Are the Characters of Juvenile Fiction
Real?, by Harry Castlemon, 4-1 BC 405

Area Map of Tutter, People, Places,
(locale of Jerry Todd boy's series
books by Leo Edwards), by Robert
L. Johnson, 2-3 TBN 1

ARGOSY Index Commencing 1930, by John
C. Nitka, 63 PU 44; 64 PU 34

Aristotle's Operative, or, The Case of
the Classic Barzun, (rational premise
in detective fiction), by Newton
Baird, 8-1 TAD 15

(Ark, Simon, detective: Edward D. Hoch),
A Simon Ark Bibliography, by
Edward D. Hoch, 3-4 TAD 248

(Ark, Simon, detective: Edward D. Hoch),
Simon Ark Stories Published by
Leisure Books, 5-3 MR 14

Arkham House and Its Eldritch English
Visitants, by Malcolm M. Ferguson,
3-1 AD 1

(Arkham House), A Non-definitive
Price Guide to Out-of-Print Arkham
House Titles, by W.K.Schoonmaker,
18 X 21

(Arkham House), Ronald Clyne, A
Portrait, by Victor Dricks, 18 X 20

(Arkham House), The Derleth Difference
(Derleth responsible for success
of Arkham House), by Steve Eng,
4-4 AD 12

(Arkham House), Supplement to THIRTY
YEARS OF ARKHAM HOUSE, (titles
published 1970 to June 1981), by
Gunter E. Swain, 5-1 AD 9

(Arkham House), The Wood Engraver
From Mazomanie, (biog. sketch of
Frank Utpatel, illustrator), by
Kay Price, 4-3 AD 1

Armato, Douglas M.: Charlie Chan in
Books and in Motion Pictures,
7-2 TAD 97

Armato, Douglas M.: letter of comment,
7-4 TAD 299

Armbruster, J.H.: The Good, the Bad,
and the Pipe, (on pipe-smoking
sleuths), 5-2 MR 29

Armchair Criminal, The, (villainy by
mastermind criminals), by Frank
D. McSherry, Jr., 14-1 TAD 58

ARMCHAIR DETECTIVE, THE, The Past,
Present and Hopeful Future of
This Journal, by Allen J. Hubin
(as editor), 1-1 TAD 28

(ARMCHAIR DETECTIVE, THE), All You
Need is a Comfortable Chair, or
Did You Hear the One About the
Two Tadpolls?, (results of "TAD"
polls for "best" in several mystery
categories), by Jon L. Breen,
6-2 TAD 78

(ARMCHAIR DETECTIVE, THE), Index to
Vols. 1 & 2, 2-4 TAD 281

(ARMCHAIR DETECTIVE, THE), Index to
Vols. 3 & 4, 4-4 TAD 259

(ARMCHAIR DETECTIVE, THE), Index to
Vols. 5 & 6, 6-4 TAD 281

(ARMCHAIR DETECTIVE, THE), Index to
Vols. 7 & 8, 8-4 TAD 326

(ARMCHAIR DETECTIVE, THE), TAD: THe
First Decade, (David Hellyer
interview with Allen J. Hubin,
editor), 10-2 TAD 142

(Armed Services Editions), Collecting
Armed Services Editions (paperbacks), by Charlotte Laughlin,
1-2 PQ 31

Armstrong, Charlotte: letter of
comment, 1-3 QC 21

(Armstrong, Charlotte), Checklist, by Audrey I. Pacheco, 5-4 MR 24

(Armstrong, Charlotte), Checklist, by Francis M. Nevins, Jr., 5-5 MR 18

(Armstrong, Charlotte), Three Ladies of the Quasi-Gothic: The Films of Armstrong, Lofts, and White, by Jack Edmund Nolan, 5-2 MR 23

(Armstrong, Charlotte: LAY ON, MACDUFF!) The First Appearance, MacDougall Duff, by Maryell Cleary, 3-1 PP 27

Army Boys, The, (boys' book series discussed), by Robert Jennings, 2 BB 4

Arnold, Armin: Zadig as a Jew, An Early German Tale of Detection by Wilhelm Hauff, 13-2 TAD 173

Arnold Bennett - As a Writer of Crime Fiction, by N.C.Ravenscroft, 10-2 TAD 182

Arnoldsmith, Anson: "Boy Swindlers Series by Dexter Itty" (satire on boys' book series), 1-4 YB 20

Arnott, Ian: *La Filza Di Thorndyke*, (foreign translations of the Dr. Thorndyke stories by R. Austin Freeman), 3 TF 28

Arnstein, Felix: The "Adventures" of Arthur Conan Doyle, 3-3 TAD 166

Arrington, Bob: letter of comment, 28 X 79

"Art in the Blood..." (Sherlockiana), by Peter E. Blau, 2-2 PDA 68

Art of the Detective Story, The, (claims rarity of good detective fiction), by R. Austin Freeman, 10 TF 12

Art Work of the Leo Edwards' Books, (dust jackets discussed), by Julius R. Chenu, 1-2 TBN 1

(art), Art portfolio, "Air War 1914-18" by Dave Prosser, 66 PU 16; 67 PU 83

(art), Art portfolio based on "Flight to Yesterday"(by Poul Anderson), by Jim Cawthorn, 64 PU 18

(art), Portfolio, fantasy, by George Barr, 63 PU 17

(art), Portfolio, science-fiction, by Eddie Jones, 60 PU 18

Arthur B. Reeve and the American Sherlock Holmes, (detective: Prof. Craig Kennedy), by John Harwood, 10-4 TAD 354

Arthur William Upfield 1888-1964, (biog. sketch), by Estelle Fox, 3-2 TAD 89

Arthur W. Upfield, A Checklist, by Estelle Fox, Francis M. Nevins,Jr. and Charles Shibuk, 3-2 TAD 90

Arthur William Upfield, September 1, 1888 - February 13, 1964, (biog. sketch), by Betty Donaldson, 8-1 TAD 1

Article I Couldn't Publish, The, (Ian Fleming and J.D.Salinger's "The Laughing Man"), by Guy M. Townsend, 1-1 MF 18

Articles and Books on Paperbacks, (general discussion), by Lance C. Casebeer, 3-5 CP 3

Artist Behind Doc Savage, (sketch of Walter Baumhofer), by Frank Hamilton, 9 DS 6

"As Far As I'm Concerned, You're Out of It": Wolfe and Archie Apart, (Nero Wolfe, Archie Goodwin), by David R. Anderson, 1-2 G 28

Asdell, Philip T.: A Thorndyke Examination, (quiz, Dr. Thorndyke oriented), 1 TF 32

Asdell, Philip T.: Australian Words and Expressions in Upfield's Novels (Arthur W. Upfield, with Inspector Bonaparte as detective), 1 BY 5

Asdell, Philip T.: Bony Was There, (locales of stories, Inspector Bonaparte's investigations in Arthur W. Upfield's mystery novels) 1 BY 2

Asdell, Philip T.: CLERIHEWS COMPLETE (by E.C.Bentley), a Rambling Book Review, 1-3 PP 21

Asdell, Philip T.: Freeman Books in Print 1976, (R. Austin Freeman), 1 TF 50

Asdell, Philip T.: The Great Melbourne Cup Mystery, (on FOLLOW MY DUST by Arthur W. Upfield), 1 BY 3

Asdell, Philip T.: In Search of a Hansom Cab, (on THE MYSTERY OF A HANSOM CAB by Fergus Hume), 1-2 PP 10

Asdell, Philip T.: John Evelyn Who? (possible origin of Thorndyke's names), 7 TF 35

Asdell, Philip T.: John W. Vandercook and His Tropical Murders, 3-2 PP 3

Asdell, Philip T.: letter of comment, 4-1 MF 40; 2-1 PP 45; 9-1 TAD 82

Asdell, Philip T.: THE PRESIDENT'S MYSTERY STORY, a review, 2-4 PP 11

Asdell, Philip T.: The Whodunit's Who's Who, (on Jessia Hawke's FOLLOW MY DUST, Ngaio Marsh's BLACK BEECH AND HONEYDEW, 3-4 PP 11

Asdell, Philip T., and John H. Dirckx: Nathaniel Polton, Artificer Extraordinary, (character in Dr. Thorndyke stories by Freeman), 6 TF 25

Asey Mayo - Cape Cod Sleuth, by Lance Casebeer and Bruce Taylor, 3-1 CP 20

Asey Mayo: "The Hayseed Sherlock" (character detective of Phoebe Atwood Taylor), by Fred Dueren, 10-1 TAD 21

(Ashe, Gordon), Crime Haters Series,
Checklist, (pseud. of John Creasey),
by R.E.Briney and John Creasey,
2-1 TAD 12
(Ashe, Gordon), Patrick Dawlish Series,
Checklist, (pseud. of John Creasey),
by R.E.Briney and John Creasey,
2-1 TAD 11
Ashforth, Albert: letter of comment,
9 JD 6; 12 JD 13; 15 JD 21
Ashley, L.F.: letter of comment,
7-4 TAD 299
Ashley, Mike: Annotated Listing of works
of E.C.Tubb, 7 SF 7
Ashley, Mike: Bibliography of Weird
Fiction of Oscar Cook and Christine
Campbell Thomson, 3 WT 13
Ashley, Mike: Checklist of works of
H.S.Chibbet, 4 WT 7
Ashley, Mike: The Fiction of William
Hope Hodgson, A Working Bibliography,
15 SF 15
Ashley, Mike: H.S.Chibbet, (sketch),
4 WT 7
Ashley, Mike: letter of comment, 5 WT 31;
6 WT 31
Ashley, Mike: The Perils of Bibliography,
A Look at the Writings of E.C. Tubb,
7 SF 5
Ashley, Mike: Unlocking the Night, (on
Oscar Cook and Christine Campbell
Thomson, comments), 3 WT 8
(Asimov, Isaac), The Science Fiction
Mystery Novels of Asimov, Bester and
Lem, Fusions and Foundations, by
Steven R. Carter, 1-1 C 109
(Asimov, Isaac: THE 13 CRIMES OF SCIENCE
FICTION), Mystery Plus: Getting There
May Be More Than Half the Fun, by
R. Jeff Banks, 3-5 PP 15
Ask Mr. Mystery: Writing for ELLERY
QUEEN'S MYSTERY MAGAZINE, (anonymous),
27 JD 12
Aspects of the Unknown Gardner, (on Erle
Stanley Gardner), by Francis M. Nevins,
Jr., 5-4 MR 13; 5-5 MR 27
Astin, J.T.: letter of comment, 1-2 M 3
Astonishers! or, Just Who Are You,
Anyway?, (dime novel characters), by
Gil O'Gara, 1-2 YB 8
Astrological Guide to Murder, by Sydney
Sonar, 1-3 M 15
At the Movies: Doc Savage, The Man of
Bronze, 1 BSA 15
Ath, D.E., ("D.E.Ath"): letter of comment,
1-6 PP 29; 2-3 PP 40; 2-6 PP 11
Athanason, Arthur Nicholas: The Mousetrap
Phenomenon, (THE MOUSETRAP: Agatha
Christie, stage production), 12-2 TAD
152
Athey, Forrest T., Jr.: letter of comment,
2-5 MR 12; 1-3 QC 21; 6-3 TAD 195;
9-4 TAD 296

Atkey, Bertram: The Adventure of the
House with the Baboons, (fiction,
Classic Corner rare tales), 13-2
TAD 125
Atkinson, Michael: Virginity Preserved
and the Secret Marriage of Sherlock
Holmes, (Sherlockiana), 2-1 C 62
Atlas Reviews, (book reviews), 1-1 WA 9;
1-2 WA 7
Atmosphere of Houses, (verse), by
Steve Eng, 2-2 AD 12
Attic Dawn, (verse), by Jayne Fawcett,
4-1 AD 12
Aucott, Robert: letter of comment,
1-1 MF 43; 5-1 MF 45; 5-2 MF 47;
1-1 PP 28; 3-1 PP 48; 2-1 TAD 62;
2-4 TAD 277; 3-2 TAD 140; 3-3 TAD 209;
4-1 TAD 60; 5-3 TAD 189; 5-4 TAD 236;
6-3 TAD 205; 7-1 TAD 75; 7-2 TAD 146;
10-3 TAD 278
Aucott, Robert: To Those Mysteriously
Murdered in Books, (verse), 12-1 TAD
68
Aucott, Robert: When was the Golden Age,
Anyway?, 5-4 TAD 207
Aucott, Robert: Where Have I Read That?
(quiz), 12-2 TAD 187
Aucott, Robert, and Amnon Kabatchnik: A
Readers' Supplementary List to the
Haycraft/Queen Definitive Library of
Detective-Crime-Mystery Fiction,
9-2 TAD 87
(Audley, David & Colonel Price Series:
Anthony Price), Checklist, annotated,
by Barry Van Tilburg, 4-6 MF 6
Augie vs. The United States Post Office,
(reminiscences on August Derleth), by
Bill Dutch, 2-2 AD 10
August Derleth (as published in 1936), by
Raymond Palmer, 2 WT 12
August Derleth: A Giant Remembered, by
Basil Copper, 1-2 AD 1
August Derleth: Biographical, Personal,
Bibliographical, (notes written by
Derleth in 1941), 5-1 AD 1
August Derleth on Literature: Summary
of a Correspondence, by Harry James
Cargas, 2 3/4 AD 1
August Derleth: Pre-Romantic, by
Frederick Shroyer, 1-2 PDA 49
August Derleth Society, activities of
members, 3-4 AD 6; 4-1 AD 13;
4-3 AD 10; 4-4 AD 3
August Derleth Society, April 1980
Meeting Report, 3-4 AD 7
August Derleth Society, Charter members,
1-1 AD 3; 1-2 AD 6; 1-3 AD 8;
1-4 AD 10
August Derleth Society, July 1980
Meeting Report, 4-1 AD 3
August Derleth Society, October 1980
Meeting Report, 4-3 AD 8

August Derleth Society: Some Thoughts
     on the Future of the Newsletter,
     by Richard H. Fawcett, 2-2 AD 9
August Derleth Society of Wisconsin -
     A Milestone, 1-3 AD 1
August Derleth's Reply to "The Sac
     of Fortune" of Sinclair Lewis,
     4-3 AD 4
August Derleth's Wisconsin Diary, (on
     Derleth's weekly column in the
     Madison Capitol Times, by Bill
     Dutch, 4-4 AD 7
(Austen, Jane), From Howtoits to Whodunits,
     Jane Austen to Agatha Christie, (an
     exploration of background settings)
     by Rosemary DePaolo, 2-2 C 8
(Austin, Steve), The Real Steve Austin,
     (series character), by Sue Hagen
     and "Operative 1701", 6 U 15
(Austin, Steve), Steve Austin: Story
     or Authentic?, by Albert Tonik,
     5 U 3
(Australia), Australian Words and
     Expressions in Upfield's Novels,
     (Arthur W. Upfield: Inspector
     Bonaparte), by Philip T. Asdell,
     1 BY 5
(Australia), Bony Was There, (locales
     of stories, Arthur W. Upfield's
     detective, Inspector Bonaparte), by
     Philip T. Asdell, 1 BY 2
(Australia), The Great Melbourne Cup
     Mystery, (comments on FOLLOW MY
     DUST by Arthur W. Upfield), by
     Philip T. Asdell, 1 BY 3
(Australia), Under the Southern Star,
     (paperback books of Whitman Press
     of Australia), by Dave & Su Bates,
     3-3 CP 18
Australian Words and Expressions in
     Upfield's Novels, by Philip T.
     Asdell, 1 BY 5
Author of "The Boy Travellers" series,
     (Thomas W. Knox, biog. sketch;
     boys' book series), by B.B.Vallentine,
     4-1 BC 400
Author Checklist, Ace Books, (paperbacks)
     by J. Grant Thiessen, 1 SF 21
(author collections), The "Best of"
     Phenomenon, by J. Grant Thiessen,
     4 SF 32; 5 SF 47
Author Index, Ballantine Books,
     Science-Fiction, Fantasy and Weird
     Fiction 1953-1976, by Carl Bennett,
     6 SF 34
Author Index, BIZARRE FANTASY TALES,
     by Gene Marshall & Carl F. Waedt,
     3 SF 20
Author Index, Defunct Paperback
     Publishers, (science-fiction), by
     J. Grant Thiessen, 2 SF 14
Author Index, FAMOUS SCIENCE FICTION,
     by Gene Marshall and Carl F. Waedt,
     3 SF 20

Author Index, MAGAZINE OF HORROR, by
     Gene Marshall and Carl F. Waedt,
     3 SF 20
Author Index, THE ROHMER REVIEW,
     Issues Nos. 1-10, 10 R 15
Author Index, STARTLING MYSTERY
     STORIES, by Gene Marshall and
     Carl F. Waedt, 3 SF 20
Author Index, WEIRD TERROR TALES,
     by Gene Marshall and Carl F. Waedt,
     3 SF 20
Author Under the Microscope, The, by
     R. Austin Freeman, 2 TF 33
Avallone, Mike: Another Chapter from
     DEATH OF A .300 HITTER, 1-1 MF 3
Avallone, Mike: Another Chapter from
     DEATH OF A .300 HITTER, 1-2 MF 11
Avallone, Mike: Avallone's Avocados,
     12 MN 3
Avallone, Mike: Children of the Night,
     (Sherlockiana fiction), 2-2 PDA 56
Avallone, Mike: Denise is on the
     Phone, (fiction), 8 U 100
Avallone, Mike: The 11 Best Private
     Eye Novels of Them All, 38 X 130
Avallone, Mike: For Mystery Critics
     Only, Hard-Boiled Detective
     Division, 21 X 10
Avallone, Mike: God Save Ian Fleming,
     A Long Overdue Thank You to a
     Master Storyteller, 12-1 TAD 31
Avallone, Mike: Kiss My Deadly
     Typewriter #539, ("old truths"),
     2-2 QC 9; 3-1 QC 17 (Note: rebuttals
     by Marvin Lachman, Francis M.
     Nevins, Jr., Charles MacDonald,
     Stanley A. Carlin, Jon L. Breen,
     Joe Gores, and, cross-rebuttal by
     Avallone, 3-1 QC 14
Avallone, Mike: The Legless Runner,
     (Excerpt from DEATH OF A .300
     HITTER), 6 X 8
Avallone, Mike: letter of comment,
     11 DS 6; 11 DS 19; 9 JD 10; 9 MN 35;
     2-1 QC 16; 4 SF 45; 4-4 TAD 253;
     5-1 TAD 55; 9-3 TAD 239; 10-2 TAD
     160; 13-1 TAD 76; 13-2 TAD 162;
     5 U 65; 5 U 66; 6 U 51; 7 U 57;
     38 X 144; 43 X 6
Avallone, Mike: The Little Dread
     Schoolhouse, (fiction), 9 X 19
Avallone, Mike: Lonely Are the Great,
     (comments on Cornell Woolrich),
     11 X 7
Avallone, Michael: Marie Corelli,
     Vendetta! (on Corelli's VENDETTA),
     9-4 TAD 270
Avallone, Mike: Ms. Found in the
     Bottles, Vintage Wine Department,
     (puzzle mysteries), 28 X 6
Avallone, Mike: Robert Fish: In
     Memorium, (memorial tribute),
     14-2 TAD 119

Avallone, Mike: The Robeson Syndrome,
    (discussion), 2 PW 1
Avallone, Mike: This Little Paperback
    Went to Market, or Kiss My Deadly
    Typewriter, (on paperback publishing
    fallacies), 3-2 MR 27
Avallone, Mike: Two Short Chapters from
    DEATH OF A .300 HITTER, 1A MF 11
Avallone, Mike: The Violencers,
    (prospectus for unwritten series)
    5 U 21
Avallone, Mike: When Pulp Was Gold,
    (writing for the pulps), 7 X 68
(Avallone, Mike), A Tribute to, 1-1 MF 5
(Avallone, Mike), Adventures in
    Noonland, (verse), 2-2 MR 14
(Avallone, Mike), Avallone's Avocados,
    (extract of letter from Avallone
    to Bob Bloch, 1966), 11 MN A10
(Avallone, Mike), Ave Avallone!, by
    Robert Bloch, 8 U 77
(Avallone, Mike), Checklist of full
    length works, 8 U 95
(Avallone, Mike), Ed Noon's Quickest
    Caper, or Revenge, Italian Style,
    by R.T.Karlinchak, 38 X 139
(Avallone, Mike), Fading Shadows:
    Avallone, (biog. sketch), by Tom
    Johnson, 9 SF 21
(Avallone, Mike), Interview with
    Michael Avallone, by Michael S.
    Barson, 3-1 PQ 10
(Avallone, Mike), Michael Avallone, A
    Checklist, by Stephen Mertz,
    9-2 TAD 132
(Avallone, Mike), Mike Avallone, One
    of the Un-Angry Young Men, by
    Kelly Adrian, 1-5 MR 3
(Avallone, Mike), Paperback Writers,
    Michael Avallone, by Bill Crider,
    3-1 PQ 7
(Avallone, Mike), Partial Checklist,
    by Kelly Adrian, 1-5 MR 5
(Avallone, Mike), Michael Avallone-
    Writer Extraordinaire!, by Michael
    L. Cook, 8 U 76
(Avallone, Mike: Ed Noon series), Spy
    Series Characters in Hardback, Pt.
    IX, by Barry Van Tilburg, 5-5 MF 16
Avalon Books, Checklist, (science-
    fiction), by Stuart W. Wells III
    and Dick Spelman, 5 SF 29
Avante-Garde Writing in the Detective
    Story, by Frank D. McSherry, Jr.,
    3-2 TAD 96
Avati, James: "Dutch Diary", (report
    on Paperbacks U.S.A. exhibition
    in Holland), 4-1 PQ 15
(Avati, James), Soft Cover Sketches-
    James Avati, (paperback cover
    artist), by Thomas L. Bonn,
    3-3 PQ 40
Ave Avallone! (Mike Avallone), by
    Robert Bloch, 8 U 77

Avenger, The, (pulp hero character),
    by Wooda Nicholas Carr, 3-6 MR 13
Avenger's Aides, The, (pulp hero
    character's sidekicks), by Nick
    Carr, 5 P 6
(Avenger, The), A Coffin for the
    Avenger, (fiction), by Kenneth
    Robeson, 9 P 13
(Avenger, The), A Recurring Little
    Villain, (Cadwiller Olden in
    Doc Savage and The Avenger stories)
    by Bill Laidlaw, 5 DQ 9
(Avenger, The), Adieu to the Avenger,
    by Nick Carr, 11 X 123
(Avenger, The), The Avenger's First
    Appearance, (in first issue of
    pulp magazine THE ADVENGER), by
    Bob Jones, 8 BS 17
(Avenger, The), Death to the Avenger,
    (fiction), by Kenneth Robeson,
    8 P 16
(Avenger, The), Goulart's Version of
    The Avenger: New Wine, Old Bottles,
    and Something Extra, (stories by
    Ron Goulart), by R. Jeff Banks,
    9-2 TAD 122
(Avenger, The), The Great Escape Artist,
    by Bob Jones, 9 BS 19
(Avenger, The), The Red Baron, The
    Avenger, and Doc Savage, (comparison
    discussion), by Bill Laidlaw, 3 DQ 4
(Avenger, The), Trivia Quiz on the
    Avenger, by Kirk McConnell, 1-1 WA 11
(Avenger, The), Vengeance on the
    Avenger, (fiction), by Kenneth Robeson,
    10 P 12
AVENGER, THE, Checklist, pulp magazine,
    by Wooda Nicholas Carr, 3-6 MR 16
(aviation), The War in the Air 1914-18,
    (historical review of the aviation
    aspects, with art portfolio), by
    Dave Prosser, 66 PU 29; 67 PU 83
(aviation pulps), Bill Barnes - Air
    Adventurer, by B.W.Overn, 3 BS 14
(aviation pulps), Death in the Skies,
    by Robert Weinberg, 4 P 20
(aviation pulps), Dusty Ayres, by
    Robert Weinberg, 1 P 22
(aviation pulps), FLYING ACES, (in-
    depth discussion of pulp magazine)
    by Dean A. Grennell, 66 PU 9
(aviation pulps), The Flying Spy,
    (on G-8 pulp magazines), by Nick
    Carr, 6 DS 15
(aviation pulps), Fokker Joker, (on
    FLYING ACES pulp magazine), by
    Bud Overn, 10 P 7
(aviation pulps), Heroes of the Flying
    Pulps, (character heroes), by Herm
    Schreiner, 22 X 38
(aviation pulps), How I Got Into
    Aviation Writing, by Arch Whitehouse,
    22 X 36

(aviation pulps), Terence X. O'Leary's
War Birds, (on the pulp magazine
of this title, by Robert A. Madle,
69 PU 5
Avon and DAW Problem, The, (on the
identification of first and subsequent
editions of the Avon and DAW paperbacks)
by Richard Bilyeu, 11 SF 25
Avon Classic Crime, (on the Avon
paperbacks), by Jeff Meyerson,
1-4 CP 5; 1-5 MF 19
Avon Classic Crime Checklist, (on
the paperback crime series), by
Jeff Meyerson, 1-4 CP 6; 1-5 MF 20
Avon Doubles, Checklist (of paperback
books), by Lance Casebeer, 1-6 CP 8
AVON FANTASY AND SCIENCE FICTION MAGAZINE,
Index, by Brian Perry, 9 X 11; 10 X 5
AVON FANTASY NOVELS, Checklist of
paperback (digest-size) series, by
J. Grant Thiessen, 2 SF 6
AVON MURDER MYSTERY MONTHLY,
(AVON MURDER MYSTERY MONTHLY), Remembering
Avon Murder Mystery Monthly, with
Checklist, (magazine), by Francis
M. Nevins, Jr., 7 MY 3
(awards), see: Mystery Writers of
America, and International Crime
Writers
Axelrod, Martha: A Matter of Relative
Importance, (fiction), 1-2 M 43
Axelrod, Nancy: letter of comment,
3-6 PP 39; 4-6 MF 48
(Ayer, Frederick, Jr.), Department of
Unknown Mystery Writers, (biog.
sketch), by Marvin Lachman, 1-5 PP 17
(Ayres, Dusty), Contemplating Seven of
the Pulp Heroes, (comparisons and
characteristics), by Nick Carr and
Herman S. McGregor, 12 BS 3
(Ayres, Dusty), Dusty Ayres, (pulp hero
character), by Robert Weinberg,
1 P 22
(Ayres, Dusty), Dusty Ayres, (pulp hero
character now in Corinth paperbacks)
by Bruce Cervon, 3-2 CP 18

Babener, Liahna K.: California Babylon,
The World of American Detective
Fiction, 1-2 C 77
Baby, I Could Plot! (keynote talk at
Florida Suncoast Writers' Conference
by Harry Whittington), 2-2 PQ 25
Backbone of BLACK MASK, The, (Frederick
Nebel's detective stories in the
the pulp magazine), with checklist,
by Dave Lewis, 2-2 C 118
Background and Checklist, Don Elliott/
Robert Silverberg Erotic Fiction
Titles, by Keith L. Justice,
13 SF 18
Background of First Andy Blake Book,
(boys' book series by Leo Edwards)
by Julius R. Chenu, 1-3 TBN 1

Bacon, Martha: Destry and Dionysus,
(literary essay on Frederick
Faust), 2-2 FC 1
(Bagley, Desmond), A Word With Desmond
Bagley, by Deryck Harvey,
7-4 TAD 258
(Bailey, H.C.), Bibliography of
(Reggie) Fortune Short Stories, by
Thomas D. Waugh, 6-2 TAD 76
(Bailey, H.C.), Checklist, Joshua
Clunk Series, by Maryell Cleary,
3-5 PP 20
(Bailey, H.C.), In Defense of Mr. Fortune,
(discussion of Reggie Fortune,
detective character of Bailey)
by William Antony S. Sarjeant,
14-4 TAD 302
(Bailey, H.C.), The Parables of H.C.
Bailey, by Thomas D. Waugh, 6-2 TAD
75
(Bailey, H.C.), The Reggie Fortune
Short Stories, An Appreciation and
Partial Bibliography, by Mark
Purcell, (additional listings by
Francis M. Nevins, Jr.), 5-4 MR 1
(Bailey, H.C.: THE GARSTON MURDER
CASE), The First Appearance, Joshua
Clunk, by Maryell Cleary, 3-5 PP 19
Bailey, Ken: Doc Savage - Why They
Call Him Doc, (literary supposition)
1 MB 17
Baird, Newton: Aristotle's Operative,
or, The Case of the Classic Barzun,
(rational premise in detective
fiction), 8-1 TAD 15
Baird, Newton: Checklist, annotated,
Fredric Brown, 10-4 TAD 370;
11-1 TAD 86
Baird, Newton: Conrad's Probe to
Absolute Zero, (on Joseph Conrad's
THE SECRET AGENT), 9-1 TAD 43
Baird, Newton: letter of comment,
8-1 TAD 71; 8-3 TAD 235; 9-3 TAD
233; 10-3 TAD 277; 11-3 TAD 308
Baird, Newton: Paradox and Plot: The
Fiction of Fredric Brown, 9-4 TAD
282; 10-1 TAD 33; 10-2 TAD 151;
10-3 TAD 249; 10-4 TAD 370; 11-1
TAD 86
(Baker, Samm Sinclair), Checklist, by
Marvin Lachman, 4-2 PP 19
(Baker, Samm Sinclair), Department of
Unknown Mystery Writers, by
Marvin Lachman, 4-1 PP 17
(Baker, Samm Sinclair), Samm Sinclair
Baker Revisited, by Marvin Lachman,
4-2 PP 19
(Baker Street Irregulars), An Irregular
History, (Sherlockiana), by Sean M.
Wright, 2-2 M 24
Bakerman, Jane S.: A View from Wall
Street, Social Criticism in the
Mystery Novels of Emma Lathen,
9-3 TAD 213

Bakerman, Jane S.: Advice Unheeded,
Shakespeare in Some Modern Mystery
Novels, (Shakespeare associations
in crime fiction), 14-2 TAD 134

Bakerman, Jane S.: Bowlers, Beer, Bravado,
and Brains, Anthony Gilbert's Arthur
Crook, 2-4 MF 5

Bakerman, Jane S.: Explorations of Love,
An Examination of Some Novels by Ruth
Rendell, 11-2 TAD 139

Bakerman, Jane S.: "From the Time I Could
Read, I Always Wanted to be a Writer",
Interview with P.D.James, 10-1 TAD 55

Bakerman, Jane S.: Gene Stratton-Porter,
Mistress of the Mini-Mystery, 3-1 MF 3

Bakerman, Jane S.: Humor, Horror and
Intellect, Giles Mont of Ruth Rendell's
A JUDGEMENT IN STONE, 5-4 MF 5

Bakerman, Jane S.: Hunter and Hunted,
Comparison and Contrast in Tony
Hillerman's PEOPLE OF DARKNESS,
5-1 MF 3

Bakerman, Jane S.: Joe Leaphorn and the
Navajo Way, Tony Hillerman's Indian
Detective Fiction, 2-1 C 9

Bakerman, Jane S.: letter of comment,
2-2 MF 42; 2-3 MF 71; 4-1 MF 40

Bakerman, Jane S.: Meeting Menendes, An
Analysis of Three Detective Novels
of Suzanne Blanc, 10-3 TAD 227

Bakerman, Jane S.: One in Two, Some
Personality Studies by Ruth Rendell,
5-6 MF 21

Bakerman, Jane S.: Patterns of Guilt and
Isolation in Five Novels by "Tucker
Coe", 12-2 TAD 118

Bakerman, Jane S.: Piercing the Closed
Circle, The Technique of Point of
View in Works by P.D.James, 1-5 MF 3

Bakerman, Jane S.: Rendell Territory,
(on Ruth Rendell), 10 MN A1

Bakerman, Jane S.: Tension and Duality,
Daphne du Maurier's "Don't Look
Now", 3-4 MF 8

Bakerman, Jane S.: Vera Caspary's Fascinating Females, Laura, Evvie and
Bedelia, 1-1 C 46

Bakerman, Jane S.: Women and Wall Street,
Portraits of Women in Novels by
Emma Lathen, 8-1 TAD 36

Bakerman, Jane S.: The Writer's Probe,
Ruth Rendell as Social Critic,
3-5 MF 3

(Bakerman, Jane S.), People, (short
biog. sketch), by Jim Huang, 10 CL 11

Bakka Bookshop: letter of comment,
17 X 61

Balderston, Jean: Agatha Christie,
(verse), 12-3 TAD 210

Balderston, Jean: Midnight Visitor,
(verse), 12-3 TAD 208

Baldwin, F. Lee: letter of comment,
33 X 113; 38 X 145

Baldwin, John: letter of comment,
1-2 BC 62

Bales, Jack: Horatio Alger, or The
Man Behind the Great American
Dream, 2-4 BC 226

Bales, Jack: Charles Pierce Burton
and the Boys of Bobs Hill, (boys'
series books), 5 BB 5

Bales, Jack: Horatio Alger, Jr. and
the Horatio Alger Society,
1-3 TBN 6

Bales, Jack: letter of comment,
6 MA 28; 1-3 TBN 5; 1-4 YB 10

Ball, John: A Visit with Dame Ngaio
Marsh, 3-1 M 23

Ball, John: letter of comment,
1-3 MF 51; 10-1 TAD 41

Ball, John: My Hero - Fu Manchu,
11 R 5

(Ball, John), Biographical Sketch,
11 R 4

(Ball, John), Books by John Ball, by
Robert E. Briney, 5-6 MR 14

(Ball, John), John Ball Interview,
by Karen Bornstein, 1-3 M 31

(Ball, John), John Ball: View and
Interview, by Robert E. Briney,
5-6 MR 9

(Ball, John: Virgil Tibbs, detective)
Virgil Tibbs and the American Negro
in Mystery Fiction, by Marvin
Lachman, 1-3 TAD 86

Ball, Ted: Bibliographic Notes on some
HPL Books, (H.P.Lovecraft), 4 SF 18

Ballard of Lucifer, The, (verse),
by Lucile Coleman, 1 U 9

Ballantine Books, a Checklist of
Science Fiction, Fantasy and Weird
Fiction 1953-1976, by Carl Bennett,
6 SF 3

(Ballard, Willis Todhunter), W.T.Ballard,
An Interview, by Stephen Mertz,
12-1 TAD 14

(Ballard, Willis Todhunter), Checklist
of works, by Stephen Mertz, 12-1 TAD
19

Ballinger, John: letter of comment,
4-1 MF 44

(Ballinger, Bill S.) Bill Ballinger, His
Work, His Women and His World, by
Pat Erhardt, with checklist, 4-6 MR 3

(Ballinger, Bill S.: Joaquin Hawks
series), The Rivals of James Bond,
by Larry Rickert, 4-2 PP 7

(ballistics, audio), Sounds of Gunshots,
by Lawrence Heming, 15 JD 8

Ballooning, A Hobby of Serenity,
4 DQ 5

Balmer, Edwin, and William MacHarg:
The Eleventh Hour, (fiction, Classic
Corner rare tales), 12-1 TAD 40

Balopole, Donna: letter of comment,
6/7 LR 17

Balow, Tom: letter of comment, 6-2 TAD 131

Balrog Awards, The, (science-fiction), 6 U 47

Bama Legacy, The, (on James Bama, cover artist for Doc Savage pulp magazines) by Dafydd Neal Dyar, 7 DQ 6

(Bama, James), The Bama Legacy, by Dafydd Neal Dyar, 7 DQ 6

(Bama, James), James Bama, An Interview, (cover artist for Doc Savage pulp magazines), 1 BSA 3

(Bama, James), James Bama and His Man of Bronze, by Mark J. Golden, 1 DR 4

(Bama, James), Jim Bama and the Artistic Doc Savage, by Mark J. Golden, 2/3 DR 11

(Bama, James), Letter and Comment from Bama, Today's Doc Savage Illustrator, 2 BS 3

Bander, Elaine: Dorothy L. Sayers and the Apotheosis of Detective Fiction (social vs. puzzle), 10-4 TAD 362

Bander, Elaine: The English Detective Novel Between the Wars, 1919-1939, 11-3 TAD 262

Banks, R. Jeff: A Modesty Blaise Appreciation, 8 MN 3

Banks, R. Jeff: Carmody, Sagebrush Detective, (detective character created by Peter McCurtin), 8-1 TAD 42

Banks, R. Jeff: Checklist, annotated, of Modesty Blaise books (written by Peter O'Donnell), 4-2 MF 8

Banks, R. Jeff: Checklist, The Joe Gall series, annotated, 3-2 MF 28

Banks, R. Jeff: Detecting the Sponsors, (quiz), 12-2 TAD 190

Banks, R. Jeff: The Distaff Detectives, (quiz), 8 MN 2

Banks, R. Jeff: Dogging the Detectives, A Quiz, 7 MN 3

Banks, R. Jeff: Double-Duty Detectives, (quiz), 9-2 TAD 111

Banks, R. Jeff: Favorite Magazine Issues, MANHUNT (Vol.3, No.6) June 1955, 4-6 MF 7

Banks, R. Jeff: Goulart's Version of the Avenger, New Wine, Old Bottles and Something Extra, (The Avenger, as by Goulart, in paperback books), 9-2 TAD 122

Banks, R. Jeff: I Remember...B-Movies, 4-5 MF 13

Banks, R. Jeff: I Remember...Pulp Mysteries - Mystery Pulps, 3-4 MF 19

Banks, R. Jeff: I Remember...Radio Mysteries, 3-5 MF 17

Banks, R. Jeff: Immoderate Homage to Modesty (books featuring Modesty Blaise by Peter O'Donnell), 4-2 MF 8

Banks, R. Jeff: Lawrence Block, Annotated Checklist of the Tanner Series Books, 5/6 MN 7

Banks, R. Jeff: letter of comment, 1-2 MF 51;1-3 MF 56; 1-4 MF 55; 2-1 MF 52; 2-2 MF 41; 2-3 MF 59; 2-4 MF 53; 2-5 MF 51; 2-6 MF 43; 3-1 MF 51; 4-1 MF 43; 5-1 MF 42; 5-4 MF 41; 5/6 MN 11; 5/6 MN 13; 7 MN 5; 8 MN 30; 9 MN L2; 2 PE 37; 3 PE 35; 4 PE 29; 4 PE 35; 5 PE 37; 1-2 PP 27; 1-3 PP 32; 1-5 PP 28; 1-6 PP 33; 2-1 PP 38; 2-2 PP 44; 2-6 PP 42; 3-1 PP 41; 3-5 PP 50; 4-2 PP 46; 4-3 PP 36; 7-1 TAD 65; 7-2 TAD 149; 7-4 TAD 303; 8-1 TAD 74; 8-2 TAD 154; 8-3 TAD 244; 8-4 TAD 315; 9-1 TAD 82; 9-2 TAD 160; 9-3 TAD 232; 11-4 TAD 316; 4 U 51

Banks, R. Jeff: Mark Twain, Detective Story Writer, an Appreciation, 7-3 TAD 176

Banks, R. Jeff: Mr. & Mrs. North, (detective characters of Frances and Richard Lockridge), 9-3 TAD 182

Banks, R. Jeff, Mystery Plus, (series of columns of commentary, reviews, and bibliographical data),

Mystery Plus #1, (elusive mysteries), 1-1 PP 17

Mystery Plus: A Contemporary Science Fiction Pair, (TIME AFTER TIME by Karl Alexander, and THE WOLFEN by Whitley Strieber), 3-1 PP 16

Mystery Plus: A Different Perspective, 2-1 PP 20

Mystery Plus: A Movie Review (THE LEGACY: Jimmy Sangster), 3-3 PP 17

Mystery Plus: A Pair of Parodies, (SPACE FOR HIRE by William F. Nolan, and THE CHEAP DETECTIVE by Robert Grossbach), 1-5 PP 10

Mystery Plus: A Pair of Triple Threats (commentary on mystery novels involving mystery-magic-western and mystery-SF-magic), 4-4 PP 14

Mystery Plus: THE ADVENTURE OF THE HOLMES-DRACULA FILE, 2-4 PP 16

Mystery Plus: The Demolished Man, (Alfred Bester: THE DEMOLISHED MAN), 1-2 PP 11

Mystery Plus: Getting There May Be More Than Half the Fun (THE 13 CRIMES OF SCIENCE FICTION by Asimov-Greenberg-Waugh, and THE SPIRIT by Thomas Page), 3-5 PP 15

Mystery Plus: The Hawk, (THE HAWK: Milton J. Shapiro), 2-3 PP 24

Mystery Plus: The Holmes Pastiche of the Decade, (ENTER THE LION: Michael P. Hodel and Sean M. Wright), 4-1 PP 21

Banks, R. Jeff: Mystery Plus, (continued)
  Mystery Plus: Image of the Beast,
    (Philip Jose Farmer: IMAGE OF
    THE BEAST), 3-2 PP 15
  Mystery Plus: Incubus, (Ray Russell:
    INCUBUS), 1-3 PP 9
  Mystery Plus: John Reese Revisited,
    1-6 PP 18
  Mystery Plus: On Mystery Magazines,
    4-2 PP 13
  Mystery Plus: Poe Must Die, (POE
    MUST DIE: Mark Oldham), 2-2 PP 12
  Mystery Plus: R-Rated Double Feature,
    (reviews), 2-6 PP 13
  Mystery Plus: Series Shots, (comments
    on recently published series
    characters and books), 4-5/6 PP 40
  Mystery Plus: (SHADOW OF A BROKEN
    MAN: George C. Chesbro), 4-1 PP 22
  Mystery Plus: Old Friends Break New
    Ground, (AN OLD FRIEND OF THE
    FAMILY by Fred Saberhagen, and
    GHOSTS by Ed McBain), 3-6 PP 15
  Mystery Plus: Short Notices of Various
    Books, 2-5 PP 13
  Mystery Plus: The Spear, (THE SPEAR:
    James Herbert), 3-4 PP 14
  Mystery Plus: Weapon Heavy, (on
    Jeff Hewitt, Western Private Eye)
    1-4 PP 21
  Mystery Plus: What's-Its, 4-3 PP 11
Banks, R. Jeff: Mystery Theme Match-Up,
  (quiz), 11-3 TAD 305
Banks, R. Jeff: Old Movie Expert (mini-
  mystery parody), 7 PE 10
Banks, R. Jeff: Radio Detectives Tag-Line
  Quiz, 11-4 TAD 395
Banks, R. Jeff: Radio Mystery Quiz,
  12-3 TAD 211
Banks, R. Jeff: The Round Robin Caper,
  or, The Too Long Goodbye, part 3,
  (round robin story, pt.1 by Joe R.
  Lansdale 5 PE 5; pt.2 by Ralph
  Diffinetti 5 PE 7; pt.4 by David
  Rose 8 PE 9), 6 PE 26
Banks, R. Jeff: Spillane and the Critics,
  (treatment in literary criticism),
  12-4 TAD 300
Banks, R. Jeff: The Tiger Mann Series,
  (by Mickey Spillane), 2-3 MF 32
Banks, R. Jeff: Two-Detective Mysteries,
  (quiz), 12-4 TAD 378
Banks, R. Jeff: Visiting Firemen, (mini-
  mystery parody), 7 PE 11
Banks, R. Jeff, and Harry D. Dawson:
  Checklist, the Len Deighton series,
  annotated, 3-1 MF 12
Banks, R. Jeff, and Harry D. Dawson:
  Checklist, the Quiller novels of
  Adam Hall, annotated, 4-1 MF 8
Banks, R. Jeff, and Harry D. Dawson:
  Checklist, the spy novels of John
  LeCarre, annotated, 2-5 MF 22

Banks, R. Jeff, and Harry D. Dawson:
  LeCarre's Spy Novels, 2-5 MF 22
Banks, R. Jeff, and Harry D. Dawson:
  The Len Deighton Series, 3-1 MF 10
Banks, R. Jeff, and Harry D. Dawson:
  The Quiller Report, (on Quiller
  series by Adam Hall), 4-1 MF 8
Banks, R. Jeff, and Leslie M. Thompson:
  When Is This Stiff Dead? Detective
  Stories and Definitions of Death,
  2-6 MF 11
Banks, R. Jeff, and Guy M. Townsend:
  Checklist, the Matt Helm series,
  annotated, 2-2 MF 3
Banks, R. Jeff, and Guy M. Townsend:
  The Matt Helm Series (by Donald
  Hamilton), 2-2 MF 3
(Bannon, Carlos, detective), Carlos
  Bannon, The Private Detective
  Fiction of Kenneth Gravell, with
  Checklist, by Randy Himmel, 12 LR 8
(Bantam Books), Los Angeles editions,
  (paperbacks), by Paul Payne,
  1-3 CP 10
(Bantam Publications), Los Angeles
  (editions of Bantam books), by
  J. Grant Thiessen, 2 SF 6
(Bantan series), Checklist by author,
  Maurice B. Gardner, (Tarzan-like
  juvenile series), 62 PU 22
(Bantan series), Why I Wrote the
  Bantan Novels, by Maurice B.
  Gardner, 62 PU 19; 1 U 12
Barbarino, John: letter of comment,
  2-2 CP 2
Barbato, Joseph: The Mysteries of the
  Pseudonymous Professors (anonymity
  required), 1-4 MF 3
Barber Shop, The, by Ray Bradbury.
  36 X R26
Barbero, Kevin: A Wolfean Quiz, (quiz
  oriented to Nero Wolfe), 1-1 G 31
Barbless Arrow, The, (mystery-action
  fiction reprinted from a pulp
  magazine), by Herman Petersen,
  2-2 C 78
(Barbour, Ralph Henry), Ralph Henry
  Barbour's Books, (boys' series
  books), by Julius R. Chenu,
  1-4 BC 118; 6 YB 17
(Barbour, Ralph Henry), Some Further
  Addenda to Ralph Henry Barbour data,
  by Julius R. Chenu, 3-2 BC 317
Bards, The, (verse), by Frederick
  Faust, 1-4 FC 6; 2-1 FC 9
Bargainnier, Earl F.: Agatha Christie's
  Other Detectives, Parker Pyne and
  Harley Quin, 11-2 TAD 110
Bargainnier, Earl F.: Another Watson,
  Captain Hastings, (Capt. Arthur
  Hastings, character in Agatha
  Christie), 13-4 TAD 354

Bargainnier, Earl F.: letter of comment, 11-3 TAD 212; 14-1 TAD 73

Bargainnier, Earl F.: The Mysteries of Edgar Box (a.k.a. Gore Vidal), 2-1 C 45

Bargainnier, Earl F.: Ngaio Marsh's "Theatrical" Murders, 10-2 TAD 175

Bargainnier, Earl F.: The Playful Mysteries of Peter Dickinson, 13-3 TAD 185

Bargainnier, Earl F.: Roderick Alleyn, Ngaio Marsh's Oxonian Superintendent, 11-1 TAD 63

Baring-Gould, William S.: "I Shall Live When You Are Smoke" (on Dr. Fu Manchu), 1-1 TAD 2

(Baring-Gould, William S.), Meet the Author, (also Dedication), by Allen J. Hubin, 1-1 TAD 3

(Baring-Gould, William S.: NERO WOLFE OF WEST THIRTY-FIFTH STREET), The Case of the Missing Wolfe, (review) by William J. Clark, 3-4 MR 16

(Bark, Conrad Voss: Mr. Holmes series) Checklist, by Barry Van Tilburg, 4-2 MF 11

Barker, Jonathan M.: letter of comment, 1-2 M 3

(Barkley, James), An Informal Survey of Cover Art of the Seventies, Pt.2, Tribute to Maj Sjowall and Per Wahloo, (Barkley, artist), by Frank Eck, 10-1 TAD 46

(Barlow, R.H.), R.H.Barlow, (biog. and literary sketch), by Kenneth Faig, Jr., 1 HP 3

(Barnes, Bill), Bill Barnes, (aviation pulp hero), by Al Grossman, 11 P 17

(Barnes, Bill), Index to Bill Barnes Novels, (aviation stories in pulp magazine of that name), by Will Murray, 22 X 40

(Barnes, Dallas), Interview with Dallas Barnes, by Paul Bishop, 2-1 M 36

(Barnes, Detective Berkeley: Eugene Franklin), The Case of the Hypochrondriac Detective, by Larry L. French, 1-2 PP 9

(Barnes, Elmer Tracey), The Motion-Picture Comrades, (boys' series books by Barnes), by Robert Jennings, 6 BB 24

(Baron series: J.J. Marric), Checklist, (Marric pseud. for John Creasey), by R.E.Briney and John Creasey, 2-1 TAD 16

Barr, George: Art Portfolio, fantasy, 63 PU 17

Barr, George: letter of comment, 62 PU 15

Barrett, Mervyn: letter of comment, 15 JD 21

Barry, Jeremy: letter of comment, 10 BS 21; 8 JD 16; 10 JD 8; 11 JD 19

Barry, Jerome: letter of comment, 67 PU 60

(Barry, Mike: The Lone Wolf series), Checklist of paperback titles, by George Kelley, 1-5 MF 18

(Barry, Mike: The Lone Wolf series) Fear and Loathing with the Lone Wolf Series, by George Kelley, 1-5 MF 18

Barson, Michael: Checklist, Gil Brewer paperbacks, 3-4 PQ 11

Barson, Michael S.: Fires That Create, The Versatility and Craft of Harry Whittington, (discussion of works) 4-2 PQ 13

Barson, Michael S.: First Printing, Two Million, (on John Jakes books) 3-3 PQ 7

Barson, Michael S.: Gil Brewer's Fables of Evil Women, Driven Men and Doom, (novels by Brewer) 3-4 PQ 3

Barson, Michael S.: Interview with Gil Brewer, 3-4 PQ 6

Barson, Michael S.: Interview with Harry Whittington, 4-2 PQ 17

Barson, Michael S.: Interview with John D. MacDonald, 4-1 PQ 5

Barson, Michael S.: Interview with John Jakes, 3-3 PQ 9

Barson, Michael S.: Interview with Michael Avallone, 3-1 PQ 10

Barson, Michael S.: Interview with Robert Bloch, 4-1 PQ 18

Barson, Michael S.: John D. MacDonald, The Greatest Paperbacker of Us All, (on MacDonald's place in paperback book writing), 4-1 PQ 3

Barson, Michael S.: Just a Writer Working for a Buck, (on Mickey Spillane, with interview), 12-4 TAD 293

Barson, Michael S.: letter of comment, 3-2 CP 1; 2 U 59

Barson, Michael S.: Paperback Originals by John D. MacDonald, (checklist), 4-1 PQ 10

Barson, Michael S.: The Paperback Original Novels of John Jakes, (with checklist), 3-3 PQ 20

Barson, Michael S.: Paperback Originals by Robert Bloch, (checklist), 4-1 PQ 24

Barson, Michael S.: Paperback Originals by Harry Whittington, (with checklist), 4-2 PQ 23

Barson, Michael S.: "There's No Sex in Crime", The Two-Fisted Homilies of Race Williams, (pulp magazine detective), 2-2 C 103

Barson, Michael S.: Two Lonely Nights With Mickey Spillane, (interview), 2-3 PQ 13

Barson, Michael S.: Yours Truly, Bloch the Ripper, (Robert Bloch's macabre taste in writing), 4-1 PQ 17

(Barstow, Kent, series: Rutherford Montgomery), Boys' Series Bibliography, by Harry K. Hudson, 1-5 YB 13

Bart House, (publisher, checklist of titles), by J. Grant Thiessen, 2 SF 6

Barte, G.R., Jr.: letter of comment, 24 JD 40; 26 JD 46

Barton, Billy: letter of comment, 4-3 PP 37; 4-4 PP 34; 4-5/6 PP 85

Barton, Billy: Speaking With Myself, (author, self-interview), 5-4 MF 13

Barzun, Jacques: A Critical Vocabulary for Crime Fiction, 4-2 TAD 75

Barzun, Jacques: Books About Books of Crime, and the Criticism Thereof, 5-1 TAD 15

Barzun, Jacques: Disposing of a Pair of Ghosts, (T.L.Davidson; Cornell Woolrich: DARK CITY, DARK MEN), 6-4 TAD 248

Barzun, Jacques: In Memorial: Edmund Crispin, 12-1 TAD 13

Barzun, Jacques: letter of comment, 4-1 TAD 52; 10-2 TAD 163

(Barzun, Jacques), Aristotle's Operative, or, The Case of the Classic Barzun, (rational premise in detective fiction), 8-1 TAD 15

Barzun, Jacques, and Wendell Hertig, Supplement to A CATALOGUE OF CRIME, 9-2 TAD 93; 9-3 TAD 209; 9-4 TAD 271; 10-2 TAD 126; 10-3 TAD 224; 11-1 TAD 92; 11-2 TAD 203; 11-3 TAD 281; 11-4 TAD 394; 12-1 TAD 32; 12-3 TAD 262; 13-3 TAD 208; 13-4 TAD 308; 14-1 TAD 88; 14-2 TAD 142; 14-3 TAD 228; 14-4 TAD 328

Baseball Bat, The, (verse), by Frederick Faust, 1-3 FC 3

Bashaw, S.J., Jr.: letter of comment, 8 X 38

Basic Nancy Drew, (collecting Nancy Drew girl's series books), by Dave Farah, 6 YB 6

Basil Rathbone as Sherlock Holmes, by Leonard Maltin, 1-4 MR 12

Bass, Henry: letter of comment, 7 MA 22

Bates, David: Can Such Things Be? (mystery related items, collecting), 2 PE 25

Bates, David: Checklist, Harry Stephen Keeler, 4-2 PP 4

Bates, David: Epitaph for an Unrepentent Murderer, (verse), 3-3 PP 16

Bates, David: Harry Stephen Keeler, (on works; biog.), 4-2 PP 3

Bates, David: letter of comment, 1-6 CP 4; 2-1 CP 1; 3-1 CP 10; 3-4 CP 1; 1-1 MF 47; 13 MN L3; 4 PE 29; 6 PE 36; 1-1 PP 26; 1-3 PP 31; 4-2 PP 47; 4-3 PP 39; 4-5/6 PP 98; 36 X 74

Bates, David: Magazine Reprints of Kendell Foster Crossen, 13 MN 1

Bates, David: The Unabated Storm, Sacco & Vanzetti, 2-6 PP 23

Bates, David & Su: A Bow to Cartographers, (biog./article on Richard Sharpe Shaver), 1-6 CP 24

Bates, David & Su: BATS IN THE BELFRY by Norman Matson, (discussion), 2-1 CP 24

Bates, David & Su: Columbia's Science Fiction Paper Books, 1-4 CP 25

Bates, David & Su: The Gothic Magazines, 1-5 CP 29

Bates, David & Su: The Health Knowledge Publications, (magazines, mystery and horror), 2-3 CP 28

Bates, David & Su: letter of comment, 1-4 CP 1; 3-3 CP 1; 3-6 PP 39

Bates, David & Su: New England Mystery Dealer, (memorial tribute to Howard Waterhouse), 3-3 PP 10

Bates, David & Su: Sailing Uncharted Seas, (on Ray Palmer and the Shaver Mystery), 2-2 CP 35

Bates, David & Su: Under the Southern Star, (Whitman Press of Australia paperback publications), 3-3 CP 18

Bates, Dave & Su: When Fantasy Trod the Boards (fantasy and science-fiction paperback plays), 2-4 CP 16

Bates, David & Su, and Lance Casebeer: Who Drew That Girl? (paperback cover artists), 2-3 CP 36

Bates, David & Su: Zane Grey's Western (on the ZANE GREY MAGAZINE), 1-3 CP 20

Bates, Susannah: Paperback Editions of Robert Graves, with checklist, 3-5 CP 25

Bates, Capt.Gordon: Khaki Boys boys' series books; see: Josephine Chase

(Batman), The Case of Commissioner James Gordon, (Gordon was the Whisperer - pulp character - and the ancestor of Batman?), by Arn McConnell, 1-3 WA 14

Batory, Dana Martin: A Dead Ringer, 5 U 25

Batory, Dana Martin: The Biblical War of the Worlds, (biblical associations with WAR OF THE WORLDS), 8 U 46

Batory, Dana Martin: The Burroughs-Doyle Connection, (comparison of passages, Edgar Rice Burroughs and Arthur Conan Doyle works), 15 SF 10

Batory, Dana Martin: Conan Doyle Shows His Hand, 8 U 104

Batory, Dana Martin: Dating the War of the Worlds, 8 U 40

Batory, Dana Martin: Dr. Doyle's Doppelganger, 8 U 109

Batory, Dana Martin: First Annual Cumulative Index to Volume One of THE AGE OF THE UNICORN, 7 U 32

Batory, Dana Martin: Frankenstein a la Doyle, 8 U 114

Batory, Dana Martin: Genesis of the War of the Worlds, 8 U 34

Batory, Dana Martin: Hiatus in Paradise, (Sherlock Holmes in Shangri-La), 11 SF 29

Batory, Dana Martin: Notes on the Lost World, 2 U 9

Batory, Dana Martin: Operation England, The Martian Maelstrom (on WAR OF THE WORLDS), 8 U 58

Batory, Dana Martin: Orifice Into Hell, (macabre fiction of A. Conan Doyle), 3 U 11

Batory, Dana Martin: The Other War of the Worlds, 8 U 50

Batory, Dana Martin: The Real Professor Challenger, (a la A. Conan Coyle), 13 SF 42

Batory, Dana Martin: Watch That Man?, (A. Conan Doyle syndrome), 9 SF 40

Batory, Dana Martin: Where was Maple White Land?, (locates setting of Doyle's THE LOST WORLD), 6 U 16

Bats in the Belfry, (discusses BATS IN THE BELFRY by Norman Matson), by David and Su Bates, 2-1 CP 24

Batt, James R.: letter of comment, 4-1 AD 14

(Baum, L. Frank), L. Frank Baum and His Teen-Age Serials, A Biblio graphical Checklist, by Justin G. Schiller, 2-3 BC 194

(Baum, L. Frank), Sam Steele... (boys' series books by Baum as Capt. Hugh Fitzgerald), by George Holmes, 6 YB 8

Baum, Nelson: letter of comment, 2-4 TAD 278

Baumhofer, Walter M.: letter of comment, 6 U 51

Baumhofer, Walter M.: Doc Savage's First Cover Artist (Baumhofer), 14 BS 3

(Baumhofer, Walter M.), A Pulp Cover Gallery, 42 X 23

(Baumhofer, Walter M.), Artist Behind Doc Savage, by Frank Hamilton, 9 DS 6

(Baumhofer, Walter M.), Interview with the King of the Pulp Artists, Walter M. Baumhofer, by Frank Lewandowski, 9 DS 12

Baunsgaard, Hilmar: A Defense for Crime Fiction, (literary quality), 10-4 TAD 358

Bauska, Barry: Endure and Prevail, The Novels of Dick Francis, 11-3 TAD 238

(Baxter, Roger, series), The Roger Baxter Series, (boys' books), by Bob Ybarra, 3 MA 23

Bayer, Palmer: letter of comment, 7 JD 2

Bayport's Famous Sleuths, (on the Hardy Boys boys' series), by Fred Woodworth, 4 MA 3

Beal, Tita: letter of comment, 24 JD 40

Beaman, Bruce R.: Checklist, S.S.Van Dine works, 8-2 TAD 134

Beaman, Bruce R.: Checklist, Willard Huntington Wright works, 8-2 TAD 134

Beaman, Bruce R.: letter of comment, 3-4 TAD 306; 8-2 TAD 156; 8-3 TAD 238; 8-4 TAD 317; 9-1 TAD 82; 9-4 TAD 296

Beaman, Bruce R.: S.S.Van Dine, A Biographical Sketch, 8-2 TAD 133

(Bean, Tuffy, series: Leo Edwards), Checklist of boys' books, by Julius R. Chenu, 3 BB 10

(Bean, Tuffy, series: Leo Edwards) Checklist, 1-1 TB 4

(Bean, Tuffy, series: Leo Edwards), Checklist, by Julius R. Chenu, 1-2 YB 18

(Bean, Tuffy, series: Leo Edwards), Further Data on the Tuffy Bean Series, 2-1 TB 6

(Bean, Tuffy, series: Leo Edwards), Tuffy Bean Stories Last Edward's Stories, 1-4 TB 1

(Beane, Sawney), Sawney Beane, An Incident from the Casebook of a Royal Detective, (British classic true crime), by Veronica M.S. Kennedy, 9-2 TAD 126

(Beard, Jason, character), The Education of Jason Beard, A.B. Guthrie's Western Suspense Stories, 1-2 C 126

Beast Imagery and Stereotypes in the Novels of John D. MacDonald, by George S. Peek, 2-1 C 91

("Beat Generation" paperbacks), Mass Market Murmurings, by Barry Bernard, 2-3 CP 14

Beauchesne, Bernard: Corrections and Additions to Mundell's ERLE STANLEY GARDNER, A CHECKLIST, 3-5 MR 35

Beauchesne, Bernard: letter of comment, 9 JD 15; 13 JD 20; 3-5 MR 35; 5-3 MR 15; 1-2 TAD 66; 2-1 TAD 68; 3-4 TAD 280

Beauchesne, Bernard: H.S.Keeler, A Checklist, 1-4 TAD 147

Beauchesne, Bernard: Harry Stephen Keeler, Mystery Writer Extraordinary, 1-4 TAD 143

(Beauchesne, Bernard), Meet the Author, by Allen J. Hubin, 1-4 TAD 150

Beaupre, Lee: Espionage Fights Off Boredom (on spy films), 1-5 MR 12

(Beck, Martin, detective), Martin Beck, the Swedish Version of Barney Miller Without the Canned Laughter, by Thomas E. Williams, 1-1 C 123

Bedell, Jeanne F.: Melodrama and Manners, Changing Attitude Toward Class Distinction in English Detective Fiction 1868-1939, 1-1 C 15

(Bedford-Jones, H.), in PEOPLES MAGAZINE, (pulp), by William J. Clark, 30 X 147

Beebel, Charles: Driving Through the Wisconsin Valley on a Summer Evening, (verse), 4-1 AD 10

(Beeding, Francis: Colonel Alistair Granby series), checklist, by Barry Van Tilburg, 4-2 MF 11

(Beef, Sergeant, series: Leo Bruce), My Favourite Detectives, Pt.3, by Robert C.S.Adey, 5-3 MR 20

Behind the Eight Ball, (fiction), by Joseph Allen, 1-1 M 40

Behind the Scenes at Bouchercon 9, or, It was Murder at the Bismarck! (report on Bouchercon 9), by Mary Ann Grochowski, 2-6 MF 3

Behind These Eyes, (verse), by Michael Kase, 1-4 AD 5

Being an Examination of the Ponsian and Holmesian Secret Deductive Systems, (methods, Solar Pons and Sherlock Holmes), by A.E.Van Vogt, 1-2 PDA 52

Beitz, Les: A Very Sad Book Story, (boys' books), 1-1 BC 26

Beitz, Les: Illustrated by... (boys' books illustrators), 3-4 BC 366

Beitz, Les: J.T.Trowbridge, Youth Fiction Trailblazer, (early boys' book author), 1-4 BC 104

Beitz, Les, and Alan S. Dikty: Is It Valuable? (values in boys' books collecting), 2-4 BC 233

Bela Lugosi - A Meeting Remembered, by Jack A. Miller, 1 CD 31

Bela Lugosi - A Scrapbook, (photo article), by Gordon R. Guy, 1 CD 16

Bela Lugosi and "Mark of the Vampire" (film), by Dr. Carroll Borland Parten, 1 CD 34

Bela Lugosi in Murder by Television, (film), by Gordon R. Guy, 1 CD 12

Belcher, Joseph: letter of comment, 7 U 45

Bell, John: letter of comment, 2 SF 40

Bellem, Robert Leslie: Break It Up! (how to write for the pulps), 2-2 C 50

(Bellem, Robert Leslie), Ante-Bellem Days, or, "My Roscoe Sneezed Ka-chee!" (Bellem's influence on pulp detective fiction), by Bill Pronzini, 2-2 C 41

(Bellem, Robert Leslie), The Further Adventures of Robert Leslie Bellem, or, the Bellem-Adams Connection, by Stephen Mertz, 38 X 138

(Bellem, Robert Leslie), Robert Leslie Bellem, The Great Unknown, (pulp detective writer), by Stephen Mertz, 21 X 49

(Bellem, Robert Leslie: Dan Turner series), Investigating Dan Turner, by Stephen Mertz, 5 PE 9

Bemporad, Harriet: letter of comment, 4 BS 16

(Bencolin, Henri, detective: Jeff Marle), Henri Bencolin, by Fred Dueren, 8-2 TAD 98

Benedict, W. Ritchie: Case File, Canada (book reviews), 6 U 38

Bengis, Nathan L.: John Jasper's Devotion (on Dickens' THE MYSTERY OF EDWIN DROOD), 8-3 TAD 165; 8-4 TAD 257; 9-1 TAD 25

Bengis, Nathan L.: letter of comment, 2-1 TAD 65; 9-2 TAD 155

Bengis, Nathan L.: Plots for Sale, Cheap! Apply, 221B, (Holmes' influence on detective fiction), 1-4 TAD 116

Bengis, Nathan L.: Sherlocko-Pontine Parallels, (comparisons, Solar Pons and Sherlock Holmes), 1-4 PD 3

(Bengis, Nathan L.), Meet the Author, by Allen J. Hubin, 1-4 TAD 118

(Bennett, Arnold), Arnold Bennett - As a Writer of Crime Fiction, by N.C. Ravenscroft, 10-2 TAD 182

Bennett, Carl: Ballantine Books, a Checklist of Science Fiction, Fantasy and Weird Fiction 1953-1976, 6 SF 3

(Bennett, Jay), An Interview with Jay Bennett, by Paul B. Janeczko, 10-4 TAD 342

Bennett, Ron: letter of comment, 26 JD 46

Bennett, Ron: Pale Leman for Psychosis, (parody on Travis McGee of John D. MacDonald), 11 JD 4

(Benson, Ben), Checklist, mystery novels, by Bob Briney, 3-2 MR 8

Bentcliffe, Eric: Scents of Wonder, (space opera in the pulps), 60 PU 13

Bentley, Christopher: Murder by Client, A Reworked Theme in Dashiell Hammett, 14-1 TAD 78

(Bentley, Edmund Clerihew), Edmund
   Clerihew Bentley, (biog./literary
   sketch), by Charles Shibuk, 4-1 TAD
   30
(Bentley, E.C.), Ernest Bramah to E.C.
   Bentley, An Unpublished Letter,
   2-3 MR 8
(Bentley, E.C.), Satirist and Sleuth,
   or, Trent versus Toff, (on Bentley's
   parody of Lord Peter Wimsey), 2-1 PDA
   28
(Bentley, E.C.: CLERIHEWS COMPLETE),
   A Rambling Book Review, by Philip
   T. Asdell, 1-3 PP 21
(Benton, Kenneth: Peter Craig series),
   Checklist, by Barry Van Tilburg,
   4-2 MF 12
Benton, Mike: How to Succeed in Collecting
   Paperbacks, 3-2 CP 21
Benton, Mike: letter of comment, 2-1 CP 3
Berch, Victor: letter of comment,
   14-4 TAD 381
Berg, Valerie: letter of comment, 10 JD 8;
   11 JD 18
Berg, Stanton O.: Sherlock Holmes, Father
   of Scientific Crime Detection,
   5-2 TAD 81
(Berg, Trigger, series: Leo Edwards),
   (boys' series books), Checklist,
   by Julius R. Chenu, 3 BB 10
(Berg, Trigger, series: Leo Edwards),
   Checklist, 1-1 TB 4
(Berg, Trigger, series: Leo Edwards),
   Checklist, by Julius R. Chenu,
   1-2 YB 18
(Berg, Trigger, series: Leo Edwards),
   Trigger Berg, Leo's Jr. Series, by
   Julius R. Chenu, 2-4 TBN 1
(Berger, Thomas: WHO IS TEDDY VILLANOVA?)
   Thomas Berger's Comic-Absurd Vision
   in WHO IS TEDDY VILLANOVA?, by David
   Madden, 14-1 TAD 37
(Bergey, Earle), Checklist, paperback
   cover artist, 1-2 CP 23
Berglund, E.P.: The Work of Clark
   Ashton Smith, 18 X 35
Berland, A. Lance: letter of comment,
   25 JD 37
Berman, Alex: letter of comment, 38 X 145
Bernard, Barry: Mass Market Murmurings,
   (column of various paperback book
   discussions),
   "Beat Generation" paperbacks, 2-3 CP 14
   Cartoon paperbacks, 1939-1959,
      1-4 CP 8
   Cartoon paperbacks, 1960-1969,
      1-6 CP 20
   Crossword Puzzle paperbacks, 1-5 CP 12
   E.C. Artists in paperback, the MAD
      artists, 2-4 CP 18
   Edward Gorey and Anchor Books,
      1-3 CP 5
   JUNKIE, by William S. Burroughs,
      1-1 CP 6

Bernard, Barry: Mass Market Murmurings,
   (continued)
   Paperback Publisher's Colophons,
      1-2 CP 6
   Paperback Magazines, 2-2 CP 32
Berry, George W.: letter of comment,
   1-2 G 69
Berryman, George R.: An Evening with
   John D. MacDonald, 22 JD 4
Berryman, George R.: letter of comment,
   6 JD 10; 7 JD 9; 10 JD 18;
   19 JD 11; 24 JD 39; 25 JD 39
Bertin, Eddy C.: The Harry Dickson
   Detective Stories of Jean Ray,
   1-1 MR 7
Best Books of 1978 - Fiction, (mystery)
   by George Kelley, 2-2 PP 19
Best Crime and Mystery Books of
   1980, by George Kelley, 4-1 PP 11
Best Crime Fiction and Non-Fiction
   of 1979, by George Kelley, 3-1 PP
   25
Best of Hitchcock, The, (Alfred
   Hitchcock books), by Raymond
   Onstfeld, 14-3 TAD 248
"Best of" Phenomenon, The, (author
   collections), by J. Grant Thiessen,
   4 SF 32; 5 SF 47
Best of Dink, or Stover Revisited,
   (Dink Stover, boys' books),
   1-2 BC 47
Best of John Creasey, The, by Deryck
   Harvey, 7-1 TAD 42
Best Selling American Detective
   Fiction, (dissertation), by Joan
   M. Mooney, (Purpose and Method;
   The Detective Story - Some Whys;
   The Emergence of Detective Fiction;
   The Detective's World, The 19th
   Century View; The World View in
   the 20th Century Detective Novel),
   3-3 TAD 141; (The Social Scene in
   the 20th Century), 3-4 TAD 215;
   (The Detective), 4-1 TAD 12; (The
   Detective and the Women), 4-2 TAD
   87
(Best Selling American Detective
   Fiction, by Joan M. Mooney),
   Commentary on, by Joe R. Christopher,
   5-1 TAD 11
(Best Selling American Detective
   Fiction, by Joan M. Mooney), The
   Detective Story: Pertinent?, by
   Bruce L. Monblatt, 4-3 TAD 170
Best TV Eyes of the 80's, The, (on
   television private eye detectives)
   by Robert J. Randisi, 2-1 M 11
(Bester, Alfred), The Science Fiction,
   Mystery Novels of Asimov, Bester
   and Lem: Fusions and Foundations,
   by Steven R. Carter, 1-1 C 109
(Bester, Alfred: THE DEMOLISHED MAN)
   Mystery Plus: The Demolished Man,
   by R. Jeff Banks, 1-2 PP 13

Bestseller Mystery Checklist, by Jeff
  Meyerson, 1-5 PP 33
Bestseller Mysteries, Checklist Addendum,
  by Jim Tinsman, 1-6 PP 27; 2-1 PP 31
Betz, Arthur: letter of comment, 8-4
  TAD 313
Beyond This Horizon, (verse), by James
  Grant Thiessen, 4 SF 25
Biblical War of the Worlds, The, (bible
  associations in WAR OF THE WORLD),
  by Dana Martin Batory, 8 U 46
Biblio-File, (bibliographical data on
  var. pulp magazines), by Nils Hardin,
  7 X 9; 8 X 4; 9 X 9; 10 X 11; 11 X 9;
  14 X 6
Bibliographic Notes on Some HPL Books
  (on Howard Philips Lovecraft), by
  Ted Ball, 4 SF 18
Bibliographica Rohmeriana, (bibliographic
  data on works of Sax Rohmer), by
  Robert E. Briney, 8 R 25; 9 R 13;
  11 R 17; (Sax Rohmer in French)
  12 R 17; (The Paul Harley series)
  17 R 15
Biblio Addendum/Errata, (to Hudson's
  BIBLIOGRAPHY OF HARD-COVER BOYS'
  BOOKS), by Harry K. Hudson, 6 BB 19;
  7 BB 20
Bibliography: Craig Rice, by David R.
  Jasen, 5-1 TAD 26
Bibliography and Checklist, James H.
  Schmitz, by J. Grant Thiessen,
  12 SF 13
Bibliography and English Language Index
  to Georges Simenon's Maigret Novels,
  by Norman J. Shaffer, 3-1 TAD 31
Bibliography, Jack Williamson, by
  Uwe Luserke, 13 SF 29
Bibliography of American Mystery Novels
  Associated with Railroads, by Frank
  P. Donovan, 1-4 TAD 126
Bibliography of English Railway Novels
  of Detection and Mystery, and
  Translations, by Frank P. Donovan,
  2-2 TAD 105
Bibliography of English Railway Short
  Stories of Detection and Mystery,
  and Translations, by Frank P. Donovan,
  2-3 TAD 178
Bibliography of Railroad Short Stories
  of Detection in America, by Frank P.
  Donovan, 2-1 TAD 47
Bibliography of Secondary Sources, A,
  (mystery and related reference), for:
  1972, 7-1 TAD 46   (by Walter Albert)
  1973, 7-4 TAD 266
  1974, 8-4 TAD 290
  1975, 9-4 TAD 316
  1976, 11-2 TAD 196
  1977, 12-2 TAD 125
  1978, 13-1 TAD 43
  1979, 13-4 TAD 313
  1980, 14-4 TAD 346

Bibliography of Weird Fiction of
  Oscar Cook and Christine Campbell
  Thomson, by Mike Ashley, 3 WT 13
Bibliography of Works of August
  Derleth, (list of corrections),
  by Bill Dutch, 4-4 AD 11
(bibliography), see also: Checklists,
  Indexes
(bibliography), A Selective Critical
  Bibliography of the Genre in the
  Sixties, (mystery novels), by
  Rev. Robert E. Washer, 2-1 MR 18;
  2-2 MR 3
(bibliography), Catastrophe Fiction,
  by Robert L. Brown, 20 X 10
(bibliography), Culver, Grace (series
  character), by Roswell Brown,
  17 X 8
(bibliography), Giesy, J.U. (w/ Junius
  B. Smith), The Occult Detector
  Series, 17 X 55
(bibliography), Mass Market Paperback
  Publishing 1939-Present, An Annotated
  Bibliography, by Thomas Bonn,
  1-4 PQ 3
(bibliography), Smith, Clark Ashton,
  by E.P. Berglund, 18 X 35
(BIBLIOGRAPHY OF HARD-COVER BOYS' BOOKS:
  Harry K. Hudson), Addendum and
  Errata, by author, 6 BB 19;
  7 BB 20
Bibliophile, The - Sooner or Later,
  (collecting Rex Stout), by Judson
  C. Sapp, 6 U 31
Biederstadt, Lynn: Robert Fish, In
  Memorium, (memorial tribute)
  14-2 TAD 119
Biederstadt, Lynn: "To the Very Last,
  The Dying Message" (in detective
  fiction), 12-3 TAD 209
Biegel, Andy, Jr.: CONFESSIONS OF A
  THUG by Col. Philip Meadows Taylor,
  An Appreciation, 11 SF 37
Biegel, Andy, Jr.: Thrills, Spills and
  Cliff-Hanging Adventures Supreme
  in a Calvacade of Famous "Chapter-
  Play" Serials: King of Entertainment,
  (on old movie serials), 5 U 11
Biegel, Andy, Jr.: letter of comment,
  5 U 63; 24 X 12
("big brother" police state), Hard
  Touch, by Bill Wilson, 19 JD 9
Big Game Series, (boys' series books,
  checklist and bibliography), by
  Harry K. Hudson, 3 BB 25
(Big Little books), The Hows, Whys, Ifs
  and Buts of Collecting Big Little
  Books, by Randall Zbiciak, 4 BB 7
(BIG MAGAZINE, THE), Checklist, pulp
  magazine, by Lynn Hickman, 75 PU 7
Big Sell, The: An Interview with
  Allen Hubin, by Gary Warren Niebuhr,
  4-5/6 PP 24

58

(Biggers, Earl Derr), Checklist, by
Charles Shibuk, 2-6 MR 21
(Biggers, Earl Derr: CHARLIE CHAN CARRIES
ON), Charlie Chan Carries On, by
Neil Ellman, 10-2 TAD 183
Biggers, Julian L.: A Note on Dovelands
Cottage, (re: Sax Rohmer), 14 R 23
Biggers, Julian L.: A Walking Tour of
Sax Rohmer's London, (descriptive
essay), 18 R 13
Biggers, Julian L.: Letter to Sherlock,
and Annotations, 6 R 7
Biggers, Julian L.: letter of comment,
8 R 31
Biggers, Julian L.: Locating Dr. Petrie's
Practice, (Sax Rohmer character),
7 R 17
Biggers, Julian L.: Sax Rohmer, An
Astrological Analysis, 8 R 19
Biggers, Julian L.: Zagazig, Zagazig,
Z.A.Gazig (re: Dr. Fu Manchu), 5 R 25
(Biggers, Julian L.), Biograpical Sketch
of Biggers, 7 R 25
Bill Ballinger, His Work, His Women and
His World, with checklist of works,
by Pat Erhardt, 4-6 MR 3
Bill Barnes - Air Adventurer, (aviation
pulp hero character), by B.W.Overn,
3 BS 14
Bill Barnes, (aviation pulp hero character
dissected), by Al Grossman, 11 P 17
Bill Pronzini: A Checklist (and introduction)
by Bill Pronzini and Francis M. Nevins,
Jr., 13-4 TAD 345
Bill Pronzini Revisited, by George Kelley,
2-5 MF 5
Bill S. Ballinger Checklist, by Harold
Knott, 4-6 MR 9
(Billy To-Morrow Series), Boys' Series
Bibliography, by Harry K. Hudson,
1-3 YB 9
Bilyeu, Richard: The Avon and DAW Problem,
(identification of first and subsequent
editions, paperback publishers), 11 SF 25
Binocular Eyes, Cross-Cultural Detectives,
(story contact between different
cultural spheres), by Margaret J. King,
13-3 TAD 253
Birns, Margaret Boe: Agatha Christie's
Portrait of the Artist, (self-revelation)
1-2 C 31
Birth and Growth of the Crime Writers'
Association, The, (British organization
of mystery writers), by Rona Randall,
5-3 MR 25
Birth of (Dr.) Death, (pulp character first
in ALL DETECTIVE MAGAZINE), by Dick
Myers, 6 BS 5
Birth of Dr. Fu Mancu, The, (by the author),
by Sax Rohmer, 17 R 1
Bishop, Dan: Doc's Adventures Search, (Doc
Savage oriented puzzle), 5 DS 22
Bishop, Paul: The Book Detective, (collecting
mystery novels), 6 PE 29

Bishop, Paul: The Daily Occurrence
Sheet, (fiction), 1-2 M 39
Bishop, Paul: The Enigma of the
Policeman/Writer, (police
procedurals written by police
officers), 2-1 M 34
Bishop, Paul: Interview with Dallas
Barnes, 2-1 M 36
Bishop, Paul: The Ladies of the Rube,
(television mysteries), 3-1 M 53
Bishop, Paul: Lady Cop, (women in
law enforcement), 3-1 M 18
Bishop, Paul: letter of comment,
2 PE 46; 2-1 PP 36
Bishop, Paul: The Longest Goodbye,
or, The Search for Chandler's
Los Angeles, (explores locale
of Raymond Chandler stories),
1-2 M 33
Bishop, Paul: Man in a Suitcase,
(television series with checklist)
7 PE 15
Bishop, Paul: Mongo?, (detective
sketch by George Chesbro, character
creator), 2 PE 28
Bishop, Paul: Mystery Fandom, (on
organizations and publications),
1-3 M 24
Bishop, Paul: Playedback...or
Chandler's Los Angeles Revisited,
(locales of Raymond Chandler
stories), 5 PE 29
Bishop, Paul: Testing Your Eye-Q,
(quiz oriented to private eye
detectives), 1-1 M 12
Bishop, Paul: The Trenchcoat Files,
James Hazell, the Toughest Bastard
to Ever Push Your Bell Button,
(private eye detective), 4 PE 17
Bishop, Paul: The Trenchcoat Files,
Meet Joe Goodey - San Francisco
Will Never Be the Same, (series
by Charles Alverson), 6 PE 31
Bishop, Paul: The Trenchcoat Files,
(Zach Rolfe series by J.J.Lamb),
3 PE 15
Bits and Pieces, (mystery news), by
Allen J. Hubin, 6-1 TAD 43
("Bitter End": Rex Stout), The "Lost"
Nero Wolfe Tale, by Art Scott,
9 MN A14
BIZARRE FANTASY TALES, Checklist and
Index, by Gene Marshall and Carl
F. Waedt, 3 SF 19
Bjornsen, (verse), by Frederick
Faust, 2-4 FC 6
(BLACK BEECH AND HONEYDEW: Ngaio
Marsh), The Whodunit's Who's Who,
(on autobiography of Ngaio Marsh),
by Philip T. Asdell, 3-4 PP 11
(BLACK BOX MURDER, THE: Maarten
Maartens), Chance and Illogic and
THE BLACK BOX MURDER, by E.F.
Bleiler, 2-1 MF 8

Black, Cary Joseph: letter of comment,
1-1 MF 43
Black Cops and/or Robbers, The Detective
Fiction of Chester Himes, by Frank J.
Campenni, 8-3 TAD 206
Black, Louis: Film Note on "The President
Vanishes" (by Rex Stout), 9 MN A60
Black, Louis: letter of comment, 1-2 CP 4
(Black Magic series: Dennis Wheatley),
Checklist, by Iwan Hedman, 2-4 TAD 236
(BLACK MASK), Annotated Raoul Whitfield
Checklist, (author's works in pulp
magazine), by E.R.Hagemann, 13-3 TAD
183
(BLACK MASK), The Backbone of Black Mask,
(Frederick Nebel's detective stories
in the pulp magazine, with checklist)
by Dave Lewis, 2-2 C 118
(BLACK MASK), Excerpts from "The Boys in
the Black Mask" (exhibit, UCLA Library,
1961, with checklist of hardboiled
detective fiction), 3-2 MR 23
(BLACK MASK), The Black Mask Boys Go
Legit, (discussion of Dashiell
Hammett and Raymond Chandler), by
William F. Nolan, 13-1 TAD 23
(BLACK MASK), Gardner and Black Mask -
Incomplete? (Erle Stanley Gardner
in the pulp magazine), by Stewart
Kemble, 73 PU 4
(BLACK MASK), Lester Dent, The Last of
the Joe Shaw's Black Mask Boys,
(Dent's work in the pulp magazine
under editor Shaw), by Will Murray,
2-2 C 128
Black Murder and Gold Medal, (mysteries
published by Gold Medal Books, an
English publisher), by Frank D.
McSherry, Jr., 4-3 TAD 156
Black Orchid Banquet Quiz, The, (quiz
oriented to Rex Stout), by Marjorie
Mortensen, 1-1 G 13
Black Orchid Banquet Theme Songs,
(re: Rex Stout and the Wolfe Pack)
by Marjorie Mortensen, 1-1 G 9
Black Sounds, ("Duende" magazine and
the pulps), by Will Murray, 1 D 2
Blackbeard, Bill: Fore Shadowings,
Genesis of The Shadow, (forerunners
to The Shadow character), 17 X 6;
22 X 30
Blackbeard, Bill: letter of comment,
4-1 TAD 56; 13 X 58; 30 X 150
Blackbeard, Bill: What Was That Zine
Again, 28 X 77
Blackbeard, Bill, and Rich Register:
How to Make Your Pulps Last
Forever, (idea on preservation),
26 X 70
(Blackburn, John), Six Britons the
Movies Ignored, (seldom filmed),
by Jack Edmund Nolan, 3-5 MR 9

(Blackburn, John: General Kirk series),
Checklist, by Barry Van Tilburg,
4-2 MF 12
(Blackmore, Richard D.: CLARA VAUGHAN)
Inspector Bucket's Rival, by
Clifford Jiggens, 12-3 TAD 270
BLACKOUT, Hubert Aquin's Surreal Mystery,
by Russell M. Brown, 13-1 TAD 58
Blaine, John: A Rick Brant Reminiscence,
(on Rick Brant boys' series books
by their author), 3 MA 3
(Blaine, John), Not Forgotten, (on
the Rick Brant boys' series), 2 MA 1
(Blaine, John), The Rick Brant Crossword
Puzzle, (boys' book character
oriented), 4 MA 28
(Blaine, John), The Roger Baxter Series,
(boys' books series), by Bob Ybarra,
3 MA 23
(Blaine, John), Spindrift Revisited,
(on Rick Brant boys' series books)
by Kent Winslow, 3 MA 1
(Blair, Peter, series: J.R.L.Anderson)
Checklist, by Barry Van Tilburg,
4-2 MF 11
Blair, Stanley R.: Never to be Forgotten!
(reminiscences, pulp magazines),
11 X 19
(Blaise, Modesty, series: Peter O'Donnell)
A Modesty Blaise Appreciation, by
R. Jeff Banks, 8 MN 3
(Blaise, Modesty, series: Peter O'Donnell)
Checklist, annotated, by R. Jeff Banks,
4-2 MF 8
(Blaise, Modesty, series: Peter O'Donnell)
Immoderate Homage to Modesty, by
R. Jeff Banks, 4-2 MF 8
(Blake, Andy, series: Leo Edwards),
Andy Blake First Leo Edwards Book,
(boys' series), by Julius R. Chenu,
1-1 TB 1
(Blake, Andy, series: Leo Edwards),
Background of First Andy Blake Book,
(boys' series), by Julius R. Chenu,
1-3 TBN 1
(Blake, Andy, series: Leo Edwards),
Checklist, by Julius R. Chenu,
3 BB 10; 1-2 YB 17
(Blake, Andy, series: Leo Edwards),
Checklist, 1-1 TB 4
(Blake, Andy, series: Leo Edwards),
More Information on Andy Blake
Series, by Julius R. Chenu, 1-3 TB 3
(Blake, Andy, series: Leo Edwards),
More on Andy Blake, Printing History
of (Appleton edition), 1-4 TB 1
(Blake, Andy, series: Leo Edwards),
Printing Variations in the Andy
Blake Series, by Julius R. Chenu,
1-1 TBN 5
(Blake, Andy, series: Leo Edwards),
That First Andy Blake, by Ray H.
Zorn, 1-3 TB 3

(Blake, Andy & Arabella, series: Richard Powell), Checklist, annotated (espionage genre), by Barry Van Tilburg, 4-6 MF 6

(Blake, Nicholas), A Conversation with Nicholas Blake, by Jan Broberg, 2-3 MR 3

(Blake, Nicholas), Checklist of books, by Jan Broberg, 2-3 MR 3

(Blake, Nicholas: A QUESTION OF PROOF), The First Appearance: Nigel Strangeways, by Maryell Cleary, 2-5 PP 25

Blake, Robert: letter of comment, 14-1 TAD 71

(Blake, Sexton), Sexton Blake, the Office Boys' Sherlock Holmes, (detective character, British, in dime novels) by Fr. Francis Hertzberg, 7 X 5

(Blake, Sexton, series: John Creasey), Checklist, by R.E.Briney and John Creasey, 2-1 TAD 20

Blame Stephen Sondheim (regarding Frederick Hazleton's SWEENEY TODD, THE DEMON BARBER OF FLEET STREET, British villain), by E.F.Bleiler, 5-1 MF 15

(Blanc, Suzanne), Traveler with Crime, Suzanne Blanc, by Winn Kearns, 8-3 TAD 194

(Blanc, Suzanne: Inspector Miguel Menendes) Meeting Menendes, An Analysis of Three Detective Novels of Suzanne Blanc, by Jane S. Bakerman, 10-3 TAD 227

Blau, Peter E.: "Art in the Blood..." (Sherlockiana), 2-2 PDA 68

Blau, Peter E.: letter of comment, 2-2 M 2; 7 MN 7; 12 MN L10; 13 MN L1; 2-5 PP 41; 3-6 PP 32; 5-1 TAD 47; 5-2 TAD 115; 5-4 TAD 234; 7-1 TAD 66; 9-2 TAD 156; 11-4 TAD 316; 12-4 TAD 353

Blau, Peter E.: The Rivals of Sherlock Holmes, a Reference List (contemporary detective stories), 11-2 TAD 193

Blau, Peter E.: The Sherlockian EQMM, (Sherlockiana stories in ELLERY QUEEN'S MYSTERY MAGAZINE), 2-1 QC 15

Blau, Peter E.: Sherlockiana, (related items published),(in 1975) 8 MN 39; (in 1976) 1-11 MM 8; (in 1978) 12 MN 2; 13 MN 1

Blei, Norbert: letter of comment, 2-1 AD 12

Blei, Norbert: Sac Prairie Looked the Same (but August Derleth wasn't there), 3-4 AD 1

Bleiler, E.F.: A Chinese Detective in San Francisco, (Chan To, Chan Tow) 5-3 MF 2

Bleiler, E.F.: The Apocryphalization of Holmes, (article review on SHERLOCK HOLMES, THE PUBLISHED APOCRYPHA by Jack Tracy), 4-5 MF 3

Bleiler, E.F.: Blame Stephen Sondheim, (on Frederick Hazleton's SWEENEY TODD, THE DEMON BARBER OF FLEET STREET, British villain), 5-1 MF 15

Bleiler, E.F.: Chance and Illogic and THE BLACK BOX MURDER, 2-1 MF 8

Bleiler, E.F.: Chinese Detectives in Poland, (Polish translations and introduction), 11-4 TAD 343

Bleiler, E.F.: The Dilemma of Datchery, (on Dickens' THE MYSTERY OF EDWIN DROOD), 4-4 MF 7

Bleiler, E.F.: Female Detectives, Ghost Books and the Relative Importance of it All, (re: EXPERIENCES OF A LADY DETECTIVE, anonyma), 8-3 TAD 202

Bleiler, E.F.: His Own Desert , (authentification of literary works in article review of A.Q. Morton's LITERARY DETECTION, HOW TO PROVE AUTHORSHIP AND FRAUD IN LITERATURE AND DOCUMENTS), 3-4 MF 11

Bleiler, E.F.: John B. Williams, M.D., Forgotten Writer of Detective Stories, 10-4 TAD 353

Bleiler, E.F.: letter of comment, 2-1 MF 60; 2-5 MF 46; 3-5 MF 50; 4-6 MF 42; 5-1 MF 36; 5-4 TAD 249; 6-3 TAD 201; 6-4 TAD 278; 7-1 TAD 69; 8-1 TAD 72; 8-4 TAD 317; 9-3 TAD 169; 10-2 TAD 160; 10-3 TAD 278; 10-4 TAD 292; 12-1 TAD 92; 13-2 TAD 159

Bleiler, E.F.: Marmelahd or Marmelade, (on the name Lestrade in the Sherlock Holmes stories), 13-4 TAD 334

Bleiler, E.F.: Recent European Works on the Detective Story, 2-3 MF 23

Bleiler, E.F.: Sweden's Commitment to Mystery Fiction, 2-5 MF 7

Bleiler, E.F.: Try to Find It, (rare detective fiction), 6-2 TAD 97

Bleiler, E.F.: Vincent Starrett vs. Arthur Machen, or, How Not to Communicate Over Eight Years of Correspondence, 3-6 MF 11

"Bless You, Tom Swift", (Tom Swift boys' series), by Andrew E. Svenson, 2-1 BC 130

(Blessington, Charles, detective: John Sherwood), Checklist, by Barry Pike, 2-3 PP 23

(Blessington, Charles, detective: John Sherwood), Pen Profile, (sketch), by Barry Pike, 2-3 PP 23

(BLIND SPOT: Joseph Harrington), Joseph Harrington's First Three Books, by R.W.Hays, 4-2 TAD 104

(Blish, James), Killians Memoranda,
    (on science fiction works in
    paperback), by Dave Killian,
    2-3 CP 8
Bloch, Robert: Ave Avallone! (on
    Mike Avallone), 8 U 77
Bloch, Robert: Crumbs for a Toast to
    Solar Pons, (verse), 1-2 PDA 42
Bloch, Robert: Inside the Outsider,
    (discusses H.P.Lovecraft), 18 X 4
Bloch, Robert: letter of comment,
    1-1 AD 1; 1-3 AD 3; 2-2 AD 9;
    21 JD 15; 4 MA 24; 1-1 MF 40;
    3/4 MN 11; 12 MN L11; 2 U 48;
    5 U 66; 6 U 50; 7 U 45; 4 WT 12;
    13 X 59; 15 X 13; 22 X 50;
    24 X 45; 26 X 73; 28 X 78;
    33 X 113; 38 X 143; 40 X 85;
    43 X 6
Bloch, Robert: Robert Bloch on Crime
    Fiction, 1-6 MR 15
(Bloch, Robert), An Interview with
    Robert Bloch, 1 FM 9
(Bloch, Robert), Avallone's Avocados,
    (extract of letter from Avallone
    to Bloch, 1966), 11 MN A10
(Bloch, Robert), The Derleth Connection,
    Robert Bloch, by Richard H. Fawcett
    (with introduction by Bloch),
    3-1 AD 3
(Bloch, Robert), Interview with Robert
    Bloch, by Michael S. Barson, 4-1
    PQ 18
(Bloch, Robert), Paperback Originals
    of Robert Bloch, checklist, by
    Michael S. Barson, 4-1 PQ 24
(Bloch, Robert), Some Thoughts About
    Robert Bloch, by Bruce Walker,
    7 X 72
(Bloch, Robert), Yours Truly, Bloch
    the Ripper, (Bloch's macabre taste
    in writing), by Michael S. Barson,
    4-1 PQ 17
Blochman, Lawrence G.: letter of comment,
    6-1 TAD 59; 6-3 TAD 194; 7-1 TAD 71
(Blochman, Lawrence G.: Dr. Coffee
    series), Coffee in the Lab, A
    Preliminary Bibliography, by James
    Mark Purcell, 4-3 MR 29
Block, Don Z.: Collecting Paperback
    First Editions of Philip Jose Farmer,
    2-3 CP 18
Block, Don Z.: Hancer's Price Guide,
    (discussed), 2-5 CP 24
Block, Don Z.: I, LIBERTINE, Shepherd's
    Crook or Bony Sturgeon?, (comments
    on paperback title), 2-4 CP 27
Block, Don Z.: letter of comment,
    3-1 CP 6; 3-3 CP 5
Block, Don Z.: Why I Love the American
    Comic Book Company's 1980 Paperback
    Catalog, (value), 2-2 CP 7

(Block, Lawrence: Matt Scudder series)
    Series Synopses, by Jeff Meyerson,
    12-1 TAD 62
(Block, Lawrence: Tanner series),
    Lawrence Block, Annotated Checklist
    of the Tanner Series Books,
    5/6 MN 7
Blohm, Ed H., Jr.: letter of comment,
    16 X 77; 24 X 47
Blom, K. Arne, and Jan Broberg:
    Detective Fiction in Sweden,
    9-4 TAD 272
Blood and Thunder on Stage, by James
    Keddie, Jr., 1-4 TAD 119
Blood Chronicle, (Richard Curtis van
    Loam as The Phantom Detective, and
    on THE PHANTOM DETECTIVE magazine)
    by Robert Sampson, 3-3 MR 3
Bloody But Readable, (on mysteries
    1914-1918), by Mary Groff, 11-3
    TAD 234
Blosser, Fred: letter of comment,
    15 JD 22; 17 JD 32; 19 JD 11;
    4-1 MR 18; 4-6 MR 17; 5-2 MR 16;
    3-3 TAD 207; 4-1 TAD 59; 4-2 TAD
    131; 5-1 TAD 45; 5-3 TAD 182
Blosser, Fred: The Man From Miami,
    Lester Dent's Oscar Sail (detective
    character), 5-2 TAD 93
Blowing Out the Boy's Brains, (on
    boys' books), by Franklin R. Mathiews,
    1-4 BC 106
Blue & Gold 1916, (Frederick Faust in
    Univ. of California Yearbook), by
    Paul S. Latimer, 2-1 FC 9
"Blue Max, The", (observations on the
    World War I aircraft used in the
    film), by Dave Prosser, 66 PU 5
Blue Mountain, (verse), by George Gott,
    2-3/4 AD 11
Blue Scorpion, The, by Robert Weinberg,
    10 R 20
(BLUE-BOOK), H. Bedford-Jones in BLUE-
    BOOK, (pulp magazine), by William
    J. Clark, 22 X 42
Blue Seal Books, (checklist of paperback
    series), by Bill O'Connell, 3-3 CP 23
Blum, Emarie R.: letter of comment,
    1-2 AD 8
Blumenthal, Hope: letter of comment,
    1-3 PP 33
Blythe, Hal: letter of comment,
    4-1 PP 40; 4-2 PP 35; 4-4 PP 33;
    4-5/6 PP 96
(Bobbsey Twins series), Whatever
    Happened to...? (juvenile series)
    by Sidney Fields, 4-1 BC 393
(Bob's Hill Boys series), Charles Pierce
    Burton and The Boys of Bob's Hill,
    (Boy Scout boys' series books by
    Burton), by Jack Bales, 5 BB 5
Bodnar, Louis, Jr.: letter of comment,
    1-4 YB 9

Body in the Library, The: TWENTIETH
CENTURY CRIME AND MYSTERY WRITERS
and the Mystery World in Our Time,
by Martin Morse Wooster, 5-1 MF 11
Boehm, John, and Mark Justice: Death
Flies in Silver Circles, (fiction,
Doc Savage pastiche), 1 MB 7
(Bogart, Humphrey), Garfield for the
Defense, Purcell vs. Bogart,
(rebuttal, see 11-1 TAD 6), by
Brian Garfield, 11-2 TAD 186
(Bogart, Humphrey), Humphrey Bogart,
Some Remarks on the Canonization
Process, (developing popularity)
by J.M. Purcell, (see rebuttal
11-2 TAD 186), 11-1 TAD 6
(Bogart, Humphrey), Play It Again,
Sam Spade, (as film actor), by
Steve Fisher, 5-2 TAD 79
(Bogart, Humphrey), Spade - Bogart,
(Bogart as Sam Spade in film)
by Mark MacDonald, 4 MT 31
(Bogart, William G.), The Secret
Kenneth Robesons, (Bogart as
Doc Savage author), by Will Murray,
2 D 3
(Bognor, Simon, series: Tim Heald)
Checklist, annotated, by Barry
Van Tilburg, 4-4 MF 17
(Bolton, Judy, series), A Judy Bolton
Mystery - "Blacklisted Classics"
(Judy Bolton girls' series books)
by Luana Russell, 2-1 C 35
(Bolton, Judy, series), Checklist,
by Julius R. Chenu, 1-1 YB 4
(Bolton, Judy, series), The Judy Bolton
Series by Margaret Sutton, by
Julius R. Chenu, 1-1 YB 3
Bomba, the Jungle Boy, (boys' book
series, Tarzan-like adventure),
by Robert Jennings, 5 BB 9
(Bonaparte, Inspector Napoleon: Arthur
W. Upfield), A Preliminary Chronology
of the Documented Cases of Napoleon
Bonaparte, by William Antony S.
Sarjeant, 12-4 TAD 358
(Bonaparte, Inspector Napoleon: Arthur
W. Upfield), Arthur William Upfield
1888-1964, by Estelle Fox, 3-2 TAD 89
(Bonaparte, Inspector Napoleon: Arthur
W. Upfield), Australian Words and
Expressions in Upfield's Novels, by
Philip T. Asdell, 1 BY 5
(Bonaparte, Inspector Napoleon: Arthur
W. Upfield), Bony Was There, (locales
of stories), by Philip T. Asdell,
1 BY 2
(Bonaparte, Inspector Napoleon: Arthur
W. Upfield), The Great Melbourne Cup
Mystery, (on FOLLOW MY DUST), by
Philip T. Asdell, 1 BY 3

(Bonaparte, Inspector Napoleon: Arthur
W. Upfield), Too Right Bony, by
M.C.Hill, 3-2 PQ 7
(Bond, Christopher, series: Wyndham
Martin), Checklist, annotated, by
Barry Van Tilburg, 4-5 MF 23
(Bond, James, series: Ian Fleming),
007-Type Tarzan, (comparison of
Bond and Tarzan), by John Harwood,
4-6 MR 11
(Bond, James, series: Ian Fleming),
The Rivals of James Bond, Commander
Esmonde Shaw, (espionage series
checklist and profile), by Larry
Rickert, 4-4 PP 17
(Bond, James, series: Ian Fleming),
Checklist, annotated, by Barry Van
Tilburg, 4-3 MF 26
(Bond, James, series: Ian Fleming),
God Save Ian Fleming, A Long Over-
Due Thank You to a Master Story-
teller, by Michael Avallone,
12-1 TAD 31
(Bond, James, series: Ian Fleming),
Ian Fleming, Alias James Bond,
(literary sketch of Fleming) by
Billy C. Lee, 4-1 PQ 41
(Bond, James, series: Ian Fleming),
The Ian Fleming Films and TV, by
Jack Edmund Nolan, 5-1 MR 24
(Bond, James, series: Ian Fleming)
The Rivals of James Bond, by
Larry Rickert, 4-2 PP 7
Bond-Charteris Enterprises and Saint
Enterprises, (publishers),
Checklist, by Michael Masliah,
12-4 TAD 354
Bond-Charteris Publishing Company,
Checklist, by J. Grant Thiessen,
2 SF 7
(Bonded Publications), in The Killian
Memoranda, (paperbacks), by David
Killian, 1-4 CP 23
Bonetta, Deborah: Murder Can Happen
Anywhere, (discussion on locales
of mystery stories), 14-3 TAD 257
(Bonibooks), Checklist, (paperbacks),
by Peter Manesis, 2-4 PQ 26
Bonn, Thomas: letter of comment,
1-6 CP 5; 2-2 CP 1; 2-3 CP 2;
3-1 CP 2; 1-3 PQ 3; 1-3 PQ 14;
2-1 PQ 3; 2-3 PQ 5; 2-3 PQ 8
Bonn, Thomas: Mass Market Paperback
Publishing 1939 to Present, An
Annotated Bibliography, 1-4 PQ 3
Bonn, Thomas: Soft Cover Sketches,
(paperback cover art), (Introduction) 3-3 PQ 39; (James Avati)
3-3 PQ 40; (Lou Marchetti) 4-2 PQ
32; (Robert Jones) 3-4 PQ 19

Bonner, Jack: letter of comment, 10 JD 12
Bonner, Jean: letter of comment, 14 JD 21
Bonner, Paul H., Jr.: A Second Round for
   Doc, (background of paperback books
   publication of Doc Savage novels),
   9 BS 4
Bonner, Paul H., Jr.: letter of comment,
   3 BS 2; 4 BS 16; 8 BS 5; 15 BS 15;
   5 DQ 6; 6 DQ 3
Bonnett, Hal Murray: It Was Never That
   Much Fun! (pulp author on writing for
   pulp magazines), 38 X 141
Bony Was There, (locales of Inspector
   Bonaparte stories of Arthur W. Upfield)
   by Philip T. Asdell, 1 BY 2
(book clubs), An Old Friend, The Detective
   Book Club, by Michael L. Cook, 8-2 TAD
   77
(book clubs), The Detective Book Club,
   Alphabetical Listing by Author, by
   Michael L. Cook, 10 MN 11
(book clubs), The Detective Book Club,
   Checklist in order of publication,
   by Michael L. Cook, 10 MN 121
(book clubs), The Detective Book Club,
   Supplement to Checklist in TAD 8-1,
   by Michael L. Cook, 9 MN I1
(book clubs), Collecting Book Club
   Editions, by Michael L. Cook,
   3 U 19
(book clubs), Hans Stefan Santesson and
   the Unicorn Mystery Book Club, by
   Edward D. Hoch, 8-3 TAD 185
(book clubs), Murder by Mail, Update,
   (listing of books published by the
   book clubs, May 1979 - August 1981)
   by Michael L. Cook, 4-5/6 PP 51
(book clubs), The Mystery Guild - New
   Selections and Major Alternates for
   1975, by Don Miller, 8 MN 53
(book clubs), Rex Stout in Mystery Guild
   Editions, (checklist), by Michael L.
   Cook, 9 MN A27
(book clubs), The Unicorn Mystery Book
   Club, Checklist by author and in
   order of publication, by Michael
   L. Cook, 12 MN I1
(book clubs), Unicorn Mystery Book Club,
   Complete Checklist, by Edward D. Hoch,
   8-3 TAD 187
(book clubs), The Unicorn Mystery Book
   Club, (partial list, with short
   history), by Michael L. Cook, 5 MY 3
Book Collecting, (collecting boys' books),
   by Denis R. Rogers, 1-3 BC 79
(book collecting), see also "mystery
   collecting", "paperback collecting",
   "boys' book collecting"
(book collecting), Cardboard Shelves,
   (housing your collection), by Eddy
   Thomas, 10 SF 32
(book collecting), How to File Your
   Science Fiction Collection, by J.
   Grant Thiessen, 2 SF 42

(BOOK COLLECTOR, THE), Ian Fleming:
   BOOK COLLECTOR, (Fleming as editor)
   by William White, 6-3 TAD 181
Book Detective, The, (collecting mystery
   books), by Andy Jaysnovitch, 2 PE 33
Book Detective, The, (collecting mystery
   books), by Paul Bishop, 6 PE 29
Book News, (pulp oriented), 60 PU 33;
   62 PU 26
Book Nook, The, (reviews), 1-5 MM 9;
   1-6 MM 9; 1-7 MM 7; 1-8 MM 5;
   1-9 MM 5; 1-10 MM 7; 1-11 MM 3;
   2-1 MM 3; 2-2 MM 3; 2-3 MM 3;
   2-4 MM 3; 2-5 MM 5
Book Nook, The, (reviews), 1 MN 7;
   2 MN 5; 3/4 MN 7; 5/6 MN 19;
   5/6 MN 22; 7 MN 9; 8 MN 11;
   9 MN R1; 10 MN R1; 11 MN R1;
   12 MN R1
Book Notes, (on mysteries), by Jim
   Huang, 8 CL 7; 9 CL 9; 10 CL 10;
   13/14 CL 1
(book repair), How to Keep Dust and
   Soil off Books of a Collection, by
   Jack R. Schorr, 1-2 BC 63
(book repair), How to Restore a Book,
   by Jack R. Schorr, 1-1 BC 29
Book Review Extracts, (from the press)
   by Don Miller, 1-1 MM 10; 1-2 MM 7;
   1-3 MM 9; 1-4 MM 7; 1-5 MM 5; 1-6
   MM 5; 1-7 MM5; 1-8 MM 8; 1-9 MM 8;
   1-10 MM 10; 1-11 MM 6; 2-1 MM 7;
   2-2 MM 9; 2-3 MM 7; 2-4 MM 8
Book Reviews, 2-2 C 154; 16 CD 9, (see
   also "Reviews")
Book Sellers, (list of dealers in
   paperback books), 4-1 PQ 48
   (see also "booksellers")
Book Sellers Under the Big Top, (boys'
   books), 3-3 BC 322
(book selling), The Last Thousand, (a
   collector's experience in disposing
   of collection), by Basil Wells,
   5 U 24
Books, (reviews) (see also "Reviews")
   1 PE 12; 2 PE 17; 3 PE 19; 4 PE 11;
   5 PE 15; 6 PE 17; 7 PE 11
Books About Books of Crime and the
   Criticism Thereof, by Jacques
   Barzun, 5-1 TAD 15
Books About J.R.R.Tolkien and His
   Works, including list, by David S.
   Bratman, 5 SF 26
Books by E. Phillips Oppenheim, check-
   list, 4-3 MR 23
Books by John D. MacDonald Through
   1979, (original editions), by Ed
   Hirshberg, 24 JD 35
Books of Edgar Rice Burroughs, The,
   a Checklist, by John F. Sullivan,
   3-3 BC 349
Books of Geoffrey Homes, The, by
   Theodore P. Dukeshire, 3-3 MF 19

Books of Nicholas Luard, The, by Theodore
P. Dukeshire, 4-1 MF 12

Books of Sax Rohmer, The, (a Chronological
List), by Robert E. Briney, 1 R 25

Booksellers, (paperback specalists),
list, 2-3 PQ 29; 2-4 PQ 31; 3-1 PQ 50;
3-2 PQ 54; 3-3 PQ 56; 3-4 PQ 56

(booksellers), Literary Sleuths, Alias
Your Friendly Neighborhood Book
Detectives, by Mary Ann Grochowski,
2-3 PP 3

(booksellers), Murder by Mail, A Dealer
Checklist, by Walter Albert, 3-5 MF 7

(Borden, Lizzie), The Great Lizzie Borden
T-Shirt Media Event and Mystery Quiz,
(on Univ. of Calif.,San Diego, 1978)
5-6 MF 7

(Borden, Lizzie), Lament for a Legend,
Lizzie Borden Revisited, by Mary D.
Smith, 11-2 TAD 132

Borgo Press, The, (publisher), by Robert
Reginald, 2-1 PQ 14

(Borgo Press), Checklist of publications,
by Robert Reginald, 2-1 PQ 20

Boris! Boris! Boris! (on Boris Vallejo,
paperback cover artist for Doc Savage
books), by Robert Woo, 1 DS 11

Bornstein, Karen: Do You Hear What I
Hear? (or, Play It Again, George),
(voice and sound analysis in
detection), 1-2 M 13

Bornstein, Karen: John Ball Interview,
1-3 M 31

Bornstein, Karen, and Douglas Christensen:
A Day in the Life of a Real Private
Investigator, 1-3 M 52

Borowitz, Albert I.: Innocence and
Arsenic, The Literary and Criminal
Careers of C.J.L.Almquist, 9-1 TAD 17

Borowitz, Albert I.: The Many Rises and
Falls of J. Rufus Wallington,
(detective character of George R.
Chester), 12-1 TAD 28

Borowitz, Albert I.: The Mystery of
Edwin Drood, 10-1 TAD 14

Borowitz, Albert I.: New Gaslight on
Jack the Ripper, 9-3 TAD 175

Borowitz, Albert I.: Night Must Fall,
The Sinister Behind the Ordinary,
(discusses NIGHT MUST FALL by
Emlyn Williams), 14-3 TAD 284

(Boston Blackie), Old-Time Radio Lives,
(Boston Blackie radio serials),
by Carl Larsen, 5-6 MF 3

(Boston Blackie), Radio Shows, checklist, by Ray Stanich, 3 PE 17

Boston, John: letter of comment,
62 PU 11

Boswell, Bill: letter of comment,
10 JD 12; 11 JD 32

Bottiggi, William D.: The Importance of
"C--ing" in Earnest, A Comparison
of THE MALTESE FALCON and CHINATOWN
(films), 14-1 TAD 86

Boucher, Anthony: letter of comment,
7 JD 2; 1-2 TAD 63; 1-3 TAD 109

(Boucher, Anthony), A. Boucher
Bibliography, by J.R.Christopher
with D.W.Dickensheet and R.E.
Briney, 2-2 TAD 77; 2-3 TAD 143;
2-4 TAD 263

(Boucher, Anthony), A Boucher Portrait,
Anthony Boucher as Seen by his
Friends and Colleagues, 2-2 TAD 69

(Boucher, Anthony), Anthony Boucher,
(sketch and checklist), by Francis
M. Nevins, Jr., 3-2 M 18

(Boucher, Anthony), The Case of the
Triple Bouchers, by Luther Norris,
1-5 MR 10

(Boucher, Anthony), Dell Paperback
Bibliography, (Dell Pub. Co.), by
Bill Lyles, 1-4 CP 26

(Boucher, Anthony), In Memoriam:
Anthony Boucher, by Len and June
Moffatt, 10 JD 1

(Bouchercon), Of Fans and Bouchercons,
(comments in general), by Guy M.
Townsend, 5-5 MF 11 (conventions)

(Bouchercon I), A Report, by Pat Erhardt,
3-6 MR 25

(Bouchercon I), A report, by Leo Rand,
14 JD 7

(Bouchercon I), The First Bouchercon, a
report by Jon L. Breen, 3-4 TAD 250

(Bouchercon II), A report, by Leo Rand,
17 JD 15

(Bouchercon III), a report, by Robert E.
Briney, 6-2 TAD 98

(Bouchercon III), a report, by Leo Rand,
18 JD 5

(Bouchercon IV), announcement, 6-1 MR 29

(Bouchercon IV), Bouchercon East, a
Report, by Robert E. Briney, 7-1 TAD
48

(Bouchercon IV), Notice of Convention,
6-3 TAD 186

(Bouchercon IV), Report, by Ed Demchko,
6-2 MR 34

(Bouchercon V), a report, by Marvin
Lachman, 8-2 TAD 131

(Bouchercon V), A report, by Leo Rand,
20 JD 17

(Bouchercon VI), A Second Look, by
Robert E. Briney, 5/6 MN 3

(Bouchercon VI), A Short Report, by
George Fergus, 2 MN 3

(Bouchercon VII), A report, by Art Scott,
1A MF 18

(Bouchercon VII), Criminalists, Clergypersons & Others, a Report, by R.E.
Briney, 10-1 TAD 53

(Bouchercon VII), notice, 9-3 TAD 207

(Bouchercon VIII), a report, by Marvin
Lachman, 2-5 MM 3

(Bouchercon VIII), Murder at the Waldorf,
A Report, by Robert E. Briney, 11-1
TAD 53

(Bouchercon VIII), Murder at the Waldorf, Bouchercon VIII, October 7-9, 1977, by Mary Ann Grochowski, 2-2 MF 15

(Bouchercon IX), A Personal View, by Jeff Meyerson, 1-6 PP 20

(Bouchercon IX), Behind the Scenes at Boucheron 9, or It Was Murder at the Bismarck!, by Mary Ann Grochowski, 2-6 MF 3

(Bouchercon IX), Bouchercon 1978, IX and Counting, by Donald A. Yates, 3-1 MF 15

(Bouchercon X), report, by Mary Ann Grochowski, 2-5 PP 27

(Bouchercon X), report, by Diane Wiseman, 1-1 M 17

(Bouchercon X), Two Views, by (1) Marvin Lachman, and (2) Mary Ann Grochowski, 3-5 MF 11

(Bouchercon XI), Bouchercon Scrapbook, (photo report), 4-6 MF 19

(Bouchercon XI), Pow-Wow on the Potomac, A Report on, by John Nieminski, 4-6 MF 12

(Bouchercon XI), "Where Crime Was Our Government's Business", by "Michelle Grant", 3-5 PP 33

BOUCHERCONsense, Bouchercon Notes in Verse, by Walter & Jean Shine, 4-5/6 PP 35

Bound to Win Series, (boys' series sports stories by var. authors), by Gil O'Gara, 1-1 YB 8

Bourgeau, Art: East Coast (Mystery) News, 1-1 M 32; 1-2 M 17

Bourke, Alice: letter of comment, 5-2 TAD 109

Bourne, Michael: Rex Stout, (memorial tribute), 21 X 8

Bovard, Barbara: letter of comment, 66 PU 64

Bovee, Steve: letter of comment, 2 MA 29; 4 MA 25

(Bowen, Robert Sidney), obituary of author, 10 P 4

Bowlers, Beer, Bravado, and Brains: Anthony Gilbert's Arthur Crook (Arthur Crook, detective), by Jane S. Bakerman, 2-4 MF 5

(Box, Edgar), The Edgar Box Mystery Novels, by George Kelley, 4 U 30

(Box, Edgar), The Mysteries of Edgar Box (a.k.a Gore Vidal), by Earl F. Bargainnier, 2-1 C 45

Box 35, (letters of comment), 2 FM 18

Boy Allies, or Who Won World War I, The, (boys' series war stories), by John T. Dizer, Jr., 3-1 BC 270

(Boy Allies, The, series), Checklist of various series/authors), by John T. Dizer, Jr., 3-1 BC 270

Boy Aviators, The, (boys' series books) by Robert Jennings, 3 BB 13

Boy Detectives, (boys' books), by J. Randolph Cox, 1-3 TB 4

Boy Scouts in Old Udolpho, (on August Derleth's MOON TENDERS), by Frederick Shroyer, 2-2 PDA 43

"Boy Swindler Series by Dexter Itty", (satire on boys' series books, by Anson Arnoldsmith, 1-4 YB 20

(Boy Travellers series), The Author of "The Boy Travellers" (Thomas W. Knox; boys' series), 4-1 BC 400

Boyd, Richard D.: letter of comment, 10 JD 12; 15 JD 23; 19 JD 11

(Boyer, Brian, and John Weisman: The Headhunters Series), Series Synopses, by Bill Crider, 11-4 TAD 365

Boyles, John: A Word for John Creasey, J.J.Marric's GIDEON'S RISK, (commentary), 11-3 TAD 282

Boys' Book Author Checklist, 1-1 BC 30

Boys' Bookman, (biog. sketch of John T. Dizer, Jr.), 2-3 BC 220

Boys' Books and the American Dream, by John T. Dizer, Jr., 1-1 BC 3; 1-2 BC 52

Boys' Book Oddities, (variants), by Harry K. Hudson, (Tom Swift) 1-2 BC 43; (The Rover Boys) 1-4 BC 112;)Dave Porter Series), 3-1 BC 285

Boys' Books and the Times, (patriotism and prejudice), by Alan S. Dikty, 1-1 BC 11

Boys' Books and the Times, (boys' books and motion pictures), by Alan S. Dikty, 1-2 BC 50

Boys' Books Written by Roy Judson Snell, by Julius R. Chenu, 1-1 BC 12

Boys' Fiction Written by Leo Edwards, by Julius R. Chenu, 1-2 BC 35

Boys Go to War, The, (war adventures in the boys' series books), by Robert Jennings, 2 BB 9

Boys' Series Bibliographies, by Harry K. Hudson, 1-3 YB 8; 1-4 YB 23; 1-5 YB 13; 1-6 YB 15

Boys Who Used Their Brains: The Boy Who Was Always Looking Ahead, (Leo Edwards boys' series books), by Judson D. Stuart, 2-2 TBN 1

(boys' book collecting), A Representative Collection, by Jack R. Schorr, 3-1 BC 287

(boys' book collecting), A Very Sad Book Story, by Les Beitz, 1-1 BC 26

(boys' book collecting), Adventures in the Mail, by Jack R. Schorr, 2-2 BC 192

(boys' book collecting), Among the Book
Stalls, by Jack E. Schorr, 3-3 BC 330
(boys' book collecting), Book Collecting
by Denis R. Rogers, 1-3 BC 79
(boys' book collecting), Book Sellers
Under the Big Top), 3-3 BC 322
(boys' book collecting), Building a
Collection of Boys' Books, by Jack
R. Schorr, 1-1 BC 32
(boys' book collecting), Chapter One,
by Fred Woodworth, 1 MA 1
(boys' book collecting), Chasing "Will-
o'-the-Wisps", (hard-to-find), by
M.E.Owen, 1-2 BC 64
(boys' book collecting), Collecting
Inside Outside, by Jack Schorr,
1 BB 24
(boys' book collecting), Collecting the
Things, by Julius R. Chenu, 6 BB 5
(boys' book collecting), Discovered
Treasure, by J. Curtis Frymoyer,
3-2 BC 311
(boys' book collecting), From the Dealer's
View, by Ivor A. Rogers, 2-4 BC 236
(boys' book collecting), From Tutter
to Oz- and Back Again!, by Dick
Martin, 2-5 TBN 1
(boys' book collecting), The Great Book
Bubble, by Alan S. Dikty, 1-4 BC 110
(boys' book collecting), How I Found My
Inferior Decorators (Poppy Ott
series book by Leo Edwards), by Jack
R. Schorr, 4-1 TB 1
(boys' book collecting), How I Got
Started Collecting, by Jack Schorr,
1-3 BC 71
(boys' book collecting), The Hows, Whys,
Ifs, and Buts of Collecting Big
Little Books, by Randall Zbiciak,
4 BB 7
(boys' book collecting), Hunting for
Hidden Books, by Kent Winslow,
1 MA 3; 2 MA 21; 5 MA 22; 6 MA 10
(boys' book collecting), Is It Valuable?
by Les Beitz and Alan S. Dikty,
2-4 BC 233
(boys' book collecting), "Is Your
Collection Costing Too Much?", by
Jack Schorr, 1-4 BC 117
(boys' book collecting), Juvenalia,
(var. topics discussed), by Julius
R. Chenu, 1-1 YB 9; 1-2 YB 12;
1-3 YB 16; 1-5 YB 11; 1-6 YB 11
(boys' book collecting), Letters to a
Collector, (advice), by S.E.Wallen,
3-1 BC 265; 3-2 BC 303; 3-3 BC 331;
3-4 BC 380; 4-1 BC 396
(boys' book collecting), Looking Back,
by Jack R. Schorr, 1-2 TBN 4
(boys' book collecting), Loose Ends,
by Fred Woodworth, 6 MA 2
(boys' book collecting), Memories on
Which I Dwell Fondly, by Harry
Pulfer, 1-3 BC 89

(boys' book collecting), Now They're
Collectors' Items, (on the early
boys' books and authors), by J.
Edward Leithead, 1-1 BC 13; 1-2
BC 44; 1-3 BC 72; 1-4 BC 114;
2-1 BC 154; 2-2 BC 187; 2-3 BC 205
(boys' book collecting), Phantom
Titles, (titles announced but
never published), by Harry K.
Hudson, 3 BB 11
(boys' book collecting), Rambling
With Jack, (comments on various
boys' series), by Jack Tornquist,
1-2 TBN 8; 1-3 TBN 7; 1-4 TBN 7
(boys' book collecting), Rantings and
Ravings of a Book Collector, by
George Holmes, 1-3 YB 12
(boys' book collecting), Sam Steele...
(Sam Steele boys' series by L.
Frank Baum writing as Capt. Hugh
Fitzgerald), by George Holmes,
1-6 YB 8
(boys' book collecting), Taking Care
of Your Collection, by Jack R.
Schorr, 2-4 BC 254
(boys' book collecting), What to Do
With Your Duplicates, by Jack R.
Schorr, 3-3 BC 344
(boys' book collecting), Where Do You
Get All That Stuff?, by Robert
Jennings, 6 BB 10
(boys' book collecting), "Where to Look
for Books", by Jack R. Schorr,
2-1 BC 139
(boys' book collecting), You Find Them
in the Oddest Places, by Jack R.
Schorr, 4-1 BC 409
(boys' books - illustrators), Artist,
Clemens Gretter, by Fred Woodworth,
6 MA 5
(boys' books - illustrators), Illustrated
by..., by Les Beitz, 3-4 BC 366
(boys' books - publishers), The Grain
and Salt Printing Company, (essay on
imaginary series), by Robert Jennings
1 BB 12
(boys books - publishers), The Grain and
Salt Printing Company - Update, (more
on the imaginary series), by D.W.
Howard, 2 BB 15
(boys' books - publishers), Whitman, The
Authorized Edition series, by Andrew
Zerbe, 1 BB 17
(boys' books - special collections),
University of Missouri collection,
news note, 1-1 BC 9
(boys' books - value), What Makes a
Juvenile Book Valuable?, by Jack R.
Schorr, 1-1 BC 10
(Boys of Columbia High), Checklist of,
(boys' series books), by Julius R.
Chenu, 5 BB 8; 5 BB 9
(boys papers/magazines), A Quick Look
at the YOUTH'S COMPANION, by Walter
H. McIntosh, 4-1 BC 394

(boys' papers/magazines), Letters to a Collector, by S.E.Wallen, 3-3 BC 331

(boys' papers/magazines), The OPEN ROAD FOR BOYS Goes to War, (wartime issues discussed), by Michael L. Cook, 6 YB 3

(Brackett, Leigh), see Leigh Brackett Hamilton

(Brackett, Leigh), In Memoriam, (memorial tribute to writer), by Robert E. Briney, 11-3 TAD 258

Bradbury, Ray: The Barber Shop, 36 X R26

Bradbury, Ray: Emily Dickinson, Where Are You?, (verse), 13 X 6

Bradbury, Ray: Groon, (verse), 18 X 25

Bradbury, Ray: letter of comment, 14 X 62; 40 X 85

Bradbury, Ray: Why Viking-Lander? Why the Planet Mars?, (verse), 26 X 3

Bradbury in the Pulps, (pulp magazine writings by Ray Bradbury), by William F. Nolan, 36 X R21

(Bradbury Building), Inside Gumshoe Haven, A Look at LA's Bradbury Building, ("home" of fictional private eyes), by Joseph Allen, 1-2 M 27

(Bradbury, Ray), An Index, by Donn Albright, 13 X 9; 26 X 4; 36 X R2; (pulp stories: see Index by Wm. F. Nolan)

(Bradbury, Ray), Index to Pulp Stories, by William F. Nolan, 36 X R22

(Bradbury, Ray), Bradbury in the Pulps, by William F. Nolan, 36 X R21

(Bradbury, Ray), Bradbury's First Book Appearances, by William F. Nolan, 36 X R8

(Bradbury, Ray), Bradbury's Textbook Appearances 1955-1972, by William F. Nolan, 36 X R28

(Bradbury, Ray), The Crime/Suspense Fiction of Ray Bradbury, A Listing, by William F. Nolan, 4-3 TAD 155

(Bradbury, Ray), "The Chronicles" on Stage, (stage production), by Bruce Francis, 36 X R19

(Bradbury, Ray), The Chronicles Remembered, 36 X R36

(Bradbury, Ray), Joke Submitted to George Burns and Gracie Allen (1936) 36 X R16

(Bradbury, Ray), Lights! Camera! - Inaction, Unfilmed Film Scripts of Ray Bradbury, by Ben P. Indick, 36 X R25

(Bradbury, Ray), Ray Bradbury, Fantasist, Visionary, Moralist, by Nils Hardin, 36 X R1

(Bradbury, Ray), The Trip, by Donn Albright, 36 X R13

(Bradbury, Ray), Uncle Ray, by Philip A. Shreffler, 36 X R30

(Bradbury, Ray: FAHRENHEIT 451), Reprints/Reprints, by Bill Crider, 3-3 PQ 22

(Bradbury, Ray: LONG AFTER MIDNIGHT), review by Bruce Francis, 26 X 12

Bradbury's First Book Appearances, by William F. Nolan, 36 X R8

Bradbury's Textbook Appearances, 1955-1972, by William F. Nolan, 36 X R28

Bradd, Sidney H.: Donald E. Keyhole and the Brain Devil of G-2, 22 X 34

Bradd, Sidney H.: G-8, Flying Spy of the Pulps, (pulp hero character) 11 X 11

(Bradfield, Detective-Constable Peter: Clifford Witting), Pen Profile, (biog. & literary sketch), by Barry Pike, 2-6 PP 25

(Brady, Old King), Old King Brady, His Rise and Decline, (dime novels detective character), by Gil O'Gara, 7 U 19

Brahce, Jack D.: letter of comment, 4 MA 25

Bramah, A Footnote to Carrados, by William White, 2-4 MR 19

(Bramah, Ernest), Bramah, A Footnote to Carrados (discusses Bramah and his detective), 2-4 MR 19

(Bramah, Ernest), Ernest Bramah in Anthologies 1914-1972, by William White, 10-1 TAD 30

(Bramah, Ernest), Ernest Bramah to E.C.Bentley, An Unpublished Letter, 2-3 MR 8

(Bramah, Ernest), Ernest Bramah's Max Carrados, (Bramah and his detective Carrados), by William White, 2-2 MR 7

(Bramah, Ernest), An Unpublished Ernest Bramah Letter on Max Carrados (his detective creation), by William White, 3-2 TAD 92

(Bramah, Ernest), What's in a Name?, or, Playfully on a Tangent, (on Max Carrados, his detective character) by Joshua Goldberg, 7-2 TAD 122

Branche, Calvin L.: letter of comment, 9-3 TAD 236; 11-1 TAD 4

(Brand, Christianna: HEADS YOU LOSE), The First Appearance, Inspector Cockrill, by Maryell Cleary, 3-2 PP 6

Brand, H.S.: letter of comment, 14-2 TAD 185

(Brand, Max), see also Frederick Faust

(Brand, Max), King of the Pulps, (on Frederick Faust/Max Brand in the pulp magazines), by Stewart Kimble, 69 PU 25

(Brand, Max), Max Brand and the Mystery Story, by Bill Clark, 2-4 TAD 255

(Brand, Max), Max Brand, Pulp King, by William F. Nolan, 32 X 2

Brandner, Gary: letter of comment, 11-1 TAD 4

Brandon, Carl J., Jr.: letter of comment, 64 PU 40

Brandshaft, Richard: letter of comment, 13-2 TAD 160

(Brandstetter, David, series: Joseph Hansen), Series Synopses, by Fred Dueren, 11-4 TAD 365

Brandt, Dave: letter of comment, 5-6 MR 18

Brandt, Larry: letter of comment, 2-2 TAD 135; 3-1 TAD 67

(Brant, Rick, series: John Blaine) A Rick Brant Reminiscence, by John Blaine (author, boys' book series), 3 MA 3

(Brant, Rick, series: John Blaine) Not Forgotten, by Fred Woodworth, 2 MA 1

(Brant, Rick, series: John Blaine) Spindrift Revisited, (on the boys' series), by Kent Winslow, 3 MA 1

Bratman, David S.: Books About J.R.R. Tolkien and His Works, (bibliography), 5 SF 26

(Braun, Lilian Jackson), The Case of the Quivering Mustache, (commentary) by Mary Ann Grochowski, 3-6 PP 3

Braveman, David: Good Old Petrie (re: Sax Rohmer), 3 R 18

Bravoes of Market-Drayton, The, (fiction, Classic Corner, rare tales) by Arthur Conan Doyle, 14-2 TAD 144

(Bray, Detective-Inspector Bernard: St.John Sprigg), Pen Profile, (biog. and literary sketch), by Barry Pike, 2-5 PP 23

Break a Leg, Break a Neck: The Mystery on Stage, by Tim Kelly, 2-2 M 14

Break It Up!, (how to write for the pulps, by a veteran pulp writer), by Robert Leslie Bellem, 2-2 C 50

Breaking Into the Mystery Market, (advice on writing mystery fiction) by Hal Charles, 4-1 PP 9

Breen, Florence: letter of comment, 10 DS 5; 10 DS 6

Breen, Jon L.: About the Murders of Anthony Abbott, (author's mystery works), 3-1 TAD 1

Breen, Jon L.: All You Need is a Comfortable Chair, or, Did You Hear the One About the Two Tadpolls? (results of "TAD" polls for "best" in several mystery categories), 6-2 TAD 78

Breen, Jon L.: Charlie Chan in Qui Nhon, (on Armed Forces TV in Vietnam), 2-2 TAD 114

Breen, Jon L.: Checklist, Lee Thayer, works, 5-3 TAD 149

Breen, Jon L.: Commentaries for the Curious, (tributes and comments on John Dickson Carr), 1 NC 13

Breen, Jon L.: Cortland Fitzsimmons and the Sports Mystery, (literary sketch), 14-2 TAD 129

Breen, Jon L.: Dedications, A Detective Story Quiz, (quiz), 1-2 TAD 59

Breen, Jon L.: Detective Fiction and the Turf, (racing in mysterys), 5-1 TAD 24

Breen, Jon L.: The Detective Novels of Carolyn Wells, A Chronological Bibliography, 3-2 TAD 78

Breen, Jon L.: The Fantastic World-Wide Ellery Queen Poll, 3-1 QC 7

Breen, Jon L.: The First Bouchercon, A Report, (mystery writers/fans convention), 3-4 TAD 250

Breen, Jon L.: The Idea Man, (fiction, Ellery Queen pastiche), 1-4 QC 11

Breen, Jon L.: The Invisible Man Revisited, (on G.K.Chesterton's THE INVISIBLE MAN), 4-3 TAD 154

Breen, Jon L.: letter of comment, 10 JD 15; 11 JD 20; 13 JD 21; 14 JD 21; 16 JD 17; 17 JD 26; 21 JD 15; 2-1 MF 54; 2-3 MF 66; 2-5 MF 45; 2-6 MF 43; 3-1 MF 47; 3-2 MF 54; 3-3 MF 52; 3-4 MF 53; 4-2 MF 58; 5-1 MF 34; 5-2 MF 46; 5-3 MF 43; 9 MN L5; 11 MN L14; 3-2 MR 16; 2-2 PP 35; 3-2 PP 33; 3-3 PP 37; 3-5 PP 47; 4-2 PP 37; 4-3 PP 33; 1-1 QC 12; 3-1 TAD 69; 3-3 TAD 206; 3-4 TAD 275; 3-4 TAD 306; 4-1 TAD 64; 4-1 TAD 69; 4-2 TAD 125; 5-1 TAD 55; 5-4 TAD 240; 7-3 TAD 228; 9-3 TAD 236; 10-3 TAD 275; 3 U 48; 5 U 62

Breen, Jon L.: On Carolyn Wells, (mystery writer), 3-2 TAD 77

Breen, Jon L.: On Lee Thayer, (mystery writer), 5-3 TAD 148

Breen, Jon L.: On the Passing of MANHUNT, (lament for cessation of MANHUNT magazine), 1-3 TAD 89

Breen, Jon L.: The Pun Detective and the Great Seal Mystery, (fiction), 7 CL 3

Breen, Jon L.: Rebuttal to "Kiss My Deadly Typewriter #539" (Mike Avallone), 3-1 QC 16

Breen, Jon L.: Series Characters, A Detective Story Matching Quiz, (quiz), 3-2 TAD 122

Breen, Jon L.: The Thatcher Colt Novels of Anthony Abbott, A Bibliography, 3-1 TAD 5

Breen, Jon L.: Who Killed Charlie Chan?, (updated Chan), 7-2 TAD 100

Breen, Jon L.: Interview, Mary Roberts
    Rinehart, 1-3 MR 11
Brener, Carol: letter of comment,
    11-2 TAD 206
Brennan, Joseph Payne: The Derleth
    Connection, Joseph Payne Brennan
    in Brief (an autobiography and
    relation with August Derleth),
    2-1 AD 6
Brennan, Joseph Payne: letter of comment,
    1-4 AD 9
Brennan, Lorin: TV Reviews, (reviews
    of television mystery programs),
    (Mystery on PBS) 2-3 M 16; 3-1 M 42;
    3-2 M 50
(Brewer, Gil), Checklist, paperback
    books, by Michael S. Barson, 3-4 PQ 11
(Brewer, Gil), Gil Brewer's Fables of
    Evil Women, Driven Men and Doom
    (Brewer in paperback), by Michael
    S. Barson, 3-4 PQ 3
(Brewer, Gil), Interview with Gil
    Brewer, by Michael S. Barson,
    3-4 PQ 6
Brian Lumley Talks About August Derleth,
    (by Brian Lumley), 2-2 AD 1
Brice, Harvey: letter of comment,
    3 BS 2
(Bridge, Ann: Julia Probyn series),
    Checklist, annotated, by Barry
    Van Tilburg, 5-3 MF 20
Brief Loves, The Early Short Stories
    of Cornell Woolrich, (humor and
    romance short stories), by Francis
    M. Nevins, Jr., 14-2 TAD 168
Briley, Alice: Two Fungi from Yuggoth,
    (verse), 4-3 AD 9
Brimmell, R.A.: letter of comment,
    7-1 TAD 66
Briney, Robert E.: A Mysterious Quiz,
    (mystery quiz), 7-1 TAD 24
Briney, Robert E.: A Rohmer Miscellany,
    (Sax Rohmer), 11 R 8
Briney, Robert E.: Addenda to John
    Creasey Checklists, 2-2 TAD 123;2-4 TAD 276
Briney, Robert E.: An Informal Survey
    of the Works of Sax Rohmer, 1 R 3
Briney, Robert E.: Bibliographica
    Rohmeriana, (bibliographical data,
    various, Sax Rohmer and his works),
    8 R 25; 9 R 13; 11 R 17; (Sax
    Rohmer in French) 12 R 17; (The
    Paul Harvey series) 17 R 15
Briney, Robert E.: Books by John Ball,
    5-6 MR 14
Briney, Robert E.: The Books of Sax
    Rohmer, a Chronological List, 1 R 25
Briney, Robert E.: Bouchercon III, a
    report (convention), 6-2 TAD 98
Briney, Robert E.: Bouchercon VI, A
    Second Look, (convention), 5/6 MN 3
Briney, Robert E.: Bouchercon East,
    (report on Bouchercon IV, convention)
    7-1 TAD 48

Briney, Robert E.: Checklist, Ben
    Benson mystery novels, 3-2 MR 8
Briney, Robert E.: Checklist, Clayton
    Rawson works, 3-1 MR 8
Briney, Robert E.: Checklist, Jack
    Mann works, 6-2 MR 21
Briney, Robert E.: Checklist, Pyramid
    reprints of Fu Manchu series,
    9-4 TAD 247
Briney, Robert E.: Commentary on Sax
    Rohmer's A TALE OF SECRET EGYPT
    (see 7 R 11); 7 R 12
Briney, Robert E.: Criminalists,
    Clergypersons, & Others, (Report
    on Bouchercon VII, convention),
    10-1 TAD 53
Briney, Robert E.: Dell Great Mystery
    Library, a Checklist, (Dell Pub.
    Co. series), 7 MN 4
Briney, Robert E.: The Early Chronicles
    of Fu Manchu, 15 R 9
Briney, Robert E.: Fu Manchu (by Sax
    Rohmer) checklist, 7 R 21
Briney, Robert E.: In Memoriam, Leigh
    Brackett, (memorial tribute),
    11-3 TAD 258
Briney, Robert E.: John Ball, View
    and Interview, 5-6 MR 9
Briney, Robert E.: John Dickson Carr,
    A Tribute, 1 NC 1 (memorial tribute)
Briney, Robert E.: letter of comment,
    3-3 CP 2; 7 JD 8; 9 JD 15; 11 JD 22;
    13 JD 21; 15 JD 23; 17 JD 29; 19 JD
    11; 6/7 LR 16; 1-3 MF 52; 1-1 MF
    45; 1-6 MF 56; 1-5 MF 56; 2-1 MF 55;
    2-2 MF 45; 2-3 MF 70; 2-4 MF 52;
    2-6 MF 53; 3-1 MF 46; 3-2 MF 55;
    5-2 MF 42; 5-5 MF 45; 3/4 MN 15;
    7 MN 6; 9 MN L1; 11 MN L1; 12 MN
    L1; 12 MN L2; 2-5 MR 12; 2-6 MR 14;
    3-1 MR 16; 4-1 MR 19; 4-3 MR 19;
    4-5 MR 17; 4-6 MR 17; 5-2 MR 18;
    5-3 MR 16; 5-4 MR 12; 5-5 MR 20;
    6-2 MR 17; 7 MY 12; 3-4 PQ 46;
    1-1 PP 26; 1-2 PP 28; 1-3 PP 33;
    2-1 PP 40; 2-2 PP 39; 4-2 PP 34;
    4-4 PP 37; 4-1 PQ 51; 4-2 PQ 52;
    64 PU 41; 70 PU 29; 2 R 22; 4 SF
    42; 1-3 TAD 106; 1-3 TAD 108;
    1-4 TAD 153; 2-2 TAD 123; 2-3 TAD
    201; 2-4 TAD 275; 3-1 TAD 66; 3-2
    TAD 137; 3-3 TAD 206; 3-4 TAD 279;
    4-1 TAD 68; 4-3 TAD 189; 5-3 TAD
    181; 5-4 TAD 238; 7-2 TAD 145;
    7-4 TAD 302; 8-4 TAD 320; 9-1 TAD
    82; 9-2 TAD 155; 9-4 TAD 247;
    10-2 TAD 159; 10-3 TAD 283; 10-4
    TAD 390; 11-2 TAD 206; 13 X 59;
    36 X 74
Briney, Robert E.: The Line-Up, (on
    mystery-detective fanzines),
    1A MF 22
Briney, Robert E.: The Lost "Eye"
    (re: Sax Rohmer), 6 R 9; 7 R 10

Briney, Robert E.: Murder at the Waldorf,
A Report on Bouchercon VIII, 11-1 TAD
53

Briney, Robert E.: The Mysterious Arthur
H. Ward, (Sax Rohmer character), 12 R 5

Briney, Robert E.: MYSTERY BOOK MAGAZINE,
An Appreciation and Index, 8-4 TAD 245

Briney, Robert E.: 1972 "Edgar" Awards -
Winners and Nominees, (Mystery Writers
of America), 5-3 MR 29

Briney, Robert E.: Obituary, John Dickson
Carr, 10-2 TAD 137

Briney, Robert E.: The Paul Harley Series,
(by Sax Rohmer), 17 R 15

Briney, Robert E.: Pyramid reissues of
Fu Manchu Paperbacks, 15 R 29

Briney, Robert E.: RED STAR MYSTERY, Don
Diavolo, (on the pulp and principal
story character, with index to the
magazine), 64 PU 14

Briney, Robert E.: Sax Rohmer, George
Robey, and "Round in Fifty", 8 R 11

Briney, Robert E.: Sax Rohmer in Dutch,
(Dutch translations), 11 R 17

Briney, Robert E.: Sax Rohmer in French,
(French translations), 12 R 17

Briney, Robert E.: Sax Rohmer in Wartime,
9 R 32

Briney, Robert E.: The Smith Letters,
(Rohmer - correspondence "by" Sir
Nayland Smith), 12 R 9

Briney, Robert E.: Subject Index to
THE ARMCHAIR DETECTIVE's Letter
Columns, Vols. 1-3, 3-4 TAD 282

Briney, Robert E.: The (Very Temporary)
Return of Skull-Face, (re: THE RETURN
OF SKULL-FACE by Robert E. Howard &
Richard A. Lupoff), 2-2 MF 21

Briney, Robert E., and J.R.Christopher
& D.W.Dickensheet: A. Boucher
Bibliography, 2-2 TAD 77; 2-3 TAD 143;
2-4 TAD 263

Briney, Robert E., and John Creasey:
A John Creasey Bibliography, incld.
summary of series and pseudonyms,
2-1 TAD 5

Briney, Robert E., and W.O.G.Lofts:
Musette, Max and Sumuru, (Rohmer
radio serials), 15 R 5

Briney, Robert E., and W.O.G.Lofts:
Sh-h-h! Dr. Fu Manchu is on the
Air! (radio programs), 11 R 9

(Briney, Robert E.), Biographical Sketch,
8 R 30

(Briney, Robert E.), Meet the Author,
(biographical sketch), 2-4 TAD 273

(British current mysteries), Current
Crime, The British Scene, by Rona
Randall, 5-1 MR 29; 5-2 MR 31;
5-3 MR 31

British Pocket Books, (British paperback editions), by Piet Schreuders,
3-1 CP 11

Broberg, Jan: A Conversation with
Nicholas Blake, 2-3 MR 3

Broberg, Jan: Checklist, Nicholas
Blake works, 2-3 MR 3

Broberg, Jan, and K. Arne Blom:
Detective Fiction in Sweden,
9-4 TAD 272

(Brock, Detective-Inspector David:
R.J.White), Pen Profile, (biog.
and literary sketch), by Barry
Pike, 2-2 PP 24

Brockowski, Joe: letter of comment,
1-6 CP 2 (see "Brokowski")

Brodsky, Hal: letter of comment,
6-2 TAD 128; 7-2 TAD 149

Brody, Howard: A Guide to Thorndykean
Pilopathology, (medico-legal
importance of the skin and hair
in the Thorndyke stories by
Freeman), 11 TF 3

Brody, Howard: An Inquiry Into Circular
Heels, ("circular heel" footprints
in the Thorndyke stories of Freeman)
12 TF 8

Broecker, Jay: letter of comment,
2-3 MF 57

Brokowski, Joe: letter of comment,
3-4 CP 1 (see "Brockowski")

Bronze Shadows Presents: Conan, (review
of the Conan stories and publications)
by Fred S. Cook, 13 BS 19

(Brook, Roger, series: Dennis Wheatley)
Checklist, by Iwan Hedman, 2-4 TAD
235

(BROOKLYN MUDERS, THE: G.D.H.Cole),
The First Appearance, Superintendent
Wilson, by Maryell Cleary, 3-6 PP 13

Brooks, Barry M.: letter of comment,
26 JD 47

Brooks, C.W., Jr.: letter of comment,
1-3 TBN 4

(Brooks, Edna: Khaki Girls series), see
Josephine Chase

(Brooks, Kevin), An Informal Survey of
Cover Art of the Seventies, Pt.1,
Tribute to Agatha Christie, (Kevin
Brooks, artist), by Frank Eck,
9-3 TAD 170

Brooks, Lawrence F.: letter of comment,
26 JD 48

Brooks, Lawrence F.: Nero Wolfe,
Logomachizer, 1-1 G 21

Brooks, Ned: letter of comment, 38 X 143

Broom, Leonard: letter of comment,
7 JD 9; 9 JD 17

Brosey, Myrtis: letter of comment,
1-6 CP 2; 1-2 MF 48; 1-6 MF 58;
2-1 MF 59; 2-2 MF 42; 2-2 MF 59;
2-3 MF 72; 2-5 MF 56; 4-6 MF 47;
5-1 MF 45; 3/4 MN 13; 7 MN 6; 8 MN 32;
9 MN L1; 12 MN L12; 6 MY 8; 7 MY 13;
2 PE 40; 1-2 PP 30; 1-5 PP 27; 2-3
PP 39; 2-6 PP 44; 3-1 PP 39; 3-5 PP 48
4 5/6 PP 88

Brother Officers...Be Damned, The Police
    Procedural, Pt.III, by George N. Dove,
    10-4 TAD 320
Brotherhood Makes History, The, (Popular
    Culture Association), by Francis M.
    Nevins, Jr., 5-1 TAD 28
Brothers Are Reunited, (Jerry Todd, boys'
    series, "news item"), by "Cassibum
    Kepp", 2-3 TBN 1
Brown, Bob: letter of comment, 2-2 TBN 6
(Brown, Charles Brocken: WIELAND), The
    First Locked-Room Mystery, by Peter
    J. Christensen, 10-4 TAD 368
Brown, Charlie: letter of comment,
    10 JD 17
(Brown, Fredric), Checklist, by J. Grant
    Thiessen, 2 SF 26
(Brown, Fredric), Checklist, (novels),
    by William F. Nolan, 5-4 TAD 193
(Brown, Fredric), Fredric Brown, An
    Appreciation, by J. Grant Thiessen,
    2 SF 26
(Brown, Fredric), Paradox and Plot, The
    Fiction of Fredric Brown, by Newton
    Baird, 9-4 TAD 282; 10-1 TAD 33;
    10-2 TAD 151; 10-3 TAD 249; 10-4 TAD
    370; 11-1 TAD 86
(Brown, Fredric), Thoughts on Fredric
    Brown, by William F. Nolan, 5-4 TAD
    191
(Brown, Fredric), The Uncollected Fiction
    of Fredric Brown, by Dennis McMillan,
    3-1 CP 15; 3-2 CP 25
Brown, John Stanley: letter of comment,
    15 X 14
(Brown, Quiribus, detective: Harry Stephen
    Keeler), Hick Dick From the Sticks,
    Harry Stephen Keeler's Quiribus Brown,
    by Francis M. Nevins, Jr., 7-4 TAD 251
Brown, Ray: letter of comment, 26 JD 47
Brown, Robert L.: Catastrophe Fiction
    Bibliography, 20 X 10
Brown, Robert L.: The End of the World
    and the Day After, (catastrophe
    fiction commentary), 20 X 9
Brown, Robert L.: letter of comment,
    28 X 79
(Brown, Roswell: Gracie Culver detective
    series), Grace Note, by Robert
    Sampson, 17 X 8
(Brown, Roswell: Gracie Culver detective
    series), Notes of a Pulp Collector,
    (on series in THE SHADOW magazine)
    by G. Alan, 15 BS 14
Brown, Russell M.: BLACKOUT, Hubert Aquin's
    Surreal Mystery, 13-1 TAD 58
(Brown, Mrs. Zenith), see Leslie Ford,
    David Frome
(Browne, Howard), Interview with Howard
    Browne, by Caleb A. Lewis, 11-2 TAD
    172
(Browne, Howard: Paul Pine, detective),
    The Return of Paul Pine, by Caleb A.
    Lewis, 11-1 TAD 79

Browne, John T.: letter of comment,
    67 PU 57; 1-4 QC 17; 2-3 TAD 201;
    3-4 TAD 280; 5-2 TAD 116; 7-1 TAD
    67; 7-3 TAD 229; 8-1 TAD 75; 11 JD
    25
Brownell, David: Checklist, Sheridan
    LeFanu, 9-3 TAD 197
Brownell, David: Comic Construction in
    the Novels of Emma Lathen and R.B.
    Dominic, 9-2 TAD 91
Brownell, David: John Fowles' Experi-
    ments with the Form of the Mystery
    Story, 10-2 TAD 184
Brownell, David: K.C. Constantine,
    9-1 TAD 42
Brownell, David: letter of comment,
    8 JD 10; 11 JD 26; 6-1 TAD 52;
    7-1 TAD 73; 9-2 TAD 157; 10-4
    TAD 371
Brownell, David: Wicked Dreams, The
    World of Sheridan LeFanu, 9-3 TAD
    191
Bruccoli, Matthew J.: letter of comment,
    6-3 TAD 194; 10-1 TAD 4; 10-2 TAD
    161
(Bruccoli, Matthew J.: RAYMOND CHANDLER,
    A DESCRIPTIVE BIBLIOGRAPHY), The
    Black Mask Boys Go Legit, by William
    F. Nolan, 13-1 TAD 23
Bruce, David W.: Mystery Suspense Home
    Entertainment, (video cassettes,
    film, discs), 1-2 M 11
Bruce, David W.: Mystery/Suspense on
    Screen, 1-1 M 10
(Bruce, Jean: Hubert Bonisseur de la
    Bath series), Checklist, by Barry
    Van Tilburg, 4-2 MF 13
(Bruce, Leo: Sergeant Beef series), My
    Favourite Detectives, Pt.3, by
    Robert C.S.Adey, 5-3 MR 20
(Brundage, Margaret), A Visit with
    Margaret Brundage, (WEIRD TALES
    cover artist), by Forrest J. Ackerman,
    3 WT 17
(Brundage, Margaret), Margaret Brundage,
    (sketch on WEIRD TALES cover artist)
    by Robert Weinberg, 2 WT 3
Bruns, Rebecca: Arabian Nights and Art
    Nouveau, (discussion of Edmund
    Dulac's works), 6 YB 23
Brust, Toby: letter of comment,
    4-2 PP 40; 4-5 MF 45
(Buchan, John), A Checklist of the
    Fiction of John Buchan, (1875-
    1940), by J. Randolph Cox, 2-4 TAD
    213
(Buchan, John), A John Buchan Checklist,
    by Theodore P. Dukeshire, 7-3 TAD
    201
(Buchan, John), Checklist, by J. Randolph
    Cox, 6-2 MR 18
(Buchan, John), John Buchan, (discussion)
    by Theodore P. Dukeshire, 7-3 TAD 198

(Buchan, John), John Buchan, A Philosophy
of High Adventure, by J. Randolph Cox,
2-4 TAD 207

Buck, Dave: Ishmael Reed's Neo-Hoodooism,
11 X 9

Buckner, Vance: letter of comment,
28 X 80

Buckskins and Ballistics, William Leggett
and the American Detective Story, by
John Seelye, 1-3 MR 3

Buhr, Robert: A Fight to the Death, (fiction,
Tarzan style), 4 SF 25

Buhrer, Barbara: A Look at Dell Shannon,
3/4 MN 3

Buhrer, Barbara: Checklist of Mystery
Awards, (Mystery Writers of America),
11 MN A1; 12 MN L4

Buhrer, Barbara A.: Georgette Heyer,
(literary sketch), 13 MN 1

Buhrer, Barbara A.: letter of comment,
20 JD 19; 8 MN 29; 9 MN L4; 12 MN L10;
12 MN L12; 13 MN L3; 7-3 TAD 223;
8-1 TAD 68; 8-4 TAD 313; 9-2 TAD 156

Buhrer, Barbara A., and J. Clyde Stevens:
Checklist Bibliography of Dell
Shannon, 3/4 MN 4

Building a Collection of Boys' Books, by
Jack R. Schorr, 1-1 BC 32

Bull Pen, The, (letters), 1-2 CP 2; 1-3 CP 1;
1-4 CP 1; 1-5 CP 1; 1-6 CP 1; 2-1 CP 1;
2-2 CP 1; 2-3 CP 1; 2-4 CP 1; 2-5 CP 1;
3-1 CP 2; 3-2 CP 1; 3-3 CP 1; 3-4 CP 1;
3-5 CP 1

(BULL'S EYE WESTERN), Checklist, pulp
magazine, by Lynn Hickman, 75 PU 7

Bullis, John: Stark Reality, (Donald E.
Westlake's Richard Stark novels)
1-5 CP 5

(Bulmer, Kenneth), Checklist, by Ian
Covell, 4 SF 28

Bumudemutomuro, (Tarzan discussion article
in depth), by Robert Sampson, 8 U 3

Bundles From Britain, Spy Anthologies, by
Frank D. McSherry, Jr., 3-3 TAD 176

Bundy, Franklin: Robert Fish, In Memorium,
(memorial tribute), 14-2 TAD 119

Burger, Knox: letter of comment, 9 JD 6;
13 JD 11; 19 JD 12

Burger, Knox: Lines to a Man Who Should
Know Better, (verse, re: John D.
MacDonald), 11 JD 8

Burgess, Gelett: London's Ha'Penny
Comics, 1-1 YB 19

(Burgess, Thornton W.), Thornton W.
Burgess Books for Older Boys, by
Julius R. Chenu, 1-2 BC 42

Burglaring Joke and Other Occasional
Pieces, (fiction, Classic Corner
rare tales), by Anthony Berkeley
Cox, 14-3 TAD 239

Burks, Arthur J.: On Pulpsmithing, (on
writing for the pulps), 69 PU 10

(BURL IVES SONG BOOK, THE), Spotlight,
2-1 PQ 37

(Burleigh, Clarence B.), About "The
Smugglers of Chestnut", by Maurice
Owen, 1-1 BC 17

Burn, Barbara: Recipe for a Cookbook,
(Nero Wolfe article), 1-1 G 34

Burnell, Ken: letter of comment,
25 JD 38

(Burnett, W.R.), A Literary Exile
Comes Home, (interview with
Burnett), by David Wilson, 3-2 M 26

Burning of Doc Savage, The, (DOC SAVAGE
magazine collecting experiences),
by Dickson Thorpe, 7 DQ 13

(Burns, George & Gracie Allen), Joke
Submitted by Ray Bradbury, 36 X R16

Burns, Stan: letter of comment,
5 LR 6; 6/7 LR 27; 5/6 MN 15;
8 MN 33

Burns, T. Carrington (pseud. of John
D. MacDonald): World-Size Bottleneck
(on Cuban missiles), 26 JD 7

Burr, R.C.: letter of comment, 3-1 M 2

Burroughs the Fantastic, (Edgar Rice
Burroughs in the pulp magazines)
by John Harwood, 69 PU 13

(Burroughs, Edgar Rice), Bumudemutomuro,
(in-depth study of Tarzan), by
Robert Sampson, 8 U 3

(Burroughs, Edgar Rice), Burroughs the
Fantastic, (Burroughs in the pulps)
by John Harwood, with checklist,
69 PU 13

(Burroughs, Edgar Rice), The Burroughs-
Doyle Connection, (comparison of
passages, Edgar Rice Burroughs and
Arthur Conan Doyle), by Dana Martin
Batory, 15 SF 10

(Burroughs, Edgar Rice), Checklist of
Books, by John F. Sullivan, 3-3 BC
349

(Burroughs, Edgar Rice), Edgar Rice
Burroughs, a Short Biography, by
John F. Sullivan, 3-3 BC 346

(Burroughs, Edgar Rice), Edgar Rice
Burroughs and the Action Pulps,
by John Harwood, 75 PU 12

(Burroughs, Edgar Rice), Tarzan's
Greater, A Historical View, by
Bill Laidlaw, 7 DQ 16

(Burroughs, William S.: JUNKIE),
Junkie: A Personal Reminiscence,
by Jeff Chambers, 3-3 CP 11

(Burroughs, William S.: JUNKIE)
Mass Market Murmurings, by Barry
Bernard, 1-1 CP 6

Burroughs-Doyle Connection, The,
(comparison of passages from
Edgar Rice Burroughs and Arthur
Conan Doyle), by Dana Martin Batory,
15 SF 10

Burt, Jesse: letter of comment, 13 JD 16

(Burton, Charles Pierce) Charles Pierce
Burton and the Boys of Bobs Hill,
(boys books), Jack Bales, 5 BB 5

Busch, Lloyd: Checklist of the Paperback
    Editions of John Dickson Carr, 2-2 CP
    9
Busch, Lloyd: letter of comment, 1-4 CP 1;
    2-1 CP 5; 2-2 CP 1; 3-1 CP 8; 3-3 CP 2;
    3-1 PQ 4
Buscho, Dale: letter of comment, 5 X 41
Bush, Geoffrey: The Last Meeting of the
    Butlers Club, (Dr. Thorndyke pastiche)
    12 TF 13
Bustin, Malcolm: letter of comment,
    36 X 70
Butler, Richard C.: Dell "Map-Back"
    Checklist, Nos. 1-300 (Dell Pub.
    co.'s "map-back" paperbacks),
    1-2 MF 17
Butler, Richard C.: letter of comment,
    1-2 MF 47
Butler, Richard C.: Popular Library
    Paperback Checklist, Nos. 1-200,
    1-3 MF 5

(CADAVER OF GIDEON WYCK: Alexander Laing)
    Horror, Detection and Footnotes, by
    Edward Lauterbach, 3-1 TAD 12
(Cadee, Don, series: Spencer Dean),
    Series Synopses, by John Vining,
    9-2 TAD 113
(Cain, James M.) Hard Cain, The Paperback
    Original Novels of James M. Cain,
    by George Kelley, 4-3 PP 9
(Cain, Paul: FAST ONE), Introducing Paul
    Cain and His FAST ONE, A Forgotten
    Hard-Boiled Writer and a Forgotten
    Gangster Novel, by E.R.Hagemann,
    12-1 TAD 72
Caine, Hamilton T.: Ace Carpenter,
    Detective, (fiction), 1-1 M 33;
    1-2 M 47; 1-3 M 54
Caine, Hamilton T.: An Interview with
    Stephen J. Cannell, 2-1 M 5
Caine, Hamilton T.: The Case of the
    Empty Fortune Cookies, (fiction),
    2-3 M 10
Caine, Hamilton T.: Hollywood Highness,
    (fiction), 2-1 M 46
Calculated Man, The, (fiction), by
    John McNamara, 1 MT 2
Caldwell, T.E.: letter of comment,
    12 SF 29
(Calhoun, Frances Boyd: Miss Minerva
    series), Miss Minerva and Kinfolks,
    (juvenile series, books), by
    Julius R. Chenu, 1-4 YB 3
California Babylon, The World of American
    Detective Fiction, by Liahna K. Babener
    1-2 C 77
(California), California Babylon, The
    World of American Detective Fiction,
    by Liahna K. Babener, 1-2 C 77
(California), The American Regional
    Mystery, (locales of mystery fiction),
    by Marvin Lachman, (Northern Calif.)
    9-4 TAD 260; (So.Calif.) 10-4 TAD 294

Call to Conclave, (founding of
    organization devoted to Solar
    Pons, detective created by
    August Derleth), by Alvin F.
    Germeshausen, 1-1 PD 1
(Callan series: James Mitchell),
    Checklist, annotated, by Barry
    Van Tilburg, 5-3 MF 19
Calling Justice Inc., (fiction), by
    Kenneth Robeson, 11 P 19
Call of Lovecraft, The, (H.P.Lovecraft)
    by Willis Conover, 18 X 16
Calls to Glory, (verse), by Frederick
    Faust, 1-3 FC 7
Camarota, C.: letter of comment,
    10 JD 13
Cameo Edition Nancy Drews, (girls'
    series books, bibliographical
    data), by Dave Farah, 1-5 YB 3
Campagna, Bob: letter of comment,
    1-4 YB 9
Cameron, Mary S.: The University of
    North Carolina Crime Fiction
    Collection, 1-2 TAD 51
(Cameron, Mary S.) Meet the Author,
    (short biog. sketch), by Allen
    J. Hubin, 1-2 TAD 52
Cammett, Stephen: James Otis, Writer
    of Over One Hundred Boys' Books,
    (biog.sketch), 2-3 BC 210
Campanaro, Andy R.: letter of comment,
    11 JD 31
(Campbell, Bruce: Ken Holt series)
    The Ken Holt Crossword Puzzle
    (oriented to the boys' books series)
    3 MA 28
(Campbell, Bruce: Ken Holt series)
    The Ken Holt Mystery Stories,
    (boys' series), by Fred Woodworth,
    2 MA 7
Campbell, Forrest: A Visit to Hi-Lee,
    (home of Leo Edwards, author of
    boys' books), 2-1 TB 3
Campbell, Forrest: letter of comment,
    1-3 TB 10
Campbell, Gary W.: letter of comment,
    2-3 M 2
(Campbell, John Franklin), Department
    of Unknown Mystery Writers, by
    Marvin Lachman, 2-3 PP 22
(Campbell, John W., Jr.) A Doc Savage
    Adventure Rediscovered, ("Who Goes
    There" by Don A. Stuart, pseud. of
    Campbell), by Albert Tonik, 4 DS 10
Campbell, Ramsey: Derleth As I Knew
    Him, (August Derleth), 1-1 AD 4;
    1-3 AD 4; 1-4 AD 5; 2-1 AD 8
Campbell, Robert: letter of comment,
    40 X 85
Campbell, Scott: letter of comment,
    11 SF 48
Campbell, W.T.: letter of comment,
    28 JD 40

Campenni, Frank J.: Black Cops and/or Robbers, The Detective Fiction of Chester Himes, 8-3 TAD 206

(Campion, Albert, series: Margery Allingham), Margery Allingham's Albert Campion, A Chronological Examination of the Novels in Which He Appears, (in-depth study), by B.A.Pike, 9-1 TAD 1; 9-2 TAD 95; 10-1 TAD 25; 10-2 TAD 117; 10-4 TAD 324; 11-1 TAD 34; 11-2 TAD 177; 11-3 TAD 279; 11-4 TAD 408; 12-1 TAD 34; 12-4 TAD 348; 12-2 TAD 168

Can Such Things Be? (collecting mystery related items), by David Bates, 2 PE 25

Can You Match This?, (quiz, Leo Edward's boys' books oriented), 1-3 TB 1; 1-4 TB 6

Cancellari, Mike: letter of comment, 30 X 148

(Canfield, Flavia A.: The Kidnapped Campers series), Boys' Series Bibliography, by Harry K. Hudson, 1-5 YB 14

(Cannell, Stephen J.), An Interview with Stephen J. Cannell, by Hamilton T. Caine, 2-1 M 6

Cap Shaw and His "Great and Regular Fellows", The Making of THE HARD-BOILED OMNIBUS, 1945-1946, (Jos. Shaw, editor and his contributors) by E.R.Hagemann, 2-2 C 143

(Capek, Karel), A Discovery in Capek, by Josef Skvorecky, 8-3 TAD 180

Caper Novel, The, (commentary), by George Kelley, 7 U 61

Caper Novels of James Hadley Chase, The, by Theodore P. Dukeshire, 10-2 TAD 128

Caper Novels of Tony Kendrick, The, by George Kelley, 2-4 MF 3

(Capp, Andy, cartoon character), Andy Capp - Gold Medal/Fawcett PIBS, (Gold Medal and Fawcett paperback books), by Raymond Torrence, 1-6 CP 13

Cappadonna, M.S.: A Checklist of Mystery, Detective and Suspense Fiction Published in the U.S., (comprehensive bibliography),
June - December 1975, 9-2 TAD 137
January - March 1976, 9-3 TAD 210
April-June 1976, 9-4 TAD 322
July-September 1976, 10-1 TAD 93
October-December 1976, 10-2 TAD 131
January-April 1977, 10-3 TAD 261
April-June 1977, 10-4 TAD 366
July-September 1977, 11-2 TAD 190
October-December 1977, 11-3 TAD 287
January-March 1978, 11-3 288
April-June 1978, 11-4 346
July-September 1978, 12-1 TAD 89

Cappadonna, M.S.: Checklist of Mystery, Detective and Suspense Fiction Published in the U.S. (continued)
October-December 1978, 12-2 TAD 132
January-March 1979, 12-3 TAD 244
April-June 1979, 12-4 TAD 360
July-September 1979, 13-1 TAD 25
October-December 1979, 13-2 TAD 110
January-March 1980, 13-3 TAD 210
April-June 1980, 13-4 TAD 336
July-September 1980, 14-1 TAD 76
October-December 1980, 14-2 TAD 150
January-March 1981, 14-3 TAD 234
April-July 1981, 14-4 TAD 372

(CAPTAIN COMBAT), Checklist, pulp magazine, by Lynn Hickman, 75 PU 7

CAPTAIN FUTURE, Paperback Readers Guide and Checklist, by Bruce Cervon, 2-5 CP 17

(Captain Future), An Inside Look at Captain Future, (pulp hero character) by Edmond Hamilton, 3 P 3

(Captain O'Hagan), The Incredible Captain O'Hagan, by Alvin F. Germeshausen, 1 R 27

Captain Satan, (on the pulp magazine character from CAPTAIN SATAN magazine), by Dean A. Grennell, 72 PU 15

(CAPTAIN SATAN), A Minor Mystery Finally Resolved (pulp magazine) 2 P 31

(CAPTAIN SATAN), Checklist, pulp magazine, by Lynn Hickman, 75 PU 11

(CAPTAIN SATAN), How Are the Fallen Mighty Department, (pulp magazine and character), by Dean A. Grennell, 42 X 9

Captain Shaw's Hard-Boiled Boys, (authors contributing to Joseph Shaw's THE HARD-BOILED OMNIBUS) by Stephen Mertz, 12-3 TAD 264

Capwell Wyckoff - A Hardy Author? (on possibility Wyckoff wrote some of the Hardy Boys boys' series books), by Fred Woodworth, 4 MA 19

Cardboard Shelves, (on housing your collection), by Eddy Thomas, 10 SF 32

Carew, Donald: TV Reviews (mystery), 2-2 M 47

Cargas, Harry James: August Derleth on Literature, Summary of a Correspondence, 2-3/4 AD 1

Cargas, Harry James: letter of comment, 2-2 AD 9

Cargill, Jennifer: letter of comment, 3-2 M 2

Cargo of Doom, (fiction), by Kenneth Robeson, 12 P 18

Carlin, Lianne: An Interview with Catherine Aird, 4-2 MR 29

Carlin, Lianne: Comments and Queries,
(questions and answers on mystery
fiction), 1-5 MR 13
Carlin, Lianne: For Your Investigation,
(news and comments on new mystery
fiction), 1A MR 2; 1-1 MR 2;
1-2 MR 2; 1-3 MR 2; 1-4 MR 2;
1-5 MR 2; 1-6 MR 2; 2-1 MR 2;
2-2 MR 2; 2-3 MR 2; 2-4 MR 2;
2-5 MR 2; 2-6 MR 2
Carlin, Lianne: In the Spotlight,
(mystery news), 1-1 MR 8
Carlin, Lianne: I've Been Reading
(comments on new mystery fiction),
2-4 MR 8
Carlin, Lianne: Julian Symons, An
Interview, 3-4 MR 24
Carlin, Lianne: Movies on TV and in
Theatres, (general review article
on current mystery productions)
3-2 MR 15
Carlin, Lianne: News and Some Future
Books, (mystery announcements),
4-3 MR 2
Carlin, Lianne: News Roundup, (mystery
fiction and in general, news),
1-1 MR 4; 1-2 MR 6; 1-3 MR 10;
1-4 MR 6; 1-5 MR 9; 1-6 MR 7;
2-1 MR 10; 2-2 MR 11
Carlin, Lianne: Reviews, 3-1 MR 7
Carlin, Lianne, and Ruth Withee:
Recent Paperbacks Reviewed, (new
paperback mysteries reviews),
3-2 MR 10
Carlin, Stanley A.: A Justly Celebrated,
Elusive, American, (on Quentin Locke,
detective, on screen), 3-2 MR 31
Carlin, Stanley A.: Chandler-Hammett-
Hemingway, Teachers in the "Tough
School", (hard-boiled detective
fiction), 2-5 MR 15
Carlin, Stanley A.: The Corpse Tells
the Tale, (on forensic medicine)
3-1 MF 25
Carlin, Stanley A.: Film review of
WAIT UNTIL DARK, 1-3 MR 6
Carlin, Stanley A.: letter of comment,
3-3 MR 12
Carlin, Stanley A.: Rebuttal to "Kiss
My Deadly Typewriter #359" of
Mike Avallone, 3-1 QC 16
Carlin, Stanley A.: Reviews (var. new
mystery fiction), 1-3 MR 6; 1-5 MR 6
Carlin, Stanley A.: Who's Who? (mystery
puzzle), 4-6 MR 14
Carlos Bannon: The Private Detective
Fiction of Kenneth Gravell (with
Bannon as detective character), by
Randy Himmel, with checklist,
12 LR 8
Carmody: Sagebrush Detective, (on
Carmody, detective, character created
by Peter McCurtin), by R. Jeff Banks,
8-1 TAD 42

(CARNACKI, THE GHOST FINDER: William
Hope Hodgson), in article by same
name, 12-2 TAD 122
Carney, Raymond: John MacDonald and
the Technologies of Knowledge,
26 JD 16
Carpenter, John: Harlequin, (fiction),
15 SF 3
Carpenter, Margaret Haley: Legacy,
(verse), 2-3/4 AD 9
Carr Chronology, The, (chronology of
vital and literary statistics of
John Dickson Carr), by Larry L.
French, 1 NC 29
(Carr, Freddy, boys' series), Boys'
Series Bibliographies, by Harry
K. Hudson, 1-4 YB 24
Carr, G.M.: Georgette Heyer's "Who-
dunnits", with checklist, 13 MN
15
(Carr, Glyn), Detection Among the
Mountains, The Writings of Glyn
Carr, by William A.S.Sarjeant,
4-5/6 PP 3
Carr, John Dickson: John Dickson
Carr's Solution to THE MYSTERY OF
EDWIN DROOD, 14-4 TAD 291
Carr, John Dickson: letter of comment,
1-3 QC 20; 2-4 TAD 279
(Carr, John Dickson), A John Dickson
Carr Checklist, by Rick Sneary,
3-4 MR 13
(Carr, John Dickson), Addenda to
Checklist by Rick Sneary, by J.R.
Christopher, 4-1 MR 20
(Carr, John Dickson), Addendum to
article "The Baker Street -
Carrian Connection" by Larry L.
French, 1 NC 5 (Sherlockiana)
(Carr, John Dickson), Adolf Hitler
and John Dickson Carr's Least-
Known Locked Room, by Douglas
G. Greene, 14-4 TAD 295
(Carr, John Dickson), Alternate Titles
of Stories, by Michael F. Wahl,
1-6 CP 4
(Carr, John Dickson), The Carr
Chronology, (vital and literary
statistics), by Larry L. French,
1 NC 29
(Carr, John Dickson), Carrian Canon for
the Curious, (bibliography of Carr),
by Larry L. French, 1 NC 20
(Carr, John Dickson), The Cases of
Gideon Fell, (commentary), by Marvin
Lachman, 2-3 MF 4
(Carr, John Dickson), Checklist of the
Paperback Editions of John Dickson
Carr, by Lloyd Busch, 2-2 CP 9
(Carr, John Dickson), Checklist of
Paperback Books, in Rare Books Are
Getting Scarce, by Bruce Taylor,
1-2 CP 15

(Carr, John Dickson), Commentaries for
the Curious, (var. tributes to Carr)
1 NC 11

(Carr, John Dickson), Epilogue: Culprit
Confesses, (John Dickson Carr's
autobiography in process at time
of death), 1 NC 27

(Carr, John Dickson), John Dickson Carr,
A Tribute, by Robert E. Briney,
1 NC 1

(Carr, John Dickson), John Dickson Carr,
Alias Roger Fairbairn, and the
Historical Novel, by Douglas G.
Greene, 11-4 TAD 339

(Carr, John Dickson), John Dickson Carr
and the Aura of Genius (minor
aberrations in the Carr stories),
by James Kingman, 14-2 TAD 166

(Carr, John Dickson), John Dickson Carr
1906-1977, (tribute and comments)
by Wooda Nicholas Carr II, 1-3 MF 3

(Carr, John Dickson), John Dickson Carr
on British Radio, with checklist, by
Douglas G. Greene, 12-1 TAD 69

(Carr, John Dickson), The Life and Times
of Gideon Fell, (detective), by
Marvin Lachman, 2-3 MF 3

(Carr, John Dickson), The Man Who Read
(and Published) John Dickson Carr/
Carter Dickson, (Ellery Queen), by
Larry L. French, 1 NC 8

(Carr, John Dickson), The Man Who Was
John Dickson Carr, (biographical
tribute), by Larry L. French, 1 NC 3

(Carr, John Dickson), The Most Dangerous
Man in Europe, (on early Carr stories)
2-4 TAD 253

(Carr, John Dickson), The Murder Club
(in Carr stories), by Larry L. French,
1 NC 30

(Carr, John Dickson), The Mysterious John
Dickson Carr, by Larry L. French,
1-6 MF 13

(Carr, John Dickson) Obituary, by Robert
E. Briney, 10-2 TAD 137

(Carr, John Dickson), The Sound of
Suspense, John Dickson Carr as a
Radio Writer, by Francis M. Nevins,
Jr., 11-4 TAD 335

(Carr, John Dickson), Stanislaw Lem and
John Dickson Carr, Critics of the
Scientific World-View, (comparison
and viewpoint), by Edmund Miller,
14-4 TAD 341

(Carr, John Dickson: PAPA LA-BAS),
review, in verse, by Len Moffatt,
2-2 MR 6

(Carr, John Dickson: Sir Henry Merrivale,
detective), My Favourite Detectives,
No.1, by Robert C.S. Adey, with
checklist, 3-2 MR 11

Carr, Wooda Nicholas: A Comment from
Nick Carr's Typewriter, (Star Wars
and the pulps), 1 PW 2

Carr, Wooda Nicholas: A Visit to No
Man's Land, (war stories in the
pulp magazines), 10 DS 11

Carr, Wooda Nicholas: Adieu to The
Avenger, (pulp hero character),
11 X 123

Carr, Wooda Nicholas: The Avenger,
(on pulp hero character), 3-6
MR 13

Carr, Wooda Nicholas: The Avenger's
Aides, (assistants to the pulp
hero character in the stories),
5 P 6

Carr, Wooda Nicholas: Checklist,
THE AVENGER magazine (pulp)
3-6 MR 15

Carr, Wooda Nicholas: Checklist,
Dusty Ayres series, (pulp
magazines), 10 SF 45

Carr, Wooda Nicholas: The Chronicle
of Christopher Syn, (Dr. Syn,
pulp magazine villain), 7 X 7;
9 X 5; 10 X 8

Carr, Wooda Nicholas: Cole Wilson,
(series character, The Avenger)
17 X 56

Carr, Wooda Nicholas: Contemplating
Jim Harmon's Novel, THE GREAT
RADIO HEROES, 69 PU 28

Carr, Wooda Nicholas: Contemplating
the Pulp Westerns, (discussion)
12 P 10

Carr, Wooda Nicholas: Dan Turner,
(detective pulp character),
21 X 51

Carr, Wooda Nicholas: Deadlier Than
the Male, (female villains in
Operator 5 stories, pulp magazines)
11 P 3

Carr, Wooda Nicholas: The Devil You
Say, (on G-8, pulp hero character)
3 X 6

Carr, Wooda Nicholas: The Emperor of
the World, (from Dusty Ayres series
in pulp magazines), 10 SF 42

Carr, Wooda Nicholas: Emperor Rudolph,
(re: Operator 5 and the Purple
Empire series, pulp magazines),
10 P 22

Carr, Wooda Nicholas: The Flying Spy,
(G-8, pulp hero, pulp magazines)
6 DS 15

Carr, Wooda Nicholas: The Fright
Syndrome, (on weird menace pulp
magazines), 10 BS 19

Carr, Wooda Nicholas: From the Typewriter of Nick Carr, (pulp items,
various), 2 PW 2

Carr, Wooda Nicholas: G-8 Versus Chu
Ling, (pulp hero character and
villain, pulp magazines), 4 P 3

Carr, Wooda Nicholas: G-8 Versus
Stahlmaske, (pulp hero character
and villain, pulp magazines), 6 P 10

Carr, Wooda Nicholas: Harold F. Cruick-shank, (memorial tribute to author), 8 DS 2

Carr, Wooda Nicholas: Incident at the Grand Canyon, (Operator 5 and the Purple Invasion, pulp magazines) 30 X 131

Carr, Wooda Nicholas: Introducing the Yellow Peril, (Dr. Yen Sin, pulp magazine villain), 12 SF 39

Carr, Wooda Nicholas: John Dickson Carr 1906-1907, (reminiscences), 1-3 MF 3

Carr, Wooda Nicholas: Ki-Gor, King of the Jungle, (commentary, JUNGLE STORIES pulp magazine), 2 P 22

Carr, Wooda Nicholas: "Let's Face It!" A Look at the Disguises of Operator 5 During the Purple Invasion, (pulp hero character's use of disguises), 3 U 3

Carr, Wooda Nicholas: letter of comment, 3 BS 2; 6 BS 21; 7 DQ 3; 5 DS 5; 11 DS 28; 12 DS 8; 2 U 48; 4 U 51; 5 U 63; 5 U 66; 8 X 38; 14 X 63; 21 X 56

Carr, Wooda Nicholas: The Masked Detective, (detective pulp hero) 8 P 3

Carr, Wooda Nicholas: The Masked Detective, Checklist, pulp magazines, 8 P 7

Carr, Wooda Nicholas: Mistress of Violence, (on Sheena, Queen of the Jungle, in pulp magazine stories), 22 X 24

Carr, Wooda Nicholas: My Favorite Jungle Stories Magazine Covers, (descriptive commentary on pulp magazine cover art), 8 U 30

Carr, Wooda Nicholas: The Mysterious Wu Fang, (pulp villain), 8 DS 5

Carr, Wooda Nicholas: Operator 5, (espionage pulp hero), 1 P 3

Carr, Wooda Nicholas: Operator 5 Bounds Out of the Thirties, (a close look at Jimmy Christopher, alias Operator 5, in the pulp magazine stories), 6 BS 8; 7 BS 7

Carr, Wooda Nicholas: Operator 5 Speaks, (pulp hero character), 5A P 8

Carr, Wooda Nicholas: Portrait of a Pulpster, (Ryerson Johnson, author of pulp stories, biog. sketch), 14 SF 2

Carr, Wooda Nicholas: The Pulp Reincarnation, 10 X 10

Carr, Wooda Nicholas: The Pulp Villains, 42 X 126

Carr, Wooda Nicholas: The Pulp Villains, Tang-Akhmut, The Man from the East, (in The Spider pulp stories) 5 DS 10

Carr, Wooda Nicholas: The Quest, (pulp magazine collecting experiences), 6-4 MR 1

Carr, Wooda Nicholas: Quoth the Raven, "Nevermore", (on G-8, pulp character, in pulp magazines) 6 X 29

Carr, Wooda Nicholas: Ryerson Johnson and the Phantom Detective, (an interview with pulp author), 6 U 9

Carr, Wooda Nicholas: The Shadow Speaks, (exchange between Nick Carr and Shadow author, Walter B. Gibson), 5 P 3

Carr, Wooda Nicholas: Some Pulp Contemplations, 6 DS 8; 7 DS 16; 9 DS 18; 10 DS 27; 11 DS 16; 12 DS 16

Carr, Wooda Nicholas: The Spider, a Personal View, (comments on The Spider, pulp hero character), 8 U 62

Carr, Wooda Nicholas: The Subject was Death, (Operator 5, pulp hero, and the "Army of the Dead") 15 SF 9

Carr, Wooda Nicholas: The Tepperman Quest, (search for Emile Tepperman, pulp author), 4 U 28

Carr, Wooda Nicholas: That Which Brings Death, (fiction), 2 FM 11

Carr, Wooda Nicholas: The Two Faces of Herr Matzu, (villain in G-8 pulp magazine stories), 5 X 4

Carr, Wooda Nicholas: The Weird Adventures of The Shadow (on The Shadow, pulp hero character, and his author, Walter B. Gibson), 9 BS 16

Carr, Wooda Nicholas: "What Evil Lurks in the Hearts of Men?" (difficulties in conceiving pulp heroes in today's world), 8 BS 9

Carr, Wooda Nicholas, and Tom Johnson: The Silver Witch, (villainess in stories in pulp magazine JUNGLE STORIES), 11 DS 8

Carr, Wooda Nicholas, and Herman S. McGregor: Contemplating Seven of the Pulp Heroes, (comparisons and characteristics), 12 BS 3

Carr, Wooda Nicholas, and Robert Sampson: The Pulp Corner, Memoirs of a Doc Savage Reader, 14 SF 21

Carr, Wooda Nicholas, and Robert Sampson: The Pulp Corner, (reminiscences, collecting experiences, other), 15 SF 8

(Carr, Sarah Pratt), Billy To-Morrow Series, Boy's Series Bibliographies, (boys' books), by Harry K. Hudson, 1-3 YB 9

(Carrados, Max, detective: Ernest Bramah)
An Unpublished Ernest Bramah Letter
on Max Carrados, by William White,
3-2 TAD 92

(Carrados, Max, detective: Ernest Bramah)
Bramah: A Footnote to Carrados,
2-4 MR 19

(Carrados, Max, detective: Ernest Bramah)
Ernest Bramah's Max Carrados, by
William White, 2-2 MR 7

(Carrados, Max, detective: Ernest Bramah)
What's in a Name? or, Playfully, on a
Tangent, by Joshua Goldberg, 7-2 TAD
122

Carrian Canon for the Curious, (bibliography, John Dickson Carr), by Larry
L. French, 1 NC 20

Carrick, J.D.: letter of comment,
26 X 72; 28 X 79

Carroll, Barry M.: letter of comment,
18 R 29

Carroll John Daly, The Forgotten Pioneer
of the Private Eye, (prolific pulp
writer of detective stories), by
William F. Nolan, 4-1 TAD 1

Carroll, John E.: The Imperial Dragon,
(re: Sax Rohmer stories), 10 R 5

Carroll, John E.: letter of comment,
2 R 22; 3 R 28; 4 R 24; 5 R 32;
17 R 25

Carroll, John E.: Limehouse and the
River Police, (on Rohmer's Fu Manchu
stories), 5 R 13

Carroll, John E.: The Manor of Stepney,
(re: Rohmer's stories), 6 R 17

Carroll, John E.: The Romance of the
Middle East, (in Sax Rohmer), 4 R 7

Carroll, John E.: The Thugs and Dacoits
of India, 8 R 1

(Carroll, John E.), biographical sketch,
8 R 29

(Carroll, Lewis), A Note About Lewis
Carroll, (mystery elements in his
writings), by R.W.Hays, 7-2 TAD 95

(Carroll, Lewis: "The Unknown One"),
The Unknown One, (discusses story
of that title), by J.R.Christopher,
3-4 TAD 247

(Carter, John Franklin), Obituary,
1-2 TAD 44

(Carter, John Franklin: Dennis Tyler
series), Checklist, annotated,
by Barry Van Tilburg, 4-3 MF 25

Carter, J.M.: A Second John D.?
(comparison of authors, John D.
MacDonald and Charles Williams),
18 JD 15

Carter, J.M.: letter of comment, 18 JD 23;
7-2 TAD 150; 8-4 TAD 314; 10-3 TAD 278;
19 JD 12; 22 JD 20

(Carter, John, of Mars), The Mysterious
Case of the Carters, ("genealogy"
of the Carters in the Burroughs
stories), by Todd Rutt and Arn
McConnell, 1-2 WA 3

(Carter, Lin: Zarkon Novels), Lord
of the Unknown, the Zarkon Novels
of Lin Carter, by Link Hullar,
8 U 141

(Carter, Nick, detective), The
Adventures of Nick Carter, (review
of television show), by J. Randolph
Cox, 5-2 MR 35

(Carter, Nick, detective), The Many
Lives of Nick Carter, (literary
discussion of the span of the
Nick Carter stories), by J. Randolph
Cox, 71 PU 8

(Carter, Nick, detective), The Pulp
Career of Nicholas Carter, by J.
Randolph Cox, 22 X 15

(Carter, Nick, detective), The Mysterious
Case of the Carters, ("genealogy"
of the Carter family, including
John Carter of Mars), by Todd Rutt
and Arn McConnell, 1-2 WA 3

(Carter, Nick, detective), Nick Carter,
The Man and the Myth, by J. Randolph
Cox, 2-3 MR 15

(Carter, Nick, detective), Nick
Crider: Killmaster? (on writing a
Nick Carter story), by Bill Crider,
7 PE 9

Carter, Steven R.: Freedom and Mystery
in John Fowles' THE ENIGMA, 3-5 MF
14

Carter, Steven R.: Julian Symons and
Civilization's Discord, (social
stress in works), 12-1 TAD 57

Carter, Steven R.: Karma and Spiritual
Responsibility in James Jones' A
TOUCH OF DANGER, 13-3 TAD 230

Carter, Steven R.: The Science Fiction
Mystery Novels of Asimov, Bester
and Lem: Fusions and Foundations,
1-1 C 109

Carter, Steven R.: Spenserian Ethics,
The Unconventional Morality of
Robert B. Parker's Traditional
American Hero, 1-2 C 109

(cartoon paperback books), Andy Capp,
Gold Medal/Fawcett PIBS, (Andy
Capp in Gold Medal and Fawcett
paperback books), by Raymond
Torrence, 1-6 CP 13

(cartoon paperback books), Mass
Market Murmurings, (general
discussion), (1939-1959) 1-4 CP 8;
(1960-1969) 1-6 CP 20

(Carvic, Heron), Checklist of works,
by Audrey I. Pacheco, 5-4 MR 23

Casandra, (verse), by Lucile Coleman,
28 X 2

Case of the Blind Clairaudient, A
Critical Study, (Solar Pons story)
by Bruno Lumbroso, 3-1 PDA 32

Case of the Canonical Collector, The,
(on collecting Sherlockiana), by
Jackie Geyer, 11-3 TAD 290

Case of the Cheshire Cat's Paw, The, (fiction, Sherlock Holmes pastiche), by G. Arthur Rahman and James A. McKraken, 10 CL 3

Case of Commissioner James Gordon, The, (Gordon was the Whisperer, pulp magazine character, and ancestor of Batman?), by Arn McConnell, 1-3 WA 14

Case of the Elusive Author, The, (on R.T.M. Scott, pulp hero author) by Dick Myers, 9 BS 5

Case of the Elusive Author, The, (on Frank S. Lawton, pulp hero author), by Dick Myers, 10 BS 14

Case of the Empty Fortune Cookies, The, (fiction), by Hamilton T. Caine, 2-3 M 10

Case of the Hypochrondriac Detective, (discusses Detective Berkeley Barnes, character creation of Eugene Franklin) by Larry L. French, 1-2 PP 9

Case of John D. MacDonald, The, Introduction and Comment, by John D. MacDonald, 1-1 C 63

Case of the Missing Article, The, (Ellery Queen in GOOD HOUSEKEEPING) by J.R.Christopher, 2-1 QC 14

Case of the Missing Criminal, The, Crime Fiction's Unpaid Debt to It's Ne'er-do-wells, (the criminal character in mystery fiction), by Connie Fletcher, 10-1 TAD 17

Case of the Missing End, The, by Richard Moskowitz, 6/7 LR 6

Case of the Missing Memorial, The, (discusses why few public memorials to Sherlock Holmes), by Rev.Fr. Francis Hertzberg, 3-5 MR 15

Case of the Missing Wolfe, The, (review of NERO WOLFE OF WEST THIRTY-FIFTH STREET by William S. Baring-Gould), by William J. Clark, 3-4 MR 16

Case of the Moonlighting Physicians, The, (on Dr. de Grandin and Dr. Trowbridge) by Chet Williamson, 6 WT 14

Case of the Quivering Mustache, The, (re: Lilian Jackson Braun, author) by Mary Ann Grochowski, 3-6 PP 3

Case of the Triple Couchers, The, (on Anthony Boucher), by Luther Norris, 1-5 MR 10

Case of the Unbeaten Attorney, The, or the Secret Life of Perry Mason, (lawyer-detective of Erle Stanley Gardner), by Marvin Lachman, 4-3 TAD 147

Case of the Underground Man, Evolution or Devolution, The, ? (discusses Ross Macdonald's THE UNDERGROUND MAN) by G.A.Finch, 6-4 TAD 210

Case of the Vanishing Locomotives, The, or, A Hell of a Way to Run a Railroad, (impossible crimes: vanishing locomotives as a theme), by J.R. Christopher, 1-2 TAD 56

Case File: Canada, (book reviews), by W. Ritchie Benedict, 6 U 38

Casebeer, Lance: A Diversey Checklist, (Diversey paperback books), 3-3 CP 10

Casebeer, Lance: Articles and Books on Paperbacks, (general discussion), 3-5 CP 3

Casebeer, Lance: Avon Doubles, (Avon paperbacks, two-in-one, checklist) 1-6 CP 8

Casebeer, Lance: Checker Books, a Checklist, (paperback books under that trademark), 1-3 CP 15

Casebeer, Lance: Checklist, Freeman Eliot, paperback cover artist, 1-1 CP 20

Casebeer, Lance: Chicago Paperback Books, Checklist, (paperbacks under that tradename), 1-5 CP 20

Casebeer, Lance: I Wonder? (questions and answers of bibliographic nature on paperback collecting), 1-2 CP 8; 1-3 CP 2; 1-4 CP 3; 1-5 CP 3; 1-6 CP 8; 2-1 CP 5; 2-3 CP 5; 2-5 CP 3

Casebeer, Lance: Paperback Talk, (questions and answers on paperbacks, continued as column "I Wonder", see) 1-1 CP 12

Casebeer, Lance: Puzzled? (paperback book collecting acrostic puzzle), 1-2 CP 24

Casebeer, Lance: Who Drew That Girl? (paperback book cover art and artists), (general) 1-1 CP 20; 1-2 CP 22; (Wallace Wood, artist) 1-3 CP 26; (Robert McGuire, artist) 1-5 CB 31; 1-6 CP 28; (Popular Library cover artists) 2-1 CP 21; 2-3 CP 36; (Bill Wenzel, artist) 2-4 CP 30; 3-1 CP 25

Casebeer, Lance, and Bruce Taylor: Asey Mayo, Cape Cod Sleuth, (in paperbacks), 3-1 CP 20

(Caspary, Vera), Vera Caspary's Fascinating Females, Laura, Evvie, and Bedelia (in mystery fiction) by Jane S. Bakerman, 1-1 C 46

Casting a Little Light Among the Shadows, (on The Shadow, pulp hero character, and his past) by Arn McConnell, 2-1 WA 3

Castlemon, Harry: Are the Characters of Juvenile Fiction Real? (on boys' books, by prolific author) 4-1 BC 406

Castlemon, Harry: How I Came to Write
My First Book, (boys' books author),
1-1 BC 28
Castlemon, Harry: How to Write Stories
for Boys, (boys' book author),
4-1 BC 404
(Castlemon, Harry), A Talk with Harry
Castlemon, (boys' books author)
by Carabel Lewis Munger, 2-4 BC 250
(Castlemon, Harry), Checklist, (boys'
books), 1-1 BC 20
(Castlemon, Harry), Chronology of Books
(boys' books), by Maurice Owen,
1-3 BC 75
(Castlemon, Harry), Favorite Juvenile
Authors: What Publishers Said About
Their Old Stand-bys, by Gil O'Gara,
1-2 YB 19
(Castlemon, Harry), Thank You Harry
Castlemon, (tribute), 1-4 TB 2
Catastrophe Stories, The, (bibliography
of fiction), by Robert L. Brown,
20 X 10
Cats in Mysteries, by Jane Merrill
Filstrup, 11-1 TAD 59; 11-2 TAD 134
Cattaneo, Larry: letter of comment,
2-2 M 2
Cavallo, Charles: letter of comment,
15 X 14; 24 X 47; 40 X 85; 43 X 5
Caves, Gas and The Great Transfer
Theory, (provides possible answer
to disappearances of popular fiction
characters), by Todd Rutt and Arn
McConnell, 1-2 WA 11
Cawthorn, Jim: Art Portfolio based on
"Flight to Yesterday" of Poul
Anderson, 64 PU 18
Ceia, Dr. Mario: letter of comment,
2-1 TAD 63
(Cellini, Dr. Emmanuel, series: Michael
Halliday), Checklist, by Robert E.
Briney and John Creasey, 2-1 TAD 13
Century Books, Checklist (science-
fiction), by J. Grant Thiessen,
2 SF 7
Certo, Nick: letter of comment, 26 X 77;
30 X 148
Cervon, Bruce: Captain Future, Paperback
Readers Guide and Checklist, 2-5 CP 17
Cervon, Bruce: Dusty Ayres (pulp hero
character now in Corinth paperbacks)
3-2 CP 18
Cervon, Bruce: G-8 and His Battle Aces,
(pulp hero character now in paperback
books), 3-5 CP 24
Cervon, Bruce: Hard Boiled is Hard to
Find, (hard-boiled detective mysteries
in paperback books), 3-2 CP 23
Cervon, Bruce: The Phantom Detective in
Paperback, (paperback books), 2-4 CP 7
Cervon, Bruce: Reader's Guide to Doctor
Death, (Doctor Death series in
paperback books), 3-3 CP 30

Cervon, Bruce: Secret Agent X, (pulp
hero character in paperback books)
3-1 CP 14
Cervon, Bruce: The Shadow Known,
(pulp hero character in paperback
books), 2-3 CP 31
Cervon, Bruce: The Spider, (discussion
of the pulp hero magazine and the
paperback book series, with checklist)
3-4 CP 11
(Chaber, M.E.), see Kendell F. Crossen
(Chaber, M.E.), Checklist, Milo March
novels, by Dickson Thorp, 1-2 MF 6
(Chadwick, Lester), The College Life
Series, boys' books by Chadwick, by
Jack R. Schorr, 2-4 TBN 6
Challenges to the Listener, (Ellery
Queen on radio), by Chris Steinbrunner,
12-3 TAD 214
Challenge to the Reader, (Ellery Queen
a bigamist?), by J.R.Christopher,
1-2 QC 11
Challenge to the Reader, (link to
HALFWAY HOUSE?), by Donald A. Yates,
1-3 QC 12
(Challis, Bart, series: William F. Nolan)
Of Hammett, Chandler, Brand and
Bradbury - and an Eye Named Challis,
by William F. Nolan, 2-2 TAD 86
Chambers, Jeff: Junkie, A Personal
Reminiscence, (on JUNKIE by William
Burroughs and other paperback
collecting comments), 3-3 CP 11
Champion of Catastrophe and Son of the
East, A Short "Genealogy" of Victor
von Doom, (Dr. Doom), by Scott
Koeller, 1-4 WA 5
(Chan, Charlie), Charlie Chan, A
Biography, by Fred Dueren, 7-4 TAD
263
(Chan, Charlie), Charlie Chan Carries
On, (discusses Earl Derr Biggers'
CHARLIE CHAN CARRIES ON), by Neil
Ellman, 10-2 TAD 183
(Chan, Charlie), Charlie Chan in Books
and in Motion Pictures, by Douglas
M. Armato, 7-2 TAD 97
(Chan, Charlie), Charlie Chan in Qui
Nhon, (on Armed Forces TV in Vietnam)
by Jon L. Breen, 2-2 TAD 114
(Chan, Charlie), Who Killed Charlie
Chan, (the updated Chan), by Jon L.
Breen, 7-2 TAD 100
(Chan To, detective), A Chinese
Detective in San Francisco, by E.F.
Bleiler, 5-3 MF 2
Chance and Illogic and THE BLACK BOX
MURDER, by E.F.Bleiler, 2-1 MF 8
(Chance, George, as The Ghost, Super
Detective), Ghost Story,(pulp
hero character), by Robert Sampson,
5 P 20

Chandler on Screen, TV and Radio - With a Look at the Many Marlowes, with checklist, by William F. Nolan, 3-1 TAD 23

Chandler-Hammett-Hemingway, Teachers in the "Tough School" (of hard-boiled detective fiction), by Stanley A. Carlin, 2-5 MR 15

(Chandler, Raymond), The Black Mask Boys Go Legit, (re: BLACK MASK pulp magazine), by William F. Nolan, 13-1 TAD 23

(Chandler, Raymond), Chandler-Hammett-Hemingway, Teachers in the "Tough School" (of hard-boiled detective fiction), by Stanley A. Carlin, 2-5 MR 15

(Chandler, Raymond), Chandler on Screen, TV and Radio - With a Look at the Many Mr. Marlowes, with checklist, by William F. Nolan, 3-1 TAD 23

(Chandler, Raymond), The Complex Art of Raymond Chandler (literary quality and method), by George N. Dove, 8-4 TAD 271

(Chandler, Raymond), Ideology and Narrative Stereotyping, The Case of Raymond Chandler, by K.A. MacDermott, 2-1 C 77

(Chandler, Raymond), The Longest Goodbye, or, The Search for Chandler's Los Angeles, (locales of stories), by Paul Bishop, 1-2 M 33

(Chandler, Raymond), Marlowe's Long Goodbye, (Chandler's Philip Marlowe), by G.A.Finch, 6-1 TAD 7

(Chandler, Raymond), Morality and the Detective Hero, Raymond Chandler's Philip Marlowe, by Jay G. Milner, 1-1 C 116

(Chandler, Raymond), More Chandlerisms, by Thea Taylor, 1-4 CP 29

(Chandler, Raymond), Play It Again, Sam Spade, (Bogart as Spade, film) by Steve Fisher, 5-2 TAD 79

(Chandler, Raymond), Playedback...or Chandler's Los Angeles Revisited, by Paul Bishop, 5 PE 29

(Chandler, Raymond), Portrait of a Tough Guy, by William F. Nolan, 28 X 13

(Chandler, Raymond), Raymond Chandler 1888-1959, Checklist, by Charles Shibuk, 1-3 MR 9

(Chandler, Raymond), Raymond Chandler and the Detective, by Mark MacDonald, 3 MT 2

(Chandler, Raymond), Raymond Chandler, Novelist, by James W. Thompson, 21 X 52

(Chandler, Raymond), Raymond Chandler on Film, An Annotated Checklist, by Peter Pross, 1-6 MF 3

(Chandler, Raymond), Raymond Chandler on Film, Screenplays Written by Chandler, An Annotated Checklist, by Peter Pross, 2-3 MF 27

(Chandler, Raymond), Raymond Chandler on Film, Addendum by Charles Shibuk, 2-4 MF 14

(Chandler, Raymond), Raymond Chandler on the Screen, by Charles Shubuk, 1-3 MR 7

(Chandler, Raymond), Raymond Chandler's Self-Parody (as found in his various works), by Randall R. Mawer, 14-4 TAD 355

(Chandler, Raymond), 24 Stories and 7 Novels, (commentary on DOWN THESE MEAN STREETS A MAN MUST GO by Philip Durham), by Stewart Kemble, 72 PU 18

(Chandler, Raymond), Where Have All the Values Gone?, The Private Eye's Vision of America in the Novels of Raymond Chandler and Ross Macdonald, by Etta C. Abrahams, 9-2 TAD 128

(Chandler, Raymond: Continental Op series), Checklist, by William F. Nolan, 1-4 TAD 153

Chang Monster, The, (on Mr. Chang, pulp magazine villain), by Robert Sampson, 14 SF 41

Chant Royal of the Sodality of Praed Street Irregulars, (verse), by Michael Harrison, 1-1 PDA 2

Chapter One, (on boys' books), by Fred Woodworth, 1 MA 1

Charet, Larry: letter of comment, 3-2 M 2

Charles, Hal: Breaking Into the Mystery Market (advice on writing mystery fiction), 4-1 PP 9

Charles, Hal ("Mother"): letter of comment, 28 JD 41

Charles, Hal: The Perspiration Factor, (discipline for would-be authors) 4-5/6 PP 43

Charles, Hal: Two Heads Are Better Than One, (co-authorship of mysteries discussed; advantages), 4-2 PP 9

Charles, Hal: What Happened to the 29th Pilgrim, or, Inspiration, No, -- Perspiration, Yes, (comments on writing mystery fiction), 4-3 PP 3

Charles, Hal: The Whole Versus the Sum of the Parts, or, Using Personal Experience in Fiction (advice on writing), 4-4 PP 9

(Charles, Hal), A Reply to Hal Charles, by Gary Warren Niebuhr, 4-2 PP 12

Charles L. Harness, a Bibliography, by William D. Vernon, 14 SF 30

Charles L. Harness, The Paradox Man, by William D. Vernon, 14 SF 25

Charles Pierce Burton, The Bob's Hill Boys, (boys' series), by Jack Bales, 5 BB 5

Charlie Chan: A Biography, by Fred
Dueren, 7-4 TAD 263
Charlie Chan Carries On (on Earl Derr
Biggers' CHARLIE CHAN CARRIES ON)
by Neil Ellman, 10-2 TAD 183
Charlie Chan in Qui Nhon, (on Armed
Forces TV in Vietnam), by Jon L.
Breen, 2-2 TAD 114
Charlie Chan in Books and in Motion
Pictures, by Douglas M. Armato,
7-2 TAD 97
(CHARLIE CHAN MYSTERY MAGAZINE), Who
Killed Charlie Chan?, (discussion
on the magazine), by Jon L. Breen,
7-2 TAD 100
(Charlton, Detective-Inspector Henry:
Clifford Witting), Pen Profile,
(biog. & literary sketch), by
Barry Pike, 2-6 PP 25
(Chartered Publications), The Killian
Memoranda, by Dave Killian, 1-4 CP 23
Charteris, Leslie: letter of comment,
17 R 23; 13 X 60
Charteris, Leslie: The Sound of Fu Manchu,
6 R 19
(Charteris, Leslie), Bond-Charteris
Enterprises and Saint Enterprises,
checklist of publications, by
Michael Masliah, 12-4 TAD 354
(Charteris, Leslie), Leslie Charteris
and The Saint, Five Decades of
Partnership, (The Saint, detective,
by Charteris), by Jan Alexandersson
and Iwan Hedman, 4-4 MF 21
(Charteris, Leslie), Notes on Very Early
Leslie Charteris, by Charles Shibuk,
4-4 TAD 230
(Charteris, Leslie), Prolegomena to a
Bibliography of the Immortal Works
of Leslie Charteris, by J. Randolph
Cox, 5-2 MR 9
(Charteris, Leslie), The Saint on Film,
by J. Randolph Cox, 5-2 MR 14
(Charteris, Leslie), The Saint's Boston
Caper, by John A. Dinan, 11 X 17
(Charteris, Leslie: The Saint),
Series Synopses, by John Vining,
10-2 TAD 187
Chase - The Private Eye Novels of
James Hadley Chase, by Theodore P.
Dukeshire, 7 PE 7
Chase, Frederick: letter of Comment,
5 BB 23
(Chase, James Hadley), The Caper Novels
of James Hadley Chase, by Theodore
P. Dukeshire, 10-2 TAD 128
(Chase, James Hadley), Chase: The
Private Eye Novels of James Hadley
Chase, by Theodore P. Dukeshire,
7 PE 7
(Chase, James Hadley), Checklist of
works, by Theodore P. Dukeshire,
5-1 TAD 33

(Chase, James Hadley), The Films of
James Hadley Chase, by Jack Edmund
Nolan, 3-6 MR 30
(Chase, James Hadley), James Hadley
Chase, by Theodore P. Dukeshire,
5-1 TAD 32
(Chase, James Hadley: NO ORCHIDS FOR
MISS BLANDISH), No Orchids for
George Orwell, (Orwell's criticism)
by Susan Harris Smith, 9-2 TAD 114
(Chase, Josephine), Checklist, series
books under various pseudonyms,
by Roy B. Van Devier, 1-2 BC 40
(Chase, Josephine), Josephine Chase
and Her Pen Names, by Roy B. Van
Devier, 1-2 BC 39
Chasing "Will-o'-the-Wisps", (boys'
book collecting experiences), by
M.E.Owen, 1-2 BC 64
Chastain, Thomas: Robert Fish, In
Memorium, (memorial tribute),
14-2 TAD 119
(Chastain, Thomas), Thomas Chastain
and the New Police Procedural,
by Larry L. French, 2-4 MF 17
Chatterbox Feature Unique and Infor-
mative Innovation (discusses the
"forum" feature as important part
of the Leo Edward's boys' books)
by Julius R. Chenu, 2-4 TB 1
Chats With Big Americans for Young
Americans, (re: boys' books), by
Hugh C. Weir, 3-1 BC 278
(Chavasse, Paul, series: Martin
Fallon), Checklist, annotated,
by Barry Van Tilburg, 4-3 MF 28
(Chayse, Dr. Sarah, detective: Lynn
Meyer), Feminists as Detectives,
Harriet Vane, Kate Fansler, Sarah
Chayse, by Kathleen Gregory Klein,
13-1 TAD 31
(CHEAP DETECTIVE, THE: Robert Grossbach),
A Pair of Parodies, by R. Jeff
Banks, 1-5 PP 10
Checker Books, checklist of titles under
that trademark, paperbacks, by Lance
Casebeer, 1-3 CP 15
Checklists (see also Indexes, Biblio-
graphies)
A. MERRITT'S FANTASY, (pulp magazine)
by Herman S. McGregor, 74 PU 15
Abbott, Anthony: Thatcher Colt
Novels, by Jon L. Breen, 3-1
TAD 5
Ace Books, paperbacks, by author, by
J. Grant Thiessen, 1 SF 21
Ace Books, paperbacks, numerical
sequence, by J. Grant Thiessen,
1 SF 3
Ace Books, (additions and errata)
by J. Grant Thiessen, 2 SF 35
Ace Double Mysteries, paperbacks,
by Steve Lewis, 7 MY 3

Checklists, (continued)

ACE G-MAN, pulp magazine, index
of issues, by Lynn Hickman,
75 PU 6

ACE-HIGH DETECTIVE, pulp magazine,
by Lynn Hickman, 75 PU 7

ACE-HIGH MAGAZINE, pulp magazine,
by Lynn Hickman, 75 PU 9

ACE-HIGH WESTERN, pulp magazine,
by Lynn Hickman, 75 PU 8

Ace Science Fiction Specials,
paperbacks, by William Trojan,
5 SF 21

Acre, Ethridge, boys' mystery
series, by Harry K. Hudson,
1-4 YB 24

Adair, Arnold, boys' series books,
by Harry K. Hudson, 1-3 YB 8

Adams, Cleve F., works, by Francis
M. Nevins, Jr. and William J.
Clark, 8-3 TAD 200

Aiken, Joan, works, by Audrey I.
Pacheco, 5-4 MR 25

Alexander, David, works, by Jim
McCahery, 1-6 PP 23

ALL-ACES, pulp magazine, by Lynn
Hickman, 75 PU 7

Allingham, Margery, works, by B.A.
Pike, 6-3 TAD 198

Allingham, Margery, works, by Mrs.
Kathy Hoble, 1-3 MR 13

Allingham, Margery, additions to
checklist, 1-4 MR 10

American Detective series, early
thick paperbacks, by Howard
Waterhouse, 2-3 PQ 36

Among the Sioux, boys' series books,
by Harry K. Hudson, 1-3 YB 8

Anderson, J.R.L.: Peter Blair
series, by Barry Van Tilburg,
4-2 MF 11

Armstrong, Charlotte, works, by
Audrey I. Pacheco, 5-4 MR 24

Armstrong, Charlotte, works, by
Francis M. Nevins, Jr.,
5-5 MR 18

Ashe, Gordon: Crime Haters Series,
by Robert E. Briney and John
Creasey, 2-1 TAD 12

Ashe, Gordon: Patrick Dawlish
Series, by Robert E. Briney and
John Creasey, 2-1 TAD 11

Avallone, Michael, works, by
Stephen Mertz, 8 PE 2; 9-2 TAD 132

Avallone, Michael, works (full-
length), 8 U 95

Avallone, Michael, in MIKE SHAYNE
MYSTERY MAGAZINE, by Tom Johnson,
9 SF 23

Avallone, Michael, partial list of
works, by Kelly Adrian, 1-5 MR 5

Avalon Books, paperbacks, by Stuart
W. Wells and Dick Spelman, 5 SF 29

Checklists, continued)

Avenger, The, in THE AVENGER
MAGAZINE, by Wooda Nicholas
Carr, 3-6 MR 16

Avenger, The, (magazine series),
by Jack Irwin, 2 BS 2

Avon Clasic Crime, paperbacks,
by Jeff Meyerson, 1-4 CP 6;
1-5 MF 20

Avon Doubles, paperbacks, 1-6 CP 8

AVON FANTASY NOVELS, science-
fiction/fantasy magazine,
by J. Grant Thiessen, 2 SF 6

AVON MURDER MYSTERY MONTHLY, by
Francis M. Nevins, Jr., 7 MY 3

Bailey, H.C.: Reggie Fortune
short stories, by Thomas D.
Waugh, 6-2 TAD 76

Baker, Samm Sinclair, works, by
Marvin Lachman, 4-2 PP 19

Ball, John, works, by Robert E.
Briney, 5-6 MR 14

Ballantine Books, Science-Fiction,
Fantasy and Weird fiction 1953-
1976, by Carl Bennett, 6 SF 3

Ballard, W.T., works, by Stephen
Mertz, 12-1 TAD 19

Ballinger, Bill S., works, by
Harold Knott, 4-6 MR 9

Bantam Publications (Los Angeles),
paperbacks, science-fiction,
by J. Grant Thiessen, 2 SF 6

Bantan novels series by Maurice
B. Gardner (author), 62 PU 22

Barbour, Ralph Henry, boy's books,
by Julius R. Chenu, 1-4 BC 118

Barbour, Ralph Henry, various
boys' series, by Julius R. Chenu,
6 YB 17

Bark, Conrad Voss: Mr. Holmes
series, by Barry Van Tilburg,
4-2 MF 11

Bart House, paperback publications,
by J. Grant Thiessen, 2 SF 7

Basic Mystery Fiction, revised
"indefinite" list by various
contributors, by Charles Shibuk
and Marvin Lachman, 9-3 TAD 203

Baum, L. Frank, Teen-age serials,
by Justin G. Schiller, 2-3 BC
194

Bean, Tuffy, series, of Leo Edwards,
boy's books, 1-1 TB 4

Bean, Tuffy, series, of Leo Edwards,
by Julius R. Chenu, 3 BB 10;
1-2 YB 18

Beeding, Francis: Colonel Alistair
Granby series, by Barry Van
Tilburg, 4-2 MF 11

Benson, Ben, mystery novels, by
Robert E. Briney, 3-2 MR 8

Benton, Kenneth: Peter Craig series,
by Barry Van Tilburg, 4-2 MF 12

84

Checklists, (continued)

Berg, Trigger, series, boys' books,
by Julius R. Chenu, 3 BB 10

Berg, Trigger, series, boys' books,
1-1 TB 4

Berg, Trigger, series, boys' books,
by Julius R. Chenu, 1-2 YB 18

Bergey, Earle, (paperback cover
artist), by Lance Casebeer, 1-2 CP
23

Bestseller Mysteries, digest-size
paperback series, by Jeff Meyerson
1-5 PP 33

Bestseller Mysteries, addendum, by
Jim Tinsman, 1-6 PP 27; 2-1 PP 31

Big Game Series, boys' books, by
Harry K. Hudson, 3 BB 25

BIG MAGAZINE, THE, pulp magazine, by
Lynn Hickman, 75 PU 7

Biggers, Earl Derr, works, by Charles
Shubuk, 2-6 MR 21

Billy To-Morrow series, boys' books,
by Harry K. Hudson, 1-3 YB 9

BIZARRE FANTASY TALES, magazine, by
Gene Marshall and Carl F. Waedt,
3 SF 19

Blackburn, John: General Kirk series,
by Barry Van Tilburg, 4-2 MF 12

Blake, Andy, series, boys' books, by
Julius R. Chenu, 3 BB 10; 2-2 YB 17

Blake, Andy, series, boys' books,
1-1 TB 4

Blake, Nicholas, works, by Jan Broberg,
2-3 MR 3

Blessington, Charles, detective,
series, by Barry Pike, 2-3 PP 23

Bloch, Robert, paperback originals,
by Michael S. Barson, 4-1 PQ 24

Blochman, Lawrence: Dr. Coffee series,
by James Mark Purcell, 4-3 MR 29

Block, Lawrence: Tanner series,
annotated, by R. Jeff Banks,
5/6 MN 7

Blue Seal Books, paperbacks, by Bill
O'Connell, 3-3 CP 23

Bolton, Judy, girls' series books,
by Julius R. Chenu, 1-1 YB 3

Bonaparte, Napoleon, detective: Arthur
W. Upfield, by William Antony S.
Sarjeant, 12-4 TAD 358

Bond-Charteris Books, paperbacks, by
J. Grant Thiessen, 2 SF 7

Bond-Charteris Enterprises and Saint
Enterprises, paperbacks, by Michael
Masliah, 12-4 TAD 354

Bonded Publications, paperbacks, by
Dave Killian, 1-4 CP 23

Bonibooks, paperbacks, by Peter Manesis,
2-4 PQ 28

Borgo Press publications, 2-1 PQ 20

Boucher, Anthony, works, by Francis M.
Nevins, Jr., 3-2 M 63

Checklists, (continued)

Boucher, Anthony, works, by J.R.
Christopher, D.W.Dickensheet
& Robert E. Briney, 2-2 TAD 77;
2-3 TAD 143; 2-4 TAD 263

Boy Allies Series, boys' books,
by John T. Dizer, Jr., 3-1 BC
270

Boy's book authors, 1-1 BC 30

Boy's Papers & Magazines, by S.E.
Wallen, 3-3 BC 333

Boys of Columbia High, boys' book
series, by Julius R. Chenu,
5 BB 8

Bradbury, Ray, crime-suspense
fiction, by William F. Nolan,
4-3 TAD 155

Bramah, Ernest, in anthologies
1914-1972, by William White,
10-1 TAD 30

Brewer, Gil, works in paperbacks,
by Michael S. Barson, 3-4 PQ
11

Bridge, Ann: Julia Probyn series,
annotated, by Barry Van Tilburg,
5-3 MF 20

Brown, Fredric, works, by J. Grant
Thiessen, 2 SF 26

Brown, Fredric, works, annotated,
by Newton Baird, 10-4 TAD 370;
11-1 TAD 86

Brown, Fredric, works (novels),
by William F. Nolan, 5-4 TAD 193

Brown, Fredric, the uncollected
fiction, in paperbacks, by
Dennis McMillan, 3-1 CP 15;
3-2 CP 25

Bruce, Jean: Hubert Bonisseur de la
Bath series, by Barry Van Tilburg
4-2 MF 13

Buchan, John, works, by J. Randolph
Cox, 6-2 MR 18

Buchan, John, works of fiction, by
J. Randolph Cox, 2-4 TAD 213

Buchan, John, works, by Theodore P.
Dukeshire, 7-3 TAD 201

Bulmer, Kenneth, works, by Ian
Covell, 4 SF 28

Burroughs, Edgar Rice, books, by
John F. Sullivan, 3-3 BC 349

Burroughs, Edgar Rice, in pulp
magazines, by John Harwood,
69 PU 13

BULL'S EYE WESTERN, pulp magazine,
by Lynn Hickman, 75 PU 7

Calhoun, Frances Boyd, juvenile
series books, by Julius R.Chenu
1-4 YB 4

Canfield, Flavia A.: The Kidnapped
Campers series, (boys' books),
1-5 YB 14

Checklists, (continued)

Capp, Andy, (cartoon character paperbacks, by Raymond Torrence,
1-6 CP 13

CAPTAIN COMBAT, pulp magazine, by
Lynn Hickman, 75 PU 7

Captain Future in paperback books,
by Bruce Cervon, 2-5 CP 17

CAPTAIN SATAN, pulp magazine, by
Lynn Hickman, 75 PU 11

Carr, Freddy, boy's series books,
by Harry K. Hudson, 1-4 YB 24

Carr, Glyn, works, by William A.S.
Sarjeant, 4 5/6 PP 14

Carr, John Dickson, works, by Rick
Sneary, 3-4 MR 13

Carr, John Dickson, addenda to
checklist of Rick Sneary, by
J.R.Christopher, 4-1 MR 20

Carr, John Dickson, on British
radio, by Douglas G. Greene,
12-1 TAD 69

Carr, John Dickson, works, by
Larry L. French, 1 NC 20

Carr, John Dickson, paperback
book editions, by Lloyd Busch,
2-2 CP 9

Carr, John Dickson, paperback
book editions, 1-2 CP 16

Carr, John Dickson: Gideon Fell
series, by Marvin Lachman,
2-3 MF 4

Carter, John Franklin ("Diplomat"):
Dennis Tyler series, annotated,
by Barry Van Tilburg, 4-3 MF 25

Carvic, Heron, works, by Audrey I.
Pacheco, 5-4 MR 23

Castlemon, Harry, boys' books,
1-1 BC 29

Castlemon, Harry, chronology of
books, by Maurice Owen, (boys'
books), 1-3 BC 75

Century Books, paperbacks, by J.
Grant Thiessen, 2 SF 7

Chandler, Raymond, works, by Charles
Shibuk, 1-3 MR 9

Chandler, Raymond: Continental Op
series, by William F. Nolan,
1-4 TAD 153

Chandler, Raymond, on film, by
Peter Pross, 1-6 MF 3

Chandler, Raymond, film, TV, radio,
by William F. Nolan, 3-1 TAD 24

Chandler, Raymond, screenplays by,
by Peter Pross, 2-3 MF 27

Chartered Publications, paperbacks,
by Dave Killian, 1-4 CP 23

Chase, James Hadley, works, by
Theodore P. Dukeshire, 5-1 TAD 33

Chase, Josephine, boys' series books
under var. pseudonyms, by Roy B.
Van Devier, 1-2 BC 40

Checker Books, paperbacks, by Lance
Casebeer, 3-3 CP 15

Checklists, (continued)

Cheyney, Peter, works, by Theodore
P. Dukeshire, 4-4 MR 9

Cheyney, Peter, works, by Iwan
Hedman, 4-2 TAD 111

Chibbet, H.S., works, by Mike
Ashley, 4 WT 7

Chicago Paperback Books (trade
name), publications, by Lance
Casebeer, 1-5 CP 20

Christie, Agatha, paperback book
editions, by Richard P. Hall,
3-3 CP 27

Christie, Agatha, short mystery
stories, by Paul McCarthy,
6-1 TAD 16

Classics of Mystery Fiction: The
Silver Fifty, by Gerald
Tomlinson, 10-2 TAD 165

Cloud Country, boys' book series,
by Harry K. Hudson, 1-3 YB 9

Clunk, Joshua, detective: H.C.
Bailey, by Maryell Cleary,
3-5 PP 20

Coe, Tucker: Mitch Tobin series,
by Maryell Cleary, 4 5/6 PP 32

Coe, Tucker, works, by Jim McCahery,
2 PE 18

Cole, G.D.H., works, by Maryell
Cleary, 3-6 PP 13

Coles, Manning: Thomas Elphinstone
Hambledon series, by Barry Van
Tilburg, 4-3 MF 23

Collier Books, paperbacks, by Ellen
Nehr, 3-5 CP 19

Columbia Science Fiction, paperback
series, by David & Su Bates,
1-4 CP 25

Comicbook artists in paperback books,
by Barry Bernard, 2-4 CP 18

Cooper, John R.: Mel Martin Baseball
Series, boys' books, by Harry K.
Hudson, 6 YB 15

Corinth Paperbacks, by Tom Johnson,
10 SF 37

Cory, Desmond: Johnny Fedora series,
annotated, by Barry Van Tilburg,
4-3 MF 23

Counselman, Mary Elizabeth, stories
in WEIRD TALES, 6 WT 21

Cox, Anthony Berkeley, works, by
Paul R. Moy, 14-3 TAD 236

Coxe, George Harmon, chronological
list of writings, by J. Randolph
Cox, 7-1 TAD 16

Creasey, John, works, by Robert E.
Briney and John Creasey, 2-1 TAD
5; 2-2 TAD 123; 2-4 TAD 276

Creasey, John: Department Z series,
by R.E.Briney & John Creasey,
2-1 TAD 9

Creasey, John: Dr. Palfrey series,
by R.E.Briney & John Creasey,
2-1 TAD 8

Checklists, (continued)

Creasey, John: Dr. Palfrey series,
by Barry Van Tilburg, 4-2 MF 12

Creasey, John: Gordon Craigie and
Dept.Z series, annotated, by
Barry Van Tilburg, 4-3 MF 24

Creasey, John, paperback originals,
by R.E. Briney and John Creasey,
2-1 TAD 20

Creasey, John, pseudonyms, by
R.E.Briney & John Creasey, 2-1
TAD 5

Creasey, John: Roger West series,
by R.E.Briney & John Creasey,
2-1 TAD 8

Creasey, John: The Toff series,
by R.E.Briney & John Creasey,
2-1 TAD 10

Crime Club, paperback editions, by
M.C.Hill, 2-5 CP 15

Crispin, Edmund: Gervase Fen
stories, by William A.S.Sarjeant,
14-3 TAD 196

Crispin, Edmund, works, by Charles
Shibuk, 2-1 MR 15

Crispin, Edmund, works, by William
A.S.Sarjeant, 3-3 PP 9

Crofts, Freeman Wills, works, by
Charles Shibuk, 1-4 MR 14

Crofts, Freeman Wills, works, by
James Keddie, Jr., 2-3 TAD 140

Crossen, Kendell Foster, works, by
Don Miller, 12 MN B1

Crossen, Kendell Foster, reviews
of works, with abstracts, by
Don Miller, 12 MN A5

Crossen, Kendell Foster, short stories,
by Dickson Thorpe, 1-2 MF 7

Curtis Books, paperbacks, by
Dennis Lien, 14 SF 7

Daly, Carroll John, works, by
William F. Nolan, 4-1 TAD 4

Daly, Carroll John, selected list
of works, by Stephen Mertz,
2-3 MF 22

Daly, Elizabeth, works, by Charles
Shibuk, 1-6 MR 16

Daly, Elizabeth, works, by Jim
McCahery, 2-1 PP 28

Davidson, Avram, works, by Richard
Grant, 9 SF 4

Davis, Mildred, works, by Marvin
Lachman, 2-5 PP 16

Davison, Gilderoy: Colonel Royston
and Peter Castle series, annotated,
by Barry Van Tilburg, 5-3 MF 20

Deane, Norman: Bruce Murdoch series,
by R.E.Briney & John Creasey,
2-1 TAD 12

Deane, Norman: Liberator series, by
R.E.Briney & John Creasey, 2-1 TAD
13

Checklists, (continued)

Decolta, Ramon, stories in BLACK
MASK pulp magazine, by E.R.
Hagemann, 14-1 TAD 8

Deer Lodge, boys' book series,
by Harry K. Hudson, 1-3 YB 10

Deering (Deal) boys' book
series, by Harry K. Hudson,
1-3 YB 10

Defunct paperback publishers, by
J. Grant Thiessen, 2 SF 6

Deighton, Len; series, annotated,
by R. Jeff Banks and Harry
D. Dawson, 3-1 MF 12

Deighton, Len; unnamed character
series, annotated, by Barry
Van Tilburg, 4-3 MF 24

de la Torre, Lillian, works, by
James Mark Purcell, 4-5 MR 25

Dell Publishing Company, paperbacks,
1st series, 1st editions, by
William Lyles, 1-5 CP 26;
1-6 CP 17

Dell Great Mystery Library series,
by Bruce Taylor, 3-1 CP 24

Dell Great Mystery Library series,
by Robert E. Briney, 7 MN 4

Dell "Mapback" paperbacks, Nos.
1-300, by Richard C. Butler,
1-2 MF 17

Dell Mysteries, (Murder Ink and
Scene of the Crime series), by
Charlotte Laughlin, 3-4 PQ 15

Dell Paperbacks, early, by William
Lyles, 2-4 CP 13

Dell Paperbacks, variant editions,
by William Lyles, 3-2 CP 31

Dell 10¢ Paperback series, by M.C.
Hill, 2-2 PQ 15

Dell 10¢ Paperback series, by Steve
Lewis, 5 MY 6; 6 MY 7

Derleth, August, works, and list of
corrections, by Bill Dutch,
4-4 AD 11

Derleth, August, works, as prepared
by Derleth in 1941, 5-1 AD 4

Derleth, August: The Mill Creek
Irregulars series, (boys' books)
by Harry K. Hudson, 6 YB 16

Detection Club's Collaborations
(British mystery writer's club)
by Paul R. Moy, 4 5/6 PP 17

Detective Book Club, by Michael L.
Cook, 8-2 TAD 79

Detective Book Club, alphabetical
listing by author, by Michael
L. Cook, 10 MN I1

Detective Book Club, in order of
publication, by Michael L. Cook,
10 MN I21

Detective Book Club, supplemental
list of additions, 9 MN I1

Checklists, (continued)
Detectives (unconventional) in pulp
magazines (in DETECTIVE FICTION
WEEKLY), by Bernard A. Drew,
2-2 C 98
Dickson, Carter, works, by Stanley D.
Doremus, 2-4 MR 9
Diversey Paperback publications, by
Lance Casebeer, 3-3 CP 10
Doc Savage, stories in alphabetical
order, by Bill Laidlaw, 2 DQ 3
Doc Savage, Bantam paperback editions,
1 DS 8
Doc Savage, comparison list of the
original pulp novels and the
paperback book reprints, by Bill
Laidlaw, 1 DQ 6
Doc Savage, The DUENDE Doc Savage
Index, by Will Murray, 2 D 28
DOC SAVAGE magazine, 1933-1949,
pulp magazine, 1 BSA 25
Doc Savage Novels, chronological
order of appearance, 1 DR 9;
2 BS 22
Doc Savage, radio serials, by Will
Murray, 3-4 CP 13
Don Sturdy series, boys' books, by
Robert Jennings, 1 BB 11
Double-Action Pocketbook paperback
book series, by J. Grant Thiessen,
2 SF 7
Double-C series: Edward D. Hoch, by
James Mark Purcell, 5-2 MR 43
Dr. Thorndyke series: R. Austin Freeman,
by George T. Hamilton, 4-2 AD 10;
4-3 AD 6
Dr. Who, books, by Ian Covell, 5 SF 42
DR. YEN SIN, pulp magazine, by Lynn
Hickman, 75 PU 11
Dramatizations of the Great Literary
Detectives and Criminals, (Radio)
1-2 TAD 48; (Television) 1-3 TAD
94; (Theatre) 1-4 TAD 132; (Film)
2-3 TAD 183
DUSTY AYRES, pulp magazine, by Robert
Weinberg, 1 P 23
Dusty Ayres series in pulp magazines,
by Wooda Nicholas Carr, 10 SF 45
Eberhart, Mignon G., works, by Jim
McCahery, 2-3 PP 25
Eliot, Freeman, (paperback book cover
artist), by Lance Casebeer, 1-1
CP 20
Ellin, Stanley, works, by Pat Erhardt,
2-3 MR 14
English Railway Novels of Detection
and Mystery, and Translations, by
Frank P. Donovan, 2-2- TAD 105
English Railway Short Stories of
Detection and Mystery, and Trans-
lations, by Frank P. Donovan,
2-3 TAD 178

Checklists, (continued)
Every Boys' Library, boys'
books, by Charles P. Fisk,
2-1 BC 141
Fallon, Martin: Paul Chavasse
series, annotated, by Barry
Van Tilburg, 4-3 MF 28
FAMOUS FANTASTIC MYSTERIES, pulp
magazine, by Herman S. McGregor,
74 PU 6
FAMOUS SCIENCE FICTION, magazine,
by Gene Marshall and Carl F.
Waedt, 3 SF 17
FANTASTIC NOVELS, pulp magazine,
by Gary Shaheen, 7 X 69
FANTASTIC NOVELS, pulp magazine,
by Herman S. McGregor, 74 PU 6
Farmer, Philip Jose, works, by
Paul Whitney, 5 SF 4
Farmer, Philip Jose, "A Different
Kind of Checklist", by Bruce
Doering, 2-2 CP 24
Faust, Frederick, stories in
MAX BRAND'S WESTERN MAGAZINE,
pulp magazine, by William J.
Clark, 1-1 FC 7
Faust, Frederick, writings in
THE OCCIDENT (high school
paper), by William J. Clark,
1-3 FC 10
Fish, Robert L., works, by Luther
Norris, 2-5 MR 11
Fischer, Bruno, in Gold Medal
paperback editions, by Bill
Crider, 1-4 PQ 23; 2-1 PQ 7
Fitzhugh, Percy Keese, boys'
books, by John F. Sullivan,
3-2 BC 300
Fitzhugh, Percy Keese, works,
(boys' books),by John F.
Sullivan, 4-2 TB 1
Flagship Books, paperbacks, partial
checklist, by Jim Sanderson,
2-3 PQ 48
Flagship Books, addition to check-
list, 3-1 PQ 3
Fleming, Ian: James Bond series,
annotated, by Barry Van Tilburg,
4-3 MF 26
Fleming, Ian, works, by Iwan Hedman,
5-4 TAD 217
Flower, Jesse Graham, boys' series
books, by Roy B. Van Devier,
1-2 BC 40
Footner, Hubert: Rosika Storey
series, by Howard Waterhouse,
2-4 PP 3
Forbes, Stanton, works, 2-2 MR 21
Ford, Leslie, works, by Maryell
Cleary, 3-4 PP 24
Fortune, Dan, stories: Michael
Collins, by John Edwards,
9 SF 38

Checklists, (continued)
Fortune, Reggie, detective: H.C.
    Bailey, short stories, by Mark
    Purcell, with additions by
    Francis M. Nevins, Jr., 5-4 MR 1
Fowler, Dan, detective; novels in
    G-MEN magazine, by Robert Weinberg
    1 P 19
Fox, Gardner F., in paperback editions,
    by Edwin L. Murray, 3-5 CP 7
Frazer, Robert Caine: Mark Kilby series,
    by Robert E. Briney & John Creasey,
    2-1 TAD 12
Freeman, R. Austin, works, by Norman
    Donaldson, 1-2 TAD 35
Freeman, R. Austin, works, by Ruth
    D. McAleer, 11 TF 12
Freeman, R. Austin, works, by R.
    Narasimhan, 8 TF 41
French, Paul: Lucky Starr series,
    (boys' books), 1-5 YB 14
Fu Manchu, list of stories by Sax
    Rohmer, by Robert E. Briney, 7 R 21
Fu Manchu, "early chronicles" by
    Sax Rohmer, by Robert E. Briney,
    15 R 9
Fu Manchu, on radio, by Ray Stanich,
    12 R 11
Fu Manchu, on Radio Luxembourg, 11 R 15
Gaddis, Peggy, in paperback editions,
    by Charles Culpepper, 3-2 CP 5
GALAXY SCIENCE-FICTION NOVELS,
    paperback series, by Stuart W.
    Wells III & J. Grant Thiessen,
    3 SF 44
Gardner, John: Brian "Boysie" Oakes
    series, annotated, by Barry Van
    Tilburg, 4-3 MF 25
Gault, William Campbell, works, by Bill
    Crider, 2 PE 21
Gault, William Campbell, in paperback
    book editions, by Bill Crider,
    2-2 PQ 6
Gerard, Francis: John Meredith series,
    annotated, by Barry Van Tilburg,
    5-3 MF 21
Gilbert, Anthony, works, by Estelle
    Fox, 2-6 MR 18
Gilman, Dorothy, works, by Audrey I.
    Pacheco, 5-4 MR 23
Gilman, Dorothy: Emily Pollifax series,
    annotated, by Barry Van Tilburg,
    5-3 MF 19
Gold Seal Books, paperbacks, by
    Bill O'Connell, 3-3 CP 23
Golden Age Detective stories, by
    Neville Wood, 1-1 PP 11
Golden Amazon series, science-
    fiction paperback series by
    Harlequin Books, by John Russell
    Fearn, 2 SF 24
Gravell, Kenneth: Carlos Bannon
    series, by Randy Himmel, 12 LR 8

Checklists, (continued)
Graves, Robert, in paperback
    book editions, by Susannah
    Bates, 3-5 CP 25
Great Britain, crime fiction
    published January-March 1977,
    by Allen J. Hubin, 10-3 TAD
    270
Great Marvel Series, boys' science
    fiction series by Roy Rockwood,
    by Robert Jennings, 7 BB 19
Green Door Mysteries, paperback
    series, by Howard Waterhouse,
    1-2 PQ 40
Green Door Mysteries, paperback
    series, by Bruce Taylor,
    3-2 CP 29
Green Lama, The: Richard Foster,
    pulp hero character stories,
    by Dickson Thorpe, 1-2 MF 7
Greene, Graeme, works, by Pat
    Erhardt, 1-5 MR 15
Grey, Zane (ZANE GREY'S WESTERN
    MAGAZINE), by David & Su
    Bates, 1-3 CP 21
Gruber, Frank, works, by Bill
    Clark, 67 PU 31
Haggard, William: Col. Charles
    Russell series, annotated,
    by Barry Van Tilburg, 4-3 MF
    27
Halfaday Creek book series: James
    B. Hendryx, by John Harwood,
    3-6 MF 7
Hall, Adam: Quiller series,
    annotated, by Barry Van Tilburg,
    4-3 MF 26
Halliday, Michael, works, by R.E.
    Briney & John Creasey, 2-1 TAD
    14
Halliday, Michael: Dr. Emmanuel
    Cellini series, by R.E.Briney
    & John Creasey, 2-1 TAD 13
Halliday, Michael: Fane Brothers
    series, by R.E.Briney and
    John Creasey, 2-1 TAD 13
Hamilton, Edmond, in WEIRD TALES
    pulp magazine, by Robert
    Weinberg, 1 WT 9
Hammer, Mike, TV series, by Andy
    Jaysnovitch, 4 PE 5
Hammett, Dashiell: Continental Op
    stories, by William F. Nolan,
    8-1 TAD 121
Hammett, Dashiell, paperbound
    novels and short stories, by
    William Lyles, 1-3 CP 9
Hammett, Dashiell, "Checklist
    Revisited" by William F. Nolan,
    6-4 TAD 249; 9-4 TAD 292
Handi-Books, paperback publications,
    science-fiction, by J. Grant
    Thiessen, 2 SF 9

Checklists, (continued)

Hard-Boiled Detective, in paperbacks,
by Bruce Taylor and Dave Lewis,
2-5 CP 22

Hard-Boiled Detective, short stories
in paperbacks, by Bruce Cervon,
3-2 CP 23

Hardboiled Dick, The, a Personal
Checklist, by James Sandoe,
1-2 TAD 38

Harlequin Science-Fiction paperbacks,
by J. Grant Thiessen, 2 SF 9

Harness, Charles L., works, by William
D. Vernon, 14 SF 30

Harvester, Simon: Dorian Silk series,
annotated, by Barry Van Tilburg,
4-4 MF 16

Hawks, Joaquin, series: Bill S.
Ballinger, by Larry Rickert,
4-2 PP 7

Haycraft, Howard, works, 5-1 MR 13

Haycraft/Queen List Supplement, by
Amnon Kabatchnik and Robert
Aucott, 9-2 TAD 87

Hazard, Glenn, boys' & girls' mystery
series, by Harry K. Hudson,
1-4 YB 25

Heald, Tim: Simon Bognor series,
annotated, by Barry Van Tilburg,
4-4 MF 17

Helm, Matt, series, annotated, by
R. Jeff Banks and Guy M. Townsend,
2-2 MF 3

Henty, G.A., works, additions to a
bibliography, by Jared C. Lobdell,
1-4 BC 125

Hersey Pulp Magazines, (Hersey as
publisher), 68 PU 10

Heyer, Georgette, works, by Don
Miller, 13 MN B1

Heyer, Georgette, checklist of
reviews, by Don Miller, 13 MN 27

Heyer, Georgette, mystery novels, by
G.M.Carr, 13 MN 15

Heyer, Georgette, Regency Romances,
by Jo Ann Vicarel, 13 MN 17

Hillman Publications, science-fiction
paperback books, by J. Grant
Thiessen, 2 SF 10

Hitchcock, Alfred, films, by Richard
Moskowitz, 6/7 LR 41

Hitchcock, Alfred, paperbacks to
1960, by Bruce Taylor, 2-4 CP 10

Hoch, Edward D., works, by William
J. Clark, Edward D. Hoch, and
Francis M. Nevins, Jr., 9-2 TAD 102

Hoch, Edward D.: Double-C spy stories,
addendum, 5-3 MR 13

Hoch, Edward D.: Simon Ark stories, by
Edward D. Hoch, 3-4 TAD 248

Hoch, Edward D.: Simon Ark stories
published by Leisure Press, 5-3 MR 14

Checklists, (continued)

Hodgson, William Hope, a Working
Bibliography, by Mike Ashley,
15 SF 15

Holmes, Sherlock, stories in
ELLERY QUEEN'S MYSTERY MAGAZINE,
by Peter E. Blau, 2-1 QC 15

Holmes, Sherlock, Rivals of,
(contemporary detective fiction)
by Peter E. Blau, 11-2 TAD 193

Homes, Geoffrey, works, by
Theodore P. Dukeshire, 3-3 MF 21

Hood, Mark, series: James Dark,
by Larry Rickert, 4 5/6 PP 39

Hossent, Harry: Max Heald series,
annotated, by Barry Van Tilburg,
5-3 MF 19

Howard, Robert E.; Howard's Library,
an annotated checklist, by
Charlotte Laughlin, 1-1 PQ 23;
1-2 PQ 51; 1-3 PQ 43; 1-4 PQ 55

Hull, Richard, works, by Charles
Shibuk, 2-6 MR 21

Hunter, Evan, works, by Bill
Pronzini, 5-3 TAD 131

Impossible ("miraculous") crimes
fiction, partial list, by
Robert C.S.Adey, 5-3 TAD 168

Innes, Hammond, works, by Don Cole,
4-1 MR 7; 1-4 PP 8

Jakes, John, original paperback
novels, by Michael S. Barson,
3-3 PQ 20

James, Laurence, works, by Ian
Covell, 4 SF 29

Japanese Mystery Fiction in English
Translation, by John L. Apostolou,
13-4 TAD 311

Johnson, E. Richard, works, 2-6 MR
13

Jonathan Press Mysteries, digest-
size paperback series, by Jeff
Meyerson, 1-3 PP 35

Jonathan Press Mysteries, Addendum,
by Jim Tinsman, 1-6 PP 27; 2-1
PP 31

Kane, Frank, works, by George Kelley,
2 PE 31

Keating, H.R.F., works, by Sven-
Ingmar Pettersson, 8-4 TAD 279

Keeler, Harry Stephen, works, by
David Bates, 4-2 PP 4

Keeler, Harry Stephen, works by
Bernard Beauchesne, 1-4 TAD 147

Keeler, Harry Stephen, novels, a
preliminary checklist, by Francis
M. Nevins, Jr., 3-2 TAD 74

Kellogg, Elijah, books, (boys'
books), by Walter H. McIntosh,
3-2 BC 309

Kelton, Elmer, paperback books,
1-2 PQ 16

Checklists, (continued)

King, Rufus, series short stories,
by J.M.Purcell, 12-4 TAD 380

Kingston, William H.G., works,
(English boys' books), by
Walter H. McIntosh, 3-4 BC 357

Krasner, William, works, by Marvin
Lachman, 1-2 PP 11

Lancer Publications, paperback books,
by Bill Denholm, 1-2 CP 26;
1-4 CP 16

Lancer Publications, Science-Fiction
paperbacks cover artists, by
William J. Denholm, 10 SF 25

Lancer Publications, Science-Fiction
paperback books, by William
J. Denholm III, 10 SF 4

Laser Books, Science-Fiction paperback
books series, by Keith L. Justice,
15 SF 4

Latimer, Jonathan W., works, by Jim
McCahery, 11 SF 20

Latimer, Jonathan W., filmography,
by Jim McCahery, 11 SF 21

Latimer, Jonathan W.: William Crane
series, by Jim McCahery, 1 PE 6;
2 PE 13

Leasor, James: Dr. Jason Love series,
annotated, by Barry Van Tilburg,
4-4 MF 16

LeCarre, John: George Smiley series,
annotated, by Barry Van Tilburg,
4-3 MF 27

LeCarre, John, Spy Novels, annotated,
by R. Jeff Banks and Harry D.
Dawson, 2-5 MF 22

LeFanu, Sheridan, works, by David
Brownell, 9-3 TAD 197

Leonard, Charles: Paul Kilgerrin series,
annotated, by Barry Van Tilburg,
4-4 MF 17

Levin, Ira, works, 3-1 MR 11

Lion paperback books, science-fiction,
by J. Grant Thiessen, 2 SF 10

Lockridge, Frances and Richard, works,
by Kathy Hobel, 2-5 MR 6

Lodestone Books, paperbacks, by Bill
Denholm, 1-4 CP 16

Lodestone Books, science-fiction paperbacks, by William J. Denholm III,
10 SF 4

Logos of Publishers, identifying mystery
series, illustrated, by Robert C.S.
Adey, 3-4 MR 27

Lone Wolf series: Mike Barry, (paperback
series), by George Kelley, 1-5 MF 18

Long, Amelia Reynolds, works in the
weird fiction magazines, by Chet
Williamson, 2 WT 9

Lustgarten, Edgar, works, by Mary Groff,
12-3 TAD 286

Lutz, John, works, by Mary Ann
Grochowski, 12-3 TAD 278; 1-2 PP 8

Checklists, (continued)

Lynds, Dennis, works, by John
Edwards, 4 U 21

MacDonald, John D., current novels,
by Len and June Moffatt, 1 JD 1

MacDonald, John D., Detective Pulp
Stories, publication identification, by Bill Clark, 6 JD 15

MacDonald, John D., Detective Pulp
Stories, synopsis and list,
6 JD 1; 7 JD 13

MacDonald, John D., Hardcover and
paperback books, by Len J.
Moffatt, 1-6 MR 13

MacDonald, John D., his list of
stories in DOC SAVAGE and THE
SHADOW (pulp magazines), with
data (by MacDonald), 7 BS 4

MacDonald, John D., magazine
stories, 3 JD 5; 4 JD 1; 5 JD 1;
5 JD 4; 7 JD 13; 8 JD 2; 8 JD 18

MacDonald, John D., novels, 1 JD 1

MacDonald, John D., novels, by Len
& June Moffatt, 2 JD 6

MacDonald, John D., paperback
original books, by Michael S.
Barson, 4-1 PQ 10

MacDonald, John D., science-fiction
stories, alphabetical checklist,
28 JD 25

MacDonald, Philip, on the screen,
by Jack Edmund Nolan, 3-3 MR 33

MacDonald, Philip, works, by Norman
Donaldson, 3-1 TAD 10

MacLean, Alistair, works, by Iwan
Hedman, 4-5 MR 31

Maquire, Robert, paperback book cover
art, by Lance Casebeer, 1-6 CP 28

McCutchan, Philip: Commander Esmond
Shaw series, annotated, by Barry
Van Tilburg, 4-5 MF 21

McCutchan, Philip: Simon Shard series,
annotated, by Barry Van Tilburg,
4-5 MF 21

McGinnis, - , paperback book cover
art, by Bill Denholm, 1-3 CP 12;
1-5 CP 23

McGuire, Robert, paperback book cover
art (Who Drew That Girl?), by
Lance Casebeer, 1-5 CP 31

McLeod, Robert: Talos Cord series,
annotated, by Barry Van Tilburg,
4-5 MF 22

MAGAZINE OF HORROR, by Gene Marshall
and Carl F. Waedt, 3 SF 6

Magnum science-fiction books, paperbacks, by William J. Denholm III,
10 SF 4

Mair, George B.: Dr. David Grant
series, annotated, by Barry Van
Tilburg, 4-4 MF 16

Man in a Suitcase, TV series, by
Paul Bishop, 7 PE 15

Checklists, (continued)

Mann, Jack, works, by R.E.Briney,
6-2 MR 21

Manton, Peter, works, by R.E.Briney
and John Creasey, 2-1 TAD 15

March, Milo, series: M.E.Chaber,
by Dickson Thorpe, 1-2 MF 6

Marquand, John Phillips: Mr. Moto
series, annotated, by Barry Van
Tilburg, 4-5 MF 22

Marric, J.J.: The Baron series, by
Robert E. Briney & John Creasey,
2-1 TAD 16

Marric, J.J.: Commander Gideon
series, by Robert E. Briney &
John Creasey, 2-1 TAD 15

Marsh, Ngaio, works, by Charles
Shibuk, 1-5 MR 16

Martin, A.E., works, by Marvin
Lachman, 1-3 PP 11

Martyn, Wyndham: Christopher Bond
series, annotated, by Barry Van
Tilburg, 4-5 MF 23

Masked Detective, The, series, (in
pulp magazines), by Wooda Nicholas
Carr, 8 P 7

Mason, Francis Van Wyck: Hugh North
series, annotated, by Barry Van
Tilburg, 4-6 MF 4

Mather, Berkeley: Idwal Rees series,
annotated, by Barry Van Tilburg,
4-6 MF 4

Mayo, James: Charles Hood series,
annotated, by Barry Van Tilburg,
4-6 MF 5

Mercer Boys series: Capwell Wyckoff,
boys' books, by Don Holbrook,
5 MA 8

Mercury Mysteries, digest-size paperbacks, by Jeff Meyerson, 1-4 PP 33

Mercury Mysteries, addendum, by Jim
Tinsman, 1-6 PP 27; 2-1 PP 31

Merit Books, science-fiction paperback series, by J. Grant Thiessen,
2 SF 11

Merrivale, Sir Henry, detective: John
Dickson Carr, by Robert C.S.Adey,
3-2 MR 11

Michel, Scott, works, by Jim McCahery,
4-4 PP 3

Millar, Margaret, (an "unknown" mystery
writer), by Marvin Lachman, 3-2 TAD
85

Milne, A.A., short tales of crime and
detection, by J. Randolph Cox,
9-4 TAD 269

Mitchell, Gladys, works, by B.A.Pike,
9-4 TAD 259

Mitchell, James: Callan series, annotated,
by Barry Van Tilburg, 5-3 MF 19

Modern Fantasy in paperback books,
selected list, by Dave Killian,
2-5 CP 12

Checklists, (continued)

Modesty Blaise series: Peter O'Donnell,
annotated, by R. Jeff Banks, 4-2 MF
8

Modern Age Books, paperbacks, by Bill
O'Connell, 3-3 CP 24

Modern Age Publishing Company, by
Robert C.S.Adey, 4-1 PP 4

Monarch Books, paperbacks, by Steve
Woolfolk, 14 SF 35

Monig, Christopher: Kim Locke stories,
by Dickson Thorpe, 1-2 MF 7

Moon Man stories in TEN DETECTIVE ACES
of Frederick Davis, by Robert
Weinberg, 2 P 19

Montgomery, R.G.: Golden Stallion
series, boys' books, 1-5 YB 13

Montgomery, R.G.: Kent Barstow
series, boys' books, 1-5 YB 13

Mr. Chang, pulp villain, in magazine
appearances, by Robert Sampson,
14 SF 46

Mr. Moto, on film, 3-2 MR 7

Munsey Magazines, commencements of
publication, by John Harwood,
3-5 MF 49

MURDER MYSTERY MONTHLY, by Steve
Lewis, 2-1 PQ 5

MYSTERIOUS WU FANG, THE, pulp magazine,
by Lynn Hickman, 75 PU 11

Mystery Awards, by Mystery Writers of
America; by Barbara A. Buhrer,
11 MN A1; 12 MN L4

Mystery book dealers, (Murder by Mail)
by Walter Albert, 3-5 MF 7

MYSTERY BOOK MAGAZINE, digest-size
magazine, by Robert E. Briney,
8-4 TAD 245

Mystery, Detective and Suspense
Fiction Published in the U.S.
monthly, June 1968 through July
1981, see listing under (1) George
J. Rausch, Jr., (2) Robert Breyfogle
Green, (3) M.S.Cappadonna

Mystery Hunters series: Capwell
Wyckoff, boys' books, by Don
Holbrook, 5 MA 8

Mystery League, Inc., The., book
publisher, by Ellen Nehr, 2-6 PP 5

Mysteries with beasts, (A Beastly
Case of Murder), by Mary Ann
Grochowski, 1-6 PP 7

Mystery Writers of America, annual
volumes published, by Charles
MacDonald, 5-4 TAD 252

Nebel, Frederick, detective stories
in BLACK MASK pulp magazine, by
Dave Lewis, 2-2 C 118

Novel Library, paperback books, by
Craig Henry, 2-3 CP 27

OCTOPUS, THE, pulp magazine, by
Lynn Hickman, 75 PU 11

Checklists, (continued)

O'Malley, Patrick: Harrigar and Hoeffler series, annotated, by Barry Van Tilburg, 4-6 MF 5

Oppenheim, E. Phillips, works, 4-3 MR 25

Oppenheim, E. Phillips, addendum, by J. Randolph Cox, 5-3 MR 17

Ott, Poppy, series: Leo Edwards, (boys' series), by Julius R. Chenu, 3 BB 10; 1-2 YB 17

Ott, Poppy, series: Leo Edwards, (boys' series), 1-1 TB 4

Owen, Frank, works, by Lemuel Nash, 28 X 12

Owen, Frank, works, by Richard Minter, 30 X 3

Paperback originals, (mystery and crime fiction), by Bill Crider, 5-1 MR 20

Patten, Gilbert, in clothbound editions, (boys' books), by Harry K. Hudson, 1-3 BC 86

Permabooks, paperback science-fiction books, by J. Grant Thiessen, 2 SF 12

Perry, Ritchie: Philis series, annotated, by Barry Van Tilburg, 4-6 MF 5

Pettee, Florence Mae: Dr. Nancy Dayland, detective, stories in pulp magazines, by Robert Sampson, 5-6 MF 13

PHANTOM DETECTIVE, THE, pulp magazine (1933-1953), by Bernie Wermers, 11 BS 4

PHANTOM DETECTIVE, THE, pulp magazine, (1933-1953), by Robert Sampson, 3-3 MR 8

Phantom, The, in Avon paperback editions, (pulp hero character), by Melville C. Hill, 12 SF 22

Phantom Detective, The, in paperback, by Bruce Cervon, 2-4 CP 8

Philips, Judson P., partial bibliography, by Tim Dumont, 4 MY 4

Pocket Books, Nos. 1-500, (paperback books), by Hal Knott and Marvin Lachman, 1-6 MF 29

Pocket Books (British editions), by Piet Schreuders, 3-1 CP 12

Poggioli stories: T.S.Stribling, (detective series), by Robert Sampson, 2-2 C 74

Pony Books, paperbacks, by Lance Casebeer, 1-1 CP 21

Popular Library, cover art, (paperbacks) by Bill Denholm, 2-1 CP 25

Popular Library Nos. 1-200, paperbacks, by Richard C. Butler, 1-3 MF 5

Popular Publications, chronological list of titles of this publisher with comments, by Harry Steeger, 67 PU 39

Popular Publications, titles 1930-1955, by Nils Hardin and George Hocutt, 33 X 21

Checklists, (continued)

Powell, Richard: Andy & Arabella Blake series, annotated, by Barry Van Tilburg, 4-6 MF 6

Price, Anthony: David Audley & Colonel Butler series, annotated, by Barry Van Tilburg, 4-6 MF 6

Prize Science-Fiction Novels, paperback series, by J. Grant Thiessen, 2 SF 13

Pronzini, Bill, works, by Francis M. Nevins, Jr. and Bill Pronzini, 13-4 TAD 345

Propper, Milton, novels, by Francis M. Nevins, Jr., 10-3 TAD 203

Pyramid Reprint series of Fu Manchu novels, by Robert E. Briney, 9-4 TAD 247

Queen, Ellery, works, by John J. Newton, 1-3 QC 13

Queen, Ellery, works, (partial list) by Rev. Robert E. Washer, 1-4 MR 9

Queen, Ellery, on television 1955-76, by Francis M. Nevins, Jr., 12-3 TAD 216

Queen, Ellery, Jr., mystery stories, (boys' series), by Harry K. Hudson 1-4 YB 23

Quick-Reader series, paperbacks, by Dave Killian, 1-1 CP 18

Quiller series: Adam Hall, annotated, by R. Jeff Banks and Harry D. Dawson, 4-1 MF 8

Railroads, mystery novels associated with, by Frank P. Donovan, 1-4 TAD 126

Ransom, in mystery plots, (The Ultima Hi-Jacking Novel), by Marvin Lachman, 2-2 PP 17

Raven House Mysteries, paperbacks, by Michael L. Cook, 4-5/6 PP 27

Rawson, Clayton, works, by Robert E. Briney, 3-1 MR 8

Rawson, Clayton, paperback editions, by Bruce Taylor, 1-6 CP 10

Red Seal Books, paperbacks, by Bill O'Connell, 3-3 CP 23

Reeve, Arthur B., works, by J. Rando Cox, 11-1 TAD 29

Reilly, Helen, works, by Francis M. Nevins, Jr., 5-5 MR 18

Reilly, Helen, works, by Audrey I. Pacheco, 5-4 MR 23

Rendell, Ruth, works, by Jim McCaher 2-3 PP 28

Rendell, Ruth, novels through 1974, by Jo Ann Genaro Vicarel, 9-3 TAD 198

Rendell, Ruth, works, by J. Clyde Stevens, 7 MY 8

Rendell, Ruth, works, by Don Miller, 10 MN A27

Checklists, (continued)

Rendell, Ruth, checklist of reviews, by Don Miller, 10 MN A23

Rice, Craig, works, by Mary Ann Grochowski, 13-3 TAD 267

Rice, Craig, works, by David A. Jasen, 5-1 TAD 26

Risteen, H.L., works, (boys' books) by H.L.Risteen, 3-1 BC 263

Rohmer, Sax: Denis Nayland Smith series, annotated, by Barry Van Tilburg, 5-1 MF 2

Rohmer, Sax, works in Dutch translation, by Robert E. Briney, 11 R 17

Rohmer, Sax, works in French translation, by Robert E. Briney, 12 R 17

Rohmer, Sax: Paul Harley series, by Robert E. Briney, 17 R 15

Rohmer, Sax, paperback reprint editions, by Richard Paul Hall, 3-4 CP 15

Roscoe, Theodore, in pulp magazines, by Bill Clark, 65 PU 15

Ross, Angus: Marcus Farrow series, annotated, by Barry Van Tilburg, 5-2 MF 2

Russell, Eric Frank, works, by Lemuel Nash, 28 X 12

Russell, Martin, works, by Sven-Ingmar Petersson, 8-1 TAD 49

Saint, The: Leslie Charteris, Prolegomena to a Bibliography, by J. Randolph Cox, 5-2 MR 9

Saint Mystery Library, paperbacks, by M.C.Hill, 2-4 PQ 6

Sampson, Emma Speed, juvenile books, by Julius R. Chenu, 1-4 YB 4

San Francisco Mysteries (locale), by Don Herron, 3-2 M 8

Sapper: Bulldog Drummond series, annotated, by Barry Van Tilburg, 4-5 MF 22

Saunders, Norman, paperback cover art, 1-3 PQ 41

Sayers, Dorothy L., works, by Charles Shibuk, 2-2 MR 10

Schmitz, James H., works, by J. Grant Thiessen, 12 SF 13

Science Fiction Pornography, by Kenneth R. Johnson, 4 SF 4; 5 SF 45

SCORPION, The, pulp magazine, by Lynn Hickman, 75 PU 11

Seal Books, paperback publisher, by Bill O'Connell, 3-3 CP 24

Secondary Sources, annual compilation of reference sources in mystery and crime fiction, by Walter Albert, 1972-1980, see listing under Walter Albert

Secret Agent X, paperback editions of pulp hero stories, by Bruce Cervon, 3-1 CP 14

Checklists, (continued)

Secret Service Smith stories in the pulp magazines, by John Harwood, 67 PU 63

SECRET SIX, THE, pulp magazine, by Lynn Hickman, 75 PU 11

Shadow, The, in comic books, by Mark MacDonald, 1 MT 43

Shadow, The, paperback editions of the pulp stories, by Bruce Cervon, 2-3 CP 33

SHADOW, THE, pulp magazine, list by chronological order, by Fred Cook, 1 BS 5

Shadow, The, Pyramid editions of paperback books, 1 DS 8

Shadow, The, Pyramid editions of paperback books, by Mark MacDonald 1 MT 43

Shadow, The, the Tinsley novels, by Robert Weinberg, 1 P 33

Shannon, Dell, works, by Barbara A. Buhrer and J. Clyde Stevens, 3/4 MN 4

Shaw, Commander Esmonde, series, profile and checklist, by Larry Rickert, 4-4 PP 17

Sherwood, John, works, by Barry Pike, 2-3 PP 23

Simenon, Georges: Inspector Maigret series, short cases, by Gary L. Gannett, 10-4 TAD 347

Simenon, Georges: Inspector Maigret series, novels, by Norman J. Shaffer, 3-1 TAD 31

Sinclair, Fiona, works, by Barry Pike, 4-5/6 PP 50

SINISTER STORIES, pulp magazine, by Lynn Hickman, 75 PU 11

Slot-Machine Kelly series: Michael Collins, 9 SF 38

Smith, Aurelius, detective;stories in pulp magazines , by John Harwood, 67 PU 63

Smith, Thorne, paperback editions, by Don Sprague, 3-2 CP 20

SOUTH SEA STORIES, pulp magazine, with separate author index, by Robert Weinberg, 8 P 12

Speed, Nell, juvenile series, by Julius R. Chenu, 1-4 YB 5

SPIDER, THE, pulp magazine, 67 PU 73

Spider, The, paperback reprint editions, by Bruce Cervon, 3-4 CP 11

SPIDER, THE, pulp magazine, by John Steinkuhl, 1 U 17

Stableford, Brian: paperback puzzle novels, by George Kelley, 1-2 CP 19

Stagge, Jonathan, works, by Barry Pike, 3-3 PP 21

Standish, Burt L., short stories in TIP TOP WEEKLY (dime novels) by Gerald J.McIntosh, 2-2 BC 168

Checklists, (continued)
STAR MAGAZINE, pulp magazine, by Nils
    Hardin, 7 X 66
Stark, Richard, series: Donald E.
    Westlake, by John Bullis, 1-5 CP 9
STARTLING MYSTERY STORIES, magazine,
    by Gene Marshall and Carl F. Waedt,
    3 SF 14
Stephens, C.A.: Old Farm Series, (boys'
    books), by Harry K. Hudson, 1-6 YB
    16
Steranko, James, paperback cover art,
    by M.C.Hill, 4-1 PQ 37
Stewart, Mary, works, by Audrey I.
    Pacheco, 5-4 MR 25
Stout, Rex, works, by Don Miller,
    9 MN A65
Stout, Rex, in ELLERY QUEEN'S MYSTERY
    MAGAZINE, by Don Miller, 9 MN A24
Stout, Rex, in ELLERY QUEEN'S
    ANTHOLOGIES, by Don Miller, 9 MN A29
Stout, Rex, in Mystery Guild (book
    club) editions, by Michael L. Cook,
    9 MN A27
Stout, Rex, works, (partial list), by
    Don Miller, 9 MN A45
Stout, Rex, editor: REX STOUT MYSTERY
    MAGAZINE, by Frank D. McSherry, Jr.,
    9 MN A21
Stribling, T.S.: Professor Poggioli
    series, by John Nieminski, 6-1 TAD
    55
Subject Guide to Mystery Fiction, by
    Richard Emery, 3-1 PP 3; 3-3 PP 43;
    3-4 PP 41; 3-6 PP 41
SUPER SCIENCE STORIES, Canadian series,
    magazine, by J. Grant Thiessen,
    4 SF 21
Superior Reprints, paperback books,
    by James Tinsman, 2-3 PQ 45
Swift, Tom, series: Victor Appleton,
    (boys' series), by John T.Dizer,
    Jr., 2-1 TBN 5
Symons, Julian, works, by Charles Shibuk,
    2-3 MR 19
Tey, Josephine, works, by Catherine
    Aird, 2-3 TAD 157
Thayer, Lee, works, by Barry Pike,
    3-5 PP 27
Thayer, Lee, works, by Jon L. Breen,
    5-3 TAD 149
Thomson, Sir Basil, works, by Barry
    Pike, 3-6 PP 18
Thomson, June, works, by Barry Pike,
    3-4 PP 17
Thriller Novel Classics, science-
    fiction paperback books, by
    J. Grant Thiessen, 2 SF 13
THRILLING WESTERN MAGAZINE, by Gene
    Marshall and Carl F. Waedt, 3 SF 41
Thunder Jim stories: Charles Stoddard,
    by Will Murray, 1 D 22
Tiger Mann series: Mickey Spillane,
    by R. Jeff Banks, 2-3 MF 32

Checklists, (continued)
Toby Press, paperback books, by
    J. Grant Thiessen, 2 SF 13
Todd, Jerry, series: Leo Edwards,
    (boys' books), by Julius R.
    Chenu, 3 BB 10; 1-2 YB 17
Todd, Jerry, series: Leo Edwards,
    (boys' books), 1-1 TB 4
Tolkien, J.R.R., books about Tolkien
    and his works, by David S.
    Bratman, 5 SF 26
True crimes in film, by Mary Groff,
    4-5/6 PP 59
True crimes, mysteries suggested by,
    by Mary Groff; see listing under
    Mary Groff
Tubb, E.C., works, by Mike Ashley,
    7 SF 7
Tubb, E.C.: The Dumarest Saga series,
    by Bob Stuart, 1-5 CP 28
Tute, Warren: George Mado series,
    annotated, by Barry Van Tilburg,
    5-2 MF 2
Uhnak, Dorothy, works, by Audrey I.
    Pacheco, 5-4 MR 23
Unicorn Mystery Book Club, checklist
    by author,and in chronological
    order of publication, by Michael
    L. Cook, 12 MN I1
Unicorn Mystery Book Club, complete
    selections, by Edward D. Hoch,
    8-3 TAD 187
Unicorn Mystery Book Club, partial
    listing, by Michael L. Cook,
    5 MY 3
Upfield, Arthur W., works, by Estelle
    Fox, Francis M. Nevins,Jr. and
    Charles Shibuk, 3-2 TAD 90
Upfield, Arthur W., works, (and
    review), by Betty Donaldson,
    8-1 TAD 4
Urquhart, MacGregor: Chief-Inspector
    Joshua Smarles series, Pen
    Profile and checklist, by Barry
    Pike, 4-4 PP 19
Van der Valk series: Nicolas Freeling
    by William Ruble, 5-2 MR 5
Van Dine, S.S., works, by Bruce R.
    Beaman, 8-2 TAD 134
Van Vogt, A.E., works, by J. Grant
    Thiessen, 8 SF 7
Varley, John, works, by Fred Isajenko
    12 SF 29
Vega Books, paperback science-fiction
    by Ronald W. Spitzer, 4 SF 19
Vickers, Roy: The Department of Dead
    Ends series, partial list, by Mark
    Purcell, 4-1 MR 29
Vickers, Roy, short stories, by Howard
    Waterhouse, 1-3 PP 7
Wade, Henry, works, by Barry Pike,
    4-5/6 PP 46
Wade, Henry, works, by Charles Shibuk
    1-4 TAD 112

Checklists, (continued)

Wade, Jerry, and The Crimson Mask
    stories in DETECTIVE NOVELS,
    pulp magazine, by Robert Weinberg,
    2 P 21
Wallace, Edgar, works, 1-3 TAD 72
Ward, Peter, novels by David St.John,
    by Larry Rickert, 4-3 PP 8
Watson, Colin, works, by Barry Pike,
    4-2 PP 22
WEIRD TERROR TALES magazine, by Gene
    Marshall and Carl F. Waedt,
    3 SF 18
Wellman, Manly Wade, works, by Karl
    Edward Wagner & Edwin Murray,
    7 X 12
Wells, Angus, works, by Ian Covell,
    4 SF 29
Wells, Carolyn: chronological list of
    detective novels, by Jon L. Breen,
    3-2 TAD 78
Wentworth, Patricia, works, by Nancy
    Blue Wynne, 14-1 TAD 92
Wessolowski, H.W., pulp magazine
    cover artist, 6 P 16
WESTERN ACE-HIGH STORIES, pulp
    magazine, by Lynn Hickman,
    75 PU 10
Westlake, Donald E., works, by
    Nobumitsu Kodaka & Donald E.
    Westlake, 8-3 TAD 203
Wheatley, Dennis, works, by Iwan
    Hedman, 2-4 TAD 231
Wheatley, Dennis, works, with a biog.
    sketch, by Iwan Hedman, 2-4 TAD
    227
Wheatley, Dennis: Black Magic series,
    by Iwan Hedman, 2-4 TAD 236
Wheatley, Dennis: Duke DeRichleau
    series, by Iwan Hedman,
    2-4 TAD 235
Wheatley, Dennis: Gregory Sallust
    series, annotated, by Barry
    Van Tilburg, 5-3 MF 18
Wheatley, Dennis: Gregory Sallust
    series, by Iwan Hedman,
    2-4 TAD 235
Wheatley, Dennis: Julian Day series,
    by Iwan Hedman, 2-4 TAD 236
Wheatley, Dennis: Roger Brook series,
    by Iwan Hedman, 2-4 TAD 235
White, Ethel Lina, works, by Barry
    Pike, 4-5/6 PP 48
Whitfield, Raoul F., stories in
    BLACK MASK pulp magazine, by
    E.R.Hagemann, 13-3 TAD 183
Whitman Authorized Editions, (boys'
    books), by Andrew Zerbe, 1 BB 21
Whitman Publishing Company, The
    Western Heroes books, (juvenile)
    by I.R.Ybarra, 6 MA 19

Checklists, (continued)

Whitney, Phyllis A., works, by
    Pat Erhardt, 2-4 MR 5
Whittington, Harry, paperback
    originals, by Michael S. Barson,
    4-2 PQ 23
Wilcox, Collin, works, by Jeff
    Pierce, 3-2 M 23
Wilde, Carney, series: Bart Spicer,
    by Jim McCahery, 4 PE 23
Williamson, Jack, works, by Uwe
    Luserke, 13 SF 29
Wodehouse, P.G., works, by David
    A. Jasen, 3-1 TAD 38
Wolfe, Nero, first edition publi-
    cation data, by Don Miller,
    9 MN A43
Wolfe, Nero, in paperback editions,
    by Bruce Taylor, 2-2 CP 27
Wollheim, Donald A., works, in
    paperback editions, 1-3 PQ 20
Woodhouse, Martin: Giles Yeoman
    series, annotated, by Barry
    Van Tilburg, 5-3 MF 18
Woods, Sara, works, by Estelle Fox,
    4-3 TAD 153
Woolrich, Cornell, works, by Pat
    Erhardt, 1-2 MR 4
Woolrich, Cornell, works, by Harold
    Knott, Francis M. Nevins, Jr., &
    William Thailing, 2-4 TAD 237
Woolrich, Cornell, in paperback
    editions, by Bruce Taylor,
    1-1 CP 9
Worell, Everil, stories in WEIRD
    TALES pulp magazine, by Jeanne
    Eileen Murphy, 1 WT 15
WORLD WIDE ADVENTURE magazine, by
    Gene Marshall and Carl F. Waedt,
    3 SF 40
Wright, Willard Huntington, works,
    by Bruce R. Beaman, 8-2 TAD 134
Wuorio, Eva-Lis, works, by Audrey
    I. Pacheco, 5-4 MR 23
Wyckoff, Capwell, boys' books, by
    Don Holbrook, 5 MA 8
Wylie, Philip Gordon, in paperback
    editions, by Raymond Torrence,
    2-4 CP 25
Wyndham, John, works, by Philip
    Stephenson-Payne, 8 SF 31
York, Andrew: Jonas Wilde series,
    annotated, by Barry Van Tilburg,
    5-3 MF 18
Yates, Dornford, mystery novels and
    short stories, by J. Randolph
    Cox, 14-2 TAD 186
York, Jeremy: Superintendent Folly
    series, by Robert E. Briney &
    John Creasey, 2-1 TAD 17

Checklists, (continued)
    York, Jeremy, suspense novels, by
        Robert E. Briney and John Creasey,
        2-1 TAD 17
    Yorke, Margaret, works, by Barry
        Pike, 3-4 PP 17
Cheesborough, John: letter of comment,
    7 JD 8; 10 JD 13
Chenu, Bob, see: Julius R. Chenu
Chenu, Julius R.: Andy Blake First Leo
    Edwards Book, (first book by author
    of Jerry Todd, Poppy Ott, Tuffy Bean
    and other boys' series), 1-1 TB 1
Chenu, Julius R.: Art Work of the Leo
    Edward's Books, (dust jackets),
    1-2 TBN 1
Chenu, Julius R.: Background of First
    Andy Blake Book, (boys' series by
    Leo Edwards), 1-3 TBN 1
Chenu, Julius R.: Boys' Books Written
    by Roy Judson Snell, (discussion),
    1-1 BC 12
Chenu, Julius R.: Boys' Fiction Written
    by Leo Edwards, (discussion),
    1-2 BC 35
Chenu, Julius R.: The Boys of Columbia
    High, (boys' series books), 5 BB 9
Chenu, Julius R.: Chatterbox Feature
    Unique and Informative Innovation
    ("club" forum in the books of Leo
    Edwards, boys' series), 2-4 TB 1
Chenu, Julius R.: Checklist, Andy Blake
    Series, (boys' series by Leo Edwards),
    3 BB 10; 1-2 YB 17
Chenu, Julius R.: Checklist, Jerry Todd
    Series, (boys' series by Leo Edwards),
    3 BB 10; 1-2 YB 17
Chenu, Julius R.: Checklist, Poppy Ott
    Series, (boys' series by Leo Edwards),
    3 BB 10; 1-2 YB 17
Chenu, Julius R.: Checklist, Trigger
    Berg Series, (boys' series by Leo
    Edwards), 3 BB 10; 1-2 YB 18
Chenu, Julius R.: Checklist, Tuffy Bean
    Series, (boys' series by Leo Edwards),
    3 BB 10; 1-2 YB 18
Chenu, Julius R.: Chief Mummy Inspector's
    Quiz, (quiz based on Jerry Todd boys'
    books), 1-4 YB 10
Chenu, Julius R.: Collecting the Things,
    (collecting boys' books), 6 BB 5
Chenu, Julius R.: Dedications in Leo's
    Books, (boys' series by Leo Edwards),
    1-4 TB 3
Chenu, Julius R.: Edition Variations of
    Leo Edwards Books Published by Grosset
    & Dunlap, (boys' series books),
    3-1 BC 282
Chenu, Julius R.: Edwards' Magazine
    Illustrators, artists for stories by
    Leo Edwards), 2-1 TBN 1
Chenu, Julius R.: Edwards' Plot Ideas,
    (Leo Edwards, boys' series books),
    2-6 TBN 1

Chenu, Julius R.: The Hal Keene and
    Skippy Dare Series, (boys' books)
    1-1 BC 12
Chenu, Julius R.: Jerry Todd, (on
    Jerry Todd series, boys' books
    by Leo Edwards), 4 BB 3
Chenu, Julius R.: Jerry Todd, Detective,
    (fiction), 1-1 TBN 7; 1-2 TBN 11;
    1-3 TBN 13; 1-4 TBN 15; 2-1 TBN 6;
    2-2 TBN 7; 2-3 TBN 7
Chenu, Julius R.: The Judy Bolton
    Series by Margaret Sutton, (girls'
    mystery series books), 1-1 YB 3
Chenu, Julius R.: Juvenalia, (various
    on boys' book series and collecting),
    1-1 YB 9; 1-2 YB 12; 1-3 YB 16;
    1-4 YB 14; 1-5 YB 11; 1-6 YB 11
Chenu, Julius R.: Leo Edwards and His
    Books, (commentary on boys' series
    by Edwards), 1-2 YB 15; 3 BB 7
Chenu, Julius R.: Leo Edwards' Bird
    Watchers Society, 2-2 TB 1
Chenu, Julius R.: letter of comment,
    2 BB 21; 2 MA 28; 1-1 TBN 3;
    2-3 TBN 6; 2-4 TBN 4; 2-5 TBN 3
Chenu, Julius R.: Magazine Serial is
    Background for Two Books (of Leo
    Edwards, boys' book author),
    2-5 TB 1
Chenu, Julius R.: Miss Minerva and
    Kinfolks, (on Miss Minerva juvenile
    series written by Frances Boyd
    Calhoun, Nell Speed, and Emma
    Speed Sampson), 1-4 YB 3
Chenu, Julius R.: More Information on
    Andy Blake Series, (boys' series by
    Leo Edwards), 1-3 TB 3
Chenu, Julius R.: Mummy Itchers, (humor
    relating to Leo Edwards' Jerry Todd
    boys' series books), 2-4 TBN 1
Chenu, Julius R.: Mummy Plot Fact
    Believe It or Not, (basis for Leo
    Edwards' book JERRY TODD AND THE
    WHISPERING MUMMY), 1-3 TB 1
Chenu, Julius R.: Poppy Ott Sequel to
    Popular Todd Series, (on Jerry Todd
    and Poppy Ott series, boys' books,
    by Leo Edwards), 1-3 TB 1
Chenu, Julius R.: Printing Variations
    in the Andy Blake Series, (by Leo
    Edwards; boys' series), 1-1 TBN 5
Chenu, Julius R.: Ralph Henry Barbour's
    Books, (boys' books), 1-4 BC 118;
    1-6 YB 17; 3-2 BC 317
Chenu, Julius R.: The Sorak Series by
    Harvey D. Richards, (boys' books),
    1-3 YB 5
Chenu, Julius R.: Thornton W. Burgess
    Books for Older Boys, 1-2 BC 42
Chenu, Julius R.: Todd Series Tops Pop,
    More Titles and More Printings,
    (Jerry Todd boys' series by Leo
    Edwards), 1-4 TBN 1

Chenu, Julius R.: Tom Slade and Friends, (boys' series books), 1-5 YB 16

Chenu, Julius R.: Trigger Berg, Leo's Junior Series, (Trigger Berg boys' book series by Leo Wards), 2-4 TBN 1

Chenu, Julius R.: Utica, Illinois is Setting for Other (Leo Edwards) Stories, (locales, boys' books), 1-4 TB 1

(Chesbro, George), Mongo? (detective series character), by Paul Bishop, 2 PE 28

(Chesbro, George C.), Mongo the Magnificent series, Series Synopses, by Robert J. Randisi, 12-4 TAD 366

(Chesbro, George C.: SHADOW OF A BROKEN MAN), Mystery Plus, (discussion), by R. Jeff Banks, 4-1 PP 22

Chess in the Detective Story, by R.W. Hays, 5-1 TAD 19

(Chester, George Randolph: J. Rufus Wallington, character), The Many Rises and Falls of J. Rufus Wallington, by Albert Borowitz, 12-1 TAD 28

(Chester, George Randolph: GET-RICH-QUICK WALLINGFORD), Rogues for the New Century, by Fred Dueren, 5-3 MF 11

(Chesterton, G.K.), The Private Life of Father Brown, by R.W.Hays, 4-3 TAD 135

(Chesterton, G.K.), G.K.Chesterton's Father Brown, by Robert A.W.Lowndes, 9-3 TAD 184

(Chesterton, G.K.: THE INVISIBLE MAN), The Invisible Man Revisited, by Jon L. Breen, 4-3 TAD 154

(Chesterton, G.K.: Mr. Pond series), A Lesser Chesterton Detective, Mr. Pond, by R.W.Hays, 9-2 TAD 125

(Chetwynd-Hayes, Ronald), Ronald Chetwynd-Hayes, Horror Story Author Extraordinaire!, by John Dinan, 6 U 6

(Cheyney, Peter), Checklist of works, by Iwan Hedman, 4-2 TAD 111

(Cheyney, Peter), Filmed Misogyny, The Screen Adaptations of Peter Cheyney and Lionel White (filmed mysteries) by Jack Edmund Nolan, 4-6 MR 27

(Cheyney, Peter), Peter Cheyney (literary discussion), by Iwan Hedman, 4-2 TAD 111

(Cheyney, Peter), Peter Cheyney, (discussion with checklist), by Theodore P. Dukeshire, 4-4 MR 8

(Chibbet, H.S.), H.S.Chibbet, (discussion) by Mike Ashley, 4 WT 7

(Chibbet, H.S.), Checklist of Works, by Mike Ashley, 4 WT 7

(Chicago Paperback books), Checklist, by Lance Casebeer, 1-5 CP 20

(Chidsey, Donald Barr), Pulpster Profile, Visit with Donald Barr Chidsey, by Alvin H. Lybeck, 5 U 17

Chief Mummy Inspector's Quiz, (quiz based on Jerry Todd boys' books of Leo Edwards) by Julius R. Chenu, 1-4 YB 10

Children of the Night, (Sherlockian fiction), by Michael Avallone, 2-2 PDA 56

(CHILL, THE: Ross Macdonald), The Detective as Both Tortoise and Achilles: Archer Gets the Feel of the Case in THE CHILL, by William W. Combs, 2-1 C 98

Chinese Detectives in Poland, (Polish translation and introduction) by Everett F. Bleiler, 11-4 TAD 343

Chow, George Daniel: letter of comment, 14 X 62; 24 X 45

Christ No, Hell Yes, (on censorship in paperback books), by Dave Lewis, 2-4 CP 6

Christensen, Douglas, and Karen Bornstein: A Day in the Life of a Real Private Investigator, 1-3 M 52

Christensen, Peter J.: The First Locked-Room Mystery? (Charles Brockden Brown's WIELAND), 10-4 TAD 368

Christensen, Peter J.: letter of comment, 12-4 TAD 355; 14-1 TAD 71

Christensen, Peter J.: William Hope Hodgson, CARNACKI THE GHOST FINDER, (discussion), 12-2 TAD 122

Christian, Pete: Angela, A Chat with Angela Lansbury, Star of Stage, Screen and Television, 3-1 M 32

Christian, Pete: The World of Mystery (New York Mystery Beat; news), 2-1 M 33; 2-2 M 14; 2-3 M 21; 3-1 M 48; 3-2 M 32

(Christie, Agatha), A Teacher Meets Agatha Christie, by Gordon C. Ramsey, 1-1 TAD 13

(Christie, Agatha), A Tribute to the Crowned Queen of Misdirection, Dame Agatha Christie, with checklist of paperbacks, by Richard P. Hall, 3-3 CP 26

(Christie, Agatha), Agatha Christie, (verse), by Jean Balderston, 12-3 TAD 210

(Christie, Agatha), Agatha Christie in the Dell Mapbacks, (paperback editions of the Dell Pub. Co.'s "mapback" series), by William Lyles, 3-3 PQ 26

(Christie, Agatha), Agatha Christie is Still Alive and Well, by Amnon Kabatchnik, 2-6 MF 9

(Christie, Agatha), Agatha Christie's Alter Ego, Ariadne Oliver, by Sylvia W. Patterson, 14-3 TAD 222

(Christie, Agatha), Agatha Christie's Other Detectives, Parker Pyne and Harley Quin, by Earl F. Bargainnier, 11-2 TAD 110

(Christie, Agatha), Agatha Christie's Portrait of the Artist, (self-revelation), by Margaret Boe Birns, 1-2 C 31

(Christie, Agatha), Another Watson, Captain Hastings, (Captain Arthur Hastings, Christie character), by Earl F. Bargainnier, 13-4 TAD 354

(Christie, Agatha), Dame Agatha's Admirable Addleheads (characters), by Mary F. Lindsley, 1-2 PDA 73

(Christie, Agatha), Dell Paperback Bibliography, (Dell Pub. Company paperback editions), by William Lyles, 1-4 CP 26

(Christie, Agatha), End of the Golden Age, (memorial to Christie), by George Wuyek, 10-3 TAD 263

(Christie, Agatha), Exclusive! The Detection Club's First Collaborations, Unpublished Christie and Others, with checklist, by Paul R. Moy, 4-5/6 PP 15

(Christie, Agatha), Fame Surprises Agatha Christie, (newspaper item), 4-1 MR 2

(Christie, Agatha), From Howtoits to Whodunits, Jane Austen to Agatha Christie, (exploration of background settings), by Rosemary DePaolo, 2-2 C 8

(Christie, Agatha), Hercule Poirot, The Private Life of a Private Eye, by Fred Dueren, 7-2 TAD 111

(Christie, Agatha), Miss Jane Marple and Aging in Literature, by Mary S. Weinkauf, 1-1 C 32

(Christie, Agatha), Shadow Gallery, An Informal Survey of Cover Art of the Seventies, Pt.1: Tribute to Agatha Christie, by Frank Eck, 9-3 TAD 170

(Christie, Agatha), The Short Mystery Stories of Agatha Christie, with a checklist, by Paul McCarthy, 6-1 TAD 16

(Christie, Agatha), Some Agatha Christie Films, (discussion), by Jack Edmund Nolan, 4-2 MR 19

(Christie, Agatha), The Solving Six (Solving Six series of short stories by Christie), by Robert Sampson, 5-5 MF 3

(Christie, Agatha: THE MOUSETRAP), The Mousetrap Phenomenon, (on the stage production), by Arthur Nicholas Athanason, 12-2 TAD 152

Christie, Gene: letter of comment, 8-2 TAD 159

Christie, Gene: Savage Comments, (on Doc Savage, pulp hero character), (an abbreviation code) 4 DR 4; (on numbering the series) 2/3 DR 12

Christmas Assassin, The, (fiction), by Randy Himmel, 9 LR 2

(Christopher, Jimmy, pulp character), see: Operator 5

Christopher, Joe R.: A Sherlock-Pontine Addendum, (Sherlock Holmes/ Solar Pons), 2-1 PD 3

Christopher, Joe R.: A Detective Searches for a Clue in THE HEART OF THE MATTER (by Graham Greene, 1948), 4-1 TAD 32

Christopher, Joe R.: Addenda to Rick Sneary's Checklist of John Dickson Carr, 4-1 MR 20

Christopher, Joe R.: An Unsolved Mystery, (Ngaio Marsh: CLUTCH OF CONSTABLES), 3-2 TAD 93

Christopher, Joe R.: The Case of the Missing Article, (Ellery Queen in GOOD HOUSEKEEPING magazine), 2-1 QC 14

Christopher, Joe R.: The Case of the Vanishing Locomotives, or, A Hell of a Way to Run a Railroad, (impossible crimes: vanishing locomotives themes), 1-2 TAD 56

Christopher, Joe R.: Challenge to the Reader, (Ellery Queen a bigamist?) 1-2 QC 11

Christopher, Joe R.: Commentary on Joan M. Mooney's "Best Selling American Detective Fiction"(see), 5-1 TAD 11

Christopher, Joe R.: Cross Trumps, (Ellery Queen and Rex Stout), 2-2 QC 6

Christopher, Joe R.: Dantean Allusions in "The Trail of Fu Manchu", 5 R 27

Christopher, Joe R.: Detective Fiction in the Wade Collection (Wheaton College), 9-4 TAD 274

Christopher, Joe R.: The Female Private Eye Ponders Where to Carry Her Gat, (verse), 9-2 TAD 101

Christopher, Joe R.: Future Inversions, 6-1 MR 34

Christopher, Joe R.: Last Nut Not Least, (stories in which last words are the name of the killer), 4-1 TAD 11

Christopher, Joe R.: letter of comment, 1-6 MR 8; 2-1 MR 11; 3-1 MR 15; 4-1 MR 20; 4-3 MR 18; 5-2 MR 18; 1-1 TAD 30; 1-3 TAD 106; 1-4 TAD 156; 2-2 TAD 132; 2-3 TAD 200; 2-4 TAD 279; 303 TAD 204; 4-1 TAD 60; 4-3 TAD 190; 5-2 TAD 109; 5-4 TAD 249; 13-2 TAD 160

Christopher, Joe R.: The Literary Tradition of Brow Spraying, 3 R 23

Christopher, Joe R.: Lord Peter Views the Telly, (Lord Peter Wimsey on BBC television), 12-1 TAD 20

Christopher, Joe R.: The Marble Faun, a Whydunit, (on THE MARBLE FAUN of Nathaniel Hawthorne), 11-1 TAD 78

Christopher, Joe R.: Murder at the Cross-
roads; or, Oedipus the Detective, (on
classics mystery), 2-4 TAD 225
Christopher, Joe R.: The Mystery of Robert
Eustace, (author commentary), 13-4 TAD
365
Christopher, Joe R.: The Mystery of Social
Reaction, Two Novels of Ellery Queen,
6-1 TAD 28
Christopher, Joe R.: On LOLITA as a Mystery
Story, (Vladimir Nabokov: LOLITA),
7-1 TAD 29
Christopher, Joe R.: Poe and the Detective
Story, 2-1 TAD 49
Christopher, Joe R.: The Retirement of
Richard Queen, (Inspector Queen of the
Ellery Queen canon), 1-1 QC 3
Christopher, Joe R.: The Rites of a Mystery
Cult, (social function), 5-3 TAD 152
Christopher, Joe R.: "The Unknown One", (on
Lewis Carroll's "The Unknown One"), 3-4
TAD 247
Christopher, Joe R., and D.W.Dickensheet &
Robert E. Briney: A. Boucher Bibliography,
2-2 TAD 77; 2-3 TAD 143; 2-4 TAD 263
(Christopher, Joe R.), Meet the Author, Joe
R. Christopher, by Allen J. Hubin,
1-2 TAD 58; 2-4 TAD 273
(Christopher, Jumping Jimmy), Jumping Jimmy
Christopher, (on Operator 5, pulp hero
character), by Dean A. Grennell, 30 X 17
(Christopher, Jumping Jimmy), see also:
Operator 5
Chronicle of Christopher Syn, The, (Dr. Syn,
pulp villain), by Wooda Nicholas Carr,
7 X 7; 8 X (np); 9 X 5; 10 X 8
Chronicles on Stage, The, (Ray Bradbury), by
Bruce Francis, 36 X R19
Chronicles Remembered, The, (Ray Bradbury),
36 X R36
Chronology of The Man of Bronze, (Doc Savage
novels), by Albert Tonik, 7 DS 6
Chronology of the Travis McGee Novels, The,
(by John D. MacDonald), by Allan D. Pratt,
13-2 TAD 83
Chukman, L.D.: letter of comment, 5/6 MN 15;
3 MY 1; 6 MY 2
Cinemania, (mystery on screen), by Charles
Shibuk, 2-2 TAD 112
Clairmonte, Mrs. Glenn: letter of comment,
11 JD 15
(Clancy, Peter, detective: Lee Thayer), Pen
Profile No.14, (literary & biog.sketch)
by Barry Pike, 3-5 PP 25
(CLARA VAUGHAN: Richard D. Blackmore),
Inspector Bucket's Rival, by Clifford
Jiggens, 12-3 TAD 270
Clark, Bob: letter of comment, 1-2 M 3
Clark, James D.: **letter of comment,**
4-4 TAD 259; 5-3 TAD 175; 6-3 TAD 193
Clark, Jim: letter of comment, 1-2 MF 50
Clark, Meera: Book Reviews, 2-1 C 123
Clark, Meera: Detective Fiction and Social
Realism, H.R.F.Keating's India, 2-1 C 1

Clark Savage, the Early Years, (on
Doc Savage, pulp hero character),
by "Doc Savage, Jr.", 7 DQ 10
Clark Savage, Sr., Retired British
Secret Agent, (Doc Savage pastiche)
by Bill Laidlaw, 2 DQ 7; 3 DQ 10;
4 DQ 10; 5 DQ 15; 6 DQ 11
Clark, William J.: H. Bedford-Jones in
PEOPLE'S, on author's works in pulp
magazine), 30 X 147; BLUE BOOK, 22 X 42
Clark, William J.: Bibliography,
Theodore Roscoe, (pulp author, with
checklist), 65 PU 15
Clark, William J.: The Case of the
Missing Wolfe, (review of NERO WOLFE
OF WEST THIRTY-FIFTH STREET by
William S. Baring-Gould), 3-4 MR 16
Clark, William J.: Debunking the
Legends, (commentary on Frederick
Faust), 1-2 FC 8
Clark, William J.: Detective Pulp
Stories of John D. MacDonald,
publication identification, 6 JD 15
Clark, William J.: Did He or Didn't
He? (Frederick Faust as possible
author of THE GREY CHARTERIS by
Robert Simpson), 1-1 FC 5
Clark, William J.: Faust and the
Western Story Magazine (Frederick
Faust's western stories in dime
novels and pulp magazines), 1-3 FC 9
Clark, William J.: Faust in THE
OCCIDENT (writings of Frederick
Faust in high school paper), 1-3
FC 10
Clark, William J.: Frank Gruber,
(literary comments and bibliographical
checklist), 67 PU 31
Clark, William J.: In Memory of Frank
Gruber, (memorial tribute to author)
2-1 FC 4
Clark, William J.: letter of comment,
2-2 TAD 132; 24 X 44
Clark, William J. The Long History of
Short Stories, 20 X 41
Clark, William J.:Max Brand and the
Mystery Story, (Frederick Faust
writing as Max Brand), 2-4 TAD 255
Clark, William J.: MAX BRAND'S WESTERN
MAGAZINE, checklist of stories by
Frederick Faust writing as Max Brand,
1-1 FC 7
Clark, William J.: The Occult Detector,
(THE OCCULT DETECTOR by J.U.Giesy
and Junius B. Smith), 17 X 55
Clark, William J.: The Scarcest Title,
(THE VILLAGE STREET AND OTHER POEMS
by Frederick Faust), 1-4 FC 9
Clark, William J.: The Shadowers, (THE
SHADOWERS, by "David Fox"), 28 X 75
Clark, William J.: Taxi, Speedy and
Silvertip, (on Frederick Faust's
western stories), 2-1 FC 5

Clark, William J., and Edward D. Hoch & Francis M. Nevins, Jr.: Edward D. Hoch, a Checklist, 9-2 TAD 102

Clark, William J., and Francis M. Nevins, Jr.: Checklist, Cleve F. Adams, 8-3 TAD 200

Classic and Hard-Boiled Detective Fiction (hard-boiled vs. classic mystery discussion), by John M. Reilly, 9-4 TAD 289

Classic Corner, Rare Tales, (fiction):
A Classic Forgery, from THE EXPLOITS OF FIDELITY DOVE, by Roy Vickers, 11-4 TAD 357

The Adventure of the House with the Baboons, by Bertram Atkey, 13-2 TAD 125

The Bravoes of Market-Drayton, by Arthur Conan Doyle, 14-2 TAD 144

Donovan of Whitehall, by William LeQueux, 14-1 TAD 44

The Burglaring Joke and Other Occasional Pieces, by Anthony Berkeley Cox, 14-3 TAD 239

Garroted, by Frank Pierce, 14-4 TAD 336

The Eleventh Hour, by Edwin Balmer and William MacHarg, 12-1 TAD 40

The Happy Land, by James M'Levy, 13-3 TAD 219

Kesho Naik, Dacoit, by Sir Edmund C. Cox, 13-4 TAD 319

Lingo Dan, by Percival Pollard, 12-3 TAD 238

Madame Sara, The Sorceress of the Strand, by L.T.Meade, 12-2 TAD 136

Peter Crane's Cigar, by Victor L. Whitechurch, 12-4 TAD 332

The Twelve Green Russian Garnets, by Arthur Sherburne Hardy, 13-1 TAD 48

Classics of Science Fiction, by Marvin Morrison, 30 X 12

Clayton Rawson and the Flexible Formula, (illusory nature of the formula puzzle mystery), by Fred Erisman, 14-2 TAD 173

Clayton, Tom: Travis McGee Quiz, (quiz based on John D. MacDonald's character Travis McGee), 26 JD 19

Cleary, Maryell: Checklist, G.D.H. Cole, 3-6 PP 14

Cleary, Maryell: Checklist, Joshua Clunk, detective (by H.C.Bailey), 3-5 PP 20

Cleary, Maryell: Checklist, Leslie Ford, 3-4 PP 24

Cleary, Maryell: Face-to-Face with P.D. James, (commentary on author), 4-1 PP 8

Cleary, Maryell: The First Appearance, Colonel John Primrose (in THE STRANGLED WITNESS by Leslie Ford), 3-4 PP 23

Cleary, Maryell: The First Appearance, Grace Latham, (in ILL MET BY MOON-LIGHT, by Leslie Ford), 2-4 PP 27

Cleary, Maryell: The First Appearance, Inspector Cockrill, (in HEADS YOU LOSE by Christianna Brand), 3-2 PP 6

Cleary, Maryell: The First Appearance, Joshua Clunk, (in THE GARSTON MURDER CASE by H.C.Bailey), 3-5 PP 19

Cleary, Maryell: The First Appearance, MacDougall Duff, (in LAY ON, MacDUFF! by Charlotte Armstrong), 3-1 PP 27

Cleary, Maryell: The First Appearance, Nigel Strangeways, (in A QUESTION OF PROOF, by Nicholas Blake), 2-5 PP 25

Cleary, Maryell: The First Appearance, Roderick Alleyn, (in A MAN LAY DEAD, by Ngaio Marsh), 2-6 PP 12

Cleary, Maryell: The First Appearance, Superintendent Wilson, (in THE BROOKLYN MURDERS, by G.D.H.Cole), 3-6 PP 13

Cleary, Maryell: letter of comment, 2-3 PP 42; 2-4 PP 43; 3-1 PP 40; 3-1 PP 42; 3-4 PP 37; 4-1 PP 42; 4-3 PP 32

Cleary, Maryell: Mitch Tobin's Healing, (discussion of Tobin as detective in series by Donald E. Westlake writing as Tucker Coe), 4-5/6 PP 31

Cleary, Maryell: Reminiscences of Cases Past, The Books of Elizabeth Daly, 2-1 PP 3; 2-2 PP 3

Cleary, Michael: letter of comment, 27 JD 34

Clements, William M.: The Red Herring as Folklore, (the misleading clue in mystery fiction), 12-3 TAD 255

(CLERIHEWS COMPLETE: E.C.Bentley), A Rambling Book Review, by Philip T. Asdell, 1-3 PP 21

Cliff Edge Memory, (verse), by Debbie Denaro, 3-6 MR 5

(Clifford, Francis), Six Britons the Movies Ignored, (mystery author seldom filmed), by Jack Edmund Nolan, 3-5 MR 9

Clingan, Chet: letter of comment, 2 SF 40

Clipjoint, (book review extracts from the press), 13A MN 3; 13B MN 1; 13C MN 3

(CLOAK AND DAGGER), Cloak Survey Results on Poll, (readers' preference poll by fanzine), by Jim Huang, 8 CL 2

(CLOAK AND DAGGER), Index to Issues Nos. 1 to 13/14, (fanzine), 15 CD 10

Cloak Looks at Books, (reviews in CLOAK and DAGGER mystery fanzine), by Jim Huang, 6 CL 3; 9 CL 3; 12 CL 3; 15 CL 4

Cloos, George: letter of comment,
    3-6 PP 37; 3-2 TAD 134; 401 TAD 54;
    4-3 TAD 187; 5-2 TAD 128; 5-3 TAD
    188; 9-2 TAD 161
Cloud Country, boys' series, Boys'
    Series Bibliography, by Harry K.
    Hudson, 1-3 YB 9
Clue in the Old Library, The, (on the
    Hardy Boys boys' mystery series)
    by John M. Enright, 4 MA 23
Clue of the Dying Message, The, (as
    used in mystery fiction) by R.W. Hays,
    7-1 TAD 1
(CLUES OF THE CARIBEES: T.S.Stribling)
    Rare Vintages from the Tropics, by
    Frank D. McSherry, Jr., 6-3 TAD 172
(Clunk, Joshua, detective: H.C.Bailey),
    Checklist, by Maryell Cleary,
    3-5 PP 20
(Clunk, Joshua, detective: H.C.Bailey)
    The First Appearance, Joshua Clunk,
    (in THE GARSTON MURDER CASE), 3-5
    PP 19
(CLUTCH OF CONSTABLES: Ngaio Marsh)
    An Unsolved Mystery, by Joe R.
    Christopher, 3-2 TAD 93
Clyne, Ronald, A Portrait (biog. and
    literary sketch), by Victor Dricks,
    18 X 20
(Cobb, Professor Ira, detective), The
    Professional Sleuth of Roy Winsor,
    by Larry L. French, 2-1 MF 3
Cobb, Owen R.: letter of comment,
    2-2 TBN 6
Cobert, Carlton S.: letter of comment,
    5-4 TAD 243
Cockcroft, T.G.: letter of comment,
    65 PU 20
Cockney, Charles: letter of comment,
    28 X 79
Cochran, Leonard: Readers in Search of
    an Author (visit to the home of
    August Derleth), 1-3 PD 1
(Cockrill, Inspector, detective), The
    First Appearance, Inspector Cockrill,
    (in HEADS YOU LOSE by Christianna
    Brand), by Maryell Cleary, 3-2 PP 6
Codes and Ciphers, by Robert C.S.Adey,
    2-6 MR 11
Codicil, The, (verse), by Jayne Fawcett,
    4-2 AD 5
(Coe, Tucker), Checklist (Donald E.
    Westlake pseud.), by Jim McCahery,
    2 PE 18
(Coe, Tucker), Mitch Tobin's Healing,
    (discussion of Tobin as detective
    in series by Donald E. Westlake
    writing as Tucker Coe), by Maryell
    Cleary, 4-5/6 PP 31
(Coe, Tucker), Patterns of Guilt and
    Isolation in Five Novels by "Tucker
    Coe", by Jane S. Bakerman, 12-2 TAD
    118

(Coe, Tucker), Walls of Guilt,
    Donald E. Westlake as Tucker Coe,
    by Francis M. Nevins, Jr., 7-3
    TAD 163
Coffee in the Lab, A Preliminary
    Bibliography, (Dr. Coffee series
    by Lawrence Blochman), by James
    Mark Purcell, 4-3 MR 29
Coffey, Joseph J.: A Song for the
    Unsung, (discusses Harry Horne,
    detective character of John
    Gonzales), 13-1 TAD 67
Coffey, Joseph J.: letter of comment,
    11 JD 15; 7 PE 16; 2-3 TAD 199;
    4-3 TAD 183; 11-3 TAD 213
Cohen, Regina: letter of comment,
    7-2 TAD 151
Cohen, Stanley: Robert Fish, In
    Memorium, (memorial tribute to
    Fish), 14-2 TAD 119
Cole, Don: Checklist, Hammond Innes,
    1-4 PP 8
Cole, Don: Conversation, (interviews),
    with:
    Bill Pronzini, 1-6 PP 11
    Arthur Maling, 2-1 PP 11
    Collin Wilcox, 2-2 PP 15
    Joe L. Hensley, 2-3 PP 19
    Joe Gores, 3-1 PP 19
    Arthur Lyons, 3-2 PP 10
    Michael Z. Lewin, 3-3 PP 13
Cole, Don: High Adventure Fiction,
    (adventure in mystery/suspense
    novels, with Hammond Innes
    checklist), 4-1 MR 3; 1-4 PP 8
Cole, Don: letter of comment, 6/7 LR
    16; 1-5 MF 59; 3-1 MF 48; 2-5 MR
    13; 5-3 MR 16; 1-1 PP 27; 1-2 PP
    25; 1-3 PP 31; 1-6 PP 30; 2-3 PP
    44; 2-6 PP 44; 3-3 TAD 206
(Cole, Don), Don Cole's Underrated
    Books, by George Kelley, 1-5 PP 8
(Cole, G.D.H.), Checklist, by Maryell
    Cleary, 3-6 PP 14
(Cole, G.D.H.: THE BROOKLYN MURDERS)
    The First Appearance, Superintendent
    Wilson, by Maryell Cleary, 3-6 PP 13
Cole, Jud: letter of comment, 4 LW 1
Coleman, Lucile: The Ballad of Lucifer,
    (verse), 1 U 9
Coleman, Lucile: Casandra, (verse),
    28 X 2
Coleman, Lucile: letter of comment,
    38 X 143
Coleman, Lucile: Little Egypt Swings
    It, (fiction), 3 U 16
Coleman, Lucile: To a Scholar, (verse),
    30 X 134
Coleman, Lucile: The Unicorn, (verse),
    1 U 8
(Coles, Manning: Thomas Elphinstone
    Hambledon series), Annotated Check-
    list, by Barry Van Tilburg, 4-3
    MF 23

(Colicos, John), Fading Shadows: John Colicos, (sketch), by Tom Johnson, 1 PW 2

(collaborations), Exclusive! The Detection Club's First Collaborations, Unpublished Christie and Others, with checklist, by Paul R. Moy, 4-5/6 PP 15

Collecting Armed Services Editions (of paperback books), by Charlotte Laughlin, 1-2 PQ 31

Collecting Book Club Editions, by Michael L. Cook, 3 U 19

Collecting Inside Outside, (boys' series books), by Jack R. Schorr, 1 BB 24

Collecting Mania, The, (comments), by Gerry de la Ree, 20 X 6

Collecting Original Paperback Cover Art, by Robert Weinberg, 3-3 PQ 44

Collecting Paperback First Editions of Philip Jose Farmer, by Don Block, 2-3 CP 18

COLLECTING PAPERBACKS?, Index to Volume I, 2-1 CP (no pages)

Collecting Science Fiction (paperbacks) by Dean Smith, 1-4 CP 21

Collecting the Things, (boys' series books) by Julius R. Chenu, 6 BB 5

Collecting Thoughts, (various, on paperback book collecting), by Ron Tatar, 2-3 CP 7; (DAW science-fiction paperbacks), 2-4 CP 9; (new paperbacks), 3-3 CP 29

(collecting), see (1) Mystery collecting, (2) Paperback collecting, (3) Boys' Book collecting

Collector's Bag, The: letter of comment, 40 X 85

Collector's Corner, (A. Talbot Mundy, bibliography), by Robert Weinberg, 6 P 24

Collector's Crossword, (based on boys' series books), by Herb L. Risteen, 1-3 BC 67; 2-1 BC 134

Collector's Items, (on mystery fiction), by Bonita Summers, 4-3 MR 11

College Life Series, The, (boys' books), by Jack R. Schorr, 2-4 TBN 6

Collier Books, (paperbacks), with checklist, by Ellen Nehr, 3-5 CP 19

Collins, Allan: letter of comment, 5-6 MR 15

Collins, Kreigh: letter of comment, 4 BS 16

Collins, Max: Dat's Mike Ham-muh? (Mickey Spillane's Mike Hammer in the popular media), 12-4 TAD 308

(Collins, Max), An Interview with Max Collins, by Robert J. Randisi, 11-3 TAD 300

(Collins, Max), Meet Nolan, (discussion of "heist artist"/detective Nolan in series by Collins), by Robert J. Randisi, 4-5/6 PP 29

Collins, Max Alllan: letter of comment, 7 PE 17; 11-3 TAD 213; 13-3 TAD 238; 13-4 TAD 342

(Collins, Michael: Dan Fortune series), Dan Fortune, Private Eye, by John Edwards, 9 SF 38

(Collins, Michael: Slot Machine Kelly series), Checklist, 9 SF 38

Colombo, John Robert: letter of comment, 2 R 24

Color Him Quixote - MacDonald's Strategy in the Early McGee Novels, by Michael J. Tolley, 10-1 TAD 6

(Colt, Thatcher: Anthony Abbott) The Thatcher Colt Novels of Anthony Abbott, A Bibliography, by Jon L. Breen, 3-1 TAD 5

(Columbia Publications), The Columbia Pulps, (magazines), by Robert A.W. Lowndes, 67 PU 5

Columbia Pulps, The, (on the pulp magazines of Columbia Publications) by Robert A.W.Lowndes, 67 PU 5

Columbia's Science Fiction Paper Books, by Dave & Su Bates, 1-4 CP 25

Combs, William W.: The Detective as Both Tortoise and Achilles, Archer Gets the Feel of the Case in THE CHILL (novel by Ross Macdonald), 2-1 C 98

Comedy-Detective Film is Alive and Well, The, (short reviews), by Jim Huang, 5 CL 1

COMET Magazine, an Index, by Jerry Alexander, 8 U 139

Comic Book Adventures of Ellery Queen, The, (Queen in comic books), by Ron Goulart, 12-3 TAD 197

Comic Capers and Comic Eyes (on humorous mystery fiction), by David Geherin, 13-4 TAD 276

Comic Construction in the Novels of Emma Lathen and R.B.Dominick, by David Brownell, 9-2 TAD 91

(comics), The Comic Book Adventures of Ellery Queen, (Queen in comic books), by Ron Goulart, 12-3 TAD 197

(comics), Doc Defeated, or Doc Savage in the Comics, by A. Grossman, 2/3 DR 5

(comics), Doc Savage and the Comics, by Tony Isabella, 14 BS 18

(comics), Duck Savage, The Mallard of Bronze, (comic strip, pastiche of Doc Savage), by Todd R. Rutt and Timothy J. Rutt, 1-2 WA 9; 1-3 WA 11; 1-4 WA 11; 2-1 WA 18

(comics), The Gold Key Doc Savage Comic Book, by Wayne Vucenic, 14 BS 18

(comics), "Judge Perkins" comic strip of 1935 (by Bert Salg) reproduced, 2-5 TBN 7

(comics), Mickey Spillane Comic Strip, 12-4 TAD 317

(comics), What's Up, Doc? (on Doc Savage comic book series by Marvel Pub.) by Shelby L. Peck, 2/3 DR 3

Comment from Cover Artist on Rex Stout Memorial Issue (of THE MYSTERY NOOK fanzine), by Frank D. McSherry,Jr., 9 MN A10

Commentaries for the Curious, (comments from various on John Dickson Carr), 1 NC 11

Commentary, (on Sax Rohmer), by Douglas A. Rossman, 6 R 5

Commentary on Joan M. Mooney's "Best Selling American Detective Fiction" (see), by Joe R. Christopher, 5-1 TAD 11

Comments and Queries, (commentary on mystery fiction, and letters from readers), LA MR 4; 1-1 MR 6; 1-2 MR 5; 1-3 MR 5; 1-5 MR 13; 1-6 MR 8; 2-1 MR 11; 2-2 MR 15; 2-3 MR 11; 2-4 MR 17; 2-5 MR 12; 2-6 MR 14; 3-1 MR 15; 3-2 MR 16; 3-3 MR 11; 3-4 MR 33; 3-5 MR 35; 3-6 MR 9; 4-1 MR 18; 4-2 MR 14; 4-3 MR 18; 4-4 MR 14; 4-5 MR 16; 4-6 MR 16; 5-1 MR 14; 5-2 MR 16; 5-3 MR 13; 5-4 MR 9; 5-5 MR 16; 5-6 MR 15; 6-1 MR 19; 6-2 MR 15

Comments on the Corpus, (letters from readers), 1-2 QC 12; 1-3 QC 19; 1-4 QC 17; 2-1 QC 16; 2-2 QC 12

Commodore, Helen: letter of comment, 8-2 TAD 154

Common Heard, The, (quiz based on Nero Wolfe), by Richard Oldberg, 1-2 G 60

Common Law, The, (essay), by Frederick Faust, 2-1 FC 8

"Common Practice" in Science Fiction, The: Aspects on the Writing of Henry Kuttner, by Leon James, 42 X 147

Compleat Poisoner, The, (on Dr. Thorndyke stories of Freeman involving poisons) by John H. Dirckx, 7 TF 3

(COMPLETE UNCLE ABNER, THE: Melville Davisson Post), Special review article, by Martin Morse Wooster, 2-5 MF 9

Complex Art of Raymond Chandler, The, (literary quality discussion), by George N. Dove, 8-4 TAD 271

Comprehensive Survey of THE SPIDER novels, (in-depth study of each novel), by Herman S. McGregor (see listing under Herman S. McGregor)

Compton, Ethel D.: Lady in Waiting, (verse,re: John D. MacDonald and Travis McGee), 24 JD 41

Compton, Ethel D.: letter of comment, 24 JD 41

Compton, Loyal G.: For Travis McGee Fans, (crossword puzzle), 26 JD 13

Compton, Loyal G.: letter of comment, 25 JD 39

Conan Doyle and Sherlock Holmes, The Creator versus The Creation, by Jack Tracy, 2-2 M 26

Conan Doyle Shows His Hand, by Dana Martin Batory, 8 U 104

(Conan series: Robert E. Howard), Bronze Shadows Presents Conan (general review of the Conan stories and publications), by Fred S. Cook, 13 BS 19

Conarton, Warner: Confessions from a JDM Addict, (comments on works of John D. MacDonald), 27 JD 16

Concerning NENA SAHIB (by Sir John Retcliffe), by Paul Plass, 6-3 TAD 157

Concerning the Problem of the Man With the Broken Face, (Solar Pons article), by Roger Johnson, 1-1 PDA 32

(CONDOMINIUM: John D. MacDonald), Early "Condominium" Hurricane Warning, by Jean & Walter Shine, 22 JD 15

Cone, Chaz: letter of comment, 24 JD 41

Cone, Susan: letter of comment, 26 JD 47

Confessions from a JDM Addict (on works of John D. MacDonald), by Warner Conarton, 27 JD 16

Confessions of a Pulp Eater (on fiction, pulp style), by Sam Potts, 13 BS 3

Confessions of a Pulp Western Hack, by Walker Tompkins, 32 X 13

Confessions of a Reluctant Bibliophile, (collecting Nero Wolfe), by John McAleer, 1-1 G 47

(CONFESSIONS OF A THUG: Col. Philip Meadows Taylor), An Appreciation, by Andy Biegel, Jr., 11 SF 37

Conner, Wilkie: Konner's Korner, (pulp magazine reminiscences) 63 PU 33; 64 PU 11; 65 PU 3

Conner, Wilkie: letter of comment, 60 PU 31; 62 PU 12; 64 PU 41; 70 PU 29

Conner, Wilkie: Pulp Fiction - Yesterday and Today, (change in quality noted), 67 PU 45

Conner, Edward: The Films of Ellery Queen, 3-1 QC 10

Conover, Willis: The Call of Lovecraft, (on H.P.Lovecraft), 18 X 15

Conquering the Stereotypes, On Reading the Novels of John D. MacDonald, (female stereotyped characters), by George S. Peck, 13-2 TAD 90

(Conquest of the U.S., series: H.Irving Hancock), Future Shock, 1916, (boys' books),by Robert Jennings, 4 BB 15

(Conrad, Joseph: THE SECRET AGENT),
    Conrad's Probe to Absolute Zero,
    by Newton Baird, 0-1 TAD 43
Conrad's Probe to Absolute Zero, by
    Newton Baird, 9-1 TAD 43
(Constantine, K.C.), K.C. Constantine,
    sketch, by David Brownell,
    9-1 TAD 42
Contemplating Jim Harmon's Novel,
    THE GREAT RADIO HEROES, by Wooda
    Nicholas Carr, 69 PU 28
Contemplating the Pulp Westerns,
    (magazines), by Wooda Nicholas
    Carr, 12 P 10
Contemplating Seven of the Pulp Heroes,
    (comparisons and characteristics),
    by Wooda Nicholas Carr and Herman
    S. McGregor, 12 BS 3
(Continental Op series: Dashiell Hammett)
    Checklist of stories, by William F.
    Nolan, 1-4 TAD 153
(Continental Op series: Dashiell Hammett)
    Shadowing the Continental Op, with
    checklist, by William F. Nolan,
    8-1 TAD 121
Controversy: Townsend, Tey and Richard
    III, A Rebuttal, (on Josephine Tey's
    THE DAUGHTER OF TIME; see also
    10-4 TAD 211), by M.J. Smith,
    10-4 TAD 317 (see next item)
Controversy, (see also 10-3 TAD 211,
    10-3 TAD 237; 10-4 TAD 317), by
    Guy M. Townsend, 11-2 TAD 105;
    (by Myrna J. Smith) 11-3 TAD 236;
    (by J.M. Purcell) 11-4 TAD 398
Conversation, (interviews), by Don
    Cole, with:
    Bill Pronzini, 1-6 PP 11
    Arthur Maling, 2-1 PP 11
    Collin Wilcox, 2-2 PP 15
    Joe L. Hensley, 2-3 PP 19
    Joe Gores, 3-1 PP 19
    Arthur Lyons, 3-2 PP 10
    Michael Z. Lewin, 3-3 PP 13
Conway, Peter W.: letter of comment,
    7-2 TAD 150; 8-3 TAD 243
Cook, Fred S.: A Cook's Tour of the Pulps,
    (literary reminiscences), 67 PU 43
Cook, Fred S.: A Full Length "Shadow"
    Novel as Told to... (novels of
    The Shadow, pulp hero character,
    written by Theodore Tinsley and
    Bruce Elliott), 3 BS 12
Cook, Fred S.: Bronze Shadows Presents,
    Conan, (general review of the Conan
    stories and publications; as created
    by Robert E. Howard), 13 BS 19
Cook, Fred S.: Checklist, THE SHADOW
    magazine, chronological date list,
    1 BS 5
Cook, Fred S.: Kenneth Robeson's Alter
    Egos, (Doc Savage novels written by
    other than Lester Dent), 2 BS 14

Cook, Fred S.: Ki-Gor and the Fiction
    House Monster, (JUNGLE STORIES,
    pulp magazines, and Fiction House
    as publisher), 5 BS 18
Cook, Fred S.: letter of comment,
    64 PU 41
Cook, Fred S.: Notes of a Pulp Collector,
    (first advertisement for DOC SAVAGE
    magazine, comments), 10 BS 13
Cook, Fred S.: Pulp Heroes, Incidental
    Information, (news and letters from
    readers), 2 BS 2; 3 BS 2; 4 BS 2;
    5 BS 3; 6 BS 20; 7 BS 2; 8 BS 3;
    10 BS 21; 15 BS 15
Cook, Fred S.: World of Entertainment,
    pulp hero related news and reviews,
    4 BS 19
Cook, Fred S. & Gordon Huber: Index to
    NEW MYSTERY ADVENTURES, pulp
    magazine, 30 X 146
Cook, Katherine E.: letter of comment,
    5-3 TAD 189
Cook, Kevin: letter of comment,
    5 SF 47; 6 U 49; 14 X 64; 17 X 61;
    26 X 77; 43 X 5
Cook, Michael L.: An Old Friend, The
    Detective Book Club, 8-2 TAD 77
Cook, Michael L.: Collecting Book Club
    Editions, 3 U 19
Cook, Michael L.: Complete Checklist,
    The Detective Book Club, 8-2 TAD 79
Cook, Michael L.: Crime After Crime,
    (news column, mystery), 2 PW 1
Cook, Michael L.: The Detective Book
    Club, Alphabetical Listing by Author,
    10 MN I1
Cook, Michael L.: The Detective Book
    Club, Checklist in order of publi-
    cation, 10 MN I21
Cook, Michael L.: The Detective Book
    Club, Supplement to Checklist in
    TAD 8-1, 9 MN I1
Cook, Michael L.: The Legend of the
    Unicorn, 1 U 4
Cook, Michael L.: letter of comment,
    1-4 AD 8; 7 DQ 5; 12 DS 8; 25 JD 39;
    3-1 MF 54; 4-1 MF 47; 5-2 MF 48;
    5-4 MF 46; 5/6 MN 13; 11 MN L13;
    4-2 PP 33; 4-3 PP 36; 4-4 PP 32;
    1-2 YB 24; 1-3 YB 11; 1-4 YB 10;
    1-5 YB 21
Cook, Michael L.: Michael Avallone,
    Writer Extraordinaire! (sketch),
    8 U 76
Cook, Michael L.: Murder by Mail -
    Update, (bibliographical listing of
    books published by the book clubs
    May 1979 - August 1981), 4-5/6 PP 51
Cook, Michael L.: THE OPEN ROAD FOR
    BOYS Goes to War, (wartime issues
    of magazine discussed), 1-6 YB 3
Cook, Michael L.: Prey and Tell,
    (mystery news column), 12 LR 18

Cook, Michael L.: Raven House Mysteries, Forever More! (checklist and introduction to the Raven House line of mystery paperbacks), 4-5/6 PP 27

Cook, Michael L.: Recent Arrivals, (book reviews), 7 U 31

Cook, Michael L.: Red-Blooded Mysteries Are Now Blue-Blooded, (mystery reference books, and acceptance of detective literature now), 14 SF 38

Cook, Michael L.: Rex Stout in Mystery Guild Editions, (editions of book club), 9 MN A27

Cook, Michael L.: Smokerings and Things, (review of books, periodicals, and news of forthcoming), 1 U 25; 2 U 20; 3 U 22; 4 U 34; 5 U 32; 6 U 80; 7 U 41

Cook, Michael L.: Solar Pons and Basil Copper, (Copper's new Solar Pons paperback books, pastiches of Sherlock Holmes), 7 U 29

Cook, Michael L.: The Unicorn Mystery Book Club, checklist by author, and list in chronological order, 12 MN I1

Cook, Michael L.: The Unicorn Mystery Book Club, (partial list of, with brief history), 5 MY 3

(Cook, Oscar), Bibliography of Weird Fiction of Oscar Cook and Christine Campbell Thomson, by Mike Ashley, 3 WT 13

(Cook, Oscar), Unlocking the Night, by Mike Ashley, 3 WT 8

Cook, Paul H.: letter of comment, 11 DS 5

Cook, Wister: John D. MacDonald, A Little Ecology Goes a Long Way, 1-1 C 57

Cooksey, Paul: letter of comment, 24 JD 40

Cooper, Anice Page: Sax Rohmer and the Art of Making Villains, 5 R 8

(Cooper, John R.: Mel Martin Baseball series), Boys' Series Bibliographies, by Harry K. Hudson, 1-6 YB 15

Cooper, Raymond D.: letter of comment, 12-2 TAD 186

Cooper-Clark, Diana: An Interview with Peter Lovesey, 14-3 TAD 210

Cooper-Clark, Diana: An Interview with Ruth Rendell, 14-2 TAD 108

Cooper-Clark, Diana: Patricia Highsmith, Interview, 14-4 TAD 313

Copper, Basil: August Derleth, a Giant Remembered, 1-2 AD 1

Copper, Basil: letter of comment, 2-2 AD 9

(Copper, Basil), Solar Pons and Basil Copper, (Copper's new Solar Pons paperback books, pastiches of Sherlock Holmes), by Michael L. Cook, 7 U29

(COP OUT: Ellery Queen), The Mystery of Social Reaction, Two Novels of Ellery Queen, by J.R.Christopher, 6-1 TAD 28

Cops and Cop-Haters, The, The Police Procedural (type of mystery), by George N. Dove, 10-3 TAD 241

Cops and Detectives, by Etta C. Abrahams, 1-1 C 96

(Cord, Talos, series: Robert McLeod) Checklist, annotated, by Barry Van Tilburg, 4-5 MF 22

Cordes, Jack: letter of comment, 15 BS 16; 30 X 148

Corduan, Winn: White Tea, (fiction), 13 MN F1

(Corelli, Marie: VENDETTA), Marie Corelli, Vendetta!, by Michael Avallone, 9-4 TAD 270

Coriell, Vern: letter of comment, 6 P 29; 33 X 114; 15 BS 15; 60 PU 32

Corinth Paperbacks, Checklist, by Tom Johnson, 10 SF 37

(Corinth Paperbacks), Fading Shadows, Corinth/Regency Paperbacks, by Tom Johnson, 10 SF 36

(Corinth Paperbacks), Paperback Reprints of The Phantom Detective (series), by Robert Sampson, 3-3 MR 6

Corkey, Gerald J.: Edwards and His Characters, (discusses the boys' books by Leo Edwards), 2-3 TBN 3

Corkey, Gerald J.: letter of comment, 1-2 TBN 6; 2-1 TBN 4; 2-4 TBN 5; 2-5 TBN 3

Cornell Woolrich, A Bibliography, by Harold Knott, Francis M. Nevins, Jr. and William Thailing, 2-4 TAD 237

Cornell Woolrich, "...I Had Nobody" by Steve Fisher, 3-3 TAD 164

Cornell Woolrich, The Years Before Suspense, (early writings), by Francis M. Nevins, Jr., 12-2 TAD 106

Corpse Tells the Tale, The, (forensic medicine in crime solutions), by Stanley A. Carlin, 3-1 MR 25

Correspondence Between Hornung and Doyle, (E.W.Hornung, A. Conan Doyle), 4 MT 28

Cortland Fitzsimmons and the Sports Mystery, by Jon L. Breen, 14-2 TAD 129

(Cory, Desmond: Johnny Fedora series) Checklist, annotated, by Barry Van Tilburg, 4-3 MF 23

Coryell, Percelle: letter of comment, 11 R 23

Cosgriff, John: Alive and Doing Well in New York City, (fiction, Doc Savage pastiche), 1 DR 5

Costello, Sid, Jr.: letter of comment, 68 PU 26

(Cotterell, Martin, detective: John Trench), Pen Profile No.16, (biog. & literary sketch), 4-1 PP 19

Cotton, Trevor: letter of comment,
4-5/6 PP 87
Coulson, Bob: letter of comment, 68 PU 25
Counselman, Mary Elizabeth: A Derleth
Tribute (to August Derleth), 1-4 AD 1
(Counselman, Mary Elizabeth), An Inter-
view with Mary Elizabeth Counselman,
by Stephen Gresham, 6 WT 11
(Counselman, Mary Elizabeth), Mary
Elizabeth Counselman in WEIRD TALES
(pulp magazine), 6 WT 21
Covell, Ian: Checklist, Dr. Who in
book form, 5 SF 42
Covell, Ian: letter of comment, 2 SF 40
Covell, Ian: Some Notes on British
Authors, with checklists, 4 SF 28
(cover art), A Visit with Margaret
Brundage, (WEIRD TALES cover artist)
by Forrest J. Ackerman, 3 WT 17
(cover art), Letter and Comment from
James E. Bama, "Today's Doc Savage
Illustrator", 2 BS 4
(cover art), Letter and Comment from
Paul Orban, "Yesterday's Doc Savage
Illustrator", 2 BS 5
(cover art), Margaret Brundage, (WEIRD
TALES cover artist), by Robert
Weinberg, 2 WT 3
(cover art), Paperbacks with dust-
jackets of different design), by
Peter Manesis, 4-1 PQ 26
(cover Art), Shadow Gallery, An Informal
Survey of Cover Art of the Seventies,
by Frank Eck; (Tribute to Agatha
Christie), 9-3 TAD 170; (Tribute to
Maj Sjowall and Per Wahloo), 10-1
TAD 46
Cowell, Eugene: letter of comment,
11-3 TAD 311
Cox, Anthony Berkeley: The Burglaring
Joke and Other Occasional Pieces,
(fiction; Classic Corner rare tales)
14-3 TAD 239
(Cox, Anthony Berkeley), A Bibliography
of the Works of Anthony Berkeley Cox
(and as Francis Iles), by Paul R.
Moy, 14-3 TAD 236
(Cox, Anthony Berkeley), The Literary
Career of Mr. Anthony Berkeley Cox,
by Charles Shibuk, 2-3 TAD 164
Cox, Arthur J.: Dickens' Last Book, More
Mysteries Than One (on THE MYSTERY OF
EDWIN DROOD), 14-1 TAD 31
Cox, Ed: Early J.D. (early writings of
John D. MacDonald), 9 JD 19; (in
DOC SAVAGE and THE SHADOW pulp
magazines), 2 JD 3
Cox, Ed: letter of comment, 7 JD 6;
11 JD 29; 16 JD 23
Cox, Sir Edmund C.: Kesho Naik, Dacoit,
(fiction; Classic Corner rare tales)
13-4 TAD 319

Cox, J. Randolph: A Checklist of the
Fiction of John Buchan, 1875-1940
2-4 TAD 213
Cox, J. Randolph: A Chronological
Bibliography of the Books cf
Arthur B. Reeve, 11-1 TAD 29
Cox, J. Randolph: A Reading of Reeve,
Some Thoughts on the Creator of
Craig Kennedy, (Arthur B. Reeve)
11-1 TAD 28
Cox, J. Randolph: The Adventures of
Nick Carter, (television review)
5-2 MR 35
Cox, J. Randolph: Boy Detectives,
(in boys' books), 1-3 TB 4
Cox, J. Randolph: Checklist, Dornford
Yates, 14-2 TAD 186
Cox, J. Randolph: Checklist, John
Buchan, 6-2 MR 18
Cox, J. Randolph: Checklist, E.Phillips
Oppenheim, addendum, 5-3 MR 17
Cox, J. Randolph: Detection in the
Guilt-Age, (rational premise in
mystery fiction), 8-1 TAD 111
Cox, J. Randolph: The Detective
Story - Its Study and Appreciation,
4-4 MR 3; 4-5 MR 19
Cox, J. Randolph: George Harmon Coxe,
A Chronological List of His Writings,
7-1 TAD 16
Cox, J. Randolph: John Buchan, A
Philosophy of High Adventure,
2-4 TAD 207
Cox, J. Randolph: letter of comment,
3 BB 25; 3-1 MF 54; 3-2 MF 52;
1-6 MR 8; 2-2 MR 16; 3-2 MR 17;
4-6 MR 18; 5-1 MR 14; 5-3 MR 17;
5-6 MR 17; 6-1 MR 21; 1-4 PP 42;
1-5 PP 26; 2-1 PP 32; 2-2 PP 43;
2-4 PP 44; 3-6 PP 34; 1-4 QC 17;
2-2 QC 12; 13 R 32; 2-2 TAD 135;
2-3 TAD 202; 3-1 TAD 60; 3-2 TAD
138; 3-3 TAD 207; 4-2 TAD 127;
4-3 TAD 182; 5-1 TAD 47; 5-2 TAD 113;
5-3 TAD 185; 5-4 TAD 235; 6-1 TAD 45;
6-2 TAD 131; 6-3 TAD 202; 6-4 TAD
273; 7-2 TAD 148; 7-4 TAD 303; 8-3
TAD 242; 8-4 TAD 325; 9-1 TAD 79;
9-2 TAD 158; 9-3 TAD 167; 10-3
TAD 195; 10-4 TAD 381; 11-4 TAD
400; 12-3 TAD 267; 12-4 TAD 355;
14-2 TAD 185; 26 X 76; 30 X 148;
43 X 5
Cox, J. Randolph: The Many Lives of
Nick Carter, (literary discussion
of the span of Nick Carter stories)
71 PU 8
Cox, J. Randolph: More Mystery for a
Dime, Street & Smith and the First
Pulp Detective Magazine (on pulp
magazine, DETECTIVE STORY MAGAZINE)
2-2 C 52

Cox, J. Randolph: Mystery Master, A
Survey and Appreciation of the
Fiction of George Harmon Coxe,
6-2 TAD 63; 6-3 TAD 160; 6-4
TAD 232; 7-1 TAD 11
Cox, J. Randolph: Notes of a Pulp
Collector, (background of THE
SHADOW, pulp magazine), 14 BS 17
Cox, J. Randolph: Prolegomena to a
Bibliography of the Immortal Works
of Leslie Charteris, 5-2 MR 9
Cox, J. Randolph: Nick Carter, The
Man and the Myth, (dime novel
and pulp detective character)
2-3 MR 15
Cox, J. Randolph: The Pulp Career
of Nicholas Carter, (Nick
Carter, detective, in pulp magazines)
22 X 15
Cox, J. Randolph: The Saint on Film
(The Saint, detective-rogue),
5-2 MR 14
Cox, J. Randolph: The Smiling Corpse
Revisited, (re: THE SMILING CORPE,
anon.), 3-3 TAD 170
Cox, J. Randolph: Some Errors in
Fiction Factory, (re: THE FICTION
FACTORY by Quentin Reynolds),
74 PU 31
Cox, J. Randolph: Some Notes Toward a
Checklist of A.A.Milne's Short Tales
of Crime and Detection, 9-4 TAD 269
Cox, J. Randolph: That Mysterious Aide
to the Forces of Law and Order, (on
THE SHADOW, pulp character), 4-4
TAD 221
Cox, J. Randolph: Tutt and Monsieur
Donaque, Some Notes on the Crime
Fiction of Arthur Train, 2-4 PP 9
(Cox, J. Randolph), Meet the Author,
J. Randolph Cox, by Allen J. Hubin,
2-4 TAD 214
Cox, Jean: Dogging the Footsteps of
Solar Pons, (August Derleth's
Sherlockian character, Solar Pons)
1-1 PDA 9
(Cox, William Robert), Tracking Tom
Buchan, by Bernard A. Drew, 8 U 135
(Coxe, George Harmon), George Harmon
Coxe, A Chronological List of His
Writings, by J. Randolph Cox,
7-1 TAD 16
(Coxe, George Harmon), Mystery Master,
A Survey and Appreciation of the
Fiction of George Harmon Coxe,
by J. Randolph Cox, 6-2 TAD 63;
6-3 TAD 160; 6-4 TAD 232; 7-1
TAD 11
Coyle, James E.: letter of comment,
6-1 MR 19
(Craig, Linda, girls' series),
Juvenalia, by Julius R. Chenu,
1-4 YB 14

Craig, Noel: The World of Mystery
Fiction, (on the series, The
Mystery Library), 1-1 M 27
(Craig, Peter, series: Kenneth Benton)
Checklist, by Barry Van Tilburg,
4-2 MF 12
Craig Rice, Merry Mistress of Mystery
and Mayhem, by Mary Ann Grochowski,
13-3 TAD 265
(Craigie, Gordon & Department Z,
series: John Creasey), Checklist,
annotated, by Barry Van Tilburg,
4-3 MF 24
Cramer, Susan: letter of comment,
2-1 MF 55
Crandall, Rick: A Leo Edwards Imitation,
(on the Fun Loving Gang series by
Harold M. Sherman, boys' books),
1-3 YB 7
Crandall, Rick: An Overlooked Boys
Series Best Seller, (books by Zane
Grey), 1-2 YB 14
Crandall, Rick: letter of comment,
1-2 YB 23; 1-4 YB 9; 1-6 YB 9
(Crane, William, series: Jonathan
Latimer), Checklist, by Jim McCahery,
1 PE 6; 2 PE 13
(Crane, William, series: Jonathan
Latimer), Series Spotlight, Jonathan
Latimer's William Crane, by Jim
McCahery, 1 PE 5; 2 PE 5
Creasey, John: John Creasey, Fact or
Fiction, A Candid Commentary in
Third Person, 2-1 TAD 1
Creasey, John: letter of comment,
4-6 MR 16; 5-1 MR 16; 1-4 TAD 155;
2-2 TAD 127
Creasey, John: The Social Consequences
of Crime Writing, 4-1 TAD 38
(Creasey, John), Addenda to Checklist,
by Robert E. Briney, 2-2 TAD 123;
2-4 TAD 276
(Creasey, John), The Best of John
Creasey, by Deryck Harvey, 7-1
TAD 42
(Creasey, John), Checklist, Paperback
Originals, by Robert E. Briney and
John Creasey, 2-1 TAD 20
(Creasey, John), Checklist of Pennames,
by Robert E. Briney and John Creasey,
2-1 TAD 5
(Creasey, John), Checklist of Series,
by Robert E. Briney and John Creasey,
2-1 TAD 5
(Creasey, John), Dedication and Tribute,
by Allen J. Hubin, 6-4 TAD 209
(Creasey, John), John Creasey Biblio-
graphy, with summary of series and
pennames, by Robert E. Briney and
John Creasey, 2-1 TAD 5
(Creasey, John), Meet the Author: John
Creasey, 2-1 TAD 3

(Creasey, John), The Mini Screen Career of John Creasey, (discusses filmed Creasey mystery novels), by Jack Edmund Nolan, 4-5 MR 11

(Creasey, John), Obituary, 6-1 MR 38

(Creasey, John), Prolificity Pays: John Creasey, by Granville Wilson, 4-5 MR 8

(Creasey, John), Remembering John Creasey, by Francis M. Nevins, Jr., 4 X 37

(Creasey, John: Department Z series), Checklist, by Robert E. Briney and John Creasey, 2-1 TAD 9

(Creasey, John: Dr. Palfrey series), Checklist, by Robert E. Briney and John Creasey, 2-1 TAD 8

(Creasey, John: Dr. Palfrey series), Checklist, by Barry Van Tilburg, 4-2 MF 12

(Creasey, John: Gordon Craigie and Department Z series), Checklist, annotated, by Barry Van Tilburg, 4-3 MF 24

(Creasey, John: Roger West series), Checklist, by Robert E. Briney and John Creasey, 2-1 TAD 7

(Creasey, John: Sexton Blake series), Checklist, by Robert E. Briney and John Creasey, 2-1 TAD 20

(Creasey, John: The Toff series), Checklist, by Robert E. Briney and John Creasey, 2-1 TAD 10

Created, The Destroyer, An Interview with Warren Murphy, (The Destroyer series, paperbacks), by Dick Lochte, 11-3 TAD 284

Creative Compulsion, The, (on writing, by John D. MacDonald), by William L. Rohde, 10 JD 7

Creative Order in Rex Stout, by David R. Anderson, 9 MN Al

Crew, Gary: letter of comment, 3-2 MF 54; 1-5 PP 24

Crider, Bill: Ace Science Fiction Doubles, (paperback 2-in-1 volumes),3-4 PQ 25

Crider, Bill: "Archie O'Neill" - Jim Henaghan, The Jeff Pride Series, 4 PE 15

Crider, Bill: Bruno Fischer's Gold Medal, (Fischer in paperback editions, annotated), 1-4 PQ 23; 2-1 PQ 7

Crider, Bill: Checklist, Paperback Originals, (mystery fiction), 5-1 MR 20

Crider, Bill: Checklist, William Campbell Gault, works, 2 PE 21

Crider, Bill: Here Comes the Judge, The "Nero" Award, (fiction award), 3-6 MF 8

Crider, Bill: letter of comment, 8 JD 14; 11 JD 28; 12 JD 14; 14 JD 22; 16 JD 19; 5 LR 8; 6/7 LR 17; 2-4 MF 58; 2-5 MF 56; 2-6 MF 44; 3-1 MF 55; 3-2 MF 50; 3-3 MF 52; 3-4 MF 57; 4-1 MF 43; 4-3 MF 50; 5-1 MF 36; 5-2 MF 41;

Crider, Bill: letter of comment, (continued), 5-4 MF 39; 5-6 MF 53; 5-1 MR 14; 2 PE 36; 5 PE 34; 1-5 PP 29; 1-6 PP 30; 2-1 PP 34; 2-2 PP 35; 2-3 PP 41; 2-4 PP 43; 2-5 PP 39; 206 PP 41; 3-1 PP 46; 3-2 PP 33; 3-3 PP 40; 3-6 PP 33; 4-1 PP 49; 4-2 PP 41; 4-3 PP 35; 4-4 PP 37; 8-4 TAD 315; 9-1 TAD 80; 9-4 TAD 323; 10-1 TAD 3; 10-2 TAD 163; 10-3 TAD 274; 11-2 TAD 108

Crider, Bill: Nick Crider, Killmaster? (on writing a Nick Carter story) 7 PE 9

Crider, Bill: Paperback Bodies, (sex in paperback cover art), 2-4 PQ 32

Crider, Bill: Paperback Originals, 1-1 PQ 3; (mysteries) 5-1 MR 19

Crider, Bill: Paperback Writers, (of paperback originals), 1-1 PQ 9; (John Faulkner) 1-2 PQ 8; (on collecting) 1-3 PQ 16; (Bruno Fischer) 1-4 PQ 22; (E.Howard Hunt) 2-1 PQ 9; (Mickey Spillane) 2-3 PQ 9; (Michael Avallone) 3-1 PQ 7; (Richard Wormser) 4-1 PQ 31; (William Campbell Gault) 2-2 PQ 5

Crider, Bill: Reprints/Reprints, Ray Bradbury's FAHRENHEIT 451, (in paperback), 3-3 PQ 22

Crider, Bill: See What the Boys in the Backwoods Will Have (and Tell Them I'm Having the Same), (paperback novels, backwoods settings), 2-3 PQ 22

Crider, Bill: Series Synopses, The Headhunters series by John Weisman and Brian Boyer, 11-4 TAD 365

Crider, Bill, and Charlotte Laughlin: Paperback Blurbs, (advertisements on book covers), 4-2 PQ 3

Crider, Bill, and Billy C. Lee: Some Notes on Movie Editions (paperback books), 2-1 PQ 29

Crime After Crime, (mystery news column), by Michael L. Cook, 2 PW 1

Crime and Character, Notes on Rex Stout's Early Fiction, by David R. Anderson, 13-2 TAD 169

(CRIME BUSTERS MAGAZINE), Street & Smith's Crime Busters, (pulp magazine) with index, by Will Murray, 38 X 132

Crime Crossword, (crossword puzzle) by Louis C. Mandes, Jr., 11-1 TAD 100; 11-2 TAD 194; 11-3 TAD 293; 11-4 TAD 397; 12-1 TAD 82; 12-2 TAD 165; 12-4 TAD 382

(CRIME,DETECTIVE,ESPIONAGE,MYSTERY AND THRILLER FICTION & FILM: David & Ann Skene Melvin),The Skene Melvin Bibliography of Critical Writing, (review article), by Walter Albert, 5-3 MF 5

Crime Fiction: Some Varieties of Historical Experience, by Fred Erisman, 1-1 C 1

(Crime Haters series: Gordon Ashe), Checklist, by Robert E. Briney and John Creasey, 2-1 TAD 12

Crime Hunt: Real Life Cases, (The Wallace Case discussed), by T.M. McDade, 14-4 TAD 374

Crime Novel, The, v. The Whodunit, (Julian Symons and Michael Gilbert, comparison of styles) by Rona Randall, 5-6 MR 25

Crime Novels of Harold R. Daniels, The, by George Kelley, 3-4 MF 13

Crime Pays for TV, But Less, by Harry S. Glover, 6/7 LR 10

Crime/Suspebse Fiction of Ray Bradbury, The; A Listing, by William F. Nolan, 4-3 TAD 155

Crime Undercover, (on The Shadow, pulp hero character), by Frank P. Eisgruber, Jr., 4 P 15

Crime With a Smile, (interview with author Joyce Porter), by Luther Norris, 3-2 MR 18

(Crime Writers' Association), Awards 1955-1970, (British organization of crime writers), by Rona Randall, 5-3 MR 28

(Crime Writers' Association), The Birth and Growth of the Crime Writers' Association, (British organization of crime writers) by Rona Randall, 5-3 MR 25

(Crime Writers' Association), 1973 Crime Writers' Association Conference, (report on annual meeting, British organization of crime writers), by Deryck Harvey, 6-4 TAD 255

(Crime Writers' Association), Report on the Crime Writers' Third International Congress, (in Stockholm, 1981), by Iwan Hedman, 5-6 MF 10

(Crime Writers' Association), Stockholm in June, Crime Writers 3rd International Congress, (report), by Edward D. Hoch, 14-4 TAD 323

(Crime Writers' Association), Crime Writers' International Conference, (report, first international), by Daniel P. King, 9-3 TAD 207

(Crime Writers' Congress), announcement of 2nd international meeting, 11-1 TAD 96

("Crimefiles" series), Seven "Crimefiles" of the 1930s: The Purest Puzzles of the Golden Age, (books with actual clues pasted in), by William Reynolds, 1-2 C 42

Criminal Quiz, (quiz), by Richard Emery, 3-5 PP 18

Criminalists, Clergypersons, and Others, Report on Bouchercon 7, (mystery fans and writers convention), by Robert E. Briney, 10-1 TAD 53

Criminous Christmases, (mystery fiction with Christmas theme), by Jane Gottschalk, 13-4 TAD 281

(Crimson Mask), Checklist, detective stories in DETECTIVE NOVELS pulp magazine, by Robert Weinberg, 2 P 21

(Crispin, Edmund), Checklist of Published Writings, by William A.S. Sarjeant, 3-3 PP 9

(Crispin, Edmund), Checklist of Works, by Charles Shibuk, 2-1 MR 15

(Crispin, Edmund), Edmund Crispin, (autobiographical sketch), by Robert Bruce Montgomery, 12-2 TAD 183

(Crispin, Edmund), Edmund Crispin, A Memorial and Appreciation, by William A.S.Sarjeant, 3-3 PP 3

(Crispin, Edmund), In Memorium - Edmund Crispin, by Jacques Barzun, 12-1 TAD 13

(Crispin, Edmund), Is the Detective Story Dead? (recorded dialogues between Julian Symons and Edmund Crispin), by Julian Symons, 4-2 MR 3

(Crispin, Edmund), Obituary, by Julian Symons, 1-5 PP 23

(Crispin, Edmund), Obsequies About Oxford, The Investigations and Eccentricities of Gervase Fen, (detective character of Edmund Crispin), by William A.S.Sarjeant, with bibliography, 14-3 TAD 196

(criticism), Don't Tell Me I Won't Like It, (on literary criticism) by David Marshall Lewis, 12 LR 12

Criticism and the Detective Story (detective fiction as second-class literature), by G.C.Ramsey, 1-3 TAD 90

Critic's Clew, The...to Miss Drew, (discusses various authorships of Nancy Drew series, girls' books) by Kent Winslow, 7 MA 16

Croft, Bill: letter of comment, 14 X 64

(Crofts, Freeman Wills), Checklist of works, by Charles Shibuk, 1-4 MR 14

(Crofts, Freeman Wills), Freeman Wills Crofts 1/6/69 - 4/11/57, obituary, 2-3 TAD 137

(Crofts, Freeman Wills), Freeman Wills
  Crofts, A Checklist, 2-3 TAD 140
(Crook, Arthur, detective: Anthony Gilbert)
  Bowlers, Beer, Bravado and Brains,
  Anthony Gilbert's Arthur Crook,
  by Jane S. Bakerman, 2-4 MF 5
(Crook, Arthur, detective: Anthony Gilbert)
  Lucy Beatrice Malleson, by Estelle
  Fox, 2-6 MR 16
Cropper, Fred: letter of comment, 20 JD 19;
  24 JD 41; 27 JD 34
Cropper, Fred: Limerick, Travis McGee,
  20 JD 18
Cropper, Fred: Waiting for McGee (on
  collecting the Travis McGee books
  by John D. MacDonald), 22 JD 13
Cropper, Michael: letter of comment,
  3-1 AD 7; 3-4 MF 57
Crosby, John: Miss Wonderly, Killer,
  (hardboiled detective stories)
  5-4 MR 8
(Cross, Amanda), The "Amanda Cross" Case,
  Sociologizing the U.S.Academic
  Mystery, (campus locale mystery
  fiction), by J.M.Purcell, 13-1 TAD 36
(Cross, Amanda: Kate Fansler, detective)
  Feminists as Detectives, Harriet
  Vane, Kate Fansler, Sarah Chayse,
  by Kathleen Gregory Klein, 13-1
  TAD 31
Cross, Barry, Jr.: letter of comment,
  3-3 CP 2
(Cross, James), Department of Unknown
  Writers, James Cross, by Marvin
  Lachman, 2-6 PP 17
Cross Trumps, (on Ellery Queen and
  Rex Stout), by J.R.Christopher,
  2-2 QC 6; 1-1 TAD 9(by A.J.Hubin)
(Crossen, Kendell F.), A Partial Index
  to Reviews of Crossen Books, by
  Don Miller, 12 MN A5
(Crossen, Kendell F.) A Selection of
  Reviews of Crossen Books, by Don
  Miller, 12 MN A11
(Crossen, Kendell F,), Excerpts from
  Crossen's Letters, 12 MN A17
(Crossen, Kendell F.), Interview,
  by Steve Lewis, 12 MN A1
(Crossen, Kendell F.), Kendell Foster
  Crossen, A Bibliography, by Don
  Miller, 12 MN B1
(Crossen, Kendell F.) Magazine Reprints
  (of Crossen), by David Bates,
  13 MN O1
(Crossen, Kendell F.), Short Stories
  Checklist, by Dickson Thorpe,
  1-2 MF 6
(Crossen, Kendell F.), Special Issue,
  THE MYSTERK NOOK, June 1979, (#12),
  entire
(Crossen, Kendell F.), Will the Real
  Ken Crossen Please Stand Up, by
  Dickson Thorpe, 1-2 MF 5

(crossword puzzle), A Wolfean
  Double-Cross Tick, (based on
  Nero Wolfe), by Tenby Storm,
  1-2 G 34
(crossword puzzle), Acrostic,
  2-2 M 42
(crossword puzzle), All About Henty,
  (based on G.A.Henty, boys'
  author), by Herb L. Risteen,
  3-1 BC 277
(crossword puzzle), (based on boys'
  books), by Herb L. Risteen,
  1-3 BC 67
(crossword puzzle), Collector's
  Crossword, (based on boys' books)
  by Herb L. Risteen, 2-1 BC 134
(crossword puzzle), Crime Crossword,
  by Louis C, Mandes, Jr., 11-1 TAD
  100; 11-2 TAD 194; 11-3 TAD 293;
  11-4 TAD 397; 12-1 TAD 82; 12-2
  TAD 165; 12-4 TAD 382
(crossword puzzle), Digging for Gold,
  Call About Alger, (based on
  Horatio Alger, Jr.), by Herb L.
  Risteen, 2-3 BC 222
(crossword puzzle), Doublecrossed,
  by Sutherland, 2-5 CP 29
(crossword puzzle), For Travis McGee
  Fans, by Loyal G. Compton, 26 JD 13
(crossword puzzle), (based on juvenile
  books), by Harry K. Hudson, 1-4
  YB 8
(crossword puzzle), The Ken Holt Puzzle,
  (Ken Holt boys' series books),
  3 MA 28
(crossword puzzle), The Maltese Puzzle,
  2-3 M 25
(crossword puzzle), Mystery-Adventure
  Series Puzzle, (based on boys'
  series books), by Kent Winslow,
  7 MA 26
(crossword puzzle), Mystery Crossword,
  by Mrs. Miriam Fibish, 4-3 MR 12
(crossword puzzle), Mystery and Adventure Crossword Puzzle (boys' series
  books), by Kent Winslow, 5 MA 30
(crossword puzzle), The Rick Brant
  Puzzle, (boys' series), 4 MA 28
(crossword puzzle), The Tom Quest
  Cro-sword, (based on Tom Quest
  boys' series books), 2 MA 30
(crossword puzzle), (mystery basis),
  by Marilyn Fibish, 2-1 MR 16
Crossword Puzzle Metaphor and Some
  Crossword Puzzle Mysteries, The,
  by Edward & Karen Lauterbach,
  10-2 TAD 167
Crossword Puzzle Paperback Books,
  Mass Market Murmurings, by Barry
  Bernard, 1-5 CP 12
Crostic Puzzle, (based on Nero Wolfe)
  by Robert Lopresti, 1-2 G 17

Cruickshank, Harold F.: letter of comment, 12 P 4

(Cruickshank, Harold F.), A letter from, (pulp author), 12 P 4

(Cruickshank, Harold F.), A Tribute - Portrait, by Dickson Thorpe, 3 U 18

(Cruickshank, Harold F.), Harold F. Cruickshank, a Memorial, by Wooda Nicholas Carr, 8 DS 2

Crumbs for a Toast to Solar Pons, (verse), by Robert Bloch, 1-2 PDA 42

Crump, Bob: letter of comment, 2-5 TBN 5

(Crump, J. Irving), The Father of Og, (Crump as author of Og series of tales), by Gerry de la Ree, 3 BS 5

Cryptograms, by Dafydd Neal Dyar, 7 U 25

Crystal, Tamar: Which Doorbell Rang? (on Nero Wolfe), 1-1 G 38

Cthulhu Mythos, The, (mythos created by H.P.Lovecraft), by Steve Miller, 3 MT 5

Cuffman, Frank: letter of comment, 3 LW 3; 4 LW 1

Culiver, Mrs. Newell: letter of comment, 1-3 TB 12

Culpepper, Charles: letter of comment, 3-1 CP 2; 3-3 CP 8; 3-4 CP 3; 3-2 PQ 4

Culpepper, Charles: The Temptations of Peggy Gaddis, 3-2 CP 3

Cult of Sherlock Holmes, The, by John Bennett Shaw, 1-2 TAD 53

(Culver, Grace, series: Roswell Brown), Grace Note, by Robert Sampson, 17 X 8

(Culver, Grace, series: Roswell Brown), Notes of a Pulp Collector, (on detective series in THE SHADOW pulp magazine), by G. Alan, 15 BS 14

(Cummings, Ray), Note Thoughts on Ray Cummings, (his works), by Winston Dawson, 30 X 3

Curious Case of the Croyden Crossing, The, (re: Solar Pons), by David Galerstein, 1-1 PDA 18

Curious Route of the Orient Express, The, (re: Solar Pons), by David Galerstein, 3-1 PDA 24

Curlee, Mrs. Arthur: letter of comment, 8 JD 11

Curmudgeon in the Corner, The, by William R. Loeser, 3-2 MF 3; 3-4 MF 16

Current Bits and Pieces, (mystery news), by Allen J. Hubin, 6-2 TAD 112

Current Crime - The American Crime Scene, (mystery news and happenings), by Rona Randall, 5-2 MR 33; 5-4 MR 27; 6-1 MR 37

(CURRENT CRIME), Nigel Morland, Fifty Years of Crime Writing, (editor of CURRENT CRIME), by Pearl G. Aldrich, 13-3 TAD 194

Current Crime - The British Crime Scene, (mystery news and happenings), by Rona Randall, 5-1 MR 29; 5-2 MR 31; 5-3 MR 31

Curtis Books, Checklist, by Dennis Lien, 14 SF 7

Curtis Books, (discussion, paperbacks), by Dennis Lien, 14 SF 5

Curtis, Betty: letter of comment, 10-1 TAD 39; 11-4 TAD 317; 12-2 TAD 186

(Curtiss, Ursula), An Interview with Ursula Curtiss, by Ann Waldron, 4-3 TAD 140

Cushon, Allan: letter of comment, 10-1 TAD 3

Cuthbert, Chester D.: letter of comment, 5 SF 46; 2-1 TB 4

Cuthbert, Jack: Another Side of Harry Stephen Keeler, (with letters written by Keeler), 7-2 TAD 101

Cuthbert, Jack: letter of comment, 7 JD 8; 8 JD 11; 9 JD 15; 10 JD 14; 13 JD 20; 18 JD 29; 21 JD 15; 4-2 MR 15

Cykman, Greg: letter of comment, 1-4 CP 1

Daily Occurance Sheet, The, (fiction), by Paul Bishop, 1-2 M 39

Dahl, Marge: letter of comment, 1-2 TBN

Dahl, Marge: Who was Leslie Quirk? (boys' books author), 2-2 TBN 6

Dahlen, Roald: letter of comment, 2-4 TBN 3

(DAIN CURSE, THE: Dashiell Hammett), The Problem of Moral Vision in Dashiell Hammett's Detective Novels, by George J. Thompson, 7-1 TAD 32

(Dale, Jimmie, series), Jimmie Dale, Pulp Archtype, by Don Hutchison, 22 X 12

("Dallas" TV series), A Settling of Accounts, by Emma Lathen, 9 LR 25

("Dallas" TV series), Heavyweight Contenders, by Collin Wilcox, 9 LR 26

("Dallas" TV series), J.R. Eats Humble Pie, by John D. MacDonald, 9 LR 24

("Dallas" TV series), Mother Knows Best, by P.D.James, 9 LR 22

("Dallas" TV series), One Name on the Contract, by Nan & Ivan Lyons, 9 LR 23

Daly, Carroll John: The Ambulating Lady, (how to write for the pulp magazines), 2-2 C 113

(Daly, Carroll John), A Fatal Attraction, (on the fiction of Daly), by G.A.Finch, 13-2 TAD 112

(Daly, Carroll John), Carroll John Daly, The Forgotten Pioneer of the Private Eye, by William F. Nolan, 4-1 TAD 1

(Daly, Carroll John), Checklist, by
William F. Nolan, 4-1 TAD 4

(Daly, Carroll John), Checklist of
Selected Titles, by Stephen Mertz,
2-3 MF 22

(Daly, Carroll John), In Defense of
Carroll John Daly, by Stephen Mertz,
2-3 MF 19

(Daly, Carroll John: Race Williams
series), "There's No Sex in Crime",
The Two-Fisted Homilies of Race
Williams, pulp detective, by
Michael S. Barson, 2-2 C 103

(Daly, Elizabeth), A Profile of Henry
Gamadge and an Elizabeth Daly
Checklist, (Henry Gamadge a
detective created by Daly), by
Estelle Fox, 4-4 MR 27

(Daly, Elizabeth), Checklist of works,
by Charles Shibuk, 1-6 MR 16

(Daly, Elizabeth), Checklist of works,
by Jim McCahery, 2-1 PP 28

(Daly, Elizabeth), The Golden Years
of Elizabeth Daly, by Ann Waldron,
7-1 TAD 25

(Daly, Elizabeth), Reminiscences of
Cases Past, The Books of Elizabeth
Daly, by Maryell Cleary, 2-1 PP 3;
2-2 PP 3

(Daly, Elizabeth), Whodunit Writer Began
Career at 50, by Estelle Fox,
4-4 MR 25

Dame Agatha's Admirable Addleheads, (on
the characters created by Agatha
Christie), by Mary F. Lindsley,
1-2 PDA 73

(Dame Beatrice: Gladys Mitchell), In
Praise of Gladys Mitchell, by Barry
A. Pike, 9-4 TAD 255

D'Ammassa, Don: letter of comment,
5/6 MN 14; 9 MN L5; 11 MN L14;
4 SF 46

D'Ammassa, Don: Murder for Heyer, (on
the mystery novels of Georgette
Heyer), 13 MN 9

Dan Fortune - Private Eye, (detective
created by Michael Collins), by
John Edwards, 9 SF 38

Dan J. Marlowe, Who Said He Would and He
Did, (on Marlowe and his works, with
checklist), by Kelly Adrian, 3-3
MR 25

(Danberg, Norman), see Norman Daniels

Dancing Girl of Egypt, by Sax Rohmer,
15 R 1

(Daniel, Roland), Roland Daniel, Prolific
Mystery Writer, by W.O.G.Lofts,
6-4 TAD 242

(Daniels, Harold R.), The Crime Novels of
Harold R. Daniels, by George Kelley,
3-4 MF 13

(Daniels, Norman), The Secret Kenneth
Robesons, (on authorship of Doc Savage)
by Will Murray, 2 D 3

(Dannay, Frederic), A Case of Double
Identity, (Dannay and Lee as
Ellery Queen), 3-2 QC 11

(Dannay, Frederic), Frederic Dannay,
Doctor of Humane Letters, (award
by Carrol College), 12-3 TAD 236

(Dannay, Frederic), Fred Dannay and
EQMM (ELLERY QUEEN'S MYSTERY
MAGAZINE), by Eleanor Sullivan,
12-3 TAD 201

Dantean Allusions in "The Trail of
Fu Manchu", by Joe R. Christopher,
5 R 27

Danzoli, C.G.: letter of comment,
11 JD 25

(Dare, Skippy, series), The Hal Keene
and Skippy Dare series, (boys'
books), by Julius R. Chenu,
1-1 BC 12

(DARK CITY, DARK MEN: Cornell Woolrich)
Disposing of a Pair of Ghosts, by
Jacques Barzun, 6-4 TAD 248

Dark Forces at Work, (verse), by
Nicholas Howard, 4-3 AD 7

(Dark, James: Mark Hood, detective),
Rivals of James Bond, No.4: Mark
Hood, (profile and review of
series), by Larry Rickert,
4-5/6 PP 38

Dashiell, Alan: letter of comment,
10 JD 15

(DASHIELL HAMMETT: A CASEBOOK: William
F. Nolan), Hammett, A Reaction
Report (on author's book), by
William F. Nolan, 3-3 TAD 162

(DASHIELL HAMMETT: A DESCRIPTIVE
BIBLIOGRAPHY: Richard Layman)
The Black Mask Boys Go Legit,
by William F. Nolan, 13-1 TAD 23

(DAST Magazine), The History and
Activities of Mystery Fans in
Sweden (and Scandinavia), by
Iwan Hedman, 3-4 MF 12

(DAST Magazine), Iwan Hedman, An
Interview,(Hedman, editor), by
Caleb A. Lewis, 13-2 TAD 166

Dating the Travis McGee Stories,
(establishing time chronology
of John D. MacDonald's books
on Travis McGee), by Dean
Grennell, 22 JD 11

Dating the War of the Worlds,
(establishing time chronology
of events in WAR OF THE WORLDS)
by Dana Martin Batory, 8 U 40

Dat's Mike Ham-muh? (Mickey Spillane's
Mike Hammer in the popular media),
by Max Collins, 12-4 TAD 308

(DAUGHTER OF TIME, THE: Josephine
Tey), Richard III and Josephine
Tey, Partners in Crime, by Guy
M. Townsend, 10-3 TAD 211 (see
rebuttals 10-4 TAD 317; 11-2 TAD
105; 11-3 TAD 237)

Dave Dixon's Strawberry Magic, (A Dixon
    Farm Story); (1926 fiction by Edward
    Edson Lee, later known as Leo Edwards),
    3-5 TB 5; 4-1 TB 2
David (Pudd'nhead) Wilson, The Missing
    Figure in a Detective's Group, (a la
    Mark Twain), by Louise Saylor, 13-1
    TAD 8
(Davidson, Avram), A Bibliography of Avram
    Davidson, by Grant Grant, 9 SF 4
Davidson, Donald S.: letter of comment,
    2 FM 18; 15 X 13
Davidson, Gene, and John Knoerle: Ross
    Macdonald Interview, 1-1 M 5
(Davidson, T.L.), Disposing of a Pair
    of Ghosts, by Jacques Barzun, 6-4
    TAD 248
Davis, Mrs. Allene J.: letter of comment,
    8-2 TAD 153
Davis, Dorothy Salisbury: Robert Fish,
    In Memorium, (memorial tribute to
    Fish), 14-2 TAD 120
(Davis, Dorothy Salisbury), Interview,
    Dorothy Salisbury Davis, by Shelly
    Lewis, 1-2 M 8
Davis, Elizabeth: Treachery, (fiction),
    3-1 M 55
(Davis, Frederick), The Moon Man Stories
    in TEN DETECTIVE ACES, Checklist,
    (pulp magazine detective stories by
    Davis), by Robert Weinberg, 2 P 19
Davis, Hank: Mr. and Mrs. North, and
    Mr. and Mrs. Lockridge, (the North
    mystery novels by Frances and
    Richard Lockridge), 1-1 MF 21
(Davis, Harold A.), The Secret Kenneth
    Robesons, (authorship of Doc Savage
    stories by other than Robeson), by
    Will Murray, 2 D 3
Davis, Jada: letter of comment, 1-3 PQ 7
(Davis, Jada), A PQ Interview with Jada
    Davis (interview by PAPERBACK
    QUARTERLY), 1-2 PQ 45
(Davis, Martha Wirt: THE PROFESSOR KNITS
    A SHROUD), The Adventure of the
    Purloined Red Herring, by Edward
    Lauterbach, 3-5 PP 3
(Davis, Mildred), An Unknown Mystery
    Writer Revisited, Mildred Davis,
    by Marvin Lachman, 3-5 PP 12
(Davis, Mildred), Checklist of works,
    by Marvin Lachman, 2-5 PP 16
(Davis, Mildred), Department of Unknown
    Mystery Writers, Mildred Davis, by
    Marvin Lachman, 2-5 PP 16
(Davis, Mildred), Mildred Davis Revisited,
    by Marvin Lachman, 3-6 PP 12
Davis, Monte: letter of comment, 6 JD 11
Davis, Phil: letter of comment, 27 JD 35
Davis, Richard: letter of comment,
    1-1 AD 2
(Davison, Gilderoy: Colonel Royston &
    Peter Castle series), Checklist,
    annotated, by Barry Van Tilburg,
    5-3 MF 20

(DAW books), A PQ Interview with Donald
    A Wolheim, (PAPERBACK QUARTERLY
    interviews founder of DAW paperback
    books), 1-3 PQ 23
(DAW books), Collecting Thoughts, (on
    science fiction paperbacks published
    by DAW), by Ron Tatar, 2-4 CP 9
(Dawlish, Patrick, series: John Creasey
    as Gordon Ashe), Checklist, by Robert
    E. Briney and John Creasey, 2-1 TAD 11
Dawson, Harry D.: The Fathers and Sons
    of John LeCarre, (espionage fiction),
    5-3 MF 15
Dawson, Harry D.: John LeCarre's Circus,
    (espionage fiction), 13-2 TAD 150
Dawson, Harry D., and R. Jeff Banks:
    Checklist, The Len Deighton series,
    annotated, (espionage fiction),
    3-1 MF 12
Dawson, Harry D., and R. Jeff Banks:
    Checklist, The Quiller novels of
    Adam Hall, annotated, (espionage
    fiction), 4-1 MF 8
Dawson, Harry D., and R. Jeff Banks:
    Checklist, Spy Novels, John LeCarre,
    annotated, 2-5 MF 22
Dawson, Harry D., and R. Jeff Banks:
    LeCarre's Spy Novels, (discussion),
    2-5 MF 22
Dawson, Harry D., and R. Jeff Banks:
    The Len Deighton Series, (discussion,
    espionage novels), 3-1 MF 10
Dawson, Harry D., and R. Jeff Banks:
    The Quiller Report, (Quiller spy
    novels by ADam Hall), 4-1 MF 8
Dawson, Winston: letter of comment,
    22 X 49
Dawson, Winston: Some Thoughts on Ray
    Cummings, 30 X 3
Day, Bruce: letter of comment, 5 DS 6;
    12 DS 6
Day, Charles C.: letter of comment,
    11 R 24
(Day, Julian, series: Dennis Wheatley),
    Checklist, by Iwan Hedman, 2-4 TAD
    236
(DAY OF THE JACKAL, THE: Frederick
    Forsyth), Stalking Forsyth's Jackal,
    7-3 TAD 165
D.E.Ath Suggests, (reviews, mystery),
    2-1 PP 14; 2-2 PP 14; 2-4 PP 28
(DEAD HAND, THE: R. Austin Freeman)
    The Dead Hand...and How It Grew,
    (notes on formulation of story),
    by Norman Donaldson, 7 TF 18
Dead of Winter Views, (on Murder Ink
    Bookstore weekend at Mohonk Mountain
    House), by Jane Merrill Filstrup,
    10-3 TAD 235
Deadlier Than the Male, (female villains
    in Operator 5 pulp magazine stories),
    by Wooda Nicholas Carr, 11 P 3
(Dean, Graham M.: Agent Nine series),
    A "G" Man Series (juvenile), by
    Robert L. George, 1-3 YB 3

(Dean, Spencer: Don Cadee series), Series Synopses, by John Vining, 9-2 TAD 113

DeAndrea, William L.: Paper Crimes, (reviews of paperback mystery books), 14-3 TAD 265; 14-4 TAD 378

(Deane, Norman: Bruce Murdoch series), Checklist, by Robert E. Briney and John Creasey, 2-1 TAD 12

(Deane, Norman: Liberator series), Checklist, by Robert E. Briney and John Creasey, 2-1 TAD 13

Dear Me, Mr. Van Dine, (on S.S.Van Dine and his mystery works), by Robert A.W.Lowndes, 7-1 TAD 30

Death and JDM, (treatment of death in the John D. MacDonald stories), by June M. Moffatt, 5 JD 3

Death Flies in Silver Circles, (fiction, Doc Savage pastiche), by John Boehm and Mark Justice, 1 MB 7

Death in the Skies, (on aviation pulp magazines), by Robert Weinberg, 4 P 20

Death Inside the Cow: A Few Notes on the Novels of Lee Thayer, by Francis M. Nevins, Jr., 5-3 TAD 151

Death of a "John Dee" Fan, (on the acceptance of violence in the John D. MacDonald novels), by Dave Stewart, 17 JD 5

Death of a Magazine, (THE SAINT Mystery Magazine), by Allen J. Hubin, 1-2 TAD 47

DEATH OF A .300 HITTER, Another Chapter from, by Mike Avallone, 1-1 MF 3; 1-2 MF 11

DEATH OF A .300 HITTER, Two Short Chapters from, by Mike Avallone, 1A MF 11

Death to the Avenger, (fiction), by Kenneth Robeson, 8 P 16

Death Wears a Necktie, (fiction), by John Knoerle, 2-1 M 55

(Death), When is This Stiff Dead?, (definitions of death, and the detective story), by R. Jeff Banks and Leslie M. Thompson, 2-6 MF 11

Debunking the Legends, (on Frederick Faust), by William J. Clark, 1-2 FC 8

deCamp, L. Sprague: H.P.Lovecraft and Edmund Wilson, (discussion of authors), 1 FM 5

deCamp, L. Sprague: letter of comment, 13 X 59

deCamp, L. Sprague: Young Man Lovecraft, (H.P.Lovecraft as a young man), 18 X 8

(deCamp, L.Sprague and Catherine), A Conversation with the de Camps, (interview), by Charlotte Laughlin, 1-1 PQ 16

deCaro, F.A.:letter of comment, 8-4 TAD 323

Decline and Fall of the Detective Story, (excerpt from essay), by W. Somerset Maugham, 1-5 MR 7

(Decolta, Ramon), Checklist of Stories in BLACK MASK magazine, by E.R. Hagemann, 14-1 TAD 8

(Decolta, Ramon), Ramon DeColta aka Raoul Whitfield, and His Diminutive Brown Man, Jo Gar, The Island Detective, by E.R.Hagemann, 14-1 TAD 3

(DECOY: Michael Morgan), The Worst Mystery Novel of All Time, by Bill Pronzini, 13-2 TAD 137

Dedication and Tribute, (to John Creasey), by Allen J. Hubin, 6-4 TAD 209

Dedications: A Detective Story Quiz, (quiz), by Jon L. Breen, 1-2 TAD 59

Dedications in Leo's Books, (in books of Leo Edwards; boys' books), by Julius R. Chenu, 1-4 TB 3

Deeck, William: letter of comment, 4-1 TAD 60

Deems, Paul: Tom Swift and the Great Nostalgia, (appeal of the Tom Swift boys' books), 4-1 BC 386

(Deer Lodge series), Boys' Series Bibliography, by Harry K. Hudson, 1-3 YB 10

(Deering Deal series), Boys' Series Bibliography, by Harry K. Hudson, 1-3 YB 10

Defective Detectives, The, (detective characters with "defects" from the pulp magazines), by Bob Jones, 2-4 MR 7; 68 PU 21

(definitions), Living With a Paperback Book Collector, (paperback book terms for a collector), by M.Kirklin, 1-5 CP 18

Degeneration of Donald Hamilton, The, (his books), by George Kelley, 1-6 MF 11

(deGrandin, Jules, series), Jules deGrandin Returns, by Robert Weinberg, 18 X 33

(deGrandin, Jules, series), The Very Much So Clever Fellow, by Robert Sampson, 5 WT 3

(Deighton, Len), Checklist, annotated, by R. Jeff Banks and Harry D.Dawson, 3-1 MF 12

(Deighton, Len), LeCarre, Deighton, Hall and the Screen's Tired Spies (spy fiction on screen), by Jack Edmund Nolan, 4-1 MR 23

(Deighton, Len), The Len Deighton Series, by R. Jeff Banks and Harry D. Dawson, 3-1 MF 10

(Deighton, Len), Romantic Reality in the Spy Stories of Len Deighton, by Fred Erisman, 10-2 TAD 101

(Deighton, Len: unnamed series character),
Checklist, annotated, by Barry Van
Tilburg, 4-3 MF 24

(de la Bath, Hubert Bonisseur series: Jean
Bruce), Checklist, by Barry Van Tilburg,
4-2 MF 13

de la Ree, Gerry: The Collecting Mania,
20 X 6

de la Ree, Gerry: The Father of Og,
(J. Irving Crump, author of the
Og books), 3 BS 5

de la Ree, Gerry: letter of comment,
2 BS 3; 8 X 38; 15 X 13; 24 X 46;
26 X 76

de la Torre, Lillian: letter of comment,
12-4 TAD 355

de la Torre, Lillian: The Pleasures of
Histo-Detection, (writing historical
mysteries), 7-3 TAD 155

(de la Torre, Lillian), Lillian de la
Torre, Preliminary Bibliography:
Blood on the Periwigs, by James Mark
Purcell, 4-5 MR 25

(Dell Books), Murder Ink and Scene of the
Crime books series announced, 16 CD 1

Dell Dimers, on Dell paperback 10¢ books),
by M.C.Hill, 2-2 PQ 14

Dell Great Mystery Library, (paperback
series), Checklist, by Robert E. Briney,
7 MN 4

(Dell Great Mystery Library), Rare Books
are Getting Scarce, by Bruce Taylor,
3-1 CP 23

(Dell Map-back series), Agatha Christie
in the Mapbacks, (paperback series),
by William Lyles, 3-3 PQ 26

(Dell Map-back series), Rex Stout in the
Dell Mapbacks, (paperback series),
by William Lyles, 2-4 PQ 14

(Dell Map-back series), Checklist,
Nos. 1-300, by Richard C. Butler,
1-2 MF 17

Dell Mysteries: Murder Ink and Scene of
the Crime, (paperback mystery series
by Dell Pub. Co.), by Charlotte
Laughlin, 3-4 PQ 13

(Dell paperbacks), Alfred Hitchcock, in
Dell Paperbacks, by Billy C. Lee and
Charlotte Laughlin, 3-1 PQ 23

(Dell paperbacks), "Map Back" Checklist
Nos. 1-300, by Richard C. Butler,
1-2 MF 17

(Dell paperbacks), Keyhole Confidential,
(on early paperbacks of Dell Pub.Co.)
by William Lyles, 2-4 CP 13

(Dell paperbacks), Dell 1st series,
1st editions, checklist, by William
Lyles, 1-5 CP 26; 1-6 CP 17

(Dell paperbacks), Dell Paperback
Variant Editions, in Keyhole Confidential, by William Lyles, 3-2 CP 10

(Dell paperbacks), Checklist, Dell 10¢
paperbacks, by M.C.Hill, 2-2 PQ 15

(Dell paperbacks), Checklist, Dell 10¢
paperbacks, by Steve Lewis, 5 MY 6;
6 MY 7

Delpino, Louis: letter of comment,
6-2 MR 15

Demarest, Michael: JDM BIBLIOPHILE,
(review in TIME magazine), 25 JD 14

DeMarr, Mary Jean: Kay Cleaver Strahan,
A Forgotten Detective Novelist,
2-1 C 53

DeMarr, Mary Jean: Three Gentle Men,
Doris Miles Disney's Continuing
Detectives, 3-3 MF 5

Demchko, Ed: A Report on Bouchercon IV,
(mystery fans and writers convention)
6-2 MR 34

(DEMOLISHED MAN, THE: Alfred Bester)
Mystery Plus: The Demolished Man,
by R. Jeff Banks, 1-2 PP 13

Demon in a Lunchbox, An Appreciation of
Horror Fiction, by Chelsea Quinn
Yarbro, 2-2 M 43

Denaro, Debbie: Cliff Edge Memory,
(verse), 3-6 MR 5

Denholm, William J., III: A Lancer
Science Fiction Checklist, (paper-
back books, including Lodestone &
Magnum paperbacks), 10 SF 4

Denholm, William J., III: Denholm's
Law, (column on various aspects of
paperback books and collecting),
No.1, (paperback books) 1-2 CP 25
No.2, (McGinnis' artwork on paper-
back book covers), 1-3 CP 11
No.3, (Lodestone and Lancer Books
checklists; Standard Book Numbers;
Ace Books), 1-4 CP 15
No.4, (more, McGinnis' art), 1-5
CP 23
No.5, (Popular Library cover art),
2-1 CP 25

Denholm, William J., III: Lancer Books,
Checklist, 1-2 CP 26

Denholm, William J., III: Lancer science-
fiction paperbacks, artists checklist,
10 SF 25

Denholm, William J., III: letter of
comment, 1-2 PQ 6; 1-4 CP 1; 2-1 CP 3;
14 SF 47

Denholm, William J., III: We Can All Be
Joe Friday, (identifying paperback
books cover art), 1-6 CP 14

Denise is on the Phone, (fiction), by
Michael Avallone, 8 U 100

Denison, Mary Ann: letter of comment,
27 JD 34

(Dennis, Ralph: Hardman series), Have
You Met Hardman? (discussion of
series), by G.A.Finch, 8-4 TAD 275

Dennis Wheatley: A Biographical Sketch
and Bibliography, by Iwan Hedman,
2-4 TAD 227

Dent, Lester: Incidentals 9, (Dent as guest columnist, pulp reminiscences) 3-5 CP 23

Dent, Lester: The Pulp Paper Master Fiction Plot, (formula for writing pulp fiction), 12 BS 15

(Dent, Lester), Dent's Detectives, (in pulp and subsequent fiction), by Will Murray, 1 D 8

(Dent, Lester), Doc Savage's Creator, Lester Dent, (personal reminiscences), by Billy G. Smith, 2 BS 6

(Dent, Lester), InciDENTals, (various facets on Lester Dent and Doc Savage), by Will Murray, 2-2 CP 30; 2-3 CP 12; 2-4 CP 21; 2-5 CP 9; 3-1 CP 21; 3-2 CP 7; 3-3 CP 17; 3-4 CP 13

(Dent, Lester), Kenneth Robeson's Alter Egos, (on Doc Savage novels written by other than Lester Dent), by Fred S. Cook, 2 BS 14

(Dent, Lester), Lester Dent, by Frank Gruber, 2-4 TAD 215

(Dent, Lester), Lester Dent, Adventurer, (commentary), 1 BSA 21

(Dent, Lester), Lester Dent, The Last of the Joe Shaw's BLACK MASK Boys, (Dent in pulp magazine BLACK MASK), by Will Murray, 2-2 C 128

(Dent, Lester), The Man of Bronze - and His Creator, (Lester Dent, and Doc Savage), by Samuel W. Pitts, 2 BS 8

(Dent, Lester), The Secret Kenneth Robesons, (authors writing the Doc Savage novels under the name Robeson) by Will Murray, 2 D 3

(Dent, Lester), Some Unusual Facts About Lester Dent, by Frank Lewandowski, 1 DS 6

(Dent, Lester), Who is Doc Savage?, (on Doc Savage and his authors), by Frank Lewandowski, 1 DS 3

(Dent, Lester: Oscar Sail series), The Man from Miami - Lester Dent's Oscar Sail, (detective pulp character), by Fred Blosser, 5-2 TAD 93

(Dent, Mrs. Lester), A Visit with "Mrs. Doc Savage", by Bill Smith, 6 BS 3

Dent, Mrs. Norma: letter of comment, 6 DS 7; 8 BS 4; 7 DQ 3

Dent's Detectives, (Lester Dent's detective characters in pulp and subsequent fiction), by Will Murray, 1 D 8

Denton, Frank: letter of comment, 5 LR 5; 6/7 LR 25; 2-2 PP 37

DePaolo, Rosemary: From Howtoits to Whodunits, Jane Austen to Agatha Christie, (exploration of background locales and settings), 2-2 C 8

(Department of Dead End series: Roy Vickers), An Open-Ended Search for Dead Ends, by Howard Waterhouse, 1-3 PP 7

Department of Unmitigated Mishmosh, (on Mike Hammer and Mickey Spillane), by Francis M. Nevins, Jr., 3-1 MR 21

Department of Unknown Mystery Writers, (biog. and literary sketch), by Marvin Lachman,
William Krasner, 1-2 PP 11
A.E.Martin, 1-3 PP 11
Julian F. Thompson, Linda Villesvik, Sidney Rowland, Howard F. Aldridge, Hughes Allison, 1-4 PP 15
Frederick Ayer, Jr., 1-5 PP 17
Thomas Walsh, 2-1 PP 15
John Franklin Campbell, 2-3 PP 22
L.A.G.Strong, 2-4 PP 13
Mildred Davis, 2-5 PP 16
James Cross, 2-6 PP 17
Pat Stadley, 3-1 PP 23
Peter Godfrey, 3-2 PP 13
James O'Hanlon, 3-3 PP 15
Roy Huggins, 3-4 PP 20
Donald McNutt Douglass, 3-6 PP 11
Samm Sinclair Baker, 4-1 PP 17
Babette Rosmond, 4-2 PP 19
Ernest Savage, 4-4 PP 11
(Ernest Savage Responds), 4 5/6 PP 33

Department of Unrelated Miscellanea, (various facets on mystery fiction and authors), by Francis M. Nevins, Jr., (Ian Fleming, Harry Stephen Keeler, Brett Halliday) 4-1 MR 21; 4-3 MR 28; 4-5 MR 18; 5-2 MR 28

Department of Unreprinted Masterworks, (mystery fiction), by Francis M. Nevins, Jr., 2-2 MR 12; 2-4 MR 14; 2-5 MR 14

(Department Z series: John Creasey), Checklist, by Robert E. Briney and John Creasey, 2-1 TAD 9

(DeRichleau, Duke, series: Dennis Wheatley), Checklist, by Iwan Hedman, 2-4 TAD 235

Derleth, August: More from Dr. Parker's Notebooks, (Solar Pons), 1-2 PDA 43

Derleth, August: Some Further Jottings from the Notebooks of Dr. Lyndon Parker, (Solar Pons), 1-1 PDA 3

Derleth, August: Weird Tales, A Memoir, (recalls WEIRD TALES pulp magazine) 60 PU 7

Derleth and the Morel Season, (reminiscences, of August Derleth), by Bill Dutch, 2 3/4 AD 9

Derleth As I Knew Him, (August Derleth), by Ramsey Campbell, 1-1 AD 4; 1-3 AD 4; 1-4 AD 5; 2-1 AD 8

Derleth Connection, The, Joseph Payne Brennan in Brief, an Autobiography, by Joseph Payne Brennan, 2-1 AD 6

Derleth Connection, The, Frank Belknap Long, (Introduction by Long), 2-2 AD 3

Derleth Connection, The, Edna Meudt,
    by Edna Meudt, 2 3/4 AD 6
Derleth Connection, The, Robert Bloch,
    by Richard H. Fawcett with intro-
    duction by Bloch, 3-1 AD 3
Derleth Connection, The; I Remember
    Moskowitz, by Sam Moskowitz, 3-2
    AD 6; 3-3 AD 3
Derleth Connection, The, E. Hoffman
    Price, 3-4 AD 10; 4-1 AD 8
Derleth Connection, The, Manly Wade
    Wellman, 4-1 AD 4
Derleth Connection, The, Carl Jacobi,
    by Carl Jacobi, 4-4 AD 3
Derleth Difference, The, (on August
    Derleth and his Arkham House,
    Publishers), by Steve Eng, 4-4
    AD 12
Derleth Legend, The, by Bill Dutch,
    3-1 AD 9
Derleth on Art, by Bill Dutch, 3-3 AD 7
Derleth on Education, by Bill Dutch,
    3-4 AD 12; 4-1 AD 11; 4-2 AD 4
Derleth/Sister Anaclete Letters, The,
    (correspondence by August Derleth
    with Sister Anaclete), 2-2 AD 5;
    2-3/4 AD 3
(Derleth, August), A.D., (thoughts and
    comments), by Frederick Shroyer,
    2-1 PDA 7; 3-3 AD 1
(Derleth, August), A Derleth Tribute,
    by Mary Elizabeth Counselman,
    1-4 AD 1
(Derleth, August), A Double Memorial,
    (memorial tribute, by (1) A.E.Van
    Vogt, and (2) Colin Wilson,
    2-1 PDA 3
(Derleth, August), A Flat in Paddington,
    (verse, re: Solar Pons and Praed
    Street), by Steve Eng, 3-3 AD 3
(Derleth, August), A List of August
    Derleth's Works in Print, 1-1 AD 2
(Derleth, August), A Visit with August
    Derleth, (recalled), by John Davenport
    Dixon, 4-1 AD 1
(Derleth, August), The Adventures of the
    Pastiche Craftsman, (Derleth writing
    the Solar Pons stories), by A.E.Van
    Vogt, 2-1 PD 1
(Derleth, August), Arkham House and Its
    Eldritch English Visitants (Arkham
    House, Publishers), by Malcolm M.
    Ferguson, 3-1 AD 1
(Derleth, August), Augie vs. The United
    States Post Office, by Bill Dutch,
    2-2 AD 10
(Derleth, August), August Derleth (in
    1936), by Raymond Palmer, 2 WT 12
(Derleth, August), August Derleth, A
    Giant Remembered, by Basil Copper,
    1-2 AD 1
(Derleth, August), August Derleth Award
    Given to Frances Hamerstrom, 5-1 AD 7

(Derleth, August), August Derleth,
    Biographical, Personal, Biblio-
    graphical, (notes by Derleth
    written 1941), 5-1 AD 1
(Derleth, August), August Derleth
    on Literature, Summary of a
    Correspondence, by Harry James
    Cargas, 2-3/4 AD 1
(Derleth, August), August Derleth,
    Pre-Romantic, by Frederick Shroyer,
    1-2 PDA 49
(Derleth, August), August Derleth
    Society, Activities of Members,
    3-4 AD 6; 4-1 AD 13; 4-3 AD 10
(Derleth, August), August Derleth
    Stamp, (proposed), 4-4 AD 10
(Derleth, August), August Derleth's
    Reply to "The Sac of Fortune" of
    Sinclair Lewis, 4-3 AD 4
(Derleth, August), August Derleth's
    Wisconsin Dairy, (on weekly news-
    paper column), by Bill Dutch,
    4-4 AD 7
(Derleth, August), Bibliography of
    the Works of August Derleth
    (list of corrections), by Bill
    Dutch, 4-4 AD 11
(Derleth, August), Brian Lumley Talks
    About August Derleth, by Brian
    Lumley, 2-2 AD 1
(Derleth, August), Chart of Derleth's
    "First Spring Sightings" 1936-65,
    5-1 AD 8
(Derleth, August), Comic Strips (on
    Derleth collecting comic strips),
    3-4 AD 8
(Derleth, August), Derleth and the
    Morel Season, by Bill Dutch,
    2-3/4 AD 9
(Derleth, August), Derleth As I Knew
    Him, by Ramsey Campbell, 1-1 AD 4;
    1-3 AD 4; 1-4 AD 5; 2-1 AD 8
(Derleth, August), The Derleth
    Connection, (relationships and
    reminiscences by various authors),
    Joseph Payne Brennan, 2-1 AD 6
    Frank Belknap Long, 2-2 AD 3
    Edna Meudt, 2-3/4 AD 6
    Robert Bloch, (by Richard H.Fawcett),
        3-1 AD 3
    Sam Moskowitz, 3-2 AD 6; 3-3 AD 3
    E. Hoffman Price, 3-4 AD 10;
        4-1 AD 8
    Manly Wade Wellman, 4-1 AD 4
    Carl Jacobi, 4-4 AD 4
(Derleth, August), The Derleth Differ-
    ence, (on Derleth and his Arkham
    House, Publishers), by Steve Eng,
    4-4 AD 12
(Derleth, August), The Derleth Legend,
    by Bill Dutch, 3-1 AD 9
(Derleth, August), Derleth on Art, by
    Bill Dutch, 3-3 AD 7

(Derleth, August), Derleth on Education,
by Bill Dutch, 3-4 AD 12; 4-1 AD 11;
4-2 AD 4

(Derleth, August), The Derleth/Sister
Anaclete Letters, (correspondence
between Derleth and Sister Anaclete)
2-2 AD 5; 2-3/4 AD 3

(Derleth, August), Derleth Writes Own
Review of THE HOUSE ON THE MOUND,
1958, 1-2 AD 7

(Derleth, August) Derleth's "Wisconsin
Diary", by Bill Dutch, 1-4 AD 5

(Derleth, August), "D'Erlette", (verse),
by Brian Lumley, 1-1 AD 4

(Derleth, August), Elegy for August
Derleth, (verse), by T.V.Olsen,
2-3/4 AD 8

(Derleth, August), Hello Wisconsin,
(reminiscences), by Miles McMillin,
1-4 AD 3

(Derleth, August), In Re: August Derleth,
by William Wingfield, 3-2 PDA 16

(Derleth, August), In Re: August Derleth,
A Tribute, by Malcolm Ferguson,
1-3 AD 7

(Derleth, August), In Re: Judge Peck,
(discusses detective character
created by Derleth), by George J.
Marx, 1-1 PDA 24

(Derleth, August), Letter to August
Derleth, (verse), by Jesse Stuart,
2-1 AD 1

(Derleth, August), Life in One Small
American Town, (with Derleth),
2-3/4 AD 4

(Derleth, August), Microcosm, (verse),
by Steve Eng, 2-1 AD 3

(Derleth, August), My Auctorial Friend,
August Derleth, by George J. Marx,
1-1 PD 4

(Derleth, August), My Homily, August
Derleth, (verse), 2-3/4 AD 10

(Derleth, August), On Keeping a Journal
(after reading VILLAGE YEAR by
Derleth), (verse), by Steve Eng,
2-1 AD 12

(Derleth, August), Photo Article,
2-1 AD 10

(Derleth, August), Posthumous Citation
to Derleth by Wisconsin Academy of
Science,Arts and Letters (April
1981), 4-4 AD 1

(Derleth, August), Praed Street, East
of the Sun and West of the Moon,
(on Derleth's Solar Pons), by
Frederick Shroyer, 3-2 AD 1

(Derleth, August), The Praed Street
Irregulars, (Solar Pons), 1-2 MR 7

(Derleth, August), Readers in Search
of an Author, (visit to home of
Derleth), by Leonard Cochran,
1-3 PD 1

(Derleth, August), Recommended Reading
(Derleth's works), 1-2 AD 7

(Derleth, August), Reminiscences,
by Bill Dutch, 2-1 AD 4

(Derleth, August), Reminiscences and
a Caution, by E. Hoffman Price,
2-3/4 AD 11

(Derleth, August), Return to Place of
Hawks, (verse, re: Derleth), by
Edna Meudt, 2-3/4 AD 8

(Derleth, August), The Sac of Fortune,
4-2 AD 1

(Derleth, August), Sac Prairie Looked
the Same (But August Derleth
Wasn't There), by Norbert Blei,
3-4 AD 1

(Derleth, August), Sac Prairie People,
(verse), by Steve Eng, 2-3/4 AD 8

(Derleth, August), Sauk Prairie -
First Impressions, 2-1 AD 3

(Derleth, August), Self-Appraisal,
(best books), 1-4 AD 6

(Derleth, August), Some Thoughts on
the Future of the August Derleth
Society Newsletter, by Richard H.
Fawcett, 2-2 AD 9

(Derleth, August), Stories Filmed for
TV, 1-3 AD 2

(Derleth, August), To August Derleth,
by Gahan Wilson, 3-1 AD 7

(Derleth, August), Toward October 10th,
August Derleth Festival Plans,
(1981), 4-4 AD 1; 4-4 AD 3

(Derleth, August), The Unpublished
Derleths, (discussion of titles
mentioned by Derleth but not
published), 5-1 AD 6

(Derleth, August), The Wood Engraver
from Mazomanie, (on Frank Utpatel
and his work for Arkham House), by
Kay Price, 4-3 AD 1

(Derleth, August), Works in Progress,
(on Derleth) by various authors,
1-3 AD 5

(Derleth, August: THE HOUSE ON THE
MOUND), Derleth Writes Own Review,
(1958), 1-2 AD 7

(Derleth, August: Mill Creek Irregulars
series), Boys' Series Bibliographies
by Harry K. Hudson, 1-6 YB 16

(Derleth, August: MOON TENDERS), The
Boy Scouts in Old Udolpho, (on a
boys' book by Derleth), by Frederick
Shroyer, 2-2 PDA 43

(Derleth, August: WALDEN WEST), Walden
West as Viewed Through an Eastern
Window, 1-3 AD 6

(Derleth, August, Society), August
Derleth Society of Wisconsin, A
Milestone, 1-3 AD 1

(Derleth, August, Society), August Derleth
Society, Activities of Members,
3-4 AD 6; 4-1 AD 13; 4-3 AD 10

(Derleth, August, Society, Charter
Members, 1-1 AD 3; 1-2 AD 6; 1-3 AD 8;
1-4 AD 10

(Derleth, August, Society), Meeting Report, (April 1980), 3-4 AD 7; July 1980) 4-1 AD 3; (October 1980) 4-3 AD 8

(Derleth, August, Society), The Society is Born, 1-1 AD 1

Derleth, Mrs Rosella, obituary, 3-1 AD 12

D'Erlette, (verse, re: August Derleth), by Brian Lumley, 1-1 AD 4

Derry, Charles F.: letter of comment, 1-3 BC 85

DeSimone, Desi: letter of comment, 6 MA 29

DeSimone, R.A.: letter of comment, 5 X 41

deSoto, Rafael: letter of comment, 6 P 30

Destiny of the House, The, (on "The Specialty of the House" by Ellin), by Stanley Ellin, 12-3 TAD 195

Destroy Secret Agent X, (on pulp hero character), by Tom Johnson, 9 P 3

(Destroyer series: Warren Murphy & Richard Sapir), Created, The Destroyer, An Interview with Warren Murphy, 11-3 TAD 284

Destry and Dionysus, (literary essay on Frederick Faust), by Martha Bacon, 2-2 FC 1

Detecting the Sponsors, (mystery quiz), by R. Jeff Banks, 12-2 TAD 190

Detection Among the Mountains, The Writings of Glyn Carr, by William A.S.Sarjeant, 4-5/6 PP 3

(Detection Club), Exclusive! The Detection Club's First Collaborations, Unpublished Christie and Others, by Paul R. Moy, with checklist, 4-5/6 PP 15

Detection in the Guilt-Age, (rational premise in the crime fiction), by J. Randolph Cox, 8-1 TAD 111

Detective as Both Tortoise and Achilles, The: Archer Gets the Feel of the Case in THE CHILL (of Ross Macdonald), by William W. Combs, 2-1 C 98

(Detective Book Club), The Detective Book Club, An Alphabetical Listing by Author, by Michael L. Cook, 10 MN I1

(Detective Book Club), An Old Friend, The Detective Book Club, by Michael L. Cook, 8-2 TAD 77

(Detective Book Club), The Detective Book Club, Checklist, in order of Publication, by Michael L. Cook, 10 MN I21

(Detective Book Club), Complete Checklist, by Michael L. Cook, 8-2 TAD 79

(Detective Book Club), The Detective Book Club, Supplement to Checklist in TAD 8:1, by Michael L. Cook, 9 MN I1

(Detective Book Club), Murder by Mail, Update (bibliographical listing of books published by the book clubs May 1979-August 1981), by Michael L. Cook, 4-5/6 PP 51

Detective Fiction, (general essay), by W.B.Stevenson, 1A MR 3; 1-1 MR 9

Detective Fiction and Ernest Hemingway, by S. Carl Linn, 1-1 MR 3

Detective Fiction and Social Realism, H.R.F.Keating's India, by Meera T. Clark, 2-1 C 1

Detective Fiction and the Turf, (on horse racing backgrounds and settings), by Jon L. Breen, 5-1 TAD 24

Detective Fiction and Things Shakespearean, (Shakespeare associations in mystery novels), by Jane Gottschalk, 14-2 TAD 100

Detective Fiction in Sweden, by K. Arne Blom and Jan Broberg, 9-4 TAD 272

Detective Fiction in the Wade Collection, (at Wheaton College), by Joe R. Christopher, 9-4 TAD 274

(DETECTIVE FICTION WEEKLY), Hoh-Hoh to Satan, DETECTIVE FICTION WEEKLY'S Nutty Series Heroes of the 1930's, (unconventional detectives in the pulps), by Bernard A. Drew, 2-2 C 88

Detective Literature of the Americas, The, (mystery fiction in Latin America), by Donald A. Yates, 4-1 TAD 5

Detective Novels of Carolyn Wells, The, (chronological bibliography), by Jon L. Breen, 3-2 TAD 78

Detective Novels of Ronald A. Knox, The, by William Reynolds, 14-3 TAD 275

(DETECTIVE NOVELS Magazine), A Snappy Hero, Jerry Wade, with checklist of Jerry Wade and The Crimson Mask stories), by Robert Weinberg, 2 P 20

Detective Pulp Stories of John D. MacDonald, (list and synopsis), by Len & June Moffatt, 6 JD 15

Detective Short Story Quiz, (quiz), by R.W.Hays, 3-1 TAD 11

Detective Story Aspects of the Nouveau Roman, (search for meaning), by Erica M. Eisinger, 12-4 TAD 362

(detective story), Recent European Works on the Detective Story, by E.F.Bleiler, 2-3 MF 23

Detective Story, The - Its Study and Appreciation, by J. Randolph Cox, 4-4 MR 3; 4-5 MR 19

120

(DETECTIVE STORY MAGAZINE), More Mystery for a Dime, Street & Smith and the First Detective Story Magazine, by J. Randolph Cox, 2-2 C 52

Detective Story, The: Pertinent?, (a commentary on Joan L. Mooney's "Best Selling American Detective Fiction"), by Bruce L. Monblatt, 4-3 TAD 170

(DETECTIVE STORY CORNERSTONES: Haycraft-Queen), In the Wake of Haycraft-Queen, (possible additions to basic list), by Norman Donaldson, 5-3 TAD 137

(DETECTIVE, OR THE SECRETS OF A PRIVATE ENQUIRY OFFICE, FROM ORIGINAL SOURCES, THE: by an Ex-Detective), Try to Find It, by E.F.Bleiler, 6-2 TAD 97

(DETECTIVE'S ALBUM, TALES OF THE AUSTRALIAN POLICE: by W.W.), Try to Find It, by E.F.Bleiler, 6-2 TAD 97

Detectives and Geology, (geological clues used in mystery fiction), by William A.S.Sarjeant, 11-3 TAD 294

Detectives in Disguise, (quiz), by Veronica M.S.Kennedy, 4-2 TAD 103; 9-1 TAD 6

Dettman, Bruce: In the Master's Footsteps, (Solar Pons), 1-2 PD 1

Dettman, Bruce: letter of comment, 2-2 TAD 127

Dettman, Bruce: The Most Dangerous Man in Europe, (on early stories of John Dickson Carr), 2-4 TAD 253

Dettman, Bruce: Singular Malady of Septimus Grayle, (on Solar Pons in Tottenham Werewolf), 2-3 PD 1

Deuel, Jack: letter of comment, 1-6 CP 2

Deveny, Jack: letter of comment, 9 DS 23

DeVet, Charles V.: letter of comment, 64 PU 28

Devil You Say, The, (discussion on G-8, pulp aviation hero character), by Wooda Nicholas Carr, 3 X (np)

(deVilliers, Gerard), The Anatomy of a Spy Novel, Gerald deVilliers and the Modern French Roman D'Espionnage, (spy fiction by deVilliers), by Lance K. Donaldson-Evans, 2-2 C 28

DeVoto, Bernard: The Easy Chair, "Alias Nero Wolfe", 1-2 G 37

DeWaal, Ronald: letter of comment, 2-2 MR 15

DeWaal, Ronald, and Peter A. Ruber: The Solar System (code identifi-cations for Solar Pons stories of August Derleth), 2-1 PDA 2

Dewes, Joyce Lynch: An Interview with Stephen King, 2-2 M 6

DeWitt, Jack: Johnny Wasn't Always Superamalgamated, (on Doc Savage character), 3 BS 7

DeWitt, Jack: The Return of Doctor Death, (on the pulp magazine DR. DEATH and the paperback reprints) 5 BS 4

Dialogue Between Author and Publisher, (humorous fiction), by David Rose, 10 LR 1

Diamond, Ruth: letter of comment, 4-1 TAD 67

Diavolo Quartet, The, (Don Diavolo series: Stuart Towne), by Francis M. Nevins, Jr., 3-4 TAD 243

Diavolo Quartet, The, (Don Diavolo series: Stuart Towne, in RED STAR MYSTERY MAGAZINE, pulp), by Francis M. Nevins, Jr., 3 X (np)

(Dick, Philip K.), The Time Machine, Philip K. Dick, The Middle Period, by George Kelley, 2-1 PQ 23

Dicks on Stage, Form and Formula in Detective Drama, by Charles LaBorde, 11-3 TAD 215; 11-4 TAD 348; 12-1 TAD 83; 12-2 TAD 158; 12-3 TAD 246; 12-4 TAD 341; 13-1 TAD 69; 13-2 TAD 150; 13-3 TAD 240

Dickens' Last Book: More Mysteries Than One, (THE MYSTERY OF EDWIN DROOD), by Arthur J. Cox, 14-1 TAD 31

(Dickens, Charles: THE MYSTERY OF EDWIN DROOD), Dickens' Last Book, More Mysteries Than One, by Arthur J. Cox, 14-1 TAD 31

(Dickens, Charles: THE MYSTERY OF EDWIN DROOD), The Dilemma of Datchery, by E.F.Bleiler, 4-4 MF 7

(Dickens, Charles: THE MYSTERY OF EDWIN DROOD), Drood the Oscure, The Evidence of the Names, by Robert F. Fleissner, 13-1 TAD 12

(Dickens, Charles: THE MYSTERY OF EDWIN DROOD), Edwin and Angelina (R.Austin Freeman's MYST OF ANGELINA FROOD), by Norman Donaldson, 2 TF 2

(Dickens, Charles: THE MYSTERY OF EDWIN DROOD), Edwin's Mystery and Its History, or, Another Look at Datchery, by Ben Fisher, 4-5 MF 6

(Dickens, Charles: THE MYSTERY OF EDWIN DROOD), John Dickson Carr's Solution to, 14-4 TAD 291

(Dickens, Charles: THE MYSTERY OF EDWIN DROOD), John Jasper's Devotion, by Nathan L. Bengis, 8-3 TAD 165; 8-4 TAD 257; 9-1 TAD 25

(Dickens, Charles: THE MYSTERY OF EDWIN DROOD), The Mystery of Edwin Drood, by Albert I. Borowitz, 10-1 TAD 14

Dickensheet, D.W., with J.R.Christopher
and Robert E. Briney: A. Boucher
Bibliography, 2-2 TAD 77; 2-3 TAD 143;
2-4 TAD 263

Dickensheet, Dean & Shirley: The Profession
of Henry Baker, (Sherlockiana),
1-1 PDA 36

(Dickensheet, Dean W.), Meet the Author:
Dean W. Dickensheet, by Allen J.
Hubin, 2-4 TAD 273

Dickinson, D.C.: News Note from the
University of Missouri, (Special
Collection, boys' books), 1-1 BC 9

(Dickinson, Peter), The Playful Mysteries
of Peter Dickinson, by Earl F.
Bargainnier, 13-3 TAD 185

Dickson, Carl Byron: Edmund Wilson and
the Detective Story, 9-3 TAD 189

Dickson, Carl Byron: letter of comment,
6-3 TAD 202; 8-4 TAD 314

(Dickson, Carter), Checklist of works,
by Stanley D. Doremus, 2-4 MR 9

(Dickson, Harry, detective character),
The Harry Dickson Detective Stories
by Jean Ray, by Eddy C. Bertin,
1-1 MR 7

Did It All Start With Ellery? (mystery
authors as characters in stories),
by Ellen Nehr, 3-4 PP 3

Difference Between Us, The, (absence
of a "pulp era" in Britain), by
John Phillifent, 61 PU 3

Different Jerry Todd Editions, (Jerry
Todd boys' books by Leo Edwards),
by Robert L. Johnson, 2-2 TBN 1

Diffinetti, Ralph: The Round Robin Caper,
or, The Too Long Goodbye, pt.2,
(pt.1, by Joe R. Lansdale, 5 PE 5;
pt.3, by R. Jeff Banks, 6 PE 26;
pt.4, by David Rose, 8 PE 9), 5 PE 7

Diffinetti, Ralph: Sex and the Single
Sleuth, 3 PE 3

Digests Not in Hancer, (additions of
digest-size paperbacks not in
Hancer's price guide), by Scott
Edwards, 3-4 CP 22

Digging for Gold - Call About Alger,
(crossword puzzle based on Alger
stories), by Herb L. Risteen, 2-3 BC 222

Dignity in the Detective Novel, by Thomas
D. Lane, 1-1 C 119

Dikty, Alan S.: Boy's Books and the
Times, (patriotism and prejudice
in boys' books), 1-1 BC 11;
(boys' books and motion pictures),
1-2 BC 50

Dikty, Alan S.: The Great Book Bubble,
(collecting boys' books), 1-4 BC 110

Dikty, Alan S.: Hi-Lee Hello, (visit
to home of Leo Edwards, boys' books
author), 1-4 BC 113

Dikty, Alan S.: William A. Rogers,
Cartoonist-Illustrator, (boys'
books artist), 4-1 BC 411

Dikty, Alan S. & Les Beitz: Is It
Valuable? (boys' books), 2-4 BC 233

Dilemma of Datchery, The, (Dickens'
THE MYSTERY OF EDWIN DROOD), by
E.F.Bleiler, 4-4 MF 7

Dillon, Perry C.: letter of comment,
2-6 MF 51; 3-2 MF 60

(DIME DETECTIVE magazine), Speaking
of Pulp, by Steve Lewis, 5 PE 27

(DIME MYSTERY magazine), The
Defective Detectives, (eccentric
and odd detectives in pulp magazine)
by Bob Jones, 68 PU 21

(DIME MYSTERY magazine), The Weird
Menace Magazines, (pulp), by Bob
Jones, 10 BS 3; 11 BS 7; 12 BS 7;
13 BS 7; 14 BS 13; 15 BS 4

Dime Novel Makers, by George C. Jenks,
8 U 119; 1-3 YB 18; 1-4 YB 11

(Dime Novels), Astonishers! or, Just
Who Are You, Anyway?, by Gil
O'Gara, 1-2 YB 8

Dinan, John: Graveyard Walking and
Gravewatching, (on H.P.Lovecraft),
2 FM 14

Dinan, John: letter of comment,
18 R 20; 13-4 TAD 343; 6 U 49;
24 X 46; 28 X 78

Dinan, John: Mr. Chang, a Minor Pulp
Villain, 12 R 21

Dinan, John: Ronald Chetwynd-Hayes,
Horror Story Author Extraordinaire,
6 U 6

Dinan, John: The Saint's Boston Caper,
11 X 17

Dinosaur! (on Doc Savage), by Robert
Sampson, 11 X 110

(Diplomat, aka John Franklin Carter),
Obituary, 1-2 TAD 44

Dirckx, John H.: A Museum of Thorndykean Pathology, (medical oddities
in the Thorndyke stories of R.Austin
Freeman), 5 TF 2

Dirckx, John H.: The Compleat Poisoner,
(poison as factor in Thorndyke
stories by R.Austin Freeman), 7 TF 3

Dirckx, John H.: Dr. Thorndyke's
Library, (as mentioned in stories
by R.Austin Freeman), 2 TF 35

Dirckx, John H.: Dr. Thorndyke's
Pockets, (comment on pocket content
as in various R.Austin Freeman
stories), 4 TF 25

Dirckx, John H.: The Inquest: An Inquiry
(use of an inquest in Thorndyke
stories by R.Austin Freeman), 9 TF 22

Dirckx, John H.: Jonathan Faldish,
Lately Departed: A Thorndyke
Pastiche, 6 TF 3

Dirckx, John H.: letter of comment,
3 TF 52

Dirckx, John H.: Literary Quotations
and Allusions in the Dr. Thorndyke
Novels and Short Stories, 1 TF 3

Dirckx, John H.: Thorndyke the Linguist,
(knowledge of languages in the R.
Austin Freeman stories of Dr. Thorndyke), 10 TF 24

Dirckx, John H., and Philip T. Asdell:
Nathaniel Polton, Artificer Extraordinary, (character in Thorndyke
stories by R.Austin Freeman), 6 TF 25

Discher, Don: letter of comment,
8 X 38

Discovered Treasure, (on boys' books),
by J. Curtis Frymoyer, 3-2 BC 311

(Disney, Doris Miles), Three Gentle
Men: Doris Miles Disney's Continuing
Detectives, by Mary Jean DeMarr,
3-3 MF 5

Disposing of a Pair of Ghosts, (T.L.
Davidson, Cornell Woolrich, DARK
CITY, DARK MEN), by Jacques Barzun,
6-4 TAD 248

Distaff Detectives, The, (quiz on
female detective characters), by
R.Jeff Banks, 8 MN 2

Dixon, Bill: letter of comment,
8-3 TAD 233

(Dixon Farm series: Leo Edwards),
Dixon Farm Data, (boys' books),
1-4 TB 6

(Dixon, Franklin W.), A Laughing Ghost,
(GHOST OF THE HARDY BOYS: Leslie
McFarlane), by Kent Winslow, 4 MA 15

(Dixon, Franklin W.), Bayport's Famous
Sleuths (Hardy Boys boys' books),
by Fred Woodworth, 4 MA 3

(Dixon, Franklin W.), The Dust-Jacketed
Era, 1927-1961, (bibliographical
data, Hardy Boys boys' books), by
John M. Enright, 4 MA 12

(Dixon, Franklin W.), Hardy Boys Series:
Dates of Originals and Rewrites
(bibliographical data), 4 MA 11

(Dixon, Franklin W.), The Hardy Boys:
A Few Criticisms of the Series and
Its Background (boys' books), by
I.R.Ybarra, 4 MA 22

(Dixon, Franklin W.), Hardy Boys
Illustrators: Paul Laune, 4 MA 22

(Dixon, Franklin W.), Hardy Boys Tie-Ins,
by John M. Enright, 4 MA 9

(Dixon, Franklin W.), Mr.McFarlane's
Magic, (Hardy Boys series boys'
books), by John M. Enright, 4 MA 5

Dixon, John Davenport: A Visit with
August Derleth, 4-1 AD 1

Dizer, John T., Jr.: The Boy Allies,
or Who Won World War I, (on Boy
Allies series, boys' books),
3-1 BC 270

Dizer, John T., Jr.: Boys' Bookman,
(biographical sketch), 2-3 BC 220

Dizer, John T., Jr.: Boy's Books and
the American Dream, 1-1 BC 3; 1-2
BC 52

Dizer, John T., Jr.: Checklist, Tom
Swift Series by Victor Appleton,
(boys' books), 2-1 TBN 5

Dizer, John T., Jr.: Fortune and the
Syndicate, (Stratemeyer Syndicate
and boys' books), 2-1 BC 146; 2-2
BC 178

Dizer, John T., Jr.: Leo Edwards
and the First Person Singular,
(hero in boys' books writing
as first person singular),
1-4 YB 6

Dizer, John T., Jr.: letter of comment,
1-3 TBN 5; 2-3 TBN 3; 2-4 TBN 6

Dizer, John T., Jr.: Ode to Hadley's
Flivver, (verse), 2-2 TB 6;
2-4 TBN 4

Dizer, John T., Jr., Shopton, Home
of the Swifts, (locale of Tom
Swift boys' series), 1-3 TBN 11;
1-4 TBN 8

Dizer, John T., Jr., and William D.
Dizer: Series Books, Their
Influence on Children, 1-3 BC 67;
1-4 BC 98

Dizer, William D., and John T. Dizer,
Jr.: Series Books, Their Influence
on Children, 1-3 BC 68; 1-4 BC 98

Do Good Boys and the Grave Peril, The,
or Percy Keese Hits the Trail,
(boys' series books), by John F.
Sullivan, 3-2 BC 290

Do You Hear What I Hear?, or Play It
Again, George, (voice and sound
analysis in crime fiction), by
Karen Bornstein, 1-2 M 13

Dobin, Art: letter of comment,
33 X 115

Dobish, Paul: letter of comment,
3-3 CP 6; 3-4 CP 4

Doc in Digest, (Doc Savage magazines
in digest format), by Robert
Sampson, 2 P 3

Doc Defeated, or Doc Savage in the
Comics, (failure of comic book
format Doc Savage stories), by
A. Grossman, 2/3 DR 5

Doc Garbage in The Demon of Dayton,
(Doc Savage pastiche), by David
McDonnell, 1 DR 6; 2/3 DR 6

Doc in the Movies? Nope, on Radio!
(Doc Savage radio serials),
2/3 DR 9

Doc Savage and the Comics, (stories
in comic book format), by Tony
Isabella, 14 BS 18

Doc Savage and the Great Depression,
by Link Hullar, 7 DS 18

Doc Savage at 75, an Informal Interview
with Clark Savage, Jr. (simulated
interview), by Dafydd Neal Dyar,
12 DS 18

Doc Savage Comic #1: A Belated Epitaph,
by Steve Wawrzenski, 6 DQ 14

Doc Savage Diet, The, (food habits as
found in the Doc Savage novels), by
Bill Laidlaw, 3 DQ 9

Doc Savage in Alphabetical Order,
(checklist of novels), by Bill
Laidlaw, 2 DQ 3

Doc Savage Lives!, by Frank Lewandowski,
1 DS 7

DOC SAVAGE Magazine Checklist, (1933-49), 1 BSA 25

Doc Savage: Man of Bronze? (critique on Doc Savage Comic Books), by Gene Klein, 65 PU 29

Doc Savage Method of Self-Defense, (in various Doc Savage novels) by Kenneth Robeson, 4 DQ 6

Doc Savage Movie Review, by Albert Manachino, 3 DS 8

Doc Savage Novels, The, (checklist as they appeared in DOC SAVAGE magazine, chronological order), 1 DR 9

Doc Savage on the Air, (radio serials), by George Hocutt, 9 X 7

Doc Savage Pulps and Books, (comparison checklist of the original magazine novels and the reprints), by Bill Laidlaw, 1 DQ 6

Doc Savage Returns, (reminiscences on original stories and the reissues by Bantam Books), by Gerald Weales, 4 BS 3

Doc Savage in Shadow Comic #1, by Steve Wawrzenski, 7 DQ 18

Doc Savage: The Beginning, (birth and youth of Doc Savage), 1 BSA 12

Doc Savage: The Self-Appointed Avenger of Crime, by Robert Weinberg, 5 P 17

Doc Savage Story That Wasn't, The, by Daryl S. Herrick, 6 U 19

Doc Savage: Suspended! (suspension of Bentam Books reissue program), by Frank Lewandowski, 2 DS 5

Doc Savage Title Challenge, (quiz), by Will Murray, 9 DS 20

Doc Savage - Why They Call Him Doc, by Ken Bailey, 1 MB 17

(Doc Savage), A Brief Bibliographic Essay on Doc Savage, by Link Hullar, 6 U 22

(Doc Savage), A Critical Analysis of the Doc Savage Novels, (individual magazine treatment of stories), by Herman S. McGregor, 2 BS 10 (Vol.1, Nos.1-3); 3 BS 8 (Vol.1,Nos.4-6); 4 BS 8 (Vol.2, Nos.1-4); 5 BS 6 (Vol.2, Nos.5-6; Vol.3, No.1); 6 BS 15 (Vol.3, Nos.2-4); 7 BS 13 (Vol.3, Nos.5-6; Vol.4, No.1); 8 BS 11 (Vol.4, Nos.2-4); 9 BS 8 (Vol.4, Nos.5-6; Vol.5, No.1); 10 BS 9 (Vol.5, Nos.2-4); 11 BS 14 (Vol.6, Nos.2-4); 12 BS 11 (Vol.5, Nos.5-6; Vol.6, No.1); 13 BS 13 (Vol.6, Nos.5-6; Vol.7,No.1); 14 BS 5 (Vol.7, Nos.2-4); 15 BS 9 (Vol.7, Nos.5-6; Vol.8, No.1); 2/3 DR 13 (Vol.1, Nos.1-3)

(Doc Savage), A Critical "Savage" Artist, (cover art), by Albert Manachino, 4 DR 2

(Doc Savage), A Doc Savage Adventure Rediscovered, ("Who Goes There" by Don A. Stuart), by Albert Tonik, 4 DS 10

(Doc Savage), A Recurring Little Villain, (Cadwiller Olden in Doc Savage and The Avenger stories), by Bill Laidlaw, 5 DQ 9

(Doc Savage), A Second Round for Doc, (background of paperback publication of Doc Savage novels), by Paul H. Bonner, Jr., 9 BS 4

(Doc Savage), A Visit with "Mrs. Doc Savage", (interview, Mrs. Lester Dent), by Bill Smith, 6 BS 3

(Doc Savage), Alive and Doing Well in New York City, (fiction, a la Doc Savage), by John Cosgriff, 1 DR 5

(Doc Savage), Announcement of the Doc Savage Annual, (never published), by Dave Funnell, 3 BS 13

(Doc Savage), Artist Behind Doc Savage (commentary on Walter Baumhofer), 9 DS 6

(Doc Savage), At the Movies - Doc Savage: The Man of Bronze, (review), 1 BSA 15

(Doc Savage), The Bama Legacy, (on James Bama, cover artist), by Dafydd Neal Dyar, 7 DQ 6

(Doc Savage), Boris! Boris! Boris! (Boris Vallejo, paperback cover artist for Doc Savage reprints), by Robert Woo, 1 DS 11

(Doc Savage), Checklist, Bantam Paperback reprints, 1 DS 8

(Doc Savage), Checklist, DOC SAVAGE Magazine, 1933-1949, 1 BSA 25

(Doc Savage), Chronology of The Man of Bronze, by Albert Tonik, 7 DS 6

(Doc Savage), Clark Savage, the Early Years, by "Clark Savage, Jr.", 7 DQ 10

(Doc Savage), Clark Savage, Sr., Retired British Secret Agent, (Doc Savage speculative pastiche), by Bill Laidlaw, 2 DQ 7; 3 DQ 10; 4 DQ 10; 5 DQ 15; 6 DQ 11

(Doc Savage), Contemplating Seven of the Pulp Heroes, (comparisons and characteristics)1 by Wooda Nicholas Carr and Herman S. McGregor, 12 BS 3

(Doc Savage), Cryptograms, by Dafydd Neal Dyar, 7 U 26

(Doc Savage), Death Flies in Silver Circles, (pastiche, Doc Savage), by John Boehm and Mark Justice, 1 MB 7

(Doc Savage), Dinosaur!, by Robert Sampson, 11 X 110

(Doc Savage), Doc Defeated, or Doc Savage in the Comics, (failure of comic book format), by A. Grossman, 2/3 DR 5

(Doc Savage), Doc Garbage in The Demon of Dayton, (pastiche), by David McDonnell, 1 DR 6; 2/3 DR 6

(Doc Savage), Doc in the Movies? Nope, on Radio! (radio serials), 2/3 DR 9

(Doc Savage), Doc Savage and the Comics, (comic book format), by Tony Isabella, 14 BS 18

(Doc Savage), Doc Savage Award, from the DOC SAVAGE pulp magazine, 4 BS 18

(Doc Savage), Doc Savage Club, from the DOC SAVAGE pulp magazine, 4 BS 17

(Doc Savage), Doc Savage Comic #1: A Belated Epitaph, by Steve Wawrzenski, 6 DQ 14

(Doc Savage), The Doc Savage Diet, (food habits, from the novels), by Bill Laidlaw, 3 DQ 9

(Doc Savage), Doc Savage in Alphabetical Order, Checklist, by Bill Laidlaw, 2 DQ 3

(Doc Savage), The Doc Savage Method of Self-Defense, by Kenneth Robeson, 4 DQ 6

(Doc Savage), The Doc Savage Novels: Checklist in chronological order from DOC SAVAGE magazine, 2 BS 22

(Doc Savage), Doc Savage Pulps and Books, (comparison checklist of the original magazine novels and the reprint paperbacks), by Bill Laidlaw, 1 DQ 6

(Doc Savage), Doc Savage Returns, (reminiscences on the original stories, and the Bantam paperback reprints), 4 BS 3

(Doc Savage), Doc Savage in Shadow Comic #1, by Steve Wawrzenski, 7 DQ 18

(Doc Savage), Doc Savage: The Beginning (birth and youth of Doc Savage), 1 BSA 12

(Doc Savage), Doc Savage - Why They Call Him Doc, by Ken Bailey, 1 MB 17

(Doc Savage), Doc's Adventures Search Puzzle, (puzzle), by Dan Bishop, 5 DS 22

(Doc Savage), Doc Savage's Creator: Lester Dent, (personal reminiscences), by Billy G. Smith, 2 BS 6

(Doc Savage), Doc's Fabulous Physique, by Robert Woo, 3 DS 16

(Doc Savage), Doc Savage's First Cover Artist: Walter M. Baumhofer, by Walter Baumhofer, 14 BS 3

(Doc Savage), Doc's Villianous Foes Search Puzzle, (puzzle), by Jerry Schneiderman, 3 DS 15

(Doc Savage), Doc Savage and Crew Reborn as Stars of Star Trek and Star Wars, (speculative), by "Operative 1701," 5 DS 14

(Doc Savage), Doc Savage, The (Space) Man of Bronze, (speculative), by Dafydd Neal Dyar, 7 U 6

(Doc Savage), Doc Savage: Suspended!, (suspension of Bantam paperback reprint program), by Frank Lewandowski, 2 DS 5

(Doc Savage), Duck Savage: The Mallard of Bronze, (comic strip, pastiche), by Todd R. & Timothy J. Rutt, 1-2 WA 9; 1-3 WA 11; 1-4 WA 11; 2-1 WA 18

(Doc Savage), The Duende Doc Savage Index, by Will Murray, 2 D 28

(Doc Savage), The Eye of Day: A Speculation on the Maternity of John Sunlight, (Doc Savage villain), by Dafydd Neal Dyar, 6 DQ 6

(Doc Savage), The First Doc Savage: The Apocryphal Life of Clark Savage Jr. (birth and youth speculation), by Timithy J. Rutt, 1-3 WA 3

(Doc Savage), The Girl Who Loved Doc Savage, ("Monja"), by Will Murray, 4 DR 6

(Doc Savage), The Girl Who Loved Monk Mayfair, (Doc Savage aide), 7 DS 13

(Doc Savage), The Gold Key Doc Savage Comic Book, by Wayne Vucenic, 14 BS 18

(Doc Savage), The Gold Mine of Dust, (Doc Savage pastiche featuring Doc Aborigine), by Gary Zachrich, 63 PU 10

(Doc Savage), The Golden Boys, by Will Murray, 10 DS 16

(Doc Savage), The Hildalgo Trading Corporation of America in 1979, (pastiche), by "Operative 1701," 1 DQ 8

(Doc Savage), His Name, by Bruce Guthrie, 6 DS 4

(Doc Savage), How Much Do You Know? (quiz), by Bill Laidlaw, 3 DQ 15; 4 DQ 9

(Doc Savage), "I'll Save the World in a Minute, But First How About Something to Eat?, (eating habits of Doc Savage), by Albert Manachino, 4 DS 7

(Doc Savage), Incidentals, (Lester Dent and Doc Savage), by Will Murray, 2-2 CP 30; 2-3 CP 12; 3-2 CP 7; 3-3 CP 17; (radio serials) 3-4 CP 13; (Dent as guest columnist) 3-5 CP 23

(Doc Savage), James Bama, An Interview (magazine cover artist), 1 BSA 3

(Doc Savage), James Bama and His Man of Bronze, (cover artist), by Mark J. Golden, 1 DR 4

(Doc Savage), Jim Bama and the Artistic Doc Savage, (cover artist), by Mark J. Golden, 2/3 DR 11

(Doc Savage), John D. MacDonald's List of His Stories in DOC SAVAGE and THE SHADOW magazines, with data), 7 BS 4

(Doc Savage), John D. MacDonald vs. Doc Savage, (on writing pulp stories), by John D. MacDonald, 3 BS 3

(Doc Savage), Johnny Wasn't Always Super-amalgamated, (on Doc Savage aide), by Jack DeWitt, 3 BS 7

(Doc Savage), Kenneth Robeson's Alter Egos, (Doc Savage novels written by other than Lester Dent), by Herman S. McGregor, 2 BS 14

(Doc Savage), Lester Dent, Adventurer, (Doc Savage author), 1 BSA 21

(Doc Savage), The Man of Bronze - and His Creator, (Doc Savage, and Lester Dent), by Samuel W. Potts, 2 BS 8

(Doc Savage), The Man of Mystery, (John Montague as the real Doc Savage speculation), by Bill Laidlaw, 2 DQ 5

(Doc Savage), Monk, Ham and Their Private War, (from DOC SAVAGE magazine, October 1937), 5 BS 5

(Doc Savage), Never Fear, Doc Savage Fans Are Here, (on fan organizations), 1 MB 21

(Doc Savage), The Never-Was Adventure (speculative meeting between The Shadow and Doc Savage), by Will Murray, 6 DQ 16

(Doc Savage), Notes for a Pulp Collector, (first advertisement for DOC SAVAGE magazine), by Fred S. Cook, 10 BS 13

(Doc Savage), Notes on an Ideal Library (hardback Doc Savage series by Ideal) by Robert Sampson, 2/3 DR 2

(Doc Savage), Original Illustrations From DOC SAVAGE Magazine, 5 BS 10

(Doc Savage), Pat Savage, the Original Supergirl, 1 BSA 20

(Doc Savage), The Phantom Airship: The Truth Behind the Fuction, by Dafydd Neal Dyar, 12 SF 32

(Doc Savage), The Pulp Corner: Memoirs of a Doc Savage Reader, by Robert Sampson and Wooda Nicholas Carr, 14 SF 21

(Doc Savage), The Red Baron, The Avenger, and Doc Savage, (comparison essay), by Bill Laidlaw, 3 DQ 4

(Doc Savage), Reflections in a Flame-Gold Eye, (changes in Doc Savage during the magazine series), by Will Murray, 2/3 DR 16

(Doc Savage), Related Movie Reviews, 6 DQ 19

(Doc Savage), The Resurrection of "IN HELL, MADONNA," by Will Murray, 5 DS 8

(Doc Savage), The Robeson Syndrome, by Michael Avallone, 2 PW 1

(Doc Savage), Savage Comments, by Gene Christie, (suggested abbreviation code for Doc Savage stories) 4 DR 4; (on numbering the series) 2/3 DR 12

(Doc Savage), The Self Appointed Avenger of Crime, by Robert Weinberg, 5 P 17

(Doc Savage), The Shadow or Doc Savage?, by Ed Noonchester, 2 DS 13

(Doc Savage), The Secret Kenneth Robesons, (authors using the house name), by Will Murray, 2 D 3

(Doc Savage), Sunlight, Son Bright, (on John Sunlight, villain in Doc Savage stories), by Dafydd Neal Dyar, 8 DS 22

(Doc Savage), Superman of Bronze, by Will Murray, 5 DS 17

(Doc Savage), The Terrible Beekeeper, (pastiche involving The Shadow, Doc Savage, The Spider, Sherlock Holmes), by Arn McConnell and Todd Rutt, 1-2 WA 6; 1-3 WA 7; 1-4 WA 7; 2-1 WA 5

(Doc Savage), Thoughts on Doc Savage, by Leo Giroux, Jr., 4 DS 16

(Doc Savage), Today's Doc Savage Illustrator: Letter and Comments, by James E. Bama, 2 BS 3

(Doc Savage), Top Secret, (Doc Savage type code), by Dafydd Neal Dyar, 6 U 28

(Doc Savage), The Top 10 Doc Savage Novels and One Stinker, (analysis and descriptive comments by var. contributors), by Will Murray, 8 U 22

(Doc Savage), Welcome Back Doc Savage and Crew, (paperback reprints), by John Keasler, 3 BS 6

(Doc Savage), What Will TV Do to Doc Savage?, (difficulty in depicting), by Samuel Potts, 6 BS 6

(Doc Savage), What's Up, Doc?, (on Doc Savage Marvel Comics series), by Shelby L. Peck, 2/3 DR 3

(Doc Savage), What's Up, Doc? (Doc Savage, from the pulps to the present), by Shelby L. Peck, 1 DR 3

(Doc Savage), Who is Doc Savage? (speculative essay), by Dafydd Neal Dyar, 12 DS 9

(Doc Savage), Who is Doc Savage? (speculative essay), by Frank Lewandowski, 1 DS 3

(Doc Savage), Writing the Biography of Doc Savage, by Philip Jose Farmer, 5A P 2

(Doc Savage), Yesterday's Doc Savage Illustrator: Letter and Comments, by Paul Orban, 2 BS 5

(Doc Savage association item), Alis Big Bad John, by Dafydd Neal Dyar, 6 U 13

DOC SAVAGE CLUB READER Interview with Brigadier General Theodore Marley Brooks, May 1978, ("Ham," Doc Savage aide, comments on Doc Savage), 3 DS 11

DOC SAVAGE CLUB READER News, by Frank Lewandowski, 2 DS 12; 5 DS 9; 6 DS 8; 7 DS 16

(DOC SAVAGE magazine), The Burning of Doc
Savage, (collecting experiences), by
Dickson Thorpe, 7 DQ 13

(DOC SAVAGE magazine), Chronological
appearance of Doc Savage novels,
checklist, 1 DR 9

(DOC SAVAGE magazine), Doc in Digest,
(digest-format issues), by Robert
Sampson, 2 P 3

(DOC SAVAGE magazine), The Doc Savage
Novels,(checklist in chronological
order), 2 BS 22

(DOC SAVAGE magazine), Early JDM: in
Doc Savage, (stories in magazine
by John D. MacDonald), by Francis
M. Nevins, Jr., 19 JD 8

(DOC SAVAGE magazine), Early J.D.,
(John D.MacDonald stories in
Doc Savage and The Shadow magazines),
by Ed Cox, 2 JD 3

(DOC SAVAGE magazine), Pulp Notes,
by Tom Johnson, 7 DQ 15

(DOC SAVAGE magazine), Savage Views,
(comments on first two issues),
by Mark Justice, 1 MB 23

Doc Savage's Creator: Lester Dent,
(personal reminiscences), by Billy
G. Smith, 2 BS 6

Doc Savage's First Cover Artist: Walter
M. Baumhofer, by Baumhofer, 14 BS 3

(DOCTOR DEATH magazine), The Return of
Doctor Death, (on the original pulp
magazine and the paperback reprints),
by Jack DeWitt, 5 BS 4

Doctor's Blade, The, (interview with Sax
Rohmer, 1947), 9 R 19

(Doctor Satan series), The World's
Weirdest Criminal, (on Doctor Satan
series in WEIRD TALES magazine), by
Bob Jones, 72 PU 12

Doctor Wonderful, (Dr. Nancy Dayland,
pulp detective, with partial checklist)
by Robert Sampson, 5-6 MF 13

Doctors in Crime, (quiz), by Mr. & Mrs.
W.H.J.Kennedy, 1-5 MR 4

Documents in the Case, The, (letters
column), 1-1 MF 39; 1-2 MF 47; 1-3
MF 51; 1-4 MF 55; 1-5 MF 53; 1-6 MF
55; 2-1 MF 50; 2-2 MF 41; 2-3 MF 57;
2-4 MF 49; 2-5 MF 45; 2-6 MF 43; 3-1
MF 46; 3-2 MF 50; 3-3 MF 50; 3-4 MF 53;
3-5 MF 46; 4-1 MF 37; 4-2 MF 54; 4-3
MF 47; 4-4 MF 49; 4-5 MF 44; 4-6 MF 40;
5-1 MF 30; 5-2 MF 39; 5-3 MF 41; 5-4
MF 38; 5-5 MF 44; 5-6 MF 49

Dodge, Margaret R.: Mystery's Palette,
(verse), 3-3 MR 12

Doehla, Rick: letter of comment,
2 BS 2

Doering, Bruce: Philip Jose Farmer, A
Different Kind of Checklist, 2-2 CP
24

Doerrer, David H.: Additional Bibliography
of Richard Stark, 2-4 MF 51

Doerrer, David H.: Index of Books Reviewed
in Vol.2, THE MYSTERY FANCIER, 3-1 MF 26

Doerrer, David H.: Index of Books
Reviewed in Vol.3, THE MYSTERY
FANCIER, 4-2 MF 3

Doerrer, David H.: Index of Books
Reviewed in Vol.4, THE MYSTERY
FANCIER, 5-2 MF 3

Doerrer, David H.: Lachman's Reviews,
(Index to Marvin Lachman's "It's
About Crime", reviews in THE
MYSTERY FANCIER, Vols.2-4), 5-2
MF 6

Doerrer, David H.: letter of comment,
5 LR 5; 6/7 LR 28; 2-2 MF 51;
2-2 MF 56; 2-3 MF 63; 2-4 MF 49;
2-6 MF 54; 3-1 MF 50; 3-3 MF 55;
3-4 MF 62; 4-1 MF 44; 4-2 MF 54;
4-5 MF 47; 5-1 MF 37; 3 PE 34;
1-4 PP 30; 1-5 PP 31; 1-6 PP 32;
2-1 PP 42; 2-2 PP 42; 2-3 PP 44;
2-5 PP 40; 3-1 PP 43; 4-1 PP 47;
4-5/6 PP 95; 11-4 TAD 401; 12-1
TAD 91; 5 U 66

Doerrer, David H.: Miss Marple She
Isn't, (on female sleuths), 2-6
MF 7

Dogging the Detectives: A Quiz,
(quiz), by R. Jeff Banks, 7 MN 3

Dogging the Footsteps of Solar Pons,
by Jean Cox, 1-1 PDA 9

(Dominic, R.B.), Comic Construction
in the Novels of Emma Lathen and
R.B.Dominic, by David Brownell,
9-2 TAD 91

Don Cole's Underrated Books, (mystery
fiction author), by George Kelley,
1-5 PP 8

(Don Diavolo), RED STAR MYSTERY: Don
Diavolo, (on the pulp magazine
and principal story character,
with index to the magazine), by
Robert E. Briney, 64 PU 14

Don Sturdy and the Great Search for
Adventure (Don Sturdy series boys'
books by Victor Appleton), by
Robert Jennings, 1 BB 5

Donald E. Westlake: A Checklist, by
Nobumitsu Kodaka and Donald E.
Westlake, 8-3 TAD 203

Donaldson, Betty: Arthur William
Upfield, September 1, 1888 -
February 13, 1964, (tribute),
8-1 TAD 1

Donaldson, Betty: The Novels of
Arthur W. Upfield, Bibliography
and Review, 8-1 TAD 4

Donaldson, Norman: Checklist of
Philip MacDonald, 3-1 TAD 10

Donaldson, Norman: Checklist of
R. Austin Freeman, 1-2 TAD 35

Donaldson, Norman: THE DEAD HAND by
R. Austin Freeman...and How It
Grew, (notes on formulation),
7 TF 18

Donaldson, Norman: Edwin and Angelina
(Freeman's THE MYSTERY OF ANGELINA
FROOD, w/comments), 2 TF 2

Donaldson, Norman: The First Thorndyke Story, ("The Blue Sequi" in 1908 by R. Austin Freeman), 10 TF 2

Donaldson, Norman: In the Wake of Haycraft-Queen, (possible additions suggested for basic crime fiction list), 5-3 TAD 137

Donaldson, Norman: letter of comment, 1-2 TAD 65; 1-3 TAD 107; 1-4 TAD 155; 2-1 TAD 64; 3-3 TAD 207

Donaldson, Norman: The Penrose Mystery Mystery, (Dr.Thorndyke story by R. Austin Freeman), 2-2 TAD 108

Donaldson, Norman: Perk Stone and the Thorndyke Quiz, (1936 interrogatory on Dr. Thorndyke of R. Austin Freeman) 1 TF 26

Donaldson, Norman: Philip MacDonald: Gethryn and Others, 3-1 TAD 6; (addenda) 3-2 TAD 95

Donaldson, Norman: R. Austin Freeman, (biblio-biographical comments), 1-2 TAD 32

Donaldson, Norman: Ronald Arbuthnott Knox, 7-4 TAD 235

Donaldson, Norman: Social and Political Images in American Crime Fiction, (panel discussion, Popular Culture Association 1971), 5-2 TAD 61

Donaldson, Norman: Thorndyke and the Plumber's Oddments, (use of true crime in DR.THORNDYKE INTERVENES by R. Austin Freeman), 4 TF 8

Donaldson, Norman: Winifred Duke: A Preliminary Survey, 2-2 TAD 94

(Donaldson, Norman), Meet the Author: Norman Donaldson, by Allen J.Hubin, 1-2 TAD 37

Donaldson-Evans, Lance K.: The Anatomy of a Spy Novel, Gerard deVilliers and the Modern French *Roman d'Espionnage*, (spy fiction of deVilliers), 2-2 C 28

Donovan, Frank P.: Checklist, Railroad Short Stories of Detection in America, 2-1 TAD 47

Donovan, Frank P.: Bibliography of American Mystery Novels Associated with Railroads, 1-4 TAD 126

Donovan, Frank P.: Bibliography of English Railway Novels of Detection and Mystery, and Translations, 202 TAD 105

Donovan, Frank P.: Bibliography of English Railway Short Stories of Detection and Mystery, and Translations, 2-3 TAD 178

Donovan, Frank P.: Mystery Rides the Rails, Pt.1, American Railroad Novels of Detection and Mystery, 1-4 TAD 124; Pt.2, Railroad Short Stories of Detection and Mystery in America, 2-1 TAD 46; Pt.3, English Railway Novels of Detection and Mystery and Translations, 2-2 TAD 103; Pt.4, English Railway Short Stories and Translations, 2-3 TAD 176

(Donovan, Frank P.), Meet the Author, Frank P. Donovan, by Allen J.Hubin, 1-4 TAD 128

(Donovan, Laurence), The Secret Kenneth Robesons, (author under house name), by Will Murray, 2 D 3

Donovan, Pauline: letter of comment, 7-2 TAD 154

Donovan of Whitehall, by William LeQueux, (fiction, Classic Corner Rare Tales), 14-1 TAD 44

Don't Guess, Let Me Tell You, (verse), Ogden Nash, 3-1 CP 26

(DON'T LOOK NOW: Daphne duMaurier), Tension and Duality in Daphne duMaurier's "Don't Look Now") by Jane S. Bakerman, 3-4 MF 8

Don't Tell Me I Won't Like It, (on literary criticism), by David Marshall Lewis, 12 LR 12

Doran, Michael: letter of comment, 2-2 MF 43; 2-4 MF 56; 2-5 MF 48; 2-6 MF 46; 3-1 MF 50; 3-2 MF 62; 3-4 MF 54

Doremus, Stanley D.: Checklist, Carter Dickson, 2-4 MR 9

Doremus, Stanley D.: letter of comment, 5-1 TAD 59

Dorinson, Zahava K.: Ross Macdonald, The Personal Paradigm and Popular Fiction, 10-1 TAD 43

Dorothy L. Sayers: A Brief Addendum, by William White, 3-1 MR 12

Dorothy L. Sayers: A Second Brief Addendum, by Mary Ann Whitten, 3-3 MR 2

Dorothy L. Sayers and the Apotheosis of Detective Fiction, (social v. puzzle), by Elaine Bander, 10-4 TAD 362

Dorothy L. Sayers' Detective Short Fiction, (literary study), by William Reynolds, 14-2 TAD 176

Double-Action Pocketbooks, Checklist, (science-fiction paperbacks), by J. Grant Thiessen, 2 SF 8

(Double-C spy stories: Edward D.Hoch), Checklist, by James Mark Purcell, 5-2 MR 43

Double Death: A Retrospective Commentary, (mysteries of which each chapter is by a different author), by Neville Wood, 1-3 PP 20

Double-Duty Detectives, (quiz), by R. Jeff Banks, 9-2 TAD 111

Double Jeopardy: Husband and Wife Teams in Detective Fiction, by Gail Adams, 8-4 TAD 251

Double Life of Gloria Amoury, The, (interview), by Pat Erhardt, 3-5 MR 3

Dougherty, Graham: letter of comment, 27 JD 34

(Douglass, Donald McNutt), Department of Unknown Mystery Writers, by Marvin Lachman, 3-6 PP 11

Douty, Robert W.: Ellery Queen, First
  Impressions, 12-3 TAD 196
Dove, George N.: Brother Officers...
  Be Damned, The Police Procedural
  III, 10-4 TAD 320
Dove, George N.: The Complex Art of
  Raymond Chandler, (literary
  quality), 8-4 TAD 271
Dove, George N.: The Cops and Cop-Haters,
  The Police Procedural II, 10-3 TAD 241
Dove, George N.: Intruder in the Rose
  Garden, (private eye v. classic
  mystery), 9-4 TAD 278
Dove, George N.: letter of comment,
  8-4 TAD 324; 9-2 TAD 156
Dove, George N.: The Police Are Always
  There, The Police Procedural IV,
  11-1 TAD 74
Dove, George N.: "Realism, Routine,
  Stubborness and System," The
  Police Procedural I, 10-2 TAD 133
Dove, George N.: The Rookie Type, The
  Police Procedural VI, 11-3 TAD 249
Dove, George N.: "Shades of Dupin!"
  Fictional Detectives on Detective
  Fiction, 8-1 TAD 12
Dove, George N.: The Tangled Emotions,
  The Police Procedural V, 11-2 TAD 150
Dove, George N.: The Weevil in Beancurd,
  or The Cop Abroad, (police procedural
  analysis), 2-6 MF 17
(Dowling, Fr.Roger, series: Ralph
  McInerny), Father Roger of Fox River,
  by Jim McCahery, 2-5 PP 8
Down Grey, Wet Streets, (private eye
  mysteries discussed), by Mary Groff,
  3 PE 9
Down Memory-Bank Lane, (reminiscences
  on science-fiction early magazines),
  by Terry Jeeves, 61 PU 7; 62 PU 3;
  63 PU 7; 64 PU 4; 65 PU 8; 68 PU 16;
  70 PU 5; 71 PU 2; 72 PU 8
(DOWN THESE MEAN STREETS A MAN MUST GO:
  Philip Durham), commentary on book
  about Raymond Chandler, by Stewart
  Kemble, 72 PU 18
(Doyle, Arthur Conan), The "Adventures"
  of Arthur Conan Doyle, by Felix
  Arnstein, 3-3 TAD 166
(Doyle, Arthur Conan), The Burroughs-
  Doyle Connection, (comparison of
  passages, Edgar Rice Burroughs and
  Doyle), by Dana Martin Batory,
  15 SF 10
(Doyle, Arthur Conan), Classic Corner
  Rare Tales, "The Bravoes of Market-
  Drayton," 14-2 TAD 144
(Doyle, Arthur Conan), Conan Doyle and
  Sherlock Holmes: The Creator versus
  The Creation, by Jack Tracy, 2-2 M
  26
(Doyle, Arthur Conan), Conan Doyle Shows
  His Hand, by Dana Martin Batory,
  8 U 104

(Doyle, Arthur Conan), Correspondence
  between Hornung and Doyle, (E.W.
  Hornung), 4 MT 28
(Doyle, Arthur Conan), Dr. Doyle's
  Doppelganger, by Dana Martin
  Batory, 8 U 109
(Doyle, Arthur Conan), Frankenstein
  a la Doyle, by Dana Martin Batory,
  8 U 114
(Doyle, Arthur Conan), Holmes Was a
  Sideline, by Julian Symons, 9 LR
  21
(Doyle, Arthur Conan), Information
  Center - Sherlock Holmes, (various
  data), 2 MT 33
(Doyle, Arthur Conan), Orifice Into
  Hell, by Dana Martin Batory,
  3 U 11
(Doyle, Arthur Conan), The Real
  Professor Challenger, by Dana
  Martin Batory, 13 SF 42
(Doyle, Arthur Conan), Watch That Man?
  (Doyle's Syndrome), by Dana Martin
  Batory, 9 SF 40
(Doyle, Arthur Conan: THE HOUND OF
  THE BASKERVILLES), Narrative Vision
  in The Hound of the Baskervilles,
  by Paul F. Ferguson, 1-2 C 24
(Doyle, Arthur Conan: THE LOST WORLD),
  The Land That Maple White Found,
  by Arn McConnell, 1-1 WA 7
(Doyle, Arthur Conan: THE LOST WORLD),
  Notes on The Lost World, by Dana
  Martin Batory, 2 U 9
(Doyle, Arthur Conan: THE LOST WORLD),
  Where was Maple White Land?, by
  Dana Martin Batory, 6 U 16
(Doyle, Arthur Conan: THE RING OF
  THOTH), A Dead Ringer, by Dana
  Martin Batory, 5 U 25
(Dr. Coffee series: Lawrence Blochman),
  Coffee in the Lab: A Preliminary
  Bibliography, by James Mark Purcell,
  4-3 MR 29
(Dr. Death), Reader's Guide to Doctor
  Death, (Dr.Death series paperbacks)
  by Bruce Cervon, 3-3 CP 30
(Dr. Death), Jimmy Holm, Supernatural
  Detective v. Dr. Death, (on the
  pulp magazine and characters), by
  Tom Johnson, 10 DS 8
(Dr. deGrandin), The Case of the Moon-
  lighting Physicians, by Chet
  Williamson, 6 WT 14
(Dr. Doom), Champion of Catastrophe
  and Son of the East: A Short
  "Genealogy" of Victor von Doom,
  by Scott Koeller, 1-4 WA 5
Dr. Doyle's Doppelganger, (Arthur
  Conan Doyle), by Dana Martin
  Batory, 8 U 109
Dr. Kildare's Dilemma, (fiction by
  Max Brand/Frederick Faust),
  3-1 FC 1; 3-2 FC 1

(Dr. Nancy Dayland, pulp detective), Doctor Wonderful, (discussion with partial checklist), by Robert Sampson, 5-6 MF 13

(Dr. No), The Article I Couldn't Publish, (Ian Fleming and J.D.Salinger's "The Laughing Man"), by Guy M. Townsend, 1-1 MF 18

(Dr. Palfrey series: John Creasey), Checklist, by Robert E. Briney and John Creasey, 2-1 TAD 8

(Dr. Sax), in Fore Shadowings, by Bill Blackbeard, 17 X 6

(Dr. Sax), The Other Shadow, by Will Murray, 10 X 2

(Dr. Syn), The Chronicle of Christopher Syn, (series character), by Wooda Nicholas Carr, 7 X 7; 8 X (np); 9 X 5; 10 X 8

(Dr. Thorndyke), A Glass of Wine Within the Meaning of the Act, (use of wine in the Thorndyke stories by Freeman), 7 TF 30

(Dr. Thorndyke), A Guide to Thorndykean Pilopathology, (medico-legal importance of the skin and hair in the Thorndyke stories by Freeman), by Howard Brody, 11 TF 3

(Dr. Thorndyke), A Museum of Thorndykean Pathology, (medical oddities in the Thorndyke stories by Freeman), by John H. Dirckx, 5 TF 2

(Dr. Thorndyke), A Note on the Chronology of the Dr. Thorndyke Novels, by Michael G. Heenan, 9-1 TAD 52

(Dr. Thorndyke), A Thorndyke Examination, (quiz), by Philip T. Asdell, 1 TF 32

(Dr. Thorndyke), An Inquiry Into Circular Heels, (circular heel footprints in the Thorndyke stories of Freeman), by Howard Brody, 12 TF 8

(Dr. Thorndyke), ...And Great Virtue in a Really Good Feed, (hospitality to Thorndyke in stories by Freeman), by Michael G. Heenan, 10 TF 9

(Dr. Thorndyke), The Compleat Poisoner, (poison as used in the Thorndyke stories by Freeman), by John H. Dirckx, 7 TF 3

(Dr. Thorndyke), THE DEAD HAND by R. Austin Freeman...and How It Grew, (notes on story formulation), by Norman Donaldson, 7 TF 18

(Dr. Thorndyke), Dr. Thorndyke's Library (as mentioned in stories by Freeman) by John H. Dirckx, 2 TF 35

(Dr. Thorndyke), Dr. Thorndyke's Pockets, (on pocket contents in various stories by Freeman), by John H. Dirckx, 4 TF 25

(Dr. Thorndyke), "The Eye of Osiris" and the Webster-Parkman Case, by John McAleer, 12 TF 2

(Dr. Thorndyke), The First Thorndyke Story, ("The Blue Sequin" 1908 by R.Austin Freeman), by Norman Donaldson, 10 TF 2

(Dr. Thorndyke), 5A King's Bench Walk, (residence of Thorndyke in Freeman stories), by P.M.Stone, 3 TF 37

(Dr. Thorndyke), Golden Beetles or Blue Bugs?, (Freeman's "The Blue Scarab" as a commentary on Poe's "The Gold-Big"), by Oliver Mayo, 11 TF 13

(Dr. Thorndyke), Great Detectives, by George T. Hamilton, 4-2 AD 6

(Dr. Thorndyke), The Inquest: An Inquiry, (use of the inquest in the Thorndyke stories by Freeman), by John H. Dirckx, 9 TF 22

(Dr. Thorndyke), John Evelyn Who? (possible origin of Thorndyke's names), by Philip T. Asdell, 7 TF 35

(Dr. Thorndyke), Jonathan Faldish, Lately Departed, a Thorndyke Pastiche, by John H. Dirckx, 6 TF 3

(Dr.Thorndyke), La Filza Di Thorndyke, (foreign translations of the Thorndyke stories by Freeman), by Ian Arnott, 3 TF 28

(Dr. Thorndyke), The Last Meeting of the Butlers Club, (Dr. Thorndyke pastiche), by Geoffrey Bush, 12 TF 13

(Dr. Thorndyke), Literary Quotations and Allusions in the Dr. Thorndyke Novels and Short Stories, by John H. Dirckx, 1 TF 3

(Dr. Thorndyke), Meet Dr. Thorndyke, by R. Austin Freeman, 4-2 AD 6; 4 TF 31

(Dr. Thorndyke), Mr. R. Austin Freeman: A Review of His Early Fiction, (1913), by John Adams, 6 TF 34

(Dr. Thorndyke), The Names of Characters in the Thorndyke Stories, by Michael G. Heenan, 4 TF 2

(Dr. Thorndyke), Nathaniel Polton, Artificer Extraordinary, (character in Thorndyke stories), by John H. Dirckx and Philip T. Asdell, 6 TF 25

(Dr. Thorndyke), Notes on a Freeman Bibliography, by R. Narasimhan, 8 TF 41

(Dr. Thorndyke), On the Trails of Dr. Freeman and Dr. Thorndyke, or A Guide to Thorndykean England, by Michael G. Heenan and Philip T. Asdell, 8 TF 4

(Dr. Thorndyke), The Penrose Mystery Mystery, by Norman Donaldson, 2-2 TAD 108

(Dr. Thorndyke), Perk Stone and the Thorndyke Quiz, (1936 interrogatory) by Norman Donaldson, 1 TF 26

(Dr. Thorndyke), The Silent Sickle, a Thorndyke Pastiche, by Oliver Mayo, 3 TF 2

(Dr. Thorndyke), Thorndyke the Linguist, (knowledge of languages in the stories by Freeman), by John H. Dirckx, 10 TF 24

(Dr. Thorndyke), Thorndyke's Topography, (locales of Thorndyke stories, by Freeman), by Michael G. Heenan, 5 TF 23

(Dr. Thorndyke), The Thorny Way to Heaven, a Thorndyke Pastiche, by Oliver Mayo, 9 TF 5

(DR. THORNDYKE INTERVENES: R. Austin Freeman), Thorndyke and the Plumber's Oddments, (use of true crime by Freeman), by Norman Donaldson, 4 TF 6

(Dr. Trowbridge), The Case of the Moon-lighting Physicians, by Chet Williamson, 6 WT 14

(Dr. Who), Checklist, by Ian Covell, 5 SF 42

(Dr. Yen Sin), Introducing the Yellow Peril, (pulp magazine villain), by Wooda Nicholas Carr, 12 SF 39

(DR. YEN SIN magazine), An Index, by Joseph Lewandowski, 4 U 32

(DR. YEN SIN magazine), Checklist, by Lynn Hickman, 75 PU 11

Dragon Murder Case, First National, 1934, a Cinematography, (S.S.Van Dine), by Jon Tuska, 6-1 TAD 20

Dragoo, Kent V.: letter of comment, 24 X 12

Drained, (verse), by Steve Eng, 1-3 AD 5

(Drake, Earl, series: Dan J. Marlowe), Series Synopses, by Robert J. Randisi, 10-2 TAD 181

Dramatis Personae, (Nero Wolfe quiz), by Richard Oldberg, 1-1 G 55

Dramatizations of the Great Literary Detectives and Criminals, Pt.1, Radio, 1-2 TAD 48; Pt.2, Television, 1-3 TAD 94; Pt.3, Theatre, 1-4 TAD 132; Pt.4, Film, 2-1 TAD 31; 2-3 TAD 183, by C.Shibuk and M. Lachman

Dream-Vista, (verse), by Steve Eng, 4-4 AD 2

Dressed to Kill: An Appreciation, ("Dressed to Kill," a Brian DePalma film), by Stuart M. Kaminsky, 14-1 TAD 14

Drew, Bernard A.: A Conversation with Judson Philips, (interview), 13-4 TAD 325

Drew, Bernard A.: A Visit with Walter Gibson, 7 U 23

Drew, Bernard A.: Hoh-Hoh to Satan, DETECTIVE FICTION WEEKLY'S Nutty Series Heroes of the 1930's, (the unconventional detectives in this pulp magazine), 2-2 C 88

Drew, Bernard A.: letter of comment, 6 U 51

Drew, Bernard A.: The Mike Shayne Caper, 3-1 PQ 51

Drew, Bernard A.: Secretaries in the Pulps, (comments on role of secretaries in pulp stories), 2 U 7

Drew, Bernard A.: Spenser, Hardboiled Roots, 21 X 7

Drew, Bernard A.: Tracking Tom Buchanan, 8 U 135

Drew, Bernard A.: The Vanishing Resource - Old Pulp Writers (on the need to interview now), 2 U 2

(Drew, Nancy, girls' series), Cameo Edition Nancy Drews, (biblio-graphic data), by Dave Farah, 1-5 YB 3

(Drew, Nancy, girls' series), The Critic's Clew...to Miss Drew, (discusses various writers who wrote the series), by Kent Winslow, 7 MA 16

(Drew, Nancy, girls' series), Nancy Drew in Japanese, (on Japanese editions and translations), by Don Holbrook, 7 MA 13

(Drew, Nancy, girl's series), Nancy Drew in Review, by John M. Enright, 7 MA 6

(Drew, Nancy, girls' series), Nancy Drew on the Screen, by David Zinman, 6-2 MR 3

(Drew, Nancy, girls' series), Series Move to New Publisher, (change in publishers for Nancy Drew series), by Fred Woodworth, 2 MA 24

(Drew, Nancy, girls' series), TV's Nancy Drew, by John M. Enright, 7 MA 14

Drews, Bob: letter of comment, 11 JD 23

Dricks, Victor: Group Controlling Pulp Prices Arrested! (humour), 30 X 136

Dricks, Victor: Ronald Clyne, A Portrait, (biographical sketch), 18 X 20

Dricks, Victor: Why I Collect Science Fiction, (commentary), 20 X 5

(Driggs, Laurence LaTourette), Arnold Adair Boy's Books Series: Biblio-graphy, by Harry K. Hudson, 1-3 YB 8

Driven to Death, (verse), by Margaret B. Maron, 13-1 TAD 68

Driving Through the Wisconsin Valley on a Summer Evening, (verse), by Charles Beebel, 4-1 AD 10

(Drood, Edwin), The Dilemma of Datchery, (MYSTERY OF EDWIN DROOD by Charles Dickens), by E.F.Bleiler, 4-4 MF 7

(Drood, Edwin), Edwin's Mystery and Its History, or, Another Look at Datchery, (MYSTERY OF EDWIN DROOD by Dickens), by Ben Fisher, 4-5 MF 6

(Drood, Edwin), John Dickson Carr's Solution to THE MYSTERY OF EDWIN DROOD (by Dickens), 14-4 TAD 291

(Drood, Edwin), Drood the Obscure: The Evidence of the Names (MYSTERY OF EDWIN DROOD by Dickens), by Robert F. Fleissner, 13-1 TAD 12

Drood the Obscure: The Evidence of the Names, (THE MYSTERY OF EDWIN DROOD by Dickens), by Robert F. Fleissner, 13-1 TAD 12

Drucker, Thomas: letter of comment,
2-3 TAD 202; 3-4 TAD 280
(Drummond, Bulldog, series, by "Sapper"),
Checklist, annotated, by Barry
Van Tilburg, 4-5 MF 22
(Drummond, Bulldog, series, by "Sapper"),
Reminiscences, (script-writing Holmes
and Bulldog Drummond), by Frank
Gruber, 2-1 TAD 56
duBoucher, Andres: letter of comment,
1-2 G 68
Dubourg, Maurice: Maigret & Co., The
Detectives of the Simenon Agency,
(translated by Francis M. Nevins,
Jr.), 4-2 TAD 79
Duck Savage: The Mallard of Bronze,
(comic strip, pastiche of Doc
Savage), by Todd R. & Timothy J.
Rutt, 1-2 WA 9; 1-3 WA 11; 1-4 WA
11; 2-1 WA 18
Dueren, Fred: Asey Mayo, "The Hayseed
Sherlock," (detective character
created by Phoebe Atwood Taylor),
10-1 TAD 21
Dueren, Fred: Charlie Chan, A Biography,
(character created by Earl Derr
Biggers), 7-4 TAD 263
Dueren, Fred: Evan Pinkerton, (detective
character created by David Frome),
7-3 TAD 193
Dueren, Fred: The Great Merlini(magician
detective created by Clayton Rawson),
4-4 MF 28
Dueren, Fred: Henri Bencolin, (detective
character created by Jeff Marle),
8-2 TAD 98
Dueren, Fred: Hercule Poirot, The
Private Life of a Private Eye
(Agatha Christie's Poirot), 7-2 TAD
111
Dueren, Fred: John J. Malone (and
Cohorts), (detective created by
Craig Rice), 8-1 TAD 44
Dueren, Fred: letter of comment, 12 MN L2;
4-3 MF 49; 5-3 MF 44; 7-1 TAD 64;
8-1 TAD 75; 8-3 TAD 231; 10-4 TAD 292;
14-2 TAD 185
Dueren, Fred: Paper Crimes , (reviews of
mystery paperback books), 8-4 TAD 295;
9-1 TAD 50; 9-2 TAD 140; 9-3 TAD 212;
9-4 TAD 277; 10-1 TAD 51; 10-2 TAD
130; 10-4 TAD 340; 11-2 TAD 192; 11-3
TAD 306; 11-4 TAD 396; 12-2 TAD 135;
12-3 TAD 287; 13-1 TAD 65; 13-2 TAD
136; 13-3 TAD 251; 13-4 TAD 361; 14-1
TAD 80; 14-2 TAD 183
Dueren, Fred: Philo Vance, (detective
created by S.S.Van Dine), 9-1 TAD 23
Dueren, Fred: Rogues for the New Century,
(comparison of Grant Allen's AN
AFRICAN MILLIONAIRE and George
Randolph Chester's GET-RICH-QUICK
WALLINGFORD), 5-3 MF 11
Dueren, Fred: Series Synopses, David
Brandstetter Series by Joseph
Hansen, 11-4 TAD 365

Dueren, Fred: Was the Old Man in the
Corner an Armchair Detective?
(detective character created by
Baroness Orczy), 14-3 TAD 232
(Durrenmatt, Friedrich), The Failure
of Two Swiss Sleuths, (in mystery
fiction of Durrenmatt), by Kay
Herr, 13-2 TAD 163
(Durrenmatt, Friedrich), Friedrich
Durrenmatt: The Detective Story
as Moral Parable, by Orley I.
Holtan, 5-3 TAD 133
(Duff, MacDougal, detective), The
First Appearance: MacDougal Duff,
(in LAY ON MacDUFF! by Charlotte
Armstrong), by Maryell Cleary,
3-1 PP 27
(Duffield, J.W.), Bert Wilson Series,
(boys' books), by Jack Schorr,
2-1 TBN 2
Duffield, Marcus: The Pulps, Day Dreams
for the Masses, 33 X 108
Duke, Terry: letter of comment,
27 JD 34
(Duke, Winifred), Winifred Duke, A
Preliminary Survey, by Norman
Donaldson, 2-2 TAD 94
Dukeshire, Theodore P.: The Books of
Geoffrey Homes, 3-3 MF 19
Dukeshire, Theodore P.: The Books of
Nicholas Luard, 4-1 MF 12
Dukeshire, Theodore P.: The Caper
Novels of James Hadley Chase,
10-2 TAD 126
Dukeshire, Theodore P.: Chase, The
Private Eye Novels of James Hadley
Chase, 7 PE 7
Dukeshire, Theodore P.: Checklist,
Geoffrey Homes, 3-3 MF 21
Dukeshire, Theodore P.: James Hadley
Chase, 5-1 TAD 32 ; (checklist)
5-1 TAD 33
Dukeshire, Theodore P.: John Buchan,
7-3 TAD 198; (checklist) 7-3 TAD
201
Dukeshire, Theodore P.: Kim Philby,
Master Spy in Fact and Fiction,
3-1 MF 14
Dukeshire, Theodore P.: letter of
comment, 5-1 MR 16; 4-3 TAD 183;
5-3 TAD 175; 5-4 TAD 251
Dukeshire, Theodore P.: Peter Cheyney,
(with checklist), 4-4 MR 8
Dukeshire, Theodore P.: Robert Rostand
and Mike Locken, 2-4 MF 4
(Dulac, Edmund), Arabian Nights and
Art Nouveau, (books by Dulac), by
Rebecca Bruns, 6 YB 23
Dumarest Saga, a Checklist, (by E.C.
Tubb), by Bob Stuart, 1-5 CP 28
(duMaurier, Daphne: DON'T LOOK NOW),
Tension and Duality in Daphne
duMaurier's "Don't Look Now" by
Jane S. Bakerman, 3-4 MF 8
Dumbfounded in Keelerland, (Harry
Stephen Keeler), by Art Scott,
1-1 MF 12

"Dummy" in Museum was Oltime Outlaw,
(news item, Los Angeles), 1-2 MF 55
Dumont, Tom: Fifty Years of Mysteries,
(biog. sketch of Judson Philips,
with checklist), 4 MY 2
(Duncan, W. Murdoch), W. Murdoch Duncan,
Master of Mystery, An Appreciation,
by Donald Ireland, 9-2 TAD 116
Dunn, Bill: Interview with William X.
Kienzle, 6/7 LR 22
(Dunning, John: LOOKING FOR GINGER
NORTH), Looking for Rachel Wallace
and Ginger North, by George Kelley,
4-3 MF 29
(Dupin, C.Auguste, detective), A Look
at Dupin, by Steve Miller, 2 MT 20
(Durbridge, Francis: Paul Temple series),
The Paul Temple Saga, (British
radio), by Derek Adley, 9-4 TAD 267
(Durham, Philip: DOWN THESE MEAN STREETS
A MAN MUST GO), Commentary on book
about Raymond Chandler, by Stewart
Kemble, 72 PU 18
(Durrell, Sam, series: Edward S.Aarons),
Spy Series Characters in Hardback,
Pt.IX, by Barry Van Tilburg, 5-5
MF 15
Dust-Jacketed Era, The, 1927-1961, (on
Hardy Boys boys' series, biblio-
graphical data), by John M. Enright,
4 MA 12
Dust Jackets, (commentary on values of
dust jackets for collectible books),
by Basil Wells, 2 U 16
Dusty Ayres, (pulp air/spy hero), by
Robert Weinberg, 1 P 22
Dusty Ayres, (in Corinth paperback
books), by Bruce Cervon, 3-2 CP 18
(Dusty Ayres series), Checklist,
(in pulp magazines), by Wooda Nicholas
Carr, 10 SF 45
(Dusty Ayres series), The Emperor of
the World, by Wooda Nicholas Carr,
10 SF 42
Dutch, Bill: Augie vs. the United States
Post Office, (August Derleth's
experiences with postal service),
2-2 AD 10
Dutch, Bill: August Derleth's Wisconsin
Diary, (on Derleth's weekly column
in Madison newspaper), 4-4 AD 7
Dutch, Bill: Bibliography of the Works
of August Derleth, (list of corrections)
4-4 AD 11
Dutch, Bill: Derleth and the Morel
Season, (August Derleth's love for
mushrooms), 2-3/4 AD 9
Dutch, Bill: The Derleth Legend,
3-1 AD 9
Dutch, Bill: Derleth on Art, (August
Derleth), 3-3 AD 7
Dutch, Bill: Derleth on Education,
(August Derleth), 3-4 AD 12; 4-1
AD 11; 4-2 AD 4
Dutch, Bill: Derleth's "Wisconsin Diary"
(newspaper column), 1-4 AD 5

Dutch, Bill: letter of comment,
1-4 AD 8; 3-2 AD 10
Dutch, Bill: Reminiscences, (of
August Derleth), 2-1 AD 4
Dutch Diary, (report on "Paperbacks
U.S.A."exhibition in Holland),
by James Avati, 4-1 PQ 15
Dutcher, Roger: letter of comment,
22 X 52; 26 X 72; 30 X 148;
33 X 115; 36 X 70; 40 X 85
Dyar, Dafydd Neal: Alias Big Bad John,
(Doc Savage association article),
6 U 13
Dyar, Dafydd Neal: The Bama Legacy,
(James Bama, Doc Savage artist),
7 DQ 6
Dyar, Dafydd Neal: Cryptograms,
(code), 7 U 26
Dyar, Dafydd Neal: Doc Savage at 75,
An Informal Interview with Clark
Savage, Jr. (simulated), 12 DS 18
Dyar, Dafydd Neal: Doc Savage, The
(Space) Man of Bronze, (Doc
Savage, speculative article),
7 U 6
Dyar, Dafydd Neal: The Eye of Day:
A Speculation on the Maternity
of John Sunlight, (speculative
article on Doc Savage villain),
6 DQ 6
Dyar, Dafydd Neal: letter of comment,
6 DQ 4; (as Clark Savage,Jr.) 6 DQ 5;
7 DQ 4; 7 DS 5; (as Clark Savage,
Jr.) 9 DS 23; (as Clark Savage,Jr.)
12 DS 5; 6 U 51; 7 U 40
Dyar, Dafydd Neal: Who is Doc Savage?
(speculative essay), 12 DS 9
Dyar, Dafydd Neal: The Phantom Airship,
The Truth Behind the Fiction,
(re: Doc Savage), 12 SF 32
Dyar, Dafydd Neal: Sunlight, Son
Bright, (John Sunlight, pulp Doc
Savage villain), 8 DS 22
Dyar, Dafydd Neal: Top Secret, (Doc
Savage type cryptogram), 6 U 28
Dynamics of the Brothers Moriarty, The,
(Sherlockiana), by Timothy J. Rutt,
1-1 WA 5

Early Chronicles of Fu Manchu, The,
by Robert E. Briney, 15 R 9
Early "Condominium" Hurricane Warning,
(John D. MacDonald), by Jean and
Walter Shine, 22 JD 15
Early Hurst Books, The, (Hurst & Co.,
publisher of boys' books), by
Harry K. Hudson, 1-2 YB 3
Early J.D., (John D. MacDonald in
the pulp magazines), by Ed Cox,
2 JD 3; 9 JD 19
Early JDM in EQMM, (John D. MacDonald
in ELLERY QUEEN'S MYSTERY MAGAZINE)
by Francis M. Nevins,Jr., 18 JD 10
Early JDM: Pulp Thought & Pulp Action,
(John D. MacDonald in pulps), by
Francis M. Nevins,Jr., 14 JD 14

Early JDM: Three Pulps from '49, (John D. MacDonald in magazine stories), by Francis M. Nevins, Jr., 15 JD 19

Early JDM: Woolrich Touches, (John D. MacDonald and Cornell Woolrich similarities in early work), by Francis M. Nevins, Jr., 16 JD 12

Early JDM: To Any Lengths, (John D. MacDonald, magazine stories), by Francis M. Nevins, Jr., 17 JD 18

Early JDM: In Doc Savage, (John D. MacDonald stories in DOC SAVAGE pulp magazine), 19 JD 8, by Francis M. Nevins, Jr.

Early JDM: Four from Early '49, (John D. MacDonald, magazine stories), by Francis M. Nevins, Jr., 21 JD 11

East, Andy: For Your Spy's Eyes Only, (discusses paperback spy novels of 1960's), 1-3 M 44

East Coat Mystery News, (general news column), by Art Bourgeau, 1-1 M 32; 1-2 M 17

(East Coast Pulp and Paperback Convention), A Report on...First Convention, by Albert Tonik, 11 SF 34

(Eastwood, Clint), The Siegel-Eastwood Quest, (film, Don Siegel and Clint Eastwood), by Kathy Esselman, 7-4 TAD 253

Easy Chair, The - "Alias Nero Wolfe," by Bernard DeVoto, 1-2 G 37

Eaton, Herbert: letter of comment, 14-2 TAD 186

Eberhardt, Dorothy: letter of comment, 1-2 M 3

Eck, Frank: letter of comment, 5/6 MN 13; 9 MN L5; 8 R 31; 8-3 TAD 231; 9-1 TAD 77; 9-1 TAD 80

Eck, Frank: Shadow Gallery, An Informal Survey of Cover Art of the Seventies, Pt.1, (Tribute to Agatha Christie) 9-3 TAD 170; Pt.2, (Tribute to Maj Sjowall and Per Wahloo) 10-1 TAD 46

Ecology and the Detective Novel, The Contribution of John D. MacDonald, by Donald C. Wall, 21 JD 3

Economic Despair Fueled Miami Riots, (essay), by John D. MacDonald, 26 JD 10

Ed McBain, (interview), by David Harlequin, 2-1 M 14

Ed Noon's Quickest Caper, or, Revenge: Italian Style, (Ed Noon, detective created by Mike Avallone), by R.T. Karlinchak, 38 X 139

Edgar Award Winners, (for 1977), by Jim Huang, 7 CL 1

Edgar Box Mystery Novels, The, by George Kelley, 4 U 30

Edgar Lustgarten 1970-1978, (memorial and checklist), by Mary Groff, 12-3 TAD 286

Edgar Rice Burroughs, a Short Biography, by John F. Sullivan, 3-3 BC 346

Edgar Rice Burroughs and the Action Pulps, by John Harwood, 75 PU 12

Edgar Wallace I Knew, The, by Nigel Morland, 1-3 TAD 68

Edgars, The, (34th Annual MWA Awards Banquet report), by Thomas Godfrey, 2-1 M 22

Edgars, Anyone?, (choosing the MWA awards), by Hillary Waugh, 2-1 TAD 52

Editor at Work: Ellery Queen and EQMM, (ELLERY QUEEN'S MYSTERY MAGAZINE), by Francis M. Nevins, Jr., 14 X 4

(edition identification), The Avon and DAW problem, (identification of 1st and subsequent editions), by Richard Bilyeu, 11 SF 25

(edition identification), Publishers' Codes and Collecting Contemporary Editions, (identification of 1st and subsequent editions), by Keith L. Justice, 11 SF 23

Edition Variations of Leo Edwards Books Published by Grosset & Dunlap, (Leo Edwards' boys' books), by Julius R. Chenu, 3-1 BC 282

Edmond Hamilton, ("by himself, 1934") 2 WT 10

Edmond Hamilton, by Robert Weinberg, 1 WT 7

Edmund Clerihew Bentley, (biog. and literary sketch), by Charles Shibuk, 4-1 TAD 30

Edmund Crispin, A Memorial and Appreciation, by William A.S. Sarjeant, 3-3 PP 3

Edmund Crispin, (autobiographical sketch), by Robert Bruce Montgomery, 12-2 TAD 183

Edmund Wilson and the Detective Story, by Carl Byron Dickson, 9-3 TAD 189

Education of Jason Beard, A.B. Guthrie's Western Suspense Stories, by Fred Erisman, 1-2 C 126

Edward D. Hoch, A Chec-list, by William J. Clark, Edward D. Hoch, and Francis M. Nevins, Jr., 9-2 TAD 102

Edwards and His Characters, (on the books of Leo Edwards; boys' books), by Gerald J. Corkey, 2-3 TBN 3

Edwards' Magazine Illustrators, (on artists for Leo Edwards and his juvenile stories in magazines), by Julius R. Chenu, 2-1 TBN 1

Edwards' Plot Ideas, (boys' books, Leo Edwards), by Julius R. Chenu, 2-6 TBN 1

Edwards, John: Dan Fortune - Private Eye, (stories by Michael Collins), 9 SF 38

Edwards, John: From Shadow to Superman, (heroes of popular fiction), 7 U 10

Edwards, John: The Story of Dennis Lynds, 4 U 21; 5 U 20; 6 U 36

(Edwards, Leo), A Leo Edwards Imitation, (Fun Loving Gang series by Harold M. Sherman, boys' books), by Rick Crandall, 1-3 YB 7

(Edwards, Leo), A Stranger Visits "The Land of Leo Edwards," (boys' books author), by Ed Mulford, 2-6 TBN 5

(Edwards, Leo), A Visit to Hi-Lee, (home of Leo Edwards, boys' books author), by Forrest Campbell, 2-1 TB 3

(Edwards, Leo), Andy Blake First Leo Edwards Book, by Julius R. Chenu, 1-1 TB 1

(Edwards, Leo), Area Map of Tutter, People, Places, (locale of Jerry Todd books by Leo Edwards, boys' books), by Robert L. Johnson, 2-3 TBN 1

(Edwards, Leo), Art Work of the Leo Edwards' Books: Dust Jackets, (boys' books), by Julius R. Chenu, 1-2 TBN 1

(Edwards, Leo), Background of First Andy Blake Book, (boys' books), by Julius R. Chenu, 1-3 TBN 1

(Edwards, Leo), Boys' Fiction Written by Leo Edwards, by Julius R. Chenu, 1-2 BC 35

(Edwards, Leo), Boys Who Used Their Brains: The Boy Who Was Always Looking Ahead (Leo Edwards' books characters, boys' books), by Judson D. Stuart, 2-2 TBN 1

(Edwards, Leo), Brothers are Reunited! ("news item" by "Cassibum Kepp" re: books by Leo Edwards), 2-3 TBN 1

(Edwards, Leo), Can You Match This?, (quiz), 1-4 TB 6

(Edwards, Leo), Chatterbox Feature Unique and Informative Innovation ("club" columns in Leo Edwards books), by Julius R. Chenu, 2-4 TB 1

(Edwards, Leo), Dave Dixon's Strawberry Magic, (fiction, a Dixon Farm story, 1926 reprint from boys' paper), by Edward Edson Lee (Leo Edwards), 3-5 TB 5; 4-1 TB 2

(Edwards, Leo), Dedications in Leo's Books, (boys' books by Leo Edwards), by Julius R. Chenu, 1-4 TB 3

(Edwards, Leo), Different Jerry Todd Editions, (bibliographical data on Jerry Todd boys' books series by Edwards), by Robert L. Johnson, 2-2 TBN 1

(Edwards, Leo), Dixon Farm Data, (on series of stories by Edwards published in boys' papers), 1-4 TB 6

(Edwards, Leo), Edition Variations of Leo Edwards Books Published by Grosset & Dunlap, (boys' books), by Julius R. Chenu, 3-1 BC 282

(Edwards, Leo), Edwards and His Characters (boys' books), by Gerald J. Corkey, 2-3 TBN 3

(Edwards, Leo), Edwards Fans Unite (to form Juvenile Jupiter Detective Association; boys' books), by Robert L. Johnson, 1-1 TB 1

(Edwards, Leo), Edwards' Magazine Illustrators, (artwork for stories for boys published in boys' papers), by Julius R. Chenu, 2-1 TBN 1

(Edwards, Leo), Edwards' Plot Ideas, (boys' books by Leo Edwards), by Julius R. Chenu, 2-6 TBN 1

(Edwards, Leo), The Flannigans Achieve a Victory, (fiction by Edwards as Edward Edson Lee, 1923), 1-3 TB 5

(Edwards, Leo), The Flannigan Flock, (fiction by Edwards as Edward Edson Lee, 1923), 1-2 TB 4; (publication data 1-4 TB 2)

(Edwards, Leo), Further Data on the Tuffy Bean Series, (by Edwards, boys' books), 2-1 TB 6

(Edwards, Leo), Hi-Lee Cottage 1970 Get-Together Report, (visit to home of Edwards, boys' books author), 3-4 TB 1

(Edwards, Leo), Hi-Lee Hello, (visit to home of Edwards, boys' books author), by Alan S. Dikty, 1-4 BC 113

(Edwards, Leo), How I Found My Inferior Decorators (collecting experience in acquiring POPPY OTT: INFERIOR DECORATOR, by Edwards, boys' book) by Jack R. Schorr, 4-1 TB 1

(Edwards, Leo), How to Tell First G&D Editions in Edwards Books, (on identification of 1st editions by Grosset & Dunlap, boys' books by Edwards), 3-1 TB 1; 3-2 TB 3

(Edwards, Leo), "Illustrated by Bert Salg," (on artist for Edwards books, boys' series), 1-2 TB 1; 1-3 TBN 11

(Edwards, Leo), In Appreciation of Leo Edwards, (boys' books author), by Gil O'Gara, 1-1 YB 13

(Edwards, Leo), Interesting Parallels Between Books by Margaret Sutton and Edward Edson Lee, (comparisons, series by Sutton for girls, and Leo Edwards books for boys), 2-3 TB 1

(Edwards, Leo), Is There a Comet Coaster Around? (re: Jerry Todd books by Edwards), 1-1 TB 4

(Edwards, Leo), Jerry Todd, (boys' books series), by Julius R. Chenu, 4 BB 3

(Edwards, Leo), Jerry Todd, Detective, (fiction using character created by Leo Edwards, boys' book series), by Julius R. Chenu, 1-1 TBN 7; 1-2 TBN 11; 1-3 TBN 13; 1-4 TBN 15; 2-1 TBN 6; 2-2 TBN 7; 2-3 TBN 7

(Edwards, Leo), Jerry Todd Stories Edwards' Most Popular, (Jerry Todd boys' series books), by Julius R. Chenu, 1-2 TB 1

(Edwards, Leo), Leo Edwards, (sketch of author by his son), by Eugene Lee, 1-3 BC 92

(Edwards, Leo), Leo Edwards and His Books, (biographical and literary sketch, boys' books author), by Julius R. Chenu, 3 BB 7; 1-2 YB 15

(Edwards, Leo), Leo Edwards and the First Person Singular (hero writes as first person singular in boys' books series by Edwards), by John T. Dizer, 1-4 YB 6

(Edwards, Leo), Leo Edwards' Bird Watchers Society, (involvement of youth by author of boys' books), 2-2 TB 1

(Edwards, Leo), Earliest Picture of Leo Edwards, (as provided by his son), by Eugene E. Lee, 3-4 BC 360

(Edwards, Leo), Leo Edwards Magazine Stories, (pre-book writings of boys' books author), by Eugene Lee, 1-2 BC 63

(Edwards, Leo), Letters and Photos of Leo Edwards, (from boys' books author's son), by Eugene Lee, 3-2 BC 314

(Edwards, Leo), The Lost Fortune, A Dixon Farm Story, (as by Edward Edson Lee, fiction in boy's papers) 2-1 TB 2; 2-2 TB 2; 2-3 TB 3; 2-5 TB 2; 3-4 TB 2; 3-5 TB 1

(Edwards, Leo), Magazine Serial is Background for Two Books (Leo Edwards' use of pre-books serial) by Julius R. Chenu, 2-5 TB 1

(Edwards, Leo), More Information on Andy Blake Series, (boys' books), by Julius R. Chenu, 1-3 TB 3

(Edwards, Leo), More on Andy Blake: Printing History of Appleton Edition, (first Leo Edwards boys' book), by Ray H. Zorn, 1-4 TB 1

(Edwards, Leo), Mummy Itchers, (a humorous depiction of item in JERRY TODD AND THE WHISPERING MUMMY by Leo Edwards), by Julius R. Chenu, 2-4 TBN 1

(Edwards, Leo), Mummy Plot Fact Believe It or Not, (basis of Leo Edwards' JERRY TODD AND THE WHISPERING MUMMY boys' book), by Julius R. Chenu, 1-3 TB 1

(Edwards, Leo), Ode to Hadley's Flivver, (verse), by Jack Dizer, 2-2 TB 6; 2-4 TBN 4

(Edwards, Leo), Our Chatterbox, (in THE TUTTER BUGLE, a la columns in Edwards' boys' books), 1-1 TB 2

(Edwards, Leo), Photo (of Edwards) Distributing Newest book, 1-2 TB 3

(Edwards, Leo), Poppy Ott Sequel to Popular Todd Series, (sequential series by Leo Edwards), by Julius R. Chenu, 1-3 TB 1

(Edwards, Leo), Printing Variations in the Andy Blake Series, (bibliographical data on editions), by Julius R. Chenu, 1-1 TBN 5

(Edwards, Leo), Quiz: Can You Match This?, (quiz), 1-3 TB 1

(Edwards, Leo), Rebirth of the Bugle, (THE TUTTER BUGLE), by Robert L. Johnson, 1-1 TB 1

(Edwards, Leo), The Secret and Mysterious Order of the Freckled Goldfish, (readers' club of boys' books by Leo Edwards), 1-1 TB 4

(Edwards, Leo), The Secret of the Jade Throne, (fiction, as by Edward Edson Lee, 1921), 2-6 TBN 7

(Edwards, Leo), Stranger Visits the Land of Leo Edwards, (visit to home of Leo Edwards, boys' books author), by Ed Mulford, 1-1 TB 3; 1-2 TB 2

(Edwards, Leo), That First Andy Blake, (printing history of first Leo Edwards' series book, in rare edition), by Ray H. Zorn, 1-3 TB 3

(Edwards, Leo), Todd Book Editions, (bibliographical data, Jerry Todd boys' books series by Edwards), 2-5 TBN 4

(Edwards, Leo), Todd Series Tops Pop: More Titles and More Printings, (popularity of Jerry Todd series boys' books), by Julius R. Chenu, 1-4 TBN 1

(Edwards, Leo), Trigger Berg, Leo's Junior Series, (Trigger Berg boys' series by Edwards), by Julius R. Chenu, 2-4 TBN 1

(Edwards, Leo), Troubles in Doubles, (fiction, as Edward Edson Lee), 2-4 TBN 7

(Edwards, Leo), Tuffy Bean Stories Last Edwards' Stories, (Tuffy Bean boys' series books by Edwards), 1-4 TB 1

(Edwards, Leo), Tutter Business Establishments, (as mentioned in Jerry Todd boys' series books by Edwards), 1-3 TB 9

(Edwards, Leo), Utica, Ill. is Setting for Other Stories, (locale of some boys' books by Edwards), by Julius R. Chenu, 1-4 TB 1

Edwards, Scott: Digests Not in Hancer, (additional digest-size paperbacks not listed in Hancer's Price Guide), 3-4 CP 22

Edwin and Angelina, (THE MYSTERY OF ANGELINA FROOD by R. Austin Freeman, and THE MYSTERY OF EDWIN DROOD by Dickens), by Norman Donaldson, 2 TF 2

Edwin's Mystery and It's History, or Another Look at Datchery, (re: Charles Dickens' THE MYSTERY OF EDWIN DROOD), by Ben Fisher, 4-5 MF 6

Eggling, John: letter of comment, 5 X 42; 33 X 114

Ehrman, Tom: letter of comment, 24 JD 38

Eisendrath, David & Barbara: letter of comment, 11 JD 21

Eisgruber, Frank, Jr.: A Few Shadow Oddities, (on The Shadow character), 10 P 35

Eisgruber, Frank, Jr.: Crime Undercover, (on The Shadow character), 4 P 15

Eisgruber, Frank, Jr.: letter of comment, 66 PU 64; 74 PU 28

Eisgruber, Frank, Jr.: Only The Shadow Knows, (on The Shadow character), 3 P 28

Eisinger, Erica M.: Detective Story Aspects of the Nouveau Roman, (search for meaning), 12-4 TAD 362

Eldridge, D.W.: letter of comment, 10 JD 19

Elegy for August Derleth, (verse), by T.V.Olsen, 2-3/4 AD 8

Eleven Best Private Eye Novels of Them All, The, (commentary), by Michael Avallone, 38 X 130

Eleventh Hour, The, (fiction, Classic Corner Rare Tales), by Edwin Balmer and William MacHarg, 12-1 TAD 40

(ELEVENTH JUROR, THE: Vincent Starrett), An Eleventh-Hour Reassessment of The Eleventh Juror, Revealing the Germination of a Successful Mystery Tale, by Vincent Starrett, 2-2 PDA 48

Elijah Kellogg, Maine Boy's Writer, (sketch of author), by Walter H. McIntosh, 3-2 BC 309

(Eliot, Freeman), Checklist of Paperback Book Cover Art, by Lance Casebeer, 1-1 CP 20

Ellery Queen, A Checklist, by John J. Newton, 1-3 QC 13

Ellery Queen and His New York, by Marvin Lachman, 1-3 QC 8

Ellery Queen, First Impressions, by Robert W. Douty, 12-3 TAD 196

Ellery Queen in Wrightsville, (locale of series of mystery novels), by Francis M. Nevins, Jr., 7-1 TAD 4

Ellery Queen on the Small Screen, (television series 1955-76), by Francis M. Nevins, Jr., 12-3 TAD 216

Ellery Queen Pilot Show on TV, by Don Hutchison, 7 MY 10

(Ellery Queen Anthologies), EQA 30: An Author/Title Index to ELLERY QUEEN'S ANTHOLOGY 1960-1975, by John Nieminski, 11 MN I1

(Ellery Queen Anthologies), Rex Stout in ELLERY QUEEN'S ANTHOLOGY, checklist, by Don Miller, 9 MN A29

(ELLERY QUEEN'S MYSTERY MAGAZINE), Fred Dannay and EQMM, by Eleanor Sullivan, 12-3 TAD 201

(ELLERY QUEEN'S MYSTERY MAGAZINE), The Magazine, (with chronology, outstanding writers, and circulation) by Marvin Lachman, 2-1 QC 6

(ELLERY QUEEN'S MYSTERY MAGAZINE), 1975 Index, by Don Miller, 8 MN 45

(ELLERY QUEEN'S MYSTERY MAGAZINE), Rex Stout in Ellery Queen's Mystery Magazine, (checklist), by Don Miller, 9 MN A24

(ELLERY QUEEN'S MYSTERY MAGAZINE), The Sherlockian EQMM, (Sherlock Holmes stories/pastiches in Ellery Queen's Mystery Magazine), by Peter E. Blau, 2-1 QC 15

Ellin, Stanley: The Destiny of the House, (comments on Ellin's "The Specialty of the House"), 12-3 TAD 195

Ellin, Stanley: letter of comment, 3-3 MR 12; 1-2 QC 13; 1-3 QC 19; 2-2 QC 12; 10-3 TAD 273

(Ellin, Stanley), Checklist of Works, by Pat Erhardt, 2-3 MR 14

(Ellin, Stanley), Stanley Ellin Talks About Himself and His Writing, by Pat Erhardt, 2-3 MR 13

(Elliott, Bruce), A Full Length Shadow Novel as Told to... (Shadow stories written by Theodore Tinsley and Bruce Elliott), by Fred S. Cook, 3 BS 12

(Elliott, Don), Background and Checklist, Don Elliott/Robert Silverberg Erotic Fiction Titles, by Keith L. Justice, 13 SF 18

Ellis, Charles B.: letter of comment, 2-1 MR 11; 3-2 MR 16

(Ellis, Edward S.), An Introduction to SETH JONES OF NEW HAMPSHIRE (boys' book), 3-3 BC 336

(Ellis, Edward S.), Edward S. Ellis, An Introduction, (biographical and literary sketch of boys' books author), by Edward S. Ellis, 3-3 BC 336

(Ellis, Edward S.), Favorite Juvenile Authors: What Publishers Said About Their Old Stand-bys, by Gil O'Gara, 1-2 YB 19

Ellis, James: A Remembrance of FN, (on FANTASTIC NOVELS pulp magazine), 20 X 37

Ellis, James: Leigh Brackett, Story-teller, (sketch), 42 X 27

Ellis, James: letter of comment, 22 X 49; 22 X 52; 24 X 12; 24 X 46; 43 X 6

Ellis, James: Will F. Jenkins (memorial tribute), 15 X 5

Ellman, Neil: Charlie Chan Carries On, (on CHARLIE CHAN CARRIES ON by Earl Derr Biggers), 10-2 TAD 183

Elston, James I., Jr.: letter of comment, 8-4 TAD 324

Elves in the Shelves, (reviews), 1 D 20

Emery, Richard: Criminal Quiz, (quiz), 3-5 PP 18

Emery, Richard: letter of comment, 2-1 PP 32; 2-2 PP 32; 3-1 PP 49; 3-2 PP 40; 3-3 PP 42; 3-4 PP 38; 4-2 PP 42; 4-5/6 PP 96

Emery, Richard: Subject Guide to Mystery Fiction, 3-1 PP 3

Emily Dickinson, Where Are You?, (verse), by Ray Bradbury, 13 X 6

Emmens, Tom: letter of comment, 27 JD 35

Emperor of the World, The, (discussion of segment of Dusty Ayres series, pulp magazine hero), by Wooda Nicholas Carr, 10 SF 42

Emperor Rudolph, (Operator 5, pulp magazine hero, and the Purple Empire, an enemy villain), by Wooda Nicholas Carr, 10 P 22

(ENCYCLOPEDIC GUIDE TO MYSTERY, DETECTIVE AND SUSPENSE FICTION: Ordean Hagen), How I "Done" It, (on writing the book), by Ordean Hagen, 1-2 TAD 45

End of the Golden Age, (memorial tribute to Agatha Christie), by George Wuyek, 10-3 TAD 263

(END OF THE NIGHT, THE: John D. MacDonald), The Prophet Before the Fact: A Note on The End of the Night by John D. MacDonald, by Veronica M.S.Kennedy, 7-1 TAD 41

End of the World and the Day After, The, by Robert L. Brown, 20 X 9

Ending of ROSEMARY'S BABY and Other Comments from Ira Levin, (interview with Levin), 3-1 MR 9

Endure and Prevail, The Novels of Dick Francis, by Barry Bauska, 11-3 TAD 238

Eng, Steve: A Flat in Paddington, (verse, re: Praed Street and Solar Pons), 3-3 AD 3

Eng, Steve: Atmosphere of Houses, (verse), 2-2 AD 12

Eng, Steve: The Derleth Difference, (on August Derleth and Arkham House), 4-4 AD 12

Eng, Steve: Drained, (verse), 1-3 AD 5

Eng, Steve: Dream-Vista, (verse), 4-4 AD 2

Eng, Steve: Evening in Spring, (verse), 2-3/4 AD 10

Eng, Steve: The Forest Gift, (verse), 4-2 AD 10

Eng, Steve: Knock?, (verse), 4-1 AD 9

Eng, Steve: letter of comment, 1-3 AD 3; 2-2 AD 9

Eng, Steve: Microcosm, (verse, re: August Derleth), 2-1 AD 3

Eng, Steve: Nostalgia, (verse), 1-4 AD 5

Eng, Steve: On Keeping a Journal, (after reading VILLAGE YEAR by August Derleth; verse), 2-1 AD 12

Eng, Steve: Sac Prairie People, (verse, re: August Derleth), 2-3/4 AD 8

Eng, Steve: Silence, (verse), 3-1 AD 9

Eng, Steve: Tavern Bill, (verse), 1-2 AD 7

Eng, Steve: Upon Reading of Lovecraft's Death, (verse), 3-1 AD 2

Eng, Steve: Vanished, (verse), 3-4 AD 11

Engineer and Me, The, (relationship to author's works and Robert D. Heinlein), by Arthur D. Hlavaty, 11 SF 3

Engkent, Garry: letter of comment, 11 JD 26

English Detective Novel Between the Wars, The, 1919-1939, by Elaine Bander, 11-3 TAD 262

(ENIGMA, THE: John Fowles), Freedom and Mystery in John Fowles' THE ENIGMA, by Steven R. Carter, 3-5 MF 14

Enigma of the Policeman/Writer, The, (police procedurals written by police personnel), by Paul Bishop, 2-1 M 34

Enright, John M.: The Clue in the Old Library, (on Hardy Boys boys' books series), 4 MA 23

Enright, John M.: The Dust-Jacketed Era, 1927-1961, (Hardy Boys boys' books series), 4 MA 12

Enright, John M.: Hardy Boys Tie-Ins, (Hardy Boys boys' book series), 4 MA 9

Enright, John M.: letter of comment, 4 MA 24

Enright, John M.: Mr. McFarlane's Magic, (Hardy Boys boys' books series), 4 MA 5

Enright, John M.: NancyDrew in Review, (Nancy Drew girls' books series) 7 MA 6

Enright, John M.: Other Writings by Leslie McFarlane, (one of the authors of Hardy Boys boys' books series), 4 MA 18

Enright, John M.: TV's Nancy Drew, (Nancy Drew on television), 7 MA 14

Epilogue, Culprit Confesses, (John Dickson Carr's autobiography in process at time of death), 1 NC 27

Epitaph for An Unrepentant Murderer, (verse), by David Bates, 3-3 PP 16

Epstein, Marvin P.: letter of comment, 14-1 TAD 74

EQA 30: An Author/Title Index to Ellery Queen's Anthology 1960-1975, by John Nieminski, 11 MN I1

EQMM Cover Murders, The, (fiction), by Marvin S. Lachman, 1-1 MF 6; (pt.2) by Rik Thompson, 1-2 MF 3

Erhardt, Pat: A Report on Bouchercon I, (mystery author and fans convention), 3-6 MR 25

Erhardt, Pat: Bill Ballinger, His Work, His Women and His World, (with checklist), 4-6 MR 3

Erhardt, Pat: Checklist for Graham Greene Mysteries, 1-5 MR 15

Erhardt, Pat: Checklist, Stanley Ellin, Works, 2-3 MR 14

Erhardt, Pat: Checklist, Phyllis A. Whitney, 2-4 MR 5

Erhardt, Pat: Double Life of Gloria Amoury, The, (interview), 3-5 MR 3

Erhardt, Pat: letter of comment, 12 JD 13; 3-1 MR 16; 1-2 QC 13; 2-2 QC 12; 2-1 TAD 64; 2-2 TAD 127; 3-2 TAD 139

Erhardt, Pat: Meet Phyllis A. Whitney, (interview), 2-4 MR 3

Erhardt, Pat: Mystery Writer of Merit, Cornell Woolrich, 1-2 MR 3

Erhardt, Pat: Stanley Ellin Talks About Himself and His Writing, 2-3 MR 13

Erhardt, Pat: Woolrich Check List, (Cornell Woolrich), 1-2 MR 4

Erickson, Bengt: letter of comment, 7 BS 2; 8 BS 3

Erisman, Fred: Clayton Rawson and the Flexible Formula, (illusory nature of the formula puzzle mystery), 14-2 TAD 173

Erisman, Fred: Crime Fiction, Some Varieties of Historical Experience, 1-1 C 1

Erisman, Fred: The Education of Jason Beard, A.B.Guthrie's Western Suspense Stories, 1-2 C 126

Erisman, Fred: Romantic Reality in the Spy Stories of Len Deighton, 10-2 TAD 101

(Erlika, Daughter of Satan), Fading Shadows, Erlika, Daughter of Satan, (in G.T.Fleming-Roberts' Secret Agent X series), by Tom Johnson, 11 DS 24

Ernest Bramah in Anthologies 1914-1972, by William White, 10-1 TAD 30

Ernest Bramah to E.C.Bentley, An Unpublished Letter, by William White, 2-3 MR 8

Ernest Bramah's Max Carrados, (Carrados, detective creation of Bramah), by William White, 2-2 MR 7

(erotic fiction, paperback), Background and Checklist, Don Elliott/Robert Silverberg Erotic Fiction Titles, by Keith L. Justice, 13 SF 18

Escude, R.: letter of comment, 3 DS 7

Eskestrand, W. Del: letter of comment, 11 JD 20, 4-3 TAD 181

Espionage Fights Off Boredom, (spy films), by Lee Beaupre, 1-5 MR 12

Esselman, Kathy: The Siegel-Eastwood Quest, (film, Don Siegel, Clint Eastwood), 7-4 TAD 253

(Esteven, John), Modern Age Books and the John Esteven Mystery, (the identification of Esteven), by Angela Andrews, 4-2 PQ 29

Estrada, Joseph: Writers for the Record, Authors Reply to Questions on Series Characters, 3-2 M 36

Estrada, Joseph: Writers for the Record, the Changing Role of Women as Influence on Mystery Fiction,(by var. writers), 3-1 M 40

(Ethan, John B.: Victor Grant series), Series Synopses, by John Vining, 10-2 TAD 187

European Paperback Prelude, The, (discussion on early European paperback books), by Piet Schreuders, 4-2 PQ 38

(Eustace, Robert), The Mystery of Robert Eustace, by Joe R.Christopher, 13-4 TAD 365

Evan Pinkerton, (detective character created by David Frome), by Fred Dueren, 7-3 TAD 193

Evans, T. Jeff: Robert B. Parker and the Hardboiled Tradition of American Detective Fiction, 1-2 C 100

Evening in Spring, (verse), by Steve Eng, 2-3/4 AD 10

Everett, E.: letter of comment, 14 R 27

Everil Worrell, (pulp author, sketch and comments), by Jeanne Eileen Murphy, 1 WT 13

Evernden, Margery: America, Ou est-vous? Speculations on Exbrayat, (Charles Hubert Exbrayat-Durivaux, author), 11-3 TAD 254

Everson, William K.: letter of comment, 4-2 TAD 130; 10-3 TAD 274; 14-1 TAD 71

Everts, R. Alain: The Lovecraft Family in America, (on H.P.Lovecraft), 18 X 7

Every Bad Boy's Bad Boy, (literary discussion of George Wilbur Peck's THE BAD BOY with reprint of a portion), by Gil O'Gara, 1-5 YB 4

(Every Boy's Library), Checklist, by Charles P. Fisk, 2-1 BC 141

Evil as Illusion in the Detective Story, by Bill Nelson, 1-1 C 9

Evil Lotus, The, (on the pulp villainess) by Will Murray, 11 DS 20

Evolution of the Great American Detective, The - The Reader as Detective Hero, by William Kittredge and Steven M. Krauzer, 11-4 TAD 319

(Ewing, Frederick R.), I,LIBERTINE, Shepherd's Crook or Bony Sturgeon? by Don Z. Block, 2-4 CP 27

(Exbrayat-Durivaux, Charles Hubert), America,
Ou est-vous?, Speculations on Exbrayat,
by Margery Evernden, 11-3 TAD 254

Excerpt From the Files of Shot Scott:
Private Eye, (report on annual paperback
book collectors party), by Art Scott,
2-5 CP 5

Excerpts from THE BOYS IN THE BLACK MASK
(exhibit, UCLA Library, 1961, with
checklist of hardboiled fiction),
3-2 MR 23

Exclusive! The Detection Club's First
Collaborations, Unpublished Christie
and Others, (with checklist), by
Paul R. Moy, 4-5/6 PP 15

(Executioner, The, series: Don Pendleton),
Series Synopses, by John Vining,
9-2 TAD 113

Experience Will Out, (verse), by Margaret
B. Maron, 13-1 TAD 68

(EXPERIENCES OF A LADY DETECTIVE: Anonyma),
Female Detectives, Ghost Books and
the Relative Importance of It All,
by E.F.Bleiler, 8-3 TAD 202

Expiatory Symbolism in Lawrence Sanders'
THE FIRST DEADLY SIN, by Bill Nelson,
1-2 C 71

Explaining Ellery Queen (Who is Ellery
Queen?), by William Ruble, 2-2 QC 8

Explaining the Mystery Story, (as social
function), by R. Gordon Kelly, 5-4
TAD 214

Explorations of Love, An Examination of
Some Novels by Ruth Rendell, by Jane
S. Bakerman, 11-2 TAD 139

Explosive Novels of Richard L. Garves, The,
by George Kelley, 3-6 MF 9

Expressionism and American Popular
Literature, Hammett as a Continental
Op - Eye, by Margaret Lamb, 2-1 C 26

Exquisite Perquisite, (Solar Pons), by
Helen Halbach, 2-5 PD 4

Eye Appeal, (reviews), by Marlowe Archer,
4 PE 24; 5 PE 16

"Eye of Osiris, The" and the Webster-
Parkman Case, (re: R. Austin Freeman),
by John McAleer, 12 TF 2

Eye of Day, The, A Speculation on the
Maternity of John Sunlight, (Doc
Savage villain), by Dafydd Neal Dyar,
6 DQ 6

Eye Q II, (private eye quiz), by Jonathon
Harrow, 1-2 M 4

Eye-Q 3, (private eye quiz), 1-3 M 42

Eye-Q 4, Tour of Duty, (police procedural
quiz), by Jonathon Harrow, 2-1 M 42

(EYE OF SIVA, THE: Sax Rohmer), The
Lost "Eye" by Robert E. Briney,
6 R 9; 7 R 10

EYEclopedia, (private eye "dictionary"),
by F.E.Perine, 1 PE 22

Eyes on the Screen, (mystery and crime
shows on television), by Mary Croff,
13-3 TAD 261

Face-to-Face with P.D.James, (mystery
author), by Maryell Cleary, 4-1
PP 8

Faces from the Shadows, (pulp heroes
discussed), by Robert Sampson,
6-2 MR 7

Fading Shadows: The Adjustor, (pulp
detective hero), by Tom Johnson,
8 U 137

Fading Shadows: Corinth/Regency
Paperbacks, (The Phantom Detective,
The Spider, and other paperback
reprints of pulp magazine stories),
by Tom Johnson, 10 SF 36

Fading Shadows: Erlika, Daughter of
Satan, (pulp villainess in G.T.
Fleming-Roberts Secret Agent X
series), by Tom Johnson, 11 DS 24

Fading Shadows: Fantastic Fighting
Men of Fiction, (pulp heroes), by
Tom Johnson, 8 U 66

Fading Shadows: Fighting Men Extraordinary, (pulp heroes), by Tom
Johnson, 22 X 26

Fading Shadows: Harold Sherman, (pulp
author), by Tom Johnson, 7 U 26

Fading Shadows: James Reasoner,
(author), by Tom Johnson, 2 PW 3

Fading Shadows: John Colicos, (author),
by Tom Johnson, 1 PW 2

Fading Shadows: Lady X, (female
villains in pulp magazine stories),
by Tom Johnson, 6 U 24

Fading Shadows: Madame Death, (G.T.
Fleming-Roberts' female villainess
in Secret Agent X series), by Tom
Johnson, 11 DS 12

Fading Shadows: Michael Avallone,
(author), by Tom Johnson, 9 SF 21

Fading Shadows: The Story of G.T.
Fleming-Roberts, (pulp magazine
author), by Tom Johnson, 2 U 14

(FAHRENHEIT 451: Ray Bradbury),
Reprints/Reprints, (reprint editions
of Bradbury's book), by Bill Crider,
3-3 PQ 22

Faig, Kenneth, Jr.: HPL, The Book That
Nearly Was, (H.P.Lovecraft), 11 X 118

Failure of Two Swiss Sleuths, The,
(fiction of Friedrich Durrenmatt),
by Kay Herr, 13-2 TAD 163

(Fairbairn, Roger), John Dickson Carr,
Alias Roger Fairbairn, and the
Historical Novel, by Douglas G.
Greene, 11-4 TAD 339

Fairchild, W.R.: letter of comment,
7 DQ 3

Fake Plow Case, The, (Before Midnight
Contest, The Wolfe Pack), by James
R. Skelton, 1-2 G 45

Falina, Peter: letter of comment,
10 BS 21

Fall Highlights, (mystery reviews), by
Amnon Kabatchnik, 11 CL 7

Fallen Mighty, The, (on The Shadow pulp
    character), by Dean A. Grennell,
    22 X 20
(Fallon, Martin: Paul Chavasse series),
    Checklist, annotated, by Barry
    Van Tilburg, 4-3 MF 28
Fame Surprises Agatha Christie, (news-
    paper article), 4-1 MR 2
(FAMOUS FANTASTIC MYSTERIES), The
    Fantastic Sisters - Literature and
    Lovely, (on the pulp magazines
    FAMOUS FANTASTIC MYSTERIES and
    FANTASTIC NOVELS, with checklist
    and index), by Herman S. McGregor,
    74 PU 6
FAMOUS SCIENCE FICTION, Checklist and
    Index, (pulp magazine), by Gene
    Marshall and Carl F. Waedt, 3 SF 17
(fan organizations), Never Fear, Doc
    Savage Fans Are Here, (fan clubs),
    by Daryl S. Herrick, 1 MB 21
(fan organizations), Mystery Fandom,
    (clubs and publications), by Paul
    Bishop, 1-3 M 24
(Fane Brothers series: Michael Halliday),
    Checklist, by Robert E. Briney and
    John Creasey, 2-1 TAD 13
(Fansler, Kate, detective: Amanda Cross),
    Feminists as Detectives, Harriet
    Vane, Kate Fansler, Sarah Chayse,
    by Kathleen Gregory Klein, 13-1
    TAD 31
(FANTASTIC NOVELS), A Remembrance of
    FN, (pulp magazine), by James Ellis,
    20 X 37
(FANTASTIC NOVELS), The Fantastic
    Sisters - Literature and Lovely,
    (on the pulp magazines FANTASTIC
    NOVELS and FAMOUS FANTASTIC
    MYSTERIES, with checklist and
    index), by Herman S. McGregor,
    74 PU 6
(FANTASTIC NOVELS), Index to FANTASTIC
    NOVELS, (pulp magazine), by Gary
    Shaheen, 7 X 69
Fantastic Sisters, The - Literature and
    Lovely, (on FAMOUS FANTASTIC
    MYSTERIES and FANTASTIC NOVELS,
    pulp magazines, with checklist
    and index), by Herman S. McGregor,
    74 PU 6
Fantastic World-Wide Ellery Queen Poll,
    The, by Jon L. Breen, 3-1 QC 7
Fanzines, (on mystery and related
    amateur publications), by Jim Huang,
    12 CL 9
(fanzines), Mystery Fandom, (on clubs
    and publications), by Paul Bishop,
    1-3 M 24
Farah, Dave: Basic Nancy Drew (Nancy
    Drew girls' series books), 1-6
    YB 6
Farmer, Philip Jose: letter of comment,
    7 DQ 3; 6 P 31; 24 X 45; 33 X 115;
    1-1 WA 10

Farmer, Philip Jose: Oft Have I
    Travelled, (on Solar Pons),
    2-2 PD 1
Farmer, Philip Jose: Writing the
    Biography of Doc Savage, 5A P 2
(Farmer, Philip Jose), A Different
    Kind of Checklist, by Bruce Doering,
    2-2 CP 24
(Farmer, Philip Jose), An Interview
    with Philip Jose Farmer, by
    Philip A. Shreffler, 42 X 7
(Farmer, Philip Jose), Collecting
    Paperback First Editions of
    Philip Jose Farmer, by Don
    Block, 2-3 CP 18
(Farmer, Philip Jose), Philip Jose
    Farmer, An Appreciation, 5 SF 3
(Farmer, Philip Jose), Philip Jose
    Farmer, A Checklist, by Paul
    Whitney, 5 SF 4
(Farmer, Philip Jose), The Up-Dated
    Farmer, by "These Ven," 42 X 17
(Farmer, Philip Jose: IMAGE OF THE
    BEAST), Mystery Plus, Image of
    the Beast, by R. Jeff Banks,
    3-2 PP 15
Farnsworth, Linda: letter of comment,
    1-2 M 3
Farrah, Dave: Cameo Edition Nancy
    Drews, (bibliographic article on
    girls' series books), 1-5 YB 3
(Farrow, Marcus, series: Angus Ross),
    Checklist, annotated, by Barry
    Van Tilburg, 5-2 MF 2
Farsace, Larry: letter of comment,
    38 X 145
Farsh, Dave: letter of comment,
    3 MA 26
(FAST ONE: Paul Cain), Introducing Paul
    Cain and His FAST ONE, A Forgotten
    Hard-Boiled Writer and a Forgotten
    Gangster Novel, by E.R.Hagemann,
    12-1 TAD 72
Fatal Glance, The, (on Solar Pons),
    by Bruno Lumbroso, 3-2 PDA 24
Fate of Llewellyn Cadmon, The, (fiction),
    by Frederick Faust, 1-2 FC 1
(Father Brown series: G.K.Chesterton),
    G.K.Chesterton's Father Brown,
    by Robert A.W.Lowndes, 9-3 TAD 184
(Father Brown series: G.K.Chesterton),
    The Private Life of Father Brown,
    by R.W.Hays, 4-3 TAD 135
(Father Dowling series: Ralph McInerny),
    Series Synopses, by Dan Andriacco,
    12-2 TAD 133
Father of Og, The, (J. Riving Crump,
    author of the Og books), by Gerry
    de la Ree, 3 BS 5
Father Roger of Fox River, (on Father
    Roger Dowling series by McInerny),
    by Jim McCahery, 2-5 PP 8
Fatherly, Mrs. Jo Anne: letter of
    comment, 4-1 TAD 62; 5-1 TAD 53;
    5-4 TAD 255; 11-4 TAD 316

Fathers and Sons of John LeCarre, The, (spy fiction of LeCarre), by Harry D. Dawson, 5-3 MF 15

(Faulkner, John), Paperback Writers, by Bill Crider, 1-2 PQ 8

Faulkner, Thomas C.: letter of comment, 12 MN L12

Faust and the Western Story Magazine, (Frederick Faust's western stories in dime novels and pulps), by William J. Clark, 1-3 FC 9

Faust, Frederick: The Bards, (verse), 1-4 FC 6; 2-1 FC 9

Faust, Frederick: The Baseball Bat, (verse), 1-3 FC 3

Faust, Frederick: Bjornsen, (verse), 2-4 FC 6

Faust, Frederick: Calls to Glory, (verse), 1-3 FC 7

Faust, Frederick: The Common Law, (essay), 2-1 FC 8

Faust, Frederick: Dr. Kildare's Dilemma, (fiction, as by Max Brand), 3-1 FC 1; 3-2 FC 1

Faust, Frederick: The Fate of Llewellyn Cadmon, (fiction), 1-2 FC 1

Faust, Frederick: Fellowship, (verse), 3-2 FC 8

Faust, Frederick: Follow the Herd, (fiction), 2-1 FC 1

Faust, Frederick: The Garden, (fiction), 2-4 FC 1

Faust, Frederick: Guenevere, (verse), 1-4 FC 6

Faust, Frederick: Hastings, (verse), 1-4 FC 6

Faust, Frederick: I Am the Emperor, (fiction), 1-2 FC 8

Faust, Frederick: Judgment, (verse), 2-2 FC 5

Faust, Frederick: The Magic Draught, (verse), 1-2 FC 5

Faust, Frederick: Mercy Anne, (fiction, as by Max Brand), 1-4 FC 1

Faust, Frederick: Ode to a Beer Opener, (verse), 1-3 FC 7

Faust, Frederick: The Paragon, (verse), 1-2 FC 9

Faust, Frederick: The Plow and the Horse, (fiction), 1-3 FC 1

Faust, Frederick: Strange Things are Found, (verse), 2-4 FC 8

Faust, Frederick: Summer Night at a Tavern, (verse), 3-1 FC 9

Faust, Frederick: The Three Arts, (verse), 1-2 FC 7

(Faust, Frederick), A Farewell to Max Brand, (literary reminiscences), by Steve Fisher, 1-3 FC 4

(Faust, Frederick), Blue & Gold 1916, (Faust in Yearbook, University of California), by Paul S. Latimer, 2-1 FC 9

(Faust, Frederick), Debunking the Legends, by William J. Clark, 1-2 FC 8

(Faust, Frederick), Destry and Dionysus, (literary essay on Faust), by Martha Bacon, 2-2 FC 1

(Faust, Frederick), Did He or Didn't He?, (Faust as possible author of THE GREY CHARTERIS by "Robert Simpson"), by William J. Clark, 1-1 FC 5

(Faust, Frederick), Faust and the Western Story Magazine (western stories in dime novels and pulp magazines), by William J. Clark, 1-3 FC 9

(Faust, Frederick), Faust in THE OCCIDENT, (writings in high school paper), by William J. Clark, 1-3 FC 10

(Faust, Frederick), The Faust Papers, A Visit to the Faust Collection at the University of California in Berkeley), by William F. Nolan, 1-4 FC 4

(Faust, Frederick), Faust Published in Sweden Through 1968, (and Hungarian reprints), by Gosta Gillberg, 1-4 FC 10

(Faust, Frederick), Faust Stories in MAX BRAND'S WESTERN MAGAZINE, (checklist), by William J. Clark, 1-1 FC 7

(Faust, Frederick), Heinie and the Chicken, (personal essay on Faust), by Frank Gruber, 1-1 FC 11

(Faust, Frederick), How Many Words? (extent of writings of Frederick Faust), by William F. Nolan, 1-1 FC 2

(Faust, Frederick), The King is Dead, (fiction, as by "Schiller Faust"), 1-1 FC 6

(Faust, Frederick), King of the Pulps, (on Frederick Faust/Max Brand in the pulp magazines), by Stewart Kemble, 69 PU 25

(Faust, Frederick), news items, var., 1-2 FC 6; 1-3 FC 8; 1-3A FC 1; 1-4 FC 7; 2-1 FC 7; 2-2 FC 6; 2-3 FC 7; 2-4 FC 7; 3-1 FC 10; 3-2 FC 9

(Faust, Frederick), Seven Years with Heinie Faust, (literary reminiscences on Faust), 2-3 FC 1

(Faust, Frederick), Taxi, Speedy and Silvertip, (on Faust's western stories), by William J. Clark, 2-1 FC 5

(Faust, Frederick: THE VILLAGE STREET AND OTHER POEMS), The Scarcest Title, (on collecting Faust books), by William J. Clark, 1-4 FC 9

Faust Papers, The, A Visit to the Faust Collection at the University of California in Berkeley, (Frederick Faust), by William F. Nolan, 1-4 FC 4

Faust Published in Sweden Through 1968,
(Frederick Faust foreign translations,
including Hungarian), by Gosta Gillberg,
1-4 FC 10

(Faust, Ron), Running Hot and Cold with
Ron Faust, (discussion of mystery
novels by Ron Faust), by George Kelley,
5-4 MF 11

Faust, Schiller: The King is Dead, (fiction
by Frederick Faust as Schiller Faust),
1-1 FC 6

Favorite Juvenile Authors: What Publishers
Said About Their Old Stand-bys, (re:
Horatio Alger, Jr., Harry Castlemon,
Edward S. Ellis, J.T.Trowbridge), by
Gil O'Gara, 1-2 YB 19

Favorite Magazine Issues: MANHUNT (3:6) June
1955, (commentary and review), by R. Jeff
Banks, 4-6 MF 7

Fawcett, Jayne: Attic Dawn, (verse), 4-1
AD 12

Fawcett, Jayne: The Codicil, (verse),
4-2 AD 5

Fawcett, Jayne: Pan's Song, (verse), 3-4
AD 6

Fawcett, Richard H.: The Derleth Connection,
Robert Bloch, (with introduction by
Bloch), 3-1 AD 3

Fawcett, Richard H.: Some Thoughts on the
Future of the AUGUST DERLETH SOCIETY
NEWSLETTER, 2-2 AD 9

Fear and Loathing with the Lone Wolf,
(The Lone Wolf series by Mike Barry
aka Barry Malzberg), by George Kelley,
1-5 MF 17

Fearn, John Russell:The Golden Amazon,
(science fiction series by Harlequin
paperbacks, with checklist, 2 SF 24

Featherstone, Jim: letter of comment,
1-2 TBN 7

(FEDERAL AGENT magazine), G-77 in Public
Enemy #1, (pulp magazine discussion),
by Bryan James Kelley, 2 P 14

(Fedora, Johnny, series: Desmond Cory),
Checklist, annotated, by Barry
Van Tilburg, 4-3 MF 23

Feegel, John R.: A Tribute to JDM,
(tribute to John D. MacDonald),
24 JD 22

Feetnote to Fleming, (gun characteristics),
by Dean A. Grennell, 15 JD 10

Feir, Ike: letter of comment,
8 X 38

(Fell, Gideon, detective), The Cases
of Gideon Fell, by Marvin Lachman,
2-3 MF 4

(Fell, Gideon, detective), The Life and
Times of Gideon Fell, by Marvin
Lachman, 2-3 MF 3

Fellowship, (verse), by Frederick Faust,
3-2 FC 8

Female Detectives, Ghost Books and
the Relative Importance of It All,
(on EXPERIENCES OF A LADY DETECTIVE,
Anonyma), by E.F.Bleiler, 8-3 TAD 202

Female Private Eye Ponders Where to
Carry Her Gat, The, (verse), by
J.R.Christopher, 9-2 TAD 101

(female sleuths), Little Old Ladies
I Have Known and Loved, by Ellen
Nehr, 3-4 MF 3

Feminists as Detectives, Harriet Vane,
Kate Fansler, Sarah Chayse, by
Kathleen Gregory Klein, 13-1
TAD 31

(Fen, Gervase, detective: Edmund
Crispin), Obsequies About Oxford,
The Investigations and Eccentri-
cities of Gervase Fen, (with
bibliography), by William A.S.
Sarjeant, 14-3 TAD 196

Fenady, Andrew J.: letter of comment,
1-3 M 4

(Fenton, Lawrie, series: Michael
Annesley), Spy Series Characters
in Hardback, IX, by Barry Van
Tilburg, 5-5 MF 15

Fergus, George: A Short Report on
Bouchercon VI, (mystery authors
and fans convention), 2 MN 3

Fergus, George: letter of comment,
4-4 MR 14

Ferguson, Malcolm M.: Arkham House
and Its Eldritch English Visitants,
3-1 AD 1

Ferguson, Malcolm M.: In Re: August
Derleth, A Tribute, 1-3 AD 7

Ferguson, Malcolm M.: letter of comment,
1-3 AD 3; 3-4 AD 9; 4-1 AD 14

Ferguson, Malcolm W.: Literature with
a Capital Hell, (writing and
publishing imaginative fiction),
3 WT 4

Ferguson, Paul F.: Narrative Vision
in "The Hound of the Baskervilles,"
(Sherlockiana), 1-2 C 24

Fialcowitz, Brice: The Freckled Gold-
fish is Here - New Goldfish Club
Started, (boys' readers' club of
Leo Edwards for his books), 2-5
TB 1

Fialcowitz, Ron: letter of comment,
1-2 TBN 7; 1-2 TBN 8; 1-2 TBN 10;
2-2 TBN 4

Fibish, Marilyn: Mystery Crossword
Puzzle, (crossword puzzle), 2-1
MR 16

Fick, Alvin S.: letter of comment,
1-2 PQ 4; 24 X 47

Ficker, Robin: letter of comment,
1-5 YB 20

(FICTION FACTORY, THE: Quentin
Reynolds), Some Errors in Fiction
Factory, by J. Randolph Cox,
74 PU 31

(FICTION FACTORY, THE: Quentin
Reynolds), Street & Smith Pulps,
(commentary on Reynolds' book),
by Stewart Kemble, 74 PU 29

(Fiction House Publishers), Ki-Gor and the Fiction House Monster, by Fred S. Cook, 5 BS 18

Fiction of William Hope Hodgson, The: A Working Bibliography, by Mike Ashley, 15 SF 15

(fictional detectives on detective fiction), More "Shades of Dupin!" by R.W.Hays, 8-4 TAD 288

Field, Albert: Harry Stephen Keeler, (literary sketch), 3-5 PP 10

Fields, Sidney: Whatever Happened to...?, (on Bobbsey Twins, juvenile series), 4-1 BC 393

Fiene, Judith: letter of comment, 2-3 MF 73

Fifty Rarest and Most Uniquest Pulps in the Whole Wide World, The, by Karl Edward Wagner, 24 X 6

Fifty Years of Mysteries, (biog.sketch with checklist of Judson P.Philips), by Tim Dumont, 4 MY 2

Fighting Fury, The, (on The Skipper, pulp character, and THE SKIPPER magazine), by Link Hullar and Will Murray, 12 SF 3

Film Note: The President Vanishes (based on Rex Stout story), by Louis Black, 9 MN A60

Film Notes, (mystery films), by Jim Huang, 9 CL 9; 10 CL 1; 11 CL 1; 12 CL 11

Film Notes, (Sax Rohmer films), by W.O.G.Lofts, 9 R 23

Filmed Misogyny, The Screen Adaptations of Peter Cheyney and Lionel White, by Jack Edmund Nolan, 4-6 MR 27

Films and TV Work of Eric Ambler, The, by Jack Edmund Nolan, 3-1 MR 13

Films of Ellery Queen, The, by Edward Connor, 3-1 QC 10

Films of James Hadley Chase, The, by Jack Edmund Nolan, 3-6 MR 30

(films, spy), Espionage Fights Off Boredom, by Lee Beaupre, 1-5 MR 12

Filstrup, Chris and Janie: An Interview with a Black Sheep of Amsterdam, Janwillem van de Wetering, 13-2 TAD 98

Filstrup, Chris and Janie: An Interview with Richard Lockridge, 11-4 TAD 382

Filstrup, Jane Merrill: A KAHNfidential Interview, (interview with Joan Kahn, mystery book editor), 2-2 C 15

Filstrup, Jane Merrill: Cats in Mysteries, 11-1 TAD 59; 11-2 TAD 134

Filstrup, Jane Merrill: Dead of Winter Views, (on Murder Ink weekend at Mohonk Mountain House), 10-3 TAD 235

Filstrup, Jane Merrill: letter of comment, 1-1 PP 28; 2-1 PP 43; 2-4 PP 40

(Finch, Detective-Inspector), Pen Profile No.12, June Thomson, by Barry Pike, 3-4 PP 17

Finch, G.A.: A Fatal Attraction, (on the fiction of Carroll John Daly), 13-2 TAD 112

Finch, G.A.: The Case of the Underground Man, Evolution or Devolution?, (THE UNDERGROUND MAN by Ross Macdonald), 6-4 TAD 210

Finch, G.A.: From Spade to Marlowe to Archer, (commentary on private eye detectives), 4-2 TAD 107

Finch, G.A.: Have You Met Hardman? (Hardman private eye series by Ralph Dennis), 8-4 TAD 275

Finch, G.A.: Marlowe's Long Goodbye, (on Raymond Chandler's character, Philip Marlowe), 6-1 TAD 7

Finch, G.A.: letter of comment, 5-3 TAD 187

Find the Name Puzzle, (mystery puzzle), by Linda Gambino, 9-1 TAD 58

Finzel, Jim: letter of comment, 3-6 PP 35; 4-1 PP 47; 4-2 PP 35; 14-2 TAD 185

Fires That Create, The Versatility and Craft of Harry Whittington, (author), by Michael S. Barson, 4-2 PQ 13

First Annual PSI Dinner, (report, Solar Pons fan organization), 1-2 PD 1

First Appearance, The, (discussion of first in print appearance of detective and related characters), by Maryell Cleary;
Colonel John Primrose (in THE STRANGLED WITNESS:Leslie Ford), 3-4 PP 23
Grace Latham (in ILL MET BY MOONLIGHT: Leslie Ford), 2-4 PP 27
Inspector Cockrill (in HEADS YOU LOSE: Christianna Brand), 3-2 PP 6
Joshua Clunk (in THE GARSTON MURDER CASE: H.C.Bailey), 3-5 PP 19
MacDougal Duff (in LAY ON, MacDUFF!: Charlotte Armstrong), 3-1 PP 27
Nigel Strangeways (in A QUESTION OF PROOF: Nicholas Blake), 2-5 PP 25
Roderick Alleyn (in A MAN LAY DEAD: Ngaio Marsh), 2-6 PP 12
Superintendent Wilson (in THE BROOKLYN MURDERS: G.D.H.Cole), 3-6 PP 13

First Bouchercon, The, A Report, (mystery author and fan convention), by Jon L. Breen, 3-4 TAD 250

First Class Transportation in the 1930's: The Lone Survivor (on "the last locomotive") by Bill Laidlaw, 5 DQ 7

(FIRST DEADLY SIN, THE: Lawrence Sanders), Expiatory Symbolism in Lawrence Sanders' THE FIRST DEADLY SIN, by Bill Nelson, 1-2 C 71

First Doc Savage, The: The Apocryphal Life of Clark Savage, Jr., (speculative birth and youth of Doc Savage), by Timothy J. Rutt, 1-3 WA 3

First Locked-Room Mystery?, The: Charles Brockden Brown's WIELAND, by Peter J. Christensen, 10-4 TAD 368

First Printing, Two Million, (comments on series by John Jakes), by Michael S. Barson, 3-3 PQ 7

First Thorndyke Story, The, (on "The Blue Sequin" by R. Austin Freeman, 1908), by Norman Donaldson, 10 TF 2

Fiscella, Joan B.: A Sense of the Under Toad, Play in Mystery Fiction, 1-2 C 1

(Fischer, Bruno), Bruno Fischer's Gold Medal Books, (annotated checklist of Gold Medal paperback books), by Bill Crider, 1-4 PQ 23; 2-1 PQ 7

(Fischer, Bruno), Paperback Writers, Bruno Fischer, by Bill Crider, 1-4 PQ 22

(Fischer, Bruno), PQ Interview with Bruno Fischer, (interview by PAPERBACK QUARTERLY magazine), 1-4 PQ 26

(Fish, Robert L.), Checklist, by Luther Norris, 2-5 MR 11

(Fish, Robert L.), Interview with Robert L. Fish, by Luther Norris, 2-5 MR 8

(Fish, Robert L.), Obituary, 3-1 M 29

(Fish, Robert L.), Robert Fish, In Memorium, (tributes by various persons), 14-2 TAD 119

(Fish, Robert L.), Some Memories, (literary memories and tribute to Fish), 14-2 TAD 121

Fisher, Ben: Edwin's Mystery and Its History, or, Another Look at Datchery, (THE MYSTERY OF EDWIN DROOD, by Charles Dickens), 4-5 MF 6

Fisher, Ben: letter of comment, 2-1 PP 34; 4-6 MF 46; 5-1 MF 48; 4-4 PP 33; 4-5/6 PP 92

Fisher, Carla J.: letter of comment, 3-1 MF 57

Fisher, Steve: A Farewell to Max Brand, (literary reminiscences on Frederick Faust aka Max Brand), 1-3 FC 4

Fisher, Steve: Cornell Woolrich, "...I Had Nobody," 3-3 TAD 164

Fisher, Steve: Frank Grundy - I Loved You, Too, Buddy, 3-3 TAD 170

Fisher, Steve: Is Deductive Fiction Unfilmable?, 3-4 TAD 240

Fisher, Steve: letter of comment, 4-1 TAD 70

Fisher, Steve: Play It Again, Sam Spade, (Humphrey Bogart in film), 5-2 TAD 79

Fisher, Steve: Pulp Literature, Sub-culture Revolution in the Late 1930s, (and Roger Torrey, author), 5-2 TAD 91

Fisher, Tom: Pulpy Eyes, (various comments on private eye detectives, 3 PE 30; 4 PE 25; 6 PE 23

Fisher, Tom: letter of comment, 3 PE 32; 4 PE 33; 6 PE 33

Fishman, Charles: Another Peacock Cry, Heraldic Birds in Five Lew Archer Novels, (on Ross Macdonald), 2-1 C 106

Fisk, Charles P.: Checklist of Every Boy's Library, (boys' books), 2-1 BC 141

Fitch, Lynda: letter of comment, 27 JD 35

Fitzhugh, Percy Keese: For the Honor of Uncle Sam, (fiction by boys' books author), 1-2 BC 57

(Fitzhugh, Percy Keese), Checklist of Books, (boys' books), by John F. Sullivan, 3-2 BC 300; 4-2 TB 1

(Fitzhugh, Percy Keese), The Do Good Boys and the Grave Peril, or Percy Keese Hits the Trail, (boys' books adventures), 3-2 BC 290

(Fitzhugh, Percy Keese), Tom Slade - Paper Saint, (boys' books of Tom Slade series), by John F. Sullivan, 4-2 TB 1

Fitzpatrick, Al: letter of comment, 13 MN L1

(Fitzsimmons, Cortland), Cortland Fitzsimmons and the Sports Mystery, (literary sketch, boys' books), by Jon L. Breen, 14-2 TAD 129

5A King's Bench Walk, (Dr. Thorndyke's residence in mystery novels by R. Austin Freeman), by P.M.Stone, 3 TF 37

(Flagship Books), Partial Checklist, (paperback publisher), by Jim Sanderson, 2-3 PQ 48; 3-1 PQ 3

Flannigans Achieve a Victory, The, (fiction, 1923, by Edward Edson Lee, aka Leo Edwards), 1-3 TB 5

Flannigan Flock, The, (fiction, 1923, by Edward Edson Lee, aka Leo Edwards), 1-2 TB 4; (publication data) 1-4 TB 2

Fleet Street Report, (items, Sax Rohmer), by Andrew Jay Peck, 2 R 18; 3 R 24; 4 R 20; (with Robert E. Briney) 5 R reverse cover

Fleissner, Robert F.: Drood the Obscure, The Evidence of the Names (THE MYSTERY OF EDWIN DROOD, by Charles Dickens), 13-1 TAD 12

Fleissner, Robert F.: letter of comment, 14-4 TAD 383

Fleissner, Robert F., (translator: Name as Symbol: On Sherlock Holmes and the Nature of the Detective Story, by Richard Gerber), 8-4 TAD 280

(Fleming, Ian), An Ian Fleming Bibliography, by Iwan Hedman, 5-4 TAD 217

(Fleming, Ian), The Article I Couldn't Publish, (Ian Fleming, and J.D. Salinger's THE LAUGHING MAN), by Guy M. Townsend, 1-1 MF 18

(Fleming, Ian), Checklist, James Bond series, annotated, by Barry Van Tilburg, 4-3 MF 26

(Fleming, Ian), Department of Unrelated Miscellanea, by Francis M. Nevins, Jr., 4-1 MR 21

(Fleming, Ian), God Save Ian Fleming, A Long Over-due Thank You to a Master Storyteller, (tribute), by Michael Avallone, 12-1 TAD 31

(Fleming, Ian), Ian Fleming, (biographical, literary sketch), by Iwan Hedman, 5-4 TAD 216

(Fleming, Ian), Ian Fleming, Alias James Bond, (literary sketch), by Billy C. Lee, 4-1 PQ 41

(Fleming, Ian), Ian Fleming, Book Collector, (as editor of THE BOOK COLLECTOR), by William White, 6-3 TAD 181

(Fleming, Ian), The Ian Fleming Films and TV, by Jack Edmund Nolan, 5-1 MR 24

Fleming, Lawrence: About Critical Essays on Books by JDM, (comments on literary criticisms of works of John D. MacDonald) 16 JD 11

Fleming, Lawrence: letter of comment, 14 JD 23; 17 JD 31; 20 JD 19

Fleming, Lawrence: On the Invention of Villainy, Speculations by a Mystery Fan, 17 JD 19

Fleming, Lawrence: The Uses of Astonishment, (as ingredient in mystery fiction), 18 JD 11

(Fleming-Roberts, G.T.), Fading Shadows, Erlika, Daughter of Satan, (villainess in Secret Agent X pulp stories by Fleming-Roberts), by Tom Johnson, 11 DS 24

(Fleming-Roberts, G.T.), Fading Shadows, Madame Death, (female villainess in Secret Agent X pulp stories by Fleming-Roberts), by Tom Johnson, 11 DS 12

(Fleming-Roberts, G.T.), Fading Shadows, The Story of G.T.Fleming-Roberts, (pulp author), by Tom Johnson, 2 U 14

(Fleming-Roberts, G.T.), The Leopard Lady, (female villainess in Secret Agent X pulp stories by Fleming-Roberts), by Tom Johnson, 8 DS 16

Flemming, Nate: letter of comment, 2-5 TBN 6

Fletcher, Connie: The Case of the Missing Criminal, Crime Fiction's Unpaid Debt to Its Ne'er-do-wells, (the criminal in mystery fiction), 10-1 TAD 17

(Fletcher, Johnny, & Sam Cragg, series: Frank Gruber), Johnny Fletcher and Sam Cragg, by Peter Harris, 4-4 MR 12

Fletcher, Robert: letter of comment, 36 X 70

Flight 54 - Not Quite First Class (travel essay), by John D. MacDonald, 25 JD 7

Flinchbaugh, Dick: letter of comment, 65 PU 20

FLOATING ADMIRAL, THE, and Some Thoughts About Its Authors, by Neville Wood, 2-4 PP 7

(Florida, regional mysteries), The American Regional Mystery, Pt. VIII, (locales of crime fiction), by Marvin Lachman, 5-5 MR 1

(Florida Suncoast Writer's Conference), Keynote Speech, by Harry Whittington, January 1978, 2-2 PQ 25

(Flower, Jessie Graham), Checklist of Series Books, (Grace Harlowe books author), by Roy B. Van Devier, 1-2 BC 40

(Flower, Jessie Graham), see Josephine Chase

Floyd, Frank: letter of comment, 3-5 MF 47; 4-1 MF 37; 4-6 MF 44; 5-4 MF 43; 5-6 MF 49

FLYING ACES, (discussion of the contents of this aviation pulp magazine), by Dean A. Grennell, 66 PU 9

(FLYING ACES), Fokker Joker, (on pulp character in FLYING ACES magazine) by Bud Overn, 10 P 7

Flying Spy, The, (G-8, pulp hero), by Wooda Nicholas Carr, 6 DS 15

Fogaris, Michael: letter of comment, 65 PU 20; 4-3 TAD 184

Foiled By a Hat, (comments on a true crime), by R. Austin Freeman, 6 TF 31

Fokker Joker, (pulp character discussion from FLYING ACES magazine), by Bud Overn, 10 P 7

(Foley,Rae: Hiram Potter series), Series Synopses, by John Vining, 10-2 TAD 188

(FOLLOW MY DUST: Jessica Hawke), Biography of Arthur W. Upfield in The Whodunit's Who's Who, by Philip T. Asdell, 3-4 PP 11

(FOLLOW MY DUST: Arthur W. Upfield), The Great Melbourne Cup Mystery, (discussion of book), by Philip T. Asdell, 1 BY 3

Follow the Herd, (fiction), by Frederick Faust, 2-1 FC 1

Fool-Con II, (science fiction and fantasy convention report), by W. Paul Ganley, 2 FM 10

(Footner, Hubert), Checklist, Rosika Storey series, by Howard Waterhouse, 2-4 PP 3

(Footner, Hubert), Super Detective Person: Rosika Storey, (on series), by Howard Waterhouse, 2-4 PP 3

Footsteps on the Golden Road, Addenda to The Golden Road to Samarkand, (exotic mystery locale), by Frank D. McSherry, Jr., 7-4 TAD 264

For Mystery Critics Only: Hard-Boiled Detective Division, by Michael Avallone, 21 X 10

For Mystery Readers: The Newest Must-Have Book (on TWENTIETH CENTURY CRIME AND MYSTERY WRITERS ed. by John M. Reilly), Steve Miller, 3-4 PP 9

For the Honor of Uncle Sam, (fiction), by
    Percy Keese Fitzhugh, 1-2 BC 57
For Us, A Child, (Rex Stout and the times
    of his birth), by Mary Grodd, 9 MN A15
For Your Investigation, (reviews and
    announcements of new mystery books),
    by Lianna Carlin, 1A MR 2; 1-1 MR 2;
    1-2 MR 2; 1-3 MR 2; 1-4 MR 2; 1-5
    MR 2; 1-6 MR 2; 2-1 MR 2; 2-2 MR 2;
    2-3 MR 2; 2-4 MR 2; 2-5 MR 2; 2-6
    MR 2
For Your Spy's Eyes Only, (paperback spy
    novels of 1960s), by Andy East,
    1-3 M 44
(Forbes, Graham B.), The Boys of Columbia
    High (boys' series books), by Julius
    R. Chenu, 5 BB 9
(Forbes, Stanton), An Interview with
    Stanton Forbes/Tobias Wells, 2-2 MR 19
(Forbes, Stanton), Checklist of works,
    2-2 MR 21
Ford, Esther: letter of comment, 8 BS 5
(Ford, Leslie), A Brief Encounter with
    Leslie Ford and David Frome, by Bill
    Lyles, 2-4 PP 15
(Ford, Leslie), An Interview with Leslie
    Ford, by Ann Waldron, 4-1 TAD 33
(Ford, Leslie), Checklist of works, by
    Maryell Cleary, 3-4 PP 24
(Ford, Leslie: ILL MET BY MOONLIGHT), The
    First Appearance, Grace Latham, by
    Maryell Cleary, 2-4 PP 27
(Ford, Leslie: THE STRANGLED WITNESS),
    The First Appearance, Colonel John
    Primrose, by Maryell Cleary, 3-4
    PP 23
Fore Shadowings, (genesis of The Shadow),
    by Bill Blackbeard, 17 X 6; 22 X 30
Forest Gift, The, (verse), by Steve Eng,
    4-2 AD 10
FORGOTTEN FANTASY, (magazine, with
    checklist and index), by Paul Allen,
    5 SF 23
Forgotten Ferrets, (Patrick Mulligan),
    by Alvin F. Germeshausen, 1-2 PDA 69
Forgotten Men, (forgotten detectives and
    criminals in mystery fiction), by
    Marvin Lachman, 2-4 TAD 217
(Forsyth, Frederick: THE DAY OF THE
    JACKAL), Stalking Forsyth's Jackal,
    by Peter Wolfe, 7-3 TAD 165
Fortune and the Syndicate (Stratemeyer
    Syndicate, boys & girls' books,
    discussed), by John T. Dizer,Jr.,
    2-1 BC 146; 2-2 BC 178
(Fortune, Dan, series: Michael Collins),
    Dan Fortune, Private Eye, by
    John Edwards, 9 SF 38
(Fortune, Reggie, series: H.C.Bailey),
    Bibliography of Fortune Short
    Stories, by Thomas D. Waugh, 6-2
    TAD 76
(Fortune, Reggie, series: H.C.Bailey),
    In Defense of Mr. Fortune, by
    William Antony S. Sarjeant, 14-4
    TAD 302

(Fortune, Reggie, series: H.C.Bailey),
    The Reggie Fortune Short Stories,
    An Appreciation and Partial Biblio-
    graphy, (with additional biblio-
    graphy by Francis M. Nevins, Jr.),
    by Mark Purcell, 5-4 MR 1
(Fosdick, Charles A.), see Harry
    Castlemon
Foster, Brad: letter of comment, 6 PE
    36
Foster, Frank: letter of comment, 3-2
    M 2
(Foster, Richard), Checklist, The Green
    Lama Stories, (pulp detective), by
    Dickson Thorpe, 1-2 MF 6
(Foster, Richard), see Kendell F.
    Crossen
Foster, Richard A.: letter of comment,
    17 X 62
Fourteen Issues, (descriptive commentary
    on pulp magazine, SCOTLAND YARD, and
    index), by Robert Sampson, 22 X 4
(Fowler, Dan, detective), Dan Fowler
    Novels in G-MEN magazine, by
    Robert Weinberg, 1 P 19
(Fowles, John), John Fowles' Experiments
    With the Form of the Mystery Story,
    by David Brownell, 10-2 TAD 184
(Fowles, John), Threats to Rationalism,
    John Fowles, Stanislaw Lem, and
    the Detective Story, (inexplicable
    unsolved), by Frank Occhiogrosso,
    13-1 TAD 4
(Fowles, John: THE ENIGMA), Freedom
    and Mystery in John Fowles' THE
    ENIGMA, by Steven R. Carter, 3-5
    MF 14
Fox, David: The Shadowerers, (by William
    J. Clark writing as Fox), 28 X 75
Fox, Estelle: A Frivolity (I Would
    Like to...), 5-1 TAD 10
Fox, Estelle: A Profile of Henry Gamadge
    and an Elizabeth Daly checklist,
    (Henry Gamadge, detective created
    by Daly), 4-4 MR 27
Fox, Estelle: Arthur William Upfield,
    1888-1964, (biographical and literary
    sketch), 3-2 TAD 89
Fox, Estelle: Checklist, Anthony Gilbert,
    2-6 MR 18
Fox, Estelle: Checklist, Sara Woods,
    4-3 TAD 153
Fox, Estelle: letter of comment, 8 JD 12;
    3-6 MR 9; 1-4 TAD 156; 3-2 TAD 136;
    8-2 TAD 154
Fox, Estelle: Lucy Beatrice Malleson
    (Anthony Gilbert), sketch, 2-6 MR 16
Fox, Estelle: My Whodunit File, A
    Collection of Scrapbooks Devoted to
    the Mystery Story Field, 2-1 TAD 29
Fox, Estelle: Sara Woods (sketch),
    4-3 TAD 152
Fox, Estelle: Whodunit Writer Began
    Career at 50, (on Elizabeth Daly),
    4-4 MR 25

Fox, Estelle: (with Francis M. Nevins, Jr., and Charles Shibuk), Arthur W. Upfield, a Checklist, 3-2 TAD 90

(Fox, Gardner F.), The Versatile Gardner F. Fox, (on his various fields in paperback, with checklist), by Edwin L. Murray, 3-5 CP 5

Foxworth, Walter: letter of comment, 15 BS 17

Fragasso, Dina: letter of comment, 25 JD 38

Fragments of the Indian Scene, (travel essay and experiences), by John D. MacDonald, 27 JD 9

Francis, Bruce: The Chronicles on Stage (re: Ray Bradbury; staged production) 36 X R19

Francis, Bruce: Review of LONG AFTER MIDNIGHT, (by Ray Bradbury), 26 X 12

Francis Plot Key, The, (plot guide to books by Dick Francis), by Jeffrey D. Smith, 4-5/6 PP 19

(Francis, Dick), A Word with Dick Francis, (interview) by Deryck Harvey, 6-3 TAD 151

(Francis, Dick), Endure and Prevail, The Novels of Dick Francis, by Barry Bauska, 11-3 TAD 238

(Francis, Dick), The Francis Plot Key, (plot guide to books of Dick Francis), by Jeffrey D. Smith, 4-5/6 PP 19

Frandsen, Niels H.: letter of comment, 5-3 TAD 173

Frank Gruber, (literary comments on Gruber with bibliographic checklist), by William J. Clark, 67 PU 31

Frank Gruber, A Dedication, by Allen J. Hubin, 3-2 TAD 95

Frank Gruber, I Loved You, Too, Buddy, by Steve Fisher, 3-3 TAD 170

Frank, R.A.: letter of comment, 67 PU 59; 15 BS 17

Frank Tinsley, Prophet With a Brush, (on Tinsley as pulp magazine cover artist), by Bud Overn, 67 PU 68

Frankenstein a la Doyle, by Dana Martin Batory, 8 U 114

(Franklin, Eugene: Berkeley Barnes, detective), The Case of the Hypochondriac Detective, by Larry L. French, 1-2 PP 9

Frauenglas, Robert A.: Law, Lawyers and Justice in the Novels of Joe L. Hensley, 4-1 MF 3

Frauenglas, Robert A.: Minus One, (fiction), 10 LR 14

Frayne, Mr. & Mrs. Trent: letter of comment, 7 JD 2

(Frazer, Robert Caine: Mark Kilby series), Checklist, by Robert E. Briney and John Creasey, 2-1 TAD 12

Frazier, Gerie: Introducing Alexandra Roudybush, (author), 3-3 MF 2

Frazier, Gerie: letter of comment, 1-6 MF 55; 2-1 MF 59; 2-4 MF 59; 2-6 MF 53; 3-1 MF 58

(Freas, Kelly), Interview with Kelly Freas, (artist), 3-2 PQ 12

Freck, Nelson: letter of comment, 2-2 CP 3; 4-1 PP 49

(Freckled Goldfish Club), The Freckled Goldfish is Here, New Goldfish Club Started, (readers' club, Leo Edwards books, boys' series), by Brice Fialcowitz, 2-5 TB 1

(Freckled Goldfish Club), The Secret and Mysterious Order of the Freckled Goldfish, (readers' club, Leo Edwards' boys' series books, 1-1 TB 4

Fred Dannay and EQMM, (Dannay's association with ELLERY QUEEN'S MYSTERY MAGAZINE), by Eleanor Sullivan, 12-3 TAD 201

Frederic Dannay, Doctor of Gumane Letters, (award, Carrol College), by Allen J. Hubin, 12-3 TAD 236

Fredericks, Alice: letter of comment, 1-2 TBN 5

Frederic Brown, An Appreciation, (with checklist), by J. Grant Thiessen, 2 SF 26

Freedom and Mystery in John Fowles' THE ENIGMA, by Steven R. Carter, 3-5 MF 14

(Freeling, Nicolas), Van der Valk, (detective character created by Freeling), by William Ruble, 5-2 MR 1

Freeman, Lucy: Robert Fish, In Memorium, 14-2 TAD 120

Freeman Bibliophile, The, (notes on collectible items by R. Austin Freeman), by Ruth D. McAleer, 11 TF 33

Freeman, Marjorie: Vast Collection of Books Requires Separate Handling, (on Jack Schorr's collection of boys' books), 3-4 BC 374

Freeman, Mildred: letter of comment, 2-2 MR 16

Freeman Books in Print, (R. Austin Freeman, as of 1976), by Philip T. Asdell, 1 TF 50

Freeman, R. Austin: The Art of the Detective Story, (rarity of good detective fiction), 10 TF 12

Freeman, R. Austin: The Author Under the Microscope, 2 TF 33

Freeman, R. Austin: Foiled By a Hat, (comments on a true crime), 6 TF 31

Freeman, R. Austin: Hospital London, (descriptive essay), 9 TF 28

Freeman, R. Austin: Meet Dr. Thorndyke, 4-2 TAD 6; 4 TF 31

Freeman, R. Austin: Victims of Circumstance, (fiction), 5 TF 28

(Freeman, R. Austin), A Glass of Wine Within the Meaning of the Act, (use of wine in the Thorndyke stories), by Oliver Mayo, 7 TF 30

148

(Freeman, R. Austin), A Guide to Thorn-
dykean Pilopathology (medico-legal
importance of the hair and skin
in the Thorndyke stories), by Howard
Brody, 11 TF 3
(Freeman, R. Austin), A Museum of
Thorndykean Pathology, (medical oddities
in the Thorndyke stories), by John H.
Dirckx, 5 TF 2
(Freeman, R. Austin), A Note on the
Chronology of the Dr. Thorndyke Novels,
by Michael G. Heenan, 9-1 TAD 52
(Freeman, R. Austin), A Thorndyke
Examination, (quiz on Thorndyke stories),
by Philip T. Asdell, 1 TF 32
(Freeman, R. Austin), An Inquiry Into
Circular Heels, (circular heel-prints
in the Thorndyke stories), by Howard
Brody, 12 TF 8
(Freeman, R. Austin), ...And Great Virtue
in a Really Good Feed, (hospitality to
Thorndyke in the stories by Freeman),
by Michael G. Heenan, 10 TF 9
(Freeman, R. Austin), Checklist, by
Norman Donaldson, 1-2 TAD 35
(Freeman, R. Austin), The Compleat
Poisoner, (stories of Thorndyke
involving poisons), by John H. Dirckx,
7 TF 3
(Freeman, R. Austin), Dr. Thorndyke's
Library, (books of Thorndyke as mentioned
in the stories by Freeman), by John H.
Dirckx, 2 TF 35
(Freeman, R. Austin), Dr. Thorndyke's
Pockets, (comments on pocket contents
of Thorndyke in various stories by
Freeman), by John H. Dirckx, 4 TF 25
(Freeman, R. Austin), "The Eye of Osiris"
and the Webster-Parkman Case, by
John McAleer, 12 TF 2
(Freeman, R. Austin), The First Thorndyke
Story, ("The Blue Sequin" 1908), by
Norman Donaldson, 10 TF 2
(Freeman, R. Austin), 5A King's Bench Walk,
(residence of Dr. Thorndyke), by P.M.
Stone, 3 TF 37
(Freeman, R. Austin), The Freeman Biblio-
phile, (notes on collectible items by
Freeman), by Ruth D. McAleer, 11 TF 33
(Freeman, R. Austin), Freeman Books in
Print, (1976), by Philip T. Asdell,
1 TF 50
(Freeman, R. Austin), The Freeman Memorial
Ceremony, (dedication of grave marker),
by Kathleen D. Heenan, 9 TF 2
(Freeman, R. Austin), Freeman Memorial
Fund, (to purchase grave marker),
12-1 TAD 68
(Freeman, R. Austin), Ross Freeman and
the Aetiology of Malaria, (R.Austin
Freeman's investigation of malaria),
by Oliver Mayo and John Mayo, 5 TF 16
(Freeman, R. Austin), Golden Beetles or
Blue Bugs?, (Freeman's "The Blue
Scarab" as a commentary on Poe's
"The Goldbug"), by Oliver Mayo, 11 TF 13

(Freeman, R. Austin), The Inquest, An
Inquiry, (use of the inquest in the
Thorndyke stories), by John H.
Dirckx, 9 TF 22
(Freeman, R. Austin), John Evelyn Who?,
(possible origin of Thorndyke's
names), by Philip T. Asdell, 7 TF
35
(Freeman, R. Austin), Jonathan Faldish,
Lately Departed, A Thorndyke Pastiche,
by John H. Dirckx, 6 TF 3
(Freeman, R. Austin), La Filza Di
Thorndyke, (foreign translations
and editions), by Ian Arnott,
3 TF 28
(Freeman, R. Austin), Literary Quotations
and Allusions in the Dr. Thorndyke
Novels and Short Stories, by John
H. Dirckx, 1 TF 3
(Freeman, R. Austin, Memorial Appeal
for Grave Marker, 6 TF 2; (report)
7 TF 2; 8 TF 2
(Freeman, R. Austin), Mr. R. Austin
Freeman, A Review of His Early
Fiction, (1913), by John Adams,
6 TF 34
(Freeman, R. Austin), The Names of
Characters in the Thorndyke Stories,
by Michael G. Heenan, 4 TF 2
(Freeman, R. Austin), Nathaniel Polton,
Artificer Extraordinary, (character
in Dr. Thorndyke stories), by John
H. Dirckx and Philip T. Asdell,
6 TF 25
(Freeman, R. Austin), Notes for a
Freeman Bibliography, by Ruth D.
McAleer, 11 TF 12
(Freeman, R. Austin), Notes on a
Freeman Bibliography, by R. Narasimhan,
8 TF 41
(Freeman, R. Austin), On the Trails of
Dr. Freeman and Dr. Thorndyke, or,
A Guide to Thorndykean England, by
Michael G. Heenan and Philip T.
Asdell, 8 TF 4
(Freeman, R. Austin), The Penrose
Mystery Mystery, by Norman
Donaldson, 2-2 TAD 108
(Freeman, R. Austin), Perk Stone and
the Thorndyke Quiz, (interrogatory
of 1936), by Norman Donaldson,
1 TF 26
(Freeman, R. Austin), R. Austin Freeman,
(bibliographical, literary sketch),
by Norman Donaldson, 1-2 TAD 32
(Freeman, R. Austin), R. Austin Freeman,
A Bibliography, by George T.Hamilton,
4-2 TAD 10; 4-3 TAD 6
(Freeman, R.Austin), R.Austin Freeman
and the Improvement of Mankind, by
Oliver Mayo, 1 TF 34; 2 TF 18
(Freeman, R. Austin), R. Austin Freeman,
Toward a Definite Biography, by
John McAleer, 11 TF 19

(Freeman, R. Austin), The Silent Sickle, a Thorndyke pastiche, by Oliver Mayo, 3 TF 2

(Freeman, R. Austin), Thorndyke, the Linguist, (Dr.Thorndyke's knowledge of languages in the stories by Freeman), by John H. Dirckx, 10 TF 24

(Freeman, R. Austin), Thorndyke's Topography, (locales of Thorndyke stories), by Michael G. Heenan, 5 TF 23

(Freeman, R. Austin), The Thorny Way to Heaven, a Thorndyke Pastiche, by Oliver Mayo, 9 TF 5

(Freeman, R. Austin), Was "Jack Wylde" Really R. Austin Freeman?, by W.O.G.Lofts and Derek J. Adley, 7-4 TAD 247

(Freeman, R. Austin: THE DEAD HAND), ...And How It Grew, (notes on story formulation), by Norman Donaldson, 7 TF 18

(Freeman, R. Austin: DR. THORNDYKE INTERVENES), Thorndyke and the Plumber's Oddments, (use of true crime in the story), by Norman Donaldson, 4 TF 8

(Freeman, R. Austin: THE MYSTERY OF ANGELINA FROOD), Edwin and Angelina, (w/comments on Dickens' MYSTERY OF EDWIN DROOD), by Norman Donaldson, 2 TF 2

Freeman Wills Crofts, 1-6-79 - 4-11-57, (biog. and literary sketch), by James Keddie, Jr., 2-3 TAD 137

French, Bill: letter of comment, 8 JD 9; 11 JD 20

French, Larry L.: Addendum to The Baker Street - Carrian Connection, (Sherlockian writings by John Dickson Carr), 1 NC 15

French, Larry L.: The Carr Chronology, (chronology of John Dickson Carr, vital and literary statistics), 1 NC 29

French, Larry L.: Carrian Canon for the Curious, (bibliography of John Dickson Carr), 1 NC 20

French, Larry L.: The Case of the Hypochondriac Detective, (Detective Berkeley Barnes, created by Eugene Franklin), 1-2 PP 9

French, Larry L.: letter of comment, 1-6 MF 58; 2-1 MF 50; 2-2 MF 47; 2-4 MF 57; 1-2 PP 26; 1-4 PP 31; 11-1 TAD 5; 11-4 TAD 317

French, Larry L.: The Man Who Read (and Published) John Dickson Carr/ Carter Dickson, (Ellery Queen), 1 NC 8

French, Larry L.: The Man Who Was John Dickson Carr, (biographical tribute), 1 NC 3

French, Larry L.: The Murder Club, (in John Dickson Carr stories), 1 NC 30

French, Larry L.: The Mysterious John Dickson Carr, 1-6 MF 13

French, Larry L.: The Professional Sleuth of Roy Winsor, (Professor Ira Cobb), 2-1 MF 3

French, Larry L.: Professor Without a Pseudonym, (on Robert B. Parker), 2-2 MF 12

French, Larry L.: Thomas Chastain and the New Police Procedural, 2-4 MF 17

(French, Paul: Lucky Starr series), Bibliography, (boys' books series), by Harry K. Hudson, 1-5 YB 14

Freund, Bella: letter of comment, 12 JD 20

Friday, February 25, 1955, (news item from The London TIMES LITERARY SUPPLEMENT on mystery fiction), by Mary Groff, 10-3 TAD 232

Fright Syndrome, The, (weird menace pulp magazines), by Wooda Nicholas Carr, 10 BS 19

Fritch, Charles E.: letter of comment, 3-2 PQ 3

Friedrich Duerrenmatt, The Detective Story as Moral Parable, by Orley I. Holtan, 5-3 TAD 133

From Blue Swastika to the Ace of Spades, (history of the Ace pulp magazines), by Donald Wollheim, 68 PU 5

From Howtoits to Whodunits, Jane Austen to Agatha Christie, (exploration of background settings in crime fiction), by Rosemary DePaolo, 2-2 C 8

From the Dealer's View, (boys' books), by Ivor A. Rogers, 2-4 BC 236

From the Press: The Early Non-Nero Wolfe Books, (review extracts), by Don Miller, 9 MN A57

"From the Time I Could Read, I Always Wanted to be a Writer," Interview with P.D.James, by Jane S. Bakerman, 10-1 TAD 55

From the Typewriter of Nick Carr, (column on pulp magazines and stories), by Wooda Nicholas Carr, 2 PW 2

From...TQCB, (Queen Canon Bibliophile on Ellery Queen), by Nils Hardin, 14 X 55

From Shadow to Superman, (heroes in the popular literature), by John Edwards, 7 U 10

From Spade to Marlowe to Archer, (private eye detective fiction), by G.A.Finch, 4-2 TAD 107

From Tutter to Oz - and Back Again!, (on collecting boys' books), by Dick Martin, 2-5 TBN 1

(Frome, David), A Brief Encounter with Leslie Ford and David Frome, by Bill Lyles, 2-4 PP 15

(Frome, David: Evan Pinkerton series), Evan Pinkerton, by Fred Dueren, 7-3 TAD 193

(Frost, Robert), Frostwatching, (reminiscences, Robert Frost), by Anne MacDonald, 25 JD 15

Frostwatching, (reminiscences of Robert Frost), by Anne MacDonald, 25 JD 15

Frundt, Mary: letter of comment, 2-1 PQ 5

Frymoyer, J. Curtis: Discovered Treasure, (boys' books), 3-2 BC 311

Fu Chin Chow, (comic strip), by Jack Gaughan, 13 R 11

Fu (Manchu), by Henry E. Wenden, 8 R 27

Fu Manchu, by Cay Van Ash, 9 R 15

Fu Manchu Checklist, by Robert E. Briney, 7 R 21

Fu Manchu Speaks, by Sidney Petty, 11 R 12

Fu Manchu Thinks Kindly of Sir Denis Nayland Smith, (verse), by Ed Lauterbach, 1-2 PDA 48

(Fu Manchu), A Curious Interview, (simulation), by James Wade, 13 R 8

(Fu Manchu), A Note on Dovelands Cottage, by J.L.Biggers, 14 R 23

(Fu Manchu), A Question of Time, by Cay Van Ash, 17 R 7

(Fu Manchu), Dantean Allusions in "The Trail of Fu Manchu," by J.R.Christopher, 5 R 27

(Fu Manchu), The Doctor's Blade, (interview with Sax Rohmer, 1947), 9 R 19

(Fu Manchu), The Early Chronicles of Fu Manchu, by Robert E. Briney, 15 R 9

(Fu Manchu), Fu Chin Chow, (comic strip), by Jack Gaughan, 13 R 11

(Fu Manchu), Fu Manchu Thinks Kindly of Sir Denis Nayland Smith, (verse), by Ed Lauterbach, 1-2 PDA 48

(Fu Manchu), Good Old Petrie, by David Braveman, 3 R 18

(Fu Manchu), The Hand of Dr. Insidious, by Ron Goulart, 13 R 1

(Fu Manchu), How Fu Manchu Was Born, by Sax Rohmer, 2 R 3

(Fu Manchu), "I Shall Live When You Are Smoke," by William S. Baring-Gould, 1-1 TAD 2

(Fu Manchu), The Immortal Enemy, by Robert A.W.Lowndes, 7 R 1

(Fu Manchu), The Last Encounter, (with Sir Denis Nayland Smith), by James Wade, 1-2 PDA 66

(Fu Manchu), Letter to Sherlock, and Annotations, by Julian L. Biggers, 6 R 7

(Fu Manchu), Meet Dr. Fu Manchu, by Sax Rohmer, 10 R 1

(Fu Manchu), Musette, Max and Sumuru, (radio serials), by Robert E. Briney and W.O.G.Lofts, 15 R 5

(Fu Manchu), My Hero - Fu Manchu, by John Ball, 11 R 5

(Fu Manchu), The Old Doctor of Limehouse, (Solar Pons association), vy Charles R.L.Power, 2-2 PD 4

(Fu Manchu), On Finding Petrie's Correct Name, (Fu Manchu story character), by Evelyn A. Herzog, 18 R 25

(Fu Manchu), The Papyrocunabula of Sax Rohmer, (paperback reprints, with checklist), by Richard Paul Hall, 3-4 CP 15

(Fu Manchu), Petrie Letter, by Bruce Pelz, 3 R 16

(Fu Manchu), The Politics of Fu Manchu, by Jim Pobst, 10 R 9

(Fu Manchu), Pyramid Reissues of Fu Manchu Paperbacks, (paperback books by Pyramid Books), by Robert E. Briney, 15 R 29; (checklist) 9-4 TAD 247

(Fu Manchu), Radio Fu Manchu, (radio serials), by Ray Stanich, 12 R 11

(Fu Manchu), Radio Luxembourg Dr. Fu Manchu Series, (serials on Luxembourg radio, with checklist), 11 R 15

(Fu Manchu), Sh-h-h! Dr. Fu Manchu is on the Air, (radio serials on B.B.C.), by W.O.G.Lofts and Robert E. Briney, 11 R 9

(Fu Manchu), The Sound of Fu Manchu, by Leslie Charteris, 6 R 19

(Fu Manchu), Speculations on the Origin of Dr. Fu Manchu, by John Harwood, 2 R 6

(Fu Manchu), The Third Eyelid, by Marvin L. Morrison, 14 R 19

(Fu Manchu), Those Mysterious Mandolins (Fu Manchu on the screen), by Robert W. Shurtleff, 18 R 9

(Fu Manchu), The Thugs and Dacoits of India, by John E. Carroll, 8 R 1

(Fu Manchu), Zagazig, by Jeffrey N. Weiss, 4 R 22

(Fu Manchu), Zagazig, Zagazig, by Evelyn Herzog, 5 R 22

(Fu Manchu), Zagazig, Zagazig, Z.A. Gazid, 5 R 25

Fuchs, Edna: letter of comment, 1-2 TBN 9

Fuchs, Edna: Wishful Thinking, (verse), (boys' books related), 1-2 TBN 3

Fulcher, James: Melville's "Benito Cereno" - an American Mystery (by Herman Melville), 2-1 C 116

Fulton, Al: letter of comment, 8 BS 6

Fulwiler, William: letter of comment, 24 X 46

(Fun Loving Gang series), A Leo Edwards Imitation, (boys' book series patterned after Jerry Todd series by Leo Edwards, written by Harold M. Sherman), by Rick Crandall, 1-3 YB 7

Funk, Howard: letter of comment, 10 BS 21

Funk, Raymond M.: The Lighted Bridge of Detection, (on the name, Solar Pons), 2-1 PDA 25

Funk, Raymond, Jr.: letter of comment, 2 R 24

Funnell, Dave: Accouncement of the Doc Savage Annual, (never published), 3 BS 13

Funnell, Dave: letter of comment, 8 BS 6

Further Adventures of Robert Leslie Bellem, or, The Bellem-Adams Connection, (pulp author), by Stephen Mertz, 38 X 138

Further Data on the Tuffy Bean Series, (boys' books by Leo Edwards), 2-1 TB 6

Further Excursions Into the Wacky World of Harry Stephen Keeler, (author), by Art Scott, 1-4 MF 13

Future Inversions, (inverted mysteries), by Joe R. Christopher, 6-1 MR 34

Future Shock: 1916, (boys' books, Conquest of the U.S. series by H. Irving Hancock), by Robert Jennings, 4 BB 15

(G-2), Donald E. Keyhole and the Brain Devil of G-2, by Sidney H. Bradd, 22 X 34

G-8, Flying Spy of the Pulps, (pulp aviation/espionage hero), by Sidney H. Bradd, 11 X 11

G-8 and His Battle Aces, (paperback reprint books), by Bruce Cervon, 3-5 CP 24

G-8 Rags the Scale, (G-8, pulp hero), by James E. Parten, 12 DS 13

G-8 Versus Chu Ling, (pulp hero and villain), by Wooda Nicholas Carr, 4 P 3

G-8 Versus Stahlmaske, (pulp hero and villain), by Wooda Nicholas Carr, 6 P 10

(G-8), Contemplating Seven of the Pulp Heroes, (comparisons and characteristics), by Wooda Nicholas Carr and Herman S. McGregor, 12 BS 3

(G-8), The Devil You Say, (pulp master spy hero), by Wooda Nicholas Carr, 3 X 4

(G-8), The Flying Spy, (pulp master spy/aviation hero), by Wooda Nicholas Carr), 6 DS 15

(G-8), Quoth the Raven, "Nevermore," (pulp hero aviation spy), by Wooda Nicholas Carr, 6 X 29

(G-8), The Strange Case of Philip Strange, or, Will the Real G-8 Please Stand Up, (similarity of the pulp heroes), by Bud Overn, 5 BS 16; 2 P 15

(G-8), The Two Faces of Herr Matzu, (pulp villain vs. G-8, master spy, in the pulps), by Wooda Nicholas Carr), 5 X 4

G-77 in Public Enemy #1, (secret service agent in pulp gangster magazine) by Bryan James Kelley, 2 P 14

G.K.Chesterton's Father Brown, (Father Brown, layman detective, series),by Robert A.W.Lowndes, 9-3 TAD 184

(G-MEN MAGAZINE), Dan Fowler Novels in G-Men Magazine, (pulp detective), by Robert Weinberg, 1 P 19

(Gaddis, Peggy), The Temptations of Peggy Gaddis, (with checklist of paperback digest-size novels), by Charles Culpepper, 3-2 CP 3

Gaddy, Mark W.: letter of comment, 6 DQ 3

Gadziola, David S.: letter of comment, 11 JD 26

Gagnon, Louise: letter of comment, 5-2 MF 49

Galaxy Science Fiction Novels, (in digest-size paperbacks), by Stuart W. Wells III and J. Grant Thiessen, 3 SF 44

Galbreath, Robert: letter of comment, 4-1 TAD 62

Galbreath, Robert: The Well of Zem-Zem, (re: Sax Rohmer), 9 R 18

Galerstein, David: The Curious Case of the Croyden Crossing, (Solar Pons), 1-1 PDA 18

Galerstein, David: The Curious Route of the Orient Express, (Solar Pons), 3-1 PDA 24

(Gall, Joe, series), Checklist chart, annotated, by R. Jeff Banks, 3-2 MF 28

(Gall, Joe, series), The Joe Gall Series, (commentary), by George Kelley, 3-2 MF 26

Galpern, Frank" letter of comment, 1-5 CP 1

(Gamadge, Henry, detective: Elizabeth Daly), A Profile of Henry Gamadge and An Elizabeth Daly Checklist, by Estelle Fox, 4-4 MR 27

Gambino, Linda: Find the Name Puzzle, 9-1 TAD 58

Gambino, Linda: letter of comment, 5-1 TAD 54

Gameroff, Marvin: letter of comment, 24 JD 38

Games of Detective Fiction, The, (plot games in crime fiction), by Jane Gottschalk, 10-1 TAD 74

Gammell, Leon: letter of comment, 24 X 12

Gamso, Jeffrey M.: letter of comment, 3-2 M 62

Gamso, Jeffrey M.: The Would-Be Psycho, (fiction), 1-3 M 36

Ganley, W. Paul: Fool-Con II, (science fiction and fantasy convention report), 2 FM 10

Ganley, W. Paul: The Incinerator, (reviews), 2 FM 16; 5 U 29; 6 U 26

Ganley, W. Paul: letter of comment, 3 U 48

Gannett, Gary L.: All the Short Cases of Inspector Maigret,(by Georges Simenon), 10-4 TAD 347

(Gar, Jo, detective: Raoul Whitfield),
Ramon Decolta, aka Raoul Whitfield,
and His Diminutive Brown Man, Jo Gar,
The Island Detective, by E.R.Hagemann,
14-1 TAD 3

Garasha, Robert: letter of comment, 2-4
TAD 277

Garbarino, John: letter of comment, 1-5
CP 2; 2-5 CP 1; 3-1 CP 10; 3-3 CP 4

Garbarino, John: The TV Tie-in Affair, or
Matt Dillon Meets Emma Peel, (paperback
use of TV publicity), 3-4 CP 5

Garden, The, (fiction), by Frederick Faust,
2-4 FC 1

Gardner and BLACK MASK - Incomplete?
(Erle Stanley Gardner writings in
BLACK MASK pulp detective magazine),
by Stewart Kemble, 73 PU 4

(Gardner, Erle Stanley), Aspects of the
Unknown Gardner, by Francis M. Nevins,
Jr., 5-4 MR 13; 5-5 MR 27

(Gardner, Erle Stanley), The Case of the
Unbeaten Attorney, or the Secret Life
of Perry Mason, by Marvin Lachman,
4-3 TAD 147

(Gardner, Erle Stanley), Corrections and
Additions to Mundell's ERLE STANLEY
GARDNER, A CHECKLIST, by Bernard
Beauchesne, 3-5 MR 35

(Gardner, Erle Stanley), Gardner and
BLACK MASK - Incomplete?, by Stewart
Kemble, 73 PU 4

(Gardner, John: Brian "Boysie" Oakes
series), Checklist, Annotated, by
Barry Van Tilburg, 4-3 MR 25

Gardner, Maurice: letter of comment,
62 PU 14; 24 X 47

Gardner, Maurice: Why I Wrote the Bantan
Novels, (series like Tarzan), 62 PU 19;
1 U 12

Garfield for the Defense, Purcell vs.
Bogart, by Brian Garfield, 11-2 TAD
186, (rebuttal, 11-1 TAD 6)

Garfield, Brian: letter of comment,
1-3 M 4; 11-4 TAD 317; 12-3 TAD 268;
13-1 TAD 76

Garfield, Brian: The Wild Bunch Revisited,
(THE WILD BUNCH, western-crime film),
13-2 TAD 141

(Garfield, Brian), The Vengeance Novels
of Brian Garfield, by George Kelley,
2-1 MF 5

Gargiso, John: letter of comment, 14 X 63;
24 X 46

Garion, Paul: letter of comment, 3-4 CP 1

Garrett, Gary L.: letter of comment,
11-1 TAD 98

Garroted! (Classic Corner Rare Tales,
fiction), by Frank Pierce, 14-4 TAD 336

(GARSTON MURDER CASE, THE: H.C.Bailey),
The First Appearance, Joshua Clunk,
(first appearance of Clunk in novel)
by Maryell Cleary, 3-5 PP 19

(Garve, Andrew), Six Britons the Movies
Ignored, (seldom filmed), by Jack
Edmund Nolan, 3-5 MR 9

Gary, Robert: letter of comment,
24 JD 39

Gas-Fitters' Ball, The, (annual event
of the Non-Canonical Calabashes,
a Sherlock Holmes scion society),
photo report, 2-2 M 29

Gatto, John: letter of comment, 8 X 38

Gaudet, Jim: letter of comment,
10 JD 16; 12 JD 19; 14 JD 23

Gaughan, Jack: Fu Chin Chow, (comic
strip based on Fu Manchu), 13 R 11

Gaughan, Jack: letter of comment,
13 R 31

(Gault, William Campbell), Checklist,
by Bill Crider, 2 PE 21

(Gault, William Campbell), Paperback
Writers, William Campbell Gault,
(sketch, with checklist), by Bill
Crider, 2-2 PQ 5

(Gault, William Campbell), PQ Interview
with William Campbell Gault, (by
PAPERBACK QUARTERLY magazine),
2-2 PQ 8

Geherin, David J.: Archer in Hollywood,
The "Barbarous Coast" of Ross
Macdonald, (comments on locales of
Lew Archer series), 9-1 TAD 55

Geherin, David J.: Comic Capers and
Comic Eyes, (humorous mystery
fiction and private detectives),
13-4 TAD 276

Geherin, David J.: The Hard-Boiled
Detective Hero in the 1970's, Some
New Candidates, 11-1 TAD 49

Gehman, Richard: A Name is a Name,
(on pseudonyms), 1-4 MR 16

Geist, Christopher D.: The Plantation
Novel, Paperback Genre of the
1970s, 3-1 PQ 42

Gene Stratton-Porter, Mistress of the
Mini-Mystery, by Jane S. Bakerman,
3-1 MF 3

Generations Have Marveled at Frank
Merriwell, (dime novel and book
boys' hero), 1-2 BC 56

Genesis of the War of the Worlds, by
Dana Martin Batory, 8 U 34

George, Robert L.: Agent Nine, A "G"
Man Series, (boys' book series),
1-3 YB 3

George, Robert L.: The Lend-a-Hand
Boys Series, A Review, (boys'
books series), 3-2 BC 312

George Smiley, The Reluctant Hero,
(spy character of John LeCarre),
by Holly Beth King, 2-1 C 70

(George, Theodore), Unknown Authors,
Theodore George, by Robert Adey,
4-3 PP 19

Georgette Heyer, (literary sketch), by
Barbara A. Buhrer, 13 MN 1

Georgette Heyer, A Partial Bibliography,
by Don Miller, 13 MN B1

Georgette Heyer Fandom (fan and
convention activities of Heyer fans)
by Suford Lewis, 13 MN 7

Georgette Heyer's "Whodunits" (the mystery
    novels of Georgette Heyer), by G.M. Carr,
    13 MN 15
(Gerard, Francis: John Meredith series),
    Checklist, Annotated, by Barry Van
    Tilburg, 5-3 MF 21
Gerber, Richard: Name as Symbol, On
    Sherlock Holmes and the Nature of the
    Detective Story, translated by Robert
    F. Fleissner, (interpretation of name),
    8-4 TAD 280
Germeshausen, Alvin F.: Call to Conclave,
    (founding of the Solar Pons society),
    1-1 PD 1
Germeshausen, Alvin F.: Forgotten Ferrets,
    Patrick Mulligan, 1-2 PDA 69
Germeshausen, Alvin F.: The Incredible
    Captain O'Hagan, 1 R 27
Germeshausen, Alvin F.: letter of comment,
    3-1 TAD 66
(Gernsback, Hugo), The Unique Magazine,
    Hugo Gernsback's SCIENTIFIC DETECTIVE
    MONTHLY, by Robert A.W.Lowndes,
    14-1 TAD 24; 14-2 TAD 157; 14-3 TAD
    243; 14-4 TAD 367; 15-1 TAD 18
(GET-RICH-QUICK WALLINGFORD: George
    Randolph Chester), Rogues for the
    New Century, by Fred Dueren, 5-3 MF 11
(Gethryn, Col. Anthony, series: Philip
    MacDonald), Philip MacDonald, Gethryn
    and Others, (characters created by
    MacDonald), by Norman Donaldson,
    3-1 TAD 6
Geyer, Jackie: The Case of the Canonical
    Collector, (collecting Sherlockiana),
    11-3 TAD 290
Ghost of Ec'h-Pi-El, (visual puzzle,
    re: H.P.Lovecraft), 18 X 18
Ghost of Lin San Fu, The, (fiction),
    by Clifford Goodrich, 7 P 20
(GHOST OF THE HARDY BOYS: Leslie McFarlane),
    A Laughing Ghost, (comments on book
    about author of many of the Hardy
    Boys boys' series), by Kent Winslow,
    4 MA 15
Ghost Story, (George Chance as The Ghost,
    Super Detective, in pulp magazines)
    by Robert Sampson, 5 P 20
(GHOSTS: Ed McBain), Mystery Plus, Old
    Friends Break New Ground, by R. Jeff
    Banks, 3-6 PP 15
(Ghote, Inspector, series: H.R.F.Keating),
    Detective Fiction and Social Realism,
    H.R.F.Keating's India, by Meera T.
    Clark, 2-1 C 1
(Ghote, Inspector, series: H.R.F.Keating),
    Inspector Ghote Takes a Bow, by
    Rona Randall, 5-4 MR 17
Giangregorio, Alan: letter of comment,
    2 MA 26
Gibbs, Kim: letter of comment, 5 SF 28
Gibson, Dave: letter of comment,
    3-1 CP 10
Gibson, Walter B.: Out of the Shadows,
    (on The Shadow, by character's
    creator), 2 D 32

Gibson, Walter B.: The Shadow Speaks,
    (exchange between Walter B. Gibson
    and Wooda Nicholas Carr, on The
    Shadow), 5 P 3
(Gibson, Walter), A Visit with Walter
    Gibson, (interview), by Bernard A.
    Drew, 7 U 23
(Gibson, Walter), Gibson's Non-Shadow
    Detective, (Gibson's other writings),
    by Edward Lauterbach, 6-1 TAD 33
(Gibson, Walter), The Shadow Known,
    (paperback editions of The Shadow
    novels), by Bruce Cervon, 2-3 CP 31
(Gibson, Walter), The Shadow Speaks,
    (writing techniques of Walter B.
    Gibson), by George Wolf, 14 BS 11
(Gibson, Walter), Walter Gibson,
    (sketch), by Frank Gruber, 17 X 5
(Gibson, Walter), The Weird Adventures
    of The Shadow, (on Gibson and his
    creation, The Shadow), by Wooda
    Nicholas Carr, 9 BS 16
Gibson's Non-Shadow Detective, (other
    than The Shadow writings of Walter
    B. Gibson), by Edward Lauterbach,
    6-1 TAD 33
(GIDEON'S RISK: J.J.Marric), A Word
    for John Creasey, by John Boyles,
    11-3 TAD 282
Gierlowski, Regina J.: letter of comment,
    5 DS 7
(Giesy, J.U.), The Occult Detector,
    (Giesy, pulp author), by William
    J. Clark, 17 X 55
Gil Brewer's Fables of Evil Women,
    Driven Men and Doom, by Michael S.
    Barson, 3-4 PQ 3
(Gilbert, Anthony), Bowlers, Beer,
    Bravado and Brains, Anthony Gilbert's
    Arthur Crook (Arthur Crook, detective
    created by Gilbert), by Jane S.
    Bakerman, 2-4 MF 5
(Gilbert, Anthony), Checklist, by
    Estelle Fox, 2-6 MR 18
(Gilbert, Anthony), see also Lucy
    Beatrice Malleson
Gilbert, G.F., Jr.: letter of comment,
    5-1 TAD 54
Gilbert, Jack: The Law and The Shadow,
    (legal position of selling tape
    recording of radio shows), 4 BS 6
Gilbert, Joseph: letter of comment,
    8 BS 7
(Gilbert, Michael), The Crime Novel
    v. The Whodunit, by Rona Randall,
    5-6 MR 25
Gilbert Patten in Clothbound Editions,
    (boys' books), by Harry K. Hudson,
    1-3 BC 86
Gilbert Patten, The Man and The Magic,
    (on dime novels and boys' books by
    Patten), by Frank C. Acker, 2-2 BC
    162
Gill, Julian: A Hitherto Undiscovered
    Reminiscence of Dr. John H. Watson,
    M.D., (Sherlockiana), 2-1 PDA 33

Gill, Peter R.: letter of comment, 11 JD 24

Gillberg, Gosta: Faust Published in Sweden Through 1968, (Frederick Faust, Swedish editions), 1-4 FC 10

Gilliam, Richard H.: letter of comment, 4 SF 46; 8 SF 48

(Gilman, Dorothy), Checklist, by Audrey I. Pacheco, 5-4 MR 23

(Gilman, Dorothy: Emily Pollifax series), Checklist, Annotated, by Barry Van Tilburg, 5-3 MF 19

Ginsburg, David D.: letter of comment, 15 X 14

(Giovanni, Jose), A Great Contemporary, Jose Giovanni, (French author's mystery films), by Jack Edmund Nolan, 4-4 MR 19

Girl Who Loved Doc Savage, The, (on Monja, in the Doc Savage stories), by Will Murray, 4 DR 6

Girl Who Loved Monk Mayfair, (re: Doc Savage stories), by Will Murray, 7 DS 13

(GIRL ON THE BEST SELLER LIST,THE: Vin Packer), Spotlight, 3-3 PQ 54

Girls, The, (secretaries to detective characters), by Marvin Lachman, 2-3 MR 6

(girls' series books), A Judy Bolton Mystery - "Blacklisted Classics," by Luana Russell, 2-1 C 35

(girls' series books), Basic Nancy Drew, (collecting Nancy Drew books), by Dave Farah, 1-6 YB 6

(girls' series books), The Critic's Clew... to Miss Drew, (discusses various authorships of Nancy Drew series), by Kent Winslow, 7 MA 16

(girls' series books), Nancy Drew in Japanese, (Japanese editions), by Don Holbrook, 7 MA 13

(girls' series books), Nancy Drew in Review, by John M. Enright, 7 MA 6

(girls' series books), TV's Nancy Drew, by John M. Enright, 7 MA 14

Giroux, Leo, Jr.: letter of comment, 2 DS 8; 4 DS 4

Giroux, Leo, Jr.: Thoughts on Doc Savage, 4 DS 16

Gladney, Graves: letter of comment, 2 D 48

(Gladney, Graves), Graves Gladney Speaks, (pulp artist, interview), by Will Murray, 1 D 23

Glantz, Dorothy: letter of comment, 2-1 MF 54; 2-3 TAD 234; 9-3 TAD 238; 10-1 TAD 39; 11-1 TAD 98; 12-2 TAD 186

(GLASS KEY, THE: Dashiell Hammett), The Problem of Moral Vision in Dashiell Hammett's Detective Novels, by George J. Thompson, 7-4 TAD 270

(GLASS VILLAGE,THE: Ellery Queen), The Mystery of Social Reaction, Two Novels of Ellery Queen, by J.R.Christopher, 6-1 TAD 28

Glassner, Bertram: letter of comment, 10-4 TAD 381

Glover, Carl: letter of comment, 38 X 145

Glover, Harry S.: Crime Pays for TV, But Less, (writing for television), 6/7 LR 10

Gobbett, Daniel: letter of comment, 11 DS 19; 2 FM 18; 3 U 48

God Save Ian Fleming, A Long Over-due Thank You to a Master Storyteller, by Michael Avallone, 12-1 TAD 31

Godfredsen, Dick: letter of comment, 2-3 MR 11

Godfrey, Lydia: Old Sleuth, Nineteenth Century "Nipper," America's First Serialized Detective and His World, (Old Sleuth, detective, in dime novels), 1-1 C 53

(Godfrey, Peter), Department of Unknown Mystery Writers, Peter Godfrey, by Marvin Lachman, 3-2 PP 13

(Godfrey, Peter), Peter Godfrey, A Reprise, by Robert Adey, 3-5 PP 9

Godfrey, Thomas: The Edgars, (report, 34th Annual Mystery Writers of America Awards Banquet), 2-1 M 22

Godfrey, Thomas: The Lamp of God, (on Ellery Queen's THE LAMP OF GOD), 12-3 TAD 212

Godfrey, Thomas: MYSTERY at the Movies, (reviews), 2-1 M 24

Godfrey, Thomas: MYSTERY Moviegoer, (reviews), 2-2 M 59; 2-3 M 44; 3-1 M 44; 3-2 M 46

Godfrey, Thomas: TAD at the Movies, (The Armchair Detective, movie review columns), 12-3 TAD 260; 12-4 TAD 367; 13-2 TAD 134; 13-3 TAD 226; 13-4 TAD 331; 14-1 TAD 84; 14-2 TAD 152; 14-3 TAD 253; 14-4 TAD 330

Godwin, David L.: letter of comment, 4-2 TAD 131; 4-3 TAD 187; 5-1 TAD 47; 6-2 TAD 129; 6-3 TAD 194

Goggin, Joe: letter of comment, 8 X 38; 24 X 47

Gold Key Doc Savage Comic Book, The, (Doc Savage in comic book published by Gold Key), by Wayne Vucenic, 14 BS 18

(Gold Medal Books, England), Black Murder and Gold Medal, by Frank D. McSherry, Jr., 4-3 TAD 156

Gold Mine of Dust, The, (Doc Savage type fiction featuring Doc Aborigine; pastiche), by Gary Zachrich, 63 PU 10

Goldberg, Mrs. B.D.: letter of comment, 7 R 27

Goldberg, Joshua: What's In a Name? or, Playfully on a Tangent (Max Carrados, detective of Ernest Bramah), 7-2 TAD 122

(Goldberg, Len), Rohmer Artist Len Goldberg, A Capsule Biography, by Douglas A. Rossman, 2 R 18

Golden Age of the Detective Story, The, by Neville Wood, 1-1 PP 11

Golden Age of the Detective Story, Its Rise and Fall, by Charles Shibuk, 1-4 QC 14

Golden Amazon, The, (science fiction series published by Harlequin in paperback, with checklist), by John Russell Fearn, 2 SF 24

Golden Beetles or Blue Bugs?, (Freeman's "The Blue Scarab" as a commentary on Poe's "The Goldbug"), by Oliver Mayo, 11 TF 13

Golden Boys, The, (in Doc Savage), by Will Murray, 10 DS 16

Golden, Mark J.: James Bama and His Man of Bronze, (Bama as cover artist for Doc Savage books), 1 DR 4

Golden, Mark J.: Jim Bama and the Artistic Doc Savage, (cover art for Doc Savage books), 2/3 DR 11

Golden Road to Samarkand, The; The Arabian Nights in Detective Fiction, (exotic locales of discussed crime fiction), by Frank D. McSherry,Jr., 7-2 TAD 77

(Golden Stallion series: Rutherford G. Montgomery), Boys' Series Bibliographies, by Harry K. Hudson, 1-5 YB 13

Golden Years of Elizabeth Daly, The, (author), by Ann Waldron, 7-1 TAD 25

Goldman, Amy E.: letter of comment, 2-4 MF 56

Goldsmith, Ilse: letter of comment, 1-1 MF 44; 2-1 MF 58; 4-2 MF 59; 4-1 TAD 69

Goldstone, Adrian Homer: A Detective Story Reference Library, 3-1 MR 17

Goldstone, Adrian Homer: letter of comment, 1-1 MF 46; 2-5 MR 13; 2-6 MR 14; 4-4 MR 16; 7 MY 13; 1-4 QC 17

Goldstone, Adrian Homer: The Quacks in the Quorum, (fugitive books in QUEEN'S QUORUM), 12-3 TAD 226

Gombert, Rene: letter of comment, 13 X 59; 22 X 51

Gone But Not Forgotten, (defunct paperback publishers, with checklist), J. Grant Thiessen, 2 SF 6

(Gonzales, John: Harry Horne, detective), A Song for the Unsung, by Joseph J. Coffey, 13-1 TAD 67

Good, John A.: letter of comment, 5 DQ 5; 10 DS 5; 11 DS 6; 11 DS 28

Good Old Jack, (Jack Harkaway, dime novels and boys' books hero), by Gil O'Gara, 1-1 YB 22

Good Old Petrie, (re: Sax Rohmer), by David Braveman, 3 R 18

Good, the Bad and the Pipe, The, (pipe-smoking sleuths), by J.J.Armbruster, 5-2 MR 29

Goode, Greg: letter of comment, 5-6 MF 50; 4-3 PP 32; 4-5/6 PP 85; 14-1 TAD 74

(Goodey, Joe, series: Charles Alverson), The Trenchcoat Files, Meet Joe Goodey/San Francisco Will Never Be the Same, by Paul Bishop, 6 PE 31

(Goodman, Abe), An Interview with Abe Goodman, (publisher, Red Circle pulp magazines), by Robert Weinberg, 10 P 2

Goodman, Dan: letter of comment, 15 JD 24; 17 JD 27; 18 JD 25

Goodman, Jonathan: Trials Series, Some Notable, Some Not, (on various British book series reporting trials), 7-2 TAD 116

Goodman, Philip: letter of comment, 28 JD 40

Goodrich, Clifford: The Ghost of Lin San Fu, (fiction), 7 P 20

Goodrich, James R.: letter of comment, 8 BS 6; 8 BS 7; 15 BS 16; 11 JD 18; 13 JD 21; 22 JD 19; 1-2 MF 49; 2-1 MF 56; 4-2 MF 59; 4-4 MF 49; 5-1 MF 41; 5-3 MF 15; 9 MN L3; 4-2 PP 41; 4-3 PP 31; 62 PU 15; 63 PU 49; 64 PU 28; 2-3 TAD 200; 3-4 TAD 278; 4-3 TAD 181; 4-4 TAD 253; 5-2 TAD 113; 5-4 TAD 251; 11-1 TAD 98; 24 X 46; 36 X 73

(Goodwin, Archie, detective: Rex Stout), An Appreciation of Archie Goodwin, by Arden Knight, 12-4 TAD 328

(Goodwin, Archie, detective: Rex Stout), The Goodwin Document, by "Archie Goodwin" 1-2 G 49

Goodwin, Art: letter of comment, 2-2 TAD 131; 4-1 TAD 59; 6-2 TAD 129; 13-2 TAD 158

Goodwin Document, The, (re: Nero Wolfe), by "Archie Goodwin," 1-2 G 49

Goodwin, Hal: letter of comment, 4 MA 25

Goolsby, James: letter of comment, 4-3 PP 37

Gordon, John S.: letter of comment, 36 X 72

Gore Vidal, Mystery Writer, by Francis M. Nevins, Jr., 4-2 MR 25

Gores, Joe: Hammett the Writer, (on Dashiell Hammett), 38 X 5

Gores, Joe: letter of comment, 5-2 MR 19; 6-1 MR 22; 3-4 TAD 305; 7-3 TAD 223; 9-1 TAD 83

Gores, Joe: Rebuttal to "Kiss My Deadly Typewriter #539" (of Michael Avallone), 3-1 QC 16

(Gores, Joe), Conversation, (interview with Joe Gores), by Don Cole, 3-1 PP 19

(Gores, Joe), Joe Gores Clears Up Some Mysteries, (interview), by Erik Jendresen, 3-2 M 42

Gores, Roger J.: letter of comment, 2-4 TAD 277

(Gorey, Edward), Mass Market Murmurings, (Gorey as artist for paperback books published by Anchor Books), by Barry Bernard, 1-3 CP 5

Gorman, Dave: letter of comment, 6/7 LR 17; 2-2 MF 48; 3 MT 25

Gormley, Eunice: letter of comment, 6 MY 8; 2-1 PP 33; 3-1 PP 42; 5-4 TAD 241; 6-4 TAD 275; 8-3 TAD 235

(Goss, Nathaniel, detective: Colin Willock), Pen Profile No.10, Colin Willock, by Barry Pike, 3-2 PP 17

Gothic Magazines, The, by David and Su Bates, 1-5 CP 29

Gothics, Ghastly, Gruesome and Romantic, by Veronica M.S.Kennedy, 9-4 TAD 276

(Gothics), Let's Look at Gothics, by Miriam Lynch, 2-2 MR 13

(Gothics), Three Ladies of the Quasi-Gothic, The Films of Armstrong, Lofts, and White, by Jack Edmund Nolan, 5-2 MR 23

(Gothics), Cothics: Ghastly, Gruesome and Romantic, by Veronica M.S. Kennedy, 9-4 TAD 276

(Gothics), The Gothic Magazines, by David & Su Bates, 1-5 CP 29

Gott, George: Blue Mountain, (verse), 2-3/4 AD 11

Gottschalk, Jane: Criminous Christmases, (mysteries with Christmas themes), 13-4 TAD 281

Gottschalk, Jane: Detective Fiction and Things Shakespearean, (Shakespere associations in mystery novels), 14-2 TAD 100

Gottschalk, Jane: The Games of Detective Fiction, (plot games), 10-1 TAD 74

Gottschalk, Jane: letter of comment, 3-1 MF 58; 3-3 MF 59; 4-1 MF 39; 5-1 MF 42; 2-1 PP 37; 3-1 PP 37; 3-3 PP 40; 4-1 PP 42; 13-4 TAD 343

Gottschalk, Jane: Quirky Quatrains, (verse), 13-4 TAD 335

Gottschalk, Jane: Mystery, Murder and Academe, (academic scene mystery fiction), 11-2 TAD 159

Goulart, Ron: The Hand of Dr. Insidious, (fiction), 13 R 1

Coulart, Ron: The Comic Book Adventures of Ellery Queen, (Queen in comics), 12-3 TAD 197

Coulart, Ron: letter of comment, 8-2 TAD 153; 22 X 51

(Goulart, Ron), Coulart's Version of The Avenger, New Wine, Old Bottles and Something Extra, (The Avenger in paperback by Goulart), by R.Jeff Banks, 9-2 TAD 122

Goulart's Version of The Avenger: New Wine, Old Bottles and Something Extra, (The Avenger in paperback by Goulart), by R. Jeff Banks, 9-2 TAD 122

Grace, Robert B.: letter of comment, 3-6 MR 9

(Grafton, C.W.), C.W.Grafton, (biog. and literary sketch), by Bill Lyles, 3-6 PP 7

Grage, Mrs. Theodore: letter of comment, 2-1 TAD 64; 5-1 TAD 47

(Graham, John Alexander), Introducing John Alexander Graham, (interview), 2-4 MR 16

Graham, Ronald E.: letter of comment, 8-2 TAD 161

Grain and Salt Printing Company, The, (tongue-in-cheek essay on boys' book publisher), by Robert Jennings, 1 BB 12

Grain and Salt Printing Company, The, Update, (humour on boys' book publisher, imaginary), by D.W. Howard, 2 BB 15

Grammatical Boy, The, (humorous essay), by Bill Nye, 1-1 YB 11

(Granby, Col. Alistair, series: Francis Beeding), Checklist, by Barry Van Tilburg, 4-2 MF 11

Grand, Mitchell: letter of comment, 2-6 MF 45; 3-1 MF 48; 1-5 PP 26; 2-1 PP 41; 2-3 PP 41; 3-3 PP 37; 4-5/6 PP 99; 5-4 TAD 253; 9-4 TAD 249

(Grant, Dr. David, series: George B. Mair), Checklist, Annotated, by Barry Van Tilburg, 4-4 MF 16

Grant, Mary: letter of comment, 2-2 TAD 128

"Grant, Michelle": Bouchercon XI, "Where Crime was Our Government's Business," (mystery fan and author convention report), 3-5 PP 33

Grant, Nik: Review of THE MARTIAN CHRONICLES by Ray Bradbury, 26 X 12

Grant, Nik: Review of "The Syncopated, Tennis-Shoed, Beast Within Our Shower" by Ray Bradbury, 36 X R17

(Grant, Dr. Patrick, detective: Margaret Yorke), Pen Profile No.13, Margaret Yorke, by Barry Pike, 3-4 PP 18

Grant, Richard: A Bibliography of Avram Davidson, 9 SF 4

Grant, Richard: letter of comment, 11 SF 48

(Grant, Victor, series: John B. Ethan), Series Synopses, by John Vining, 10-2 TAD 187

(Gravell, Kenneth), Carlos Bannon, The Private Detective Fiction of Kenneth Gravell, (with checklist), by Randy Himmel, 12 LR 8

Graves, Douglas: Hand of Glory, 7 X 10

Graves Gladney Speaks, (interview with pulp artist), by Will Murray, 1 D 23

(Graves, Richard L.), The Explosive Novels of Richard L. Graves, by George Kelley, 3-6 MF 9

(Graves, Robert), Paperback Editions of Robert Graves, (with checklist), by Susannah Bates, 3-5 CP 25

Graveyard Walking and Gravewatching, (on H.P.Lovecraft), by John Dinan, 2 FM 14

Gray, Leonard P.: letter of comment, 12 R 23

Great Australian Detective, The, (on Detective-Inspector Napoleon Bonaparte, by Arthur W. Upfield), by William Antony S. Sarjeant, 12-2 TAD 99

Great Book Bubble, The, (on collecting boys' books), by Alan S. Dikty, 1-4 BC 110

Great Detectives, (discussion of Solar Pons and Dr. Thorndyke), by George T. Hamilton, 4-2 TAD 6

Great Escape Artist, The, (on the pulp hero, The Avenger), by Robert Kenneth Jones, 9 BS 19

Great Lizzie Borden T-Shirt Media Event and Mystery Quiz, The, (report on convention, University of California San Diego, 1978), by Francis M. Nevins, Jr., 5-6 MF 7

Great Marvel Series, The, (boys' books, science fiction), by Robert Jennings, 7 BB 5; (checklist) 7 BB 19

Great Melbourne Cup Mystery, The, (FOLLOW MY DUST: Arthur W. Upfield), by Philip T. Asdell, 1 BY 3

Great Merlini, The, (on the master magician-detective by Clayton Rawson), by Fred Dueren, 4-4 MF 28

Great Mystery Series, The, (study and checklist, Collin Wilcox), by Jeff Pierce, 3-2 M 20

(GREAT RADIO HEROES, THE: Jim Harmon), Contemplating Jim Harmon's Novel, "The Great Radio Heroes," by Wooda Nicholas Carr, 69 PU 28

Green, David: letter of comment, 10 DS 5

Green, Robert Breyfogle: A Checklist of Mystery, Detective and Suspense Fiction Published in the U.S., (bibliography), (July-September 1973) 7-1 TAD 50; (October-December 1973) 7-2 TAD 125; (January-March 1974) 7-3 TAD 206; (April-June 1974) 7-4 TAD 283; (July-September 1974) 8-1 TAD 52; (October-December 1974) 8-2 TAD 136; (January-March 1975) 8-3 TAD 217; (April-June 1975) 8-4 TAD 294

Green, Robert Breyfogle: letter of comment, 3-3 TAD 207; 5-3 TAD 174

(Green, Robert Breyfogle), Obituary, 9-1 TAD 24

Green Door Mystery, The, (Green Door Mysteries, paperback book series), by Howard Waterhouse, 1-2 PQ 39

(Green Door Mysteries), The Green Door Mystery, (paperback book series), by Howard Waterhouse, 1-2 PQ 39; (checklist) 1-2 PQ 40

(Green Door Mysteries), Rare Books Are Getting Scarce, (paperback book series), by Bruce Taylor, 3-2 CP 29

(Green Hornet series), Mystery Dial II, The Green Hornet (radio serials), by Steve Lewis, 2-2 PP 10

(Green Lama series: Richard Foster), Checklist, pulp magazine stories, by Dickson Thorpe, 1-2 MF 7

Green Spider, The, (fiction), by A. Sarsfield Ward (Sax Rohmer), 3 R 3

Greenbaum, Michael: letter of comment, 4-2 MF 57

(Greenberg, Martin H.: THE 13 CRIMES OF SCIENCE Fiction, w/ Asimov and Waugh), Mystery Plus: Getting There May Be More Than Half the Fun, by R. Jeff Banks, 3-5 PP 15

Greenberg, Robyn: Mystery Writers Honor Their Own, 32nd Annual Edgar Allen Poe Awards (Mystery Writers of America Award Banquet report), 11-2 TAD 156

Greene, Douglas G.: A Reader's Supplement to QUEEN'S QUORUM, (basic mystery list), 12-3 TAD 228

Greene, Douglas G.: Adolf Hitler and John Dickson Carr's Least-Known Locked Room, 14-4 TAD 295

Greene, Douglas G.: John Dickson Carr, Alias Roger Fairbairn, and the Historical Novel, 11-4 TAD 339

Greene, Douglas G.: John Dickson Carr on British Radio, (w/checklist), 12-1 TAD 69

Greene, Douglas G.: letter of comment, 3-2 PP 36; 3-3 PP 41; 3-5 PP 45; 3-5 PP 50; 3-6 PP 36; 4-1 PP 41; 4-2 PP 36; 4-2 PP 45; 4-4 PP 40; 4-5/6 PP 89; 3 R 28; 12-4 TAD 355; 13-1 TAD 77; 13-4 TAD 342; 14-4 TAD 381

Greene, Douglas G.: Pronzini, Nameless, and a Limited Edition, (Bill Pronzini's detective, Nameless, in A KILLING IN XANADU), 4-2 PP 11

(Greene, Graham), A Checklist for Graham Greene Mysteries, by Pat Erhardt, 1-5 MR 15

(Greene, Graham: THE HEART OF THE MATTER), A Detective Searches for a Clue in THE HEART OF THE MATTER, by J.R.Christopher, 4-1 TAD 32

Greene, Paulette: letter of comment, 6 U 50

Grella, George: letter of comment, 13-3 TAD 237

Grella, George: Murder and the Mean Streets, The Hard-Boiled Detective Novel, 5-1 TAD 1

Grella, George: Pulp Tradition in Mystery Fiction, (panel discussion, Popular Culture Association, 1972), 6-3 TAD 133

Gremlins, (unexplained facts regarding pulps), by Will Murray, 1 D 31; 2 D 47

Grennell, Dean A.: A Tan & Sandy Thirteenth, (on A TAN AND SANDY SILENCE by John D. MacDonald), 17 JD 11

Grennell, Dean A.: Captain Satan (pulp magazine character in magazine of that title), 72 PU 15

Grennell, Dean A.: Dating the Travis McGee Stories, (books by John D. MacDonald), 22 JD 11

Grennell, Dean A.: The Fallen Mighty, (on The Shadow), 22 X 20

Grennell, Dean A.: Feetnote to Fleming, (gun characteristics, Ian Fleming's James Bond stories), 15 JD 10

Grennell, Dean A.: FLYING ACES, (literary discussion of the aviation pulp magazine), 66 PU 9

Grennell, Dean A.: How Are the Fallen Mighty Department - Captain Satan (pulp character), 42 X 9

Grennell, Dean A.: Jumping Jimmy Christopher, (Operator 5, pulp hero), 30 X 17

Grennell, Dean A.: Not Vibgyor, Bpprgoaygbilstl, (acronym for Travis McGee series, John D. MacDonald), 20 JD 5

Grennell, Dean A.: The Shadow, (literary discussion of pulp hero), 61 PU 13

Grennell, Dean A.: Shadow of the Shadow, (on RETURN OF THE SHADOW), 62 PU 6

Grennell, Dean A.: Sunday Supplements in Retrospect, 28 X 11

Gresham, Stephen: An Interview with Mary Elizabeth Counselman, 6 WT 11

(Gretter, Clemens), Artists: Clemens Gretter, (boys' books illustrator), by Fred Woodworth, 6 MA 5

Gretter, Clemens: letter of comment, 5 MA 26

(GREY CHARTERIS, THE: Robert Simpson), Did He or Didn't He? (Frederick Faust as possible author), by William J. Clark, 1-1 FC 5

(Grey, Zane), An Overlooked Boys Series Best Seller, by Rick Crandall, 1-2 YB 14

(Grey, Zane), Zane Grey's Western Magazine, by David and Su Bates, 1-3 CP 20

(GREY FACE: Sax Rohmer), "She Who Loveth Silence," by Stephen Shutt, 15 R 25

Grijze, Jan: letter of comment, 5 X 41

Grimes, Larry E.: The Reluctant Hero, Reflections on Vocation and Heroism in the Travis McGee Novels of John D. MacDonald, 1-1 C 103

Grippo, Evelyn B.: letter of comment, 5-5 MR 17

Grissom, Bob: letter of comment, 12 JD 17

(Griswold, Lotta), Deering (Deal) Series, Boys' Series Bibliographies, (boys' books), by Harry K. Hudson, 1-3 YB 10

Grochowski, Mary: A Beastly Case of Murder, (crime fiction involving various beasts, with checklist), 1-6 PP 3

Grochowski, Mary: A Bit of a Twist, The Writings of John Lutz, 1-2 PP 5

Grochowski, Mary: A Hazardous Occupation, (fiction), 4 MT 1

Grochowski, Mary: The Adventure of the Elusive Vanardy, (Sherlockiana), 1-1 PP 7

Grochowski, Mary: An Interview with John Lutz, 12-3 TAD 276

Grochowski, Mary: Behind the Scenes at Bouchercon 9, or, It Was Murder at the Bismarck! (report on mystery fans and authors convention), 2-6 MF 3

Grochowski, Mary: Bouchercon X, (report on mystery fans and authors convention), 3-5 MF 13; 2-5 PP 27

Grochowski, Mary: The Case of the Quivering Mustache, (regarding Lilian Jackson Braun), 3-6 PP 3

Grochowski, Mary: Checklist of Craig Rice Books, 13-3 TAD 267

Grochowski, Mary: Checklist of John Lutz Books, 12-3 TAD 278

Grochowski, Mary: Craig Rice, Merry Mistress of Mystery and Mayhem, 13-3 TAD 265

Grochowski, Mary: letter of comment, 6/7 LR 24; 2-3 MF 66; 4-2 MF 56; 3 PE 32; 2-1 PP 39; 1-3 PP 34; 2-2 PP 42; 2-4 PP 46; 2-6 PP 40; 11-3 TAD 308

Grochowski, Mary: Literary Sleuths, Alias Your Friendly Neighborhood Book Detectives, (mystery book-sellers experiences), 2-3 PP 3

Grochowski, Mary: Murder at the Waldorf, Bouchercon VIII, October 7-9, 1977, (report of mystery fans and authors convention), 2-2 MF 15

Grochowski, Mary: Partial Checklist, John Lutz, short stories and novels, 1-2 PP 8

Grochowski, Mary: Private Eyes, Who or What Are They?, 5 PE 13

Grochowski, Mary: The Solution of the Elusive Vanardy, (Sherlockiana), 2-5 PP 3

(Grochowski, Mary), Biographical Sketch, 2-3 PP 7

Groff, Mary: All Too True, (books suggested by true crimes), 1-1 PP 3; 1-2 PP 15; 1-3 PP 16; 1-4 PP 17; 1-5 PP 13; 1-6 PP 14; 2-1 PP 23; 2-2 PP 20; 2-3 PP 15; 2-4 PP 21; 2-5 PP 19; 2-6 PP 19; 3-1 PP 29; 3-2 PP 19; 3-3 PP 22; 3-4 PP 25; 3-5 PP 21; 3-6 PP 21; 4-1 PP 24; 4-2 PP 15; 4-3 PP 15; 4-4 PP 21; 4-5/6 PP 59

Groff, Mary: Bloody But Readable, (1914-1918 mystery fiction), 11-3 TAD 234

Groff, Mary: Down Grey, Wet Streets, (private eye mystery stories), 3 PE 9

Groff, Mary: Edgar Lustgartem 1970-78, (memorial tribute and checklist), 12-3 TAD 286

Groff, Mary: Eyes on the Screen, (mystery and crime shows on television), 13-3 TAD 261

Groff, Mary: For Us, a Child, (Rex Stout and the times of his birth), 9 MN A15

Groff, Mary: Friday, February 25, 1955, (The London TIMES LITERARY SUPPLEMENT on mystery fiction), 10-3 TAD 232

Groff, Mary: It's a Novel World, (social periods reflected in mystery novels), 9-4 TAD 314

Groff, Mary: The Last Year, (the Golden Age of Mystery fiction), 11-2 TAD 145

Groff, Mary: letter of comment, 6 CL 10; 1-2 MF 51; 5/6 MN 14; 7 MN 7; 8 MN 34; 8 MN 38; 9 MN L5; 11 MN L12; 5-1 MR 17; 5-6 MR 16; 2 PE 41; 1-1 PP 28; 1-2 PP 27; 2-1 PP 33; 2-2 PP 30; 3-3 PP 35; 4-1 PP 41; 4-3 PP 30; 6-2 TAD 122; 8-1 TAD 70; 8-3 TAD 236; 10-3 TAD 274; 10-4 TAD 378; 11-2 TAD 207

Groff, Mary: Obituary, Edgar Lustgarten, 2-1 PP 13

Groff, Mary: P.D.James, (sketch), 3-3 PP 11

Groff, Mary: Some Necessary Needs, (survey of mystery reference books), 10 CL 5; 11 CL 3

Groff, Mary: Some of My Best Friends Are Books, (on Bruce & Carol Taylor and The San Francisco Mystery Bookshop), 13-2 TAD 171

Groff, Mary: This Dark Night, (fiction), 8 MN 9

Gronauer, John: letter of comment, 14 X 63

Groon, (verse), by Ray Bradbury, 18 X 25

(Grossbach, Robert: THE CHEAP DETECTIVE), A Pair of Parodies, by R. Jeff Banks, 1-5 PP 10

Grossman, Al: Bill Barnes, (aviation pulp hero), 11 P 17

Grossman, Al: Doc Defeated, or Doc Savage in the Comics, (unsuccessful attempt to use Doc Savage in comic books), 2/3 DR 5

Grossman, Al: letter of comment, 8 BS 6; 3-2 TAD 135; 4 U 53; 30 X 148

Group Controlling Pulp Prices Arrested! (humourous essay on high prices of pulp magazines), 30 X 136, by Victor Dricks

Grove, Ellis: letter of comment, 4-1 TAD 65

Growing Up With Ellery Queen, by Edward D. Hoch, 12-3 TAD 200

Grub Street Beat, The, ("World of Mystery" news column), by Martha Hudson, 3-2 M 32

Gruber, Frank: Heinie and the Chicken, (personal reminiscences on Frederick Faust), 1-1 FC 11

Gruber, Frank: The Horatio Alger Paperback First Editions, 2-4 BC 242

Gruber, Frank: Lester Dent, (comments and reminiscences), 2-4 TAD 215

Gruber, Frank: letter of comment, 67 PU 56; 2-3 TAD 204

Gruber, Frank: Reminiscences, (of Harry Stephen Keeler), 2-1 TAD 55

Gruber, Frank: Reminiscences, (of script-writing Holmes and Bulldog Drummond), 2-1 TAD 56

Gruber, Frank: Walter Gibson, (comments and reminiscences), 3-2 TAD 94; 17 X 5

(Gruber, Frank), Frank Gruber, (literary comments with bibliographic checklist 67 PU 31

(Gruber, Frank), Frank Gruber, a Dedication, by Allen J. Hubin, 3-2 TAD 95

(Gruber, Frank), Frank Gruber, I Loved You, Too, Buddy, by Steve Fisher, 3-3 TAD 170

(Gruber, Frank), In Memory of Frank Gruber, by William J. Clark, 2-1 FC 4

(Gruber, Frank), Johnny Fletcher and Sam Cragg, (detective series by Gruber), by Peter Harris, 4-4 MR 12

(Gruber, Frank), Meet the Author, Frank Gruber, by Allen J. Hubin, 2-4 TAD 216

Guenevere, (verse), by Frederick Faust, 1-4 FC 6

(Gull, Vladimir, series: Anthony Stuart), Vladimir Gull, by Theodore P. Dukeshire, 4-3 MF 22

(Gunn, James: THE MAGICIAN), Mystery Plus, A Pair of Triple Threats (magic plus mystery plus science fiction), by R. Jeff Banks, 4-4 PP 14

Guthery, Tom R., IV: letter of comment, 9 DS 21

(Guthrie, A.B.), The Education of Jason Beard, A.B.Guthrie's Western Suspense Stories, 1-2 C 126, by Fred Erisman

Guthrie, Bruce: His Name, (on Doc Savage), 5 DS 4

Guy, Gordon R.: Bela Lugosi, (sketch), 1 CD 6

Guy, Gordon R.: Bela Lugosi, A Scrapbook, (photo article), 1 CD 16

Guy, Gordon R.: Bela Lugosi in Murder by Television, (film), 1 CD 12

Guymon, E.T.: letter of comment, 9-4 TAD 297; 10-1 TAD 39

Gwilt, Peter R. & John R.: The Use of Poison in Detective Fiction, 1-2 C 8

H. Douglas Thomson, A Brief Appreciation, by Howard Haycraft, 8-4 TAD 256

HPL: The Book That Nearly Was, (H.P.
Lovecraft), by Kenneth Faig, Jr.,
11 X 118
H.P.Lovecraft, (verse), by Vincent
Starrett, 18 X 9
H.P.Lovecraft and Edmund Wilson, by
L. Sprague de Camp, 1 FM 5
H.P.Lovecraft, Rabid Racist, or,
Compassionate Gentleman?, by
Dirk W. Mosig, 18 X 13
H.R.F.Keating, (sketch with bibliography)
by Sven-Ingmar Pettersson, 8-4 TAD 277
H.S.Chibbet, (sketch), by Mike Ashley,
4 WT 7
H.S.Keeler, A Checklist, by Bernard
Beauchesne, 1-4 TAD 147
Hacker, Prof. Andrew: letter of comment,
6 JD 12; 11 JD 22
Hadji, R.S.: letter of comment, 4 SF 42;
43 X 6
Hadley, Bill: letter of comment, 2-4
TBN 4
Hagemann, E.R.: An Annotated Raoul F.
Whitfield BLACK MASK Checklist,
11-3 TAD 183
Hagemann, E.R.: Cap Shaw and His "Great
and Regular Fellows" - The Making of
THE HARD-BOILED OMNIBUS, 1945-46,
(Joseph Shaw as editor), 2-2 C 143
Hagemann, E.R.: Introducing Paul Cain
and His FAST ONE, A Forgotten Hard-
Boiled Writer and a Forgotten Gangster
Novel, 12-1 TAD 72
Hagemann, E.R.: The Jo Gar Stories of
Ramon Decolta in BLACK MASK Magazine,
14-1 TAD 8
Hagemann, E.R.: letter of comment,
3-2 M 2
Hagemann, E.R.: Philo Vance's Sunday
Nights at the Old Stuyvesant Club,
1-2 C 35
Hagemann, E.R.: Ramon Decolta aka Raoul
Whitfield, and His Diminutive Brown
Man, Jo Gar, The Island Detective,
14-1 TAD 3
Hagemann, E.R.: Raoul F. Whitfield, A
Star with the MASK, (on stories in
BLACK MASK pulp magazine), 13-3 TAD
179
Hagen, Ordean: How I "Done" It, (writing
the ENCYCLOPEDIC GUIDE TO MYSTERY,
DETECTIVE AND SUSPENSE FICTION),
1-2 TAD 45
Hagen, Ordean: letter of comment,
11 JD 19
(Hagen, Ordean), Meet the Author, Ordean
Hagen, by Allen J. Hubin, 1-2 TAD 47
(Hagen, Ordean: WHO DONE IT?), Who Done
It - Additions, Subtractions and
Alterations to Hagen's book, by
various, 3-1 TAD 44; 3-2 TAD 123;
3-3 TAD 184; The Mystery Novel on
the Screen, addenda, by Charles
Shubuk, 3-4 TAD 255; 4-2 TAD 125
Hagen, Sue, and Operative 1701: The
Real Steve Austin ("The Million Dollar
Man"), 6 U 15

(Haggard, H. Rider: SHE), Her, (on the
Corinth paperback reprints), by
J.X.Williams, 2 SF 34
(Haggard, William: Col. Charles Russell
series), Checklist, Annotated, by
Barry Van Tilburg, 4-3 MF 27
Hahn, Robert W.: The Passing of Third
Floor Back, (Vincent Starrett),
7-3 TAD 204
Haiku, (verse), by John D. MacDonald,
15 JD 20
Hal Keene and Skippy Dare Series, The,
(boys' books), by Julius R. Chenu,
1-1 BC 12
Halbach, Helen: Apostle Apostle,
(verse), 7 X 68
Halbach, Helen: Exquisite Persquisite,
(Solar Pons), 2-5 PD 4
Hale, John: letter of comment, 10 JD 9
(Halfaday Creek Books: James B. Hendryx),
The Appearances of Black John Smith
of Halfaday Creek, and Checklist of
the Halfaday Creek Books, by John
Harwood, 3-6 MF 7
(Hall, Adam), LeCarre, Deighton, Hall,
and the Screen's Tired Spies,
(filmed spy fiction), by Jack
Edmund Nolan, 4-1 MR 23
(Hall, Adam: Quiller series), Checklist,
Annotated, by R. Jeff Banks and
Harry D. Dawson, 4-1 MF 8
(Hall, Adam: Quiller series), Checklist,
Annotated, by Barry Van Tilburg,
4-3 MF 26
(Hall, Adam: Quiller series), The
Quiller Report, by R. Jeff Banks
and Harry D. Dawson, 4-1 MF 8
Hall, John: letter of comment, 14-1
TAD 71
Hall, Kyle: letter of comment, 5 MA 29;
6 MA 29
Hall, Molly: letter of comment, 2-1
TB 4
Hall, Natalie: Upfield Collector, A
Mystery Buff of the Purest Sort,
(Michael Masliah as collector of
the Arthur W. Upfield works),
11-1 TAD 72
Hall, R.L.: Some Touch of the Artist,
(Sherbockiana), 2-2 M 30
Hall, Richard P.: A Tribute to the
Crowned Queen of Misdirection,
Dame Agatha Christie, (with
paperback checklist), 3-3 CP 26
Hall, Richard P.: Papyrocunabole, or
There's One Now!, (paperback book
collectors), 1-4 CP 12
Hall, Richard P.: The Papyrocunabula
of Sax Rohmer, (paperback reprints
with checklist), 3-4 CP 15
(Halliday, Brett), Department of
Unrelated Miscellanea, by Francis
M. Nevins, Jr., 4-1 MR 21
(Halliday, Brett), The Mike Shayne
Caper, by Bernard A. Drew, 3-1
PQ 51

(Halliday, Brett), The Return of Michael
Shayne, (commentary on Shayne occasioned
by announcement of new reprints), by
Helen McCloy, 14-4 TAD 344
(Halliday, Michael), Checklist, by Robert
E. Briney and John Creasey, 2-1 TAD 14
(Halliday, Michael: Dr. Emmanuel Cellini
series), Checklist, by Robert E.
Briney and John Creasey, 2-1 TAD 13
(Halliday, Michael: Fane Brothers series),
Checklist, by Robert E. Briney and
John Creasey, 2-1 TAD 13
Halpern, Frank: letter of comment,
1-1 MF 40; 3-1 PQ 4; 6-1 TAD 56;
8-3 TAD 240
("Ham" in Doc Savage stories), DSCR
Interview with Brig. Gen. Theodore
Marley Brooks ("Ham") May 1976,
simulation, 3 DS 11
(Hambledon, Thomas Elphinstone, series:
Manning Coles), Checklist, Annotated,
by Barry Van Tilburg, 4-3 MF 23
(Hamerstrom, Frances), Recipient of
August Derleth Award, 5-1 AD 7
Hamill, Pete: We Tell Stories, A Talk
Given at a Monthly MWA Meeting in
New York, (Mystery Writers of America),
12-1 TAD 3
Hamilton, Alex: I Comma Mickey, (Mickey
Spillane talking), 1-2 MR 9
(Hamilton, Donald), The Degeneration of
Donald Hamilton, by George Kelley,
1-6 MF 11
(Hamilton, Donald), The Matt Helm Series,
with Annotated Checklist, by R. Jeff
Banks and Guy M. Townsend, 2-2 MF 3
Hamilton, Edmond: An Inside Look at
Captain Future, (pulp hero character),
3 P 3
(Hamilton, Edmond), Edmond Hamilton,
(literary sketch), by Robert Weinberg,
1 WT 7
(Hamilton, Edmond), Edmond Hamilton: By
Himself, (1934), 2 WT 10
(Hamilton, Edmond), Eulogy, by Forrest
J. Ackerman, 30 X 13
(Hamilton, Edmond), Fiction by Edmond
Hamilton, by Joseph Kankowski, 30 X 14
(Hamilton, Edmond), Edmond Hamilton in
WEIRD TALES, Checklist, by Robert
Weinberg, 1 WT 9
Hamilton, Frank: Artist Behind Doc Savage,
(on Walter Baumhofer, pulp cover
artist), 9 DS 6
Hamilton, Frank: letter of comment,
4 DS 4; 10 DS 6; 12 DS 8; 2-2 MF 44;
7 MY 13; 15 R 27; 2 U 48; 4 U 51;
4 U 53; 5 U 63; 5 U 64; 6 U 49;
7 U 46; 13 X 60
Hamilton, George T.: Great Detectives,
(on Solar Pons and Dr. Thorndyke),
4-2 AD 6
Hamilton, George T.: R. Austin Freeman,
A Bibliography, 4-2 AD 10; 4-3 AD 6

(Hamilton, Leigh Brackett), Leigh
Brackett, Storyteller, by James
Ellis, 42 X 27
(Hamilton, Leigh Brackett), Obituary,
38 X 3
(Hamilton, Patrick), Six Britons the
Movies Ignored, (seldom filmed),
by Jack Edmund Nolan, 3-5 MR 9
Hamilton, Robert M.: The Orchidology
of Nero Wolfe, (Wolfe's passion
for growing orchids), 1-2 G 18
Hammel, Kathy: letter of comment,
3 U 49
(Hammer, Mike, detective: Mickey
Spillane), Another Mike Hammer,
Pre-Spillane, by Richard S. Lochte
II, 2-1 TAD 24
(Hammer, Mike, detective: Mickey
Spillane), Dat's Mike Ham-muh?
(Hammer in the popular media),
by Max Collins, 12-4 TAD 308
(Hammer, Mike, detective: Mickey
Spillane), Department of
Unmitigated Mishmosh, by Francis
M. Nevins, Jr., 3-1 MR 21
(Hammer, Mike, detective: Mickey
Spillane), Mike Hammer, (series on
television, checklist), by Andy
Jaysnovitch, 4 PE 5
(Hammer, Mike, detective: Mickey
Spillane), Mickey Spillane
Comic Strip, 12-4 TAD 317
Hammett, A Reaction Report, (re:
DASHIELL HAMMETT: A CASEBOOK, by
William F. Nolan), by William F.
Nolan, 3-3 TAD 162
Hammett Checklist, The: Revisited,
(Dashiell Hammett), by William F.
Nolan, 6-4 TAD 249
Hammett in Hollywood, (Dashiell
Hammett), by William F. Nolan,
21 X 5
Hammett, Postscript, (Dashiell Hammett),
by William White, 3-3 TAD 175
(Hammett, Dashiell), About Dashiell
Hammett, by William White, 3-3
TAD 171
(Hammett, Dashiell), The BLACK MASK
Boys Go Legit, by William F.
Nolan, 13-1 TAD 23
(Hammett, Dashiell), Chandler-Hammett-
Hemingway, Teachers in the "Tough
School," by Stanley A. Carlin,
2-5 MR 15
(Hammett, Dashiell), Expressionism
and American Popular Literature,
Hammett as a Continental Op-Eye,
by Margaret Lamb, 2-1 C 26
(Hammett, Dashiell), Hammett, A
Reaction Report (re: DASHIELL
HAMMETT: A CASEBOOK by William F.
Nolan), by William F. Nolan, 3-3
TAD 162

(Hammett, Dashiell), The Hammett Checklist Revisited, by William F. Nolan, 6-4 TAD 249

(Hammett, Dashiell), Hammett in Hollywood, by William F. Nolan, 21 X 5

(Hammett, Dashiell), Hammett, Postscript, by William White, 3-3 TAD 175

(Hammett, Dashiell), Hammett the Writer, by Joe Goes, 38 X 5

(Hammett, Dashiell), The Importance of "C--ing" in Earnest, A Comparison of THE MALTESE FALCON and CHINATOWN, (film), by William D. Bottiggi, 14-1 TAD 86

(Hammett, Dashiell), Including Murder, An Unpublished Hammett Collection (manuscripts), by Robert S. Powell, 2-2 C 135

(Hammett, Dashiell), Murder by Client, A Reworked Theme in Dashiell Hammett, by Christopher Bentley, 14-1 TAD 78

(Hammett, Dashiell), Mystery Puzzle, (puzzle), 3-2 M 24

(Hammett, Dashiell), Mystery Reviewers Handbook, Dashiell Hammett 1894-1961, (verse), by Mark Purcell, 7-4 TAD 282

(Hammett, Dashiell), Paperback Editions of Novels and Short Stories, by William Lyles, 1-3 CP 9

(Hammett, Dashiell), The Problem of Moral Vision in Dashiell Hammett's Detective Novels, by George J. Thompson, 6-3 TAD 153; 6-4 TAD 214; 7-1 TAD 32; 7-3 TAD 178; 7-4 TAD 270; 8-1 TAD 27; 8-2 TAD 124

(Hammett, Dashiell), Revisiting the Revised Hammett Checklist, by William F. Nolan, 9-4 TAD 292

(Hammett, Dashiell), Sam Spade, Lover, (Sam Spade, detective), by Peter Wolfe, 11-4 TAD 366; 38 X 21

(Hammett, Dashiell), Sam Spade Talking, by John M. Reilly, 1-2 C 119

(Hammett, Dashiell), The Short Stories and Novels of Hammett, (in Dell Map Back paperback books and ELLERY QUEEN'S MYSTERY MAGAZINE), by M.C. Hill, 3-2 CP 9

(Hammett, Dashiell), Spade - Bogart, (Hammett's works filmed), by Mark MacDonald, 4 MT 31

(Hammett, Dashiell), The Stuff Nightmares Are Made Of: A Hammett Update, by Erik Jendresen, 3-2 M 45

(Hammett, Dashiell: Continental Op series) Shadowing the Continental Op, (with checklist), by William F. Nolan, 8-1 TAD 121

(Hammett, Dashiell: THE DAIN CURSE), The Problem of Moral Vision in Dashiell Hammett's Detective Novels, Pt.3, by George J. Thompson, 7-1 TAD 32

(Hammett, Dashiell: THE GLASS KEY), The Problem of Moral Vision in Dashiell Hammett's Detective Novels, Pt.5, by George J. Thompson, 7-4 TAD 270

(Hammett, Dashiell: THE MALTESE FALCON), Order and Disorder in The Maltese Falcon, by Donald J. Pattow, 11-2 TAD 171

(Hammett, Dashiell: THE MALTESE FALCON), The Problem of Moral Vision in Dashiell Hammett's Detective Novels, Pt.4, by George J. Thompson, 7-3 TAD 178

(Hammett, Dashiell: THE MALTESE FALCON), The Projected Detective, (filmed version), by Andy Jaysnovitch, 12 CL 8

(Hammett, Dashiell: RED HARVEST), The Problem of Moral Vision in Dashiell Hammett's Detective Novels, Pt.2, by George J. Thompson, 6-4 TAD 213

(Hammett, Dashiell: THE THIN MAN), One Britisher;s View of Hammett, (review of book in a London paper), by Edward S. Lauterbach, 4-5/6 PP 44

(Hammett, Dashiell: THE THIN MAN), The Problem of Moral Vision in Dashiell Hammett's Detective Novels, Pt.6, by George J. Thompson, 8-1 TAD 27

Hammonds, Paul: Index of Paperback Imprints in Publishers' Weekly for 1950, 1-3 PQ 28; (1952 & 1953) 2-1 PQ 38; (1954) 2-2 PQ 43

Hancer, Kevin: letter of comment, 6 BB 29; 2 MA 26; 7 MA 24; 4-1 PQ 51; 4 SF 44

(Hancer, Kevin: PAPERBACK PRICE GUIDE), Omissions from Guide, Digest Size Paperbacks, by Norral Johnson, 3-3 CP 9; by Scott Edwards, 3-4 CP 22

Hancer's Price Guide, (PAPERBACK PRICE GUIDE by Kevin Hancer), by Don Z. Block, 2-5 CP 24

(Hancock, H. Irving), Future Shock: 1916, (Conquest of the U.S. boys' books series), by Robert Jennings, 4 BB 15

Hand of Dr. Insidious, The, by Ron Goulart, 13 R 1

Hand of Glory, by Douglas Graves, 7 X 10

Handi-Books Checklist, (science-fiction published in paperback by Handi-Books), by J. Grant Thiessen, 2 SF 9

Hanos, Dimitrios-James: letter of comment, 21 X 56

Hans Stefan Santesson and the Unicorn Mystery Book Club, (with list), by Edward D. Hoch, 8-3 TAD 185

(Hansen, Joseph: David Brandstetter series), Series Synopses, by Fred Dueren, 11-4 TAD 365

(Hanson, Joseph Mills), Among the Sioux, (boys' books), Boys' Series Bibliography, by Harry K. Hudson, 1-3 YB 8

(Ha'Penny Comics), London's Ha'penny Comics, by Gelett Burgess, 1-1 YB 19

Happy Land, The, (Classic Corners Rare Tales fiction), by James M'Levy, 13-3 TAD 219

Hard-Boiled Detective in the Fallen World, The, by Jeffrey H. Mahan, 1-2 C 90

Hard-Boiled Detective Hero in the 1970's, Some New Candidates, by David J. Geherin, 11-1 TAD 49

Hard-Boiled Dick, The: A Personal Checklist, by James Sandoe, 1-2 TAD 38

Hard Boiled is Hard to Find, comments on hard-boiled detective fiction in paperback), by Bruce Cervon, 3-2 CP 23

Hardboiled Lingo, (glossary), by John Knoerle, 1-1 M 9

(HARD-BOILED OMNIBUS, THE: Joseph Shaw), Cap Shaw and His "Great and Regular Fellows": The Making of THE HARD-BOILED OMNIBUS, 1945-46, by E.R. Hagemann, 2-2 C 143

(HARD-BOILED OMNIBUS, THE: Joseph Shaw), Captain Shaw's Hard-Boiled Boys, by Stephen Mertz, 12-3 TAD 264

Hard Cain, The Paper Original Novels of James M. Cain, (paperback), by George Kelley, 4-3 PP 9

Hard Touch, (crime and social reaction), by Bill Wilson: ("big brother") 19 JD 9; (fair judicial trials) 17 JD 21; (justice for the victim) 13 JD 8; (marijuana) 14 JD 17; (police departments) 15 JD 15; (police point of view) 16 JD 8; (prison systems) 18 JD 7

Hardin, Nils: An Interview with Harry Steeger, (President and co-founder, Popular Publications, on the pulp magazines published by his firm), 33 X 3

Hardin, Nils: Biblio-File, (bibliographical data on pulp magazines), 8 X 4; 10 X 11; 9 X 9; 11 X 9

Hardin, Nils: From...TQCB, (THE QUEEN CANON BIBLIOPHILE, on Ellery Queen), 14 X 55

Hardin, Nils: How Fred Gray Found Happiness with a Pulp Price Guide, (humorous treatment of price guides), 22 X 3

Hardin, Nils: letter of comment, 8 MN 36; 6 P 30; 17 R 21

Hardin, Nils: Mini-Books of Basil Wells, 9 X 16

Hardin, Nils: MYSTERY LEAGUE (Magazine), A Summary, (literary discussion of the magazine founded by Ellery Queen), 14 X 8

Hardin, Nils: Popular Publications, A Brief Analysis, (on the pulp magazines of Popular Publications), 33 X 2

Hardin, Nils: Popular Publications, A Pictorial History, (pulp magazines), 33 X 25

Hardin, Nils: Pulpcon 4, (photo report of pulp magazine convention), 15 X 46

Hardin, Nils: Ray Bradbury, Fantasist, Visionary, Moralist, (literary tribute), 36 X R1

Hardin, Nils: STAR MAGAZINE, (Index and Checklist),(pulp magazine), 7 X 66

Hardin, Nils, and George Hocutt: A Checklist of Popular Publications Titles 1930-1955, (bibliographical checklist), 33 X 21

(Hardman series: Ralph Dennis), Have You Met Hardman?, by G.A.Finch, 8-4 TAD 275

Hardy, Arthur Sherburne: The Twelve Green Russian Garnets, (Classic Corners Rare Tales, fiction), 13-1 TAD 48

Hardy Boys, The - A Few Criticisms of the Series and Its Background, (boys' books), by I.R.Ybarra, 4 MA 22

Hardy Boys Illustrators, Paul Laune, (boys' books), 4 MA 22

Hardy Boys Tie-Ins, (boys' books), by John M. Enright, 4 MA 9

(Hardy Boys series), An Incorrect Theory, Capwell Wyckoff Not a Hardy Boys Author, by Fred Woodworth, 5 MA 9

(Hardy Boys series), Bayport's Famous Sleuths, (boys' books), by Fred Woodworth, 4 MA 3

(Hardy Boys series), Capwell Wyckoff, A Hardy Author? (speculation of Wyckoff writing some of the Hardy Boys books, boys' series), by Fred Woodworth, 4 MA 19

(Hardy Boys series), The Clue in the Old Library, (boys' books), by John M. Enright, 4 MA 23

(Hardy Boys series), Dates of Originals and Rewrites, (chronology of original editions and rewritten editions, boys' book series), 4 MA 11

(Hardy Boys series), The Dist-Jacket Era, 1927-1961, (boys' books series that were issued with dust-jackets), by John M. Enright, 4 MA 12

(Hardy Boys series), The Hardy Boys - A Few Criticisms of the Series and Its Background, by I.R.Ybarra, 4 MA 22

(Hardy Boys series), Hardy Boy Illustrators, Paul Laune, (boys' books), 4 MA 22

(Hardy Boys series), Hardy Boys Tie-Ins, (boys' series), by John M. Enright, 4 MA 9

(Hardy Boys series), Mr. McFarlane's Magic, (Leslie McFarlane, one of authors of series), by John M. Enright, 4 MA 5

(Hardy Boys series), Series Move to New Publisher, (change to Simon & Schuster from Grosset & Dunlap), by Fred Woodworth, 2 MA 24

(Hardy Boys series: THE MASKED DONKEY),
Review, by Karen Rockow, 3-3 BC 328
(Hare, Cyril), Cyril Hare, (with check-
list), by Charles Shibuk, 3-1 TAD 28
Hark! Is That You, Donn?...All Cloaked
in Glendale Dark?, (verse), 36 X R15
(Harkaway, Jack), Good Old Jack, (boys'
books and dime novels hero), by Gil
O'Gara, 1-1 YB 22
Harker, Horace: Sherlockian Dinner,
(report, The Non-Canonical Calabashes,
January 5, 1980), 1-3 M 22
Harker, Horace: Upon Distinguishing Among
140 (or More) Pastiches, (Sherlockiana)
1-3 M 14
Harkins, Peter: letter of comment, 4 MA 25
Harlequin, (fiction from Harlequin Books),
by John Carpenter, 15 SF 3
Harlequin - The Beginning, (paperback
book publisher), by J. Grant Thiessen,
9 SF 48; 10 SF 47
Harlequin Science Fiction Checklist,
(paperback science fiction from
Harlequin Books), by J. Grant Thiessen,
2 SF 9
(Harlequin Books), Golden Amazon, (science
fiction series from Harlequin Books)
by John Russell Fearn, 2 SF 24
(Harlequin Books), Romance, Checklist of
First 25 Paperbacks, by J. Grant
Thiessen, 9 SF 48
Harlequin, David: Ed McBain, (interview),
2-1 M 14
(Harley, Paul, series: Sax Rohmer), The
Paul Harley Series, by Robert E.
Briney, 17 R 15
Harmon, Jim: letter of comment, 62 PU 17
(Harmon, Jim: THE GREAT RADIO HEROES),
Contemplating Jim Harmon's Novel
"The Great Radio Heroes," by Wooda
Nicholas Carr, 69 PU 28
(Harness, Charles L.), Charles L. Harness,
A Bibliography, by William D. Vernon,
14 SF 30
(Harness, Charles L.), Charles L. Harness,
The Paradox Man, by William D. Vernon,
14 SF 25
Harold F. Cruickshank, (memorial tribute),
by Wooda Nicholas Carr, 8 DS 2
Harrell, Phil: letter of comment, 64 PU 40
(Harrigan and Hoeffler series: Patrick
O'Malley), Checklist, Annotated,
by Barry Van Tilburg, 4-6 MF 5
(Harrington, Joseph), Joseph Harrington's
First Three Books (THE LAST KNOWN
ADDRESS, BLIND SPOT, THE LAST DOORBELL),
by R.W.Hays, 4-2 TAD 104
Harris, Ernest: letter of comment, 6 SF 48
Harris, Margaret E.: letter of comment,
14-2 TAD 186
Harris, Peter: Johnny Fletcher and Sam
Cragg, (detective series by Frank Gruber),
4-4 MR 12
Harrison, Michael: Chant Royal of the
Sodality of Praed-Street Irregulars,
(verse,re:Solar Pons), 1-1 PDA 2

Harrison, Michael: Commentaries for
the Curious, (on John Dickson Carr),
1 NC 17
Harrison, Michael: The Language of
the Praed Street Irregulars,
(glossary, re: Solar Pons), 2-4
PD 1
Harrison, Michael: The Praed of Praeds,
(biographical sketch of Winthrop
Mackworth Praed), 1-1 PD 1
(Harrison, Michael), Michael Harrison,
An Interview, by Luther Norris,
3-6 MR 17
Harrod, Judge Sam: letter of comment,
25 JD 37
Harrow, Jonathon: Eye Q II, (private
eye quiz), 1-2 M 4
Harrow, Jonathon: Eye-Q 4, Tour of
Duty, (police procedural quiz),
2-1 M 42
Harry Dickson Detective Stories by Jean
Ray, The, by Eddy C. Bertin, 1-1
MR 7
Harry Stephen Keeler, Mystery Writer
Extraordinary, (pulp detective
author), by Bernard Beauchesne,
1-4 TAD 143
Harry Stphen Keeler's Screwball
Circus, (Angus MacWhoter detective
series in pulp magazines), by
Francis M. Nevins, Jr., 5-4 TAD
209
Harry Whittington - Still a Winner
(pulp author), 2-3 PQ 53
Harter, Maurice: letter of comment,
13 X 60
Hartwig, Bill: letter of comment,
1-4 AD 8; 2-2 AD 9; 2-3/4 AD 14
(Harvester, Simon: Dorian Silk series),
Checklist, Annotated, by Barry
Van Tilburg, 4-4 MF 16
Harvey, Deryck: A Word with Desmond
Bagley, (interview, mystery author),
7-4 TAD 258
Harvey, Deryck: A Word with Dick
Francis, (interview, mystery author),
6-3 TAD 151
Harvey, Deryck: The Best of John
Creasey, 7-1 TAD 42
Harvey, Deryck: letter of comment,
6-3 TAD 196; 6-4 TAD 276; 7-1
TAD 66
Harvey, Deryck: 1973 Crime Writers
Association Conference, (report,
British association of published
crime writers), 6-4 TAD 255
Harwitz, Paul: A Night's Work,
(fiction), 1-3 M 46
Harwitz, Paul: Uninvited Night Callers,
(verse), 8 U 103
Harwitz, Paul: World of Mystery,
(West Coast news), 2-2 M 20; 2-3 M 20;
3-1 M 49; 3-2 M 32
Harwood, John: A Frivolity (I Would
Like to...), 6-2 TAD 103

Harwood, John: Arthur B. Reeve and the American Sherlock Holmes, (Prof. Craig Kennedy, detective), 10-4 TAD 354

Harwood, John: Burroughs the Fantastic, (Edgar Rice Burroughs in the pulp magazines, with checklist), 69 PU 13

Harwood, John: Checklist of Aurelius Smith, Detective, (pulp magazines) 67 PU 63

Harwood, John: Checklist, The Halfaday Creek Books by James B. Hendryx, 3-6 MF 7

Harwood, John: Checklist of Secret Service Smith Stories, (in pulp magazines), 67 PU 63

Harwood, John: Edgar Rice Burroughs and the Action Pulps, 75 PU 12

Harwood, John: Houdini to the Rescue, 4 R 13

Harwood, John: It'll Never Happen! (ideas for mystery fiction), 9-2 TAD 121

Harwood, John: letter of comment, 3-2 MF 56; 3-3 MF 53; 3-4 MF 59; 3-5 MF 49; 4-1 MF 41; 4-4 MR 15; 4-5 MR 16; 5-3 MR 13; 5-4 MR 11; 5-5 MR 19; 5-6 MR 18; 2-2 PP 40; 2-6 PP 40; 64 PU 29; 67 PU 62; 68 PU 25; 69 PU 27; 2 R 25; 3 R 29; 4 R 24; 8 R 32; 4-4 TAD 251; 5-1 TAD 51; 5-1 TAD 53; 5-3 TAD 175; 5-4 TAD 241; 6-2 TAD 120; 6-3 TAD 204; 7-3 TAD 228; 8-2 TAD 161; 8-3 TAD 240; 9-1 TAD 85; 9-2 TAD 162; 9-4 TAD 296; 10-2 TAD 164; 10-4 TAD 378; 11-2 TAD 108; 11-4 TAD 399; 12-1 TAD 92

Harwood, John: The Man Who Never Said Anything, (Sir Denis Nayland Smith in Sax Rohmer stories), 6 R 20

Harwood, John: The Munsey Magazines, (checklist of commencements, pulp magazines), 3-5 MF 49

Harwood, John: Nero Wolfe vs. The Master Criminal, 6-1 MR 15

Harwood, John: 007-Type Tarzan, (on comparisons of Tarzan and James Bond), 4-6 MR 11

Harwood, John: The Saint of the North, Black John Smith of Halfaday Creek, 3-6 MF 3

Harwood, John: Speculations on the Origin of Dr. Fu Manchu, 2 R 6

(Harwood, John), Biographical Sketch, 7 R 26

Haslam, Charles P.: letter of comment, 26 JD 48

Hass, Stan: letter of comment, 2-3 CP 1; 3-5 CP 1

Hasselrooth, Glenn: letter of comment, 4-1 TAD 64

Hastings, (verse), by Frederick Faust, 1-4 FC 6

Hatch, Robert: letter of comment, 9-2 TAD 157; 10-1 TAD 89

(Hathway, Alan), The Secret Kenneth Robesons, (writer under house name), by Will Murray, 2 D 3

(Hauff, Wilhelm), Zadig as a Jew, An Early German Tale of Detection, by Armin Arnold, 13-2 TAD 173

(HAUNT OF HORROR magazine), An Index to the HAUNT OF HORROR, by Dr. Roger C. Schlobin, 1 U 5

Haunted Temple, The, by Sax Rohmer, 9 R 1

Havard, James C.: letter of comment, 10 R 33

Have You Met Hardman?, (Hardman private eye series by Ralph Dennis), by G.A.Finch, 8-4 TAD 275

(Hawaii), The American Regional Mystery, Pt.XII, (Hawaii as locale for crime fiction), by Marvin Lachman, 9-4 TAD 260

Hawes, Phil: letter of comment, 25 JD 37

(HAWK, THE: Milton J. Shapiro), Mystery Plus: The Hawk, by R. Jeff Banks, 2-3 PP 24

(Hawke, Jessia: FOLLOW MY DUST), Biography of Arthur W. Upfield, The Whodunit's Who's Who, by Philip T. Asdell, 3-4 PP 11

(Hawks, Joaquin, series: Bill S. Ballinger), The Rivals of James Bond, by Larry Rickert, 4-2 PP 7

(Hawthorne, Nathaniel: THE MARBLE FAUN), The Marble Faun, A Whydunit, by J.R.Christopher, 11-1 TAD 78

Haycraft, Howard: H. Douglas Thomson, A Brief Appreciation, 8-4 TAD 256

Haycraft, Howard: letter of comment, 2-5 MR 13; 1-2 TAD 63; 3-3 TAD 209

(Haycraft, Howard), An Interview with Howard Haycraft, 5-1 MR 11; (with checklist of works) 5-1 MR 13

(Haycraft-Queen: DETECTIVE STORY CORNERSTONES), Readers' Supplementary List(of basic detective fiction), by Amnon Kabatchnik and Robert Aucott, 9-2 TAD 87

(Haycraft-Queen: DETECTIVE STORY CORNERSTONES), In the Wake of Haycraft-Queen, (possible additions to the basic crime fiction list), by Norman Donaldson, 5-3 TAD 137

(Haycraft: MURDER FOR PLEASURE), What the World Waited For (updated library checklist by various contributors), by Charles Shibuk and Marvin Lachman, 9-3 TAD 203

Hayman, Robert G.: letter of comment, 7 JD 6; 10 JD 14; 1-2 QC 13; 1-4 TAD 152; 2-2 TAD 134; 7-4 TAD 300

Hays, R.W.: A Lesser Chesterton Detective, Mr. Pond, (G.K.Chesterton, author), 9-2 TAD 125

Hays, R.W.: A Note About Lewis Carroll, (mystery elements in his writing), 7-2 TAD 95

Hays, R.W.: A Note from Francis Parkman, 5-4 TAD 193

Hays, R.W.: A Note on Medieval Detection, (forerunners of the modern detective), 5-2 TAD 88

Hays, R.W.: Addenda to "Chess in the Detective Story," 7-3 TAD 203

Hays, R.W.: Chess in the Detective Story, (chess used as plot or background), 5-1 TAD 19

Hays, R.W.: The Clue of the Dying Message, (in mystery fiction), 7-1 TAD 1

Hays, R.W.: Detective Short Story Quiz, 3-1 TAD 11

Hays, R.W.: Joseph Harrington's First Three Books, (THE LAST KNOWN ADDRESS, BLIND SPOT, THE LAST DOORBELL), 4-2 TAD 104

Hays, R.W.: letter of comment, 4-3 TAD 184; 5-1 TAD 47; 5-1 TAD 51; 5-3 TAD 189; 5-4 TAD 255; 6-1 TAD 52; 6-2 TAD 121; 6-3 TAD 192; 6-3 TAD 195; 6-3 TAD 198; 7-1 TAD 43; 7-2 TAD 144; 7-4 TAD 298; 8-4 TAD 324; 9-2 TAD 160;

Hays, R.W.: More "Shades of Dupin," (fictional detectives on detective fiction), 8-4 TAD 288

Hays, R.W.: Poetry Quiz, (mystery quiz), 5-4 TAD 215

Hays, R.W.: The Private Life of Father Brown, (layman detective by G.K. Chesterton), 4-3 TAD 135

Hays, R.W.: Religion and the Detective Story, 8-1 TAD 24

Hays, R.W.: Shakespeare Quiz, (mystery quiz), 8-1 TAD 41

Hays, R.W.: Traitor's Purse, a Double-Dactyl, (verse), 7-1 TAD 10

(Hays, R.W.), In Memory of R.W.Hays, (obituary), 9-3 TAD 235

(Hazard, Glen, series), Boys' Series Bibliographies, (boys' and girls' mystery series), by Harry K. Hudson, 1-4 YB 25

Hazard, Johannine Brown: letter of comment, 5-6 MR 17

(Hazell, James, TV series), The Trenchcoat Files: James Hazell, The Toughest Bastard to Ever Push Your Bell Button, by Paul Bishop, 4 PE 17

Hazen, Ruth: letter of comment, 1-2 G 67

(Hazleton, Frederick: SWEENEY TODD, THE DEMON BARBER OF FLEET STREET), Blame Stephen Sondheim, by E.F.Bleiler, 5-1 MF 15

(Headhunters series: John Weisman and Brian Boyer), Series Synopses, by Bill Crider, 11-4 TAD 365

Head, Ron: letter of comment, 2- JD 20

(HEADS YOU LOSE: Christianna Brand), The First Appearance - Inspector Cockrill, by Maryell Cleary, 3-2 PP 6

(Heald, Max, series: Harry Hossent), Checklist, Annotated, by Barry Van Tilburg, 5-3 MF 19

(Heald, Tim: Simon Bognor series), Checklist, Annotated, by Barry Van Tilburg, 4-4 MF 17

Healing Under the Bare Bulb, The Detective as Therapist, (methodology in the modus operandi), by Rob Whaley and George A. Antonelli, 2-2 C 1

Health Knowledge Publications, (digest-size mystery, horror and supernatural magazines published by Health Knowledge), by Dave & Su Bates, 2-3 CP 28

Heap, George R.: letter of comment, 10 JD 13

(HEART OF THE MATTER, THE: Graham Greene), A Detective Searches for a Clue in THE HEART OF THE MATTER, by J.R.Christopher, 4-1 TAD 32

Heavyweight Contenders, (on the television series "Dallas"), by Collin Wilcox, 9 LR 26

Hedman, Iwan: A Report on the Crime Writers Third International Congress, Stockholm, 1981 (the British published-author crime fiction association), 5-6 MF 10

Hedman, Iwan: Alistair MacLean, A Bibliography and Biography, 4-5 MR 29

Hedman, Iwan: An Ian Fleming Bibliography, 5-4 TAD 217

Hedman, Iwan: Dennis Wheatley, A Biographical Sketch and Bibliography, 2-4 TAD 227

Hedman, Iwan: Checklist, Peter Cheyney, 4-2 TAD 111

Hedman, Iwan: The History and Activities of Mystery Fans in Sweden (and Scandinavia), 3-4 MF 12

Hedman, Iwan: Ian Fleming, (biography) 5-4 TAD 216

Hedman, Iwan: letter of comment, 15 JD 25; 1-3 M 4; 2-5 MF 57; 4-2 MF 60; 5-2 MF 44; 5-5 MF 46; 1-1 PP 26; 4-2 PP 43; 3-2 TAD 135; 10-4 TAD 291; 3 U 48; 24 X 45

Hedman, Iwan: Mystery Fiction in Scandinavia, 3-3 TAD 173

Hedman, Iwan: Peter Cheyney, (biographical sketch), 4-2 TAD 111

Hedman, Iwan: Swedish Mystery Writers, (status of mystery fiction in Sweden), 3-4 MR 7

(Hedman, Iwan), Iwan Hedman, An Interview, by Caleb A. Lewis, 13-2 TAD 166

(Hedman, Iwan), Meet the Author, Iwan
Hedman, by Allen J. Hubin, 2-4 TAD 236
(Hedman, Iwan), Sweden's Commitment to
Mystery Fiction, by E.F.Bleiler,
2-5 MF 7
Hedman, Iwan, and Jan Alexandersson:
Leslie Charteris and The Saint,
Five Decades of Partnership,
4-4 MF 21
Heenan, Kathleen D.: The Freeman Memorial
Ceremony, (dedication of grave marker
for R. Austin Freeman), 9 TF 2
Heenan, Michael G.: A Note on the
Chronology of the Dr. Thorndyke
Novels, (of R. Austin Freeman),
9-1 TAD 52
Heenan, Michael G.: ...And Great Virtue
in a Really Good Feed, (hospitality
to Dr. Thorndyke in the stories by
R.Austin Freeman), 10 TF 9
Heenan, Michael G.: letter of comment,
9-1 TAD 79; 2 TF 32; 10 TF 30
Heenan, Michael G.: The Names of Characters
in the Thorndyke Stories, (by R.Austin
Freeman), 4 TF 2
Heenan, Michael G.: Thorndyke's Topography,
(locales, in the R.Austin Freeman
stories of Dr. Thorndyke), 5 TF 23
Heenan, Michael G., and Philip T. Asdell:
On the Trails of Dr. Freeman and Dr.
Thorndyke, or, A Guide to Thorndykean
England, 8 TF 4
Hehner, Barbara: letter of comment,
10-4 TAD 385
Heideman, Gerald: letter of comment,
2-3/4 AD 14
Heinie and the Chicken, (personal essay
of reminiscences on Frederick
Faust), by Frank Gruber, 1-1 FC 11
(Heinlein, Robert D.), The Engineer and
Me, (relationship to authors' works
with reference to Heinlein), by
Arthur D. Hlavaty, 11 SF 3
Hello Wisconsin, (re: August Derleth),
by Miles McMillin, 1-4 AD 3
Hellyer, C. David: Mysteries Make Headlines,
(recognition of mystery fiction as
literature), 11-3 TAD 260
Hellyer, C. David: TAD, The First Decade,
Interview with Allen J. Hubin, (as
editor, THE ARMCHAIR DETECTIVE),
10-2 TAD 142
Heming, Lawrence: Sounds of Gunshots,
(audio characteristics of ballistics
in mystery fiction), 15 JD 8
(Hemingway, Ernest), Chandler-Hammett-
Hemingway, Teachers in the "Tough
School," by Stanley A. Carlin,
2-5 MR 15
(Hemingway, Ernest), Detective Fiction and
Ernest Hemingway, by S. Carl Linn,
1-1 MR 3
(Hemingway, Ernest), Oak Park Revisited,
by Michael Murphy, 5 X 6

(Henaghan, Jim: Jeff Pride series),
"Archie O'Neill" - Jim Henaghan,
The Jeff Pride Series, by Bill
Crider, 4 PE 15
Henderson, Craig: letter of comment,
5-6 MR 15
Hendra, Barbara J.: letter of comment,
8 JD 8
Hendrix, Chester E.: letter of comment,
6 U 50
(Hendryx, James B.), The Saint of the
North, Black John Smith of Halfaday
Creek, by John Harwood, 3-6 MF 3
Henige, David: letter of comment,
12-1 TAD 93; 13-2 TAD 162
Henri Bencolin, (detective character
of Jeff Marle), by Fred Dueren,
8-2 TAD 98
Henry, Craig: I Await You, (collecting
paperback books), 2-3 CP 22
Henry Kitchell Webster, The Emergence
of an American Mystery-Writer,
by Wendell Hertig Taylor, 5-4 TAD
199
Henry Wade Revisited, by Charles Shubuk,
2-1 TAD 45
Hensley, Joe L.: letter of comment,
18 JD 24; 9 LR 19; 2-4 MF 59;
2-6 MF 49; 3-1 MF 55; 5-1 MR 17;
5-4 MF 38; 2-4 PP 40; 3-1 PP 43;
3-2 PP 35; 3-5 PP 49; 3-6 PP 32;
4-1 PP 50; 4-3 PP 35; 7-1 TAD 74;
4 U 52; 7 U 46
(Hensley, Joe L.), Interview with Joe
L. Hensley, Conversations Pt.IV, by
Don Cole, 2-3 PP 19
(Hensley, Joe L.), Law, Lawyers and
Justice in the Novels of Joe L.
Hensley, by Robert A. Frauenglas,
4-1 MF 3
Henty Hints, (G.A.Henty, boys' books),
by William B. Poage, 1-2 BC 38
(Henty, G.A.), Additions to a Biblio-
graphy of G.A.Henty and Hentyana,
by Jared C. Lobdell, 1-4 BC 125
(Henty, G.A.), All About Henty,
(crosswood puzzle), by Herb L.
Risteen, 3-1 BC 277
(Henty, G.A.), Henty Hints, by William
B. Poage, 1-2 BC 38
Her, (on H. Rider Haggard's SHE in
Corinth paperbacks), by J.X.Williams,
2 SF 34
(Herbert, James: THE SPEAR), Mystery
Plus: The Spear, by R. Jeff Banks,
3-4 PP 14
Hercule Poirot, The Private Life of a
Private Eye, (detective character of
Agatha Christie), by Fred Dueren,
7-2 TAD 111
Here and There, (anecdotes), by Sax
Rohmer, 11 R 1
Here Comes the Judge, The "Nero" Award,
by Bill Crider, 3-6 MF 8

Herink, Curtis: letter of comment, 16 CD 12

Herman, Linda: letter of comment, 4-1 TAD 72

Herndon, Larry: letter of comment, 9 DS 22; 64 PU 30; 63 PU 43

Herndon, Larry: Shadow Comic Book Author, Jerry Siegel, 3 BS 11

Hero Pulp Quiz, (quiz), by Robert Weinberg, 1 P 21

Heroes of the Flying Pulps, (pulp heroes in aviation genre), by Herm Schreiner, 22 X 38

Herpick, William H.: letter of comment, 36 X 74

Herr, Kay: The Failure of Two Swiss Sleuths, (fiction of Friedrich Duerrenmatt), 13-2 TAD 163

Herrick, Daryl S.: The Doc Savage Story That Wasn't, 6 U 19

Herrick, Daryl S.: letter of comment, 5 U 64; 36 X 74

Herrick, Daryl S.: Never Fear, Doc Savage Fans Are Here (Doc Savage fan organizations), 1 MB 21

Herring, Albert: Suicidio!, (fiction), 3-2 M 52

Herron, Don: San Francisco Mysteries, (crime fiction with San Francisco as locale), 3-2 M 8

(Hersey, Harold B.), Hersey Pulps, (on Hersey as editor and publisher of pulp magazines), 68 PU 10

Hersey Pulps, (on Harold B. Hersey, pulp magazine editor and publisher), by Stewart Kemble, 68 PU 10

Hertzberg, Father Francis: A Preliminary Study in the Literature of Nero Wolfe, 2-4 MR 11

Hertzberg, Father Francis: The Case of the Missing Memorial, (comments on the few public memorials to Sherlock Holmes), 3-5 MR 15

Hertzberg, Father Francis: Sexton Blake, the Office Boys' Sherlock Holmes, 7 X 5

Hertzberg, Father Francis: THE STRAND, (with particular note of Sherlock Holmes stories), 4-5 MR 23

Herzel, Roger: Commentaries for the Curious, (tribute to John Dickson Carr), 1 NC 16

Herzog, Evelyn: letter of comment, 14 R 28; 18 R 17; 6-4 TAD 278; 9-4 TAD 321; 11-3 TAD 308; 17 R 23

Herzog, Evelyn: Not Too Many Clients, (commentary on Nero Wolfe), 1-1 G 28

Herzog, Evelyn A.: On Finding Petrie's Correct Name, (from Fu Manchu tales by Sax Rohmer), 18 R 25

Herzog, Evelyn: Zagazig, Zagazig, (re: Sax Rohmer stories of Fu Manchu), 5 R 22

Herzog, John E.: letter of comment, 1-4 TAD 156; 2-2 TAD 127; 5-1 TAD 57; 5-4 TAD 249

Hevlin, Rusty: letter of comment, 68 PU 25

Hevlin, Rusty: Pulp Collecting, for Fun or Fortune?, 24 X 5

(Hewitt, Jeff, series: John Reese), Mystery Plus: Weapon Heavy, by R. Jeff Banks, 1-4 PP 21

(Heyer, Georgette), A Partial Index of Reviews of the Books of Georgette Heyer, by Don Miller, 13 MN 27

(Heyer, Georgette), Georgette Heyer, (literary sketch), by Barbara A. Buhrer, 13 MN 1

(Heyer, Georgette), Georgette Heyer, A Partial Bibliography, by Don Miller, 13 MN B1

(Heyer, Georgette), Georgette Heyer Fandom, (fan and convention activities for author), by Suford Lewis, 13 MN 7

(Heyer, Georgette), Georgette Heyer's "Whodunnits" (on the mystery novels of Heyer,, with checklist), by G.M.Carr, 13 MN 15

(Heyer, Georgette), Murder for Heyer, (commentary on the mystery novels by Georgette Heyer), by Don D'Ammassa, 13 MN 9

(Heyer, Georgette), Regency Lady, (literary sketch), by Lesleigh Luttrell, 13 MN 3

(Heyer, Georgette), Regency Romances of Georgette Heyer, (with checklist), by Jo Ann Vicarel, 13 MN 17

(Heyer, Georgette), Review Extracts of Books, 13 MN 23

(Heyliger, William), The Jerry Hicks Series by William Heyliger, (boys' books), by Joseph A. Rutter, 1-4 YB 17

(Heyliger, William), William Heyliger, Biographical Sketch from Book Jacket, 1-4 BC 128

Hiatus in Paradise, (Sherlock Holmes in Shangri-La), by Dana Martin Batory, 11 SF 29

High Dick From the Sticks: Harry Stephen Keeler's Quiribus Brown, (detective character, pulp magazines), by Francis M. Nevins, Jr., 7-4 TAD 251

Hickey, J.A.: letter of comment, 28 X 78

Hickman, Lynn A.: ACE HIGH MAGAZINE, (on the pulp magazine of this title), 66 PU 3

Hickman, Lynn A.: Checklist, ACE G-MAN, (pulp magazine), 75 PU 6

Hickman, Lynn A.: Checklist, ACE-HIGH DETECTIVE, (pulp magazine), 75 PU 7

Hickman, Lynn A.: Checklist, ACE-HIGH MAGAZINE, (pulp magazine), 75 PU 9

Hickman, Lynn A.: Checklist, ACE-HIGH WESTERN, (pulp magazine), 75 PU 8

Hickman, Lynn A.: Checklist, ALL ACES, (pulp magazine), 75 PU 7

Hickman, Lynn A.: Checklist, THE BIG MAGAZINE, (pulp magazine), 75 PU 7

Hickman, Lynn A.: Checklist, BULL'S EYE WESTERN, (pulp magazine), 75 PU 7

Hickman, Lynn A.: Checklist, CAPTAIN COMBAT, (pulp magazine), 75 PU 7

Hickman, Lynn A.: Checklist, CAPTAIN SATAN, (pulp magazine), 75 PU 11

Hickman, Lynn A.: Checklist, DR.YEN SIN, (pulp magazine), 75 PU 11

Hickman, Lynn A.: Checklist, THE MYSTERIOUS WU FANG, (pulp magazine), 75 PU 11

Hickman, Lynn A.: Checklist, THE OCTOPUS, (pulp magazine), 75 PU 11

Hickman, Lynn A.: Checklist, THE SCORPION, (pulp magazine), 75 PU 11

Hickman, Lynn A.: Checklist, SECRET SIX, (pulp magazine), 75 PU 11

Hickman, Lynn A.: Checklist, SINISTER STORIES, (pulp magazine), 75 PU 11

Hickman, Lynn A.: Checklist, WESTERN ACE-HIGH STORIES, (pulp magazine), 75 PU 10

Hickman, Lynn A.: letter of comment, 4 BS 14; 6 BS 20; 8 BS 4; 15 BS 15; 8 X 38

Hickman, Lynn A.: The Pulp Review, Comments on an Issue of TEXAS RANGERS, (pulp magazine), 71 PU 7

Hickman, Lynn A., and Gary Zachrich: News and Views, (book notes), 63 PU 51; 64 PU 31; 65 PU 24; 66 PU 53; 67 PU 128; 68 PU 31; 69 PU 31; 70 PU 6; 71 PU 18; 72 PU 6; 73 PU 31; 74 PU 16; 75 PU 21

(Hicks, Jerry, series), The Jerry Hicks Series by William Heyliger, (boys' books), by Joseph A. Rutter, 1-4 YB 17

Hidalgo Trading Corporation of America in 1979, The, (Doc Savage pastiche), by "Operative 1701," 1 DQ 8

Higgins, Walter A.: letter of comment, 1-2 BC 62

Higgledy-Piggledies, (verse), by Mark Purcell, 5-4 TAD 203

High Adventure Fiction, (crime adventure), by Don Cole, 1-4 PP 8; (adventure in mystery/suspense novels, with Hammond Innes checklist), 4-1 MR 3

(HIGH SEAS ADVENTURES), Pirates on the High Seas, (piracy tales in pulp magazine with index to magazine), by Darrell Richardson, 63 PU 38

(Highsmith, Patricia), Patricia Highsmith, Interview, by Diana Cooper-Clark, 14-4 TAD 313

(Highsmith, Patricia), Patricia Highsmith On the Screen, by Jack Edmund Nolan, 4-3 MR 15

Hi-Lee Cottage 1970 Get-Together Report, (visit to home of Leo Edwards, boys' book author), 3-4 TB 1

Hi-Lee Hello, (visit to home of Leo Edwards, boys' book author), 1-4 BC 113

Hill, Kenneth: Semi-Mean, (verse), 3-2 M 45

Hill, Melville C.: A Crime Club Selection, (in paperbacks), 2-5 CP 14

Hill, Melville C.: Checklist, The Phantom in Avon Paperbacks, (paperback reprints), 12 SF 22

Hill, Melville C.: Checklist, The Saint Mystery Library, (paperbacks), 2-4 PQ 6

Hill, Melville C.: Dell Dimers, (Dell paperback 10¢ series, with checklist), 2-2 PQ 14

Hill, Melville C.: Inner Sanctum, (discussion on the mystery paperback series, "Inner Sanctum Mysteries"), 3-4 CP 9

Hill, Melville C.: James Steranko, Extraordinary, (as paperback cover artist), 4-1 PQ 34

Hill, Melville C.: letter of comment, 2-4 CP 2; 1-5 CP 1; 1-3 PQ 4; 14-4 TAD 381; 6 U 50

Hill, Melville C.: Ramblings of a Rare Paperback Book Fiend, (on collecting paperback editions), 2-2 CP 38

Hill, Melville C.: Ramblings of a Rare Paperback Book Fiend, (a discussion of paperback book movie tie-ins), 3-5 CP 17

Hill, Melville C.: THE SAINT MYSTERY LIBRARY, (comments on this paperback series), 2-4 PQ 4

Hill, Melville C.: The Short Stories and Novels of Hammett, (Dell Map Backs paperback books and ELLERY QUEEN'S MYSTERY MAGAZINE), 3-2 CP 9

Hill, Melville C.: Steranko Art on Paperbacks, (covers by James Steranko, checklist), 4-1 PQ 37

Hill, Melville C.: The Story of The Phantom, (pulp and paperback hero), 12 SF 21

Hill, Melville C.: Too Right Bony, (Arthur W. Upfield's Inspector Bonaparte novels in paperback), 3-2 PQ 7

(Hillerman, Tony), Interview with Tony Hillerman), by Bruce Taylor, 14-1 TAD 93

(Hillerman, Tony: Joe Leaphorn, detective), Joe Leaphorn and the Navajo Way, Tony Hillerman's Indian Detective Fiction, by Jane S. Bakerman, 2-1 C 9

(Hillerman, Tony: PEOPLE OF DARKNESS), Hunter and Hunted, Comparison and Contract in Tony Hillerman's PEOPLE OF DARKNESS, by Jane S. Bakerman, 5-1 MF 3

(Hillman paperbacks), Checklist, (science-fiction), by J. Grant Thiessen, 2 SF 10

(Hilton, James), Three British Experiments from the Mainstream, (mainstream authors as mystery writers), by Charles Shubuk, 3-2 TAD 80

(Hilton, James: LOST HORIZON), Reprints/
Reprints, (paperback editions), by
Billy C. Lee, 3-1 PQ 37

(Himes, Chester), Black Cops and/or Robbers,
The Detective Fiction of Chester Himes,
by Frank J. Campenni, 8-3 TAD 206

(Himes, Chester), Killian's Memoranda,
(paperback editions of mystery novels
by Himes), by Dave Killian, 3-3 CP 19

Himmel, Randy: Carlos Bannon, The Private
Detective Fiction of Kenneth Gravell,
(Bannon, detective; with checklist),
12 LR 8

Himmel, Randy: The Christmas Assassin,
(fiction), 9 LR 2

Himmel, Randy: letter of comment, 9 LR 14

Hinman, Richard: letter of comment, 28 X
78

Hirshberg, Edgar W.: Books by John D.
MacDonald Through 1979, (original
editions bibliography), 24 JD 35

Hirshberg, Edgar W.: From the Editor's
Dreadful Grey Typewriter, (miscellaneous
news and items re: John D. MacDonald),
23 JD 2; 24 JD 1; 25 JD 1; 26 JD 1;
27 JD 1

Hirshberg, Edgar W.: John D. MacDonald as
Social Critic, (emphasis on Travis
McGee books), 1-1 C 129

Hirst, Joe: letter of comment, 5 SF 48

His Name, (on Doc Savage), by Bruce
Guthrie, 5 DS 4

His Own Desert, (authentification of literary
works, with special review of A.Q.Morton's
LITERARY DETECTION, HOW TO PROVE AUTHOR-
SHIP AND FRAUD IN LITERATURE AND DOCUMENTS)
by Everett F. Bleiler, 3-4 MF 11

History and Activities of Mystery Fans in
Sweden (and Scandinavia), by Iwan
Hedman, 3-4 MF 12

Hitchcock the Anthologer, (Alfred Hitchcock),
by Norma LeValley, 2-3 M 36

(Hitchcock, Alfred), Alfred Hitchcock,
Dell Paperbacks, (Dell Publishing Co.
and Hitchcock books in paperback),by
Billy C. Lee and Charlotte Laughlin,
3-1 PQ 23

(Hitchcock, Alfred), Alfred Hitchcock on
Television, (survey study), by David
Steier, 2-3 M 30

(Hitchcock, Alfred), The Alfred Hitchcock
Theater at Universal Studios, 2-3 M 38

(Hitchcock, Alfred), Alfred Hitchcock's
TV Shows: A Footnote on Scripters
and Literary Sources, by Jack Edmund
Nolan, 3-4 MR 17

(Hitchcock, Alfred), The Best of Hitchcock,
(literary commentary), by Raymond
Obstfeld, 14-3 TAD 248

(Hitchcock, Alfred), Hitchcock the Anthologer,
by Norma LeValley, 2-3 M 36

(Hitchcock, Alfred), The Mystery Films of
Alfred Hitchcock, by Charles Shibuk,
2-1 MR 3

(Hitchcock, Alfred), Mystery's Loss,
(Obituary, film checklist), by Richard
Moskowitz, 6/7 LR 41

(Hitchcock, Alfred), The Mystery of
Alfred Hitchcock, (an in-depth
study of his works), by Stuart
J. Kaminsky, 2-3 M 26

(Hitchcock, Alfred), Paperbacks to
1960, (checklist, in Rare Books
are Getting Scarce), by Bruce
Taylor, 2-4 CP 10

(Hitchcock, Alfred), The Quotable
Hitchcock, (quotable comments),
2-3 M 32

(Hitchcock, Alfred), Short Biography,
1-1 MR 5

(Hitler, Adolf), Adolf Hitler and
John Dickson Carr's Least-Known
Locked Room, by Douglas G. Greene,
14-4 TAD 295

Hittel, Robert A.: letter of comment,
10-1 TAD 39

Hlavaty, Arthur D.: The Engineer and
Me, (relationship of author's works
and Robert D. Heinlein), 11 SF 3

Hlavaty, Arthur D.: letter of comment,
4 SF 46

Hobel, Kathy: Checklist, Frances and
Richard Lockridge, 2-5 MR 6

Hobel, Kathy: Checklist, Margery
Allingham, 1-3 MR 13

Hobel, Kathy: letter of comment,
7 JD 6

Hoch, Edward D.: A Mirror to Our
Crimes, (true crimes as mystery
fiction), 12-3 TAD 280

Hoch, Edward D.: Complete Checklist,
The Unicorn Mystery Book Club,
8-3 TAD 187

Hoch, Edward D.: Growing Up With
Ellery Queen, 12-3 TAD 200

Hoch, Edward D.: Hans Stefan Santesson
and the Unicorn Mystery Book Club,
8-3 TAD 185

Hoch, Edward D.: letter of comment,
5-3 MR 13; 4-5/6 PP 99; 2-2 TAD
135; 2-3 TAD 202; 3-2 TAD 138;
3-4 TAD 275; 4-1 TAD 59; 4-2
TAD 126; 4-3 TAD 182; 4-4 TAD
256; 5-4 TAD 250; 7-4 TAD 303;
8-4 TAD 321; 11-3 TAD 308

Hoch, Edward D.: Stockholm in June,
Crime Writers 3rd International
Congress,(report on convention
of Crime Writers Association,
British published-authors group),
14-4 TAD 323

Hoch, Edward D.: THE UNICORN NEWS,
(newsletter of Unicorn Mystery
Book Club), 8-3 TAD 192

Hoch, Edward D.: The Vorpel Blade,
(fiction), 2-2 M 10

Hoch, Edward D., William J. Clark,
and Francis M. Nevins, Jr.:
Edward D. Hoch, A Checklist,
9-2 TAD 102

(Hoch, Edward D.), Checklist, Double-C
Spy Stories, by James Mark Purcell,
5-2 MR 43; (addendum) 5-3 MR 13

(Hoch, Edward D.), Edward D. Hoch, A Checklist, by William J. Clark, Edward D. Hoch, and Francis M. Nevins, Jr., 9-2 TAD 102

(Hoch, Edward D.), Simon Ark Stories Published by Leisure Books (paperbacks) in letter from Hoch, 5-3 MR 14

(Hoch, Edward D.), Simon Ark Bibliography, by Edward D. Hoch, 3-4 TAD 248

Hocutt, George: Doc Savage on the Air, (radio), 9 X 7

Hocutt, George: letter of comment, 6 U 53; 13 X 60

Hocutt, George and Nils Hardin: A Checklist of Popular Publications Titles 1930-1955, (pulp magazines bibliography), 33 X 21

Hodel, Michael: Holmes and the Ladies, (Sherlockiana), 3-1 M 30

Hodel, Michael: Inspector Lestrade's Lament, (verse), 2-2 M 19

Hodel, Michael: Under the Jack-Knife, (Sherlockiana column), 2-1 M 30; 2-3 M 23; (John Bennett Shaw and Holmes collecting) 3-2 M 34

Hodel, Michael, and Sean M. Wright: Under the Jack-Knife, (The Great Sherlockian Centennial 1881-1981), 3-1 M 51

(Hodel, Michael, and Sean M. Wright: ENTER THE LION), Mystery Plus, The Holmes Pastiche of the Decade), by R. Jeff Banks, 4-1 PP 21

(Hodgson, William Hope: CARNACKI THE GHOST FINDER), William Hope Hodgson, CARNACKI THE GHOST FINDER, by Peter Christensen, 12-2 TAD 122

Hodska, Nicholas S.: letter of comment, 11 JD 21

(Hoffman), Poe on "trial" (whether Poe or Hoffman was "father of mystery story"), by Sam Moskowitz, 4-1 TAD 10

Hoffman, Lee: letter of comment, 9 JD 17

Hogan, John A.: An Exhumation of THE TOMB OF TS'IN, (by Edgar Wallace), 6-3 TAD 167

Hogan, John A.: letter of comment, 5-3 MR 13; 6-1 MR 19; 5-1 TAD 52; 5-4 TAD 251; 6-4 TAD 279; 8-1 TAD 74

Hogan, John A.: Stranger Than Fiction, (authors' use of true crime), 9-2 TAD 119

Hogan, John A.: Waffling Again About Wallace, (THE MAN WHO KNEW: Edgar Wallace), 4-3 TAD 167

(Hogan, Robert J.), G-8 Versus Stahlmaske, (G-8, pulp hero, and villain, in stories by Hogan), 6 P 10

(Hogan, Robert J.), Notes of a Pulp Collector: Robert J. Hogan, (pulp author), by Bernie Wermers, 6 BS 19

Hoh-Hoh to Satan, DETECTIVE FICTION WEEKLY'S Nutty Series Heroes of the 1930's, (unconventional detectives in pulp magazine),by Bernard A. Drew, 2-2 C 88

Holbrook, Don: Missing Mercer Musings, (Mercer Boys boys' series by Capwell Wyckoff), 6 MA 6

Holbrook, Don: Nancy Drew in Japanese, (Japanese editions of girls' series books), 7 MA 13

Holbrook, Don: Wyckoff's Stories of Adventure, (boys' books by Wyckoff), 5 MA 6

Holland, Elevanda: letter of comment, 2-2 CP 1

Hollywood Highness, (fiction), by Hamilton T. Caine, 2-1 M 46

(Holm, Jimmy), Jimmy Holm, Supernatural Detective vs. Dr. Death, (pulp detective character), by Tom Johnson, 10 DS 8

Holmes and the Ladies, (Sherlockiana), by Michael Hodel, 3-1 M 30

Holmes, George: letter of comment, 2 MA 29; 5 MA 27; 1-2 TBN 9; 1-3 TBN 9; 1-5 YB 20

Holmes, George: Rantings and Ravings of a Book Collector, (collecting boys' books), 1-3 YB 12

Holmes, George: Sam Steele... (on collecting Sam Steele boys' books by L. Frank Baum writing as Capt. Hugh Fitzgerald), 1-6 YB 8

(Holmes, Mr., series: Conrad Voss Bark), Checklist, by Barry Van Tilburg, 4-2 MF 11

(Holmes, Mycroft), Mycroft Holmes and Ian Murdock's Case, ("The Adventure of the Lion's Mane") by J.W.Scheideman, 9-1 TAD 14

(Holmes, Sherlock), A Case of Identity, Being a Trifling Monograph Upon the similarities Between Sir Denis Nayland Smith and Sherlock Holmes, by Andrew Jay Peck, 2 R 9

(Holmes, Sherlock), A Hitherto Undiscovered Reminiscence of Dr. John H. Watson, M.D., (Sherlockiana) by Julian Gill, 2-1 PDA 33

(Holmes, Sherlock), A Latter Holmes, (Solar Pons), by Bruce Kennedy. 1-3 PD 1

(Holmes, Sherlock), A Sherlocko-Pontine Addendum, by J.R.Christopher, 2-1 PD 3

(Holmes, Sherlock), A Visit to Baker Street, by W.O.G.Lofts, 6-1 TAD 15

(Holmes, Sherlock), The Adventures of Chubblock Homes, (comic strip parodies), by W.O.G.Lofts, 8-3 TAD 193

(Holmes, Sherlock), Addendum to Article in THE BAKER STREET JOURNAL 1978: The Baker Street-Carrian Connection, (Sherlockiana by John Dickson Carr), by Larry L. French, 1 NC 15

(Holmes, Sherlock), The ADventure of the Elusive Vanardy, (fiction), by Mary Ann Grochowski, 1-1 PP 7

(Holmes, Sherlock), The Adventure of the Purloined Red Herring, (THE PROFESSOR KNITS A SHROUD: Martha Wirt Davis), by Edward Lauterbach, 3-5 PP 3

(Holmes, Sherlock), The American Sherlock Holmes, A Study in Scarlet Impersonation, (Holmes and Watson protesting Craig Kennedy and Walter Jameson's reputation as the "American Sherlock Holmes"), by Marvin Lachman, 3-2 MR 2

(Holmes, Sherlock), An Irregular History, (Sherlockiana, the Baker Street Irregulars), by Sean M. Wright, 2-2 M 24

(Holmes, Sherlock), Annotating the Holmes Saga, by Edward Lauterbach, 7-2 TAD 119

(Holmes, Sherlock), The Apocryphalization of Holmes, (article review of SHERLOCK HOLMES: THE PUBLISHED APOCRYPHA by Jack Tracy), by E.F.Bleiler, 4-5 MF 3

(Holmes, Sherlock), "Art in the Blood..." by Peter E. Blau, 2-2 PDA 68

(Holmes, Sherlock), Basil Rathbone as Sherlock Holmes, by Leonard Maltin, 1-4 MR 12

(Holmes, Sherlock), Being an Examination of the Ponsian and Holmesian Secret Deductive Systems, (Sherlock Holmes, Solar Pons), by A.E.van Vogt, 1-2 PDA 52

(Holmes, Sherlock), The Case of the Canonical Collector, (collecting Sherlockiana), by Jackie Geyer, 11-3 TAD 290

(Holmes, Sherlock), The Case of the Cheshire Cat's Pat, (fiction, Sherlock Holmes pastiche), by G. Arthur Rahman and James A. McKraken, 10 CL 3

(Holmes, Sherlock), The Case of the Missing Memorial, (comments on why so few public memorials to Sherlock Holmes), by Fr. Francis Hertzberg, 3-5 MR 15

(Holmes, Sherlock), Children of the Night, (fiction), by Michael Avallone, 2-2 PDA 56

(Holmes, Sherlock), Conan Doyle and Sherlock Holmes, The Creator versus The Creation, by Jack Tracy, 2-2 M 26

(Holmes, Sherlock), The Cult of Sherlock Holmes, by John Bennett Shaw, 1-2 TAD 53

(Holmes, Sherlock), The Dynamics of the Brothers Moriarty, by Timothy J. Rutt, 1-1 WA 5

(Holmes, Sherlock), The Easy Chair - "Alias Nero Wolfe", (speculation on Wolfe being son of Mycroft Holmes), by Bernard DeVoto, 1-2 G 37

(Holmes, Sherlock), The Gas-Fitters' Ball, (annual event of the Non-Canonical Calabashes, a Holmes scion society; report), Photos, 2-2 M 9

(Holmes, Sherlock), Hiatus in Paradise, (Holmes in Shangri-La), by Dana Martin Batory, 11 SF 29

(Holmes, Sherlock), Holmes and the Ladies, by Michael Hodel, 3-1 M 30

(Holmes, Sherlock), Holmes versus Wolfe, (letter from Joel Rosenberg to N.Y.TIMES BOOK REVIEW), 6/7 LR 14

(Holmes, Sherlock), Holmes Was a Sideline, by Julian Symons, 9 LR 21

(Holmes, Sherlock), Information Center, (various items), 2 MT 33

(Holmes, Sherlock), Inspector Lestrade's Lament, (verse), by Michael Hodel, 2-2 M 19

(Holmes, Sherlock), Jamison and Lestrade, A Comparative Study, (Sherlock Holmes and Solar Pons), by John McGoldrick, 1-4 PD 1

(Holmes, Sherlock), The Legend of Crimpen Mire, (verse), by Fred Jaeger, 2-1 PDA 27

(Holmes, Sherlock), Letter to Sherlock, and Annotations, by Julian L. Biggers, 6 R 7

(Holmes, Sherlock), Marmelahd or Marmelade, (on the name Lestrade), by E.F.Bleiler, 13-4 TAD 334

(Holmes, Sherlock), The Missing Golf Balls, (fiction, pastiche), by Wex Jones, 7-3 TAD 177

(Holmes, Sherlock), My Good Name... (fiction, pastiche), 2-2 M 40

(Holmes, Sherlock), Mystery Plus: The Holmes Pastiche of the Decade, (ENTER THE LION, by Michael P. Hodel and Sean M. Wright), by R. Jeff Banks, 4-1 PP 21

(Holmes, Sherlock), Name as Symbol: On Sherlock Holmes and the Nature of the Detective Story, (interpretation of name), by Richard Gerber, translated by Robert F. Fleissner, 8-4 TAD 280

(Holmes, Sherlock), Narrative Vision in The Hound of the Baskervilles, by Paul F. Ferguson, 1-2 C 24

(Holmes, Sherlock), Oscar Wilde and Sherlock Holmes, A Literary Mystery, by Randy Roberts, 1-1 C 41

(Holmes, Sherlock), Plots For Sale - Cheap; Apply 221B, (Holmes influence on other writers), by Nathan L. Bengis, 1-4 TAD 116

(Holmes, Sherlock), The Profession of Henry Baker, by Dean & Shirley Dickensheet, 1-1 PDA 36

(Holmes, Sherlock), Quiz on Silver Blaze, (quiz), 3 MT 26

(Holmes, Sherlock), Reminiscences (of script writing Holmes, and Bulldog Drummond), by Frank Gruber, 2-1 TAD 56

(Holmes, Sherlock), The Rivals of Sherlock Holmes, A Reference List, (contemporary detective fiction), by Peter E. Blau, 11-2 TAD 193

(Holmes, Sherlock), Sexton Blake, the
Office Boys' Sherlock Holmes, by
Father Francis Hertzberg, 7 X 5
(Holmes, Sherlock), Sherlock Holmes,
Father of Scientific Crime Detection,
by Stanton O. Berg, 5-2 TAD 81
(Holmes, Sherlock), Sherlockian Dinner,
(report, The Non-Canonical Calabashes,
January 5, 1980), by Horace Harker,
1-3 M 22
(Holmes, Sherlock), The Sherlockian
EQMM, (Holmes stories in ELLERY QUEEN'S
MYSTERY MAGAZINE, checklist), by Peter
E. Blau, 2-1 QC 15
(Holmes, Sherlock), The Sherlockian Quiz,
(quiz), by John Bennett Shaw, 10-1
TAD 77
(Holmes, Sherlock), Sherlockiana, (items
published in 1975), by Peter E. Blau,
8 MN 39; (1976) 11 MN 8; (1978) 12 MN
02;(1980) 13 MN 01
(Holmes, Sherlock), Sherlocko-Pontine
Parallels, (Sherlock Homes, Solar Pons),
1-4 PD 3
(Holmes, Sherlock), Some Touch of the
Artist, by R.L.Hall, 2-2 M 30
(Holmes, Sherlock), THE STRAND, (with note
of Sherlock Holmes stories published),
by Father Francis Hertzberg, 4-5 MR 23
(Holmes, Sherlock), Under the Jack-Knife,
(column on Sherlock Holmes), by Michael
Hodel, 2-1 M 30; 2-3 M 23; (John
Bennett Shaw and collecting) 3-2 M 34
(Holmes, Sherlock), Under the Jack-Knife,
(The Great Sherlockian Centennial
1881-1981), by Michael Hodel and Sean
Wright, 3-1 M 51
(Holmes, Sherlock), Upon Distinguishing
Among 140 (or More) Pastiches, by
Horace Harker, 1-3 M 14
(Holmes, Sherlock), Virgnity Preserved and
the Secret Marriage of Sherlock Holmes,
by Michael Atkinson, 2-1 C 62
(Holmes, Sherlock), Was Watson Jack the
Ripper?, by Eileen Snyder, 8-3 TAD 211
(Holmes, Sherlock), Watch That Man? (Conan
Doyle Syndrome), by Dana Martin Batory,
9 SF 40
(Holmes, Sherlock), Why Sherlock Holmes?,
Nostalgia for the Absolute, (the
appeal of Holmes), by Nancy Senter,
2-2 M 39
(Holmes, Sherlock), The Worcester Enigma,
(fiction, pastiche), by James Mines,
2-2 M 34
Holmes versus Wolfe, (letter from Joel
Rosenberg to N.Y.TIMES BOOK REVIEW),
6/7 LR 14
Holmes Was a Sideline, by Julian Symons,
9 LR 21
(Holt, Ken), The Ken Holt Puzzle,
(crossword puzzle, on Ken Holt boys'
series books), 3 MA 28
(Holt, Ken), The Ken Holt Mystery Stories,
(boys' books), by Fred Woodworth,
2 MA 7

(Holt, Ken), Not Forgotten, (on the
Ken Holt boys' series books), by
Fred Woodworth, 2 MA 1
Holtan, Orley I.: Friedrich Duerrenmatt,
The Detective Story as Moral Parable,
5-3 TAD 133
Holtsmark, Erling B.: letter of comment,
26 JD 2
Holtsmark, Erling B.: Travis McGee as
Traditional Hero, (John D. MacDonald
books on Travis McGee), 1-1 C 99
Homage to Bela, (verse, re: Bela Lugosi),
by Helen Ruggieri, 1 CD 43
Homel, Leonard: letter of comment,
1-2 YB 24
(Homes, Chubblock), The Adventures of
Chubblock Homes, (comic strip parodies
of Sherlock Holmes), by W.O.G.Lofts,
8-3 TAD 193
(Homes, Geoffrey), Checklist of works,
by Theodore P. Dukeshire, 3-3 MF 21
(Homes, Geoffrey), The Books of
Geoffrey Homes, by Theodore P.
Dukeshire, 3-3 MF 19
(Hood, Charles, series: James Mayo)
Checklist, Annotated, by Barry
Van Tilburg, 4-6 MF 5
(Hood, Mark, series: James Dark), Rivals
of James Bond #4: Mark Hood, by
Larry Rickert, 4-5/6 PP 38
Hood, Victor: letter of comment,
2 DS 6
Hook, John: letter of comment, 7 DQ 5
Hopkins, Bill: letter of comment,
17 X 61
(Hopley, George), see Cornell Woolrich
Horatio Alger, or The Man Behind the
Great American Dream, (sketch), by
Jack Bales, 2-4 BC 226
Horatio Alger Paperback First Editions,
The, by Frank Gruber, 2-4 BC 242
Horatio Alger, Jr. and the Horatio
Alger Society, (fan organization),
by Jack Bales, 1-3 TBN 6
(Horne, Harry, detective: John Gonzales)
A Song for the Unsung, by Joseph
J. Coffey, 13-1 TAD 67
(Hornung, E.W.), Correspondence Between
Hornung and Doyle, 4 MT 28
Horrendous Headlines, (quiz), by
Veronica M.S.Kennedy, 9-2 TAD 124
Horrible Hunchbacks, The, (in pulp
magazines), by Will Murray, 6 DS 13
(horror anthologies), An Index to
the "Not at Night" Series, by
Darrell Schweitzer, 10 SF 45
Horror, Detection and Footnotes,
(Alexander Laing: THE CADAVER OF
GIDEON WYCK), by Edward Lauterbach,
3-1 TAD 12
(horror fiction), Demon in a Lunchbox,
An Appreciation of Horror Fiction,
by Chelsea Quinn Yarbro, 2-2 M 43

(HORROR STORIES), The Weird Menace Magazines, (pulp, various), by Robert Kenneth Jones, 10 BS 3; 11 BS 7' 12 BS 7; 13 BS 7; 14 BS 13; 15 BS 14

Hoskins, Bob: letter of comment, 11-2 TAD 108

Hospital London, (descriptive essay), by R. Austin Freeman, 9 TF 28

(Hossent, Harry: Max Heald series), Checklist, Annotated, by Barry Van Tilburg, 5-3 MF 19

Hot Story, by Basil Wells, 28 X 5

Houdini to the Rescue, by John Harwood, 4 R 13

(Houdini), Were Houdini's Feats Supernatural?, by Sax Rohmer, 5 R 1

Houghton, Michael: letter of comment, 12 SF 28

("Hound of the Baskervilles, The": A. Conan Doyle), Narrative Vision in The Hound of the Baskervilles, by Paul F. Ferguson, 1-2 C 24

(HOUSE ON THE MOUND, THE: August Derleth), Derleth Writes His Own Review, (1958), 1-2 AD 7

(Household, Geoffrey), Six Britons the Movies Ignored, (seldom filmed), by Jack Edmund Nolan, 3-5 MR 9

How Are the Fallen Mighty Department - Captain Satan, (pulp character), by Dean A. Grennell, 42 X 9

How Fred Gray Found Happiness With a Pulp Price Guide, (humourous treatment of price guide discussion), by Nils Hardin, 22 X 3

How Fu Manchu Was Born, by Sax Rohmer, 2 R 3

How I Came to Write My First Book, (boys' book author), by Harry Castlemon, 1-1 BC 28

How I "Done" It, (writing ENCYCLOPEDIC GUIDE TO MYSTERY, DETECTIVE AND SUSPENSE FICTION), by Ordean Hagen, 1-2 TAD 45

How I Found My Inferior Decorators, (collecting experience in locating POPPY OTT: INFERIOR DECORATOR, by Leo Edwards), by Jack R. Schorr, 4-1 TB 1

How I Got Into Aviation Writing, (pulps), by Arch Whitehouse, 22 X 36

How I Got Started Collecting, (boys' books), by Jack Schorr, 1-3 BC 71

How I Write, (by pulp author of The Spider and other characters), by Norvell W. Page, 6 P 5

How Many Words?, (extent of writing of Frederick Faust), by William F. Nolan, 1-1 FC 2

How Much Do You Know?, (Doc Savage quiz), by Bill Laidlaw, 3 DQ 15; 4 DQ 9

How to File Your SF Collection, by J. Grant Thiessen, 2 SF 42

How to Keep Dust and Soil Off Books of a Collection, by Jack R. Schorr, 1-2 BC 63

How to Make Your Pulps Last Forever, Sell Your Valuable Pulps at Top Dollar, Have Them, and Acquire All Rare Pulps Cheap, by Bill Blackbeard and Rich Reguster, 26 X 70

How to Organize Your Collection, Your Way!, (mystery book collecting), by Ellen Nehr, 2-3 PP 9

How to Restore a Book, by Jack R.Schorr, 1-1 BC 29

How to Succeed in Collecting Paperbacks, by Mike Benton, 3-2 CP 21

How to Tell First G&D Editions in Edwards Books, (identifying first editions by Grosset & Dunlap, books of Leo Edwards; boys' books), 3-1 TB 1; 3-2 TB 3

How to Write Stories for Boys, by Harry Castlemon, 4-1 BC 404

Howard, Carole A.: letter of comment, 2 BS 3; 8 BS 7

Howard, D.W.: The Grain and Salt Printing Company, (imaginary series of books by imaginary publisher; boys' books), 2 BB 15

Howard, Nicholas: Dark Forces at Work, (verse), 4-3 AD 7

(Howard, Robert E.), Bronze Shadows Presents Conan, (general review of the Conan stories and publications), by Fred S. Cook, 13 BS 19

(Howard, Robert E.),Checklist, Robert E. Howard's Library, 1-2 PQ 51

(Howard, Robert E.), Letters by Howard, 18 X 42

(Howard, Robert E.), Robert E. Howard's Library, An Annotated Checklist, by Charlotte Laughlin, 1-1 PQ 23; 1-2 PQ 51; 1-3 PQ 43; 1-4 PQ 55

(Howard, Robert E.), Underwood/Miller Release, New Howard Editions, 1-3 PQ 46

(Howard, Robert E.: ALMURIC), Almuric, or, "Edgar Rice Burroughs Visits the Huborian Age," by Michael T. Smith, 1-2 PQ 48

(Howard, Robert E.: THE LAST CELT), New Book Released About Robert E. Howard, by Tevis Clyde Smith, 1-1 PQ 33

(Howard, Robert E., and Richard A. Lupoff: THE RETURN OF SKULL FACE), The (Very Temporary) Return of Skull-Face, by Robert E. Briney, 2-2 MF 21

Howard, Wendell V.: letter of comment, 6 JD 12; 7 JD 10; 8 JD 14; 9 JD 6; 10 JD 8

(Howard, Wendell V.), In Memoriam, (obituary), by Len & June Moffatt, 14 JD 10

(Howitt, John Newton), John Newton Howitt, American Artist/Illustrator, A Discussion, by William Papalia, 33 X 87

Hows, Whys, Ifs and Buts of Collecting
Big Little Books, The, by Randall
Zbiciak, 4 BB 7
Hoyt, Charles L.: letter of comment,
6 JD 11; 8 JD 13
Hoyt, George C., Jr.: letter of comment,
9 JD 17; 2-6 MR 15; 1-4 TAD 156
Huang, Jim: Book Notes, (mystery),
8 CL 7; 9 CL 9; 10 CL 10;
13/14 CL 1
Huang, Jim: Cloak Survey Results, (of
survey poll by CLOAK AND DAGGER
magazine), 8 CL 2
Huang, Jim: The Comedy-Detective Film
is Alive and Well, (short reviews),
5 CL 1
Huang, Jim: Edgar Award Winners 1977,
(Mystery Writers of America Awards
report), 7 CL 1
Huang, Jim: Fanzines, (on mystery and
related fanzines), 12 CL 9
Huang, Jim: Film Notes, (mystery),
9 CL 9; 10 CL 1; 11 CL 1; 12 CL 11
Huang, Jim: Mystery Previews, 9 CL 1
Huang, Jim: People, Jane S. Bakerman,
(short biographical sketch),
10 CL 11
Huang, Jim: Television, (comments on
mystery television shows), 8 CL 1;
12 CL 1
(Hubbard, L. Ron), L. Ron Hubbard. A
Living Legend, by Virgil Wilhite
and Patricia Barnes Mintz, 42 X 133
Huber, Gordon, and Fred Cook: Index to
NEW MYSTERY ADVENTURES, (pulp
magazine), 30 X 146
Huber, Gordon: letter of comment,
65 PU 19
Hubin, Allen J.: The Academic Respect-
ability of Detective Fiction, An
Editor's Introduction to Thesis
Best-selling American Detective
Fiction of Joan M. Mooney, 3-2
TAD 97
Hubin, Allen J.: THE ARMCHAIR DETECTIVE,
The Past, Present and Hopeful Future
of This Journal, 1-1 TAD 28
Hubin, Allen J.: AJH Reviews, (book
reviews), 11-1 TAD 17; 11-2 TAD
116; 11-3 TAD 230; 11-4 TAD 331;
12-1 TAD 6; 12-2 TAD 111; 12-3
TAD 203; 12-4 TAD 320; 13-1 TAD 26;
13-2 TAD 94; 13-3 TAD 199; 13-4
TAD 294; 14-1 TAD 17; 14-2 TAD
123; 14-3 TAD 218; 14-4 TAD 298
Hubin, Allen J.: Bits and Pieces,
(mystery news), 6-1 TAD 43
Hubin, Allen J.: Cecil Day Lewis Named
Poet Laureate of England, 1-2 TAD 62
Hubin, Allen J.: Chaotic Notes in Rapid
Passing, (mystery news), 2-4 TAD 262
Hubin, Allen J.: Checklist of Crime
Fiction Published in Great Britain
January 1, 1977 - March 31, 1977,
10-3 TAD 270

Hubin, Allen J.: Commentaries for the
Curious, (on John Dickson Carr),
1 NC 18
Hubin, Allen J.: Conjectural Cross
Trumps, A Note on Rex Stout and
Ellery Queen, 1-1 TAD 9
Hubin, Allen J.: Current Bits and
Pieces, (mystery news), 6-2 TAD
112
Hubin, Allen J.: Death of a Magazine,
(on THE SAINT MYSTERY MAGAZINE
discontinuance), 1-2 TAD 47
Hubin, Allen J.: Dedication and
Tribute, (to John Creasey), 6-4
TAD 209
Hubin, Allen J.: Frank Gruber, a
Dedication, 3-2 TAD 95
Hubin, Allen J.: Frederic Dannay,
Doctor of Humane Letters, (award,
Carrol College), 12-3 TAD 236
Hubin, Allen J.: letter of comment,
8 JD 12; 15 JD 32; 1-3 MF 56;
5-1 MF 39; 505 MF 44; 4-1 MR 19;
4-3 MR 19; 5A MY 3; 2-5 PP 41;
1-1 QC 12; 2 U 15; 36 X 74
Hubin, Allen J.: Meet the Author,
(biographical short sketch),
Robert C.S.Adey, 2-4 TAD 261
Catherine Aird, 2-3 TAD 157
William S. Baring-Gould, 1-1
TAD 3
Bernard Beauchesne, 1-4 TAD 150
Nathan L. Bengis, 1-4 TAD 118
Robert E. Briney, 2-4 TAD 273
Mary S. Cameron, 1-2 TAD 52
J.R.Christopher, 1-2 TAD 58;
2-4 TAD 273
J. Randolph Cox, 2-4 TAD 214
John Creasey, 2-1 TAD 3
Dean W. Dickensheet, 2-4 TAD 273
Norman Donaldson, 1-2 TAD 37
Frank P. Donovan, 1-4 TAD 128
Frank Gruber, 2-4 TAD 216
Ordean Hagen, 1-2 TAD 47
Iwan Hedman, 2-4 TAD 236
Joan Kahn, 2-3 TAD 170
James Keddie, Jr., 1-1 TAD 9
Marvin Lachman, 1-1 TAD 24
Bruce L. Monblatt, 4-3 TAD 171
Nigel Morland, 1-3 TAD 72
Francis M. Nevins, Jr., 1-3 TAD 85
Lenore Glen Offord, 2-2 TAD 76
Gordon C. Ramsey, 1-1 TAD 18
Dr. George J. Rausch, Jr., 2-1
TAD 60
James Sandoe, 1-2 TAD 42
John Bennett Shaw, 1-2 TAD 55
Charles Shibuk, 1-1 TAD 12
Hillary Waugh, 2-1 TAD 54
Hubin, Allen J.: THE MYSTERY LEAGUE
MAGAZINE, 3-1 TAD 64
Hubin, Allen J.: Mystery News Notes,
1-1 TAD 4; 2-1 TAD 60; 2-4 TAD 226;
Hubin, Allen J.: Mystery Notes of
Recent and Forthcoming Publications,
1-3 TAD 99

Hubin, Allen J.: Mystery Writer Deaths,
(obituaries of recently deceased
mystery authors, 1968), 1-3 TAD 104
Hubin, Allen J.: Organizations/Publi-
cations for Mystery Fans, 1-2 TAD 37
Hubin, Allen J.: Reviews - Capsule Comments,
1-4 TAD 131
Hubin, Allen J.: Some Notes on the Current
Crop, (reviews), 6-3 TAD 191; 6-4 TAD
265; 7-1 TAD 61; 7-2 TAD 141; 7-3 TAD
220; 7-4 TAD 293; 8-1 TAD 65; 8-2 TAD
146; 8-3 TAD 225; 8-4 TAD 308; 9-1
TAD 72; 9-2 TAD 152; 9-3 TAD 223;
9-4 TAD 310; 10-1 TAD 5
(Hubin, Allen J.), The Big Sell, An
Interview with Allen Hubin, by
Gary Warren Niebuhr, 4-5/6 PP 24
(Hubin, Allen J.) Social and Political
Images in American Crime Fiction,
(panel discussion, Popular Culture
Association, 1971), 5-2 TAD 61
(Hubin, Allen J.) TAD: The First Decade,
Interview with Allen J. Hubin (as
editor of THE ARMCHAIR DETECTIVE),
by C. David Hellyer, 10-2 TAD 142
Hudson, Harry K.: Biblio Addendum/Errata
(to Hudson's BIBLIOGRAPHY OF HARD-
COVER BOYS' BOOKS), 6 BB 19; 7 BB 20
Hudson, Harry K.: Bibliographies, Boys'
Books, (Golden Stallion series by
R.G.Montgomery; Kent Barstow series
by R.G.Montgomery; Kidnapped Campers
series by Flavia A. Canfield, and
Lucky Starr series by Paul French),
1-5 YB 13
Hudson, Harry K.: The Big Game Series,
(checklist and bibliography, boys'
books), 3 BB 25
Hudson, Harry K.: Boys' Series Biblio-
graphies, 1-3 YB 8; 1-4 YB 23;
1-5 YB 13; 1-6 YB 15
Hudson, Harry K.: Boys' Book Oddities,
(Tom Swift) 1-2 BC 43; (The Rover
Boys) 1-4 BC 112; (Dave Porter)
3-1 BC 285
Hudson, Harry K.: Checklist, Among the
Sioux series, (boys' books), 1-3
YB 8
Hudson, Harry K.: Checklist, Arnold Adair
series, (boys' books), 1-3 YB 8
Hudson, Harry K.: Checklist, Billy
To-Morrow series, (boys' books),
1-3 YB 9
Hudson, Harry K.: Checklist, Deer Lodge
series, (boys' books), 1-3 YB 10
Hudson, Harry K.: Checklist, Deering
(Deal) series, (boys' books), 1-3
YB 10
Hudson, Harry K.: Checklist, Cloud Country
series, (boys' books), 1-3 YB 9
Hudson, Harry K.: Crossword Puzzle,
(boys' books oriented), 1-4 YB 8
Hudson, Harry K.: The Early Hurst Books,
(Hurst & Co. as boys' books pub-
lisher), 1-2 YB 3

Hudson, Harry K.: letter of comment,
3 BB 25; 1-3 TB 11; 33 X 115;
1-2 YB 23
Hudson, Harry K.: Phantom Titles,
(boys' books in series announced
but never published), 3 BB 11
Hudson, Martha: World of Mystery, The
Grub Street Beat, (mystery news),
2-2 M 18; 3-2 M 32
Huff, William H.: letter of comment,
69 PU 27
(Huggins, Roy), Department of Unknown
Writers, Roy Huggins, by Marvin
Lachman, 3-4 PP 20
Hughes, B.: letter of comment,
10-3 TAD 195
Hughes, David and Jeanne: letter of
comment, 24 JD 39
Hughes, John: letter of comment,
1-6 CP 1
(Hull, Richard), Checklist, by
Charles Shubuk, 2-6 MR 21
Hullar, Link: A Brief Bibliographic
Essay on Doc Savage, 6 U 22
Hullar, Link: Doc Savage and The Great
Depression, 7 DS 18
Hullar, Link: letter of comment,
7 DQ 5; 4 DS 3; 11 DS 19; 12 DS 30;
5 U 62; 6 U 49; 7 U 45
Hullar, Link: Lord of the Unknown,
The Zarkon Novels of Lin Carter,
8 U 141
Hullar, Link: The Pulps and American
History, An Informal Comment, (on
the place of the pulp magazines
in literary history), 6 DS 10
Hullar, Link: The Thinking Machine,
30 X 133
Hullar, Link, and Will Murray: The
Fighting Fury, (on The Skipper,
pulp character, in THE SKIPPER
magazine), 12 SF 3
Humbugging of Solar Pons, The,
(Mycroft & Moran, publishers,
revisions), by Ebenezer Snawley
(Jon L. Lellenberg), 3-2 PDA 11
(Hume, Fergus: THE MYSTERY OF A
HANSOM CAB), In Search of a
Hansom Cab, by Philip T. Asdell,
1-2 PP 10
Humor, Horror and Intellect, Giles
Mont of Ruth Rendell's A JUDGEMENT
IN STONE, by Jane S. Bakerman,
5-4 MF 5
Humphrey Bogart, Some Remarks on the
Canonization Process, (developing
popularity), by James Mark Purcell,
11-1 TAD 6; (see 11-2 TAD 186 also)
Hunsburger, H. Edward: Minor Offenses,
(mystery/suspense short stories
discussed), 14-2 TAD 163; 14-3
TAD 268; 14-4 TAD 380
Hunt, David A.: letter of comment,
28 JD 40

(Hunt, E. Howard), Paperback Writers,
E. Howard Hunt, (sketch), by Bill
Crider, 2-1 PQ 9

(Hunt, E. Howard), PQ Interview with
E. Howard Hunt, (interview by
PAPERBACK QUARTERLY), 2-1 PQ 11

Hunt, Roy: letter of comment, 1-4 WC 18;
2 R 26; 8 R 32; 12 R 25; 5-1 TAD 54

Hunter, Evan: letter of comment,
2-2 M 2

(Hunter, Evan), Checklist, by Bill
Pronzini, 5-3 TAD 131

(Hunter, Evan), The "Mystery" Career of
Evan Hunter, by Bill Pronzini, 5-3
TAD 129

Hunter and Hunted, Comparison and Contrast
in Tony Hillerman's PEOPLE OF DARKNESS,
by Jane S. Bakerman, 5-1 MF 3

(HUNTER, THE: Richard Stark), What Happens
in "Point Blank" (film), by Francis M.
Nevins, Jr., 9-1 TAD 7

Hunting for Hidden Books, (boys' books
collecting), by Kent Winslow, 1 MA 3;
2 MA 21; 5 MA 22; 6 MA 10

(Hurst & Co.) The Early Hurst Books,
(Hurst & Co. as boys' books publisher),
by Harry K. Hudson, 1-2 YB 3

Hutchison, Don: Comment on Pulp Prices,
(pulp magazines), 24 X 43

Hutchison, Don: Ellery Queen Pilot Show
on TV, 7 MY 10

Hutchison, Don: Jimmie Dale, Pulp Archtype,
(series character), 22 X 12

Hutchison, Don: letter of comment, 6 DS 7;
11 DS 6; 6 P 30; 64 PU 29; 65 PU 21;
67 PU 58; 70 PU 29; 74 PU 28; 8-1
TAD 68; 9-1 TAD 81; 3 U 49; 13 X 60;
15 X 13; 36 X 74

Hymerling, Madelyn: letter of comment,
10-4 TAD 291

I Am the Emperor, (fiction), by Frederick
Faust, 1-2 FC 8

I Await You, (collecting paperback books),
by Craig Henry, 2-3 CP 22

I Comma Mickey, (Mickey Spillane talking),
by Alex Hamilton, 1-2 MR 9

I, LIBERTINE: Shepherd's Crook or Bony
Sturgeon?, (on the paperback book of
that title), by Don Z. Block, 2-4 CP 27

I Remember...B-Movies, (film reminiscences),
by R. Jeff Banks, 4-5 MF 13

I Remember...Pulp Mysteries-Mystery Pulps,
(pulp magazine comments), by R. Jeff
Banks, 3-4 MF 19

I Remember...Radio Mysteries, (reminiscences)
by R. Jeff Banks, 3-5 MF 17

"I Shall Live When You Are Smoke," (on Dr.
Fu Manchu), by William S. Baring-Gould,
1-1 TAD 2

I, the Spillane, or, My Spillane is Quick,
or, Vengeance is Spillane, or, One
Lonely Spillane, or, The Big Spillane,
(parody on Mickey Spillane), by John D.
MacDonald, 14 JD 16

I Wonder?, (questions and answers on
paperback book collecting, with
bibliographical data), by Lance
Casebeer, 1-2 CP 8; 1-3 CP 2;
1-4 CP 3; 1-5 CP 3; 1-6 CP 8;
2-1 CP 5; 2-3 CP 5; 2-5 CP 3

"I'll Save the World in a Minute, But
First How About Something to Eat?",
(eating habits of Doc Savage), by
Albert Manachino, 4 DS 7

I've Been Reading, (new books, mystery),
by Lianne Carlin, 2-4 MR 8

Ian Fleming, (literary sketch), by
Iwan Hedman, 5-4 TAD 216

Ian Fleming, Alias James Bond, (literary
essay), by Billy C. Lee, 4-1 PQ 41

Ian Fleming, Book Collector, (sketch
as editor of THE BOOK COLLECTOR), by
William White, 6-3 TAD 179

Ian Fleming Films and TV, The, by Jack
Edmund Nolan, 5-1 MR 24

Idea Man, The, (fiction, Ellery Queen
pasticle), by Jon L. Breen,
1-4 QC 11

(Ideal Library series), Notes on an
Ideal Library, (hardback Doc Savage
series by Ideal), by Robert Sampson,
2/3 DR 2

Ideology and Narrative Stereotyping,
The Case of Raymond Chandler, by K.A.
MacDermott, 2-1 C 77

(Iles, Francis), A Bibliography of the
Works of Anthony Berkeley Cox
(Francis Iles), by Paul R. Moy,
14-3 TAD 236

(ILL MET BY MOONLIGHT: Leslie Ford),
The First Appearance, Grace Latham
(as character by Ford), by Maryell
Cleary, 2-4 PP 27

Illustrated by..., (on boys' books
illustrators), by Les Beitz, 3-4
BC 366

"Illustrated by Bert Salg," (illustrator
of boys' books written by Leo Edwards),
1-2 TB 2; 1-3 TBN 11

(IMAGE OF THE BEAST: Philip Jose Farmer),
Mystery Plus: Image of the Beast,
by R. Jeff Banks, 3-2 PP 15

Immoderate Homage to Modesty, (Modesty
Blaise books by Peter O'Donnell), by
R. Jeff Banks, 4-2 MF 8

Immortal Enemy, The, (on Fu Manchu), by
Robert A.W.Lowndes, 7 R 1

Immortals Do Die: Cornell Woolrich,
1903-1968, A Memoriam, by Bill
Thailing, 2-3 TAD 161

Imperial Dragon, The, by John E. Carroll,
10 R 5

Importance of "C--ing" in Earnest, A
Comparison of THE MALTESE FALCON and
CHINATOWN (film), by William D.
Bottiggi, 14-1 TAD 86

In Appreciation of Leo Edwards, (boys'
books author), by Gil O'Gara, 1-1
YB 13

In Defense of Carroll John Daly, (pulp detective author), by Stephen Mertz, 2-3 MF 19

In Defense of Mr. Fortune, (Reggie Fortune, detective character of H.C.Bailey), by William Antony S. Sarjeant, 14-4 TAD 302

In Defense of Ronald Knox, (author), by James Kingman, 11-3 TAD 299

(IN HELL, MADONNA: Kenneth Robeson), The Resurrection of IN HELL, MADONNA, (Doc Savage story to be published), by Will Murray, 5 DS 8

In Memoriam: Anthony Boucher, by Len & June Moffatt, 10 JD 1

In Memoriam: Leigh Brackett, by Robert E. Briney, 11-3 TAD 258

In Memoriam: Edmund Crispin, by Jacques Barzun, 12-1 TAD 13

In Memoriam: Wendell V. Howard, by Len & June Moffatt, 14 JD 10

In Memoriam: Dennis Wheatley, by Veronica M.S.Kennedy, 11-2 TAD 129

In Memory of Frank Gruber, by William J. Clark, 2-1 FC 4

In Praise of Gladys Mitchell, (including interview), by B.A.Pike, 9-4 TAD 250

In Re: August Derleth, (tribute), by William Wingfield, 3-2 PDA 16

In Re: August Derleth, A Tribute, by Malcolm Ferguson, 1-3 AD 7

In Re: Judge Peck, (August Derleth's detective character), by George J. Marx, 1-1 PDA 24

In Search of the "Con Man," (con men in mystery fiction), by Robert C.S.Adey, 2-4 TAD 259

In Search of the Dame Protagonist, (female sleuths), by Audrey I. Pacheco, 5-4 MR 23

In Search of a Hansom Cab, (Fergus Hume: THE MYSTERY OF A HANSOM CAB), by Philip T. Asdell, 1-2 PP 10

In the Master's Footsteps, (Solar Pons following Sherlock Holmes traditions), by Bruce Dettman, 1-2 PD 1

In the Matter of Stephen King, (literary sketch of author), by Michele Slung, 14-2 TAD 147

In the Moons of Borea, (unpublished prologue to the book of that time), by Brian Lumley, 6 U 3

In the Press: A Few Review Extracts of Nero Wolfe Books, by Don Miller, 9 MN A56

In the Spotlight, (mystery news), by Lianne Carlin, 1-1 MR 8

In the Wake of Haycraft-Queen, (possible additions to basic mystery list), by Norman Donaldson, 5-3 TAD 137

Incident at Nor-Um-Bega, (fiction), by H. Warner Munn, 2 FM 3

Incident at the Grand Canyon, (Purple Invasion pulp stories), by Wooda Nicholas Carr, 30 X 131

InciDENTals, (various on Lester Dent, pulp author), by Will Murray, 2-2 CP 30; 2-3 CP 12; 2-4 CP 21; 2-5 CP 9; 3-1 CP 21; 3-2 CP 7; 3-3 CP 17; (Doc Savage radio serials, w/checklist) 3-4 CP 13; (Lester Dent as guest columnist) 3-5 CP 23

Incinerator, The, (book reviews), by W. Paul Ganley, 2 FM 16; 5 U 29; 6 U 26

Including Murder: An Unpublished Hammett Collection, (manuscripts), by Robert S. Powell, 2-2 C 135

Incredible Captain O'Hagan, The, by Alvin F. Germeshausen, 1 R 27

(INCUBUS: Ray Russell), Mystery Plus: Incubus, by R. Jeff Banks, 1-3 PP 9

(Index)
A. MERRITT'S FANTASY, by Herman S. McGregor, 74 PU 15

AGE OF THE UNICORN, THE, First Annual Cumulative Index to Vol.1, by Dana Martin Batory, 7 U 32

Anthology Index (various mystery anthologies), by Don Miller, 2-4 MM Q1

ARGOSY, (commencing 1930), by John C. Nitka, 63 PU 44; 64 PU 34

ARMCHAIR DETECTIVE, THE, (Vols. 1-2) 2-4 TAD 281; (Vols. 3-4) 4-4 TAD 259; (Vols.5-6) 6-4 TAD 281; (Vols.7-8) 8-4 TAD 326

ARMCHAIR DETECTIVE, THE, Index to Letter Columns by Subject, Vols.1-3, by Robert E. Briney, 3-4 TAD 282

Bedford-Jones, H., in BLUE BOOK, 22 X 42

Bedford-Jones, H., in PEOPLE's (pulp magazine), 30 X 147

Bill Barnes novels, (in pulp magazines), by Will Murray, 22 X 40

Bradbury, Ray, works and pulp stories, (by William F.Nolan), (by Donn Albright), 26 X4; 36 X R2; 36 X R22

Carter, Nick, Stories, by J. Randolph Cox, 22 X 19

CLOAK AND DAGGER Magazine, Nos.1-13/14, 15 CD 10

COLLECTING PAPERBACKS, Vol.1, 2-1 CP (np)

COMET MAGAZINE, by Jerry Alexander, 8 U 139

CRIME BUSTERS MAGAZINE, by Will Murray, 38 X 134

DR. YEN SIN, (pulp magazine), by Joseph Lewandowski, 4 U 32

(Index), continued

ELLERY QUEEN'S MYSTERY MAGAZINE, 1975, by Don Miller, 8 MN 45

ELLERY QUEEN'S ANTHOLOGY: EQA 30, An Author/Title Index to Anthologies, by John Nieminski, 11 MN I1

FAMOUS FANTASTIC MYSTERIES, (pulp magazine), by Herman S. McGregor, 74 PU 6

FANTASTIC NOVELS, (pulp magazine), by Herman S. McGregor, 74 PU 6

HAUNT OF HORROR Magazine, (digest-size), by Dr. Robert C. Schlobin, 1 U 5

Health Knowledge Magazines, (horror, mystery, supernatural), by Gene Marshall and Carl F. Waedt, 3 SF 3

HIGH SEAS ADVENTURE, (pulp magazine), by Darrell Richardson, 63 PU 38

MASKED RIDER MAGAZINE, THE, by Tom Land, 42 X 137

MURDER MYSTERY MONTHLY, Index by author, by Howard Waterhouse, 1-4 PQ 34

MYSTERY FANCIER, THE, Index of Books Reviewed,(Vol.1) 2-1 MF 9, by Jeff Meyerson; (Vol.2) 3-1 MF 26 (by David H. Doerrer); (Vol.3) 4-2 MF 3 (by Doerrer); (Vol.4) 5-2 MF 3 (by Doerrer)

MYSTERY LOVERS NEWSLETTER, THE, (Vol.1) 1-6 MR 17; (Vol.2) 2-6 MR 20

MYSTERY READERS NEWSLETTER, THE, (Vol.3) 3-6 MR 34; (Vol.4) 4-6 MR 42

NERO WOLFE MYSTERY MAGAZINE, by Frank D. McSherry, Jr., 9 MN A25

NEW MYSTERY ADVENTURES/MYSTERY ADVENTURE MAGAZINE/MYSTERY ADVENTURES MAGAZINE, by Fred Cook and Gordon Huber, 22 X 47; 30 X 146

"Not At Night" series horror anthologies, by Darrell Schweitzer, 10 SF 46

Paperback Imprints in Publishers Weekly, by Paul Hammonds, (1950), 1-3 PQ 28; (1952-53) 2-1 PQ 38; (1954) 2-2 PQ 43

PIRATE STORIES, (pulp magazine), by Darrell Richardson, 63 PU 38

PLANET STORIES, by Robert O'Malley, 20 X 42; 21 X 55; 22 X 48; 26 X 13

PQ, (PAPERBACK QUARTERLY), Vols. 1-3, 3-4 PQ 48

RED STAR MYSTERY, (pulp magazine), by Robert E. Briney, 64 PU 16

Reviews, "It's About Crime" by Marvin Lachman, in THE MYSTERY FANCIER, Vols.2-4, by David H. Doerrer, 5-2 MF 6

REX STOUT MYSTERY MAGAZINE, by Frank D. McSherry, Jr., 9 MN A21

REX STOUT'S MYSTERY QUARTERLY, by David Killian, 1-5 CP 21

(Index), continued

STAR MAGAZINE, (pulp magazine), by Nils Hardin, 7 X 66

SCOTLAND YARD, (pulp magazine), by Robert Sampson, 22 X 10

SOUTH SEA STORIES, Index by author, by Robert Weinberg, 8 P 12

STRANGE DETECTIVE STORIES, (pulp magazine), by Glenn Lord, 65 PU 12

STRANGE STORIES, Author index, by Robert Weinberg, 6 WT 26

STRANGE STORIES, Issue index, by Robert Weinberg, 6 WT 23

THORNDYKE FILE, THE, Issues Nos.1-10, by Philip T. Asdell, 10 TF 33

THRILL BOOK, THE, (pulp magazine), by Robert Kenneth Jones, 30 X 9

UNCANNY TALES, (Canadian pulp magazine), by Dennis Lien, 9 SF 23

UNKNOWN Magazine, (pulp magazine), by Will Murray, 42 X 12

VOID Magazine, by Darrell Schweitzer, 2 U 18

WEIRD TALES Magazine, (pulp magazine), by Robert Weinberg, 1 WT 16; 2 WT 17; 3 WT 18; 4 WT 18; 5 WT 24

WORLDS OF FANTASY Magazine, by Dr. Roger C. Schlobin, 2 U 12

(Indexes), see also: Checklists

Indick, Ben P.: letter of comment, 5 X 41; 24 X 47

Indick, Ben P.: Lights! Camera! - Inaction, (unfilmed film scripts of Ray Bradbury), 36 X R25

Indick, Ben P.: Lovecraft's Ladies, (on H.P.Lovecraft), 18 X 10

Infallible Boswell, The - Lyndon Parker, M.D. (Solar Pons), by Cecil A. Ryder, 3-1 PDA 15

Information Center, (re: Sherlock Holmes), 2 MT 33; (mystery items) 3 MT 23; 3 MT 41

Information, Please, (questions and answers on science fiction paperbacks) by J. Grant Thiessen, 4 SF 39; 5 SF 41; 10 SF 35

Influences on a Writer, by William F. Nolan, 11 JD 11

Inner Sanctum, (discussion on the Inner Sanctum mystery paperback series), by M.C.Hill, 3-4 CP 9

(Innes, Hammond), Checklist, by Don Cole, 1-4 PP 8; 4-1 MR 7

(Innes, Hammond), High Adventure Fiction, by Don Cole, 4-1 MR 3

Innocence and Arsenic, The Literary and Criminal Careers of C.J.L. Almquist, by Albert I. Borowitz, 9-1 TAD 17

Innsmouth Revisited, (verse), by Frank Belknap Long, 18 X 17

Inouye, Jon: The Smell on Pulps, (on pulp magazines), 11 X 8

Inquest, The: An Inquiry, (the use of the inquest in the Dr. Thorndyke stories by R. Austin Freeman), by John H. Dirckx, 9 TF 22

Inside Gumshoe Haven, A Look at LA's Bradbury Building, by Joseph Allen, 1-2 M 27

Inside Mystery, (letter column), 2-2 M 2

Inside the Outsider, (on H.P.Lovecraft's "The Outsider"), by Robert Bloch, 18 X 4

Inspector Bucket's Rival, (Richard D. Blackmore: CLARA VAUGHAN), by Clifford Jiggens, 12-3 TAD 270

Inspector Ghote Takes a Bow, (detective created by H.R.F.Keating), by Rona Randall, 5-4 MR 17

Inspector Lestrade's Lament, (verse), by Michael Hodel, 2-2 M 19

(Inspector Maigret, detective: Georges Simenon), All the Short Cases of Inspector Maigret, by Gary L. Gannett, 10-4 TAD 347

Interesting Parallels Between Books by Margaret Sutton and Edward Edson Lee, (comparisons, girl's detective series by Sutton, and the boy's series by Lee writing as Leo Edwards), 2-3 TB 1

Interior Paperback Art, by Mark Schaffer, 3-2 PQ 43

(International Congress of Crime Writers II), Whowunit? International Crime Spree Rocks New York, (report), by Caleb A. Lewis, 11-2 TAD 153

Interview with Michael Avallone, by Michael S. Barson, 3-1 PQ 10

Interview with Dallas Barnes, by Paul Bishop, 2-1 M 36

Interview with the King of the Pulp Artists, Walter M. Baumhofer, by Frank Lewandowski, 9 DS 12

Interview with Robert Bloch, by Michael S. Barson, 4-1 PQ 18

Interview with Gil Brewer, by Michael S. Barson, 3-4 PQ 6

Interview with Howard Browne, by Caleb A. Lewis, 11-2 TAD 172

Interview with Kendell Foster Crossen, by Steve Lewis, 12 MN A1

Interview with Dorothy Salisbury Davis, by Shelly Lewis, 1-2 M 8

Interview with Robert L. Fish, by Luther Norris, 2-5 MR 8

Interview with Stanton Forbes/Tobias Wells, 2-2 MR 19

Interview with Kelly Freas, (artist), 3-2 PQ 12

Interview with Tony Hillerman, by Bruce Taylor, 14-1 TAD 93

Interview with John Jakes, by Michael S. Barson, 3-3 PQ 9

Interview with William X. Kienzle, by Bill Dunn, 6/7 LR 22

Interview with John D. MacDonald, by Michael S. Barson, 4-1 PQ 5

Interview with John Nanovic, by Albert Tonik, 9 SF 44

Interview with Lillian O'Donnell, by Patricia Maida, 14-2 TAD 164

Interview with Otto Penzler, 4 MT 7

Interview with Mary Roberts Rinehart, by Harvey Breit, 1-3 MR 11

Interview with Ruth Rendell, by Diana Cooper-Clark, 14 TAD 108

Interview with Aaron Marc Stein, by Shelly Lewis, 1-2 M 23

Interview with Mary Stewart, by Roy Newquist, 1-4 MR 3

Interview with Harry Whittington, by Michael S. Barson, 4-2 PQ 17

Introducing Alexandra Roudybush, (mystery author), by Gerie Frazier, 3-3 MF 2

Introducing John Alexander Graham, (interview), 2-4 MR 16

Introducing Paul Cain and His Fast One, A Forgotten Hard-Boiled Writer, and a Forgotten Gangster Novel, (Paul Cain: FAST ONE), by E.R.Hagemann, 12-1 TAD 72

Introducing the Yellow Peril, (Dr. Yen Sin, pulp villain), by Wooda Nicholas Carr, 12 SF 39

Intruder in the Rose Garden, (private eye vs. classic mystery), by George N. Dove, 9-4 TAD 278

Investigating Dan Turner, (pulp detective created by Robert Leslie Bellem), by Stephen Mertz, 5 PE 9

Investigation, The: Fiction and Fact, (THE INVESTIGATION: Dorothy Uhnak), by Jo Ann Vicarel, 3-3 MF 15

(INVESTIGATION, THE: Dorothy Uhnak), The Investigation: Fiction and Fact, by Jo Ann Vicarel, 3-3 MF 15

(INVISIBLE MAN, THE: G.K.Chesterton), The Invisible Man Revisited, by Jon L. Breen, 4-3 TAD 154

Invisible Man Revisited, The, (THE INVISIBLE MAN: G.K.Chesterton), by Jon L. Breen, 4-3 TAD 154

Invisible Man, U.S.A., Some Pulp Prototypes, by Edward S. Lauterbach, 3-4 TAD 241

Ireland, Donald: W.Murdoch Duncan, Master of Mystery, An Appreciation, 9-2 TAD 116

(Irish, William), see Cornell Woolrich

Irwin, Jack: letter of comment, 2 BS 2; 8 BS 6; 10 BS 21

Irwin, John C.: letter of comment, 19 JD 13

Is Deductive Fiction Unfilmable?, by Steve Fisher, 3-4 TAD 240

Is It True What They Say About Travis?
(notes on Travis McGee, character of
John D. MacDonald), by Len & June Moffatt,
2 JD 8
Is It Valuable?, (on boys' books
collecting), by Alan S. Dikty and
Les Beitz, 2-4 BC 233
Is the Detective Story Dead? (recorded
dialogue between Julian Symons and
Edmund Crispin), by Julian Symons,
4-2 MR 3
"Is Your Collecting Costing Too Much?"
(boys' book collecting), by Jack
Schorr, 1-4 BC 117
Isabella, Tony: Doc Savage and the
Comics, 14 BS 18
Isadore, Raymond: letter of comment,
38 X 143
Isajenko, Fred: Checklist, John Varley,
12 SF 29
Isham, Lucille M.: letter of comment,
1-2 TBN 5; 3-2 TB 1
(Israel, Peter, detective), Lonesome
Cage, Private Investigator a la
Peter Israel, by Jim McCahery,
4 PE 3
It, (fiction), by Robert L. Moore,
12 LR 21
It Was Never That Much Fun! (pulp
writing), by Hal Murray Bonnett,
38 X 141
It'll Never Happen! (ideas for mystery
fiction), by John Harwood, 9-2 TAD
121
It's a Novel World, (social periods
reflected in mystery fiction), by
Mary Groff, 9-4 TAD 314
It's About Crime, (books about mystery
fiction), by Marvin Lachman,
2-4 MF 15; (reviews) 2-5 MF 3;
(notes on recent reading) 2-6 MF 27;
3-2 MF 21; 3-3 MF 17; 3-4 MF 23;
4-1 MF 13; 4-3 MF 31; 4-4 MF 18;
4-5 MF 24; 5-1 MF 17; 5-2 MF 10·
5-3 MF 22; (new books of and about
mystery) 5-4 MF 18; 5-5 MF 17;
(business and the mystery story)
5-6 MF 29
(It's About Crime, column by Marvin
Lachman), Index to reviews in
THE MYSTERY FANCIER, Vols.2-4,
by David H. Doerrer, 5-2 MF 6
It's All in the Faces, (face
characterizations), by W.O.G.Lofts,
7-2 TAD 109
It's All in the Family, (listing of
"first families" in the mystery
field), by Marvin Lachman, 1-6
MR 9
It's For You, Inspector, You've Been
Cancelled, (mystery on television),
by John Ury, 7-4 TAD 265
Items of Interest - Mystery, by
Richard Moskowitz, 6/7 LR 8;
6/7 LR 10

Iwan Hedman, An Interview, by Caleb
A. Lewis, 13-2 TAD 166
JDM, A Critique, (on John D. MacDonald)
by Elijah Stern, 10 JD 4
JDM BIBLIOPHILE, Review in TIME
Magazine, by Michael Demarest,
25 JD 14
(JDM BIBLIOPHILE), ...& Everything,
(background on publishing the
JDM BIBLIOPHILE), by Len and
June Moffatt, 28 JD 31
JDM Gives Commencement Adddress,
(commencement address, Sarasota,
Fla., June 1981, by John D.
MacDonald), 28 JD 6
JDM in Perspective, (on John D.
MacDonald), by Marvin Lachman,
11 JD 9
JDM Popularity Poll Results, (on
John D. MacDonald), by Clarence
G. Petersen, 13 JD 5
JDM Responds, (on atomic bombings
of Japan), by John D. MacDonald,
27 JD 24
JDM's Images of the Inhuman, (on
John D. MacDonald), by Francis
M. Nevins, Jr., 11 JD 6
J.R. Eats Humble Pie, (on "Dallas"
television show), by John D.
MacDonald, 9 LR 24
J.T.Trowbridge, Youth Fuction Trail-
blazer, (sketch on boys' books
author), by Les Beitz, 1-4 BC 104
Jabre, Shakrallah C.: letter of
comment, 22 X 51
Jack Ritchie, An Interview, by Ray
Puechner, 6-1 TAD 12
Jack of Many Trades - Some Uses of
the Ripper on the Screen, (Jack
the Ripper), by Jack Edmund
Nolan, 6-1 MR 25
Jack the R.I.P., (verse), by Edward
Lauterbach, 1-2 PDA 79
Jack the Ripper, Some Ruminations
on the Whitechapel Fiend, by
Raymond Jones, 2-2 PDA 73
(Jack the Ripper), Jack of Many
Trades, Some Uses of the Ripper
on the Screen, by Jack Edmund
Nolan, 6-1 MR 25
(Jack the Ripper), Jack the R.I.P.,
(verse), by Edward Lauterbach,
1-2 PDA 79
(Jack the Ripper), Jack the Ripper,
Some Ruminations on the White-
chapel Fiend, by Raymond Jones,
2-2 PDA 73
(Jack the Ripper), Mystery on Stage,
by Tim Kelly, 3-2 M 55
(Jack the Ripper), New Gaslight on
Jack the Ripper, by Albert I.
Borowitz, 9-3 TAD 175

(Jack the Ripper), The Stalker in the Dark: Jack the Ripper and Wold Newton, by Timothy J. Rutt, 1-3 WA 5

(Jack the Ripper), Was Watson Jack the Ripper?, by Eileen Snyder, 8-3 TAD 211

Jack Vance's Planet of Adventure Series, (science-fiction paperbacks), by George Kelley, 2-2 PQ 20

Jackson, Mrs. Donald: letter of comment, 8-2 TAD 152

Jackson, Gregory, Jr.: letter of comment, 6 BB 30; 5 MA 27

Jackson, Jon A.: letter of comment, 11-2 TAD 207

Jacobi, Carl: The Derleth Connection, (reminiscences by Jacobi), 4-4 AD 4

Jacobs, David L.: Photo Detection, The Image as Evidence, 1-2 C 18

Jacobs, Irv: letter of comment, 66 PU 64; 67 PU 59

Jacoby, Margaret: letter of comment, 9-4 TAD 249

Jaeger, Frederick J.: A Portrait of Poe and His Tales, 4-6 MR 20

Jaeger, Frederick J.: The Legend of Crimpen Mire, (Sherlockiana verse), 2-1 PDA 27

Jaffe, Marc: letter of comment, 2 DS 6

Jakes, John: letter of comment, 6 U 50

(Jakes, John), First Printing, Two Million, (comments on a paperback series), by Michael S. Barson, 3-3 PQ 7

(Jakes, John), Interview with John Jakes, by Michael S. Barson, 3-3 PQ 9

(Jakes, John), The Paperback Original Novels of John Jakes, by Michael S. Barson, 3-3 PQ 20

James Bama, An Interview, (cover artist, Doc Savage paperback books), 1 BSA 3

James Bama and His Man of Bronze, (Bama as cover artist, Doc Savage books), by Mark J. Golden, 1 DR 4

James E. Bama, Today's Doc Savage Illustrator; Letter and Comments from Bama, 2 BS 4

James, Bill: letter of comment, 3-1 M 2

James, Edgar: Mystery Writers Meet in La Jolla, (Third Annual Mystery Writers Convention report), 1-1 M 14

James, Edgar: World of Mystery, The Stockholm Story, (current news), 2-3 M 20

James Hadley Chase, (sketch), by Theodore P. Dukeshire, 5-1 TAD 32

(James, Laurence), Checklist, by Ian Covell, 4 SF 29

James, Leon: The "Common Practice" in Science Fiction, Aspects on the Writing of Henry Kuttner, 42 X 147

James Otis, Writer of Over One Hundred Boys' Books, (sketch), by Stephen Cammett, 2-3 BC 210

James, P.D.: Mother Knows Best, (on "Dallas" television show), 9 LR 22

(James, P.D.), Face-to-Face with P.D.James, by Maryell Cleary, 4-1 PP 8

(James, P.D.), "From the Time I Could Read, I Always Wanted to Be a Writer" - Interview with P.D.James, by Jane S. Bakerman, 10-1 TAD 55

(James, P.D.), P.D.James, (literary sketch), by Mary Groff, 3-3 PP 11

(James, P.D.), Piercing the Closed Circle, The Technique of Point of View in Works by P.D.James, by Jane S. Bakerman, 1-5 MF 3

James Sandoe, A Retrospective, (and memorial tribute), by Tom and Enid Schantz, 13-4 TAD 288

James Steranko...Extraordinary, (as paperback cover artist), by M.C. Hill, 4-1 PQ 34

Jamison and Lestrade, A Comparative Study, (Sherlock Holmes/Solar Pons), by John McGoldrick, 1-4 PD 1

Janeczko, Paul B.: An Interview with Jay Bennett, 10-4 TAD 342

(Japan), Mystery Stories in Japan, by Katsuo Jinka, 9-2 TAD 112

Japanese Mystery Fiction in English Translation, (with checklist), by John L. Apostolou, 13-4 TAD 310

Jarrett, Pete: letter of comment, 16 JD 15; 18 JD 29

Jasen, David A.: Bibliography, Craig Rice, 5-1 TAD 26

Jasen, David A.: letter of comment, 4-1 TAD 56; 4-3 TAD 180; 5-4 TAD 252

Jasen, David A.: The Mysterious Craig Rice, 5-1 TAD 25

Jasen, David A.: The Mysterious Wodehouse, (bibliography, P.G. Wodehouse), 3-1 TAD 38

Jason, Ben: letter of comment, 3-5 CP 1

(Jaxon, Wood, series: M. Scott Michel), Series Spotlight, M. Scott Michel's Wood Jaxon, by Jim McCahery, 6 PE 3

Jaysnovitch, Andy: A Reel Mystery, (film reviews), 13/14 CL 13

Jaysnovitch, Andy: The Book Detective, (collecting crime fiction), 2 PE 33

Jaysnovitch, Andy: letter of comment, 7 CL 11; 6/7 LR 19; 2-2 M 2; 2-1 PP 41; 4-5/6 PP 99

Jaysnovitch, Andy: The Lost B Movie, (mystery films), 7 PE 3

Jaysnovitch, Andy: Mike Hammer, (on television, checklist), 4 PE 5

Jaysnovitch, Andy: Murder in Miami, (Mike Shayne on television), 1 PE 23

Jaysnovitch, Andy: Naked City, (on the
    television series of that title),
    6 PE 10
Jaysnovitch, Andy: The Projected Detective,
    (detective series, various, on
    television), 8 CL 6; (on the film of
    Hammett's THE MALTESE FALCON) 12 CL 8
Jaysnovitch, Andy: Vegas- The First Season,
    (on the television series of that
    title), 6 PE 16
Jeeves, B.T.: letter of comment, 64 PU 41
Jeeves, Terry: Down Memory-Bank Lane,
    (reminiscences on early science
    fiction magazines), 61 PU 7; 62 PU 3;
    63 PU 7; 64 PU 4; 65 PU 8; 68 PU 16;
    70 PU 5; 71 PU 2; 72 PU 8
Jeeves, Terry: letter of comment, 68 PU 24
Jeffery, Mrs.R.E., Jr.: letter of comment,
    3-2 TAD 138
Jeffrey, David K.: The Mythology of Crime
    and Violence, 1-1 C 75
(Jeffreys, J.G.: Jeremy Sturrock series),
    Sturrock's "Duty", by Edward
    Lauterbach, 3-6 PP 5
Jeffries, Jay: letter of comment,
    5/6 MN 14; 8-4 TAD 312
Jeffries, Jay: Nuggets (and Otherwise)
    From the Golden Age, (mystery book
    reviews), 6 MY 10; 7 MY 6
Jendresen, Erik: Joe Gores Clears Up Some
    Mysteries, (interview), 3-2 M 42
Jendresen, Erik: The Stuff Nightmares Are
    Made Of, A Hammett Update, (film:
    "Hammett"), 3-2 M 45
Jendresen, Erik: World of Mystery, The
    San Francisco Beat, (current news),
    3-1 M 48
Jendresen, Erik: World of Mystery, The
    Burritt Street Beat, (on San Francisco
    Mystery Bookstore party April 1981),
    3-2 M 30
Jenkins, Will: An Interview with Murray
    Leinster, from FANTASY magazine 1934;
    (note: Leinster is pseudonym of
    Will Jenkins), 15 X 6
Jenkins, Will F.: "Why I Use a Pen Name,"
    from FANTASY Magazine October-November
    1934 (writes as Murray Leinster)
(Jenkins, Will F.), Memorial, (tribute)
    by James Ellis, 15 X 5
Jenks, George C.: Dime Novel Makers,
    8 U 119; 1-3 YB 18; 1-4 YB 11
Jennings, Robert: The Army Boys, (boys'
    series), 2 BB 4
Jennings, Robert: Bomba, the Jungle Boy,
    (juvenile Tarzan-like series), 5 BB 9
Jennings, Robert: The Boy Aviators,
    (boys' series books), 3 BB 13
Jennings, Robert: The Boys Go to War,
    (World War I settings for boys'
    series books), 2 BB 9
Jennings, Robert: Checklist, Don Sturdy
    Series, (boys' series by Victor
    Appleton), 1 BB 11
Jennings, Robert: Checklist, The Great
    Marvel Series, (boys' science-fiction
    series by Roy Rockwood), 7 BB 19

Jennings, Robert: Don Sturdy and the
    Great Search for Adventure, (Don
    Sturdy 'oys' series by Victor
    Appleton), 1 BB 5
Jennings, Robert: Future Shock, 1916,
    (Conquest of the U.S. boys' series
    by H. Irving Hancock), 4 BB 15
Jennings, Robert: The Great Marvel
    Series, (boys' science-fiction
    series by Roy Rockwood), 7 BB 5
Jennings, Robert: letter of comment,
    24 X 12
Jennings, Robert: The Motion-Picture
    Comrades, (boys' series books),
    6 BB 24
Jennings, Robert: Where Do You Get All
    That Stuff?, (collecting boys'
    books), 6 BB 10
Jennings, Thomas J.: letter of comment,
    5 X 41
Jensen, Paul M.: letter of comment,
    9-1 TAD 80
Jerry Hicks Series by William Heyliger,
    The, (boys' series books), by
    Joseph A. Rutter, 1-4 YB 17
Jerry Todd, Detective, (fiction, a la
    Leo Edwards' Jerry Todd boy's book
    series), by Julius R. Chenu,
    1-1 TBN 7; 1-2 TBN 11; 1-3 TBN 13;
    1-4 TBN 15; 2-1 TBN 6; 2-2 TBN 7;
    2-3 TBN 7
Jerry Todd Stories Edwards' Most
    Popular, (Jerry Todd series boys'
    books by Leo Edwards), by Julius
    R. Chenu, 1-2 TBN 1
Jessen, Connie: letter of comment,
    4-1 TAD 73; 9-4 TAD 323
Jewell, Hank: letter of comment,
    5/6 MN 12; 5/6 MN 15; 8 MN 38;
    12 MN L2
Jiggens, Clifford: Inspector Bucket's
    Rival, (Richard D. Blackmore: CLARA
    VAUGHAN), 12-3 TAD 270
Jim Bama and the Artistic Doc Savage,
    (cover arrist of Doc Savage book
    reprint series), by Mark J. Golden,
    2/3 DR 11
Jim Thompson, A Walk in the Jungle,
    Addendum to Judge Crater and His
    Fellow Travellers, (mysterious
    disappearances), by Frank D. McSherry,
    Jr., 8-1 TAD 99
Jimmy Holm, Supernatural Detective vs.
    Dr. Death, (pulp detective), by
    Tom Johnson, 10 DS 8
Jinka, Katsuo: Mystery Stories in
    Japan, 9-2 TAD 112
Jobst, James A.: letter of comment,
    2-1 MF 57
Joe Gall Series, The, by George Kelley,
    3-2 MF 26
Joe Gall Series, The, Checklist chart,
    annotated, by R. Jeff Banks, 3-2
    MF 28
Joe Gores Clears Up Some Mysteries,
    (interview), by Erik Jendresen,
    3-2 M 42

Joe Leaphorn and the Navajo Way, Tony
   Hillerman's Indian Detective Fiction,
   by Jane S. Bakerman, 2-1 C 9
John B. Williams, M.D., Forgotten Writer
   of Detective Stories, by E.F.Bleiler,
   10-4 TAD 353
John Ball Interview, by Karen Bornstein,
   1-3 M 31
John Ball, View and Interview, by Robert
   E. Briney, 5-6 MR 9
John Buchan, (sketch), by Theodore P.
   Dukeshire, 7-3 TAD 198
John Buchan, A Philosophy of High Adventure,
   (literary sketch), by J. Randolph Cox,
   2-4 TAD 207
John Creasey, Fact or Fiction, A Candid
   Commentary in Third Person, by John
   Creasey, 2-1 TAD 1
John D. MacDonald, A Little Ecology Goes
   a Long Way, by Wister Cook, 1-1 C 57
John D. MacDonald, A Sonnet, (verse), by
   Dave Stewart, 16 JD 5
John D. MacDonald and the Technologies of
   Knowledge, (essay), by Raymond Carney,
   26 JD 16
John D. MacDonald as Social Critic, by
   Edgar W. Hirshberg, 1-1 C 129
John D. MacDonald, The Greatest Paperbacker
   of Us All, (on MacDonald's role in
   paperback book mystery originals), by
   Michael S. Barson, 4-1 PQ 3
John D. MacDonald vs. Doc Savage, (on writing
   for the pulps), by John D. MacDonald,
   3 BS 3
John D. MacDonald, The Writer's Writer, by
   Len J. Moffatt, 1-6 MR 11
John D. and the Critics, with JDM's Response,
   by John D. MacDonald, 24 JD 4
John Dickson Carr, A Tribute, by Robert
   E. Briney, 1 NC 1
John Dickson Carr, Alias Roger Fairbairn,
   and the Historical Novel, by Douglas
   G. Greene, 11-4 TAD 339
John Dickson Carr and the Aura of Genius,
   (minor aberrations in the Carr stories),
   by James Kingman, 14-2 TAD 166
John Dickson Carr on British Radio, (with
   checklist), by Douglas G. Greene, 12-1
   TAD 69
John Dickson Carr's Solution to THE MYSTERY
   OF EDWIN DROOD, 14-4 TAD 291
John Evelyn Who?, (origin speculation on
   the name of Dr. Thorndyke), by Philip
   T. Asdell, 7 TF 35
John Fowles' Experiments With the Form of
   the Mystery Story, by David Brownell,
   10-2 TAD 184
John J. Malone (and Cohorts), (detective
   character created by Craig Rice), by
   Fred Dueren, 8-1 TAD 44
John Jasper's Devotion, (re: Dickens' THE
   MYSTERY OF EDWIN DROOD), by Nathan L.
   Bengis, 8-3 TAD 165; 8-4 TAD 257;
   9-1 TAD 25
John LeCarre's Circus, (on the spy fiction
   of LeCarre), by Harry D. Dawson, 13-2
   TAD 150

John P. Marquand and Espionage Fiction,
   by George J. Rausch, 5-4 TAD 194
John W. Vandercook and His Tropical
   Murders, by Philip T. Asdell,
   3-2 PP 3
(Johnny Dollar radio mystery series),
   Mystery Dial I: Johnny Dollar,
   by Steve Lewis, 2-1 PP 9
Johnny Fletcher and Sam Cragg, (detective
   series by Frank Gruber), by Peter
   Harris, 4-4 MR 12
Johnny Wasn't Always Superamalgamated,
   (on Doc Savage aide), by Jack
   DeWitt, 3 BS 7
Johns, S.B.: letter of comment,
   8 MN 38; 3-2 TAD 134
(Johnson, E. Richard), An Interview
   With E. Richard Johnson), 2-6 MR 12
(Johnson, E. Richard), Checklist of
   Books, 2-6 MR 13
Johnson, Ginger: letter of comment,
   5 U 63
Johnson, Ginger: Pulpsters, Ltd., (on
   a coterie of pulp fans), 2 PW 2
Johnson, Kenneth R.: letter of comment,
   2 SF 40; 4 SF 41; 6 U 53
Johnson, Kenneth R.: Science Fiction
   Pornography, (with checklist),
   4 SF 4; 5 SF 45
Johnson, Norral: letter of comment,
   3-3 CP 4; 3-4 CP 3
Johnson, Norral: Omissions of Digest-
   size Paperbacks from Kevin Hancer's
   PAPERBACK PRICE GUIDE, 3-3 CP 9
(Johnson, Owen), The Best of Dink, or
   Stover Revisited, (Dink Stover
   boys' series), 1-2 BC 47
Johnson, P.H.: letter of comment,
   1-3 TBN 7
Johnson, Robert L.: Area Map of Tutter,
   People, Places, (populated locale
   of Leo Edwards' Jerry Todd boys'
   series), 2-3 TBN 1
Johnson, Robert L.: Different Jerry
   Todd Editions, (bibliographical
   data on identifying editions of
   Jerry Todd boys' series of Leo
   Edwards), 2-2 TBN 1
Johnson, Robert L.: Edwards Fans United
   to Form Juvenile Jupiter Detective
   Association, (re: Jerry Todd boys'
   series by Leo Edwards), 1-1 TB 1
Johnson, Robert L.: Rebirth of the
   Bugle, (THE TUTTER BUGLE, re: Leo
   Edwards' boys' series books),
   1-1 TB 1
Johnson, Robert L.: Todd Book Editions,
   (bibliographical data on editions
   of Jerry Todd series, boys' books
   by Leo Edwards), 2-5 TBN 4
Johnson, Roger: A Selection from the
   Pontine Weapon Gallery (re: Solar
   Pons stories by August Derleth),
   2-1 PDA 15
Johnson, Roger: Concerning the Problem
   of the Man With the Broken Face,
   (Solar Pons), 1-1 PDA 32

Johnson, Roger: The Pontine Canon, A Selective Commentary, (comments on the Solar Pons stories of August Derleth), 3-1 PDA 37

Johnson, Seth: letter of comment, 63 PU 49; 64 PU 27

Johnson, Tom: Checklist, Michael Avallone Stories in MIKE SHAYNE MYSTERY MAGAZINE 9 SF 23

Johnson, Tom: Destroy Secret Agent X, (on the pulp hero character), 9 P 3

Johnson, Tom: Fading Shadows, The Adjustor, (on the pulp detective, The Adjustor), 8 U 137

Johnson, Tom: Fading Shadows, Corinth/ Regency Paperbacks, (paperback book reprints of various pulp hero characters), 10 SF 36

Johnson, Tom: Fading Shadows, Erlika, Daughter of Satan, (pulp villainess in G.T. Fleming-Roberts' Secret Agent X stories), 11 DS 24

Johnson, Tom: Fading Shadows, Fantastic Fighting Men of Fiction, (on various pulp hero characters), 8 U 66

Johnson, Tom: Fading Shadows, Fighting Men Extraordinary, (on various pulp hero characters), 22 X 26

Johnson, Tom: Fading Shadows, Harold Sherman, (pulp author), 7 U 26

Johnson, Tom: Fading Shadows, James Reasoner, (contemporary author), 2 PW 3

Johnson, Tom: Fading Shadows, John Colicos, (author), 1 PW 2

Johnson, Tom: Fading Shadows, Lady X, (pulp villainesses), 6 U 24

Johnson, Tom: Fading Shadows, Madame Death, (pulp villainess in G.T. Fleming-Roberts' Secret Agent X stories), 11 DS 12

Johnson, Tom: Michael Avallone, (contemporary author), 9 SF 21

Johnson, Tom: Fading Shadows, The Story of G.T. Fleming-Roberts, (pulp author), 2 U 14

Johnson, Tom: Jimmy Holm, Supernatural Detective vs. Dr. Death, (pulp hero) 10 DS 8

Johnson, Tom: The Leopard Lady, (pulp villainess, vs. Agent X, by G.T. Fleming-Roberts), 8 DS 16

Johnson, Tom: letter of comment, 2 DS 7; 12 DS 7; 3 U 48; 4 U 53; 5 U 65; 6 U 49; 7 U 40

Johnson, Tom: Pulp Notes - Doc Savage Magazine, 7 DQ 15

Johnson, Tom: Mike Shayne Author Former Area Resident, (Clayton Matthews as writer of some of the Mike Shayne stories), 5 U 30

Johnson, Tom: The Phantom Fed, (Agent G-X, pulp detective), 10 P 5

Johnson, Tom, and Wooda Nicholas Carr: The Silver Witch, (villainess in JUNGLE STORIES pulp magazine), 11 DS 8

Johnson, Tom, and Albert Tonik: U.N.C.L.E., (on the U.N.C.L.E. espionage series), 10 DS 20

(Johnson, W. Ryerson), Portrait of a Pulpster, (pulp author sketch), by Wooda Nicholas Carr, 14 SF 2

(Johnson, W. Ryerson), Ryerson Johnson and The Phantom Detective, (interview), by Wooda Nicholas Carr, 6 U 9

(Johnson, W. Ryerson), The Secret Kenneth Robesons, (Johnson as author using house name), by Will Murray, 2 D 3

Jonathan Faldish, Lately Departed, A Thorndyke pastiche, (fiction), by John H. Dirckx, 6 TF 3

Jonathan Press Checklist, by Jeff Meyerson, 1-3 PP 35

Jonathan Press Checklist Addendum, by Jim Tinsman, 1-6 PP 27; 2-1 PP 31

Jonathan W. Latimer, An Interview, by Jim McCahery, 11 SF 16

Jones, Robert Kenneth: The Avenger's First Adventure, (first issue of THE AVENGER pulp magazine), 8 BS 17

Jones, Robert Kenneth: The Defective Detectives, (unconventional and eccentric detectives from the pulps) 2-4 MR 7; 68 PU 21

Jones, Robert Kenneth: The Great Escape Artist, (on The Avenger, pulp hero), 9 BS 19

Jones, Robert Kenneth: letter of comment, 4 BS 15; 33 X 113; 36 X 71; 38 X 144; 40 X 86; 43 X 5

Jones, Robert Kenneth: Masterpieces of the Macabre, 42 X 127

Jones, Robert Kenneth: The Thrill Book Semi-Monthly, (pulp magazine), 30 X 4; (index) 30 X 9

Jones, Robert Kenneth: The Weird Menace Magazines, (pulp), 10 BS 3; 11 BS 7; 12 BS 7; 13 BS 7; 14 BS 13; 15 BS 4

Jones, Robert Kenneth: Who Liked the Pulps Besides 10 Million Readers?, 67 PU 21

Jones, Robert Kenneth: The World's Weirdest Criminal, (on the Doctor Satan series in WEIRD TALES), 72 PU 12

Jones, Eddie: Art Portfolio, (science-fiction subjects), 60 PU 18

(Jones, H. Bedford), H. Bedford-Jones in BLUE BOOK, (pulp magazine), by William J. Clark, 22 X 42

(Jones, H. Bedford), H. Bedford-Jones in PEOPLE'S, (pulp magazine), by William J. Clark, 30 X 147

(Jones, James: A TOUCH OF DANGER), Karma and Spiritual Responsibility in A TOUCH OF DANGER, by Steven R. Carter, 13-3 TAD 230

Jones, Jim: letter of comment, 74 PU 28; 15 R 27; 24 X 47; 26 X 72

Jones, Raymond: Jack the Ripper, Some Ruminations on the Whitechapel Fiend, 2-2 PDA 73

(Jones, Robert), Soft Cover Sketches, Robert Jones, (paperback book cover artist), by Thomas Bonn, 3-4 PQ 19

Jones, Rudolph C.: letter of comment, 2-1 PP 36

Jones, Tommy: letter of comment, 2 MA 26

Jones, Wex: The Missing Golf Balls, (Sherlock Holmes pastiche, fiction), 7-3 TAD 177

Jordan, Charles: letter of comment, 1-2 TBN 5; 1-4 TBN 6

Joseph Harrington's First Three Books, by R.W.Hays, 4-2 TAD 104

Joseph, Robert: letter of comment, 8 BS 4

Josephine Chase and Her Pen Names, by Roy B. Van Devier, 1-2 BC 39

Joyner, Samuel: letter of comment, 3 DS 6

Judge Crater and His Fellow Travellers, ("vanishers" in mystery fiction), by Frank D. McSherry, Jr., 4-4 TAD 195

Judgment, (verse), by Frederick Faust, 2-2 FC 5

Judy Bolton Series, The, (girls' detective series by Margaret Sutton) by Julius R. Chenu, 1-1 YB 3

Jules deGrandin Returns, by Robert Weinberg, 18 X 33

Julian Symons, An Interview, by Lianne Carlin, 3-4 MR 24

Julian Symons and Civilization's Discord, (social stress reflected in mystery fiction), by Steven R. Carter, 12-1 TAD 57

Jumping Jimmy Christopher, (on the pulp hero, Operator 5), by Dean A. Grennell, 30 X 17

(JUNGLE STORIES magazine), Ki-Gor, King of the Jungle, (pulp magazine), by Wooda Nicholas Carr, 2 P 22

(JUNGLE STORIES magazine), My Favorite Jungle Stories Magazine Covers, (pulp magazine), 8 U 30

(JUNGLE STORIES magazine), The Silver Witch, (villainess in pulp magazine), by Wooda Nicholas Carr and Tom Johnson, 11 DS 8

Junket, (essay on Apollo 9 launch), by John D. MacDonald, 12 JD 3

Junkie: A Personal Reminiscence, (on JUNKIE, paperback, by William Burroughs), by Jeff Chambers, 3-3 CP 11

(JUNKIE: William Burroughs), Junkie: A Personal Reminiscence, by Jeff Chambers, 3-3 CP 11

(JUNKIE: William Burroughs), Mass Market Murmurings, (on the paperback by Burroughs), by Barry Bernard, 1-1 CP 6

Jurena, Louis: letter of comment, 2 FM 18

Juri, Dorothy: letter of comment, 1-5 MF 53; 2-1 MF 57; 4-5/6 PP 94

Just a Little Matter of Doom, (on The Shadow, pulp hero), by Robert Sampson, 4 X 7

Just a Writer Working for a Buck, (on Mickey Spillane, with interview), by Michael S. Barson, 12-4 TAD 293

Justice, Keith L.: A Failed Experiment, The Laser Books, History and Checklist, (analysis and bibliography of short-lived science-fiction paperback line), 15 SF 4

Justice, Keith L.: Background and Checklist, Don Elliott/Robert Silverberg Erotic Fiction Titles, 13 SF 18

Justice, Keith L.: Publishers' Codes and Collecting Contemporary Editions, (identification of first and subsequent editions), 11 SF 23

Justice, Mark, and John Boehm: Death Flies in Silver Circles, (fiction, Doc Savage pastiche), 1 MB 7

Justice, Mark: Savage Views, (comments on Doc Savage Magazine Nos.1 & 2), 1 MB 23

Juvenalia, (collecting comments, boys' books), by Julius R. Chenu, 1-1 YB 9; 1-2 YB 12; 1-3 YB 16; 1-4 YB 14; 1-5 YB 11; 1-6 YB 11

(Juvenile Jupiter Detective Association) Edwards' Fans Unite to Form Juvenile Jupiter Detective Association, (re: Jerry Todd series by Leo Edwards, boys' books), by Robert L. Johnson, 1-1 TB 1; (list of members) 1-2 TB 7; 1-3 TB 12; 2-1 TB 1

K.C.Constantine, (literary sketch), by David Brownell, 9-1 TAD 42

Kabatchnik, Amnon: Agatha Christie is Still Alive and Doing Well, 2-6 MF 9

Kabatchnik, Amnon: Fall Highlights, (mystery reviews), 11 CL 7

Kabatchnik, Amnon: letter of comment, 3-1 MR 15; 4-5 MR 16; 5-5 MR 19; 1-6 PP 29; 2-2 PP 34; 4-1 PP 43; 4-2 PP 43; 1-4 QC 18; 1-4 TAD 156; 2-4 TAD 279; 3-1 TAD 67; 4-1 TAD 70; 4-2 TAD 133; 5-2 TAD 118; 5-3 TAD 176; 6-1 TAD 53; 6-2 TAD 120; 6-3 TAD 203; 8-4 TAD 322; 5 U 62

Kabatchnik, Amnon: Reprints of Mystery and Detective Fiction Offered in 1978, 1-1 PP 19

Kabatcknik, Amnon: The Suspense Novel, and The Middle East, (suspense novels with Middle East locales), 3-4 MR 3

Kabatchnik, Amnon, and Robert Aucott: A Readers' Supplementary List to the Haycraft/Queen Definitive Librar of Detective-Crime-Mystery Fiction, (basic mystery list additions), 9-2 TAD 87

(Kabatchnik, Amnon), Profile, (biographical
    sketch), by Jim Huang, 8 CL 11
Kafer, Susan: letter of comment, 5 MA 28
Kahl, Richard: letter of comment,
    14 X 62; 24 X 12
Kahn, Joan: Commentaries for the
    Curious, (on John Dickson Carr),
    1 NC 19
Kahn, Joan: No Rules for a Suspense
    Editor, (editing crime fiction),
    2-3 TAD 169
(Kahn, Joan), A Conversation with Joan
    Kahn, (crime fiction editor), by
    Robert Randisi, 3-1 M 16
(Kahn, Joan), A KAHNfidential Interview,
    (interview with Kahn as crime fiction
    editor), by Jane Merrill Filstrup,
    2-2 C 15
(Kahn, Joan), Meet the Author, Joan
    Kahn, 2-3 TAD 170
Kaiser, Harold D.: letter of comment,
    12-4 TAD 357
Kallan, Susan: letter of comment,
    11-1 TAD 4
Kamerow, Allan L.: letter of comment,
    19 JD 13
Kaminsky, Stuart J.: The Mystery of Alfred
    Hitchcock, (in-depth study of his
    works), 2-3 M 26
Kaminsky, Stuart M.: Mystery on Film,
    (general commentary), 16 CD 10
Kaminsky, Stuart M.: Dressed to Kill, An
    Appreciation, (on "Dressed to Kill,"
    a Brian DePalma film), 14-1 TAD 14
Kaminsky, Stuart M.: letter of comment,
    1-3 M 4
(Kaminsky, Stuart M.) An Interview with
    Stuart Kaminsky, by Robert J.
    Randisi, 13-4 TAD 338
(Kaminsky, Stuart M.), short note on
    writing, in "People" column, 16 CD 8
Kanarr, Dave: letter of comment,
    3 BB 23
(Kane, Frank), Frank Kane, (checklist),
    by George Kelley, 2 PE 31
Kankowski, Joseph: Fiction by Edmond
    Hamilton, (literary commentary),
    30 X 14
Karlinchak, R.T.: Ed Noon's Quickest
    Caper, or, Revenge, Italian Style,
    38 X 139
Karlson, Kate: letter of comment,
    14 R 28
Karpowitz, William A., Jr.: letter of
    comment, 9 LR 19
Karma and Spiritual Responsibility in
    James Jones' A TOUCH OF DANGER, by
    Steven R. Carter, 13-3 TAD 230
Kase, Michael: Behind These Eyes, (verse),
    1-4 AD 5
Katsuta, Yasuhiko: letter of comment,
    1-3 M 4
Kay Cleaver Strahan, A Forgotten
    Detective Novelist, by Mary Jean
    DeMarr, 2-1 C 53

Kaye, Marvin: letter of comment,
    10-3 TAD 195
Kearns, Winn: Traveler With Crime,
    Suzanne Blanc, 8-3 TAD 194
Keasler, John: letter of comment,
    2 BS 21
Keasler, John: Welcome Back, Doc
    Savage...and Crew, (reappearance
    in paperback book reprints),
    3 BS 6
Keating, H.R.F.: letter of comment,
    5-5 MR 16; 10 TF 32
Keating, H.R.F.: Mrs. Craggs and a
    Certain Lady's Town House,
    (fiction), 3-1 M 26
(Keating, H.R.F.), Detective Fiction
    and Social Realism, H.R.F.Keating's
    India, by Meera T. Clark, 2-1 C 1
(Keating, H.R.F.), H.R.F.Keating,
    (sketch, with bibliography), by
    Sven-Ingmar Pettersson, 8-4 TAD
    277
(Keating, H.R.F.), Inspector Ghote
    Takes a Bow, by Rona Randall,
    5-4 MR 17
Keddie, James, Jr.: Blood and Thunder
    on Stage, 1-4 TAD 119
Keddie, James, Jr.: Freeman Wills
    Crofts, 1-6-69/4-11-57, (tribute
    and sketch), 2-3 TAD 137
Keddie, James, Jr.: Freeman Wills
    Crofts, A Checklist, 2-3 TAD 140
Keddie, James, Jr.: letter of comment,
    1-2 TAD 65; 1-3 TAD 104; 3-1
    TAD 59; 7-1 TAD 73; 7-3 TAD
    228
Keddie, James, Jr.: Rambling Thoughts
    on a 'Tec Collection, (collecting
    crime fiction), 1-1 TAD 5
(Keddie, James, Jr.), Meet the Author,
    James Keddie, Jr., by Allen J.
    Hubin, 1-1 TAD 9
(Keeler, Harry Stephen), A Note on
    Harry Stephen Keeler as Filmed,
    by Francis M. Nevins, Jr., 3-3
    TAD 165
(Keeler, Harry Stephen), Another Side
    of Harry Stephen Keeler, (with
    letters from Keeler), by Jack
    Cuthbert, 7-2 TAD 101
(Keeler, Harry Stephen), Checklist, by
    David Bates, 4-2 PP 4
(Keeler, Harry Stephen), Department
    of Unrelated Miscellanea, by Francis
    M. Nevins, Jr., 4-1 MR 21
(Keeler, Harry Stephen), Dumbfounded
    in Keelerland, by Art Scott,
    1-1 MF 12
(Keeler, Harry Stephen), Further
    Excursions Into the Wacky World of
    Harry Stephen Keeler, by Art Scott,
    1-4 MF 13
(Keeler, Harry Stephen), H.S.Keeler, A
    Checklist, by Bernard Beauchesne,
    1-4 TAD 147

188

(Keeler, Harry Stephen), Harry Stephen Keeler, (sketch), by David Bates, 4-2 PP 3

(Keeler, Harry Stephen), Harry Stephen Keeler, (sketch), by Albert Field, 3-5 PP 10

(Keeler, Harry Stephen), Harry Stephen Keeler, Mystery Writer Extraordinary, by Bernard Beauchesne, 1-4 TAD 143

(Keeler, Harry Stephen), The Late Novels of Harry Stephen Keeler, A Preliminary Checklist, by Francis M. Nevins, Jr., 3-2 TAD 74

(Keeler, Harry Stephen), Reminiscences, (of Keeler), by Frank Gruber, 2-1 TAD 55

(Keeler, Harry Stephen), The Wild and Woolly World of Harry Stephen Keeler, Scenes from the Last Act, by Francis M. Nevins, Jr., 3-2 TAD 71

(Keeler, Harry Stephen: THE AMAZING WEB), The Worst Legal Mystery in the World, by Francis M. Nevins, Jr., 1-3 TAD 82

(Keeler, Harry Stephen: Angus MacWhorter series), Harry Stephen Keeler's Screwball Circus, by Francis M. Nevins, Jr., 5-4 TAD 209

(Keeler, Harry Stephen: Quiribus Brown, detective), Hick Dick from the Sticks, Harry Stephen Keeler's Quiribus Brown, by Francis M. Nevins, Jr., 7-4 TAD 251

Keeley, Mrs.Larry L. (Peggy): letter of comment, 7 JD 7; 9 JD 16; 11 JD 20

Keeley, Peggy: Minute Quiz, (mystery quiz), 1-6 MR 12

(Keene, Hal, series), The Hal Keene and Skippy Dare Series, (boys' books), by Julius R. Chenu, 1-1 BC 12

Keffer, Willametta: letter of comment, 1-5 MR 14

Keit, Mildred: letter of comment, 3-4 PP 38

Keleher, Catharine: letter of comment, 27 JD 35

(Kelley, Bryan James), G-77 in PUBLIC ENEMY #1, (pulp), 2 P 14

Kelley, George: Best Books of 1978 - (Mystery) Fiction, (overview), 2-2 PP 19

Kelley, George: Best Crime and Mystery Books of 1980, (overview), 4-1 PP 11

Kelley, George: Best Crime Fiction and Non-Fiction of 1979, (overview), 3-1 PP 25

Kelley, George: Bill Pronzini Revisited, 2-5 MF 5

Kelley, George: The Caper Novel, 7 U 61

Kelley, George: The Caper Novels of Tony Kendrick, 2-4 MF 3

Kelley, George: Checklist, Lone Wolf Series by Mike Barry (Barry Malzberg), 1-5 MF 18

Kelley, George: The Crime Novels of Harold R. Daniels, 3-4 MF 13

Kelley, George: The Degeneration of Donald Hamilton, 1-6 MF 11

Kelley, George: Don Cole's Underrated Books, 1-5 PP 8

Kelley, George: The Edgar Box Mystery Novels, 4 U 30

Kelley, George: The Explosive Novels of Richard L. Graves, 3-6 MF 9

Kelley, George: Fear and Loathing with the Lone Wolf, (Lone Wolf series by Mike Barry/Barry Malzberg), 1-5 MF 17

Kelley, George: Frank Kane, (checklist), 2 PE 31

Kelley, George: Hard Cain, The Paperback Original Novels of James M. Cain, 4-3 PP 9

Kelley, George: Jack Vance's Planet of Adventure Series, (science fiction paperback series), 2-2 PQ 20

Kelley, George: The Joe Gall Series, 3-2 MF 26

Kelley, George: letter of comment, 6/7 LR 19; 1-1 MF 39; 1-4 MF 56; 1-5 MF 57; 2-2 MF 51; 4-1 MF 48; 4-2 MF 57; 2-1 PP 44; 2-3 PP 42; 3-1 PP 44; 3-3 PP 38

Kelley, George: Looking for Rachel Wallace and Ginger North, (re: LOOKING FOR RACHEL WALLACE by Robert B. Parker, and LOOKING FOR GINGER NORTH, by John Dunning), 4-3 MF 29

Kelley, George: The Programmed Writing of Dean R. Koontz, 1-4 MF 11

Kelley, George: Running Hot and Cold with Ron Faust, (discussion of Faust's crime fiction), 5-4 MF 11

Kelley, George: Sinning with Lawrence Sanders, (discussion of Sanders' crime fiction), 3-5 MF 20

Kelley, George: Skullduggery, File No.1: So You Want to be a Crime Collector, (on collecting mystery fiction), 3 U 20

Kelley, George: The Suspense Novels of Bill Pronzini, 1-2 MF 15

Kelley, George: Ten Books, (science fiction paperbacks), 1-4 PQ 44

Kelley, George: Ten Books, Poul Anderson and the Best, ("Best" anthologies), 1-3 PQ 33

Kelley, George: The Time Machine, Philip K. Dick, The Middle Period, (science fiction paperbacks), 2-1 PQ 23

Kelley, George: Vault of the Ages, (Brian Stableford's puzzle novels) 1-2 CP 19; 1-4 CP 27; (Stableford's The Realms of Tartarus) 1-3 CP 16; (Survey of Science Fiction Literature,ed.by Magill) 2-2 CP 20

Kelley, George: The Vengeance Novels of
Brian Garfield, 2-1 MF 5
(Kellogg, Elijah), Checklist of Books,
by Walter H. McIntosh, (boys'
books), 3-2 BC 309
(Kellogg, Elijah), Elijah Kellogg,
Maine Boy's Writer, by Walter H.
McIntosh, 3-2 BC 309
(Kelly, Aloysius, detective: Barbara
Worsley-Gough), Pen Profile No.6,
by Barry Pike, 2-5 PP 24
Kelly, R. Gordon: Explaining the Mystery
Story, (as social function), 5-4
TAD 214
Kelly, R. Gordon: letter of comment,
17 JD 25; 5-1 TAD 43
(Kelly, Slot-Machine, series: Michael
Collins), Checklist, by John
Edwards, 9 SF 38
Kelly, Tim: Break a Leg, Break a Neck,
The Mystery on Stage, 2-2 M 14
Kelly, Tim: MYSTERY on Stage, 2-3 M
24; (Jack the Ripper) 3-2 M 55
Kelton, Elmer: letter of comment,
1-3 PQ 7
(Kelton, Elmer), A PQ Interview with
Elmer Kelton, 1-2 PQ 18
(Kelton, Elmer), Elmer Kelton, Paperback
Writer, (with checklist), 1-2 PQ 16
Kemble, Stewart: Gardner and Black Mask -
Incomplete? (Erle Stanley Gardner in
BLACK MASK magazine), 73 PU 4
Kemble, Stewart: Hersey Pulps, (on Harold
B. Hersey, pulp editor and publisher),
68 PU 10
Kemble, Stewart: King of the Pulps, (on
Frederick Faust/Max Brand), 69 PU 25
Kemble, Stewart: Notes of a Pulp Collector,
(abstract from VOR by James Blish),
15 BS 8
Kemble, Stewart: Street & Smith Pulps,
(comments on THE FICTION FACTORY by
Quentin Reynolds), 74 PU 29
Kemble, Stewart: 24 Stories and 7 Novels,
(commentary on DOWN THESE MEAN STREETS
A MAN MUST GO, by Philip Durham, about
Raymond Chandler), 72 PU 18
Kemp, Earl: letter of comment, 15 BS 16
Ken Holt Mystery Stories, The, (boys'
series), by Fred Woodworth, 2 MA 7
Kendell Foster Crossen, A Bibliography,
by Don Miller, 12 MN B1
(Kendrick, Tony), The Caper Novels of
Tony Kendrick, by George Kelley,
2-4 MF 3
KenKnight, Brian: letter of comment,
1-4 CP 2; 6/7 LR 16; 11-2 TAD 109
Kennedy, Bruce: A Latter Holmes, (the
Solar Pons series by August Derleth),
1-3 PD 1
(Kennedy, Craig, detective: Arthur B.
Reeve), A Reading of Reeve, Some
Thoughts on the Creator of Craig
Kennedy, by J. Randolph Cox, 11-1
TAD 28
(Kennedy, Craig, detective: Arthur B.
Reeve), The American Sherlock
Holmes, A Study in Scarlet Imper-
sonation, (Holmes and Watson
protesting Craig Kennedy and Walter
Jameson's reputation as the American
Sherlock Holmes), by Marvin Lachman,
3-2 MR 2
(Kennedy, Craig, detective: Arthur B.
Reeve), Arthur B. Reeve and the
American Sherlock Holmes, by John
Harwood, 10-4 TAD 354
(Kennedy, Craig, detective: Arthur B.
Reeve), Craig Kennedy Radio Shows,
(checklist), by Ray Stanich, 3 PE 18
Kennedy, Margaret: letter of comment,
11 JD 19
Kennedy, Veronica M.S.: A Chaucerian
Fragment, (re; Charlie Chan), 5-1
TAD 23
Kennedy, Veronica M.S.: A Possible
Source for the Opening of "Sleuth",
(play by Anthony Shaffer), 7-3
TAD 175
Kennedy, Veronica M.S.: Detectives in
Disguise, (mystery quiz), 4-2 TAD
103; 9-1 TAD 6
Kennedy, Veronica M.S.: Gothics -
Ghastly, Gruesome and Romantic,
9-4 TAD 276
Kennedy, Veronica M.S.: Horrendous
Headlines, (mystery quiz), 9-2
TAD 124
Kennedy, Veronica M.S.: In Memoriam
Dennis Wheatley, 11-2 TAD 129
Kennedy, Veronica M.S.: Ladies in
Crime, (mystery quiz), 7-2 TAD 94
Kennedy, Veronica M.S.: letter of
comment, 3-1 TAD 66; 3-1 TAD 67;
4-1 TAD 54; 4-2 TAD 133; 5-4 TAD
239; 6-2 TAD 127; 6-3 TAD 206;
8-1 TAD 68; 10-4 TAD 381
Kennedy, Veronica M.S.: The Prophet
Before the Fact, A Note on John
D. MacDonald's THE END OF THE
NIGHT, 7-1 TAD 41
Kennedy, Veronica M.S.: Sawney Beane,
An Incident from the Casebook of
a Royal Detective, (British classic
true crime), 9-2 TAD 126
Kennedy, Mr. & Mrs. W.H.J.: Doctors
in Crime, (mystery quiz), 1-5
MR 4
Kennedy, Mrs. W.H.J.: letter of comment,
11 JD 15
Kenneth Robeson's Alter Egos, (Doc
Savage novels written by other than
Lester Dent), by Fred S. Cook,
2 BS 14
Kenny, Nancy Zoole: letter of comment,
4 DS 5
(Kersh, Gerald: THE SECRET MASTERS),
Smorgasbord Thriller, by Edward
S. Lauterbach, 4-3 TAD 165

Kesho Naik, Dacoit, (Classic Corner Rare
    Tales, fiction), by Sir Edmund C. Cox,
    13-4 TAD 319
(Keyhoe, Donald E.), Donald E. Keyhoe and
    the Brain Devil of G-2, by Sidney H.
    Bradd, 22 X 34
Keyhole Confidential, (paperback books,
    various data), by William Lyles,
    1-2 CP 10; 1-3 CP 7; (Dell author
    bibliography, Anthony Boucher and
    Agatha Christie) 1-4 CP 26; (Dell
    1st editions, 1st series, checklist)
    1-5 CP 26; 1-6 CP 17; (paperback
    female cover art) 2-2 CP 22; (early
    Dell paperbacks) 2-4 CP 13; (Dell
    variant editions) 3-2 CP 30
Kid Glove Kid, The, (mystery puzzle),
    12-1 TAD 62
(Kidnapped Campers series: Flavia A.
    Canfield), Boys' Series Bibliography,
    by Harry K. Hudson, 1-5 YB 14
Kienzle, William X.: letter of comment,
    14-1 TAD 71
(Kienzle, William X.), Interview with
    William X. Kienzle, by Bill Dunn,
    6/7 LR 22
Ki-Gor and the Fiction House Monster,
    (Fiction House, pulp publisher),
    by Fred S. Cook, 5 BS 18
Ki-Gor, King of the Jungle, (JUNGLE
    STORIES pulp magazine), by Wooda
    Nicholas Carr, 2 P 22
(Kilby, Mark, series: Robert Caine
    Frazer), Checklist, by Robert E.
    Briney and John Creasey, 2-1 TAD 12
(Kilgerrin, Paul, series: Charles Leonard),
    Checklist, Annotated, by Barry Van
    Tilburg, 4-4 MF 17
(Killain, Johnny, series: Dan J. Marlowe),
    Checklist, by Kelly Adrian, 3-3 MR 25
Killian, Dave: Killian's Memoranda,
    (column on paperback book data),
    (on Quick-Reader paperback series)
    1-1 CP 17; (a partial list of Bonded
    and Chartered publications) 1-4 CP
    23; (Rex Stout's Mystery Quarterly
    index) 1-5 CP 21; (Popular Library
    science fiction paperbacks) 2-1 CP
    17; (paperbacks of James Blish,
    science fiction), 2-3 CP 8; (mystery
    paperbacks of Chester Himes), 3-3
    CP 19
Killian, Dave: letter of comment,
    2-2 CP 5; 1-2 PQ 3
Killian, Dave: Modern Fantasy, (in
    paperbacks), 2-5 CP 11
Killian's Memoranda, see: Dave Killian
Kim Philby, Master Spy, in Fact and
    Fiction, by Theodore P. Dukeshire,
    3-1 MF 14
Kimball, Clay: letter of comment,
    1-2 CP 2; 7 JD 2; 9 JD 9; 10 JD 17;
    13 JD 18; 14 JD 24; 16 JD 18; 20 JD
    20; 3/4 MN 12; 5/6 MN 14; 8 MN 34;
    4-1 TAD 60; 8-1 TAD 76; 8-4 TAD 322

Kimura, Jiro: letter of comment,
    1-2 G 69; 3-1 M 2; 9-3 TAD 169;
    14-3 TAD 247; 5 U 64
Kimura, Jiro: 34th Edgar Allen Poe
    Awards Dinner, (Mystery Writers
    of America), 13-3 TAD 205
King, Betty J.: letter of comment,
    4-1 MF 43; 3-1 PP 40
King, Daniel P.: First Crime Writers
    International Conference, (report),
    9-3 TAD 207
King, Harvey: letter of comment,
    15 X 14; 26 X 72
King, Holly Beth: George Smiley, The
    Reluctant Hero, (spy character of
    John LeCarre), 2-1 C 70
King is Dead, The, (fiction), by
    Schiller Faust (Frederick S. Faust),
    1-1 FC 6
King, J.P.: letter of comment,
    2-2 TAD 132
(King Kong), Kong, His Life and Fall,
    (speculative essay), by Arn
    McConnell, 1-4 WA 3
King, Margaret J.: An Interview with
    Elizabeth Linington, 13-4 TAD 299
King, Margaret J.: Binocular Eyes,
    Cross-Cultural Detectives, (contact
    in crime fiction between different
    cultural spheres), 13-3 TAD 253
King of the Pulps, (on Frederick
    Faust/Max Brand), by Stewart Kemble,
    69 PU 25
(King, Rufus), A Note on Rufus King's
    Series Short Stories, (with check-
    list), by J. Mark Purcell, 12-4 TAD
    380
(King, Stephen), An Interview with
    Stephen King), by Joyce Lynch Dewes,
    2-2 M 6
(King, Stephen), In the Matter of
    Stephen King, (literary sketch), by
    Michele Slung, 14-2 TAD 147
King of the Dime Novels, (Gilbert
    Patten/Burt L. Standish), by Gil
    O'Gara, 3 U 17
Kingman, James: In Defense of Ronald
    Knox, 11-3 TAD 299
Kingman, James: John Dickson Carr and
    the Aura of Genius, (minor aberrations
    in the Carr stories), 14-2 TAD 166
Kingman, James: letter of comment,
    10-2 TAD 100
(Kingston, William H.G.), Checjlist
    of Books, by Walter H. McIntosh,
    3-4 BC 357
(Kingston, William H.G.), William H.G.
    Kingston, English Boys' Writer,
    by Walter H. McIntosh, 3-4 BC 355
Kinney, Harold: letter of comment,
    2-1 CP 1; 13 SF 48
Kirby, Brian: letter of comment,
    8 JD 9; 9 JD 8
Kirde, Kalju: letter of comment,
    30 X 148

(Kirk, General, series: John Blackburn),
Checklist, by Barry Van Tilburg,
4-2 MF 12

Kirklin, Mardi: Living With a Paperback
Book Collector, 1-1 CP 15; 1-2 CP 13;
(shelving) 1-3 CP 3; (definitions)
1-5 CP 18; (collecting Popular Library
editions) 2-1 CP 19

Kiss My Deadly Typewriter #539, ("old
truths"), by Michael Avallone,
2-2 QC 9; 3-1 QC 17; (rebuttals,
by Marvin Lachman, Francis M.
Nevins,Jr., Charles MacDonald,
Stanley A. Carlin, Jon L. Breen,
Joe Gores, and reply by Avallone)
3-1 QC 14

Kittredge, William, and Steven M. Krauzer:
The Evolution of the Great American
Detective - The Reader as Detective
Hero, 11-4 TAD 319

Klein, Gene: Doc Savage, Man of Bronze?,
(critique on Doc Savage Comic),
65 PU 29

Klein, Kathleen Gregory: Feminists as
Detectives, Harriet Vane, Kate
Fansler, Sarah Chayse, 13-1 TAD 31

Klein, Kathleen Gregory: letter of
comment, 1-2 M 3; 12-1 TAD 93

Kleinberg, Allan: letter of comment,
9 MN L5; 5/6 MN 13; 5/6 MN 14;
7 MN 7; 1-2 PP 29; 7-3 TAD 227;
8-3 TAD 233; 9-1 TAD 81; 9-3
TAD 167; 10-3 TAD 195

(Kleinberg, Allan), Biographical
Sketch, 2-3 PP 7

Kniepp, Paul: letter of comment,
6 JD 12; 11 JD 17

Knight, Arden: An Appreciation of Archie
Goodwin, (detective, Nero Wolfe
novels by Rex Stout), 12-4 TAD 328

Knight, Don: letter of comment,
12-2 TAD 186; 13-2 TAD 159

Knock?, (verse), by Steve Eng,
4-1 AD 9

Knoerle, John: Death Wears a Necktie,
(fiction), 2-1 M 55

Knoerle, John: Hardboiled Lingo,
(glossary), 1-1 M 9

Knoerle, John, and Gene Davidson:
Ross Macdonald Interview,
1-1 M 5

Knott, Harold: Bill S. Ballinger
Checklist, 4-6 MR 9

Knott, Harold: Some Important Detective
First Editions in Paperback Books,
3-1 MR 2

Knott, Harold: Who Really Wrote?
(pseudonyms of authors), 3-6 MR 2

Knott, Harold, and Marvin Lachman:
Pocket Books Checklist 1-500
(Pocket Books as publisher),
1-6 MF 29

Knott, Harold, and Francis M. Nevins,
Jr., William Thailing: Cornell
Woolrich, A Bibliography,
2-4 TAD 237

Knowledge of the Occult - Immense,
(Solar Pons, in stories by August
Derleth), by Jon L. Lellenberg,
2-2 PDA 52

(Knox, Ronald A.) The Detective Novels
of Ronald A. Knox, by William
Reynolds, 14-3 TAD 275

(Knox, Ronald A.), In Defense of Ronald
Knox, by James Kingman, 11-3 TAD
299

(Knox, Ronald A.), Ronald Arbuthnott
Knox, (literary sketch), by Norman
Donaldson, 7-4 TAD 235

(Knox, Thomas W.), The Author of "The
Boy Travellers", (boys' series),
by B.B.Vallentine, 4-1 BC 400

Koch, George: letter of comment,
4-2 MR 15

Koch, Pat: letter of comment,
3-5 PP 50

Kochell, Leo: letter of comment,
2-3 CP 1

Kodaka, Nobumitsu, and Donald E.
Westlake: Donald E. Westlake, A
Checklist, 8-3 TAD 203

Koeller, Scott: Champion of Catastrophe
and Son of the East, A Short
"Genealogy" of Victor von Doom,
(re: Dr. Doom stories, a speculative
essay), 1-4 WA 5

Koeller, Scott: letter of comment,
1-2 WA 13

Koenig, Mary Louise: letter of comment,
3-3 TAD 206; 5-4 TAD 251

Kohl, Barbara: letter of comment,
7 JD 2; 11 JD 20

Kojak, The Godfather and the City,
by Jack E. Wallace, 1-1 C 25

Kolesnik, Robert: letter of comment,
3-4 TAD 306; 6-3 TAD 202;
7-1 TAD 75; 7-3 TAD 232; 8-1
TAD 74; 8-2 TAD 160; 8-4 TAD
325; 9-1 TAD 82

Kong: His Life and Fall, (King Kong),
by Arn McConnell, 1-4 WA 3

Konigsberg, E.P.H.: letter of comment,
11 JD 18

Konner's Korner, (pulp magazine data
and reminiscences), by Wilkie Conner,
63 PU 33; 64 PU 11; 65 PU 3

(Koontz, Dean R.), The Programmed
Writing of Dean R. Koontz, by
George Kelley, 1-4 MF 11

Koopmann, Werner: letter of comment,
4-1 TAD 64; 5-4 TAD 241

Korzenowski, Rob: letter of comment,
4 DS 3

Koutek, Judy: letter of comment,
6/7 LR 26; 3-1 PP 39

Krabacher, Thomas: letter of comment,
2-1 AD 12

Krankkala, Judith L.: letter of comment,
24 JD 39

(Krasner, William), Department of
Unknown Mystery Writers: William
Krasner, by Marvin Lachman, 1-2 PP 11

Krause, Terri: letter of comment,
6/7 LR 21; 2-3 PP 43; 3-2 PP 32
Kraushar, Charles: letter of comment,
6 MY 8
Krauzer, Steven: letter of comment,
3-1 MF 53; 5 PE 33; 10-1 TAD 41;
10-3 TAD 283; 38 X 145
Krauzer, Steven M., and William Kittredge:
The Evolution of the Great American
Detective, The Reader as Detective
Hero, 11-4 TAD 319
Krelle, Lloyd F.: letter of comment,
3 U 48
Krements, Jill: Photo Article, Rex
Stout, 6-2 MR 36
Krieger, Ellen: Werowance in the Wold,
(on Nero Wolfe), 1-2 G 54
Kroker, Alan: letter of comment,
1-3 QC 21
Krostiansen, Ralph: letter of comment,
22 X 52
Kufus, Patricia: letter of comment,
10 LR 24
Kulisheck, Patricia: letter of comment,
2-1 TAD 62
Kurzman, Dave: letter of comment,
30 X 148; 43 X 6
Kusske, John F.: letter of comment,
8 JD 14; 10 JD 12
(Kuttner, Henry), The "Common Practice"
in Science Fiction, Aspects on the
Writing of Henry Kuttner, by Leon
James, 42 X 147
Kutzner, Carl: letter of comment,
2-5 MF 58

L. Frank Baum and His Teen-Age Serials,
A Bibliographical Checklist, by
Justin G. Schiller, 2-3 BC 194
L. Ron Hubbard, a Living Legend,
(laudatory sketch), by Virgil Wilhite
and Patricia Barnes Mintz, 42 X 133
Laaksonen, Reijo: letter of comment,
21 JD 15; 22 JD 19
LaBorde, Charles: Dicks on Stage, Form
and Formula in Detective Drama,
11-3 TAD 215; 11-4 TAD 348;
12-1 TAD 83; 12-2 TAD 158; 12-3
TAD 246; 12-4 TAD 341; 13-1 TAD
69; 13-2 TAD 150; 13-3 TAD 240
Lachman, Marvin: The American Regional
Mystery, (geographical locales of
crime fiction), (New York City)
3-2 MR 23; 4-1 MR 8; (New England)
3-3 MR 13; 3-4 MR 22; (New York State)
4-3 MR 3; (New Jersey and Pennsylvania)
4-5 MR 2; (Washington D.C. and
Maryland) 5-1 MR 3; (The South) 5-3
MR 1; (Florida) 5-5 MR 1; (The Middle
West) 6-1 MR 1; (The Southwest) 6-2 MR
23; (The Mountain States, Pacific Northwest, and Alaska) 9-1 TAD 11; (Hawaii
and Northern California) 9-4 TAD 260;
(Southern California) 10-4 TAD 294

Lachman, Marvin: The American Sherlock
Holmes, A Study in Scarlet Imper-
sonation, (Holmes and Watson
protesting Craig Kennedy and Walter
Jameson's reputation as the
American Sherlock Holmes), 3-2
MR 2
Lachman, Marvin: An Unknown Mystery
Writer Revisited, Mildred Davis,
3-5 PP 12
Lachman, Marvin: Bouchercon V, (mystery
authors and fans convention report),
8-2 TAD 131
Lachman, Marvin: Bouchercon VIII,
(mystery authors and fans convention
report), 2-5 MM 3
Lachman, Marvin: Bouchercon X, (mystery
authors and fans convention report),
3-5 MF 11
Lachman, Marvin: The Case of the
Unbeaten Attorney, or, The Secret
Life of Perry Mason, 4-3 TAD 147
Lachman, Marvin: The Cases of Gideon Fell
(character of John Dickson Carr),
2-3 MF 4
Lachman, Marvin: Checklist, A.E.Martin
works, 1-3 PP 11
Lachman, Marvin: Mildred Davis, 2-5
PP 16
Lachman, Marvin: Checklist, Samm
Sinclair Baker, 4-2 PP 19
Lachman, Marvin: Commentaries for the
Curious, (on John Dickson Carr),
1 NC 13
Lachman, Marvin: Department of Unknown
Mystery Writers, (sketch),
William Krasner, 1-2 PP 11
A.E.Martin, 1-3 PP 11
Julian F. Thompson, Linda Villesvik,
Sidney Rowland, Howard F.
Aldridge, Hughes Allison,
1-4 PP 15
Frederick Ayer, Jr., 1-5 PP 17
Thomas Walsh, 2-1 PP 15
John Franklin Campbell, 2-3 PP 22
L.A.G.Strong, 2-4 PP 13
Mildred Davis, 2-5 PP 16
James Cross, 2-6 PP 17
Pat Stadley, 3-1 PP 23
Peter Godfrey, 3-2 PP 13
James O'Hanlon, 3-3 PP 15
Roy Huggins, 3-4 PP 20
Donald McNutt Douglass, 3-6 PP 11
Samm Sinclair Baker, 4-1 PP 17
Babette Rosmond, 4-2 PP 19
Ernest Savage, 4-4 PP 11; (author
response to article) 4-5/6 PP 33
Lachman, Marvin: Dramatizations of the
Great Literary Detectives and
Criminals, Pt.II (television),1-3
TAD 94; Pt.III (theatre) 1-4 TAD 132
Lachman, Marvin: Ellery Queen and His
New York, 1-3 QC 8

Lachman, Marvin: Hughes Allison Revisited, 4-1 PP 18

Lachman, Marvin: The EQMM Cover Murders, (fiction), 1-1 MF 6

Lachman, Marvin: Forgotten Men, (obscure detectives and criminals in crime fiction), 2-4 TAD 217

Lachman, Marvin: The Girls, (on secretaries to fictional detectives), 2-3 MR 6

Lachman, Marvin: It's About Crime, (books about mystery fiction) 2-4 MF 15; (reviews) 2-5 MF 3; (notes on recent reading) 2-6 MF 27; 3-2 MF 21; 3-3 MF 17; 3-4 MF 23; 4-1 MF 13; 4-3 MF 31; 4-4 MF 18; 4-5 MF 24; 4-6 MF 31; 5-1 MF 17; 5-2 MF 10; 5-3 MF 22; (new books of and about mystery) 5-4 MF 18; (notes on recent reading) 5-5 MF 17; (business and the mystery story) 5-6 MF 29

Lachman, Marvin: It's All in the Family, (a listing of first families in the mystery field), 1-6 MR 9

Lachman, Marvin: JDM in Perspective, (on John D. MacDonald), 11 JD 9

Lachman, Marvin: letter of comment, 7 JD 4; 8 JD 12; 18 JD 27; 19 JD 13; 1-1 MF 42; 1-2 MF 51; 1-4 MF 58; 1-6 MF 57; 2-2 MF 53; 2-5 MF 48; 3-1 MF 47; 3-3 MF 59; 3-4 MF 57; 4-2 MF 56; 4-5 MF 44; 5-1 MF 30; 1-6 MR 8; 2-1 MR 11; 2-3 MR 11; 4-1 MR 15; 4-3 MR 18; 4-5 MR 16; 5-4 MR 11; 1-2 PP 29; 1-4 PP 29; 3-2 PP 37; 3-3 PP 36; 3-5 PP 48; 3-6 PP 35; 4-1 PP 44; 1-1 QC 12; 1-2 QC 13; 1-4 QC 18; 1-3 TAD 107; 2-1 TAD 64; 2-3 TAD 204; 3-1 TAD 69; 3-4 TAD 306; 4-1 TAD 53; 4-4 TAD 257; 6-1 TAD 49; 7-3 TAD 223; 8-2 TAD 154; 8-4 TAD 322; 9-2 TAD 160; 9-4 TAD 321; 10-2 TAD 159; 10-4 TAD 378

Lachman, Marvin: The Life and Times of Gideon Fell, (detective character created by John Dickson Carr), 2-3 MF 3

Lachman, Marvin: The Magazine, (on ELLERY QUEEN'S MYSTERY MAGAZINE, with chronology, outstanding writers, and circulation data), 2-1 QC 6

Lachman, Marvin: The Man Who was Thursday, (Max Thursday, detective created by Wade Miller), 8-3 TAD 179

Lachman, Marvin: Margaret Millar, The Checklist of an "Unknown" Mystery Writer, 3-2 TAD 85

Lachman, Marvin: Mildred Davis Revisited, 3-6 PP 12

Lachman, Marvin: The Misadventures of Ellery Queen, (pastiches about Ellery Queen), 1-4 QC 7

Lachman, Marvin: Miscellaneous Mystery Mish-Mash, 2-1 MF 7; (California locales of filmed mysteries) 2-2 MF 19

Lachman, Marvin: Mystery Stories and the Presidency, 2-1 MR 8

Lachman, Marvin: The President and the Mystery Story, (Presidents as readers, authors, fans, and as characters), 2-3 M 6

Lachman, Marvin: Quotations from the Mysteries, 2-5 MR 18; 2-6 MR 3

Lachman, Marvin: The Real Fourth Side of the Triangle, (speculative, Della Street's affair with Archie Goodwin), 9 MN A11

Lachman, Marvin: Rebuttal to Michael Avallone's "Kiss My Deadly Typewriter #539," 3-1 QC 14

Lachman, Marvin: Religion and Detection, (religion as mystery background), 1-1 TAD 19

Lachman, Marvin: Samm Sinclair Baker Revisited, 4-2 PP 19

Lachman, Marvin: Sports and the Mystery Story, (tennis) 6-1 TAD 1; (prize-fighting and bull-fighting) 6-2 TAD 83; (baseball and basketball) 6-4 TAD 243; (football) 7-3 TAD 195; (golf) 7-4 TAD 261; (cricket) 8-1 TAD 108

Lachman, Marvin: The Ultimate Hi-Jacking Novel, (ransom in mystery plots, with checklist), 2-2 PP 17

Lachman, Marvin: Virgil Tibbs and the American Negro in Mystery Fiction, 1-3 TAD 86

Lachman, Marvin: The Wit and Wisdom of the Mystery Story, Quotations from the Mysteries, 1A MF 3; 1-4 MF 7

Lachman, Marvin, and Harold Knott: Pocket Books, Checklist 1-500, (paperbacks published by Pocket Books), 1-6 MF 20

Lachman, Marvin, and Charles Shibuk: What the World Waited For, (revised "indefinite" checklist of basic mystery fiction), 9-3 TAD 203

(Lachman, Marvin), Lachman's Reviews in THE MYSTERY FANCIER Volumes 2-4, by David H. Doerrer, 5-2 MF 6

(Lachman, Marvin), Meet the Author: Marvin Lachman, by Allen J. Hubin, 1-1 TAD 24

Lackritz, Richard M.: letter of comment, 7-3 TAD 232; 8-2 TAD 160; 8-4 TAD 313; 13-1 TAD 78; 30 X 149

LaCross, John K.J.: letter of comment, 28 JD 40

Ladies in Crime, (mystery quiz), by Veronica M.S.Kennedy, 7-2 TAD 94

Ladies of the Tube, (mystery on television), by Paul Bishop, 3-1 M 53

Lady Cop, (women in law enforcement), by Paul Bishop, 3-1 M 18

Lady in a Straightjacket, (on MYSTERY BOOK Magazine), by Frank D. McSherry, Jr., 9-3 TAD 201

Lady in Waiting, (verse re: John D. MacDonald), by Ethel D. Compton, 24 JD 41

La Filza di Thorndyke, (foreign translations and editions of Dr. Thorndyke stories by R. Austin Freeman), by Ian Arnott, 3 TF 28

Laidlaw, Bill: A Few Non-Medical Thoughts, 1 DQ 5

Laidlaw, Bill: A Recurring Little Villain, (Cadwiller Olden in Doc Savage and The Avenger stories, pulp magazines), 5 DQ 9

Laidlaw, Bill: All in One World, (legendary facts), 7 DQ 9

Laidlaw, Bill: Clark Savage, Sr., Retired British Secret Agent, (Doc Savage pastiche, fiction), 2 DQ 7; 3 DQ 10; 4 DQ 10; 5 DQ 15; 6 DQ 11

Laidlaw, Bill: The Doc Savage Diet, (food and eating habits of Doc Savage in the stories), 3 DQ 9

Laidlaw, Bill: Doc Savage in Alphabetical Order, (checklist of stories), 2 DQ 3

Laidlaw, Bill: Doc Savage Pulps and Books, (comparison checklist of the original novels and the reprint paperbound books), 1 DQ 6

Laidlaw, Bill: First Class Transportation in the 1930's - The Lone Survivor, (on "the last locomotive"), 5 DQ 7

Laidlaw, Bill: How Much Do You Know? (quiz, Doc Savage), 3 DQ 15; 4 DQ 9

Laidlaw, Bill: The Man of Mystery, (John Montague as the real Doc Savage?), 2 DQ 5

Laidlaw, Bill: The Red Baron, The Avenger, and Doc Savage, (hero comparison essay) 3 DQ 4

Laidlaw, Bill: Tarzan's Greater - A Historical View, (commentary), 7 DQ 16

Laidlaw, Bill: Terror for the Navy, (the mysterious ocean current changes in 1923), 4 DQ 3

(Laing, Alexander: THE CADAVER OF GIDEON WYCK), Horror, Detection and Footnotes, by Edward Lauterbach, 3-1 TAD 12

Lamb, J.J.: letter of comment, 1-3 M 4; 3 PE 33

(Lamb, J.J.: Zach Rolfe series), The Trenchcoat Files, by Paul Bishop, 3 PE 15

Lamb, Margaret: Expressionism and American Popular Literature, Hammett as a Continental Op-Eye, 2-1 C 26

Lament for a Legend - Lizzie Borden Revisited, (famous true crime discussed), by Mary D. Smith, 11-2 TAD 132

Lamont, Joyce H.: letter of comment, 1-3 PQ 8

(L'Amour, Louis), Louis L'Amour's Pseudonymous Works, by John D. Nesbitt, 3-3 PQ 3

Lamp of God, The, (Ellery Queen's "The Lamp of God"), by Thomas Godfrey, 12-3 TAD 212

(LAMP OF GOD, THE: Ellery Queen), The Lamp of God, by Thomas Godfrey, 12-3 TAD 212

Lancer Books - Checklist, (paperbound book publisher), by Bill Denholm, 1-2 CP 26; (additions), 1-4 CP 16

Lancer Science Fiction Checklist, (bibliography of Lancer SF, Lodestone, and Magnum paperbacks), by William J. Denholm III, 10 SF 4

Lancer Science Fiction Artists, (list of cover artists, Lancer Books), by William J. Denholm III, 10 SF 25

Land That Maple White Found, The, (THE LOST WORLD: A.Conan Doyle), by Arn McConnell, 1-1 WA 7

Landau, Jan: letter of comment, 1-4 CP 1; 2-2 PQ 4; 3-1 PQ 4; 4-2 PQ 52; 40 X 85

Landers, Edward J.: letter of comment, 2-1 TBN 5

Lane, Thomas D.: Dignity in the Detective Novel, 1-1 C 119

Landfried, Paul: letter of comment, 6-3 TAD 201

Lang, Brad: letter of comment, 9-4 TAD 297

(Lang, Fritz), Obituary, by J. Mark Purcell, 9-4 TAD 288

Language of the Praed Street Irregulars, The, (Solar Pons, glossary), by Michael Harrison, 2-4 PD 1

Lanham, Cathryn: A Dream of Reason, The Great Detective as True Believer, (classic detectives and logical thinking), 2-2 C 23

(Lansbury, Angela), Angela, A Chat With Angela Lansbury, Star of Stage, Screen and Television, by Pete Christian, 3-1 M 32

Lansdale, Joe R.: letter of comment, 2-2 M 2; 1-5 MF 53; 2-3 MF 61; 2-4 MF 58; 2-5 MF 47; 2-6 MF 47; 3-1 MF 56; 3-2 MF 51; 3-3 MF 51; 4-2 MF 58; 2 PE 45; 3 PE 36; 4 PE 32; 5 PE 33; 6 PE 35; 4-1 PP 45; 4-3 PP 31; 4-4 PP 36

Lansdale, Joe R.: The Round Robin Caper, or, The Too Long Goodbye, (round robin fiction) Pt.1, 5 PE 5; Pt.2 by Ralph Diffinetti, 5 PE 5; Pt.3 by R. Jeff Banks, 6 PE 26; Pt.4 by David Rose, 8 PE 9

LaPorte, Karen: letter of comment, 4-3 MF 47

Larsen, Carl: letter of comment, 3-3 MF 54; 4-1 MF 46; 4-6 MF 50; 5-1 MF 46

Larsen, Carl: Old Time Radio Lives, (Look for It in the Morning Express!) 4-6 MF 9; ("Saints Preserve Us, Mr. Keen!") 4-5 MF 18; (Boston Blackie radio serials) 5-6 MF 3

Larsen, Hans: letter of comment, 6-1 TAD 59

(Larkin, Bob), The Newest Doc Savage Cover Artist, by Frank Lewandowski, 1 DS 12

(Laser Books), A Failed Experiment: The
Laser Books, History and Checklist,
(analysis and bibliography of short-
lived science-fiction paperback line),
by Keith L. Justice, 15 SF 4

Lassner, Allan S.: letter of Comment.
10 JD 17

Last But Not Least, (discusses stories
in which the last words are the name
of the killer), by J.R.Christopher,
4-1 TAD 11

(LAST CELT, THE: Glenn Lord), New Book
Released about Robert E. Howard, by
Tevis Clyde Smith, 1-1 PQ 33

(LAST DOORBELL, THE: Joseph Harrington),
Joseph Harrington's First Three
Books, by R.W.Hays, 4-2 TAD 104

Last Encounter, The, (Fu Manchu and
Sir Denis Nayland Smith), by James
Wade, 1-2 PDA 66

(LAST KNOWN ADDRESS, THE: Joseph
Harrington), Joseph Harrington's
First Three Books, by R.W.Hays,
4-2 TAD 104

Last Meeting of the Butlers Club, The,
(Dr. Thorndyke pastiche), by Geoffrey
Bush, 12 TF 13

Last Thousand, The, (experiences in
selling personal book collection),
by Basil Wells, 5 U 24

Last Year, The, (the "Golden Age" of
mystery fiction), by Mary Groff,
11-2 TAD 145

Late Novels of Harry Stephen Keeler, The;
A Preliminary Checklist, by Francis
M. Nevins, Jr., 3-2 TAD 74

(Latham, Grace, series: Leslie Ford),
The First Appearance, Grace Latham,
(ILL MET BY MOONLIGHT), by Maryell
Cleary, 2-4 PP 27

Latham, Larry: letter of comment,
26 X 77

Lathen, Emma: A Settling of Accounts,
(re: "Dallas" television show),
9 LR 25

(Lathen, Emma), A View from Wall Street:
Social Critcism in the Mystery
Novels of Emma Lathen, by Jane S.
Bakerman, 9-3 TAD 213

(Lathen, Emma), Comic Construction in
the Novels of Emma Lathen and R.B.
Dominic, by David Brownell, 9-2
TAD 91

(Lathen, Emma), Women and Wall Street:
Portraits of Women in Novels by
Emma Lathen, by Jane S. Bakerman,
8-1 TAD 36

(Latimer, Jonathan W.), Bibliography
and Checklist, by Jim McCahery,
11 SF 20

(Latimer, Jonathan W.), Filmography
Checklist, by Jim McCahery,
11 SF 21

(Latimer, Jonathan W.), Jonathan W.
Latimer, An Interview, by Jim
McCahery, 11 SF 16

(Latimer, Jonathan W.: William Crane
series), Checklist, by Jim McCahery,
1 PE 6; 2 PE 13

(Latimer, Jonathan W.: William Crane
series), Series Spotlight,
Jonathan Latimer's William Crane,
by Jim McCahery, 1 PE 5; 2 PE 5

Latimer, Paul S.: Blue and Gold 1916
(Frederick Faust in University of
California Yearbook), 2-1 FC 9

(Latin-America), The Detective Literature of the Americas, by Donald A.
Yates, 4-1 TAD 5

Laughlin, Charlotte: A Conversation
with the de Camps (L. Sprague de
Camp & Catherine Crook de Camp),
1-1 PQ 16

Laughlin, Charlotte: Checklist, Dell
Publishing Company's Murder Ink
& Scene of the Crime Series,
(paperback), 3-4 PQ 15

Laughlin, Charlotte: Collecting Armed
Services Editions (paperbacks),
1-2 PQ 31

Laughlin, Charlotte: Dell Mysteries,
Murder Ink and Scene of the Crime
(paperback series), 3-4 PQ 13

Laughlin, Charlotte: Robert E.Howard's
Library, An Annotated Checklist,
1-1 PQ 23; 1-2 PQ 51; 1-3 PQ 43;
1-4 PQ 55

Laughlin, Charlotte: Zebra Stinks!
(criticism of the Zebra Books
paperback series), 2-3 PQ 49

Laughlin, Charlotte, and Bill Crider:
Paperback Blurbs, (book cover
advertising, paperbacks), 4-2
PQ 3

Laughlin, Charlotte, and Billy C. Lee:
Alfred Hitchcock - Dell Paperbacks,
(Hitchcock in Dell paperback
editions), 3-1 PQ 23

(Laune, Paul), Hardy Boys Illustrators,
Paul Laune, (boys' books), 4 MA 22

Lauritzen, Robert L.: letter of
comment, 4-1 TAD 60; 5-1 TAD 58;
6-1 TAD 47; 10-2 TAD 163

Lauterbach, Edward S.: The Adventure
of the Purloined Red Herring, (THE
PROFESSOR KNITS A SHROUD: Martha
Wirt Davis), 3-5 PP 3

Lauterbach, Edward S.: Annotating the
Holmes Saga, 7-2 TAD 119

Lauterbach, Edward S.: Fu Manchu Thinks
Kindly of Sir Denis Nayland Smith,
(verse), 1-2 PDA 48

Lauterbach, Edward S.: Gibson's Non-
Shadow Detective, (fiction by Walter
Gibson other than The Shadow), 6-1
TAD 33

Lauterbach, Edward S.: Horror, Detection
and Footnotes, (Alexander Laing:
THE CADAVER OF GIDEON WYCK), 3-1
TAD 12

Lauterbach, Edward S.: Invisible Man,
U.S.A., Some Pulp Prototypes,
3-4 TAD 241

Lauterbach, Edward S.: Jack the R.I.P.,
(verse), 1-2 PDA 79
Lauterbach, Edward S.: letter of comment,
4-2 MR 14; 5-2 MR 21; 5-4 MR 9;
6-2 MR 16; 1-6 PP 30; 2-1 PP 34;
2-2 PP 34; 2-5 PP 43; 3-2 PP 37;
3-3 PP 39; 3-6 PP 34; 4-1 PP 49;
13 R 31; 2-1 TAD 65; 2-4 TAD 278;
3-3 TAD 206; 4-2 TAD 132; 4-4 TAD
257; 5-1 TAD 42; 5-3 TAD 182; 5-4
TAD 244; 6-1 TAD 57; 7-1 TAD 47;
7-2 TAD 147; 8-3 TAD 233; 9-1
TAD 81; 9-2 TAD 160; 10-3 TAD
283; 12-3 TAD 269; 2-1 TB 4
Lauterbach, Edward S.: Lovecraft in the
British Thriller, (H.P.Lovecraft),
2-2 TAD 102
Lauterbach, Edward S.: The Mysterious
Card Unsealed, (THE MYSTERIOUS CARD
UNSEALED: Cleveland Moffett), 4-1
TAD 41
Lauterbach, Edward S.: One Britisher's
View of Hammett, (review of Dashiell
Hammett's THE THIN MAN in a London
paper), 4-5/6 PP 44
Lauterbach, Edward S.: Our Heroes in
Motley, (crime humor), 9-3 TAD 178
Lauterbach, Edward S.: Smorgasbord
Thriller, (THE SECRET MASTERS: Gerald
Kersh), 4-3 TAD 165
Lauterbach, Edward S.: Sturrock's Duty,
(Jeremy Sturrock series: J.G.
Jeffreys), 3-6 PP 5
Lauterbach, Edward S.: Those Lovely,
Detailed Paperback Covers, 4-1 PP 16
Lauterbach, Edward S.: Wise Detective
Stories, (by Thomas J. Wise), 5-3
TAD 146
Lauterbach, Edward S.: Wolfe and the
Law, (on Nero Wolfe), 3-2 TAD 114
Lauterbach, Edward S., and Karen
Lauterbach: The Crossword Puzzle
Metaphor and Some Crossword Puzzle
Mysteries, 10-2 TAD 167
Lauterbach, Karen:letter of comment,
4-4 TAD 252; 8-2 TAD 156
Law and the Shadow, The, (legal position
of selling tape recordings of radio
shows), by Jack Gilbert, 4 BS 6
Law, Lawyers and Justice in the Novels
of Joe L. Hensley, by Robert A.
Frauenglas, 4-1 MF 3
Lawrence Block, Annotated Checklist of
the Tanner Series Books, by R. Jeff
Banks, 5/6 MN 7
(Lawrence, John), Partial Checklist,
by Francis M. Nevins, Jr., 21 X 4
(Lawrence, John), The Marquis of
Unremembered Manhunters, by Francis
M. Nevins, Jr., 21 X 3
(Lawton, Frank S.), The Case of the
Elusive Author, by Dick Myers,
10 BS 14
(Lawton, Capt. Wilbur), The Boy Aviators,
(boys series by Lawton), by Robert
Jennings, 3 BB 13

(LAY ON, MacDUFF!: Charlotte Armstrong),
The First Appearance, MacDougall
Duff, by Maryell Cleary, 3-1 PP 27
Layman, Richard: letter of comment,
8-1 TAD 74
(Layman, Richard: DASHIELL HAMMETT, A
DESCRIPTIVE BIBLIOGRAPHY), The
BLACK MASK Boys Go Legit, by William
F. Nolan, 13-1 TAD 23
(Leasor, Paul: Dr. Jason Love series),
Checklist, Annotated, by Barry
Van Tilburg, 4-4 MF 16
LeBlanc, Edward T.: letter of comment,
2 MA 26
LeCarre, Deighton, Hall and the
Screen's Tired Spies, (filmed spy
fiction), by Jack Edmund Nolan,
4-1 MR 23
(LeCarre, John), Checklist, Spy Novels,
Annotated List, by R. Jeff Banks
and Harry D. Dawson, 2-5 MF 22
(LeCarre, John), The Fathers and Sons
of John LeCarre, by Harry D. Dawson,
5-3 MF 15
(LeCarre, John), John LeCarre's Circus,
(spy fiction novels), by Harry D.
Dawson, 13-2 TAD 150
(LeCarre, John), LeCarre, Deighton,
Hall and the Screen's Tired Spies,
(filmed spy fiction), by Jack
Edmund Nolan, 4-1 MR 23
(Le Carre, John), LeCarre's Spy Novels,
by R.Jeff Banks and Harry D.Dawson,
2-5 MF 22
(LeCarre, John), The Spy Fiction of
John LeCarre, by Richard W. Noland,
1-2 C 54
(LeCarre,John: George Smiley series),
Checklist, Annotated, by Barry
Van Tilburg, 4-3 MF 27
(LeCarre,John: George Smiley series),
George Smiley - The Reluctant Hero,
by Holly Beth King, 2-1 C 70
LeCarre's Spy Novels, by R.Jeff Banks
and Harry D. Dawson, 2-5 MF 22
Lee, Billy C.: Ian Fleming, Alias
James Bond, (literary sketch on
Fleming), 4-1 PQ 41
Lee, Billy C.: letter of comment,
1-2 PQ 7
Lee, Billy C.: Reprints/Reprints - LOST
HORIZON by James Hilton (paperback
editions), 3-1 PQ 37
Lee, Billy C.: The War Over Middle
Earth, (re: LORD OF THE RINGS by
J.R.R.Tolkien, in paperback editions),
1-4 PQ 37
Lee, Billy C., and Bill Crider: Some
Notes on Movie Editions (paperbacks),
2-1 PQ 29
Lee, Billy C., and Charlotte Laughlin:
Alfred Hitchcock - Dell Paperbacks,
(paperback editions), 3-1 PQ 23
Lee, Dan: letter of comment, 24 X 47;
36 X 72
(Lee, Edward Edson), see Leo Edwards

Lee, Eugene E.: Earliest Picture of Leo Edwards, (boys' books author; by his son), 3-4 BC 360

Lee, Eugene E.: Leo Edwards, (sketch by son of boys' books author), 1-3 BC 92

Lee, Eugene E.: Leo Edwards Magazine Stories, (writings of Leo Edwards pre-book series), 1-2 BC 63

Lee, Eugene E.: Letters and Photo of Leo Edwards, (reminiscent photo article and sketch by son of boys' books author), 3-2 BC 314

Lee, Eugene E.: letter of comment, 1-2 BC 62; 1-4 TBN 5; 2-4 TBN 5

Lee, Manfred B.: letter of comment, 1-2 QC 14; 1-3 TAD 107; 2-3 TAD 202; 4-2 TAD 129

(Lee, Manfred B.), Memorial Tribute, by Robert E. Washer, 4-4 MR 2

(Lee, Manfred B.), see Ellery Queen

Lee, Timothy Jason: letter of comment, 1-2 M 3

Lee, William G.: letter of comment, 5-3 MR 13

Legacy, (verse), by Margaret Haley Carpenter, 2-3/4 AD 9

(LEGACY, THE: Jimmy Sangster), Mystery Plus: A Movie Review, by R. Jeff Banks, 3-3 PP 17

Legal Lunacy, (odd laws), by Richard Moskowitz, 6/7 LR 3; 8 LR 4

Legend of Crimpen Mire, The, (verse, Sherlockiana), by Fred Jaeger, 2-1 PDA 27

Legend of the Unicorn, The, by Michael L. Cook, 1 U 4

Leg Work, (mystery news), 1-3 M 5; 2-1 M 3; 2-2 M 4; 2-3 M 4; 3-1 M 4; 3-2 M 4

(LeFanu, J. Sheridan), Checklist, by David Brownell, 9-3 TAD 197

(LeFanu, J. Sheridan), Wicked Dreams, The World of Sheridan LeFanu, by David Brownell, 9-3 TAD 191

(LEGEND OF THE LONE RANGER: Gary McCarthy), Recent Lone Ranger Story a Mess, (critical comments), by I.R.Ybarra, 6 MA 8

(Leggett, William), Buckskins and Ballistics, William Leggett and the American Detective Story, by John Seelye, 1-3 MR 3

Legless Runner, The, (excerpt from DEATH OF A .300 HITTER, by Michael Avallone), 6 X 8

Leiber, Fritz: Lovecraft in My Life, (reminiscences of H.P.Lovecraft), 1 HP 5

Leiber, Fritz: The Stage in My Stories, (frequent use of stage as background discussed by author), 1 HP 11

Leigh Brackett, Storyteller, by James Ellis, 42 X 27

Leimbacher, Ed: letter of comment, 5 PE 35

(Leinster, Murray), An Interview with Murray Leinster, by Will Jenkins, (Leinster is pseudonym of Jenkins) from FANTASY Magazine, Sept.1934, 15 X 6

(Leinster, Murray), Some Bibliographic Listings in American Pulp Magazines, 15 X 9

Leithead, J. Edward: Now They're Collector's Items, (on boy's book collecting, and authors), 1-1 BC 13; 1-2 BC 44; 1-3 BC 72; 1-4 BC 114; 2-1 BC 154; 2-2 BC 187; 2-3 BC 205

Leithead, J. Edward: Prolific, (on boys' books author, Harry St.George Rathborne), 2-1 BC 142

(Leithead, J. Edward), In Memoriam, (obituary), 2-1 BC 133

Leland, Doc: letter of comment, 2-4 TBN 4

Lellenberg, Jon L.: Commentaries for the Curious, (on John Dickson Carr), 1 NC 15

Lellenberg, Jon L.: The Humbugging of Solar Pons, (as by Ebenezer Snawley, on Mycroft & Moran, Publishers' revisions), 3-2 PDA 11

Lellenberg, Jon L.: Knowledge of the Occult - Immense, (on Solar Pons in stories by August Derleth), 2-2 PDA 52

(Lem, Stanislaw), The Science Fiction Mystery Novels of Asimov, Bester and Lem, Fusions and Foundations, by Steven R. Carter, 1-1 C 109

(Lem, Stanislaw), Stanislaw Lem and John Dickson Carr, Critics of the Scientific World-View, (comparison of works of the two authors), by Edmund Miller, 14-4 TAD 341

(Lem, Stanislaw), Threats to Rationalism, John Dowles, Stanislaw Lem, and the Detective Story, (the inexplicable solved), by Frank Occhiogrosso, 13-1 TAD 4

Leman, Bob: Paint the Coffin Fuchsia, (John D. MacDonald parody), 9 JD 26

Len Deighton Series, The, by R. Jeff Banks and Harry D. Dawson, 3-1 MF 10

(Lend-a-Hand Boys), The Lend-a-Hand Boys Series, A Review, by Robert L. George, (boys' books), 3-2 BC 312

Lent, Stephen L.: letter of comment, 11 JD 26

Lenzi, Linda: letter of comment, 6 MA 29

Leo Edwards, (sketch of boys' books author by his son), by Eugene E. Lee, 1-3 BC 92

Leo Edwards and His Books, (commentary on boys' books author), by Julius R. Chenu, 3 BB 7; 1-2 YB 15

Leo Edwards and the First Person Singular, (hero writes as first person singular in boys' books by Edwards), by John T. Dizer, 1-4 YB 6

Leo Edwards' Bird Watchers Society, (boys' books by Edwards, club), by Julius R. Chenu, 2-2 TB 1

Leo Edwards Magazine Stories, (pre-books writings by Edwards discussed by his son), by Eugene E. Lee, 1-2 BC 63

Leon, Steven J.: letter of comment, 40 X 86

(Leonard, Charles: Paul Kilgerrin series), Checklist, Annotated, by Barry Van Tilburg, 4-4 MF 17

Leonard, Mark R.: letter of comment, 11 DS 19

Leopard Lady, The, (pulp villainess in Secret Agent X stories by G.T.Fleming-Roberts), by Tom Johnson, 8 DS 16

LeQueux, William: Donovan of Whitehall, (Classic Corner Rare Tales, fiction), 14-1 TAD 44

Leslie Charteris and the Saint, Five Decades of Partnership, by Jan Alexandersson and Iwan Hedman, 4-4 MF 21

Lesser, Tom: letter of comment, 2-1 CP 5

Lesser, Tom: Paperback Collector's Con III, (report on paperback book collectors' convention), 1-5 CP 34

Lester Dent, (reminiscent sketch), by Frank Gruber, 2-4 TAD 215

Lester Dent, Adventurer, (sketch on Doc Savage author), 1 BSA 21

Lester Dent, The Last of the Joe Shaw's BLACK MASK Boys, (Dent in BLACK MASK pulp detective magazine), by Will Murray, 2-2 C 128

(Lester, Pauline), see Josephine Chase

Let There Be Music, (verse), by Sister M. Anaclete, 2-2 AD 7

"Let's Face It!" - A Look at the Disguises of Operator 5 During the Purple Invasion, (pulp magazine series), by Wooda Nicholas Carr, 3 U 3

Let's Look at Gothics, by Miriam Lynch, 2-2 MR 13

Letson, Russell: letter of comment, 36 X 71

Letter to August Derleth, (verse), by Jesse Stuart, 2-1 AD 1

Letter to Sherlock, and Annotations, (Sherlockiana), by Julian L. Biggers, 6 R 7

Letters, (of comment from readers), 1-4 AD 8; 2-1 AD 12; 2-2 AD 9; 2-3/4 AD 14; 2 BB 21; 3 BB 23; 5 BB 21; 6 BB 29; 1-2 BC 62; 1-3 BC 85; 16 CD 12; 7 CL 10; 9 CL 10; 10 CL 11; 12 CL 10; 7 DQ 3; 2 DS 6; 3 DS 5; 4 DS 3; 5 DS 5; 6 DS 6; 7 DS 5; 9 DS 21; 10 DS 5; 11 DS 5; 12 DS 5; 1-2 G 67; 5 LR 5; 6/7 LR 16; 8 LR 7; 2 LW 1; 3 LW 3; 4 LW 1; 5 LW 1; 1-2 M 3; 1-3 M 4; 2-3 M 2; 3-1 M 2; 3 MA 25; 6 MA 28;

Letters, (continued), 7 MA 22; 2 MA 26; 4 MA 24; 5 MA 26; 3 MT 25; 6 P 29; 1-2 PQ 3; 1-3 PQ 3; 2-1 PQ 3; 2-2 PQ 3; 2-3 PQ 3; 3-1 PQ 3; 3-2 PQ 3; 3-3 PQ 51; 3-4 PQ 46; 4-1 PQ 51; 60 PU 31; 62 PU 10; 63 PU 42; 64 PU 25; 65 PU 19; 66 PU 64; 67 PU 54; 68 PU 24; 69 PU 27; 70 PU 29; 74 PU 28; 18 R 17; 2 SF 39; 4 SF 41; 5 SF 28; 6 SF 48; 8 SF 44; 11 SF 48; 12 SF 28; 14 SF 47; 1-1 TAD 29; 1-2 TAD 63; 1-3 TAD 104; 1-4 TAD 152; 2-1 TAD 62; 2-2 TAD 123; 2-3 TAD 199; 2-4 TAD 275; 3-1 TAD 59; 3-2 TAD 134; 3-3 TAD 203; 3-4 TAD 275; 4-1 TAD 52; 4-2 TAD 124; 4-3 TAD 180; 4-4 TAD 246; 5-1 TAD 42; 5-2 TAD 106; 5-3 TAD 167; 5-4 TAD 234; 6-1 TAD 45; 6-2 TAD 119; 6-3 TAD 192; 6-4 TAD 272; 7-1 TAD 43; 7-1 TAD 64; 7-2 TAD 144; 7-3 TAD 223; 7-4 TAD 298; 8-1 TAD 68; 8-2 TAD 152; 8-3 TAD 231; 8-4 TAD 312; 9-1 TAD 75; 9-2 TAD 155; 9-3 TAD 167; 9-4 TAD 247; 9-3 TAD 232; 9-3 TAD 236; 9-3 TAD 238; 10-3 TAD 195; 11-2 TAD 108; 11-3 TAD 212; 11-4 TAD 316; 12-1 TAD 91; 12-2 TAD 186; 12-3 TAD 266; 12-4 TAD 353; 13-1 TAD 76; 13-2 TAD 158; 13-3 TAD 237; 13-4 TAD 342; 14-1 TAD 71; 14-2 TAD 185; 14-3 TAD 247; 14-4 TAD 381; 2 TF 32; 3 TF 52; 10 TF 30; 2 U 48; 5 U 62; 6 U 48; 1-1 WA 10; 4 WT 12; 5 WT 31; 6 WT 31; 5 X 41; 13 X 58; 14 X 62; 15 X 13; 16 X 5; 17 X 61; 22 X 49; 24 X 12; 24 X 44; 26 X 72; 28 X 78; 30 X 148; 33 X 113; 36 X 70; 38 X 143; 40 X 85; 43 X 5; 1-2 YB 23; 1-3 YB 11; 1-4 YB 9; 1-5 YB 20; 1-6 YB 9

(Letters), Box 35, (letters of comment from readers), 2 FM 18

(Letters), The Bull Pen, (letters of comment from readers), 1-2 CP 2; 1-4 CP 1; 1-5 CP 1; 1-6 CP 1; 2-1 CP 1; 2-2 CP 1; 2-3 CP 1; 2-4 CP 1; 2-5 CP 1; 3-1 CP 2; 3-2 CP 1; 3-3 CP 1; 3-4 CP 1; 3-5 CP 1

(Letters), Comments and Queries, (letters of comment from readers), 1-5 MR 14; 1-6 MR 8; 2-1 MR 11; 2-2 MR 15; 2-3 MR 11; 2-5 MR 12; 2-6 MR 14; 3-1 MR 15; 3-2 MR 16; 3-3 MR 11; 3-4 MR 33; 3-5 MR 35; 3-6 MR 9; 4-1 MR 18; 4-2 MR 14; 4-3 MR 18; 4-4 MR 14; 4-5 MR 16; 4-6 MR 16; 5-1 MR 14; 5-2 MR 16; 5-3 MR 13; 5-4 MR 9; 5-5 MR 16; 5-6 MR 15; 6-1 MR 19; 6-2 MR 15

(Letters), Comments on the Corpus, (letters of comment from readers), 1-2 QC 12; 1-3 QC 19; 1-4 QC 17; 2-1 QC 16; 2-2 QC 12

(Letters), The Documents in the Case,
(letters of comment from readers),
1-1 MF 39; 1-2 MF 47; 1-3 MF 51;
1-4 MF 55; 1-5 MF 53; 1-6 MF 55;
2-1 MF 50; 2-2 MF 41; 2-3 MF 57;
2-4 MF 49; 2-5 MF 45; 2-6 MF 43;
3-1 MF 46; 3-2 MF 50; 3-3 MF 50;
3-4 MF 53; 3-5 MF 46; 4-1 MF 37;
4-2 MF 54; 4-3 MF 47; 4-4 MF 49;
4-5 MF 44; 4-6 MF 40; 5-1 MF 30;
5-2 MF 39; 5-3 MF 41; 5-4 MF 38;
5-5 MF 44; 5-6 MF 49

(Letters), Inside Mystery, (letters
of comment from readers), 2-2 M 2

(Letters), Letters to/from Limehouse,
(letters of comment from readers),
2 R 22; 3 R 28; 4 R 24; 5 R 31;
6 R 21; 7 R 27; 8 R 31; 9 R 31;
10 R 31; 11 R 23; 12 R 23; 13 R
23; 14 R 27; 15 R 27; 17 R 21

(Letters), Meteor Writes, (letters of
comment from readers), 1-2 WA 13

(Letters), Mystery Views, (letters of
comment from readers), 6 MY 2;
7 MY 11

(Letters), see Our Chatterbox

(Letters), Pen Letters, (letters of
comment from readers), 1-1 PP 26;
1-2 PP 25; 1-2 PP 31; 1-3 PP 31;
1-4 PP 29; 1-5 PP 24; 1-6 PP 27;
2-2 PP 30; 2-3 PP 37; 2-4 PP 38;
2-5 PP 39; 2-6 PP 40; 3-1 PP 37;
3-2 PP 32; 3-3 PP 35; 3-4 PP 37;
3-5 PP 45; 3-6 PP 32; 4-1 PP 40;
4-2 PP 33; 4-3 PP 30; 4-4 PP 32;
4-5/6 PP 82

(Letters), Please Write for Details,
(letters of comment from readers),
6 JD 9; 7 JD 3; 8 JD 5; 9 JD 5;
10 JD 8; 11 JD 13; 12 JD 13;
13 JD 11; 14 JD 21; 15 JD 21;
16 JD 15; 17 JD 23; 18 JD 21;
19 JD 11; 20 JD 19; 21 JD 15;
22 JD 19; 24 JD 38; 25 JD 37;
26 JD 46; 27 JD 34; 28 JD 40

(Letters), Ragged Edges, (letters
of comment from readers), 2 D 48

(Letters), Strictly Private,
(letters of comment from readers),
2 PE 36; 3 PE 32; 4 PE 28; 5 PE
33; 6 PE 33; 7 PE 16

(Letters), Things That Go Bump in
the Mailbox, (letters of comment
from readers), 5/6 MN 11; 7 MN 5;
8 MN 29; 9 MN L1;11 MN L1; 12 MN
L1; 13 MN L1

(Letters), Subject Index to TAD's
Letters Columns, Vol.1-5, (in
THE ARMCHAIR DETECTIVE), by
Robert E. Briney, 3-4 TAD 282

Letters to a Collector, (advice on
boys' books collecting), by S.E.
Wallen, 3-1 BC 265; 3-2 BC 303;
3-3 BC 331; 3-4 BC 380; 4-1 BC
396

LeValley, Norma: Hitchcock the
Anthologer, 2-3 M 36

Levang, Helen: letter of comment,
5-1 TAD 58

Leventhal, Steve: letter of comment,
26 X 73

Leventhal, Steve: Why I Collect Science
Fiction, 20 X 7

(Levin, Ira), Checklist of works,
3-1 MR 11

(Levin, Ira), The Ending of ROSEMARY'S
BABY and Other Comments from Ira
Levin, (interview), 3-1 MR 9

Levitt, Dan: letter of comment,
1-5 CP 1

Levy, Mark: The Most Wanted Man,(on
Solar Pons), 2-4 PD 1

Levy, Vivian: letter of comment,
28 JD 41

Lew Archer's "Moral Landscape" (social
atmosphere of detective character
of Ross Macdonald), by Elmer R.
Pry, Jr., 8-1 TAD 104

Lewandowski, Frank: Doc Savage Lives!
(commentary), 1 DS 7

Lewandowski, Frank: Doc Savage -
Suspended! (on the cessation of
Doc Savage paperback reprints),
2 DS 5

Lewandowski, Frank: Interview with
the King of the Pulp Artists,
Walter M. Baumhofer, 9 DS 12

Lewandowski, Frank: The Newest Doc
Savage Artist, (on Bob Larkin),
1 DS 12

Lewandowski, Frank: Some Unusual Facts
about Lester Dent, 1 DS 6

Lewandowski, Frank: Who is Doc Savage?
(speculative essay), 1 DS 3

Lewandowski, Joseph: An Index to DR.
YEN SIN, (pulp magazine), 4 U 32

Lewandowski, Joseph: Cover Montage of
Photos of The Shadow, 4 U 18

Lewandowski, Joseph: letter of comment,
7 DQ 5; 4 U 52; 6 U 48; 38 X 144;
43 X 6

Lewandowski, Joseph: The Telephone (an
association item, The Shadow),
6 U 2

(Lewin, Michael Z.), Conversation, Pt.
VII, (interview with Lewin), by Don
Cole, 3-3 PP 13

Lewis, Caleb A.: Interview with Howard
Browne, 11-2 TAD 172

Lewis, Caleb A.: Iwan Hedman, An Interview, 13-2 TAD 166

Lewis, Caleb A.: Mystery Stories -
Report to the Stockholders, (on
The Mystery Library book series),
10-1 TAD 50

Lewis, Caleb A.: The Return of Paul
Pine, (Paul Pine, detective: Howard
Browne), 11-1 TAD 79

Lewis, Caleb A.: Whowunit? International Crime Spree Rocks New York (report of 2nd International Congress of Crime Writers), 11-2 TAD 153

(Lewis, Cecil Day), Cecil Day Lewis Named Poet Laureate of England, by Allen J. Hubin, 1-2 TAD 62

Lewis, Dave: The Backbone of Black Mask, (Frederick Nebel's detective stories in BLACK MASK pulp magazine, with checklist), 2-2 C 118

Lewis, Dave: Christ No, Hell Yes, (on censorship in paperbacks), 2-4 CP 6

Lewis, Dave: letter of comment, 2-1 CP 5; 2-2 CP 4; 3-3 CP 3

Lewis, Dave, and Bruce Taylor: Rare Books are Getting Scarce, (on defunct detective characters), 2-5 CP 19

Lewis, David Marshall: Don't Tell Me I Won't Like It, (on critics and literary criticism), 12 LR 12

Lewis, Shelly: Interview, Dorothy Salisbury Davis, 1-2 M 8

Lewis, Shelly: Interview with Aaron Marc Stein, 1-2 M 23

Lewis, Sinclair: The Sac of Fortune, (re: August Derleth), 4-2 AD 1

(Lewis, Sinclair), August Derleth's Reply to "The Sac of Fortune" by Sinclair Lewis, 4-3 AD 4

Lewis, Steve: Ace Double Mysteries, (discussion of the paperback line with checklist), 6 MY 3

Lewis, Steve: Books Announced, (mystery and crime fiction, August 1975), 7 MN 8

Lewis, Steve: Corrections to MURDER MYSTERY MONTHLY Checklist, 2-1 PQ 5

Lewis, Steve: Interview, Kendell Foster Crossen, 12 MN A1

Lewis, Steve: letter of comment, 5 LR 7; 2-2 MR 16; 2-3 MR 11; 2-5 MR 12; 1-2 PP 26; 2-2 PP 41; 69 PU 27; 2-3 TAD 202; 3-1 TAD 60; 6-2 TAD 119; 8-2 TAD 160; 8-4 TAD 322; 17 X 62

Lewis, Steve: Mystery Dial, (comments on old radio mystery shows), 2 MY 3; 3 MY 3; 4 MY 6; 5 MY 9; 6 MY 12; 7 MY 9; (Johnny Dollar) 2-1 PP 9; (The Green Hornet) 2-2 PP 10; (locked rooms) 2-3 PP 11; (Mr. & Mrs. North) 2-4 PP 25; (Lights Out, and others) 2-6 PP 28

Lewis, Steve: Mystery*File, (reviews), 1A MF 23; 1-1 MF 27; 1-2 MF 23; 1-3 MF 37; 1-4 MF 37; 1-5 MF 21; 1-6 MF 38; 2-1 MF 21; 2-2 MF 33; 2-3 MF 41; 2-4 MF 30; 2-5 MF 26; 2-6 MF 30; 3-1 MF 31; 3-2 MF 36; 3-3 MF 31; 3-4 MF 38; 3-5 MF 35; 3-6 MF 27; 4-2 MF 31; 4-3 MF 34; 4-4 MF 33; 4-5 MF 27; 5-1 MF 20; 5-2 MF 13; 5-3 MF 27; 5-4 MF 21; 5-5 MF 20; 5-6 MF 33

Lewis, Steve: Mystery Quiz, (quiz), 5 MY 8; 5a MY 3

Lewis, Steve: News and Comments, 2 MY 1; 3 MY 1; 4 MY 1; 5 MY 1; 5a MY 1; 6 MY 1; 7 MY 1

Lewis, Steve: Paperback Mysteries Announced for July 1975, 3/4 MN 17; (August 1975) 5/6 MN 8

Lewis, Steve: Paperback Mysteries Issued in June 1974, 2 MY 7; (July 1974) 3 MY 5

Lewis, Steve: Reviews, 5a MY 1

Lewis, Steve: Son of Mystery*File, (news and comments), 1 MN 3; 3/4 MN 11

Lewis, Steve: Speaking of Pulp, (on THRILLING DETECTIVE magazine), 4 PE 9; (DIME DETECTIVE) 5 PE 27

Lewis, Suford: Georgette Heyer Fandom (fan and convention activities for author Georgette Heyer), 13 MN 7

(Liberator series: Norman Deane), Checklist, by Robert E. Briney and John Creasey, 2-1 TAD 13

Library Display, (on housing and displaying boys' book collection) 3-4 BC 379

Lien, Dennis: Checklist, Curtis Books, (paperback Curtis line), 14 SF 7

Lien, Dennis: Curtis Books, (notes on Curtis Books paperback line), 14 SF 5

Lien, Dennis: letter of comment, 2-3 CP 1; 4 SF 44; 8 SF 48

Lien, Dennis: UNCANNY TALES, (on the Canadian pulp magazine with checklist and index), 9 SF 25

Life and Times of Gideon Fell, (detective character of John Dickson Carr), by Marvin Lachman, 2-3 MF 3

Life as a Series of Abstract Analyses, (discussion of Professor Poggioli as detective, created by T.S. Stribling, with checklist in pulp magazines and otherwise), by Robert Sampson, 2-2 C 61

Life in One Small American Town, (re: August Derleth), 2-3/4 AD 4

Lighted Bridge of Detection, The, (on the name, Solar Pons), by Raymond M. Funk, 2-1 PDA 25

Lights! Camera! - Inaction, (unfilmed film scripts of Ray Bradbury), by Ben P. Indick, 36 X R25

(Lights Out, radio mystery series), Mystery Dial V: Lights Out and Others, by Steve Lewis, 2-6 PP 28

Lillian de la Torre, Preliminary Bibliography: Blood on the Periwigs, by James Mark Purcell, 4-5 MR 25

Limehouse and the River Police, (in association with Sax Rohmer stories), by John E. Carroll, 5 R 13

Linard, Jean: letter of comment, 19 JD 13; 20 JD 21; 25 JD 38

Lindsay, Ethel: letter of comment, 3-5 PP 46; 4-2 PP 35; 4-3 PP 38; 4-4 PP 41; 4-5/6 PP 87

Lindsay, Ethel: Some Thoughts on Josephine Tey, (retribution as a motive), 3-6 MR 7

Lindsley, Mary F.: Dame Agatha's Admirable Addleheads, (on the characters of Agatha Christie), 1-2 PDA 73

Lindsley, Mary F.: Mrs. Pinkerton as Frankenstein, 1-1 PDA 27

Lindsley, Mary F.: Satirist and Sleuth, or Trent versus Toff, (on E.C. Bentley's parody of Lord Peter Wimsey), 2-1 PDA 28

Lines to a Man Who Should Know Better, (verse, re: John D. MacDonald), by Knox Burger, 11 JD 8

Line-Up, The, (mystery-detective fanzines), by Robert E. Briney, 1A MF 22; 2-1 MF 20; by Walter Albert: 4-5 MF 9

Lingo Dan, (Classic Corner Rare Tales, fiction), by Percival Pollard, 12-3 TAD 238

Linington, Elizabeth: letter of comment, 3-6 MR 11

(Linington, Elizabeth), An Interview with Elizabeth Linington, by Margaret J. King, 13-4 TAD 299

(Linington, Elizabeth), Past-Mistress of the Police Procedural, by Ann Waldron, 3-5 MR 32

Linn, S. Carl: Detective Fiction and Ernest Hemingway, 1-1 MR 3

Linzner, Gordon: letter of comment, 2 FM 18

Lion Paperbacks, (checklist of science fiction paperback line), by J. Grant Thiessen, 2 SF 10

(Lipman, David & Judi), Sketch, 2-3 PP 8

Literary Career of Mr. Anthony Berkeley Cox, The, by Charles Shibuk, 2-3 TAD 164

Literary Quotations and Allusions in the Dr. Thorndyke Novels and Short Stories, (of R. Austin Freeman), by John H. Dirckx, 1 TF 3

Literary Sleuths, Alias Your Friendly Neighborhood Book Detectives, (notes and experiences of a bookseller), by Mary Ann Grochowski, 2-3 PP 3

Literary Tradition of Brow Spraying, The, by J.R.Christopher, 3 R 23

Literary Works of Fictional Detectives and "Watsons," The, (quiz), by Barry A. Pike, 7-4 TAD 260

(LITERARY DETECTION: A.Q.Morton), Article review, by E.F.Bleiler, 3-4 MF 11

Literature with a Capital Hell, (on publishing imaginative fiction, and writing notes), by Malcolm W. Ferguson, 3 WT 4

Little Dread Schoolhouse, The, (fiction), by Michael Avallone, 9 X 19

Little Egypt Swings It, (fiction), by Lucile Coleman, 3 U 16

Little Old Ladies I Have Known and Loved, (feminine sleuths), by Ellen Nehr, 3-4 MF 3

Little Old Men With Whom I'm Only Slightly Acquainted, (little-known male sleuths), by Ellen Nehr, 4-4 MF 2

Live Instruments of Villainy, by Sax Rohmer, 6 R 3

Livezey, Bob: letter of comment, 15 X 14

Living With a Paperback Book Collector, (comments, some humourous), by M. Kirklin, 1-1 CP 15; 1-2 CP 13; (shelving) 1-3 CP 3; (definitions) 1-5 CP 18; (collecting Popular Library editions) 2-1 CP 19

Livingstone, Don: letter of comment, 6-1 MR 20

Lobdell, Jared C.: Additions to a Bibliography of G.A.Henty and Hentyana, 1-4 BC 125

Locating Dr. Petrie's Practice, (re: Fu Manchu), by Julian Biggers, 7 R 17

Lochte, Richard S., II: Another Mike Hammer, Pre-Spillane, 2-1 TAD 24

Lochte, Richard S., II: Created, The Destroyer, An Interview with Warren Murphy (The Destroyer paperback series), 11-3 TAD 284

Lochte, Richard S., II: letter of comment, 1-3 TAD 108; 1-4 TAD 153; 3-4 TAD 278; 5-1 TAD 51; 5-1 TAD 58; 5-2 TAD 109; 6-1 TAD 58; 7-1 TAD 75

Lochte, Richard S., II: The Private Eye, Enduring as a $1.29 Steak, (characteristics of a private detective), 3-2 TAD 117

Lochte, Richard S., II: Reviews of Mystery and Crime Films, 5-3 TAD 158; 5-4 TAD 231; 6-1 TAD 39

Lochte, Richard S.,II: Reviews of Various Television Detective Series, 5-2 TAD 104

Lochte, Richard S., II: Rogue's Gallery, (con-men in crime fiction), 2-3 TAD 158

Lochte, Richard S., II: Who's Afraid of Nero Wolfe?, (interview with Rex Stout), 3-4 TAD 211

Locke, David: letter of comment, 11 JD 31; 14 JD 24; 16 JD 20; 18 JD 27; 21 JD 15

Locke, G.W.: letter of comment, 4 SF 45

Locke, George: letter of comment,
9 JD 6; 9-2 TAD 160

(Locke, Kim, adventures), Checklist,
Christopher Monig, by Dickson Thorpe,
1-2 MF 7

(Locke, Quentin, detective), A Justly
Celebrated, Elusive, American,
(on screen), by Stanley A. Carlin,
3-2 MR 31

Locked House, The, An Essay on Locked
Rooms, by Donald A. Yates, 3-2 TAD 81

(Locked Rooms, radio), Mystery Dial
III: Locked Rooms, by Steve Lewis,
2-3 PP 11

Lockhart, Brian: letter of comment,
26 X 77; 28 X 80; 38 X 145

(Locken, Mike, detective), Robert Rostand
and Mike Locken, by Theodore P.
Dukeshire, 2-4 MF 4

(Lockridge, Frances & Richard), Checklist
by Kathy Hobel, 2-5 MR 6

(Lockridge, Frances & Richard), Mr. & Mrs.
North, and Mr. & Mrs. Lockridge, by
Hank Davis, 1-1 MF 21

(Lockridge, Frances & Richard), Mr. & Mrs.
North, (detectives, created by the
Lockridges), by R. Jeff Banks, 9-3
TAD 182

(Lockridge, Richard), An Interview with
Richard Lockridge, by Chris and Janie
Filstrup, 11-4 TAD 382

Lodestone Books, Checklist, (paperbacks
published by Lodestone), by Bill
Denholm, 1-4 CP 16

Loeser, William R.: The Curmudgeon in the
Corner, 3-2 MF 3; 3-4 MF 16

Loeser, William R.: letter of comment,
3-2 MF 58; 3-4 MF 59; 4-1 MF 43;
4-6 MF 46; 5-1 MF 47; 1-2 PP 30;
2-2 PP 31; 2-4 PP 46; 6-1 TAD 55;
6-3 TAD 200; 7-2 TAD 146; 7-2 TAD
150; 7-3 TAD 229; 13-1 TAD 78;
33 X 114

(Lofts, Norah), Three Ladies of the
Quasi-Gothic, The Films of Armstrong,
Lofts, and White, by Jack Edmund
Nolan, 5-2 MR 23

Lofts, W.O.G.: A Visit to Baker Street,
6-1 TAD 15

Lofts, W.O.G.: The Adventures of Chubblock
Homes, (comic strip parodies of
Sherlock Holmes), 8-3 TAD 193

Lofts, W.O.G.: Film Notes, (on Sax Rohmer
works), 9 R 23

Lofts, W.O.G.: It's All in the Face, (on
face characterizations) 7-2 TAD 109

Lofts, W.O.G.: On the Trail of the
Mysterious "Jack Mann", (author),
6-2 MR 19

Lofts, W.O.G.: letter of comment,
6-2 MR 15; 8 R 31; 5-2 TAD 126;
5-3 TAD 174; 6-2 TAD 123; 6-2 TAD
128; 7-2 TAD 147; 7-3 TAD 226;
8-1 TAD 76; 8-4 TAD 315

Lofts, W.O.G.: Roland Daniel, Prolific
Mystery Writer, 6-4 TAD 242

Lofts, W.O.G.: Secret Egypt Unveiled,
(a la Sax Rohmer), 8 R 23

Lofts, W.O.G.: Thoughts on the Master
of Villainy, (Sax Rohmer), 10 R 27

Lofts, W.O.G., and Derek J. Adley:
Was "Jack Wylde" Really R. Austin
Freeman?, 7-4 TAD 247

Lofts, W.O.G., and Robert E. Briney:
Sh-h-h! Dr. Fu Manchu is On the
Air! (radio serials), 11 R 9

Lofts, W.O.G., and Robert E. Briney:
Musette, Max and Sumuru, (radio
serials from Sax Rohmer), 15 R 5

(Lofts, W.O.G.), Biographical Sketch,
8 R 29

Logan, John: letter of comment,
1-4 TAD 152

(LOLITA: Vladimir Nabokov), On LOLITA
as a Mystery Story, by J.R.
Christopher, 7-1 TAD 29

London's Ha'penny Comics, by Gelett
Burgess, 1-1 YB 19

(Lone Ranger), A Look at the Lone
Ranger, by Fred Woodworth, 1 MA 11

(Lone Ranger), Recent Lone Ranger
Story a Mess, (critical review on
LEGEND OF THE LONE RANGER by Gary
McCarthy), by I.R.Ybarra, 6 MA 8

(Lone Ranger), UpDate, Tom Quest and
the Lone Ranger, (book series for
boys by Fran Striker), by Fred
Woodworth, 6 MA 13

(Lone Ranger), The Writings of Fran
Striker, (boys' books), by Kent
Winslow, 1 MA 7

(Lone Wolf series: Mike Barry), Checklist of Paperbacks, by George
Kelley, 1-5 MF 18

(Lone Wolf series: Mike Barry), Fear
and Loathing with the Lone Wolf,
by George Kelley, 1-5 MF 17

Lonely Are the Great, (commentary on
writers), by Mike Avallone, 11 X 7

Lonesome Cage, Private Investigator
a la Peter Israel, by Jim McCahery,
4 PE 3

("Long After Midnight": Ray Bradbury),
Article review by Bruce Francis,
26 X 12

Long History of Short Stories, The, by
William J. Clark, 20 X 41

(LONG LAVENDER LOOK, THE: John D.
MacDonald), An Interesting Book, This
Lavender Look, (review in verse),
by Dave Stewart, 15 JD 17

(Long, Amelia Reynolds), Amelia Reynolds
Long, (sketch, WEIRD TALES author),
by Chet Williamson, 2 WT 7

(Long, Amelia Reynolds), Amelia Reynolds
Long in the Weird Fiction Magazines,
(chronological listing of stories),
by Chet Williamson, 2 WT 9

Long, Bob: letter of comment, 15 BS 15

Long, Frank Belknap: Innsmouth Revisited, (verse, re: H.P.Lovecraft's mythos), 18 X 17

Long, Frank Belknap: letter of comment, 1-1 AD 1

(Long, Frank Belknap), The Derleth Connection, Frank Belknap Long, (with introduction by Long), 2-2 AD 3

Longest Goodbye, The, or The Search for Chandler's Los Angeles, (Raymond Chandler), by Paul Bishop, 1-2 M 33

Looking Back, (reminiscences on collecting boys' books), by Jack R. Schorr, 1-2 TBN 4

Looking for Rachel Wallace and Ginger North, (on LOOKING FOR RACHEL WALLACE by Robert B. Parker, and LOOKING FOR GINGER NORTH, by John Dunning), by George Kelley, 4-3 MF 29

(LOOKING FOR GINGER NORTH: John Dunning), Looking for Rachel Wallace and Ginger North, by George Kelley, 4-3 MF 29

(LOOKING FOR RACHEL WALLACE: Robert B. Parker), Looking for Rachel Wallace and Ginger North, by George Kelley, 4-3 MF 29

Loose Ends, (boys' books collecting notes), by Fred Woodworth, 6 MA 2

Lopresti, Robert: Crostic Puzzle, (on Nero Wolfe), 1-2 G 17

Lopresti, Robert: letter of comment, 1-2 G 68

(Loraine, Philip), Philip Loraine on the Screen, or, Where Did the Mysteries Go?, by Jack Edmund Nolan, 5-3 MR 18

Lord of the Unknown, The Zarkon Novels of Lin Carter, by Link Hullar, 8 U 141

Lord, Glenn: letter of comment, 4 BS 20; 1-3 PQ 13; 14 SF 48

Lord, Glenn: STRANGE DETECTIVE STORIES, (on the pulp magazine of this title, with index), 65 PU 12

(Lord, Glenn: THE LAST CELT), New Book Released about Robert E. Howard, by Tevis Clyde Smith, 1-1 PQ 33

(LORD OF THE RINGS: J.R.R.Tolkien), The War Over Middle Earth, by Billy C. Lee, 1-4 PQ 37

Lord Peter Views the Telly, (Lord Peter Wimsey on BBC television), by J.R.Christopher, 12-1 TAD 20

Lord Peter Wimsey of Piccadilly, His Lordship's Life and Times, (detective character of Dorothy L. Sayers), by William M. Scott, 13-1 TAD 17; 13-3 TAD 212

Lost and Found - L.A.Bantam, (on Bantam Books, paperline line, Los Angeles editions), by Paul Payne, 1-3 CP 10

Lost B Movie, The, (mysteries), by Andy Jaysnovitch, 7 PE 3

Lost Eye, The, by Robert E. Briney, 6 R 9; 7 R 10

Lost Fortune, The, a Dixon Farm Story by Edward Edson Lee, (serialized magazine fiction by boys' books author Leo Edwards), 2-1 TB 2; 2-2 TB 2; 2-3 TB 3; 2-5 TB 2; 3-4 TB 2; 3-5 TB 1

"Lost" Nero Wolfe Tale, The, (on "Bitter End" by Rex Stout), by Art Scott, 9 MN A14

(LOST HORIZON: James Hilton), Reprints/Reprints, (on paperback editions), by Billy C. Lee, 3-1 PQ 37

(LOST WORLD, THE: A. Conan Doyle), Where was Maple White Land?, by Dana Martin Batory, 6 U 16

(LOST WORLD, THE: A. Conan Doyle), The Land That Maple White Found, by Arn McConnell, 1-1 WA 7

(LOST WORLD, THE: A. Conan Doyle), Notes on the Lost World, by Dana Martin Batory, 2 U 9

Louis L'Amour's Pseudonymous Works, by John D. Nesbitt, 3-3 PQ 3

Louis, Robert: Tom Loved Mary... Remember That?, (on Tom Swift boys' books), 4-1 BC 402

(Love, Dr. Jason, series: Paul Leasor), Checklist, Annotated, by Barry Van Tilburg, 4-4 MF 16

Lovecraft Family in America, The, by R. Alain Everts, 18 X 7

Lovecraft in My Life, (literary reminiscences, H.P.Lovecraft), by Fritz Leiber, 1 HP 5

Lovecraft in the British Thriller, (H.P.Lovecraft), by Edward Lauterbach, 2-2 TAD 102

Lovecraft's Ladies, (in stories by H.P.Lovecraft), by Ben P. Indick, 18 X 10

(Lovecraft, H.P.), Bibliographic Notes on Some HPL Books, by Ted Ball, 4 SF 18

(Lovecraft, H.P.), The Call of Lovecraft, by Willis Conover, 18 X 15

(Lovecraft, H.P.), The Cthulhu Mythos, by Steve Miller, 3 MT 5

(Lovecraft, H.P.), The Ghost of Ec'h-Pi-El, (visual puzzle), 18 X 18

(Lovecraft, H.P.), Graveyard Walking and Gravewatching, by John Dinan, 2 FM 14

(Lovecraft, H.P.), HPL: The Book That Nearly Was, 11 X 118

(Lovecraft, H.P.), H.P.Lovecraft and Edmund Wilson, 1 FM 5

(Lovecraft, H.P.), H.P.Lovecraft, (verse), by Vincent Starrett, 18 X 9

(Lovecraft, H.P.), H.P.Lovecraft, Rabid Racist, or Compassionate Gentleman?, by Dirk W. Mosig, 18 X 13

(Lovecraft, H.P.), In Re: August Derleth,
    by William Wingfield, 3-2 PDA 16
(Lovecraft, H.P.), Innsmouth Revisited,
    (verse), by Frank Belknap Long,
    18 X 17
(Lovecraft, H.P.), Inside the Outsider,
    (concerning Lovecraft's "The
    Outsider"), by Robert Bloch, 18 X 4
(Lovecraft, H.P.), Lovecraft in My Life,
    (literary reminiscences), by Fritz
    Leiber, 1 HP 5
(Lovecraft, H.P.), Lovecraft in the British
    Thriller, by Edward Lauterbach, 2-2
    TAD 102
(Lovecraft, H.P.), Lovecraft's Ladies,
    (in his stories), by Ben P. Indick,
    18 X 10
(Lovecraft, H.P.), The Pseudonymous
    Lovecraft, by George Wetzel, 28 X 3
(Lovecraft, H.P.), Clark Ashton Smith,
    a Postcard from Lovecraft, 1927,
    18 X 14
(Lovecraft, H.P.), Two Fungi From Yuggoth,
    (verse), by Alice Briley, 4-3 AD 9
(Lovecraft, H.P.) Upon Reading of Love-
    craft's Death, (verse), by Steve Eng,
    3-1 AD 2
(Lovecraft, H.P.), Young Man Lovecraft,
    (reminiscences), by L. Sprague de
    Camp, 18 X 8
Lovelace, Craven: Trivia Quiz, The
    Biographers, (quiz), 2-1 WA 19
(Lovesey, Peter), An Interview with Peter
    Lovesey, by Diana Cooper-Clark,
    14-3 TAD 210
Lowder, Christopher: letter of comment,
    2 SF 39; 4 SF 45
Lowndes, Robert A.W.: The Columbia Pulps,
    (Lowndes, as editor, discusses the
    pulp magazines of Columbia Publi-
    cations), 67 PU 5
Lowndes, Robert A.W.: Dear Mr. Mr. Van
    Dine, (on author, S.S.Van Dine),
    7-1 TAD 30
Lowndes, Robert A.W.: G.K.Chesterton's
    Father Brown, 9-3 TAD 184
Lowndes, Robert A.W.: The Immortal Enemy,
    (commentary on Dr. Fu Manchu),
    7 R 1
Lowndes, Robert A.W.: letter of comment,
    4-3 TAD 193; 5-2 TAD 106; 6-3 TAD
    196; 6-4 TAD 279; 8-1 TAD 71; 9-2
    TAD 161; 8 SF 45; 5 WT 31
Lowndes, Robert A.W.: Readers Choice,
    (excerpts from the readers' columns
    of WEIRD TALES, "The Eyrie"), 5 WT
    20; 6 WT 16
Lowndes, Robert A.W.: The Unique Magazine,
    Hugo Gernsback's SCIENTIFIC DETECTIVE
    MONTHLY, 14-1 TAD 24; 14-2 TAD 157;
    14-3 TAD 243; 14-4 TAD 367; 15-1 TAD
    18
(Lowndes, Robert A.W.), Biographical
    Sketch, 7 R 25
(Luard, Nicholas), The Books of Nicholas
    Luard, by Theodore P. Dukeshire,
    4-1 MF 12

Lubelski, Amy: Mysteries for Children,
    12 SF 24
(Lucky Starr series: Paul French),
    Boys' Series Bibliography, by
    Harry K. Hudson, 1-5 YB 14
(Ludlum, Robert), An Interview with
    Robert Ludlum, by Stephen L.
    Smoke, 1-3 M 8
(Lugosi, Bela), Bela Lugosi, (sketch
    and commentary), by Gordon R. Guy,
    1 CD 6
(Lugosi, Bela), Bela Lugosi - A
    Meeting Remembered, by Jack A.
    Miller, 1 CD 31
(Lugosi, Bela), Bela Lugosi - A Scrap
    Book, (photo article, movie stills)
    by Gordon R. Guy, 1 CD 16
(Lugosi, Bela), Bela Lugosi and Mark
    of the Vampire, (film), by Dr.
    Carroll Borland Parten, 1 CD 34
(Lugosi, Bela), Bela Lugosi in Murder
    by Television, (film), 1 CD 12
(Lugosi, Bela), Homage to Bela,
    (verse), by Helen Ruggieri,
    1 CD 43
Lumbroso, Bruno: The Case of the Blind
    Clairaudient, A Critical Study,
    (Solar Pons), 3-1 PDA 32
Lumbroso, Bruno: The Fatal Glance,
    (Solar Pons), 3-2 PDA 24
Lumley, Brian: Brian Lumley Talks
    About August Derleth, 2-2 AD 1
Lumley, Brian: D'Erlette, (verse about
    August Derleth), 1-1 AD 4
Lumley, Brian: In the Moons of Borea,
    (unpublished Prologue to book of
    same title), 6 U 3
Lund, Robert: letter of comment,
    2 BS 3; 3 BS 2; 6 BS 22
(Lupoff, Richard A., and Robert E.
    Howard: THE RETURN OF SKULL FACE),
    The (Very Temporary) Return of
    Skull-Face, by Robert E. Briney,
    2-2 MF 21
Luserke, Uwe: Jack Williamson
    Bibliography, 13 SF 29
Lusk, Homer: letter of comment,
    3-5 CP 1
(Lustgarten, Edgar), Edgar Lustgarten
    1970-1978, (memorial and checklist),
    by Mary Groff, 12-3 TAD 286
(Lustgarten, Edgar), Obituary, by
    Mary Groff, 2-1 PP 13
Luttrell, Lesleigh: letter of comment,
    3/4 MN 12
Luttrell, Lesleigh: Regency Lady,
    (literary sketch, Georgette Heyer),
    13 MN 3
Lutz, John, and Bill Pronzini:
    Tiger, Tiger, (fiction), 3-2 M 14
(Lutz, John), A Bit of a Twist, The
    Writings of John Lutz, by Mary Ann
    Grochowski, 1-2 PP 5
(Lutz, John), An Interview with John
    Lutz, by Mary Ann Grochowski,
    12-3 TAD 276; (checklist) 12-3 TAD
    278

(Lutz, John), A Checklist of the Short
Stories of John Lutz, by Francis M.
Nevins, Jr., 1-3 PP 13
(Lutz, John), Partial Checklist, Short
Stories and Novels, by Mary Ann
Grochowski, 1-2 PP 8
Lybeck, Al: letter of comment,
7 U 45; 22 X 49
Lybeck, Alvin H.: Pulpster Profile,
Visit with Donald Barr Chidsey,
(author), 5 U 17
Lyles, William: A Brief Encounter with
Leslie Ford and David Frome
(authors), 2-4 PP 15
Lyles, William: Agatha Christie in the
Dell Mapbacks, (paperback series),
3-3 PQ 26
Lyles, William: C.W.Grafton, (sketch),
3-6 PP 7
Lyles, William: Dashiell Hammett, (on
paperback editions of novels and
short stories), 1-3 CP 9
Lyles, William: Keyhole Confidential,
(paperback books, general comments
and data) 1-2 CP 10; 1-3 CP 7;
(Dell bibliography for Anthony
Boucher and Agatha Christie) 1-4
CP 26; (Dell 1st editions, 1st
series, checklist) 1-5 CP 26;
1-6 CP 17; (paperback female cover
art) 2-2 CP 22; (early Dell paperbacks), 2-4 CP 13; (Dell, variant
editions) 3-2 CP 30
Lyles, William: letter of comment,
1-4 CP 2; 1-6 CP 1; 2-1 CP 3;
3-4 CP 3; 3-4 MF 57; 1-1 PP 28;
2-1 PP 31; 2-2 PP 30; 2-4 PP 42;
4-5/6 PP 82; 1-3 PQ 5; 2-3 PQ 3;
2-2 PQ 3; 2-3 PQ 8; 3-1 PQ 5;
3-2 PQ 4; 4-2 PQ 52
Lyles, William: Lyles Column #1,
(paperback collecting, sources
of information), 1-1 CP 4
Lyles, William: Rex Stout in the Dell
Mapbacks, (paperback series), 2-4
PQ 14
Lyman, Jim: letter of comment,
1-4 YB 9
Lynch, Miriam: Let's Look at Gothics,
2-2 MR 13
(Lynds, Dennis), Checklist of works,
by John Edwards, 4 U 21; 6 U 36
(Lynds, Dennis), More on "The Story of
Dennis Lynds," by John Edwards,
5 U 20
(Lynds, Dennis), Private Eye in an Evil
Time, Mark Sadler's Paul Shaw,
(Lynds under Sadler pseudonym),
by Francis M. Nevins, Jr., 38 X 11
(Lynds, Dennis), The Story of Dennis
Lynds, by John Edwards, 4 U 21
(Lyons, Arthur), Conversation Part VI,
(interview with Arthur Lyons), by
Don Cole, 3-2 PP 10
Lyons, Nan and Ivan: One Name on the
Contract, (re: Dallas" television
series), 9 LR 23

(Maartens, Maarten: THE BLACK BOX
MURDERS), Chance and Illogic and
THE BLACK BOX MURDER, by E.F.
Bleiler, 2-1 MF 8
(Machen, Arthur), Starrett versus
Machen, (correspondence, Vincent
Starrett and Machen), by Michael
Murphy, 18 X 24
(Machen, Arthur), Vincent Starrett
vs. Arthur Machen, or, How Not to
Communicate Over Eight Years of
Correspondence, by E.F.Bleiler,
3-6 MF 11
M'Levy, James: The Happy Land, (Classic
Corners Rare Tales, fiction), 13-3
TAD 219
MacDermott, Aubrey: letter of comment,
6 U 50
MacDermott, K.A.: Ideology and Narrative
Stereotyping, The Case of Raymond
Chandler, 2-1 C 77
MacDonald, Anne: Frostwatching, (Robert
Frost reminiscences), 25 JD 15
MacDonald, Charles: letter of comment,
13 JD 11; 5-2 MF 39; 4-5/6 PP 89;
3-2 PQ 3; 4-1 TAD 55; 4-2 TAD 129;
5-4 TAD 252
MacDonald, Charles: Mystery Writers of
America - Annual Volumes Checklist,
5-4 TAD 252
MacDonald, Charles: Rebuttal to "Kiss
My Deadly Typewriter #539" by Mike
Avallone, 3-1 QC 15
MacDonald, John D.: A Note from John
D., 25 JD 15
MacDonald, John D.: The "Aging" of
Travis McGee, 20 JD 3
MacDonald, John D.: The Case of John D.
MacDonald, Introduction and Comment,
(introductory comment to issue of
CLUES: A JOURNAL OF DETECTION which
was dedicated to MacDonald), 1-1 C 63
MacDonald, John D.: Economic Despair
Fueled Miami Riots, (essay),
26 JD 10
MacDonald, John D.: Flight 54 - Not
Quite First Class, (travel experiences),
25 JD 7
MacDonald, John D.: Fragments of the
Indian Scene, (travel essay), 27 JD 9
MacDonald, John D.: Haiku, (verse),
15 JD 20
MacDonald, John D.: I, the Spillane, or,
My Spillane is Quick, or, Vengeance
is Spillane, or, One Lonely Spillane,
or, The Big Spillane, (parody),
14 JD 16
MacDonald, John D.: JDM Responds, (on
atomic bombings of Japan), 27 JD 24
MacDonald, John D.: J.R.Eats Humble Pie,
(on "Dallas" television series),
9 LR 24
MacDonald, John D.: John D. and the
Critics, (with JDM's responses),
24 JD 4

MacDonald, John D.: John D. MacDonald
vs. Doc Savage, (on writing for
the pulp magazines), 3 BS 3

MacDonald, John D.: Junket(to Apollo
9 launch), 12 JD 3

MacDonald, John D.: letter of comment,
3 JD 1; 8 JD 3; 8 JD 5; 9 JD 4;
10 JD 8; 11 JD 13; 13 JD 11;
14 JD 26; 21 JD 17; 26 JD 48

MacDonald, John D.: Reflections on
China, (travel experiences),
24 JD 13

MacDonald, John D.: Secrets from the
CBI, (China-Burma-India area),
16 JD 6

MacDonald, John D.: The Spiralled Myth,
(fiction), 3 JD 3; 9 JD 24

(MacDonald, John D.), A Checklist of
Hardcover and Paperback Books,
by Len J. Moffatt, 1-6 MR 13

(MacDonald, John D.), A Day in the
Life of the Wife of An Amachoor
Skoller, by June M. Moffatt,
6 JD 13

(MacDonald, John D.), A Letter from
John D. MacDonald, (on acceptance
of violence), 17 JD 9

(MacDonald, John D.), A Pile of Pointy
Polka Dots, (parody on Travis McGee),
by Bailey Phelps, 26 JD 35

(MacDonald, John D.), A Second John
D.?, (comparison of authors John
D. MacDonald and Charles Williams),
by J.M.Carter, 18 JD 15

(MacDonald, John D.), A Stern Look
at McGee, (Travis McGee, series
character), by Elijah Stern, 15 JD 5

(MacDonald, John D.), A Tribute to
JDM, by John R. Feegel, M.D.,
24 JD 22

(MacDonald, John D.), About Critical
Essays on Books by JDM, by Lawrence
Fleming, 16 JD 11

(MacDonald, John D.), Additions and
Corrections to the JDM Master List,
(bibliography), 24 JD 45

(MacDonald, John D.), Alphabetical
Checklist of the Science-Fiction
Stories of John D. MacDonald, by
Jean and Walter Shine, 28 JD 25

(MacDonald, John D.), An Evening with
John D. MacDonald, by George R.
Berry, 22 JD 4

(MacDonald, John D.), The Anatomy of
"Romance" (as ingredient in the
fiction of John D. MacDonald), by
Stan Woolston, 18 JD 13

(MacDonald, John D.), Author's List
of Stories in Street & Smith Publications, DOC SAVAGE and THE SHADOW,
with bibliographical data, 7 BS 4

(MacDonald, John D.), Beast Imagery
and Stereotypes in the Novels of
John D. MacDonald, by George S.
Peek, 2-1 C 91

(MacDonald, John D.), Checklist of Novels,
by Len & June Moffatt, 1 JD 1

(MacDonald, John D.), Confessions
From a JDM Addict, by Warner
Conarton, 27 JD 16

(MacDonald, John D.), Dating the
Travis McGee Stories, by Dean
Grennell, 22 JD 11

(MacDonald, John D.), Death and JDM,
(treatment of death in the
fiction of MacDonald), by June M.
Moffatt, 5 JD 3

(MacDonald, John D.), Death of a
"John Dee" Fan, (on acceptance of
violence), by Dave Stewart, 17 JD 5

(MacDonald, John D.), Detective Pulp
Stories of John D. MacDonald,
Publication and Identification,
by Bill Clark, 6 JD 5

(MacDonald, John D.), Detective Pulp
Stories - Synopsis and Checklist,
6 JD 1; 7 JD 13

(MacDonald, John D.), Early "Condo-
minium" Hurricane Warning, (on
CONDOMINIUM), by Jean and Walter
Shine. 22 JD 15

(MacDonald, John D.), Early J.D.,
(pulp writings), by Ed Cox,
9 JD 19

(MacDonald, John D.), Early J.D.,
(stories in DOC SAVAGE and THE
SHADOW magazines), by Ed Cox,
2 JD 3

(MacDonald, John D.), Early JDM:
Four From Early '49, (pulp stories),
by Francis M. Nevins, Jr., 21 JD 11

(MacDonald, John D.), Early JDM:
In Doc Savage, (stories in the pulp
magazine DOC SAVAGE), by Francis M.
Nevins, Jr., 19 JD 8

(MacDonald, John D.), Early JDM in
EQMM, (John D. MacDonald in ELLERY
QUEEN'S MYSTERY MAGAZINE), by
Francis M. Nevins, Jr., 18 JD 10

(MacDonald, John D.), Early JDM: Pulp
Thought and Pulp Action, (writings
in pulp magazines), by Francis M.
Nevins, Jr., 14 JD 14

(MacDonald, John D.), Early JDM: Three
Pulps From '49, (pulp stories), by
Francis M. Nevins, Jr., 15 JD 19

(MacDonald, John D.), Early JDM: To
Any Lengths (pulp stories), by
Francis M. Nevins, Jr., 17 JD 18

(MacDonald, John D.), Early JDM:
Woolrich Touches, (pulp writings),
by Francis M. Nevins, Jr., 16 JD 12

(MacDonald, John D.),Ecology and the
Detective Novel, The Contribution
of John D. MacDonald, by Donald C.
Wall, 21 JD 3

(MacDonald, John D.), For Travis Mcgee
Fans, (crossword puzzle), by Loyal
G. Compton, 26 JD 13

(MacDonald, John D.), Influence on a
a Writer, by William F. Nolan,
11 JD 11

(MacDonald, John D.), Interview with
John D. MacDonald, by Michael S.
Barson, 4-1 PQ 5

(MacDonald, John D.), Is It True What They
Say About Travis? (notes on Travis
McGee, series character of McDonald),
by Len and June Moffatt, 2 JD 8
(MacDonald, John D.), JDM: A Critique, by
Elijah Stern, 10 JD 4
(MacDonald, John D.), JDM BIBLIOPHILE,
(review in TIME Magazine), by Michael
Demarest, 25 JD 14
(MacDonald, John D.), JDM Gives Commence-
ment Address, (Sarasota, Florida,
June 1981), 28 JD 6
(MacDonald, John D.), JDM in Perspective,
by Marvin Lachman, 11 JD 9
(MacDonald, John D.), The JDM Popularity
Poll Results, by Clarence G. Petersen,
13 JD 5
(MacDonald, John D.), JDM's Images of the
Inhuman, by Francis M. Nevins, Jr.,
11 JD 6
(MacDonald, John D.), John D. MacDonald,
A Little Ecology Goes a Long Way,
by Wister Cook, 1-1 C 57
(MacDonald, John D.), John D. MacDonald,
A Sonnet, (verse), 16 JD 5
(MacDonald, John D.), John MacDonald and
the Technologies of Knowledge, (essay),
by Raymond Carney, 26 JD 16
(MacDonald, John D.), John D. MacDonald
as Social Critic (in his books), by
Edgar W. Hirshberg, 1-1 C 129
(MacDonald, John D.), John D. MacDonald,
The Greatest Paperbacker of Us All,
(on MacDonald's place in paperback
mysteries and paperback originals),
by Michael S. Barson, 4-1 PQ 3
(MacDonald, John D.), John D. MacDonald,
The Writer's Writer, by Len J. Moffatt,
1-6 MR 11
(MacDonald, John D.), Lady in Waiting,
(verse), by Ethel D. Compton, 24 JD 41
(MacDonald, John D.), Letters to McGee,
(Travis McGee, series character), by
Bob Allison, 25 JD 5
(MacDonald, John D.), Limerick, Travis
McGee, by Fred Cropper, 20 JD 18
(MacDonald, John D.), Lines to a Man Who
Should Know Better, (verse), by Knox
Burger, 11 JD 8
(MacDonald, John D.), McGee Gets a
Fan(atic!) Letter, (letter to Travis
McGee and reply regarding social
reaction to murder suspects), 28
JD 10
(MacDonald, John D.), McGee's Girls,
(on the female characters in the
Travis McGee stories), by Peggy
Moran, 1-1 C 82
(MacDonald, John D.), Magazine Stories,
by Len & June Moffatt, (checklist),
3 JD 5; 4 JD 1; 5 JD 1; 5 JD 4;
7 JD 13; 8 JD 2; 8 JD 18
(MacDonald, John D.), The Making of a
Tale-Spinner, John D. MacDonald's
Early Pulp Mystery Stories, by
Francis M. Nevins, Jr., 1-1 C 89

(MacDonald, John D.), From the Editor's
Dreadful Grey Typewriter, (news and
comments), 23 JD 2; 24 JD 1; 25 JD 1;
26 JD 1; 27 JD 1, by Edgar W. Hirsh-
berg
(MacDonald, John D.), News and Previews,
8 JD 4; 18 JD 4
(MacDonald, John D.), Not Vibgyor:
Bpprgoaygbiltstl, (acronym for
Travis McGee series), by Dean A.
Grennell, 20 JD 5
(MacDonald, John D.), Notes from the
Funeral Black Typewriter, (news
and comments), 28 JD 28
(MacDonald, John D.), Notes on Two
Shadows of JDM, (detective stories
in THE SHADOW), by Francis M. Nevins,
Jr., 13 JD 10
(MacDonald, John D.), Novels of John D.
MacDonald, (checklist), 1 JD 1
(MacDonald, John D.), Novels of John D.
MacDonald, (checklist), by Len &
June Moffatt, 2 JD 6
(MacDonald, John D.), Paint the Coffin
Fuchsia, (John D. MacDonald parody),
by Bob Leman, 9 JD 26
(MacDonald, John D.), Pale Leman for
Psychosis, (parody), 11 JD 4
(MacDonald, John D.), Paperback Originals
by John D. MacDonald, (checklist),
by Michael S. Barson, 4-1 PQ 10
(MacDonald, John D.), Please Write for
Details, (letters of comments from
readers), see: Letters
(MacDonald, John D.), Press Release, May
15, 1967, 6 JD 16
(MacDonald, John D.), Previews from the
Publisher, by David Stewart, 18 JD 9
(MacDonald, John D.), Pulp Perspective
Plus, (on pulp writing), 7 BS 3
(MacDonald, John D.), Random Thoughts
on JDM and the Frustration of the
Expected, by Francis M. Nevins, Jr.,
7 JD 11
(MacDonald, John D.), The Real McGee,
(a synthesis of puzzle and hero type
mystery fiction in Travis McGee
series), by Bailey P. Phelps, 28 JD
13
(MacDonald, John D.), The Reluctant
Hero, Reflections on Vocation and
Heroism in the Travis McGee Novels
of John D. MacDonald, by Larry E.
Grimes, 1-1 C 103
(MacDonald, John D.), The "Shine"
Section, (various notes and comments
on MacDonald and his works), by
Walter & Jean Shine, 22 JD 7; 23 JD
17; 24 JD 30; 25 JD 24; 26 JD 29;
27 JD 18; 28 JD 20
(MacDonald, John D.), Travis McGee as
Traditional Hero, by Erling B.
Holtsmark, 1-1 C 99
(MacDonald, John D.), Travis McGee
Quiz, (quiz), by Tom Clayton,
26 JD 19

(MacDonald, John D.), Untitled Opinion,
by Edward A. Nickerson, 18 JD 20
(MacDonald, John D.), Waiting for McGee,
(on collecting the Travis McGee
series), by Fred Cropper, 22 JD 13
(MacDonald, John D.: A TAN AND SANDY
SILENCE), A Tan & Sandy Thirteenth,
by Dean A. Grennell, 17 JD 11
(MacDonald, John D.: CONDOMINIUM)
Early "Condominium" Hurricane
Warning, by Jean & Walter Shine,
22 JD 15
(MacDonald, John D.: THE END OF THE NIGHT),
The Prophet Before the Fact, by
Veronica M.S.Kennedy, 7-1 TAD 41
(MacDonald, John D.: THE LONG LAVENDER
LOOK), An Interesting Book, This
Lavender Look, (review in verse),
by Dave Stewart, 15 JD 17
(MacDonald, John D.: Travis McGee series),
The Chronology of the Travis McGee
Novels, by Allan D. Pratt,
13-2 TAD 83
(MacDonald, John D.: Travis McGee series),
Color Him Quixote, MacDonald's
Strategy in the Early McGee Novels,
by Michael J. Tolley, 10-1 TAD 6
(MacDonald, John D.: Travis McGee series),
Conquering the Stereotypes: On
Reading the Novels of John D.
MacDonald, (on female stereotyped
characters), by George S. Peck,
13-2 TAD 90
(MacDonald, John D.), see T. Carrington
Burns (pseudonym)
MacDonald, Mark: Checklist, The Shadow
Series Comic Books, 1 MT 43
MacDonald, Mark: Checklist, The Shadow
Series, Pyramid Paperbacks,
1 MT 43
MacDonald, Mark: Raymond Chandler and the
Detective, 3 MT 2
MacDonald, Mark: Spade - Bogart, (Bogart's
role as Sam Spade in filmed Dashiell
Hammett), 4 MT 31
MacDonald, Mark: Who Knows What Evil Lurks...
("The Shadow Secret Society"), 1 MT 41
MacDonald, Maynard: letter of comment,
26 JD 48
(MacDonald, Philip), Checklist, by
Norman Donaldson, 3-1 TAD 10
(MacDonald, Philip), Obituary, 3-1 M 29
(MacDonald, Philip), Philip MacDonald -
Gethryn and Others, by Norman
Donaldson, 3-1 TAD 6; (addenda)
3-2 TAD 95
(MacDonald, Philip), Philip MacDonald on
the Screen, (with checklist), by Jack
Edmund Nolan, 3-3 MR 33
MacDonald, Mrs. Ronan G.: letter of
comment, 13 JD 18
(Macdonald, Ross), Ross Macdonald
Interview, by Gene Davidson and John
Knoerle, 1-1 M 6

(Macdonald, Ross), Ross Macdonald,
The Personal Paradigm and Popular
Fiction, by Zahava K. Dorinson,
10-1 TAD 43
(Macdonald, Ross), Where Have All the
Values Gone? - The Private Eye's
Vision of America in the Novels of
Raymond Chandler and Ross Macdonald,
by Etta C. Abrahams, 9-2 TAD 128
(Macdonald, Ross: THE CHILL), The
Detective as Both Tortoise and
Achilles - Archer Gets the Feel of
the Case in THE CHILL, by William
W. Combs, 2-1 C 98
(Macdonald, Ross: Lew Archer, detective),
Another Peacock Cry: Heraldic Birds
in Five Lew Archer Novels, by
Charles Fishman, 2-1 C 106
(Macdonald, Ross: Lew Archer, detective),
Archer in Hollywood, The "Barbarous
Coast" of Ross Macdonald, by David
J. Geherin, 9-1 TAD 55
(Macdonald, Ross: Lew Archer, detective),
Lew Archer's "Moral Landscape" by
Elmer R. Pry, Jr., 8-1 TAD 104
(Macdonald, Ross: THE UNDERGROUND MAN),
The Case of the Underground Man,
Evolution or Devolution?, by G.A.
Finch, 6-4 TAD 210
MacHarg, William, and Edwin Balmer:
The Eleventh Hour, (Classic Corner
Rare Tales, fiction), 12-1 TAD 40
(MacLean, Alistair), Alistair MacLean,
A Bibliography and Biography, by
Iwan Hedman, 4-5 MR 29
(MacWhorter, Angus, series: Harry
Stephen Keeler), Harry Stephen
Keeler's Screwball Circus, by
Francis M. Nevins, Jr., 5-4 TAD 209
(Madame Death), Fading Shadows: Madame
Death, (villainess in Secret Agent X
pulp series by G.T.Fleming-Roberts),
by Tom Johnson, 11 DS 12
Madame Sara, The Sorceress of the Strand,
(Classic Corner Rare Tales, fiction),
by L.T.Meade, 12-2 TAD 136
Madden, David: Thomas Berger's Comic-
Absurd Vision in WHO IS TEDDY
VILLANOVA?, 14-1 TAD 37
Maddren, Gerry: The Shuffle, (fiction),
1-2 M 57
Madel, Melvin: letter of comment,
22 X 52
Mader, Tom & Sue: letter of comment,
7 JD 5
Madison, George H.: letter of comment,
5-1 TAD 46
Madison, (Mr. & Mrs.) George H.: letter
of comment, 3-6 MR 11; 9-3 TAD 168
Madle, Robert A.: Terence X. O'Leary's
War Birds, (on the pulp magazine
WAR BIRDS), 69 PU 5
Madle, Robert A.: Why I Collect Science
Fiction, 20 X 7

(Mado, George, series: Warren Tute),
Checklist, Annotated, by Barry
Van Tilburg, 5-2 MF 2
Madzak, Stanley: letter of comment,
36 X 74
Magazine, The, (on ELLERY QUEEN'S MYSTERY
MAGAZINE, with chronology, outstanding
writers, and circulation data), by
Marvin Lachman, 2-1 QC 6
(MAGAZINE OF HORROR), Checklist and
Index, by Gene Marshall and Carl F.
Waedt, 3 SF 6
Magazine Serial is Background for Two
Books, (by Leo Edwards, boys' books),
by Julius R. Chenu, 2-5 TB 1
Magazine Stories of John D. MacDonald,
by Len & June Moffatt, 3 JD 5;
4 JD 1; 5 JD 1; 5 JD 4; 7 JD 13;
8 JD 2; 8 JD 18
(Magee, Alan), An Informal Survey of
Cover Art of the Seventies, Pt.1,
Tribute to Agatha Christie, by
Frank Eck, 9-3 TAD 170
Magic Draught, The, (verse), by Frederick
Faust, 1-2 FC 5
(MAGICIAN, THE: James Gunn), Mystery
Plus: A Pair of Triple Threats,
(magic, mystery, and science fiction),
by R. Jeff Banks, 4-4 PP 14
(Magill, Frank N., ed.: SURVEY OF SCIENCE
FICTION LITERATURE), Vault of the Ages,
by George Kelley, 2-2 CP 20
Magnus Stronghold, The, (fiction), by
John McNamara, 2 MT 2
Mahan, Jeffrey H.: The Hard-Boiled Detective
in the Fallen World, 1-2 C 90
Mahoney, Ed: letter of comment,
4-2 PP 48; 5-1 MF 46
Maida, Patricia: Interview with Lillian
O'Donnell, 14-2 TAD 164
(Maigret, Inspector, detective: Georges
Simenon), A Bibliography and English
Language Index to Georges Simenon's
Maigret Novels, by Norman J. Shaffer,
3-1 TAD 31
(Maigret, Inspector, detective: Georges
Simenon), Maigret & Co., The Detectives
of the Simenon Agency, (translated by
Francis M. Nevins, Jr.), by Maurice
Dubourg, 4-2 TAD 79
Maigret & Co.- The Detectives of the
Simenon Agency, (translated by
Francis M. Nevins, Jr.), by Maurice
Dubourg, 4-2 TAD 79
Main, R.W.: letter of comment, 4 SF 45;
5 SF 47
Mainstream Mysteries and Novels of Crime,
(reviews), by Gary Warren Niebuhr,
3-2 PP 23; 3-6 PP 17; (bestsellers
1980) 4-1 PP 13; 4-3 PP 5; (mystery-
related books reviewed) 4-5/6 PP 63
Maio, Kathi: letter of comment,
6/7 LR 19
(Mair, George B.: Dr. David Grant series),
Checklist, Annotated, by Barry Van
Tilburg, 4-4 MF 16

Making of a Tale-Spinner, The: John
D. MacDonald's Early Pulp Mystery
Stories, by Francis M. Nevins, Jr.,
1-1 C 89
(Maling, Arthur), Conversation,
(interview with Maling), by Don
Cole, 2-1 PP 11
Mallaber, Paul: letter of comment,
3-2 CP 1
(Malleson, Lucy Beatrice), Lucy
Beatrice Malleson, (sketch), by
Estelle Fox, 2-6 MR 16
(Malone, John J., series: Craig Rice),
John J. Malone (and Cohorts),
by Fred Dueren, 8-1 TAD 44
Maloney, Martin: The Radio Mystery
Program, 2-5 MR 3
(MALTESE FALCON, THE: Dashiell Hammett),
Order and Disorder in The Maltese
Falcon, by Donald J. Pattow,
11-2 TAD 171
(MALTESE FALCON, THE: Dashiell Hammett),
The Problem of Moral Vision in
Dashiell Hammett's Detective
Novels, Pt.4, by George J.Thompson,
7-3 TAD 178
(MALTESE FALCON, THE: Dashiell Hammett),
The Projected Detective, (on the
film), by Andy Jaysnovitch,
12 CL 8
Maltese Puzzle, The, (crossword
puzzle), 2-3 M 25
Maltin, Leonard: Basil Rathbone as
Sherlock Holmes, 1-4 MR 12
Malzberg, Barry N.: letter of comment,
5 SF 28
Man From Miami, The - Lester Dent's
Oscar Sail, (on detective character
of Dent), by Fred Blosser, 5-2
TAD 93
Man From the East, The, (on The Spider,
pulp hero character), by Robert
Weinberg, 10 P 32
Man in a Suitcase, (television series,
with checklist), by Paul Bishop,
7 PE 15
Man of Bronze - and His Creator, (on
pulp hero character Doc Savage
and author Lester Dent), by Samuel
W. Potts, 2 BS 8
Man of Mystery, The, (John Montague
as the real Doc Savage?), by Bill
Laidlaw, 2 DQ 5
Man Who Never Said Anything, The, (on
Sir Denis Nayland Smith, in Dr. Fu
Manchu stories), by John Harwood,
6 R 20
(MAN WHO KNEW, THE: Edgar Wallace),
Waffling Again About Wallace, by
John A. Hogan, 4-3 TAD 167
Man Who Read (and Published) John
Dickson Carr, The, (Ellery Queen),
by Larry L. French, 1 NC 8
Man Who Was John Dickson Carr, The,
(biographical tribute), by Larry
L. French, 1 NC 3

Man Who was Thursday, The, (Wade Miller's detective character, Max Thursday), by Marvin Lachman, 8-3 TAD 179

Manacher, Gary P.: letter of comment, 3 BS 20

Manachino, Albert: A Critical "Savage" Artist, (on cover art for Doc Savage), 4 DR 2

Manachino, Albert: "I'll Save the World in a Minute, But First How About Something to Eat?" (on eating habits of Doc Savage in the stories), 4 DS 7

Manachino, Albert: letter of comment, 3 DS 6; 4 DS 3; 11 DS 19

Mandes, Louis C., Jr.: Crime Crossword, (crossword puzzle), 11-1 TAD 100; 11-2 TAD 194; 11-3 TAD 293; 11-4 TAD 397; 12-3 TAD 82; 12-2 TAD 165; 12-4 TAD 382

Manesis, Peter: The Bonibooks, (on the Bonibooks line of paperback books), 2-4 PQ 26; (checklist) 2-4 PQ 28

Manesis, Peter: Cover-Up! (paperbacks with dust-jackets of different designs), 4-1 PQ 26

(MANHUNT magazine), Favorite Magazine Issues: MANHUNT (3:6) June 1955, by R. Jeff Banks, 4-6 MF 7

(MANHUNT magazine), On the Passing of MANHUNT, by Jon L. Breen, 1-3 TAD 89

(MANHUNT magazine), Requiem for a Magazine, by Robert Turner, 1-6 MR 5

(Mann, Jack), Checklist, by Robert E. Briney, 6-2 MR 21

(Mann, Jack), On the Trail of the Mysterious "Jack Mann", (author), by W.O.G.Lofts, 6-2 MR 19

Mann, Rich: letter of comment, 7 JD 3

Manor of Stepney, The, (re: Sax Rohmer), by John E. Carroll, 6 R 17

(Manton, Peter), Checklist, by Robert E. Briney and John Creasey, 2-1 TAD 15

Many Faces of the Whisperer, The, (on Street & Smith's pulp magazine THE WHISPERER), by Will Murray, 7 P 3

Many Lives of Nick Carter, The, (on the span of the Nick Carter stories in various formats), by J. Randolph Cox, 71 PU 8

Many Rises and Falls of J. Rufus Wallington, (detective character of George R. Chester), by Albert Borowitz, 12-1 TAD 28

(Maguire, Robert), Who Drew That Girl? (paperback cover art), by Lance Casebeer, 1-6 CP 28

Marble Faun, The: A Whydunit, (on THE MARBLE FAUN: Nathaniel Hawthorne), by J.R.Christopher, 11-1 TAD 78

(MARBLE FAUN, THE: Nathaniel Hawthorne), The Marble Faun: A Whydunit, by J.R.Christopher, 11-1 TAD 78

(March, Milo, detective: M.E.Chaber), Checklist, by Dickson Thorpe, 1-2 MF 6

Marchenkoff, P.R.: letter of comment, 63 PU 42

(Marchetti, Lou), Soft Cover Sketches, Lou Marchetti, (paperback cover art), by Thomas L. Bonn, 4-2 PQ 32

Marciniak, Ms. N.: letter of comment, 2 PE 42

Margaret Brundage, (sketch on WEIRD TALES cover artist), by Robert Weinberg, 2 WT 3

Margaret Millar, The Checklist of an "Unknown" Mystery Writer, by Marvin Lachman, 3-2 TAD 85

Margery Allingham's Albert Campion, A Chronological Examination of the Novels in Which He Appears, by B.A.Pike, 9-1 TAD 1; 9-2 TAD 95; 10-1 TAD 25; 10-2 TAD 117; 10-3 TAD 245; 10-4 TAD 324; 11-1 TAD 34; 11-2 TAD 177; 11-3 TAD 274; 11-4 TAD 372; 11-4 TAD 408; 12-1 TAD 34; 12-2 TAD 168; 12-4 TAD 348

Marie Corelli, Vendetta! (Marie Corelli: VENDETTA), by Michael Avallone, 9-4 TAD 270

(marijuana), Hard Touch, by Bill Wilson, 14 JD 17

Marinakis, Steve: letter of comment, 10 JD 20

Marine, Gene: letter of comment, 24 JD 41

(Marle, Jeff: Henri Bencolin, detective), Henry Bencolin, by Fred Dueren, 8-2 TAD 98

Mark Twain, Detective Story Writer, An Appreciation, by R. Jeff Banks, 7-3 TAD 176

Marley, Linward C.: letter of comment, 13-3 TAD 239

Marlowe, Dan J.: letter of comment, 4-2 MR 16

(Marlowe, Dan J.), Checklist, by Kelly Adrian, 3-3 MR 25

(Marlowe, Dan J.), Dan J. Marlowe, Who Said He Would and He Did, (on Marlowe and his books, with checklist), by Kelly Adrian, 3-3 MR 25

(Marlowe, Dan J.: Earl Drake series), Series Synopses, by Robert J. Randisi, 10-2 TAD 181

(Marlowe, Dan J.: John Killain series), Checklist, by Kelly Adrian, 3-3 MR 25

(Marlowe, Philip, detective), Marlowe's Long Goodbye, (character of Raymond Chandler), by G.A.Finch, 6-1 TAD 7

(Marlowe, Philip, detective), Morality
  and the Detective Hero: Raymond
  Chandler's Philip Marlowe, by Jay
  G. Milner, 1-1 C 116
Marlowe's Long Goodbye, (on Raymond
  Chandler's detective, Philip
  Marlowe), by G.A.Finch, 6-1 TAD 7
Marmelahd or Marmelade, (on the name
  Lestrade in the Sherlock Holmes
  stories), by E.F.Bleiler, 13-4 TAD
  334
Marohl, David: letter of comment,
  8-3 TAD 236; 9-3 TAD 169
Maron, Margaret B.: Driven to Death,
  (verse), 13-1 TAD 68
Maron, Margaret B.: Experience Will
  Out, (verse), 13-1 TAD 68
Maron, Margaret B.: letter of comment,
  10-4 TAD 386
Maroui, Lawrence: letter of comment,
  6 JD 11
(Marquand, John P.), John P. Marquand
  and Espionage Fiction, by George
  J. Rausch, 5-4 TAD 194
(Marquand, John P.: Mr. Moto Series),
  Checklist, Annotated, by Barry
  Van Tilburg, 4-5 MF 22
Marquardt, Ralph R.: letter of comment,
  1-4 AD 8
(Marric, J.J.: Commander Gideon series),
  Checklist, by Robert E. Briney
  and John Creasey, 2-1 TAD 15
(Marric, J.J.: GIDEON'S RISK), A Word
  for John Creasey, by John Boyles,
  11-3 TAD 282
(Marsh, Ngaio), A Visit with Dame Ngaio
  Marsh, by John Ball, 3-1 M 23
(Marsh, Ngaio), Checklist, by Charles
  Shibuk, 1-5 MR 16
(Marsh, Ngaio), Ngaio Marsh's "Theatrical"
  Murders, by Earl F. Bargainnier,
  10-2 TAD 175
(Marsh, Ngaio: A MAN LAY DEAD), The
  First Appearance, Roderick Alleyn,
  by Maryell Cleary, 2-6 PP 12
(Marsh, Ngaio: BLACK BEECH AND HONEYDEW),
  The Whodunit's Who's Who, (auto-
  biography of Marsh), by Philip T.
  Asdell, 3-4 PP 11
(Marsh, Ngaio: CLUTCH OF CONSTABLES),
  An Unsolved Mystery, by J.R.
  Christopher, 3-2 TAD 93
(Marsh, Ngaio: Roderick Alleyn, detective),
  The First Appearance (in A MAN LAY
  DEAD), by Maryell Cleary, 2-6 PP 12
(Marsh, Ngaio: Roderick Alleyn, detective),
  Roderick Alleyn, Ngaio Marsh's
  Oxonian Superintendent, by
  Earl F. Bargainnier, 11-1 TAD 63
Marshall, Gene: letter of comment,
  2 SF 40
Marshall, Gene, and Carl F. Waedt:
  An Index to the Health Knowledge
  Magazines, 3 SF 3
Marshall, Vincent R.: letter of comment,
  1-3 YB 11
Marsuzaka, (Mr. & Mrs.) Ken: letter
  of comment, 8-4 TAD 315
Martin, A.: letter of comment,
  14-1 TAD 73
(Martin, A.E.), Checklist, by Marvin
  Lachman, 1-3 PP 11
(Martin, A.E.), Department of Unknown
  Mystery Writers, A.E.Martin, by
  Marvin Lachman, 1-3 PP 11
Martin Beck, The Swedish Version of
  Barney Miller Without the Canned
  Laughter, by Thomas E. Williams,
  1-1 C 123
Martin, Dick: letter of comment,
  2-4 TBN 3
Martin, Dick: From Tutter to Oz - And
  Back Again, (collecting boys'
  books), 2-5 TBN 1
Martin, Don: letter of comment,
  63 PU 43
Martin, Lew: letter of comment,
  67 PU 56; 5-3 TAD 174
Martin Russell, A Profile, by
  Sven-Ingmar Petersson, 8-1 TAD 48
Martin, Walker: letter of comment,
  4-2 MF 59; 11 MN L13; 4-4 MR 14;
  9-1 TAD 85; 13 X 60; 22 X 51;
  36 X 73
(Martyn, Wyndham: Christopher Bond
  series), Checklist, Annotated,
  by Barry Van Tilburg, 4-5 MF 23
Martz, David: letter of comment,
  4-2 PP 38
(Marvel Comics), What's Up Doc? (on
  the Doc Savage Marvel Comics
  series), by Shelby L. Peck,
  2/3 DR 3
Marx, George J.: In Re: Judge Peck,
  (detective character of August
  Derleth), 1-1 PDA 24
Marx, George J.: letter of comment,
  3-2 AD 10
Marx, George J.: My Auctorial Friend,
  August Derleth, 1-1 PD 4
(Maryland), The American Regional
  Mystery, Maryland, Pt.Vi, by
  Marvin Lachman, 5-1 MR 3
Marzolf, Sister Florence: letter of
  comment, 1-4 AD 9
Masked Detective, The, (on the pulp
  magazine stories), by Wooda
  Nicholas Carr, 8 P 3; (checklist)
  8 P 7
Masked Rider, The, (on the MASKED
  RIDER Magazine stories), by Tom
  Land, 42 X 137; (index) 42 X 137
(MASKED RIDER, THE, magazine), The
  Masked Rider, by Tom Land, 42 X
  137; (index) 42 X 137
Masliah, Michael: Bond-Charteris
  Enterprises and Saint Enterprises,
  Checklist of Publications,
  12-4 TAD 354
Masliah, Michael L.: letter of comment,
  8-2 TAD 152; 12-2 TAD 186; 12-4
  TAD 354

(Masliah, Michael L.), Upfield Collector,
A Mystery Buff of the Purest Sort,
(collection of works of Arthur W.
Upfield), by Natalie Hall, 11-1 TAD 72
Mason, Ellsworth: letter of comment,
27 JD 35
(Mason, Francis Van Wyck: Hugh North series),
Checklist, Annotated, by Barry Van
Tilburg, 4-6 MF 4
(Mason, Perry, detective: Erle Stanley
Gardner), The Case of the Unbeaten
Attorney, or, The Secret Life of
Perry Mason, by Marvin Lachman,
4-3 TAD 147
(Mason, Perry, detective: Erle Stanley
Gardner), The Real Fourth Side of
the Triangle, (speculation, Della
Street's affair with Archie Goodwin),
by Marvin Lachman, 8 MN A11
Mass Market Murmurings, (column on
various data on paperback books),
by Barry Bernard, (JUNKIE by
William S. Burroughs) 1-1 CP 6;
(paperback book colophons) 1-2
CP 6; (Edward Gorey and Anchor
Books), 1-3 CP 5; (cartoon paper-
backs, 1939-59) 1-4 CP 8; (cross-
word puzzle paperbacks) 1-5 CP 12;
(cartoon paperbacks, 1960-69), 1-6
CP 20; (paperback magazines) 2-2
CP 32; ("Beat Generation" paperbacks),
2-3 CP 14; (E.C. artists in paper-
back, Pt.1, MAD magazine) 2-4 CP 18
Mass Market Paperback Publishing 1939-
Present, An Annotated Bibliography,
by Thomas Bonn, 1-4 PQ 3
Masser, Helmuth: letter of comment,
2-2 MF 60
Master of Mystery, (on Edgar Wallace,
by his daughter), by Penelope Wallace,
1-1 PDA 19
Masterpieces of the Macabre, by Robert
Kenneth Jones, 42 X 127
Masur, Harold Q.: Robert Fish, In Memorium,
(tribute), 14-2 TAD 120
(Mather, Berkeley: Idwal Rees series),
Checklist, Annotated, by Barry
Van Tilburg, 4-6 MF 4
Matisik, Ed: letter of comment,
3-2 M 2
Matt Helm Series, The, (adventure spy
series by Donald Hamilton), by R.
Jeff Banks and Guy M. Townsend,
2-2 MF 3
(Mattern, Jimmie), Cloud Country,
Boys' Series Bibliography, by
Harry K. Hudson, 1-3 YB 9
Matteson, Archibald C.: letter of comment,
13 JD 16
Matthews, Clayton: letter of comment,
3-1 TAD 68
(Matthews, Clayton), Mike Shayne Author
Former Area Resident, by Tom
Johnson, 5 U 30
Matthews, Earl M.: letter of comment,
11 JD 19

Matthews, Michael S.: letter of comment,
2-3 TAD 200
Mathiews, Franklin K.: Blowing Out the
Boy's Brains, (on boys' adventure
series books), 1-4 BC 106
(Matson, Norman: BATS IN THE BELFRY),
Bats in the Belfry, by Dave and Su
Bates, 2-1 CP 24
Mauel, Carole: letter of comment,
24 JD 39
Maugham, W. Somerset: Decline and Fall
of the Detective Story, (excerpt
from essay), 1-5 MR 6
(Maugham, W. Somerset), W. Somerset
Maugham as a Mystery Writer, (literary
study), by F. Shropshire, 14-2
TAD 190
Mauriac, Claude: Review of THE COMPLETE
WORKS OF GEORGES SIMENON, (article
review, translated by Francis M.
Nevins, Jr.), 2-3 TAD 162
Mawer, Randall R.: Raymond Chandler's
Self-Parody, (as found in various
works), 14-4 TAD 355
Max Brand and the Mystery Story, by
William J. Clark, 2-4 TAD 255
(MAX BRAND'S WESTERN MAGAZINE), Check-
list of Frederick Faust stories, by
William J. Clark, 1-1 FC 7
Maxims of Solar Pons, The, by Brian
Rountree, 1-1 PDA 21; 1-2 PDA 56;
2-1 PDA 24; 2-2 PDA 62
Maxwell, J.A.: letter of comment,
1-4 YB 9
May I Say a Few Well-Chosen Words,
(on the Praed Street Irregulars and
Solar Pons), by Alfred Peake,
2-5 PD 1
May, R.F.: letter of comment,
3 LW 3
Mayer, Les: letter of comment,
8 BS 4; 15 BS 16; 4-1 TAD 52
(Mayo, Asey, detective: Phoebe Atwood
Taylor), Asey Mayo - Cape Cod
Sleuth, by Lance Casebeer and Bruce
Taylor, 3-1 CP 20
(Mayo, Asey, detective: Phoebe Atwood
Taylor), Asey Mayo, "The Hayseed
Sherlock", by Fred Dueren,
10-1 TAD 21
(Mayo, James: Charles Hood series),
Checklist, Annotated, by Barry
Van Tilburg, 4-5 MF 5
Mayo, M.G.: letter of comment,
3-4 PP 38
Mayo, Oliver: A Glass of Wine Within
the Meaning of the Act, (use of
wine in the Dr. Thorndyke stories
of R. Austin Freeman), 7 TF 30
Mayo, Oliver: Golden Beetles or Blue
Bugs? (Freeman's "The Blue Scarab"
as a commentary on Poe's "The Gold-
Bug"), 11 TF 13
Mayo, Oliver: R. Austin Freeman and the
Improvement of Mankind, 1 TF 34;
2 TF 18

Mayo, Oliver: The Silent Sickle, a Thorndyke Pastiche, 3 TF 2

Mayo, Oliver: The Thorny Way to Heaven, a Thorndyke Pastiche, 9 TF 5

Mayo, Oliver, and John Mayo: Ross Freeman and the Aetiology of Malaria, (R. Austin Freeman's investigation of malaria), 5 TF 16

(McAfee, Maria), An Informal Survey of Cover Art of the Seventies, Pt.1, Tribute to Agatha Christie, (Maria McAfee, artist), by Frank Eck, 9-3 TAD 170

McAleer, John J.: A Welcome to the Wolfe Pack, (organization of Nero Wolfe fans), 1-1 G 15

McAleer, John J.: Confessions of a Reluctant Bibliophile, (comments on collecting works of Nero Wolfe and other by Rex Stout), 1-1 G 47

McAleer, John J.: "The Eye of Osiris" and the Webster-Parkman Case, (re: R. Austin Freeman), 12 TF 2

McAleer, John J.: letter of comment, 1-1 MF 40; 3-5 MR 36; 3-6 PP 38

McAleer, John J.: Nero Wolfe's Legacy of Books, 1-2 G 8

McAleer, John J.: R. Austin Freeman, Toward a Definite Biography, 11 TF 19

McAleer, John J.: Rex Stout, A Creator's World, 9 MN A7

McAleer, John J.: Rex Stout Newsletter, (column on Rex Stout, and on Nero Wolf particularly), 11-3 TAD 257; 12-1 TAD 66; 12-2 TAD 130; 12-3 TAD 224; 12-4 TAD 330; 13-1 TAD 41; 13-2 TAD 108; 13-3 TAD 224; 13-4 TAD 286; 14-1 TAD 22; 14-2 TAD 140; 14-3 TAD 230; 14-4 TAD 321

McAleer, John J.: West Thirty-Fifth Street, (verse, re: Nero Wolfe), 1-1 G 20

McAleer, Ruth D.: The Freeman Bibliophile, (notes on collectable items by R. Austin Freeman), 11 TF 33

McAleer, Ruth D.: Notes for a Freeman Bibliography, (R. Austin Freeman), 11 TF 12

(McBain, Ed), Ed McBain, Interview, by David Harlequin, 2-1 M 14

(McBain, Ed: GHOSTS), Mystery Plus: Old Friends Break New Ground, by R. Jeff Banks, 3-6 PP 15

McCaffrey, Valerie: letter of comment, 27 JD 36

McCahery, Jim: Checklist, Catherine Aird, 1-2 PP 22

McCahery, Jim: Checklist, David Alexander, 1-6 PP 23

McCahery, Jim: Checklist, Tucker Coe, 2 PE 18

McCahery, Jim: Checklist, Elizabeth Daly, 2-1 PP 28

McCahery, Jim: Checklist, Mignon G. Eberhart, 2-3 PP 25

McCahery, Jim: Checklist, Jonathan Latimer (William Crane series), 1 PE 6; 2 PE 13

McCahery, Jim: Checklist, Ruth Rendell, 2-3 PP 28

McCahery, Jim: Checklist, Bart Spicer (Carney Wilde series), 4 PE 23

McCahery, Jim: Father Roger of Fox River, (Father Roger Dowling series by Ralph McInerny), 2-5 PP 8

McCahery, Jim: Jonathan W. Latimer, An Interview, 11 SF 16

McCahery, Jim: Jonathan W. Latimer, Bibliography, 11 SF 20

McCahery, Jim: Jonathan W. Latimer, Filmography, 11 SF 21

McCahery, Jim: letter of comment, 5 LR 7; 6/7 LR 25; 2-5 MF 55; 3-4 MF 53; 2 PE 42; 3 PE 33; 4 PE 34; 6 PE 33; 1-2 PP 30; 1-3 PP 32; 1-4 PP 31; 1-5 PP 30; 1-6 PP 28; 2-1 PP 43; 2-2 PP 43; 2-4 PP 39; 2-5 PP 41; 3-1 PP 40; 3-1 PP 46; 3 U 48; 4 U 51; 5 U 62; 6 U 53

McCahery, Jim: Lonesome Cage, Private Investigator a la Peter Israel, 4 PE 3

McCahery, Jim: Pen Puzzler #1, The Personal Touch, (quiz mystery puzzle), 1-4 PP 7

McCahery, Jim: Scott Michel, An Interview, (with bibliography), 4-4 PP 3

McCahery, Jim: Series Spotlight, Bart Spicer's Carney Wilde (series), 3 PE 24; 4 PE 20; 5 PE 21

McCahery, Jim: Series Spotlight, Jonathan Latimer's William Crane, 1 PE 5; 2 PE 5

McCahery, Jim: Series Spotlight, M. Scott Michel's Wood Jaxon (series), 6 PE 3

(McCarthy, Gary: LEGEND OF THE LONE RANGER), Recent Lone Ranger Story a Mess, (critical article review), by I.R.Ybarra, 6 MA 8

McCarthy, John V., Jr.: letter of comment, 33 X 115

McCarthy, Paul: letter of comment, 1-4 PP 29; 2-5 PP 44; 3-1 PP 37; 3-1 PP 45; 4-2 PP 42; 7-4 TAD 300

McCarthy, Paul: The Short Mystery Stories of Agatha Christie, A Checklist, 6-1 TAD 16

McCarty, Clifford: letter of comment, 2-3 TAD 202; 5-1 TAD 57

McCauley, T.J.: Who Killed Kelly?, 14 R 11

McCloy, Helen: letter of comment, 4-2 MR 14

McCloy, Helen: The Return of Michael Shayne, (commentary on Shayne occasioned by announcement of new reprints, paperbacks), 14-4 TAD 344

(McClure, James), Apartheid in the Novels of James McClure, by Donald C. Wall, 10-4 TAD 348

McConnell, Arn: The Case of Commissioner
James Gordon, (Gordon was The Whisperer,
and the ancestor of Batman??), 1-3
WA 14

McConnell, Arn: Casting a Little Light
Among the Shadows, (speculation on
the Shadow and his past), 2-1 WA 3

McConnell, Arn: Kong, His Life and Fall,
(speculative essay on King Kong),
1-4 WA 3

McConnell, Arn: The Land that Maple White
Found, (THE LOST WORLD: A. Conan
Doyle), 1-1 WA 7

McConnell, Arn: Trivia Quiz - A Living
Shadow! (quiz) 1-4 WA 18

McConnell, Arn, and Todd Rutt: Caves,
Gas, and The Great Transfer Theory,
(speculative solution to the
disappearance of popular fiction
characters), 1-2 WA 11

McConnell, Arn, and Todd Rutt: The
Mysterious Case of the Carters,
or How Hirohito Became Nick
Carter's Aide, (imaginative
speculation), 1-2 WA 3

McConnell, Arn, and Todd Rutt: The
Terrible Beekeeper, (fiction,
pastiche on The Spider, Doc
Savage, The Shadow, Sherlock
Holmes), 1-2 WA 6; 1-3 WA 7;
1-4 WA 7; 2-1 WA 5; 1-1 WA 3

McConnell, Kirk: Trivia Quiz - The
Avenger, (quiz), 1-1 WA 11

McConnell, (Mrs.) Fran: letter of
comment, 3-3 PP 38

McCormick, John: letter of comment,
4 SF 45; 5 SF 28

(McCurtin, Peter), Carmody, Sagebrush
Detective, by R. Jeff Banks,
8-1 TAD 42

(McCurtin, Peter: THE SAVAGE), Mystery
Plus: A Pair of Triple Threats,
("a magical western mystery"), by
R. Jeff Banks, 4-4 PP 14

(McCutchin, Philip: Commander Esmond
Shaw series), Checklist, Annotated,
by Barry Van Tilburg, 4-5 MF 21

(McCutchin, Philip: Simon Shard series),
Checklist, Annotated, by Barry
Van Tilburg, 4-5 MF 21

McDade, T.M.: Crime Hunt, Real Life Cases,
(discussion of the Wallace Case),
14-4 TAD 374

McDade, Terrence J.: letter of comment,
25 JD 39

McDaniel, Ken: letter of comment,
3-2 CP 2; 4 PE 34; 5 PE 36;
38 X 144

McDearmon, L.H.: letter of comment,
4-1 TAD 73

McDole, Gary: letter of comment,
10-3 TAD 195

McDonald, Brian: letter of comment,
2 DS 9

(Mcdonald, Gregory), An Interview
with Gregory Mcdonald, by Robert
Randisi, 12-2 TAD 134

McDonnell, David: Doc Garbage in The
Demon of Dayton, (fiction, Doc
Savage pastiche), 1 DR 6; 2/3
DR 6

McFarland, Orin S.: letter of comment,
1-1 MF 40; 8-2 TAD 152

McFarlane, Leslie: letter of comment,
1-4 YB 10

(McFarlane, Leslie), Not Forgotten,
(on the Ken Holt and Rick Brant
boys' books series), by Fred
Woodworth, 2 MA 1

(McFarlane, Leslie), Other Writings
by Leslie McFarlane, by John M.
Enright, 4 MA 18

(McFarlane, Leslie: GHOST OF THE
HARDY BOYS), A Laughing Ghost,
(commentary on the book by
author of many of the Hardy Boys
boys' series books), by Kent
Winslow, 4 MA 15

McGee Gets a Fan(atic!) Letter,
(letter to Travis McGee, John
D. MacDonald character, and
reply, regarding social reaction
to murder suspects), by
Kenneth-Lorin Darby, 28 JD 10

(McGee, Travis, series: John D.
MacDonald), A Pile of Pointy
Polka Dots, (parody on McGee),
by Bailey Phelps, 26 JD 35

(McGee, Travis, series: John D.
MacDonald), A Stern Look at
McGee, by Elijah Stern, 15 JD 5

(McGee, Travis, series: John D.
MacDonald), The Aging of Travis
McGee, by John D. MacDonald,
20 JD 3

(McGee, Travis, series: John D.
MacDonald), The Chronology of
the Travis McGee Novels, by
Allan D. Pratt, 13-2 TAD 83

(McGee, Travis, series: John D.
MacDonald), Color Him Quixote,
MacDonald's Strategy in the
Early McGee Novels, by Michael
J. Tolley, 10-1 TAD 6

(McGee, Travis, series: John D.
MacDonald), Conquering the
Stereotypes, On Reading the
Novels of John D. MacDonald,
(comments on the female characters),
by George S. Peck, 13-2 TAD 90

(McGee, Travis, series: John D.
MacDonald), Dating the Travis
McGee Stories, by Dean Grennell,
22 JD 11

(McGee, Travis, series: John D.
MacDonald), For Travis McGee
Fans, (crossword puzzle), by
Loyal G. Compton, 26 JD 13

(McGee, Travis, series: John D. MacDonald),
Is It True What They Say About Travis?
(comments and notes), by Len & June
Moffatt, 2 JD 8
(McGee, Travis, series: John D. MacDonald),
John D. MacDonald - A Little Ecology
Goes a Long Way, by Wister Cook,
1-1 C 57
(McGee, Travis, series: John D. MacDonald),
Lady in Waiting, (verse), by Ethel
D. Compton, 24 JD 41
(McGee, Travis, series: John D. MacDonald),
Letters to McGee, by Bob Allison,
25 JD 5
(McGee, Travis, series: John D. MacDonald),
Limerick, by Fred Cropper, 20 JD 18
(McGee, Travis, series: John D. MacDonald),
McGee Gets a Fan(atic!) Letter, (social
reaction to murder suspects, and reply),
by Kenneth-Lorin Darby, 28 JD 10
(McGee, Travis, series: John D. MacDonald),
McGee's Girls, by Peggy Moran,
1-1 C 82
(McGee, Travis, series: John D. MacDonald),
Not Vibgyor: Bpprgoaygbiltstl, (acronym
for McGee series), by Dean A. Grennell,
20 JD 5
(McGee, Travis, series: John D. MacDonald),
The Real McGee, (a synthesis of puzzle
and hero type mystery fiction), by
Bailey P. Phelps, 28 JD 13
(McGee, Travis, series: John D. MacDonald),
The Reluctant Hero - Reflections
on Vocation and Heroism in the Travis
McGee Novels of John D. MacDonald, by
Larry E. Grimes, 1-1 C 103
(McGee, Travis, series: John D. MacDonald),
Travis McGee as Traditional Hero, by
Erling B. Holtsmark, 1-1 C 99
(McGee, Travis, series: John D. MacDonald),
Travis McGee Quiz, (quiz), by Tom
Clayton, 26 JD 19
McGee's Girls, (on Travis McGee series by
John D. MacDonald), by Peggy Moran,
1-1 C 82
McGerr, Patricia: letter of comment,
8-1 TAD 70; 10-2 TAD 100
(McGinnis),Denholm's Law #2, (on
McGinnis as paperback cover artist),
1-3 CP 11; 1-5 CP 23
McGoldrick, John: Jamison and Lestrade,
A Comparative Study, (Sherlock
Holmes and Solar Pons), 1-4 PD 1
McGonigle, Jack: letter of comment,
26 X 77
McGregor, Herman S.: A Critical Analysis
of the Doc Savage Novels, (individual
treatment of stories in depth; magazine)
2 BS 10 (Vol.1, #1,2,3);3 BS 8 (Vol.1,
#4,5,6); 4 BS 8 (Vol.2, #1,2,3,4);
5 BS 6 (Vol.2, #5,6; Vol.3, #1);
6 BS 15 (Vol.3, #2,3,4); 7 BS 13
(Vol.3, #5,6; Vol.4, #1);8 BS 11
(Vol.4, #2,3,4); 9 BS 8 (Vol.4,
#5,6; Vol.5, #1); 10 BS 9 (Vol.5,

McGregor, Herman S.: A Critical Analysis
of the Doc Savage Novels, (continued),
#2,3,4); 11 BS 14 (Vol.6, #2,3,4);
12 BS 11 (Vol.5, #5,6; Vol.6, #1);
13 BS 13 (Vol.6, #5,6; Vol.7, #1);
14 BS 5 (Vol.7, #2,3,4); 15 BS 9
(Vol.7, #5,6; Vol.8, #1); 2/3 DR
13 (Vol.1, #1,2,3)
McGregor, Herman S.: Comprehensive Survey
of The Spider Novels, (in-depth
treatment of each story in magazine
THE SPIDER), 66 PU 41 (Vol.1, #1,2,3);
67 PU 77 (Vol.1, #4; Vol.2, #1);
68 PU 29 (Vol.2, #2); 70 PU 13
(Vol.2, #3,4; Vol.3, #1,2); 71 PU 15
(Vol.3, #3)
McGregor, Herman S.: The Fantastic
Sisters - Literature and Lovely,
(on FAMOUS FANTASTIC MYSTERIES and
FANTASTIC NOVELS, pulp magazines,
with checklist and index), 74 PU 7
McGregor, Herman S.: letter of comment,
4 BS 16; 5 BS 3; 7 BS 2; 8 BS 6;
8 BS 8; 68 PU 24
McGregor, Herman S.: The Pulps? I Loved
Them! (reminiscences of the pulp
magazines), 67 PU 36
McGregor, Herman S.: The Scheme of
Things, (fiction), 15 BS 19
McGregor, Herman S., and Wooda Nicholas
Carr: Contemplating Seven of the
Pulp Heroes, (comparisons and
characteristics), 12 BS 3
(McGuire, Robert), Who Drew That Girl?,
(McGuire as paperback cover artist),
by Lance Casebeer, 1-5 CP 31
(McInerny, Ralph: Father Roger Dowling
series), Father Roger of Fox River,
by Jim McCahery, 2-5 PP 8
(McInerny, Ralph: Father Roger Dowling
series), Series Synopses, by Dan
Andriacco, 12-2 TAD 133
McIntosh, Gerald J.: The Short Short
Stories of Burt L. Standish (pseud.
of Gilbert L. Patten, writing in
TIP TOP WEEKLY, dime novel),
2-2 BC 168
McIntosh, Walter H.: A Quick Look at
THE YOUTH'S COMPANION, (boy's
paper), 4-1 BC 394
McIntosh, Walter H.: An Aid to Historical
Fiction - Boys' Books, 3-3 BC 326
McIntosh, Walter H.: Checklist, Elijah
Kellogg (boys' books), 3-2 BC 309
McIntosh, Walter H.: Checklist,
William H.G.Kingston, (boys' books),
3-4 BC 357
McIntosh, Walter H.: Elijah Kellogg,
Maine Boy's Writer, 3-2 BC 309
McIntosh, Walter H.: William H.G.King-
ston, English Boys' Writers,
3-4 BC 355
McKearnan, Robert T.: letter of comment,
21 JD 17
McKimmey, James: letter of comment,
7-2 TAD 152

McKinstry, Lohr: letter of comment,
69 PU 27

McKraken, James A., and G. Arthur Rahman:
The Case of the Cheshire Cat's Paw,
(fiction, Sherlock Holmes pastiche),
10 CL 3

McLaughlin, Arthur: letter of comment,
1-2 M 3

McLaughlin, Mary & Jerry: letter of
comment, 27 JD 36

McLaughlin, Patrick: letter of comment,
7 JD 7; 10 JD 15

McLeish, Stewart C.: letter of comment,
5 BB 21

(McLeod, Robert: Talos Cord series),
Checklist, Annotated, by Barry
Van Tilburg, 4-5 MF 22

McManus, Allen: letter of comment,
7-1 TAD 74

McMilian, Peter L.: letter of comment,
8 X 38

McMillan, Dennis: The Uncollected Fiction
of Fredric Brown, 3-1 CP 15; 3-2
CP 25

McMillin, Miles: Hello Wisconsin,
(regarding August Derleth), 1-4
AD 3

McNabb, Edward J.: letter of comment,
1-3 BC 85

McNamara, John: The Calculated Man,
(fiction), 1 MT 2

McNamara, John: The Magnus Stronghold,
(fiction), 2 MT 2

McPhail, Dan: letter of comment,
62 PU 13

McSherry, Frank D., Jr.: A New Category
of the Mystery Story, (plots with
two possible solutions - mundane
or supernatural), 2-1 TAD 23

McSherry, Frank D., Jr.: A Study in
Black, (supernatural themes in
crime fiction), 5-5 MR 23;
5-6 MR 3; 6-1 MR 29; 6-2 MR
39

McSherry, Frank D., Jr.: The Amateur's
Hour, (amateur detectives in crime
fiction), 3-1 TAD 14

McSherry, Frank D., Jr.: The Armchair
Criminal, (villainy by mastermind
criminals), 14-1 TAD 58

McSherry, Frank D., Jr.: Avante-Garde
Writing in the Detective Story,
3-2 TAD 95

McSherry, Frank D., Jr.: Black Murder
and Gold Medal, (Gold Medal line
of mystery fiction, England),
4-3 TAD 156

McSherry, Frank D., Jr.: Bundles from
Britain - Spy Anthologies, 3-3 TAD
176

McSherry, Frank D., Jr.: Comment from
Cover Artist on Rex Stout Memorial
Issue of THE MYSTERY NOOK, 9 MN A10

McSherry, Frank D., Jr.: Footsteps on
the Golden Road, (addenda to "The
Golden Road to Samarkand"), 7-4 TAD
264

McSherry, Frank D., Jr.: The Golden
Road to Samarkand - The Arabian
Nights in Detective Fiction, (on
exotic locales used in some crime
fiction), 7-2 TAD 77

McSherry, Frank D., Jr.: Index, NERO
WOLFE MYSTERY MAGAZINE, 9 MN A25

McSherry, Frank D., Jr.: Rex Stout
as Editor, (index to REX STOUT
MYSTERY MAGAZINE), 9 MN A21

McSherry, Frank D., Jr.: Jim Thompson,
A Walk in the Jungle, (addenda to
"Judge Crater and His Fellow
Travellers" on mysterious dis-
appearances), 8-1 TAD 99

McSherry, Frank D., Jr.: Judge Crater
and His Fellow Travellers,
("vanishers" in mystery fiction),
4-4 TAD 195

McSherry, Frank D., Jr.: Lady in a
Straightjacket, (MYSTERY BOOK
MAGAZINE), 9-3 TAD 201

McSherry, Frank D., Jr.: letter of
comment, 2-1 MF 52; 11 MN L4;
1-5 PP 31;2-3 PP 37; 74 PU 28;
14 R 28; 1-3 TAD 108; 1-4 TAD
154; 2-1 TAD 57; 2-2 TAD 133;
3-1 TAD 62; 3-3 TAD 203; 3-4
TAD 276; 4-1 TAD 52; 4-1 TAD
54; 4-3 TAD 184; 4-4 TAD 258;
5-1 TAD 48; 5-2 TAD 110; 5-3
TAD 177; 5-4 TAD 244; 6-1 TAD
60; 6-2 TAD 125; 6-3 TAD 206;
6-4 TAD 280; 7-1 TAD 68; 7-2
TAD 144; 7-3 TAD 230; 7-4 TAD
301; 8-1 TAD 73; 8-2 TAD 157;
8-3 TAD 232; 8-4 TAD 319; 9-1
TAD 76; 9-2 TAD 158; 9-3 TAD
238; 9-4 TAD 299; 10-1 TAD 4;
10-2 TAD 99; 10-3 TAD 276;
10-4 TAD 379; 11-2 TAD 206;
11-3 TAD 309; 12-1 TAD 91;
12-1 TAD 93; 12-3 TAD 266;
12-4 TAD 356; 13-2 TAD 159;
13-3 TAD 238; 14-4 TAD 382;
5 U 62; 36 X 70

McSherry, Frank D., Jr.: Now It Can Be
Told - The Secret of the Pons
(Solar Pons), 1-2 PDA 57

McSherry, Frank D., Jr.: Rare Vintages
From the Tropics - T.S.Stribling's
CLUES OF THE CARRIBEES, (Poggioli),
6-3 TAD 172

McSherry, Frank D., Jr.: The Shadow
of Ying Ko, (re: Sax Rohmer), 16 R 1

McSherry, Frank D., Jr.: The Smallest
Sub-Genre, (the reader as detective),
10-3 TAD 267

McSherry, Frank D., Jr.: Under Two
Flags - The Detective Story in
Science Fiction, 2-3 TAD 171

McSherry, Frank D., Jr.: Watch This
Space! (article review of SPACE
FOR HIRE by William F. Nolan),
5-4 TAD 226

McSherry, Frank D., Jr.: Who-Really-Dun-It?,
    Two Sub-Branches of the Detective Story,
    (clues make the story), 2-2 TAD 88
Mead, David: letter of comment,
    9 JD 18
Meade, L.T.: Madame Sara, The Sorceress
    of the Strand, (Classic Corners Rare
    Tales, fiction), 12-2 TAD 136
Mean Streets Revisited, Seven Hardboiled
    Authors at the Scene of the Crime
    Bookshop, by Ray Zone, 2-3 M 18
Medoff, Randy: letter of comment,
    26 X 72
Meeder, (Mrs.) Pam: letter of comment,
    3-3 PP 39; 3-4 PP 39
Meet Dr. Fu Manchu, (by creator), by
    Sax Rohmer, 10 R 1
Meet Dr. Thorndyke, (by creator; origin
    and characteristics), by R. Austin
    Freeman, 4 TF 31
Meet Nolan, (discussion of "heist artist"/
    detective Nolan in series by Max
    Collins), by Robert J. Randisi,
    4-5/6 PP 29
Meet Phyllis A. Whitney, (interview),
    by Pat Erhardt, 2-4 MR 3
Meet the Author, (biographical data),
    by Allen J. Hubin,
    Robert C.S.Adey, 2-4 TAD 261
    Catherine Aird, 2-3 TAD 157
    Bernard Beauchesne, 1-4 TAD 150
    Nathan L. Bengis, 1-4 TAD 118
    Robert E. Briney, 2-4 TAD 273
    Mary S. Cameron, 1-2 TAD 52
    J.R.Christopher, 1-2 TAD 58; 2-4 TAD 273
    J. Randolph Cox, 2-4 TAD 214
    John Creasey, 2-1 TAD 3
    Dean W. Dickensheet, 2-4 TAD 273
    Norman Donaldson, 1-2 TAD 37
    Frank P. Donovan, 1-4 TAD 128
    Frank Gruber, 2-4 TAD 216
    Ordean Hagen, 1-2 TAD 47
    Iwan Hedman, 2-4 TAD 236
    Joan Kahn, 2-3 TAD 170
    James Keddie, Jr., 1-1 TAD 9
    Bruce L. Monblatt, 4-3 TAD 171
    Marvin Lachman, 1-1 TAD 24
    Nogel Morland, 1-3 TAD 72
    Francis M. Nevins, Jr., 1-3 TAD 85
    Lenore Glen Offord, 2-2 TAD 76
    Gordon C. Ramsey, 1-1 TAD 18
    Dr. George J. Rausch, Jr., 2-1 TAD 60
    James Sandoe, 1-2 TAD 42
    John Bennett Shaw, 1-2 TAD 55
    Charles Shibuk, 1-1 TAD 12
    Hillary Waugh, 2-1 TAD 54
Meet the Author, Joe Archibald, by Joe
    Archibald, 10 P 10
Meet the Collector, Tom Kelly, by Tom
    Kelly, 2-3 FC 5
Meeting Menendes, An Analysis of Three
    Detective Novels by Suzanne Blanc,
    by Jane S. Bakerman, 10-3 TAD 227
(Mel Martin Baseball series: John R.
    Cooper), Boys' Series Bibliography,
    by Harry K. Hudson, 1-6 YB 15

Melerault, Mme. B.: letter of comment,
    27 JD 36
Melodrama and Manners, Changing
    Attitudes Toward Class Distinctions
    in English Detective Fiction 1868-
    1939, by Jeanne F. Bedell, 1-1 C 15
Meltzer, Edmund S.: letter of comment,
    1-4 MF 60; 11-1 TAD 5
(Melville, Herman), Melville's "Benito
    Cereno" - An American Mystery,
    by James Fulcher, 2-1 C 116
Melville's "Benito Cereno" - An American
    Mystery, (by Herman Melville), by
    James Fulcher, 2-1 C 116
Memoir, by E. Hoffman Price, 1 WT 4
Memoir of Mayne Reid, (boys' books
    author), by R.H.Stoddard, 2-2 BC
    172
Memorial, Rex Stout, by Michael Bourne,
    21 X 8
Memories of Ngai, (verse), by Walter
    Shedlofsky, 15 X 45
Memories Upon Which I Dwell Fondly,
    (reminiscences of boys' books),
    by Harry Pulfer, 1-3 BC 89
Menasce, Gianni: letter of comment,
    7 MY 11; 8-2 TAD 163; 8-3 TAD
    236
Mendelson, Bob: letter of comment,
    13 R 30
(Menendes, Inspector Miguel, detective:
    Suzanne Blanc), Meeting Menendes,
    An Analysis of Three Detective
    Novels by Suzanne Blanc, by Jane
    S. Bakerman, 10-3 TAD 227
Menshikoff, Natasha: letter of comment,
    11-3 TAD 212
(Mercer Boys series: Capwell Wyckoff),
    Missing Mercer Musings, (boys'
    series books), by Don Holbrook,
    6 MA 6
(Mercer Boys series: Capwell Wyckoff),
    Wyckoff's Stories of Adventure,
    (boys' series books), by Don
    Holbrook, 5 MA 6
Mercury Mystery Checklist, (digest-
    sized paperback mystery series),
    by Jeff Meyerson, 1-4 PP 33;
    (addendum by Jim Tinsman) 1-6 PP
    27; 2-1 PP 31
Mercy Anne, (fiction), by Max Brand
    (pseud. for Frederick Faust),
    1-4 FC 1
(Meredith, John, series: Francis
    Gerard), Checklist, Annotated,
    by Barry Van Tilburg, 5-3 MF 21
Merit Books, Checklist, (paperback
    line), by J. Grant Thiessen,
    2 SF 11
Merrill, Bruce: letter of comment,
    1-2 CP 3; 1-5 CP 1; 2-1 CP 2
Merrill, Bruce: Popular Library vs.
    Art, (paperback coverart),
    2-1 CP 20
(Merritt, Abraham), A. Merritt's
    Mysteries, by Walter J. Wentz,
    5-4 TAD 204

(Merrivale, Sir Henry, detective: John Dickson Carr), My Favourite Detectives, Sir Henry Merrivale, (with checklist), by Robert C.S.Adey, 3-2 MR 11

(Merriweather Girls, series), Juvenalia, (girls' series books), by Julius R. Chenu, 1-4 YB 14

(Merriwell, Frank), Generations Have Marveled at Frank Merriwell, (boys' hero in dime novels and books), 1-2 BC 56

(Merriwell, Frank), King of the Dime Novels, (Frank Merriwell in dime novels), by Gil O'Gara, 3 U 17

Mertz, Stephen: Captain Shaw's Hard-Boiled Boys, (authors in THE HARD BOILED OMNIBUS, edited by Joseph Shaw), 12-3 TAD 264

Mertz, Stephen: Checklist, Carroll John Daly, A Selective List, (author), 2-3 MF 22

Mertz, Stephen: The Further Adventures of Robert Leslie Bellem, of the Bellem-Adams Connection, (pulp author), 38 X 138

Mertz, Stephen: In Defense of Carroll John Daly, (pulp author), 2-3 MF 19

Mertz, Stephen: Investigating Dan Turner, (detective character created by Robert Leslie Bellem, pulp magazines), 5 PE 9

Mertz, Stephen: letter of comment, 2-3 MF 58; 2-4 MF 59; 2-5 MF 49; 3-5 MF 46; 1 MN 5; 5 PE 36; 6-4 TAD 275; 7-3 TAD 227; 8-1 TAD 71; 8-2 TAD 159; 9-4 TAD 298; 10-1 TAD 4; 11-3 TAD 310; 11-4 TAD 399; 40 X 86

Mertz, Stephen: Michael Avallone, A Checklist, 9-2 TAD 132

Mertz, Stephen: Rapping With Mike, A Michael Avallone Appreciation, Interview, and Checklist, 8 PE 2

Mertz, Stephen: Robert Leslie Bellem, The Great Unknown, (pulp author), 21 X 49

Mertz, Stephen: W.T.Ballard, An Interview, (pulp author), 12-1 TAD 14; (checklist), 12-1 TAD 19

Messecar, C.L.: "American Boy" Reviews, (reviews of boys' books), 3-2 BC 318; 3-3 BC 351; 3-4 BC 371

Messer, Gordon: letter of comment, 2 DS 7

Meteor Writes, (letters column), 1-2 WA 13

Metzger, Albert: letter of comment, 5 X 41; 8 X 38

Meudt, Edna: The Derleth Connection, Edna Meudt, 2-3/4 AD 6

Meudt, Edna: Return to Place of Hawks, (re: August Derleth, verse), 2-3/4 AD 8

Meudt, Edna: Summer 1971, (verse), 2-3/4 AD 7

Meyer, Daniel R.: letter of comment, 1-6 YB 9

(Meyer, Lynn: Dr. Sarah Chayse, detective), Feminists as Detectives, Harriet Vane, Kate Fansler, Sarah Chayse, by Kathleen Gregory Klein, 13-1 TAD 31

Meyers, Richard S.: letter of comment, 13-3 TAD 237

Meyers, Richard S.: TAD on TV, (mystery television shows, reviews and comment in THE ARMCHAIR DETECTIVE), 13-3 TAD 228; 13-4 TAD 332; 14-1 TAD 82; 14-2 TAD 153; 14-3 TAD 254; 14-4 TAD 332

Meyerson, Jeffrey: Avon Classic Crime, (mystery fiction published in Avon line of paperbacks), 1-4 CP 5; 1-5 MF 19; (checklist) 1-5 MF 20

Meyerson, Jeffrey: Bouchercon IX - A Personal View, (report on mystery fans and authors convention), 1-6 PP 20

Meyerson, Jeffrey: Checklist, Best-seller Mysteries, (paperback series), 1-5 PP 33

Meyerson, Jeffrey: Checklist, Mercury Mysteries, (paperback series), 1-4 PP 33

Meyerson, Jeffrey: Index of Books Reviewed in Vol.1, THE MYSTERY FANCIER, 2-1 MF 9

Meyerson, Jeffrey: Jonathan Press Checklist, (paperback series), 1-3 PP 35

Meyerson, Jeffrey: letter of comment, 9 CL 10; 1-2 CP 2; 22 JD 21; 6/7 LR 27; 1-2 MF 48; 1-3 MF 56; 1-4 MF 58; 1-5 MF 55; 1-6 MF 57; 2-2 MF 46; 2-3 MF 69; 2-4 MF 54; 2-5 MF 54; 2-6 MF 48; 3-1 MF 57; 3-2 MF 53; 3-4 MF 60; 11 MN L10; 11 MN L11; 12 MN L2; 12 MN L12; 2 PE 44; 5 PE 35; 3-4 TAD 305; 9-1 TAD 78; 9-2 TAD 156; 10-1 TAD 3; 10-2 TAD 163; 11-1 TAD 4; 13-1 TAD 77; 4 U 52

Meyerson, Jeffrey: Series Synopses, Matt Scudder Series by Lawrence Block, 12-1 TAD 62

(Meyerson, Jeffrey), Biographical Sketch, 2-3 PP 8

Michael Avallone, A Checklist, by Stephen Mertz, 9-2 TAD 132

Michael Avallone, Writer Extra-ordinaire!, by Michael L. Cook, 8 U 76

Michael Harrison, An Interview, by Luther Norris, 3-6 MR 17

(Michel, M. Scott), Scott Michel, An Interview, (with bibliography), by Jim McCahery, 4-4 PP 3

(Michel, M. Scott), Series Spotlight, M. Scott Michel's Wood Jaxon, by Jim McCahery, 6 PE 3

Mickey Spillane Comic Strip, 12-4 TAD 317
Microcosm, (verse, re: August Derleth), by
    Steve Eng, 2-1 AD 3
(Middle East locale), The Suspense Novel -
    and the Middle East, by Amnon Kabatchnik,
    3-4 MR 3
Midnight Visitor, (verse), by Jean
    Balderston, 12-3 TAD 208
(Midwest locale), The American Regional
    Mystery, Pt.IX, (locales of crime
    fiction), by Marvin Lachman), 6-1 MR 1
Mighty, Miraculous Murder Mystery Monthly,
    (on MURDER MYSTERY MONTHLY), by Howard
    Waterhouse, 1-4 PQ 31
Mike Avallone, One of the Un-Angry Young
    Men, by Kelly Adrian, 1-5 MR 3
Mike Hammer, (on television, checklist),
    by Andy Jaysnovitch, 4 PE 5
Mike Shayne Author Former Area Resident,
    (on Clayton Matthews), by Tom Johnson,
    5 U 30
(Mill Creek Irregulars series: August
    Derleth), Boys' Series Bibliography,
    by Harry K. Hudson, 1-6 YB 16
(Millar, Margaret), Margaret Millar, The
    Checklist of an "Unknown" Mystery
    Writer, by Marvin Lachman, 3-2 TAD 85
Miller, Chuck: letter of comment,
    1-3 PQ 10
Miller, Don: A Look at the Novels of Ruth
    Rendell, 10 MN A7
Miller, Don: A Look at the Short Stories
    of Ruth Rendell, 10 MN A19
Miller, Don: A Partial Checklist of Reviews
    of Books by Rex Stout, 9 MN A45
Miller, Don: A Partial Checklist of Reviews
    of Books by Ruth Rendell, 10 MN A23
Miller, Don: A Partial Index to Reviews of
    Crossen Books, (Kendell F. Crossen,
    with abstracts from reviews), 12 MN A5
Miller, Don: A Partial Index of Reviews of
    the Books of Georgette Heyer, 13 MN 27
Miller, Don: The Amateur Press, (on fan
    magazines), 1 MN 2; 5/6 MN 9; 8 MN 43
Miller, Don: Anthology Index, (index to
    various mystery anthologies), 2-4
    MM Q1
Miller, Don: Book Review Extracts, (from
    various newspapers), 1-1 MM 10; 1-2
    MM 7; 1-3 MM 9; 1-4 MM 7; 1-5 MM 5;
    1-6 MM 5; 1-7 MM 5; 1-8 MM 8; 1-9
    MM 8; 1-10 MM 10; 1-11 MM 6; 2-1
    MM 7; 2-2 MM 9; 2-3 MM 7; 2-4 MM 8
Miller, Don: ELLERY QUEEN'S MYSTERY MAGAZINE,
    1975 Index, 8 MN 45
Miller, Don: From the Press - The Early
    Non-Nero Wolfe Books, (review extracts),
    9 MN A57
Miller, Don: Georgette Heyer, A Partial
    Bibliography, 13 MN B1
Miller, Don: In the Press, A Few Review
    Extracts of Nero Wolfe Books, 9 MN A56
Miller, Don: Kendell Foster Crossen, A
    Bibliography, 12 MN B1
Miller, Don: The Mystery Guild - New
    Selections and Major Alternates for
    1975, (book club), 8 MN 53

Miller, Don: The Mystery of the
    Publishers' Taste, (new books
    announced), 1-3 MM 7; 1-4 MM 5;
    1-5 MM 4; 1-6 MM 4; 1-7 MM 2;
    1-8 MM 4; 1-9 MM 3; 1-10 MM 5;
    1-11 MM 10; 2-1 MM 10; 2-2 MM
    10; 2-3 MM 6; 2-4 MM 15; 2-5
    MM 19
Miller, Don: Nero Wolfe on Film,
    9 MN A26
Miller, Don: The Nero Wolfe Saga,
    A Chronology, (1st edition
    publishers' data), 9 MN A43
Miller, Don: The Nero Wolfe Saga,
    Three at Random, (reviews),
    9 MN A61
Miller, Don: Odds & Ends, (short crime
    fiction reviews and comments),
    1-1 MM 2; 1-2 MM 2; 1-3 MM 2;
    1-4 MM 2; 1-5 MM 2; 1-6 MM 4;
    1-7 MM 2; 1-8 MM 2; 1-9 MM 2;
    1-10 MM 2; 1-11 MM 2; 2-1 MM 2;
    2-2 MM 2; 2-3 MM 2; 2-4 MM 2;
    2-5 MM 2
Miller, Don: Rex Stout, A Bibliography,
    9 MN A65
Miller, Don: Rex Stout, A Capsule
    Biography, 9 MN A63
Miller, Don: Rex Stout in Ellery
    Queen's Anthologies, (checklist),
    9 MN A29
Miller, Don: Rex Stout in ELLERY
    QUEEN'S MYSTERY MAGAZINE, (check-
    list), 9 MN A24
Miller, Don: Ruth Rendell, A Biblio-
    graphy, 10 MN A27
Miller, Don: The Steady Stream, (short
    reviews of crime fiction), 1-1
    MM 3; 1-2 MM 3; 1-4 MM 3; 1-5
    MM 3; 1-6 MM 3; 1-7 MM 3; 1-8
    MM 3; 1-9 MM 3; 1-10 MM 3; 1-11
    MM 9; 2-1 MM 8; 2-2 MM 7; 2-3
    MM 9; 2-4 MM 11; 2-5 MM 13;
    2-5 MM 21
Miller, Edmund: Stanislaw Lem and
    John Dickson Carr, Critics of the
    Scientific World-View, (comparison
    of the work of the two authors),
    14-4 TAD 341
Miller, Jack A.: Bela Lugosi, A Meeting
    Remembered, 1 CD 31
Miller, P. Schuyler: letter of comment,
    3-4 TAD 278; 6-1 TAD 50; 7-1
    TAD 74; 8-1 TAD 72
Miller, Richard W.: letter of comment,
    63 PU 49; 67 PU 60
Miller, Robert L.: letter of comment,
    14 X 62
Miller, Steven: A Collector's Obser-
    vations, (on mystery fiction),
    3-5 PP 13
Miller, Steven: A Look at Dupin, (C.
    Auguste Dupin, detective), 2 MT 20
Miller, Steven: The Cthulhu Mythos
    (of H.P.Lovecraft), 3 MT 5

Miller, Steven: For Mystery Readers, The
    Newest Must-Have Book, (on TWENTIETH
    CENTURY CRIME AND MYSTERY WRITERS, by
    John M. Reilly, ed.), 3-4 PP 9
Miller, Steven: letter of comment,
    3-2 PP 32
Miller, Thomas Kent, and Gary von Tersch:
    The Raconteur of Emerald Lake, (on
    E. Hoffman Price), 6 WT 3
(Miller, Wade: Max Thursday, detective),
    The Man Who Was Thursday, by Marvin
    Lachman, 8-3 TAD 179
(Milne, A.A.), Some Notes Toward a Checklist
    of A.A.Milne's Short Tales of Crime and
    Detection, by J. Randolph Cox, 9-4
    TAD 269
Milne, Terry: letter of comment, 3-3 CP 5
Milner, Jay G.: Morality and the Detective
    Hero, Raymond Chandler's Philip Marlowe,
    1-1 C 116
Milton, Tom: letter of comment, 64 PU 40
Mines, James: Wearing of the Green,
    (fiction), 2-3 M 50
Mines, James: The Worcester Enigma, (a
    "new" Sherlock Holmes adventure;
    fiction, pastiche), 2-2 M 34
Mini-Books of Basil Wells, by Nils Hardin,
    9 X 16
Mini Screen Career of John Creasey, The,
    (filmed Creasey mysteries), by Jack
    Edmund Nolan, 4-5 MR 11
Minor Offenses, (on mystery/suspense
    short stories, reviews and comments),
    by H. Edward Hunsburger, 14-2 TAD
    163; 14-3 TAD 268; 14-4 TAD 380
Minter Speaks Up!, by Richard H. Minter,
    24 X 11
Minter, Richard H.: A Checklist of Books
    by Frank Owen, 30 X 3
Minter, Richard H.: letter of comment,
    4 U 52; 5 U 63; 4 WT 12; 8 X 38;
    13 X 60; 14 X 62; 28 X 80; 30 X
    149; 33 X 114; 36 X 71; 43 X 6
Minter, Richard H.: Minter Speaks Up!,
    24 X 11
Mintz, Patricia Barnes, and Virgil Wilhite:
    L. Ron Hubbard, a Living Legend,
    42 X 133
Minus One, (fiction), by Robert A.
    Frauenglas, 10 LR 14
Minute Quiz, (mystery quiz), by Peggy
    Keeley, 1-6 MR 12
Miranda, Vincent J.: letter of comment,
    11 R 25
Miranda, Vincent J.: Revenge a la Mode,
    (re: Sax Rohmer's stories), 13 R 23
Misadventures of Ellery Queen, (pastiches
    about Ellery Queen), by Marvin S.
    Lachman, 1-4 QC 7
Miscellaneous Mystery Mish-Mash, by
    Marvin S. Lachman, 2-1 MF 7; (The
    California Switch, California locales
    of filmed mysteries), 2-2 MF 19
Miss Jane Marple and Aging in Literature,
    by Mary S. Weinkauf, 1-1 C 32

Miss Marple She Isn't, (on feminine
    sleuths), by David H. Doerrer,
    2-6 MF 7
Miss Minerva and Kinfolks, (Miss
    Minerva juvenile series, by Frances
    Boyd Calhoun, Nell Speed, and
    Emma Speed Sampson), by Julius
    R. Chenu, 1-4 YB 3
Miss Wonderly, Killer, (hardboiled
    detective stories), by John Crosby,
    5-4 MR 8
Missal, Ruth R. (Mrs. M.E.): letter
    of comment, 25 JD 39; 27 JD 36;
    1-3 TAD 108; 3-2 TAD 135; 9-3
    TAD 236
Missing Golf Balls, The, (fiction,
    Sherlock Holmes pastiche), by
    Wex Jones, 7-3 TAD 177
Missing Mercer Musings, (Mercer Boys
    boys' series by Capwell Wyckoff),
    by Don Holbrook, 6 MA 6
Missing Years of Nero Wolfe, The,
    (speculative essay), by Thomas
    D. Waugh, 5-1 TAD 16
Mistress of Violence, (on Sheena,
    Queen of the Jungle, pulp
    heroine), by Wooda Nicholas Carr,
    22 X 24
Mitch Tobin's Healing, (discussion
    of Tobin as detective in series
    by Donald E. Westlake writing as
    Tucker Coe), by Maryell Cleary,
    4-5/6 PP 31
Mitchell, Christine: letter of comment,
    9-4 TAD 298; 11-4 TAD 401
(Mitchell, Gladys), Checklist, by
    Barry A. Pike, 9-4 TAD 259
(Mitchell, Gladys), In Praise of Gladys
    Mitchell, (including interview),
    by Barry A. Pike, 9-4 TAD 250
(Mitchell, James: Callan series),
    Checklist, Annotated, by Barry
    Van Tilburg, 5-3 MF 19
Mobley, Chris: letter of comment,
    11 JD 32; 16 JD 23
Modern Age Books, (on Modern Age
    paperback line, and hardbacks,
    with checklist), by Bill O'Connell,
    3-3 CP 22
Modern Age Books and the John Esteven
    Mystery, (unraveling identity of
    Esteven), by Angela Andrews,
    4-2 PQ 29
Modern Fantasy, (in paperback), by
    Dave Killian, 2-5 CP 11
Modern Publishing Company, The, (mystery
    publisher, with checklist), by
    Robert C.S.Adey, 4-1 PP 3
Moffatt, June M.: A Day in the Life of
    the Wife of an Amachoor Skoller,
    (John D. MacDonald related),
    6 JD 13
Moffatt, June M.: Death and JDM,
    (treatment of death in the fiction
    of John D. MacDonald), 5 JD 3

Moffatt, Len J.: A Checklist of Hardcover and Paperback Books of John D. MacDonald, 1-6 MR 13

Moffatt, Len J.: John D. MacDonald, The Writer's Writer, 1-6 MR 11

Moffatt, Len J.: letter of comment, 1-1 MF 43; 2-2 TAD 132; 4-2 TAD 124

Moffatt, Len J.: Review in Verse of PAPA LA-BAS by John Dickson Carr, 2-2 MR 6

Moffatt, Len J.: What is Mystery Story Fandom?, 14 JD 3

Moffatt, Len J. & June: Checklist of Current Novels, John D. MacDonald, 1 JD 1

Moffatt, Len J. & June: Is It True What They Say About Travis?, (notes on Travis McGee, character of John D. MacDonald), 2 JD 8

Moffatt, Len J. & June: John D. MacDonald Detective Pulp Stories, Synopsis and List, 6 JD 1; 7 JD 13

Moffatt, Len J. & June: In Memoriam, Anthony Boucher, 10 JD 1

Moffatt, Len J. & June: In Memoriam, Wendell V. Howard, 14 JD 10

Moffatt, Len J. & June: letter of comment, 1-2 QC 14

Moffatt, Len J. & June: Magazine Stories, John D. MacDonald, 7 JD 13

Moffatt, Len J. & June: News & Previews ...& Everything, (John D. MacDonald related), 7 JD 12; 9 JD 4; 10 JD 6; 10 JD 21; 11 JD 3; 12 JD 2; 13 JD 2; 14 JD 5; 15 JD 4; 16 JD 4; 17 JD 4; 19 JD 3; 20 JD 25; 21 JD 12; 22 JD 2; 23 JD 12; 24 JD 25; 25 JD 31; 26 JD 21; 27 JD 29; 28 JD 31

Moffatt, Len J. & June: Novels of John D. MacDonald, (checklist), 2 JD 6

(Moffett, Cleveland: THE MYSTERIOUS CARD), The Mysterious Card Unsealed, by Edward S. Lauterbach, 4-1 TAD 41

Monarch Books, Checklist, (paperback line), by Steve Woolfolk, 14 SF 35

(Monarch Books), The World of Monarch, (paperback line), by Bill Pronzini, 1-4 CP 13

Monblatt, Bruce L.: The Detective Story, Pertinent?, (on Mooney's "Best-Selling American Detective Fiction"), 4-3 TAD 170

Monblatt, Bruce L.: letter of comment, 3-2 TAD 135; 4-1 TAD 73; 5-3 TAD 175

(Monblatt, Bruce L.), Meet the Author, Bruce L. Monblatt, by Allen J. Hubin, 4-3 TAD 171

Mogensen, Harald: letter of comment, 7 JD 3

Mongiovi, Gary: letter of comment, 1-2 WA 13

Mongo?, (on the detective character of George Chesbro), by Paul Bishop, 2 PE 28

(Mongo the Magnificent series: George C. Chesbro), Mongo?, by Paul Bishop, 2 PE 28

(Mongo the Magnificent series: George C. Chesbro), Series Synopses, by Robert J. Randisi, 12-4 TAD 366

Mongold, Harry E.: letter of comment, 5-1 TAD 57; 6-2 TAD 129

(Monig, Christopher), Checklist of Kim Locke Stories, by Dickson Thorpe, 1-2 MF 6

(Monig, Christopher), see: Kendell F. Crossen

(Montague, John), The Man of Mystery, (Montague as the real Doc Savage?) by Bill Laidlaw, 2 DQ 5

Montgomery, Richard: letter of comment, 2-2 TBN 5

Montgomery, Robert Bruce: Edmund Crispin, (autobiographical sketch), 12-2 TAD 183

(Montgomery, Rutherford: Kent Barstow series), Boys' Series Bibliography, by Harry K. Hudson, 1-5 YB 13

(Montgomery, Rutherford: Golden Stallion series), Boys' Series Bibliography, by Harry K. Hudson, 1-5 YB 13

Moon Man Stories in TEN DETECTIVE ACES, The, (series by Frederick Davis in pulp magazine, checklist), by Robert Weinberg, 2 P 19

(MOON TENDERS: August Derleth), The Boy Scouts in Old Udolpho, (boys' book discussed), by Frederick Shroyer, 2-2 PDA 43

Mooney, Joan M.: Best-Selling American Detective Fiction, a Dissertation, Pt. 1-3, (Purpose and Method; The Detective Story - Some Whys; The Emergence of Detective Fiction) 3-2 TAD 97; Pt.4, (The Detective's World, The 19th Century View) and Pt.5 (The World View in the 20th Century Detective Novel) 3-3 TAD 141; Pt.6, (The Social Scene in the 20th Century) 3-4 TAD 215; Pt.7, (The Detective) 4-1 TAD 12; Pt.8, (The Detective and the Women) 4-2 TAD 87

Mooney, Joan M.: letter of comment, 4-4 TAD 246; 5-2 TAD 118

(Mooney, Joan L.: "Best-Selling American Detective Fiction"), Commentary, by Joe R. Christopher, 5-1 TAD 11

(Mooney, Joan L.: "Best-Selling American Detective Fiction"), The Detective Story: Pertinent?, by Bruce L. Monblatt, 4-3 TAD 170

Moore, Richard A.: letter of comment, 43 X 6

Moore, Robert L.: It, (fiction) 12 LR 21

Morality and the Detective Hero, Raymond Chandler's Philip Marlowe, by Jay G. Milner, 1-1 C 116

Moran, Peggy: McGee's Girls, (on the women in Travis McGee stories by John D. MacDonald), 1-1 C 82

More Chanderisms, (Raymond Chandler), by Thea Taylor, 1-4 CP 29

More From Dr. Parker's Notebooks, (re: Solar Pons), by August Derleth, 1-2 PDA 43

More Information on Andy Blake Series, (boys' books by Leo Edwards), by Julius R. Chenu, 1-3 TB 3

More Mystery for a Dime - Street & Smith and the First Pulp Detective Magazine, (DETECTIVE STORY MAGAZINE), by J. Randolph Cox, 2-2 C 52

More Notes on C.E.Vulliamy, by Charles Shibuk, 5-3 TAD 145

More on Andy Blake - Printing History, (of the Appleton edition, boys' book series, by Leo Edwards), by Ray H. Zorn, 1-4 TB 1

More on the Story of Dennis Lynds, by John Edwards, 5 U 20

More "Shades of Dupin!" (fictional detectives on detective fiction), by R.W.Hays, 8-4 TAD 288

(Morgan, Michael: DECOY), The Worst Mystery Novel of All Time, by Bill Pronzini, 13-2 TAD 137

Moriarty, Thomas M.: letter of comment, 65 PU 22; 33 X 115

Moritz, Mike: letter of comment, 1-6 YB 9

Morland, Nigel: The Edgar Wallace I Knew, (personal reminiscences and literary discussion), 1-3 TAD 68

Morland, Nigel: letter of comment, 1-2 TAD 64; 14-1 TAD 73

(Morland, Nigel), Meet the Author, Nigel Morland, by Allen J. Hubin, 1-3 TAD 72

(Morland, Nigel), Nigel Morland - Fifty Years of Crime Writing, by Pearl G. Aldrich, 13-3 TAD 194

(Morley, Christopher, ed.: MURDER WITH A DIFFERENCE), A Different Kind of Murder, (article review), by William White, 3-5 MR 7

Morris, Harry, Jr.: letter of comment, 15 X 14

Morrison, Marvin: A Review from the Microcosm, (comments and review of Resnick's Price Guide, pulps), 28 X 7

Morrison, Marvin: Classics of Science Fiction, 30 X 12

Morrison, Marvin: The Third Eyelid, 14 R 19

Morrow, Thomas G.: letter of comment, 2 LW 1

Morse, Irv: letter of comment, 7 JD 6

Mortensen, Marjorie: A Special Report on Shad Roe, (a la Nero Wolfe), 1-2 G 51

Mortensen, Marjorie: The Black Orchid Banquet Quiz, (quiz, Nero Wolfe), 1-1 G 13

Mortensen, Marjorie: Black Orchid Banquet Theme Songs, (Nero Wolfe/Rex Stout fans' The Wolfe Pack annual banquet activities), 1-1 G 9

Mortensen, Marjorie: Notes on the First Annual Black Orchid Banquet, (of the Wolfe Pack, Nero Wolfe/Rex Stout fans' organization), 1-1 G 4

Mortensen, Marjorie: The Second First Annual Wolfe Pack Event, 1-2 G 58

(Morthoe, Sir Julian, detective: P.W. Wilson), Pen Profile #8: P.W.Wilson, by Barry Pike, 3-1 PP 28; 3-2 PP 18

(Morton, A.Q.: LITERARY DETECTION - HOW TO PROVE AUTHORSHIP AND FRAUD IN LITERATURE AND DOCUMENTS), Special review by E.F.Bleiler, 3-4 MF 11

(Morton, Anthony: The Baron series), Checklist, by Robert E. Briney and John Creasey, 2-1 TAD 16

Morton, Robert D.: letter of comment, 11 JD 28

Mosig, Dirk W.: H.P.Lovecraft, Rabid Racist, or Compassionate Gentleman? 18 X 13

Moskowitz, Richard: The Case of the Missing End, 6/7 LR 6

Moskowitz, Richard: Items of Interest, (mystery news and comments), 6/7 LR 8; 6/7 LR 10

Moskowitz, Richard: Legal Lunacy, (unusual laws), 6/7 LR 3; 6/7 LR 4; 8 LR 4

Moskowitz, Richard: Mystery's Loss, (Obituary, Albert Hitchcock, with film checklist), 6/7 LR 41

Moskowitz, Richard: Publishing, Current Events (crime fiction), 10 LR 12

Moskowitz, Richard: letter of comment, 16 CD 13; 10 CL 11; 2-5 MF 45; 3-3 MF 61;4-2 MF 62; 2 PE 41

Moskowitz, Sam: The Derleth Connection, I Remember Moskowitz, (biog. sketch), 3-2 AD 6; 3-3 AD 3

Moskowitz, Sam: letter of comment, 3-1 AD 10; 4-1 TAD 72; 6-2 TAD 130; 22 X 49

Moskowitz, Sam: Poe on "Trial", (whether Poe or Hoffman was "father of the mystery story", 4-1 TAD 10

Most Dangerous Man in Europe, The, (on early John Dickson Carr stories), by Bruce Dettman, 2-4 TAD 253

Most Wanted Man, The, (re: Solar Pons), by Mark Levy, 2-4 PD 1

Mother Knows Best, ("Dallas" television series), by P.D.James, 9 LR 22

Motion-Picture Comrades, The, (boys' book series), by Robert Jennings, 6 BB 24

(Moto, Mr., series: John P. Marquand), Checklist, Annotated, by Barry Van Tilburg, 4-5 MF 22

Motsinger, Thomas L.: letter of comment, 2-6 MF 47

Moulton, David A.: Mr. Trowbridge and Our
Young Folks, (John T. Trowbridge,
boys' books author), 3-1 BC 258
(Mountain States), The American Regional
Mystery, Pt.XI, (locales of crime
fiction), by Marvin Lachman, 9-1
TAD 11
Mousetrap Phenomenon, The, ("The Mousetrap": Agatha Christie, stage
production), by Arthur Nicholas Athanason,
12-2 TAD 152
Movie Quiz, (mystery quiz), 2-3 MR 10
(movie serials), I Remember...B Movies,
by R. Jeff Banks, 4-5 MF 13
(movie serials), Thrills, Spills and
Cliff-Hanging Adventures Supreme in
a Calvacade of Famous "Chapter-Play"
Serials, King of Entertainment, by
Andy Biegel, Jr., 5 U 11
Movies on TV and in Theatres, (general
review article on current mystery
productions), by Lianne Carlin,
3-2 MR 15
Moy, Paul R.: A Bibliography of the Works
of Anthony Berkeley Cox, (pseudonym of
Francis Iles), 14-3 TAD 236
Moy, Paul R.: Exclusive! The Detection
Club's First Collaborations, Unpublished
Christie and Others, (with checklist),
4-5/6 PP 15
Moy, Paul R.: letter of comment,
3-6 PP 40; 4-4 PP 32; 4-5/6 PP 93;
14-4 TAD 381
Mr. Chang, a Minor Pulp Villain, by
John A. Dinan, 12 R 21
(Mr. Chang, pulp villain), The Chang
Monster, by Robert Sampson, 14 SF 41;
(partial checklist of magazine
appearances) 14 SF 46
Mr. Hitchcock, (short biography of Alfred
Hitchcock), 1-1 MR 5
Mr. J.G.Reeder, (detective series character
created by Edgar Wallace), by Penelope
Wallace, 2-2 PDA 63
Mr. McFarlane's Magic, (author of a number
of the Hardy Boys boys' series books),
by John M. Enright, 4 MA 5
Mr. Moto on Film, (with checklist),
3-2 MR 7
Mr. and Mrs. North, and Mr. and Mrs.
Lockridge, (the Norths, detectives of
Frances and Richard Lockridge), by
Hank Davis, 1-1 MF 21
Mr. and Mrs. North, (detective characters
created by Frances and Richard Lock-
ridge), by R. Jeff Banks, 9-3 TAD 182
(Mr. Pond: G.K.Chesterton), A Lesser
Chesterton Detective, by R.W.Hays,
9-2 TAD 125
Mr. R. Austin Freeman, A Review of His
Early Detective Fiction, (1913), by
John Adams, 6 TF 34
Mr. Trowbridge and Our Young Folks, (John
T. Trowbridge, boys' books author), by
David A. Moulton, 3-1 BC 258

(Mr.Verily, detective: Peter Antony),
My Favourite Detectives, Pt.2,
by Robert C.S.Adey, 4-3 MR 21
Mrs.Craggs and a Certain Lady's Town
House, (fiction), by H.R.F.Keating,
3-1 M 26
Mrs.Pinkerton as Frankenstein, by
Mary F. Lindsley, 1-1 PDA 27
Mrs. Steeger Recalls... (comments on
Harry Steeger, editor and publisher,
Popular Publications pulps), by
Shirley Steeger, 33 X 20
Ms. Found in the Bottles, Vintage Wine
Department, (puzzle mysteries), by
Mike Avallone, 28 X 6
(Mulcaheney, Norah, series: Lillian
O'Donnell), Series Synopses, by Jo
Ann Vicarel, 10-1 TAD 80; 11-4 TAD
365
Mulcahy, Kay: letter of comment,
2-3/4 AD 14; 3-2 AD 10
Mulford, Ed: letter of comment,
1-3 TB 10; 1-4 TBN 5; 2-3 TBN 3;
2-4 TBN 3
Mulford, Ed: Stranger Visits Land of
Leo Edwards, (visit to Wisconsin
and home of Edwards, boys' books
author), 1-1 TB 3; 1-2 TB 2; 2-6
TBN 5
Mullan, W.C.: letter of comment,
27 JD 36
(Mulligan, Patrick), Forgotten Ferrets,
Mr. Patrick Mulligan, by Alvin F.
Germeshausen, 1-2 PDA 69
Mullinix, Jim: letter of comment,
5 LW 1
Mummy Itchers, (simulation of items
found in Jerry Todd story by Leo
Edwards, boys' book series), by
Julius R. Chenu, 2-4 TBN 1
Mummy Plot Fact Believe It or Not,
(basis for JERRY TODD AND THE
WHISPERING MUMMY, boys' book by
Leo Edwards), by Julius R. Chenu,
1-3 TB 1
Mundell, Elmore, Jr.: letter of
comment, 1-1 TAD 30; 2-1 TAD 63;
4-6 MF 49; 5-1 MF 45; 5-3 TAD 181;
7-3 TAD 227
(Mundy, A. Talbot), Collectors'
Corner, Bibliography of Mundy, by
Robert Weinberg, 6 P 24
Munger, Carabel Lewis: A Talk With
Harry Castlemon, (boys' book author),
2-4 BC 250
Munn, H. Warner: Incident at Nor-Um-
Bega, (fiction), 2 FM 3
(Munsey Magazines), Checklist of
commencements, pulp magazines, by
John Harwood, 3-5 MF 49
Murder at the Waldorf: A Report on
Bouchercon VIII, (mystery fans and
authors convention), by Robert E.
Briney, 11-1 TAD 53

Murder at the Waldorf, Bouchercon VIII, October 7-9, 1977, (mystery authors and fans convention), by Mary Ann Grochowski, 2-2 MF 15

Murder at the Crossroads, or, Oedipus the Detective, (classic mystery discussed), by J.R.Christopher, 2-4 TAD 225

Murder and the Mean Streets, The Hard-Boiled Detective Novel, by George Grella, 5-1 TAD 1

Murder by Client, A Reworked Theme in Dashiell Hammett, by Christopher Bentley, 14-1 TAD 78

Murder by Mail, A Dealer Checklist, (list of book dealers), by Walter Albert, 3-5 MF 7

Murder by Mail - Update, (bibliographical listing of books published by the book clubs, May 1979 - August 1981), by Michael L. Cook, 4-5/6 PP 51

(MURDER BY TELEVISION - film), Bela Lugosi in Murder by Television, by Gordon R. Guy, 1 CD 12

Murder Can Happen Anywhere, (discussion on the locale of crime fiction), by Deborah Bonetti, 14-3 TAD 257

Murder Club, The, (in John Dickson Carr stories), by Larry L. French, 1 NC 30

Murder for Heyer, (on the mystery novels of Georgette Heyer), by Don D'Ammassa, 13 MN 9

Murder in Miami, (Mike Shayne on television), by Andy Jaysnovitch, 1 PE 23

(Murder Ink Bookshop), Dead of Winter Views, (on Murder Ink weekend at Mohonk Mt. House), by Jane Merrill Filstrup, 10-3 TAD 235

(Murder Ink, Dell Mystery series), Dell Mysteries, Murder Ink and Scene of the Crime paperback series, by Charlotte Laughlin, 3-4 PQ 13

Murder Multiplied, Detection Detained, (survey of Garland's Fifty Crime Classics books edited by Barzun & Taylor), by Michael Murphy, 30 X 135

Murder Mystery, (verse), by Ross H. Spencer, 14-2 TAD 133

(MURDER MYSTERY MONTHLY), Index by Author, Murder Mystery Monthly, by Howard Waterhouse, 1-4 PQ 34

(MURDER MYSTERY MONTHLY), Correction to Checklist, by Steve Lewis, 2-1 PQ 5

(MURDER MYSTERY MONTHLY), Mighty, Miraculous Murder Mystery Monthly, by Howard Waterhouse, 1-4 PQ 31

(MURDER WITH A DIFFERENCE: Christopher Morley, ed.), A Different Kind of Murder, (article review), by William White, 3-5 MR 7

(Murdoch, Bruce, series: Norman Deane), Checklist, by Robert E. Briney and John Creasey, 2-1 TAD 12

Murphy, C. Ray: letter of comment, 4-1 PP 51

Murphy, Jeanne Eileen: Everil Worrell, (author), 1 WT 13

Murphy, Jeanne Eileen: Everil Worrell in WEIRD TALES, Checklist, 1 WT 15

Murphy, Michael: A Queen Quandary Quickly Quavered in Quondam Quixotic Quotations, (re: Ellery Queen), 14 X 2

Murphy, Michael:A Tribute to Vincent Starrett, 2-2 PDA 70

Murphy, Michael: letter of comment, 40 X 86

Murphy, Michael: Murder Multiplied, Detection Detained, (survey of Garland's Fifty Crime Classics books, ed. by Barzun & Taylor), 30 X 135

Murphy, Michael: Oak Park Revisited, (Ernest Hemingway), 5 X 6

Murphy, Michael: Starrett versus Machen, (correspondence and dispute between Vincent Starrett and Arthur Machen), 18 X 24

Murphy, Michael: Vincent Starrett on the Hard-Boiled School, 21 X 47

(Murphy, Warren: The Destroyer series), Created, The Destroyer, An Interview with Warren Murphy, by Dick Lochte, 11-3 TAD 284

Murray, Edwin L.: letter of comment, 1-1 MF 45; 3-4 PQ 46

Murray, Edwin L.: The Versatile Gardner F. Fox, (on his works in paperback, with checklist), 3-5 CP 5

Murray, Edwin L., and Karl Edward Wagner: A Bibliography of Manly Wade Wellman, 7 X 12

Murray, John E.: letter of comment, 2-1 MR 11

Murray, Will: A Thunder Jim Checklist, (character in the THRILLING ADVENTURES pulp magazine), 1 D 22

Murray, Will: Black Sounds, (the pulp magazines and the word "duende"), 1 D 2

Murray, Will: Dent's Detectives, (on detectives of Lester Dent), 1 D 8

Murray, Will: Doc Savage Title Challenge, (quiz), 9 DS 20

Murray, Will: The Duende Doc Savage Index, (index of DOC SAVAGE pulp magazines), 2 D 28

Murray, Will: The Evil Lotus, (pulp villainess), 11 DS 20

Murray, Will: The Girl Who Loved Doc Savage, (Monja, in Doc Savage novels), 4 DR 6

Murray, Will: The Girl Who Loved Monk Mayfair, (aide to Doc Savage), 7 DS 13

Murray, Will: The Golden Boys, (re: Doc Savage novels), 10 DS 16

Murray, Will: Gremlins in the Pulps, 1 D 31; 2 D 47

Murray, Will: The Horrible Hunchbacks, (in pulp magazines, various villains), 6 DS 13

Murray, Will: InciDENTals, (column on Lester Dent, author, and Doc Savage), 2-2 CP 30; 2-3 CP 12; 2-4 CP 21; 2-5 CP 9; 3-1 CP 21; 3-2 CP 7; 3-3 CP 17; (radio serials of Doc Savage with checklist) 3-4 CP 13; (Dent as guest columnist) 3-5 CP 23

Murray, Will: Index, Bill Barnes Novels (pulp aviation/espionage hero), 22 X 40

Murray, Will: Index to UNKNOWN pulp magazine, 42 X 12

Murray, Will: Lester, Dent, The Last of the Joe Shaw's Black Mask Boys, (Dent as author of stories in BLACK MASK pulp detective magazine), 2-2 C 128

Murray, Will: letter of comment, 2-4 CP 5; 5 DQ 5; 6 DQ 3; 3 DS 5; 11 DS 28; 2 U 48; 3 U 48; 4 U 52; 7 U 47; 38 X 145; 43 X 6

Murray, Will: The Many Faces of The Whisperer, (Street & Smith's pulp magazine, THE WHISPERER), 7 P 3

Murray, Will: The Never-Was Adventure, (speculative meeting between The Shadow and Doc Savage), 6 DQ 16

Murray, Will: Odyssey Column #1, (on Odyssey Publications), 1 PW 1; 2 PW 3

Murray, Will: The Old Pulp Writers, 33 X 38

Murray, Will: The Other Shadow, (on the pulp hero-villain, Dr. Sax), 10 X 2

Murray, Will: Reflections in a Flame-Gold Eye, (changes in the character of Doc Savage during the series), 2/3 DR 16

Murray, Will: The Resurrection of IN HELL, MADONNA, (a hitherto unpublished Doc Savage story), 5 DS 8

Murray, Will: The Secret Kenneth Robesons, (various authors using the house name), 2 D 3

Murray, Will: Street & Smith's Crime Busters, (on pulp magazine CRIME BUSTERS), 38 X 132

Murray, Will: Superman of Bronze, (comments on Doc Savage), 5 DS 17

Murray, Will: The Ten Top Spider Novels, and One Stinker, (THE SPIDER, pulp magazine, commentary on novels by Murray and various others), 13 SF 5

Murray, Will: The Top Ten Doc Savage Novels, and One Stinker, (commentary on Doc Savage novels by Murray and others), 8 U 22

Murray, Will: The Top Twenty-Five Shadow Novels, and One Stinker, (on THE SHADOW magazine stories of the hero character by Murray and others), 4 U 3

Murray, Will: The Unknown UNKNOWN, (the pulp magazine UNKNOWN), 42 X 11

Murray, Will: Zanigew, Napoleon of Crime, (pulp villain vs. The Shadow), 8 DS 19

Murray, Will, and Link Hullar: The Fighting Fury, (on The Skipper, from THE SKIPPER pulp magazine), 12 SF 3

Musemeche, Rocco: letter of comment, 2-2 TBN 4; 2-3 TBN 3; 24 X 44; 38 X 143; 1-2 YB 23

Musette, Max and Sumuru, (radio serials based on Sax Rohmer tales), by Robert E. Briney and W.O.G. Lofts, 15 R 5

Muth, Tom: letter of comment, 1-2 G 69

My Auctorial Friend, August Derleth, by George J. Marx, 1-1 PD 4

My Favourite Detectives, (commentary with checklists), by Robert C.S. Adey, (Sir Henry Merrivale, by John Dickson Carr) 3-2 MR 11; (Sergeant Beef by Leo Bruce) 5-3 MR 20; (Mr. Verily, by Peter Antony), 4-3 MR 21

My Good Name...(Sherlock Holmes pastiche), by Lucy Chase Williams, 2-2 M 40

My Hero - Fu Manchu, by John Ball, 11 R 5

My Homily, August Derleth, (verse), by Raymond Roseliep, 2-3/4 AD 10

My Favorite Jungle Stories Magazine Covers, (covers of JUNGLE STORIES, pulp magazine), by Wooda Nicholas Carr, 8 U 30

My Fourth Trip to the U.S., (account of trip by author promoting his book, PAPERBACKS U.S.A.), by Piet Schreuders, 3-4 CP 17

My Whodunit File, A Collection of Scrapbooks Devoted to the Mystery Story Field, by Estelle Fox, 2-1 TAD 29

Myers, Dick: The Birth of (Dr.) Death, (in ALL DETECTIVE magazine, pulp), 5 BS 5

Myers, Dick: The Case of the Elusive Author, (R.T.M.Scott, pulp-hero writer), 9 BS 5; (Frank S. Lawton, pulp author) 10 BS 14

Myers, Dick: letter of comment, 4 BS 15; 7 BS 2

Myers, John T.: letter of comment, 13 JD 12

Mycroft Holmes and Ian Murdock's Case, (on Sherlock Holmes in "The Adventure of the Lion's Mane"), by J.W. Scheideman, 9-1 TAD 14

(Mycroft & Moran, Publishers), The Humbugging of Solar Pons, (as by Ebenezer Snawley as pseudonym for Jon L. Lellenberg on revisions made by publisher), 3-2 PDA 11

Mysteries for Children, by Amy Lubelski, 12 SF 24

Mysteries Make Headlines, (recognition of crime fiction), by C. David Hellyer, 11-3 TAD 260

Mysteries of Edgar Box, The, (crime
fiction of Gore Vidal writing as
Edgar Box), by Earl F. Bargainnier,
2-1 C 45

Mysteries of the Pseudonymous Professors,
(pseudonyms used when anonymity
required), by Joseph Barbato,
1-4 MF 3

Mysterious Arthur H. Ward, The, by
Robert E. Briney, 12 L 5

Mysterious Case of the Carters, or How
Hirohito Became Nick Carter's Aide,
("genealogy" of the Carter family
in a speculative essay), by Todd
Rutt and Arn McConnell, 1-2 WA 3

Mysterious Card Unsealed, The, (THE
MYSTERIOUS CARD: Cleveland Moffett),
by Edward S. Lauterbach, 4-1 TAD 41

Mysterious Craig Rice, The, (author),
by David A. Jasen, 5-1 TAD 25

Mysterious John Dickson Carr, The,
(author), by Larry L. French,
1-6 MF 13

Mysterious Wodehouse, The, (P.G. Wodehouse, with bibliography), by David
A. Jasen, 3-1 TAD 38

Mysterious Wu Fang, The, (pulp villain),
by Wooda Nicholas Carr, 8 DS 5

(MYSTERIOUS WU FANG, THE), Checklist
of pulp magazine, by Lynn Hickman,
75 PU 11

(mystery - academic scene), The "Amanda
Cross" Case: Sociologizing the U.S.
Academic Mystery, by James Mark
Purcell, 13-1 TAD 36

(mystery - academic scene), Mystery,
Murder and Academe, by Jane
Gottschalk, 11-2 TAD 159

(mystery - academic scene), Obsequies
About Oxford: The Investigations
and Eccentricities of Gervase Fen,
(detective character of Edmund
Crispin, with bibliography), by
William A.S.Sarjeant, 14-3 TAD 196

(mystery - adventure), High Adventure
Fiction, (mystery/suspense with
Hammond Innes checklist), by Don
Cole, 14-1 MR 3

MYSTERY ADVENTURE MAGAZINE Index,
(pulp magazine), 22 X 47

Mystery-Adventure Series Puzzle,
(crossword puzzle, boys' series
books related), by Kent Winslow,
7 MA 26

(mystery - amateur detectives), The
Amateur's Hour, by Frank D.
McSherry, Jr., 3-1 TAD 14

(mystery - American Indian), Joe
Leaphorn and the Navajo Way,
Tony Hillerman's Indian Detective
Fiction, by Jane S. Bakerman,
2-1 C 9

Mystery and Adventure Crossword Puzzle,
(oriented boys' series books), by
Kent Winslow, 5 MA 30

Mystery Appreciation Course, University
of California San Diego, 10-3 TAD
226

MYSTERY at the Movies, (MYSTERY
magazine review column), by Thomas
Godfrey, 2-1 M 24

(mystery - Australia), The Great
Australian Detective, (Napoleon
Bonaparte, detective, by Arthur W.
Upfield), by William Antony S.
Sarjeant, 12-2 TAD 99

(mystery - Australia), Arthur William
Upfield 1888-1964, by Estelle Fox,
3-2 TAD 89

(mystery - Australia), Arthur William
Upfield, September 1, 1888 - February
13, 1964, by Betty Donaldson, 8-1
TAD 1

(mystery - Australia), Australian Words
and Expressions in Upfield's Novels,
by Philip T. Asdell, 1 BY 5

(mystery - Australia), FOLLOW MY DUST,
by Jessica Hawke, (biography of
Upfield, in The Whodunit's Who's
Who by Philip T. Asdell, 3-4 PP 11)

(mystery - Australia), Bony Was There,
(locales of stories by Arthur W.
Upfield, with Inspector Bonaparte),
by Philip T. Asdell, 1 BY 2

(mystery - Australia), Checklist,
Arthur W. Upfield, by Estelle Fox,
Francis M. Nevins, Jr., and Charles
Shibuk, 3-2 TAD 90

(mystery - Australia), The Great
Melbourne Cup Mystery (FOLLOW MY
DUST; Arthur W. Upfield), by Philip
T. Asdell, 1 BY 3

(mystery - Australia), The Novels of
Arthur W. Upfield, Bibliography
and Review, by Betty Donaldson,
8-1 TAD 4

(mystery - Australia), Too Right Bony,
(paperbacks of Inspector Bonaparte,
by Arthur W. Upfield), by M.C.Hill,
3-2 PQ 7

(mystery - Australia), Upfield Collector,
A Mystery Buff of the Purest Sort,
(Michael Masliah as collector of
works of Arthur W. Upfield), by
Natalie Hall, 11-1 TAD 72

(mystery authors as characters in
stories), Did It All Start with
Ellery?, by Ellen Nehr, 3-4 PP 3

(mystery - avante-garde writing),
Avante-Garde Writing in the Detective
Story, by Frank D. McSherry, Jr.,
3-2 TAD 95

(mystery - baseball theme), Sports and
the Mystery Story, Pt.3, by Marvin
Lachman, 6-4 TAD 243

(mystery - basketball theme), Sports
and the Mystery Story, Pt.3, by
Marvin Lachman, 6-4 TAD 243

(mystery - beasts theme), A Beastly Case
of Murder, (with checklist), by Mary
Ann Grochowski, 1-6 PP 3
(mystery - bestsellers), Best-Selling
American Detective Fiction, A
Dissertation, by Joan M. Mooney,
Pts.1-3 (Purpose and Method; The
Detective Story - Some Whys; The
Emergence of Detective Fiction)
3-2 TAD 97; Pts.4-5 (The Detective's
World, The 19th Century View; The
World View in the 20th Century
Detective Novel) 3-3 TAD 141; Pt.6
(The Social Scene in the 20th
Century) 3-4 TAD 215; Pt.7 (The
Detective) 4-1 TAD 12; Pt.8 (The
Detective and the Women) 4-2 TAD
87; (commentary by Joe R.Christopher)
5-1 TAD 11; (commentary by Bruce
L. Monblatt) 4-3 TAD 170; (pertinent
letters by Mooney) 4-4 TAD 246;
5-2 TAD 118
(mystery - bestsellers), Mainstream
Mysteries and Novels of Crime
(1980), by Gary Warren Niebuhr,
4-1 PP 13
(mystery - book editors), A Conversation
with Joan Kahn, (interview), by
Robert J. Randisi, 3-1 M 16
MYSTERY BOOK MAGAZINE: An Appreciation
and Index, by Robert E. Briney,
8-4 TAD 245
(MYSTERY BOOK MAGAZINE), Lady in a
Straightjacket, by Frank D. McSherry,
Jr., 9-3 TAD 201
(mystery - booksellers), Biographical
Short Sketches: Mary Ann Grochowski,
Allan Kleinberg, David & Judi Lipman,
Jeff Meyerson, Scott Owen, Peter
Pross, and Howard Waterhouse, 2-3
PP 7
(mystery - booksellers), Literary
Sleuths, Alias Your Friendly
Neighborhood Book Detectives,
by Mary Ann Grochowski, 2-3 PP 3
(mystery - bullfighting theme), Sports
and the Mystery Story, Pt.2, by
Marvin Lachman, 6-2 TAD 83
(mystery - business theme), A View
From Wall Street, Social Criticism
in the Mystery Novels of Emma
Lathen, by Jane S. Bakerman,
9-3 TAD 213
(mystery - business theme), Comic
Construction in the Novels of
Emma Lathen and R.B.Dominic,
by David Brownell, 9-2 TAD 91
(mystery - business theme), It's About
Crime, (business and the mystery
story), by Marvin Lachman,
5-6 MF 29
(mystery - business theme), Women
and Wall Street, Portraits of
Women in Novels by Emma Lathen,
by Jane S. Bakerman, 8-1 TAD 36

(mystery - California), The American
Regional Mystery, Pt.12 (Hawaii
and Northern California) 9-4 TAD
260; Pt.13 (Southern California)
10-4 TAD 294, by Marvin Lachman
(mystery - California), Archer in
Hollywood, The "Barbarous Coast"
of Ross Macdonald, by David J.
Geherin, 9-1 TAD 55
(mystery - California), San Francisco
Mysteries, by Don Herron, 3-2 M 8
(mystery - California), see Dashiell
Hammett; Raymond Chandler
(mystery - caper novels), The Caper
Novel, by George Kelley, 7 U 61
(mystery - caper novels), The Caper
Novels of James Hadley Chase, by
Theodore P. Dukeshire, 10-2 TAD 128
(mystery - caper novels), The Caper
Novels of Tony Kendrick, by George
Kelley, 2-4 MF 3
"Mystery" Career of Evan Hunter, The,
(author), by Bill Pronzini, 5-3
TAD 129
(mystery - cats in), Cats in Mysteries,
by Jane Merrill Filstrup, 11-1 TAD
59; 11-2 TAD 134
(mystery - chess theme), Chess in the
Detective Story, by R.W.Hays, 5-1
TAD 19; (addenda) 7-3 TAD 203
(mystery - Chinese detectives), Charlie
Chan, A Biography, by Fred Dueren,
7-4 TAD 263
(mystery - Chinese detectives), Charlie
Chan Carries On (CHARLIE CHAN CARRIES
ON: Earl Derr Biggers), by Neil
Ellman, 10-2 TAD 183
(mystery - Chinese detectives), Charlie
Chan in Books and in Motion Pictures,
by Douglas M. Armato, 7-2 TAD 97
(mystery - Chinese detectives), Charlie
Chan in Qui Nhon, (on Armed Forces
TV in Vietnam), by Jon L. Breen,
2-2 TAD 114
(mystery - Chinese detectives), Chinese
Detectives in Poland, (Polish editions
and translations), by Everett F.
Bleiler, 11-4 TAD 343
(mystery - Chinese detectives), Who Killed
Charlie Chan, (the updated Chan
stories), by Jon L. Breen, 7-2 TAD
100
(mystery - Chinese detectives), A
Chinese Detective in San Francisco,
(Chan To), by E.F.Bleiler, 5-3 MF 2
(mystery - Christmas theme), Criminous
Christmases, by Jane Gottschalk,
13-4 TAD 281
(mystery - classic), Classic and Hard-
Boiled Detective Fiction (hardboiled
vs. classic mystery), by John M.
Reilly, 9-4 TAD 289
(mystery - classic), The Golden Age of
the Detective Story, (with checklist)
by Neville Wood, 1-1 PP 11

(mystery - classic), A Woman's Intuition:
Wives and Lovers in British Golden
Age Detective Novels, by Helaine
Ross, 2-1 C 17

(mystery - classic), End of the Golden
Age, (memorial to Agatha Christie),
by George Wuyek, 10-3 TAD 263

(mystery - classic), The Golden Age of
the Detective Story, Its Rise and
Fall, by Charles Shibuk, 1-4 QC 14

(mystery - classic), Intruder in the
Rose Garden, (private eye fiction
vs. classic mystery), by George N.
Dove, 9-4 TAD 278

(mystery - classic), The Last Year, by
Mary Groff, 11-2 TAD 145

(mystery - classic), Murder at the
Crossroads, or, Oedipus the Detective,
by J.R.Christopher, 2-4 TAD 225

(mystery - classic), The Silver Fifty
(checklist of classic crime fiction),
by Gerald Tomlinson, 10-2 TAD 165

(mystery - classic), When was the Golden
Age, Anyway?, by Robert Aucott,
5-4 TAD 207

(mystery - clues as major factor),
Who-Really-Dun-It?: Two Sub-Branches
of the Detective Story, by Frank D.
McSherry, Jr., 2-2 TAD 88

(mystery - collecting), A Collector
Reminisces, by Neville Wood, 3-2 PP 7

(mystery - collecting), A Collector's
Observations, by Steven Miller,
3-5 PP 13

(mystery - collecting), The Book
Detective, by Paul Bishop, 6 PE 29

(mystery - collecting), The Book
Detective, by Andy Jaysnovitch,
2 PE 33

(mystery - collecting), Can Such Things
Be?, by David Bates, 2 PE 25

(mystery - collecting), The Case of the
Canonical Collector, (collecting
Sherlockiana), by Jackie Geyer,
11-3 TAD 290

(mystery - collecting), How to Organize
Your Collection Your Way!, by Ellen
Nehr, 2-3 PP 9

(mystery - collecting), On Compiling a
Sax Rohmer Collection, by Alan
Warren, 13-2 TAD 148

(mystery - collecting), Rambling Thoughts
on a 'tec Collection, by James
Keddie, Jr., 1-1 TAD 5

(mystery - collecting), Skullduggery: So
You Want to be a Crime Collector,
by George Kelley, 3 U 20

(mystery - collecting), Try to Find It,
(on rare detective fiction), by
E.F.Bleiler, 6-2 TAD 97

(mystery - collecting), Upfield Collector,
A Mystery Buff of the Purest Sort,
(Michael Masliah's collection of
Arthur W. Upfield works), by
Natalie Hall, 11-1 TAD 72

(mystery - collections), The University
of North Carolina Crime Fiction
Collection, by Mary S. Cameron,
1-2 TAD 51

(mystery - con-men), In Search of the
"Con Man", by Robert C.S.Adey,
2-4 TAD 259

(mystery - con-men), Rogues' Gallery,
by Richard S. Lochte II, 2-3 TAD
158

Mystery Contest, (quiz), 3-1 M 52

(mystery - cricket theme), Sports and
the Mystery Story, Pt.6, by Marvin
Lachman, 8-1 TAD 108

(mystery - criminal character), The
Case of the Missing Criminal,
Crime Fiction's Unpaid Debt to
Its Ne'er-Do-Wells, by Connie
Fletcher, 10-1 TAD 17

(mystery - cross-cultural), Binocular
Eyes: Cross-Cultural Detectives,
(contact between different cultural
spheres), by Margaret J. King,
13-3 TAD 253

Mystery Crossword Puzzle, by Marilyn
Fibish, 2-1 MR 16; 4-3 MR 12

Mystery Dial, (comments on old radio
mystery shows), by Steve Lewis,
2 MY 3; 3 MY 3; 4 MY 6; 5 MY 9;
6 MY 12; 7 MY 9

Mystery Dial I - Johnny Dollar, (radio
mystery series), by Steve Lewis,
2-1 PP 9

Mystery Dial II - The Green Hornet,
(radio mystery series), by Steve
Lewis, 2-2 PP 10

Mystery Dial III - Locked Rooms, (radio
mystery programs), by Steve Lewis,
2-3 PP 11

Mystery Dial IV - Mr. & Mrs. North, (on
radio), by Steve Lewis, 2-4 PP 25

Mystery Dial V - Lights Out and Others,
(radio mystery programs), by Steve
Lewis, 2-6 PP 28

(mystery - dying message clue), The
Clue of the Dying Message, by
R.W.Hays, 7-1 TAD 1

(mystery - dying message clue), "To
the Very Last: The Dying Message,"
by Lynn Biederstadt, 12-3 TAD 209

(mystery - editing), No Rules for a
Suspense Editor, by Joan Kahn,
2-3 TAD 169

(mystery - English), A Woman's Intuition,
Wives and Lovers in British Golden
Age Detective Novels, by Helaine
Ross, 2-1 C 17

(mystery - English), Checklist of Crime
Fiction Published in Great Britain
January 1, 1977 - March 31, 1977,
by Allen J. Hubin, 10-3 TAD 270

(mystery - English), The English
Detective Novel Between the Wars,
1919-1939, by Elaine Bander, 11-3
TAD 262

(mystery - evolution of the detective),
The Evolution of the Great American
Detective: The Reader as Detective
Hero, by William Kittredge and Steven
M. Krauzer, 11-4 TAD 319
(mystery - exotic locales), The Golden
Road to Samarkand: The Arabian Nights
in Detective Fiction, by Frank D.
McSherry, Jr., 7-2 TAD 77
(mystery - exotic locales), Footsteps on
the Golden Road, Addenda to "The
Golden Road to Samarkand," by Frank
D. McSherry, Jr., 7-4 TAD 264
(mystery - face characteristics), It's
All in the Face, by W.O.G.Lofts,
7-2 TAD 109
(mystery - fan organizations), Organizations/
Publications for Mystery Fans, by
Allen J. Hubin, 1-2 TAD 37
(MYSTERY FANCIER, THE), Index of Books
Reviewed in Vol.I, by Jeff Meyerson,
2-1 MF 9; (by David H. Doerrer),
Vol.2, 3-1 MF 26; Vol.3, 4-2 MF 3;
Vol.4, 5-2 MF 3
Mystery Fandom, (organizations and
publications), by Paul Bishop,
1-3 M 24
(mystery - fandom), Of Fans and
Bouchercons, (mystery fans and the
conventions), by Guy M. Townsend,
5-5 MF 11
(mystery - fandom), On Mystery and
Science Fiction Fandom, (general
comparisons), by David Rose,
16 CD 3
(mystery - fandom), What is Mystery
Story Fandom?, by Len Moffatt,
14 JD 3
(mystery - fandom), see various entries
under Bouchercon
(mystery - fanzines), The Line-Up, by
Robert E. Briney, 1A MF 22; 2-1
MF 20
(mystery - fanzines), PQ Recommends,
2-1 PQ 56
Mystery Feature Films Made-for-TV:
Work in Progress, (1972), by Jack
Edmund Nolan, 5-2 MR 30
(mystery - female authors & sleuths),
Women in Detective Fiction, by
Michele Slung
(mystery - female supporting characters),
The Girls, (secretaries to detectives),
by Marvin Lachman, 2-3 MR 6
Mystery Fiction in Scandinavia, by
Iwan Hedman, 3-3 TAD 173
(mystery - fictional detectives on
detective fiction), "Shades of
Dupin", by George N. Dove, 8-1 TAD 12
(mystery - fictional detectives on
detective fiction), More "Shades of
Dupin!", by R.W.Hays, 8-4 TAD 288
Mystery*File, (reviews), by Steve Lewis,
1A MF 23; 1-1 MF 27; 1-2 MF 23;
1-3 MF 37; 1-4 MF 37; 1-5 MF 29;

Mystery*File, (continued), 1-6 MF 38;
2-1 MF 21; 2-2 MF 33; 2-3 MF 41;
2-4 MF 30; 2-5 MF 26; 2-6 MF 30;
3-1 MF 31; 3-2 MF 36; 3-3 MF 31;
3-4 MF 38; 3-5 MF 35; 3-6 MF 27;
4-2 MF 31; 4-3 MF 34; 4-4 MF 33;
4-5 MF 27; 5-1 MF 20; 5-2 MF 13;
5-3 MF 27; 5-4 MF 21; 5-5 MF 20;
5-6 MF 33
(mystery - film), A Great Contemporary:
Jose Giovanni, (French author's
mystery films), by Jack Edmund
Nolan, 4-4 MR 19
(mystery - film), A Justly Celebrated
Elusive American, (Quentin Locke,
detective, on screen), by Stanley
A. Carlin, 3-2 MR 31
(mystery - film), A Note on Harry
Stephen Keeler, (as filmed), by
Francis M. Nevins, Jr., 3-3 TAD 165
(mystery - film), A Reel Mystery
(film reviews), by Andy Jaysnovitch,
12/14 CL 13
(mystery - film), The Alfred Hitchcock
Theater at Universal Studios,
2-3 M 38
(mystery - film), All Too True, (a
partial list of films based on true
mysteries and crimes), by Mary
Groff, 4-5/6 PP 59
(mystery - film), At the Movies, Doc
Savage: The Man of Bronze, 1 BSA 15
(mystery - film), Bela Lugosi and
Mark of the Vampire, by Dr. Carroll
Borland Parten, 1 CD 34
(mystery - film), Bela Lugosi in Murder
by Television, by Gordon R. Guy,
1 CD 12
(mystery - film), Chandler on Screen,
TV and Radio - With a Look at the
Many Mr. Marlowes, (w/checklist),
by William F. Nolan, 3-1 TAD 23
(mystery - film), Charlie Chan in
Books and in Motion Pictures, by
Douglas M. Armato, 7-2 TAD 97
(mystery - film), Charlie Chan in
Qui Nhon, (on Armed Forces TV in
Vietnam), by Jon L. Breen, 2-2 TAD
114
(mystery - film), Cinemania, by Charles
Shibuk, 2-2 TAD 112
(mystery - film), The Comedy-Detective
Film is Alive and Well, (short
reviews), by Jim Huang, 5 CL 1
(mystery - film), Dat's Mike Ham-muh?
(Mickey Spillane's Mike Hammer in
the popular media), by Max Collins,
12-4 TAD 308
(mystery - film), Death on the Nile -
Leisurely Peril, by Donald A. Yates,
3-1 MF 45
(mystery - film), The Dragon Murder
Case, (based on book by S.S.Van Dine,
First National, 1934, a Cinematograph),
by Jon Tuska, 6-1 TAD 20

(mystery - film), Dramatizations of the Great Literary Detectives and Criminals, Pt.4, Film, by Charles Shibuk, 2-1 TAD 31; 2-3 TAD 183

(mystery - film), "Dressed to Kill," An Appreciation, (film by Brian DePalma), by Stuart M. Kaminsky, 14-1 TAD 14

(mystery - film), The Films and TV Work of Eric Ambler, by Jack Edmund Nolan, 3-1 MR 13

(mystery - film), Film Notes, by Jim Huang, 9 CL 9; 10 CL 1; 11 CL 1; 12 CL 11; 15 CD 1

(mystery - film), Film Notes, (on Sax Rohmer), by W.O.G.Lofts, 9 R 23

(mystery - film), Filmed Misogyny, The Screen Adaptations of Peter Cheyney and Lionel White, (filmed mysteries), by Jack Edmund Nolan, 4-6 MR 27

(mystery - film), The Films of Ellery Queen, by Edward Connor, 3-1 QC 10

(mystery - film), The Films of James Hadley Chase, by Jack Edmund Nolan, 3-6 MR 30

(mystery - film), I Remember...B-Movies, by R. Jeff Banks, 4-5 MF 13

(mystery - film), The Ian Fleming Films and TV, by Jack Edmund Nolan, 5-1 MR 24

(mystery - film), The Importance of "C--ing" in Earnest: A Comparison of "The Maltese Falcon" and "China-town", by William D. Bottiggi, 14-1 TAD 86

(mystery - film), Inside Gumshoe Haven: A Look at LA's Bradbury Building, by Joseph Allen, 1-2 M 27

(mystery - film), Is Deductive Fiction Unfilmable?, by Steve Fisher, 3-4 TAD 240

(mystery - film), Jack of Many Trades: Some Uses of the Ripper on the Screen, by Jack Edmund Nolan, 6-1 MR 25

(mystery - film), LeCarre, Deighton, Hall and the Screen's Tired Spies, (filmed espionage fiction), by Jack Edmund Nolan, 4-1 MR 23

(mystery - film), The Lost B Movie, by Andy Jaysnovitch, 7 PE 3

(mystery - film), The Mini Screen Career of John Creasey, (filmed mysteries from Creasey books), by Jack Edmund Nolan, 4-5 MR 11

(mystery - film), Miscellaneous Mystery Mish-Mash, (The California Switch: California locales for filmed mysteries), by Marvin Lachman, 2-2 MF 19

(mystery - film), Movies on TV and in Theatres, (general review on current mystery productions), by Lianne Carlin, 3-2 MR 15

(mystery - film), Mr. Moto on Film, (with checklist), 3-2 MR 7

(mystery - film), MYSTERY at the Movies, (reviews in MYSTERY Magazine), by Thomas Godfrey, 2-1 M 24

(mystery - film), Mystery Feature Films Made-for-TV: Work in Progress (1972), by Jack Edmund Nolan, 5-2 MR 30

(mystery - film), The Mystery Films of Alfred Hitchcock, by Charles Shibuk, 2-1 MR 3

(mystery - film), MYSTERY Moviegoer, (reviews in MYSTERY Magazine), by Thomas Godfrey, 2-2 M 59; 3-2 M 46

(mystery - film), Mystery on Film, (general commentary), by Stuart M. Kaminsky, 16 CD 10

(mystery - film), Mystery on the 1972-73 TV Schedule: The Outlook, by Jack Edmund Nolan, 5-5 MR 13

(mystery - film), Mystery/Suspense on Screen, by David W. Bruce, 1-1 M 10

(mystery - film), Nancy Drew on the Screen, (filmed Nancy Drew girls' series books characters), by David Zinman, 6-2 MR 3

(mystery - film), Notes on the Film and the Detective Story, by Charles Shibuk, 5-4 TAD 202

(mystery - film), Old Movie Expert, (mini-mystery parody), by R. Jeff Banks, 7 PE 10

(mystery - film), Patricia Highsmith On the Screen, by Jack Edmund Nolan, 4-3 MR 15

(mystery - film), Philip Loraine on the Screen, or, Where Did the Mysteries Go?, by Jack Edmund Nolan, 5-3 MR 18

(mystery - film), Philip MacDonald on the Screen, (with checklist), by Jack Edmund Nolan, 3-3 MR 33

(mystery - film), Philo Vance on the Screen, by Jack Edmund Nolan, 2-4 MR 18

(mystery - film), Play It Again, Sam Spade, (with Humphrey Bogart, filmed) by Steve Fisher, 5-2 TAD 79

(mystery - film), The Projected Detective, (on film of Dashiell Hammett's THE MALTESE FALCON), by Andy Jaysnovitch, 12 CL 8

(mystery - film), Reviews, 1 PE 17

(mystery - film), Reviews of Mystery and Crime Films, by Richard S. Lochte II, 5-3 TAD 158; 5-4 TAD 231; 6-1 TAD 39

(mystery - film), The Saint on Film, by J. Randolph Cox, 5-2 MR 14

(mystery - film), The Siegel-Eastwood Quest, (Don Siegel - Clint Eastwood), by Kathy Esselman, 7-4 TAD 253

(mystery - film), Six Britons the Movies Ignored: Tey, Household, Hamilton, Garve, Clifford, and Blackburn, (authors whose works were seldom filmed), by Jack Edmund Nolan, 3-5 MR 9

(mystery - film), Some Agatha Christie
Films, by Jack Edmund Nolan,
4-2 MR 19

(mystery - film), Some Themes in the
Film Work of Jimmy Sangster, by
Jack Edmund Nolan, 5-6 MR 21

(mystery - film), The Stuff Nightmares
Are Made Of: A Hammett Update,
by Erik Jendresen, 3-2 M 45

(mystery - film), TAD at the Movies,
(THE ARMCHAIR DETECTIVE reviews),
by Thomas Godfrey, 12-3 TAD 260;
12-4 TAD 367; 13-2 TAD 134; 13-3
TAD 226; 13-4 TAD 331; 14-1 TAD 84;
14-2 TAD 152; 14-3 TAD 253; 14-4
TAD 330

(mystery - film), Three Ladies of the
Quasi-Gothic: The Films of Armstrong,
Lofts and White, by Jack Edmund
Nolan, 5-2 MR 23

(mystery - film), Visiting Firemen,
(mini-mystery parody), by R. Jeff
Banks, 7 PE 11

(mystery - film), What Happens in "Point
Blank", (film based on Richard
Stark's THE HUNTER), by Francis M.
Nevins, Jr., 9-1 TAD 7

(mystery - film), "The Wild Bunch"
Revisited, (western-crime film),
by Brian Garfield, 13-2 TAD 141

Mystery Films of Alfred Hitchcock, The,
by Charles Shibuk, 2-1 MR 3

(mystery - football theme), Sports and
the Mystery Story, Pt.4, by Marvin
Lachman, 7-3 TAD 195

(mystery - forensic medicine), The
Corpse Tells the Tale, by Stanley
A. Carlin, 3-1 MF 25

(mystery - forerunners), A Note on
Medieval Detection, by R.W.Hays,
5-2 TAD 88

(mystery - formula plots), Ross
Macdonald, The Personal Paradigm
and Popular Fiction, by Zahava K.
Dorinson, 10-1 TAD 43

Mystery Genre Gets Literary Status Boost,
(with the Mystery Library and the
University of California), by Paul
B. Scranton, 10-4 TAD 336

(mystery - geological clues), Detectives
and Geology, by William A.S.Sarjeant,
11-3 TAD 294

(mystery - German), Zadig as a Jew: An
Early German Tale of Detection,
(by Wilhelm Hauff), by Armin Arnold,
13-2 TAD 173

(mystery - glossary), A Critical Vocabulary
for Crime Fiction, by Jacques Barzun,
4-2 TAD 75

(mystery - Golden Age), see: mystery -
classic

(mystery - golf theme), Sports and the
Mystery Story, Pt.5, by Marvin
Lachman, 7-4 TAD 261

(mystery - Gothics), Gothics, Ghastly,
Gruesome & Romantic, by Veronica
M.S.Kennedy, 9-4 TAD 276

(mystery - gun characteristics),
Feetnote to Fleming, by Dean A.
Grennell, 15 JD 10

(mystery - hair and skin pathology),
A Guide to Thorndykean Pilo-
pathology, (medico-legal impor-
tance of the skin and hair in the
Dr. Thorndyke stories by R.Austin
Freeman), by Howard Brody, 11 TF 3

(mystery - hardboiled), Captain Shaw's
Hard-Boiled Bous, (authors in the
HARD-BOILED OMNIBUS by Joseph Shaw),
by Stephen Mertz, 12-3 TAD 264

(mystery - hardboiled), Excerpts from
"The Boys in the Black Mask" (the
exhibit, UCLA, 1961, with checklist
of hardboiled crime fiction), 3-2
MR 23

(mystery - hardboiled), Chandler-
Hammett-Hemingway: Teachers in the
"Tough School," by Stanley A. Carlin,
2-5 MR 15

(mystery - hardboiled), Checklist, by
Dave Lewis and Bruce Taylor,
2-5 CP 22

(mystery - hardboiled), Classic and
Hard-Boiled Detective Fiction, by
John M. Reilly, 9-4 TAD 289

(mystery - hardboiled), The Hard-Boiled
Detective Hero in the 1970's: Some
New Candidates, by David J. Geherin,
11-1 TAD 49

(mystery - hardboiled), The Hardboiled
Dick: A Personal Checklist, by
James Sandoe, 1-2 TAD 38

(mystery - hardboiled), Hard-Boiled is
Hard to Find, (paperback editions),
3-2 CP 23

(mystery - hardboiled), Hardboiled
Lingo, (glossary), by John Knoerle,
1-1 M 9

(mystery - hardboiled), Introducing
Paul Cain and His FAST ONE: A For-
gotten Hard-Boiled Writer and a
Forgotten Gangster Novel, by E.R.
Hagemann, 12-1 TAD 72

(mystery - hardboiled), Mean Streets
Revisited: Seven Hardboiled Authors
at the Scene of the Crime Bookshop,
by Ray Zorn, 2-3 M 18

(mystery - hardboiled), Miss Wonderly,
Killer, by John Crosby, 5-4 MR 8

(mystery - hardboiled), Murder and the
Mean Streets: The Hard-Boiled
Detective Novel, by George Grella,
5-1 TAD 1

(mystery - hardboiled), Robert B. Parker
and the Hardboiled Tradition of
American Detective Fiction, by
T. Jeff Evans, 1-2 C 100

(mystery - high adventure), High
Adventure Fiction, by Don Cole,
1-4 PP 8

(mystery - historical theme), John
Dickson Carr, Alias Roger Fairbairn,
and the Historical Novel, by Douglas
G. Greene, 11-4 TAD 339

(mystery - horse racing theme), A Word
with Dick Francis, (interview), by
Deryck Harvey, 6-3 TAD 151

(mystery - horse racing theme), Detective
Fiction and the Turf, by Jon L. Breen,
5-1 TAD 24

(mystery - horse racing theme), Endure
and Prevail, The Novels of Dick
Francis, by Barry Bauska, 11-3
TAD 238

(mystery - horse racing theme), The
Francis Plot Key, (guide to books
of Dick Francis), by Jeffrey D.
Smith, 4-5/6 PP 19

(mystery - humor), Comic Capers and
Comic Eyes, by David Geherin,
13-4 TAD 276

(mystery - humor), Our Heroes in Motley,
by Edward Lauterbach, 9-3 TAD 178

(mystery 0 humor), The Unspeakable in
Search of the Inedible Among the
Unfindable, by Mike Wharton,
5-2 TAD 89

(Mystery Hunter series: Capwell Wyckoff),
Wyckoff's Stories of Adventure,
(boys' books series), by Don
Holbrook, 5 MA 6

(mystery - husband and wife detectives),
Checklist, Frances & Richard
Lockridge, by Kathy Hobel,
2-5 MR 6

(mystery - husband and wife detectives),
Double Jeopardy - Husband and Wife
Teams in Detective Fiction, by
Gail Adams, 8-4 TAD 251

(mystery - husband and wife detectives),
Mr. & Mrs. North, and Mr. & Mrs.
Lockridge, by Hank Davis, 1-1
MF 21

(mystery - husband and wife detectives),
Mr. & Mrs. North, (detective team
created by Frances and Richard
Lockridge), by R. Jeff Banks,
9-3 TAD 182

(mystery - ideas for stories), It'll
Never Happen!, by John Harwood,
9-2 TAD 121

(mystery - impossible crimes), The Case
of the Vanishing Locomotives, or, A
Hell of a Way to Run a Railroad,
(vanishing locomotives theme),
by J.R.Christopher, 1-2 TAD 56

(mystery - impossible crimes), Partial
Checklist, "miraculous crime" novels
and short stories, by Robert C.S.
Adey, 5-3 TAD 168

(mystery - impossible crimes), The First
Locked Room Mystery?: Charles
Brockden Brown's WIELAND, by
Peter J. Christensen, 10-4 TAD 368

(mystery - impossible crimes), The
Locked House: An Essay on Locked
Rooms, by Donald A. Yates,
3-2 TAD 81

(mystery - India), Detective Fiction
and Social Realism: H.R.F.Keating's
India, by Meera T. Clark, 2-1 C 1

(mystery - Indian), see: mystery:
American Indian

(mystery - inexplicable unsolved),
Threats to Rationalism: John Fowles,
Stanislaw Lem, and the Detective
Story, by Frank Occhiogrosso,
13-1 TAD 4

(mystery - inverted), Future Inversions,
by Joe R. Christopher, 6-1 MR 34

(mystery - Japan), Japanese Mystery
Fiction in English Translation,
(with checklist), by John L.
Apostolou, 13-4 TAD 310

(mystery - Japan), Mystery Stories in
Japan, by Katsuo Jinka, 9-2 TAD 111

(mystery - judicial trials), Hard
Touch: "Fair Trials", by Bill
Wilson, 17 JD 21

(mystery - Latin-America), The
Detective Literature of the
Americas, by Donald A. Yates,
4-1 TAD 5

Mystery League, A Summary, (on the
origin and life of MYSTERY LEAGUE
MAGAZINE, with index), by Nils
Hardin, 14 X 8

Mystery League, Inc., (discussion of
the "Mystery League" series of
books and the publisher, with
checklist), by Ellen Nehr, 2-6
PP 3

(MYSTERY LEAGUE MAGAZINE), Mystery
League, A Summary, (with index),
by Nils Hardin, 14 X 8

(MYSTERY LEAGUE MAGAZINE), The Mystery
League Magazine, by Allen J. Hubin,
3-1 TAD 64

(Mystery Library, The), Mystery Stories:
Report to the Stockholder, by Caleb
A. Lewis, 10-1 TAD 50

(Mystery Library, The), The World of
Mystery Fiction, by Noel Craig,
1-1 M 27

Mystery Library Writers Conference
(announcement), 2 CD 1

(mystery - literary criticism), A
Fatal Attraction, by G.A.Finch,
13-2 TAD 112

(mystery - literary criticism), Don't
Tell Me I Won't Like It, by David
Marshall Lewis, 12 LR 12

(mystery - literary quality), A Defense
for Crime Fiction, by Hilmar
Baunsgaard, 10-4 TAD 358

(mystery - literary quality), Mysteries
Make Headlines, by C. David Hellyer,
11-3 TAD 260

(mystery - locked rooms), The First
Locked Room Mystery?: Charles
Brockden Brown's WIELAND, by Peter
J. Christensen, 10-4 TAD 368

(mystery - locked rooms), The Locked House, An Essay on Locked Rooms, by Donald A. Yates, 3-2 TAD 81

(mystery - logic), A Dream of Reason, The Great Detective as True Believer, (classic detectives and logical reasoning), by Cathryn Lanham, 2-2 C 23

(mystery - logos), Symbolic Motifs, (mystery-identifying logos of various publishers, with illustrated checklist), by Robert C.S.Adey, 3-4 MR 27

MYSTERY LOVERS NEWSLETTER, THE, Index to Vol.1, 1-6 MR 17; Vol.2, 2-6 MR 20

(mystery - magazines), Mystery Plus: On Mystery Magazines, by R. Jeff Banks, 4-2 PP 13

(mystery - magazines), The Not-So-Literary Digests, (digest-size mystery magazines), by Robert Turner, 38 X 19

(mystery - magazines), see: fanzines; specific titles

(mystery - mainstream authors), Three British Experiments from the Mainstream, by Charles Shibuk, 3-2 TAD 80

(mystery - mainstream authors), Mainstream Mysteries and Novels of Crime, (reviews), by Gary Warren Niebuhr, 3-2 PP 23; 3-6 PP 17; 4-1 PP 13; 4-3 PP 5; 4-5/6 PP 63

Mystery Master: A Survey and Appreciation of the Fiction of George Harmon Cox, by J. Randolph Cox, 6-2 TAD 63; 6-3 TAD 160; 6-4 TAD 232; 7-1 TAD 11

(mystery - methods of operation), Healing Under the Bare Bulb: The Detective as Therapist, by Rob Whaley and George A. Antonelli, 2-2 C 1

(mystery - misleading clues), The Red Herring as Folklore, by William M. Clements, 12-3 TAD 255

MYSTERY MONTHLY MAGAZINE, by Robert J. Randisi, 9-4 TAD 307

(mystery - morality), The Unconventional Morality of Robert B. Parker's Traditional American Hero, by Steven R. Carter, 1-2 C 109

(mystery - motive development), Opus in G Minor for Blunt Instruments: The Development of Motive in Detective Fiction, by Raymond Obstfeld, 14-1 TAD 9

MYSTERY Moviegoer, (reviews in MYSTERY magazine), by Thomas Godfrey, 2-2 M 59; 2-3 M 44; 3-1 M 44; 3-2 M 46

Mystery, Murder and Academe, (academic scene crime fiction), by Jane Gottschalk, 11-2 TAD 159

(mystery - Negro detectives), Black Cops and/or Robbers: The Detective Fiction of Chester Himes, by Frank J. Campenni, 8-3 TAD 206

(mystery - Negro detectives), Virgil Tibbs and the American Negro in Mystery Fiction, by Marvin Lachman, 1-3 TAD 86

(mystery - New England), The American Regional Mystery, Pt.1, by Marvin Lachman, 3-3 MR 13; 3-4 MR 22

(mystery - New Jersey), The American Regional Mystery, Pt.5, by Marvin Lachman, 4-5 MR 2

(mystery - New York City), The American Regional Mystery, Pt.2, by Marvin Lachman, 3-2 MR 23; 4-1 MR 8

(mystery - New York State), The American Regional Mystery, Pt.4, by Marvin Lachman, 4-3 MR 3

Mystery News, Chaotic Notes in Rapid Passing, by Allen J. Hubin, 2-4 TAD 262

Mystery News Notes, (news and comments), by Allen J. Hubin, 1-1 TAD 4; 2-1 TAD 60; 2-4 TAD 226

Mystery Nook Poll Results, The, (of a readers' poll by MYSTERY NOOK magazine), by Jo Ann Vicarel, 9 MN P1

Mystery Notes of Recent and Forthcoming Publications, by Allen J. Hubin, 1-3 TAD 99

(MYSTERY OF A HANSOM CAB, THE: Fergus Hume), In Search of a Hansom Cab, by Philip T. Asdell, 1-2 PP 10

Mystery of Alfred Hitchcock, The, (in-depth study and survey of his works), by Stuart J. Kaminsky, 2-3 M 26

(MYSTERY OF ANGELINA FROOD, THE: R. Austin Freeman), Edwin and Angelina, (with comments on THE MYSTERY OF EDWIN DROOD), by Norman Donaldson, 2 TF 2

Mystery of Edwin Drood, The, by Albert I. Borowitz, 10-1 TAD 14

(MYSTERY OF EDWIN DROOD, THE: Charles Dickens), Dickens' Last Book: More Mysteries Than One, by Arthur J. Cox, 14-1 TAD 31

(MYSTERY OF EDWIN DROOD, THE: Charles Dickens), The Dilemma of Datchery, by E.F.Bleiler, 4-4 MF 7

(MYSTERY OF EDWIN DROOD, THE: Charles Dickens), Drood the Obscure: The Evidence of the Names, by Robert F. Fleissner, 13-1 TAD 12

(MYSTERY OF EDWIN DROOD, THE: Charles Dickens), Edwin's Mystery and Its History, or, Another Look at Datchery, by Ben Fisher, 4-5 MF 6

(MYSTERY OF EDWIN DROOD, THE: Charles Dickens), John Dickson Carr's Solution to "The Mystery of Edwin Drood", 14-4 TAD 291

(MYSTERY OF EDWIN DROOD, THE: Charles Dickens), John Jasper's Devotion, by Nathan L. Bengis, 8-3 TAD 165; 8-4 TAD 257; 9-1 TAD 25

(MYSTERY OF EDWIN DROOD, THE: Charles Dickens), The Mystery of Edwin Drood, by Albert I. Borowitz, 10-1 TAD 14

Mystery of the Publishers' Taste, The,
(forthcoming mystery books, January-
June 1976), by Martin Morse Wooster,
1-1 MM 5; 1-2 MM 5

Mystery of the Publishers' Taste, The,
(forthcoming mystery books), by Don
Miller, 1-3 MM 7; 1-4 MM 5; 1-5 MM 4;
1-6 MM 4; 1-7 MM 2; 1-8 MM 4; 1-9
MM 3; 1-10 MM 5; 1-11 MM 10; 2-1
MM 10; 2-2 MM 10; 2-3 MM 6; 2-4 MM
15; 2-5 MM 19

Mystery of Robert Eustace, The, (author),
by Joe R. Christopher, 13-4 TAD 365

Mystery of Social Reaction, The: Two
Novels of Ellery Queen, by J.R.
Christopher, 6-1 TAD 28

Mystery on Film, (general commentary),
by Stuart M. Kaminsky, 16 CD 10

MYSTERY on Stage, (stage production
reviews in MYSTERY Magazine), by
Tim Kelly, 2-3 M 24; (Jack the
Ripper) 3-2 M 55

Mystery on the 1972-73 TV Schedule:
The Outlook, by Jack Edmund Nolan,
5-5 MR 13

(mystery - paperback), A Crime Club
Selection, 2-5 CP 14

(mystery - paperback), Ace Double
Mysteries, (discussion with checklist), by Steve Lewis, 6 MY 3

(mystery - paperback), Ace Paperback
Books, (checklist by author), by
J. Grant Thiessen, 1 SF 21; 2 SF 35

(mystery - paperback), Ace Paperback
Books, (numerical checklist), by
J. Grant Thiessen, 1 SF 3; 2 SF 35

(mystery - paperback), Ace Books and
Standard Book Numbers, by Bill
Denholm, 1-4 CP 17

(mystery - paperback), Ace Double
Mysteries, A Pair of Aces, (Letter
from Donald A. Wolheim as editor),
7 MY 5

(mystery - paperback), Murder Ink and
Scene of the Crime Books Series
Announced, (Dell paperbacks),
16 CD 1

(mystery - paperback), Dell Dimers,
(Dell 10¢ series), by M.C.Hill,
2-2 PQ 14

(mystery - paperback), Dell Great
Mystery Library, by Bruce Taylor,
3-1 CP 23

(mystery - paperback), Dell Mapback
Series, Agatha Christie in the
Mapbacks, by William Lyles,
3-3 PQ 26

(mystery - paperback), Dell Mapback
Series, Rex Stout in the Dell
Mapbacks, by William Lyles,
2-4 PQ 14

(mystery - paperback), Dell Mapback
Series, Checklist, Nos.1-300, by
Richard C. Butler, 1-2 MF 17

(mystery - paperback), Dell Mysteries:
Murder Ink and Scene of the Crime,
by Charlotte Laughlin, 3-4 PQ 13

(mystery - paperback), Alfred Hitchcock
in Dell Paperbacks, by Billy C. Lee
and Charlotte Laughlin, 3-1 PQ 23

(mystery - paperback), Keyhole Confidential, (on early Dell paperbacks),
by William Lyles, 2-4 CP 13

(mystery - paperback), Dell 1st Series,
1st Editions, (checklist), by William
Lyles, 1-5 CP 25; 1-6 CP 17

(mystery - paperback), Dell Paperback
Variant Editions, by William Lyles,
3-2 CP 10

(mystery - paperback), Inner Sanctum,
(Inner Sanctum mystery series), by
M.C.Hill, 3-4 CP 9

(mystery - paperback), Keyhole Confidential, (various data, regular
column), by William Lyles, 1-2 CP 10;
1-3 CP 7 (Dell author bibliography,
Anthony Boucher and Agatha Christie)
1-4 CP 26; 1-5 CP 26; 1-6 CP 17;
(paperback female cover art) 2-2 CP
22.

(mystery - paperback), Killian's Memoranda, (column on paperback book
data), by Dave Killian, 1-1 CP 17;
(partial list of Bonded and Chartered
Publications) 1-4 CP 23; (Rex Stout's
Mystery Quarterly) 1-5 CP 21; 2-1
CP 17; 2-3 CP 8; (mystery paperbacks
of Chester Himes) 3-3 CP 19

(mystery - paperback), Paperbacks
Announced for July 1975, by Steve
Lewis, 3/4 MN 17; (August 1975) 5/6
MN 8

(mystery - paperback), Paperback
Mysteries Issued in June 1974, by
Steve Lewis, 2 MY 7; (July) 3 MY 5

(mystery - paperback), Paper Crimes,
(reviews of mystery paperback books),
8-4 TAD 295; 9-1 TAD 50; 9-2 TAD
140; 9-3 TAD 212; 9-4 TAD 277; 10-1
TAD 51; 10-2 TAD 130; 10-4 TAD 340;
11-2 TAD 192; 11-3 TAD 306; 11-4 TAD
396; 12-2 TAD 135; 12-3 TAD 287;
13-1 TAD 65; 13-2 TAD 136; 13-3 TAD
251; 13-4 TAD 361; 14-1 TAD 80; 14-2
TAD 183

(mystery - paperback), The Paperback
Revolution, (reviews of mystery
paperback books), by Charles Shubuk,
1-1 TAD 10; 1-2 TAD 41; 1-3 TAD 96;
1-4 TAD 129; 2-1 TAD 44; 2-2 TAD 97;
2-3 TAD 174; 2-4 TAD 251; 3-1 TAD
40; 3-2 TAD 115; 3-3 TAD 179; 3-4
TAD 245; 4-1 TAD 37; 4-2 TAD 115;
4-3 TAD 168; 4-4 TAD 219; 5-1 TAD
30; 5-2 TAD 94; 5-3 TAD 154; 5-4
TAD 220; 6-1 TAD 35; 6-2 TAD 102;
6-3 TAD 179; 6-4 TAD 246; 7-1 TAD
44; 7-2 TAD 120; 7-3 TAD 205; 7-4

(mystery - paperback), The Paperback Revolution, (continued), TAD 281; 8-1 TAD 50; 8-2 TAD 132; 8-3 TAD 210; 8-4 TAD 276; 9-1 TAD 41; 9-2 TAD 135; 9-3 TAD 208; 9-4 TAD 281; 10-1 TAD 71; 10-2 TAD 149; 10-3 TAD 239; 10-4 TAD 360; 11-1 TAD 96; 11-2 TAD 189; 11-3 TAD 298; 11-4 TAD 379; 12-1 TAD 30; 12-2 TAD 166; 12-3 TAD 255; 12-4 TAD 368; 13-1 TAD 75; 13-2 TAD 135; 13-3 TAD 250; 13-4 TAD 362; 14-1 TAD 79; 14-2 TAD 182; 14-3 TAD 266; 14-4 TAD 376

(mystery - paperback), Random Thoughts on Writing "The Paperback Revolution" by Charles Shibuk, 4-3 TAD 172

(mystery - paperback), Raven House Mysteries - Forever More! (checklist and introduction to the Raven House line of mystery paperbacks), by Michael L. Cook, 4-5/6 PP 27

(mystery - paperback), Remembering Avon Murder Mystery, with Checklist, by Francis M. Nevins, Jr., 7 MY 3

(mystery - paperback), The Sales Score on Mystery Authors, (paperback bestsellers), 3-6 MR 29

(mystery - paperback), see individual publishers

(mystery - Pennsylvania), The American Regional Mystery, Pt.5, by Marvin Lachman, 4-5 MR 2

(mystery - photography), Photo Detection: The Image as Evidence, by David L. Jacobs, 1-2 C 18

(mystery - plot games), The Games of Detective Fiction, by Jane Gottschalk, 10-1 TAD 74

Mystery Plus, (on elusive mysteries), by R. Jeff Banks, 1-1 PP 17

Mystery Plus: A Contemporary Science Fiction Pair, (TIME AFTER TIME by Karl Alexander, and THE WOLFEN by Whitley Strieber), 3-1 PP 16

Mystery Plus: A Different Perspective, by R. Jeff Banks, 2-1 PP 20

Mystery Plus: A Movie Review, ("The Legacy": Jimmy Sangster), 3-3 PP 17

Mystery Plus: A Pair of Parodies, (SPACE FOR HIRE by William F. Nolan, and THE CHEAP DETECTIVE by Robert Grossbach), 1-5 PP 10

Mystery Plus: A Pair of Triple Threats, (commentary on mystery novels involving mystery-magic-western and mystery-SF-magic), 4-4 PP 14

Mystery Plus: THE ADVENTURE OF THE HOLMES-DRACULA FILE, (commentary), by R. Jeff Banks, 2-4 PP 15

Mystery Plus: The Demolished Man, (on Alfred Bester's THE DEMOLISHED MAN), by R. Jeff Banks, 1-2 PP 11

Mystery Plus: Getting There May Be More Than Half the Fun, (THE 13 CRIMES OF SCIENCE FICTION by Asimov-Greenberg-Waugh, and THE SPIRIT by Thomas Page), by R. Jeff Banks, 3-5 PP 15

Mystery Plus: The Hawk, (THE HAWK: Milton J. Shapiro), by R. Jeff Banks, 2-3 PP 24

Mystery Plus: The Holmes Pastiche of the Decade, (ENTER THE LION: Michael P. Hodel and Sean M. Wright), by R. Jeff Banks, 4-1 PP 21

Mystery Plus: Image of the Beast, (IMAGE OF THE BEAST: Philip Jose Farmer), by R. Jeff Banks, 3-2 PP 15

Mystery Plus: Incubus, (INCUBUS: Ray Russell), by R. Jeff Banks, 1-3 PP 9

Mystery Plus: John Reese Revisited, by R. Jeff Banks, 1-6 PP 18

Mystery Plus: On Mystery Magazines, by R. Jeff Banks, 4-2 PP 13

Mystery Plus: Poe Must Die, (POE MUST DIE: Mark Oldham), by R. Jeff Banks, 2-2 PP 12

Mystery Plus: R-Rated Double Feature, (reviews), by R. Jeff Banks, 2-6 PP 13

Mystery Plus: Series Shots, (comments on recently published series books and characters), by R. Jeff Banks, 4-5/6 PP 40

Mystery Plus: Shadow of a Broken Man, (SHADOW OF A BROKEN MAN: George C. Chesbro), by R. Jeff Banks, 4-1 PP 22

Mystery Plus: Old Friends Break New Ground, (AN OLD FRIEND OF THE FAMILY by Fred Saberhagen, and GHOSTS by Ed McBain), by R. Jeff Banks, 3-6 PP 15

Mystery Plus: Short Notices of Various Books, by R. Jeff Banks, 2-5 PP 13

Mystery Plus: The Spear, (THE SPEAR: James Herbert), by R. Jeff Banks, 3-4 PP 14

Mystery Plus: Weapon Heavy, (on Jeff Hewitt, Western Private Eye), by R. Jeff Banks, 1-4 PP 21

Mystery Plus: What's-Its, by R. Jeff Banks, 4-3 PP 11

(mystery - poison), The Use of Poison in Detective Fiction, by Peter R. Gwilt and John R. Gwilt, 1-2 C 8

(mystery - police procedurals), The Enigma of the Policeman/Writer, (novels written by police personnel) by Paul Bishop, 2-1 M 34

(mystery - police procedurals), Eye-Q 4: Tour of Duty, (quiz), by Jonathon Harrow, 2-1 M 42

(mystery - police procedurals), "Realism, Routine, Stubborness and System:: The Police Procedural I, by George N. Dove, 10-2 TAD 133

(mystery - police procedurals), The Cops and the Cop-Haters: The Police Procedural II, by George N. Dove, 10-3 TAD 241

(mystery - police procedurals), Brother Officers...Be Damned: Police Procedural III, by George N. Dove, 10-4 TAD 320

(mystery - police procedurals), Past-Mistress of the Police Procedural, (Elizabeth Linington), by Ann Waldron, 3-5 MR 32

(mystery - police procedurals), The Police Are Always There: The Police Procedural IV, by George N. Dove, 11-1 TAD 74

(mystery - police procedurals), The Tangled Emotions: The Police Procedural V, by George N. Dove, 11-2 TAD 150

(mystery - police procedurals), The Rookie Type: The Police Procedural VI, by George N. Dove, 11-3 TAD 249

Mystery Poll, (by The San Francisco Mystery Bookstore), by Bruce Taylor, 3-5 PP 31

(mystery - popular aesthetics), On Reading Detective Fiction, by John M. Reilly, 12-1 TAD 64

Mystery Previews, by Jim Huang, 9 CL 1

(mystery - private eye), A Day in the Life of a Real Private Investigator, by Douglas Christensen and Karen Bornstein, 1-3 M 52

(mystery - private eye), A Fatal Attraction, by G.A.Finch, 13-2 TAD 112

(mystery - private eye), The Best TV Eyes of the 70's, by Robert J. Randisi, 2-1 M 11

(mystery - private eye), Carroll John Daly: The Forgotten Pioneer of the Private Eye, by William F. Nolan, 4-1 TAD 1

(mystery - private eye), Chase: The Private Eye Novels of James Hadley Chase, by Theodore P. Dukeshire, 7 PE 7

(mystery - private eye), Down Grey, Wet Streets, by Mary Groff, 3 PE 9

(mystery - private eye), The 11 Best Private Eye Novels of Them All, by Michael Avallone, 38 X 130

(mystery - private eye), EYEclopedia, (glossary), by F.E.Perine, 1 PE 22

(mystery - private eye), From Spade to Marlowe to Archer, by G.A.Finch, 4-2 TAD 107

(mystery - private eye), Have You Met Hardman? (Hardman series: Ralph Dennis), by G.A.Finch, 8-4 TAD 275

(mystery - private eye), Intruder in the Rose Garden, (private eye vs. classic mystery), by George N. Dove, 9-4 TAD 278

(mystery - private eye), The Private Eye - Enduring as a $1.29 Steak, by Richard S. Lochte II, 3-2 TAD 117

(mystery - private eye), The Private Eye on Radio, by David Pollard, 2 PE 14

(mystery - private eye), Private Eyes-Who or What Are They?, by Mary Ann Grochowski, 5 PE 13

(mystery - private eye), Sex and the Single Sleuth, by Ralph Diffinetti, 3 PE 3

(mystery - prizefighting theme),Sports and the Mystery Story, Pt.2, by Marvin Lachman, 6-2 TAD 83

Mystery Puzzle, (on Dashiell Hammett), 3-2 M 24

(mystery - questions & answers), Comments and Queries, 1A MR 4; 1-1 MR 6; 1-2 MR 5; 1-3 MR 5; 1-6 MR 8; 2-4 MR 17

Mystery Quiz, by Steve Lewis, 5 MY 8; 5A MY 3

Mystery Quiz on Cats, 6/7 LR 15

(mystery - radio), Boston Blackie, (with checklist), by Ray Stanich, 3 PE 17

(mystery - radio), Challenges to the Listener, (Ellery Queen on radio), by Chris Steinbrunner, 12-3 TAD 214

(mystery - radio), Chandler on Screen, TV and Radio - With a Look at the Many Mr. Marlowes, (with checklist), by William F. Nolan, 3-1 TAD 23

(mystery - radio), Craig Kennedy, (with checklist), by Ray Stanich, 3 PE 18

(mystery - radio), Doc in the Movies? Nope, on Radio!, (Doc Savage), 2/3 DR 9

(mystery - radio), Dramatizations of the Great Literary Detectives and Criminals, Pt.1: Radio, by Charles Shibuk, 1-2 TAD 48

(mystery - radio), I Remember...Radio Mysteries, by R. Jeff Banks, 3-5 MF 17

(mystery - radio), John Dickson Carr on British Radio, (with checklist), by Douglas G. Greene, 12-1 TAD 69

(mystery - radio), Mystery Dial, (comments on old radio mystery shows), 2 MY 3; 3 MY 3; 4 MY 6; 5 MY 9; 6 MY 12; 7 MY 9, by Steve Lewis

(mystery - radio), Mystery Dial I: Johnny Dollar, by Steve Lewis, 2-1 PP 9

(mystery - radio), Mystery Dial II: The Green Hornet, by Steve Lewis, 2-2 PP 10

(mystery - radio), Mystery Dial III: Locked Rooms, by Steve Lewis, 2-3 PP 11

(mystery - radio), Mystery Dial IV: Mr. & Mrs. North, by Steve Lewis, 2-4 PP 25

(mystery - radio), Mystery Dial V: Lights Out and Others, by Steve Lewis, 2-6 PP 28

(mystery - radio), Nero Wolfe is "On the Air", by Judson C. Sapp, 9 MN A19

(mystery - radio), The Paul Temple Saga, (Temple series, Francis Durbridge, on British radio), by Derek J. Adley, 9-4 TAD 267

(mystery - radio), Old Time Radio Lives- Look for It in the Morning Express! by Carl Larsen, 4-6 MF 9

(mystery - radio), Old Time Radio Lives: "Saints Preserve Us, Mr. Keen!" by Carl Larsen, 4-5 MF 18

(mystery - radio), The Private Eye on Radio, by David Pollard, 2 PE 14

(mystery - radio), Quickie Radio Trivia Quiz, (mystery quiz), 9 MN Q1

(mystery - radio), Radio Detectives Tag-Line Quiz, (quiz), by R. Jeff Banks, 11-4 TAD 395

(mystery - radio), The Radio Murder Hour, by Chris Steinbrunner, 14-2 TAD 156; 14-3 TAD 229; (The Shadow) 14-4 TAD 335

(mystery - radio), Radio Mystery Quiz, (quiz), by R. Jeff Banks, 12-3 TAD 211

(mystery - radio), The Sound of Suspense: John Dickson Carr as a Radio Writer, by Francis M. Nevins, Jr., 11-4 TAD 335

(mystery - radio), Wolfe on the Air, (Nero Wolfe), by Art Scott, 9 MN A17

(mystery - railroad theme), Bibliography of American Mystery Novels Associated with Railroads, by Frank P. Donovan, 1-4 TAD 126

(mystery - railroad theme), Bibliography of English Railway Novels of Detection and Mystery, and Translations, by Frank P. Donovan, 2-2 TAD 105

(mystery - railroad theme), Bibliography of English Railway Short Stories of Detection and Mystery, and Translations, by Frank P. Donovan, 2-3 TAD 178

(mystery - railroad theme), The Case of the Vanishing Locomotives, or, A Hell of a Way to Run a Railroad, by J.R. Christopher, 1-2 TAD 56

(mystery - railroad theme), Mystery Rides the Rails: American Railroad Novels of Detection and Mystery, by Frank P. Donovan, 1-4 TAD 119

(mystery - railroad theme), Mystery Rides the Rails: Railroad Short Stories of Detection and Mystery in America, by Frank P. Donovan, 2-1 TAD 26

(mystery - railroad theme), Mystery Rides the Rails: English Railway Novels of Detection and Mystery, and Translations, by Frank P. Donovan, 2-2 TAD 103

(mystery - railroad theme), Mystery Rides the Rails: English Railway Short Stories of Detection and Mystery, and Translations, by Frank P. Donovan, 2-3 TAD 176

(mystery - ransom plots), The Ultimate Hi-Jacking Novel, by Marvin Lachman, 2-2 PP 17

(mystery - rational premise), Aristotle's Operative, or, The Case of the Classic Barzun, by Newton Baird, 8-1 TAD 15

(mystery - rational premise), Detection in the Guilt-Age, by J. Randolph Cox, 8-1 TAD 111

MYSTERY READERS NEWSLETTER, THE, Index to Volume III, 3-6 MR 34; Volume IV, 4-6 MR 42

(mystery - reference books), A Bibliography of Secondary Sources, by Walter Albert, (1972) 7-1 TAD 46; (1973) 7-4 TAD 266; (1974) 8-4 TAD 290; (1975) 9-4 TAD 316; (1976) 11-2 TAD 196; (1977) 12-2 TAD 125; (1978) 13-1 TAD 43; (1979) 13-4 TAD 313; (1980) 14-4 TAD 346

(mystery - reference books), A Detective Story Reference Library, by Adrian Goldstone, 3-1 MR 17

(mystery - reference books), It's About Crime, by Marvin Lachman, 2-4 MF 15

(mystery - reference books), Red-Blooded Mysteries Are Now Blue-Blooded, by Michael L. Cook, 14 SF 38

(mystery - reference books), Some Necessary Needs, (survey of reference books), by Mary Croff, 10 CL 5; 11 CL 4

(mystery - religion theme), Religion and Detection, by Marvin Lachman, 1-1 TAD 19

(mystery - religion theme), Religion and the Detective Story, by R.W. Hays, 8-1 TAD 24

(mystery - respectability), The Academic Respectability of Detective Fiction, An Editor's Introduction to thesis "Best-Selling American Detective Fiction" by Joan M. Mooney, by Allen J. Hubin, 3-2 TAD 97

(mystery - review criticism), Books about Books of Crime and the Criticism Thereof, by Jacques Barzun, 5-1 TAD 15

(mystery - review criticism), Don't Tell Me I Won't Like It, by David Marshall Lewis, 12 LR 12

(mystery - review extracts), A Partial Index to Reviews of Crossen Books, (Kendell F. Crossen, with extracts), by Don Miller, 12 MN A5

(mystery - review extracts), Book Review
Extracts, (from various newspapers),
1-1 MM 10; 1-2 MM 7; 1-3 MM 9; 1-4
MM 7; 1-5 MM 5; 1-6 MM 5; 1-7 MM 5;
1-8 MM 8; 1-9 MM 8; 1-10 MM 10; 1-11
MM 6; 2-1 MM 7; 2-2 MM 9; 2-3 MM 7;
2-4 MM 8, by Don Miller

(mystery - review extracts), From the Press:
The Early Non-Nero Wolfe Books,
9 MN A57, by Don Miller

(mystery - review extracts), In the Press:
A Few Review Extracts of Nero Wolfe
Books, by Don Miller, 9 MN A56

(mystery - review extracts), Review
Extracts from the Press, by Don
Miller, 1 MN 9; 2 MN 9; 3/4 MN 5;
5/6 MN 19; 5/6 MN 22; 8 MN 18;
8 MN 28; 9 MN A56; 10 MN A6;
10 MN A18; 10 MN 22; 10 MN 25;
10 MN 29; 12 MN R8

Mystery Reviewers Handbook - Dashiell
Hammett (1894-1961), (verse), by
James Mark Purcell, 7-4 TAD 282

Mystery Rides the Rails: American Railroad
Novels of Detection and Mystery, by
Frank P. Donovan, 1-4 TAD 124

Mystery Rides the Rails: Railroad Short
Stories of Detection and Mystery in
America, by Frank P. Donovan,
2-1 TAD 46

Mystery Rides the Rails: English Railway
Novels of Detection and Mystery, and
Translations, by Frank P. Donovan,
2-2 TAD 103

Mystery Rides the Rails: English Railway
Short Stories of Detection and Mystery,
and Translations, by Frank P. Donovan,
2-3 TAD 176

(mystery - Scandinavia), Mystery Fiction
in Scandinavia, by Iwan Hedman,
3-3 TAD 173

(mystery - scientific detection),
Sherlock Holmes, Father of
Scientific Crime Detection, by
Stanton O. Berg, 5-2 TAD 81

(mystery - scientific detection), The
Unique Magazine, Hugo Gernsback's
SCIENTIFIC DETECTIVE MONTHLY, by
Robert A.W.Lowndes, 14-1 TAD 24;
14-2 TAD 157; 14-3 TAD 243; 14-4
TAD 367; 15-1 TAD 18

(mystery - Shakespeare theme), Advice
Unheeded: Shakespeare in Some Modern
Mystery Novels, by Jane S. Bakerman,
14-2 TAD 134

(mystery - Shakespeare theme), Detective
Fiction and Things Shakespearean, by
Jane Gottschalk, 14-2 TAD 100

(mystery - social context), Lew Archer's
"Moral Landscape", by Elmer R. Pry,
Jr., 8-1 TAD 104

(mystery - social context), The Problem
of Moral Vision in Dashiell Hammett's
Detective Novels, by George J. Thompson,
6-3 TAD 153; 6-4 TAD 214; 7-1 TAD 32;
7-3 TAD 178; 7-4 TAD 270; 8-1 TAD 27;
8-2 TAD 124

(mystery - social context), A View
From Wall Street: Social Criticism
in the Mystery Novels of Emma
Lathen, by Jane S. Bakerman, 9-3
TAD 213

(mystery - social context), see Travis
McGee series by John D. MacDonald

(mystery - social function), Explaining
the Mystery Story, by R. Gordon
Kelly, 5-4 TAD 214

(mystery - social function), The Mystery
of Social Reaction: Two Novels of
Ellery Queen, by J.R.Christopher,
6-1 TAD 28

(mystery - social function), The Rites
of a Mystery Cult, by J.R.Christopher,
5-3 TAD 152

(mystery - social periods reflected),
It's a Novel World, by Mary Groff,
9-4 TAD 314

(mystery - social stress), Julian
Symons and Civilization's Discord,
by Steven R. Carter, 12-1 TAD 57

(mystery - social vision), Where Have
All the Values Gone?: The Private
Eye's Vision of America in the
Novels of Raymond Chandler and
Ross Macdonald, by Etta C. Abrahams,
9-2 TAD 128

(mystery - social vs. puzzle), Dorothy
L. Sayers and the Apotheosis of
Detective Fiction, by Elaine Bander,
10-4 TAD 362

(mystery - sound analysis), Do You Hear
What I Hear?, Or, Play It Again,
George, by Karen Bornstein, 1-2 M 13

(mystery - sports), Cortland Fitzsimmons
and the Sports Mystery, (literary
sketch), by Jon L. Breen, 14-2 TAD
129

(mystery - sports), Sports and the
Mystery Story, by Marvin Lachman,
(tennis) 6-1 TAD 1; (prizefighting
and bull-fighting) 6-2 TAD 83;
(baseball and basketball) 6-4 TAD
243; (football) 7-3 TAD 195; (golf)
7-4 TAD 261; (cricket) 8-1 TAD 108

(mystery - stage), Blood and Thunder
On Stage, by James Keddie, Jr.,
1-4 TAD 119

(mystery - stage), Break a Leg, Break
a Neck: The Mystery on Stage, by
Tim Kelly, 2-2 M 14

(mystery - stage), Dicks on Stage: Form
and Formula in Detective Drama, by
Charles LaBorde, 11-3 TAD 215; 11-4
TAD 348; 12-1 TAD 83; 12-2 TAD 158;
12-3 TAD 246; 12-4 TAD 341; 13-1
TAD 69; 13-2 TAD 150; 13-3 TAD 240

(mystery - stage), Dramatizations of
the Great Literary Detectives and
Criminals, Pt.III: Theatre, by
Marvin Lachman, 1-4 TAD 132

(mystery - stage), The Mousetrap
Phenomenon, ("The Mousetrap: Agatha
Christie), by Arthur Nicholas
Athanason, 12-2 TAD 152

(mystery - stage), MYSTERY on Stage,
(reviews in MYSTERY magazine), by Tim
Kelly, 2-3 M 24; (Jack the Ripper)
3-2 M 55

(mystery - stage), Ngaio Marsh's "Theatrical"
Murders, (mystery novels with stage
theme), by Earl F. Bargainnier,
10-2 TAD 175

(mystery - stage), West End Notes, (on
mystery plays in London), 4-2 TAD 114

Mystery Stories and the Presidency,
by Marvin Lachman, 2-1 MR 8

Mystery Stories in Japan, by Katsuo
Jinka, 9-2 TAD 112

(mystery - subject guide), Subject Guide
to Mystery Fiction, by Richard
Emery, 3-1 PP 3; 3-3 PP 43;
3-4 PP 41; 3-6 PP 41

(mystery - supernatural theme), A Study
in Black, by Frank D. McSherry, Jr.,
5-5 MR 23; 5-6 MR 3; 6-1 MR 29;
6-2 MR 39

(mystery - supernatural theme), Mystery
Plus: Incubus, (INCUBUS: Ray Russell),
by R. Jeff Banks, 1-3 PP 9

Mystery Suspense Home Entertainment, (on
video cassettes, film, discs), by
David Bruce, 1-2 M 11

Mystery/Suspense on Screen, by David
Bruce, 1-1 M 10

(mystery - television), The Adventures
of Nick Carter, (article review), by
J. Randolph Cox, 5-2 MR 35

(mystery - television), Alfred Hitchcock
on Television, (survey study),
2-3 M 30

(mystery - television), Alfred Hitchcock's
TV Shows: A Footnote on Scripters and
Literary Sources, by Jack Edmund
Nolan, 3-4 MR 17

(mystery - television), The Best TV Eyes
of the 70's, by Robert J. Randisi,
2-1 M 11

(mystery - television), Chandler on Screen,
TV and Radio - With a Look at the Many
Mr. Marlowes, (with checklist), by
William F. Nolan, 3-1 TAD 23

(mystery - television), Crime Pays for TV,
But Less, by Harry S. Glover, 6/7 LR 10

(mystery - television), Dat's Mike Ham-muh?
(Mickey Spillane's Mike Hammer on
television), by Max Collins, 12-4
TAD 308

(mystery - television), Ellery Queen on
the Small Screen, (television 1955-
1976, with checklist), by Francis M.
Nevins, Jr., 12-3 TAD 216

(mystery - television), Dramatizations of
the Great Literary Detectives and
Criminals, Pt.II: Television, by
Marvin Lachman, 1-3 TAD 94

(mystery - television), Ellery Queen
Pilot Show on TV, by Don Hutchison,
7 MY 10

(mystery - television), Eyes on the
Screen, by Mary Groff, 13-3 TAD 261

(mystery - television), It's For you,
Inspector, You've Been Cancelled,
by Jon Ury, 7-4 TAD 265

(mystery - television), The Ladies of
the Tube, by Paul Bishop, 3-1 M 53

(mystery - television), Lord Peter
Views the Telly, (Lord Peter
Wimsey on BBC TV), by J.R.Christopher,
12-1 TAD 20

(mystery - television), Man in a
Suitcase, (series, with checklist),
by Paul Bishop, 7 PE 15

(mystery - television), Mystery on the
1972-73 TV Schedule: The Outlook,
by Jack Edmund Nolan, 5-5 MR 13

(mystery - television), "Mystery" TV
Series on PBS, by Lorin Brennan,
2-3 M 16

(mystery - television), The Projected
Detective, by Andy Jaysnovitch,
8 CL 6

(mystery - television), Requiem for a
Detective: The Strange Death of
Ellery Queen, (cancellation of
television series), by Paul A.
Sukys, 10-1 TAD 81

(mystery - television), Reviews of
Various Detective Series, by Richard
S. Lochte II, 5-2 TAD 104

(mystery - television), TAD on TV,
(commentary and reviews in THE
ARMCHAIR DETECTIVE), by Richard
Meyers, 13-3 TAD 228; 13-4 TAD 332;
14-1 TAD 82; 14-2 TAD 153; 14-3 TAD
254; 14-4 TAD 332

(mystery - television), Television,
(comments on mystery shows), by
Jim Huang, 8 CL 1; 12 CL 1

(mystery - television), TV Notes, by
Jack Edmund Nolan, 4-2 MR 32

(mystery - television), TV Reviews, by
Lorin Brennan, 3-2 M 50

(mystery - television), TV Reviews, by
Donald Carew, 2-2 M 47

(mystery - television), Two From the
Telly, (British TV detective series,
"Sapphire and Steel" and "The
Professionals"), by Robert C.S.Adey,
5-6 MF 19

(mystery - television), What Will TV
Do to Doc Savage? (difficulty of
depicting the Doc Savage of books
on television), by Samuel Potts,
6 BS 6

(mystery - television), Wolfe a Howler,
(comments on the Nero Wolfe television series), by Bob Napier,
5-5 MF 7

(mystery - television writers), An
Interview with Stephen J. Cannell,
by Hamilton T. Caine, 2-1 M 6

(mystery - tennis theme), Sports and the
Mystery Story, Pt.1, by Marvin Lachman,
6-1 TAD 1

Mystery Theme Match-Up, (mystery quiz), by
R. Jeff Banks, 11-3 TAD 305

(mystery - trials series), Trials Series,
Some Notable, Some Not, (various books
and series on British classic trials),
by Jonathan Goodman, 7-2 TAD 116

(mystery - true crimes as fiction), A
Mirror to Our Crimes, by Edward D.
Hoch, 12-3 TAD 280

(mystery - true crimes as fiction), All
Too True, (books and stories suggested
by true crimes), by Mary Groff, 1-1
PP 3; 1-2 PP 15; 1-3 PP 16; 1-4 PP 17;
1-5 PP 13; 1-6 PP 14; 2-1 PP 23; 2-2
PP 20; 2-3 PP 15; 2-4 PP 21; 2-5 PP
19; 2-6 PP 19; 3-1 PP 29; 3-2 PP 19;
3-3 PP 22; 3-4 PP 25; 3-5 PP 21; 3-6
PP 21; 4-1 PP 24; 4-2 PP 15; 4-3 PP
15; 4-4 PP 21; (films based on true
mysteries and crimes) 4-5/6 PP 59

(mystery - true crimes as fiction), Crime
Hunt: Real Life Cases, (discussion of
The Wallace Case), by T.M.McDade,
14-4 TAD 374

(mystery - true crimes as fiction), Stranger
Than Fiction, by John A. Hogan, 9-2
TAD 119

(mystery - vanishers), Jim Thompson: A
Walk in the Jungle, Addendum to "Judge
Crater and His Fellow Travellers," by
Frank D. McSherry, Jr., 8-1 TAD 99

(mystery - vanishers), Judge Crater and
His Fellow Travellers, by Frank D.
McSherry, Jr., 4-4 TAD 195

(mystery - video), Mystery Suspense Home
Entertainment, (cassettes, film, discs),
by David Bruce, 1-2 M 11

Mystery Views, (letters of comment from
readers), 6 MY 2; 7 MY 11

(mystery - villainy), On the Invention
of Villainy: Speculations By a Mystery
Fan, by Lawrence Fleming, 17 JD 19

Mystery Writer Beware!, (lack of markets
for novice authors), by B.F.Watkinson,
16 CD 6

Mystery Writer Deaths, (various recent
deaths of mystery authors, 1968), by
Allen J. Hubin, 1-3 TAD 104

Mystery Writer of Merit - Cornell Woolrich,
by Pat Erhardt, 1-2 MR 3

Mystery Writers Honor Their Own: 32nd
Annual Edgar Allan Poe Awards, (report,
Mystery Writers of America), by Robyn
Greenberg, 11-2 TAD 156

Mystery Writers Meet in LaJolla, (Third
Annual Mystery Writers Convention,
report), by Edgar James, 1-1 M 14

(Mystery Writers of America), Announcement
of Awards Nominees for 1969, 3-4 MR 8

(Mystery Writers of America), Annual MWA
"Edgars" Awarded, (Award Dinner report),
10-3 TAD 240

(Mystery Writers of America), Checklist:
Annual Volumes, by Charles MacDonald,
5-4 TAD 252

(Mystery Writers of America), Checklist
of Mystery Awards, by Barbara
Buhrer, 11 MN A1; 12 MN L4

(Mystery Writers of America), Edgar
Award Winners, (1977), by Jim Huang,
7 CL 1

(Mystery Writers of America), The Edgars,
(report on 34th Annual Awards banquet)
by Thomas Godfrey, 2-1 M 22

(Mystery Writers of America), Edgars,
Anyone?, (choosing the MWA awards),
by Hillary Waugh, 2-1 TAD 52

(Mystery Writers of America), Mystery
Writers Honor Their Own - 32nd Annual
Edgar Allan Poe Awards, (report), by
Robyn Greenberg, 11-2 TAD 156

(Mystery Writers of America), 1972
"Edgar" Awards - Winners and Nominees,
by Robert E. Briney, 5-3 MR 29

(Mystery Writers of America), Special
Announcement of New England Chapter,
(formation), 5-2 MR 15

(Mystery Writers of America), 34th Edgar
Allan Poe Awards Dinner, (report),
by Jiro Kimura, 13-3 TAD 205

(Mystery Writers of America), We Tell
Stories: A Talk Given at a Monthly
MWA Meeting in New York, by Pete
Hamill, 12-1 TAD 3

(mystery writing), A Reply to Hal
Charles, by Gary Warren Niebuhr,
4-2 PP 12

(mystery writing), The Ambulating Lady,
(how to write for the pulps), by
Carroll John Daly, 2-2 C 113

(mystery writing), Ask Mr. Mystery:
Writing for ELLERY QUEEN'S MYSTERY
MAGAZINE, (anon.), 27 JD 12

(mystery writing), Break It Up! (how to
write for the pulps), by Robert
Leslie Bellem, 2-2 C 50

(mystery writing), Breaking Into the
Mystery Market, by Hal Charles,
4-1 PP 9

(mystery writing), The Creative Compulsio
by William L. Rohde, 1- JD 7

(mystery writing), How I "Done" It,
(writing the ENCYCLOPEDIC GUIDE TO
MYSTERY, DETECTIVE AND SUSPENSE
FICTION), by Ordean Hagen, 1-2 TAD
45

(mystery writing), Influences on a
Writer, by William F. Nolan,
11 JD 11

(mystery writing), John D. MacDonald
vs. Doc Savage, (on writing for the
pulps), by John D. MacDonald, 3 BS 3

(mystery writing), Mystery Writer Beware!
(lack of markets for novice authors)
by B.F.Watkinson, 16 CD 3

(mystery writing), Nelson Keys and
Captain Kettle, (essay on collaborations), by Sax Rohmer, 18 R 1

(mystery writing), Nick Crider, Killmaster?
(on writing a Nick Carter story), by
Bill Crider, 7 PE 9

(mystery writing), On Pulpsmithing, (on
writing for the pulps), by Arthur J.
Burks, 69 PU 10

(mystery writing), The Perspiration Factor,
(discusses the importance of discipline
for novice authors), by Hal Charles,
4-5/6 PP 43

(mystery writing), The Pleasures of
Histo-Detection, (writing historical
mysteries), by Lillian de la Torre,
7-3 TAD 155

(mystery writing), The Pulp Paper Master
Fiction Plot, (formula for writing
pulp fiction), by Lester Dent, 12 BS 15

(mystery writing), Pulp Perspective Plus,
(on pulp writing), 7 BS 3

(mystery writing), The Shadow Speaks,
(writing techniques of Walter B.
Gibson), by George Wolf, 14 BS 11

(mystery writing), The Social Consequences
of Crime Writing, by John Creasey,
4-1 TAD 38

(mystery writing), Tips on Breaking Into
the Pro Ranks, by Ralph Roberts,
12 SF 26

(mystery writing), We Tell Stories: A Talk
Given at a Monthly MWA Meeting in New
York, by Pete Hamill, 12-1 TAD 2

(mystery writing), What Happened to the
29th Pilgrim; or, Inspiration, No --
Perspiration, Yes, by Hal Charles,
4-3 PP 3

(mystery writing), The Whole Versus the
Sum of the Parts, or, Using Personal
Experience in Fiction, by Hal Charles,
4-4 PP 3

(mystery writing), Writers for the Record:
The Changing Role of Women as Influence
on Mystery Fiction, by various writers,
Joseph Estrada, ed., 3-1 M 40

(mystery writing: co-authorship), Two Heads
Are Better Than One, by Hal Charles,
4-2 PP 9

Mystery's Loss, (obituary of Alfred
Hitchcock, with film checklist),
6/7 LR 41

Mystery's Palette, (verse), by Margaret R.
Dodge, 3-3 MR 12

Mythology of Crime and Violence, The,
by David K. Jeffrey, 1-1 C 75

(Nabokov, Vladimir: LOLITA), On LOLITA
as a Mystery Story, by J.R.Christopher,
7-1 TAD 29

Naked City, (television series), by Andy
Jaysnovitch, 6 PE 10

Name as Symbol: On Sherlock Holmes and the
Nature of the Detective Story (with
interpretation of name), by Richard
Gerber, translated by Robert F.
Fleissner, 8-4 TAD 280

Names of Characters in the Thorndyke
Stories,)of R. Austin Freeman), by
Michael G. Heenan, 4 TF 2

Nancy Drew in Japanese, (Japanese
editions of Nancy Drew girls'
series books), by Don Holbrook,
7 MA 13

Nancy Drew in Review, (Nancy Drew
girls' series books), by John M.
Enright, 7 MA 6

Nancy Drew on the Screen, (filmed
versions of girls' series books),
by David Zinman, 6-2 MR 3

(Nanek), A Rembrance of Early Pulp
Collecting and Fandom 1938-43 by
Virginia Combs Anderson ("Nanek")
with William Papalia, 40 X 3

(Nanek), Dwellers in the Mirage,
(verse), by Virginia Combs Anderson
("Nanek"), 40 X 121

Nanovic, John: letter of comment,
2 D 48

(Nanovic, John), Interview with John
Nanovic, by Albert Tonik, 9 SF 44

Napier, Bob: letter of comment,
6/7 LR 25; 5-1 MF 34; 3-2 PP 34;
3-3 PP 40; 4-3 PP 34

Napier, Bob: Wolfe a Howler! (on the
television series portraying Nero
Wolfe), 5-5 MF 7

Napolitano, Joseph: letter of comment,
26 X 77

Narasimhan, R.: Notes on a Freeman
Bibliography, (works of R. Austin
Freeman), 8 TF 41

Narrative Vision in The Hound of the
Bakervilles, (Sherlockiana), by
Paul F. Ferguson, 1-2 C 24

Nash, Lemuel: Checklist of books by
Frank Owen and Eric Frank Russell,
28 X 12

Nash, Lemuel: letter of comment,
13 X 60; 22 X 51; 24 X 12;
30 X 149

Nash, Ogden: Don't Guess, Let Me Tell
You, (verse), 3-1 CP 26

Nash, Ogden: Paperback, Who Made Thee?
Dost Thou Know Who Made Thee?,
(verse), 1-4 CP 7

Nash, Ogden: The Trouble With Shakespeare, You Remember Him, (verse),
1-5 CP 11

Nathan, Dorothy: letter of comment,
6/7 LR 18

Nathaniel Polton, Artificer Extraordinary, (character in Dr.Thorndyke
stories by R. Austin Freeman), by
John H. Dirckx and Philip T.Asdell,
6 TF 25

Nathanson, Philip D.: letter of comment,
1-6 CP 6

(Nebel, Frederick), The Backbone of
Black Mask, (Nebel's detective
stories in BLACK MASK pulp magazine,
with checklist), by Dave Lewis,
2-2 C 118

Necrology, (death notices of various
mystery authors), 2-2 TAD 113

Necrology of Mystery-Crime Writers
1975-76, by George Wuyek, 10-3 TAD
264

Nedza, Frank M.: letter of comment,
27 JD 36
Nehr, Ellen: Checklist, The Mystery
League, (series of crime fiction
published by The Mystery League,
Inc.), 2-6 PP 5
Nehr, Ellen: Collier Books, (line of
paperback books, with checklist),
3-5 CP 19
Nehr, Ellen: Did It All Start With Ellery?
(mystery authors as characters in
their stories), 3-4 PP 3
Nehr, Ellen: How to Organize Your
Collection Your Way, (on collecting
mystery fiction), 2-3 PP 9
Nehr, Ellen: letter of comment, 1-2 CP 2;
6/7 LR 17; 2-3 MF 75; 2-4 MF 60;
2-6 MF 43; 3-2 MF 59; 3-3 MF 54;
3-5 MF 50; 3-1 PP 38; 3-1 PP 45;
3-6 PP 34
Nehr, Ellen: Little Old Ladies I Have
Known and Loved, (feminine sleuths),
3-4 MF 3
Nehr, Ellen: Little Old Men With Whom I'm
Only Slightly Acquainted, (on little-
known male sleuths), 4-4 MF 2
Nehr, Ellen: Mystery League, Inc.,
(publisher of series of crime fiction
in 1930's), 2-6 PP 3
Nelson, Bill: Evil as Illusion in the
Detective Story, 1-1 C 9
Nelson, Bill: Expiatory Symbolism in
Lawrence Sanders' THE FIRST DEADLY
SIN, 1-2 C 71
Nelson, Jeff: letter of comment,
2-4 CP 5
Nelson Keys and Captain Kettle, (essay
on collaborations by authors), by
Sax Rohmer, 18 R 1
(NENA SAHIB: Sir John Retcliffe),
Concerning Nena Sahib, by Paul Plass,
6-3 TAD 157
("Nero" Award), Here Comes the Judge:
The "Nero" Award, (annual awards by
The Wolfe Pack, Nero Wolfe fans
organization), by Bill Crider,
3-6 MF 8
Nero Wolfe, Logomachizer, (on Nero Wolfe,
detective created by Rex Stout), by
Lawrence F. Brooks, 1-1 G 21
Nero Wolfe is "On the Air", (radio
programs featuring Nero Wolfe,
detective, based on Rex Stout
books), by Judson C. Sapp, 9 MN A19
Nero Wolfe on Film, (screened versions
of Nero Wolfe, detective), by Don
Miller, 9 MN A26
Nero Wolfe Quiz, (mystery quiz based on
Nero Wolfe books), by Lee Poleske,
1 LW 1; 2 LW 1; 3 LW 1; 4 LW 2;
5 LW 1; 6 LW 1
Nero Wolfe Saga, The, (commentary and
synopsis of each novel by Rex Stout
featuring Nero Wolfe as detective),
by Guy M. Townsend, 1-3 MF 13; 1-4

Nero Wolfe Saga, The, (continued),
MF 25; 1-5 MF 21; 1-6 MF 15;
2-1 MF 15; 2-2 MF 25; 2-3 MF 34;
2-4 MF 19; 2-5 MF 13; 2-6 MF 20;
3-1 MF 21; 3-2 MF 13; 3-3 MF 22;
3-4 MF 25; 3-5 MF 22; 3-6 MF 15;
4-1 MF 17; 4-2 MF 14; 4-3 MF 3
Nero Wolfe Saga, The, A Chronology,
(first edition publication data
of Nero Wolfe novels by Rex Stout),
by Don Miller, 9 MN A43
Nero Wolfe Saga: The Early Years,
(Nero Wolfe series: Rex Stout), by
Guy M. Townsend, 9 MN A31
Nero Wolfe Saga, The: The First Four
(commentary on four of Rex Stout's
Nero Wolfe novels), by Jo Ann
Vicarel, 9 MN A42
Nero Wolfe Saga, The: Three at Random,
(commentary of three of Rex Stout's
Nero Wolfe novels), by Don Miller,
9 MN A61
Nero Wolfe vs. The Master Criminal,
by John Harwood, 6-1 MR 15
(NERO WOLFE MYSTERY MAGAZINE), Index,
by Frank D. McSherry, Jr.,
9 MN A25
(NERO WOLFE OF WEST THIRTY-FIFTH
STREET: William S. Baring-Gould),
The Case of the Missing Wolfe,
(commentary and review), by William
J. Clark, 3-4 MR 16
Nero Wolfe's Legacy of Books, by
John J. McAleer, 1-2 G 8
Nesbitt, John D.: Louis L'Amour's
Pseudonymous Works, 3-3 PQ 3
Nestor, Graham: letter of comment,
1-2 M 3
Never Fear, Doc Savage Fans Are Here,
(Doc Savage, pulp character, fan
organizations), by Daryl S. Herrick,
1 MB 21
Never to be Forgotten!, by Stanley
R. Blair, 11 X 19
Never-Ending Bookshelf, The, (on rare
paperbacks and collecting), by
J. Grant Thiessen, 8 SF 23
Never-Was Adventure, The, (speculative
meeting between The Shadow and Doc
Savage), by Will Murray, 6 DQ 16
Nevins, Francis M., Jr.: A Checklist
of the Short Stories of John Lutz,
1-3 PP 13
Nevins, Francis M., Jr.: A Note on
Harry Stephen Keeler as Filmed
(pulp author), 3-3 TAD 165
Nevins, Francis M., Jr.: A Woolrich
Preview, (on uncompleted works of
Cornell Woolrich), 4-3 TAD 145
Nevins, Francis M., Jr.: About the
Output of Anthony Abbot, 2-1 MR 12
Nevins, Francis M., Jr.: Additions and
Corrections to Checklist by Mark
Purcell of Roy Vickers' works,
4-2 MR 17

Nevins, Francis M., Jr.: Anthony Boucher, (literary sketch and checklist), 3-2 M 18

Nevins, Francis M., Jr.: Aspects of the Unknown Gardner, (Erle Stanley Gardner), 5-4 MR 13; 5-5 MR 27

Nevins, Francis M., Jr.: Brief Loves: The Early Short Stories of Cornell Woolrich, (humor and romance short stories discussed), 14-2 TAD 168

Nevins, Francis M., Jr.: The Brotherhood Makes History, (Popular Culture Association), 5-1 TAD 28

Nevins, Francis M., Jr.: Checklist, Charlotte Armstrong, 5-5 MR 18

Nevins, Francis M., Jr.: Checklist, Helen Reilly, 5-5 MR 18

Nevins, Francis M., Jr.: Checklist, Novels of Milton Propper, 10-3 TAD 203

Nevins, Francis M., Jr.: Commentaries for the Curious, (comments on John Dickson Carr), 1 NC 14

Nevins, Francis M., Jr.: Cornell Woolrich, (literary sketch and commentary), 2-1 TAD 25; 2-2 TAD 99; 2-3 TAD 180

Nevins, Francis M., Jr.: Cornell Woolrich, The Years Before Suspense, (early writings), 12-2 TAD 106

Nevins, Francis M., Jr.: Death Inside the Cow: A Few Notes on the Novels of Lee Thayer, 5-3 TAD 151

Nevins, Francis M., Jr.: Department of Unmitigated Mishmosh, (comments on Mike Hammer and Mickey Spillane), 3-1 MR 21

Nevins, Francis M., Jr.: Department of Unrelated Miscellanea, (comments on Ian Fleming, Harry Stephen Keeler, and Brett Halliday), 4-1 MR 21; 4-3 MR 25; 4-5 MR 18; 5-2 MR 28

Nevins, Francis M., Jr.: Department of Unreprinted Masterworks, (crime fiction), 2-2 MR 12; 2-4 MR 14; 2-5 MR 14

Nevins, Francis M., Jr.,: (translator), Maigret & Co., The Detectives of the Simenon Agency, by Maurice Dubourg, 4-2 TAD 79

Nevins, Francis M., Jr.: The Diavolo Quartet, (Don Diavolo series, by Stuart Towne, pulp magician detective), 3-4 TAD 243

Nevins, Francis M., Jr.: The Diavolo Quartet, (Don Diavolo stories by Stuart Towne in RED STAR MYSTERY magazine; magician-detective), 3 X 2

Nevins, Francis M., Jr.: Early JDM, Four From Early '49, (pulp fiction of John D. MacDonald), 21 JD 11

Nevins, Francis M., Jr.: Early JDM, In Doc Savage, (fiction by John D. MacDonald in DOC SAVAGE pulp magazine), 19 JD 8

Nevins, Francis M., Jr.: Early JDM in EQMM, (stories by John D. MacDonald in ELLERY QUEEN'S MYSTERY MAGAZINE), 18 JD 10

Nevins, Francis M., Jr.: Early JDM, Pulp Thought and Pulp Action, (pulp fiction by John D. MacDonald), 14 JD 14

Nevins, Francis M., Jr.: Early JDM, Three Pulps from '49, (pulp stories of John D. MacDonald), 15 JD 19

Nevins, Francis M., Jr.: Early JDM, To Any Lengths, (pulp stories of John D. MacDonald), 17 JD 18

Nevins, Francis M., Jr.: Early JDM, Woolrich Touches, (Cornell Woolrich influence on pulp fiction of John D. MacDonald), 16 JD 12

Nevins, Francis M., Jr.: Editor at Work - Ellery Queen, 14 X 4

Nevins, Francis M., Jr.: Ellery Queen in Wrightsville, (stories with Wrightsville locale), 7-1 TAD 4

Nevins, Francis M., Jr.: Ellery Queen on the Small Screen, (television shows 1955-1976, with checklist), 12-3 TAD 216

Nevins, Francis M., Jr.: Core Vidal, Mystery Writer, (sketch), 4-2 MR 25

Nevins, Francis M., Jr.: The Great Lizzie Borden T-Shirt Media Event and Mystery Quiz, (report, University of California San Diego 1978), 5-6 MF 7

Nevins, Francis M., Jr.: Harry Stephen Keeler's Screwball Circus, (on the unconventional MacWhorter series in pulps), 5-4 TAD 209

Nevins, Francis M., Jr.: Hick Dick From the Sticks - Harry Stephen Keeler's Quiribus Brown, (Brown, detective, in pulp fiction of Keeler), 7-4 TAD 251

Nevins, Francis M., Jr.: The Horn Blows at Noon #76 3/4, (rebuttal to Michael Avallone's "Kiss My Deadly Typewriter #539"), 3-1 QC 14

Nevins, Francis M., Jr.: JDM's Images of the Inhuman, (in stories of John D. MacDonald), 11 JD 6

Nevins, Francis M., Jr.: The Late Novels of Harry Stephen Keeler - A Preliminary Checklist, 3-2 TAD 74

Nevins, Francis M., Jr.: letter of comment, 9 JD 11; 10 JD 19; 11 JD 15; 12 JD 14; 13 JD 12; 14 JD 27; 15 JD 26; 17 JD 23; 19 JD 14; 21 JD 18; 26 JD 1; 1-2 MF 47; 1-3 MF 55; 1-4 MF 57; 2-5 MF 50; 3-1 MF 55; 3-2 MF 59; 3-4 MF 56; 3-5 MF 46; 4-2 MF 59; 4-5 MF 45; 4-6 MF 47; 5-1 MF 44; 5-2 MF 50; 5-4 MF 43; 1 MN 4; 3/4 MN 15; 11 MN L13; 12 MN L12; 13 MN L3; 1-5 MR 14; 2-2 MR 16; 2-5 MR 13; 2-6 MR 15; 3-2 MR 17; 3-3 MR 11; 3-4 MR 33; 4-1 MR 18; 4-5 MR 17; 4-6 MR 19;

Nevins, Francis M., Jr.: letters of
comment, (continued) 5-1 MR 17;
5-3 MR 14; 5-4 MR 12; 5-5 MR 17;
6-2 MR 17; 6 MY 8; 1-3 PP 31;
2-2 PP 32; 2-4 PP 41; 2-5 PP 44;
3-1 PP 41; 3-2 PP 35; 3-5 PP 47;
3-6 PP 32; 4-1 PP 44; 4-2 PP 34;
4-3 PP 30; 4-4 PP 37; 4-5/6 PP 88;
1-4 QC 17; 12 R 23; 14 R 27; 18 R
17; 1-1 TAD 29; 1-3 TAD 106; 1-4
TAD 157; 2-1 TAD 66; 2-2 TAD 131;
2-4 TAD 280; 3-1 TAD 66; 3-2 TAD
137; 3-3 TAD 204; 3-4 TAD 275;
4-1 TAD 70; 4-3 TAD 192; 4-4 TAD
254; 5-1 TAD 57; 5-2 TAD 125; 5-3
TAD 184; 5-4 TAD 234; 6-1 TAD 58;
6-2 TAD 121; 6-3 TAD 203; 6-4 TAD
277; 7-1 TAD 67; 7-2 TAD 148; 7-3
TAD 232; 8-1 TAD 71; 8-2 TAD 159;
8-3 TAD 237; 9-1 TAD 84; 9-2 TAD
157; 10-1 TAD 39; 10-2 TAD 159;
10-3 TAD 274; 10-4 TAD 291; 11-4
TAD 401; 12-3 TAD 267; 13-1 TAD
76; 13-2 TAD 158; 14-2 TAD 185
Nevins, Francis M., Jr.: The Making of
a Tale-Spinner, John D. MacDonald's
Early Pulp Mystery Stories, 1-1
C 89
Nevins, Francis M., Jr.: The Marquis
of Unremembered Manhunters, (on
John Lawrence, author), 21 X 3
Nevins, Francis M., Jr.: Notes on Two
Shadows of JDM, (two stories by
John D. MacDonald in THE SHADOW
pulp magazine), 13 JD 10
Nevins, Francis M., Jr.: Paperback
Reviews, (crime fiction), 1-6 MR 3
Nevins, Francis M., Jr.: Private Eye
in an Evil Time, Mark Sadler's
Paul Shaw, 38 X 11
Nevins, Francis M., Jr.: Pulp Tradition
in Mystery Fiction, (panel discussion,
Popular Culture Association, 1972)
6-3 TAD 133
Nevins, Francis M., Jr.: Random Thoughts
on JDM and the Frustration of the
Expected, (fiction of John D.
MacDonald), 7 JD 11
Nevins, Francis M., Jr.: The Reggie
Fortune Short Stories, An Appreciation
and Partial Bibliography, by James
Mark Purcell, with Additional Biblio-
graphy by Nevins, 5-4 MR 1
Nevins, Francis M., Jr.: Remembering
AVON MURDER MYSTERY MONTHLY, (with
checklist), 7 MY 3
Nevins, Francis M., Jr.: Remembering
John Creasey, 4 X 37
Nevins, Francis M., Jr.: Review of THE
COMPLETE WORKS OF GEORGES SIMENON
by Claude Mauriac, translated by
Nevins, 2-3 TAD 162
Nevins, Francis M., Jr.: Royal Bloodline,
The Biography of the Queen Canon,
1-1 QC 6; 1-2 QC 2; 1-3 QC 2; 1-4
QC 2; 2-1 QC 2; 2-2 QC 1; 3-1 QC 2,
3-2 QC 2

Nevins, Francis M., Jr.: Social and
Political Images in American
Crime Fiction, (panel discussion,
Popular Culture Association,1971),
5-2 TAD 61
Nevins, Francis M., Jr.: The Sound
of Suspense, John Dickson Carr
as a Radio Writer, 11-4 TAD 335
Nevins, Francis M., Jr.: Walls of
Guilt - Donald E. Westlake as
Tucker Coe, 7-3 TAD 163
Nevins, Francis M., Jr.: What Happens
in POINT BLANK, (film, from
Richard Stark's THE HUNTER),
8-1 TAD 7
Nevins, Francis M., Jr.: The Wild and
Woolly World of Harry Stephen
Keeler, Scenes From the Last Act,
(unconventional detectives in pulp
fiction), 3-2 TAD 71
Nevins, Francis M., Jr.: The World of
Cleve F. Adams, (pulp author),
8-3 TAD 195
Nevins, Francis M., Jr.: The World of
Milton Propper, (author), 10-3
TAD 197
Nevins, Francis M., Jr.: The Worst
Legal Mystery in the World, (Harry
Stephen Keeler: THE AMAZING WEB),
1-3 TAD 82
Nevins, Francis M., Jr., and William
J. Clark: Checklist, Cleve F.
Adams, 8-3 TAD 200
Nevins, Francis M., Jr., William J.
Clark, and Edward D. Hoch:
Checklist, Edward D. Hoch, 9-2
TAD 102
Nevins, Francis M., Jr., Estelle Fox,
and Charles Shibuk: Checklist,
Arthur W. Upfield, 3-2 TAD 90
Nevins, Francis M., Jr., Harold Knott,
and William Thailing: Cornell
Woolrich, a Bibliography, 2-4
TAD 237
Nevins, Francis M., Jr., and Bill
Pronzini: Checklist, Bill Pronzini,
(with introduction), 13-4 TAD 345
(Nevins, Francis M., Jr.), Meet the
Author: Francis M. Nevins, Jr., by
Allen J. Hubin, 1-3 TAD 85
New Book Released About Robert E.
Howard (Glenn Lord: THE LAST CELT),
by Tevis Clyde Smith, 1-1 PQ 33
New Books, (comments), by David
Turner, 30 X 22; 32 X 14
New England Mystery Dealer, (tribute
to Howard Waterhouse), by David
& Su Bates, 3-3 PP 10
(New England), The American Regional
Mystery, Pt.1, by Marvin Lachman,
3-3 MR 13; 3-4 MR 22
New Gaslight on Jack the Ripper, by
Albert I. Borowitz, 9-3 TAD 175
(New Jersey), The American Regional
Mystery, Pt.5, by Marvin Lachman,
4-5 MR 2

NEW MYSTERY ADVENTURES, (pulp magazine, index), by Fred Cook and Gordon Huber, 22 X 47; 30 X 146

(New York City), The American Regional Mystery, Pt.2 & 3, by Marvin Lachman, 3-2 MR 23; 4-1 MR 8

(New York State), The American Regional Mystery, Pt.4, by Marvin Lachman, 4-3 MR 3

New York Mystery Beat: World of Mystery, (news column), by Pete Christian, 3-2 M 32

Newest Doc Savage Artist, The, (comments on Bob Larkin and his work), by Frank Lewandowski, 1 DS 12

Newlander, Hellgate: letter of comment, 5-2 TAD 113

Newquist, Roy: Interview, Mary Stewart, 1-4 MR 3

News and Comments, (news of mystery scene and publications), by Steve Lewis, 2 MY 1; 3 MY 1; 4 MY 1; 5 MY 1; 5A MY 1; 6 MY 1; 7 MY 1

News and Previews, (John D. MacDonald and related items), by Len and June Moffatt, 7 JD 12; 8 JD 4; 9 JD 4; 10 JD 6; 10 JD 21; 11 JD 3; 12 JD 2; 13 JD 2; 14 JD 5; 15 JD 4; 16 JD 4; 17 JD 4; 18 JD 4; 19 JD 3; 20 JD 25; 21 JD 12; 22 JD 2; 23 JD 12; 24 JD 25; 25 JD 31; 26 JD 21; 27 JD 29

News and Reviews From the Lair, (on various publications of the genre), by Michael L. Cook, 1 U 6

News and Some Future Books, (crime fiction), by Lianne Carlin, 4-3 MR 2

News and Views, (book notes), by Gary Zachrich and Lynn Hickman, 63 PU 51; 64 PU 31; 65 PU 24; 66 PU 53; 67 PU 128; 68 PU 31; 69 PU 31; 70 PU 6; 71 PU 18; 72 PU 6; 73 PU 31; 74 PU 16; 75 PU 21

News From the Editor's Dreadful Grey Typewriter, (re: John D. MacDonald), by Ed Hirshberg, 23 JD 2; 24 JD 1; 25 JD 1; 26 JD 1; 27 JD 1

News Item, "Dummy in Museum was Oldtime Outlaw," (from Los Angeles), 1-2 MF 55

News Item, "Wax Dummy Gives Police Bizarre Case," (Los Angeles), 1-1 MF 48

News Note from the University of Missouri, (on special collection of boys' books), by D.C.Dickinson, 1-1 BC 9

News Roundup, (mystery items), by Lianne Carlin, 1-1 MR 4; 1-2 MR 6; 1-3 MR 10; 1-4 MR 6; 1-5 MR 9; 1-6 MR 7; 2-1 MR 10; 2-2 MR 11; 2-3 MR 14; 2-4 MR 6; 2-5 MR 7; 2-6 MR 17

Newsletter Observer, The: Reading Around, (news items), 2-1 MR 20

Newton, John J.: Ellery Queen, A Checklist, 1-3 QC 13

Newton, John J.: letter of comment, 1-2 QC 13; 1-3 TAD 108

Ngaio Marsh's "Theatrical" Murders, (stage background of mystery novels), by Earl F. Bargainnier, 10-2 TAD 175

Nichols, Lewis: Comment, The Shadow, NEW YORK TIMES BOOK REVIEW, 3-1 MR 20

Nichols, Melvin J.: letter of comment, 1-2 BC 62

Nick Carter, The Man and the Myth, (pulp and dime novel hero), by J. Randolph Cox, 2-3 MR 15

Nick Crider, Killmaster?, (on writing a Nick Carter story), by Bill Crider, 7 PE 9

Nickerson, Edward A.: Untitled Opinion, (on John D. MacDonald), 18 JD 20

Niebuhr, Cary Warren: A Reply to Hal Charles, (on mystery writing), 4-2 PP 12

Niebuhr, Gary Warren: The Big Sell, An Interview with Allen Hubin, 4-5/6 PP 24

Niebuhr, Gary Warren: letter of comment, 3-1 PP 38; 3-5 PP 49; 4-3 PP 33; 4-4 PP 35

Niebuhr, Gary Warren: Mainstream Mysteries and Novels of Crime, (commentary and review), 3-2 PP 23; 3-6 PP 17; (bestsellers of 1980) 4-1 PP 13; 4-3 PP 5; 4-5/6 PP 63

Nielsen, Bjorne: A Bit of Inspiration from Denmark, (verse), 14-1 TAD 30

Nieminski, John: Checklist, T.S. Stribling, Professor Poggioli Series, 6-1 TAD 55

Nieminski, John: EQA 30, An Author/ Title Index to Ellery Queen's Anthology 1960-1975, 11 MN I1

Nieminski, John: letter of comment, 22 JD 19; 6/7 LR 26; 11 MN L2; 2-5 MF 46; 3-2 MF 50; 3-3 MF 51; 4-6 MF 40; 5-1 MF 30; 2-2 PP 37; 7 R 28; 2-2 TAD 128; 5-1 TAD 56; 6-1 TAD 55

Nieminski, John: Pow-Wow on the Potomac, A Report on Bouchercon XI, (mystery fans and authors convention), 4-6 MF 12

Nieminski, John: Sax Rohmer in Chicago, 14 R 5

Nigel Morland - Fifty Years of Crime Writing, by Pearl G. Aldrich, 13-3 TAD 194

(NIGHT MUST FALL: Emlyn Williams), Night Must Fall: The Sinister Behind the Ordinary, (literary discussion), by Albert I. Borowitz, 14-3 TAD 284

Night Shift, (fiction), by Melissa Sitter, 2-3 M 40

Nippy Weston, Girl Flyer, (female aviation
    ace of pulp magazine G-8 and His Battle
    Aces), by John Sullivan, 11 X 115
Nitka, John C.: Index to ARGOSY Magazine,
    (commencing 1930), 63 PU 44; 64 PU 34
Nitka, John C.: letter of comment,
    64 PU 25
No Orchids for George Orwell, (commentary
    on Orwell's criticism of NO ORCHIDS FOR
    MISS BLANDISH by James Hadley Chase),
    by Susan Harris Smith, 9-2 TAD 114
(NO ORCHIDS FOR MISS BLANDISH: James Hadley
    Chase), No Orchids for George Orwell,
    (commentary on Orwell's criticism),
    by Susan Harris Smith, 9-2 TAD 114
No Rules for a Suspense Editor, (book
    editing comments), by Joan Kahn,
    2-3 TAD 169
Noble, Don: letter of comment, 13 X 59;
    24 X 47
(Nolan, detective: Max Collins), Meet Nolan,
    (discussion of heist artist/detective
    in series by Collins), by Robert J.
    Randisi, 4-5/6 PP 29
Nolan, Jack Edmund: A Great Contemporary,
    Jose Giovanni, (French author's mystery
    films), 4-4 MR 19
Nolan, Jack Edmund: Alfred Hitchcock's TV
    Shows, A Footnote on Scripters and
    Literary Sources, 3-4 MR 17
Nolan, Jack Edmund: Filmed Misogyny, The
    Screen Adaptations of Peter Cheyney
    and Lionel White, (filmed mystery
    stories), 4-6 MR 27
Nolan, Jack Edmund: The Films and TV Work
    of Eric Ambler, 3-1 MR 13
Nolan, Jack Edmund: The Films of James
    Hadley Chase, 3-6 MR 30
Nolan, Jack Edmund: The Ian Fleming Films
    and TV, 5-1 MR 24
Nolan, Jack Edmund: Jack of Many Trades -
    Some Uses of the Ripper on the Screen,
    6-1 MR 25
Nolan, Jack Edmund: LeCarre, Deighton,
    Hall and the Screen's Tired Spies,
    (filmed espionage fiction), 4-1 MR 23
Nolan, Jack Edmund: letter of comment,
    3-6 MR 10; 4-2 MR 16; 4-6 MR 17;
    5-2 MR 18; 5-3 MR 14; 5-5 MR 20;
    6-2 MR 16
Nolan, Jack Edmund: The Mini Screen Career
    of John Creasey, (filmed mysteries),
    4-5 MR 11
Nolan, Jack Edmund: Mystery Feature Films
    Made-for-TV, Work in Progress, (1972),
    5-2 MR 30
Nolan, Jack Edmund: Mystery on the 1972-73
    TV Schedule, The Outlook, 5-5 MR 13
Nolan, Jack Edmund: Patricia Highsmith -
    On the Screen, 4-3 MR 15
Nolan, Jack Edmund: Philip Loraine on the
    Screen, or, Where Did the Mysteries
    Go?, 5-3 MR 18
Nolan, Jack Edmund: Philip MacDonald on
    the Screen, (with checklist), 3-3 MR 33

Nolan, Jack Edmund: Six Britons the
    Movies Ignored, Tey, Household,
    Hamilton, Garve, Clifford, and
    Blackburn, (authors whose works
    were seldom filmed), 3-5 MR 9
Nolan, Jack Edmund: Some Agatha
    Christie Films, 4-2 MR 19
Nolan, Jack Edmund: Some Themes in
    the Film Work of Jimmy Sangster,
    5-6 MR 21
Nolan, Jack Edmund: Three Ladies of
    the Quasi-Gothic, The Films of
    Armstrong, Lofts, and White,
    5-2 MR 23
Nolan, Jack Edmund: TV Notes, (on
    mystery shows), 4-2 MR 32
Nolan, Norman: letter of comment,
    4-2 TAD 125
Nolan, Richard W.: The Spy Fiction
    of John LeCarre, 1-2 C 54
Nolan, William F.: A Walk in the
    Pulpwoods, Random Recollections,
    (pulp magazine reminiscences),
    2-2 C 38
Nolan, William F.: The Black Mask Boys
    Go Legit, (re: Dashiell Hammett and
    Raymond Chandler), 13-1 TAD 23
Nolan, William F.: Bradbury in the
    Pulps, (Ray Bradbury), 36 X R21
Nolan, William F.: Bradbury's First
    Book Appearances, (Ray Bradbury),
    36 X R8
Nolan, William F.: Bradbury's Textbook
    Appearances 1955-1972, (Ray Bradbury)
    36 X R28
Nolan, William F.: Carroll John Daly,
    The Forgotten Pioneer of the
    Private Eye, (pulp author), 4-1
    TAD 1
Nolan, William F.: Chandler on Screen,
    TV and Radio - With a Look at the
    Many Mr. Marlowes, (with checklist),
    3-1 TAD 23
Nolan, William F.: Checklist, Carroll
    John Daly, 4-1 TAD 4
Nolan, William F.: Checklist, Conti-
    nental Op Stories by Raymond
    Chandler, 1-4 TAD 153
Nolan, William F.: Checklist, Fredric
    Brown novels, 5-4 TAD 193
Nolan, William F.: The Crime/Suspense
    Fiction of Ray Bradbury, A Listing,
    4-3 TAD 155
Nolan, William F.: The Faust Papers,
    A Visit to the Faust Collection
    At the University of California
    in Berkeley, (Frederick Faust
    Special Collection), 1-4 FC 4
Nolan, William F.: Hammett, A Reaction
    Report, (re: DASHIELL HAMMETT, A
    CASEBOOK by Nolan), 3-3 TAD 162
Nolan, William F.: The Hammett Check-
    list Revisited, 6-4 TAD 249
Nolan, William F.: Hammett in
    Hollywood, 21 X 5

Nolan, William F.: Hark! Is That You, Donn?...All Cloaked in Glendale Dark?, (verse), 36 X R15

Nolan, William F.: How Many Words? (extent of writings of Frederick Faust, aka Max Brand), 1-1 FC 2

Nolan, William F.: Influences on a Writer, 11 JD 11

Nolan, William F.: letter of comment, 2-2 QC 12; 1-3 TAD 105; 1-4 TAD 153; 2-2 TAD 128; 2-3 TAD 204; 2-4 TAD 278; 3-3 TAD 208; 3-4 TAD 281; 4-1 TAD 67; 4-3 TAD 188; 4-4 TAD 251; 5-1 TAD 42; 5-3 TAD 183; 5-4 TAD 253; 6-1 TAD 54; 6-2 TAD 122; 6-3 TAD 202; 6-4 TAD 272; 9-1 TAD 78; 9-4 TAD 297; 10-3 TAD 274; 11-2 TAD 109; 11-4 TAD 400; 12-4 TAD 353; 14-1 TAD 72; 15 X 14; 40 X 85

Nolan, William F.: Max Brand, Pulp King, (pulp fiction of Frederick Faust writing as Max Brand), 32 X 2

Nolan, William F.: Of Hammett, Chandler, Brand, and Bradbury - and An Eye Named Challis, (Bart Challis series by Nolan), 2-2 TAD 86

Nolan, William F.: Portrait of a Tough Guy, (sketch of Raymond Chandler), 38 X 13

Nolan, William F.: Revisiting the Revised Hammett Checklist, (Dashiell Hammett), 9-4 TAD 292

Nolan, William F.: Sam Space, An Eye on Mars, (comments on SPACE FOR HIRE: William F. Nolan), 1-3 M 28

Nolan, William F.: Shadowing the Continental Op, (Dashiell Hammett series, with checklist), 8-1 TAD 121

Nolan, William F.: Thoughts on Fredric Brown, 5-4 TAD 191

(Nolan, William F.), About the Author, William F. Nolan, 32 X 15

(Nolan, William F.), The Trip, by Donn Albright, 36 X R13

(Nolan, William F.: Bart Challis series), Of Hammett, Chandler, Brand, and Bradbury - and An Eye Named Challis, by William F. Nolan, 2-2 TAD 86

(Nolan, William F.: DASHIELL HAMMETT, A CASEBOOK), Hammett: A Reaction Report, by William F. Nolan, 3-3 TAD 162

(Nolan, William F.: SPACE FOR HIRE), A Pair of Parodies, by R. Jeff Banks, 1-5 PP 10

(Nolan, William F.: SPACE FOR HIRE), Sam Space, An Eye on Mars, (comments by author), by William F. Nolan, 1-3 M 28

(Nolan, William F.: SPACE FOR HIRE), Watch This Space! (article review), by Frank D. McSherry, Jr., 5-4 TAD 226

Nom De Loup, (on the names used in the Nero Wolfe novels by Rex Stout), by Terry Abraham, 3 LW 5

(Non-Canonical Calabashes, The), The Gas-Fitters' Ball, (annual event of Sherlock Holmes scion society, report), 2-2 M 29

(Non-Canonical Calabashes, The), Sherlockian Dinner, (annual event of Sherlock Holmes scion society; January 5, 1980), by Horace Harker, 1-3 M 22

(Noon, Ed, detective: Mike Avallone), Adventures in Noonland, (verse), 2-2 MR 14

(Noon, Ed, detective: Mike Avallone), Checklist of Stories in MIKE SHAYNE MYSTERY MAGAZINE, by Tom Johnson, 9 SF 23

(Noon, Ed, detective: Mike Avallone), Ed Noon's Quickest Caper, or, Revenge: Italian Style, by R.T. Karlinchak, 38 X 139

(Noon, Ed, detective: Mike Avallone), Spy Series Characters in Hardback, Pt. IX, by Barry Van Tilburg, 5-5 MF 16

"Noonchester, Ed": The Shadow or Doc Savage?, (comparisons and comments), by Mike Avallone writing as Ed Noonchester, 2 DS 13

Norris, Luther: The Case of the Triple Bouchers, (on Anthony Boucher), 1-5 MR 10

Norris, Luther: Checklist, Robert L. Fish, 2-5 MR 11

Norris, Luther: Crime With a Smile, (interview with Joyce Porter), 3-2 MR 18

Norris, Luther: Interview with Robert L. Fish, 2-5 MR 8

Norris, Luther L.: letter of comment, 2-2 MR 18; 1-2 QC 13; 3 R 30; 4 R 27; 1-1 TAD 30

Norris, Luther: Michael Harrison, An Interview, 3-6 MR 17

Norris, Luther: Pontine Patter - Letter from "Dr. John Watney", (re:Solar Pons), 2-1 PDA 12

Norris, Luther: Pontine Patter, (report of 3rd annual meeting of Praed Street Irregulars, re: Solar Pons), 2-1 PD 4

Norris, Luther: The Romance of Scarabs (Sax Rohmer association article), 1 R 30

(North, Hugh, series: Francis Van Wyck Mason), Checklist, Annotated, by Barry Van Tilburg, 4-6 MF 4

(North, Mr. & Mrs., series: Frances and Richard Lockridge), Checklist, by Kathy Hobel, 2-5 MR 6

(North, Mr. & Mrs., series: Frances and Richard Lockridge), Mr. & Mrs. North, and Mr. & Mrs. Lockridge, by Hank Davis, 1-1 MF 21

(North, Mr. & Mrs., series: Frances and Richard Lockridge), Mr. & Mrs. North, by R. Jeff Banks, 9-3 TAD 182

(North, Mr. & Mrs., series: Frances and Richard Lockridge), Mystery Dial IV, (radio serials), by Steve Lewis, 2-4 PP 25

Norton, Charles A.: The Randolph Mason Stories, (by Melville Davisson Post), 6-2 TAD 86

Nostalgia, (verse), by Steve Eng, 1-4 AD 5

Nostalgia and the Pulp Collector, by James W. Thompson, 42 X 5; 44 X 33

("Not at Night" series, anthologies), An Index to the "Not at Night" Series, by Darrell Schweitzer, 10 SF 45

Not Forgotten, (Ken Holt and Rick Brant boys' series books), by Fred Woodworth, 2 MA 1

Not-So-Secret-Six, The, (on the pulp magazine of that title, and the stories), by Robert Weinberg, 4 P 18

Not Too Many Clients, (re: Nero Wolfe), by Evelyn Herzog, 1-1 G 28

Not Vibgyor: Bpprgoaygbiltstl, (acronym for Travis McGee series by John D. MacDonald), by Dean A. Grennell, 20 JD 5

Not-So-Literary Digests, The, (on the digest-sized mystery magazines), by Robert Turner, 38 X 19

Notes and Queries, (paperback bibliographical and other data and comments) 1-1 PQ 42; 1-2 PQ 56; 1-3 PQ 53; 1-4 PQ 54; 2-3 PQ 42

Notes for a Freeman Bibliography, (works of R. Austin Freeman), by Ruth D. McAleer, 11 TF 12

Notes from the Funeral Black Typewriter, (news and comments re: John D. MacDonald), 28 JD 28

Notes of a Pulp Collector: Robert J. Hogan, (pulp author), by Bernie Wermers, 6 BS 19

Notes of a Pulp Collector, (first advertisement for DOC SAVAGE magazine), by Fred S. Cook, 10 BS 13

Notes of a Pulp Collector, (background of The Shadow, pulp hero character), by J. Randolph Cox, 14 BS 17

Notes of a Pulp Collector, (abstract from VOR by James Blish), by Stewart Kemble, 15 BS 8

Notes of a Pulp Collector, (Gracie Culver detective stories in THE SHADOW pulp magazine), by G. Alan, 15 BS 14

Notes on a Freeman Bibliography, (R. Austin Freeman), by R. Narasimhan, 8 TF 41

Notes on an Ideal Library, (Doc Savage novels in hardback), by Robert Sampson, 2/3 DR 2

Notes on C.E.Vulliamy, by Charles Shibuk, 3-3 TAD 161

Notes on the Film and the Detective Story, by Charles Shibuk, 5-4 TAD 202

Notes on the First Annual Black Orchid Banquet, (annual event of The Wolfe Pack, fan organization honoring Nero Wolfe), by Marjorie Mortensen, 1-1 G 4

Notes on The Lost World, (THE LOST WORLD: A. Conan Doyle), by Dana Martin Batory, 2 U 9

Notes on Two Shadows of JDM, (pulp fiction of John D. MacDonald in THE SHADOW magazine), by Francis M. Nevins, Jr., 13 JD 10

Notes on Very Early Leslie Charteris, by Charles Shibuk, 4-4 TAD 230

Novel Library Paperbacks, (Novel Library line of paperbacks, checklist), by Craig Henry, 2-3 CP 27

Novels of Arthur W. Upfield, The: Bibliography and Review, by Betty Donaldson, 8-1 TAD 4

Novels of John D. MacDonald, (checklist of current novels), by Len and June Moffatt, 1 JD 1; 2 JD 6

Now It Can Be Told: The Secret of the Pons, (re: Solar Pons), by Frank D. McSherry, Jr., 1-2 PDA 57

Now They're Collector's Items, (boys' books collecting), by J. Edward Leithead, 1-1 BC 13; 1-2 BC 44; 1-3 BC 72; 1-4 BC 114; 2-1 BC 154; 2-2 BC 187; 2-3 BC 205

Nuggets (and Otherwise) From the Golden Age, (mystery reviews), by Jay Jeffries, 6 MY 10; 7 MY 6

Nyberg, Bart: letter of comment, 2-3 TBN 3

Nye, Bill: The Grammatical Boy, (humorous essay), 1-1 YB 11

Nylander, Dick: letter of comment, 5 X 42; 22 X 50

Oak Park Revisited, (re: Ernest Hemingway), by Michael Murphy, 5 X 6

(Oakes, Brian "Boysie", series: John Gardner), Checklist, Annotated, by Barry Van Tilburg, 4-3 MF 25

O'Boyle Report, The, (the "genealogy" of Nero Wolfe, detective), 1-2 G 2

Obsequies About Oxford: The Investigations and Eccentricities of Gervase Fen, (detective character of Edmund Crispin; with bibliography), by William A.S.Sarjeant, 14-3 TAD 196

Obstfeld, Raymond: The Best of Hitchcock, (literary commentary), 14-3 TAD 248

Obstfeld, Raymond: Opus in G Minor for Blunt Instruments: Development of Motive in Detective Fiction, 14-1 TAD 9

Obstfeld, Raymond: Someone's in the
Kitchen with Dinah, (fiction), 2-1 M 18

Occhiogrosso, Frank: The Police in Society,
The Novels of Maj Sjowall and Per Wahloo,
12-2 TAD 174

Occhiogrosso, Frank: Threats to Rationalism,
John Fowles, Stanislaw Lew, and the
Detective Story, (the inexplicable still
unsolved), 13-1 TAD 4

Occult Detector, The, (pulp magazine
character in series of stories by J.U.
Giesy and Junius B. Smith; with checklist of stories), by William J. Clark,
17 X 55

O'Connell, William: letter of comment,
3-1 CP 9; 3-4 CP 4

O'Connell, William: Modern Age Books,
(paperbacks and hardcovers published
by Modern Age, with checklist), 3-3 CP 22

O'Connor, Liam: letter of comment, 6/7 LR 24

(OCTOPUS, THE), Checklist, (pulp magazine),
by Lynn Hickman, 75 PU 11

Odds and Ends, (short mystery reviews and
comments), by Don Miller, 1-1 MM 2;
1-2 MM 2; 1-3 MM 2; 1-4 MM 2; 1-5
MM 2; 1-6 MM 4; 1-7 MM 2; 1-8 MM
2; 1-9 MM 2; 1-10 MM 2; 1-11 MM 2;
2-1 MM 2; 2-2 MM 2; 2-3 MM 2; 2-4
MM 9; 2-5 MM 2

Ode to a Beer Opener, (verse), by Frederick
Faust, 1-3 FC 7

Ode to Hadley's Flivver, (verse), by Jack
Dizer, 2-2 TB 6; 2-4 TBN 4

O'Donnell, Jim: letter of comment,
4-2 MF 62; 4-4 MF 49

(O'Donnell, Lillian), Interview with Lillian
O'Donnell, by Patricia Maida, 14-2 TAD
164

(O'Donnell, Lillian: Norah Mulcaheney
series), Series Synopses, by Jo Ann
Vicarel, 10-1 TAD 80; 11-4 TAD 365

(O'Donnell, Peter: Modesty Blaise series),
A Modesty Blaise Appreciation, by
R. Jeff Banks, 8 MN 3

(O'Donnell, Peter: Modesty Blaise series),
Checklist, Annotated, by R. Jeff
Banks, 4-2 MF 8

(O'Donnell, Peter: Modesty Blaise series),
Immoderate Homage to Modesty, by
R. Jeff Banks, 4-2 MF 8

Odyssey Column, (comments and announcements
of Odyssey Publications), by Will
Murray, 1 PW 1; 2 PW 3

(Odyssey Publications), Odyssey Column,
(comments and announcements), by
Will Murray, 1 PW 1; 2 PW 3

Of Hammett, Chandler, Brand and Bradbury -
and An Eye Named Challis, (Bart Challis
series by William F. Nolan), by William
F. Nolan, 2-2 TAD 86

Offord, Lenore Glen: A Boucher Portrait,
Anthony Boucher as Seen by His Friends
and Colleagues, 2-2 TAD 69

(Offord, Lenore Glen), Meet the Author,
Lenore Glen Offord, by Allen J. Hubin,
2-2 TAD 76

Oft Have I Travelled, (concerning
Solar Pons case and other locales),
by Philip Jose Farmer, 2-2 PD 1

O'Gara, Gil: Astonishers! Just Who
Are You, Anyway?, (dime novels),
1-2 YB 8

O'Gara, Gil: Bound to Win Series,
(boys' books series by various
authors published by M.A.Donohue
& Company), 1-1 YB 8

O'Gara, Gil: Every Bad Boy's Bad
Boy, (on George Wilbur Peck's
THE BAD BOY, literary discussion
with reprint of portion), 1-5 YB 4

O'Gara, Gil: Favorite Juvenile
Authors - What Publishers Said
About Their Old Stand-Bys, (Horatio
Alger, Jr., Harry Castlemon, Edward
S. Ellis, J.T. Trowbridge - comments
by publishers), 1-2 YB 19

O'Gara, Gil: Good Old Jack, (Jack
Harkaway, dime novels and boys'
books - juvenile hero), 1-1 YB 22

O'Gara, Gil: In Appreciation of Leo
Edwards, (boys' books author),
1-1 YB 13

O'Gara, Gil: King of the Dime Novels,
(Frank Merriwell, boys' hero)
3 U 17

O'Gara, Gil: Old King Brady, His Rise
and Decline, (dime novel detective),
7 U 19; 1-1 YB 5

O'Gara, Gil: Tom Slade - and Friends,
(boys' series books), 1-4 YB 21

Ogden, Willard: letter of comment,
15 BS 15

(O'Hanlon, James), Department of
Unknown Mystery Writers - James
O'Hanlon, by Marvin Lachman,
3-3 PP 15

(O'Hara, John: TEN NORTH FREDERICK),
Spotlight, (discussion of book),
2-4 PQ 11

O'Herin, Tim: letter of comment,
5 MA 29

Ohtsuka, Kanji: letter of comment,
8-3 TAD 239

O'Keeffe, Patrick: letter of comment,
7-3 TAD 232

Old Doctor of Limehouse, The, (Dr. F.
in Solar Pons stories), by Charles
R.L.Power, 2-2 PD 4

(Old Farm series: C.A.Stephens),
Boys' Series Bibliography, by
Harry K. Hudson, 1-6 YB 16

Old King Brady - His Rise and Decline,
(detective series in dime novels),
by Gil O'Gara, 7 U 19; 1-1 YB 5

Old Movie Expert, (mini-mystery
parody), by R. Jeff Banks, 7 PE 10

Old Pulp Writers, The, by Will
Murray, 33 X 38

Old Rope Trick, The, (verse), by
Frank Schweitzer, 3-5 MR 14

Old-Time Radio Lives, (Boston Blackie),
by Carl Larsen, 5-6 MF 3

Old Time Radio Lives - Look for It in the Morning Express!, by Carl Larsen, 4-6 MF 9

Old Time Radio Lives - "Saints Preserve Us, Mr. Keen!", by Carl Larsen, 4-5 MF 18

Old Sleuth, Nineteenth Century "Nipper" America's First Serialized Detective and His World, (the Old Sleuth, detective, in dime novels), by Lydia Godfrey, 1-1 C 53

Old Werner Publishing Company of Akron, Ohio, The, (publisher of boys' books), by Roy B. Van Devier, 2-4 BC 246

Oldberg, Richard: The Common Heard, (mystery quiz based on Nero Wolfe), 1-2 G 60

Oldberg, Richard: Dramatis Personae, (mystery quiz, based on Nero Wolfe), 1-1 G 55

(Olden, Marc), An Interview with Marc Olden, by Robert J. Randisi, 12-4 TAD 324

(Oldham, Mark: POE MUST DIE), Mystery Plus: Poe Must Die, (discussion of book), by R. Jeff Banks, 2-2 PP 12

Oldewarris, Hans: letter of comment, 1-3 PQ 11

Olsen, T.V.: Elegy for August Derleth, (verse), 2-3/4 AD 8

Olson, Mark L.: letter of comment, 5 X 41

O'Malley, Don: letter of comment, 3 DS 7

(O'Malley, Patrick: Harrigan and Hoeffler series), Checklist, Annotated, by Barry Van Tilburg, 4-6 MF 5

O'Malley, Robert: An Index to PLANET STORIES, (science fiction pulp magazine), 20 X 42; 21 X 55; 22 X 48; 26 X 13

O'Malley, Robert: letter of comment, 28 X 79

On Carolyn Wells, (author), by Jon L. Breen, 3-2 TAD 77

On Compiling a Sax Rohmer Collection, by Alan Warren, 13-2 TAD 148

On Fans and Bouchercons, (mystery fandom and the Bouchercon conventions), by Guy M. Townsend, 5-5 MF 11

On Finding Petrie's Correct Name, (Dr. Petrie, in Fu Manchu stories by Sax Rohmer), by Evelyn A. Herzog, 18 R 25

On Lee Thayer, (author), by Jon L. Breen, 5-3 TAD 148

On LOLITA as a Mystery Story, (Vladimir Nabokov: LOLITA), by J.R.Christopher, 7-1 TAD 29

On Mystery & Science Fiction Fandom, (generalized comparisons), by David Rose, 16 CD 3

On Pulpsmithing, (writing for the pulp magazines), by Arthur J. Burks, 69 PU 10

On Reading Detective Fiction, (the popular aesthetics of the form), by John M. Reilly, 12-1 TAD 64

On the Invention of Villainy, Speculations by a Mystery Fan, by Lawrence Fleming, 17 JD 19

On the Keeping of a Journal, (after reading August Derleth's VILLAGE YEAR; verse), by Steve Eng, 2-1 AD 12

On the Passing of MANHUNT, (the demise of the mystery magazine), by Jon L. Breen, 1-3 TAD 89

On the Trail of the Mysterious "Jack Mann," (author), by W.O.G.Lofts, 6-2 MR 19

On the Trails of Dr. Freeman and Dr. Thorndyke, or, A Guide to Thorndykean England, (locales in the Thorndyke stories by Freeman), by Michael G. Heenan and Philip T. Asdell, 8 TF 4

On the Warpath, (comments on boys' series books), by H.L.Risteen, 3-1 BC 263

One Britisher's View of Hammett, (review of Dashiell Hammett's THE THIN MAN in a London paper), by Edward S. Lauterbach, 4-5/6 PP 44

One in Two: Some Personality Studies by Ruth Rendell, by Jane S. Bakerman, 5-6 MF 21

One Name on the Contract, (re: the television series "Dallas"), by Nan & Ivan Lyons, 9 LR 23

O'Neil, Dennis: letter of comment, 9 JD 8

O'Neill, Robert: letter of comment, 7 JD 5

Ong, (Mrs.) P.: letter of comment, 3/4 MN 16; 9 MN L5

Only the Shadow Knows, (commentary, The Shadow, pulp character), by Frank P. Eisgruber, Jr., 3 P 28

007-Type Tarzan, (comparisons, James Bond and Tarzan), by John Harwood, 4-6 MR 11

OPEN ROAD FOR BOYS Goes to War, The, (on the wartime issues of the boys' magazine), by Michael L. Cook, 1-6 YB 3

Operation England - The Martian Maelstrom (documentation for THE WAR OF THE WORLDS by H.G. Wells), by Dana Martin Batory, 8 U 58

Operative 1701: Doc Savage & Crew Reborn as Stars of Star Trek and Star Wars, 5 DS 14

Operator 5, (pulp magazine espionage hero), by Wooda Nicholas Carr, 1 P 3

Operator 5 Speaks, (pulp magazine espionage hero), by Wooda Nicholas Carr, 5A P 8

(Operator 5 pulp series), Contemplating Seven of the Pulp Heroes, (comparisons and characteristics), by Wooda Nicholas Carr and Herman S. McGregor, 12 BS 3

(Operator 5 pulp series), Deadlier Than the Male, (female villains in the Operator 5 stories), by Wooda Nicholas Carr, 11 P 3

(Operator 5 pulp series), Emperor Rudolph, (Operator 5 and the Purple Empire sub-series), by Wooda Nicholas Carr, 10 P 22

(Operator 5 pulp series), Jumping Jimmy Christopher, by Dean A. Grennell, 30 X 17

(Operator 5 pulp series), "Let's Face It!" - A Look at the Disguises of Operator 5 During the Purple Invasion, (Operator 5 and the Purple Empire sub-series), by Wooda Nicholas Carr, 3 U 3

(Operator 5 pulp series), Operator 5, by Wooda Nicholas Carr, 1 P 3

(Operator 5 pulp series), Operator 5 Bounds Out of the Thirties, (close look at Jimmy Christopher, aka Operator 5), by Wooda Nicholas Carr, 6 BS 8; 7 BS 7

(Operator 5 pulp series), Operator 5 Speaks, by Wooda Nicholas Carr, 5A P 8

(Operator 5 pulp series), The Subject was Death, (Operator 5 and the "Army of the Dead"), by Wooda Nicholas Carr, 15 SF 9

(Oppenheim, E. Phillips), Books by E. Phillips Oppenheim, 4-3 MR 23

(Oppenheim, E. Phillips), Checklist Addendum, by J. Randolph Cox, 5-3 MR 17

(Optic, Oliver), Oliver Optic, (boys' books author), by Roy B. Van Devier, 2-3 BC 215

Opus in G Minor for Blunt Strument - The Development of Motive in Detective Fiction, by Raymond Obstfeld, 14-1 TAD 9

Orban, Paul: letter of comment, 6 BS 2

(Orban, Paul), Letter and Comment from Orban, "Yesterday's Doc Savage Illustrator", 2 BS 5

Orchidology of Nero Wolfe, The, (orchids in the Nero Wolfe stories by Rex Stout), by Robert M. Hamilton, 1-2 G 18

Orchids to the Wolfe Pack: The Second Annual Black Orchid Banquet, (report of meeting of The Wolfe Pack, Nero Wolfe fan group), by Judson C. Sapp, 6 U 29

(Orczy, Baroness: THE OLD MAN IN THE CORNER), Was the Old Man in the Corner an Armchair Detective?, by Fred Dueren, 14-3 TAD 232

Order and Disorder in THE MALTESE FALCON, (Dashiell Hammett: THE MALTESE FALCON), by Donald J. Pattow, 11-2 TAD 171

Organizations/Publications for Mystery Fans, by Allen J. Hubin, 1-2 TAD 37

Orifice Into Hell, (macabre fiction of A. Conan Doyle), by Dana Martin Batory, 3 U 11

Origlio, David: letter of comment, 5 MA 29

Orth, Paul: letter of comment, 11-2 TAD 205

Orton, Vrest: letter of comment, 27 JD 36

(Orwell, George), No Orchids for George Orwell, (comments on Orwell's criticism of NO ORCHIDS FOR MISS BLANDISH by James Hadley Chase), by Susan Harris Smith, 9-2 TAD 114

Osborn, Pauline W.: letter of comment, 5-2 MF 45

Oscar Wilde and Sherlock Holmes - A Literary Mystery, by Randy Roberts, 1-1 C 41

Osheroff, Alex: letter of comment, 13 X 60

Osida, Joseph: letter of comment, 14 JD 23

O'Spelin, C. MacLean: letter of comment, 5-6 MR 16

Osterman, Bob: letter of comment, 15 BS 17

Osterman, Robert: Where are the Pulp Fictioneers, (comment on pulp magazine writers), 2 BS 15

(Otis, James), Writer of Over One Hundred Boys' Books, (sketch of James Otis), by Stephen Cammett, 2-3 BC 210

(Ott, Poppy, series: Leo Edwards), Checklist, (boys' books), J.R.Chenu, 1-1 TB 4; 3 BB 10; 1-2 YB 17

(Ott, Poppy, series: Leo Edwards), How I Found My Inferior Decorators, (search for POPPY OTT: INFERIOR DECORATOR title), by Jack R. Schorr, 4-1 TB 1

(Ott, Poppy, series: Leo Edwards), Poppy Ott Sequel to Popular Todd Series, (refers to Jerry Todd boys' series by Edwards as predecessor), by Julius R. Chenu, 1-3 TB 1

Other Shadow, The, (Dr. Sax, pulp character), by Will Murray, 10 X 2

OTHER TIMES MAGAZINE, Index, by Darrell Schweitzer, 8 U 146

Other War of the Worlds, The, (re: H.G.Wells: THE WAR OF THE WORLDS), by Dana Martin Batory, 8 U 50

Other Writings by Leslie McFarlane, by John M. Enright, 4 MA 18

(Ottolengui, Rodrigues), Rodrigues
Ottolengui, A Forgotten American
Mystery Writer, by Wendell Hertig
Taylor, 9-3 TAD 181
Our Chatterbox, (letters of comment from
readers, with introductory comments
in first entry by Julius R. Chenu),
1-1 TB 2; 1-2 TB 7; 1-3 TB 10;
1-4 TB 6; 2-1 TB 4; 2-4 TB 2;
2-5 TB 4; 3-1 TB 3; 1-1 TBN 3;
1-2 TBN 5; 1-3 TBN 4; 1-4 TBN
5; 2-1 TBN 3; 2-2 TBN 4; 2-3
TBN 3; 2-4 TBN 3; 2-5 TBN 2;
2-6 TBN 4
Our Heroes in Motley, (crime humor), by
Edward S. Lauterbach, 9-3 TAD 178
Ourselves and Gaston Max, (Sax Rohmer
character), by Cay Van Ash, 15 R 23
Out of the Shadows, (commentary on The
Shadow by the creator), by Walter B.
Gibson, 2 D 32
Overn, B.W.: Bill Barnes - Air Adventurer,
(aviation pulp hero), 3 BS 14
Overn, B.W.: Fokker Joker, (on characters
in FLYING ACES pulp magazine), 10 P 7
Overn, B.W.: Frank Tinsley, Prophet With
a Brush, (pulp magazine cover artist),
67 PU 68
Overn, B.W.: letter of comment, 2 BS 3;
6 BS 20; 64 PU 27; 67 PU 54
Overn, B.W.: The Strange Case of Philip
Strange, or, Will the Real G-8 Please
Stand Up?, (similarity of pulp heroes),
6 BS 16; 2 P 15
(Owen, Frank), Checklist of Books, by
Richard Minter, 30 X 3
(Owen, Frank), Checklist of Books, by
Lemuel Nash, 28 X 12
Owen, Maurice E.: About "The Smugglers of
Chestnut", (boys' fiction), 1-1 BC 17
Owen, Maurice E.: Chasing "Will-o'-the-
Wisps", (boys' books collecting),
1-2 BC 64
Owen, Maurice E.: Harry Castlemon, A
Chronology of Books, (boys' books by
Castlemon), 1-3 BC 75
Owen, Scott: letter of comment, 1-3 PQ 7;
2 U 48
(Owen, Scott), short biographical sketch,
2-3 PP 8

Paccassi, Frank: letter of comment,
4-6 MR 16
Pacheco, Audrey I.: Checklist, Joan Aiken,
5-4 MR 25
Pacheco, Audrey I.: Checklist, Charlotte
Armstrong, 5-4 MR 24
Pacheco, Audrey I.: Checklist, Heron
Carvin, 5-4 MR 23
Pacheco, Audrey I.: Checklist, Helen
Reilly, 5-4 MR 24
Pacheco, Audrey I.: Checklist, Mary
Stewart, 5-4 MR 25
Pacheco, Audrey I.: Checklist, Dorothy
Uhnak, 5-4 MR 23

Pacheco, Audrey I.: Checklist,
Eva-Lis Wuorio, 5-4 MR 23
Pacheco, Audrey I.: In Search of the
Female Protagonist, (on female
sleuths), 5-4 MR 23
Pacheco, Audrey I.: letter of comment,
6-1 MR 22
Pachon, Stanley A.: letter of comment,
1-2 BC 62; 4 BS 2; 8 BS 7;
18 JD 30; 5 MA 28; 1-6 MR 8;
61 PU 12; 65 PU 19; 68 PU 25
(Pacific Northwest), The American
Regional Mystery, Pt. XI, by
Marvin Lachman, 9-1 TAD 11
(Packer, Vin: THE GIRL ON THE BEST
SELLER LIST), Spotlight, (review
and commentary), 3-3 PQ 54
Padgett, Carolyn: letter of comment,
5 BB 24; 6 BB 32
Page, Norvell W.: How I Write, 6 P 5
(Page, Thomas: THE SPIRIT), Mystery
Plus: Getting There May Be More
Than Half the Fun, (discussion of
book), by R. Jeff Banks, 3-5 PP 15
Paint the Coffin Fuchsia, (John D.
MacDonald parody), by Bob Leman,
9 JD 26
(Palacios, Rafael), Rafael Palacios,
(paperback cover artist), by
Piet Schreuders, 3-3 CP 32
Pale Leman for Psychosis, (parody of
John D. MacDonald fiction), by Ron
Bennett, 11 JD 4
(Palfrey, Dr., series: John Creasey),
Checklist, by Barry Van Tilburg,
4-2 MF 12
Palmer, Raymond: August Derleth (sketch
and reminiscences 1936) 2 WT 12
(Palmer, Raymond), Sailing Uncharted
Seas, (on the "Shaver Mystery"),
by David and Su Bates, 2-2 CP 35
Pan's Song, (verse), by Jayne Fawcett,
3-4 AD 6
Panagos, Angelo: letter of comment,
10-4 TAD 292; 11-3 TAD 213
Panshin, Alexei: letter of comment,
15 JD 26
(PAPA LA-BAS: John Dickson Carr),
Review in Verse, by Len Moffatt,
2-2 MR 6
Papalia, William: John Newton Howitt,
American Artist/Illustrator, A
Discussion, (pulp artist), 33 X 87
Papalia, William, and Virginia Combs
("Nanek") Anderson: A Remembrance
of Early Pulp Collecting and Fandom
1938-43, 40 X 3
Paper Crimes, (reviews of paperback
mystery books), by Fred Dueren,
8-4 TAD 295; 9-1 TAD 50; 9-2 TAD
140; 9-3 TAD 212; 9-4 TAD 277;
10-1 TAD 51; 10-2 TAD 130; 10-4
TAD 340; 11-2 TAD 192; 11-3 TAD
306; 12-2 TAD 135; 12-3 TAD 287;
13-1 TAD 65; 13-2 TAD 136; 13-3

Paper Crimes, (continued), TAD 251;
13-4 TAD 361; 14-1 TAD 80; 14-2
TAD 183
Paper Crimes, (reviews of paperback
mystery books), by William L. DeAndrea,
14-3 TAD 265; 14-4 TAD 378
Paperback Art Comes Into It's Own, (on
covert art), by Robert Weinberg,
2-5 CP 28
(paperback - art), A Partial List of
Paperback Covers Painted by Norman
Saunders, 1-3 PQ 41
(paperback - art), American Paperback
Cover Art Exhibition, 3-3 PQ 53
(paperback - art), Aphrodisia, Here is
Your Hat, (sex in paperback cover
art), by Tamsen Stocking, 3-4 PQ 28
(paperback - art), Boris! Boris! Boris!,
(Boris Vallejo, cover artist for
Doc Savage series), by Robert Woo,
1 DS 11
(paperback - art), Checklist, Dealers
of Original Paperback Cover Art,
4-1 PQ 49
(paperback - art), Collecting Original
Paperback Cover Art, by Robert
Weinberg, 3-3 PQ 44
(paperback - art), Cover-Up!, (paperbacks with dust-jackets of different
designs), by Peter Manesis, 4-1 PQ
26
(paperback - art), Interior Paperback
Art, by Mark Schaffer, 3-2 PQ 43
(paperback - art), Interview with Kelly
Freas, 3-2 PQ 12
(paperback - art), James Steranko...
Extraordinary, (cover artist), by
M.C.Hill, 4-1 PQ 34
(paperback - art), Lancer SF Paperback
Artists, (checklist, cover artists
for Lancer line of science fiction
paperbacks), by William J. Denholm
III, 10 SF 25
(paperback - art), The Newest Doc Savage
Artist, (Bob Larkin as cover artist),
by Frank Lewandowski, 1 DS 12
(paperback - art), Paperback Art Comes
Into Its Own, by Robert Weinberg,
2-5 CP 28
(paperback - art), Paperback Bodies,
(sex in paperback cover art), by
Bill Crider, 2-4 PQ 32
(paperback - art), Rafael Palacios,
(sketch as cover artist), by Piet
Schreuders, 3-3 CP 32
(paperback - art), Selling Culture With
Paperback Covers, by Mark Schaffer,
2-4 PQ 42
(paperback - art), Soft Cover Sketches:
Introduction, by Thomas L. Bonn,
3-3 PQ 39; (on James Avati) 3-3 PQ
40; (on Robert Jones), 3-4 PQ 19;
(on Lou Marchetti) 4-2 PQ 32
(paperback - art), Steranko Art on Paperbacks, (checklist, James Steranko),
by M.C.Hill, 4-1 PQ 37

(paperback - art), Those Lovely,
Detailed Paperback Covers, by
Edward Lauterbach, 4-1 PP 16
(paperback - art), We Can All Be
Joe Friday, (identifying artists
of paperback covers), 1-6 CP 14
(paperback - backwoods novels), See
What the Boys in the Backwoods
Will Have (and Tell Them I'm
Having the Same), (discusses
various backwoods theme paper-
backs), by Bill Crider, 2-3 PQ 22
Paperback Blurbs, (on book cover
advertising), by Charlotte Laughlin
and Bill Crider, 4-2 PQ 3
Paperback Bodies, (sex in paperback
cover art), by Bill Crider, 2-4
PQ 32
Paperback Book Party, (report of
gathering at home of Bruce and
Carol Taylor, San Francisco), by
"Secret Agent X-9", 1-2 CP 30
(paperback - booksellers), List of
Bookdealers, 2-3 PQ 29; 2-4 PQ
31; 3-1 PQ 50; 3-2 PQ 54; 3-3
PQ 56; 3-4 PQ 56
(paperback - censorship), Christ No,
Hell Yes, by Dave Lewis, 2-4 CP 6
(paperback - collecting), Articles
& Books on Paperbacks, (reference
material), by Lance C. Casebeer,
3-5 CP 3
(paperback - collecting), Collecting
Armed Services Editions, by
Charlotte Laughlin, 1-2 PQ 31
(paperback - collecting), Collecting
Thoughts, (comments), by Ron Tatar,
2-3 CP 7
(paperback - collecting), How to
Succeed in Collecting Paperbacks,
by Mike Benton, 3-2 CP 21
(paperback - collecting), I Await
You, by Craig Henry, 2-3 CP 22
(paperback - collecting), Junkie, A
Personal Reminiscence, (on editions
of JUNKIE by William Burroughs), by
Jeff Chambers, 3-3 CP 11
(paperback - collecting), Rare Books
Are Getting Scarce, (on collecting
mystery and detective fiction), by
Bruce Taylor, 1-1 CP 8; 3-5 CP 12
(paperback - collecting), Paperback
Writers, by Bill Crider, 1-3 PQ 16
(paperback - collecting), Ramblings
of a Rare Paperback Book Fiend,
by M.C.Hill, 2-2 CP 38
(paperback - collecting), Sources of
Information, in Lyles Column No.1,
by William Lyles, 1-1 CP 4
(paperback - collecting), Survey
Results, by Larry Rickert, 3-2
CP 35
Paperback Collector's Con III, (report
on convention), by Tom Lesser,
1-5 CP 34

254

(paperback - colophons), Mass Market
Murmurings, by Barry Bernard,
1-2 CP 6
(paperback - comicbook artists), Mass
Market Murmurings, (on artists of
MAD magazine), by Barry Bernard,
2-4 CP 18
(paperback - detective first editions),
Some Important Detective Fiction
First Editions in Paperback Books,
by Harold Knott, 3-1 MR 2
(paperback - digest size), Digests Not
in Hancer's (additional listing of
digest-size paperback books not in
Hancer's Price Guide), by Scott
Edwards, 3-4 CP 22
(paperback - early), The American
Detective Series, by Howard Waterhouse,
2-3 PQ 32, (checklist) 2-3 PQ 36
Paperback Editions of Robert Graves,
(with checklist), by Susannah Bates,
3-5 CP 25
(paperback - European), The European
Paperback Prelude, (discussion of
early paperbacks in Europe), by
Piet Schreuders, 4-2 PQ 38
(paperback - exhibitions), "Dutch
Diart" (report on Paperbacks U.S.A.
Exhibition in Holland), by James
Avati, 4-1 PQ 15
(paperback - exhibitions), Paperbacks
U.S.A.: The Exhibition, (held in
Holland), by Piet Schreuders,
4-1 PQ 13
Paperback Firsts, by Agatha Taylor,
2-1 PQ 53; 2-2 PQ 40
(paperback - female cover art), Aphrodisia,
Here is Your Hat, (sex in paperback
cover art), by Tamsen Stocking,
3-4 PQ 28
(paperback - female cover art), Paperback
Bodies, (sex in paperback cover art),
by Bill Crider, 2-4 PQ 32
(paperback - fantasy), Modern Fantasy,
(selected checklist of publisher),
by Dave Killian, 2-5 CP 11
(paperback - fantasy, When Fantasy
Trod the Boards, (fantasy and science
fiction plays in paperback books),
by David and Su Bates, 2-4 CP 16
(paperback - history), A Glance at Paperback History, by Mark Schaffer,
2-2 PQ 31
(paperback - movie editions), Some Notes
on Movie Editions, by Billy C. Lee
and Bill Crider, 2-1 PQ 29
Paperback Mysteries Issued in June 1974,
(comments and reviews), by Steve
Lewis, 2 MY 7; (July 1974) 3 MY 5
Paperback Mystery Directory, (authors
and publishers), 5-2 MR 6
Paperback Original Novels of John Jakes,
The, (checklist), by Michael S. Barson,
3-3 PQ 20

Paperback Originals, (original editions
in paperback), by Bill Crider,
1-1 PQ 3; (mysteries) 5-1 MR 19;
(addendum by Bill Pronzini) 5-2
MR 17
Paperback Originals by John D.
MacDonald, (checklist), by Michael
S. Barson, 4-1 PQ 10
Paperback Originals by Harry Whittington
(checklist), by Michael S. Barson,
4-2 PQ 23
Paperback Originals by Robert Bloch,
(checklist), by Michael S. Barson,
4-1 PQ 24
(paperback - originals), Hard Cain -
The Paperback Original Novels of
James M. Cain, by George Kelley,
4-3 PP 9
(paperback - originals), Paperback
Writers, by Bill Crider, 1-1 PQ 9
(paperback - plantation novels),
The Plantation Novel: Paperback
Genre of the 1970s?, by Christopher
D. Geist, 3-1 PQ 42
(paperback - promotion), Paperback
Firsts: Nose, Nose, Anything Goes,
(perfumed books as promotion),
2-2 PQ 42
(paperback - promotion), Paperback
Promotionals, (selling aids),
2-1 PQ 28; (vending machines)
2-2 PQ 28; (racks) 2-3 PQ 40
(paperback - promotion), The TV Tie-In
Affair, or, Matt Dillon Meets Emma
Peel, (paperbacks trading on other
publicity), by John Garbarino,
3-4 CP 5
Paperback Promotionals, (selling aids),
2-1 PQ 28; (vending machines) 2-2
PQ 28; (racks) 2-3 PQ 40
(paperback - publishers), Gone But
Not Forgotten, (defunct paperback
science fiction publishers, with
checklist), by J. Grant Thiessen,
2 SF 6
(paperback - publishers), Index of
Paperback Publishers in PUBLISHERS
WEEKLY for 1950, by Paul Hammonds,
1-3 PQ 28; (for 1952 & 1953) 2-1
PQ 38
(paperback - publishers), Mass Market
Paperback Publishing 1939-Present,
An Annotated Bibliography, by
Thomas L. Bonn, 1-4 PQ 4
(paperback - publishers), Paperback
Mystery Directory, 5-2 MR 6
(paperback - publishing fallacies),
This Little Paperback Went to
Market, or Kiss My Deadly Typewriter,
by Michael Avallone, 3-2 MR 27
(PAPERBACK PRICE GUIDE: Kevin Hancer)
Digests Not in Hancer's, (digest-
size paperbacks not in Price Guide)
by Scott Edwards, 3-4 CP 22

(PAPERBACK PRICE GUIDE: Kevin Hancer), Omissions from Guide, Digest-Size Paperbacks, by Norral Johnson, 3-3 CP 9

PAPERBACK QUARTERLY, Index to Volumes I-III, 3-4 PQ 48

(paperback - queries), Notes and Queries, (with answers to some), 1-1 PQ 42; 1-3 PQ 53; 1-4 PQ 54; 2-3 PQ 42; 1-2 PQ 56

(paperback - queries), I Wonder, (questions and answers when possible on paperback collecting), by Lance Casebeer, 1-2 CP 8; 1-3 CP 2; 1-4 CP 3; 1-5 CP 3; 1-6 CP 8; 2-1 CP 5; 2-3 CP 5; 2-5 CP 3

(paperback - repairing), Repairing Paperbacks, by Nicholas Willmott, 3-2 PQ 39

Paperback Reviews, (mystery fiction), by Francis M. Nevins, Jr., 1-6 MR 3

Paperback Revolution, The, (reviews of paperback crime fiction), by Charles Shibuk, 1-1 TAD 10; 1-2 TAD 41; 1-3 TAD 96; 1-4 TAD 129; 2-1 TAD 44; 2-2 TAD 97; 2-3 TAD 174; 2-4 TAD 251; 3-1 TAD 40; 3-2 TAD 115; 3-3 TAD 179; 3-4 TAD 245; 4-1 TAD 37; 4-2 TAD 115; 4-3 TAD 168; 4-4 TAD 219; 5-1 TAD 30; 5-2 TAD 94; 5-3 TAD 154; 5-4 TAD 220; 6-1 TAD 35; 6-2 TAD 102; 6-3 TAD 179; 6-4 TAD 246; 7-1 TAD 44; 7-2 TAD 120; 7-3 TAD 205; 7-4 TAD 281; 8-1 TAD 50; 8-2 TAD 132; 8-3 TAD 210; 8-4 TAD 276; 9-1 TAD 41; 9-2 TAD 135; 9-3 TAD 208; 9-4 TAD 281; 10-1 TAD 71; 10-2 TAD 149; 10-3 TAD 239; 10-4 TAD 360; 11-1 TAD 96; 11-2 TAD 189; 11-3 TAD 298; 11-4 TAD 379; 12-1 TAD 30; 12-2 TAD 166; 12-3 TAD 255; 12-4 TAD 368; 13-1 TAD 75; 13-2 TAD 135; 13-3 TAD 250; 13-4 TAD 362; 14-1 TAD 79; 14-2 TAD 182; 14-3 TAD 266; 14-4 TAD 376

(Paperback Revolution, The), Random Thoughts on Writing the "Paperback Revolution", by Charles Shibuk, 4-3 TAD 172

(paperback - SF pornography), Science Fiction Pornography, (with checklist), by Kenneth R. Johnson, 4 SF 4; 5 SF 45

Paperback Writers, (of paperback original editions), by Bill Crider, 1-1 PQ 9; (on John Faulkner) 1-2 PQ 8; (on collecting paperbacks) 1-3 PQ 16; (on Bruno Fischer) 1-4 PQ 22; (on E. Howard Hunt) 2-1 PQ 9; (on William Campbell Gault, with paperback checklist) 2-2 PQ 5; (on Mickey Spillane) 2-3 PQ 9; (on Michael Avallone) 3-1 PQ 7; (on Richard Wormser) 4-1 PQ 31

Paperback, Who Made Thee? Dost Thou Know Who Made Thee? (verse), by Ogden Nash, 1-4 CP 7

Paperbacks on Review, 1-1 PQ 35; 1-2 PQ 53; 1-3 PQ 49; 1-4 PQ 49

Paperbacks U.S.A.: The Exhibition, (report on exhibition in Holland), by Piet Schreuders, 4-1 PQ 13

(PAPERBACKS U.S.A.: Piet Schreuders) My Fourth Trip to the U.S., (account of promotional trip from Holland to promote author's book), by Piet Schreuders, 3-4 CP 17

Papyrocunabole, or, There's One Now!, (on paperback book collectors), by Richard Hall, 1-4 CP 12

Papyrocunabula of Sax Rohmer, The, (on the paperback reprint editions of Sax Rohmer, with checklist), by Richard Paul Hall, 3-4 CP 15

Parables of H.C.Bailey, The, (in his crime fiction), by Thomas D. Waugh, 6-2 TAD 75

Paradox and Plot: The Fiction of Fredric Brown, by Newton Baird, 9-4 TAD 282; 10-1 TAD 33; 10-2 TAD 151; 10-3 TAD 249; 10-4 TAD 370; 11-1 TAD 86

Paragon, The, (verse), by Frederick Faust, 1-2 FC 9

(Parker, Robert B.), Professor Without a Pseudonym, by Larry L. French, 2-2 MF 12

(Parker, Robert B.), Robert B. Parker and the Hardboiled Tradition of American Detective Fiction, by T. Jeff Evans, 1-2 C 100

(Parker, Robert B.), Spenser - Hardboiled Roots, (Spenser, detective character of Parker), by Bernard Drew, 21 X 7

(Parker, Robert B.), The Unconventional Morality of Robert B. Parker's Traditional American Hero, ("Spenserian Ethics"), by Steven R. Carter, 1-2 C 109

(Parker, Robert B.: LOOKING FOR RACHEL WALLACE), Looking for Rachel Wallace and Ginger North, by George Kelley, 4-3 MF 29

(Parker, William Gordon), Deer Lodge Series, Boys' Series Bibliography, by Harry K. Hudson, 1-3 YB 10

Parkinson, Howard: Thank You Harry Castlemon, (commentary on books by Castlemon; boys' books), 1-4 TB 2

(Parkman, Francis), A Note from Francis Parkman, by R.W.Hays, 5-4 TAD 193

Parnell, Patricia: letter of comment, 2-5 MF 59

Parrot, Edward Gray, II: letter of comment, 11 R 23

Parsons, Mike: letter of comment, 26 X 73

Parten, Dr. Carroll Borland: Bela Lugosi and Mark of the Vampire, (commentary on Lugosi in the film), 1 CD 34

Parten, James E.: G-8 Rags the Scale,
(G-8, pulp character), 12 DS 13

Passing of Third Floor Back, (on Vincent
Starrett), by Robert W. Hahn, 7-3
TAD 204

Past-Mistress of the Police Procedural,
(literary discussion of Elizabeth
Linington's crime novels), by Ann
Waldron, 3-5 MR 32

Pat Savage, The Original Supergirl,
(character in Doc Savage novels),
1 BSA 20

Patricia Highsmith, Interview, by Diana
Cooper-Clark, 14-4 TAD 313

Patricia Highsmith - On the Screen, by
Jack Edmund Nolan, 4-3 MR 15

Patricia Wentworth Revisited, by Nancy
Blue Wynne, 14-1 TAD 90

Patten, A Top Maine Author of Juveniles,
(commentary and sketch of Gilbert
L. Patten), by Jacqueline Steele,
1-3 TB 4

(Patten, Gilbert),Gilbert Patten in
Clothbound Editions, (boys' books),
by Harry K. Hudson, 1-3 BC 86

(Patten, Gilbert), Gilbert Patten:
The Man and the Magic, (comments
on prolific boys' author in books
and dime novels), 2-2 BC 162

(Patten, Gilbert), Patten, A Top Maine
Author of Juveniles, by Jacqueline
Steele, 1-3 TB 4

Pattengill, Barry: letter of comment,
2-2 CP 2; 2-3 CP 2; 3-1 CP 9;
3-1 PQ 3

Patterns of Guilt and Isolation in Five
Novels by "Tucker Coe" (Donald E.
Westlake), by Jane S. Bakerman,
12-2 TAD 118

Patterson, Sylvia W.: Agatha Christie's
Alter Ego - Ariadne Oliver, 14-3
TAD 222

Patton, Jeff: letter of comment,
2-4 CP 3; 4-2 PQ 52

Patton, Tina: letter of comment,
2-3 M 2

Pattow, Donald J.: letter of comment,
8-3 TAD 239

Pattow, Donald J.: Order and Disorder
in The Maltese Falcon (Dashiell
Hammett: THE MALTESE FALCON),
11-2 TAD 171

Paul Harley Series, The, by Robert
E. Briney, 17 R 15

Paul Orban - Yesterday's Doc Savage
Illustrator, (artist, DOC SAVAGE
magazine, pulp covers; letter and
comment from Orban), 2 BS 5

Paul Temple Saga, The, (series by
Francis Durbridge on British radio),
by Derek J. Adley, 9-4 TAD 267

Paulus, Alois: letter of comment,
40 X 86; 43 X 6

Payne, Paul: Lost and Found, L.A.
Bantam, (on Bantam paperback
book series, Los Angeles editions),
1-3 CP 10

Peake, Alfred: May I Say a Few
Well-chosen Words, (on the
Praed Street Irregulars and
Solar Pons), 2-5 PD 1

Pearce, Murray: letter of comment,
8-4 TAD 324; 9-1 TAD 86

Peck, Andrew Jay: A Case of Identity;
Being a Trifling Monograph Upon
the Similarities between Sir
Denis Nayland Smith and Sherlock
Holmes, (Smith a character in
Sax Rohmer's Fu Manchu series),
2 R 9

Peck, Andrew Jay: Fleet Street Report,
2 R 18; 3 R 24; 4 R 20

Peck, Andrew Jay: letter of comment,
8 MN 38

Peck, Andrew Jay, and Robert E. Briney:
Fleet Street Report, 5 R Cover

Peck, George S.: Conquering the
Stereotypes; On Reading the Novels
of John D. MacDonald, (comments on
female characters), 13-2 TAD 90

(Peck, George Wilbur: PECK'S BAD BOY),
Every Bad Boy's Bad Boy, (literary
discussion with reprint of portion),
by Gil O'Gara, 1-5 YB 4

(Peck, Judge, series: August Derleth)
In Re: Judge Peck, (on detective
series by Derleth), by George J.
Marx, 1-1 PDA 24

Peck, Shelby L.: What's Up, Doc?
(Doc Savage, from the pulps to the
present), 1 DR 3; (Doc Savage Marvel
Comics series) 2/3 DR 3

(PECK'S BAD BOY: George Wilbur Peck),
Every Bad Boy's Bad Boy, (literary
discussion with reprint of portion),
by Gil O'Gara, 1-5 YB 4

Peek, George S.: Beast Imagery and
Stereotypes in the Novels of John
D. MacDonald, 2-1 C 91

Peeples, Samuel: letter of comment,
4-1 TAD 65; 5-2 TAD 116; 6-2
TAD 119

Peill, Floyd: letter of comment, 8 X 38

Peirce, Hayford: letter of comment,
13-4 TAD 343

Peltier, David V.: letter of comment,
1-6 CP 6

Pelz, Bruce E.: letter of comment,
19 JD 14; 4-4 MR 17

Pelz, Bruce E.: Petrie Letter, (on
Dr. Petrie, character of Sax Rohmer)
3 R 16

Pen Letters, (letters of comment from
readers), 1-1 PP 26; 1-3 PP 31;
1-2 PP 25; 1-2 PP 31; 1-4 PP 29;
1-5 PP 24; 1-6 PP 27; 2-2 PP 30;
2-3 PP 37; 2-4 PP 38; 2-5 PP 39;
2-6 PP 40; 3-1 PP 37; 3-2 PP 32;
3-3 PP 35; 3-4 PP 37; 3-5 PP 45;
3-6 PP 32; 4-1 PP 40; 4-2 PP 33;
4-3 PP 30; 4-4 PP 32; 4-5/6 PP 82

Pen Profile, (commentary and literary
    sketch of a mystery author and his
    detective character), by Barry
    Pike,
    R.J.White (Detective-Inspector
        David Brock), 2-2 PP 24
    John Sherwood (Charles Blessington,
        detective), 2-3 PP 23
    David Williams (Mark Treasure,
        detective), 2-4 PP 19
    Marguerite Silverson (Chief-
        Inspector Christopher Adrian),
        2-4 PP 20
    St.John Sprigg (Charles Venables
        and Detective-Inspector Bernard
        Bray), 2-5 PP 23
    Barbara Worsley-Gough (Aloysius
        Kelly, detective), 2-5 PP 24
    Clifford Witting (Detective-Insp.
        Henry Charlton and Det.-Constable
        Peter Bradfield), 2-6 PP 25
    P.W.Wilson (Sir Julian Morthoe,
        detective) 3-1 PP 28; 3-2 PP 18
    Glen Trevor (pseudonym of James
        Hilton), 3-1 PP 28
    Colin Willock (Nathaniel Goss,
        detective) 3-2 PP 17
    Jonathan Stagge (Dr. Hugh Westlake,
        detective), 3-3 PP 20
    June Thomson (Detective-Inspector
        Finch), 3-4 PP 17
    Margaret Yorke (Dr. Patrick Grant,
        detective), 3-4 PP 18
    Lee Thayer (Peter Clancy, detective),
        3-5 PP 25
    Sir Basil Thomson (P.C.Richardson,
        detective), 3-6 PP 18
    John Trench (Martin Cotterell,
        detective), 4-1 PP 19
    Colin Watson (Detective-Inspector
        Purbright), 4-2 PP 21
    Anthony Weymouth (Detective-Inspector
        Treadgold), 4-3 PP 13
    T.H.White , 4-3 PP 14
    MacGregor Urquhart (Chief-Inspector
        Joshua Smarles), 4-4 PP 19
    Henry Wade (Detective-Inspector Poole
        and P.C.John Bragg), 4-5/6 PP 45
    Ethel Lina White (various), 4-5/6 PP 48
    Fiona Sinclair (Superintendent Paul
        Grainger), 4-5/6 PP 49
Pen Puzzler #1: The Personal Touch,
    (mystery quiz puzzle), by Jim McCahery,
    1-4 PP 7
(Pendleton, Don: The Executioner series),
    Series Synopses, by John Vining,
    9-2 TAD 113
Penguin Story, The, (on British Penguin
    line paperbacks), 2-3 PQ 18, by Eric Tucker
(Penguin Books, British), The Penguin
    Story, (paperback line), by Eric Tucker,
    2-3 PQ 18
(Pennsylvania), The American Regional
    Mystery, Pt.5, by Marvin Lachman,
    4-5 MR 2

Penrose Mystery Mystery, The, (Dr.
    Thorndyke story by R. Austin
    Freeman), by Norman Donaldson,
    2-2 TAD 108
Penzler, Otto: Commentaries for the
    Curious, (on John Dickson Carr),
    1 NC 11
Penzler, Otto: letter of comment,
    2-3/4 AD 14; 5-2 MF 45; 2-1
    TAD 66; 8-1 TAD 70
Penzler, Otto: Robert Fish, In
    Memorium, (tribute), 14-2 TAD 120
(Penzler, Otto), Interview, 4 MT 7
(PEOPLE OF DARKNESS: Tony Hillerman),
    Hunter and Hunted, Comparison and
    Contrast in Tony Hillerman's
    PEOPLE OF DARKNESS, by Jane S.
    Bakerman, 5-1 MF 3
People Were Real Then, The, (on the
    fictional characters in ADVENTURE
    pulp magazines), by John Phillifent,
    67 PU 25
Perchance to Dream..., (fiction), by
    Michael Seidman, 2-2 M 48
Perfect Plan, The, (fiction), by B.F.
    Watkinsyn, 13/14 CL 3
Perils of Bibliography, The: A Look
    at the Writings of E.C.Tubb, by
    Mike Ashley, 7 SF 5
Perine, F.E.: EYEclopedia, (private
    eye glossary), 1 PE 22
Perine, F.E.: letter of comment,
    4 PE 33
Perk Stone and the Thorndyke Quiz,
    (interrogatory in 1936 on Dr.
    Thorndyke and his creator, R.
    Austin Freeman), by Norman Donaldson,
    1 TF 26
Permabooks Paperbacks, (checklist),
    by J. Grant Thiessen, 2 SF 12
Perry, Brian: Index to AVON FANTASY
    AND SCIENCE FICTION Magazine,
    9 X 11; 10 X 5
Perry, Brian: letter of comment,
    30 X 148
Perry, Joseph: letter of comment,
    30 X 150
(Perry, Ritchie: Philis series),
    Checklist, Annotated, by Barry
    Van Tilburg, 4-6 MF 5
Perspiration Factor, The, (discipline
    advice for would-be writers), by
    Hal Charles, 4-5/6 PP 43
Petaja, Emil: The Weirdest Tale of
    All, (on WEIRD TALES magazine),
    11 X 124
Peter Cheyney, (literary comments),
    by Iwan Hedman, 4-2 TAD 111
Peter Cheyney, (literary sketch with
    checklist), by Theodore P.
    Dukeshire, 4-4 MR 8
Peter Crane's Cigar, (Classic Corner
    Rare Tales, fiction), by Victor
    L. Whitechurch, 12-4 TAD 332

Peter Godfrey - A Reprise, by Robert C.S.
  Adey, 3-5 PP 9
Peterman From the Old School, ("Big-Nose
  Charlie" in the early pulp "crook"
  stories), by Robert Sampson, 5-4 MF 2
Petrie Letter, (as from Dr. Petrie, Sax
  Rohmer character), by Bruce E. Pelz,
  3 R 16
Petersen, Clarence G.: The JDM Popularity
  Poll, (poll on John D. MacDonald books)
  13 JD 5
Petersen, Clarence G.: letter of comment,
  6 JD 11; 11 JD 17
Petersen, Herman: The Barbless Arrow
  (mystery-action fiction reprinted
  from pulp magazine), 2-2 C 79
Peterson, Keith: letter of comment, 3 R 30
Petersen, Sven-Ingmar: H.R.F.Keating,
  (sketch with bibliography), 8-4
  TAD 277
Petersson, Sven-Ingmar: Martin Russell,
  A Profile, (literary sketch),
  8-1 TAD 48; (checklist) 8-1 TAD 49
(Pettee, Florence Mae: Dr. Nancy Dayland,
  detective), Doctor Wonderful, (on
  the pulp detective stories with
  partial checklist), by Robert
  Sampson, 5-6 MF 13
Petty, Sidney: Fu Manchu Speaks, 11 R 12
(Phantom, The: Lee Falk), The Story of
  The Phantom, by Melville C. Hill,
  12 SF 21; (checklist, Avon paper-
  back books) 12 SF 22
Phantom Airship, The: The Truth Behind
  the Fiction, (re: Doc Savage), by
  Dafydd Neal Dyar, 12 SF 32
Phantom Detective in Paperback, The,
  (pulp novels reprinted in paperback
  books), by Bruce Cervon, 2-4 CP 7;
  (checklist) 2-4 CP 8
(Phantom Detective, The), Contemplating
  Seven of the Pulp Heroes (comparisons
  and characteristics), by Wooda Nicholas
  Carr and Herman S. McGregor, 12 BS 3
(Phantom Detective, The), The Phantom
  Detective in Paperback, (paperback
  reprints of pulp magazine series),
  by Bruce Cervon, 2-4 CP 7; (check-
  list) 2-4 CP 8
(Phantom Detective, The), The Phantom
  Detective Paperback Reprints by
  Corinth Publishers, by Robert
  Sampson, 3-3 MR 6
(Phantom Detective, The), Fading Shadows,
  Corinth/Regency Paperbacks, by Tom
  Johnson, 10 SF 36
(PHANTOM DETECTIVE, THE), Blood Chronicle,
  (on the pulp magazine), by Robert
  Sampson, 3-3 MR 3; (checklist
  1933-53 and index) 3-3 MR 8
(PHANTOM DETECTIVE, THE), Checklist for
  the Phantom Detective Magazine
  1933-1953, by Bernie Wermers, 11 BS 4
(PHANTOM DETECTIVE, THE), Ryerson Johnson
  and the Phantom Detective, (interview),
  by Wooda Nicholas Carr, 6 U 9

Phantom Fed, The, (on Agent G-X, pulp
  magazine character), by Tom
  Johnson, 10 P 5
Phantom Titles, (boys' books titles
  announced but never published),
  by Harry K. Hudson, 3 BB 11
Phelps, Bailey P.: A Pile of Pointy
  Polka Dots, (parody on John D.
  MacDonald's Travis McGee series),
  26 JD 35
Phelps, Bailey P.: letter of comment,
  26 JD 48
Phelps, Bailey P.: The Real McGee,
  (synthesis of puzzle and hero type
  mystery fiction in the Travis McGee
  series by John D. MacDonald),
  28 JD 13
(Philby, Kim), Kim Philby, Master
  Spy in Fact and Fiction, by Theodore
  P. Dukeshire, 3-1 MF 14
Philip Jose Farmer, A Checklist, by
  Paul Whitney, 5 SF 4
Philip Jose Farmer, A Different Kind
  of Checklist, by Bruce Doering,
  2-2 CP 24
Philip Jose Farmer, An Appreciation,
  by J. Grant Thiessen, 5 SF 3
Philip Loraine on the Screen, or,
  Where Did the Mysteries Go, by
  Jack Edmund Nolan, 5-3 MR 18
Philip MacDonald, Gethryn and Others,
  by Norman Donaldson, 3-1 TAD 6;
  (addenda) 3-2 TAD 95
Philip MacDonald on the Screen, (with
  checklist), by Jack Edmund Nolan,
  3-3 MR 33
(Philips, Judson P.), Fifty Years of
  Mysteries, (biographical sketch
  with checklist), by Tim Dumont,
  4 MY 2
Philips, Judson P.: letter of comment,
  2-2 M 2
(Philips, Judson P.: A Conversation
  with Judson Philips, (interview),
  by Bernard A. Drew, 13-4 TAD 325
Philips, Thomas E., Jr.: letter of
  comment, 4 MA 24
(Philis series: Ritchie Perry),
  Checklist, Annotated, by Barry
  Van Tilburg, 4-6 MF 5
Phillifent, John: The Difference
  Between Us, (absence of a "pulp
  era" in Britain), 61 PU 3
Phillifent, John: The People Were
  Real Then, (on fictional characters
  in the ADVENTURE pulp magazines),
  67 PU 25
Phillips, Louis: Alibis, (verse),
  12-1 TAD 63
Phillips, Louis: Super Sleuth,
  (mystery puzzle), 12-3 TAD 208
Phillips, Richard: letter of comment,
  2 DS 8
Phillips, Samuel R.: letter of comment,
  14 JD 27

Philo Vance, (on the detective character created by S.S.Van Dine), by Fred Dueren, 9-1 TAD 23

Philo Vance on the Screen, (detective of S.S.Van Dine, filmed), by Jack Edmund Nolan, 2-4 MR 18

Philo Vance's Sunday Nights at the Old Stuyvesant Club, (Philo Vance series: S.S.Van Dine), by E.R.Hagemann, 1-2 C 35

(Phoenix Press), The Saga of the Phoenix: That Probably Should Never Have Arisen, (Phoenix Press mysteries), by Bill Pronzini, 10-2 TAD 106

Photo Detection: The Image as Evidence, (photography used in crime detection) by David L. Jacobs, 1-2 C 18

Picard, Florence: letter of comment, 6 MY 8

Pickens, Jay J.: letter of comment, 5 DS 7

Picou, Pat: letter of comment, 24 JD 38

Pierce, Delphine: letter of comment, 27 JD 37

Pierce: Frank: Garroted! (Classic Corner Rare Tales, fiction), 14-4 TAD 336

Pierce, Jeff: The Great Mystery Series, Collin Wilcox, (study and checklist), 3-2 M 20

Piercing the Closed Circle: The Technique of Point of View in Works by P.D. James, by Jane S. Bakerman, 1-5 MF 3

Pike, Barry A.: Bibliography, Margery Allingham, 6-3 TAD 198

Pike, Barry A.: Checklist, Gladys Mitchell, 9-4 TAD 259

Pike, Barry A.: Checklist, Jonathan Stagge, 3-3 PP 21

Pike, Barry A.: Checklist, Lee Thayer, 3-5 PP 27

Pike, Barry A.: Checklist, Sir Basil Thomson, 3-6 PP 18

Pike, Barry A.: Checklist, June Thomson, 3-4 PP 18

Pike, Barry A.: Checklist, Colin Watson, 4-2 PP 22

Pike, Barry A.: Checklist, Margaret Yorke, 3-4 PP 17

Pike, Barry A.: In Praise of Gladys Mitchell, (including interview), 9-4 TAD 250

Pike, Barry A.: letter of comment, 2-1 PP 45; 2-2 PP 36; 2-5 PP 45; 2-6 PP 43; 3-1 PP 49; 3-2 PP 39; 3-3 PP 42; 3-4 PP 37; 3-4 PP 40; 3-5 PP 51; 3-6 PP 40; 4-1 PP 40; 4-2 PP 39; 4-2 PP 42; 4-4 PP 41; 4-5/6 PP 86; 4-5/6 PP 97; 6-3 TAD 198; 7-1 TAD 68; 8-1 TAD 74; 8-2 TAD 162; 8-3 TAD 236; 9-1 TAD 84; 9-3 TAD 233; 11-2 TAD 208; 11-3 TAD 212

Pike, Barry A.: The Literary Works of Fictional Detectives and "Watsons", (mystery quiz), 7-4 TAD 260

Pike, Barry A.: Margery Allingham's Albert Campion, A Chronological Examination of the Novels in Which He Appears, 9-1 TAD 1; 9-2 TAD 95; 10-1 TAD 25; 10-2 TAD 117; 10-3 TAD 245; 10-4 TAD 324; 11-1 TAD 34; 11-2 TAD 177; 11-3 TAD 279; 11-4 TAD 372; 11-4 TAD 408; 12-1 TAD 34; 12-2 TAD 168; 12-4 TAD 348

Pike, Barry A.: Pen Profile, (commentary and literary sketch of mystery author and his detective character), R.J.White (Detective-Inspector David Brock) 2-2 PP 24
John Sherwood (Charles Blessington, detective) 2-3 PP 23
David Williams (Mark Treasure, detective) 2-4 PP 19
Marguerite Silverson (Chief-Inspector Christopher Adrian) 2-4 PP 20
St.John Sprigg (Charles Venables and Detective-Inspector Bernard Bray) 2-5 PP 23
Barbara Worsley-Gough (Aloysius Kelly, detective) 2-5 PP 24
Clifford Witting (Detective-Inspector Henry Charlton and Detective-Constable Peter Bradfield) 2-6 PP 25
P.W.Wilson (Sir Julian Morthoe, detective), 3-1 PP 28; 3-2 PP 18
Glen Trevor (pseudonym of James Hilton) 3-1 PP 28
Colin Willock (Nathaniel Goss, detective) 3-2 PP 17
Jonathan Stagge (Dr. Hugh Westlake, detective), 3-3 PP 20
June Thomson (Detective-Inspector Finch) 3-4 PP 17
Margaret Yorke (Dr. Patrick Grant, detective), 3-4 PP 18
Lee Thayer (Peter Clancy, detective) 3-5 PP 25
Sir Basil Thomson (P.C.Richardson, detective) 3-6 PP 18
John Trench (Martin Cotterell, detective) 4-1 PP 19
Colin Watson (Detective-Inspector Purbright) 4-2 PP 21
Anthony Weymouth (Detective-Inspector Treadgold) 4-3 PP 13
T.H.White, 4-3 PP 14
MacGregor Urquhart (Chief-Inspector Joshua Smarles) 4-4 PP 19
Henry Wade (Detective-Inspector Poole and P.C.John Bragg), 4-5/6 PP 45
Ethel Lina White (various) 4-5/6 PP 48
Fiona Sinclair (Superintendent Paul Grainger) 4-5/6 PP 49

(Pine, Paul, detective: Howard Browne), The Return of Paul Pine, by Caleb A. Lewis, 11-1 TAD 79

(Pinkerton, Evan, series: David Frome),
Evan Pinkerton, by Fred Dueren,
7-3 TAD 193
(Pinkerton, Mrs.), Mrs. Pinkerton as
Frankenstein, by Mary F. Lindsley,
1-1 PDA 27
(pipe-smoking sleuths), The Good, the
Bad and the Pipe, by J.J.Armbruster,
5-2 MR 29
(PIRATE STORIES magazine), Pirates on
the High Seas, (index to pulp
magazine), by Darrell Richardson,
63 PU 38
Pirates on the High Seas, (index to
PIRATE STORIES pulp magazine and
HIGH SEAS ADVENTURE pulp magazine)
by Darrell Richardson, 63 PU 38
(Planet of Adventure series: Jack Vance),
Jack Vance's Planet of Adventure
Series, (science fiction paper-
backs), by George Kelley, 2-2 PQ 20
(PLANET STORIES magazine), An Index
to PLANET STORIES, (pulp magazine),
by Robert O'Malley, 20 X 42; 21 X 55;
22 X 48; 26 X 13
Plantation Novel, The: Paperback Genre
of the 1970s?, by Christopher D.
Geist, 3-1 PQ 42
Plass, Paul: Concerning Nena Sahib,
(NENA SAHIB: Sir John Retcliffe),
6-3 TAD 157
(play and games in detective fiction),
A Sense of the Under Toad: Play in
Mystery Fiction, by Joan B. Fiscella,
1-2 C 1
Play It Again, Sam Spade, (Humphrey
Bogart as Sam Spade), by Steve
Fisher, 5-2 TAD 79
Playedback...or Chandler's Los Angeles
Revisited, (Raymond Chandler), by
Paul Bishop, 5 PE 29
Playful Mysteries of Peter Dickinson,
The, by Earl F. Bargainnier, 13-3
TAD 185
Please Write for Details, (letters of
comment from readers), 6 JD 9;
7 JD 3; 8 JD 5; 9 JD 5; 10 JD 8;
11 JD 13; 12 JD 13; 13 JD 11;
14 JD 21; 15 JD 21; 16 JD 15;
17 JD 23; 18 JD 21; 19 JD 11;
20 JD 19; 21 JD 15; 22 JD 19;
24 JD 38; 25 JD 37; 26 JD 46;
27 JD 34; 28 JD 40
Pleasures of Writing Histo-Detection,
The, (writing historical mysteries),
by Lillian de la Torre, 7-3 TAD 155
PlecKovitch, (Mr. & Mrs.) Ed: letter
of comment, 1-3 TB 12
Plots for Sale - Cheap: Apply 221B,
(influence of Sherlock Holmes),
by Nathan L. Bengis, 1-4 TAD 116
Plow and the Horse, The, (fiction),
by Frederick Faust, 1-3 FC 1
Poage, William B.: Henty Hints, (on
boys' books by G.A.Henty), 1-2 BC 38

Pobst, Jim: letter of comment,
5-2 MR 16
Pobst, Jim: The Politics of Fu Manchu,
(Sax Rohmer stories), 10 R 9
(Pobst, Jim), Biographical Sketch,
10 R 30
Pocket Books, Checklist 1-500, (on
Pocket Book line of paperbacks),
by Hal Knott and Marvin Lachman,
1-6 MF 29
(Pocket Books), Spotlight: "Pockettes"
2-3 PQ 30
(Pocket Books - British), Britich
Pocket Books (Pocket Books, G.B.,
Ltd. line of paperbacks), by
Piet Schreuders, 3-1 CP 11
(Pockettes - pocket books), Spotlight:
"Pockettes", 2-3 PQ 30
Poe and the Detective Story, by J.R.
Christopher, 2-1 TAD 49
Poe on Trial, (whether Poe or Hoffman
was "father of the mystery story"),
by Sam Moskowitz, 4-1 TAD 10
(Poe, Edgar Allan), A Look at Dupin,
by Steve Miller, 2 MT 20
(Poe, Edgar Allan), A Portrait of Poe
and His Tales, by Frederick J.
Jaeger, 4-6 MR 20
(Poe, Edgar Allan), Poe and the
Detective Story, by J.R.Christopher,
2-1 TAD 49
(Poe, Edgar Allan), Poe on Trial,
(whether Poe or Hoffman was "father
of the mystery story"), by Sam
Moskowitz, 4-1 TAD 10
(Poe, Edgar Allan: "The Gold-Bug"),
Golden Beetles or Blue Bugs?
(R. Austin Freeman's "The Blue
Scarab" as a commentary on Poe's
"The Gold-Bug"), by Oliver Mayo,
11 TF 13
(POE MUST DIE: Mark Oldham), Mystery
Plus: Poe Must Die, by R. Jeff
Banks, 2-2 PP 12
Poetry Quiz, (mystery quiz), by R.W.
Hays, 5-4 TAD 215
(Poggioli, Professor, series: T.S.
Stribling), Checklist, by John
Nieminski, 6-1 TAD 55
(Poggioli, Professor, series: T.S.
Stribling), Life as a Series of
Abstract Analyses (discussion of
series with checklist), by Robert
Sampson, 2-2 C 61
(Poggioli, Professor, series: T.S.
Stribling), Rare Vintages from
the Tropics, T.S.Stribling's
CLUES OF THE CARRIBEES, by Frank
D. McSherry, Jr., 6-3 TAD 172
Pohl, Frederik: Where Have the Heroes
Gone? (on fictional heroes in the
pulp magazines), 67 PU 29
(Poirot, Hercule, series: Agatha
Christie), Hercule Poirot, The
Private Life of a Private Eye, by
Fred Dueren, 7-2 TAD 111

(Poland), Chinese Detectives in Poland,
(Polish translations and introduction),
by Everett F. Bleiler, 11-4 TAD 343

Poleske, Lee: Nero Wolfe Novels,
(commentary), 2 LW 2

Poleske, Lee: Nero Wolfe Paperbacks in
Print, (1975), 4 LW 2

Poleske, Lee: Nero Wolfe Quiz, (mystery
quiz), 1 LW 1; 2 LW 1; 3 LW 1;
4 LW 2; 5 LW 1; 6 LW 1

Poleske, Lee: Short Stories of Nero
Wolfe by Rex Stout, 3 LW 7

Police Are Always There, The: The Police
Procedural, Pt.IV, by George N. Dove,
11-1 TAD 74

Police in Society, the: The Novels of
Maj Sjowall and Per Wahloo, by Frank
Occhiogrosso, 12-2 TAD 174

(police - point of view), Hard Touch,
by Bill Wilson, 15 JD 15; 16 JD 8

Police Procedural, The, by George N.
Dove, Pt.I (Realism, Routine,
Stubbornness and System) 10-2 TAD 133;
Pt.II (The Cops and The Cop-Haters)
10-3 TAD 241; Pt.III (Brother Officers
Be Damned) 10-4 TAD 320; Pt.IV (The
Police Are Always There) 11-1 TAD 74;
Pt.V (The Tangled Emotions) 11-2 TAD
150; Pt.VI (The Rookie Type) 11-3
TAD 249

(police procedurals),The Enigma of the
Policeman/Writer, (novels written by
police personnel), by Paul Bishop,
2-1 M 34

(police procedurals),Eye-Q 4: Tour of
Duty, (mystery quiz), by Jonathon
Harrow, 2-1 M 42

(police procedurals), The Police Procedural, by George N. Dove, Pts.
I-VI, 10-2 TAD 133; 10-3 TAD 241;
10-4 TAD 320; 11-1 TAD 74; 11-2
TAD 150; 11-3 TAD 249

(police procedurals), Past-Mistress of
the Police Procedural, (on Elizabeth
Linington), by Ann Waldron, 3-5 MR 32

(police procedurals), Thomas Chastain
and the New Police Procedural, by
Larry L. French, 2-4 MF 17

(police procedurals), The Weevil in
Beancurd, or, The Cop Abroad, by
George N. Dove, 2-6 MF 17

Politics of Fu Manchu, The, (stories by
Sax Rohmer), by Jim Pobst, 10 R 9

Pollard, David: letter of comment,
7 PE 17

Pollard, David: The Private Eye on
Radio, 2 PE 14

Pollard, Percival: Lingo Dan, (Classic
Corner Rare Tales, fiction), 12-3
TAD 238

Poller, Marian: letter of comment,
5-3 TAD 172; 6-2 TAD 129

(Pollifax, Emily, series: Dorothy Gilman),
Checklist, Annotated, by Barry
Van Tilburg, 5-3 MF 19

Polyglot Mr. Rohmer, The, (Sax Rohmer),
by Jean Stafford, 14 R 1

(Pons, Solar, series: August Derleth),
A Flat in Paddington, (verse), by
Steve Eng, 3-3 AD 3

(Pons, Solar, series: August Derleth),
A Latter Holmes, by Bruce Kennedy,
1-3 PD 1

(Pons, Solar, series: August Derleth),
A Selection from the Pontine Weapon
Gallery, by Roger Johnson, 2-1
PDA 15

(Pons, Solar, series: August Derleth),
A Sherlocko-Pontine Addendum, by
J.R.Christopher, 2-1 PD 3

(Pons, Solar, series: August Derleth),
The Adventure of the Pastiche
Craftsman, (on Derleth writing the
Pons canon), by A.E.van Vogt, 2-1
PD 1

(Pons, Solar, series: August Derleth),
Being An Examination of the Ponsian
and Holmesian Secret Deductive
Systems, by A.E.van Vogt, 1-2 PDA
52

(Pons, Solar, series: August Derleth),
Call to Conclave, (founding of the
Praed Street Ireegulars), by Alvin
F. Germeshausen, 1-1 PD 1

(Pons, Solar, series: August Derleth),
The Case of the Blind Clairaudient,
A Critical Study, by Bruno Lumbroso,
3-1 PDA 32

(Pons, Solar, series: August Derleth),
Chant Royal of the Sodality of
Praed Street Irregulars, (verse),
by Michael Harrison, 1-1 PDA 2

(Pons, Solar, series: August Derleth),
Concerning the Problem of the Man with the Broken
Face, by Roger Johnson, 1-1 PDA 32

(Pons, Solar, series: August Derleth),
Crumbs for a Toast to Solar Pons,
by Robert Bloch, 1-2 PDA 42

(Pons, Solar, series: August Derleth),
The Curious Case of the Croyden
Crossing, by David Galerstein,
1-1 PDA 18

(Pons, Solar, series: August Derleth),
The Curious Route of the Orient
Express, by David Galerstein,
3-1 PDA 24

(Pons, Solar, series: August Derleth),
Dinner at the Diogenes Club,
(puzzle), by Ted Schulz, 2-1 PDA 33

(Pons, Solar, series: August Derleth),
Dogging the Footsteps of Solar
Pons, by Jean Cox, 1-1 PDA 9

(Pons, Solar, series: August Derleth),
Exquisite Perquisite, by Helen
Halbach, 2-5 PD 4

(Pons, Solar, series: August Derleth),
The Fatal Glance, by Bruno Lumbroso,
3-2 PDA 24

(Pons, Solar, series: August Derleth),
First Annual PSI Dinner, 1-2 PD 1

(Pons, Solar, series: August Derleth),
Great Detectives, by George T. Hamilton,
4-2 AD 6

(Pons, Solar, series: August Derleth),
The Humbugging of Solar Pons, (as
by "Ebenezer Snawley", revisions made
by Mycroft & Moran, publishers), by
Jon L. Lellenberg, 3-2 PDA 11

(Pons, Solar, series: August Derleth),
In the Master's Footsteps, by Bruce
Dettman, 1-2 PD 1

(Pons, Solar, series: August Derleth),
The Infallible Boswell, Lyndon
Parker, M.D., by Cecil A. Ryder,
3-1 PDA 15

(Pons, Solar, series: August Derleth),
James and Lestrade, A Comparative
Study, by John McGoldrick, 1-4 PD 1

(Pons, Solar, series: August Derleth),
Knowledge of the Occult: Immense,
by Jon L. Lellenberg, 2-2 PDA 52

(Pons, Solar, series: August Derleth),
The Language of the Praed Street
Irregulars, (glossary), by Michael
Harrison, 2-4 PD 1

(Pons, Solar, series: August Derleth),
The Lighted Bridge of Detection
(on the name: Solar Pons), by Raymond
M. Funk, 2-1 PDA 25

(Pons, Solar, series: August Derleth),
The Maxims of Solar Pons, by Brian
Rountree, 1-1 PDA 31; 1-2 PDA 56;
2-1 PDA 24; 2-2 PDA 62

(Pons, Solar, series: August Derleth),
May I Say a Few Well-Chosen Words,
(on the Praed Street Irregulars),
by Alfred Peake, 2-5 PD 1

(Pons, Solar, series: August Derleth),
More from Dr. Parker's Notebooks,
by August Derleth, 1-2 PDA 43

(Pons, Solar, series: August Derleth),
The Most Wanted Man, by Mark Levy,
2-4 PD 1

(Pons, Solar, series: August Derleth),
Now It Can Be Told: The Secret of
the Pons, by Frank D. McSherry, Jr.
1-2 PDA 57

(Pons, Solar, series: August Derleth),
Oft Have I Travelled, by Philip
Jose Farmer, 2-2 PD 1

(Pons, Solar, series: August Derleth),
The Old Doctor of Limehouse, (Dr.F
from the stories), by Charles R.L.
Power, 2-2 PD 4

(Pons, Solar, series: August Derleth),
The Pontine Canon: A Selective
Commentary, by Roger Johnson,
3-1 PDA 37

(Pons, Solar, series: August Derleth),
The Pontine Canon, (key to identify
stories), by Peter A. Ruber, 1-2
PD 4

(Pons, Solar, series: August Derleth),
Pontine Patter, by Kay Price,
1-1 PDA 16; (letter from "Dr. John
Watney") 2-1 PDA 12; 2-1 PD 4

(Pons, Solar, series: August Derleth),
Praed Street: East of the Sun and
West of the Moon, by Fredrick
Shroyer, 3-2 AD 1; 3-1 PDA 3

(Pons, Solar, series: August Derleth),
The Praed Street Irregulars, by
August Derleth, 1-2 MR 7

(Pons, Solar, series: August Derleth),
Praed Street Irregulars as Listed
in ENCYCLOPEDIA OF ASSOCIATIONS,
2-2 PDA 72

(Pons, Solar, series: August Derleth),
Praedian Reflections, by A.E.van
Vogt, 3-2 PDA 26

(Pons, Solar, series: August Derleth),
Reminiscences of Praed Street, by
Commander Cecil A. Ryder, Jr.,USNR,
2-1 PDA 38

(Pons, Solar, series: August Derleth),
The Rival of Sherlock Holmes, by
Karen Randrup, 3-1 PDA 26

(Pons, Solar, series: August Derleth),
Sherlocko-Pontine Parallels,
1-4 PD 3

(Pons, Solar, series: August Derleth),
Singular Malady of Septimus Grayle,
(in "The Tottenham Werewolf") by
Bruce Dettman, 2-3 PD 1

(Pons, Solar, series: August Derleth),
Solar Pons and Basil Copper, (on
the continuation of the canon by
Basil Copper), by Michael L. Cook,
7 U 29

(Pons, Solar, series: August Derleth),
Some Further Jottings from the
Notebooks of Dr. Lyndon Parker,
by August Derleth, 1-1 PDA 3

Pontine Canon, The: A Selective
Commentary, (on the Solar Pons
stories), by Roger Johnson, 3-1
PDA 37

Pontine Canon, The, (key to identify
Solar Pons stories), by Peter A.
Riber, 1-2 PD 4

Pontine Patter, (news and notes),
(Praed Street Irregulars) by Kay
Price, 1-1 PDA 16; (3rd Annual
PSI meeting) by Luther Norris,
2-1 PD 4; (letter from "Dr. John
Watney"), 2-1 PDA 12; (Praed Street
Irregulars listed in Encyclopedia
of Associations) 2-2 PDA 72

Pony Books Checklist, (list of paperback
line), by Lance Casebeer, 1-1 CP 21

Poole, Beula: What to Expect, (Nero
Wolfe news notes), 1-1 G 53

Popple, E.E.: letter of comment,
3-1 TAD 68; 3-3 TAD 208

Poppy Ott Sequel to Popular Todd
Series, (refers to earlier boys'
series, Jerry Todd, by Leo
Edwards), by Julius R. Chenu,
1-3 TBN 1

(Popular Culture Association) The
Brotherhood Makes History, by Francis
M. Nevins, Jr., 5-1 TAD 28

(Popular Culture Association), Pulp
    Tradition in Mystery Fiction, (panel
    discussion, 1972, Francis M. Nevins,
    Jr., Donald A. Yates, and George
    Grella), 6-3 TAD 133
(Popular Culture Association), Social
    and Political Images in American
    Crime Fiction, (panel discussion,
    1971), by Francis M. Nevins, Jr.,
    5-2 TAD 61
Popular Library Books, (Popular Library
    paperback line), by Bill Pronzini,
    2-1 CP 7
Popular Library Short Story Collections,
    by Howard Waterhouse, 2-1 CP 12
Popular Library vs. Art, (on cover art
    of Popular Library paperbacks), by
    Bruce Merrill, 2-1 CP 20
(Popular Library), A Crime Club Selection
    (paperbacks, Popular Library line),
    by M.C.Hill, 2-5 CP 14
(Popular Library), Checklist, Nos.1-200,
    (paperbacks), by Richard C. Butler,
    1-3 MF 5
(Popular Library), The Killian Memoranda,
    (Popular Library science fiction),
    by Dave Killian, 2-1 CP 17
(Popular Library), Living With the
    Paperback Book Collector, (on
    collecting Popular Library line),
    by Mardi Kirklin, 2-1 CP 19
(Popular Library), Popular Library vs.
    Art, (on cover art of Popular
    Library line), by Bruce Merrill,
    2-1 CP 20
(Popular Library), Rare Books are
    Getting Scarce, (Popular Library
    mysteries), by Bruce Taylor, 2-1
    CP 15
(Popular Library), Who Drew That Girl?
    (Popular Library cover artists), by
    Lance Casebeer, 2-1 CP 21
(Popular Library), Denholms Law #5,
    (on Popular Library cover art), by
    Bill Denholm, 2-1 CP 25
Popular Publications, The, (chronological
    list of titles of pulp magazines and
    comments by publisher Steeger), by
    Henry Steeger, 67 PU 39
Popular Publications, A Brief Analysis,
    (pulp magazine publisher), by Nils
    Hardin, 33 X 2
Popular Publications, A Checklist of
    Titles 1930-1955, (pulp magazines
    with bibliographical data), by Nils
    Hardin and George Hocutt, 33 X 21
Popular Publications, A Pictorial
    History, (pulp magazine covers
    illustrated), by Nils Hardin, 33 X 25
Popular Publications, An Interview with
    Henry Steeger, (as President and
    publisher; pulp magazines), by Nils
    Hardin, 33 X 3

(Popular Publications), The Weird
    Menace Magazines, (including those
    published by Popular Publications;
    pulp magazines), by Robert Kenneth
    Jones, 10 BS 3; 11 BS 7; 12 BS 7;
    13 BS 7; 14 BS 13; 15 BS 4
(pornography - science fiction), Science
    Fiction Pornography, (with checklist),
    by Kenneth R. Johnson, 4 SF 4;
    5 SF 45
(Porter, Dave, series), Boys' Book
    Oddities: Dave Porter Series, by
    Harry K. Hudson, 3-1 BC 285
(Porter, Joyce), Crime With a Smile,
    (interview with Joyce Porter), by
    Luther Norris, 3-2 MR 18
Portrait of a Pulpster, (sketch and
    comments of Ryerson Johnson, pulp
    author), by Wooda Nicholas Carr,
    14 SF 2
Portrait of a Tough Guy, (sketch and
    comments on Raymond Chandler), by
    William F. Nolan, 38 X 13
Portser, Elinor: letter of comment,
    2-3 MF 72; 1-1 PP 28
(Post, Melville Davisson), THE COMPLETE
    UNCLE ABNER, Special review article,
    by Martin Morse Wooster, 2-5 MF 9
(Post, Melville Davisson), The Randolph
    Mason Stories, by Charles A. Norton,
    6-2 TAD 86
(Potter, Hiram, series: Rae Foley),
    Series Synopses, by John Vining,
    10-2 TAD 188
Potter, (Mrs.) J.L.: letter of comment,
    13 JD 19; 16 JD 23; 20 JD 22
Potter, Margaret: letter of comment,
    5/6 MN 16; 7 MN 7; 6 MY 8; 7 MY 12
Potter, Nancy: letter of comment,
    7 JD 9; 11 JD 19
(Potthoff, Willis), Book Sellers Under
    the Big Top, (boys' books),
    3-3 BC 322
Potts, Sam: Confessions of a Pulp
    Eater, (fiction, pulp style),
    13 BS 3
Potts, Sam: letter of comment, 6 BS 20;
    6 BS 21; 8 BS 3
Potts, Samuel W.: The Man of Bronze -
    and His Creator, (on Lester Dent's
    Doc Savage), 2 BS 8
Potts, Samuel W.: What Will TV Do to
    Doc Savage? (difficulty in depicting),
    6 BS 6
Potts, Samuel W.: The Wonderful World
    of Street & Smith (during the pulp
    era; publishers), 4 BS 12
Powe, Bruce: letter of comment,
    21 JD 18
(Powell, Richard: Andy & Arabella Blake
    series), Checklist, Annotated, by
    Barry Van Tilburg, 4-6 MF 6

Powell, Robert S.: Including Murder, An
Unpublished Hammett Collection,
(manuscript material), 2-2 C 135

Power, Charles R.L. The Old Doctor of
Limehouse, (Dr.F of Solar Pons
stories), 2-2 PD 4

Powers, Douglas: letter of comment,
7-2 TAD 148

Pow-Wow on the Potomac, A Report on
Bouchercon XI, (mystery fans and
authors convention), by John Nieminski,
4-6 MF 12

PQ Interview with Jada Davis, (PAPERBACK
QUARTERLY magazine conducting interview), 1-2 PQ 45; (with Bruno Fischer),
1-4 PQ 26; (with William Campbell
Gault), 2-2 PQ 8; (with E. Howard Hunt),
2-1 PQ 11; (with Elmer Kelton), 1-2
PQ 18; (with Norman Saunders) 1-3
PQ 38; (with Harry Whittington),
1-1 PQ 13; (with Donald A. Wollheim),
1-3 PQ 23

PQ Recommends, (recommendations for mystery
magazines, by PAPERBACK QUARTERLY), 2-1
PQ 56

Praed of Praeds, The, (biographical sketch,
Winthrop Mackworth Praed), by Michael
Harrison, 1-1 PD 1

Praed Street - East of the Sun and West of
the Moon, (re: Solar Pons), by Frederick
Shroyer, 3-2 AD 1; 3-1 PD 3

Praed Street Irregulars, The, (group to
honor and study Solar Pons), by August
Derleth, 1-2 MR 7

(Praed Street Irregulars), An Evening
With the Praed Street Irregulars at
the Greater Los Angeles Press Club,
(Solar Pons fan society), 3-1 PDA 22

(Praed Street Irregulars), Call to
Conclave, (founding of the Praed Street
Irregulars, Solar Pons fan society),
by Alvin F. Germeshausen, 1-1 PD 1

(Praed Street Irregulars), Chant Royal of
the Sodality of Praed Street Irregulars,
(verse), by Michael Harrison, 1-1 PDA 2

(Praed Street Irregulars), First Annual
PSI Dinner, (report, Solar Pons fan
society), 1-2 PD 1

(Praed Street Irregulars), The Language
of the Praed Street Irregulars,
(glossary, Solar Pons fan society),
by Michael Harrison, 2-4 PD 1

(Praed Street Irregulars), Listed in
ENCYCLOPEDIA OF ASSOCIATIONS,
2-2 PDA 72

(Praed Street Irregulars), May I Say a
Few Well-chosen Words, by Alfred
Peake, 2-5 PD 1

(Praed Street Irregulars), Pontine Patter,
by Kay Price, 1-1 PDA 16

(Praed, Winthrop Mackworth), The Praed of
Praeds, (bio. sketch), by Michael
Harrison, 1-1 PD 1

Praedian Reflections, (Solar Pons), by
A.E.van Vogt, 3-2 PDA 26

Prael, John W., Jr., letter of comment,
3-2 TAD 138

Pratt, Allan D.: The Chronology of
the Travis McGee Novels, (of John
D. MacDonald), 13-2 TAD 83

Preliminary Regency Checklist, (on
Regency paperback books), by
Tom Whitmore, 15 SF 19

Prentice, Anna: letter of comment,
1-1 PP 27

Presidency and the Mystery Story, The,
(Presidents as readers, authors,
fans, and characters), by Marvin
Lachman, 2-3 M 6

(PRESIDENT VANISHES, THE: Rex Stout),
Film Note, by Louis Black,
9 MN A60

PRESIDENT'S MYSTERY STORY, THE - A
Review, (article commentary), by
Philip T. Asdell, 2-4 PP 11

Previews from the Publisher, (on
John D. MacDonald books), by David
Stewart, 18 JD 9

Prey and Tell, (mystery news), by
Michael L. Cook, 12 LR 18

(price guides), A Review from the
Microcosm, (re: Resnick's Price
Guide), by Marvin Morrison,28 X 7

(price guides), An Explanation of
Sorts, or, Why Your Universe Will
Not Come to An End, by Mike
Resnick, 26 X 14

(price guides), Hancer's Price Guide,
by Don Z. Block, 2-5 CP 24

(price guides), Why I Love the American
Comic Book Company's 1980 Paperback
Catalog, by Don Z. Block, 2-2 CP 7

(price guides), A Partial History of
Pulp Prices 1946-1973, 24 X 40

(price guides), Comment, by Don
Hutchison, 24 X 43

(price guides), Minter Speaks Up!,
by Richard Minter, 24 X 11

(Price, Anthony: David Audley and
Colonel Butler series), Checklist,
Annotated, by Barry Van Tilburg,
4-6 MF 6

Price, E. Hoffman: A Memoir, 1 WT 4

Price, E. Hoffman: letter of comment,
4 WT 12; 6 WT 31; 18 X 33;
26 X 76

Price, E. Hoffman: Reminiscences and
a Caution, (re: August Derleth),
2-3/4 AD 11

(Price, E. Hoffman), The Derleth
Connection: E. Hoffman Price,
3-4 AD 10; 4-1 AD 8

(Price, E. Hoffman), The Raconteur
of Emerald Lake, by Thomas Kent
Miller and Gary von Tersch, 6 WT 3

Price, Jack: letter of comment,
8 X 38

Price, Kay: Pontine Patter, (the
Praed Street Irregulars), 1-1 PDA 16

Price, Kay: The Wood Engraver from
Mazomanie, (Frank Utpatel),
4-3 AD 1

Prichard, Michael: letter of comment,
10-3 TAD 273

(Pride, Jeff, series: Jim Henaghan),
    "Archie O'Neill" - Jim Henaghan -
    The Jeff Pride Series, by Bill
    Crider, 4 PE 15
(Priestley, J.B.), Three British Experi-
    ments from the Mainstream (mainstream
    authors as mystery writers), by
    Charles Shibuk, 3-2 TAD 80
(Primrose, Col. John, detective: Leslie
    Ford), The First Appearance, (in
    THE STRANGLED WITNESS: Ford), by
    Maryell Cleary, 3-4 PP 23
Prince, J.: letter of comment, 7 JD 7;
    16 JD 19; 17 JD 24
Printing Variations in the Andy Blake
    Series, (bibliographical data,
    boys' books series by Leo Edwards),
    by Julius R. Chenu, 1-1 TBN 5
Private Eye, The: Enduring as a $1.29
    Steak, (characteristics), by Richard
    S. Lochte II, 3-2 TAD 117
Private Eye in an Evil Time: Mark
    Sadler's Paul Shaw, by Francis M.
    Nevins, Jr., 38 X 11
Private Eyes, Who or What Are They?,
    by Mary Ann Grochowski, 5 PE 13
Private Life of Father Brown, The,
    (Father Brown series by G.K.
    Chesterton), by R.W.Hays, 4-3
    TAD 135
Prize Science-Fiction Novels, (check-
    list of Prize line of paperbacks),
    by J. Grant Thiessen, 2 SF 13
Problem of Moral Vision in Dashiell
    Hammett's Detective Novels, The, by
    George J. Thompson, 6-3 TAD 153;
    6-4 TAD 214; 7-1 TAD 32; 7-3 TAD
    178; 7-4 TAD 270; 8-1 TAD 27; 8-2
    TAD 124
(Probyn, Julia, series: Ann Bridge),
    Checklist, Annotated, by Barry
    Van Tilburg, 5-3 MF 20
Profession of Henry Baker, The, (re:
    Sherlock Holmes), by Dean & Shirley
    Dickensheet, 1-1 PDA 36
Professional Sleuth of Roy Winsor, The,
    (Professor Ira Cobb, detective), by
    Larry L. French, 2-1 MF 3
Professor Without a Pseudonym, Robert
    B. Parker, author), by Larry L.
    French, 2-2 MF 12
(Professor Challenger: A. Conan Doyle),
    The Real Professor Challenger, by
    Dana Martin Batory, 13 SF 42
(PROFESSOR KNITS A SHROUD, THE: Martha
    Wirt Davis), The Adventure of the
    Purloined Red Herring, by Edward
    Lauterbach, 3-5 PP 3
Profile: ALFRED HITCHCOCK'S MYSTERY
    MAGAZINE, by Paul Taublieb, 2-3 M 34
Programmed Writing of Dean R. Koontz,
    The, by George Kelley, 1-4 MF 11
Projected Detective, The, (mystery on
    television), by Andy Jaysnovitch,
    8 CL 6; (MALTESE FALCON) 12 CL 8

Prolegomena to a Bibliography of the
    Immortal Works of Leslie Charteris,
    by J. Randolph Cox, 5-2 MR 9
Prolific, (on the works of Harry
    St.George Rathborne), by J.Edward
    Leithead, 2-1 BC 142
Prolificity Pays - John Creasey,
    (on the work of John Creasey), by
    Granville Wilson, 4-5 MR 8
Pronzini, Bill: Ante-Bellem Days, or,
    "My Roscoe Sneezed Ka-chee!",
    (Robert Leslie Bellem's influence
    on pulp detective fiction), 2-2
    C 41
Pronzini, Bill: Checklist, Evan
    Hunter, 5-3 TAD 131
Pronzini, Bill: letter of comment,
    11 MN L14; 5-2 MR 17; 7 MY 13;
    3 PE 33; 1-3 PQ 8; 2-3 PP 39;
    3-1 PP 41; 3-2 PP 32; 3-3 PP 36;
    2-2 TAD 131; 4-4 TAD 257; 5-2
    TAD 115; 5-3 TAD 184; 6-1 TAD
    60; 9-2 TAD 158; 10-3 TAD 273;
    12-3 TAD 268; 14-1 TAD 73
Pronzini, Bill: The "Mystery" Career
    of Evan Hunter, 5-3 TAD 129
Pronzini, Bill: Paperback Originals,
    Addendum, (paperbacks as original
    edition), 5-2 MR 17
Pronzini, Bill: Popular Library Books,
    (Popular Library line of paperbacks),
    2-1 CP 7
Pronzini, Bill: The Saga of the Phoenix;
    That Probably Should Never Have
    Arisen, (mysteries by Phoenix Press),
    10-2 TAD 106
Pronzini, Bill: The World of Monarch,
    (Monarch Books), 1-4 CP 13
Pronzini, Bill: The Worst Mystery
    Novel of All Time (Michael Morgan:
    DECOY), 13-2 TAD 137
Pronzini, Bill, and John Lutz: Tiger,
    Tiger, (fiction), 3-2 M 14
Pronzini, Bill, and Francis M. Nevins,
    Jr.: Bill Pronzini, A Checklist,
    (and introduction), 13-4 TAD 345
(Pronzini, Bill), An Interview with
    Bill Pronzini, by Robert J.
    Randisi, 11-1 TAD 46
(Pronzini, Bill), Bill Pronzini
    Revisited, by George Kelley,
    2-5 MF 5
(Pronzini, Bill), Bill Pronzini, A
    Checklist (and Introduction), by
    Bill Pronzini and Francis M. Nevins,
    Jr., 13-4 TAD 345
(Pronzini, Bill), Conversation,
    (interview), by Don Cole, 1-6 PP 11
(Pronzini, Bill), The Suspense Novels
    of Bill Pronzini, by George Kelley,
    1-2 MF 15
(Pronzini, Bill: A KILLING IN XANADU),
    Pronzini, Nameless, and a Limited
    Edition, by Douglas Greene,4-2
    PP 11

Pronzini, Nameless, and a Limited Edition, (Bill Pronzini: A KILLING IN XANADU), by Douglas Greene, 4-2 PP 11

Prophet Before the Fact: A Note on John D. MacDonald's THE END OF THE NIGHT, by Veronica M.S.Kennedy, 7-1 TAD 41

(Propper, Milton), Checklist of the Novels of Milton Propper, by Francis M. Nevins, Jr., 10-3 TAD 203

(Propper, Milton), The World of Milton Propper, by Francis M. Nevins, Jr., 10-3 TAD 197

Pross, Peter N.: letter of comment, 1-1 MF 46; 1-5 MF 57; 2-1 MF 57; 2-2 MF 53; 2-3 PP 43; 11-3 TAD 213

Pross, Peter N.: Raymond Chandler on Film, An Annotated Checklist, 1-6 MF 3; (screenplays written by Chandler) 2-3 MF 27

(Pross, Peter N.), Biographical Sketch, 2-3 PP 88

Prosser, Dave: Art Portfolio, "Air War 1914-18", 66 PU 17; 67 PU 83

Prosser, Dave: "The Blue Max" (observations on the World War I aircraft used in the film), 66 PU 5

Prosser, Dave: The War in the Air, 1914-1918, (historical review of the aviation aspects), 66 PU 29; 67 PU 83

Pruitt, B.H.: Georges Simenon, (sketch), 3-3 PP 12

Pry, Elmer R., Jr.: Lew Archer's "Moral Landscape", (detective character of Ross Macdonald), 8-1 TAD 104

Pry, Elmer R., Jr.: letter of comment, 8-3 TAD 239

Pseudonymous Lovecraft, The, (H.P.Lovecraft), by George Wetzel, 28 X 3

(pseudonyms), A Name is a Name, by Richard Gehman, 1-4 MR 15

(pseudonyms), List of author's pen names in letter of M.C.Hill, 14-4 TAD 381

(pseudonyms), The Mysteries of the Pseudonymous Professors, (anonymity required), by Joseph Barbato, 1-4 MF 3

(pseudonyms), Rare Books are Getting Scarce, (mystery authors and their pseudonyms), by Bruce Taylor, 1-5 CP 15

(pseudonyms), Who Really Wrote It?, (pseudonyms of mystery authors), by Harold Knott, 3-6 MR 2

(PUBLIC ENEMY magazine), G-77 in Public Enemy #1, (pulp magazine), Bryan James Kelley, 2 P 14

Publishers' Codes and Collecting Contemporary Editions, (identification of 1st and subsequent editions by use of publishers' codes), by Keith L. Justice, 11 SF 23

Puechner, Ray: Jack Ritchie, An Interview, 6-1 TAD 12

Pulfer, Harry: letter of comment, 1-2 BC 62

Pulfer, Harry: Memories on Which I Dwell Fondly, (reminiscences on reading boys' books), 1-3 BC 89

Pulp, (overview of pulp magazine entertainment in graphic assessment), by Robert Sampson, 22 X 55

Pulp Artist - Norman Saunders, (personal reminiscences by Saunders with introduction by Nils Hardin), 33 X 116

Pulp Career of Nicholas Carter, The, (Nick Carter, detective), by J. Randolph Cox, 22 X 15

Pulp Collecting - For Fun or Fortune?, by Rusty Hevelin, 24 X 5

Pulp Corner, The, (column of pulp magazine data, reminiscences, and collecting experiences), by Wooda Nicholas Carr and Robert Sampson, 15 SF 8; (Memoirs of a Doc Savage Reader) 14 SF 21

Pulp Fiction - Yesterday and Today, (change in quality of pulp prose), by Wilkie Connor, 67 PU 45

Pulp Gallery, The, (checklist, cover art by H.W.Wessolowski), 6 P 16

Pulp Hero Quiz, (quiz), by G. Alan, 11 BS 13

Pulp Information Center, (biblio. data column, with replies to submitted problems), 15 X 48; 16 X 4; 17 X 58; 18 X 28; 19 X 38; 20 X 40; 21 X 9; 22 X 46; 24 X 37; 26 X 68; 28 X 71; 30 X 137; 33 X 118; 36 X 69; 38 X 142

Pulp Library, The, (bibliographic data and detailed synopsis of various pulp magazines and pulp characters), by Robert Sampson, 30 X 21; 33 X 111; 38 X 131; 42 X 131

Pulp Literature: Subculture Revolution in the Late 1930s, (and on Roger Torrey, author), by Steve Fisher, 5-2 TAD 91

Pulp Notes, by Robert Weinberg, 3 P 38; 10 P 36

Pulp Notes: Doc Savage Magazines, by Tom Johnson, 7 DQ 15

Pulp Paper Master Fiction Plot, The, (formula for writing pulp fiction), by Lester Dent, 12 BS 15

Pulp Perspective Plus, (on writing pulp fiction), by John D. MacDonald, 7 BS 3

Pulp Quiz, (quiz based on pulp magazines) by G. Alan, 14 BS 12; 15 BS 18

Pulp Quiz, (quiz based on pulp magazines) by Robert Weinberg, 2 P 18; 3 P 27; 10 P 31; 5 P 19

Pulp Reincarnation, The, (editorial), by Wooda Nicholas Carr, 10 X 10

Pulp Review, The: Comments on an issue
of TEXAS RANGERS, (pulp magazine),
by Lynn Hickman, 71 PU 7

Pulp Tradition in Mystery Fiction, (panel
discussion, Popular Culture Association
1972), by Francis M. Nevins, Jr.,
George Grella, and Donald A. Yates,
6-3 TAD 133

Pulp Villains, The, (master villains in
the pulp magazines), by Wooda Nicholas
Carr, 42 X 126; (Tang-Akhmut, The Man
from the East, in THE SPIDER), 5 DS 10

Pulpcon 3, (convention report), 6 P 32

Pulpcon 4, (convention report, with
photos), by Nils Hardin, 15 X 47

Pulpcon 8 - The Impressions of a First
Timer, (convention report), by
Albert Tonik, 3 U 9

Pulpcon 1973, Special Issue of PULP,
(entire), 5A P entire

(Pulpcon 9), A Report on Pulpcon 9,
(convention report), by Albert Tonik,
14 SF 15

Pulps, The, I Loved Them! (literary and
personal reminiscences), by Herman S.
McGregor, 67 PU 36

Pulps and American History, The; An
Informal Comment, by Link Hullar,
6 DS 10

Pulps, Day Dreams for the Masses, by
Marcus Duffield, 33 X 108

Pulpster Profile: Visit with Donald Barr
Chidsey, (author), by Alvin H. Lybeck,
5 U 17

Pulpsters, Ltd., (coterie of pulp fans),
by Ginger Johnson, 2 PW 2

Pulpwoody News Items, (comments and news
on pulp-magazine related items),
1 PW 3; 2 PW 3

Pulpy Eyes, (various, private eye
detectives in the pulps), by Tom
Fisher, 3 PE 30; 4 PE 25; 6 PE 23

Pun Detective and the Great Seal Mystery,
The, (fiction), by Jon L. Breen,
7 CL 3

Purcell, James Mark: A Note on Rufus King's
Series Short Stories, (with checklist),
12-4 TAD 380

Purcell, James Mark: All Good Mysteries
are Short Stories, A Polemic, (the
advantages of short story form),
4-6 MR 23

Purcell, James Mark: The "Amanda Cross"
Mystery - Sociologizing the U.S.
Academic Mystery, 13-1 TAD 36

Purcell, James Mark: Checklist, Double-C
Stories by Edward D. Hoch, 5-2 MR 43

Purcell, James Mark: Coffee in the Lab,
A Preliminary Bibliongraphy, (Dr.
Coffee series: Lawrence Blochman),
4-3 MR 29

Purcell, James Mark: Controversy,11-4
TAD 398

Purcell, James Mark: Higgledy-Piggledies,
(verse), 5-4 TAD 203

Purcell, James Mark: Humphrey Bogart,
Some Remarks on the Canonization
Process, (the developing Bogart
popularity) 11-1 TAD 6; (rebuttal,
see 11-2 TAD 186)

Purcell, James Mark: letter of comment,
4-1 MR 20; 4-5 MR 17; 9-3 TAD
236; 10-1 TAD 3; 11-3 TAD 212

Purcell, James Mark: Lillian de la
Torre, Preliminary Bibliography -
Blood on the Periwigs, 4-5 MR 25

Purcell, James Mark: Mystery Reviewers
Handbook - Dashiell Hammett 1894-
1961, (verse), 7-4 TAD 282

Purcell, James Mark: Obituary of Fritz
Lang, 9-4 TAD 288

Purcell, James Mark: The Reggie Fortune
Short Stories, An Appreciation and
Partial Bibliography, (with addn'l
bibliography data by Francis M.
Nevins,Jr.), 5-4 MR 1

Purcell, James Mark: Roy Vickers, The
Department of Dead Ends Series - A
Partial Bibliography, 4-1 MR 29

(Purcell James Mark), Garfield for
the Defense: Purcell vs. Bogart,
(rebuttal to Purcell's article,
11-1 TAD 6), 11-2 TAD 186

(puzzle), Dinner at the Diogenes
Club, (based on Solar Pons), by
Ted Schulz, 2-1 PDA 33

(puzzle), Doc's Adventures Search,
(based on Doc Savage), by Dan
Bishop, 5 DS 22

(puzzle), Doc's Villainous Foes
Search Puzzle, (based on Doc
Savage), by Jerry Schneiderman,
3 DS 15

(puzzle), Find the Name Puzzle,
(mystery puzzle), by Linda Gambino,
9-1 TAD 58

(puzzle), The Kid Glove Kid, (mystery
puzzle), 12-1 TAD 62

(puzzle), Mystery Puzzle, (based on
Dashiell Hammett), 3-2 M 24

(puzzle), Pen Puzzler: The Personal
Touch, (mystery puzzle), by Jim
McCahery, 1-4 PP 7

(puzzle), Super Sleuths, (mystery
puzzle), by Louis Phillips,
12-3 TAD 208

(puzzle), This Gun for Hire, (mystery
puzzle), 14-2 TAD 143

(puzzle), Who's Who, (mystery puzzle),
by Stanley A. Carlin, 4-6 MR 14

(puzzle), see: crossword puzzle;
quiz

Puzzled?, (paperback book collecting
acrostic puzzle), by Lance
Casebeer, 1-2 CP 24

(Pyne, Parker, detective: Agatha
Christie), Agatha Christie's Other
Detectives, Parker Pyne and Harley
Quin, by Earl F. Bargainnier,
11-2 TAD 110

(Pyramid Books), Checklist, The Green Door
Mysteries, (digest-size paperback books
series by Pyramid Books), by Howard
Waterhouse, 1-2 PQ 40
(Pyramid Books), The Green Door Mystery,
(Green Door series of digest-size
paperbacks published by Pyramid),
by Howard Waterhouse, 1-2 PQ 39
(Pyramid Books), Pyramid Reissues of
Fu Manchu, (paperback reprints of
series by Pyramid Books), by Robert E.
Briney, 15 R 29
(Pyramid Books), Rare Books are Getting
Scarce: Green Door Mysteries, (Green
Door series of digest-size paperbacks
by Pyramid), by Bruce Taylor, 3-2
CP 29
(Pyramid Books), Reprints of Fu Manchu
Series, (paperback reprints of series
by Pyramid Books, checklist), by
Robert E. Briney, 9-4 TAD 247
Pyramid Reissues of Fu Manchu, (paperback
reprints of series by Pyramid Books),
by Robert E. Briney, 15 R 29

Quacks in the Quorum, The, (fugitive books
in basic mystery checklist, QUEEN'S
QUORUM), by Adrian Goldstone, 12-3
TAD 226
Queen Canon, The: A Fragmentary Fraction,
(on Ellery Queen), by Rev. Robert E.
Washer, 1-4 MR 7
(Queen, Ellery), A Case of Double Identity,
(Dannay and Lee as "Ellery Queen"
author), 3-2 QC 11
(Queen, Ellery), A Partial Check List,
by Rev. Robert E. Washer, 1-4 MR 9
(Queen, Ellery), A Queen Quandary Quickly
Quavered in Quondam Quixotic Quotations,
by Michael Murphy, 14 X 2
(Queen, Ellery), A Tribute to Ellery Queen
on His Fortieth Birthday, by Donald A.
Yates, 2-4 TAD 250
(Queen, Ellery), An Editor's Outline, by
Rev. Robert E. Washer, 1-3 QC 23
(Queen, Ellery), The Case of the Missing
Article, (Ellery Queen in GOOD HOUSE-
KEEPING magazine), by J.R.Christopher,
2-1 QC 14
(Queen, Ellery), Challenge to the Reader,
(Ellery Queen a bigamist?), by J.R.
Christopher, 1-2 QC 11
(Queen, Ellery), Challenge to the Reader
(link to HALFWAY HOUSE?), by Donald
A. Yates, 1-3 QC 12
(Queen, Ellery), Challenges to the
Listener, (Ellery Queen on radio),
by Chris Steinbrunner, 12-3 TAD 214
(Queen, Ellery), The Comic Book Adventures
of Ellery Queen, (Queen in comics), by
Ron Goulart, 12-3 TAD 197
(Queen, Ellery), Cross Trumps, (Ellery
Queen and Rex Stout), by J.R.Christopher,
2-2 QC 6

(Queen, Ellery), Cross Trumps: A
Conjectural Note on Rex Stout and
Ellery Queen, by Allen J. Hubin,
1-1 TAD 9
(Queen, Ellery), Editor at Work, Ellery
Queen and ELLERY QUEEN'S MYSTERY
MAGAZINE, by Francis M. Nevins, Jr.,
14 X 4
(Queen, Ellery), Ellery Queen: A Check-
list, by John J. Newton, 1-3 QC 13
(Queen, Ellery), Ellery Queen and His
New York, by Marvin Lachman, 1-3
QC 8
(Queen, Ellery), Ellery Queen: First
Impressions, by Robert W. Douty,
12-3 TAD 196
(Queen, Ellery), Ellery Queen in
Wrightsville, (locale series), by
Francis M. Nevins, Jr., 7-1 TAD 4
(Queen, Ellery), Ellery Queen on the
Small Screen, (television, 1955-76,
with checklist), by Francis M.
Nevins, Jr., 12-3 TAD 216
(Queen, Ellery), Ellery Queen Pilot
Show on TV, by Don Hutchison,
7 MY 10
(Queen, Ellery), Explaining Ellery
Queen (Who is Ellery Queen?), by
William Ruble, 2-2 QC 8
(Queen, Ellery), The Fantastic World-
Wide Ellery Queen Poll, by Jon L.
Breen, 3-1 QC 7
(Queen, Ellery), The Films of Ellery
Queen, by Edward Connor, 3-1 QC 10
(Queen, Ellery), From...TQCB, (Queen
Canon Bibliography), by Nils Hardin,
14 X 55
(Queen, Ellery), Growing Up with Ellery
Queen, by Edward D. Hoch, 12-3 TAD
200
(Queen, Ellery), The Idea Man, (fiction,
pastiche), by Jon L. Breen, 1-4
QC 11
(Queen, Ellery), The Man Who Read (and
Published) John Dickson Carr/Carter
Dickson, (Ellery Queen), by Larry
L. French, 1 NC 8
(Queen, Ellery), The Misadventures of
Ellery Queen, (on pastiches about
Queen), by Marvin S. Lachman, 1-4
QC 7
(Queen, Ellery), The Retirement of
Richard Queen, (Inspector Queen,
father of Ellery Queen, in early
stories), by J.R.Christopher, 1-1
QC 3
(Queen, Ellery), Royal Bloodline: The
Biography of the Queen Canon, by
Francis M. Nevins, Jr., 1-1 QC 6;
1-2 QC 2; 1-3 QC 2; 1-4 QC 2; 2-1
WC 2; 2-2 QC 1; 3-1 QC 2; 3-2 QC 2
(Queen, Ellery), The Queen Canon, A
Fragmentary Fraction, by Rev.Robert
E. Washer, 1-4 MR 7

(Queen, Ellery), Requiem for a Detective:
   The Strange Death of Ellery Queen,
   (on the television series), by Paul
   A. Sukys, 10-1 TAD 81
(Queen, Ellery), "To the Very Last: The
   Dying Message," by Lynn Biederstadt,
   12-3 TAD 209
(Queen, Ellery), Van Dine and Queen,
   (random "jottings", S.S.Van Dine and
   Ellery Queen), by Donald A. Yates,
   1-4 QC 12
(Queen, Ellery: COP OUT), The Mystery of
   Social Reaction: Two Novels of Ellery
   Queen, by J.R.Christopher, 6-1 TAD 28
(Queen, Ellery: THE GLASS VILLAGE), The
   Mystery of Social Reaction: Two Novels
   of Ellery Queen, by J.R.Christopher,
   6-1 TAD 28
(Queen, Ellery: THE LAMP OF GOD), The
   Lamp of God, (commentary), by Thomas
   Godfrey, 12-3 TAD 212
(Queen, Ellery: QUEEN'S QUORUM), A Reader's
   Supplement to QUEEN'S QUORUM, (basic
   mystery list), by Douglas G. Greene,
   12-3 TAD 228
(Queen, Ellery: QUEEN'S QUORUM), The
   Quacks in the Quorum, (fugitive books
   in basic mystery list), by Adrian
   Goldstone, 12-3 TAD 226
(Queen, Ellery, Jr., mystery series),
   Boys' Series Bibliography, by
   Harry K. Hudson, 1-4 YB 23
Quest, The, (experiences in collecting
   pulp magazines), by Wooda Nicholas
   Carr, 5-4 MR 5
Quest for Nirvana, (verse), by Walter
   Shedlofsky, 14 X 14
(Quest, Tom, series), Tom Quest Crossword,
   (puzzle based on boys' series books),
   2 MA 30
(Quest, Tom, series), The Tom Quest
   Series, (boys' books), by Fred
   Woodworth, 1 MA 20
(Quest, Tom, series), Update: Tom Quest
   & The Lone Ranger, (books by Fran
   Striker), by Fred Woodworth, 6 MA 13
(Quick Reader series), The Killian
   Memoranda, (paperback book series),
   by Dave Killian, 1-1 CP 17; (check-
   list) 1-1 CP 18
Quickie Radio Trivia Quiz, (mystery),
   9 MN Q1
Quiet Master, The, (Jack Williamson,
   author), by Joseph A. Willis,
   13 SF 26
Quiller Report, The, (Quiller series:
   Adam Hall), by R. Jeff Banks and
   Harry D. Dawson, 4-1 MF 8; (check-
   list, annotated) 4-1 MF 8
(Quiller series: Adam Hall), The
   Quiller Report, by R. Jeff Banks and
   Harry D. Dawson, 4-1 MF 8; (check-
   list, annotated) 4-1 MF 8
(Quiller series: Adam Hall), Checklist,
   Annotated, by Barry Van Tilburg,
   4-3 MF 26

(Quin, Harley, detective: Agatha
   Christie), Agatha Christie's Other
   Detectives, Parker Pyne and Harley
   Quin, by Earl F. Bargainnier, 11-2
   TAD 110
(Quirk, Leslie), Who was Leslie Quirk?,
   (sketch of boys' books author), by
   Marge Dahl, 2-2 TBN 6
Quirky Quatrains, (verse), by Jane
   Gottschalk, 13-4 TAD 335
Quiz - Can You Match This? (based on
   Leo Edwards' boys' books),1-4 TB 6
Quiz on Silver Blaze, (based on
   Sherlock Holmes story), 3 MT 26
(quiz), A Mysterious Quiz, by Robert
   E. Briney, 7-1 TAD 24
(quiz), A Thorndyke Examination, by
   Philip T. Asdell, 1 TF 32
(quiz), Can You Match This?, (based
   on Leo Edwards' boys' series books),
   1-4 TB 6
(quiz), Chief Mummy Inspector's Quiz,
   (based on Leo Edwards' boys' series
   books), by Julius R. Chenu, 1-4
   YB 10
(quiz), Criminal Quiz, by Richard
   Emery, 3-5 PP 18
(quiz), Dedications: A Detective Story
   Quiz, by Jon L. Breen, 1-2 TAD 59
(quiz), Detecting the Sponsors,
   (mystery quiz), by R. Jeff Banks,
   12-2 TAD 190
(quiz), Detective Short Story Quiz,
   by R.W.Hays, 3-1 TAD 11
(quiz), Detectives in Disguise, by
   Veronica M.S.Kennedy, 4-2 TAD 103;
   9-1 TAD 6
(quiz), The Distaff Detectives, by
   R. Jeff Banks, 8 MN 2
(quiz), Doc Savage Title Challenge,
   by Will Murray, 9 DS 20
(quiz), Doctors in Crime, by Mr. &
   Mrs. W.H.J.Kennedy, 1-5 MR 4
(quiz), Dogging the Detectives, by
   R. Jeff Banks, 7 MN 3
(quiz), Double-Duty Detectives, by
   R. Jeff Banks, 9-2 TAD 111
(quiz), Eye-Q II, (private eye quiz),
   by Jonathon Harrow, 1-2 M 4
(quiz), Eye-Q 3, (private eye quiz),
   1-3 M 42
(quiz), Eye-Q 4: Tour of Duty, (police
   procedural quiz), by Jonathon
   Harrow, 2-1 M 42
(quiz), Horrendous Headlines, by
   Veronica M.S.Kennedy, 9-2 TAD 124
(quiz), How Much Do you Know? (on
   Doc Savage), by Bill Laidlaw,
   3 DQ 15; 4 DQ 9
(quiz), Ladies in Crime, by Veronica
   M.S.Kennedy, 7-2 TAD 94
(quiz), The Literary Works of
   Fictional Detectives and "Watsons",
   by Barry A. Pike, 7-4 TAD 270
(quiz), Minute Quiz, by Peggy
   Keeley, 1-6 MR 12

(quiz), Movie Quiz, (mystery), 2-3 MR 10
(quiz), Mystery Contest, 3-1 M 52
(quiz), Mystery Quiz, by Steve Lewis,
  5 MY 8; 5A MY 3
(quiz), Mystery Quiz on Cats, 6/7 LR 15
(quiz), Mystery Theme Match-Up, by R.
  Jeff Banks, 11-3 TAD 305
(quiz), Nero Wolfe Quiz, by Lee Poleske,
  1 LW 1; 2 LW 1; 3 LW 1; 4 LW 2;
  5 LW 1; 6 LW 1
(quiz), Poetry Quiz, (mystery), by R.W.
  Hays, 5-4 TAD 215
(quiz), The Pulp Hero Quiz, by G. Alan,
  11 BS 13
(quiz), The Pulp Hero Quiz, by Robert
  Weinberg, 1 P 21; 2 P 18
(quiz), Pulp Quiz, by G. Alan, 14 BS 12;
  15 BS 18
(quiz), Pulp Quiz, by Robert Weinberg,
  3 P 27; 10 P 31; 5 P 19
(quiz), Quiz on Silver Blake, (based on
  Sherlock Holmes story), 3 MT 26
(quiz), Radio Detectives Tag-Line Quiz,
  by R. Jeff Banks, 11-4 TAD 395
(quiz), Radio Mystery Quiz, by R. Jeff
  Banks, 12-3 TAD 211
(quiz), Shakespeare Quiz, (mystery), by
  R.W.Hays, 8-1 TAD 41
(quiz), The Sherlockian Quiz, by John
  Bennett Shaw, 10-1 TAD 77
(quiz), Series Characters: A Detective
  Story Matching Quiz, by Jon L. Breen,
  3-2 TAD 122
(quiz), Supersleuth Quiz, 6/7 LR 9
(quiz), Testing Your Eye-Q, (private
  eye quiz), by Paul Bishop, 1-1 M 12
(quiz), Travis McGee Quiz, by Tom
  Clayton, 26 JD 19
(quiz), Trivia Quiz: A Living Shadow!,
  by Arn McConnell, 1-4 WA 18
(quiz), Trivia Quiz: The Avenger, by
  Kirk McConnell, 1-1 WA 11
(quiz), Trivia Quiz: The Biographers,
  by Craven Lovelace, 2-1 WA 19
(quiz), Trivia Quiz: Mostly Movies,
  1-2 WA 14
(quiz), Trivia Quiz: Nero Wolfe,
  1-3 WA 13
(quiz), Two-Detective Mysteries, by
  R. Jeff Banks, 12-4 TAD 378
(quiz), Where Have I Read That?, by
  Robert Aucott, 12-2 TAD 187
(quiz), see also: puzzle; crossword
  puzzle
Quotable Hitchcock, The, (worth-repeating
  Alfred Hitchcock quotes), 2-3 M 32
Quotations from the Mysteries, by
  Marvin Lachman, 2-5 MR 18; 2-6
  MR 3
(quotations), The Wit and Wisdom of
  the Mystery Story (as continuation
  of "Quotations from the Mysteries"),
  by Marvin Lachman, 1A MF 3; 1-4
  MF 7

Quoth the Raven, "Nevermore", (on G-8
  and His Battle Aces, pulp characters),
  by Wooda Nicholas Carr, 6 X 29

R. Austin Freeman and the Improvement of
  Mankind, by Oliver Mayo, 1 TF 34;
  2 TF 18
R. Austin Freeman, Toward a Definite
  Biography, by John J. McAleer,
  11 TF 19
Rabe, Norman: letter of comment,11 JD 27
Raconteur of Emerald Lake, The, (on
  E. Hoffman Price), by Thomas Kent
  Miller and Gary von Tersch, 6 WT 3
Radio Detectives Tag-Line Quiz, (quiz),
  by R. Jeff Banks, 11-4 TAD 395
Radio Fu Manchu, (Fu Manchu in radio
  serials), by Ray Stanich, 12 R 11
Radio Luxembourg Dr. Fu Manchu, (Fu
  Manchu radio programs in Luxembourg,
  checklist), 11 R 15
Radio Murder Hour, The, (old radio
  mystery programs discussed), by
  Chris Steinbrunner, 14-2 156;
  14-3 TAD 229; (The Shadow) 14-4
  TAD 335
Radio Mystery Program, The, (old radio
  mystery programs discussed), by
  Martin Maloney, 2-5 MR 3
Radio Mystery Quiz, (quiz), by R.Jeff
  Banks, 12-3 TAD 211
(radio - tape recordings), The Law
  and The Shadow, (legal position
  of selling tape recordings from
  radio shows), by Jack Gilbert,
  4 BS 6
Rafael Palacios, (on the paperback
  book cover artist), by Piet
  Schreuders, 3-3 CP 32
Ragan, Robert: letter of comment,
  1-5 CP 1
Ragged Edges, (letters of comment
  from readers), 2 D 48
Rahman, G. Arthur, and James A.
  McKraken: The Case of the
  Cheshire Cat's Paw, (fiction,
  Sherlock Holmes pastiche),
  10 CL 3
Rall, William J.: letter of comment,
  2-1 MF 51; 9 MN L1; 11 MN L2;
  11-1 TAD 4; 33 X 115
Ralph, David C.: letter of comment,
  1-6 MF 55; 3/4 MN 16; 5/6 MN 16;
  2-6 PP 41; 8-3 TAD 239; 9-4 TAD
  323
Ralph Henry Barbour's Books, (boys'
  books), by Julius R. Chenu,
  1-4 BC 118; 1-6 YB 17
Raman, E.: letter of comment,
  10 JD 11
Ramblin' With Jack, (boys' books
  collecting experiences), by Jack
  Tornquist, 1-2 TBN 8; 1-3 TBN 7;
  1-4 TBN 7

Rambling Thoughts on a 'tec Collection, (collecting crime fiction), by James Keddie, Jr., 1-1 TAD 5

Ramblings of a Rare Paperback Book Fiend, (various data), by M.C.Hill, 2-2 CP 38; (on movie-ins as promotion), 3-5 CP 17

Ramon Decolta aka Raoul Whitfield, and His Diminutive Brown Man: Jo Gar, The Island Detective, by E.R.Hagemann, 14-1 TAD 3

Ramsey, Gordon C.: A Teacher Meets Agatha Christie, 1-1 TAD 13

Ramsey, Gordon C.: Criticism and the Detective Story, (discusses prevalence of thought of mystery as second-class literature), 1-3 TAD 90

Ramsey, Gordon C.: letter of comment, 1-2 TAD 64; 5-3 TAD 188

(Ramsey, Gordon C.), Meet the Author: Gordon C. Ramsey, by Allen J. Hubin, 1-1 TAD 18

Ramsey, Jack: letter of comment, 14-1 TAD 71

Rand, Leo: A Report on Bouchercon I, (mystery authors and fans convention), 14 JD 7; (on Bouchercon II) 17 JD 15; (on Bouchercon III) 18 JD 5; (on Bouchercon V) 20 JD 17

(Randall, Homer), The Army Boys, (boys' series books by Randall), by Robert Jennings, 2 BB 4

Randall, Rona: The Birth and Growth of the Crime Writers' Association, (British professional authors group), 5-3 MR 25

Randall, Rona: The Crime Novel v. The Whodunit, (Julian Symons and Michael Gilbert), 5-6 MR 25

Randall, Rona: Crime Writers' Association (awards of the British professional mystery authors' group, 1955-70), 5-3 MR 28

Randall, Rona: Current Crime - The American Scene, (mystery news), 5-2 MR 33

Randall, Rona: Current Crime - The British Scene, (mystery news), 5-1 MR 29; 5-2 MR 31; 5-3 MR 31

Randall, Rona: Inspector Ghote Takes a Bow, (Inspector Ghote series: H.R.F.Keating) 5-4 MR 17

Randisi, Robert J.: A Conversation with Joan Kahn, (interview with mystery editor), 3-1 M 16

Randisi, Robert J.: An Interview with Bill Pronzini, 11-1 TAD 46

Randisi, Robert J.: An Interview with Gregory Mcdonald, 12-2 TAD 134

Randisi, Robert J.: An Interview with Marc Olden, 12-4 TAD 324

Randisi, Robert J.: An Interview with Max Collins, 11-3 TAD 300

Randisi, Robert J.: An Interview with Stuart Kaminsky, 13-4 TAD 338

Randisi, Robert J.: The Best TV Eyes of the 70's, (private eye detective television series), 2-1 M 11

Randisi, Robert J.: letter of comment, 4-1 PP 45; 4-4 PP 36; 4-5/6 PP 83; 8-2 TAD 155; 8-3 TAD 243; 8-4 TAD 324; 9-1 TAD 75; 9-2 TAD 155; 9-4 TAD 321; 9-4 TAD 337; 10-4 TAD 292; 12-3 TAD 268; 14-2 TAD 186; 14-3 TAD 247

Randisi, Robert J.: Meet Nolan, (Max Collins' Nolan as heist artist/detective), 4-5/6 PP 29

Randisi, Robert J.: MYSTERY MONTHLY Magazine, 9-4 TAD 307

Randisi, Robert J.: Series Synopses, Earl Drake series of Dan J.Marlowe, 10-2 TAD 181

Randisi, Robert J.: Series Synopses, Mongo the Magnificent by George C. Chesbro, 12-4 TAD 366

Randolph Mason Stories, The, (by Melville Davisson Post), by Charles A. Norton, 6-2 TAD 86

Random Thoughts on JDM and the Frustration of the Expected, (John D. MacDonald), by Francis M. Nevins, Jr., 7 JD 11

Random Thoughts on Writing "The Paperback Revolution" (review column in THE ARMCHAIR DETECTIVE), by Charles Shibuk, 4-3 TAD 172

Randrup, Karen: The Rival of Sherlock Holmes, (Solar Pons), 3-1 PDA 26

Rantings and Ravings of a Book Collector, (boys' books collecting), by George Holmes, 1-3 YB 12

Raoul F. Whitfield, A Star with the Mask, (author in BLACK MASK pulp magazine), by E.R.Hagemann, 13-3 TAD 179

Rapp, Howard: letter of comment, 5-1 MF 43; 3-6 PP 40; 5-4 TAD 252; 9-4 TAD 249

Rapping With Mike, A Michael Avallone Appreciation, Interview, and Checklist, by Stephen Mertz, 8 PE 2

Rare Books are Getting Scarce, (paperback book related column), by Bruce Taylor, (collecting mystery & detective fiction) 1-1 CP 6; (John Dickson Carr in paperback) 1-2 CP 15; (The Affair of the Purloined Plot) 1-3 CP 18; (crime fiction paperbacks valuable) 1-4 CP 19; (pseudonyms of mystery authors) 1-5 CP 15; (Clayton Rawson) 1-6 CP 10; (Popular Library mystery books) 2-1 CP 15; (Nero Wolfe in paperback) 2-2 CP 27; (Hitchcock in paperback) 2-4 CP 10; (defunct detectives) 2-5 CP 19; (Dell Great Mystery Library) 3-1 CP 23; (Green Door Mysteries) 3-2 CP 29; (affordable crime collection) 3-5 CP 12

Rare Vintages from the Tropics: T.S. Stribling's CLUES OF THE CARRIBEES, by Frank D. McSherry, Jr., 6-3 TAD 172

(Rason, Inspector, series: Roy Vickers), An Open-Ended Search for Dead Ends, by Howard Waterhouse, 1-3 PP 7

(Rathbone, Basil), Basil Rathbone as Sherlock Holmes, (stage), by Leonard Maltin, 1-4 MR 12

(Rathborne, Harry St.George), Prolific, (boys' books author), by J. Edward Leithead, 2-1 BC 142

Rausch, George J., Jr.: A Checklist of Mystery, Detective and Suspense Fiction Published in the U.S. June-August 1968, 2-1 TAD 57; September-November 1968, 2-2 TAD 115; December 1968-February 1969, 2-3 TAD 195; March-May 1969, 2-4 TAD 256; June-August 1969, 3-1 TAD 41; September-November 1969, 3-2 TAD 119; December 1969-February 1970, 3-3 TAD 180; March-May 1970, 3-4 TAD 251; June-August 1970, 4-1 TAD 44; September-November 1970, 4-2 TAD 118; December 1970-February 1971, 4-3 TAD 174; March-May 1971, 4-4 TAD 232; June-August 1971, 5-1 TAD 35; September-November 1971, 5-2 TAD 96; December 1971-February 1972, 5-3 TAD 156; March-May 1972, 5-4 TAD 223; June-August 1972, 6-1 TAD 36; September-November 1972, 6-2 TAD 104; December 1972-March 1973, 6-3 TAD 183; April-June 1973, 6-4 TAD 257

Rausch, George J.: John P. Marquand and Espionage Fiction, 5-4 TAD 194

Rausch, George J.,Jr.: letter of comment, 11 JD 22; 3-1 TAD 60; 5-1 TAD 48

Rausch, George J., Jr.: The Works of Eric Ambler, 2-4 TAD 260

(Rausch, Dr. George J., Jr.), Meet the Author: Dr. George J. Rausch, Jr., by Allen J. Hubin, 2-1 TAD 60

Rauth, Jerold: letter of comment, 1-4 AD 8; 8 MN 34; 14 X 64

Raven House Mysteries: Forever More! (checklist and introduction to Raven House line of mystery paperbacks), by Michael L. Cook, 4-5/6 PP 27

Ravenscroft, N.C.: Arnold Bennett, As a Writer of Crime Fiction, 10-2 TAD 182

Rawson, Clayton: letter of comment, 2-2 TAD 129

(Rawson, Clayton), Checklist, by Robert E. Briney, 3-1 MR 8

(Rawson, Clayton), Clayton Rawson and the Flexible Formula, (illusory nature of the formula puzzle mystery), by Fred Erisman, 14-2 TAD 173

(Rawson, Clayton), The Great Merlini, (series by Rawson), by Fred Dueren 4-4 MF 21

(Rawson, Clayton), Paperback Titles, in Rare Books are Getting Scarce, by Bruce Taylor, 1-6 CP 10

(Ray, Jean), The Harry Dickson Detective Stories by Jean Ray, by Eddy C. Bertin, 1-1 MR 7

Ray, Joseph M.: letter of comment, 26 JD 49

Raymond Chandler and the Detective, by Mark MacDonald, 3 MT 2

Raymond Chandler on Film: An Annotated Checklist, by Peter Pross, 1-6 MF 3; (screenplays written by Chandler), 2-3 MF 27; (addendum by Charles Shibuk) 2-4 MF 14

Raymond Chandler on the Screen, by Charles Shibuk, 1-3 MR 7

(RAYMOND CHANDLER: A DESCRIPTIVE BIBLIOGRAPHY: Matthew J. Bruccoli), The BLACK MASK Boys Go Legit, by William F. Nolan, 13-1 TAD 23

Raymond Chandler's Self-Parody, (discussion of his works), by Randall R. Mawer, 14-4 TAD 355

Readers Choice, (excerpts from the Eyrie, reader's column, of WEIRD TALES), by Robert A.W.Lowndes, 5 WT 20; 6 WT 16

Reader's Guide to Doctor Death, (Dr. Death series in paperback), by Bruce Cervon, 3-3 CP 30

Readers in Search of an Author (visit to home of August Derleth), by Leonard Cochran, 1-3 PD 1

Readers Response, (letters of comment from readers), 5 BB 21

Readers' Supplementary List to the Haycraft/Queen Definitive Library of Detective-Crime-Mystery Fiction, by Amnon Kabatchnik and Robert Aucott, 9-2 TAD 87

Reading Around, (book comments), 2-1 MR 20

(Reagan, Ronald), Thank You, Mr. President, (photos from movies), 2-2 M 5

Reagan, Thomas B.: letter of comment, 3-6 MR 11

Real Fourth Side of the Triangle, The, (Speculative, Della Street's affair with Archie Goodwin), by Marvin Lachman, 9 MN All

Real McGee, The, (a synthesis of puzzle and hero-type mystery fiction in the Travis McGee series by John D. MacDonald), by Bailey P. Phelps, 28 JD 13

Real Professor Challenger, The, (re: A. Conan Doyle's character), by Dana Martin Batory, 13 SF 42

Real Steve Austin, The, (Austin based on real person?), by Sue Hagen and Operative 1701, 6 U 15

Realism, Routine, Stubborness and System:
The Police Procedural, Pt.1, by George
N. Dove, 10-2 TAD 133
Realm of In-Between, The, (fiction), by
Walter Shedlofsky, 6 X 5
Reasoner, James: letter of comment,
3-6 PP 38; 4-2 PP 34; 4-4 PP 35
(Reasoner, James), Fading Shadows, by
Tom Johnson, 2 PW 3
Rebirth of the Bugle, (THE TUTTER BUGLE,
re: Leo Edwards' boys' books), by
Robert L. Johnson, 1-1 TB 1
Recent Arrivals, (crime fiction news),
by Michael L. Cook, 7 U 31
Recent European Works on the Detective
Story, by E.F.Bleiler, 2-3 MF 23
Recent Lone Ranger Story a Mess, (LEGEND
OF THE LONE RANGER: Gary McCarthy),
by I.R.Ybarra, 6 MA 8
Recent Paperbacks Reviewed, by Ruth
Withee and Lianne Carlin, 3-2 MR 10
Recent Releases, (reviews of paperback
crime fiction), 2-4 PQ 48; 3-1 PQ 19;
3-2 PQ 37; 3-4 PQ 55
Recipe for a Cookbook, (re: Nero Wolfe),
by Barbara Burn, 1-1 G 34
Recommended Reading, (on August Derleth
works), 3-1 AD 10
Record, George H.: letter of comment,
6 R 21
Red Baron, The Avenger, and Doc Savage,
(comparison essay of pulp heroes),
by Bill Laidlaw, 3 DQ 4
Red-Blooded Mysteries Are Now Blue-Blooded,
(mystery reference books), by Michael
L. Cook, 14 SF 38
(Red Circle Magazines), An Interview with
Abe Goodman, (publisher, pulp magazines),
by Robert Weinberg, 10 P 2
(RED HARVEST: Dashiell Hammett), The
Problem of Moral Vision in Dashiell
Hammett's Detective Novels, by George
J. Thompson, 6-4 TAD 213
Red Herring as Folklore, The, (the
misleading clue in mystery fiction),
by William M. Clements, 12-3 TAD 256
RED STAR MYSTERY: Don Diavolo, (the
pulp magazine and the principal
story character, with magazine
index), by Robert E. Briney, 64 PU 14
(RED STAR MYSTERY Magazine), The Diavolo
Quartet, (magician-detective series
by Clayton Rawson in pulp magazine),
by Francis M. Nevins, Jr., 3 X 2
Reed, Gladys L.: letter of comment,
5/6 MN 12
(Reed, Ishmael), Ishmael Reed's Neo-Hoodooism
by Dave Buck, 11 X 9
Reeder, Dave: letter of comment,
2-1 AD 12; 8 SF 47
(Rees, Idwal, series: Berkeley Mather),
Checklist, Annotated, by Barry
Van Tilburg, 4-6 MF 4
(Reese, John), Mystery Plus: John Reese
Revisited, by R. Jeff Banks, 1-6 PP 18

(Reese, John: Jeff Hewitt series),
Mystery Plus: Weapon Heavy, by
R. Jeff Banks, 1-4 PP 21
(Reeve, Arthur B.), A Chronological
Bibliography of the Books of
Arthur B. Reeve, by J. Randolph
Cox, 11-1 TAD 29
(Reeve, Arthur B.: Craig Kennedy,
detective), A Reading of Reeve,
Some Thoughts on the Creator of
Craig Kennedy, by J. Randolph Cox,
11-1 TAD 28
(Reeve, Arthur B.: Craig Kennedy,
detective), Arthur B. Reeve and the
American Sherlock Holmes, by John
Harwood, 10-4 TAD 354
(Reeve, Arthur B.: Craig Kennedy,
detective), The American Sherlock
Holmes: A Study in Scarlet Imper-
sonation, (Holmes and Watson
protesting Craig Kennedy and Walter
Jameson's reputation as "the
American Sherlock Holmes"), by
Marvin Lachman, 3-2 MR 2
Reflections in a Flame-Gold Eye, (the
changes in Doc Savage during the
course of the series), by Will
Murray, 2/3 DR 16
Reflections on China, (travel essay),
by John D. MacDonald, 24 JD 13
Reflections on Impermanence, (verse),
by Craig Rice, 2-1 TAD 51
Regency Lady, (literary sketch of
Georgette Heyer), by Lesleigh
Luttrell, 13 MN 3
(Regency Books), Fading Shadows:
Corinth/Regency Paperbacks, by
Tom Johnson, 10 SF 36
(Regency Books), Prelimary Regency
Checklist, (paperbacks), by Tom
Whitmore, 15 SF 19
Regency Romances of Georgette Heyer,
(with checklist), by Jo Ann
Vicarel, 13 MN 17
Reggie Fortune Short Stories, The:
An Appreciation and Partial
Bibliography, (with additional
bibliographic entries by Francis
M. Nevins, Jr.), by James Mark
Purcell, 5-4 MR 1
Reginald, Robert: The Borgo Press,
2-1 PQ 14; (checklist) 2-1 PQ 21
Reginald, Robert: letter of comment,
6 SF 48; 8 SF 47
Register, Richard: letter of comment,
22 X 52
Register, Richard, and Bill Blackbeard:
How to Make Your Pulps Last Forever,
26 X 70
(Reid, Mayne), Memoirs of Mayne Reid,
(boys' books author), by R.H.
Stoddard, 2-2 BC 172
(Reilly, Helen), Checklist, by Francis
M. Nevins, Jr., 5-5 MR 18
(Reilly, Helen), Checklist, by Audrey
I. Pacheco, 5-4 MR 24

Reilly, John M.: Classic and Hard-Boiled Detective Fiction, (hard-boiled vs. classic mystery), 9-4 TAD 289

Reilly, John M.: letter of comment 5-2 MF 45; 4-2 PP 33; 14-2 TAD 186

Reilly, John M.: On Reading Detective Fiction, (popular aesthetics of the form), 12-1 TAD 64

Reilly, John M.: Sam Spade Talking, 1-2 C 119

(Reilly, John M., ed.: TWENTIETH CENTURY CRIME AND MYSTERY WRITERS), The Body in the Library: Twentieth Century Crime and Mystery Writers and the Mystery World in Our Time, by Martin Morse Wooster, 5-1 MF 11

(Reilly, John M., ed.: TWENTIETH CENTURY CRIME AND MYSTERY WRITERS), For Mystery Readers: The Newest Must-Have Book, by Steve Miller, 3-4 PP 9

Reineke, Becky: letter of comment, 4-5 MF 46; 501 MF 40; 5-3 MF 41

Religion and Detection, (religion used as background for crime fiction), by Marvin Lachman, 1-1 TAD 19

Religion and the Detective Story, (religion used as background for cime fiction), by R.W.Hays, 8-1 TAD 24

Reluctant Hero, The: Reflections on Vocation and Heroism in the Travis McGee Novels of John D. MacDonald, by Larry E. Grimes, 1-1 C 103

Remembering AVON MURDER MYSTERY MONTHLY, (with checklist), by Francis M. Nevins, Jr., 7 MY 3

Remembering John Creasey, by Francis M. Nevins, Jr., 4 X 37

Reminiscences, (re: August Derleth), by Bill Dutch, 2-1 AD 4

Reminiscences, (of Harry Stephen Keeler), by Frank Gruber, 2-1 TAD 55

Reminiscences, (of script-writing Holmes and Bulldog Drummond), by Frank Gruber, 2-1 TAD 56

Reminiscences and a Caution, (on August Derleth), by E. Hoffman Price, 2-3/4 AD 11

Reminiscences of Cases Past: The Books of Elizabeth Daly, by Maryell Cleary, 2-1 PP 3; 2-2 PP 3

Reminiscences of Praed Street, (Solar Pons), by Commander Cecil A. Ryder, Jr., USNR, 2-1 PDA 38

Renard, Henry D.: letter of comment, 9 JD 7

Rendell Territory, (Ruth Rendell crime fiction), by Jane S. Bakerman, 10 MN A1

(Rendell, Ruth), A Look at the Novels of Ruth Rendell, by Don Miller, 10 MN A7

(Rendell, Ruth), A Look at the Short Stories of Ruth Rendell, by Don Miller, 10 MN A19

(Rendell, Ruth), A Partial Checklist of Reviews of Books by Ruth Rendell, by Don Miller, 10 MN A23

(Rendell, Ruth), A Rendell Dozen Plus One: An Annotated Checklist of the Rendell Novels Through 1974, by Jo Ann Genaro Vicarel, 9-3 TAD 198

(Rendell, Ruth), Explorations of Love: An Examination of Some Novels by Ruth Rendell, by Jane S. Bakerman, 11-2 TAD 139

(Rendell, Ruth), Interview with Ruth Rendell, by Diana Cooper-Clark, 14-2 TAD 108

(Rendell, Ruth), One in Two: Some Personality Studies by Ruth Rendell, by Jane S. Bakerman, 5-6 MF 21

(Rendell, Ruth), Rendell Territory, by Jane S. Bakerman, 10 MN A1

(Rendell, Ruth), Review Extracts from the Press, 10 MN A6; 10 MN A18; 10 MN A22; 10 MN A25; 10 MN A29

(Rendell, Ruth), Ruth Rendell: A Bibliography, 10 MN A27

(Rendell, Ruth), Ruth Rendell - A Bibliography, by J. Clyde Stevens, 7 MY 8

(Rendell, Ruth), The Writer's Probe: Ruth Rendell as Social Critic, by Jane S. Bakerman, 3-5 MF 3

(Rendell, Ruth: A JUDGEMENT IN STONE), Humor, Horror and Intellect: Giles Mont in Ruth Rendell's A JUDGEMENT IN STONE, by Jane S. Bakerman, 5-4 MF 5

Rendon, Rene: letter of comment, 28 X 78

Repairing Paperbacks, by Nicholas Willmott, 3-2 PQ 39

Report on Bouchercon IV, (mystery fans and authors convention), by Ed Demchko, 6-2 MR 34

Report on the Crime Writers' Third International Congress, Stockholm, 1981, by Iwan Hedman, 5-6 MF 10

Report on PulpCon 9, (pulp fans convention), by Albert Tonik, 14 SF 15

Reprints of Mystery and Detective Fiction Offered in 1978, by Amnon Kabatchnik, 1-1 PP 19

Reprints/Reprints: LOST HORIZON by James Hilton, (on paperback editions), by Billy C. Lee, 3-1 PQ 37

Reprints/Reprints: Ray Bradbury's FAHRENHEIT 451, (on paperback editions), by Bill Crider, 3-3 PQ 22

Requiem for a Detective: The Strange Death of Ellery Queen, (cessation of series on television), by Paul A. Sukys, 10-1 TAD 81

Requiem for a Magazine, (cessation of MANHUNT), by Robert Turner, 1-6 MR 5

Resnick, Mike: An Explanation of Sorts, or Why Your Universe Really Will Not Come to An End (price guide)26 X 14

Resnick's Price Guide: A Review from the Microcosm, (pulp price guide comments), by Marvin Morrison, 28 X 7

Restaino, Katherine M.: letter of comment, 11-2 TAD 205

Resurrection of IN HELL, MADONNA, The, (on the discovery and planned publication of a Doc Savage novel), by Will Murray, 5 DS 8

(Retcliffe, Sir John: NENA SAHIB), Concerning Nena Sahib, by Paul Plass, 6-3 TAD 157

Retirement of Richard Queen, The, (on Inspector Queen, of the early Ellery Queen stories), by J.R.Christopher, 1-1 QC 3

Return of Doctor Death (DOCTOR DEATH pulp magazine and the paperback book reprints), by Jack DeWitt, 5 BS 4

Return of Michael Shayne, The, (commentary on Shayne occasioned by the announcement of new reprints), by Helen McCloy, 14-4 TAD 344

Return of Paul Pine, The, (Paul Pine, detective: Howard Browne), by Caleb A. Lewis, 11-1 TAD 79

(RETURN OF SKULL-FACE, THE: Robert E.Howard and Richard A. Lupoff), The (Very Temporary) Return of Skull-Face, by Robert E. Briney, 2-2 MF 21

Return to Place of Hawks, (verse, re: August Derleth), by Edna Meudt, 2-3/4 AD 8

Revenge a la Mode, by Vincent J. Miranda, 13 R 23

Reviews, (book reviews), 1-2 C 132; 2-2 C 154; 7 CL 8; 8 CL 8; 10 CL 8; 11 CL 9; 13/14 CL 9; 12 LR 19; 1-1 M 20; 1-2 M 19; 1-3 M 16; 2-1 M 26; 2-2 M 55; 1A MF 32; 1-3 MR 6; 1-5 MR 6; 2-1 MR 7; 3-1 MR 7; 3-2 MR 9; 3-3 MR 29; 3-4 MR 9; 3-5 MR 19; 3-6 MR 21; 4-1 MR 33; 4-2 MR 34; 4-3 MR 31; 4-4 MR 33; 4-5 MR 32; 4-6 MR 31; 5-1 MR 31; 5-2 MR 37; 4-3 MR 33; 5-4 MR 28; 5-5 MR 32; 5-6 MR 30; 6-1 MR 41; 6-2 MR 45; 5A MY 1; 7 PE 11; 1-1 PP 19; 1-2 PP 19; 1-3 PP 23;1-4 PP 23; 1-5 PP 18; 1-6 PP 22; 2-1 PP 27; 202 PP 25; 2-3 PP 25; 2-4 PP 29; 2-5 PP 30; 2-6 PP 31; 3-1 PP 33; 3-2 PP 25; 3-3 PP 26; 3-4 PP 29; 3-5 PP 35; 3-6 PP 25; 4-1 PP 28; 4-2 PP 24; 4-3 PP 20; 4-4 PP 24; 4-5/6 PP 66; 4-2 PQ 46; 1-1 TAD 25; 1-2 TAD 60; 1-3 TAD 101; 2-1 TAD 60; 2-2 TAD 119; 2-3 TAD 197; 2-4 TAD 274; 3-1 TAD 57; 3-2 TAD 132; 3-3 TAD 200; 3-4 TAD 270; 4-1 TAD 47; 4-2 TAD 121; 4-3 TAD 178; 4-4 TAD 236; 5-1 TAD 38; 5-2 TAD 99; 5-3 TAD 162; 5-4 TAD 228; 6-1 TAD 40; 6-2 TAD 107; 6-3 TAD 187; 6-4 TAD 259; 7-1 TAD 53; 7-2 TAD 128;

Reviews, (continued), 7-3 TAD 208; 7-4 TAD 285; 8-1 TAD 53; 8-2 TAD 137; 8-3 TAD 219; 8-4 TAD 296; 9-1 TAD 59; 9-2 TAD 142; 9-3 TAD 218; 9-4 TAD 300; 10-1 TAD 5; 10-1 TAD 58; 10-2 TAD 138; 10-4 TAD 310; 11-2 TAD 110; 11-3 TAD 252; 11-3 TAD 245; 11-4 TAD 380; 11-4 TAD 402; 12-1 TAD 77; 12-1 TAD 94; 12-2 TAD 178; 12-2 TAD 189; 12-3 TAD 272; 12-3 TAD 274; 12-4 TAD 369; 13-1 TAD 61; 13-1 TAD 78; 13-2 TAD 145; 13-3 TAD 247; 13-3 TAD 268; 13-4 TAD 351; 14-1 TAD 53; 14-1 TAD 74; 14-3 TAD 268

Reviews, (book reviews), by Meera Clark, 2-1 C 123

Reviews, (book reviews), by Michael L. Cook, 4 U 20; 5 U 31

Reviews, (book reviews), by J. Grant Thiessen, 13 SF 3; 14 SF 18

Reviews, A Selection of Reviews of Crossen Books, (Kendell F. Crossen), 12 MN A11

(reviews), AJH Reviews, (book reviews), by Allen J. Hubin, 10-2 TAD 112; 10-3 TAD 204; 10-4 TAD 307; 11-1 TAD 17; 11-2 TAD 116; 11-3 TAD 230; 11-4 TAD 331; 12-1 TAD 6; 12-2 TAD 111; 12-3 TAD 203; 12-4 TAD 320; 13-1 TAD 26; 13-2 TAD 94; 13-3 TAD 199; 13-4 TAD 294; 14-1 TAD 17; 14-2 TAD 123; 14-3 TAD 218; 14-4 TAD 298

(reviews), "American Boy" Reviews, (boys' books), by C.L.Messecar, 3-2 BC 319; 3-3 BC 351; 3-4 BC 371

(reviews), Atlas Reviews, (reviews in THE WOLD ATLAS), 1-1 WA 9; 1-2 WA 7

(reviews), The Book Nook, 1-5 MM 9; 1-6 MM 9; 1-7 MM 7; 1-8 MM 5; 1-9 MM 5; 1-10 MM 7; 1-11 MM 3; 2-1 MM 3; 2-2 MM 3; 2-3 MM 3; 2-4 MM 3; 2-5 MM 5; 1 MN 7; 2 MN 5; 3/4 MN 7; 5/6 MN 19; 5/6 MN 22; 7 MN 9; 8 MN 11; 9 MN R1; 10 MN R1; 11 MN R1; 12 MN R1

(reviews), Books, 1 PE 12; 2 PE 17; 3 PE 19; 4 PE 11; 5 PE 15; 6 PE 17

(reviews), Capsule Comments, by Allen J. Hubin, 1-4 TAD 131

(reviews), Case File: Canada, by W. Ritchie Benedict, 6 U 38

(reviews), Cloak Looks at Books, 6 CL 3; 9 CL 3; 12 CL 3; 15 CL 4

(reviews), Current Crime: The American Crime Scene, 5-4 MR 27; 6-1 MR 37

(reviews), D.E.Ath Suggests, 2-1 PP 14; 2-2 PP 14; 2-4 PP 28

(reviews), Elves in the Shelves, 1 D 20

(reviews), Eye Appeal, (reviews of private
eye crime fiction), by Marlowe Archer,
4 PE 24; 5 PE 16
(reviews), Fall Highlights, by Amnon
Kabatchnik, 11 CL 7
(reviews), Films, 1 PE 17
(reviews), For Your Investigation, by
Lianne Carlin, 1A MR 2; 1-1 MR 2;
1-2 MR 2; 1-3 MR 2; 1-4 MR 2; 1-5
MR 2; 2-1 MR 2; 2-2 MR 2; 2-3 MR 2;
2-4 MR 2; 2-5 MR 2; 2-6 MR 2
(reviews), The Incinerator, by W. Paul
Ganley, 2 FM 16; 5 U 29; 6 U 26
(reviews), It's About Crime, by Marvin
Lachman, 2-4 MF 15; 2-5 MF 3; 2-6
MF 27; 3-2 MF 21; 3-3 MF 17; 3-4
MF 23; 4-1 MF 13; 4-3 MF 31; 4-4
MF 18; 4-5 MF 24; 4-6 MF 31; 5-1
MF 17; 5-2 MF 10; 5-3 MF 22; 5-4
MF 18; 5-5 MF 17; 5-6 MF 29
(reviews), I've Been Reading, by Lianne
Carlin, 2-4 MR 8
(reviews), Mainstream Mysteries and
Novels of Crime, by Gary Warren
Niebuhr, 3-2 PP 23; 4-1 PP 13;
4-3 PP 5
(reviews), Mini-Reviews, 3 MT 20
(reviews), Mystery*File, by Steve Lewis,
1-1 MF 27; 1-2 MF 23; 1-3 MF 37;
1-4 MF 37; 1-5 MF 29; 1-6 MF 38;
2-1 MF 21; 2-2 MF 33; 2-3 MF 41;
2-4 MF 30; 2-5 MF 26; 2-6 MF 30;
3-1 MF 31; 3-2 MF 36; 3-3 MF 31;
3-4 MF 38; 3-5 MF 35; 3-6 MF 27;
4-2 MF 31; 4-3 MF 34; 4-4 MF 33;
4-5 MF 27; 5-1 MF 20; 5-2 MF 13;
5-3 MF 27; 5-4 MF 21; 5-5 MF 20;
5-6 MF 33
(reviews), Mystery Plus, by R. Jeff
Banks, 1-1 PP 17; 1-2 PP 11;
1-3 PP 9; 1-4 PP 21; 1-5 PP
10; 1-6 PP 18; 2-1 PP 20; 2-2
PP 12; 2-3 PP 24; 2-4 PP 15;
2-5 PP 13; 2-6 PP 13; 3-1 PP
16; 3-2 PP 15; 3-3 PP 17; 3-4
PP 14; 3-5 PP 15; 3-6 PP 15;
4-1 PP 21; 4-2 PP 13; 4-3 PP
11; 4-4 PP 14; 4-5/6 PP 40
(reviews), Nuggest (and Otherwise)
From the Golden Age, by Jay Jeffries,
6 MY 10; 7 MY 6
(reviews), Odds & Ends, (short mystery
reviews), by Don Miller, 1-1 MM 2;
1-2 MM 2; 1-3 MM 2; 1-4 MM 2; 1-5
MM 2; 1-6 MM 4; 1-7 MM 2; 1-8 MM
2; 1-9 MM 2; 1-10 MM 2; 1-11 MM
2; 2-1 MM 2; 2-2 MM 2; 2-2 MM 3;
2-4 MM 9
(reviews), Paper Crimes, (paperback
reviews), by Fred Dueren, 8-4
TAD 295; 9-1 TAD 50; 9-2 TAD
140; 9-3 TAD 212; 9-4 TAD 277;
10-1 TAD 51; 10-2 TAD 130; 10-4
TAD 340; 11-2 TAD 192; 11-3 TAD
306; 12-2 TAD 135; 12-3 TAD 287;
13-1 TAD 65; 13-2 TAD 136; 13-3

(reviews), Paper Crimes, (continued),
TAD 251; 13-4 TAD 361; 14-1 TAD
80; 14-2 TAD 183
(reviews), Paper Crimes, (paperback
reviews), by William L. DeAndrea,
14-3 TAD 265; 14-4 TAD 378
(reviews), Paperbacks on Review,
1-1 PQ 35; 1-2 PQ 53; 1-3 PQ 49;
1-4 PQ 49
(reviews), Paperback Reviews, by
Francis M. Nevins, Jr., 1-6 MR 3
(reviews), The Paperback Revolution,
(paperback reviews), by Charles
Shibuk, 1-1 TAD 10; 1-2 TAD 41;
1-3 TAD 96; 1-4 TAD 129; 2-1 TAD
44; 2-2 TAD 97; 2-3 TAD 174; 2-4
TAD 251; 3-1 TAD 40; 3-2 TAD 115;
3-3 TAD 179; 3-4 TAD 245; 4-1 TAD
37; 4-2 TAD 115; 4-3 TAD 168; 4-4
TAD 219; 5-1 TAD 30; 5-2 TAD 94;
5-3 TAD 154; 5-4 TAD 220; 6-1
TAD 35; 6-2 TAD 102; 6-3 TAD 179;
6-4 TAD 246; 7-1 TAD 44; 7-2 TAD
120; 7-3 TAD 205; 7-4 TAD 281;
8-1 TAD 50; 8-2 TAD 132; 8-3 TAD
210; 8-4 TAD 276; 9-1 TAD 41;
9-2 TAD 135; 9-3 TAD 208; 9-4 TAD
281; 10-1 TAD 71; 10-2 TAD 149;
10-3 TAD 239; 10-4 TAD 360; 11-1
TAD 96; 11-2 TAD 189; 11-3 TAD
298; 11-4 TAD 379; 12-1 TAD 30;
12-2 TAD 166; 12-3 TAD 255; 12-4
TAD 368; 13-1 TAD 75; 13-2 TAD
135; 13-3 TAD 250; 13-4 TAD 362;
14-1 TAD 79; 14-2 TAD 182; 14-3
TAD 266; 14-4 TAD 376
(reviews), Reading Around, 2-1 MR 20
(reviews), Recent Arrivals, by
Michael L. Cook, 7 U 31
(reviews), Recent Paperbacks Reviewed,
by Ruth Withee and Lianne Carlin,
3-2 MR 10
(reviews), Recent Releases, (paperback books), 2-4 PQ 48; 3-1 PQ
19; 3-2 PQ 37; 3-4 PQ 55
(reviews), Short Notes on the Current
Crop/Some Notes on the Current
Crop, by Allen J. Hubin, 6-3 TAD
191; 6-4 TAD 265; 7-1 TAD 61; 7-2
TAD 141; 7-3 TAD 220; 7-4 TAD 293;
8-1 TAD 65; 8-2 TAD 146; 8-3 TAD
225; 8-4 TAD 308; 9-1 TAD 72; 9-2
TAD 152; 9-3 TAD 223; 9-4 TAD 310
(reviews), The Steady Stream, (short
mystery reviews), by Don Miller,
1-1 MM 3; 1-2 MM 3; 1-3 MM 3;
1-4 MM 3; 1-5 MM 3; 1-6 MM 3;
1-7 MM 3; 1-8 MM 3; 1-9 MM 3;
1-10 MM 3; 1-11 MM 9; 2-1 MM 9;
2-2 MM 7; 2-3 MM 9; 2-4 MM 11;
2-5 MM 13; 2-5 MM 21
(reviews), Surveillance), 2-3 M 46;
3-1 M 36; 3-2 M 38
(reviews), Ten Books, (science fiction
paperbacks), by George Kelley,
1-4 PQ 44

(reviews), Verdicts, 1-1 MF 34; 1-2 MF 29;
   1-3 MF 43; 1-4 MF 41; 1-5 MF 37; 1-6
   MF 42; 2-1 MF 31; 2-2 MF 36; 2-3 MF
   49; 2-4 MF 37; 2-5 MF 35; 2-6 MF 36;
   3-1 MF 38; 3-2 MF 42; 3-3 MF 40; 3-4
   MF 42; 3-5 MF 42; 3-6 MF 42; 4-1 MF
   29; 4-2 MF 41; 4-3 MF 42; 4-4 MF 44;
   4-5 MF 37; 4-6 MF 34; 5-2 MF 26; 5-3
   MF 34; 5-4 MF 28; 5-5 MF 28; 5-6 MF
   42
(reviews), Views and Reviews, (short
   science fiction reviews), by J. Grant
   Thiessen, 8 SF 28; 9 SF 46; 10 SF 39
(reviews), Within the Queen Tradition,
   1-2 QC 15; 1-3 QC 22; 1-4 QC 19;
   2-1 QC 17; 2-2 QC 13; 3-1 QC 18;
   3-2 QC 18
(reviews), Worlds in Print), by Sheldon
   A. Wiebe, 5 SF 38
(reviews - extracts), Book Review Extracts
   (from the press), by Don Miller,
   1-1 MM 10; 1-2 MM 7; 1-3 MM 9;
   1-4 MM 7; 1-5 MM 5; 1-6 MM 5;
   1-7 MM 5; 1-8 MM 8; 1-9 MM 8;
   1-10 MM 10; 1-11 MM 6; 2-1 MM
   7; 2-2 MM 9; 2-3 MM 7; 2-4 MM
   8
(reviews - extracts), The Clipjoint, by
   Don Miller, 13A MN 3; 13B MN 1;
   13C MN 3
(reviews - extracts), Review Extracts,
   by Don Miller, 13 MN 1
(reviews - extracts), Review Extracts
   from the Press: Books of Ruth
   Rendell, 10 MN A6; 10 MN A18;
   10 MN A22; 10 MN A25; 10 MN A29
(reviews - extracts), Review Extracts:
   The Early Non-Nero Wolfe Books,
   (of Rex Stout), 9 MN A57
(reviews - extracts), Review Extracts:
   A Few Review Extracts of Nero
   Wolfe Books (by Rex Stout), 9 MN A56
Reviews of Mystery and Crime Films, by
   Richard S. Lochte II, 5-3 TAD 158;
   5-4 TAD 231; 6-1 TAD 39
Reviewer at Work, The, by James Sandoe,
   11-1 TAD 84
Revisiting the Revised Hammett Checklist,
   (Dashiell Hammett; bibliographical),
   by William F. Nolan, 9-4 TAD 292
Rex Stout, A Bibliography, by Don
   Miller, 9 MN A65
Rex Stout, A Capsule Biography, by
   Don Miller, 9 MN A63
Rex Stout, A Creator's World, by John
   J. McAleer, 9 MN A7
Rex Stout, A Tribute, by Guy M. Townsend,
   9 MN A6
Rex Stout in Ellery Queen's Anthologies,
   (checklist), by Don Miller,
   9 MN A29
Rex Stout in ELLERY QUEEN'S MYSTERY
   MAGAZINE, (checklist), by Don
   Miller, 9 MN A24

Rex Stout in Mystery Guild Editions,
   (checklist of book club editions),
   by Michael L. Cook, 9 MN A27
Rex Stout in the Dell Mapbacks, (in
   Dell paperback series), by William
   Lyles, 2-4 PQ 13
Rex Stout Newsletter, by John J.
   McAleer, 11-3 TAD 257; 12-1 TAD
   66; 12-2 TAD 130; 12-3 TAD 224;
   12-4 TAD 330; 13-1 TAD 41; 13-2
   TAD 108; 13-3 TAD 224; 13-4 TAD
   286; 14-1 TAD 22; 14-2 TAD 140;
   14-3 TAD 230; 14-4 TAD 321
(REX STOUT MYSTERY MAGAZINE), Index
   (and checklist of magazine), by
   Frank D. McSherry, Jr., 9 MN A21
(REX STOUT'S MYSTERY QUARTERLY),
   Index, by David Killian, 1-5 CP 21
(Reynolds, Quentin: THE FICTION
   FACTORY), Some Errors in Fiction
   Factory, by J. Randolph Cox,
   74 PU 31
(Reynolds, Quentin: THE FICTION
   FACTORY), Street & Smith Pulps,
   (commentary on book), by Stewart
   Kemble, 74 PU 29
Reynolds, William: The Detective
   Novels of Ronald A. Knox,
   14-3 TAD 275
Reynolds, William: Dorothy L. Sayers'
   Detective Short Fiction, (literary
   study), 14-2 TAD 176
Reynolds, William: Seven "Crimefiles"
   of the 1930s: The Purest Puzzles
   of the Golden Age, (on the "CRIME-
   FILE" series of books containing
   actual material clues), 1-2 C 42
Rice, Craig: Reflections on
   Impermanence, (verse), 2-1
   TAD 51
(Rice, Craig), Bibliography, by David
   A. Jasen, 5-1 TAD 26
(Rice, Craig), Checklist of Craig
   Rice Books, by Mary Ann Grochowski,
   13-3 TAD 267
(Rice, Craig), Craig Rice, Merry
   Mistress of Mystery and Mayhem,
   by Mary Ann Grochowski, 13-3 TAD
   265
(Rice, Craig), The Mysterious Craig
   Rice, by David A. Jasen, 5-1 TAD
   25
(Rice, Craig: John J. Malone series),
   John J. Malone (and Cohorts), by
   Fred Dueren, 8-1 TAD 44
Rich, Ronald A.: letter of comment,
   1-4 AD 9
Richard III and Josephine Tey, Part-
   ners in Crime, (Josephine Tey:
   THE DAUGHTER OF TIME), by Guy M.
   Townsend, 10-3 TAD 211; (see also
   rebuttal, 10-4 TAD 317; 11-2 TAD
   105; 11-3 TAD 237)

Richard, Dennis: letter of comment,
9 JD 16

(Richards, Harvey D.), The Sorak Series
by Harvey D. Richards, (juvenile),
by Julius R. Chenu, 1-3 YB 5

Richardson, Darrell: Pirates on the
High Seas, (indexes to PIRATE STORIES
and HIGH SEAS ADVENTURES, pulp
magazines), 63 PU 38

Richardson, Darrell: Those Tarzan Twins,
2-1 BC 135

Richardson, Dwight J.: letter of comment,
5-4 MR 10

(Richardson, P.C., detective: Sir Basil
Thomson), Pen Profile: Sir Basil
Thomson, by Barry A. Pike, 3-6 PP 18

Richardson, Steve: letter of comment,
25 JD 40; 26 JD 49; 28 JD 41

Richman, Linda: letter of comment
1-6 CP 7

Rick Brant Crossword Puzzle, (based on
Rick Brant boys' series books),
4 MA 28

Rickert, Larry: letter of comment,
3-1 CP 6; 3-6 PP 39; 4-2 PP 37;
4-3 PP 33; 4-4 PP 39

Rickert, Larry: The Rivals of James Bond,
(espionage fiction), 4-2 PP 7;
(Peter Ward, with checklist), 4-3
PP 7; (Commander Esmond Shaw, with
checklist), 4-4 PP 17; (Mark Hood
series by James Dark), 4-5/6 PP 38

Rickert, Larry: Survey Results, (of
poll, paperback book collecting),
3-2 CP 35

Riddle, Lee: letter of comment,
62 PU 14

Riley, George: letter of comment,
27 JD 37

(Rinehart, Mary Roberts), Interview, by
Harvey Breit, 1-3 MR 11

Risteen, Herb L.: All About Henty,
(crossword puzzle based on boys'
books of G.A.Henty), 3-1 BC 277

Risteen, Herb L.: Collector's Crossword,
(crossword puzzle based on boys'
books), 1-3 BC 67; 2-1 BC 134

Risteen, Herb L.: Digging for Gold -
Call About Alger, (crossword puzzle
based on Horatio Alger, Jr. works),
2-3 BC 222

Risteen, Herb L.: On the Warpath, (on
boys' books), 3-1 BC 263

(Ritchie, Jack), Jack Ritchie, An
Interview, 6-1 TAD 12

Ritchie, Raymond E.: letter of comment,
6 DQ 3; 5 DS 7

Rites of a Mystery Cult, The, (social
fuction of crime fiction), by J.R.
Christopher, 5-3 TAD 152

Rival of Sherlock Holmes, The, (on
Solar Pons), by Karen Randrup,
3-1 PDA 26

Rivals of James Bond, The, (espionage
fiction), by Larry Rickert, 4-2

Rivals of James Bond, (continued),
PP 7; (Peter Ward, by David St.John,
with checklist) 4-3 PP 7; (on
Commander Edmond Shaw, with checklist), 4-4 PP 17; (Mark Hood series
by James Dark), 4-5/6 PP 38

Rivals of Sherlock Holmes, The: A
Reference List, (contemporary crime
fiction), by Peter E. Blau, 11-2
TAD 193

Robbins, Bruce: letter of comment,
16 JD 17; 19 JD 14; 6-2 MR 16

Roberson, Shera H.: letter of comment,
24 JD 39

Robert B. Parker and the Hardboiled
Tradition of American Detective
Fiction, by T. Jeff Evans, 1-2
C 100

Robert Bloch on Crime Fiction, by
Robert Bloch, 1-6 MR 15

Robert E. Howard's Library, An Annotated
Checklist, by Charlotte Laughlin,
1-1 PQ 23; 1-2 PQ 51; 1-3 PQ 43;
1-4 PQ 55

Robert Fish, In Memorium, (tributes by
various persons), 14-2 TAD 119

Robert Rostand and Mike Locken, by
Theodore P. Dukeshire, 2-4 MF 4

Roberts, Peter: letter of comment,
2 SF 39

Roberts, Ralph: Tips on Breaking Into
the Pro Ranks, (writing), 12 SF 26

Roberts, Randy: Oscar Wilde and
Sherlock Holmes, A Literary Mystery,
1-1 C 41

Robertson, Steve: letter of comment,
3 MA 26

Robeson, Kenneth: A Coffin for the
Avenger, (fiction), 9 P 13

Robeson, Kenneth: Cargo of Doom,
(fiction), 12 P 18

Robeson, Kenneth: Calling Justice,Inc.,
(fiction), 11 P 19

Robeson, Kenneth: Death to the Avenger,
(fiction), 8 P 16

Robeson, Kenneth: The Doc Savage Method
of Self-Defense, 4 DQ 6

Robeson, Kenneth: Vengeance on the
Avenger, (fiction), 10 P 12

(Robeson, Kenneth), The Avenger's
Aides, (pulp characters), by Wooda
Nicholas Carr, 5 P 6

(Robeson, Kenneth), Kenneth Robeson's
Alter Egos, (Doc Savage novels
written by other than Lester Dent),
by Fred S. Cook, 2 BS 14

(Robeson, Kenneth), The Secret Kenneth
Robesons, (authors using house name),
by Will Murray, 2 D 3

(Robeson, Kenneth: IN HELL, MADONNA),
The Resurrection of IN HELL, MADONNA,
(newly discovered Doc Savage novel
to be published), by Will Murray,
5 DS 8

Robeson Syndrome, The, by Michael Avallone,
2 PW 1

Robey, George: Looking Back on "Round in
Fifty", 8 R 15

(Robey, George), Sax Rohmer, George Robey
and "Round in Fifty", 8 R 11

(Rockwood, Roy), Bomba the Jungle Boy,
(boys' series books by Rockwood),
by Julius R. Chenu, 5 BB 9

(Rockwood, Roy), The Great Marvel Series,
(boys' science fiction series by
Rockwood), by Robert Jennings,
7 BB 5; (checklist) 7 BB 19

Rocky Steele Novels of John B. West, The,
by Darwin T. Turner, 6-4 TAD 226

Roderick Alleyn, Ngaio Marsh's Oxonian
Superintendent, (Roderick Alleyn,
detective), by Earl F. Bargainnier,
11-1 TAD 63

Rodgers, Walter, Jr.: letter of comment,
2 BB 21; 3 MA 26; 5 MA 28

Rodrigues, Joseph: letter of comment,
3-1 CP 6

Rodrigues Ottolengui, A Forgotten American
Mystery Writer, by Wendell Hertig
Taylor, 9-3 TAD 181

Roe, Rick: letter of comment,
13 X 59

Rogers, Denis R.: Book Collecting, (boys'
books), 1-3 BC 79

Rogers, Denis R.: letter of comment,
1-3 BC 85

Rogers, Ivor A.: From the Dealer's View,
(boys' books), 2-4 BC 236

Rogers, Ivor A.: letter of comment,
4-1 BC 416

(Rogers, William A.), William A. Rogers,
Cartoonist-Illustrator, (boys' books
artist; sketch), by Alan S. Dikty,
4-1 BC 411

Rogues Gallery, (con-men in crime fiction),
by Richard S. Lochte II, 2-3 TAD 158

Rogues for the New Century, (comparison
of Grant Allen's AN AFRICAN MILLIONAIRE
and George Randolph Chester's GET-RICH-
QUICK WALLINGFORD), by Fred Dueren,
5-3 MF 11

Rohde, William L.: The Creative Compulsion,
(John D. MacDonald and writing), 10 JD 7

Rohmer, (commentary, Sax Rohmer), by
J.C. Squire, 4 R 3

Rohmer Artist Len Goldberg, a Capsule
Biography, (illustrator, Sax Rohmer),
by Douglas A. Rossman, 2 R 18

Rohmer, Elizabeth Sax: A Sixth Sense,
(on Sax Rohmer), 9 R 25

Rohmer, Elizabeth Sax: letter of comment,
5 R 31; 9 R 31; 11 R 23

ROHMER REVIEW, THE, Author Index,
(issues #1-10), 10 R 15

Rohmer, Sax: A Tale of "Secret Egypt",
7 R 11; (commentary by Robert E.
Briney) 7 R 12

Rohmer, Sax: The Birth of Dr. Fu Manchu,
(by his creator), 17 R 1

Rohmer, Sax: Dancing Girl of Egypt,
15 R 1

Rohmer, Sax: The Haunted Temple,
9 R 1

Rohmer, Sax: Here and There, (anecdotes), 11 R 1

Rohmer, Sax: How Fu Manchu was Born,
(by his creator), 2 R 3

Rohmer, Sax: Live Instruments of
Villainy, 6 R 3

Rohmer, Sax: Meet Dr. Fu Manchu,
10 R 1

Rohmer, Sax: Nelson Keys and Captain
Kettle, (essay on collaborations),
18 R 1

Rohmer, Sax: "Shakespeare", (verse),
8 R 14

Rohmer, Sax: Were Houdini's Feats
Supernatural?, 5 R 1

(Rohmer, Sax), A Case of Identity,
Being a Trifling Monograph Upon
the Similarities between Sir Denis
Nayland Smith and Sherlock Holmes,
by Andrew Jay Peck, 2 R 9

(Rohmer, Sax), A Curious Interview,
by James Wade, 13 R 8

(Rohmer, Sax), A Note on Dovelands
Cottage, by J.L. Biggers, 14 R 23

(Rohmer, Sax), A Question of Time,
by Cay Van Ash, 17 R 7

(Rohmer, Sax), A Rohmer Miscellany,
by Robert E. Briney, 11 R 8

(Rohmer, Sax), A Sixth Sense, by
Elizabeth Sax Rohmer, 9 R 25

(Rohmer, Sax), A Walking Tour of Sax
Rohmer's London, by Julian L.
Biggers, 18 R 13

(Rohmer, Sax), An Informal Survey of
the Works of Sax Rohmer, by Robert
E. Briney, 1 R 3

(Rohmer, Sax), Bibliographica
Rohmeriana, (bibliographical data),
by Robert E. Briney, 8 R 25;
9 R 13; 11 R 17; 12 R 17; 17 R 15

(Rohmer, Sax), The Blue Scorpion,
by Robert Weinberg, 10 R 20

(Rohmer, Sax), Book News, 7 R 20;
8 R 18; 9 R 29; 10 R 25; 12 R 16;
13 R 26; 14 R 10; 17 R 19

(Rohmer, Sax), The Books of Sax Rohmer,
A Chronological List, by Robert E.
Briney, 1 R 25

(Rohmer, Sax), Commentary, by Douglas
A. Rossman, 6 R 5

(Rohmer, Sax), Dantean Allusions in
"The Trail of Fu Manchu", by J.R.
Christopher, 5 R 27

(Rohmer, Sax), The Doctor's Blade,
(interview with Rohmer, 1947),
9 R 19

(Rohmer, Sax), The Early Chronicles
of Fu Manchu, by Robert E. Briney,
15 R 9

(Rohmer, Sax), Film Notes, by W.O.G.
Lofts, 9 R 23

(Rohmer, Sax), Fleet Street Report, by Andrew Jay Peck, 2 R 18; 3 R 24; 4 R 20; (by Andrew Jay Peck and Robert E. Briney) 5 R (cover)

(Rohmer, Sax), Fu Chin Chow, (comic strip parody), by Jack Gaughan, 13 R 11

(Rohmer, Sax), Fu Manchu, by Cay Van Ash, 9 R 15

(Rohmer, Sax), Fu (Manchu), by Henry E. Wenden, 8 R 27

(Rohmer, Sax), Fu Manchu Speaks, by Sidney Petty, 11 R 12

(Rohmer, Sax), Fu Manchu Thinks Kindly of Sir Denis Nayland Smith, (verse), by Edward Lauterbach, 1-2 PDA 48

(Rohmer, Sax), Good Old Petrie, (Dr. Petrie in Fu Manchu stories) by David Braveman, 3 R 18

(Rohmer, Sax), The Hand of Dr. Insidious, by Ron Goulart, 13 R 1

(Rohmer, Sax), Houdini to the Rescue, by John Harwood, 4 R 13

(Rohmer, Sax), The Immortal Enemy (on Fu Manchu), by Robert A.W. Lowndes, 6 R 1

(Rohmer, Sax), The Imperial Dragon, 10 R 5

(Rohmer, Sax), The Incredible Captain O'Hagan, by Alvin F. Germeshausen, 1 R 27

(Rohmer, Sax), The Last Encounter, (Fu Manchu and Sir Denis Nayland Smith), by James Wade, 1-2 PDA 66

(Rohmer, Sax), Letter from Sax Rohmer to LONDON OPINION, 1919, 9 R 16

(Rohmer, Sax), Letter to Bransby Williams, 10 R 4

(Rohmer, Sax), Letter to Sherlock, and Annotations, by Julian L. Biggers, 6 R 7

(Rohmer, Sax), Limehouse and the River Police, 5 R 13

(Rohmer, Sax), The Literary Tradition of Brow Spraying, by J.R. Christopher, 3 R 23

(Rohmer, Sax), Locating Dr. Petrie's Practive, (Fu Manchu stories), 7 R 17

(Rohmer, Sax), The Lost "Eye", by Robert E. Briney, 6 R 9; 7 R 10

(Rohmer, Sax), The Man Who Never Said Anything, by John Harwood, 6 R 20

(Rohmer, Sax), The Man of Stepney, by John E. Carroll, 6 R 17

(Rohmer, Sax), Mr. Chang, A Minor Pulp Villain, by John A. Dinan, 12 R 21

(Rohmer, Sax), Musette, Max and Sumuru, (radio serials), by Robert E. Briney and W.O.G. Lofts, 15 R 5

(Rohmer, Sax), My Hero: Fu Manchu, by John Ball, 11 R 5

(Rohmer, Sax), The Mysterious Arthur H. Ward, by Robert E. Briney, 12 R 5

(Rohmer, Sax), On Compiling a Sax Rohmer Collection, by Alan Warren 13-2 TAD 148

(Rohmer, Sax), On Finding Petrie's Correct Name (Fu Manchu stories), by Evelyn A. Herzog, 18 R 25

(Rohmer, Sax), Ourselves and Gaston Max, by Cay Van Ash, 15 R 23

(Rohmer, Sax), The Papyrocunabula of Sax Rohmer, (paperback book editions, with checklist), by Richard Paul Haull, 3-4 CP 15

(Rohmer, Sax), The Paul Harley Series, by Robert E. Briney, 17 R 15

(Rohmer, Sax), Petrie Letter, by Bruce E. Pelz, 3 R 16

(Rohmer, Sax), The Politics of Fu Manchu, by Jim Pobst, 10 R 9

(Rohmer, Sax), The Polyglot Mr. Rohmer, by Jean Stafford, 14 R 1

(Rohmer, Sax), Pyramid Reissues of Fu Manchu Paperbacks, (Pyramid Books) by Robert E. Briney, 15 R 29

(Rohmer, Sax), Pyramid Reprints, (checklist of Fu Manchu series in Pyramid Books paperbacks), by Robert E. Briney, 9-4 TAD 247

(Rohmer, Sax), Radio Fu Manchu, (radio serials), by Ray Stanich, 12 R 11

(Rohmer, Sax), Radio Luxembourg Dr. Fu Manchu Series, (checklist, radio serials), 11 R 15

(Rohmer, Sax), Revenge a la Mode, by Vincent J. Miranda, 13 R 23

(Rohmer, Sax), Rohmer, by J.C. Squire, 4 R 3

(Rohmer, Sax), The Romance of the Middle East, by John E. Carroll, 4 R 7

(Rohmer, Sax), The Romance of Scarabs, by Luther Norris, 1 R 30

(Rohmer, Sax), "Round in Fifty", by George Robey, 8 R 15

(Rohmer, Sax), Sax Rohmer, An Astrological Analysis, by Julian L. Biggers, 8 R 19

(Rohmer, Sax), Sax Rohmer and the Art of Making Villains, by Anice Page Cooper, 5 R 8

(Rohmer, Sax), Sax Rohmer, George Robey and "Round in Fifty", 8 R 11

(Rohmer, Sax), Sax Rohmer in Chicago, 14 R 5

(Rohmer, Sax), Sax Rohmer in Dutch, (Dutch editions of books), by Robert E. Briney, 11 R 17

(Rohmer, Sax), Sax Rohmer in French, (French editions of books), by Robert E. Briney, 12 R 17

(Rohmer, Sax), Sax Rohmer in the 1920's: Notes on Chronology, by Cay Van Ash, 18 R 21

(Rohmer, Sax), Sax Rohmer in Wartime, by Robert E. Briney, 9 R 32

(Rohmer, Sax), The Seals of Si Fan, 11 R 21

(Rohmer, Sax), The Search for Sax Rohmer, by Cay Van Ash, 14 R 13

(Rohmer, Sax), Secret Egypt Unveiled, by W.O.G. Lofts, 8 R 23

(Rohmer, Sax), Sh-h-h! Dr. Fu Manchu is
  On the Air!, (radio serials), by
  W.O.G.Lofts and Robert E. Briney,
  11 R 9
(Rohmer, Sax), The Shadow of Ying Ko,
  by Frank D. McSherry, Jr., 16 R 1
(Rohmer, Sax), "She Who Loveth Silence",
  (from Rohmer: GREY FACE), by Stephen
  Shutt, 15 R 25
(Rohmer, Sax), Sinitic Sonnet, (verse),
  4 R 27
(Rohmer, Sax), The Smith Letters,
  ("letters" from Sir Denis Nayland
  Smith), by Robert E. Briney, 12 R 9
(Rohmer, Sax), Some Notes on Rohmer;s
  Witch-Queens, by Stephen Shutt,
  12 R 1
(Rohmer, Sax), The Sound of Fu Manchu,
  by Leslie Charteris, 6 R 19
(Rohmer, Sax), The Third Eyelid, by
  Marvin L. Morrison, 14 R 19
(Rohmer, Sax), Those Mysterious Mandolins,
  (Fu Manchu on screen), by Robert
  W. Shurtleff, 18 R 9
(Rohmer, Sax), Thoughts on the Master
  of Villainy, by W.O.G.Lofts, 10 R 27
(Rohmer, Sax), The Thugs and Dacoits
  of India, by John E. Carroll, 8 R 1
(Rohmer, Sax), The Well of Zem-Zem, by
  Robert Galbreath, 9 R 18
(Rohmer, Sax), Who Killed Kelly?, by
  T.J.McCauley, 14 R 11
(Rohmer, Sax), Zagazig, by Jeffrey N.
  Weiss, 4 R 16
(Rohmer, Sax), Zagazig, Zagazig, by
  Evelyn Herzog, 5 R 22
(Rohmer, Sax), Zagazig, Zagazig= Z.A.
  Gazig, 5 R 25
(Rohmer, Sax: Sir Denis Nayland Smith
  series), Checklist, Annotated, by
  Barry Van Tilburg, 5-1 MF 2
(Rolfe, Zach, series: J.J.Lamb), The
  Trenchcoat Files, by Paul Bishop,
  3 PE 15
Roland Daniel - Prolific Mystery Writer,
  by W.O.G.Lofts, 6-4 TAD 242
Roles, D.: letter of comment, 9 LR 19
Rollinson, Paul: letter of comment,
  3-2 CP 2
Romance of Scarabs, The, (in regard to
  Sax Rohmer novels of Egypt), by
  Luther Norris, 1 R 30
Romance of the Middle East, The, (in re:
  Sax Rohmer novels), by John E.
  Carroll, 4 R 7
Romantic Reality in the Spy Stories of
  Len Deighton, by Fred Erisman,
  10-2 TAD 101
Ronald Arbuthnott Knox, (sketch of
  author), by Norman Donaldson,
  7-4 TAD 235
Roney, Harvey: Seven Years with Heinie
  Faust, (literary reminiscences of
  Frederick Faust), 2-3 FC 1
Ronning, Harland: letter of comment,
  5/6 MN 12

Rookie Type, The; Police Procedural
  Pt.VI, by George N. Dove, 11-3
  TAD 249
(Roscoe, Theodore), Bibliography:
  Theodore Roscoe, (pulp author),
  by William J. Clark, 65 PU 15
Rose, David: Dialogue Between Author
  and Publisher, (humorous fiction),
  10 LR 1
Rose, David: letter of comment,
  7 CL 10; 12 CL 10; 6/7 LR 27;
  2 PE 46; 3 PE 33; 4 PE 28; 5 PE
  37; 1-5 PP 32; 2-1 PP 38; 2-2
  PP 31; 3-1 PP 39; 3-1 PP 41;
  3-3 PP 36; 4-1 PP 50
Rose, David: On Mystery and Science
  Fiction Fandom, (generalized
  comparisons), 16 CD 3
Rose, David: The Round Robin Caper,
  or, The Too Long Goodbye, Pt.4,
  8 PE 9; (other parts by Joe R.
  Lansdale, Ralph Diffinetti, and
  R. Jeff Banks: 5 PE 5; 5 PE 7;
  6 PE 26)
Rose, John: letter of comment,
  3 MA 26
Roseliep, Raymond: A Decade Later
  August, (verse, re: August Derleth)
  4-3 AD 8
Roseliep, Raymond: letter of comment,
  2-3/4 AD 5
Roseliep, Raymond: My Homily, August
  Derleth, (verse), 2-3/4 AD 10
(ROSEMARY'S BABY: Ira Levin), The
  Ending of ROSEMARY'S BABY and
  Other Comments from Ira Levin
  (interview), 3-1 MR 9
Rosenblatt, R.: letter of comment,
  11 R 24
(Rosmond, Babette), Department of
  Unknown Mystery Writers: Babette
  Rosmond, by Marvin Lachman,
  4-2 PP 19
(Ross, Angus: Marcus Farrow series),
  Checklist, Annotated, by Barry
  Van Tilburg, 5-2 MF 2
Ross, Helaine: A Woman's Intuition,
  Wives and Lovers in British
  Golden Age Detective Novels,
  2-1 C 17
Ross, Joe: letter of comment, 2 BS 2;
  6 BS 22
Ross Macdonald Interview, by Gene
  Davidson and John Knoerle,
  1-1 M 5
Ross Macdonald, The Personal Paradigm
  and Popular Fiction, by Zahava K.
  Dorinson, 10-1 TAD 43
Rossman, Douglas A.: Commentary, (on
  Sax Rohmer), 6 R 5
Rossman, Douglas A.: letter of comment,
  8 R 33; 11 R 25; 13 R 31
Rossman, Douglas A.: Rohmer Artist Len
  Goldberg, A Capsule Biography,
  (Sax Rohmer illustrator), 2 R 18

(Rossman, Douglas A.), Biographical
   Sketch, 7 R 25
(Rostand, Robert), Robert Rostand and
   Mike Locken, by Theodore P. Dukeshire,
   2-4 MF 4
(Roudybush, Alexandra), Introducing
   Alexandra Roudybush, (author), by
   Gerie Frazier, 3-3 MF 2
"Round in Fifty", (Sax Rohmer), by
   George Robey, 8 R 15
Round Robin Caper, or, The Too Long
   Goodbye, (round robin story by four
   authors), by Joe R. Lansdale, Ralph
   Diffinetti, R. Jeff Banks, and David
   Rose, 5 PE 5; 5 PE 7; 6 PE 26; 8 PE 9
Rountree, Brian: The Maxims of Solar Pons,
   1-1 PDA 31; 1-2 PDA 56; 2-1 PDA 24;
   2-2 PDA 62
(Rover Boys series), Boys Book Oddities:
   The Rover Boys, by Harry K. Hudson,
   1-4 BC 112
(Rowland, Sidney), Department of Unknown
   Mystery Writers, by Marvin Lachman,
   1-4 PP 15
Roy, John F.: letter of comment, 14 SF 47
Roy Vickers, The Department of Dead Ends
   Series: A Partial Bibliography, by
   James Mark Purcell, 4-1 MR 29
Royal Bloodline: The Biography of the
   Queen Canon, (Ellery Queen), by
   Francis M. Nevins, Jr., 1-1 QC 6;
   1-2 QC 2; 1-3 QC 2; 1-4 QC 2; 2-1
   QC 2; 2-2 QC 1; 3-1 QC 2; 3-2 QC 2
(Royston, Col., & Peter Castle series:
   Gilderoy Davison), Checklist,
   Annotated, by Barry Van Tilburg,
   5-3 MF 20
Ruber, Peter A.: The Pontine Canon,
   (offers a key to identify the
   Solar Pons stories of August
   Derleth), 1-2 PD 4
Ruber, Peter A., and Ronald DeWaal:
   The Solar System, (code to
   identify Solar Pons stories of
   August Derleth), 2-1 PDA 2
Ruble, William: Checklist, Van der Valk
   Mysteries of Nicolas Freeling,
   5-2 MR 5
Ruble, William: Explaining Ellery
   Queen (Who is Ellery Queen?),
   2-2 QC 8
Ruble, William: letter of comment,
   13 JD 11; 26 JD 49; 3-1 MR 16;
   6-1 MR 22; 1-1 QC 12
Ruble, William: Van der Valk, (series
   detective of Nicolas Freeling),
   5-2 MR 1
Rudd, Donald: letter of comment,
   11 MN L1
Ruggieri, Helen: Homage to Bela,
   (verse, re: Bela Lugosi),
   1 CD 43
Ruhm, Herbert: letter of comment,
   9-1 TAD 80; 12-4 TAD 356

Rumpf, Donald F.: letter of comment,
   2-4 TB 2; 2-5 TBN 6
Running Hot and Cold with Ron Faust,
   (mystery novels of Faust), by
   George Kelley, 5-4 MF 11
Runte, Robert: letter of comment,
   2 SF 40
(Russell, Col. Charles, series:
   William Haggard), Checklist,
   Annotated, by Barry Van Tilburg,
   4-3 MF 27
(Russell, Eric Frank), Checklist of
   Books, by Lemuel Nash, 28 X 12
Russell, Luana: A Judy Bolton
   Mystery - Blacklisted Classics,
   (criticism by various groups of
   girls' series books in past),
   2-1 C 35
(Russell, Martin), Martin Russell:
   A Profile, (sketch), by Sven-
   Ingmar Petersson, 8-1 TAD 48;
   (checklist) 8-1 TAD 49
(Russell, Ray: INCUBUS), Mystery
   Plus: Incubus, by R. Jeff Banks,
   1-3 PP 9
Russell, Ross: letter of comment,
   8-1 TAD 75
Ruth Rendell, A Bibliography, by
   Don Miller, 10 MN A27
Ruth Rendell, A Bibliography, by
   J. Clyde Stevens, 7 MY 8
Rutt, Timothy J.: The Dynamics of
   the Brothers Moriarty,
   (speculative Sherlockiana),
   1-1 WA 5
Rutt, Timothy J.: The First Doc Savage,
   The Apocryphal Life of Clark Savage,
   Jr. (speculative birth and death of
   Doc Savage), 1-3 WA 3
Rutt, Timothy J.: The Stalker in the
   Dark, Jack the Ripper and Wold
   Newton, 1-3 WA 5
Rutt, Todd, and Arn McConnell:
   Caves, Gas, and The Great Transfer
   Theory, (speculation on disappear-
   ance of popular fiction characters),
   1-2 WA 11
Rutt, Todd, and Arn McConnell: The
   Mysterious Case of the Carters, or
   How Hirohito Became Nick Carter's
   Aide, ("genealogy" of the Carter
   family), 1-2 WA 3
Rutt, Todd, and Arn McConnell: The
   Terrible Beekeeper, (fiction, a
   pastiche on The Spider, Doc Savage,
   The Shadow, Sherlock Holmes),
   1-1 WA 3; 1-2 WA 6; 1-3 WA 7;
   1-4 WA 7; 2-1 WA 5
Rutt, Todd, and Timothy J. Rutt: Duck
   Savage, The Mallard of Bronze,
   (comic strip pastiche on Doc
   Savage), 1-2 WA 9; 1-3 WA 11;
   1-4 WA 11; 2-1 WA 18

Rutter, Joseph: The Jerry Hicks Series by William Heyliger, (boys' series books), 1-4 YB 17

Rutter, Joseph: letter of comment, 2 MA 28

Ryder, Cecil A.: The Infallible Boswell, Lyndon Parker, M.D. (chronicler of cases of Solar Pons), 3-1 PDA 15

Ryder, Cecil A.: Reminiscences of Praed Street, (re: Solar Pons), 2-1 PDA 38

S.S.Van Dine, A Biographical Sketch, by Bruce R. Beaman, 8-2 TAD 133

(Saberhagen, Fred: THE ADVENTURE OF THE HOLMES-DRACULA FILE), Mystery Plus, by R. Jeff Banks, 2-4 PP 16

(Saberhagen, Fred: AN OLD FRIEND OF THE FAMILY), Mystery Plus: Old Friends Break New Ground, by R. Jeff Banks, 3-6 PP 16

Sac of Fortune, The, (on August Derleth), by Sinclair Lewis, 4-2 AD 1

Sac Prairie Looked the Same (but August Derleth Wasn't There), by Norbert Blei, 3-4 AD 1

Sac Prairie People, (verse, re: August Derleth), by Steve Eng, 2-3/4 AD 8

(Sacco & Vanzetti case), The Unabated Storm: Sacco & Vanzetti, by David Bates, 2-6 PP 23

Sader, Joanne: letter of comment, 22 JD 19

(Sadler, Mark), Private Eye in an Evil Time: Mark Sadler's Paul Shaw, (Dennis Lynds writing as Mark Sadler), by Francis M. Nevins, Jr., 38 X 11

Saga of the Phoenix, The: That Probably Should Never Have Arisen, (on Phoenix Press paperback mystery series), by Bill Pronzini, 10-2 TAD 106

(Sail, Oscar, series: Lester Dent), The Man from Miami - Lester Dent's Oscar Sail, by Fred Blosser, 5-2 TAD 93

Sailing Uncharted Seas, (Ray Palmer and the Shaver Mystery), by David & Sue Bates, 2-2 CP 35

Saint Mystery Library, The, (with check-list and photos), by M.C. Hill, 2-4 PQ 4

Saint Enterprises & Bond-Charteris Enterprises, (checklist of publications), by Michael Masliah, 12-4 TAD 354

Saint of the North, The: Black John Smith of Halfaday Creek, by John Harwood, 3-6 MF 3

Saint on Film, The, by J. Randolph Cox, 5-2 MR 14

(Saint, The: Leslie Charteris), Bond-Charteris Enterprises and Saint Enterprises, (checklist), by Michael Masliah, 12-4 TAD 354

(Saint, The: Leslie Charteris), Leslie Charteris and The Saint, Five Decades of Partnership, by Jan Alexandersson and Iwan Hedman, 4-4 MF 21

(Saint, The: Leslie Charteris), Prolegomena to a Bibliography of the Immortal Works of Leslie Charteris by J. Randolph Cox, 5-2 MR 9

(Saint, The: Leslie Charteris), Series Synopses, by John Vining, 10-2 TAD 187

(SAINT MYSTERY MAGAZINE, THE), Death of a Magazine, (cessation of publication), by Allen J. Hubin, 1-2 TAD 47

Saint's Boston Caper, The, by John A. Dinan, 11 X 17

Salathiel, Max: letter of comment, 15 X 14

Sales Score on Mystery Authors, The, (paperback bestsellers), 3-6 MR 29

(Salg, Bert), "Illustrated by Bert Salg", (illustrator for Leo Edwards' boys' series books), 1-2 TB 1; 1-3 TBN 11

(Salg, Bert), Judge Perkins (comic strip, 1935), 2-5 TBN 7

(Salinger J.D.), The Article I Couldn't Publish, (on Ian Fleming and J.D. Salinger's THE LAUGHING MAN), by Guy M. Townsend, 1-1 MF 18

(Sallust, Gregory, series: Dennis Wheatley), Checklist, by Iwan Hedman, 2-4 TAD 235

(Sallust, Gregory, series: Dennis Wheatley), Checklist, Annotated, by Barry Van Tilburg, 5-3 MF 18

Salmonson, Jessica Amanda: Letter of comment, 38 X 144

Sam Space, An Eye on Mars, (SPACE FOR HIRE: William F. Nolan), by William F. Nolan, 1-3 M 28

Sam Spade, Lover, by Peter Wolfe, 11-4 TAD 366; 38 X 21

Sam Spade Talking, by John M. Reilly, 1-2 C 119

Sam Steele... (Sam Steele boys' series books by Capt. Hugh Fitzgerald, pen name for L. Frank Baum), by George Holmes, 1-6 YB 8

Samoian, Robert: letter of comment, 4-6 MF 48; 5-4 MF 40; 3-6 PP 33; 4-1 PP 43; 4-2 PP 57; 4-3 PP 31; 4-4 PP 34

(Sampson, Emma Speed), Miss Minerva and Kinfolks, (juvenile series by Sampson), by Julius R. Chenu, 1-4 YB 3

Sampson, Robert: A Footnote for Shadow Collectors, (The Shadow: duplication of titles for different stories and other bibliographical data), 4-2 MR 9

Sampson, Robert: A Preliminary Inquiry
Into Initial Costs Associated with
Establishing a Secret Crime-Fighting
Identity, (do you want to be a masked
crime fighter, a la pulps?), 4-4 MR 28

Sampson, Robert: Blood Chronicle, (on
Richard Curtis van Loan as The
Phantom Detective, and THE PHANTOM
DETECTIVE magazine), 3-3 MR 3

Sampson, Robert: Bumudemutomuro, (an
in-depth study of Tarzan), 8 U 3

Sampson, Robert: The Chang Monster, (Mr.
Chang, pulp villain), 14 SF 41

Sampson, Robert: Dinosaur! (re: Doc
Savage), 11 X 110

Sampson, Robert: Doc in Digest, (the
digest-size issues of DOC SAVAGE
magazine), 2 P 3

Sampson, Robert: Doctor Wonderful, (Dr.
Nancy Dayland, pulp detective created
by Florence Mae Pettee, with partial
checklist), 5-6 MF 13

Sampson, Robert: Faces from the Shadows,
(pulp magazine heroes), 6-2 MR 7

Sampson, Robert: Fourteen Issues, (study
and descriptive essay on SCOTLAND
YARD, pulp magazine), 22 X 4

Sampson, Robert: Ghost Story, (George
Chance, The Ghost, Super Detective,
in the pulp magazines), 5 P 20

Sampson, Robert: Grace Note, (Grace
Culver, series character: Roswell
Brown), 17 X 8

Sampson, Robert: Just a Little Matter of
Doom, (commentary on The Shadow),
4 X 7

Sampson, Robert: letter of comment,
11 DS 19; 5-4 MF 44; 3-3 MR 11;
3-5 MR 35; 4-1 MR 20; 4-4 MR 14;
4-4 MR 16; 6-1 MR 19

Sampson, Robert: Life as a Series of
Abstract Analyses, (discussion of
T.S.Stribling's Professor Poggioli
stories with checklist including
pulp magazines), 2-2 C 61

Sampson, Robert: Notes on an Ideal Library,
(the Doc Savage novels in hardcover
by Ideal Library), 2/3 DR 2

Sampson, Robert: Peterman From the Old
School, ("Big-Nose Charlie" in the
early pulp "crook" stories), 5-4
MF 2

Sampson, Robert: THE PHANTOM DETECTIVE
Magazine Checklist and Index 1933-1953,
(pulp magazine), 3-3 MR 8

Sampson, Robert: Pulp, 22 X 55

Sampson, Robert: The Pulp Library, (story
snyopsis and data on pulp magazine
issues), 30 X 21; 33 X 111; 38 X 131;
42 X 131

Sampson, Robert: Shadow on the Wind, (on
dime novels), 8 U 16

Sampson, Robert: The Solving Six, (Solving
Six series of short stories by Agatha
Christie), 5-5 MF 3

Sampson, Robert: That Terrible
Sunlight, (John Sunlight, villain,
in Doc Savage stories), 10 P 26

Sampson, Robert: The Very Much So
Clever Fellow, (Jules deGrandin),
5 WT 3

Sampson, Robert: The Vulnerable Shadow,
(The Shadow, pulp hero), 1 P 24

Sampson, Robert, and Wooda Nicholas
Carr: The Pulp Corner, (memoirs
of a Doc Savage reader), 14 SF 21

Sampson, Robert, and Wooda Nicholas
Carr: The Pulp Corner, (pulp
magazine collecting experiences
and reminiscences), 15 SF 8

Samuel, Aryah R.: letter of comment,
1-4 TAD 152

(San Francisco Academy of Comic Art),
A Visit to Two Museums, by Albert
Tonik, 10 SF 34

San Francisco Mysteries, (mystery
stories with San Francisco locale),
by Don Herron, 3-2 M 8

(San Francisco Mystery Bookstore),
Mystery Poll, by Bruce Taylor,
3-5 PP 31

(San Francisco Mystery Bookstore),
World of Mystery: The Burritt
Street Beat, (report of party,
April 1981), by Erik C. Kendresen,
3-2 M 30

(San Francisco Mystery Bookstore),
Some of My Best Friends are Books,
by Mary Groff, 13-2 TAD 171

Sanders, Donald: Volland's Golden
Youth Series, (boys' books),
2-1 BC 137

(Sanders, Lawrence), Sinning with
Lawrence Sanders, (discusses
crime fiction novels by Sanders),
by George Kelley, 3-5 MF 20

(Sanders, Lawrence: THE FIRST DEADLY
SIN), Expiatory Symbolism in
Lawrence Sanders' THE FIRST
DEADLY SIN, by Bill Nelson,
1-2 C 71

Sanderson, Jim: Flagship Books,
(partial checklist, paperback
line), 2-3 PQ 48

Sanderson, Joy: letter of comment,
3-1 TAD 61

Sanderson, Ron: letter of comment,
1-5 CP 1

Sandoe, James: The Hardboiled Dick,
A Personal Checklist, 1-2 TAD 38

Sandoe, James: letter of comment,
9 JD 9; 17 JD 30; 17 R 21;
1-4 TAD 152; 2-1 TAD 67; 2-4
TAD 280; 3-2 TAD 140; 4-4 TAD
255; 7-3 TAD 223

Sandoe, James: The Reviewer at Work,
11-1 TAD 84

(Sandoe, James), Meet the Author:
James Sandoe, by Allen J. Hubin,
1-2 TAD 42

(Sandoe, James), James Sandoe: A Retrospective (and Memorial), by Tom and Enid Schantz, 13-4 TAD 288

Sandow, George: letter of comment, 2 SF 40

Sandulo, Sandy: letter of comment, 2-2 MF 56; 3-2 MF 61; 4-1 MF 39; 3-1 PP 42

(Sangster, Jimmy), Some Themes in the Film Work of Jimmy Sangster, by Jack Edmund Nolan, 5-6 MR 21

(Sangster, Jimmy: "The Legacy"), Mystery Plus: A Movie Review, by R. Jeff Banks, 3-3 PP 17

(Santesson, Hans Stefan), Hans Stefan Santesson and the Unicorn Mystery Book Club, by Edward D. Hoch, 8-3 TAD 185

(Sapir, Richard, and Warren Murphy: The Destroyer), Created, The Destroyer: An Interview with Warren Murphy, by Richard Lochte, 11-3 TAD 284

Sapp, Judson C.: The Bibliophile - Sooner or Later, (on collecting Rex Stout books and related), 6 U 31

Sapp, Judson C.: letter of comment, 2-1 CP 1; 6/7 LR 19; 3-5 MF 50; 3/4 MN 16; 11 MN L6; 11 MN L8; 2 PE 44; 4 PE 28; 1-2 PP 28; 3-3 PP 35; 15 X 14; 24 X 47

Sapp, Judson C.: Nero Wolfe is "On the Air", (radio serials), 9 MN A19

Sapp, Judson C.: Orchids to The Wolfe Pack, The Second Annual Black Orchid Banquet, (report on meeting of fan organization for Nero Wolfe stories), 6 U 29

(Sapper: Bulldog Drummond series), Checklist, Annotated, by Barry Van Tilburg, 4-5 MF 22

Sara Woods, (sketch), by Estelle Fox, 4-3 TAD 152

Sarjeant, William Antony S.: A Preliminary Chronology of the Documented Cases of Napoleon Bonaparte, (detective character created by Arthur W.Upfield), 12-4 TAD 358

Sarjeant, William Antony S.: Checklist, Edmund Crispin, 3-3 PP 9

Sarjeant, William Antony S.: Detection Among the Mountains; The Writings of Glyn Carr, 4-5/6 PP 3

Sarjeant, William Antony S.: Edmund Crispin, A Memorial and Appreciation, 3-3 PP 3

Sarjeant, William Antony S.: Detectives and Geology, (geological clues in crime fiction), 11-3 TAD 294

Sarjeant, William Antony S.: The Great Australian Detective, (Detective-Inspector Napoleon Bonaparte: Arthur W.Upfield), 12-2 TAD 99

Sarjeant, William Antony S.: In Defense of Mr. Fortune, (Reggie Fortune, detective: H.C.Bailey), 14-4 TAD 302

Sarjeant, William Antony S.: letter of comment: 3-3 PP 35; 10-2 TAD 159

Sarjeant, William Antony S.: Obsequies About Oxford; The Investigations and Eccentricities of Gervase Fen, (detective character of Edmund Crispin, with bibliography), 14-3 TAD 196

Satirist and Sleuth, or, Trent versus Toff, (on E.C.Bentley's parody of Lord Peter Wimsey), by Mary F. Lindsley, 2-1 PDA 28

Sauerwald, James K.: letter of comment, 3/4 MN 11

Sauk Prairie - First Impressions, (visit to Wisconsin re: August Derleth), 2-1 AD 3

(Saunders, Norman), A Partial List of Paperback Covers Painted by Norman Saunders, 1-3 PQ 41

(Saunders, Norman), Personal Reminiscences, (as pulp magazine cover artist), by Norman Saunders with introduction by Nils Hardin, 33 X 116

(Saunders, Norman), PQ Interview with Norman Saunders, 1-3 PQ 38

"Savage, Clark, Jr.": Clark Savage, the Early Years, (Doc Savage), 7 DQ 10

"Savage, Clark, Jr.": letter of comment, 7 DQ 3; 9 DS 23; 12 DS 5

Savage Comments, (an abbreviation code for Doc Savage stories), by Gene Christie, 4 DR 4; (numbering the Doc Savage series) 2/3 DR 12, by Gene Christie

(Savage, Ernest), Department of Unknown Mystery Writers: Ernest Savage, by Marvin Lachman, 4-4 PP 11; (Ernest Savage response to article) 4-5/6 PP 33

(Savage, Pat), Pat Savage, the Original Supergirl, (character in Doc Savage novels), 1 BSA 20

(SAVAGE, THE: Peter McCurtin), Mystery Plus: A Pair of Triple Threats ("a magical western mystery"), by R. Jeff Banks, 4-4 PP 14

Savage Views, (comments on DOC SAVAGE magazines No.1 and No.2), by Mark Justice, 1 MB 23

(Savage, Doc), see: "Doc Savage"

Sawney Beane, An Incident From the Casebook of a Royal Detective, (British classic true crime), by Veronica M.S.Kennedy, 9-2 TAD 126

Sax Rohmer, An Astrological Analysis, by Julian L. Biggers, 8 R 19

Sax Rohmer and the Art of Making Villains, by Anice Page Cooper, 5 R 8

Sax Rohmer, George Robey, and "Round in Fifty", by R.E.Briney, 8 R 11

Sax Rohmer in Chicago, by John Nieminski,
14 R 5

Sax Rohmer in Dutch, (Dutch editions of
works), by Robert E. Briney, 11 R 17

Sax Rohmer in French, (French editions of
works), by Robert E. Briney, 12 R 17

Sax Rohmer in the 1920's: Notes on
Chronology, by Cay Van Ash, 18 R 21

Sax Rohmer in Wartime, by Robert E. Briney,
9 R 32

Saxon, Claude: letter of comment,
4-5 MF 45

Saxon, Claude: Some Notes on the Detective
Element in Western Fiction, 1A MF 17

Say Hello to The Spider (for the Pulps
Are Back), on revivals of the pulp
hero stories in paperback books),
by Kenneth Turan, 1 DS 16

(Sayers, Dorothy L.), Checklist of
Detective Stories, by Charles Shibuk,
2-2 MR 10

(Sayers, Dorothy L.), Dorothy L. Sayers,
A Brief Addendum, by William White,
3-1 MR 12

(Sayers, Dorothy L.), Dorothy L. Sayers,
A Second Brief Addendum, by Mary Ann
Whitten, 3-3 MR 2

(Sayers, Dorothy L.), Dorothy L. Sayers
and the Apotheosis of Detective
Fiction, (social vs. puzzle), by
Elaine Bander, 10-4 TAD 362

(Sayers, Dorothy L.), Dorothy L. Sayers'
Detective Short Fiction, (literary
discussion), by William Reynolds,
14-2 TAD 176

(Sayers, Dorothy L.), Lord Peter Views
the Telly, (series on BBC TV), by
J.R.Christopher, 12-1 TAD 20

(Sayers, Dorothy L.), Lord Peter Wimsey
of Piccadilly, His Lordship's Life
and Times, by William M. Scott,
13-1 TAD 17; 13-3 TAD 212

(Sayers, Dorothy L.: Harriet Vane,
detective), Feminists as Detectives:
Harriet Vane, Kate Fansler, Sarah
Chayse, by Kathleen Gregory Klein,
13-1 TAD 31

Saylor, Robert: letter of comment,
30 X 149

Saylor, Louise: David (Pudd'nhead)
Wilson, The Missing Figure in a
Detective's Group, (re: Mark Twain),
13-1 TAD 8

(Scandinavia), Mystery Fiction in
Scandinavia, by Iwan Hedman, 3-3
TAD 173

Scarcest Title, The, (on THE VILLAGE
STREET AND OTHER POEMS by Frederick
Faust), by William J. Clark, 1-4
FC 9

(Scene of the Crime Bookshop), Mean
Streets Revisited: Seven Hardboiled
Authors at the Scene of the Crime
Bookshop, by Ray Zone, 2-3 M 18

Scents of Wonder, (space opera in
the pulp magazines), by Eric
Bentcliffe, 60 PU 13

Schaechter, Leslie: letter of comment,
6/7 LR 25

Schaffer, Mark: A Glance at Paperback
History, 2-2 PQ 31

Schaffer, Mark: Interior Paperback
Art, 3-2 PQ 43

Schaffer, Mark: letter of comment,
3-1 PQ 6

Schaffer, Mark: Selling Culture With
Paperback Covers, 2-4 PQ 42

Schantz, Enid: letter of comment,
4-2 TAD 129; 4-4 TAD 253

Schantz, Tom: letter of comment,
7-1 TAD 75; 7-3 TAD 233

Schantz, Tom and Enid: James Sandoe,
A Retrospective (and Memorial),
13-4 TAD 288

Scheideman, J.W.: letter of comment,
9-4 TAD 297; 10-1 TAD 3; 11-2
TAD 208; 12-1 TAD 93

Scheideman, J.W.: Mycroft Holmes
and Ian Murdock's Case, (on
Sherlock Holmes and "The Adventure
of the Lion's Mane"), 9-1 TAD 14

Scheme of Things, The, (fiction),
by Herman S. McGregor, 15 BS 19

Schenck, Remsen T.: letter of comment,
10 JD 20

Schiff, Stuart David: letter of
comment, 1-3 AD 3; 2 U 15; 5 U 63

Schiller, Justin G.: L. Frank Baum
and His Teen-Age Serials, A
Bibliographical Checklist, 2-3
BC 194

Schleret, Jean-Jacques: letter of
comment, 3-1 MF 49; 5 PE 36;
9-3 TAD 167

Schlobin, Dr. Roger C.: An Index to
THE HAUNT OF TERROR (magazine),
1 U 5

Schlobin, Dr. Roger C.: An Index to
WORLDS OF FANTASY MAGAZINE,
2 U 12

Schlobin, Dr. Roger C.: letter of
comment, 2 U 48

Schmidt, Mike: letter of comment,
4-1 TAD 62

Schmitt, K. Paul: letter of comment,
17 X 62

(Schmitz, James H.), Bibliography,
by J. Grant Thiessen, 12 SF 13

Schneiderman, Jerry: Doc's Villainous
Foes Search Puzzle, (Doc Savage
puzzle), 3 DS 15

Schoonmaker, W.K.: A Non-Definitive
Price Guide to Out-of-Print
Arkham House Titles, 18 X 21

Schorr, Jack R.: A Representative
Collection, (boys' books),
3-1 BC 287

Schorr, Jack R.: Adventures in the Mail,
(advice and comments on buying boys'
books by mail), 2-2 BC 191

Schorr, Jack R.: Among the Book Stalls,
(boys' book collecting), 3-3 BC 330

Schorr, Jack R.: Bert Wilson Series,
(boys' book series by J.W.Duffield),
2-1 TBN 2

Schorr, Jack R.: Building a Collection
of Boy's Books, 1-1 BC 32

Schorr, Jack R.: Collecting Inside Outside, (boys' book collecting), 1 BB 24

Schorr, Hack R.: The College Life Series,
(boys' book series by Lester Chadwick),
2-4 TBN 6

Schorr, Jack R.: How I Found My Inferior
Decorators, (search for POPPY OTT:
INFERIOR DECORATOR, boys' book by
Leo Edwards), 4-1 TB 1

Schorr, Jack R.: How I Got Started Collecting, (boys' books), 1-3 BC 71

Schorr, Jack R.: How to Keep Dust and Soil
Off Books of a Collection, 1-2 BC 63

Schorr, Jack R.: How to Restore a Book,
1-1 BC 29

Schorr, Jack R.: Is Your Collecting Costing
Too Much?, (boys' book collecting),
1-4 BC 117

Schorr, Jack R.: letter of comment,
1-3 YB 11

Schorr, Jack R.: Looking Back, (boys'
book collecting thoughts), 1-2 TBN 4

Schorr, Jack R.: Taking Care of Your
Collection, 2-4 BC 254

Schorr, Jack R.: What Makes a Juvenile
Book Valuable?, 1-1 BC 10

Schorr, Jack R.: What to Do with your
Duplicates, (boys' books), 3-3 BC 344

Schorr, Jack R.: Where to Look for Books,
(boys' book collecting), 2-1 BC 139

Schorr, Jack R.: You Find Them in the
Oddest Places, (boys' book collecting),
4-1 BC 409

(Schorr, Jack R.), Vast Collection of Books
Requires Separate Housing, (boys' book
collection of Jack R. Schorr), by
Marjorie Freeman, 3-4 BC 374

Schreiner, Herm: Heroes of the Flying Pulps,
(aviation story heroes in the pulp
magazines), 22 X 38

Schreiner, Herm: letter of comment,
38 X 145

Schreuders, Piet: British Pocket Books,
(British paperbacks, Pocket Book
line), 3-1 CP 11

Schreuders, Piet: The European Paperback
Prelude, (early European paperback
books), 4-2 PQ 38

Schreuders, Piet: letter of comment,
3-3 CP 4; 1-3 PQ 11; 3-3 PQ 51

Schreuders, Piet: My Fourth Trip to the
U.S., (account of promotional trip
for book PAPERBACKS U.S.A.), 3-4
CP 17

Schreuders, Piet: Paperbacks U.S.A.,
The Exhibition (in Holland), 4-1 PQ 13

Schreuders, Piet: Rafael Palacios,
(sketch, paperback artist),
3-3 CP 32

Schreuders, Piet: "Steinberg" Found!,
(paperback cover artist), 3-4
PQ 12

Schroeder, Bill: letter of comment,
10 BS 21

Schubert, Dick: letter of comment,
7 PE 16; 3-1 PP 41; 3-5 PP 49;
11 SF 48

Schultheis, Steve: letter of comment,
6-1 TAD 47

Schultheis, Stephen F., and Patricia
A. Dreyfus: A Chronology of
Crimes, (Nero Wolfe stories by
Rex Stout), 1-1 G 41

Schulz, David: letter of comment,
3 MT 25

(Schulz, Robert), An Informal Survey
of Cover Art of the Seventies,
Pt.1, Tribute to Agatha Christie,
(Schulz, artist), by Frank Eck,
9-3 TAD 170

Schulz, Ted: Dinner at the Diogenes
Club, (puzzle, based on Solar
Pons), 2-1 PDA 33

Schweitzer, Darrell: An Index to "Not
at Night" Series (horror anthologies)
10 SF 45

Schweitzer, Darrell: An Index to
OTHER TIMES Magazine, 8 U 146

Schweitzer, Darrell: An Index to
VOID Magazine, 2 U 18

Schweitzer, Darrell: An Interview with
Robert Bloch, 1 FM 9

Schweitzer, Darrell: letter of comment,
5 U 66; 6 U 50

Schweitzer, Darrell: The SF Novels of
William Sloane, (science fiction),
14 SF 33

Schweitzer, Frank: The Old Rope Trick,
(verse), 3-5 MR 14

Schweitzer, Frank: Silence, (verse),
3-3 MR 2

Schweppe, Cynthia D.: letter of comment,
7 JD 4

Science Fiction Mystery Novels of
Asimov, Bester and Lem: Fusions
and Foundations, by Steven R.
Carter, 1-1 C 109

Science Fiction Pornography, (with
checklist), by Kenneth R. Johnson,
4 SF 4; 5 SF 45

(SCIENTIFIC DETECTIVE MONTHLY), The
Unique Magazine: Hugo Gernsback's
SCIENTIFIC DETECTIVE MONTHLY, by
Robert A.W.Lowndes, 14-1 TAD 24;
14-2 TAD 157; 14-3 TAD 243; 14-4
TAD 367

(SCORPION, THE), Checklist, (pulp
magazine), by Lynn Hickman,
75 PU 11

(SCOTLAND YARD), Fourteen Issues,
(study and index of pulp magazine),
by Robert Sampson, 22 X 4

Scott, Arthur C.: A Report on Bouchercon 7,
    (mystery fans and authors convention),
    1A MF 18
Scott, Arthur C.: Dumbfounded in Keeler-
    land, (on detection fiction of Harry
    Stephen Keeler), 1-1 MF 12
Scott, Arthur C.: Excerpt From the Files
    of Shot Scott, Private Eye, (report,
    annual paperback group party), 2-5 CP 5
Scott, Arthur C.: Further Excursions Into
    the Wacky World of Harry Stephen
    Keeler, (unconventional detectives
    by Harry Stephen Keeler), 1-4 MF 13
Scott, Arthur C.: letter of comment,
    1-6 CP 3; 6/7 LR 27; 1-1 MF 41;
    1-2 MF 53; 1-3 MF 58; 8 MN 32;
    17 R 21; 9-2 TAD 159; 9-3 TAD
    233; 9-4 TAD 296; 11-3 TAD 308;
    22 X 52
Scott, Arthur C.: The "Lost" Nero Wolfe
    Tale, ("Bitter End" by Rex Stout),
    9 MN A14
Scott, Arthur C.: Wolfe on the Air,
    (Nero Wolfe, radio appearances),
    9 MN A17
Scott Michel, An Interview, (with biblio-
    graphy), by Jim McCahery, 4-4 PP 3
(Scott, R.T.M.), The Case of the Elusive
    Author, (pulp hero author), by Dick
    Myers, 9 BS 5
Scott, William M.: Lord Peter Wimsey
    of Piccadilly: His Lordship's Life
    and Times, (detective character of
    Dorothy L. Sayers), 13-1 TAD 17;
    13-3 TAD 212
Scranton, Paul B.: Mystery Genre Gets
    Literary Boost, (The Mystery Library
    published in conjunction with the
    University of California), 10-4 TAD
    336
Scroggs, Dave: letter of comment,
    17 X 62; 22 X 50
(Scudder, Matt, series: Lawrence Block),
    Series Synopses, by Jeff Meyerson,
    12-1 TAD 62
Seaberg, Lillian M.: letter of comment,
    1-1 MF 47
Seals of the Si Fan, The, (re: Fu Manchu
    stories of Sax Rohmer), by Cay Van Ash,
    11 R 21
Searce, W.C.: letter of comment, 9 LR 14
Search for Sax Rohmer, The, by Cay Van
    Ash, 14 R 13
Second First Annual Wolfe Pack Event, The,
    (The Wolfe Pack, Nero Wolfe fan
    organization), by Marjorie Mortensen,
    1-2 G 58
(SECRET AGENT, THE: Joseph Conrad),
    Conrad's Probe to Absolute Zero, by
    Newton Baird, 9-1 TAD 43
Secret Agent X, (paperback reprint editions
    of pulp hero stories), by Bruce Cervon,
    3-1 CP 14
(Secret Agent X), Chronology of Stories,
    (pulp magazine hero character),
    42 X 142

(Secret Agent X), Destroy Secret
    Agent X, (pulp magazine hero
    character), by Tom Johnson,
    9 P 3
(Secret Agent X), Fading Sgadows:
    Erlika, Daughter of Satan,(from
    Secret Agent X series in pulp
    magazines by G.T.Fleming-Roberts),
    by Tom Johnson, 11 DS 24
(Secret Agent X), Fading Shadows:
    Lady X, (female villains, Secret
    Agent X pulp series by G.T.
    Fleming-Roberts), by Tom Johnson,
    6 U 24
(Secret Agent X), Fading Shadows:
    Madame Death, (villainess in
    Secret Agent X pulp series), by
    Tom Johnson, 11 DS 12
(Secret Agent X), Secret Agent X,
    (paperback reprints of pulp
    series), by Bruce Cervon,
    3-1 CP 14
(SECRET AGENT X Magazine), Solution
    for "X" by "These Ven" (pulp
    magazine), 42 X 139
Secret Egypt Unveiled, (in re:
    Sax Rohmer), by W.O.G.Lofts,
    8 R 23
(SECRET MASTERS, THE: Gerald Kersh),
    Smorgasbord Thriller, by Edward
    S. Lauterbach, 4-3 TAD 165
Secret of the Jade Throne, The,
    (fiction, 1921, by Edward Edson
    Lee; boys' fiction), 2-6 TBN 7
(Secret Service Smith), Checklist
    of stories in pulp magazines, by
    John Harwood, 67 PU 63
(SECRET SIX, THE), Checklist, (pulp
    magazine), by Lynn Hickman,
    75 PU 11
(Secret Six, The), The Not-So-Secret-
    Six, (pulp hero characters), by
    Robert Weinberg, 4 P 18
Secrets from the CBI, (essay on the
    China-Burma-India area), by John
    D. MacDonald, 16 JD 6
Secretaries in the Pulps, (supporting
    characters in pulp detective
    stories), by Bernard A. Drew,
    2 U 7
See What the Boys in the Backwoods
    Will Have (and Tell Them I'm
    Having the Same), (on paperback
    novels, backwoods/hillbilly
    theme), by Bill Crider, 2-3 PQ 22
Seeger, Mary A.: letter of comment,
    2-6 MF 50; 3-2 MF 57; 5-6 MF 53
Seeley, Charles: letter of comment,
    4 SF 42
Seeley, E.S., Jr.: letter of comment,
    11 JD 18
Seelye, John: Buckskins and Ballistics:
    William Leggett and the American
    Detective Story, 1-3 MR 3
Seganish, Mark: letter of comment,
    5 DS 6

Seidman, Michael: letter of comment,
2-3 M 2
Seidman, Michael: Perchance to Dream...,
(fiction), 2-2 M 48
Seidman, Michael: Some Memories, (tribute
and literary reminiscences of Robert
Fish), 14-2 TAD 121
Seiler, Gary: letter of comment,
3-1 M 6; 3-2 M 62; 24 X 47
Seiler, Richard: letter of comment,
5 X 41
Self-Portrait, by Henry S. Whitehead,
4 WT 4
Self Portrait, (verse), by Farnsworth
Wright, 2 WT 6
(Sellers, Peter), Obituary, 15 CL 1
Selling Culture With Paperback Covers,
by Mark Schaffer, 2-4 PQ 42
Seltzer, Howard: letter of comment,
2-4 TBN 6
Semi-Mean, (verse), by Kenneth Hill,
3-2 M 45
Sense of Wonder, (esoteric puzzles in
pulp fiction), by Lou Tabakow,
67 PU 51
Senter, Nancy: Why Sherlock Holmes?
Nostalgia for the Absolute, (appeal
of nostalgia), 2-2 M 39
Series Books, Their Influence on
Children, (boys' books), by William
D. Dizer and John T. Dizer, Jr.,
1-3 BC 68; 1-4 BC 98
Series Characters - A Detective Story
Matching Quiz, (quiz), by Jon L.
Breen, 3-2 TAD 122
Series Move to New Publisher, (Simon
& Schuster to publish Hardy Boys
and Nancy Drew series), by Fred
Woodworth, 2 MA 24
Series Spotlight: Bart Spicer's Carney
Wilde, by Jim McCahery, 3 PE 24;
4 PE 20; 5 PE 21
Series Spotlight: Jonathan Latimer's
William Crane, by Jim McCahery,
1 PE 5; 2 PE 5
Series Spotlight: M.Scott Michel's
Wood Jaxon, by Jim McCahery,
6 PE 3
Series Synopses: David Brandstetter
Series by Joseph Hansen, by Fred
Dueren, 11-4 TAD 365; (Spencer Dean:
Don Cadee series) 9-2 TAD 113 by
John Vining; (Earl Drake series
by Dan J. Marlowe) 10-2 TAD 181
by Robert J. Randisi; (The Exe-
cutioner series by Don Pendleton)
9-2 TAD 113 by John Vining; (Father
Dowling series by Ralph McInerny)
12-2 TAD 133 by Dan Andriacco; (The
Headhunters by John Weisman and Brian
Boyer) 11-4 TAD 365 by Bill Crider;
(Hiram Potter series by Rae Foley)
10-2 TAD 188 by John Vining; (Matt
Scudder series by Lawrence Bloch)
12-1 TAD 62 by Jeff Meyerson;

Series Synopses, (continued),
(Mongo the Magnificent series by
George C. Chesbro), 12-4 TAD 366
by Robert J. Randisi; (Norah
Mulcaheney series by Lillian
O'Donnell) 10-1 TAD 80 by Jo Ann
Vicarel, (addenda) 11-4 TAD 365;
(The Saint series by Leslie
Charteris) 10-2 TAD 187 by John
Vining; (Victor Grant series by
John B. Ethan) 10-2 TAD 187 by
John Vining
Serrill, Ted: letter of comment,
10 JD 18; 2-3 TAD 202; 3-1
TAD 67; 5-4 TAD 254
Seven "Crimefiles" of the 1930s: The
Purest Puzzles of the Golden Age,
(crime fiction with actual material
clues included), by William Reynolds
1-2 C 42
Seven Years with Heinie Faust,
(literary reminiscences on Frederick
Faust, by Harvey Roney, 2-3 FC 1
Severence, Jim: letter of comment,
1-4 AD 8
Sex and the Single Sleuth, by Ralph
Diffinetti, 3 PE 3
Sexton Blake the Office Boys Sherlock
Holmes, (Sexton Blake, early
British detective hero), by
Father Francis Hertzberg, 7 X 5
Seybolt, Reva: letter of comment,
27 JD 37
SF Novels of William Sloane, The,
(science fiction), by Darrell
Schweitzer, 14 SF 33
"Shades of Dupin!": Fictional
Detectives on Detective Fiction,
by George N. Dove, 8-1 TAD 12
Shadow, The, (comment, NEW YORK TIMES
BOOK REVIEW), by Lewis Nichols,
3-1 MR 20
Shadow, The, (literary discussion,
pulp hero), by Dean A. Grennell,
61 PU 13
Shadow, The, (pulp hero reprints in
paperback books), by Bruce Cervon,
2-3 CP 33
Shadow Codes, The, (from the pulp
novels), by Walter Shedlofsky,
9 X 10
Shadow and the Hieroglyph, The,
(verse), by Walter Shedlofsky,
18 X 34
Shadow Gallery: An Informal Survey
of Cover Art of the Seventies,
Pt.1, Tribute to Agatha Christie,
by Frank Eck, 9-3 TAD 170; Pt.2,
Tribute to Maj Sjowall and Per
Wahloo, 10-1 TAD 46
Shadow Known, The, (on the paperback
reprint books from the pulps), by
Bruce Cervon, 2-3 CP 31
Shadow Knows...and Tells His Secrets,
by James Warren, 6 DS 12

(SHADOW OF A BROKEN MAN: George C. Chesbro), Mystery Plus: Shadow of a Broken Man, by R. Jeff Banks, 4-1 PP 22

Shadow of Ying Ko, by Frank D. McSherry, Jr., 16 R 1

Shadow on the Wind, (dime novels), by Robert Sampson, 8 U 16

Shadow or Doc Savage, The, (comparison of pulp hero characters), by "Ed Noonchester", 2 DS 13

Shadow Speaks, The, (exchange between Wooda Nicholas Carr and Walter B. Gibson), 5 P 3

(Shadow, The), A Few Shadow Oddities, by Frank Eisgruber, Jr., 10 P 35

(Shadow, The), A Footnote for Shadow Collectors, (duplication of titles of different stories, and other bibliographical data), by Robert Sampson, 4-2 MR 9

(Shadow, The), A Full Length "Shadow" Novel as Told to... (The Shadow novels written by Theodore Tinsley and Bruce Elliott), by Fred S. Cook, 3 BS 12

(Shadow, The), The Case of the Elusive Author, (Frank S. Lawton; original appearance of The Shadow), by Dick Myers, 10 BS 14

(Shadow, The), Casting a Little Light Among the Shadows, (The Shadow and his past, speculative), by Arn McConnell, 2-1 WA 3

(Shadow, The), Checklist, Pyramid Paper-backs, (reprints in paperback book format), 1 DS 8

(Shadow, The), Checklist, Pyramid Paper-backs, (reprints in paperback book format), by Mark MacDonald, 1 MT 43

(Shadow, The), Checklist, Shadow Comic Books, by Mark MacDonald, 1 MT 43

(Shadow, The), Contemplating Seven of the Pulp Heroes, (comparisons and characteristics), by Wooda Nicholas Carr and Herman S. McGregor, 12 BS 3

(Shadow, The), Cover Montage of Photos, by Joseph Lewandowski, 4 U 18

(Shadow, The), Crime Undercover, by Frank P. Eisgruber, Jr., 4 P 15

(Shadow, The), The Fallen Mighty, by Dean A. Grennell, 22 X 20

(Shadow, The), Fore Shadowings, (fore-runners of The Shadow), by Bill Blackbeard, 17 X 6; 22 X 30

(Shadow, The), From Shadow to Superman, (on pulp heroes), by John Edwards, 7 U 10

(Shadow, The), Graves Gladney Speaks, (interview with pulp artist), 1 D 23

(Shadow, The), John D. MacDonald's List of His Stories in DOC SAVAGE and THE SHADOW, with data, 7 BS 4

(Shadow, The), Just a Little Matter of Doom, by Robert Sampson, 4 X 7

(Shadow, The), The Law and The Shadow, (legal position of selling recordings of radio shows), by Jack Gilbert, 4 BS 6

(Shadow, The), The Never-Was Adventure, (speculative meeting between The Shadow and Doc Savage), by Will Murray, 6 DQ 16

(Shadow, The), Notes of a Pulp Collector, (background of The Shadow), by J. Randolph Cox, 14 BS 17

(Shadow, The), Only The Shadow Knows, by Frank P. Eisgruber, Jr., 3 P 28

(Shadow, The), Out of the Shadows, (by creator of The Shadow), by Walter Gibson, 2 D 32

(Shadow, The), The Radio Murder Hour, (reminiscences on The Shadow radio program), by Chris Steinbrunner, 14-4 TAD 335

(Shadow, The), The Shadow, (literary discussion), by Dean A. Grennell, 61 PU 13

(Shadow, The), Shadow Comic Book Author - Jerry Siegel, by Larry Herndon, 3 BS 11

(Shadow, The), The Shadow Known, (in paperback book format), by Bruce Cervon, 2-3 CP 31

(Shadow, The), The Shadow Knows...and Tells His Secrets, by James Warren, 6 DS 12

(Shadow, The), Shadow of the Shadow, (on RETURN OF THE SHADOW), by Dean A. Grennell, 62 PU 6

(Shadow, The), The Shadow on the Moon, (summation of an issue of Shadow Comics), by Joe Vucenic, 8 BS 20

(Shadow, The), The Shadow or Doc Savage, (comparison of pulp heroes), by "Ed Noonchester", 2 DS 13

(Shadow, The), The Shadow Speaks, (exchange between Wooda Nicholas Carr and Walter B. Gibson), 5 P 3

(Shadow, The), The Shadow Speaks, (writing techniques of Walter B. Gibson), by George Wolf, 14 BS 11

(Shadow, The), That Mysterious Aide to the Forces of Law and Order, by J. Randolph Cox, 4-4 TAD 221

(Shadow, The), The Terrible Beekeeper, (fiction, pastiche on The Shadow, Doc Savage, The Spider, Sherlock Holmes), by Arn McConnell and Todd Rutt, 1-1 WA 3; 1-2 WA 6; 1-3 WA 7; 1-4 WA 7; 2-1 WA 5

(Shadow, The), The Top Twenty-Five Shadow Novels and One Stinker, by Will Murray, 4 U 3

(Shadow, The), Trivia Quiz: A Living Shadow!, (quiz), by Arn McConnell, 1-4 WA 18

(Shadow, The), The Vulnerable Shadow, by Robert Sampson, 1 P 24

(Shadow, The), Walter Gibson, (literary sketch), by Frank Gruber, 3-2 TAD 94

(Shadow, The), The Weird Adventures of The Shadow, (on The Shadow and his creator, Walter B. Gibson), by Wooda Nicholas Carr, 9 BS 16

(Shadow, The), Who Knows What Evil Lurks...(The Shadow Secret Society), 1 MT 41

(Shadow, The), Zanigew, Napoleon of Crime, (villain), by Will Murray, 8 DS 19

(Shadow, The - association item), The Telephone, by Joseph Lewandowski, 6 U 2

(SHADOW, THE - magazine), Checklist, (by dates issued), by Fred Cook, 1 BS 5

(SHADOW, THE - magazine), Early J.D. (John D. MacDonald stories in DOC SAVAGE and THE SHADOW magazines), by Ed Cox, 2 JD 3

(SHADOW, THE - magazine), Notes on Two Shadows of JDM, (John D. MacDonald's stories in THE SHADOW), by Francis M. Nevins, Jr., 13 JD 10

Shadowers by "David Fox", The, by William J. Clark, 28 X 75

Shadowing the Continental Op, (detective character of Dashiell Hammett; with checklist), by William F. Nolan, 8-1 TAD 121

(Shaffer, Anthony: SLEUTH), A Possible Source for the Opening of SLEUTH, (play/movie), by Veronica M.S. Kennedy), 7-3 TAD 175

Shaffer, Norman J.: A Bibliography and English Language Index to Georges Simenon's Maigret Novels, 3-1 TAD 31

Shaffer, Norman J.: letter of comment, 3-3 TAD 206; 4-1 TAD 62; 5-3 TAD 185

Shaheen, Gary: An Index to FANTASTIC NOVELS, (pulp magazine), 7 X 69

Shakespeare, (verse), by Sax Rohmer, 8 R 14

Shakespeare Quiz, (mystery quiz), by R.W.Hays, 8-1 TAD 41

Shamon, T.J.: letter of comment, 13-3 TAD 239

Shaner, Alex T.: letter of comment, 1-3 TBN 4

(Shannon, Dell), A Look at Dell Shannon, by Barbara Buhrer, 3/4 MN 3

(Shannon, Dell), Checklist Bibliography, by Barbara Buhrer and J. Clyde Stevens, 3/4 MN 4

(Shapiro, Milton J.: THE HAWK), Mystery Plus: The Hawk, by R. Jeff Banks, 2-3 PP 24

(Shard, Simon, series: Philip McCutchan), Checklist, Annotated, by Barry Van Tilburg, 4-5 MF 21

Sharpe, Howard W.: letter of comment, 4-1 MF 42

(Shaver Mystery), Sailing Uncharted Seas, by Dave & Su Bates, 2-2 CP 35

(Shaver, Richard Sharpe), A Bow to Cartographers, (biography and commentary), by Dave & Su Bates, 1-6 CP 24

(Shaw, Commander Esmond, series: Philip McCutchan), Checklist, Annotated, by Barry Van Tilburg, 4-5 MF 21

(Shaw, Commander Edmond, series: Philip McCutchan), The Rivals of James Bond, (espionage series profile and checklist), by Larry Rickert, 4-4 PP 17

Shaw, John Bennett: The Cult of Sherlock Holmes, 1-2 TAD 53

Shaw, John Bennett: letter of comment, 1-4 QC 18

Shaw, John Bennett: The Sherlockian Quiz, (quiz), 10-1 TAD 77

(Shaw, John Bennett), Under the Jack Knife, (re: Shaw and Sherlockiana), by Mike Hodel, 3-2 M 34

(Shaw, John Bennett), Meet the Author, John Bennett Shaw, by Allen J. Hubin, 1-2 TAD 55

(Shaw, Joseph: THE HARD BOILED OMNIBUS) Cap Shaw and His "Great and Regular Fellows": The Making of THE HARD BOILED OMNIBUS, 1945-1946, by E.R. Hagemann, 2-2 C 143

(Shaw, Joseph: THE HARD BOILED OMNIBUS) Captain Shaw's Hard-Boiled Boys, by Stephen Mertz, 12-3 TAD 264

Shaw, Larry: letter of comment, 13 JD 4

Shaw, (Mrs.) Lawrence: letter of comment, 4-2 MR 14

(Shaw, Paul, detective: Mark Sadler), Private Eye in an Evil Time: Mark Sadler's Paul Shaw, (Dennis Lynds writing as Paul Shaw), by Francis M. Nevins, Jr., 38 X 11

Shaw, Peg: letter of comment, 2-4 TBN 3

Shaw, Thomas C.: letter of comment, 4-1 MF 41; 11 MN L12; 8-1 TAD 70; 8-4 TAD 323; 10-1 TAD 40

(Shayne, Mike, detective: Brett Halliday), Mike Shayne Author Former Area Resident, (Clayton Matthews writing under house name), by Tom Johnson, 5 U 30

(Shayne, Mike, detective: Brett Halliday), The Mike Shayne Caper, by Bernard A. Drew, 3-1 PQ 51

(Shayne, Mike, detective: Brett Halliday), Murder in Miami, (Mike Shayne on television), by Andy Jaysnovitch, 1 PE 23

(Shayne, Mike, detective: Brett Halliday), The Return of Mike Shayne (new reprints), by Helen McCloy, 14-4 TAD 344

(SHE: H. Rider Haggard), Her, (on the Corinth paperback edition), by J.X. Williams, 2 SF 34

"She Who Loveth Silence," (from Sax Rohmer's GREY FACE), by Stephen Shutt, 15 R 25

Shea, J. Vernon: letter of comment, 2-1 AD 12

Shedlofsky, Walter: Anagallery, (verse), 6 WT 22

Shedlofsky, Walter: Memories of Ngai, (verse), 15 X 45

Shedlofsky, Walter: Quest for Nirvana, (verse), 14 X 14

Shedlofsky, Walter: The Realm of In-Between, (fiction), 6 X 5

Shedlofsky, Walter: The Shadow and the Hieroglyph, (verse), 18 X 34

Shedlofsky, Walter: The Shadow Codes, 9 X 10

Shedlofsky, Walter: Space Project Valerian, (fiction), 30 X 11

Shedlofsky, Walter: Trinapulation of the Albitron, (fiction), 7 X 65

Shedlofsky, Walter: Weird Tales, (verse), 5 WT 32

Sheehan, Patrick J.: letter of comment, 2-2 TAD 132

(Sheena, Queen of the Jungle), Mistress of Violence, (pulp jungle hero), by Wooda Nicholas Carr, 22 X 24

Sheffo, Nicholas: letter of comment, 3-1 M 2

(Shellabarger, Samuel), Modern Age Books and the John Esteven Mystery, (Shellabarger writing as Esteven), by Angela Andrews, 4-2 PQ 29

Shelley, Rachel P.: letter of comment, 7-1 TAD 67

Sheppard, Nancy: letter of comment, 27 JD 38

Sher, David: letter of comment, 14 SF 47

Sherlock Holmes, Father of Scientific Crime Detection, by Stanton O. Berg, 5-2 TAD 81

(SHERLOCK HOLMES: THE PUBLISHED APOCRYPHA: Jack Tracy), The Aprocryphalization of Holmes, by E.F.Bleiler, 4-5 MF 3

Sherlockian Dinner, (The Non-Canonical Calabashes, report of meeting 1980), by Horace Harker, 1-3 M 22

Sherlockian EQMM, The, (Sherlock Holmes pastiches/stories in ELLERY QUEEN'S MYSTERY MAGAZINE), by Peter E. Blau, 2-1 QC 15

Sherlockian Quiz, The, (mystery quiz), by John Bennett Shaw, 10-1 TAD 77

Sherlockiana, (items published in 1975), by Peter E. Blau, 8 MN 39; (in 1976) 1-11 MM 8; (in 1978) 12 MN O2; (in 1980), 13 MN O1

Sherlocko-Pontine Parallels, (comparing Sherlock Holmes and Solar Pons), by Nathan L. Bengis, 1-4 PD 3

(Sherman, Harold M.), A Leo Edwards Imitation, (Fun Loving Gang by Sherman patterned after books by Edwards), by Rick Crandall, 1-3 YB 7

(Sherman, Harold), Fading Shadows, Harold Sherman, by Tom Johnson, 7 U 26

(Sherwood, John), Checklist, by Barry A. Pike, 2-3 PP 23

(Sherwood, John), Pen Profile (sketch including Sherwood's detective, Charles Blessington), by Barry A. Pike, 2-3 PP 23

Sh-h-h! Dr. Fu Manchu is On the Air! (radio serials), by W.O.G.Lofts and Robert E. Briney, 11 R 9

Shibuk, Charles: Checklist, Earl Derr Biggers, 2-6 MR 21

Shibuk, Charles: Checklist, Raymond Chandler, 1-3 MR 9

Shibuk, Charles: Checklist: Edmund Crispin, 2-1 MR 15

Shibuk, Charles: Checklist, Freeman Wills Crofts, 1-4 MR 14

Shibuk, Charles: Checklist, Elizabeth Daly, 1-6 MR 16

Shibuk, Charles: Checklist, Richard Hull, 2-6 MR 21

Shibuk, Charles: Checklist, Ngaio Marsh, 1-5 MR 16

Shibuk, Charles: Checklist, Dorothy L. Sayers, 2-2 MR 10

Shibuk, Charles: Checklist, Julian Symons, 2-3 MR 19

Shibuk, Charles: Cinemania, (mystery films), 2-2 TAD 112

Shibuk, Charles: Commentaries for the Curious, (on John Dickson Carr), 1 NC 13

Shibuk, Charles: Cyril Hare, (sketch with checklist), 3-1 TAD 28

Shibuk, Charles: Dramatizations of the Great Literary Detectives and Criminals, Pt.1, Radio, 1-2 TAD 48; Pt.4, Film, 2-1 TAD 31; 2-3 TAD 183

Shibuk, Charles: Edmund Clerihew Bentley, 4-1 TAD 30

Shibuk, Charles: The Golden Age of the Detective Story: Its Rise and Fall, 1-4 QC 14

Shibuk, Charles: Henry Wade, (tribute), 1-4 TAD 111

Shibuk, Charles: Henry Wade Revisited, 2-1 TAD 45

Shibuk, Charles: letter of comment, 1-2 MF 50; 1-4 MF 56; 2-2 MF 55; 2-5 MF 59; 3-4 MF 56; 4-5 MF 44; 4-6 MF 43; 5-6 MF 52; 1-5 MR 14; 2-1 MR 11; 2-5 MR 12; 3-2 MR 17; 3-4 MR 33; 3-6 MR 10; 3-3 PP 39; 4-1 PP 41; 4-2 PP 33; 1-2 QC 15; 1-4 QC 18; 1-3 TAD 106; 1-3 TAD

Shibuk, Charles: letter of comment,
(continued) 108; 1-4 TAD 158;
2-1 TAD 64; 2-2 TAD 134; 2-3
TAD 200; 3-1 TAD 67; 3-2 TAD
136; 4-2 TAD 125; 5-1 TAD 53;
5-3 TAD 174; 7-2 TAD 146; 7-3
TAD 227; 9-1 TAD 82; 9-3 TAD
167; 10-3 TAD 278; 13-1 TAD 77
Shibuk, Charles: The Literary Career of
Mr. Anthony Berkeley Cox, 2-3 TAD 164
Shibuk, Charles: More Notes on C.E.
Vulliamy, 5-3 TAD 145
Shibuk, Charles: The Mystery Films of
Alfred Hitchcock, 2-1 MR 3
Shibuk, Charles: Notes on C.E.Vulliamy,
3-3 TAD 161
Shibuk, Charles: Notes on the Film and
the Detective Story, 5-4 TAD 202
Shibuk, Charles: Notes on Very Early
Leslie Charteris, 4-4 TAD 230
Shibuk, Charles: The Paperback Revolution,
(reviews of paperback mystery books),
1-1 TAD 10; 1-2 TAD 41; 1-3 TAD 96;
1-4 TAD 129; 2-1 TAD 44; 2-2 TAD 97;
2-3 TAD 174; 2-4 TAD 251; 3-1 TAD 40;
3-2 TAD 115; 3-3 TAD 179; 3-4 TAD
245; 4-1 TAD 37; 4-2 TAD 115; 4-3
TAD 168; 4-4 TAD 219; 5-1 TAD 30;
5-2 TAD 94; 5-3 TAD 154; 5-4 TAD 220;
6-1 TAD 35; 6-2 TAD 102; 6-3 TAD 179;
6-4 TAD 246; 7-1 TAD 44; 7-2 TAD 120;
7-3 TAD 205; 7-4 TAD 281; 8-1 TAD 50;
8-2 TAD 132; 8-3 TAD 210; 8-4 TAD
276; 9-1 TAD 41; 9-2 TAD 135; 9-3
TAD 208; 9-4 TAD 281; 10-1 TAD 71;
10-2 TAD 149; 10-3 TAD 239; 10-4
TAD 360; 11-1 TAD 96; 11-2 TAD 189;
11-3 TAD 298; 11-4 TAD 379; 12-1
TAD 30; 12-2 TAD 166; 12-3 TAD 255;
12-4 TAD 368; 13-1 TAD 75; 13-2 TAD
135; 13-3 TAD 250; 13-4 TAD 362;
14-1 TAD 79; 14-2 TAD 182; 14-3 TAD
266; 14-4 TAD 376
Shibuk, Charles: Random Thoughts on Writing
"The Paperback Revolution" (review
column in THE ARMCHAIR DETECTIVE),
4-3 TAD 172
Shibuk, Charles: Raymond Chandler on Film,
Addendum, 2-4 MF 14
Shibuk, Charles: Raymond Chandler on the
Screen, 1-3 MR 7
Shibuk, Charles: Three British Experiments
From the Mainstream, (mainstream
authors as mystery writers), 3-2
TAD 80
Shibuk, Charles: Who Done It?: The Mystery
Novel on the Screen, Addenda (to
WHO DONE IT?: Ordean A. Hagen),
3-4 TAD 255; 4-2 TAD 125
Shibuk, Charles, with Estelle Fox and
Francis M. Nevins, Jr.: Arthur W.
Upfield, A Checklist, 3-2 TAD 90
Shibuk, Charles, and Marvin Lachman: What
the World Waited For, (revised
"indefinite" checklist, crime fiction),
9-3 TAD 203

(Shibuk, Charles), Meet the Author:
Charles Shibuk, by Allen J.Hubin,
1-1 TAD 12
Shiffrin, Susan: letter of comment,
13 JD 22
Shinabery, Matt: letter of comment,
3-2 M 2
Shine, Jean and Walter: An Alpha-
betical Checklist of the Science
Fiction Stories of John D.
MacDonald, 28 JD 25
Shine, Jean and Walter: Bouchercon-
sense, (notes on Bouchercon
convention in verse), 4-5/6 PP 35
Shine, Jean and Walter: Early
"Condominium" Hurricane Warning,
(John D. MacDonald: CONDOMINIUM),
22 JD 15
Shine, Jean and Walter: letter of
comment, 5-6 MF 51; 4-5/6 PP 89
Shine, Jean and Walter: The "Shine"
Section, (various comments and
data on John D. MacDonald),
22 JD 7; 23 JD 17; 24 JD 30;
25 JD 24; 26 JD 29; 27 JD 18;
28 JD 20
Shinner, Don: letter of comment,
1-1 TBN 3; 2-3 TBN 3; 2-6 TBN 4
Shopton, Home of the Swifts, (on
the home locale of Tom Swift,
boys' series hero), by John T.
Dizer, Jr., 1-3 TBN 11; 1-4
TBN 8
Short Mystery Stories of Agatha Christie,
The,: A Checklist, by Paul McCarthy,
6-1 TAD 16
Short Short Stories of Burt L. Standish,
The, (in TIP TOP WEEKLY; Gilbert
L. Patten writing as Burt L.Standish,
boys' stories), by Gerald J.McIntosh
2-2 BC 168
SHORT STORIES: The Long History of
SHORT STORIES, by William J. Clark,
20 X 41
Short Stories and Novels of Hammett,
The, (Dell Mapback paperbacks and
ELLERY QUEEN'S MYSTERY MAGAZINE),
by M.C.Hill, 3-2 CP 9
Shoup, Steven L.: letter of comment,
3-1 M 6
Shreffler, Philip A.: An Interview
with Philip Jose Farmer, 42 X 7
Shreffler, Philip A.: letter of
comment, 40 X 85
Shreffler, Philip A.: Uncle Ray, (on
Ray Bradbury), 36 X R30
Shropshire, F.: W. Somerset Maugham
as a Mystery Writer, (literary
study), 14-2 TAD 190
Shroyer, Fredrick: A.D. (on August
Derleth), 3-3 AD 1; 2-1 PDA 7
Shroyer, Fredrick: August Derleth,
Pre-Romantic, 1-2 PDA 49
Shroyer, Fredrick: The Boy Scouts in
Old Udolpho, (August Derleth:
MOON TENDERS), 2-2 PDA 43

Shroyer, Fredrick: Praed Street, East of
    the Sun and West of the Moon, (Solar
    Pons), 3-2 AD 1; 3-1 PDA 3
Shuffle, The, (fiction, by Gary Maddren,
    1-2 M 57
Shurtleff, Robert W.: Those Mysterious
    Mandolins, (Fu Manchu on the screen),
    18 R 9
Shutt, Stephen: letter of comment, 12 R 23;
    13 R 23; 14 R 29; 15 R 27; 17 R 22
Shutt, Stephen: "She Who Loveth Silence",
    (from Sax Rohmer's GREY FACE), 15 R 25
Shutt, Stephen: Some Notes on Rohmer's
    Witch-Queens, (Sax Rohmer), 12 R 1
Siegel-Eastwood Quest, The, (film work,
    Don Diegel, Clint Eastwood), by
    Kathy Esselman, 7-4 TAD 253
Siegel, David S.: letter of comment,
    3-1 TAD 68; 4-1 TAD 63
(Siegel, Don), The Siegel-Eastwood Quest,
    (film work, Don Siegel, Clint
    Eastwood), by Kathy Esselman,
    7-4 TAD 253
Siegel, Dora: letter of comment, 12 JD 17;
    13 JD 19
(Siegel, Jerry), Shadow Comic Book Author:
    Jerry Siegel, by Larry Herndon,
    3 BS 11
Silence, (verse), by Steve Eng, 3-1 AD 8
Silence, (verse), by Frank Schweitzer,
    3-3 MR 2
Silent Sickle, The: A Thorndyke Pastiche,
    (fiction, pastiche on Dr. Thorndyke
    stories by R. Austin Freeman), by
    Oliver Mayo, 3 TF 2
(Silk, Dorian, series: Simon Harvester),
    Checklist, Annotated, by Barry
    Van Tilburg, 4-4 MF 16
Silver Fifty, The, (classics of crime
    fiction), by Gerald Tomlinson,
    10-2 TAD 165
Silver Witch, The, (villainess of JUNGLE
    STORIES pulp magazines), by Wooda
    Nicholas Carr and Tom Johnson, 11 DS 8
(Silverberg, Robert), Background and
    Checklist Don Elliott/Robert Silverberg
    Erotic Fiction Titles, by Keith L.
    Justice, 13 SF 18
(Silverman, Marguerite: Chief-Inspector
    Christopher Adrian), Pen Profile, by
    Barry A. Pike, 2-4 PP 20
Silverman, Stuart: A Ghost Story, (verse),
    3-3 AD 6
(Simenon, Georges), A Bibliography and
    English Language Index to Georges
    Simenon's Maigret Novels, by Norman
    J. Shaffer, 3-1 TAD 31
(Simenon, Georges), All the Short Cases of
    Inspector Maigret, by Gary L. Gannett,
    10-4 TAD 347
(Simenon, Georges), Georges Simenon,
    (literary sketch), by B.H.Pruitt,
    3-3 PP 12
(Simenon, Georges), Maigret & Co., The
    Detectives of the Simenon Agency, by
    Maurice Dubourg (trans.by Francis M.
    Nevins, Jr.), 4-2 TAD 79

(Simenon, Georges), Review of THE
    COMPLETE WORKS OF GEORGES SIMENON,
    written by Claude Mauriac, trans-
    lated by Francis M. Nevins, Jr.,
    2-3 TAD 162
Simmons, Rus: letter of comment,
    6 PE 36
Simms, Bartlett: letter of comment,
    6-3 TAD 195; (as Sims) 4-4 TAD 259
(Simpson, Robert: THE GREY CHARTERIS)
    Did He, or Didn't He? (Frederick
    Faust as possible author), by
    William J. Clark, 1-1 FC 5
(Sinclair, Fiona), Pen Profile: Fiona
    Sinclair, by Barry A. Pike,
    4-5/6 PP 49
Singular Malady of Septimus Grayle,
    (as Tottenham Werewolf, with Solar
    Pons), by Bruce Dettman, 2-3 PD 1
Sinister Signposts, (traffic signs),
    by Fred Woodworth, 3 MA 30
(SINISTER STORIES), Checklist, (pulp
    magazine), by Lynn Hickman,
    75 PU 11
Sinitic Sonnet, (verse), by James Wade,
    4 R 27
Sinning With Lawrence Sanders, (on
    crime fiction by Sanders), by George
    Kelley, 3-5 MF 20
Sitter, Melissa: Night Shift, (fiction),
    2-3 M 40
Six Britons the Movies Ignored: Tey,
    Household, Hamilton, Garve,Clifford,
    and Blackburn, (authors whose works
    were seldom filmed), by Jack Edmund
    Nolan, 3-5 MR 9
(Six Million Dollar Man), The Real
    Steve Austin, (theory character
    based on real person), by Sue Hagen
    and Operative 1701, 6 U 15
(Six Million Dollar Man), Steve Austin,
    Story or Authentic? (theory story
    and character based on real event),
    by Albert Tonik, 5 U 3
(Sjowall, Maj, and Per Wahloo), The
    Police in Society: The Novels of
    Maj Sjowall and Per Wahloo, by
    Frank Occhiogrosso, 12-2 TAD 174
(Sjowall, Maj, and Per Wahloo), Shadow
    Gallery: An Informal Survey of
    Cover Art of the Seventies, Pt.2,
    Tribute to Maj Sjowall and Per
    Wahloo, by Frank Eck, 10-1 TAD 46
Skelton, James R.: The Fake Plow
    Case, (Before Midnight Contest,
    The Wolfe Pack), 1-2 G 45
Skene Melvin Bibliography of Critical
    Writing; David and Ann Skene Melvin:
    CRIME, DETECTIVE, ESPIONAGE,MYSTERY
    AND THRILLER FICTION & FILM,(special
    review article), by Walter Albert,
    5-3 MF 5
(Skene Melvin, David and Ann: CRIME,
    DETECTIVE,ESPIONAGE,MYSTERY AND
    THRILLER FICTION & FILM),The Skene
    Melvin Bibliography of Critical
    Writing, by Walter Albert, 5-3 MF 5

Skinder, Chester J.: letter of comment,
    7 JD 6; 9 JD 9
(SKIPPER, THE), The Fighting Fury, (on
    the magazine and the principal hero
    character by that name; pulp), by
    Link Hullar and Will Murray, 12 SF 3
Skovlie, Per: letter of comment,
    7 U 46
Skullduggery File #1: So You Want to be
    a Crime Collector, by George Kelley,
    3 U 20
Skvorecky, Josef: A Discovery in Capek,
    (on Karel Capek's works), 8-3 TAD 180
(Slade, Tom, series), Tom Slade - And
    Friends, (boys' series books), by
    Gil O'Gara, 1-4 YB 21
(Slade, Tom, series), Tom Slade - And
    Friends, Part II, (boys' series
    books), by Julius R. Chenu, 1-5 YB 16
Slater, George W.: letter of comment,
    8 X 38
Sleeper, William A.: letter of comment,
    7 JD 11
(SLEUTH: Anthony Shaffer), A Possible
    Source for the Opening of SLEUTH,
    (play/movie), by Veronica M.S.
    Kennedy, 7-3 TAD 175
(Sloane, William), The SF Novels of
    William Sloane, by Darrell Schweitzer,
    14 SF 33
Slung, Michele: In the Matter of Stephen
    King, (literary sketch), 14-2 TAD 147
Slung, Michele: Women in Detective
    Fiction, 3-1 M 8
Small, Lass: letter of comment, 9 DS 21
Smallest Sub-Genre, The, (the reader as
    detective), by Frank D. McSherry, Jr.,
    10-3 TAD 267
(Smarles, Chief Inspector Joshua:
    MacGregor Urquhart), Pen Profile, by
    Barry A. Pike, 4-4 PP 19
Smell of Pulps, The, by Jon Inouye,
    11 X 8
(Smiley, George, series: John LeCarre),
    Checklist, Annotated, by Barry
    Van Tilburg
(Smiley, George, series: John LeCarre),
    The Fathers and Sons of John
    LeCarre, by Harry D. Dawson,
    5-3 MF 11
(Smiley, George, series: John LeCarre),
    George Smiley - The Reluctant Hero,
    by Holly Beth King, 2-1 C 70
(Smiley, George, series: John LeCarre),
    The Spy Fiction of John LeCarre,
    by Richard W. Noland, 1-2 C 54
Smiling Corpse Revisited, The, (on THE
    SMILING CORPSE: anonymous), by J.
    Randolph Cox, 3-3 TAD 170
Smith, Anna Jean: letter of comment,
    5 DS 6; 11 DS 28
Smith, Anthony: letter of comment,
    3-1 CP 2; 21 X 56
(Smith, Aurelius, detective), Checklist
    of stories in pulp magazines, by John
    Harwood, 67 PU 63

Smith, Bill: A Visit with "Mrs. Doc
    Savage", (with Mrs. Lester Dent),
    6 BS 3
Smith, Bill: letter of comment,
    2-1 AD 12; 5 BS 3; 6 BS 22
Smith, Billy G.: Doc Savage's Creator,
    Lester Dent, (personal reminis-
    cences), 2 BS 6
(Smith, Black John, detective), The
    Saint of the North, Black John
    Smith of Halfaday Creek, by John
    Harwood, 3-6 MF 3
(Smith, Clark Ashton), The Work of
    Clark Ashton Smith, by E.P.
    Berglund, 18 X 35
Smith, Dave & Carol: letter of comment,
    3 LW 3
Smith, David R.: letter of comment,
    2-2 MR 15
Smith, Dean: Collecting Science Fiction
    (on collecting paperbacks),
    1-4 CP 21
Smith, Dean: letter of comment,
    1-3 CP 1
(Smith, Sir Denis Nayland: Sax Rohmer),
    A Case of Identity, Being a Trifling
    Monograph Upin the Similarities
    Between Sir Denis Nayland Smith and
    Sherlock Holmes, by Andrew Jay Peck,
    2 R 9
(Smith, Sir Denis Nayland: Sax Rohmer),
    Checklist, Annotated, by Barry
    Van Tilburg, 5-1 MF 2
(Smith, Sir Denis Nayland: Sax Rohmer),
    Film Notes, by W.O.G.Lofts, 9 R 23
(Smith, Sir Denis Nayland: Sax Rohmer),
    Fu Manchu Thinks Kindly of Sir
    Denis Nayland Smith, (verse), by
    Edward Lauterbach, 1-2 PDA 48
(Smith, Sir Denis Nayland: Sax Rohmer),
    The Last Encounter, (with Fu
    Manchu), by James Wade, 1-2 PDA 66
(Smith, Sir Denis Nayland: Sax Rohmer),
    Letter to Sherlock, and Annotations,
    by Julian L. Biggers, 6 R 7
(Smith, Sir Denis Nayland: Sax Rohmer),
    The Man Who Never Said Anything,
    by John Harwood, 6 R 20
(Smith, Sir Denis Nayland: Sax Rohmer),
    Petrie Letter, by Bruce Pelz,
    3 R 16
(Smith, Sir Denis Nayland: Sax Rohmer),
    The Smith Letters, (purported), by
    Robert E. Briney, 12 R 9
Smith, Dorothy Duncan: letter of
    comment, 7-2 TAD 148
Smith, Ellen: letter of comment,
    24 JD 39
Smith, Fred: letter of comment, 8 BS 3
Smith, George H.: letter of comment,
    69 PU 27
Smith, Herbert A.: letter of comment,
    1-4 TAD 157
Smith, Jeffrey D. (& Freff): The
    Francis Plot Key (guide to books of
    Dick Francis), 4-5/6 PP 19

Smith, Jeffrey D.: letter of comment,
14 JD 28; 15 JD 28; 17 JD 30; 5 LR 7;
6/7 LR 19; 7-3 TAD 232
Smith, Larry: letter of comment,
19 JD 15; 26 JD 50
Smith Letters, The, (purported to be from
Sir Denis Nayland Smith, character of
Sax Rohmer), by Robert E. Briney,
12 R 9
Smith, Myrna J.: Controversy; Townsend,
Tey and Richard III, a Rebuttal,
10-4 TAD 317; 11-3 TAD 236; (see
also 10-3 TAD 211; 10-4 TAD 317;
11-2 TAD 105; 11-4 TAD 398)
Smith, Mary D.: Lament for a Legend,
Lizzie Borden Revisited, 11-2 TAD 132
Smith, Michael: Almuric, or Edgar Rice
Burroughs Visits the Hyborian Age,
1-2 PQ 48
Smith, P.K.: letter of comment,
9-4 TAD 337
Smith, Susan Harris: No Orchids for
George Orwell, (on Orwell's criticism
of James Hadley Chase: NO ORCHIDS FOR
MISS BLANDISH), 9-2 TAD 114
Smith, Tevis Clyde: New Book Released
About Robert E. Howard, (Glenn Lord:
THE LAST CELT), 1-1 PQ 33
(Smith, Thorne), Thorne Smith (in paper-
back editions), by Don Sprague,
3-2 CP 19
Smith, Walter D.: letter of comment,
2-2 CP 1; 8 MN 38
Smith, William F.: letter of comment,
10 JD 9; 13 JD 18; 17 JD 24
Smoke, Stephen L.: An Interview with
Robert Ludlum, 1-3 M 8
Smokerings and Things, (publications
news column), by Michael L. Cook,
1 U 25; 2 U 20; 3 U 22; 4 U 34;
5 U 32; 6 U 41; 7 U 41
Smorgasbord Thriller, (on THE SECRET
MASTERS: Gerald Kersh), by Edward
S. Lauterbach, 4-3 TAD 165
"Snawley, Ebenezer": The Humbugging of
Solar Pons, (Mycroft & Moran,
publishers' revisions, by Jon L.
Lellenberg writing as Ebenezer
Snawley), 3-2 PDA 11
Sneary, Rick: A John Dickson Carr
Checklist, 3-4 MR 13
Sneary, Rick: letter of comment,
2-2 M 2; 64 PU 25; 2-1 TAD 62
(Snell, Roy Judson), Boy's Books Written
by Roy Judson Snell, by Julius R.
Chenu, 1-1 BC 12
(Snow, C.P.), Three British Experiments
From the Mainstream, (mainstream
authors as mystery writers), by
Charles Shibuk, 3-2 TAD 80
Snyder, Don: letter of comment, 26 X 77
Snyder, Eileen: Was Watson Jack the
Ripper?, 8-3 TAD 211
Social and Political Images in American
Crime Fiction, PCA discussion 1971, by
Francis M.Nevins,Jr., 5-2 TAD 61

Social Consequences of Crime Writing,
The, by John Creasey, 4-1 TAD 38
Soft Cover Sketches - Introduction,
(paperback cover art), by Thomas
L. Bonn, 3-3 PQ 39; (on James
Avati, artist) 3-3 PQ 40; (on
Robert Jones, artist), 3-4 PQ 19;
(on Lou Marchetti, artist), 4-2
PQ 32
Solar Pons and Basil Copper, (Solar
Pons stories written by Copper,
characters created by August
Derleth), by Michael L. Cook,
7 U 29
Solar System, The, (code identifi-
cation suggested for Solar Pons
stories of Derleth), by Peter A.
Ruber and Ronald DeWaal, 2-1 PDA 2
Solution for "X", (on SECRET AGENT X
pulp magazines), by "These Ven",
42 X 139
Solution of "The Elusive Vanardy," The,
by Mary Ann Grochowski, 2-5 PP 3
Solving Six, The, (Solving Six series
by Agatha Christie), by Robert
Sampson, 5-5 MF 3
Some Agatha Christie Films, by Jack
Edmund Nolan, 4-2 MR 19
Some Errors in Fiction Factory, (THE
FICTION FACTORY: Quentin Reynolds),
by J. Randolph Cox, 74 PU 31
Some Further Addenda to Ralph Henry
Barbour Data, (boys' books author),
by Julius R. Chenu, 3-2 BC 317
Some Further Jottings from the Note-
books of Dr. Lyndon Parker, (Solar
Pons' chronicler), by August
Derleth, 1-1 PDA 3
Some Important Detective Fiction First
Editions in Paperback Books, by
Harold Knott, 3-1 MR 2
Some Memories, (literary reminiscences
and tribute to Robert Fish), by
Michael Seidman, 14-2 TAD 121
Some Necessary Needs, (survey of
mystery reference books), by Mary
Groff, 10 CL 5; 11 CL 3
Some Notes on British Authors, (with
checklists), by Ian Covell, 4 SF 28
Some Notes on Movie Editions, (paper-
back books), by Bill Crider and
Billy C. Lee, 2-1 PQ 29
Some Notes on Rohmer's Witch-Queens,
(Sax Rohmer), by Stephen Shutt,
12 R 1
Some Notes on the Detective Element
in Western Fiction, by Claude
Saxon, 1A MF 17
Some Notes Toward a Checklist of
A.A.Milne's Short Tales of Crime
and Detection, by J. Randolph Cox,
9-4 TAD 269
Some of My Best Friends are Books,(on
San Francisco Mystery Bookshop and
its proprietors, Bruce & Carol
Taylor), by Mary Groff, 13-2 TAD 171

Some Pulp Contemplations, (commentary
   and data on various pulp heroes and
   magazines), by Wooda Nicholas Carr,
   6 DS 8; 7 DS 16; 9 DS 18; 10 DS 27;
   11 DS 16; 12 DS 16
Some Themes in the Film Work of Jimmy
   Sangster, by Jack Edmund Nolan,
   5-6 MR 21
Some Thoughts About Robert Bloch, by
   Bruce Walker, 7 X 72
Some Thoughts on Josephine Tey, (on
   retribution as a motive in Tey's
   novels), by Ethel Lindsay, 3-6 MR 7
Some Thoughts on Ray Cummings, by
   Winston Dawson, 30 X 3
Some Touch of the Artist, (on the Sherlock
   Holmes stories), by R.L.Hall, 2-2 M 30
Some Unusual Facts About Lester Dent,
   (pulp author), by Frank Lewandowski,
   1 DS 6
Someone's in the Kitchen with Dinah,
   (fiction), by Raymond Obstfeld,
   2-1 M 18
Son of Mystery*File, (news and comments:
   mystery fiction and related), by
   Steve Lewis, 1 MN 3; 3/4 MN 11
Sonar, Sydney: Astrological Guide to
   Murder, 1-3 M 15
Songas, John: letter of comment,
   3-5 CP 1
Sorak Series by Harvey D. Richards, The,
   (boys' book series), by Julius R.
   Chenu, 1-3 YB 5
Sorenson, Paul M.: letter of comment,
   22 X 52
Soroka, Alex: letter of comment,
   30 X 148
Sorrell, Martha: letter of comment,
   1-1 MF 39; 1-5 MF 53; 8 MN 34
Sound of Fu Manchu, The, by Leslie
   Charteris, 6 R 19
Sound of Suspense, The: John Dickson
   Carr as a Radio Writer, by Francis
   M. Nevins, Jr., 11-4 TAD 335
Sounds of Gunshots, (ballistics and
   audio aspects), by Lawrence Heming,
   15 JD 8
(South, the), The American Regional
   Mystery, Pt.VII, by Marvin Lachman,
   5-3 MR 1
SOUTH SEA STORIES, Index, (and author
   index), by Robert Weinberg, 8 P 12
(Southwest, the), The American Regional
   Mystery, Pt.X, by Marvin Lachman,
   6-2 MR 23
Sowers, Ray: letter of comment, 6 BS 22;
   68 PU 27
(SPACE FOR HIRE: William F. Nolan), A
   Pair of Parodies, by R. Jeff Banks,
   1-5 PP 10
(SPACE FOR HIRE: William F. Nolan), Sam
   Space, An Eye on Mars, by William F.
   Nolan, 1-3 M 28
(SPACE FOR HIRE: William F. Nolan), Watch
   This Space!, by Frank D. McSherry, Jr.,
   5-4 TAD 226

Space Project Valerian, (fiction),
   by Walter Shedlofsky, 30 X 11
Spade - Bogart, (Humphrey Bogart as
   Dashiell Hammett's Sam Spade in
   film), by Mark MacDonald, 4 MT 31
(Spade, Sam, detective: Dashiell
   Hammett), Play It Again, Sam
   Spade, (Humphrey Bogart as Spade
   in film), by Steve Fisher, 5-2
   TAD 79
(Spade, Sam, detective: Dashiell
   Hammett), Sam Spade, Lover, by
   Peter Wolfe, 11-4 TAD 366; 38
   X 21
(Spade, Sam, detective: Dashiell
   Hammett), Sam Spade Talking, by
   John M. Reilly, 1-2 C 119
(Spade, Sam, detective: Dashiell
   Hammett), Spade - Bogart, (Bogart
   in role of Sam Spade in film), by
   Mark McDonald, 4 MT 31
Sparks, Bob: letter of comment,
   24 X 47
Speaking of Pulp, (on THRILLING
   DETECTIVE pulp magazine), by
   Steve Lewis, 4 PE 9; (on DIME
   DETECTIVE pulp magazine) 5 PE 27
Speaking With Myself, (self-interview),
   by Billy Barton, 5-4 MF 13
(SPEAR, THE: James Herbert), Mystery
   Plus: The Spear, by R. Jeff Banks,
   3-4 PP 14
Speculations on the Origin of Dr. Fu
   Manchu, by John Harwood, 2 R 6
(Speed, Nell), Miss Minerva and
   Kinfolks, (juvenile series written
   in part by Nell Speed), by Julius
   R. Chenu, 1-4 YB 3
Spelman, Richard: letter of comment,
   30 X 149
Spelman, Richard, and Stuart W. Wells
   III: Checklist, Avalon Books,
   (paperback line), 5 SF 29
Spencer, Paul: The Unpublished
   Derleths, (discussion of titles
   mentioned by Derleth but never
   published), 5-1 AD 6
Spencer, Ross H.: Murder Mystery,
   (verse), 14-2 TAD 133
Spenser, Hardboiled Roots, (on Robert
   B. Parker's detective character,
   Spenser), by Bernard Drew, 21 X 7
(Spenser, detective: Robert B. Parker),
   Spenser, Hardboiled Roots, by
   Bernard Drew, 21 X 7
(Spenser, detective: Robert B. Parker),
   Spenserian Ethics: The Unconvent-
   ional Morality of Robert B. Parker's
   Traditional American Hero, by Steven
   R. Carter, 1-2 C 109
Spenserian Ethics: The Unconventional
   Morality of Robert B. Parker's
   Traditional American Hero, by
   Steven R. Carter, 1-2 C 109
(Spicer, Bart: Carney Wilde series),
   Checklist, by Jim McCahery, 4 PE 23

(Spicer, Bart: Carney Wilde series),
Series Spotlight: Bart Spider's
Carney Wilde, by Jim McCahery,
3 PE 24; 4 PE 20; 5 PE 21

Spider, The, (discussion of the pulp
hero, the magazine, and the paperback book reprints, with checklist),
by Bruce Cervon, 3-4 CP 11

Spider, The: A Personal View, (comments
on The Spider, pulp hero), by Wooda
Nicholas Carr, 8 U 62

Spider, The, vs. Munro, (pulp hero and
villain), by Robert Weinberg, 10 P 25

(Spider, The), Contemplating Seven of the
Pulp Heroes, (comparisons and
characteristics), by Wooda Nicholas
Carr amd Herman S. McGregor, 12 BS 3

(Spider, The), The Man From the East,
(pulp hero character), by Robert
Weinberg, 10 P 12

(Spider, The), The Pulp Villains: Tang-
Akhmut, The Man From the East, (pulp
hero vs. villain), by Wooda Nicholas
Carr, 5 DS 10

(Spider, The), The Spider vs. Munro,
(pulp hero vs. villain), by Robert
Weinberg, 10 P 25

(Spider, The), The Ten Top Sider Novels
and One Stinker, (comparison of novels
from the pulp magazine), by Will
Murray, 13 SF 5

(Spider, The), The Terrible Beekeeper,
(fiction, pastiche of The Spider,
The Shadow, Doc Savage, Sherlock
Holmes), by Arn McConnell and Todd
Rutt, 1-1 WA 3; 1-2 WA 6; 1-3 WA 7;
1-4 WA 7; 2-1 WA 5

(Spider, The), The Case of the Elusive
Author, (R.T.M.Scott), by Dick Myers,
9 BS 5

(SPIDER, THE), Checklist of novels in
the pulp magazine, by Lynn Hickman,
67 PU 73

(SPIDER, THE), Checklist of novels in
the pulp magazine, by John Steinkuhl,
1 U 17

(SPIDER, THE), Comprehensive Survey of
individual Stories, (from each
issue of the pulp magazine, an
in-depth study), by Herman S. McGregor,
(Vol.1, #1,2,3) 66 PU 41; (Vol.1,#4;
Vol.2,#1) 67 PU 77; (Vol.2,#2) 68 PU
29; (Vol.2,#3,4; Vol.3,#1,2) 70 PU 13;
(Vol.3,#3 71 PU 15

(SPIDER, THE), Excerpts from "The Web",
(excerpts from column in the pulp
magazine), 40 X 22

Spillane and the Critics, (treatment of
Spillane's works in literary criticism),
by R.Jeff Banks, 12-4 TAD 300

(Spillane, Mickey), Another Mike Hammer,
Pre-Spillane, by Richard S. Lochte II,
2-1 TAD 24

(Spillane, Mickey), Department of
Unmitigated Mishmosh, by Francis
M. Nevins, Jr., 3-1 MR 21

(Spillane, Mickey), I Comma Mickey,
(Mickey Spillane talking), by
Alex Hamilton, 1-2 MR 9

(Spillane, Mickey), I, the Spillane,
or, My Spillane is Quick, or,
Vengeance is Spillane, or, One
Lonely Spillane, or, The Big
Spillane, (parody), by John D.
MacDonald, 14 JD 16

(Spillane, Mickey), Just a Writer
Working for a Buck, (includes
interview with Spillane), by
Michael S. Barson, 12-4 TAD 293

(Spillane, Mickey), Mickey Spillane
Comic Strip, 12-4 TAD 317

(Spillane, Mickey), Mike Hammer,
(television series checklist),
4 PE 5

(Spillane, Mickey), Paperback Writers:
Mickey Spillane, by Bill Crider,
2-3 PQ 9

(Spillane, Mickey), Spillane and
the Critics, (treatment by
literary criticism), by R.Jeff
Banks, 12-4 TAD 300

(Spillane, Mickey), The Tiger Mann
Series, by R. Jeff Banks, 2-3
MF 32

(Spillane, Mickey), Two Lonely Nights
with Mickey Spillane, (interview),
by Michael S. Barson, 2-3 PQ 13

(Spillane, Mickey), Dat's Mike
Ham-muh?, (Hammer in the popular
media), by Max Collins, 12-4 TAD
308

Spindrift Revisited, (Rick Brant
boys' series), by Kent Winslow,
3 MA 1

Spiralled Myth, The, (fiction), by
John D. MacDonald, 3 JD 3;
9 JD 24

(SPIRIT, THE: Thomas Page), Mystery
Plus: Getting There May Be More
Than Half the Fun, by R.Jeff Banks,
3-5 PP 15

Spironello, Jo: letter of comment,
4-4 MR 15

Spitzer, Ronald W.: A Vega Books
Checklist, (paperback line, science
fiction), 4 SF 19

Sports and the Mystery Story, (crime
fiction with sports theme), by
Marvin Lachman, (tennis) 6-1 TAD 1;
(prizefighting and bull-fighting)
6-2 TAD 83; (baseball and basketball) 6-4 TAD 243; (football) 7-3
TAD 195; (golf) 7-4 TAD 261;
(cricket) 8-1 TAD 108

Spotlight: THE BURL IVES SONG BOOK,
(paperback edition), 2-1 PQ 37

Spotlight: THE GIRL ON THE BEST SELLER
LIST by Vin Packer, (paperback),
3-3 PQ 54

Spotlight: Pocket Books, "Pockettes",
(paperback series), 2-3 PQ 30

Spotlight: TEN NORTH FREDERICK by John
   O'Hara, (paperback edition), 2-4 PQ 11
Sprague, Don: letter of comment,
   3-2 CP 2; 3-4 CP 3
Sprague, Don: Thorne Smith, (paperback
   editions), 3-2 CP 19
Sprague, Mark E.: letter of comment,
   22 X 51; 22 X 52
(Sprigg, St.John), Pen Profile, by
   Barry A. Pike, 2-5 PP 23
Spy Fiction of John LeCarre, The, by
   Richard W. Noland, 1-2 C 54
Spy Series in Hardback, (annotated
   checklists of various authors),
   by Barry Van Tilburg,
   Pt.1 (Anderson, Bark, Beeding,
      Benton, Blackburn, Creasey,
      Bruce) 4-2 MF 11;
   Pt.2 (Coles, Cory, Deighton,
      Creasey, Carter, Gardner,
      Fleming, Hall, Haggard,
      LeCarre, Fallon), 4-3 MF 23;
   Pt.3 (Harvester, Leasor, Mair,
      Heald, Leonard), 4-4 MF 16;
   Pt.4 (McCutchan, Sapper, Marquand,
      Martyn, McLeod) 4-5 MF 21;
   Pt.5 (Mason, Mather, Mayo, Perry,
      Powell, Price, O'Malley)
      4-6 MF 4;
   Pt.6 (Sax Rohmer) 5-1 MF 2
   Pt.7 (Ross, Tute) 5-2 MF 2
   Pt.8 (Wheatley, Woodhouse, York,
      Gilman, Hossent, Mitchell,
      Bridge, Davison, Gerard)
      5-3 MF 18
   Pt.9 (Aarons, Annesley, Avallone)
      5-5 MF 15
Squire, J.C.: Rohmer, (commentary on
   Sax Rohmer), 4 R 3
Squires, John D.: letter of comment,
   17 X 61; 40 X 86
Squires, Roy A.: letter of comment,
   2 FM 18; 16 JD 15; 22 X 51;
   24 X 46
(St.John, David: Peter Ward series),
   The Rivals of James Bond: Peter
   Ward, (with checklist), by Larry
   Rickert, 4-3 PP 7
(Stableford, Brian), Checklist, Puzzle
   Paperback Novels (puzzle plot crime
   fiction), by George Kelley, 1-2
   CP 19
(Stableford, Brian), Vault of the Ages:
   The Puzzle Novels of Brian Stable-
   ford, (puzzle plot crime fiction),
   by George Kelley, 1-4 CP 27
(Stableford, Brian), Vault of the Ages,
   (Stableford: THE REALMS OF TARTARUS)
   by George Kelley, 1-3 CP 16
(Stadley, Pat), Department of Unknown
   Mystery Writers: Pat Stadley, by
   Marvin Lachman, 3-1 PP 23
Stafford, Jean: The Polyglot Mr.Rohmer,
   (literary commentary on Sax Rohmer),
   14 R 1

Stage in My Stories, The, (frequent
   use of stage as background), by
   Fritz Leiber, 1 HP 11
(Stagge, Jonathan), Checklist, by
   Barry A. Pike, 3-3 PP 21
(Stagge, Jonathan), Pen Profile:
   Jonathan Stagge, by Barry A.
   Pike, 3-3 PP 20
Stalker in the Dark, The: Jack the
   Ripper and Wold Newton, by
   Timothy J. Rutt, 1-3 WA 5
Stalking Forsyth's Jackal, (THE DAY
   OF THE JACKAL: Frederick Forsyth),
   by Peter Wolfe, 7-3 TAD 165
Stampfli, Dave: letter of comment,
   6 JD 10; 7 JD 4; 9 JD 16
Standard Book Numbers, (as used in
   Ace Books, paperbacks), Denholms
   Law #3, by Bill Denholm, 1-4
   CP 17
(Standish, Burt L.), The Short Short
   Stories of Burt L. Standish,
   (Gilbert L. Patten writing as
   Standish in TIP TOP WEEKLY, dime
   novel), by Gerald J. McIntosh,
   2-2 BC 168
Stanich, Ray: Craig Kennedy, Check-
   list of Radio Shows, 3 PE 18
Stanich, Ray: Boston Blackie,
   (checklist of radio shows),
   3 PE 17
Stanich, Ray: letter of comment,
   6 R 22; 4-3 TAD 183; 4-4 TAD 259;
   5-3 TAD 186; 6-2 TAD 129; 7-1
   TAD 64; 24 X 45
Stanich, Ray: Radio Fu Manchu,
   (radio serials), 12 R 11
Stanislaw Lem and John Dickson Carr,
   Critics of the Scientific World-
   View, (comparison of works), by
   Edmund Miller, 14-4 TAD 341
Stanley Ellin Talks About Himself and
   His Writing, (interview), by Pat
   Erhardt, 2-3 MR 13
Stanley, John: letter of comment,
   9 JD 6
STAR MAGAZINE, Checklist and Index,
   (pulp magazine), by Nils Hardin,
   7 X 66
(Star Trek & Star Wars), Doc Savage
   and Crew Reborn as Stars of Star
   Trek and Star Wars, by Operative
   1701, 5 DS 14
(Star Wars), A Comment from Nick
   Carr's Typewriter, (on Star Wars
   and the pulps), by Wooda Nicholas
   Carr, 1 PW 2
Stark Reality, (Richard Stark, aka
   Donald E. Westlake), by John
   Bullis, 1-5 CP 5
(Stark, Richard), Additional Biblio-
   graphy, by David Doerrer, 2-4
   MF 51
(Stark, Richard), The Caper Novel,
   by George Kelley, 7 U 61

(Stark, Richard), Donald E. Westlake's "Richard Stark" Novels, (Westlake writing as Stark), by John Bullis, 1-5 CP 5

(Stark, Richard: THE HUNTER), What Happens in "Point Blank", (film based on Stark's book), by Francis M. Nevins, Jr., 9-1 TAD 7

Starrett, Vincent: H.P.Lovecraft, (verse), 18 X 9

Starrett versus Machen, (correspondence dispute between Vincent Starrett and Arthur Machen), by Michael Murphy, 18 X 24

(Starrett, Vincent), A Tribute to Vincent Starrett, by Michael Murphy, 2-2 PDA 70

(Starrett, Vincent), The Passing of Third Floor Back, by Robert W. Hahn, 7-3 TAD 204

(Starrett, Vincent), Starrett versus Machen, (correspondence dispute, Starrett and Arthur Machen), by Michael Murphy, 18 X 24

(Starrett, Vincent), Vincent Starrett on the Hard-Boiled School, by Michael Murphy, 21 X 47

(Starrett, Vincent), Vincent Starrett vs. Arthur Machen, or, How Not to Communicate Over Eight Years of Correspondence, by E.F.Bleiler, 3-6 MF 11

(Starrett, Vincent: THE ELEVENTH JUROR), An Eleventh-Hour Reassessment of The Eleventh Juror: Revealing the Germination of a Successful Mystery Tale, by Vincent Starrett, 2-2 PDA 48

STARTLING MYSTERY STORIES, Checklist and Index, (digest-size magazine published by Health Knowledge, Inc.), by Gene Marshall and Carl F. Waedt, 3 SF 14

Strauch, Helen: letter of comment, 4-2 TAD 129

Stauffer, J. Michael: letter of comment, 27 JD 37

Steady Stream, The, (short mystery reviews), by Don Miller, 1-1 MM 3; 1-2 MM 3; 1-3 MM 3; 1-4 MM 3; 1-5 MM 3; 1-6 MM 3; 1-7 MM 3; 1-8 MM 3; 1-9 MM 3; 1-10 MM 3; 1-11 MM 9; 2-1 MM 9; 2-2 MM 7; 2-3 MM 9; 2-4 MM 11; 2-5 MM 13; 2-5 MM 21

Steady Stream, The, (publications received for comment), by Don Miller, 13A MN 1; 13B MN 2; 13C MN 2

Steeger, Henry: letter of comment, 2 D 48; 9 DS 21; 67 PU 58; 4 U 51; 13 X 60; 22 X 49; 26 X 73; 36 X 72; 38 X 144; 43 X 5

(Steeger, Henry), An Interview with Henry Steeger, (President and publisher of Popular Publications, pulp magazines), by Nils Hardin, 33 X 3

(Steeger, Henry), Mrs. Steeger Recalls... (on Henry Steeger and Popular Publications), by Shirley Steeger, 33 X 20

(Steeger, Henry), The Popular Publications, A Checklist of Titles 1930-1955, (checklist of titles with bibliographical data), by Nils Hardin and George Hocutt, 33 X 21

(Steeger, Henry), The Popular Publications, (chronological list of titles of pulp magazines with comments), supplied by Henry Steeger, 67 PU 39

Steeger, Shirley: Mrs. Steeger Recalls.. (on Henry Steeger and Popular Publications pulp magazines), 33 X 20

Steele, Jacqueline: Patten, A Top Maine Author of Juveniles, (on Gilbert L. Patten and his boys' books), 1-3 TB 4

(Steele, Rocky, series: John B. West), The Rocky Steele Novels of John B. West, by Darwin T. Turner, 6-4 TAD 226

Steier, David: Alfred Hitchcock on Television, (survey study), 2-3 M 30

Stein, Aaron Marc: Robert Fish, In Memorium, (tribute), 14-2 TAD 120

(Stein, Aaron Marc), Interview with Aaron Marc Stein, by Shelly Lewis, 1-2 M 23

Stein, Saul: letter of comment, 2-3 CP 1

Steinbach, Martha: letter of comment, 14-3 TAD 247

"Steinberg" Found! (on Isador N. Steinberg, paperback cover artist), by Piet Schreuders, 3-4 PQ 12

(Steinberg, Isador N.), "Steinberg" Found!, (paperback cover artist), by Piet Schreuders, 3-4 PQ 12

Steinbrunner, Chris: Challenges to the Listener, (Ellery Queen on radio), 12-3 TAD 214

Steinbrunner, Chris: Commentaries for the Curious, (on John Dickson Carr) 1 NC 12

Steinbrunner, Chris: letter of comment, 5-4 MR 9; 11 R 24; 3-2 TAD 135; 11-1 TAD 4

Steinbrunner, Chris: The Radio Murder Hour, (mystery radio serials), 14-3 TAD 229; 14-2 TAD 156; (on The Shadow) 14-4 TAD 335

Steiner, Paul: letter of comment, 5 BB 22

Steinkuhl, John: THE SPIDER, Pulp Magazine Checklist, 1 U 17

(Stephens, C.A.: Old Farm series), Boys' Series Bibliography, by Harry K. Hudson, 1-6 YB 16

Steranko Art on Paperbacks, (James Steranko, artist, checklist), by M.C.Hill, 4-1 PQ 37

(Steranko, James), James Steranko... Extraordinary, (paperback artist), by M.C.Hill, 4-1 PQ 34

Stern, Elijah: A Stern Look at McGee,
(Travis McGee series by John D.
MacDonald, 15 JD 5

Stern, Elijah: JDM, A Critique, (on
John D. MacDonald), 10 JD 4

Stern, Peter L.: letter of comment,
13-4 TAD 343

Stevens, J. Clyde: letter of comment,
7 JD 8; 6 MY 2

Stevens, J. Clyde: Ruth Rendell, A
Bibliography, 7 MY 8

Stevens, J. Clyde, and Barbara Buhrer:
Checklist Bibliography for Dell
Shannon, 3/4 MN 4

Stevenson, (Mrs.) Harriet: letter of
comment, 13 JD 19; 14 JD 28;
15 JD 29; 16 JD 26; 17 JD 26;
18 JD 23; 19 JD 15; 20 JD 22;
24 JD 38; 25 JD 38

Stevenson, W.B.: Detective Fiction,
(general essay), 1A MR 3; 1-1 MR 9

Stewart, Dave: An Interesting Book,
This Lavender Look, (John B.
MacDonald: THE LONG LAVENDER LOOK),
15 JD 17

Stewart, Dave: Death of a "John Dee"
Fan, (on acceptance of violence
in the novels of John D. MacDonald),
17 JD 5

Stewart, Dave: John D. MacDonald, A
Sonnet, (verse), 16 JD 5

Stewart, Dave: letter of comment,
12 JD 16; 17 JD 24; 18 JD 24

Stewart, Dave: Previews From the
Publisher, (John D. MacDonald
items), 18 JD 9

Stewart, Enola: letter of comment,
3-3 MF 50

Stewart, Gerald J.: letter of comment,
2-3 TAD 201

(Stewart, Mary), Checklist, by Audrey
I. Pacheco, 5-4 MR 25

(Stewart, Mary), Interview, by Roy
Newquist, 1-4 MR 3

Stilwell, Steven A.: letter of comment,
5 LR 5; 6/7 LR 18; 2-2 MF 50;
2-3 MF 38; 5-4 MF 41; 9-2 TAD
155; 13-4 TAD 343

Stockholm in June: Crime Writers'
3rd International Congress, (report),
by Edward D. Hoch, 14-4 TAD 323

Stocking, Tamsen: Aphrodisia, Here Is
Your Hat, (sex in paperback cover
art), 3-4 PQ 28

(Stoddard, Charles), A Thunder Jim
Checklist (in THRILLING ADVENTURES
pulp magazine), by Will Murray,
1 D 22

Stoddard, R.H.: Memoirs of Mayne Reid,
(boys' books author), 2-2 BC 172

Stoelting, Wally: letter of comment,
5/6 MN 12

Stone, P.M.: 5A King's Bench Walk,
(residence of Dr. Thorndyke in
stories by R. Austin Freeman),
3 TF 37

Stone, Virginia H.: letter of comment,
11 JD 32; 16 JD 23

Stooker, Richard: letter of comment,
20 JD 22

Stordahl, C.: letter of comment,
1-2 M 3

(Storey, Rosika), Super Detective
Person, Rosika Storey, by Howard
Waterhouse, 2-4 PP 3

Stories of Capwell Wyckoff, The,
(Mystery Hunter series, Mercer
Boys series, other boys' books
by Wyckoff), by Fred Woodworth,
5 MA 1

Storm, Tenby: letter of comment,
1-2 G 69

Storm, Tenby: A Wolfean Double-Cross
Tick, (Nero Wolfe acrostic puzzle),
1-2 G 34

Story of Dennis Lynds, The, (sketch
of author), by John Edwards,
4 U 21

Story of the Phantom, The, by M.C.
Hill, 12 SF 21

(Stout, Rex), A Chronology of Crimes,
by Stephen F. Schultheis and
Patricia A. Dreyfus, 1-1 G 41

(Stout, Rex), A Memorial, by Michael
Bourne, 21 X 8

(Stout, Rex), A Partial Checklist
of Reviews of Books by Rex Stout,
by Don Miller, 9 MN A45

(Stout, Rex), A Reading of Rex Stout,
(verse), by Mona Van Duyn, 1-2
G 32

(Stout, Rex), A Special Report on
Shad Roe, by Marjorie Mortensen,
1-2 G 51

(Stout, Rex), A Welcome to The Wolfe
Pack, (organization of fans of
Rex Stout), by John J. McAleer,
1-1 G 15

(Stout, Rex), A Wolfean Double-Cross
Tick, (acrostic crossword puzzle),
1-2 G 34

(Stout, Rex), A Wolfean Quiz, (quiz),
1-1 G 31

(Stout, Rex), An Appreciation of
Archie Goodwin, by Arden Knight,
12-4 TAD 328

(Stout, Rex), "As Far as I'm Concerned,
You're Out of it": Wolfe and Archie
Apart, by David R. Anderson, 1-2
G 28

(Stout, Rex), The Bibliophile - Sooner
or Later, (on collecting Rex Stout)
by Judson C. Sapp, 6 U 31

(Stout, Rex), The Black Orchid Banquet
Theme Songs, (The Wolfe Pack, Nero
Wolfe fans' organization), 1-1 G 9

(Stout, Rex), The Black Orchid Banquet
Quiz, (quiz), by Marjorie Mortensen
1-1 G 13

(Stout, Rex), Case of the Missing Wolfe
(Baring-Gould's NERO WOLFE OF WEST
THIRTY-FIFTH STREET), by William J.
Clark, 3-4 MR 16

(Stout, Rex), Checklist, Nero Wolfe series, in Rare Books are Getting Scarce, by Bruce Taylor, 2-2 CP 27

(Stout, Rex), Comment from Cover Artist on Rex Stout Memorial Issue of THE MYSTERY NOOK, by Frank D. McSherry,Jr., 9 MN A10

(Stout, Rex), The Common Heard, (Nero Wolfe quiz), by Richard Oldberg, 1-2 G 60

(Stout, Rex), Confessions of a Reluctant Bibliophile, 1-1 G 47

(Stout, Rex), Creative Order in Rex Stout, by David R. Anderson, 9 MN A1

(Stout, Rex), Crime and Character, Notes on Rex Stout's Early Fiction, by David R. Anderson, 13-2 TAD 169

(Stout, Rex), Cross Trumps: A Conjectural Note on Rex Stout and Ellery Queen, by Allen J. Hubin, 1-1 TAD 9

(Stout, Rex), Cross Trumps, (on Rex Stout and Ellery Queen), by J.R.Christopher, 2-2 QC 6

(Stout, Rex), Dramatis Personae, (quiz), 1-1 G 55

(Stout, Rex), The Easy Chair - "Alias Nero Wolfe", (Wolfe the son of Mycroft Holmes?), by Bernard DeVoto, 1-2 G 37

(Stout, Rex), The Fake Plow Case, (Before Midnight Contest, The Wolfe Pack), by James R. Skelton, 1-2 G 45

(Stout, Rex), For Us, A Child, (Rex Stout and the times of his birth), by Mary Groff, 9 MN A15

(Stout, Rex), From the Press: The Early Non-Nero Wolfe Books, (review extracts) by Don Miller, 9 MN A57

(Stout, Rex), The Goodwin Document, by "Archie Goodwin", 1-2 G 49

(Stout, Rex), In the Press: A Few Review Extracts of Nero Wolfe Books, by Don Miller, 9 MN A56

(Stout, Rex), Index, NERO WOLFE MYSTERY MAGAZINE, by Frank D. McSherry, Jr., 9 MN A25

(Stout, Rex), Index: REX STOUT MYSTERY MAGAZINE, by Frank D. McSherry, Jr., 9 MN A21

(Stout, Rex), The "Lost" Nero Wolfe Tale, ("Bitter End"), by Arthur C. Scott, 9 MN A14

(Stout, Rex), Nero Wolfe Novels, by Lee Poleske, 2 LW 2

(Stout, Rex), Nero Wolfe Paperbacks in Print, (1975), by Lee Poleske, 4 LW 2

(Stout, Rex), Nero Wolfe Quiz, (quiz), by Lee Poleske, 1 LW 1; 2 LW 1; 3 LW 1; 4 LW 2; 5 LW 1; 6 LW 1

(Stout, Rex), The Nero Wolfe Saga, (in-depth study and commentary, with story synopses, individual story treatment), by Guy M. Townsend, 1-3 MF 13; 1-4 MF 25; 1-5 MF 21; 1-6 MF 15; 2-1 MF 15; 2-2 MF 25;

(Stout, Rex), The Nero Wolfe Saga, (continued), 2-3 MF 34; 2-4 MF 19; 2-5 MF 13; 2-6 MF 20; 3-1 MF 21; 3-2 MF 13; 3-3 MF 22; 3-4 MF 25; 3-5 MF 22; 3-6 MF 15; 4-1 MF 17; 4-2 MF 14; 4-3 MF 3

(Stout, Rex), The Nero Wolfe Saga: A Chronology, (first edition publication data checklist), by Don Miller, 9 MN A43

(Stout, Rex), The Nero Wolfe Saga: The Early Years, by Guy M. Townsend, 9 MN A31

(Stout, Rex), The Nero Wolfe Saga: The First Four, (review article), by Jo Ann Vicarel, 9 MN A42

(Stout, Rex), The Nero Wolfe Saga: Three at Random, (review article), by Don Miller, 9 MN A61

(Stout, Rex), Nero Wolfe vs. The Master Criminal, by John Harwood, 6-1 MR 15

(Stout, Rex), Nom De Loup, (on the names used in the Nero Wolfe novels), by Terry Abraham, 3 LW 5

(Stout, Rex), Nero Wolfe is "On the Air", (radio programs), by Judson C. Sapp, 9 MN A19

(Stout, Rex), Nero Wolfe on Film, by Don Miller, 9 MN A26

(Stout, Rex), Nero Wolfe: Logomachizer, by Lawrence F. Brooks, 1-1 G 21

(Stout, Rex), Nero Wolfe's Legacy of Books, by John J. McAleer, 1-2 G 8

(Stout, Rex), Not Too Many Clients, by Evelyn Herzog, 1-1 G 28

(Stout, Rex), Notes on the First Annual Black Orchid Banquet, (of The Wolfe Pack, Nero Wolfe fan's organization) 1-1 G 4

(Stout, Rex), The O'Boyle Report, (on the "genealogy" of Nero Wolfe), 1-2 G 2

(Stout, Rex), The Orchidology of Nero Wolfe, by Robert M. Hamilton, 1-2 G 18

(Stout, Rex), Orchids to the Wolfe Pack, The Second Annual Black Orchid Banquet, (Nero Wolfe fans' group), by Judson C. Sapp, 6 U 29

(Stout, Rex), Photos Article, by Jill Krementz, 6-2 MR 36

(Stout, Rex), Preliminary Study in the Literature of Nero Wolfe, by Fr. Francis Hertzberg, 2-4 MR 11

(Stout, Rex), Recipe for a Cookbook, by Barbara Burn, 1-1 G 34

(Stout, Rex), Rex Stout, A Bibliography by Don Miller, 9 MN A65

(Stout, Rex), Rex Stout, A Capsule Biography, by Don Miller, 9 MN A63

(Stout, Rex), Rex Stout, A Creator's World, by John J. McAleer, 9 MN A7

(Stout, Rex), Rex Stout, A Tribute, by Guy M. Townsend, 9 MN A6

(Stout, Rex), Rex Stout in the Dell Mapbacks, (paperback series editions), by William Lyles, 2-4 PQ 14

(Stout, Rex), Rex Stout in Ellery Queen's Anthologies, (checklist), by Don Miller, 9 MN A29

(Stout, Rex), Rex Stout in ELLERY QUEEN'S MYSTERY MAGAZINE, (checklist), by Don Miller, 9 MN A24

(Stout, Rex), Rex Stout in Mystery Guild Editions, (checklist, book club publications), by Michael L. Cook, 9 MN A27

(Stout, Rex), Rex Stout Newsletter, by John J. McAleer, 11-3 TAD 257; 12-1 TAD 66; 12-2 TAD 130; 12-3 TAD 224; 12-4 TAD 330; 13-1 TAD 41; 13-2 TAD 108; 13-3 TAD 224; 13-4 TAD 286; 14-1 TAD 22; 14-2 TAD 140; 14-3 TAD 230; 14-4 TAD 321

(Stout, Rex), The Second First Annual Wolfe Pack Event, (Nero Wolfe fans' organization), by Marjorie Mortensen, 1-2 G 58

(Stout, Rex), Short Stories, by Lee Poleske, 3 LW 7

(Stout, Rex), Werowance in the Wild, by Ellen Krieger, 1-2 G 54

(Stout, Rex), West Thirty-Fifth Street, (verse), by John J. McAleer, 1-1 G 20

(Stout, Rex), What to Expect, (news notes), by Beula Poole, 1-1 G 53

(Stout, Rex), Which Doorbell Rang?, by Tamar Crystal, 1-1 G 38

(Stout, Rex), Who's Afraid of Nero Wolfe?, (interview with Rex Stout), by Richard S. Lochte II, 3-4 TAD 211

(Stout, Rex), Wolfe a Howler! (comments on Nero Wolfe television series), by Bob Napier, 5-5 MF 7

(Stout, Rex), Wolfe on the Air, (Nero Wolfe on radio), by Arthur C. Scott, 9 MN A17

(Stout, Rex: THE PRESIDENT VANISHES), Film Note, by Louis Black, 9 MN A60

(Stover, Dink, series), The Best of Dink, or Stover Revisited, (boys' books), 1-2 BC 47

(Strahan, Kay Cleaver), Kay Cleaver Strahan, A Forgotten Detective Novelist, by Mary Jean DeMarr, 2-1 C 53

STRAND, THE, (on the British magazine, with particular note of Sherlock Holmes stories), by Fr. Francis Hertzberg, 4-5 MR 23

Strange Case of Philip Strange, or, Will the Real G-8 Please Stand Up, (on the similarity of pulp heroes), by Bud Overn, 5 BS 16; 2 P 15

STRANGE DETECTIVE STORIES, (on the pulp magazine, with index), by Glenn Lord, 65 PU 12

STRANGE STORIES, Author Index, (pulp magazine), by Robert Weinberg, 6 WT 26; Issue Index, 6 WT 23

(STRANGE TALES Magazine), Masterpieces of the Macabre, (pulp magazine, commentary), by Robert Kenneth Jones, 42 X 127

Stranger Than Fiction, (author's use of true crime), by John A. Hogan, 9-2 TAD 119

Stranger Things are Found, (verse), by Frederick Faust, 2-4 FC 8

Stranger Visits Land of Leo Edwards, (visit to home of boys' books author), by Ed Mulford, 1-1 TB 3; 1-2 TB 2

(Strangeways, Nigel, detective), The First Appearance: Nigel Strangeways, (A QUESTION OF PROOF by Nicholas Blake), by Maryell Cleary, 2-5 PP 25

(STRANGLED WITNESS, THE: Leslie Ford), The First Appearance: Colonel John Primrose, by Maryell Cleary, 3-4 PP 23

(Stratemeyer, Edward), Edward Stratemeyer, (sketch and activities), by Roy B. Van Devier, 1-1 BC 21

(Stratemeyer, Edward), Fortune and the Syndicate, (boys' and girls' books), by John T. Dizer, Jr., 2-1 BC 146; 2-2 BC 178

(Stratemeyer, Edward), Reply to Criticism, (Stratemeyer Syndicate and boys' and girls' books), 3-4 BC 362

(Stratemeyer, Edward), Stratemeyer Syndicate Properties, (boys' and girls' books), 3-4 BC 377

Stratemeyer Syndicate Properties, (boys' and girls' books), 3-4 BC 377

(Stratton-Porter, Gene), Gene Strattor-Porter, Mistress of the Mini-Mystery, by Jane S. Bakerman, 3-1 MF 3

Strauch, Helen: letter of comment, 7 JD 3

(Street & Smith Publishers), More Mystery for a Dime: Street & Smith and the First Detective Story Magazine (discussion on DETECTIVE STORY MAGAZINE), by J. Randolph Cox, 2-2 C 52

(Street & Smith Publishers), Some Errors in Fiction Factory, (THE FICTION FACTORY: Quentin Reynolds), by J. Randolph Cox, 74 PU 31

(Street & Smith Publishers), Street & Smith Pulps, (THE FICTION FACTORY: Quentin Reynolds), by Stewart Kemble, 74 PU 20

(Street & Smith Publishers), Street & Smith's Crime Busters, (on CRIME BUSTERS pulp magazine), by Will Murray, 38 X 132

(Street & Smith Publishers), Where Are the Pulp Fictioneers?, (old pulp writers and Street & Smith), by Robert Osterman, 2 BS 15

(Street & Smith Publishers), The Wonderful World of Street & Smith, (during the pulp magazine era), by Samuel W. Potts, 4 BS 12

Street & Smith Pulps, (commentary on THE FICTION FACTORY: Quentin Reynolds) by Stewart Kemble, 74 PU 29

Street & Smith's Crime Busters, (on CRIME BUSTERS pulp magazine), by Will Murray, 38 X 132

(Stribling, T.S.: Professor Poggioli, detective), Life as a Series of Abstract Analyses, (with checklist), by Robert Sampson, 2-2 C 61

(Stribling, T.S.: Professor Poggioli, detective), Checklist, by John Nieminski, 6-1 TAD 55

(Stribing, T.S.: CLUES OF THE CARRIBEES) Rare Vintages from the Tropics, by Frank D. McSherry, Jr., 6-3 TAD 172

Stricker, Jim: letter of comment, 2-4 TBN 3

Strictly Private, (letters of comment from readers), 2 PE 36; 3 PE 32; 4 PE 28; 5 PE 33; 6 PE 33; 7 PE 16

(Strieber, Whitley: THE WOLFEN), Mystery Plus: A Contemporary Science Fiction Pair, by R. Jeff Banks, 3-1 PP 16

(Striker, Francis Hamilton), The Tom Quest Crossword Puzzle, (crossword based on Tom Quest boys' series), 2 MA 30

(Striker, Francis Hamilton), The Tom Quest Series, (boys' series by Striker), by Fred Woodworth, 1 MA 20

(Striker, Francis Hamilton), Update: Tom Quest and The Lone Ranger, (two boys' series by Striker), by Fred Woodworth, 6 MA 13

(Striker, Francis Hamilton), The Writings of Fran Striker, (on the Lone Ranger series, boys' books), by Kent Winslow, 1 MA 7

Strohmeier, Elise C.: letter of comment, 11 JD 19

Strøm, Ola: letter of comment, 1-5 PP 25; 8-4 TAD 312

(Strong, L.A.G.), Department of Unknown Mystery Writers: L.A.G.Strong, by Marvin Lachman, 2-4 PP 13

(Stuart, Anthony: Vladimir Gull, series) Vladimir Gull, by Theodore P. Dukeshire, 4-3 MF 22

Stuart, Bob: The Dumarest Saga, A Checklist, (series by E.C.Tubb), 1-5 CP 28

Stuart, Jesse: Letter to August Derleth, (verse), 2-1 AD 1

Stuart, Judson D.: Boys Who Used Their Brains; The Boy Who Was Always Looking Ahead, Edward Edson Lee, (on boys' books author who used pen name Leo Edwards), 2-2 TBN 1

Stuff Nightmares are Made Of, The: A Hammett Update, (on the film "Hammett"), by Erik Jendresen, 3-2 M 45

Sturdavant, Madelyne: letter of comment, 4-4 TAD 256

(Sturdy, Don, series: Victor Appleton), Checklist, (boys' books series), by Robert Jennings, 1 BB 11

(Sturdy, Don, series: Victor Appleton), Don Sturdy and the Great Search for Adventure, (on the boys' books series), by Robert Jennings, 1 BB 5

Sturrock's "Duty", (Jeremy Sturrock series: J.G.Jeffreys), by Edward Lauterbach, 3-6 PP 5

(Styles, Showell), Detection Among the Mountains: The Writings of Glyn Carr, (pseudonym for Styles), by William Anthony S. Sarjeant, 4-5/6 PP 3

Subject Guide to Mystery Fiction, (theme index), by Richard Emery, 3-1 PP 3; (supplements) 3-3 PP 43; 3-4 PP 41; 3-6 PP 41

Subject Guide to TAD'S Letter Columns, (THE ARMCHAIR DETECTIVE, Volumes 1-3), by Robert E. Briney, 3-4 TAD 282

Subject is: Detective Stories, by Peter Andrews, 6/7 LR 29

Subject Was Death, The, (Operator 5, pulp hero, and the "Army of the Dead"), by Wooda Nicholas Carr, 15 SF 9

Suicidio!, (fiction), by Albert Herring, 3-2 M 52

Sukys, Paul A.: Requiem for a Detective, The Strange Death of Ellery Queen, (cessation of television series), 10-1 TAD 81

Sullivan, Eleanor: Fred Dannay and EQMM, (Dannay, Ellery Queen writing partner, and ELLERY QUEEN'S MYSTERY MAGAZINE), 12-3 TAD 201

Sullivan, Eleanor: Robert Fish, In Memorium, (tribute), 14-2 TAD 120

Sullivan, Jim: letter of comment, 1-3 TBN 4

Sullivan, John F.: The Books of Edgar Rice Burroughs, A Checklist, 3-3 BC 349

Sullivan, John F.: Checklist, Percy Keese Fitzhugh, (boys' books), 3-2 BC 300; 4-2 TB 1

Sullivan, John F.: The Do Good Boys and the Grave Peril, or Percy Keese Hits the Trail, (boys' books of Percy Keese Fitzhugh), 3-2 BC 290

Sullivan, John F.: Edgar Rice Burroughs, a Short Biography, 3-3 BC 346

Sullivan, John F.: letter of comment, 14 X 63

Sullivan, John F.: Nippy Weston, Girl Flyer, (pulp female aviation hero), 11 X 115

Sullivan, John F.: Tarzan and the Mayas, 5 X 39

Sullivan, John F.: Tom Slade - Paper Saint, (Tom Slade boys' series by Percy Keese Fitzhugh), 4-2 TB 1

Summer Night at a Tavern, (verse), by Frederick Faust, 3-1 FC 9

Summer 1971, (verse), by Edna Meudt, 2-3/4 AD 7

Summers, Bonita: Collector's Items, (crime fiction), 4-3 MR 11

Sunday Supplements in Retrospect, by Dean A. Grennell, 28 X 11

(Sunlight, John), The Eye of Day: A Speculation on the Maternity of John Sunlight, (Doc Savage villain), by Dafydd Neal Dyar, 6 DQ 6

(Sunlight, John), Sunlight, Son Bright, (Doc Savage villain), by Dafydd Neal Dyar, 8 DS 22

(Sunlight, John), That Terrible Sunlight, (Doc Savage villain), by Robert Sampson, 10 P 26

Sunlight, Son Bright, (John Sunlight, Doc Savage villain), by Dafydd Neal Dyar, 8 DS 22

Super Detective Person, Rosika Storey, by Howard Waterhouse, 2-4 PP 3

SUPER SCIENCE STORIES, (Canadian series, science-fiction pulp magazine, with checklist and index), by J. Grant Thiessen, 4 SF 21

Super Sleuth, (puzzle), by Louis Phillips, 12-3 TAD 208

Superior Reprints, (paperback line), by James Tinsman, 2-3 PQ 43; (checklist) 2-3 PQ 45

Superman of Bronze, (commentary on Doc Savage, pulp hero), by Will Murray, 5 DS 17

(supernatural), A Study in Black, (on supernatural themes in mystery fiction), by Frank D. McSherry, Jr., 5-5 MR 23; 5-6 MR 3; 6-1 MR 29; 6-2 MR 39

(supernatural), Mystery Plus: Incubus, (as supernatural theme in mystery fiction), by R. Jeff Banks, 1-3 PP 9

(supernatural), Wicked Dreams: The World of Sheridan LeFanu, by David Brownell, 9-3 TAD 191

Supersleuth Quiz, (quiz), 6/7 LR 9

(Superintendent Folly series: Jeremy York), Checklist, by Robert E. Briney and John Creasey, 2-1 TAD 17

Surveillance, (book reviews), 2-3 M 46; 3-1 M 36; 3-2 M 38

Survey Results, (on collecting paperback books), by Larry Rickert, 3-2 CP 35

(SURVEY OF SCIENCE FICTION LITERATURE: Frank N. Magill, ed.), Vault of the Ages, by George Kelley, 2-2 CP 20

Suspense Novel, The - and the Middle East, (Middle East locales), by Amnon Kabatchnik, 3-4 MR 3

Suspense Novels of Bill Pronzini, The, by George Kelley, 1-2 MF 15

("Suspense" radio program), Mystery Dial III: Locked Rooms, by Steve Lewis, 2-3 PP 11

Sutherland: Doublecrossed, (crossword puzzle), 2-5 CP 29

(Sutton, Margaret), Checklist, The Judy Bolton Series, (girls' mystery series books), by Julius R. Chenu, 1-1 YB 4

(Sutton, Margaret), Interesting Parallels Between Books by Margaret Sutton and Edward Edson Lee, (boys' series by "Leo Edwards" compared to girls' Judy Bolton series), 2-3 TB 1

(Sutton, Margaret), The Judy Bolton Series by Margaret Sutton, (girls' mystery series books), by Julius R. Chenu, 1-1 YB 3

Svenson, Andrew E.: "Bless You, Tom Swift" (boys' series by Victor Appleton), 2-1 BC 130

(Svenson, Andrew E.), Letter in Reply to Criticism of Stratemeyer Syndicate, 3-4 BC 362

Swain, Gunter E.: A Supplement to THIRTY YEARS OF ARKHAM HOUSE, (titles published 1970 to June 1981), 5-1 AD 9

Swain, Gunter E.: letter of comment, 2 FM 18; 24 X 44; 26 X 72

Swanson, Bill: letter of comment, 27 JD 38

Swanson, Bill & Beth: letter of comment, 25 JD 39

(Sweden), Detective Fiction in Sweden, by K. Arne Blom and Jan Broberg, 9-4 TAD 272

(Sweden), Swedish Mystery Writers, (status of crime fiction in Sweden), by Iwan Hedman, 3-4 MR 7

(Sweden), The History and Activities of Mystery Fans in Sweden, (and Scandinavia), by Iwan Hedman, 3-4 MF 12

(Sweden), Sweden's Commitment to Mystery Fiction, by E.F. Bleiler, 2-5 MF 7

Sweden's Commitment to Mystery Fiction, by E.F. Bleiler, 2-5 MF 7

Swedish Mystery Writers, (status of
crime fiction in Sweden), by Iwan
Hedman, 3-4 MR 7

(SWEENEY TODD, THE DEMON BARBER OF
FLEET STREET: Frederick Hazleton),
Blame Stephen Sondheim, by E.F.
Bleiler, 5-1 MF 15

Sweet, Charlie: letter of comment,
4-1 PP 40; 4-2 PP 35; 4-4 PP 33;
4-5/6 PP 96

Swenski, Joanne: letter of comment,
8 R 32

(Swift, Tom, series: Victor Appleton),
"Bless You, Tom Swift", (boys'
books series), by Andrew E.
Svenson, 2-1 BC 130

(Swift, Tom, series: Victor Appleton),
Boys' Book Oddities: Tom Swift,
by Harry K. Hudson, 1-2 BC 43

(Swift, Tom, series: Victor Appleton),
Checklist, (boys' book series),
by John T. Dizer, Jr., 2-1 TBN 5

(Swift, Tom, series: Victor Appleton),
Shopton, Home of the Swifts, (on
home locale of boys' series), by
John T. Dizer, Jr., 1-3 TBN 11;
1-4 TBN 8

(Swift, Tom, series: Victor Appleton),
Tom Loved Mary...Remember That?,
(boys' series books), by Robert
Louis, 4-1 BC 402

(Swift, Tom, series: Victor Appleton),
Tom Swift and the Great Nostalgia,
(boys' series books), by Col.
Paul Deems, USAF, 4-1 BC 386

Symbolic Motifs, (mystery-identifying
logos of publishers, with illustrated
checklist), by Robert C.SAdey,
3-4 MR 27

Symons, Julian: Holmes was a Sideline,
9 LR 21

Symons, Julian: Is the Detective Story
Dead? (recorded dialogue between
Julian Symons and Edmund Crispin),
4-2 MR 3

Symons, Julian: letter of comment,
2-6 MR 15; 5-4 TAD 243

Symons, Julian: Obituary for Edmund
Crispin, 1-5 PP 23

(Symons, Julian), Checklist, by Charles
Shibuk, 2-3 MR 19

(Symons, Julian), The Crime Novel v.
The Whodunit, by Rona Randall,
5-6 MR 25

(Symons, Julian), Julian Symons: An
Interview, by Lianne Carlin,
3-4 MR 24

(Symons, Julian), Julian Symons and
Civilization's Discord, (social
stress depicted in crime fiction),
by Steven R. Carter, 12-1 TAD 57

Tabakow, Lou: Sense of Wonder, (esoteric
puzzles in pulp fiction), 67 PU 51

TAD at the Movies, (news, reviews), by
Thomas Godfrey, 12-3 TAD 260;

TAD at the Movies, (continued),
12-4 TAD 367; 13-2 TAD 134; 13-3
TAD 226; 13-4 TAD 331; 14-1 TAD
84; ("Eyewitness") 14-2 TAD 152;
14-3 TAD 253; 14-4 TAD 330

TAD on TV, (news and commentary on
television mystery programs and
detective shows in THE ARMCHAIR
DETECTIVE column), by Richard
Meyers, 13-3 TAD 229; 13-4 TAD
332; 14-1 TAD 82; 14-2 TAD 153;
14-3 TAD 254; 14-4 TAD 332

TAD: The First Decade, (David Hellyer
interview with Allen J. Hubin,
editor, THE ARMCHAIR DETECTIVE),
10-2 TAD 142

Taking Care of Your Collection, by
Jack R. Schorr, (boys' books
collection), 2-4 BC 254

Tangled Emotions, The: The Police
Procedural, Pt.V, by George N.
Dove, 11-2 TAD 150

Tannen, Jack: letter of comment,
3-4 TAD 281; 9-4 TAD 249; 10-4
TAD 385

(Tanner series: Lawrence Block),
Lawrence Block: Annotated Checklist
of the Tanner Series Books,
5/6 MN 7

Tarrant, Kay: letter of comment,
6 P 29

Tarzan and His Imitators, by J.Grant
Thiessen, 4 SF 26

Tarzan and the Mayas, by John F.
Sullivan, 5 X 39

Tarzan International, (bibliographic
data on Tarzan books), by Stanleigh
B. Vinson, 63 PU 4

(Tarzan), A Fight to the Death,
(fiction), by Robert Buhr, 4 SF 25

(Tarzan), Bumudemutomuro, (in-depth
commentary on Tarzan stories), by
Robert Sampson, 8 U 3

(Tarzan), The Mysterious Case of the
Carters, ("genealogy" of the Carter
family, with link to Tarzan), by
Todd Rutt and Arn McConnell,
1-2 WA 3

(Tarzan), 007-Type Tarzan, (comparison
of James Bond and Tarzan), by
John Harwood, 4-6 MR 11

(Tarzan), Tarzan's Greater: A Historical View, by Bill Laidlaw, 7 DQ 16

(Tarzan), Those Tarzan Twins, by
Darrell C. Richardson, 2-1 BC 135

Tarzan's Greater: A Historical View,
by Bill Laidlaw, 7 DQ 16

Tatar, Ron: Collecting Thoughts,
(collecting paperbacks) 2-3 CP 7;
(DAW science fiction paperbacks)
2-4 CP 9; (collecting new paperbacks), 3-3 CP 29

Tatar, Ron: letter of comment,
2-1 CP 1; 3-3 CP 2

Tauber, Larry: letter of comment,
8 JD 11; 10 JD 8; 11 JD 26; 12 JD 16

Taublieb, Paul: Profile, ALFRED HITCHCOCK'S MYSTERY MAGAZINE, 2-3 M 34

Tavern Bill, (verse), by Steve Eng, 1-2 AD 7

Taxi, Speedy and Silvertip, (on Frederick Faust's western fiction), by William J. Clark, 2-1 FC 5

Taylor, Agatha: Paperback Firsts, 2-1 PQ 53; 2-2 PQ 40

Taylor, Bruce: Checklist, John Dickson Carr (paperback editions), 1-2 CP 16

Taylor, Bruce: Interview with Tony Hillerman, 14-1 TAD 93

Taylor, Bruce: Mystery Poll, (by the San Francisco Mystery Bookstore), 3-5 PP 31

Taylor, Bruce: letter of comment, 2-2 CP 4; 2-4 CP 1; 2-5 CP 1; 3-2 CP 2; 2-6 PP 30; 3-4 PP 37; 3-5 CP 1

Taylor, Bruce: Rare Books are Getting Scarce, (collecting mystery and detective fiction in paperback editions) 1-1 CP 8; (John Dickson Carr, paperback editions) 1-2 CP 15; (The Affair of the Purloined Plot) 1-3 CP 18; (mystery & detective paperbacks of great value) 1-4 CP 18; (pseudonyms for mystery authors) 1-5 CP 15; (paperback editions of Clayton Rawson) 1-6 CP 10; (Popular Library mystery titles) 2-1 CP 15; (Nero Wolfe, paperback editions) 2-2 CP 27; (Alfred Hitchcock, paperback editions) 2-4 CP 10; (Dell Great Mystery Library) 3-1 CP 23; (Pyramid's Green Door Mysteries) 3-2 CP 29; (on forming an affordable collection) 3-5 CP 12

Taylor, Bruce: The World of Mystery, (San Francisco area news), 2-1 M 32

Taylor, Bruce, and Carol Taylor: Account of Paperback Book Party, (paperback book collectors and authors, San Francisco), by "Secret Agent X-9", 1-2 CP 30

Taylor, Bruce, and Lance Casebeer: Asey Mayo, Cape Cod Sleuth, (paperback editions), 3-1 CP 20

Taylor, Bruce, and Dave Lewis: Rare Books are Getting Scarce, (defunct detective characters), 2-5 CP 19

(Taylor, Bruce, and Carol Taylor), Some of My Best Friends are Books, (re: San Francisco Mystery Bookshop), by Mary Groff, 13-2 TAD 171

Taylor, Charlotte: letter of comment, 9 JD 18

(Taylor, Col. Philip Meadows: CONFESSIONS OF A THUG), An Appreciation, by Andy Biegel, Jr., 11 SF 37

(Taylor, Phoebe Atwood), Asey Mayo - Cape Cod Sleuth, (paperback editions), by Lance Casebeer and Bruce Taylor, 3-1 CP 20

(Taylor, Phoebe Atwood), Asey May: "The Hayseed Sherlock", by Fred Dueren, 10-1 TAD 21

Taylor, Robert Lewis: Commentaries for the Curious, (on John Dickson Carr), 1 NC 16

Taylor, Thea: More Chanderisms, (on Raymond Chandler), 1-4 CP 29

Taylor, Wendell Hertig: Henry Kitchell Webster, The Emergence of an American Mystery-Writer, 5-4 TAD 199

Taylor, Wendell Hertig: letter of comment, 5-4 TAD 239

Taylor, Wendell Hertig: Rodrigues Ottolengui, A Forgotten American Mystery Writer, 9-3 TAD 181

Taylor, Wendell Hertig: Two Recent Studies of Crime Fiction, 5-3 TAD 159

Taylor, Wendell Hertig, and Jacques Barzun: A Catalogue of Crime, (supplements to basic list of crime fiction), 9-2 TAD 93; 9-3 TAD 209; 9-4 TAD 271; 10-2 TAD 126; 10-3 TAD 224; 11-1 TAD 92; 11-2 TAD 203; 11-3 TAD 281; 11-4 TAD 394; 12-1 TAD 32; 12-3 TAD 262; 13-3 TAD 208; 13-4 TAD 308; 14-1 TAD 88; 14-2 TAD 142; 14-3 TAD 228; 14-4 TAD 328

(Teason, William), An Informal Survey of Cover Art of the Seventies, Pt.1, Tribute to Agatha Christie, (Teason, artist), by Frank Eck, 9-3 TAD 170

Telephone, The, (The Shadow, related), by Joseph Lewandowski, 6 U 2

Television, (comments on mystery - detective shows), by Jim Huang, 8 CL 1; 12 CL 1

(Temple, Paul, series: Francis Durbridge), The Paul Temple Saga, (on British radio), by Derek Adley, 9-4 TAD 267

Temple, William F.: letter of comment, 62 PU 10

Temptations of Peggy Gaddis, The, by Charles Culpepper, 3-2 CP 3

Ten Books, (commentary on science fiction paperbacks), by George Kelley, 1-4 PQ 44

Ten Books; Poul Anderson and the Best, ("Best" anthologies), by George Kelley, 1-3 PQ 33

(TEN NORTH FREDERICK: John O'Hara), Spotlight, (discussion; paperback edition), 2-4 PQ 11

Ten Top Spider Novels and One Stinker, The, (commentary on The Spider novels from pulp magazines), by Will Murray, 13 SF 5

Tension and Duality: Daphne du Maurier's "Don't Look Now", by Jane S. Bakerman, 3-4 MF 8

Tepperman Quest, The, (search for elusive pulp author), by Wooda Nicholas Carr, 4 U 28

(Tepperman, Emile C.), The Tepperman Quest, (search for elusive pulp author), by Wooda Nicholas Carr, 4 U 28

Terence X. O'Leary's War Birds, (pulp
aviation heroes and magazine), by
Robert A. Madle, 69 PU 5
Terrell, Norma C.: letter of comment,
26 X 72
Terrible Beekeeper, The, (fiction,
pastiche on The Spider, Doc Savage,
The Shadow, and Sherlock Holmes),
by Arn McConnell and Todd Rutt,
1-1 WA 3; 1-2 WA 6; 1-3 WA 7;
1-4 WA 7; 2-1 WA 5
Terror for the Navy, (mysterious ocean
current changes, 1923), by Bill
Laidlaw, 4 DQ 3
(TERROR TALES), The Weird Menace
Magazines, (pulp magazines), by
Robert Kenneth Jones, 10 BS 3;
11 BS 7; 12 BS 7; 13 BS 7; 14
BS 13; 15 BS 4
Testing Your Eye-Q, (private detective
quiz), by Paul Bishop, 1-1 M 12
(TEXAS RANGERS), The Pulp Review,
(comment on issue of pulp magazine),
by Lynn Hickman, 71 PU 7
(Tey, Josephine), Checklist, by
Catherine Aird, 2-3 TAD 157
(Tey, Josephine), Controversy: Townsend,
Tey and Richard III, A Rebuttal, by
M.J.Smith, 10-4 TAD 317; (see also
10-3 TAD 211)
(Tey, Josephine), Josephine Tey (sketch),
by Catherine Aird, 2-3 TAD 156
(Tey, Josephine), Six Britons the Movies
Ignored, (mystery authors seldom
filmed), by Jack Edmund Nolan,
3-5 MR 9
(Tey, Josephine), Some Thoughts on Josephine
Tey, (use of retribution as a motive in
crime fiction novels), by Ethel Lindsay,
3-6 MR 7
(Tey, Josephine: THE DAUGHTER OF TIME),
Richard III and Josephine Tey:
Partners in Crime, by Guy M. Townsend,
10-3 TAD 211; (see also 10-4 TAD 317;
11-2 TAD 105; 11-3 TAD 237)
Thailing, Bill: Immortals Do Die; Cornell
Woolrich 1903-1968, a Memorial,
2-3 TAD 161
Thailing, William, with Harold Knott and
Francis M. Nevins, Jr.: Cornell
Woolrich, A Bibliography, 2-4 TAD 237
Thank You, Harry Castlemon, (tribute to
boys' books author), by Howard
Parkinson, 1-4 TB 2
Thank You, Mr. President, (photo article
of Ronald Reagan in movies), 2-2 M 5
That First Andy Blake, (bibliographic data
on Appleton edition of first boys' book
by Leo Edwards), by Ray H. Zorn,
1-3 TB 3
That Mysterious Aide to the Forces of Law
and Order, (commentary on The Shadow),
by J. Randolph Cox, 4-4 TAD 221
That Terrible Sunlight, (John Sunlight,
Doc Savage villain), by Robert Sampson,
10 P 26

That Which Brings Death, (fiction), by
Wooda Nicholas Carr, 2 FM 11
(Thayer, Lee), Checklist, by Jon
L. Breen, 5-3 TAD 149
(Thayer, Lee), Checklist, by Barry
A. Pike, 3-5 PP 27
(Thayer, Lee), Death Inside the Cow:
A Few Notes on the Novels of Lee
Thayer, by Francis M. Nevins, Jr.,
5-3 TAD 151
(Thayer, Lee), On Lee Thayer, by Jon
L. Breen, 5-3 TAD 148
(Thayer, Lee), Pen Profile: Lee Thayer
by Barry A. Pike, 3-5 PP 25
Thayer, Paul: letter of comment,
27 JD 38
There's No Sex in Crime: The Two-
Fisted Homilies of Race Williams,
(detective in pulps), by Michael
S. Barson, 2-2 C 103
"These Ven": Solution for "X" (on
Secret Agent X Magazine), 42 X 139
"These Ven": The Up-Dated Farmer,
(Jose Philip Farmer), 42 X 17
Thielman, James C.: letter of comment,
3-2 M 62
Thiessen, J. Grant: A.E.van Vogt, A
Brief Checklist, 8 SF 7
Thiessen, J. Grant: A Basic Reference
Library, (science fiction), 14 SF
39
Thiessen, J. Grant: Ace Science
Fiction Specials, (paperbacks),
5 SF 21
Thiessen, J. Grant: Additions and
Errata to the Ace Checklist,
(paperback line), 2 SF 35
Thiessen, J. Grant: An Interview with
A.E.van Vogt, 8 SF 4
Thiessen, J. Grant: The "Best of"
Phenomenon, (author collections),
4 SF 32; 5 SF 47
Thiessen, J. Grant: Beyond This
Horizon, (verse), 4 SF 25
Thiessen, J. Grant: Checklist, Ace
Books, (paperback line), by
numerical chronology 1 SF 3;
by author 1 SF 21
Thiessen, J. Grant: Fredric Brown,
An Appreciation, (with checklist),
2 SF 26
Thiessen, J. Grant: Gone But Not
Forgotten, (defunct paperback
publishers, with checklist; science
fiction), 2 SF 6
Thiessen, J. Grant: Harlequin - The
Beginning, (Harlequin Books,
paperback line), 9 SF 48; 10 SF
47
Thiessen, J. Grant: Harlequin Romance
Paperbacks, Checklist of First 25,
9 SF 48
Thiessen, J. Grant: How to File Your
Science Fiction Collection,
2 SF 42

Thiessen, J. Grant: Information, Please,
(questions and answers on science
fiction), 4 SF 39; 5 SF 41; 10 SF 35
Thiessen, J. Grant: James H. Schmitz
Bibliography, 12 SF 13
Thiessen, J. Grant: The Never-Ending
Bookshelf, (on rare paperbacks),
8 SF 23
Thiessen, J. Grant: Philip Jose Farmer,
An Appreciation, 5 SF 3
Thiessen, J. Grant: Reviews and Other
Ramblings, 13 SF 3; 14 SF 18
Thiessen, J. Grant: SUPER SCIENCE
STORIES, (Canadian pulp magazine,
with checklist and index), 4 SF 21
Thiessen, J. Grant: Tarzan and His
Imitators, 4 SF 26
Thiessen, J. Grant: Views and Reviews,
(short science fiction reviews),
8 SF 28; 9 SF 46; 10 SF 39
Thiessen, J. Grant, and Stuart W. Wells
III: Galaxy Science Fiction Novels,
(digest-size paperback series, with
checklist), 3 SF 44
(THIN MAN, THE: Dashiell Hammett), One
Britisher's View of Hammett, (review
of book in a London paper), by Edward
S. Lauterbach, 4-5/6 PP 44
(THIN MAN, THE: Dashiell Hammett), The
Problem of Moral Vision in Dashiell
Hammett's Detective Novels, by George
J. Thompson, 8-1 TAD 27
Things That Go Bump in the Mailbox,
(letters of comment from readers),
5/6 MN 11; 7 MN 5; 8 MN 29; 9 MN L1;
11 MN L1; 12 MN L1; 13 MN L1
Thinking Machine, The, by Link Hullar,
30 X 133
Third Eyelid, The, (re: Sax Rohmer), by
Marvin L. Morrison, 14 R 19
(13 CRIMES OF SCIENCE FICTION, THE: Isaac
Asimov, Martin H. Greenberg, Charles
G.Waugh), Mystery Plus: Getting There
May Be More Than Half the Fun, by
R. Jeff Banks, 3-5 PP 15
(THIRTY YEARS OF ARKHAM HOUSE: August
Derleth, ed.), A Supplement, (titles
published from 1970 to June 1981),
by Gunter E. Swain, 5-1 AD 9
This Dark Night, (fiction), by Mary Groff,
8 MN 9
This Gun for Hire, (find-a-word puzzle),
14-2 TAD 143
This Little Paperback Went to Market, or
Kiss My Deadly Typewriter, (on paper-
back publishing fallacies), by Michael
Avallone, 3-2 MR 27
Thomaier, William: letter of comment,
6-2 TAD 130; 9-2 TAD 160
Thomas Berger's Comic-Absurd Vision in
WHO IS TEDDY VILLANOVA?, by David
Madden, 14-1 TAD 37
Thomas Chastain and the New Police
Procedural, by Larry L. French,
2-4 MF 17

Thomas, Eddy: Cardboard Shelves,
(suggested for housing book
collection), 10 SF 32
Thomas, Judy: letter of comment,
3-6 PP 38
Thomas, Roy: letter of comment,
6 P 31
Thompson, Bruce M.: letter of comment,
4 SF 46
Thompson, Darrel: letter of comment,
1-3 TB 11
Thompson, Don: letter of comment,
5-4 MR 10
Thompson, George: letter of comment,
8-2 TAD 158
Thompson, George J.: The Problem of
Moral Vision in Dashiell Hammett's
Detective Novels, 6-3 TAD 153;
6-4 TAD 214; 7-1 TAD 32; 7-3 TAD
178; 7-4 TAD 270; 8-1 TAD 27;
8-2 TAD 124
Thompson, James W.: Nostalgia and the
Pulp Collector, 42 X 5; 44 X 33
Thompson, James W.: letter of comment,
28 X 79
(Thompson, Jim), Jim Thompson, A Walk
in the Jungle, Addendum to Judge
Crater and His Fellow Travellers,
(on mysterious disappearances), by
Frank D. McSherry, Jr., 8-1 TAD 99
(Thompson, Julian F.), Department of
Unknown Mystery Writers: Julian F.
Thompson, by Marvin Lachman,
1-4 PP 15
Thompson, Leslie M., and R. Jeff Banks:
When Is This Stiff Dead? Detective
Stories and Definitions of Death,
2-6 MF 11
Thompson, R.: letter of comment,
8 X 38
Thompson, Rik: The EQMM Cover Story
(concluded), (fiction), 1-2 MF 3
Thompson, Rik: letter of comment,
1-2 MF 47; 8-3 TAD 236
Thomsen, Dawn: letter of comment,
19 JD 15
(Thomson, Sir Basil), Checklist, by
Barry A. Pike, 3-6 PP 18
(Thomson, Sir Basil), Pen Profile,
(sketch), by Barry A. Pike,
3-6 PP 18
(Thomson, Christine Campbell),
Bibliography of Weird Fiction of
Oscar Cook and Christine Campbell
Thomson, by Mike Ashley, 3 WT 13
(Thomson, Christine Campbell),
Unlocking the Night, (weird fiction
of Thomson), by Mike Ashley,
3 WT 8
(Thomson, H. Douglas), H. Douglas
Thomson, A Brief Appreciation, by
Howard Haycraft, 8-4 TAD 256
Thomson, James W.: letter of comment,
9-1 TAD 86

Thomson, James W.: Raymond Chandler, Novelist, 21 X 52

(Thomson, June), Checklist, by Barry A. Pike, 3-4 PP 18

(Thomson, June), Pen Profile: June Thomson, by Barry A. Pike, 3-4 PP 17

Thomson, Lila: letter of comment, 6 WT 32

Those Tarzan Twins, by Darrell C. Richardson, 2-1 BC 135

Thorndyke and the Plumber's Oddments, (use of true crime in DR. THORNDYKE INTERVENES by R. Austin Freeman), by Norman Donaldson, 4 TF 8

THORNDYKE FILE, THE, Index to Issues Nos. 1-10, by Philip T. Asdell, 10 TF 33

Thorndyke the Linguist, (knowledge of languages indicated by Dr.Thorndyke in stories by R. Austin Freeman), by John H. Dirckx, 10 TF 24

Thorndyke's Topography, (locales in the Dr.Thorndyke stories of R.Austin Freeman), by Michael G. Heenan, 5 TF 23

Thorne, Creath: letter of comment, 62 PU 16

Thorne Smith, (in paperback editions), by Don Sprague, 3-2 CP 19

Thornton W. Burgess Books for Older Boys, by Julius R. Chenu, 1-2 BC 42

Thornton, Wayne: And a New Land Shall Emerge, (verse), 8 U 140

Thorp, Katherine: letter of comment, 8-1 TAD 69

Thorpe, Dickson: The Burning of Doc Savage, (collecting experiences concerning DOC SAVAGE magazines), 7 DQ 13

Thorpe, Dickson: Checklist, The Green Lama Stories of Richard Foster, (pulp hero tales), 1-2 MF 7

Thorpe, Dickson: Checklist, Ken Crossen Short Stories, (Kendell Foster Crossen), 1-2 MF 8

Thorpe, Dickson: Checklist, Kim Locke Stories of Christopher Monig, 1-2 MF 7

Thorpe, Dickson: Checklist, Milo March Novels of M.E.Chaber, 1-2 MF 6

Thorpe, Dickson: Harold F. Cruickshank, A Tribute-Portrait, 3 U 18

Thorpe, Dickson: Those Old Detective Pulp Magazines, 1-3 MF 9

Thorpe, Dickson: Will the Real Ken Crossen Please Stand Up, (Kendell Foster Crossen), 1-2 MF 5

Thorny Way to Heaven, The: A Thorndyke Pastiche, (pastiche, Dr. Thorndyke; fiction), by Oliver Mayo, 9 TF 5

Those Lovely, Detailed Paperback Covers, (paperback cover art), by Edward Lauterbach, 4-1 PP 16

Those Mysterious Mandolins, (Fu Manchu on the screen), by Robert W. Shurtleff, 18 R 9

Those Old Detective Pulp Magazines, by Dickson Thorpe, 13 MF 9

Thoughts on Doc Savage, by Leo Giroux, Jr., 4 DS 16

Thoughts on Fredric Brown, by William F. Nolan, 5-4 TAD 191

Thoughts on the Master of Villainy, (Sax Rohmer), by W.O.G.Lofts, 10 R 27

Threats to Rationalism: John Fowles, Stanislaw Lem, and the Detective Story, (the inexplicable still unsolved), by Frank Occhiogrosso, 13-1 TAD 4

Three Arts, The, (verse), by Frederick Faust, 1-2 FC 7

Three British Experiments From the Mainstream, (mainstream authors as mystery writers), by Charles Shibuk, 3-2 TAD 80

Three Gentle Men: Doris Miles Disney's Continuing Detectives, by Mary Jean DeMarr, 3-3 MF 5

THRILL BOOK, THE, (on the pulp magazine, with index), by Robert Kenneth Jones, 30 X 4

Thriller Novel Classics, (paperback line of science fiction; checklist), by J. Grant Thiessen, 2 SF 13

(THRILLING ADVENTURES Magazine), A Thunder Jim Checklist, (series in pulp magazine), by Will Murray, 1 D 22

(THRILLING DETECTIVE Magazine), Speaking of Pulp, (commentary), by Steve Lewis, 4 PE 9

(THRILLING WESTERN Magazine), Checklist and ¬ndex, by Gene Marshall and Ca.l F. Waedt, 3 SF 41

Thrills, Spills and Cliff-Hanging Adventures Supreme in a Calvacade of Famous "Chapter-Play" Serials: King of Entertainment, (old movie serials), by Andy Biegel, Jr., 5 U 11

Thud and Blunder, Then and Now, or Now and Then, (pulp reminiscences), by Basil Wells, 67 PU 48

Thugs and Dacoits of India, The, (in relation to Sax Rohmer stories), by John E. Carroll, 8 R 1

(Thunder Jim, series), A Thunder Jim Checklist, (from THRILLING ADVENTURES pulp magazines), by Will Murray, 1 D 22

(Thursday, Max, detective: Wade Miller) The Man Who Was Thursday, by Marvin Lachman, 8-3 TAD 179

(Tibbs, Virgil, series: John Ball),
Virgil Tibbs and the American Negro
in Mystery Fiction, by Marvin
Lachman, 1-3 TAD 86
Tiger Mann Series, The, (by Mickey
Spillane), by R. Jeff Banks,
2-3 MF 32
Tiger, Tiger, (fiction), by Bill Pronzini
and John Lutz, 3-2 M 14
Tilburg, Barry Van: Spy Series Characters
in Hardback, (annotated checks and
data of series by various authors),
Pt.1 (Anderson, Bark, Beeding,
Benton, Blackburn, Creasey,
Bruce) 4-2 MF 11;
Pt.2 (Coles, Cory, Deighton,
Creasey, Carter, Gardner,
Fleming, Hall, Haggard,
LeCarre, Fallon) 4-3 MF 23;
Pt.3 (Harvester, Leasor, Mair,
Heald, Leonard) 4-4 MF 16
Pt.4 (McCutchan, Sapper, Marquand,
Martyn, McLeod) 4-5 MF 21;
Pt.5 (Mason, Mather, Mayo, Perry,
Powell, Price, O'Malley)
4-6 MF 4
Pt.6 (Sax Rohmer) 5-1 MF 2
Pt.7 (Ross, Tute) 5-2 MF 2
Pt.8 (Wheatley, Woodhouse, York,
Gilman, Hossent, Mitchell,
Bridge, Davison, Gerard)
5-3 MF 18
Pt.9 (Aarons, Annesley, Avallone)
5-5 MF 15
(TIME AFTER TIME: Karl Alexander),
Mystery Plus: A Contemporary Science
Fiction Pair), by R. Jeff Banks,
3-1 PP 16
Time Machine, The: Philip K. Dick,
The Middle Period, by George Kelley,
2-1 PQ 23
TIMES LITERARY SUPPLEMENT (London),
Friday, February 25, 1955, (the
supplement on mystery fiction,
discussed), by Mary Groff, 10-3
TAD 232
(Tinsley, Frank), Bill Barnes - Air
Adventurer, (Tinsley as illustrator
for the pulp magazines), by B.W.
Overn, 3 BS 14
(Tinsley, Frank), Frank Tinsley, Prophet
With a Brush, (pulp artist sketch),
by B.W.Overn, 67 PU 68
(Tinsley, Theodore), A Full Length "Shadow"
Novel as Told to... (Shadow stories
written by Tinsley and Bruce Elliott),
by Fred S. Cook, 3 BS 12
Tinsman, Jim: Checklist, Bestseller
Mysteries, (addendum, digest-size
paperback mystery line), 1-6 PP 27;
2-1 PP 31
Tinsman, Jim: Checklist, Jonathan Press
Mysteries, (addendum, digest-size
paperback mystery line), 1-6 PP 27;
2-1 PP 31

Tinsman, Jim: Checklist, Mercury
Mysteries, (addendum, digest-size
paperback line), 1-6 PP 27;
2-1 PP 31
Tinsman, Jim: Checklist, Superior
Reprints, (paperback line),
2-3 PQ 45
Tinsman, Jim: letter of comment,
1-6 PP 27; 2-1 PP 31
Tinsman, Jim: Superior Reprints, (on
the paperback line), 2-3 PQ 43
Tips on Breaking Into the Pro Ranks,
(on writing), by Ralph Roberts,
12 SF 26
T-K Graphics: letter of comment,
8 X 38
To a Scholar, (verse), by Lucile
Coleman, 30 X 134
To All the Late Masters of the Unknown,
(verse), by F.H.Tolman III,
3-4 AD 8; 4-1 AD 3
To August Derleth, (tribute), by
Gahan Wilson, 3-1 AD 7
To the Very Last: The Dying Message,
(as clue in crime fiction), by
Lynn Biederstadt, 12-3 TAD 209
To Those Mysteriously Murdered in
Books, (verse), by Robert Aucott,
12-1 TAD 68
(Tobin, Mitchell, series: Tucker Coe),
Mitch Tobin's Healing, (on Tobin
as detective in series by Donald
E. Westlake writing as Tucker Coe),
by Maryell Cleary, 4-5/6 PP 31
(Tobin, Mitchell, series: Tucker Coe),
Walls of Guilt: Donald E. Westlake
as Tucker Coe, by Francis M.Nevins
Jr., 7-3 TAD 163
Toby Press, (checklist, paperback line
of science fiction), by J. Grant
Thiessen, 2 SF 13
Todd Book Editions, (Jerry Todd series
by Leo Edwards; bibliographic data),
by Robert L. Johnson, 2-5 TBN 4
(Todd, Jerry, series: Leo Edwards),
Area Map of Tutter, People, Places,
(locale and people in the stories;
boys' books), 2-3 TBN 1
(Todd, Jerry, series: Leo Edwards),
Brothers are Reunited! (news item
by "Cassibum Kepp"), 2-3 TBN 1
(Todd, Jerry, series: Leo Edwards),
Checklist, (boys' books), by
Julius R. Chenu, 3 BB 10; 1-1
TB 4; 1-2 TB 17
(Todd, Jerry, series: Leo Edwards),
Different Jerry Todd Editions,
(bibliographic data, boys' books),
by Robert L. Johnson, 2-2 TBN 1
(Todd, Jerry, series: Leo Edwards),
Jerry Todd, (boys' books), by
Julius R. Chenu, 4 BB 3
(Todd, Jerry, series: Leo Edwards),
Jerry Todd Detective, (fiction), by
Julius R.Chenu,1-1 TBN 7;1-2 TBN 11;
1-3 TBN 13; 1-4 TBN 15; 2-1 TBN 6;
2-2 TBN 7; 2-3 TBN 7

(Todd, Jerry, series: Leo Edwards),
Jerry Todd Stories Edwards' Most
Popular, (boys' series), by Julius
R. Chenu, 1-2 TB 1

(Todd, Jerry, series: Leo Edwards),
Mummy Itchers, (humorous depicting
of prop in JERRY TODD AND THE
WHISPERING MUMMY; boys' book), by
Julius R. Chenu, 2-4 TBN 1

(Todd, Jerry, series: Leo Edwards),
Mummy Plot Fact Believe It or Not,
(JERRY TODD AND THE WHISPERING
MUMMY based on true fact), by
Julius R. Chenu, 1-3 TB 1

(Todd, Jerry, series: Leo Edwards),
Poppy Ott Sequel to Popular Todd
Series, (Poppy Ott and the Jerry
Todd boys' books series), by Julius
R. Chenu, 1-3 TB 1

(Todd, Jerry, series: Leo Edwards),
Todd Book Editions, (bibliographic
data; boys' books series), by
Robert L. Johnson, 2-5 TBN 4

(Todd, Jerry, series: Leo Edwards),
Todd Series Tops Pop; More Titles,
More Printings, (popularity of the
Jerry Todd series, boys' books),
by Julius R. Chenu, 1-4 TBN 1

Todd Series Tops Pop; More Titles,
More Printings, (popularity of
Jerry Todd series, boys' books),
by Julius R. Chenu, 1-4 TBN 1

(Toff series: John Creasey), Checklist,
by Robert E. Briney and John Creasey,
2-1 TAD 10

(Tolkien, J.R.R.), Books About J.R.R.
Tolkien and His Works, (bibliography), by David S. Bratman,
5 SF 26

(Tolkien, J.R.R.: LORD OF THE RINGS),
The War Over Middle Earth, by
Billy C. Lee, 1-4 PQ 37

Tolley, Michael J.: Color Him Quixote-
MacDonald's Strategy in the Early
McGee Novels, (Travis McGee series
by John D. MacDonald), 10-1 TAD 6

Tolley, Michael J.: letter of comment,
22 JD 20

Tolman, F.H., III: To All the Late
Masters of the Unknown, (verse),
3-4 AD 8; 4-1 AD 3

Tom Loved Mary...Remember That?, (on
Tom Swift series of boys' books
by Victor Appleton), by Robert
Louis, 4-1 BC 402

Tom Quest Series, The, (boys' books),
by Fred Woodworth, 1 MA 21

Tom Slade and Friends, Pt.1, (boys'
series), by Gil O'Gara, 1-4 YB 21

Tom Slade and Friends, Pt.2, (boys'
series), by Julius R. Chenu,
1-5 YB 16

Tom Slade - Paper Saint, (boys' books
series by Fitzhugh), by John F.
Sullivan, 4-2 TB 1

Tom Swift and the Great Nostalgia,
(Tom Swift boys' series by
Victor Appleton), by Col.Paul
Deems, USAF, 4-1 BC 386

Tomlinson, Gerald: The Silver Fifty,
(classics of crime fiction),
10-2 TAD 165

Tompkins, Gilbert & Juliet: The
Winning Touchdown, (song),
1-5 YB 15

Tompkins, Walker: Confessions of a
Pulp Western Hack, (writing
experiences), 32 X 13

Tompkins, Walker: letter of comment,
12 P 7; 26 X 72; 40 X 85

Tonik, Albert: A Doc Savage Adventure
Rediscovered, ("Who Goes There"
by Don A. Stuart), 4 DS 10

Tonik, Albert: A Report on PulpCon 9,
(pulp convention), 14 SF 15

Tonik, Albert: A Report on the First
East Coast Pulp and Paperback
Convention, 11 SF 34

Tonik, Albert: A Visit to Two Museums,
(libraries; Forrest J. Ackerman,
and San Francisco Academy of Comic
Art), 10 SF 34

Tonik, Albert: Chronology of The Man
of Bronze, (Doc Savage), 7 DS 6

Tonik, Albert: Interview with John
Nanovic, (pulp editor), 9 SF 44

Tonik, Albert: letter of comment,
4 DS 5; 12 DS 8; 14 SF 47;
3 U 49; 4 U 53; 5 U 64; 6 U
54; 7 U 47; 43 X 5

Tonik, Albert: PulpCon 8 - The
Impressions of a First Timer,
(report on pulp convention),
3 U 9

Tonik, Albert: Steve Austin, Story
or Authentic? (The Million Dollar
Man, possibly based on true event
and people), 5 U 3

Tonik, Albert, and Tom Johnson:
U.N.C.L.E., (espionage series),
10 DS 20

Too Right Bony, (Inspector Napoleon
Bonaparte: Arthur W. Upfield),
by M.C.Hill, 3-2 PQ 7

Tooker, Ken & Rita: letter of comment,
9 JD 17

Toole, Chuck: letter of comment,
8 JD 9; 11 JD 22; 11 JD 28;
12 JD 16

Toole, Linda: letter of comment,
4-3 MF 48; 4-5 MF 46; 5-1 MF 43;
5-2 MF 50; 5-3 MF 45; 5-4 MF 41;
5-6 MF 50; 4-1 PP 49

Top Secret, (on Doc Savage type codes)
by Dafydd Neal Dyar, 6 U 28

Top Ten Doc Savage Novels and One
Stinker, (detailed commentary),
by Will Murray, 8 U 22

Top Twenty-Five Shadow Novels and
One Stinker, (detailed comments),
by Will Murray, 4 U 3

Tornquist, Jack: letter of comment,
1-2 TBN 5; 2-2 TBN 4

Tornquist, Jack: Ramblin' With Jack,
(on boys' books and collecting),
1-2 TBN 8; 1-3 TBN 7; 1-4 TBN 7

Torrence, Raymond J.: Andy Capp, Gold
Medal/Fawcett, (Andy Capp cartoon
character in paperback books published by Gold Medal and Fawcett)
1-6 CP 13

Torrence, Raymond J.: letter of comment,
1-5 CP 2

Torrence, Raymond J.: Philip Gordon
Wylie, (paperback editions),
2-4 CP 23

(Torrey, Roger), Pulp Literature:
Subculture Revolution in the Late
1930s, by Steve Fisher, 5-2 TAD 91

Townsend, Guy M.: The Article I Couldn't
Publish, (Ian Fleming and J.D.
Salinger's THE LAUGHING MAN),
1-1 MF 18

Townsend, Guy M.: letter of comment,
6/7 LR 21; 5/6 MN 11; 8 MN 34;
11 MN L4

Townsend, Guy M.: The Nero Wolfe Saga,
(in-depth study and commentary
on Nero Wolfe novels by Rex
Stout, individual story treatment
with story synopses), 1-3 MF 13;
1-4 MF 25; 1-5 MF 21; 1-6 MF 15;
2-1 MF 15; 2-2 MF 25; 2-3 MF 34;
2-4 MF 19; 2-5 MF 13; 2-6 MF 20;
3-1 MF 21; 3-2 MF 13; 3-3 MF 22;
3-4 MF 25; 3-5 MF 22; 3-6 MF 15;
4-1 MF 17; 4-2 MF 14; 4-3 MF 3

Townsend, Guy M.: The Nero Wolfe Saga,
The Early Years, (Nero Wolfe stories
by Rex Stout), 9 MN A31

Townsend, Guy M.: Of Fans and Boucher-
Cons, (mystery fans and the
conventions), 5-5 MF 11

Townsend, Guy M.: Reviews, 1A MF 32

Townsend, Guy M.: Rex Stout, A
Tribute, 9 MN A6

Townsend, Guy M.: Richard III and
Josephine Tey: Partners in Crime,
(Tey: THE DAUGHTER OF TIME), 10-3
TAD 211; (Controversy: Rebuttal)
10-4 TAD 317; 11-2 TAD 105; 11-3
TAD 237

Townsend, Guy M., and R. Jeff Banks:
The Matt Helm Series, (of Donald
Hamilton) 2-2 MF 3; (annotated
checklist) 2-2 MF 3

Tracking Tom Buchanan, (author), by
Bernard A. Drew, 8 U 135

Tracy, Jack: Conan Doyle and Sherlock
Holmes; The Creator versus The
Creation, 2-2 M 26

(Tracy, Jack: SHERLOCK HOLMES, THE
PUBLISHED APOCRYPHA), The
Aprocryphalization of Holmes,
by E.F.Bleiler, 4-5 MF 3

(Train, Arthur), Tutt and Monsieur
Donaque: Some Notes on the Crime
Fiction of Arthur Train, by J.
Randolph Cox, 2-4 PP 9

Train, Oswald: letter of comment,
3-1 TAD 68

Trainer, Brian: letter of comment,
3-3 CP 2

Traitor's Purse, a Double-Dactyl,
(verse), by R.W.Hays, 7-1 TAD 10

Traveler With Crime: Suzanne Blanc,
by Winn Kearns, 8-3 TAD 194

Travis McGee as Traditional Hero,
(character created by John D.
MacDonald), by Erling B. Holtsmark, 1-1 C 99

Traylor, J. Barry: letter of comment,
25 JD 37; 3 MA 26; 3-1 PQ 5;
3 U 49; 14 X 62; 24 X 12;
33 X 114; 43 X 6

Treachery, (fiction), by Elizabeth
Davis, 3-1 M 55

(Treadgold, Detective-Inspector:
Anthony Weymouth), Pen Profile,
by Barry A. Pike, 4-3 PP 13

(Trench, John), Pen Profile, by
Barry A. Pike, 4-1 PP 19

(Treasure, Mark, detective: David
Williams), Pen Profile, by
Barry A. Pike, 2-4 PP 19

Trenchcoat Files, The: Zach Rolfe
Series by J.J.Lamb, by Paul
Bishop, 3 PE 15

Trenchcoat Files, The: James Hazell,
The Toughest Bastard to Ever Push
Your Bell Button, by Paul Bishop,
4 PE 17

Trenchcoat Files, The: Meet Joe
Goodey/San Francisco Will Never
Be the Same, (series by Charles
Alverson), by Paul Bishop,
6 PE 31

(Trevor, Ben), Pen Profile, by
Barry A. Pike, 3-1 PP 28

Trials Series: Some Notable, Some
Not, (British book series), by
Jonathan Goodman, 7-2 TAD 116

Tribute to Ellery Queen on His 40th
Birthday, by Donald A. Yates,
2-4 TAD 250

(Trigger Berg series: Leo Edwards),
Trigger Berg - Leo's Jr. Series,
(boys' books), by Julius R.Chenu,
2-4 TBN 1

Trimble, BJO: letter of comment,
9 JD 12

Trinapulation of the Albitron,
(fiction), by Walter Shedlofsky,
7 X 65

Trip, The, (re: Ray Bradbury and
William F. Nolan), by Donn
Allbright, 36 X R13

Trivia Quiz: The Avenger, (quiz),
by Kirk McConnell, 1-1 WA 11

Trivia Quiz - Mostly Movies, (mystery quiz), 1-2 WA 14

Trivia Quiz: Nero Wolfe, (mystery quiz based on Rex Stout's Nero Wolfe), 1-3 WA 13

Trivia Quiz: A Living Shadow, (mystery quiz based on The Shadow), by Arn McConnell, 1-4 WA 18

Trivia Quiz: The Biographers, (mystery quiz), by Craven Lovelace, 2-1 WA 19

Trojan, William: Ace Science Fiction Specials, (paperback line; checklist), 5 SF 21

Trojan, William: letter of comment, 2-1 CP 4; 22 X 52

Trombetta, Michael: letter of comment, 10-3 TAD 277

Trouble with Shakespeare, You Remember Him, (verse), by Ogden Nash, 1-5 CP 11

Troubles in Doubles, (fiction), by Edward Edson Lee, 2-4 TBN 7

(Trowbridge, John T.), Chats with Big Americans for Young Americans, (on boys' books by Trowbridge), by Hugh C. Weir, 3-1 BC 278

(Trowbridge, John T.), Favorite Juvenile Authors: What Publishers Said About Their Old Stand-Bys, (boys' books), by Gil O'Gara, 1-2 YB 19

(Trowbridge, John T.), J.T.Trowbridge, Youth Fiction Trailblazer, by Les Beitz, 1-4 BC 104

(Trowbridge, John T.), Mr. Trowbridge and Our Young Folks, (on boys' books' author), by David A. Moulton, 3-1 BC 258

Trtek, Dick: letter of comment, 17 X 62; 30 X 150; 38 X 143; 40 X 86

(true crime), A Cambridge Mystery, (1931), by Neville Wood, 1-2 PP 3; 1-3 PP 3; 1-4 PP 3; 1-5 PP 3

(true crime), A Day in the Life of a Real Private Investigator, by Douglas Christensen and Karen Bornstein, 1-3 M 52

(true crime), A Mirror ro Our Crimes, (true crimes as mystery fiction), by Edward D. Hoch, 12-3 TAD 280

(true crime), All Too True, (mystery fiction suggested by actual crimes), by Mary Groff, 1-1 PP 3; 1-2 PP 15; 1-3 PP 16; 1-4 PP 17; 1-5 PP 13; 1-6 PP 14; 2-1 PP 23; 2-2 PP 20; 2-3 PP 15; 2-4 PP 21; 2-5 PP 19; 2-6 PP 19; 3-1 PP 29; 3-2 PP 19; 3-3 PP 22; 3-4 PP 25; 3-5 PP 21; 3-6 PP 21; 4-1 PP 24; 4-2 PP 15; 4-3 PP 15; 4-4 PP 21; 4-5/6 PP 59

(true crime), Sawney Beane, An Incident from the Casebook of a Royal Detective, (British classic crime), by Veronica M.S.Kennedy, 9-2 TAD 126

(true crime), The Unabated Storm: Sacco & Vanzetti, by David Bates, 2-6 PP 23

Try to Find It, (on rare crime fiction), by E.F.Bleiler, 6-2 TAD 97

(Tubb, E.C.), Annotated Listing, (bibliography), 7 SF 7

(Tubb, E.C.), The Dumarest Saga: A Checklist, by Bob Stuart, 1-5 CP 28

(Tubb, E.C.), The Perils of Bibliography: A Look at the Writings of E.C.Tubb, by Mike Ashley, 7 SF 5

Tucker, Eric: The Penguin Story, (British paperback line), 2-3 PQ 18

Tuffy Bean Stories Last Edwards' Series, (Tuffy Bean series last to be written by Leo Edwards; boys' books), 1-4 TB 1

Turan, Kenneth: Say Hello to the Spider, For the Pulps are Back, (revival of pulp hero in paperback books), 1 DS 16

Turbiville, (Mrs.) C.F.: letter of comment, 27 JD 38

Turk, Genevieve: letter of comment, 3-4 AD 9

Turman, James: letter of comment, 22 X 52

(Turner, Dan, series: Robert Leslie Bellems), Dan Turner, (pulp detective series), by Wooda Nicholas Carr, 21 X 51

(Turner, Dan, series: Robert Leslie Bellems), Investigating Dan Turner, (pulp detective series), by Stephen Mertz, 5 PE 9

Turner, Darwin B.: The Rocky Steele Novels of John B. West, 6-4 TAD 226

Turner, David: New Books, (news and reviews), 30 X 22; 32 X 14

Turner, Edith: letter of comment, 3-3 PP 38; 8-1 TAD 69; 9-1 TAD 83

Turner, James: letter of comment, 1-3 AD 3

Turner, Robert: letter of comment, 7 JD 5; 8 JD 14; 12 JD 14; 4-3 MR 19; 26 X 74; 28 X 80; 30 X 149; 36 X 73

Turner, Robert: The Not-So-Literary Digests, (on digest-size mystery magazines), 38 X 19

Turner, Robert: Requiem for a Magazine (on cessation of MANHUNT), 1-6 MR 5

(Turner, Robert), Partial Index of Stories, 38 X 19

Tusing, Holly: letter of comment, 3-1 M 2

Tuska, Jon: The Dragon Murder Case
(S.S.Van Dine), First National 1934,
A Cinematograph, 6-1 TAD 20
Tuska, Jon: letter of comment,
5-4 TAD 243; 6-3 TAD 195
(Tute, Warren: George Mado series),
Checklist, Annotated, by
Barry Van Tilburg, 5-2 MF 2
Tutt and Monsieur Donaque: Some Notes
on the Crime Fiction of Arthur
Train, by J. Randolph Cox, 2-4
PP 9
(TUTTER BUGLE, THE), Rebirth of the
Bugle, (Leo Edwards fans' magazine),
by Robert L. Johnson, 1-1 TB 1
Tuttle, George: letter of comment,
2-3 M 2; 14-1 TAD 73
TV Notes, (mystery commentary and
reviews of television shows), by
Jack Edmund Nolan, 4-2 MR 32
TV Reviews, (mystery shows), by Donald
Carew, 2-2 M 47
TV Reviews, (mystery shows), by Lorin
Brennan, 2-3 M 16; 3-2 M 50
TV Tie-In Affair, or Matt Dillon Meets
Emma Peel, (paperback books trading
on television publicity), by John
Garbarino, 3-4 CP 5
TV's Nancy Drew, (girls' series on
television), by John M. Enright,
7 MA 14
(Twain, Mark), David (Pudd'nhead) Wilson,
The Missing Figure in a Detective's
Group, by Louise Saylor, 13-1 TAD 8
(Twain, Mark), Mark Twain, Detective
Story Writer, An Appreciation, by
R. Jeff Banks, 7-3 TAD 176
Twarog, Bill: letter of comment,
11-2 TAD 108
Twelve Green Russian Garnets, The,
(fiction, Classic Corner Rare Tales),
by Arthur Sherburne Hardy, 13-1
TAD 48
(TWENTIETH CENTURY CRIME AND MYSTERY
WRITERS: John M. Reilly, ed.), The
Body in the Library: Twentieth
Century Crime and Mystery Writers
and the Mystery World in Our Time,
by Martin Morse Wooster, 5-1 MF 11
(TWENTIETH CENTURY CRIME AND MYSTERY
WRITERS: John M. Reilly, ed.), For
Mystery Readers: The Newest Must-
Have Book, by Steve Miller, 3-4
PP 9
Two Detective Mysteries, (quiz), by
R. Jeff Banks, 12-4 TAD 378
Two Faces of Herr Matzu, The, (villain
in the G-8 pulp hero stories), by
Wooda Nicholas Carr, 5 X 4
Two From the Telly, (Sapphire and Steel,
and The Professionals, two British
television series), by Robert C.S.
Adey, 5-6 MF 19
Two Fungi From Yuggoth, (verse), by
Alice Briley, 4-3 AD 9

Two Heads are Better Than One, (on
co-authorship of mystery fiction),
by Hal Charles, 4-2 PP 9
Two Lonely Nights with Mickey Spillane,
(interview), by Michael S. Barson,
2-3 PQ 13
Two Recent Studies of Crime Fiction,
by Wendell Hertig Taylor, 5-3
TAD 159
Two Short Chapters from DEATH OF A
.300 HITTER, by Mike Avallone,
1A MF 11
Tyas, Peter H.: letter of comment,
4-5/6 PP 94
(Tyler, Dennis, series: John Franklin
Carter), Checklist, Annotated,
by Barry Van Tilburg, 4-3 MF 25
Tyson, Donald: letter of comment,
3-1 M 6

(Uhnak, Dorothy), Checklist, by
Audrey I. Pacheco, 5-4 MR 23
Ultimate Hi-Jacking Novel, The,
(ransom in mystery plots, with
checklist), by Marvin Lachman,
2-2 PP 17
U.N.C.L.E., (on the espionage series),
by Albert Tonik and Tom Johnson,
10 DS 20
Unabated Storm, The: Sacco & Vanzetti,
by David Bates, 2-6 PP 23
UNCANNY TALES Magazine, (Canadian
pulp magazine; with index and
checklist), by Dennis Lien,
9 SF 25
Uncle Ray, (on Ray Bradbury), by
Philip A. Shreffler, 36 X R30
Uncollected Fiction of Fredric Brown,
The, by Dennis McMillan, 3-1
CP 15; 3-2 CP 25
Under the Jack-Knife, (Sherlockiana
column), by Michael Hodel,
2-1 M 30; 2-3 M 23; (The Great
Sherlockian Centennial 1881-1981,
by Hodel and Sean Wright), 3-1 M
51; (on John Bennett Shaw) 3-2 M
34
Under the Southern Star, (Whitman
Press of Australia; paperback
publications), by Dave & Su Bates,
3-3 CP 18
Under Two Flags: The Detective Story
in Science Fiction, by Frank D.
McSherry, Jr., 2-3 TAD 171
(UNDERGROUND MAN, THE: Ross Macdonald)
The Case of the Underground Man,
Evolution or Devolution?, by G.A.
Finch, 6-4 TAD 210
Underwood, Tim: letter of comment,
22 X 51; 36 X 73
Unicorn, The, (verse), by Lucile
Coleman, 1 U 8
Unicorn Mystery Book Club - Checklist
by Author and in Order of Publi-
cation, by Michael L. Cook,
12 MN I1

(Unicorn Mystery Book Club), Checklist, Complete, by Edward D. Hoch, 8-3 TAD 187

(Unicorn Mystery Book Club), Hans Stefan Santesson and the Unicorn Mystery Book Club, by Edward D. Hoch, 8-3 TAD 185

(Unicorn Mystery Book Club), The Unicorn Mystery Book Club: Checklist by Author and in Order of Publication, by Michael L. Cook, 12 MN I1

(Unicorn Mystery Book Club), The Unicorn Mystery Book Club, (partial list of publications, with brief club history), Michael L. Cook, 5 MY 3

(Unicorn Mystery Book Club), THE UNICORN NEWS, (newsletter of the Unicorn Mystery Book Club), by Edward D. Hoch, 8-3 TAD 192

Uninvited Night Callers, (verse), by Paul Harwitz, 8 U 103

Unique Magazine, The: Hugo Gernsback's SCIENTIFIC DETECTIVE MONTHLY, by Robert A.W.Lowndes, 14-1 TAD 24; 14-2 TAD 157; 14-3 TAD 243; 14-4 TAD 367

(University collections), Detective Fiction in the Wade Collection, (Wheaton College), by J.R.Christopher, 9-4 TAD 274

(University collections), Pulp Collection of University of California Los Angeles, 12-2 TAD 164

(University collections), The University of North Carolina Crime Fiction Collection, by Mary S. Cameron, 1-2 TAD 51

Unknown Authors, Theodore George, by Robert C.S.Adey, 4-3 PP 19

Unknown One, The, (Lewis Carroll: THE UNKNOWN ONE), by J.R.Christopher, 3-4 TAD 247

(UNKNOWN magazine), Index, by Will Murray, 42 X 12

(UNKNOWN magazine), The Unknown UNKNOWN, (pulp magazine), by Will Murray, 42 X 11

Unknown UNKNOWN, The, (on the pulp magazine, (with index), by Will Murray, 42 X 11

Unlocking the Night, (on the weird fiction of Christine Campbell Thomson and Oscar Cook), by Mike Ashley, 3 WT 8

Unpublished Derleths, The, (discussion of titles of August Derleth mentioned but not published), by Paul Spencer, 5-1 AD 6

Unspeakable in Search of the Inedible Among the Unfindable, The, (humor), by Mike Wharton, 5-2 TAD 89

Update: Tom Quest and The Lone Ranger, (two book series by Fran Striker; boys' books), by Fred Woodworth, 6 MA 13

Up-Dated Farmer, The, (on Philip Jose Farmer), by "These Ven," 42 X 17

(Upfield, Arthur W.), Arthur William Upfield 1888-1964, by Estelle Fox, 3-2 TAD 89

(Upfield, Arthur W.), Arthur William Upfield, September 1, 1888 - February 13, 1964, (sketch), by Betty Donaldson, 8-1 TAD 1

(Upfield, Arthur W.), Australian Words and Expressions in Upfield's Novels, by Philip T. Asdell, 1 BY 5

(Upfield, Arthur W.), Biography: FOLLOW MY DUST, by Jessica Hawke, in The Whodunit's Who's Who, by Philip T. Asdell, 3-4 PP 11

(Upfield, Arthur W.), Bony Was There, (locales of stories of Inspector Napoleon Bonaparte), by Philip T. Asdell, 1 BY 2

(Upfield, Arthur W.), Checklist, by Estelle Fox, Francis M. Nevins, Jr., and Charles Shibuk, 3-2 TAD 90

(Upfield, Arthur W.), The Great Australian Detective, (on Insp. Bonaparte), by William Antony S. Sarjeant, 12-2 TAD 99

(Upfield, Arthur W.), The Novels of Arthur W. Upfield, Bibliography and Review, by Betty Donaldson, 8-1 TAD 4

(Upfield, Arthur W.), Too Right Bony, (Inspector Bonaparte, detective), by M.C. Hill, 3-2 PQ 7

(Upfield, Arthur W.), Upfield Collector A Mystery Buff of the Purest Sort, (Michael Masliah, collector of Upfield books and related), by Natalie Hall, 11-1 TAD 72

(Upfield, Arthur W.: FOLLOW MY DUST) The Great Melbourne Cup Mystery, by Philip T. Asdell, 1 BY 3

Upfield Collector: A Mystery Buff of the Purest Sort, on Michael Masliah and his Upfield collection), by Natalie Hall, 11-1 TAD 72

Upon Reading of Lovecraft's Death, (verse), by Steve Eng, 3-1 AD 2

(Urquhart, MacGregor: Chief-Inspector Joshua Smarles), Pen Profile, by Barry A. Pike, 4-4 PP 19

Ury, Jon: It's for You, Inspector, You've Been Cancelled, (on television mystery shows), 7-4 TAD 265

Use of Poison in Detective Fiction, The, by Peter R. Gwilt and John R. Gwilt, 1-2 C 8

Uses of Astonishment, The, (as ingredient in crime fiction), by Lawrence Fleming, 18 JD 11

Upon Distinguishing Among 140 (or More) Pastiches, (Sherlock Holmes), by Horace Harker, 1-3 M 14

UTOPIA - 10, (Dutch magazine), 1-4 PQ 43

(Utpatel, Frank A.B.), Obituary and Funeral Notice, 4-1 AD 10

(Utpatel, Frank A.B.), The Wood Engraver
From Mazomanie, (Arkham House
illustrator), by Kay Price, 4-3
AD 1
Utter, V.S.: letter of comment, 36 X 72

(Vallejo, Boris), Boris! Boris! Boris!
(paperback cover artist for Doc
Savage books), by Robert Woo,
1 DS 11
Vallentine, B.B.: The Author of THE BOY
TRAVELLERS, (Thomas W. Knox, boys'
books author), 4-1 BC 400
Van Achtoven, Gail: letter of comment,
14 JD 29; 15 JD 30; 16 JD 18
Van Ash, Cay: A Question of Time, (on
Sax Rohmer), 17 R 7
Van Ash, Cay: Fu Manchu, (commentary),
9 R 15
Van Ash, Cay: letter of comment,
9 R 31; 10 R 31; 12 R 8; 15 R 27;
17 R 24; 18 R 17
Van Ash, Cay: Ourselves and Gaston Max,
(Sax Rohmer character), 15 R 23
Van Ash, Cay: Sax Rohmer in the 1920's;
Notes on Chronology, 18 R 21
Van Ash, Cay: The Seals of the Si Fan,
(Fu Manchu stories by Sax Rohmer),
11 R 21
Van Ash, Cay: The Search for Sax Rohmer,
14 R 13
(Van Ash, Cay), Biographical Sketch,
11 R 4
Van Buskirk, E. Lynne: letter of
comment, 12-4 TAD 355
Van Campen, David B.: letter of comment,
10 JD 13; 11 JD 23; 18 JD 30
Van de Ven, Luc: letter of comment,
25 JD 38; 4-3 PP 34; 6-4 TAD 275;
7-1 TAD 70; 8-4 TAD 316; 10-2 TAD
162
(van de Wetering, Janwillem), An Inter-
view with a Black Sheep of Amsterdam:
Janwillem van de Wetering, by Chris
and Janie Filstrup, 13-2 TAD 98
Van der Valk, (detective created by
Nicolas Freeling), by William Ruble,
5-2 MR 1; (checklist) 5-2 MR 5
Van Devier, Roy B.: Edward Stratemeyer,
(author and syndicator, boys' series
books), 1-1 BC 21
Van Devier, Roy B.: Josephine Chase and
Her Pen Names, (juvenile author),
1-2 BC 39
Van Devier, Roy B.: The Old Werner
Publishing Company of Akron, Ohio,
(boys' books publisher), 2-4 BC 246
Van Devier, Roy B.: Oliver Optic,
(prolific boys' books author),
2-3 BC 215
Van Dine and Queen, ("random jottings"
re: S.S.Van Dine and Ellery Queen),
by Donald A. Yates, 1-4 QC 12
(Van Dine, S.S.), Checklist, by Bruce
R. Beaman, 8-2 TAD 134

(Van Dine, S.S.), The Dragon Murder
Case, First National, 1934, a
Cinematograph, by Jon Tuska,
6-1 TAD 20
(Van Dine, S.S.), Dear Me, Mr. Van
Dine, by Robert A.W.Lowndes,
7-1 TAD 30
(Van Dine, S.S.), Philo Vance, (the
detective character of Van Dine),
by Fred Dueren, 9-1 TAD 23
(Van Dine, S.S.), Philo Vance on the
Screen, (movie versions, Philo
Vance, detective), by Jack Edmund
Nolan, 2-4 MR 18
(Van Dine, S.S.), Philo Vance's
Sunday Nights at the Old Stuyve-
sant Club, (Vance, detective),
by E.R.Hagemann, 1-2 C 35
(Van Dine, S.S.), S.S.Van Dine, A
Biographical Sketch, by Bruce R.
Beaman, 8-2 TAD 133
(Van Dine, S.S.), Van Dine and Queen
("random jottings, re: Van Dine
and Ellery Queen), by Donald A.
Yates, 1-4 QC 12
Van Duyn, Mona: A Reading of Rex
Stout, (verse), 1-2 G 32
(van Loan, Richard Curtis, The
Phantom Detective), Blood Chronicle,
(The Phantom Detective and the
magazine), by Robert Sampson,
3-3 MR 3
(van Loan, Richard Curtis, The
Phantom Detective), The Phantom
Detective in Paperback, by Bruce
Cervon, 2-4 CP 7; (checklist)
2-4 CP 8
(van Loan, Richard Curtis, The
Phantom Detective), Contemplating
Seven of the Pulp Heroes, (com-
parisons and characteristics),
by Wooda Nicholas Carr and Herman
S. McGregor, 12 BS 3
(van Loan, Richard Curtis, The
Phantom Detective), Fading Shadows,
Corinth/Regency Paperbacks, by
Tom Johnson, 10 SF 36
(van Loan, Richard Curtis, The
Phantom Detective), Checklist for
THE PHANTOM DETECTIVE magazine,
1933-1953, by Bernie Wermers,
11 BS 4
(van Loan, Richard Curtis, The
Phantom Detective), Ryerson Johnson
and the Phantom Detective, (inter-
view), by Wooda Nicholas Carr,
6 U 9
Van Tilburg, Barry: letter of comment,
4-2 MF 59; 4-6 MF 49; 5-1 MF 46;
5-3 MF 41; 5-5 MF 48
Van Tilburg, Barry: Spy Series in
Hardback, (annotated checklists
of various authors),
Pt.1 (Anderson, Bark, Beeding,
Benton, Blackburn, Creasey,
Bruce) 4-2 MF 11

Van Tilburg, Barry: Spy Series in Hardback, (continued)
    Pt.2 (Coles, Cory, Deighton,
        Creasey, Carter, Gardner,
        Fleming, Hall, Haggard,
        LeCarre, Fallon) 4-3 MF 23;
    Pt.3 (Harvester, Leasor, Mair,
        Heald, Leonard) 4-4 MF 16
    Pt.4 (McCutchan, Sapper, Marquand,
        Martyn, McLeod) 4-5 MF 21
    Pt.5 (Mason, Mather, Mayo, Perry,
        Powell, Price, O'Malley)
        4-6 MF 4
    Pt.6 (Sax Rohmer) 5-1 MF 2
    Pt.7 (Ross, Tute) 5-2 MF 2
    Pt.8 (Wheatley, Woodhouse, York,
        Gilman, Hossent, Mitchell,
        Bridge, Davison, Gerard)
        5-3 MF 18
    Pt.9 (Aarons, Annesley, Avallone)
        5-5 MF 15
van Vogt, A.E.: A Double Memorial,
    (tribute to August Derleth; also
    memorial to Derleth by Colin Wilson),
    2-1 PDA 3
van Vogt, A.E.: The Adventure of the
    Pastiche Craftsman, (on August
    Derleth writing pastiches of Solar
    Pons), 2-1 PD 1
van Vogt, A.E.: Being an Examination
    of the Ponsian and Holmesian Secret
    Deductive Systems, (Solar Pons and
    Sherlock Holmes), 1-2 PDA 52
van Vogt, A.E.: Praedian Reflections,
    (Solar Pons), 3-2 PDA 26
(van Vogt, A.E.), An Interview with
    A.E.van Vogt, by J. Grant Thiessen,
    8 SF 3
(van Vogt, A.E.), Checklist, by J.
    Grant Thiessen, 8 SF 7
Van Wagner, Roy: letter of comment,
    2-5 TBN 6
(Vance, Jack: Planet of Adventure
    series), Jack Vance's Planet of
    Adventure Series, (science fiction
    paperbacks), by George Kelley,
    2-2 PQ 20
(Vance, Philo, series: S.S.Van Dine),
    Checklist, by Bruce R. Beaman,
    8-2 TAD 134
(Vance, Philo, series: S.S.Van Dine),
    The Dragon Murder Case, First
    National, 1934, A Cinematograph,
    by Jon Tuska, 6-1 TAD 20
(Vance, Philo, series: S.S.Van Dine),
    Dear Me, Mr. Van Dine, by Robert
    A.W.Lowndes, 7-1 TAD 30
(Vance, Philo, series: S.S.Van Dine)
    Philo Vance, by Fred Dueren,
    9-1 TAD 23
(Vance, Philo, series: S.S.Van Dine),
    Philo Vance on the Screen, by
    Jack Edmund Nolan, 2-4 MR 18
(Vance, Philo, series: S.S.Van Dine),
    Philo Vance's Sunday Nights at the
    Old Stuyvesant Club, by E.R.Hagemann,
    1-2 C 35

(Vandercook, John W.), John W.
    Vandercook and His Tropical
    Murders, by Philip T. Asdell,
    3-2 PP 3
(Vane, Harriet, detective: Dorothy
    L. Sayers), Feminists as Detectives,
    Harriet Vane, Kate Fansler, Sarah
    Chayse, by Kathleen Gregory Klein,
    13-1 TAD 31
Vanished, (verse), by Steve Eng,
    3-4 AD 11
Vanishing Resource, The, (Old Pulp
    Writers), (on need to interview
    living pulp writers now), by
    Bernard A. Drew, 2 U 2
(Varley, John), Checklist, by Fred
    Isajenko, 12 SF 29
Vast Collection of Books Requires
    Separate Housing, (Jack Schorr's
    collection of boys' books), by
    Marjorie Freeman, 3-4 BC 374
Vault of the Ages, (on Brian Stable-
    ford's THE REALMS OF TARTARUS), by
    George Kelley, 1-3 CP 16
Vault of the Ages, (on Brian Stable-
    ford's puzzle novels), by George
    Kelley, 1-2 CP 19; 1-4 CP 27
Vault of the Ages, (on SURVEY OF
    SCIENCE FICTION LITERATURE by
    Frank N. Magill, ed.), by George
    Kelley, 2-2 CP 20
Vega Books Checklist, (science fiction
    paperbacks line), by Ronald W.
    Spitzer, 4 SF 19
"Vegas" - The First Season, (the
    television series), by Andy
    Jaysnovitch, 6 PE 16
(Venables, Charles, detective: St.John
    Sprigg), Pen Profile, by Barry
    A. Pike, 2-5 PP 23
(VENDETTA: Marie Corelli), Marie
    Corelli, Vendetta!, by Michael
    Avallone, 9-4 TAD 270
Vengeance Novels of Brian Garfield,
    The, by George Kelley, 2-1 MF 5
Vengeance on the Avenger, (fiction),
    by Kenneth Robeson, 10 P 12
Vera Caspary's Fascinating Females:
    Laura, Evvie and Bedelia, by
    Jane S. Bakerman, 1-1 C 46
Verdicts, (book reviews), 1-1 MF 34;
    1-2 MF 29; 1-3 MF 43; 1-4 MF 41;
    1-5 MF 37; 1-6 MF 42; 2-1 MF 31;
    2-2 MF 36; 2-3 MF 49; 2-4 MF 37;
    2-5 MF 35; 2-6 MF 36; 3-1 MF 38;
    3-2 MF 42; 3-3 MF 40; 3-4 MF 42;
    3-5 MF 42; 3-6 MF 42; 4-1 MF 29;
    4-2 MF 41; 4-3 MF 42; 4-4 MF 44;
    4-5 MF 37; 4-6 MF 34; 5-2 MF 26;
    5-3 MF 34; 5-4 MF 28; 5-5 MF 28;
    5-6 MF 42
Verner, Nathanne: letter of comment,
    25 JD 40
Vernon, William D.: Charles L.
    Harness, A Bibliography, 14 SF 30
Vernon, William D.: Charles L.
    Harness, Paradox Man, 14 SF 25

Versatile Gardner F. Fox, The, (on the various fields of this author in paperback, with checklist), by Edwin L. Murray, 3-5 CP 5

Very Much So Clever Fellow, The, (on Jules deGrandin), by Robert Sampson, 5 WT 3

(Very Temporary) Return of Skull-Face, The, (re: THE RETURN OF SKULL-FACE, by Robert E. Howard and Richard A. Lupoff), by Robert E. Briney, 2-2 MF 21

Vialpando, Shirley A.: letter of comment, 24 JD 40

Vicarel, Jo Ann: A Rendell Dozen Plus One; An Annotated Checklist of the Rendell Novels Through 1974, (Ruth Rendell), 9-3 TAD 198

Vicarel, Jo Ann: The Investigation; Fiction and Fact, (on Dorothy Uhnak: THE INVESTIGATION), 3-3 MF 15

Vicarel, Jo Ann: letter of comment, 5-5 MF 48; 3/4 MN 14; 8 MN 31; 2-2 MF 55; 3-2 MF 56; 6 MY 8; 8-2 TAD 152; 8-4 TAD 324; 9-2 TAD 155

Vicarel, Jo Ann: The Mystery Nook Poll Results, (poll by MYSTERY NOOK magazine), 9 MN P1

Vicarel, Jo Ann: The Nero Wolfe Saga; The First Four, (commentary and reviews on first Nero Wolfe books by Rex Stout), 9 MN A42

Vicarel, Jo Ann: Regency Romances of Georgette Heyer, (with checklist), 13 MN 17

Vicarel, Jo Ann: Series Synopses - Norah Mulcaheney series by Lillian O'Donnell, 10-1 TAD 80; 11-4 TAD 365

Vickers, Roy: A Classic Forgery, from THE EXPLOITS OF FIDELITY DOVE, 11-4 TAD 357

(Vickers, Roy), Additions and Corrections to Checklist of Mark Purcell (on Vickers), by Francis M. Nevins, Jr., 4-2 MR 17

(Vickers, Roy), Checklist, (short stories of Vickers), by Howard Waterhouse, 1-3 PP 7

(Vickers, Roy), Roy Vickers: The Department of Dead Ends Series - A Partial Bibliography, by James Mark Purcell, 4-1 MR 29

(Vickers, Roy, Inspector Rason series), An Open-Ended Search for Dead Ends, by Howard Waterhouse, 1-3 PP 7

Victims of Circumstance, (fiction), by R. Austin Freeman, 5 TF 28

(Vidal, Gore), Gore Vidal, Mystery Writer, by Francis M. Nevins, Jr., 4-2 MR 25

(Vidal, Gore), The Mysteries of Edgar Box (pseudonym for Gore Vidal), by Earl F. Bargainnier, 2-1 C 45

Views and Reviews, (short science fiction reviews), by J. Grant Thiessen, 8 SF 28; 9 SF 46; 10 SF 39

(VILLAGE STREET AND OTHER POEMS,THE: Frederick Faust), The Scarcest Title, by William J. Clark, 1-4 FC 9

(Villesvik, Linda), Department of Unknown Mystery Writers, by Marvin Lachman, 1-4 PP 15

Vincent Starrett vs. Arthur Machen, or, How Not to Communicate Over Eight Years of Correspondence, by E.F.Bleiler, 3-6 MF 11

Vining, John: letter of comment, 7-4 TAD 302; 8-1 TAD 69; 8-2 TAD 154; 8-2 TAD 156; 8-3 TAD 238; 8-4 TAD 325; 9-1 TAD 80; 9-2 TAD 155; 9-4 TAD 249

Vining, John: Series Synopses - Don Cadee: Spencer Spean, 9-2 TAD 113

Vining, John: Series Synopses - The Executioner Series: Don Pendleton, 9-2 TAD 113

Vining, John: Series Synopses - Hiram Potter series: Rae Foley, 10-2 TAD 188

Vining, John: Series Synopses - The Saint by Leslie Charteris, 10-2 TAD 187

Vining, John: Series Synopses - Victor Grant series: John B. Ethan, 10-2 TAD 187

Vinson, Stanleigh B.: Tarzan International, (bibliographic article on Tarzan books), 63 PU 4

Violencers, The, (prospectus for proposed series and how to present to publisher), by Michael Avallone, 5 U 21

Virgil Tibbs and the American Negro in Mystery Fiction, by Marvin Lachman, 1-3 TAD 86

Virginity Preserved and the Secret Marriage of Sherlock Holmes, (Sherlockiana), by Michael Atkinson, 2-1 C 62

Visiting Firemen, (mini-mystery parody), by R. Jeff Banks, 7 PE 11

VOID MAGAZINE, An Index, by Darrell Schweitzer, 2 U 18

Volland's Golden Youth Series, (boys' books), by Donald Sanders, 2-1 BC 137

von Tersch, Gary, and Thomas Kent Miller: The Raconteur of Emerald Lake, (on E. Hoffman Price), 6 WT 3

Vorpel Blade, The, (fiction), by Edward D. Hoch, 2-2 M 10

Vosburg, Mike: letter of comment, 14 R 27

Vucenic, Joe: letter of comment, 2 BS 21;
    8 SF 44
Vucenic, Joe: The Shadow on the Moon,
    (summation of an issue of The Shadow
    Comics), 8 BS 20
Vucenic, Wayne: The Gold Key Doc Savage
    Comic Book, 14 BS 18
(Vulliamy, C.E.), More Notes on C.E.
    Vulliamy), by Charles Shibuk,
    5-3 TAD 145
(Vulliamy, C.E.), Notes on C.E.Vulliamy,
    by Charles Shibuk, 3-3 TAD 161
Vulnerable Shadow, The, (on The Shadow),
    by Robert Sampson, 1 P 24

W.Murdoch Duncan, Master of Mystery, An
    Appreciation, by Donald Ireland,
    9-2 TAD 116
W.Somerset Maugham as a Mystery Writer,
    (literary study), by F. Shropshire,
    14-2 TAD 190
W.T.Ballard, An Interview, by Stephen
    Mertz, 12-1 TAD 14
Waddington, Roger: letter of comment,
    36 X 70
(Wade, Henry), Checklist, by Charles
    Shibuk, 1-4 TAD 112
(Wade, Henry), Henry Wade, A Tribute,
    by Charles Shibuk, 1-4 TAD 111
(Wade, Henry), Henry Wade Revisited,
    by Charles Shibuk, 2-1 TAD 45
(Wade, Henry), Pen Profile: Henry
    Wade, by Barry A. Pike, 4-5/6 PP 45
Wade, James: A Curious Interview,
    (with Fu Manchu?), 13 R 8
Wade, James: The Last Encounter, (Fu
    Manchu and Sir Denis Nayland Smith,
    in fiction by Sax Rohmer), 1-2
    PDA 66
Wade, James: letter of comment,
    3 R 30; 6 R 21; 7 R 27; 13 R 31;
    14 R 27
Wade, James: Sinitic Sonnet, (verse),
    4 R 27
(Wade, Jerry, detective), A Snappy Hero,
    Jerry Wade, (from DETECTIVE NOVELS
    pulp magazine, with checklist),
    by Robert Weinberg, 2 P 20
Waedt, Carl F., and Gene Marshall: An
    Index to the Health Knowledge
    Magazines, 3 SF 3
Waffling Again About Wallace, (THE MAN
    WHO KNEW: Edgar Wallace), by John A.
    Hogan, 4-3 TAD 167
Wagner, Karl Edward, and Edwin Murray:
    A Bibliography of Manly Wade Wellman,
    7 X 12
Wagner, Karl Edward: The 50 Rarest and
    Most Uniquest Pulps in the Whole
    Wide World, 24 X 6
Wagner, Karl Edward: letter of comment,
    30 X 148
Wagner, Karl Edward: Who Fears the
    Devil (film), 11 X 128
Wahl, Michael F.: Alternate Titles of
    Stories of John Dickson Carr, 1-6 CP 4

Wahl, Michael F.: letter of comment,
    1-6 CP 4; 3-1 MR 15
(Wahloo, Per, and Maj Sjowall),
    Martin Beck, The Swedish Version
    of Barney Miller Without the
    Canned Laughter, by Thomas E.
    Williams, 1-1 C 123
(Wahloo, Per, and Maj Sjowall), The
    Police in Society: The Novels of
    Maj Sjowall and Per Wahloo, by
    Frank Occhiogrosso, 12-2 TAD 174
(Wahloo, Per, and Maj Sjowall),
    Shadow Gallery: An Informal Survey
    of Cover Art of the Seventies,
    Pt.2, Tribute to Maj Sjowall and
    Per Wahloo, by Frank Eck, 10-1
    TAD 46
Waiting for McGee, (collecting the
    Travis McGee series of John D.
    MacDonald), by Fred Cropper,
    22 JD 13
Walden West as Viewed Through an
    Eastern Window, (WALDEN WEST:
    August Derleth), 1-3 AD 6
Waldron, Ann: An Interview with
    Leslie Ford, 4-1 TAD 33
Waldron, Ann: An Interview with
    Ursuls Curtiss, 4-3 TAD 140
Waldron, Ann: The Golden Years of
    Elizabeth Daly, 7-1 TAD 25
Waldron, Ann: letter of comment,
    4-1 MR 19
Waldron, Ann: Past-Mistress of the
    Police Procedural, (Elizabeth
    Linington), 3-5 MR 32
Walker, Bruce: letter of comment,
    5 X 42
Walker, Bruce: Some Thoughts About
    Robert Bloch, 7 X 72
Wall, Donald C.: Apartheid in the
    Novels of James McClure,
    10-4 TAD 348
Wall, Donald C.: Ecology and the
    Detective Novel - The Contri-
    bution of John D. MacDonald,
    21 JD 3
Wall, Donald C.: letter of comment,
    10-1 TAD 41
Wall, Mike: letter of comment,
    3-1 CP 10; 3-3 CP 1
Wallace, Bill: letter of comment,
    26 X 72
(Wallace Case), Crime Hunt: Real
    Life Cases, (true crime, the
    Wallace case), by T.M.McDade,
    14-4 TAD 374
(Wallace, Edgar), Edgar Wallace,
    A Checklist, 1-3 TAD 72
(Wallace, Edgar), The Edgar Wallace
    I Knew, by Nigel Morland,
    1-3 TAD 68
(Wallace, Edgar), Master of Mystery,
    by Penelope Wallace, 1-1 PDA 19
(Wallace, Edgar), Mr. J.G.Reeder,
    by Penelope Wallace, 2-2 PDA 63

(Wallace, Edgar: THE MAN WHO KNEW),
Waffling Again about Wallace, by
John A. Hogan, 4-3 TAD 167
(Wallace, Edgar: THE TOMB OF TS'IN),
An Exhumation of The Tomb of
Ts'in, by John A. Hogan, 6-3
TAD 167
Wallace, Jack E.: Kojak, The Godfather
and the City, (television shows),
1-1 C 25
Wallace, Penelope: Master of Mystery,
Edgar Wallace, (by his daughter),
1-1 PDA 19
Wallace, Penelope: Mr. J.G.Reeder,
(re: Edgar Wallace, by his daughter),
2-2 PDA 63
Wallen, S.E.: Checklist, Boys' Papers/
Magazines, 3-3 BC 333
Wallen, S.E.: Letters to a Collector,
(advice, tips, data on collecting
boys' books), 3-1 BC 265; 3-2 BC
303; 3-3 BC 331; 3-4 BC 380; 4-1
BC 396
(Wallingford, J. Rufus, series: George
R. Chester), The Many Rises and Falls
of J. Rufus Wallington, by Albert
Borowitz, 12-1 TAD 28
Walls of Guilt: Donald E. Westlake as
Tucker Coe, by Francis M. Nevins,
Jr., 7-3 TAD 163
Walsh, J.R.: letter of comment,
14-3 TAD 247
(Walsh, Thomas), Department of Unknown
Mystery Writers, by Marvin Lachman,
2-1 PP 15
Walter Gibson, (sketch of author of
The Shadow and other popular
fiction), by Frank Gruber, 3-2
TAD 94
War in the Air 1914-1918, The,
(historical review of the aviation
aspects, with art folio), by Dave
Prosser, 66 PU 29; 67 PU 83
(WAR OF THE WORLDS, THE: H.G.Wells),
The Biblical War of the Worlds,
by Dana Martin Batory, 8 U 46
(WAR OF THE WORLDS, THE: H.G.Wells),
Dating the War of the Worlds,
by Dana Martin Batory, 8 U 40
(WAR OF THE WORLDS, THE: H.G.Wells),
Genesis of the War of the Worlds,
by Dana Martin Batory, 8 U 34
(WAR OF THE WORLDS, THE: H.G.Wells),
Operation England: The Martian
Maelstrom, by Dana Martin Batory,
8 U 58
(WAR OF THE WORLDS, THE: H.G.Wells),
The Other War of the Worlds,
by Dana Martin Batory, 8 U 50
War Over Middle Earth, The, (J.R.R.
Tolkien: LORD OF THE RINGS), by
Billy C. Lee, 1-4 PQ 37
(WAR STORIES), War Stories, (on
pulp magazine), by Donald A.
Wollheim, 64 PU 8

Ward, Arthur Sarsfield: The Green
Spider, (fiction), 3 R 3
(Ward, Arthur Sarsfield), Just Blame
Everything on Arthur Sarsfield
Ward, by "The Worm", 15 X 10
(Ward, Arthur Sarsfield), see Sax
Rohmer
(Ward, Arthur H.), The Mysterious
Arthur H. Ward, by Robert E.
Briney, 12 R 5
Ward, Elizabeth: letter of comment,
7-3 TAD 224
(Ward, Jonas), see William Thomas
Ard
(Ward, Peter, series: David St.John)
The Rivals of James Bond: Peter
Ward, (with checklist), by Larry
Rickert, 4-3 PP 7
Ware, Allan R.: letter of comment,
1-6 YB 10
Warner, Harry, Jr.: letter of
comment, 7 JD 10; 8 JD 15;
9 JD 9; 10 JD 15; 11 JD 23;
12 JD 18; 13 JD 12; 14 JD 31;
15 JD 30; 16 JD 21; 17 JD 28;
18 JD 24; 19 JD 15; 20 JD 23;
21 JD 18; 60 PU 31; 62 PU 11;
63 PU 50; 64 PU 26; 65 PU 22;
13 X 58; 15 X 13; 33 X 113
Warren, Alan J.: letter of comment,
13-2 TAD 161
Warren, Alan J.: On Compiling a Sax
Rohmer Collection, 13-2 TAD 148
Warren, James: The Shadow Knows...
and Tells His Secrets, 6 DS 12
Was "Jack Wylde" Really R. Austin
Freeman?, by W.O.G.Lofts and
Derek J. Adley, 7-4 TAD 247
Was the Old Man in the Corner an
Armchair Detective? (detective
character of Baroness Orczy),
by Fred Dueren, 14-3 TAD 232
Was Watson Jack the Ripper?, by
Eileen Snyder, 8-3 TAD 211
Washer, Robert E.: A Clergyman's
Irregular Crime File, (book
reviews and notes, 17 X 60;
21 X 54
Washer, Robert E.: An Editor's
Outline, (on Ellery Queen),
1-3 QC 23
Washer, Robert E.: A Selective
Critical Bibliography of the
Genre in the Sixties, (crime
fiction), 2-1 MR 18; 2-2 MR 3
Washer, Robert E.: Checklist on
Ellery Queen, (partial), 1-4
MR 9
Washer, Robert E.: letter of comment,
10 JD 11; 16 JD 18; 3-2 MR 16;
4-1 MR 19; 1-4 TAD 157
Washer, Robert E.: Memorial Tribute
to Manfred B. Lee, 4-4 MR 2
Washer, Robert E.: The Queen Canon,
A Fragmentary Fraction, (Ellery
Queen), 1-4 MR 7

(Washer, Robert E.), Social and Political Images in American Crime Fiction, (panel discussion, Popular Culture Association, 1971), 5-2 TAD 61

(Washer, Robert E.), (biographical sketch), 2-2 QC 16

(Washington, D.C.), The American Regional Mystery, Pt.VI, by Marvin Lachman, 5-1 MR 3

Watch That Man? (on the Conan Doyle syndrome), by Dana Martin Batory, 9 SF 40

Watch This Space! (SPACE FOR HIRE: William F. Nolan), by Frank D. McSherry, Jr., 5-4 TAD 226

Waterhouse, Howard: The American Detective Series, (very early paperback line), 2-3 PQ 32; (checklist) 2-3 PQ 36

Waterhouse, Howard: An Open-Ended Search for Dead Ends, (Inspector Rason and the Department of Dead Ends stories by Roy Vickers), 1-3 PP 7

Waterhouse, Howard: The Green Door Mysteries, (paperback series), 1-2 PQ 39; (checklist) 1-2 PQ 40

Waterhouse, Howard: letter of comment, 1-2 MF 50; 2-1 MF 51; 2 U 48

Waterhouse, Howard: Mighty, Miraculous MURDER MYSTERY MONTHLY, (paperback line) 1-4 PQ 31; (index by author) 1-4 PQ 34

Waterhouse, Howard: Popular Library Short Story Collections, (Popular Library line of paperbacks), 2-1 CP 12

Waterhouse, Howard: Super Detective Person, Rosika Storey, 2-4 PP 3

Waterhouse, Howard: Roy Vickers Short Stories, (checklist), 1-3 PP 7

(Waterhouse, Howard), New England Mystery Dealer, (tribute), by David & Su Bates, 3-3 PP 10

(Waterhouse, Howard), Short Sketch, 2-3 PP 8

Watkins, Russell: letter of comment, 62 PU 10

Watkinson, B.F.: Mystery Writers Beware! (lack of markets for novice authors), 16 CD 6

Watkinson, B.F.: The Perfect Plan, (fiction), 13/14 CL 3

(Watson, Colin), Checklist, by Barry A. Pike, 4-2 PP 21

(Watson, Colin), Pen Profile: Colin Watson, by Barry A. Pike, 4-2 PP 21

Watson, Harrison T., Jr.: letter of comment, 8 SF 45; 11-3 TAD 308

(Waugh, Charles G., with Isaac Asimov and Martin Greenberg: THE 13 CRIMES OF SCIENCE FICTION), Getting There May Be More Than Half the Fun, by R. Jeff Banks, 3-5 PP 15

Waugh, Hillary: Edgars, Anyone? (on the choosing of the MWA awards), 2-1 TAD 52

Waugh, Hillary: letter of comment, 13-2 TAD 160

Waugh, Hillary: Robert Fish, In Memorium, (tribute), 14-2 TAD 120

(Waugh, Hillary), Meet the Author: Hillary Waugh, by Allen J.Hubin, 2-1 TAD 54

Waugh, Thomas D.: Bibliography of Fortune Short Stories, (Reggie Fortune series: H.C.Bailey), 6-2 TAD 76

Waugh, Thomas D.: The Missing Years of Nero Wolfe, (detective of Rex Stout), 5-1 TAD 16

Waugh, Thomas D.: The Parables of H.C.Bailey, 6-2 TAD 75

Wawrzenski, Steve: Doc Savage Comic #1, A Belated Epitaph, 6 DQ 14

Wawrzenski, Steve: Doc Savage in Shadow Comic #1, 7 DQ 18

Wawrzenski, Steve: letter of comment, 5 DQ 5

Wayne, Robert S.: letter of comment, 2-3 CP 3; 2 LW 1

We Can All Be Joe Friday, (paperback cover art identification), by Bill Denholm, 1-6 CP 14

We Tell Stories: A Talk Given at a Monthly MWA Meeting in New York, by Pete Hamill, 12-1 TAD 3

Weales, Gerald: Doc Savage Returns, (on the original stories and the Bantam reprint reissues), 4 BS 3

Wearing of the Green, (fiction), by James Mines, 2-3 M 50

Weatherwax, Jack: letter of comment, 11 JD 32

Weber, Helen D.: letter of comment, 3-1 MF 60

Weber, Karl K.: letter of comment, 1-2 BC 62

Webster, Donald A.: letter of comment, 6-1 MR 22

(Webster, Henry Kitchell), Henry Kitchell Webster, The Emergence of an American Mystery-Writer, by Wendell Hertig Taylor, 5-4 TAD 199

Weeks, Ramona: letter of comment, 9 JD 6

Weel, Gordon J.: letter of comment, 11 JD 21

Weevil in Beancurd, The, or, The Cop Abroad, (police procedural analysis), by George N. Dove, 2-6 MF 17

Wein, Anota: letter of comment, 1-1 MF 47

Weinberg, Robert: An Interview with Abe Goodman, (publisher, Red Circle pulp magazines), 10 P 2

Weinberg, Robert: The Blue Scorpion 10 R 20

Weinberg, Robert: Checklist, The Jerry Wade and The Crimson Mask stories in DETECTIVE NOVELS, (pulp detective series), 2 P 21

Weinberg, Robert: Collecting Original
    Paperback Cover Art, 3-3 PQ 44
Weinberg, Robert: Collectors' Corner,
    (bibliography, A. Talbot Mundy),
    6 P 24
Weinberg, Robert: Dan Fowler Novels
    in G-MEN Magazine, (FBI series
    in pulp magazine), 1 P 19
Weinberg, Robert: Death in the Skies,
    (commentary on aviation hero
    pulp magazines), 4 P 20
Weinberg, Robert: Doc Savage, The
    Self-Appointed Avenger of Crime,
    5 P 17
Weinberg, Robert: Dusty Ayres, (pulp
    aviation hero), 1 P 22
Weinberg, Robert: Edmond Hamilton,
    (literary sketch), 1 WT 7; (in
    WEIRD TALES magazine, checklist)
    1 WT 9
Weinberg, Robert: Index to WEIRD TALES
    (complete index, pulp magazine),
    1 WT 16; 2 WT 17; 3 WT 18; 4 WT 18;
    5 WT 24
Weinberg, Robert: Jules deGrandin
    Returns, 18 X 33
Weinberg, Robert: letter of comment,
    2-1 CP 1; 2-4 CP 2; 6 P 29;
    6-3 TAD 194; 8 X 38; 13 X 60;
    22 X 50
Weinberg, Robert: The Man From the East,
    (villain in The Spider pulp hero
    series), 10 P 32
Weinberg, Robert: Margaret Brundage,
    (WEIRD TALES cover artist), 2 WT 3
Weinberg, Robert: The Moon Man Stories
    in TEN DETECTIVE ACES, (with
    checklist; series by Frederick
    Davis), 2 P 19
Weinberg, Robert: The Not-So-Secret-Six,
    (in SECRET SIX pulp magazine), 4 P 18
Weinberg, Robert: Paperback Art Comes
    Into It's Own, 2-5 CP 28
Weinberg, Robert: Pulp Notes, (pulp
    magazine bibliographic and other
    data), 3 P 28; 10 P 36
Weinberg, Robert: Pulp Hero Quiz,
    (quiz), 1 P 21; 2 P 18; 3 P 27;
    10 P 31; 5 P 19
Weinberg, Robert: SOUTH SEA STORIES,
    (checklist and author index, pulp
    magazine), 8 P 12
Weinberg, Robert: The Spider vs. Munro,
    (pulp hero and villain), 10 P 25
Weinberg, Robert: STRANGE STORIES,
    (author index to pulp magazine),
    6 WT 26; (issue index) 6 WT 23
Weinberg, Robert: The Tinsley Shadows,
    (The Shadow novels written by
    Theodore Tinsley), 1 P 33
Weinberg, Robert: Weird Whisperings,
    (on WEIRD TALES pulp magazine),
    4 WT 8
Weinberg, Robert: Why I Collect Science
    Fiction, 20 X 7

(Weinberg, Robert), Biographical
    Sketch, 10 R 30
Weinberg, Shirley: letter of comment,
    4-4 TAD 255
Weinkauf, Mary S.: Miss Jane Marple
    and Aging in Literature, 1-1 C
    32
Weins, Paula: letter of comment,
    24 JD 39
Weir, Hugh C.: Chats With Big
    Americans for Young Americans,
    (boys' books), 3-1 BC 278
Weird Adventures of The Shadow, The,
    (on The Shadow and his creator,
    Walter B. Gibson), by Wooda
    Nicholas Carr, 9 BS 16
Weird Menace Magazines, The, (pulp
    magazines), by Robert Kenneth
    Jones, 10 BS 3; 11 BS 7; 12 BS 7;
    13 BS 7; 14 BS 13; 15 BS 4
Weird Tales, (verse), by Walter
    Shedlofsky, 5 WT 32
Weird Tales: A Memoir, (WEIRD TALES
    magazine), by August Derleth,
    60 PU 7
(WEIRD TALES magazine), A Visit with
    Margaret Brundage, (cover artist)
    by Forrest J. Ackerman, 3 WT 17
(WEIRD TALES magazine), Edmond
    Hamilton in Weird Tales, (with
    checklist), by Robert Weinberg,
    1 WT 9
(WEIRD TALES magazine), Everil
    Worrell in Weird Tales, (check-
    list), by Jeanne Eileen Murphy,
    1 WT 15
(WEIRD TALES magazine), Index to
    Weird Tales, (complete index),
    by Robert Weinberg, 1 WT 16;
    2 WT 17; 3 WT 18; 4 WT 18; 5 WT
    24
(WEIRD TALES magazine), Margaret
    Brundage, (cover artist), by
    Robert Weinberg, 2 WT 3
(WEIRD TALES magazine), Mary Eliza-
    beth Counselman in Weird Tales,
    6 WT 21
(WEIRD TALES magazine), Readers
    Choice, (excerpts from letter
    column, "The Eyrie" of WEIRD
    TALES), by Robert A.W.Lowndes,
    5 WT 20
(WEIRD TALES magazine), Weird Tales:
    A Memoir, by August Derleth,
    60 PU 7
(WEIRD TALES magazine), Weird
    Whisperings, by Robert Weinberg,
    4 WT 8
Weird Whisperings, (on WEIRD TALES
    magazine), by Robert Weinberg,
    4 WT 8
Weirdest Tale of All, The, (Weird
    Tales), by Emil Petaja, 11 X 124
(WEIRD TERROR TALES), Checklist
    and Index, by Gene Marshall and
    Carl F. Waedt, 3 SF 18

Weiser, Tom: letter of comment, 1-2 M 3

(Weisman, John, and Brian Boyer: The Headhunters series), Series Synopses, by Bill Crider, 11-4 TAD 365

Weiss, Jeffrey N.: Zagazig, (re: Sax Rohmer), 4 R 16

Weissman, Shelley: letter of comment, 28 X 78

Welcome Back, Doc Savage...and Crew, (reappearance in paperback books discussed), by John Keasler, 3 BS 6

Well of Zem-Zem. The, by Robert Galbreath, 9 R 18

Wellman, Manly Wade: letter of comment, 2-3/4 AD 14

(Wellman, Manly Wade), A Bibliography of Manly Wade Wellman, by Karl Edward Wagner and Edwin Murray, 7 X 12

(Wellman, Manly Wade), The Derleth Connection: Manly Wade Wellman, 4-1 AD 4

(Wells, Angus), Checklist, by Ian Covell, 4 SF 29

Wells, Basil: Dust Jackets, (essay on value and desire), 2 U 16

Wells, Basil: Hot Story, 28 X 5

Wells, Basil: The Last Thousand, (his experiences in selling collection), 5 U 24

Wells, Basil: letter of comment, 13 X 58; 14 X 62; 30 X 150; 36 X 72; 40 X 85

Wells, Basil: Thud and Blunder, Then and Now, or Now and Then, (pulp reminiscences), 67 PU 48

(Wells, Basil), Mini-Books of Basil Wells, by Nils Hardin, 9 X 16

(Wells, Carolyn), The Detective Novels of Carolyn Wells, a Chronological Bibliography, by Jon L. Breen, 3-2 TAD 78

(Wells, Carolyn), On Carolyn Wells, by Jon L. Breen, 3-2 TAD 77

(Wells, H.G.: THE FIRST MAN IN THE MOON), The Literary Tradition of Brow Spraying, by J.R.Christopher, 3 R 23

(Wells, H.G.: THE WAR OF THE WORLDS), The Biblical War of the Worlds, by Dana Martin Batory, 8 U 46

(Wells, H.G.: THE WAR OF THE WORLDS), Dating the War of the Worlds, by Dana Martin Batory, 8 U 40

(Wells, H.G.: THE WAR OF THE WORLDS), Genesis of the War of the Worlds, by Dana Martin Batory, 8 U 34

(Wells, H.G.: THE WAR OF THE WORLDS), Operation England - The Martian Maelstrom, by Dana Martin Batory, 8 U 58

(Wells, H.G.: THE WAR OF THE WORLDS), The Other War of the Worlds, by Dana Martin Batory, 8 U 50

Wells, Helen: letter of comment, 13-3 TAD 239

Wells, Helen: Robert Fish, In Memorium, (tribute), 14-2 TAD 120

Wells, Stuart W., III, and Dick Spelman: Checklist, Avalon Books, (paperback line), 5 SF 29

Wells, Stuart W., III, and J.Grant Thiessen: Galaxy Science Fiction Novels, (digest-size paperback series, with checklist), 3 SF 44

(Wells, Tobias), see Stanton Forbes

Wenden, Henry E.: Fu (Manchu), (commentary), 8 R 27

Wenden, Henry E.: letter of comment, 6 R 22; 8-2 TAD 160

(Wenden, Henry E.), Biographical Sketch, 8 R 29

Wenstrup, Richard L.: letter of comment, 5-1 MF 45; 13-4 TAD 345

(Wentworth, Patricia), Checklist, (bibliography), by Nancy Blue Wynne, 14-1 TAD 92

(Wentworth, Patricia), Patricia Wentworth Revisited, by Nancy Blue Wynne, 14-1 TAD 90

Wentz, Walter J.: A. Merritt's Mysteries, (fantastic mystery stories by Abraham Merritt), 5-4 TAD 204

(Wenzel, Bill), Who Drew That Girl?, (paperback cover artist, Bill Wenzel), by Lance Casebeer, 2-4 CP 30; 3-1 CP 25

Were Houndini's Feats Supernatural?, by Sax Rohmer, 5 R 1

Wermers, Bernie: Checklist, THE PHANTOM DETECTIVE, (pulp magazine 1933-1953), 11 BS 4

Wermers, Bernie: letter of comment, 3 BS 2; 5 BS 3; 8 BS 3; 8 BS 5; 63 PU 42; 36 X 72

Wermers, Bernie: Notes of a Pulp Collector; Robert J. Hogan, (pulp author), 6 BS 19

Werner, Robert H., Jr.: letter of comment, 26 JD 50

(Werner Publishing Company), The Old Werner Publishing Co. of Akron, Ohio, (boys' books publisher), by Roy B. Van Devier, 2-4 BC 246

Werowance in the Wild, (on Nero Wolfe), by Ellen Krieger, 1-2 G 54

(Wessolowski, H.W.), Checklist, Pulp Covers, (cover artist), 6 P 16

West Coast Mystery Scene, (news and reviews), by Ruth Windfeldt, 1-1 M 30; 1-2 M 17; 1-3 M 27

West End Notes, (mystery plays in London), by Robert C.S.Adey, 4-2 TAD 114

West Coast Scene, ("World of Mystery" news and notes), by Paul Harwitz, 3-2 M 32

(West, John B.), The Rocky Steele Novels of John B. West, by Darwin T. Turner, 6-4 TAD 226

(West, Roger, series: John Creasey), Checklist, by Robert E. Briney and John Creasey, 2-1 TAD 7

West, Shirley: letter of comment, 6 BS 21

West Thirty-Fifth Street, (verse, re: Nero Wolfe's residence), by John J. McAleer, 1-1 G 20

(WESTERN ACE-HIGH STORIES), Checklist, (pulp magazine), by Lynn Hickman, 75 PU 10

Western Heroes, The, (Whitman boys' books series, with checklist), by I.R.Ybarra, 6 MA 19

Westgard, Gilbert K., II: letter of comment, 3 BB 23

Westlake, Donald E., and Nobumitsu Kodaka: Checklist, Donald E. Westlake, 8-3 TAD 203

(Westlake, Donald E.), Mitch Tobin's Healing, (Tobin as detective in series by Westlake writing as Tucker Coe), by Maryell Cleary, 4-5/6 PP 31

(Westlake, Donald E.), Patterns of Guilt and Isolation in Five Novels by "Tucker Coe", by Jane S. Bakerman, 12-2 TAD 118

(Westlake, Donald E.), Stark Reality, (Donald E. Westlake's novels as Richard Stark), by John Bullis, 1-5 CP 5

(Westlake, Donald E.), Walls of Guilt: Donald E. Westlake as Tucker Coe, by Francis M. Nevins, Jr., 7-3 TAD 163

(Westlake, Donald E.), Checklist, by Donald E. Westlake and Nobumitsu Kodaka, 8-3 TAD 203

(Westlake, Dr.Hugh, series: Jonathan Stagge), Pen Profile: Jonathan Stagge, by Barry A. Pike, 3-3 PP 20

Wetzel, George: The Pseudonymous Lovecraft, 28 X 3

(Weymouth, Anthony: Detective-Inspector Treadgold), Pen Profile, by Barry A. Pike, 4-3 PP 13

Whaley, Rob, and George A. Antonelli: Healing Under the Bare Bulb; The Detective as Therapist, (methodology in modus operandi), 2-2 C 1

Whalley, Allen: letter of comment, 3-3 MR 12

Wharton, Mike: letter of comment, 15 BS 16; 69 PU 27

Wharton, Mike: The Unspeakable in Search of the Inedible Among the Unfindable, (humorous sketch), 5-2 TAD 89

"What Evil Lurks in the Hearts of Men?", (difficulty in conceiving pulp heroes in today's world), by Wooda Nicholas Carr, 8 BS 9

What Happened to the 29th Pilgrim, or, Inspiration, No - Perspiration, Yes, (mystery writing), by Hal Charles, 4-3 PP 3

What Happens in "Point Blank", (film, from Richard Stark's THE HUNTERS), by Francis M. Nevins, Jr., 9-1 TAD 7

What is Mystery Story Fandom?, by Len Moffat, 14 JD 3

What Makes a Juvenile Book Valuable?, by Jack R. Schorr, 1-1 BC 10

What the World Waited For - Revised "Indefinite" Checklist of Mystery Fiction, by Charles Shibuk and Marvin Lachman, 9-3 TAD 203

What to Do With Your Duplicates, (boys' books), by Jack R. Schorr, 3-3 BC 344

What to Expect, (Nero Wolfe news notes) by Beula Poole, 1-1 G 53

What Was That Zine Again?, by Bill Blackbeard, 28 X 77

What Will TV Do to Doc Savage?, (difficulty in depicting the written Doc Savage on television), by Samuel Potts, 6 BS 6

What's In a Name, or, Playfully On A Tangent, (Max Carrados series by Ernest Bramah), by Joshua Goldberg, 7-2 TAD 122

What's Up, Doc? (Doc Savage in Marvel Comics series), by Shelby L. Peck, 2/3 DR 3; (from the pulps to the present with Doc Savage) 1 DR 3

Whatever Happened to...?, (Bobbsey Twins, juvenile series), by Sidney Fields, 4-1 BC 393

(Wheatley, Dennis), Dennis Wheatley, A Biographical Sketch and Bibliography, by Iwan Hedman, 2-4 TAD 227

(Wheatley, Dennis), In Memorial: Dennis Wheatley, by Veronica M.S. Kennedy, 11-2 TAD 129

(Wheatley, Dennis: Black Magic series), Checklist,by Iwan Hedman, 2-4 TAD 236

(Wheatley, Dennis: Roger Brook series), Checklist, by Iwan Hedman, 2-4 TAD 235

(Wheatley, Dennis: Julian Day series), Checklist, by Iwan Hedman, 2-4 TAD 236

(Wheatley, Dennis: Duke DeRichleau series), Checklist, by Iwan Hedman, 2-4 TAD 235

(Wheatley, Dennis: Gregory Sallust series), Checklist, by Iwan Hedman, 2-4 TAD 235

(Wheatley, Dennis: Gregory Sallust series), Checklist, Annotated, by Barry Van Tilburg, 5-3 MF 18

(Wheaton College), Detective Fiction in the Wade Collection, by J.R. Christopher, 9-4 TAD 274

Wheeler, (Dr.) Joe: letter of comment, 2-3 CP 4

Wheeler, Wolcott: letter of comment, 4-3 MR 18

326

When Fantasy Trod the Boards, (fantasy/
science fiction paperback plays), by
Dave & Su Bates, 2-4 CP 16

When Is This Stiff Dead? Detective Stories
and Definitions of Death, by Leslie
M. Thompson and R. Jeff Banks,
2-6 MF 11

When Pulp Was Gold, by Michael Avallone,
7 X 68

When Was the Golden Age, Anyway, (classic
crime fiction), by Robert Aucott,
5-4 TAD 207

Where Are the Pulp Fictioneers?, (on old
pulp writers), by Robert Ostermann,
2 BS 15

Where Do You Get All That Stuff? (boys'
books collecting), by Robert Jennings,
6 BB 10

Where Have the Heroes Gone? (on fictional
heroes in the pulp magazines), by
Frederik Pohl, 67 PU 29

Where Have All the Values Gone? The
Private Eye's Vision of America in
the Novels of Raymond Chandler and
Ross Macdonald, by Etta C. Abrahams,
9-2 TAD 128

Where Have I Read That?, (quiz), by
Robert Aucott, 12-2 TAD 187

Where to Look for Books, (collecting
voys' books), by Jack R. Schorr,
2-1 BC 139

Where was Maple White Land? (on A.Conan
Doyle's THE LOST WORLD), by Dana
Martin Batory, 6 U 16

Which Doorbell Rang? (re: Nero Wolfe),
by Tamar Crystal, 1-1 G 38

(Whisperer, The), The Case of Commissioner
James Gordon, (Gordon was the Whisperer,
and the ancestor of Batman?; pulp hero
in THE WHISPERER pulp magazine), by Arn
McConnell, 1-3 WA 14

(Whisperer, The), The Many Faces of The
Whisperer, (disguises of hero in THE
WHISPERER pulp magazine), by Will
Murray), 7 P 3

Whitaker, A.R.: letter of comment,
8-3 TAD 235

White, Armand: letter of comment,
26 JD 50

White, Ernest: Ernest Bramah's Max
Carrados, (Carrados, detective created
by Bramah), 2-2 MR 7

(White, Ethel Lina), Pen Profile: Ethel
Lina White, (with checklist), by Barry
A. Pike, 4-5/6 PP 48

(White, Ethel Lina), Three Ladies of the
Quasi-Gothic: The Films of Armstrong,
Lofts and White, by Jack Edmund Nolan,
5-2 MR 23

White, Gene H.: letter of comment,
38 X 144

White, Jonathan: letter of comment,
5 SF 46; 7 U 45; 36 X 71

White, Laurine: letter of comment,
13 X 59

(White, Lionel), Filmed Misogyny:
The Screen Adaptations of Peter
Cheyney and Lionel White, by
Jack Edmund Nolan, 4-6 MR 27

(White, R.J.: Detective-Inspector
David Brock), Pen Profile, by
Barry A. Pike, 2-2 PP 24

(White, T.H.), Pen Profile, by
Barry A. Pike, 4-3 PP 14

White Tea, (fiction), by Win Corduan,
13 MN F1

White, Ted: letter of comment,
13 JD 13

White, Walter: letter of comment,
1-4 TBN 6

White, William: A Different Kind of
Murder, (commentary on MURDER
WITH A DIFFERENCE, ed. by
Christopher Morley), 3-5 MR 7

White, William: About Dashiell
Hammett, 3-3 TAD 171

White, William: An Unpublished Ernest
Bramah Letter on Max Carrados,
(Carrados, detective), 3-2 TAD 92

White, William: Ernest Bramah to
E.C.Bentley; An Unpublished Letter,
2-3 MR 8

White, William: Bramah, A Footnote
to Carrados, (Max Carrados,
detective), 2-4 MR 19

White, William: Dorothy L. Sayers,
A Brief Addendum (bibliographic),
3-1 MR 12

White, William: Ernest Bramah in
Anthologies 1914-1972, 10-1 TAD 30

White, William: Hammett, Postscript,
3-3 TAD 175

White, William: Ian Fleming, Book
Collector, (as editor of THE BOOK
COLLECTOR), 6-3 TAD 179

White, William: letter of comment,
3-3 TAD 209; 5-4 TAD 250; 8-3
TAD 237; 9-1 TAD 86

Whitechurch, Victor L.: Peter Crane's
Cigar, (Classic Corner Rare Tales,
fiction), 12-4 TAD 332

Whitehead, Henry S.: Self-Portrait,
4 WT 4

Whitehouse, Arch: How I Got Into
Aviation Writing, 22 X 36

Whitfield, Allyson M.: letter of
comment, 6 DQ 3; 7 DQ 5; 6 DS 6;
12 DS 6

(Whitfield, Raoul F.), An Annotated
Checklist, BLACK MASK Magazine,
by E.R.Hagemann, 13-3 TAD 183

(Whitfield, Raoul F.), Raoul F.
Whitfield, A Star with the MASK,
(in BLACK MASK magazine), by E.R.
Hagemann, 13-3 TAD 179

(Whitfield, Raoul F.: Jo Gar series),
Ramon Decolta, aka Raoul Whitfield,
and His Diminutive Brown Man, Jo
Gar, The Island Detective, by E.R.
Hagemann, 14-1 TAD 3

(Whitman Press of Australia), Under
the Southern Star, (paperback
publications), by Dave & Su Bates,
3-3 CP 18

(Whitman Publishing Company), Checklist,
Authorized Editions, (boys' books),
by Andrew Zerbe, 1 BB 21

(Whitman Publishing Company), The Western
Heroes, (boys' books series, with
checklist), by I.R.Ybarra, 6 MA 19

Whitmore, Tom: Preliminary Regency
Checklist, (paperback books,
Regency line), 15 SF 19

Whitnell, Gale: letter of comment,
3-5 PP 47; 3-6 PP 34; 4-4 PP 38

Whitney, Paul: Philip Jose Farmer, A
Checklist, 5 SF 4

Whitney, Phyllis A.: letter of comment,
3-6 MR 10

(Whitney, Phyllis A.), Checklist, by
Pat Erhardt, 2-4 MR 5

(Whitney, Phyllis A.), Meet Phyllis A.
Whitney, (interview), by Pat Erhardt,
2-4 MR 3

Whitten, Mary Ann: Dorothy L. Sayers, A
Second Brief Addendum, 3-3 MR 2

Whittington, Harry: letter of comment,
2-1 PQ 3

(Whittington, Harry), Baby, I Could
Plot! (Keynote talk at Florida
Suncoast Writers' Conference by
Whittington), 2-2 PQ 25

(Whittington, Harry), Fires That Create:
The Versatility and Craft of Harry
Whittington, by Michael S. Barson,
4-2 PQ 13

(Whittington, Harry), Harry Whittington,
Still A Winner, 2-3 PQ 53

(Whittington, Harry), Interview With the
Author, by Michael S. Barson, 4-2
PQ 17

(Whittington, Harry), The PQ Interview
with Harry Whittington, 1-1 PQ 13

(WHO DONE IT?: Ordean A. Hagen), How I
"Done" It, (writing the book), by
Ordean A. Hagen, 1-2 TAD 45

(WHO DONE IT?: Ordean A. Hagen), Who
Done It - Additions, Subtractions
and Alterations to Hagen's book, by
various, 3-1 TAD 44; 3-2 TAD 123;
3-3 TAD 184; The Mystery Novel on
the Screen, addenda by Charles Shibuk,
3-4 TAD 255; 4-2 TAD 125

Who Drew That Girl?, (paperback book
cover art and artists), by Lance
Casebeer, 1-1 CP 20; 1-2 CP 22;
(Wallace Wood) 1-3 CP 26; (Robert
McGuire) 1-5 CP 31; 1-6 CP 28;
(Popular Library cover artists)
2-1 CP 21; 2-3 CP 36; (Bill Wenzel)
2-4 CP 30; 3-1 CP 25

Who Fears the Devil, (film), by Karl
Edward Wagner, 11 X 128

Who is Doc Savage? (speculative), by
Dafydd Neal Dyar, 12 DS 9

Who is Doc Savage?, (speculative), by
Frank Lewandowski, 1 DS 3

(WHO IS TEDDY VILLANOVA?: Thomas
Berger), Thomas Berger's Comic-
Absurd Vision in WHO IS TEDDY
VILLANOVA, by David Madden,
14-1 TAD 37

Who Killed Charlie Chan?, (the updated
Chan), by Jon L. Breen, 7-2 TAD 100

Who Killed Kelly?, by T.J.McCauley,
14 R 11

Who Knows What Evil Lurks... (The
Shadow Secret Society), by Mark
MacDonald, 1 MT 41

Who Liked the Pulps Besides 10 Million
Readers?, by Robert Kenneth Jones,
67 PU 21

Who-Really-Dun-It?: Two Sub-Branches
of the Detective Story, (clues
make the story), by Frank D.
McSherry, Jr., 2-2 TAD 88

Who Really Wrote It?, (on pseudonyms
of authors), by Harold Knott,
3-6 MR 2

Who was Leslie Quirk? (boys' books
author), by Marge Dahl, 2-2 TBN 6

Who's Afraid of Nero Wolfe?, (interview with Rex Stout), by Richard
S. Lochte III, 3-4 TAD 211

Who's Who?, (mystery puzzle), by
Stanley Carlin, 4-6 MR 14

Whodunit Writer Began Career at 50,
(on Elizabeth Daly), by Estelle
Fox, 4-4 MR 25

Whodunit's Who's Who #1, (FOLLOW MY
DUST by Jessia Hawke; BLACK BEECH
AND HONEYDEW, by Ngaio Marsh), by
Philip T. Asdell, 3-4 PP 11

Whole versus The Sum of the Parts, or
Using Personal Experience in
Fiction, (on writing), by Hal
Charles, 4-4 PP 9

Whowunit?: International Crime Spree
Rocks New York, (report of 2nd
International Congress of Crime
Writers), by Caleb A. Lewis, 11-2
TAD 153

Why I Collect Science Fiction, by
Forrest J. Ackerman, 20 X 5

Why I Collect Science Fiction, by
Don Albright, 20 X 6

Why I Collect Science Fiction, by
Victor Dricks, 20 X 5; 20 X 6

Why I Collect Science Fiction, by
Steven Leventhal, 20 X 7

Why I Collect Science Fiction, by
Robert Madle, 20 X 7

Why I Collect Science Fiction, by
Robert Weinberg, 20 X 7

Why I Love the American Comic Book
Company's 1980 Paperback Catalog,
by Don Z. Block, 2-2 CP 7

Why Viking-Lander? Why the Planet
Mars?, (verse), by Ray Bradbury,
26 X 3

Why I Wrote the Bantan Novels, (juvenile
    series a la Tarzan), by Maurice B.
    Gardner, 62 PU 19; 1 U 12
Why Sherlock Holmes?: Nostalgia for the
    Absolute, (appeal of nostalgia one
    reason for popularity), ny Nancy
    Senter, 2-2 M 39
Wicked Dreams: The World of Sheridan
    Le Fanu, by David Brownell, 9-3
    TAD 191
(Wickes, Martha), see Josephine Chase
Wiebe, Sheldon A.: Worlds in Print,
    (reviews), 5 SF 38
(WIELAND: Charles Brockden Brown), The
    First Locked-Room Mystery?, by Peter
    A. Christensen, 10-4 TAD 368
Wilcox, Collin: Heavyweight Contenders,
    (on "Dallas" television series),
    9 LR 26
(Wilcox, Collin), Conversation: Interview
    with Collin Wilcox, by Don Cole,
    2-2 PP 15
(Wilcox, Collin), The Great Mystery
    Series: Collin Wilcox, (study and
    checklist), by Jeff Pierce, 3-2 M 20
Wild and Woolly World of Harry Stephen
    Keeler, The: Scenes From the Last Act,
    (unconventional detectives and fiction
    of Keeler), by Francis M. Nevins, Jr.,
    3-2 TAD 71
Wild Bunch Revisited, The, ("The Wild
    Bunch," western-crime film), by Brian
    Garfield, 13-2 TAD 141
(Wilde, Carney, series: Bart Spicer),
    Checklist, by Jim McCahery, 4 PE 23
(Wilde, Carney, series: Bart Spicer),
    Series Spotlight: Bart Spicer's
    Carney Wilde, by Jim McCahery,
    3 PE 24; 4 PE 20; 5 PE 21
(Wilde, Oscar), Oscar Wilde and Sherlock
    Holmes: A Literary Mystery, by Randy
    Roberts, 1-1 C 41
Wilde, J.P.: letter of comment,
    6-3 TAD 195
(Wilde, Jonas, series: Andrew York),
    Checklist, Annotated, by Barry
    Van Tilburg, 5-3 MF 18
Wile, Judy: letter of comment, 3-1 M 6
Wilhite, Virgil: letter of comment,
    24 X 47
Wilhite, Virgil, and Patricia Barnes
    Mintz: L. Ron Hubbard, A Living
    Legend, 42 X 133
Wilkins, Winifred: letter of comment,
    1-6 PP 28; 3-5 PP 36
Will the Real Ken Crossen Please Stand
    Up, (Kendell Foster Crossen), by
    Dickson Thorpe, 1-2 MF 5
Willard, Oliver M.: letter of comment,
    2 TF 32
William A. Rogers, Cartoonist-Illustrator,
    (boys' books illustrator), by Alan
    S. Dikty, 4-1 BC 411
William H.G.Kingston, English Boys'
    Writer, by Walter H. McIntosh,
    3-4 BC 355

William Hope Hodgson, CARNACKI THE
    GHOST-FINDER, by Peter Christensen,
    12-2 TAD 122
(Williams, Bransby), Letter from Sax
    Rohmer to Williams, 10 R 4
(Williams, Charles), A Second John D?,
    (comparison of authors John D.
    MacDonald and Charles Williams),
    by J.M. Carter, 18 JD 15
Williams, Dave: letter of comment,
    67 PU 61
(Williams, David: Mark Treasure series)
    Pen Profile, by Barry A. Pike,
    2-4 PP 19
(Williams, Emlyn: NIGHT MUST FALL),
    Night Must Fall: The Sinister Behind
    the Ordinary, (literary discussion),
    by Albert Borowitz, 14-3 TAD 284
Williams, H.B.: letter of comment,
    2-3 TAD 200; 8-1 TAD 72
Williams, J.X.: Her, (on H. Rider
    Haggard's SHE in Corinth paperback
    edition), 2 SF 34
(Williams, John B., M.D.), John B.
    Williams, M.D.: Fprgotten Writer
    of Detective Stories, by E.F.Bleiler,
    10-4 TAD 353
Williams, Lucy Chase: My Good Name...
    (Sherlock Holmes pastiche), 2-2 M 40
(Williams, Race, detective), "There's
    No Sex in Crime": The Two-Fisted
    Homilies of Race Williams, (pulp
    detective series), by Michael S.
    Barson, 2-2 C 103
Williams, Robert M.: letter of comment,
    1-2 MF 50; 1-5 MF 57; 3-3 MF 50;
    5/6 MN 13; 9 MN L3; 8 MN 31; 12
    MN L1; 1-2 PQ 5; 3-2 PQ 6
Williams, Thomas E.: Martin Beck, The
    Swedish Version of Barney Miller
    Without the Canned Laughter,
    1-1 C 123
Williamson, Chet: Amelia Reynolds
    Long, (weird fiction writer),
    2 WT 7
Williamson, Chet: Amelia Reynolds
    Long in the Weird Fiction Magazines,
    Chronological Listing, 2 WT 9
Williamson, Chet: The Case of the
    Moonlighting Physicians, (Dr.Jules
    deGrandin and Dr. Trowbridge),
    6 WT 14
Williamson, Chet: letter of comment,
    2-4 CP 1; 3-4 CP 4; 5 MA 27;
    2-3 PQ 4; 4 SF 46; 26 X 76;
    36 X 71
Williamson, Jack: letter of comment,
    5 WT 31
(Williamson, Jack), Jack Williamson
    Bibliography, by Uwe Luserke,
    13 SF 29
(Williamson, Jack), The Quiet Master,
    by Joseph A. Willis, 13 SF 26
Williamson, (Rev.) Stephen C.: letter
    of comment, 7 JD 4; 9 JD 7

Willmott, Nicholas: Repairing Paperbacks, 3-2 PQ 39

(Willock, Colin), Pen Profile, by Barry A. Pike, 3-2 PP 17

(Wilson, Bert, series: J.W.Duffield), Bert Wilson Series, (boys' books), by Jack R. Schorr, 2-1 TBN 2

Wilson, Bill: Hard Touch, (on justice for the victim of crime); 13 JD 8, (marijuana) 14 JD 17; (police departments) 15 JD 15; (police point of view) 16 JD 8; (fair judicial trials) 17 JD 21; (prison systems) 18 JD 7; ("Big Brother") 19 JD 9

Wilson, Bill: letter of comment, 9 JD 12; 10 JD 10; 11 JD 15; 13 JD 4; 15 JD 31; 16 JD 16; 18 JD 21; 19 JD 16; 22 JD 20

(Wilson, Cole), Cole Wilson, A Portrait, (commentary and literary sketch), by Wooda Nicholas Carr, 17 X 56

Wilson, Colin: A Double Memorial, (to August Derleth; tribute also by A.E.van Vogt), 2-1 PDA 3

Wilson, Colin: letter of comment, 1-4 AD 8

Wilson, David: A Literary Exile Comes Home, (interview with W.R.Burnett), 3-2 M 26

(Wilson, Edmund), Edmund Wilson and the Detective Story, by Carl Byron Dickson, 9-3 TAD 189

(Wilson, Edmund), H.P.Lovecraft and Edmund Wilson, by L. Sprague de Camp, 1 FM 5

Wilson, Gahan: To August Derleth, (literary tribute), 3-1 AD 7

Wilson, F. Paul: letter of comment, 4 SF 42

Wilson, Granville: Prolificity Pays-John Creasey, 4-5 MR 8

Wilson, Ivan: letter of comment, 3-6 MR 9

(Wilson, P.W.: Sir Julian Morthoe, detective), Pen Profile, by Barry A. Pike, 3-1 PP 28; 3-2 PP 18

Wilson, Steve: letter of comment, 1-3 CP 1

(Wilson, Superintendent: G.D.H.Cole), The First Appearance, Superintendent Wilson, (THE BROOKLYN MURDERS), by Maryell Cleary, 3-6 PP 13

(Wimsey, Lord Peter, series: Dorothy L. Sayers), Checklist of Detective Stories, by Charles Shibuk, 2-2 MR 10

(Wimsey, Lord Peter, series: Dorothy L. Sayers), Dorothy L. Sayers, A Second Brief Addendum, by Mary Ann Whitten, 3-3 MR 2

(Wimsey, Lord Peter, series: Dorothy L. Sayers), Lord Peter Views the Telly, (series on BBC TV), by J.R. Christopher, 12-1 TAD 20

(Wimsey, Lord Peter, series: Dorothy L. Sayers), Lord Peter Wimsey of Piccadilly, His Lordship's Life and Times, by William M. Scott, 13-1 TAD 17; 13-3 TAD 212

Windfeldt, Ruth: West Coast Mystery Scene, (news and reviews), 1-1 M 30; 1-2 M 17; 1-3 M 27

Wingfield, William: In re August Derleth, 3-2 PDA 16

Winifred Duke, A Preliminary Survey, by Norman Donaldson, 2-2 TAD 94

Winning Touchdown, The, (song), by Gilbert and Juliet W. Tompkins, 1-5 YB 15

Winslow, Kent: A Laughing Ghost, (commentary on GHOST OF THE HARDY BOYS by Leslie McFarlane), 4 MA 15

Winslow, Kent: The Critic's Clew... to Miss Drew, (various authorships of Nancy Drew, girls' detective series), 7 MA 16

Winslow, Kent: Hunting for Hidden Books, (boys' books collecting), 1 MA 3; 2 MA 21; 5 MA 22; 6 MA 10

Winslow, Kent: letter of comment, 6 MA 28

Winslow, Kent: Mystery and Adventure Crossword Puzzle, (crossword puzzle based on boys' books), 5 MA 30; 7 MA 26

Winslow, Kent: Spindrift Revisited, (Rick Brant boys' books series), 3 MA 1

Winslow, Kent: The Writings of Fran Striker, (on the Lone Ranger series, boys' books), 1 MA 7

Winsor, Roy: Commentaries for the Curious, (on John Dickson Carr), 1 NC 18

(Winsor, Roy), The Professional Sleuth of Roy Winsor, (Professor Ira Cobb, detective), by Larry L. French, 2-1 MF 3

Wise Detective Stories, (crime fiction by Thomas J. Wise), by Edward S. Lauterbach, 5-3 TAD 146

(Wise, Thomas J.), Wise Detective Stories, (crime fiction by Wise), by Edward S. Lauterbach, 5-3 TAD 146

Wiseman, Diane: Bouchercon X, (report of 10th Bouchercon, mystery fans and authors convention), 1-1 M 17

Wishful Thinking, (verse, re" boys' books), by Edna Fuchs, 1-2 TBN 3

Wit and Wisdom of the Mystery Story, The; Quotations From the Mysteries, by Marvin Lachman, 1A MF 3; 1-4 MF 7

Withee, Ruth, and Lianne Carlin: Recent Paperbacks Reviewed, 3-2 MR 10

Within the Queen Tradition, (book reviews, with some connection to Ellery Queen), 1-2 QC 15; 1-3 QC 22; 1-4 QC 19; 2-1 QC 17; 2-2 QC 13; 3-1 QC 18; 3-2 QC 18

Witmer, Terry: letter of comment, 4-4 TAD 253

Witter, Dick: letter of comment, 4 BS 20

(Witting, Clifford: Detective-Inspector Henry Charlton and Detective-Constable Peter Bradfield), Pen Profile, by Barry A. Pike, 2-6 PP 25

(Wodehouse, P.G.), The Mysterious Wodehouse, (with bibliography), by David A. Jasen, 3-1 TAD 38

Wolf, George: The Shadow Speaks, (writing techniques of Walter B. Gibson, creator of The Shadow), 14 BS 11

Wolfe a Howler! (on the television series of Nero Wolfe, based on the Rex Stout novels), by Bob Napier, 5-5 MF 7

Wolfe and the Law, (Nero Wolfe, detective: Rex Stout), by Edward S. Lauterbach, 3-2 TAD 114

(Wolfe, Nero, series: Rex Stout), A Chronology of Crimes, by Stephen F. Schultheis and Patricia A. Dreyfus, 1-1 G 41

(Wolfe, Nero, series: Rex Stout), A Partial Checklist of Reviews of Books by Rex Stout, by Don Miller, 9 MN A45

(Wolfe, Nero, series: Rex Stout), A Preliminary Study in the Literature of Nero Wolfe, by Father Francis Hertzberg, 2-4 MR 11

(Wolfe, Nero, series: Rex Stout), A Reading of Rex Stout, (verse), by Mona Van Duyn, 1-2 G 32

(Wolfe, Nero, series: Rex Stout), A Special Report on Shad Roe, by Marjorie Mortensen, 1-2 G 51

(Wolfe, Nero, series: Rex Stout, A Welcome to The Wolfe Pack (Nero Wolfe fans organization), by John J. McAleer, 1-1 G 15

(Wolfe, Nero, series: Rex Stout), A Wolfean Double-Cross Tick, (cross-word puzzle), 1-2 G 34

(Wolfe, Nero, series: Rex Stout), A Wolfean Quiz, (mystery quiz), 1-1 G 31

(Wolfe, Nero, series: Rex Stout), An Appreciation of Archie Goodwin, by Arden Knight, 12-4 TAD 328

(Wolfe, Nero, series: Rex Stout), "As Far as I'm Concerned, You're Out of It": Wolfe and Archie Apart, by David R. Anderson, 1-2 G 28

(Wolfe, Nero, series: Rex Stout), The Bibliophile - Sooner or Later, (collecting Nero Wolfe), by Judson C. Sapp, 6 U 31

(Wolfe, Nero, series: Rex Stout), The Black Orchid Banquet Quiz, (mystery quiz), by Marjorie Mortensen, 1-1 G 13

(Wolfe, Nero, series: Rex Stout), The Black Orchid Banquet Theme Songs, (The Wolfe Pack, fans' organization), by Marjorie Mortensen, 1-1 G 9

(Wolfe, Nero, series: Rex Stout), The Case of the Missing Wolfe (on NERO WOLFE OF WEST THIRTY-FIFTH STREET by William S. Baring-Gould), by William J. Clark, 3-4 MR 16

(Wolfe, Nero, series: Rex Stout), Checklist, (paperback editions), by Bruce Taylor in Rare Books are Getting Scarce, 2-2 CP 27

(Wolfe, Nero, series: Rex Stout), The Common Heard, (quiz), by Richard Oldberg, 1-2 G 60

(Wolfe, Nero, series: Rex Stout), Confessions of a Reluctant Bibliophile, (collecting Nero Wolfe), by John J. McAleer, 1-1 G 47

(Wolfe, Nero, series: Rex Stout), Crime and Character: Notes on Rex Stout's Early Fiction, by David R. Anderson, 13-2 TAD 169

(Wolfe, Nero, series: Rex Stout), Crostic puzzle, (acrostic), by Robert Lopresti, 1-2 G 17

(Wolfe, Nero, series: Rex Stout), Dramatis Personae, (quiz), 1-1 G 55

(Wolfe, Nero, series: Rex Stout), The Easy Chair: "Alias Nero Wolfe", (speculative, Wolfe the son of Mycroft Holmes), by Bernard DeVoto, 1-2 G 37

(Wolfe, Nero, series: Rex Stout), The Fake Plow Case, (Before Midnight Contest, The Wolfe Pack), by James R. Skelton, 1-2 G 45

(Wolfe, Nero, series: Rex Stout), The Goodwin Document, by "Archie Goodwin", 1-2 G 49

(Wolfe, Nero, series: Rex Stout), Here Comes the Judge: The "Nero" Award, by Bill Crider, 3-6 MF 8

(Wolfe, Nero, series: Rex Stout), Holmes versus Wolfe, (letter from Joel Rosenberg to NEW YORK TIMES BOOK REVIEW), 6/7 LR 14

(Wolfe, Nero, series: Rex Stout), In the Press: A Few Review Extracts of Nero Wolfe Books, by Don Miller, 9 MN A56

(Wolfe, Nero, series: Rex Stout) The "Lost" Nero Wolfe Tale, ("Bitter End" by Stout), by Arthur C. Scott, 9 MN A14

(Wolfe, Nero, series: Rex Stout), The Missing Years of Nero Wolfe, by Thomas D. Waugh, 5-1 TAD 16

(Wolfe, Nero, series: Rex Stout), Nero
Wolfe is "On the Air", (radio serials),
by Judson C. Sapp, 9 MN A19
(Wolfe, Nero, series: Rex Stout), Nero
Wolfe: Logomachizer, by Lawrence
F. Brooks, 1-1 G 21
(Wolfe, Nero, series: Rex Stout), Nero
Wolfe Novels, by Lee Poleske, 2 LW 2
(Wolfe, Nero, series: Rex Stout), Nero
Wolfe on Film, by Don Miller, 9 MN A26
(Wolfe, Nero, series: Rex Stout), Nero
Wolfe Quiz, (quiz), by Lee Poleske,
1 LW 1; 2 LW 1; 3 LW 1; 4 LW 2;
5 LW 1; 6 LW ;
(Wolfe, Nero, series: Rex Stout), Nero
Wolfe vs. The Master Criminal, by
John Harwood, 6-1 MR 15
(Wolfe, Nero, series: Rex Stout), The
Nero Wolfe Saga, (in-depth study
and commentary on Nero Wolfe novels;
individual story treatment with
story synopses), 1-3 MF 13; 1-4 MF 25;
1-5 MF 21; 1-6 MF 15; 2-1 MF 15; 2-2
MF 25; 2-3 MF 34; 2-4 MF 19; 2-5 MF
13; 2-6 MF 20; 3-1 MF 21; 3-2 MF 13;
3-3 MF 22; 3-4 MF 25; 3-5 MF 22;
3-6 MF 15; 4-1 MF 17; 4-2 MF 14;
4-3 MF 3, by Guy M. Townsend
(Wolfe, Nero, series: Rex Stout), The
Nero Wolfe Saga: A Chronology,
(first edition publication data
checklist), by Don Miller, 9 MN A43
(Wolfe, Nero, series: Rex Stout), The
Nero Wolfe Saga: The Early Years,
by Guy M. Townsend, 9 MN A31
(Wolfe, Nero, series: Rex Stout), The
Nero Wolfe Saga: The First Four,
(commentary and review of first
four Wolfe novels), by Jo Ann
Vicarel, 9 MN A42
(Wolfe, Nero, series: Rex Stout), The
Nero Wolfe Saga: Three at Random,
(reviews and commentary), by Don
Miller, 9 MN A61
(Wolfe, Nero, series: Rex Stout), Nero
Wolfe's Legacy of Books, by John J.
McAleer, 1-2 G 8
(Wolfe, Nero, series: Rex Stout), Nom
De Loup, (on the names used in the
Wolfe novels), by Terry Abraham,
3 LW 5
(Wolfe, Nero, series: Rex Stout), Not
Too Many Clients, by Evelyn Herzog,
1-1 G 28
(Wolfe, Nero, series: Rex Stout), Notes
on the First Annual Black Orchid
Banquet, (of The Wolfe Pack, Nero
Wolfe fan's organization), by
Marjorie Mortensen, 1-1 G 4
(Wolfe, Nero, series: Rex Stout), The
O'Boyle Report, ("genealogy" of
Nero Wolfe), 1-2 G 2
(Wolfe, Nero, series: Rex Stout), The
Orchidology of Nero Wolfe, (Wolfe's
orchid hobby), by Robert M. Hamilton,
1-2 G 18

(Wolfe, Nero, series: Rex Stout),
Orchids to the Wolfe Pack, The
Second Annual Black Orchid Banquet,
(The Wolfe Pack, fan organization),
by Judson C. Sapp, 6 U 29
(Wolfe, Nero, series: Rex Stout),
Paperbacks of Nero Wolfe in Print,
(1975), by Lee Poleske, 4 LW 2
(Wolfe, Nero, series: Rex Stout), The
Real Fourth Side of the Triangle,
(Della Street's affair with Archie
Goodwin supposition), by Marvin
Lachman, 9 MN A11
(Wolfe, Nero, series: Rex Stout),
Recipe for a Cookbook, by Barbara
Burn, 1-1 G 34
(Wolfe, Nero, series: Rex Stout), Rex
Stout: A Bibliography, by Don
Miller, 9 MN A65
(Wolfe, Nero, series: Rex Stout), Rex
Stout in Ellery Queen's Anthologies
(checklist), by Don Miller, 9 MN
A29
(Wolfe, Nero, series: Rex Stout), Rex
Stout in ELLERY QUEEN'S MYSTERY
MAGAZINE, (checklist), by Don
Miller, 9 MN A24
(Wolfe, Nero, series: Rex Stout), Rex
Stout in Mystery Guild Editions,
(checklist, book club editions), by
Michael L. Cook, 9 MN A27
(Wolfe, Nero, series: Rex Stout), Rex
Stout in the Dell Mapbacks, (Dell
Publishing Company paperback book
series), by William Lyles, 2-4
PQ 14
(Wolfe, Nero, series: Rex Stout), Rex
Stout Newsletter, (notes and news
column), by John J. McAleer, 11-3
TAD 257; 12-1 TAD 66; 12-2 TAD 130;
12-3 TAD 224; 12-4 TAD 330; 13-1
TAD 41; 13-2 TAD 108; 13-3 TAD 224;
13-4 TAD 286; 14-1 TAD 22; 14-2
TAD 140; 14-3 TAD 230; 14-4 TAD
321
(Wolfe, Nero, series: Rex Stout), The
Second First Annual Wolfe Pack
Event, (fan organization), by
Marjorie Mortensen, 1-2 G 58
(Wolfe, Nero, series: Rex Stout),
Short Stories of Nero Wolfe, by
Lee Poleske, 3 LW 7
(Wolfe, Nero, series: Rex Stout),
Trivia Quiz: Nero Wolfe, 1-3 WA 13
(Wolfe, Nero, series: Rex Stout),
Werowance in the Wild, by Ellen
Krieger, 1-2 G 54
(Wolfe, Nero, series: Rex Stout),
West Thirty-Fifth Street, (verse),
by John J. McAleer, 1-1 G 20
(Wolfe, Nero, series: Rex Stout),
What to Expect, (news notes), by
Beula Poole, 1-1 G 53
(Wolfe, Nero, series: Rex Stout),
Which Doorbell Rang?, by Tamar
Crystal, 1-1 G 38

(Wolfe, Nero, series: Rex Stout), Who's Afraid of Nero Wolfe?, (interview with Rex Stout), by Richard S. Lochte II, 3-4 TAD 211

(Wolfe, Nero, series: Rex Stout), Wolfe a Howler!, (on Nero Wolfe television series), by Bob Napier, 5-5 MF 7

(Wolfe, Nero, series: Rex Stout), Wolfe and the Law, 3-2 TAD 114

(Wolfe, Nero, series: Rex Stout), Wolfe on the Air, (radio programs), by Arthur C. Scott, 9 MN A17

Wolfe Pack, The: Articles of Association and By-Laws, (Nero Wolfe fan club), 1-1 G 59

Wolfe Pack, The: Charter Members, (Nero Wolfe fan club), 1-1 G 66

Wolfe Pack, The: News and Notes, (Nero Wolfe fan club), 1-1 G 57; 1-2 G 65

Wolfe, Peter: Sam Spade, Lover, (on detective character of Dashiell Hammett), 11-4 TAD 366; 38 X 21

Wolfe, Peter: Stalking Forsyth's Jackal, (Frederick Forsyth: THE DAY OF THE JACKAL), 7-3 TAD 165

(WOLFEN, THE: Whitley Strieber), Mystery Plus: A Contemporary Science Fiction Pair, (commentary), by R. Jeff Banks, 3-1 PP 16

Wolff, C.: letter of comment, 17 X 61; 24 X 44

Wolff, Ira: letter of comment, 8 JD 9; 13 JD 18

Wolff, John: letter of comment, 24 X 12

Wolff, Julian: letter of comment, 1-2 QC 14; 1-4 QC 18

Wollheim, Donald A.: A Pair of Aces, (letter from Wollheim on Ace Double Mysteries, as editor), 7 MY 5

Wollheim, Donald A.: From Blue Swastika to the Ace of Spades, (history of the Ace pulp magazines), 68 PU 5

Wollheim, Donald A.: letter of comment, 1-2 PQ 6; 64 PU 27

Wollheim, Donald A.: WAR STORIES, (on pulp magazine of this title), 64 PU 8

(Wollheim, Donald A.), A PQ Interview with Donald A. Wollheim, 1-3 PQ 23

(Wollheim, Donald A.), Donald A. Wollheim, (sketch) 1-3 PQ 19; (checklist) 1-3 PQ 20

Women and Wall Street: Portraits of Women in Novels by Emma Lathen, by Jane S. Bakerman, 8-1 TAD 36

Women in Detective Fiction, by Michele Slung, 3-1 M 8

Wonderful World of Street & Smith, The, (publisher, during the pulp era), by Samuel W. Potts, 4 BS 12

Woo, Bengta: letter of comment, 3-3 TAD 207; 4-2 TAD 127; 6-1 TAD 47; 14 X 63

(Woo, Bengta), Biographical Sketch, 2-3 PP 10

Woo, Robert: Boris! Boris! Boris!, (Boris Vallejo, paperback cover artist for Doc Savage series), 1 DS 11

Woo, Robert: Doc's Fabulous Physique, (on Doc Savage), 3 DS 16

Wood Engraver from Mazomanie, The, (Frank Utpatel, illustrator and cover artist, Arkham House books) by Kay Price, 4-3 AD 1

Wood, Edward: letter of comment, 22 X 52; 28 X 78; 38 X 143

Wood, Neville: A Cambridge Mystery, (1931), 1-2 PP 3; 1-3 PP 3; 1-4 PP 3; 1-5 PP 3

Wood, Neville: A Collector Reminiscences, (on collecting crime fiction), 3-2 PP 7

Wood, Neville: Double Death: A Retrospective Commentary, (on mystery fiction of which each chapter is by different author), 1-3 PP 20

Wood, Neville: THE FLOATING ADMIRAL and Some Thoughts About Its Authors, (round robin mystery by Agatha Christie and others), 2-4 PP 7

Wood, Neville: The Golden Age of the Detective Story, (classic crime fiction, with checklist), 1-1 PP 11

Wood, Neville: letter of comment, 1-1 PP 27; 1-2 PP 28; 1-5 PP 32; 2-1 PP 36; 4-2 PP 44; 9-4 TAD 296

(Wood, Wallace), Who Drew That Girl? (paperback cover artist, Wallace Wood), by Lance Casebeer, 1-3 CP 26

(Woodhouse, Martin: Giles Yeoman series), Checklist, Annotated, by Barry Van Tilburg, 5-3 MF 18

(Woods, Sara), Checklist, by Estelle Fox, 4-3 TAD 153

(Woods, Sara), Sara Woods, (literary sketch), by Estelle Fox, 4-3 TAD 152

Woodworth, Fred: A Look at the Lone Ranger Books, (boys' series), 1 MA 11

Woodworth, Fred: An Incorrect Theory, Capwell Wyckoff not Hardy Boys Author, (disproving belief that Wyckoff wrote some of the Hardy Boys boys' series), 5 MA 9

Woodworth, Fred: Artists, Clemens Gretter, (boys' books artist), 6 MA 5

Woodworth, Fred: Capwell Wyckoff- A Hardy Author? (Hardy Boys boys' series), 4 MA 19

Woodworth, Fred: Chapter One, (on boys' series books), 1 MA 1

Woodworth, Fred: The Ken Holt Mystery Stories, (boys' series), 2 MA 7

Woodworth, Fred: Loose Ends, (on boys' books collecting), 6 MA 2

Woodworth, Fred: Not Forgotten, (The Ken Holt series and the Rick Brant series, boys' books), 2 MA 1

Woodworth, Fred: Series Move to New Publisher, (Simon & Schuster to assume publication of Hardy Boys and Nancy Drew series), 2 MA 24

Woodworth, Fred: Sinister Signposts, (traffic signs), 3 MA 30

Woodworth, Fred: The Stories of Capwell Wyckoff, (Mystery Hunter, Mercer Boys, and other boys' series books), 5 MA 1

Woodworth, Fred: The Tom Quest Series, (boys' series books), 1 MA 20

Woodworth, Fred: Update, Tom Quest and The Lone Ranger, (two series, boys' books, by Fran Striker), 6 MA 13

Woolfolk, Steve: A Checklist of Monarch Books, (paperback line), 14 SF 35

(Woolrich, Cornell), A Woolrich Checklist, by Pat Erhardt, 1-2 MR 4

(Woolrich, Cornell), A Woolrich Preview (on uncompleted works), by Francis M. Nevins, Jr., 4-3 TAD 145

(Woolrich, Cornell), Brief Loves; The Early Short Stories of Cornell Woolrich, (humor and romance), by Francis M. Nevins, Jr., 14-2 TAD 168

(Woolrich, Cornell), Checklist of Paperbacks, by Bruce Taylor, 1-1 CP 9

(Woolrich, Cornell), Cornell Woolrich, (literary discussion), by Francis M. Nevins, Jr., 2-1 TAD 25; 2-2 TAD 99; 2-3 TAD 180

(Woolrich, Cornell), Cornell Woolrich, A Bibliography, by Harold Knott, Francis M. Nevins, Jr. and William Thailing, 2-4 TAD 237

(Woolrich, Cornell), Cornell Woolrich: ",,,I Had Nobody", by Steve Fisher, 3-3 TAD 164

(Woolrich, Cornell), Cornell Woolrich: The Years Before Suspense, (on early writings), by Francis M. Nevins, Jr., 12-2 TAD 106

(Woolrich, Cornell), Early JDM: Woolrich Touches, (Woolrich influence on John D. MacDonald), by Francis M. Nevins, Jr., 16 JD 12

(Woolrich, Cornell), Immortals Do Die: Cornell Woolrich (1903-1968), A Memorial, by William Thailing, 2-3 TAD 161

(Woolrich, Cornell), Lonely Are the Great, by Mike Avallone, 11 X 7

(Woolrich, Cornell), Mystery Writer of Merit: Cornell Woolrich, by Pat Erhardt, 1-2 MR 3

(Woolrich, Cornell: DARK CITY, DARK MEN), Disposing of a Pair of Ghosts, by Jacques Barzun, 6-4 TAD 248

Woolston, Stan: The Anatomy of "Romance" (as ingredient in the fiction of John D. MacDonald), 18 JD 13

Woolston, Stan: letter of comment, 11 JD 28; 14 JD 32; 16 JD 24; 17 JD 24

Wooster, Martin Morse: The Body in the Library; TWENTIETH CENTURY CRIME AND MYSTERY WRITERS and the Mystery World in Our Time, 5-1 MF 11

Wooster, Martin Morse: Books Announced, (August 1975), 7 MN 8

Wooster, Martin Morse: letter of comment, 6/7 LR 25; 8 MN 33; 9 MN L5; 11 MN L14; 12 MN L10; 12 MN O4; 1-2 MF 49; 1-4 MF 56; 1-5 MF 54; 2-4 MF 55; 2-5 MF 53; 2-6 MF 50; 3-4 MF 54; 1-2 PP 27; 1-4 PP 31; 1-5 PP 29; 1-6 PP 34; 2-2 PP 45; 2-4 PP 38; 3-2 PP 33; 3-4 PP 40; 4-1 PP 46; 4-2 PP 38; 4-4 PP 38; 30 X 148

Wooster, Martin Morse: The Mystery of The Publishers' Taste, (forthcoming mystery fiction 1976) 1-1 MM 5; 1-2 MM 5

Wooster, Martin Morse: Special Review commentary, Melville Davisson Post's THE COMPLETE UNCLE ABNER, 2-5 MF 9

Worcester Enigma, The, (a "new" Sherlock Holmes adventure; pastiche, fiction), by James Mines, 2-2 M 34

Word With Desmond Bagley, by Deryck Harvey, 7-4 TAD 258

Work of Clark Ashton Smith, The, by E.P.Berglund, 18 X 35

Works in Progress, (various authors), 2-2 AD 11

Works of Eric Ambler, by George J. Rausch, Jr., 2-4 TAD 260

World Fantasy Convention, (report), 3-2 AD 5

World Fantasycon, (photo report of Third convention), 36 X R22

World of Cleve F. Adams, The, (pulp author), by Francis M. Nevins, Jr., 8-3 TAD 195

World of Entertainment, (news and reviews), by Fred S. Cook, 4 BS 19

World of Milton Propper, The, (author) by Francis M. Nevins, Jr., 10-3 TAD 197

World of Monarch, The, (Monarch Books, paperback line), by Bill Pronzini, 1-4 CP 13

World of Mystery: The Burrit Street Beat, (San Francisco Mystery Bookstore gathering April 1981), by Erik C. Jendresen, 3-2 M 30

World of Mystery: Grub Street Beat, (mystery scene news and notes) by Martha Hudson, 2-2 M 18; 3-2 M 32

World of Mystery: New York Mystery Beat (mystery scene news and notes), by Pete Christian, 2-1 M 33; 2-2 M 14; 2-3 M 21; 3-1 M 48; 3-2 M 32

World of Mystery: San Francisco Mystery Scene, (mystery news and notes), by Bruce Taylor, 2-1 M 32; by Erik C. Jendresen, 3-1 M 48

World of Mystery: The Stockholm Story, (International Crime Writers convention), by Edgar James, 2-3 M 20

World of Mystery: West Coast Scene, (mystery scene news and notes), by Paul Harwitz, 2-2 M 20; 2-3 M 20; 3-1 M 49; 3-2 M 32

World of Mystery Fiction, The, (on The Mystery Library series of books) by Noel Craig, 1-1 M 27

World-Size Bottleneck, (Cuban missiles commentary), by T. Carrington Burns (John D. MacDonald), 26 JD 7

WORLD WIDE ADVENTURE Magazine, Index and Checklist, by Gene Marshall and Carl F. Waedt, 3 SF 40

Worlds in Print, (reviews), by Sheldon A. Wiebe, 5 SF 38

(WORLDS OF FANTASY), An Index to Worlds of Fantasy Magazine, by Dr. Roger C. Schlobin, 2 U 12

World's Weirdest Criminal, The, (on the Doctor Satan series in WEIRD TALES magazine), by Robert Kenneth Jones, 72 PU 12

(Wormser, Richard), Paperback Writers: Richard Wormser, by Bill Crider, 4-1 PQ 31

(Worrell, Everil), Everil Worrell in Weird Tales, (stories in WEIRD TALES magazine), by Jeanne Eileen Murphy, 1 WT 15

(Worsley-Gough, Barbara: Aloysius Kelly, detective), Pen Profile, by Barry A. Pike, 2-5 PP 24

Worst Legal Mystery in the World, The, (Harry Stephen Keeler: THE AMAZING WEB), by Francis M. Nevins, Jr., 1-3 TAD 82

Worst Mystery Novel of All Time, The, (Michael Morgan: DECOY), by Bill Pronzini, 13-2 TAD 137

Would-Be Psycho, The, (fiction), by Jeff Gamso, 1-3 M 36

Wright, Farnsworth: Self Portrait, (verse), 2 WT 6

Wright, Sean M.: An Irregular History, (on the Baker Street Irregulars; Sherlockiana), 2-2 M 24

Wright, Sean M., and Michael Hodel: Under the Jack-Knife, (The Great Sherlockian Centennial 1881-1981), 3-1 M 51

(Wright, Sean M., and Michael Hodel: ENTER THE LION), Mystery Plus: The Holmes Pastiche of the Decade, by R. Jeff Banks, 4-1 PP 21

Wright, Stephen: letter of comment, 1-3 M 4

(Wright, Willard Huntington), Checklist, by Bruce R. Beaman, 8-2 TAD 134

(Wright, Willard Huntington), S.S. Van Dine, A Biographical Sketch by Bruce R. Beaman, 8-2 TAD 133

Writer's Probe, The: Ruth Rendell as Social Critic, by Jane S. Bakerman, 3-5 MF 3

Writers for the Record: The Changing Role of Women as Influence on Mystery Fiction, (by various, with Joseph Estrada, ed.),3-1 M 40; (authors reply to questions on series characters, by Estrada) 3-2 M 36

Writing the Biography of Doc Savage, (DOC SAVAGE:HIS APOCALYPTIC LIFE by Farmer), by Philip Jose Farmer, 5A P 2

Writings of Fran Striker, The, (on the Lone Ranger boys' series), by Kent Winslow, 1 MA 7

(Wu Fang), The Mysterious Wu Fang, (villain in the pulps), by Wooda Nicholas Carr, 8 DS 5

(Wuorio, Eva-Lis), Checklist, by Audrey I. Pacheco, 5-4 MR 23

Wuyek, George: End of the Golden Age, (memorial to Agatha Christie), 10-3 TAD 263

Wuyek, George: letter of comment, 4-1 TAD 69; 5-1 TAD 58; 7-2 TAD 152; 7-4 TAD 305; 8-1 TAD 70; 8-4 TAD 315; 8-4 TAD 317; 9-3 TAD 236

Wuyek, George: Necrology of Mystery Crime Writers 1975-1976, 10-3 TAD 264

(Wyckoff, Capwell), About the Author, (boys' books author), 5 MA 21

(Wyckoff, Capwell), An Incorrect Theory - Not Hardy Boys Author, (disproving theory Wyckoff was author of some of Hardy Boys boys' series books), by Fred Woodworth, 5 MA 9

(Wyckoff, Capwell), Capwell Wyckoff- A Hardy Boys Author?, by Fred Woodworth, 4 MA 19

(Wyckoff, Capwell), Missing Mercer Musings (Mercer Boys boys' books) by Don Holbrook, 6 MA 6

(Wyckoff, Capwell), The Stories of Capwell Wyckoff, (Mystery Hunter, Mercer Boys, and other boys' books series), by Fred Woodworth, 5 MA 1

(Wyckoff, Capwell), Wyckoff's Stories of Adventure, (boys' books), by Don Holbrook, 5 MA 6

Wyckoff's Stories of Adventure, (boys' books by Capwell Wyckoff), by Don Holbrook, 5 MA 6

(Wylde, Jack), Was "Jack Wylde" Really R. Austin Freeman?, by W.O.G.Lofts and Derek J. Adley, 7-4 TAD 247

(Wylie, Philip Gordon), Checklist, (paperback editions), by Raymond Torrence, 2-4 CP 23

(Wyndham, John), Bibliographic Checklist, by Philip Stephenson-Payne, 8 SF 31

Wynne, Nancy Blue: Patricia Wentworth, Bibliography, 14-1 TAD 92

Wynne, Nancy Blue: Patricia Wentworth Revisited, 14-1 TAD 90

Yamada, Tatsuo: letter of comment, 4-1 PP 45; 4-2 PP 41

Yarbro, Chelsea Quinn: Demon in a Lunch-box, An Appreciation of Horror Fiction, 2-2 M 43

Yates, Donald A.: A Tribute to Ellery Queen on His 40th Birthday, 2-4 TAD 250

Yates, Donald A.: Bouchercon 1978, IX and Counting, (mystery fans and authors convention), 3-1 MF 15

Yates, Donald A.: Challenge to the Reader, (a link to Ellery Queen's HALFWAY HOUSE?), 1-3 QC 12

Yates, Donald A.: The Detective Literature of the Americas, (crime fiction in Latin-America), 4-1 TAD 5

Yates, Donald A.: letter of comment, 5-1 TAD 51

Yates, Donald A.: The Locked House, An Essay on Locked Rooms, 3-2 TAD 81

Yates, Donald A.: Van Dine and Queen, ("random jottings" S.S.Van Dine and Ellery Queen), 1-4 QC 12

(Yates, Donald A.), Pulp Tradition in Mystery Fiction, (panel discussion, Popular Culture Association, 1972), 6-3 TAD 133

(Yates, Donald A.), Social and Political Images in American Crime Fiction, (panel discussion, Popular Culture Association, 1971), 5-2 TAD 61

(Yates, Dornford), Checklist, by J. Randolph Cox, 14-2 TAD 186

Ybarra, I.R.: The Hardy Boys, A Few Criticisms of the Series and Its Background, (boys' books), 4 MA 22

Ybarra, I.R.: Recent L.R.Story a Mess, (criticism of LEGEND OF THE LONE RANGER by Gary McCarthy), 6 MA 8

Ybarra, I.R.: The Roger Baxter Series, (boys' books), 3 MA 23

Ybarra, I.R.: The Western Heroes, (Whitman boys' series, with checklist), 6 MA 19

(Yeoman, Giles, series: Martin Woodhouse), Checklist, Annotated, by Barry Van Tilburg, 5-3 MF 18

Yoder, Dee: letter of comment, 24 JD 38

(York, Andrew: Jonas Wilde series), Checklist, Annotated, by Barry Van Tilburg, 5-3 MF 18

(York, Jeremy), Checklist of Suspense Novels, by Robert E. Briney and John Creasey, 2-1 TAD 17

(York, Jeremy: Superintendent Folly series), Checklist, by Robert E. Briney and John Creasey, 2-1 TAD 17

(Yorke, Margaret), Checklist, by Barry A. Pike, 3-4 PP 17

(Yorke, Margaret), Pen Profile, by Barry A. Pike, 3-4 PP 18

You Find Them in the Oddest Places, (boys' books), by Jack R. Schorr, 4-1 BC 409

Young Man Lovecraft, (on H.P.Lovecraft) by L. Sprague de Camp, 18 X 8

Young, Rachel P.: letter of comment, 5-3 MF 44; 9-3 TAD 236

Youngson, Jennie: letter of comment, 3-2 CP 2

Yours Truly, Bloch the Ripper, (on the macabre in writings of Robert Bloch), by Michael S. Barson, 4-1 PQ 17

(YOUTH'S COMPANION, THE), A Quick Look at the Youth's Companion, (boys' paper), by Walter H.McIntosh, 4-1 BC 394

Zachrich, Gary: The Gold Mine of Dust, (Doc Savage type fiction featuring Doc Aborigine) 63 PU 10

Zachrich, Gary, and Lynn Hickman: News and Views, (book notes), 63 PU 51; 64 PU 31; 65 PU 24; 66 PU 53; 67 PU 128; 68 PU 31; 69 PU 31; 70 PU 6; 71 PU 18; 72 PU 6; 73 PU 31; 74 PU 16; 75 PU 21

Zadig as a Jew: An Early German Tale of Delection, (by Wilhelm Hauff), by Armin Arnold, 13-2 TAD 173

Zagazig, Zagazig, (code in THE HAND OF FU MANCHU by Sax Rohmer), by Evelyn Herzog, 5 R 22

Zagazig, (code in THE HAND OF FU MANCHU by Sax Rohmer), by Jeffrey N. Weiss, 4 R 16

Zagazig, Zagazig: Z.A.Gazig, (code in THE HAND OF FU MANCHU by Sax Rohmer), by Julian L. Biggers, 5 R 25

Zane Grey's Western (on ZANE GREY'S
    WESTERN MAGAZINE), by David & Su
    Bates, 1-3 CP 20
Zanigew, Napoleon of Crime, (pulp villain
    in The Shadow series), by Will Murray,
    8 DS 19
(Zarkon series: Lin Carter), Lord of
    the Unknown: The Zarkon Novels of
    Lin Carter, by Link Hullar, 8 U 141
Zbiciak, Randall: The Hows, Whys, Ifs
    and Buts of Collecting Big Little
    Books, (juvenile books), 4 BB 7
Zbiciak, Randall: letter of comment,
    2 BB 22; 2 MA 27
(Zebra Books), Zebra Stinks! (criticism
    of books of paperback publisher),
    by Charlotte Laughlin, 2-3 PQ 49
Zelders, L.H.: letter of comment,
    7 JD 9
Zekas, Paul: letter of comment,
    24 X 46
Zentner, Don E.: letter of comment,
    2-5 TBN 4
Zerbe, Andrew: Checklist, Whitman
    Authorized Editions, (boys' books),
    1 BB 21
Zerbe, Andrew: letter of comment,
    2 BB 25; 4 BS 2; 8 BS 7; 15 BS 16;
    2-2 CP 4; 8 JD 11; 11 JD 27; 12 JD
    17; 13 JD 20; 16 JD 15; 3 MA 27;
    5 MA 27; 7 MA 24; 62 PU 13; 63 PU
    42; 65 PU 19; 69 PU 27; 1-4 QC 17;
    4 SF 45; 5 SF 47; 2-2 TAD 135;
    2-3 TAD 201; 4-3 TAD 187; 4-4 TAD
    253; 8 X 38; 13 X 58
Zinman, David: Nancy Drew on the Screen,
    (girls' mystery series filmed),
    8-2 MR 3
Zone, Ray: Mean Streets Revisited, Seven
    Hardboiled Authors at the Scene of
    the Crime Bookshop, 2-3 M 18
Zorn, Ray H.: letter of comment,
    2-2 TBN 4
Zorn, Ray H.: More on Andy Blake -
    Printing History, (Appleton edition
    of first Leo Edwards boys' book),
    1-4 TB 1
Zorn, Ray H.: That First Andy Blake,
    (first boys' series book by Leo
    Edwards), 1-3 TB 3

BIBLIOGRAPHY OF BOOK REVIEWS

One of the important contributions of mystery and related genre magazines is to provide commentary on both old and new books in the field, in the form of book reviews. The value of these remain constant for the use of readers and researchers, and this listing will provide a finding aid in the magazines treated in this book. Information given includes the author, title, reviewer, and location of the review.

Author	Title	Reviewer	Location
Aarons, Edward S.	ASSIGNMENT AFGHAN DRAGON	Steve Lewis	1-5 MF 32
Aarons, Edward S.	THE ART STUDIO MURDERS	Fred Dueren	8-4 TAD 295
Aarons, Edward S.	ASSIGNMENT QUAYLE QUESTION	Don D'Ammassa	1 MN 9
Aarons, Edward S.	ASSIGNMENT QUAYLE QUESTION	Steve Lewis	11 MN R16
Aarons, Edward S.	ASSIGNMENT MALTESE MAIDEN	Amnon Kabatchnik	5-6 MR 36
Aarons, Edward S.	MILLION DOLLAR MURDER	Lianne Carlin	3-3 MR 30
Abraham, Peter	THE FURY OF RACHEL MONETTE	Allen J. Hubin	14-2 TAD 123
Abrahams, Gerald	ACCORDING TO THE EVIDENCE	Barzun & Taylor	10-3 TAD 224
Ackerman, Forrest J.	AMAZING FORRIES	Michael L. Cook	3 U 25
Ackerman, Forrest J.	BORIS KARLOFF: THE FRANKEN-SCIENCE MONSTER	Gary Zachrich	74 PU 20
Ackerman, Forrest J.	METROPOLIS SOUVENIR BOOK	Michael L. Cook	3 U 25
Ackerman, Forrest J.	SOUVENIR BOOK OF MR. SCIENCE FICTION'S FANTASY MUSEUM	Michael L. Cook	3 U 25
Adams, Cleve F.	THE BLACK DOOR	Steve Lewis	1A MF 30
Adams, Cleve F.	UP JUMPED THE DEVIL	Stephen Mertz	5 PE 17
Adams, Clifton	DEATH'S SWEET SONG	Steve Lewis	2-2 MF 35
Adams, Donald, ed.	MYSTERY AND DETECTION ANNUAL 1972	Allen J. Hubin	6-2 TAD 115
Adams, Donald, ed.	MYSTERY AND DETECTION ANNUAL 1973	Allen J. Hubin	8-2 TAD 146
Adams, Herbert	BY ORDER OF THE FIVE	Charles Shibuk	7-3 TAD 211
Adams, Herbert	FATE LAUGHS	Jay Jeffries	7 MY 6
Adamson, Ewart, & Joseph Fields	THE WALKING DEAD (film)	William K. Everson	1-2 TAD 55
Adelman, Robert H.	THE BLOODY BENDERS	Jane S. Bakerman	3-6 PP 26
Adey, Robert C.S.	LOCKED ROOM MURDERS AND OTHER IMPOSSIBLE CRIMES	Allen J. Hubin	12-4 TAD 320
Adkins, Bill	PRISON AT OBREGON	Fred Dueren	9-3 TAD 212
Adler, Warren	THE CASANOVA EMBRACE	Allen J. Hubin	11-4 TAD 332
Adler, Warren	TRANS-SIBERIAN EXPRESS	Allen J. Hubin	11-1 TAD 17
Adley, Derek J. & W.O.G.Lofts	THE SAINT AND LESLIE CHARTERIS	J. Randolph Cox	5-3 MR 34
Adley, Derek J. & W.O.G.Lofts	THE SAINT AND LESLIE CHARTERIS	Marvin Lachman	6-1 TAD 41
Aickman, Robert	COLD HAND IN MINE	Barzun & Taylor	11-2 TAD 203
Aickman, Robert	COLD HAND IN MINE	Fred Dueren	13-1 TAD 65
Aickman, Robert	COLD HAND IN MINE	Steve Lewis	2-6 MF 31
Aickman, Robert, ed.	THE FIFTH FONTANA BOOK OF GREAT GHOST STORIES	Martin M. Wooster	4-3 PP 28
Aiken, Joan	A TOUCH OF CHILL: TALES FOR SLEEPLESS NIGHTS	Howard Lachtman	13-4 TAD 352
Aiken, Joan	DARK INTERVAL	Don D'Ammassa	8 MN 13
Aird, Catherine	A LATE PHOENIX	Jane S. Bakerman	5-5 MF 35
Aird, Catherine	A LATE PHOENIX	Marvin Lachman	3-4 MR 33
Aird, Catherine	A LATE PHOENIX	Jim McCahery	1-2 PP 21
Aird, Catherine	HENRIETTA WHO?	Mary Groff	1-4 PP 24
Aird, Catherine	HIS BURIAL TOO	Deryck Harvey	7-1 TAD 59
Aird, Catherine	HIS BURIAL TOO	Howard Rapp	6-2 MR 46
Aird, Catherine	PARTING BREATH	Barzun & Taylor	12-1 TAD 32

Aird, Catherine	PARTING BREATH	Allen J. Hubin	12-2 TAD 111
Aird, Catherine	PARTING BREATH	Jim McCahery	2-4 PP 34
Aird, Catherine	PASSING STRANGE	Steve Lewis	5-4 MF 21
Aird, Catherine	THE RELIGIOUS BODY	Mary Groff	1-2 PP 22
Aird, Catherine	SLIGHT MOURNING	Pearl G. Aldrich	11-2 TAD 121
Aird, Catherine	THE STATELY HOME MURDER	Mary Groff	1-4 PP 24
Aisenberg, Nadya	A COMMON SPRING: CRIME NOVEL AND CLASSIC	George Kelley	4-1 PP 39
Albert, Marvin H.	THE DARK GODDESS	Allen J. Hubin	11-4 TAD 332
Alding, Peter	MURDER AMONG THIEVES	Robert E. Briney	5-2 MR 42
Alding, Peter	MURDER IS SUSPECTED	Mary A. Grochowski	2-3 PP 34
Aldiss, Brian	NEANDERTHAL PLANET	Gary Zachrich	74 PU 22
Aldiss, Brian	STARSHIP	Gary Zachrich	74 PU 26
Aldrich, Thomas B.	OUT OF HIS HEAD	Amnon Kabatchnik	7-2 TAD 130
Aldyne, Nathan	VERMILION	Fred Dueren	14-2 TAD 183
Aldyne, Nathan	VERMILION	Elizabeth Wentworth	2-2 M 56
Alexander, David	BLOODSTAIN	Steve Lewis	9 MN R16
Alexander, David	DIE, LITTLE GOOSE	Steve Lewis	2-1 MF 30
Alexander, David	PAINT THE TOWN BLACK	Jim McCahery	2-5 PP 31
Alexander, David	TERROR ON BROADWAY	Jim McCahery	1-6 PP 22
Alexander, David M.	THE CHOCOLATE SPY	Allen J. Hubin	12-2 TAD 111
Alexander, Joan	ONE SUNNY DAY	Fred Dueren	11-3 TAD 306
Alexander, Karl, & Steve Hayes	TIME AFTER TIME (film)	Judith Claire	1-1 M 10
Alexander, Patrick	DEATH OF A THIN-SKINNED ANIMAL	Jane S. Bakerman	2-5 MF 35
Alexander, Patrick	DEATH OF A THIN-SKINNED ANIMAL	Allen J. Hubin	10-4 TAD 307
Alexander, Patrick	DEATH OF A THIN-SKINNED ANIMAL	Steve Lewis	2-4 MF 36
Alexandersson, Jan & Iwan Hedman	FOUR DECADES WITH DENNIS WHEATLEY	Allen J. Hubin	7-1 TAD 63
Alington, Adrian	THE VANISHING CELEBRITIES, OR THE ROOM IN THE WEST TOWER	Michele B. Slung	8-3 TAD 220
Allan, Francis	DEATH IN GENTLE GROVE	Steve Lewis	1A MF 29
Allan, Joan	WHO KILLED ME?	Cavendish Domremy	1-1 M 26
Allan, Stella	A MORTAL AFFAIR	Barzun & Taylor	13-4 TAD 308
Allan, Stella	A MORTAL AFFAIR	Allen J. Hubin	13-1 TAD 26
Allan, Stella	AN INSIDE JOB	Allen J. Hubin	12-1 TAD 6
Allbeury, Ted	THE LANTERN NETWORK	Robert C.S. Adey	4-4 PP 28
Allbeury, Ted	THE MAN WITH THE PRESIDENT'S MIND	Allen J. Hubin	12-2 TAD 111
Allbeury, Ted	OMEGA-MINUS	Don Miller	1-7 MM 8
Allen, Anita	THE SPELL OF CHOTI	Christine Mitchell	11-2 TAD 125
Allen, Dick, & David Chacko	DETECTIVE FICTION: CRIME AND COMPROMISE	Donald J. Pattow	7-3 TAD 218
Allen, Grant	AN AFRICAN MILLIONAIRE	Charles Shibuk	14-2 TAD 182
Allen, Grant	IVAN GREET'S MASTERPIECE: ETC.	Charles Shibuk	11-4 TAD 381
Allen, Grant	RECALLED IN LIFE	George Locke	11-4 TAD 380
Allen, Grant	THE RELUCTANT HANGMAN AND OTHER STORIES OF CRIME	Allen J. Hubin	7-2 TAD 143
Allen, Grant	THE RELUCTANT HANGMAN AND OTHER STORIES OF CRIME	James Sandoe	14-4 TAD 366
Allen, Michael	SPENCE AND THE HOLIDAY MAKERS	Allen J. Hubin	11-4 TAD 331
Allen, Michael	SPENCE AND THE HOLIDAY MAKERS	Steve Lewis	3-3 MF 34
Allen, Michael	SPENCE AT THE BLUE BAZAAR	Barzun & Taylor	13-3 TAD 208
Allen, Michael	SPENCE AT THE BLUE BAZAAR	Karen Bornstein	1-1 M 26
Allen, Michael	SPENCE AT THE BLUE BAZAAR	Mary A. Grochowski	2-6 PP 36
Allen, Michael	SPENCE AT THE BLUE BAZAAR	Allen J. Hubin	13-2 TAD 94
Allen, Michael	SPENCE AT THE BLUE BAZAAR	Steve Lewis	3-6 MF 37
Allingham, Margery	THE ALLINGHAM CASE-BOOK	Robert E. Washer	2-1 QC 17
Allingham, Margery	THE BLACK DUDLEY MURDERS	Marvin Lachman	2-1 TAD 61
Allingham, Margery	BLACK'ERCHIEF DICK	David Brownell	8-2 TAD 137
Allingham, Margery	THE CHINA GOVERNESS	Amnon Kabatchnik	5-1 MR 38
Allingham, Margery	THE FEAR SIGN	Amnon Kabatchnik	5-1 MR 38
Allingham, Margery	MR. CAMPION AND OTHERS	Arthur C. Scott	8 MN 26

Allingham, Margery	THE WHITE COTTAGE MYSTERY	David Brownell	8-2 TAD 137
Allis, Sarah	NIGHTWIND	Allen J. Hubin	9-1 TAD 74
Altick, Richard D.	VICTORIAN STUDIES IN SCARLET	Luther Norris	4-5 MR 38
Altman, Thomas	KISS DADDY GOODBYE	Richard Moskowitz	9 LR 16
Altsheler, Joseph A.	THE TEXAS STAR	C.L.Messecar	3-3 BC 351
Alverson, Charles	GOODEY'S LAST STAND	Allen J. Hubin	9-1 TAD 72
Alverson, Charles	GOODEY'S LAST STAND	Joe R. Lansdale	5 PE 18
Alverson, Charles	GOODEY'S LAST STAND	Charles Shibuk	13-2 TAD 135
Alverson, Charles	NOT SLEEPING, JUST DEAD	Steve Lewis	2-2 MF 34
Alverson, Charles	NOT SLEEPING, JUST DEAD	Charles Shibuk	13-3 TAD 250
Ambler, Eric	A COFFIN FOR DIMITRIOS	Charles Shibuk	11-3 TAD 245
Ambler, Eric	A COFFIN FOR DIMITRIOS	Martin M. Wooster	2-4 MF 39
Ambler, Eric	DOCTOR FRIGO	Charles Shibuk	9-3 TAD 208
Ambler, Eric	THE SIEGE OF THE VILLA LIPP	Allen J. Hubin	10-4 TAD 308
Ames, Delano	MURDER, MAESTRO, PLEASE	Jay Jeffries	1 MN 8
Ames, Delano	NO COFFIN FOR CHRISTOPHER	Jay Jeffries	1 MN 8
Ames, Delano	SHE WOULDN'T SAY WHO	Jay Jeffries	1 MN 8
Amis, Kingsley	DR.WATSON AND THE DARKWATER HALL MYSTERY (play)	Veronica M. Kennedy	8-2 TAD 144
Amis, Kingsley	THE RIVERSIDE VILLAS MURDER	R.Jeff Banks	3-3 MF 41
Anderson, Frederick Irving	ADVENTURES OF THE INFALLIBLE GODAHL	Ben Fisher	4-2 PP 24
Anderson, Frederick Irving	THE BOOK OF MURDER	Ben Fisher	2-2 PP 25
Anderson, Frederick Irving	THE NOTORIOUS SOPHIE LANG	Ben Fisher	4-3 PP 21
Anderson, James	THE ABOLITION OF DEATH	Allen J. Hubin	8-4 TAD 310
Anderson, James	THE AFFAIR OF THE BLOOD-STAINED EGG COSY	Robert C.S.Adey	4-3 PP 24
Anderson, James	THE AFFAIR OF THE BLOOD-STAINED EGG COSY	Allen J. Hubin	10-3 TAD 205
Anderson, James	THE AFFAIR OF THE BLOOD-STAINED EGG COSY	Jeff Meyerson	1-5 MF 42
Anderson, James	THE AFFAIR OF THE BLOOD-STAINED EGG COSY	Charles Shibuk	11-3 TAD 298
Anderson, James	THE AFFAIR OF THE MUTILATED MINK COAT	Fred Dueren	4-5/6 PP 81
Anderson, James	ANGEL OF DEATH	Robert C.S.Adey	3-1 PP 36
Anderson, James	ANGEL OF DEATH	Jon L. Breen	14-1 TAD 55
Anderson, John L.	DEATH ON THE ROCKS	Barzun & Taylor	9-4 TAD 271
Anderson, John R.L.	A SPRIG OF SEA LAVENDER	Charles Shibuk	14-2 TAD 182
Anderson, John R.L.	DEATH IN THE CHANNEL	Myrtis Broset	2-4 MM 3
Anderson, John R.L.	DEATH IN THE NORTH SEA	Stan Burns	2-5 MY 7
Anderson, John R.L.	DEATH IN THE CHANNEL	Steve Lewis	3-2 MF 36
Anderson, John R.L.	FESTIVAL	Allen J. Hubin	13-4 TAD 294
Anderson, John R.L.	FESTIVAL	Steve Lewis	4-2 MF 37
Anderson, Poul	THE DEVIL'S GAME	Paul Harwitz	2-3 M 49
Anderson, Poul	FLIGHT TO YESTERDAY	Edward Wood	64 PU 17
Anderson, Poul	MURDER BOUND	Douglas Greene	4-4 PP 25
Anderson, Poul	QUESTION AND ANSWER	Shawn Loudermilk	1-2 PQ 55
Andover, Henry	THE DENNISDALE TRAGEDY	Barzun & Taylor	11-3 TAD 281
Andress, Lesley	CAPER	Allen J. Hubin	13-3 TAD 199
Andress, Lesley	CAPER	Steve Lewis	4-4 MF 34
Andress, Lesley	CAPER	Charles Shibuk	14-3 TAD 266
Andrews, Charlton	THE RESOURCES OF MYCROFT HOLMES	Allen J. Hubin	7-1 TAD 63
Andrews, Mark	BODY RUB	Amnon Kabatchnik	1-5 MF 41
Andrews, Mark	THE RETURN OF JACK THE RIPPER	Edward Lauterbach	11-1 TAD 22
Andrews, V.C.	FLOWERS IN THE ATTIC	Fred Dueren	13-2 TAD 136
Andrews, V.C.	PETALS ON THE WIND	Joseph Terry	2-1 M 28
Andriola, Alfred	CHARLIE CHAN'S ADVENTURES (comic book)	Allen J. Hubin	10-4 TAD 309
Angus, Sylvia	DEAD TO RITES	M.S.Cappadonna	12-1 TAD 95
Angus, Sylvia	DEAD TO RITES	Allen J. Hubin	12-2 TAD 111
Anson, Jay	THE AMITYVILLE HORROR	Amnon Kabatchnik	1-3 PP 28
Anthony, David	BLOOD ON A HARVEST MOON	Stanley Carlin	5-2 MR 40

Anthony, David	THE ORGANIZATION	Bill Crider	3-4 MF 47
Anthony, David	STUD GAME	Myrtis Broset	2-6 MF 42
Anthony, David	STUD GAME	Steve Lewis	3-3 MF 35
Anthony, David	STUD GAME	Charles Shibuk	11-4 TAD 379
Anthony, Evelyn	THE ASSASSIN	Stanley Carlin	3-5 MR 20
Anthony, Evelyn	THE ASSASSIN	Robert E. Washer	3-4 TAD 270
Anthony, Evelyn	THE LEGEND	Steve Lewis	1-1 MF 32
Anthony, Evelyn	THE PERSIAN PRICE	Barbara A. Buhrer	8 MN 11
Anthony, Evelyn	THE RENDEZVOUS	Myrtis Broset	2-1 MF 39
Anthony, Evelyn	THE SILVER FALCON	Myrtis Broset	2-6 MF 42
Anthony, Evelyn	THE SILVER FALCON	Barbara A. Buhrer	12 MN R4
Anthony, Piers	MACROSCOPE	Gary Zachrich	74 PU 25
Anthony, Piers	SPLIT INFINITY	W.Ritchie Benedict	13 SF 17
Archer, Jeffrey	NOT A PENNY MORE, NOT A PENNY LESS	Barbara A. Buhrer	10 MN R1
Archer, Jeffrey	NOT A PENNY MORE, NOT A PENNY LESS	Stan Burns	2-4 MM 4
Archer, Jeffrey	NOT A PENNY MORE, NOT A PENNY LESS	Howard Lachtman	10-1 TAD 69
Archer, Jeffrey	NOT A PENNY MORE, NOT A PENNY LESS	Charles Shibuk	10-4 TAD 360
Archer, Jeffrey	SHALL WE TELL THE PRESIDENT?	Thomas L.Motsinger	2-6 MF 36
Ard, William	AS BAD AS I AM	Charles Shibuk	7-3 TAD 212
Ard, William	THE PERFECT FRAME	Stephen Mertz	2 PE 22
Ardies, Tom	THIS SUITCASE IS GOING TO EXPLODE	Stanley Carlin	5-4 MR 30
Armstrong, Anthony	THE TRAIL OF FEAR	Charles Shibuk	1-4 MF 53
Armstrong, Charlotte	A LITTLE LESS THAN KIND	Jane S.Bakerman	12 MN R1
Armstrong, Charlotte	THE CHARLOTTE ARMSTRONG READER	Robert E. Washer	3-6 MR 21
Armstrong, Charlotte	LEMON IN THE BASKET	Don D'Ammassa	8 MN 13
Armstrong, Charlotte	SEVEN SEATS TO THE MOON	Donald A. Yates	3-1 MF 39
Arnold, Armin, & Josef Schmidt	KRIMINAL ROMAN FUHRER	Allen J. Hubin	12-1 TAD 12
Arrighi, Mel	THE DEATH COLLECTION	Fred Dueren	8-4 TAD 295
Arrighi, Mel	TURKISH WHITE	Steve Lewis	2-1 MF 23
Arthur, Robert	MYSTERY AND MORE MYSTERY	Edward Lauterbach	5-3 TAD 162
Arthur, Robert	SOMEBODY WALKED OVER MY GRAVE	Don D'Ammassa	1 MN 8
Ashby, R.C.	DEATH ON TIPTOE	Mary Groff	1-1 PP 23
Ashby, R.C.	HE ARRIVED AT DUSK	Charles Shibuk	6-2 TAD 116
Ashe, Gordon	A LIFE FOR A LIFE	Allen J. Hubin	7-1 TAD 61
Ashbrook, Harriette Cora	A MOST IMMORAL MURDER	Charles Shibuk	12-2 TAD 189
Ashdown, Clifford	THE ADVENTURES OF ROMNEY PRINGLE	A.F.Germeshausen	1-2 TAD 60
Ashdown, Clifford	THE ADVENTURES OF ROMNEY PRINGLE	Allen J. Hubin	2-2 TAD 122
Ashdown, Clifford	FROM A SURGEON'S DIARY	Allen J. Hubin	10-3 TAD 206
Ashdown, Clifford	THE FURTHER ADVENTURES OF ROMNEY PRINGLE	Allen J. Hubin	4-3 TAD 180
Ashdown, Cliford	THE QUEEN'S TREASURE	Allen J. Hubin	9-2 TAD 153
Ashford, F.U.	A PACKET OF TROUBLE	Steve Lewis	5-4 MF 25
Ashford, Jeffrey	A RECIPE FOR MURDER	Howard Rapp	4-1 PP 34
Ashford, Jeffrey	HOSTAGE IN DEATH	Allen J. Hubin	11-3 TAD 230
Ashford, Jeffrey	HOSTAGE IN DEATH	Steve Lewis	2-5 MF 26
Ashford, Jeffrey	SLOW DOWN THE WORLD	Allen J. Hubin	10-2 TAD 113
Ashford, Jeffrey	SLOW DOWN THE WORLD	Steve Lewis	2-1 MF 28
Ashford, Jeffrey	THREE LAYERS OF GUILT	Allen J. Hubin	9-3 TAD 224
Asimov, Isaac	A WHIFF OF DEATH	Don Miller	9 MN R18
Asimov, Isaac	ASIMOV'S MYSTERIES	Guy M. Townsend	1-6 MF 47
Asimov, Isaac	ASIMOV'S SHERLOCKIAN LIMERICKS	C.J.Murdoch	4 MT 24
Asimov, Isaac	ASIMOV'S SHERLOCKIAN LIMERICKS	Martin M. Wooster	2-4 MF 42
Asimov, Isaac	CASEBOOK OF THE BLACK WIDOWERS	Douglas Greene	4-1 PP 35
Asimov, Isaac	THE CAVES OF STEEL	Barzun & Taylor	14-2 TAD 142
Asimov, Isaac	MURDER AT THE ABA	Pearl G.Aldrich	10-1 TAD 70
Asimov, Isaac	MURDER AT THE ABA	Barzun & Taylor	11-1 TAD 92
Asimov, Isaac	MURDER AT THE ABA	Martin M. Wooster	1-2 MF 39

Asimov, Isaac, & Greenberg & Waugh	THE THIRTEEN CRIMES OF SCIENCE FICTION	Martin M.Wooster	4-3 MF 45
Asimov, Isaac, & Greenberg & Waugh	THE TWELVE CRIMES OF CHRISTMAS	Fred Dueren	4-5/6 PP 100
Asimov, Isaac, & Alice Laurance	WHO DONE IT?	Fred Dueren	13-4 TAD 351
Asimov, Isaac, & Alice Laurance	WHO DONE IT?	F.M.Nevins, Jr.	4-4 MF 48
Asinof, Eliot	SAY IT AIN'T SO, GORDON LITTLEFIELD	Steve Lewis	2-3 MF 45
Asquith, Cynthia	THE GHOST BOOK: SIXTEEN STORIES OF THE UNCANNY	Martin M. Wooster	3-4 PP 29
Aswand, Betsy	WINDS OF THE OLD DAYS	Allen J. Hubin	14-2 TAD 123
Attiwill, Ken	NON-STOP NEW YORK (film)	Wm.K.Everson	7-2 TAD 96
Atiyah, Edward	THE THIN LINE	Charles Shibuk	8-3 TAD 222
Atkey, Bertram	THE AMAZING MR. BUNN	Douglas G. Greene	12-3 TAD 230
Atkey, Bertram	MR.DASS: A NOVEL OF PURSUIT AND PUNISHMENT	Charles Shibuk	2-5 MF 37
Atkins, Thomas	THE BLUE MAN	Barzun & Taylor	12-3 TAD 262
Atkins, Thomas	THE BLUE MAN	Allen J. Hubin	12-1 TAD 6
Atlee, Philip	THE FER-DE-LANCE CONTRACT	Fred Blosser	4-3 TAD 178
Atlee, Philip	THE MAKASSAR STRAIT	Steve Lewis	1-3 MF 40
Atlee, Philip	THE SILKEN BARONESS	Steve Lewis	5A MY 2
Atwater, James D.	TIME BOMB	Allen J. Hubin	11-2 TAD 116
Atwater, James D.	TIME BOMB	Charles Shibuk	12-3 TAD 255
Aubrey, Edmund	SHERLOCK HOLMES IN DALLAS	Mike Hodel	3-1 M 37
Audemars, Pierre	NOW DEAD IS ANY MAN	George Kelley	4-1 PP 38
Austin, Hugh	MURDER IN TRIPLICATE	Charles Shibuk	12-2 TAD 190
Avallone, Michael	ASSASSINS DON'T DIE IN BED	Robert E. Washer	1-4 QC 20
Avallone, Michael	THE BIG STIFFS	Stephen Mertz	2-5 MF 39
Avallone, Michael	THE CASE OF THE BOUNCING BETTY	Arthur C. Scott	1-2 MF 46
Avallone, Michael	THE CASE OF THE VIOLENT VIRGIN	Arthur C. Scott	1-2 MF 46
Avallone, Michael	CHARLIE CHAN AND THE CURSE OF THE DRAGON QUEEN (film)	Thomas Godfrey	3-1 M 44
Avallone, Michael	DEATH DIVES DEEP	Hellgate Newlander	4-4 TAD 242
Avallone, Michael	THE DOCTOR'S WIFE	F.M.Nevins, Jr.	3-1 MF 43
Avallone, Michael	THE DOOMSDAY BAG	Robert E. Washer	2-1 QC 18
Avallone, Michael	THE FAT DEATH	Amnon Kabatchnik	5-6 MR 35
Avallone, Michael	5-MINUTE MYSTERIES, CASES FROM THE FILES OF ED NOON	Douglas G. Greene	12-3 TAD 273
Avallone, Michael	LITTLE MISS MURDER	Hellgate Newlander	4-4 TAD 243
Avallone, Michael	MISSING!	Kelly Adrian	2-4 MR 10
Avallone, Michael	MISSING!	Robert E. Washer	1-4 QC 19
Avallone, Michael	THE TALL DOLORES	Andy Jaysnovitch	2 PE 24
Axton, David	PRISON OF ICE	George Kelley	1-6 MF 46
Babson, Marian	DANGEROUS TO KNOW	Kathi Maio	4-5/6 PP 80
Babson, Marian	THE LORD MAYOR OF DEATH	Fred Dueren	13-1 TAD 61
Babson, Marian	MURDER MURDER LITTLE STAR	Allen J. Hubin	13-4 TAD 294
Babson, Marian	MURDER MURDER LITTLE STAR	Steve Lewis	4-3 MF 34
Babson, Marian	MURDER MURDER LITTLE STAR	David Rose	3-3 PP 30
Babson, Marian	THE TWELVE DEATHS OF CHRISTMAS	Kathi Maio	3-6 PP 29
Bagby, George	BLOOD WILL TELL	Arthur C. Scott	1-8 MM 7
Bagby, George	COUNTRY AND FATAL	Steve Lewis	4-4 MF 41
Bagby, George	GUARANTEED TO FADE	Steve Lewis	3-4 MF 38
Bagby, George	I COULD HAVE DIED	Steve Lewis	3-5 MF 39
Bagby, George	INNOCENT BYSTANDER	Barzun & Taylor	11-2 TAD 203
Bagby, George	MUGGER'S DAY	Steve Lewis	3-6 MF 39
Bagby, George	MURDER ON THE NOSE	F.M.Nevins, Jr.	6-4 TAD 269
Bagby, George	THE ORIGINAL CARCASE	Steve Lewis	2-4 MF 34
Bagby, George	THE TOUGH GET GOING	Jane S. Bakerman	6 CL 5
Bagby, George	THE TOUGH GET GOING	Steve Lewis	2-6 MF 33
Bagby, George	TWO IN THE BUSH	Stan Burns	1-9 MM 5
Bagby, George	TWO IN THE BUSH	Steve Lewis	1A MF 25
Bagley, Desmond	THE ENEMY	Jane S.Bakerman	3-6 MF 43

Bagley, Desmond	THE ENEMY	Barzun & Taylor	14-1 TAD 88
Bagley, Desmond	THE ENEMY	Allen J. Hubin	11-4 TAD 333
Bagley, Desmond	THE ENEMY	Charles Shibuk	12-3 TAD 255
Bagley, Desmond	RUNNING BLIND	Iwan Hedman	4-4 MR 34
Bagley, Desmond	THE VIVERO LETTER	Jane S.Bakerman	2-3 PP 27
Bailey, F. Lee	SECRETS	Larry L. French	12-1 TAD 94
Bailey, F. Lee	SECRETS	Steve Lewis	3-3 MF 33
Bailey, H.C.	BLACK LAND, WHITE LAND	Maryell Cleary	2-4 PP 30
Bailey, H.C.	BLACK LAND, WHITE LAND	James Sandoe	8-4 TAD 297
Bailey, H.C.	BLACK LAND, WHITE LAND	Guy M. Townsend	1A MF 38
Bailey, H.C.	MR.FORTUNE: EIGHT OF HIS ADVENTURES	Jon L.Lellenberg	10-1 TAD 66
Bailey, H.C.	ORPHAN ANN	Maryell Cleary	3-5 PP 35
Bailey, H.C.	THE RED CASTLE MYSTERY	Steve Lewis	1-5 MF 35
Baker, Asa	MUM'S THE WORD FOR MURDER	John Vining	8-2 TAD 139
Baker, Carlos	THE GAY HEAD CONSPIRACY	Barzun & Taylor	9-3 TAD 209
Baker, Ivon	THE BLOOD ON MY SLEEVE	Allen J. Hubin	13-4 TAD 294
Baker, Ivon	DEATH AND VARIATIONS	Allen J. Hubin	11-3 TAD 230
Bakker, Cajus	THE LUFTWAFFE WAR DIARIES	Gary Zachrich	74 PU 20
Balchin, Nigel	THE SMALL BACK ROOM (film)	William K. Everson	5-3 TAD 145
Balderston, John L. & Hamilton Deane	DRACULA	Jackie Meyerson	1-1 PP 20
Ball, Brian	DEATH OF A LOW-HANDICAP MAN	Mary A.Grochowski	2-2 PP 29
Ball, Brian	DEATH OF A LOW-HANDICAP MAN	Steve Lewis	3-2 MF 36
Ball, Brian	THE NIGHT CREATURE	Bill Crider	1-1 PQ 36
Ball, Brian	THE NIGHT CREATURE	Veronica M.Kennedy	8-4 TAD 301
Ball, Brian	TIMEPIVOT	Gary Zachrich	75 PU 24
Ball, John	THE COOL COTTONTAIL	Maryell Cleary	2-5 PP 33
Ball, John	THE EYES OF BUDDHA	Steve Lewis	1-3 MF 40
Ball, John	THE EYES OF BUDDHA	F.M.Nevins,Jr.	1-5 MF 45
Ball, John	THE EYES OF BUDDHA	Frank Occhiogrosso	11-2 TAD 121
Ball, John	FIVE PIECES OF JADE	Greg Goode	4-5/6 PP 73
Ball, John	JOHNNY GET YOUR GUN	Lianne Carlin	3-1 MR 7
Ball, John	THE MURDER CHILDREN	Allen J. Hubin	13-1 TAD 27
Ball, John, ed.	THE MYSTERY STORY	Amnon Kabatchnik	11 MN R7
Ball, John, ed.	THE MYSTERY STORY	Arthur C. Scott	1-2 MF 32
Ball, John, ed.	THE MYSTERY STORY	Charles Shibuk	10-2 TAD 188
Ball, John, ed.	THE MYSTERY STORY	Charles Shibuk	12-2 TAD 166
Ball, John, ed.	THE MYSTERY STORY	Martin M. Wooster	1-2 MF 29
Ball, John	POLICE CHIEF	Bonnie Pollard	6 CL 7
Ball, John	THEN CAME VIOLENCE	Steve Lewis	4-3 MF 39
Ball, John	THEN CAME VIOLENCE	F.M.Nevins,Jr.	4-5 MF 37
Ball, John	TROUBLE FOR TALLON	F.M.Nevins,Jr.	5-5 MF 31
Ball, John	TROUBLE FOR TALLON	Sam Yamato	2-2 M 58
Ball, John & B.Smith	THE KILLING IN THE MARKET	Mary Groff	1-3 PP 29
Ball, John & B.Smith	THE KILLING IN THE MARKET	Andrew Stewart	4 MT 36
Ballard, W.T.	MURDER CAN'T STOP	Stephen Mertz	3-4 MF 42
Ballard, W.T.	SAY YES TO MURDER	Stephen Mertz	2-3 MF 53
Ballard, W.T.	THE SEVEN SISTERS	Stephen Mertz	2-5 MF 39
Ballinger, Bill S.	A BILL S. BALLINGER TRIPTYCH	Lianne Carlin	4-4 MR 37
Ballinger, Bill S.	THE 49 DAYS OF DEATH	Pat Erhardt	3-2 MR 9
Ballinger, Bill S.	HEIST ME HIGHER	Jeff Meyerson	1-4 MF 52
Ballinger, Bill S.	PORTRAIT IN SMOKE	Angelo Panagos	12-1 TAD 80
Ballinger, W.A.	I, THE HANGMAN	Arthur C. Scott	11 MN R19
Bandy, Franklin	THE BLACKSTOCK AFFAIR	Fred Dueren	13-4 TAD 361
Bandy, Franklin	THE BLACKSTOCK AFFAIR	Steve Lewis	4-4 MF 33
Bandy, Franklin	THE BLACKSTOCK AFFAIR	Charles Chibuk	13-4 TAD 362
Bandy, Franklin	DECEIT AND DEADLY LIES	Fred Dueren	12-2 TAD 135
Bandy, Franklin	DECEIT AND DEADLY LIES	Steve Lewis	3-3 MF 33
Bangs, John Kendrick	SHYLOCK HOMES: HIS POSTHUMOUS MEMOIRS	Allen J. Hubin	6-4 TAD 265
Banks, Carolyn	THE DARKROOM	Allen J. Hubin	14-2 TAD 123
Banks, Oliver	THE REMBRANDT PANEL	Carol Frakes	3-1 M 37
Banks, Oliver	THE REMBRANDT PANEL	Howard Lachtman	13-4 TAD 352
Banks, Oliver	THE REMBRANDT PANEL	Becky A.Reineke	4-6 MF 37

Barak, Michael	THE ENIGMA	T.P.Dukeshire	3-6 MF 44
Barak, Michael	THE ENIGMA	Steve Lewis	3-1 MF 36
Barbour, Alan G.	THE THRILL OF IT ALL	Don Miller	11 MN W1
Barbour, Ralph Henry	CHANGE SIGNALS	C.L.Messecar	3-3 BC 351
Barclay, Glen St.John	ANATOMY OF HORROR	Andy Jaysnovitch	5 PE 20
Barclay, Stephen	BLOCKBUSTER	Steve Lewis	2-1 MF 21
Bardin, John Franklin	THE JOHN FRANKLIN BARDIN OMNIBUS	Fred Dueren	10-1 TAD 52
Bardin, John Franklin	PURLOINING TINY	Allen J. Hubin	11-2 TAD 116
Baring-Gould, William	NERO WOLFE OF WEST THIRTY-FIFTH STREET	James Keddie,Jr.	2-2 TAD 121
Bark, Conrad Voss	MR. HOLMES AT SEA	Charles Shibuk	12-4 TAD 373
Barker, Albert	GIFT FROM BERLIN	George Kelley	4-2 PP 27
Barker, Dudley	G.K.CHESTERTON	Harold Hughesdon	7-1 TAD 29
Barnard, Robert	BLOOD BROTHERHOOD	Barzun & Taylor	13-4 TAD 308
Barnard, Robert	BLOOD BROTHERHOOD	Allen J. Hubin	11-4 TAD 333
Barnard, Robert	DEATH IN A COLD CLIMATE	Fred Dueren	4-5/6 PP 79
Barnard, Robert	DEATH IN A COLD CLIMATE	Allen J. Hubin	14-4 TAD 298
Barnard, Robert	DEATH IN A COLD CLIMATE	Dorothy B. Hughes	3-2 M 39
Barnard, Robert	DEATH OF A MYSTERY WRITER	Allen J. Hubin	13-2 TAD 94
Barnard, Robert	DEATH OF A PERFECT MOTHER	Steve Lewis	5-6 MF 38
Barnard, Robert	DEATH OF AN OLD GOAT	Allen J. Hubin	10-3 TAD 204
Barnard, Robert	DEATH OF A LITERARY WIDOW	Allen J. Hubin	14-2 TAD 123
Barnard, Robert	DEATH OF A MYSTERY WRITER	Fred Dueren	14-2 TAD 184
Barnard, Robert	DEATH OF A MYSTERY WRITER	Charles Shibuk	14-2 TAD 182
Barnard, Robert	DEATH ON THE HIGH C'S	Mary A.Grochowski	2-2 PP 29
Barnard, Robert	DEATH ON THE HIGH C'S	Charles Shibuk	14-4 TAD 376
Barnes, Dallas	YESTERDAY IS DEAD	Fred Dueren	9-4 TAD 334
Barnes, Melvyn	BEST DETECTIVE FICTION	Allen J. Hubin	9-2 TAD 153
Barnett, James	BACKFIRE IS HOSTILE	Allen J. Hubin	13-2 TAD 94
Barnett, James	HEAD OF THE FORCE	Robert C.S.Adey	4-4 PP 30
Barnett, James	HEAD OF THE FORCE	D.E.Ath	2-1 PP 10
Barns, Glenn M.	MURDER IS A GAMBLE	Steve Lewis	1-1 MF 28
Barr, Robert	FROM WHOSE BOURNE	Charles Shibuk	9-1 TAD 60
Barrett, James Lee	FOOL'S PARADISE (film)	Richard S.Lochte	5-1 TAD 41
Barroll, Clare	A STRANGE PLACE FOR MURDER	Allen J. Hubin	12-4 TAD 320
Barroll, Clare	A STRANGE PLACE FOR MURDER	Steve Lewis	3-6 MF 34
Barry, Mike	PHILADELPHIA BLOWUP	Bill Crider	9-3 TAD 219
Barry, Mike	PHILADELPHIA BLOWUP	Jeff Meyerson	2-1 MM 5
Barry, Nora	SHERBOURNE'S FOLLY	Steve Lewis	3-3 MF 39
Barth, Richard	THE RAG BAG CLAN	Allen J. Hubin	12-2 TAD 111
Bartram, George	THE AELIAN FRAGMENT	Steve Lewis	2-5 MF 31
Bar-Zohar, Michael	THE SPY WHO DIED TWICE	Allen J. Hubin	9-1 TAD 75
Bar-Zohar, Michael	THE SPY WHO DIED TWICE	Robert E. Washer	21 X 54
Bar-Zohar, Michael	THE THIRD TRUTH	Allen J. Hubin	6-4 TAD 267
Barzun, Jacques, ed.	BURKE AND HARE	Allen J. Hubin	8-3 TAD 230
Barzun, Jacues, & W.H.Taylor	A BOOK OF PREFACES TO FIFTY CLASSICS OF CRIME FICTION	Charles Shibuk	11-2 TAD 124
Barzun, Jacques, & W.H.Taylor	A CATALOGUE OF CRIME	William J. Clark	16 JD 14
Barzun, Jacques, & W.H.Taylor	A CATALOGUE OF CRIME	Marvin Lachman	4-5 MR 32
Barzun, Jacques, & W.H.Taylor	A CATALOGUE OF CRIME	Charles Shibuk	4-4 TAD 243
Barzun, Jacques, & W.H.Taylor	A CATALOGUE OF CRIME	Robert E. Washer	3-2 QC 18
Barzun, Jacques, & W.H.Taylor	CLASSIC STORIES OF CRIME AND DETECTION	Howard Lachtman	10-4 TAD 312
Baum, L. Frank	THE PURPLE DRAGON AND OTHER FANTASIES	Michael L. Cook	4 U 20
Baum, L. Frank	THE PURPLE DRAGON AND OTHER FANTASIES	W.Paul Ganly	6 U 28
Bax, Roger	RED ESCAPADE	Charles Shibuk	12-4 TAD 373
Baxt, George	A PARADE OF COCKEYED CREATURES, OR DID SOMEONE MURDER OUR WANDERING BOY?	Mary Jean DeMarr	3-4 MF 42

Baxt, George	THE NEON GRAVEYARD	Allen J. Hubin	13-1 TAD 27
Baxt, George	THE NEON GRAVEYARD	Steve Lewis	4-2 MF 31
Baylus, Robert F.	MIDSUMMER NIGHT'S MURDER	Allen J. Hubin	12-4 TAD 320
Baylus, Robert F.	THE PEOPLE EXCHANGE	Allen J. Hubin	13-3 TAD 199
Baynes, Jack	MOROCCO JONES IN THE CASE OF THE GOLDEN ANGEL	John Vining	9-1 TAD 62
Beagle, Peter S.	A FINE AND PRIVATE PLACE	Gary Zachrich	71 PU 22
Beahan, Charles, & Rufus King	MURDER BY THE CLOCK (film)	William K.Everson	6-3 TAD 171
Beals, Kenneth, & Richard Bojarski	THE FILMS OF BORIS KARLOFF	Veronica M. Kennedy	8-3 TAD 224
Beaman, Bruce R.	SHERLOCKIAN QUOTATIONS	Allen J. Hubin	10-3 TAD 207
Beaman, Bruce R.	SHERLOCKIAN QUOTATIONS	W.A.Karpowicz,Jr.	2 MT 25
Bearshaw, Brian	THE ORDER OF DEATH	Robert C.S.Adey	4-1 PP 39
Becker, Jens Peter, & Paul G.Buchloh	DER DETEKTIVERZAHLUNG AUF DER SPUR: ESSAYS ZUR FORM UND WERTUNG DER ENGLISHECHEN DETEKTIVLITERATUR	Barzun & Taylor	11-1 TAD 92
Bedford, Tim	SATURN OVER THE WATER	James Sandoe	7-3 TAD 211
Beechcroft, William	POSITION OF ULTIMATE	Allen J. Hubin	14-4 TAD 298
Beeding, Francis	DEATH WALKS IN EASTREPPS	James Kingman	11-1 TAD 27
Beeding, Francis	DEATH WALKS IN EASTREPPS	Charles Shibuk	14-2 TAD 182
Beeding, Francis	DEATH WALKS IN EASTREPPS	Guy M. Townsend	10 MN R20
Beeding, Francis	THE FIVE FLAMBOYS	Charles Shibuk	14-3 TAD 271
Behn, Noel	THE SHADOWBOXER	Stanley Carlin	3-5 MR 22
Behre, Frank	STUDIES IN AGATHA CHRISTIE'S WRITINGS	Mary Seeger	5-2 TAD 102
Bell, Josephine	A QUESTION OF INHERITANCE	Gary Warren Niebuhr	4-5/6 PP 79
Bell, Josephine	THE TROUBLE IN HUNTER WARD	Allen J. Hubin	10-3 TAD 204
Bell, Josephine	WOLF! WOLF!	George Kelley	4-1 PP 39
Bennett, Arnold	THE LOOT OF CITIES	Stanley Carlin	6-1 MR 48
Bennett, Arnold	THE LOOT OF CITIES	Allen J. Hubin	6-1 TAD 43
Bennett, Dorothea	THE JIGSAW MAN	Allen J. Hubin	9-4 TAD 310
Bennett, Margot	THE MAN WHO DIDN'T FLY	Helmuth Masser	5-4 MF 30
Benson, Ben	THE AFFAIR OF THE EXOTIC DANCER	Richard Moskowitz	5 LR 3
Benson, Ben	BEWARE THE PALE HORSE	Robert C.S.Adey	4-2 PP 25
Benson, Godfrey R.	TRACKS IN THE SNOW	Charles Shibuk	8-2 TAD 138
Benson, O.G.	CAIN'S WOMAN	R. Jeff Banks	1-1 PP 21
Bentley, E.C.	TRENT INTERVENES	Marvin Lachman	5-4 MF 19
Bentley, E.C.	TRENT INTERVENES	Charles Shibuk	14-4 TAD 376
Bentley, E.C.	TRENT'S LAST CASE	Charles Shibuk	11-2 TAD 123
Bentley, E.C.	TRENT'S LAST CASE	Charles Shibuk	11-3 TAD 298
Bentley, E.C.	TRENT'S OWN CASE	Charles Shibuk	14-3 TAD 266
Benton, Kenneth	CRAIG AND THE MIDAS TOUCH	Allen J. Hubin	10-1 TAD 42
Benton, Kenneth	CRAIG AND THE MIDAS TOUCH	Steve Lewis	1A MF 29
Berckman, Evelyn	A CASE IN NULLITY	Barzun & Taylor	14-1 TAD 88
Berckman, Evelyn	THE EVIL OF TIME	Don D'Ammassa	7 MN 10
Berckman, Evelyn	SHE ASKED FOR IT	Don D'Ammassa	1 MN 9
Berckman, Evelyn	STALEMATE	Don D'Ammassa	3/4 MN 20
Berckman, Evelyn	THE STRANGE BEDFELLOW	Don D'Ammassa	5/6 MN 20
Berger, Thomas	WHO IS TEDDY VILLANOVA?	Robert C.S.Adey	5-5 MF 36
Berger, Thomas	WHO IS TEDDY VILLANOVA?	Jim Huang	7 CL 10
Berger, Thomas	WHO IS TEDDY VILLANOVA?	George Kelley	1-4 MF 46
Bergman, Andrew	THE BIG KISS-OFF OF 1944	Stan Burns	3/4 MN 19
Bergman, Andrew	THE BIG KISS-OFF OF 1944	Steve Lewis	1-3 MF 38
Bergman, Andrew	HOLLYWOOD AND LEVINE	Douglas M.Armato	9-1 TAD 66
Bergman, Andrew	HOLLYWOOD AND LEVINE	Stan Burns	7 MN 9
Bergman, Andrew	HOLLYWOOD AND LEVINE	Charles Shibuk	10-2 TAD 149
Berkeley, Anthony	ASK A POLICEMAN	Paul McCarthy	3-3 PP 28
Berkeley, Anthony	THE MYSTERY AT LOVERS' CAVE	Douglas G. Greene	4-5/6 PP 67
Berkeley, Anthony	THE PUCCADILLY MURDER	Gary Warren Niebuhr	4-4 PP 24
Berkeley, Anthony	THE POISONED CHOCOLATES CASE	Charles Shibuk	12-4 TAD 370
Berkeley, Anthony	THE POISONED CHOCOLATES CASE	Charles Shibuk	14-2 TAD 182
Berkeley, Anthony	THE SECOND SHOT	James Mark Purcell	9-3 TAD 228
Berkeley, Anthony	TOP STORY MURDER	Steve Lewis	1-1 MF 32
Berkeley, Anthony	TRIAL AND ERROR	Charles Shibuk	14-4 TAD 376

Berliner, Ross	THE MANHOOD CEREMONY	Allen J. Hubin	12-2 TAD 111
Bernard, Robert	DEADLY MEETING	Barzun & Taylor	12-3 TAD 262
Bernard, Robert	THE ULLMAN CODE	Allen J. Hubin	8-4 TAD 311
Bernard, Trevor	BRIGHTLIGHT	Robert C.S.Adey	4-3 MF 42
Bernard, Trevor	BRIGHTLIGHT	R. Jeff Banks	2-1 MF 31
Bernard, Trevor	BRIGHTLIGHT	Myrtis Broset	2-1 MF 37
Bernard, Trevor	BRIGHTLIGHT	Steve Lewis	2-4 MF 32
Bernstein, Ken	INTERCEPT	Don Cole	4-4 MR 35
Berrow, Norman	THE BISHOP'S SWORD	Angelo Panagos	14-3 TAD 272
Berrow, Norman	FINGERS FOR RANSOM	Charles Shibuk	11-4 TAD 380
Berrow, Norman	THREE TIERS OF FANTASY	Angelo Panagos	14-3 TAD 272
Betcherman, Barbara	SUSPICIONS	Steve Lewis	4-4 MF 38
Biggers, Earl Derr	THE CHINESE PARROT	Maryell Cleary	4-5/6 PP 67
Biggers, Earl Derr	THE CHINESE PARROT	Don D'Ammassa	1-5 MM 9
Bill, Alfred H.	THE WOLF IN THE GARDEN	Lianne Carlin	5-3 MR 39
Bingham, John	MINISTRY OF DEATH	Allen J. Hubin	11-1 TAD 19
Bingham, John	MINISTRY OF DEATH	Steve Lewis	2-5 MF 26
Bioy-Casares, Adolfo & Jorge Luis Borges	SIX PROBLEMS FOR DON ISIDRO PARODI	Howard Lachtman	14-4 TAD 361
Bioy-Casares, Adolfo & Jorge Luis Borges	SIX PROBLEMS FOR DON ISIDRO PARODI	Gary Warren Niebuhr	4-5/6 PP 65
Bird, Al	MURDER SO REAL	Steve Lewis	3-1 MF 35
Birmingham, George A.	WILD JUSTICE	Charles Shibuk	7-1 TAD 54
Bishop, George	THE APPARITION	Mary A.Grochowski	2-5 PP 38
Bishop, Stacey	DEATH IN THE DARK	Amnon Kabatchnik	9-3 TAD 231
Black, Campbell	THE PUNCTUAL RAPE	Stanley Carlin	3-4 MR 35
Black, Gavin	A BIG WIND FOR SUMMER	Allen J. Hubin	9-3 TAD 225
Black, Gavin	THE GOLDEN COCKATRICE	Allen J. Hubin	8-3 TAD 228
Black, Ian Stuart	JOURNEY TO A SAFE PLACE	Steve Lewis	4-2 MF 39
Black, Ian Stuart	THE MAN ON THE BRIDGE	Allen J. Hubin	10-3 TAD 205
Black, Ian Stuart	THE MAN ON THE BRIDGE	Steve Lewis	2-1 MF 27
Black, Joey, & Dave Fisher	JOEY COLLECTS	Jose Mendez	2-2 M 55
Black, Lionel	THE LIFE AND DEATH OF PETER WADE	Allen J. Hubin	7-3 TAD 221
Black, Lionel	THE PENNY MURDERS	Robert C.S.Adey	5-5 MF 37
Black, Lionel	THE PENNY MURDERS	Fred Dueren	13-3 TAD 252
Black, Lionel	THE PENNY MURDERS	Steve Lewis	5-1 MF 23
Blackburn, John	BURY HIM DARKLY	Lianne Carlin	3-5 MR 21
Blackburn, John	CHILDREN OF THE NIGHT	Robert E. Washer	2-1 QC 17
Blair, Lucinda	THE PLACE OF DEVILS	Myrtis Broset	2-1 MF 37
Blake, Nicholas	A PENKNIFE IN MY HEART	Charles Shibuk	14-2 TAD 182
Blake, Nicholas	THE BEAST MUST DIE	Charles Shibuk	12-2 TAD 166
Blake, Nicholas	THE CORPSE IN THE SNOWMAN	Charles Shibuk	11-3 TAD 298
Blake, Nicholas	THE DEADLY JOKER	Barzun & Taylor	9-2 TAD 93
Blake, Nicholas	THE DREADFUL HOLLOW	Jeffery Koch	5-4 MF 33
Blake, Nicholas	END OF CHAPTER	Arthur C. Scott	9 MN R19
Blake, Nicholas	END OF CHAPTER	Charles Shibuk	10-3 TAD 239
Blake, Nicholas	THE PRIVATE WOUND	Charles Shibuk	14-3 TAD 266
Blake, Nicholas	THE SMILER WITH THE KNIFE	Charles Shibuk	12-2 TAD 166
Blake, Nicholas	THOU SHELL OF DEATH	Charles Shibuk	11-3 TAD 298
Blake, Nicholas	THE WIDOW'S CRUISE	Myrtis Broset	11 MN R2
Blake, Nicholas	THE WIDOW'S CRUISE	Charles Shibuk	10-3 TAD 239
Blake, Nicholas	THE WIDOW'S CRUISE	Arthur C. Scott	9 MN R19
Blake, Nicholas	THE WORM OF DEATH	Myrtis Broset	11 MN R2
Blanc, Suzanne	THE GREEN STONE	Robert M. Williams	1-5 MF 48
Blassingame, Wyatt	JOHN SMITH HEARS DEATH WALKING	Angelo Panagos	13-3 TAD 270
Blatty, Wm.Peter	THE EXORCIST	Len Moffatt	4-3 TAD 171
Blazer, J.S.	LEND A HAND	Allen J. Hubin	9-1 TAD 75
Bleeck, Oliver	THE BRASS Go-BETWEEN	Robert E. Washer	2-1 QC 17
Bleeck, Oliver	NO QUESTIONS ASKED	Pearl G. Aldrich	9-4 TAD 305
Bleeck, Oliver	NO QUESTIONS ASKED	Stan Burns	2-5 MM 6
Bleeck, Oliver	NO QUESTIONS ASKED	F.M.Nevins, Jr.	1-2 MF 14
Bleeck, Oliver	PROTOCOL FOR A KIDNAPPING	Robert E. Briney	5-4 MR 31

Bleiler, Everett F.	A TREASURY OF VICTORIAN DETECTIVE STORIES	Allen J. Hubin	12-3 TAD 203
Bleiler, Everett F.	BEST GHOST STORIES OF ALGERNON BLACKWOOD	Allen J. Hubin	7-3 TAD 192
Bleiler, Everett F.	THE CHECKLIST OF SCIENCE-FICTION AND SUPERNATURAL FICTION	Allen J. Hubin	12-2 TAD 117
Bleiler, Everett F.	THE CHECKLIST OF FANTASTIC LITERATURE	Lianne Carlin	5-4 MR 35
Bleiler, Everett F.	EIGHT DIME NOVELS	J.Randolph Cox	7-3 TAD 219
Bleiler, Everett F.	FIVE VICTORIAN GHOST NOVELS	Veronica M.Kennedy	7-2 TAD 139
Bloch, Robert	AMERICAN GOTHIC	Douglas M.Armato	7-4 TAD 293
Bloch, Robert	THE KING OF TERRORS	Allen J. Hubin	10-3 TAD 206
Bloch, Robert	THE KING OF TERRORS	Martin M. Wooster	1-6 MF 43
Bloch, Robert	OUT OF THE MOUTHS OF GRAVES	Allen J. Hubin	12-3 TAD 203
Bloch, Robert	SPIDERWEB	Bill Crider	1-3 PQ 49
Bloch, Robert	SUCH STUFF AS SCREAMS ARE MADE OF	Charles Shibuk	12-3 TAD 255
Bloch, Robert	SUCH STUFF AS SCREAMS ARE MADE OF	Martin M. Wooster	3-3 MF 44
Blochman, Lawrence G.	BOMBAY MAIL	F.M.Nevins, Jr.	6-4 TAD 271
Blochman, Lawrence G.	QUIET PLEASE, MURDER (film)	William K.Everson	5-4 TAD 206
Blochman, Lawrence G.	QUIET PLEASE, MURDER (film)	Andy Jaysnovitch	6 PE 19
Blochman, Lawrence G. & Hannah Lees	DEATH IN A DOLL'S HOUSE	Jay Jeffries	8 MN 23
Block, Lawrence	THE BURGLAR IN THE CLOSET	Steve Lewis	3-3 MF 38
Block, Lawrence	THE BURGLAR WHO LIKED TO QUOTE KIPLING	Mark Denning	1-3 M 21
Block, Lawrence	THE BURGLAR WHO LIKED TO QUOTE KIPLING	Allen J. Hubin	13-2 TAD 94
Block, Lawrence	THE BURGLAR WHO LIKED TO QUOTE KIPLING	Steve Lewis	3-6 MF 40
Block, Lawrence	THE BURGLAR WHO STUDIED SPINOZA	John Stevenson	3-1 M 38
Block, Lawrence	BURGLARS CAN'T BE CHOOSERS	Tamara Copenhafer	13/14 CL 12
Block, Lawrence	BURGLARS CAN'T BE CHOOSERS	Allen J. Hubin	11-2 TAD 118
Block, Lawrence	BURGLARS CAN'T BE CHOOSERS	Steve Lewis	2-4 MF 36
Block, Lawrence	IN THE MIDST OF DEATH	R. Jeff Banks	2-2 MM 3
Block, Lawrence	IN THE MIDST OF DEATH	Robert J. Randisi	11-2 TAD 121
Block, Lawrence	MONA	Steve Lewis	3-2 MF 38
Block, Lawrence	THE SINS OF THE FATHERS	Fred Dueren	10-1 TAD 52
Block, Lawrence	THE SINS OF THE FATHERS	Jeff Meyerson	1-2 MF 22
Block, Lawrence	THE SINS OF THE FATHERS	Steve Lewis	2-4 MF 30
Block, Lawrence	THE SINS OF THE FATHERS	Robert J. Randisi	11-2 TAD 121
Block, Thomas H.	MAYDAY	Richard Moskowitz	6/7 LR 4
Blom, K. Arne	THE MOMENT OF TRUTH	Allen J. Hubin	10-2 TAD 112
Blom, K. Arne	THE MOMENT OF TRUTH	Amnon Kabatchnik	1-4 MF 45
Bloodworth, Dennis	CROSSTALK	Allen J. Hubin	12-1 TAD 6
Bloom, Murray Teigh	THE 13th MAN	Allen J. Hubin	11-2 TAD 118
Blumberg, Gary	A KILLER IN MY MIND	Fred Dueren	9-1 TAD 50
Blythe, Robert C.	A BIBLIOGRAPHY OF THE WRITINGS OF EDWY SEARLES BROOKS	J.Randolph Cox	5-3 TAD 162
Bojarski, Richard, & Kenneth Beals	THE FILMS OF BORIS KARLOFF	Veronica M.Kennedy	8-3 TAD 224
Boland, John	NEGATIVE VALUE	Robert C.S.Adey	4-2 PP 27
Bond, Evelyn	THE VENETIAN SECRET	Myrtis Broset	2-5 MM 5
Bonnett, John & Emery	THE SOUND OF MURDER	Barzun & Taylor	9-3 TAD 209
Bonner, Paul, & Leonard Lewis	AGAIN - JACK THE RIPPER (TV)	Veronica M.Kennedy	7-1 TAD 58
Bonney, Joseph L.	DEATH BY DYNAMITE	Steve Lewis	8 MN 24
Booth, Charles C.	MURDER AT HIGH TIDE	Steve Lewis	3-4 MF 40
Boothby, Guy	A BID FOR FORTUNE	Douglas G. Greene	4-2 PP 24
Boothby, Guy	A BID FOR FORTUNE	Amnon Kabatchnik	6-2 TAD 117
Boothby, Guy	A BRIDE FROM THE SEA	Charles Shibuk	9-3 TAD 227
Borges, Jorge Luis & Adolfo Bioy-Casares	SIX PROBLEMS FOR DON ISIDRO PARODI	Howard Lachman	14-4 TAD 361
Borges, Jorge Luis & Adolfo Bioy-Casares	SIX PROBLEMS FOR DON ISIDRO PARODI	Gary Warren Niebuhr	4-5/6 PP 65

Borowitz, Albert	INNOCENCE AND ARSENIC	Allen J. Hubin	10-4 TAD 309
Bosworth, Allen R.	FULL CRASH DIVE	Amnon Kabatchnik	6-3 TAD 190
Boucher, Anthony	THE CASE OF THE BAKER STREET IRREGULARS	Walter Albert	4-1 PP 28
Boucher, Anthony	THE COMPLEAT WEREWOLF AND OTHER TALES OF FANTASY AND SCIENCE FICTION	J.R.Christopher	3-3 TAD 201
Boucher, Anthony	MULTIPLYING VILLAINIES	Allen J. Hubin	7-1 TAD 63
Boucher, Anthony	THE SEVEN OF CALVARY	Fred Dueren	5-5 MF 41
Bourgeau, Art	A LONELY WAY TO DIE	Steve Lewis	4-5 MF 29
Bourgeau, Art	THE MOST LIKELY SUSPECTS	William L. DeAndrea	14-4 TAD 378
Bourne, Michael, ed.	CORSAGE: A BOUQUET OF REX STOUT AND NERO WOLFE	James R. Skelton	1-1 G 52
Bova, Ben	THE MULTIPLE MAN	Myrtis Broset	2-1 MF 35
Bowen, John	AFTER THE RAIN	Gary Zachrich	62 PU 29
Bowen, Robert Sidney	BLACK LIGHTNING	Lynn Hickman	65 PU 26
Bowen, Robert Sidney	THE PURPLE TORNADO	Gary Zachrich	66 PU 55
Bowers, Dorothy	FEAR AND MISS BETONY	Jay Jeffries	3/4 MN 7
Box, Edgar	DEATH IN THE FIFTH POSITION	Amnon Kabatchnik	5-6 MR 35
Box, Roger	DEATH BENEATH JERUSALEM	Charles Shibuk	7-1 TAD 56
Boyd, Edward, & Bill Knox	THE VIEW FROM DANIEL PIKE	Robert C.S.Adey	4-5/6 PP 74
Boyd, Edward, & Bill Knox	THE VIEW FROM DANIEL PIKE	Barbara A. Buhrer	10 MN R14
Boyd, Edward, & Bill Knox	THE VIEW FROM DANIEL PIKE	Howard Waterhouse	3-1 MF 40
Boyer, Richard L.	THE GIANT RAT OF SUMATRA	Edward Lauterbach	10-1 TAD 63
Boyle, Robert	THE BABY SITTER	Allen J. Hubin	9-3 TAD 224
Bradbury, Ray	THE MARTIAN CHRONICLES	Nik Grant	26 X 12
Bradbury, Ray	THE SYNCHOPATED, TENNIS-SHOED, BEAST WITHIN OUR SHOWER	Nik Grant	36 X R17
Braddon, Mary E.	LADY AUDLEY'S SECRET	Veronica M.Kennedy	9-1 TAD 63
Bradley, Van Allen	BOOK COLLECTOR'S HANDBOOK OF VALUES	Allen J. Hubin	12-2 TAD 117
Brady, James	PARIS ONE	Jim Huang	11 CL 10
Braine, John	FINGER OF FIRE	Theodore Dukeshire	3-6 MF 45
Braine, John	THE PIOUS AGENT	Frank Denton	9 MN R5
Braine, John	THE PIOUS AGENT	Theodore Dukeshire	2-3 MF 52
Bramah, Ernest	BEST MAX CARRADOS DETECTIVE STORIES	Allen J. Hubin	6-1 TAD 45
Bramah, Ernest	BEST MAX CARRADOS DETECTIVE STORIES	William White	6-2 TAD 99
Bramah, Ernest	THE BRAVO OF LONDON	Charles Shibuk	8-2 TAD 139
Bramah, Ernest	MAX CARRADOS	William White	11-3 TAD 247
Brahms, Caryl	A BULLET IN THE BALLET	Barzun & Taylor	11-2 TAD 203
Brand, Christianna	DEATH OF JEZEBEL	Allen J. Hubin	10-1 TAD 5
Brand, Christianna	GREEN FOR DANGER	Maryell Cleary	3-2 PP 25
Brand, Christianna	GREEN FOR DANGER	Don D'Ammassa	8 MN 22
Brand, Christianna	GREEN FOR DANGER	James Mark Purcell	10-2 TAD 140
Brand, Christianna	GREEN FOR DANGER	Charles Shibuk	12-1 TAD 95
Brand, Christianna	GREEN FOR DANGER	Martin M. Wooster	2-6 MF 38
Brand, Christianna	STARRBELOW	Joe R. Christopher	12-2 TAD 180
Brand, Christianna	SUDDENLY AT HIS RESIDENCE	Maryell Cleary	3-2 PP 25
Brand, Christianna	SUDDENLY AT HIS RESIDENCE	Barry A. Pike	9-1 TAD 59
Brand, Max	INTERNES CAN'T TAKE MONEY (film)	William K.Everson	11-4 TAD 342
Brandner, Gary	THE HOWLING	Larry Rickert	4-1 PP 36
Branson, H.C.	LAST YEAR'S BLOOD	Charles Shibuk	8-1 TAD 55
Branston, Frank	AN UP AND COMING MAN	Steve Lewis	2-1 MF 25
Branston, Frank	SERGEANT RITCHIE'S CONSCIENCE	Steve Lewis	3-5 MF 35
Brautigan, Richard	WILLARD AND HIS BOWLING TROPHIES: A PERVERSE MYSTERY	Peter Wolfe	9-2 TAD 151
Brean, Herbert	THE CLOCK STRIKES THIRTEEN	Steve Lewis	3-4 MF 41
Brean, Herbert	THE TRACES OF BRILLHART	James Sandoe	8-4 TAD 299
Breen, Jon L.	THE GIRL IN THE PICTORIAL WRAPPER	Allen J. Hubin	6-1 TAD 45

Breen, Jon L.	WHAT ABOUT MURDER?	Marvin Lachman	5-4 MF 18
Breen, Jon L.	WHAT ABOUT MURDER?	Charles Shibuk	14-4 TAD 365
Breen, Jon L.	WHAT ABOUT MURDER?	Steve Stilwell	5-4 MF 28
Breen, Walter	THE DARKOVER CONCORDANCE	Michael L. Cook	6 U 40
Brennan, Joseph Payne	THE CASEBOOK OF LUCIUS LEFFING	Edward Lauterbach	6-4 TAD 259
Brennan, Joseph Payne	THE CHRONICLES OF LUCIUS LEFFING	Edward Lauterbach	11-1 TAD 24
Brennan, Joseph Payne & Donald M.Grant	ACT OF PROVIDENCE	Edward Lauterbach	12-4 TAD 370
Brent, Madeleine	STRANGER AT WILDINGS	Barbara A. Buhrer	1-10 MM 7
Breslin, Jimmy, & Dick Schapp	.44	Joe R. Lansdale	3-5 MF 43
Bretner, Reginald	A KILLING IN SWORDS	Steve Lewis	2-6 MF 31
Brett, John	WHO'D HIRE BRETT?	Steve Lewis	5-5 MF 23
Brett, Michael	DIAMOND KILL	Guy M. Townsend	2-5 MM 10
Brett, Michael	WE, THE KILLERS	Arthur C. Scott	1-10 MM 9
Brett, Simon	A COMEDIAN DIES	Allen J. Hubin	13-2 TAD 94
Brett, Simon	A COMEDIAN DIES	John Knoerle	1-1 M 21
Brett, Simon	A COMEDIAN DIES	Charles Shibuk	14-2 TAD 182
Brett, Simon	AN AMATEUR CORPSE	Barzun & Taylor	12-3 TAD 262
Brett, Simon	AN AMATEUR CORPSE	Charles Shibuk	13-4 TAD 362
Brett, Simon	CAST, IN ORDER OF DISAPPEARANCE	Steve Lewis	1-1 MF 29
Brett, Simon	CAST, IN ORDER OF DISAPPEARANCE	Charles Shibuk	12-3 TAD 255
Brett, Simon	THE DEAD SIDE OF THE MIKE	Allen J. Hubin	14-2 TAD 124
Brett, Simon	THE DEAD SIDE OF THE MIKE	F.M.Nevins, Jr.	5-2 MF 28
Brett, Simon	SO MUCH BLOOD	Allen J. Hubin	10-3 TAD 204
Brett, Simon	SO MUCH BLOOD	Charles Shibuk	12-4 TAD 368
Brett, Simon	SO MUCH BLOOD	Guy M. Townsend	1-5 MF 37
Brett, Simon	SOME DIE HARD	Bill Crider	4-4 PP 30
Brett, Simon	SOME DIE HARD	Andy Jaysnovitch	7 PE 14
Brett, Simon	STAR TRAP	Allen J. Hubin	11-4 TAD 333
Brett, Simon	STAR TRAP	Steve Lewis	2-5 MF 27
Brett, Simon	STAR TRAP	Charles Shibuk	13-3 TAD 250
Brewer, Gil	ANGEL	Bill Crider	5-6 MF 47
Briney, Robert E., & Edward Wood	SF BIBLIOGRAPHIES	Allen J. Hubin	6-1 TAD 45
Bristow, Gwen, & Bruce Manning	THE GUTENBERG MURDERS	Jim McCahery	2-6 PP 31
Bristow, Gwen, & Bruce Manning	THE INVISIBLE HOST	Barzun & Taylor	9-2 TAD 93
Bristow, Gwen, & Bruce Manning	THE INVISIBLE HOST	Jim McCahery	2-6 PP 31
Bristow, Gwen, & Bruce Manning	THE NINTH QUEST	R.L.Wenstrup	4-1 PP 29
Brobert, Jan	MORDISK FAMILJEBOK (Swedish)	Allen J. Hubin	7-2 TAD 143
Brobert, Jan, ed.	SPIONEN I SPEGELN (Swedish)	Allen J. Hubin	8-2 TAD 151
Brock, Alan	THE BROWNS OF THE YARD	Barzun & Taylor	12-1 TAD 32
Brock, Lynn	THE SLIP-CARRIAGE MYSTERY	Charles Shibuk	12-2 TAD 189
Bronte, Louisa	MOONLIGHT AT GREYSTONE	Steve Lewis	1-1 MF 31
Brookes, Owen	INHERITANCE	Joyce L. Dewes	3-1 M 39
Brosnan, John	JAMES BOND IN THE CINEMA	Lianne Carlin	5-5 MR 37
Brothers, Jay	OX	Allen J. Hubin	9-1 TAD 75
Brown, Carter	THE COFFIN BIRD	Stephen Mertz	2 PE 23
Brown, Carter	THE DEADLY KITTEN	Stephen Mertz	3-2 MF 47
Brown, Carter	DONOVAN'S DELIGHT	Stephen Mertz	3-6 MF 47
Brown, Carter	THE INVISIBLE FLAMINI	Steve Lewis	3-5 MF 38
Brown, Carter	THE MASTER	Lianne Carlin	6-1 MR 47
Brown, Carter	NEGATIVE IN BLUE	Stephen Mertz	1-4 MF 48
Brown, Carter	THE SAVAGE SISTERS	Fred Dueren	9-4 TAD 277
Brown, Carter	THE SEX CLINIC	Lianne Carlin	4-5 MR 37
Brown, Carter	THE STRAWBERRY-BLONDE JUNGLE	Steve Lewis	3-6 MF 35
Brown, Carter	THE STRIPPER	Steve Lewis	1-5 MF 34
Brown, Carter	THE WANTON	Steve Lewis	1A MF 26
Brown, Carter	WHERE DID CHARITY GO?	Stephen Mertz	12-1 TAD 77
Brown, Fredric	THE BEST OF FREDRIC BROWN	Charles Shibuk	10-4 TAD 360
Brown, Fredric	NIGHT OF THE JABBERWOCK	Steve Lewis	3-6 MF 40

Brown, Fredric	WE ALL KILLED GRANDMA	Steve Lewis	1-2 MF 24
Brown, Fredric	WHAT MAD UNIVERSE	Charles Shibuk	12-2 TAD 166
Brown, Himan	STRANGE TALES FROM CBS RADIO	Fred Dueren	10-2 TAD 130
Brown, Jerry Earl	UNDER THE CITY OF ANGELS	J.Grant Thiessen	14 SF 19
Browne, Howard	THE TASTE OF ASHES	James Sandoe	11-1 TAD 85
Browne, Pat, & Ray B. Browne, L.N.Landrum	DIMENSIONS OF DETECTIVE FICTION	Allen J. Hubin	10-1 TAD 5
Browne, Pat, & Ray B. Browne, L.N.Landrum	DIMENSIONS OF DETECTIVE FICTION	George Kelley	1-4 MF 50
Bruccoli, Matthew J.	KENNETH MILLAR/ROSS MACDONALD: A CHECKLIST	Lianne Carlin	5-2 MR 45
Bruccoli, Matthew J.	RAYMOND CHANDLER: A CHECKLIST	William White	2-1 MR 7
Bruccoli, Matthew J.	RAYMOND CHANDLER: A DESCRIPTIVE BIBLIOGRAPHY	F.M.Nevins, Jr.	1-2 C 133
Bruccoli, Matthew J.	RAYMOND CHANDLER: A DESCRIPTIVE BIBLIOGRAPHY	F.M.Nevins, Jr.	3-6 MF 49
Bruce, Leo	CASE FOR SERGEANT BEEF	Joyce L. Dewes	2-2 M 55
Bruce, Leo	CASE FOR THREE DETECTIVES	Maryell Cleary	4-5/6 PP 68
Bruce, Leo	CASE FOR THREE DETECTIVES	Fred Dueren	14-1 TAD 80
Bruce, Leo	CASE FOR THREE DETECTIVES	Charles Shibuk	14-2 TAD 182
Bruce, Leo	CASE WITH ROPES AND RINGS	Maryell Cleary	4-5/6 PP 68
Bruce, Leo	CASE WITH ROPES AND RINGS	Charles Shibuk	14-4 TAD 376
Bruce, Leo	COLD BLOOD	Barzun & Taylor	12-1 TAD 32
Bruce, Leo	COLD BLOOD	Charles Shibuk	1-1 MF 34
Bruce, Leo	DEATH IN ALBERT PARK	Allen J. Hubin	13-1 TAD 27
Bruce, Leo	DEATH IN ALBERT PARK	Steve Lewis	4-2 MF 35
Bruce, Leo	DEATH IN ALBERT PARK	Jim McCahery	3-2 PP 26
Bruce, Leo	DEATH ON ALLHALLOWE'EN	Barzun & Taylor	9-3 TAD 209
Bruce, Leo	NECK AND NECK	Barzun & Taylor	12-1 TAD 32
Bruce, Leo	SERGEANT BEEF	Elizabeth Wentworth	2-2 M 55
Brunner, John	BEDLAM PLANET	Hickman & Zachrich	69 PU 34
Bryant, Will	BLUE RUSSELL	Allen J. Hubin	10-2 TAD 113
Bryczynski, Terry	CAGED	M.S.Cappadonna	13-4 TAD 352
Bryczynski, Terry	CAGED	Allen J. Hubin	14-2 TAD 124
Bryczynski, Terry	CAGED	Samuel Sanders	2-1 M 28
Buchan, John	MOUNTAIN MEADOW	Don D'Ammassa	1 MN 8
Buchan, John	THE THIRTY-NINE STEPS	Charles Shibuk	11-4 TAD 403
Buchan, John	THE THIRTY-NINE STEPS	Martin M. Wooster	2-6 MF 36
Buchan, Stuart	FLEECED	Allen J. Hubin	8-3 TAD 226
Buchanan, Patrick	A MURDER OF CROWS	Steve Lewis	1-1 MF 28
Buchanan, Patrick	A PARLIAMENT OF OWLS	J.Randolph Cox	5-1 MR 31
Buchanan, Patrick	A REQUIEM OF SHARKS	Allen J. Hubin	7-2 TAD 142
Buchloh, Paul Gerhard & Jens P.Becker,ed.	DER DETEKTIVERSAHLUNG AUF DER SPUR: ESSAYS ZUR FORM UND WERTUNG DER ENGLISCHEN DETEKTIVLITERATUR	Barzun & Taylor	11-1 TAD 92
Buckingham, Nancy	RETURN TO VIENNA	Don D'Ammassa	3/4 MN 19
Buckley, John	BEYOND MURDER	Donna Willoby	2-1 M 26
Buckley, Robert John	THE MASTER SPY	Douglas G. Greene	12-3 TAD 230
Buckley, William F.Jr.	SAVING THE QUEEN	Amnon Kabatchnik	9 CL 3
Buckley, William F.Jr.	SAVING THE QUEEN	Amnon Kabatchnik	9-3 TAD 218
Buckley, William F.Jr.	SAVING THE QUEEN	Marvin Lachman	4-3 PP 25
Buckley, William F.Jr.	SAVING THE QUEEN	Martin M. Wooster	1-? PP 24
Buckley, William F.Jr.	STAINED GLASS	Barbara A.Buhrer	13 MN R2
Buckley, William F.Jr.	STAINED GLASS	Allen J. Hubin	11-4 TAD 333
Buckley, William F.Jr.	STAINED GLASS	Martin M. Wooster	2-6 PP 38
Bugliosi, Vincent	HELTER SKELTER: THE TRUE STORY OF THE MANSON MURDERS	Veronica M.Kennedy	8-2 TAD 144
Bugliosi, Vincent	TILL DEATH DO US PART	Mary A.Grochowski	2-6 PP 34
Bullough, Vern L. & Bonnie L.Bullough	PROSTITUTION: AN ILLUSTRATED SOCIAL HISTORY	D.E.Ath	2-1 PP 14
Bulmer, Kenneth	THE WIZARDS OF SENCHURIA	Gary Zachrich	74 PU 23
Bunn, Thomas	CLOSET BONES	Steve Lewis	2-3 MF 46
Burack, A.S.	WRITING SUSPENSE AND MYSTERY FICTION	Allen J. Hubin	10-4 TAD 308

Burack, A.S.	WRITING SUSPENSE AND MYSTERY FICTION	George Kelley	2-2 MF 39
Burger, Margaret A., & Robt.B.Harmon	AN ANNOTATED GUIDE TO THE WORKS OF DOROTHY L. SAYERS	Allen J. Hubin	10-3 TAD 206
Burger, Neal, & Geo. E. Simpson	THIN AIR	David Bates	4-4 PP 29
Burgess, M.R., & Robert Reginald	CUMULATIVE PAPERBACK INDEX 1939-1959	Charlotte Laughlin	4-2 PQ 46
Burgess, M.R., & Robert Reginald	CUMULATIVE PAPERBACK INDEX 1939-1959	Billy C. Lee	1-1 PQ 39
Burgess, M.R., & Robert Reginald	CUMULATIVE PAPERBACK INDEX 1939-1959	William Lyles	2-2 PQ 37
Burke, J.F.	DEATH TRICK	Robert E. Washer	21 X 54
Burke, J.F.	DEATH TRICK	Allen J. Hubin	91- TAD 74
Burke, J.F.	THE KAMA SUTRA TANGO	Steve Lewis	2-1 MF 22
Burke, J.F.	KELLY AMONG THE NIGHTINGALES	Jim McCahery	5 PE 40
Burke, J.F.	KELLY AMONG THE NIGHTINGALES	Jim McCahery	6 PE 21
Burke, J.F.	LOCATION SHOTS	Allen J. Hubin	7-3 TAD 221
Burke, John	THE BLACK CHARADE	Allen J. Hubin	11-1 TAD 18
Burkholz, Herbert, & Clifford Irving	THE DEATH FREAK	Carl Hoffman	13-2 TAD 147
Burleigh, Clarence B.	WITH PICKPOLE AND PEAVEY	C.L.Messecar	3-4 BC 372
Burleigh, Clarence B.	THE YOUNG GUIDE	C.L.Messecar	3-2 BC 320
Burley, W.J.	THREE-TOED PUSEY	Jeff Meyerson	1-6 MF 52
Burley, W.J.	TO KILL A CAT	Mary Groff	1-4 PP 28
Burley, W.J.	WYCLIFFE AND THE SCAPEGOAT	Steve Lewis	3-6 MF 38
Burley, W.J.	WYCLIFFE AND THE SCHOOLGIRLS	Steve Lewis	1A MF 29
Burnett, W.R.	BEAST OF THE CITY (film)	William K.Everson	8-1 TAD 110
Burnett, W.R.	DOCTOR SOCRATES (film)	William K.Everson	9-1 TAD 51
Burnett, W.R.	GOODBYE, CHICAGO	F.M.Nevins, Jr.	5-3 MF 38
Burns, Rex	THE ALVAREZ JOURNAL	Stan Burns	1-6 MM 9
Burns, Rex	THE ALVAREZ JOURNAL	Steve Lewis	1A MF 28
Burns, Rex	ANGLE OF ATTACK	Allen J. Hubin	13-1 TAD 27
Burns, Rex	ANGLE OF ATTACK	Charles Shibuk	14-2 TAD 182
Burns, Rex	THE FARNSWORTH SCORE	Steve Lewis	1-5 MF 29
Burns, Rex	SPEAK FOR THE DEAD	Allen J. Hubin	11-4 TAD 332
Burns, Rex	SPEAK FOR THE DEAD	Steve Lewis	3-1 MF 34
Burns, Rex	SPEAK FOR THE DEAD	Charles Shibuk	13-2 TAD 135
Burns, Robert	I AM A FUGITIVE FROM A CHAIN GANG (film)	James Mark Purcell	11-2 TAD 128
Burroughs, Edgar Rice	JOHN CARTER, WARLORD OF MARS (comicbook)	Kirk McConnell	1-2 WA 7
Burroughs, Edgar Rice	TARZAN, LORD OF THE JUNGLE (comicbook)	Kirk McConnell	1-2 WA 7
Burt, Michael	THE CASE OF THE ANGELS' TRUMPETS	L.F.Ashley	7-4 TAD 285
Burton, Miles	THE MAN WITH THE TATTOOED FACE	Steve Lewis	4-4 MF 41
Burton, Miles	THE SECRET OF HIGH ELDERSHAM	Amnon Kabatchnik	6-3 TAD 190
Busby, F.M.	RISSA KERGUELEN	Sheldon A.Wiebe	5 SF 38
Busby, Roger	NEW FACE IN HELL	Charles Shibuk	4-5/6 PP 75
Bush, Christopher	THE CASE OF THE COUNTERFEIT COLONEL	Steve Lewis	1-4 MF 39
Bush, Christopher	THE CASE OF THE TUDOR QUEEN	Maryell Cleary	3-2 PP 28
Butler, Ragan	CAPTAIN NASH AND THE HONOR OF ENGLAND	Stan Burns	13 MN R3
Butler, Ragan	CAPTAIN NASH AND THE HONOR OF ENGLAND	Steve Lewis	2-2 MF 34
Butler, Ragan	CAPTAIN NASH AND THE WROTH INHERITANCE	Stan Burns	13 MN R3
Butler, Ragan	CAPTAIN NASH AND THE WROTH INHERITANCE	Allen J. Hubin	10-3 TAD 205
Butler, Ragan	CAPTAIN NASH AND THE WROTH INHERITANCE	Steve Lewis	2-3 MF 46

Butler, William V.	THE DURABLE DESPERADOES: A CRITICAL STUDY OF SOME ENDURING HEROES	Allen J. Hubin	7-2 TAD 108
Butler, William V.	THE DURABLE DESPERADOES: A CRITICAL STUDY OF SOME ENDURING HEROES	F.M.Nevins, Jr.	8-1 TAD 63
Butterworth, Michael	THE MAN IN THE SOPWITH CAMEL	Allen J. Hubin	8-3 TAD 229
Butterworth, Michael	REMAINS TO BE SEEN	Steve Lewis	2-4 MF 35
Butterworth, Michael	X MARKS THE SPOT	Steve Lewis	3-1 MF 35
Byers, Charles Alma	THE INVERNESS MURDER	Hal Brodsky	9-3 TAD 230
Byfield, Barbara N.	A PARCEL OF THEIR FORTUNES	Steve Lewis	4-2 MF 38
Byfield, Barbara N.	FOREVER WILT THOU DIE	Steve Lewis	2-5 MF 32
Byfield, Barbara N.	SOLEMN HIGH MURDER	Allen J. Hubin	8-3 TAD 226
Byrd, Max	CALIFORNIA THRILLER	Steve Lewis	5-5 MF 22
Byrom, James	OR BE HE DEAD	James Sandoe	9-2 TAD 154
Caesar, Arthur	MANHATTAN MELODRAMA (film)	William K. Everson	7-1 TAD 3
Cade, Paul	DEATH SLAMS THE DOOR	Hal Brodsky	8-2 TAD 140
Caidin, Martin	THE GOD MACHINE	Gary Zachrich	71 PU 21
Caillou, Alan	DIAMONDS WILD	Fred Dueren	12-3 TAD 287
Cain, James M.	THE INSTITUTE	Amnon Kabatchnik	6 CL 8
Cain, James M.	MILDRED PIERCE	Charles Shibuk	11-3 TAD 298
Cain, James M.	OBSESSIONS (film)	James Mark Purcell	9-2 TAD 134
Cain, James M.	THE POSTMAN ALWAYS RINGS TWICE (film)	Thomas Godfrey	3-2 M 46
Cain, James M.	RAINBOW'S END	Allen J. Hubin	8-3 TAD 229
Cain, James M.	SERENADE	Charles Shibuk	11-3 TAD 298
Cain, Paul	FAST ONE	Theodore Dukeshire	6 PE 18
Cain, Paul	SEVEN SLAYERS	Theodore Dukeshire	6 PE 18
Cake, Patrick	THE PRO-AM MURDERS	Phyllis Baxter	1-2 M 21
Callison, Brian	AN ACT OF WAR	Allen J. Hubin	11-1 TAD 18
Cameron, Ian	THE WHITE SHIP	J.Randolph Cox	10-3 TAD 208
Cameron, Lou	BEHIND THE SCARLET DOOR	Lianne Carlin	5-3 MR 39
Cameron, Lou	FILE ON A MISSING REDHEAD	Charles Shibuk	3-1 MF 40
Campbell, Angus	SCOTTISH TALES OF TERROR	Veronica M.Kennedy	8-1 TAD 60
Campbell, Karen	THUNDER ON SUNDAY	Lianne Carlin	5-5 MR 35
Campbell, Keith	GOODBYE GORGEOUS	Steve Lewis	5-2 MF 18
Campbell, R.Wright	CIRCUS COURONNE	Allen J. Hubin	11-3 TAD 230
Campbell, R.Wright	CIRCUS COURONNE	Charles Shibuk	12-3 TAD 255
Campbell, R.Wright	THE SPY WHO SAT AND WAITED	Allen J. Hubin	8-3 TAD 225
Campbell, R.Wright	THE SPY WHO SAT AND WAITED	Charles Shibuk	12-3 TAD 255
Campbell, Scott	THE UNPAID RANSOM (film)	William K.Everson	2-1 TAD 28
Canler, L.	AUTOBIOGRAPHY OF A FRENCH DETECTIVE	Allen J. Hubin	10-2 TAD 114
Cannan, Joanna	BODY IN THE BECK	Mary Groff	1-4 PP 25
Cannan, Joanna	DEATH AT "THE DOG"	Maryell Cleary	3-4 PP 30
Cannan, Joanna	THEY RANG UP THE POLICE	Mary Groff	2-3 PP 26
Canning, John, ed.	50 GREAT GHOST STORIES	Veronica M.Kennedy	7-4 TAD 291
Canning, Victor	BIRDCAGE	Barbara A.Buhrer	13 MN R1
Canning, Victor	BIRDCAGE	Charles Shibuk	14-1 TAD 79
Canning, Victor	FALL FROM GRACE	Dorothy B.Hughes	3-1 M 36
Canning, Victor	THE GREAT AFFAIR	Marvin Lachman	3-4 MR 32
Canning, Victor	THE KINGSFORD MARK	Barbara A.Buhrer	2-5 MM 6
Canning, Victor	MASK OF MEMORY	Barbara A.Buhrer	1-7 MM 7
Canning, Victor	THE WHIP HAND	Fred Dueren	13-2 TAD 136
Canning, Victor	THE WHIP HAND	Charles Shibuk	13-2 TAD 135
Carey, Constance	THE CHEKHOV PROPOSAL	Barbara A.Buhrer	2-3 MM 3
Carkeet, David	DOUBLE NEGATIVE	Allen J. Hubin	14-2 TAD 124
Carmichael, Harry	NAKED TO THE GRAVE	Amnon Kabatchnik	6-1 MR 42
Carmichael, Harry	REMOTE CONTROL	Larry Shaw	4-4 MR 34
Carmichael, Harry	TWO LATE FOR TEARS	Barzun & Taylor	10-2 TAD 126
Carr, A.H.Z.	FINDING MAUBEE	Barzun & Taylor	9-2 TAD 93
Carr, Glynn	SWING AWAY, CLIMBER	James Mark Purcell	10-4 TAD 315
Carr, John Dickson	BELOW SUSPICION	Charles Shibuk	11-3 TAD 298
Carr, John Dickson	CAPTAIN CUT-THROAT	Charles Shibuk	14-1 TAD 79

Carr, John Dickson	THE CROOKED HINGE	Jeff Meyerson	1-4 MF 41
Carr, John Dickson	THE CROOKED HINGE	Charles Shibuk	11-1 TAD 23
Carr, John Dickson	THE CROOKED HINGE	Martin M. Wooster	1-4 MF 41
Carr, John Dickson	DEADLY HALL	Don Miller	11 MN R18
Carr, John Dickson	THE DOOR TO DOOM AND OTHER DETECTIONS	Allen J. Hubin	14-1 TAD 17
Carr, John Dickson	THE DOOR TO DOOM AND OTHER DETECTIONS	Steve Lewis	4-5 MF 35
Carr, John Dickson	THE DOOR TO DOOM AND OTHER DETECTIONS	David Skene-Melvin	11 SF 47
Carr, John Dickson	THE EIGHT OF SWORDS	Marvin Lachman	7-4 TAD 285
Carr, John Dickson	FIRE, BURN!	Charles Shibuk	11-3 TAD 298
Carr, John Dickson	THE GHOST'S HIGH NOON	Don Miller	2-5 MM 8
Carr, John Dickson	THE GHOST'S HIGH NOON	Robert E. Washer	2-1 QC 17
Carr, John Dickson	HAG'S NOOK	Guy M. Townsend	1A MF 35
Carr, John Dickson	HE WHO WHISPERS	Charles Shibuk	9-3 TAD 208
Carr, John Dickson	HE WHO WHISPERS	Charles Shibuk	14-1 TAD 79
Carr, John Dickson	THE HUNGRY GOBLIN: A VICTORIAN DETECTIVE NOVEL	James Sandoe	14-4 TAD 366
Carr, John Dickson	THE MEN WHO EXPLAINED MIRACLES	Lianne Carlin	3-6 MR 24
Carr, John Dickson	THE MEN WHO EXPLAINED MIRACLES	Mary A.Grochowski	1-3 PP 25
Carr, John Dickson	PAPA LA-BAS	Len Moffatt, (verse)	2-2 MR 6
Carr, John Dickson	PAPA LA-BAS	Robert E. Washer	1-4 QC 19
Carr, John Dickson	THE PROBLEM OF THE GREEN CAPSULE	Charles Shibuk	9-4 TAD 281
Carr, John Dickson	SCANDAL AT HIGH CHIMNEYS	Jeffery Koch	5-4 MF 32
Carr, John Dickson	THE SLEEPING SPHINX	Steve Lewis	2-5 MF 34
Carr, John Dickson	THE THREE COFFINS	Barzun & Taylor	13-3 TAD 208
Carr, John Dickson	THE THREE COFFINS	Douglas G. Greene	13-3 TAD 248
Carr, John Dickson, & Adrian Conan Doyle	THE EXPLOITS OF SHERLOCK HOLMES	Douglas G. Greene	12-3 TAD 233
Carr, John Dickson, & Adrian Conan Doyle	THE EXPLOITS OF SHERLOCK HOLMES	Charles Shibuk	9-4 TAD 334
Carr, Nick	AMERICA'S SECRET SERVICE ACE	Will Murray	1 D 20
Carrel, Mark	THE EMERALD	Steve Lewis	4-4 MF 36
Carroll, Robert	A DISAPPEARANCE	Barbara A. Buhrer	1-6 MM 9
Carroll, Robert	A DISAPPEARANCE	Stan Burns	1-6 MM 9
Carson, Robert	THE GOLDEN YEARS CAPER	Jon L. Breen	5-3 MR 38
Carter, Ashley	PANAMA	Judy Crider	1-4 PQ 51
Carter, Diana	GHOST WRITER	Barbara A. Buhrer	9 MN R2
Carter, Lin	INVISIBLE DEATH	Arn McConnell	1-2 WA 7
Carter, Lin	THE NEMESIS OF EVIL	Arn McConnell	1-2 WA 7
Carter, Lin	TOWER OF THE MEDUSA	Gary Zachrich	74 PU 25
Carter, Lin	THE VOLCANO OGRE	Arn McConnell	1-2 WA 7
Carter, Lin	THE VOLCANO OGRE	Martin M. Wooster	10 MN R7
Carter, Lin	THE NEMESIS OF EVIL	Martin M. Wooster	2 MN 8
Carter, Lin	THE INVISIBLE DEATH	Martin M. Wooster	9 MN R11
Carter, Nicholas	THE STOLEN PAY TRAIN	J.Randolph Cox	9-1 TAD 63
Carter, Nick	DAY OF THE DINGO	Fred Dueren	13-4 TAD 361
Carter, Nick	NICK CARTER'S 100 (DR.DEATH and RUN, SPY, RUN)	Fred Dueren	9-1 TAD 51
Carter, Nick	SUICIDE SEAT	Steve Lewis	4-5 MF 32
Carter, Youngman	MR. CAMPION'S FARTHING	James Keddie,Jr.	2-4 TAD 274
Carvic, Heron	ODDS ON MISS SEETON	Barbara A. Buhrer	10 MN R2
Carvic, Heron	ODDS ON MISS SEETON	Allen J. Hubin	9-2 TAD 153
Carvic, Heron	MISS SEETON SINGS	Allen J. Hubin	6-3 TAD 191
Carvic, Heron	PICTURE MISS SEETON	Steve Lewis	1-4 MF 38
Case, David	THE CELL	Lianne Carlin	3-1 MR 7
Casey, Robert J.	NEWS REEL	Charles Shibuk	12-2 TAD 190
Caspary, Vera	EVVIE	Jane S. Bakerman	1-4 PP 24
Caspary, Vera	LAURA	Lianne Carlin	3-3 MR 31
Cassidy, John	STATION IN THE DELTA	Allen J. Hubin	13-2 TAD 94
Casson, Stanley	MURDER BY BURIAL	Barzun & Taylor	9-3 TAD 209
Cawelti, John G.	ADVENTURE, MYSTERY, AND ROMANCE: FORMULA STORIES AS ART AND POPULAR CULTURE	J.W.Scheideman	9-4 TAD 304
Cecil, Henry	A WOMAN NAMED ANNE	Robert C.S.Adey	3-3 PP 30

Cecil, Henry	THE ASKING PRICE	Robert C.S. Adey	3-5 PP 36
Cecil, Henry	BRIEF TALES FROM THE BENCH	Robert C.S. Adey	4-4 PP 26
Cecil, Henry	NATURAL CAUSES	Barzun & Taylor	14-3 TAD 228
Cecil, Henry	TELL YOU WHAT I'LL DO	Robert E. Briney	3-4 MR 9
Cecil, Henry	TELL YOU WHAT I'LL DO	Robert E. Briney	5-5 MF 38
Chaber, M.E.	A HEARSE OF ANOTHER COLOR	Myrtis Broset	12 MN A11
Chaber, M.E.	A HEARSE OF ANOTHER COLOR	Arthur C. Scott	1-8 MM 7
Chaber, M.E.	A HEARSE OF ANOTHER COLOR	Arthur C. Scott	12 MN A11
Chaber, M.E.	THE BONDED DEAD	Arthur C. Scott	12 MN A11
Chaber, M.E.	DON'T GET CAUGHT	Arthur C. Scott	12 MN A12
Chaber, M.E.	THE FLAMING MAN	Myrtis Broset	12 MN A11
Chaber, M.E.	THE GALLOWS GARDEN	Arthur C. Scott	12 MN A11
Chaber, M.E.	HANGMAN'S HARVEST	Don Miller	12 MN A13
Chaber, M.E.	THE MAN INSIDE	Don Miller	12 MN A13
Chaber, M.E.	NO GRAVE FOR MARCH	Don Miller	12 MN A13
Chaber, M.E.	NOW IT'S MY TURN	Arthur C. Scott	12 MN A11
Chaber, M.E.	SIX WHO RAN	Arthur C. Scott	12 MN A12
Chaber, M.E.	SOFTLY IN THE NIGHT	Arthur C. Scott	12 MN A12
Chacko, David, & Dick Allen	DETECTIVE FICTION: CRIME AND COMPROMISE	Donald J. Pattow	7-3 TAD 218
Chadwick, Lester	THE WINNING TOUCHDOWN	C.L.Messecar	3-4 BC 373
Challis, Mary	CRIMES PAST	Steve Lewis	5-2 MF 24
Chambers, Dana	SOME DAY I'LL KILL YOU	Robert Samoian	4-6 MF 34
Chambers, Dana	SOME DAY I'LL KILL YOU	Charles Shibuk	7-4 TAD 288
Chambers, Robert W.	MR. KEEN, TRACER OF LOST PERSONS	J.Randolph Cox	4-4 TAD 236
Chambers, Robert	THE NEON PREACHER	Steve Lewis	2-3 MF 45
Chambers, William E.	DEATH TOLL	Robert J. Randisi	9-5 TAD 305
Champigny, Robert	WHAT WILL HAVE HAPPENED: A PHILOSOPHICAL AND TECHNICAL ESSAY ON MYSTERY STORIES	Walter Albert	5-4 MF 28
Champigny, Robert	WHAT WILL HAVE HAPPENED: A PHILOSOPHICAL AND TECHNICAL ESSAY ON MYSTERY STORIES	Gregory S.Sojka	1-2 C 132
Chandler, Raymond	THE BIG SLEEP	James Sandoe	13-4 TAD 293
Chandler, Raymond	THE BLUE DAHLIA	Barzun & Taylor	9-4 TAD 271
Chandler, Raymond	THE BLUE DAHLIA (film)	Jon L. Lellenberg	9-4 TAD 302
Chandler, Raymond:	FAREWELL, MY LOVELY (film)	Joseph W. Smith	9-1 TAD 65
Chandler, Raymond	THE LADY IN THE LAKE	Jon L. Lellenberg	9-4 TAD 302
Chandler, Raymond	THE LADY IN THE LAKE	Stephen Mertz	3-2 MF 47
Charbonneau, Louis	INTRUDER	D.E.Ath	2-2 PP 14
Charbonneau, Louis	THE LAIR	Fred Dueren	13-3 TAD 252
Charles, Robert	A CLASH OF HAWKS	Steve Lewis	1A MF 23
Charney, Hanna	THE DETECTIVE NOVEL OF MANNERS: HEDONIST MORALITY AND THE LIFE OF REASON	Meera T. Clark	2-2 C 156
Charteris, Leslie	CATCH THE SAINT	Allen J. Hubin	9-1 TAD 73
Charteris, Leslie	THE SAINT AND THE FICTION MAKERS	Don Miller	1-6 MM 10
Charteris, Leslie	THE SAINT AND THE PEOPLE IMPORTERS	J.Randolph Cox	5-3 MR 33
Charteris, Leslie	THE SAINT AND THE TEMPLAR TREASURE	Steve Lewis	3-6 MF 31
Charteris, Leslie	THE SAINT IN NEW YORK	Jeff Meyerson	1-5 MF 46
Charteris, Leslie	THE SAINT INTERVENES	Charles Shibuk	14-3 TAD 266
Charteris, Leslie	THE SAINT MEETS THE TIGER	Charles Shibuk	14-1 TAD 79
Charteris, Leslie	THE SAINT TO THE RESCUE	Charles Shibuk	13-4 TAD 362
Charteris, Leslie	THE WHITE RIDER	Maryell Cleary	3-4 PP 29
Charyn, Jerome	THE EDUCATION OF PATRICK SILVER	Paul Harwitz	3-1 M 39
Chase, James Hadley	A CAN OF WORMS	Theodore Dukeshire	3-6 MF 44
Chase, James Hadley	CONSIDER YOURSELF DEAD	Theodore Dukeshire	2-6 MF 40
Chase, James Hadley	MY LAUGH COMES LAST	Theodore Dukeshire	2-3 MF 51
Chase, James Hadley	NO ORCHIDS FOR MISS BLANDISH	Amnon Kabatchnik	8-4 TAD 298
Chase, James Hadley	NO ORCHIDS FOR MISS BLANDISH	Jim McCahery	1 PE 14
Chase, James Hadley	YOU MUST BE KIDDING	Theodore Dukeshire	3-6 MF 44
Chastain, Thomas	DIAMOND EXCHANGE	Jim Fixx	14-3 TAD 269

Chastain, Thomas	VITAL STATISTICS	Larry L. French	11-2 TAD 123
Chastain, Thomas	VITAL STATISTICS	Steve Lewis	2-3 MF 44
Chesbro, George C.	CITY OF WHISPERING STONE	Allen J. Hubin	11-4 TAD 331
Chesbro, George C.	CITY OF WHISPERING STONE	Steve Lewis	3-1 MF 33
Chesbro, George C.	SHADOW OF A BROKEN MAN	George Kelley	2-1 MF 42
Chesbro, George C.	SHADOW OF A BROKEN MAN	Charles Shibuk	12-1 TAD 30
Chesney, Kellow	THE VICTORIAN UNDERWORLD	Luther Norris	4-5 MR 39
Chesney, Kellow	THE VICTORIAN UNDERWORLD	Guy M. Townsend	1A MF 34
Chester, S. Beach	THE ARSENE LEPINE-HERLOCK SOAMES AFFAIR	Allen J. Hubin	9-4 TAD 311
Chesterton, G.K.	THE INCREDULITY OF FATHER BROWN	Jon L. Lellenberg	9-1 TAD 71
Chesterton, G.K.	THE ONNOCENCE OF FATHER BROWN	Jon L. Lellenberg	9-1 TAD 71
Chesterton, G.K.	THE SECRET OF FATHER BROWN	Jon L. Lellenberg	9-1 TAD 71
Chesterton, G.K.	THE WISDOM OF FATHER BROWN	Jon L. Lellenberg	9-1 TAD 71
Chevigny, Paul	CRIMINAL MISCHIEF	Allen J. Hubin	10-4 TAD 307
Cheyney, Peter	DARK BAHAMA	Theodore Dukeshire	4-5 MR 36
Cheyney, Peter	DARK INTERLUDE	Steve Lewis	1A MF 26
Cheyney, Peter	YOU CAN'T KEEP THE CHANGE	Stephen Mertz	2-4 MF 44
Childers, Erskine	THE RIDDLE OF THE SANDS	James Mark Purcell	9-4 TAD 310
Childers, Erskine	THE RIDDLE OF THE SANDS	Guy M. Townsend	1-6 MF 49
Childs, Timothy	COLD TURKEY	Allen J. Hubin	12-3 TAD 203
Childs, Timothy	COLD TURKEY	Steve Lewis	3-6 MF 30
Chiu, Tony	PORT ARTHUR CHICKEN	Steve Lewis	4-2 MF 36
Christie, Agatha	A MURDER IS ANNOUNCED (stage)	Jackie Meyerson	1-5 PP 18
Christie, Agatha	A POCKET FULL OF RYE	Charles Shibuk	13-1 TAD 75
Christie, Agatha	AN AUTOBIOGRAPHY	Charles Shibuk	11-1 TAD 22
Christie, Agatha	AN AUTOBIOGRAPHY	Charles Shibuk	12-2 TAD 166
Christie, Agatha	AND THEN THERE WERE NONE (film)	William K.Everson	9-2 TAD 115
Christie, Agatha	THE BIG FOUR	F.M.Nevins, Jr.	2-3 MR 5
Christie, Agatha	BY THE PRICKING OF MY THUMBS	Don Miller	2-1 MM 5
Christie, Agatha	BY THE PRICKING OF MY THUMBS	Charles Shibuk	2-2 TAD 120
Christie, Agatha	THE CARIBBEAN MYSTERY	Amnon Kabatchnik	4-1 MR 37
Christie, Agatha	CURTAIN	Amnon Kabatchnik	8 MN 14
Christie, Agatha	CURTAIN	Charles Shibuk	9-1 TAD 66
Christie, Agatha	DEATH ON THE NILE (film)	Jackie Meyerson	2-1 PP 27
Christie, Agatha	ELEPHANTS CAN REMEMBER	Charles Shibuk	6-2 TAD 112
Christie, Agatha	ENDLESS NIGHT	Charles Shibuk	1-2 TAD 61
Christie, Agatha	THE GOLDEN BALL AND OTHER STORIES	Robert E. Briney	4-6 MR 36
Christie, Agatha	THE GOLDEN BALL AND OTHER STORIES	Charles Shibuk	5-1 TAD 39
Christie, Agatha	HALLOWE'EN PARTY	Charles Shibuk	3-2 TAD 133
Christie, Agatha	THE LABOURS OF HERCULES	Douglas G. Greene	12-3 TAD 232
Christie, Agatha	LORD EDGWARE DIES (THIRTEEN AT DINNER) (film)	William K.Everson	2-1 TAD 54
Christie, Agatha	LORD EDGWARE DIES (film)	Jay Jeffries	7 MY 6
Christie, Agatha	THE MIRROR CRACK'D (film)	Thomas Godfrey	2-3 M 44
Christie, Agatha	THE MOUSETRAP AND OTHER PLAYS	Amnon Kabatchnik	12-2 TAD 179
Christie, Agatha	MR.PARKER PYNE, DETECTIVE	Charles Shibuk	14-3 TAD 266
Christie, Agatha	MURDER AT THE VICARAGE	Charles Shibuk	9-4 TAD 281
Christie, Agatha	MURDER ON THE ORIENT EXPRESS (film)	Douglas M. Armato	9-2 TAD 147
Christie, Agatha	THE MYSTERIOUS AFFAIR AT STYLES	Marvin Lachman	3-1 TAD 58
Christie, Agatha	THE MYSTERIOUS MR. QUIN	Douglas G. Greene	12-3 TAD 231
Christie, Agatha	NEMESIS	James Sandoe	14-2 TAD 189
Christie, Agatha	NEMESIS	Charles Shibuk	5-2 TAD 101
Christie, Agatha	ORDEAL BY INNOCENCE	Charles Shibuk	14-1 TAD 79
Christie, Agatha	PASSENGER TO FRANKFURT	Lianne Carlin	4-2 MR 39
Christie, Agatha	PASSENGER TO FRANKFURT	Charles Shibuk	4-2 TAD 123
Christie, Agatha	PERIL AT END HOUSE	Charles Shibuk	10-2 TAD 149
Christie, Agatha	POSTERN OF FATE	Steve Lewis	3/4 MN 20
Christie, Agatha	POSTERN OF FATE	Charles Shibuk	7-2 TAD 137
Christie, Agatha	THE REGATTA MYSTERY	Don Miller	1-8 MM 6
Christie, Agatha	SLEEPING MURDER	Charles Shibuk	10-1 TAD 64
Christie, Agatha	WHAT MRS.McGILLICUDDY SAW!	Charles Shibuk	13-2 TAD 135

Claire, Keith	THE OTHERWISE GIRL	Christine Mitchell	11-2 TAD 125
Clancy, Leo	FIX	Allen J. Hubin	13-1 TAD 27
Clapperton, Richard	THE SENTIMENTAL KILL	Robert C.S.Adey	4-3 PP 25
Clark, Curt	ANARCHAOS	Bill Crider	4-3 MF 42
Clark, Douglas	DEADLY PATTERN	F.M.Nevins, Jr.	3-3 MF 46
Clark, Douglas	PREMEDICATED MURDER	Barzun & Taylor	9-4 TAD 271
Clark, Douglas	ROAST EGGS	Robert E. Briney	5-4 MF 36
Clark, Douglas	ROAST EGGS	Steve Lewis	5-6 MF 36
Clark, Eric	SEND IN THE LIONS	Allen J. Hubin	14-4 TAD 298
Clark, Eric	THE SLEEPER	Allen J. Hubin	13-3 TAD 199
Clark, Gail	THE BARONESS OF BOW STREET	Allen J. Hubin	13-1 TAD 27
Clark, Gail	DULCIE BLIGH	Steve Lewis	2-5 MF 27
Clark, Mary Higgins	A STRANGER IS WATCHING	Allen J. Hubin	11-4 TAD 332
Clark, Mary Higgins	THE CRADLE WILL FALL	Allen J. Hubin	14-1 TAD 17
Clark, Mary Higgins	THE CRADLE WILL FALL	Charlotte Wakefield	2-1 M 29
Clark, Mary Higgins	WHERE ARE THE CHILDREN?	Barbara A. Buhrer	9 MN R1
Clark, Philip	THE DARK RIVER	Barzun & Taylor	13-4 TAD 308
Clark, William A.	THE GIRL ON THE VOLKSWAGEN FLOOR	Stanley A. Carlin	4-5 MR 38
Clark, William J.	THE FRANK GRUBER INDEX	Allen J. Hubin	3-2 TAD 134
Clark, William J., & Len & June Moffatt	THE JDM MASTER CHECKLIST	Robert E. Washer	1-3 QC 22
Clarke, Anna	THE LADY IN BLACK	Allen J. Hubin	11-4 TAD 331
Clarke, Anna	THE LADY IN BLACK	Steve Lewis	2-5 MF 30
Clarke, Anna	LETTER FROM THE DEAD	Kathi Maio	4-4 PP 31
Clarke, Anna	LETTERS FROM THE PAST	Steve Lewis	5-5 MF 21
Clarke, Anna	PLOT COUNTER PLOT	Allen J. Hubin	9-1 TAD 75
Clarke, Anna	THIS DOWNHILL PATH	Jane S. Bakerman	5-5 MF 33
Clarke, Anna	THIS DOWNHILL PATH	Mary Groff	6 CL 6
Clarke, Anna	THIS DOWNHILL PATH	Allen J. Hubin	11-1 TAD 19
Clason, Clyde B.	THE DEATH ANGEL	F.M.Nevins, Jr.	7-1 TAD 54
Clason, Clyde B.	THE MAN FROM TIBET	Jay Jeffries	1 MN 7
Clason, Clyde B.	MURDER GOES MINOAN	Jay Jeffries	1 MN 7
Clason, Clyde B.	MURDER GOES MINOAN	F.M.Nevins, Jr.	3-3 MF 46
Clason, Clyde B.	THE PURPLE PARROT	Douglas G. Greene	4-3 PP 21
Cleary, Jon	HIGH ROAD TO CHINA	Charles Shibuk	12-2 TAD 166
Cleary, Jon	THE LIBERATORS	Robert E. Washer	3-1 QC 19
Cleary, Jon	PETER'S PENCE	Fred Dueren	9-2 TAD 140
Cleary, Jon	VORTEX	Allen J. Hubin	12-2 TAD 111
Cleary, Jon	VORTEX	Charles Shibuk	13-1 TAD 75
Clements, E.H.	CHERRY HARVEST	Robert C.S.Adey	3-5 PP 36
Clifford, Charles L.	WHILE THE BELLS RANG	Steve Lewis	5-3 MF 30
Clifford, Francis	A WILD JUSTICE	Amnon Kabatchnik	5-5 MR 34
Clifford, Francis	DRUMMER IN THE DARK	Frank Eck	9-3 TAD 221
Cline, Linda	THE MIRACLE SEASON	Sheldon A. Wiebe	5 SF 38
Clinton-Baddeley,V.C.	DEATH'S BRIGHT DART	Don Miller	13 MN R5
Clinton-Baddeley,V.C.	MY FOE OUTSTRETCH'D BENEATH THE TREE	Robert E. Briney	5-5 MF 37
Clinton-Baddeley,V.C.	MY FOE OUTSTRETCH'D BENEATH THE TREE	Steve Lewis	3-1 MF 37
Clinton-Baddeley,V.C.	MY FOE OUTSTRETCH'D BENEATH THE TREE	Don Miller	13 MN R5
Clinton-Baddeley,V.C.	MY FOE OUTSTRETCH'D BENEATH THE TREE	Charles Shibuk	14-3 TAD 266
Clinton-Baddeley,V.C.	MY FOE OUTSTRETCH'D BENEATH THE TREE	Guy M. Townsend	1A MF 39
Clinton-Baddeley,V.C.	NO CASE FOR THE POLICE	Robert E. Washer	3-1 QC 18
Clinton-Baddeley,V.C.	ONLY A MATTER OF TIME	Mary A. Grochowski	2-5 PP 33
Clinton-Baddeley,V.C.	ONLY A MATTER OF TIME	Charles Shibuk	14-4 TAD 376
Clinton-Baddeley,V.C.	TO STUDY A LONG SILENCE	Mary Groff	1-6 PP 25
Clouston, J.Storer	THE MAN FROM THE CLOUDS	Amnon Kabatchnik	7-2 TAD 128
Clouston, J.Storer	THE SPY IN BLACK (film)	William K.Everson	1-1 TAD 9
Clute, Cedric E.,Jr. & Nicholas Lewin,ed.	SLEIGHT OF CRIME: FIFTEEN CLASSIC TALES OF MURDER, MAYHEM AND MAGIC	Robert E. Briney	11-1 TAD 26
Coblentz, Stanton A.	LORD OF TRANERICA	Gary Zachrich	66 PU 62

Coburn, Andrew	THE BABYSITTER	D.E.Ath	2-2 PP 14
Coe, Tucker	A JADE IN ARIES	Karen Bornstein	1-2 M 21
Coe, Tucker	A JADE IN ARIES	Lianne Carlin	4-3 MR 35
Coe, Tucker	A JADE IN ARIES	Jim McCahery	2 PE 18
Coe, Tucker	WAX APPLE	Guy M. Townsend	1A MF 21
Coffey, Brian	THE WALL OF MASKS	Allen J. Hubin	8-3 TAD 227
Coffin, Peter	THE SEARCH FOR MY GREAT-UNCLE'S HEAD	Jim McCahery	1-5 PP 20
Cohane, M.E.	MURDER ONE	Fred Dueren	9-2 TAD 140
Cohen, Octavus Roy	THE CORPSE THAT WALKED	Charles Shibuk	1-6 MF 54
Cohen, Octavus Roy	GRAY DUSK	Charles Shibuk	14-4 TAD 365
Cohen, Octavus Roy	JIM HANVEY, DETECTIVE	Charles Shibuk	11-2 TAD 127
Cohen, Stanley	THE DIANE GAME	Allen J. Hubin	7-2 TAD 143
Cohen, Stanley	TAKING GARY FELDMAN	Robert E. Briney	4-2 MR 36
Cohen, Stanley	TAKING GARY FELDMAN	Robert E. Washer	3-1 QC 19
Cohen, Terry	CANARY	Gary Warren Niebuhr	4-5/6 PP 64
Cole, G.D.H., & Margaret	LAST WILL AND TESTAMENT	James Kingman	9-3 TAD 226
Cole, G.D.H., & Margaret	MURDER AT CROME HOUSE	Michael Trombetta	11-2 TAD 125
Coleman, Lucile	THE LYRIC RETURN	Michael L. Cook	1 U 11
Coleman, Lucile	THIS LAUGHING DUST	Michael L. Cook	7 U 31
Coles, Manning	NOTHING TO DECLARE	Douglas G. Greene	12-3 TAD 234
Collins, Max	BAIT MONEY	Lianne Carlin	5-6 MR 36
Collins, Max	BAIT MONEY	George Kelley	1-6 MF 50
Collins, Max	BAIT MONEY	Jeff Meyerson	2-2 MM 5
Collins, Max	BAIT MONEY	Robert J. Randisi	14-4 TAD 361
Collins, Max	BLOOD MONEY	Lianne Carlin	5-6 MR 36
Collins, Max	BLOOD MONEY	George Kelley	1-6 MF 50
Collins, Max	BLOOD MONEY	Robert J. Randisi	14-4 TAD 361
Collins, Max	THE BROKER	George Kelley	1-6 MF 50
Collins, Max	THE BROKER	Robert J. Randisi	9-4 TAD 300
Collins, Max	THE BROKER'S WIFE	George Kelley	1-6 MF 50
Collins, Max	THE DEALER	George Kelley	1-6 MF 50
Collins, Max	HUSH MONEY	Jim Traylor	5-6 MF 45
Collins, Max	THE SLASHER	Fred Dueren	11-2 TAD 192
Collins, Max	THE SLASHER	George Kelley	2-1 MF 42
Collins, Michael	ACT OF FEAR	Charles Shibuk	13-3 TAD 250
Collins, Michael	THE BLOOD-RED DREAM	Steve Lewis	2-1 MF 27
Collins, Michael	THE BLOOD-RED DREAM	Charles Shibuk	9-4 TAD 308
Collins, Michael	THE BLOOD-RED DREAM	Charles Shibuk	14-3 TAD 266
Collins, Michael	BLUE DEATH	Charles Shibuk	8-4 TAD 301
Collins, Michael	BLUE DEATH	Charles Shibuk	13-2 TAD 135
Collins, Michael	THE BRASS RAINBOW	Steven Miller	3-6 PP 31
Collins, Michael	THE BRASS RAINBOW	Charles Shubuk	2-3 TAD 199
Collins, Michael	THE BRASS RAINBOW	Charles Shibuk	13-4 TAD 363
Collins, Michael	NIGHT OF THE TOADS	Paul Harwitz	2-3 M 49
Collins, Michael	THE NIGHTRUNNERS	Steve Lewis	2-6 MF 33
Collins, Michael	SHADOW OF A TIGER	Charles Shibuk	6-1 TAD 42
Collins, Michael	THE SILENT SCREAM	Charles Shibuk	7-2 TAD 136
Collins, Michael	THE SILENT SCREAM	Charles Shibuk	12-4 TAD 368
Collins, Michael	THE SLASHER	Allen J. Hubin	13-4 TAD 294
Collins, Michael	THE SLASHER	Rod Kassel	2-1 M 29
Collins, Michael	WALK A BLACK WIND	Charles Shibuk	5-2 TAD 99
Collins, Norman	THE HUSBAND'S STORY	D.E.Ath	2-1 PP 14
Collins, Wilkie	ARMADALE	M.S.Cappadonna	11-3 TAD 247
Collins, Wilkie	THE MOONSTONE (film)	Amnon Kabatchnik	6-4 TAD 263
Collins, Wilkie	NO NAME	Bonnie Pollard	13/14 CL 10
Collins, Wilkie	TALES OF TERROR AND THE SUPERNATURAL	Joe R. Christopher	7-1 TAD 59
Collins, Wilkie	THE WOMAN IN WHITE (film)	William K.Everson	11-4 TAD 342
Coltrane, James	TALON	Allen J. Hubin	11-3 TAD 232
Comber, Leon (trans.)	THE STRANGE TALES OF MAGISTRATE PAO: CHINESE TALES OF CRIME AND DETECTION	Douglas G. Greene	12-3 TAD 234
Conaway, J.C.	THE DEADLY SPRING	Amnon Kabatchnik	1-5 MF 41

Condon, Richard	DEATH OF A POLITICIAN	Allen J. Hubin	12-2 TAD 111
Connell, Richard	THE MOST DANGEROUS GAME (film)	William K. Everson	4-1 TAD 40
Connington, J.J.	COMMON SENSE IS ALL YOU NEED	L.F.Ashley	7-4 TAD 289
Constantine, K.C.	THE BLANK PAGE	Guy M. Townsend	1-9 MM 7
Constantine, K.C.	THE MAN WHO LIKED TO LOOK AT HIMSELF	Barzun & Taylor	11-2 TAD 203
Cook, Michael L.	MURDER BY MAIL	Allen J. Hubin	12-3 TAD 203
Cook, Robin	COMA	Guy M. Townsend	3-6 MF 45
Cook, Robin	COMA	Guy M. Townsend	12 MN R8
Cook, Robin	SPHINX	Allen J. Hubin	12-4 TAD 320
Cook, Robin	SPHINX	Guy M. Townsend	3-6 MF 46
Cook, William W.	A ROUND TRIP TO THE YEAR 2000	Allen J. Hubin	7-4 TAD 294
Cooke, Joseph Cotton	THE VERA GERARD CASE	Hal Brodsky	10-4 TAD 316
Cooney, Caroline B.	REAR-VIEW MIRROR	Allen J. Hubin	13-4 TAD 294
Cooper, Edmund	THE OVERMAN CULTURE	Robert E. Briney	5-4 MR 28
Cooper, Edmund	PRISONER OF FIRE	Allen J. Hubin	9-3 TAD 224
Cooper, Paulette	THE MEDICAL DETECTIVES: HOW MODERN SCIENCE HELPS THE DEAD TO SPEAK	Veronica M.Kennedy	7-3 TAD 217
Cooper, Will	DEATH HAS A THOUSAND DOORS	Allen J. Hubin	9-3 TAD 224
Coppel, Alfred	THIRTY-FOUR EAST	Peter Wolfe	8-1 TAD 57
Copper, Basil	THE BIG CHILL	Jon L. Breen	4-6 MF 36
Copper, Basil	THE CURSE OF THE FLEERS	Amnon Kabatchnik	2-1 MF 35
Copper, Basil	THE CURSE OF THE FLEERS	Jon L. Lellenberg	11-1 TAD 25
Copper, Basil	THE CURSE OF THE FLEERS	Steve Lewis	2-3 MF 46
Copper, Basil	THE DOSSIER OF SOLAR PONS	Fred Dueren	12-3 TAD 287
Copper, Basil	THE FURTHER ADVENTURES OF SOLAR PONS	Fred Dueren	13-2 TAD 136
Corder, Eric	THE BITE	R. Jeff Banks	5 PE 17
Corley, Edwin	THE GENESIS ROCK	Bill Crider	3-2 PP 30
Cormier, Robert	AFTER THE FIRST DEATH	Jane S. Bakerman	3-6 MF 42
Cormier, Robert	I AM THE CHEESE	Jane S. Bakerman	3-6 MF 42
Cornish, George W.	CORNISH OF SCOTLAND YARD	Hal Brodsky	8-2 TAD 138
Correll, A. Boyd, & Philip MacDonald	THE DARK WHEEL	Charles Shibuk	12-2 TAD 189
Cory, Desmond	BENNETT	Jane S. Bakerman	7 CL 8
Cory, Desmond	DEADFALL	Jane S. Bakerman	3-4 MF 46
Coulson, Robert, & Gene DeWeese	NOW YOU SEE IT/HIM/THEM...	Don Miller	8 MN 16
Counselman, Mary E.	HALF IN SHADOW	Richard H. Fawcett	2-1 AD 5
Courtier, S.H.	LIGNY'S LAKE	Robert E. Briney	5-5 MF 42
Courtier, S.H.	LIGNY'S LAKE	Robert E. Briney	4-6 MR 35
Cousins, E.G.	DEATH BY MARRIAGE	Barzun & Taylor	13-3 TAD 208
Cox, Arthur J., ed.	THE MYSTERY OF EDWIN DROOD	Edward Lauterbach	8-1 TAD 63
Cox, J.Randolph	NEW NICK CARTER WEEKLY	Allen J. Hubin	9-3 TAD 225
Cox, Richard	SAM 7	Barbara A. Buhrer	12 MN R4
Cox, Richard	SAM 7	Jeff Meyerson	2-3 MF 50
Cox, William R.	DEATH ON LOCATION	Steve Lewis	3-2 MF 38
Coxe, George Harmon	DOUBLE IDENTITY	Lianne Carlin	3-4 MR 10
Coxe, George Harmon	FENNER	Amnon Kabatchnik	4-5 MR 34
Coxe, George Harmon	THE GLASS TRIANGLE	Steve Lewis	1-5 MF 36
Coxe, George Harmon	ERROR OF JUDGMENT	John Vining	9-2 TAD 142
Coxe, George Harmon	FLASH-CASEY, DETECTIVE	Douglas G. Greene	12-3 TAD 232
Coxe, George Harmon	THE JADE VENUS	Arthur C. Scott	2-1 MM 6
Coxe, George Harmon	MURDER WITH PICTURES	Charles Shibuk	14-3 TAD 266
Coxe, George Harmon	NO PLACE FOR MURDER	Robert E. Washer	21 X 54
Coxe, George Harmon	NO PLACE FOR MURDER	J.Randolph Cox	9-3 TAD 220
Coxe, George Harmon	THE SILENT WITNESS	J.Randolph Cox	5-6 MR 30
Coxe, George Harmon	WOMAN AT BAY	Steve Lewis	1-2 MF 26
Coxe, George Harmon	WOMAN WITH A GUN	J.Randolph Cox	5-3 MR 36
Craig, Alisa	A PINT OF MURDER	Steve Lewis	4-4 MF 42
Craig, John	IF YOU WANT TO SEE YOUR WIFE AGAIN...	Bill Crider	2-3 PP 30
Craig, John	IN COUNCIL ROOMS APART	Don Cole	3-4 MR 31
Craig, Jonathan	CASE OF THE BRAZEN BEAUTY	Arthur C. Scott	1-11 MM 5

Crane, Caroline	COAST OF FEAR	Allen J. Hubin	14-4 TAD 298
Crane, Caroline	SUMMER GIRL	Allen J. Hubin	13-2 TAD 95
Crane, Frances	THE CINNAMON MURDER	Steve Lewis	1-5 MT 35
Cranston, Maurice	PHILOSOPHER'S HEMLOCK: A DETECTIVE STORY	Barzun & Taylor	14-1 TAD 88
Cranston, Maurice	TO-MORROW WE'LL BE SOBER	Barzun & Taylor	14-1 TAD 88
Cravens, Gwyneth, & John S. Marr	THE BLACK DEATH	Patricia M. Koch	3-5 PP 36
Crawford, Robert	THE SHROUD SOCIETY	Robert E. Washer	2-1 QC 17
Crawford, William	THE CHINESE CONNECTION	R. Jeff Banks	12 MN R2
Creasey, John	A BLAST OF TRUMPETS	Barbara A. Buhrer	11 MN R14
Creasey, John	A SHARP RISE IN CRIME	Barzun & Taylor	13-3 TAD 209
Creasey, John	THE EXTORTIONERS	Allen J. Hubin	8-3 TAD 227
Creasey, John	THE EXTORTIONERS	S. Jeffery Koch	5-6 MF 47
Creasey, John	THE HOUSE OF THE BEARS	Allen J. Hubin	9-1 TAD 75
Creasey, John	INSPECTOR WEST ALONE	Barbara A. Buhrer	1-9 MM 5
Creasey, John	THE MASTERS OF BOW STREET	Veronica M.Kennedy	8-1 TAD 59
Creasey, John	THE MASTERS OF BOW STREET	Denis Quane	2 MN 8
Creasey, John	THE MISTS OF FEAR	Allen J. Hubin	11-3 TAD 233
Creasey, John	SALUTE THE TOFF	John Harwood	4-6 MR 32
Creasey, John	THE SMOG	Robert E. Briney	4-6 MR 33
Creasey, John	THE THEFT OF MAGNA CARTA	Robert Kolesnik	6-4 TAD 264
Creasey, John	THE TOFF AMONG THE MILLIONS	Steve Lewis	3-2 MF 36
Creasey, John	THE TOFF AND THE FALLEN ANGELS	Scott M.Bushnell	4-1 TAD 47
Creasey, John	THE TOFF AT BUTLIN'S	Allen J. Hubin	10-2 TAD 112
Creasey, John	THE TOFF IN TOWN	Steve Lewis	1-6 MM 10
Creasey, John	TRAITOR'S DOOM	Don Miller	2-5 MM 9
Crichton, Michael	CRACKSMAN ON VELVET	Barbara A. Buhrer	5/6 MN 17
Crichton, Michael	THE GREAT TRAIN ROBBERY	Barbara A. Buhrer	5/6 MN 17
Crichton, Michael	THE GREAT TRAIN ROBBERY	Allen J. Hubin	8-4 TAD 309
Crisp, N.J.	THE GOTLAND DEAL	Charles Shibuk	11-3 TAD 298
Crisp, N.J.	THE LONDON DEAL	Frank Ballinger	4 PE 16
Crisp, N.J.	THE LONDON DEAL	Fred Dueren	14-3 TAD 269
Crisp, N.J.	THE LONDON DEAL	Paul McCarthy	3-4 MF 47
Crisp, N.J.	THE LONDON DEAL	Allen J. Hubin	12-2 TAD 112
Crisp, N.J.	THE ODD MAN JOB	Theodore Dukeshire	4-1 MF 30
Crisp, N.J.	THE ODD MAN JOB	Charles Shibuk	14-4 TAD 376
Crispin, Edmund	BEWARE OF THE TRAINS	Charles Shibuk	14-4 TAD 376
Crispin, Edmund	THE CASE OF THE GILDED FLY	Amnon Kabatchnik	4-1 MR 33
Crispin, Edmund	THE CASE OF THE GILDED FLY	James Mark Purcell	9-2 TAD 143
Crispin, Edmund	FEN COUNTRY	Robert C.S.Adey	2-6 PP 38
Crispin, Edmund	FEN COUNTRY	Douglas G. Greene	13-4 TAD 351
Crispin, Edmund	FREQUENT HEARSES	Jon L. Breen	5-1 MR 32
Crispin, Edmund	GLIMPSES OF THE MOON	Barzun & Taylor	11-1 TAD 92
Crispin, Edmund	GLIMPSES OF THE MOON	Perry Dillon	3-2 MF 47
Crispin, Edmund	GLIMPSES OF THE MOON	Steve Lewis	5-1 MF 20
Crispin, Edmund	GLIMPSES OF THE MOON	Charles Shibuk	12-4 TAD 368
Crispin, Edmund	HOLY DISORDERS	Fred Dueren	13-2 TAD 145
Crispin, Edmund	HOLY DISORDERS	David Rose	3-3 PP 26
Crispin, Edmund	THE LONG DIVORCE	Charles Shibuk	14-3 TAD 266
Crispin, Edmund	THE MOVING TOYSHOP	Paul McCarthy	2-1 MF 43
Crispin, Edmund	THE MOVING TOYSHOP	Charles Shibuk	10-4 TAD 360
Crispin, Edmund	SWAN SONG	James Sandoe	14-3 TAD 272
Crispin, Edmund	SWAN SONG	Charles Shibuk	14-4 TAD 376
Crofts, Freeman Wills	THE CASK	M.S.Cappadonna	11-1 TAD 21
Crofts, Freeman Wills	THE CASK	Charles Shibuk	10-3 TAD 239
Crofts, Freeman Wills	THE GROOTE PARK MYSTERY	Marvin Lachman	11-2 TAD 126
Crofts, Freeman Wills	INSPECTOR FRENCH'S GREATEST CASE	Charles Shibuk	11-3 TAD 298
Crofts, Freeman Wills	MURDERERS MAKE MISTAKES	Douglas G. Greene	12-3 TAD 232
Crofts, Freeman Wills	THE PURPLE SICKLE MURDERS	Howard C. Rapp	1-2 PP 20
Crofts, Freeman Wills	SIR JOHN MAGILL'S LAST JOURNEY	Guy M. Townsend	1A MF 10
Crofts, Freeman Wills	SUDDEN DEATH	Angelo Panagos	11-1 TAD 27
Cromie, Alice	LUCKY TO BE ALIVE?	Allen J. Hubin	12-2 TAD 112
Cronin, George	DEATH OF A DELEGATE	Steve Lewis	3-6 MF 38
Crosby, John	DEAR JUDGMENT	Allen J. Hubin	12-2 TAD 112

Cross, Amanda	DEATH IN A TENURED POSITION	Barzun & Taylor	14-2 TAD 142
Cross, Amanda	DEATH IN A TENURED POSITION	Meera T. Clark	2-2 C 154
Cross, Amanda	POETIC JUSTICE	Charles Shibuk	12-4 TAD 368
Cross, Amanda	THE QUESTION OF MAX	Jane S. Bakerman	11 MN R1
Cross, Amanda	THE QUESTION OF MAX	Myrtis Broset	2-5 MF 44
Cross, Amanda	THE QUESTION OF MAX	Allen J. Hubin	9-4 TAD 310
Cross, Amanda	IN THE LAST ANALYSIS	Charles Shibuk	14-4 TAD 376
Cross, Amanda	THE THEBAN MYSTERIES	Charles Shibuk	13-1 TAD 75
Crossen, Ken	MURDER OUT OF MIND	Don Miller	12 MN A12
Crossen, Ken	MURDER OUT OF MIND	Angelo Panagos	12-1 TAD 80
Crow, C.P.	NO MORE MONDAY MORNINGS	Allen J. Hubin	14-2 TAD 124
Crowe, John	CLOSE TO DEATH	Allen J. Hubin	12-3 TAD 203
Crowe, John	CLOSE TO DEATH	Steve Lewis	3-6 MF 33
Crowe, John	WHEN THEY KILL YOUR WIFE	Steve Lewis	1-6 MF 38
Crowther, Bruce	DEAD MAN'S COCKTAIL	Allen J. Hubin	11-3 TAD 232
Cruickshank, Charles	THE TANG MURDERS	Robert C.S.Adey	1-1 PP 25
Crumley, James	THE LAST GOOD KISS	Allen J. Hubin	12-1 TAD 6
Crumley, James	THE LAST GOOD KISS	Steve Lewis	3-3 MF 31
Crumley, James	THE LAST GOOD KISS	Steven Miller	4-1 PP 32
Crumley, James	THE LAST GOOD KISS	Charles Shibuk	14-3 TAD 266
Crumley, James	THE LAST GOOD KISS	Lewis Shiner	5 PE 15
Crumley, James	THE WRONG CASE	Stan Burns	2-1 MM 4
Crumley, James	THE WRONG CASE	Allen J. Hubin	8-4 TAD 309
Crumley, James	THE WRONG CASE	Steven M. Krauzer	10-1 TAD 61
Crumley, James	THE WRONG CASE	Charles Shibuk	12-2 TAD 166
Cudahy, Sheila	THE TROJAN GOLD	Allen J. Hubin	12-3 TAD 203
Cullinan, Thomas	THE EIGHTH SACRAMENT	Allen J. Hubin	11-2 TAD 118
Cumberland, Marten	THE KNIFE WILL FALL	Steve Lewis	5-2 MF 16
Cunningham, A.B.	MURDER WITHOUT WEAPONS	Steve Lewis	3-2 MF 40
Cunningham, E.V.	THE CASE OF THE ONE-PENNY ORANGE	Greg Goode	4-5/6 PP 75
Cunningham, E.V.	THE CASE OF THE POISONED ECLAIRS	Sandra Sasaki	1-1 M 21
Cunningham, E.V.	THE CASE OF THE SLIDING POOL	Steve Lewis	5-6 MF 35
Currey, L.W.	SCIENCE FICTION AND FANTASY AUTHORS: A BIBLIOGRAPHY OF FIRST PRINTINGS OF THEIR FICTION AND SELECTED NON-FICTION	Michael L. Cook	7 U 63
Curtis, Mike	THE SAVAGE WOMEN	Ammon Kabatchnik	1-5 MF 41
Curtis, Richard	STRIKE ZONE	Fred Dueren	9-1 TAD 50
Curtis, Richard	THE $3-MILLION TURN-OVER	Jeffrey Meyerson	11-3 TAD 252
Curtiss, Ursula	THE BIRTHDAY GIFT	Jane S. Bakerman	12 MN R1
Curtiss, Ursula	CHILD'S PLAY	Dorothy Glantz	11-3 TAD 253
Curtiss, Ursula	IN COLD PURSUIT	Jane S. Bakerman	2-4 PP 35
Curtiss, Ursula	IN COLD PURSUIT	Barbara A. Buhrer	13B MN 9
Curtiss, Ursula	LETTER OF INTENT	Lianne Carlin	4-4 MR 37
Curtiss, Ursula	THE MENACE WITHIN	Jane S. Bakerman	3-5 MF 42
Cushman, Dan	OPIUM FLOWER	Steve Lewis	1A MF 25
Cussler, Clive	ICEBERG	Barbara A. Buhrer	13 MN R1
Cussler, Clive	THE MEDITERRANEAN CAPER	Barbara A. Buhrer	13 MN R1
Cussler, Clive	RAISE THE TITANIC!	J.Randolph Cox	10-2 TAD 189
Cussler, Clive	RAISE THE TITANIC!	Ammon Kabatchnik	1-4 MF 45
Cussler, Clive	RAISE THE TITANIC!	Ammon Kabatchnik	2-1 PP 28
Dakin, D.Martin	HOLMESIAN CLERIHEWS	Allen J. Hubin	8-3 TAD 230
Dale, Alzina Stone	MAKER AND CRAFTSMAN: THE STORY OF DOROTHY L. SAYERS	Joe R. Christopher	12-2 TAD 180
Dalton, Moray	DEATH AT THE VILLA	Barzun & Taylor	14-2 TAD 142
Dalton, Moray	THE LONGBRIDGE MURDERS	Barzun & Taylor	14-2 TAD 142
Dalton, Moray	THE LONGBRIDGE MURDERS	Charles Shibuk	11-3 TAD 252
Dalton, Moray	THE NIGHT OF FEAR	Charles Shibuk	7-2 TAD 133
Daly, Carroll John	THE MAN IN THE SHADOWS	Ammon Kabatchnik	7-2 TAD 133
Daly, Carroll John	MURDER FROM THE EAST	Michael L. Cook	5 U 31
Daly, Carroll John	MURDER FROM THE EAST	Theodore Dukeshire	2-6 MF 40
Daly, Carroll John	MURDER FROM THE EAST	Charles Shibuk	13-3 TAD 250
Daly, Carroll John	THE SNARL OF THE BEAST	Angelo Panagos	11-2 TAD 127
Daly, Carroll John	THE SNARL OF THE BEAST	Charles Shibuk	8-4 TAD 296

Daly, Carroll John	TAINTED POWER	Stephen Mertz	12-4 TAD 376
Daly, Carroll John	THE WHITE CIRCLE	Charles Shibuk	12-3 TAD 274
Daly, Carroll John	THE WHITE CIRCLE	Charles Shibuk	12-4 TAD 372
Daly, Elizabeth	ARROW POINTING NOWHERE	Guy M. Townsend	1A MF 34
Daly, Elizabeth	DEADLY NIGHTSHADE	Guy M. Townsend	1A MF 33
Daly, Elizabeth	DEATH AND LETTERS	Steve Lewis	5-5 MF 25
Daly, Elizabeth	DEATH AND LETTERS	Charles Shibuk	14-4 TAD 376
Daly, Elizabeth	UNEXPECTED NIGHT	Jim McCahery	2-1 PP 27
D'Amato, Barbara	THE HANDS OF HEALING MURDER	Charles Jardinier	2-3 M 48
D'Amato, Barbara	THE HANDS OF HEALING MURDER	Steve Lewis	5-2 MF 21
D'Amato, Barbara	THE HANDS OF HEALING MURDER	Charles Shibuk	14-3 TAD 266
Dane, Clemence, & Helen Simpson	ENTER SIR JOHN	Paul McCarthy	3-3 PP 28
Dane, Clemence, & Helen Simpson	MURDER (film)	William K.Everson	7-1 TAD 31
Dane, Clemence, & Helen Simpson	MURDER (film)	James Mark Purcell	10-4 TAD 314
Danielle, Maria	FIELDWORK	William L.DeAndrea	14-4 TAD 378
Daniels, Les	THE BLACK CASTLE	Amnon Kabatchnik	2-4 MF 46
Dark, James	COME DIE WITH ME	Larry Rickert	4-5/6 PP 38
Dark, James	OPERATION ICE CAP	Larry Rickert	4-5/6 PP 39
Darlington, W.A.	MR. CRONK'S CASES	Allen J. Hubin	5-3 TAD 165
Datesh, John Nicholas	THE JANUS MURDER	Steve Lewis	3-5 MF 40
Davey, Jocelyn	A TREASURY ALARM	Barzun & Taylor	11-2 TAD 203
Davidson, Avram	THE ISLAND UNDER THE EARTH	Gary Zachrich	74 PU 26
Davidson, Lionel	MURDER GAMES	Allen J. Hubin	11-4 TAD 331
Davidson, Marion, & Martha Blue	MAKING IT LEGAL: A LAW PRIMER FOR THE CRAFTSMAN	D.E.Ath	2-4 PP 28
Davies, L.P.	ASSIGNMENT ABACUS	Allen J. Hubin	9-1 TAD 73
Davies, L.P.	POSSESSION	Don Miller	10 MN R7
Davies, L.P.	THE RELUCTANT MEDIUM	Don Miller	2-4 MM 5
Davies, L.P.	WHAT DID I DO TOMORROW?	Don Miller	10 MN R16
Davies, Rhys	NOBODY ANSWERED THE BELL	Rita & Jon Breen	5-1 MR 33
Davis, Dorothy S.	A GENTLE MURDERER	Howard Rapp	4-1 PP 28
Davis, Dorothy S.	SCARLET NIGHT	Allen J. Hubin	13-4 TAD 294
Davis, Dorothy S.	SCARLET NIGHT	Steve Lewis	4-4 MF 39
Davis, Frederick C.	THE DEADLY MISS ASHLEY	Steve Lewis	1-1 MF 28
Davis, Frederick C.	THURSDAY'S BLADE	Steve Lewis	5/6 MN 20
Davis, Gordon	WASHINGTON PAYOFF	Marvin Lachman	1-4 MF 51
Davis, Gordon	WHERE MURDER WAITS	Marvin Lachman	1-4 MF 51
Davis, Jada	THE OUTRAGED SECT	Bill Crider	1-2 PQ 53
Davis, Kenn	DEAD TO RIGHTS	Fred Dueren	5-6 MF 44
Davis, Kenn	THE FORZA TRAP	Fred Dueren	13-1 TAD 65
Davis, Kenn, & John Stanley	THE DARK SIDE	Fred Dueren	10-4 TAD 340
Davis, Mildred	THREE MINUTES TO MIDNIGHT	Mary Jean DeMarr	4-1 MF 29
Davis, Norbert	THE MOUSE IN THE MOUNTAIN	(not stated)	14-2 TAD 188
Davis, Norbert	OH, MURDERER MINE!	(not stated)	14-2 TAD 188
Davis, Norbert	OH, MURDERER MINE!	Angelo Panagos	13-3 TAD 270
Davis, Norbert	SALLY'S IN THE ALLEY	(not stated)	14-2 TAD 188
Davis, Phil	THE DANCER'S DEATH	Fred Dueren	14-2 TAD 183
Davis, Reginald	THE CROWING HEN	Steve Lewis	3-2 MF 40
Davis, Richard, ed.	THE YEAR'S BEST HORROR STORIES	Lianne Carlin	5-4 MR 33
Davis, Richard Harding	IN THE FOG	Amnon Kabatchnik	6-2 TAD 118
Davis, Tech	TERROR AT COMPASS LAKE	Douglas G. Greene	4-5/6 PP 68
Day, Gene	FUTURE DAY	Michael L. Cook	3 U 25
Dean, Amber	SNIPE HUNT	Steve Lewis	3-4 MF 40
DeAndrea, William L.	THE HOG MURDERS	Steven Miller	3-6 PP 30
DeAndrea, William L.	THE HOG MURDERS	Bill Crider	3-6 MF 47
DeAndrea, William L.	THE HOG MURDERS	Allen J. Hubin	13-1 TAD 27
DeAndrea, William L.	THE HOG MURDERS	Charles Shibuk	13-2 TAD 135
DeAndrea, William L.	KILLED IN THE RATINGS	Bill Crider	1 PE 14
DeAndrea, William L.	KILLED IN THE RATINGS	Mary A.Grochowski	2-2 PP 29
DeAndrea, William L.	KILLED IN THE RATINGS	Jim Huang	9 CL 8
DeAndrea, William L.	THE LUNATIC FRINGE	Steve Lewis	5-1 MF 24

Deane, Hamilton, & John L.Balderston	DRACULA	Jackie Meyerson	1-1 PP 20
DeBell, Garrett	THE ENVIRONMENTAL HANDBOOK	Gary Zachrich	74 PU 20
deBury, Richard	PHILOBIBLON	Maryell Cleary	3-3 PP 27
deCaire, Edwin	DEATH AMONG THE WRITERS	L.F.Ashley	7-4 TAD 287
deCaire, Edwin	DEATH AMONG THE WRITERS	Mary Groff	2-3 PP 30
deCamp, L.Sprague	LOVECRAFT: A BIOGRAPHY	Veronica M.Kennedy	8-4 TAD 300
Deeping, Warwick	THE MOUNTAINS WEST OF TOWN	Allen J. Hubin	9-2 TAD 152
DeFelitta, Frank	OKTOBERFEST	R. Jeff Banks	11 MN R2
Deighton, Len	AN EXPENSIVE PLACE TO DIE	Myrtis Broset	2-1 MF 39
Deighton, Len	THE BILLION DOLLAR BRAIN	Myrtis Broset	2-1 MF 38
Deighton, Len	HORSE UNDER WATER	Myrtis Broset	2-5 MF 44
Deighton, Len	SS-GB	R. Jeff Banks	2-6 PP 15
Deighton, Len	SS-GB	Theodore Dukeshire	3-4 MF 50
Deighton, Len	SS-GB	Allen J. Hubin	12-3 TAD 203
Deighton, Len	XPD	Allen J. Hubin	14-4 TAD 298
Deighton, Len	XPD	Steve Lewis	5-4 MF 26
Deindorfer, Robert G.	THE SPIES: GREAT TRUE STORIES OF ESPIONAGE	Lianne Carlin	3-3 MR 30
Dekker, Anthony	TEMPTATION IN A PRIVATE ZOO	Robert E. Washer	2-1 QC 17
Delany, Sam	BABEL 17	Gary Zachrich	64 PU 43
Delman, David	THE NICE MURDERERS	Steve Lewis	2-1 MF 22
Delmonico, Andrea	EYERIE IF AN EAGLE	Ruth Withee	3-2 MR 10
Del Rey, Lester	NERVES	Gary Zachrich	75 PU 24
Delving, Michael	BORED TO DEATH	Allen J. Hubin	8-4 TAD 309
Delving, Michael	THE CHINA EXPERT	Allen J. Hubin	10-2 TAD 113
Delving, Michael	THE CHINA EXPERT	Steve Lewis	2-1 MF 24
Delving, Michael	THE DEVIL FINDS WORK	George Kelley	1-6 MF 50
Delving, Michael	DIE LIKE A MAN	George Kelley	1-6 MF 50
Delving, Michael	DIE LIKE A MAN	Guy M. Townsend	1A MF 37
Delving, Michael	SMILING, THE BOY FELL DEAD	George Kelley	1-5 MF 50
DeMarco, Gordon	OCTOBER HEAT	Paul Bishop	2-2 M 57
Demarest, Judith	THE MODEL MURDERS	Fred Dueren	13-3 TAD 252
DeMille, Nelson	THE TERRORISTS	Bill Crider	9-2 TAD 147
Deming, Richard	SHE'LL HATE ME TOMORROW	Steve Lewis	1A MF 28
Demouzon, Alain	MOUCHE	Steve Lewis	5-2 MF 21
Demouzon, Alain	MOUCHE	Joanne Schneider	1-1 M 22
Demouzon, Alain	LE PREMIER-NE D'EGYPTE	Barzun & Taylor	11-1 TAD 92
Denbie, Roger	DEATH ON THE LIMITED	Guy M. Townsend	1A MF 38
Denbow, William	CHANDLER	Myrtis Broset	2-5 MM 5
Denham, Bertie	THE MAN WHO LOST HIS SHADOW	Ariadne Blackfriar	1-3 M 16
Denham, Bertie	THE MAN WHO LOST HIS SHADOW	Allen J. Hubin	13-3 TAD 199
Denning, Mark	BEYOND THE PRIZE	Bill Crider	3-3 MF 43
Denning, Mark	DIE FAST, DIE HAPPY	Bill Crider	10-1 TAD 65
Denning, Mark	DIE FAST, DIE HAPPY	Fred Dueren	10-1 TAD 52
Denning, Mark	SHADES OF GRAY	Bill Crider	10-1 TAD 65
Denning, Mark	THE SWISS ABDUCTION	Joyce L. Dewes	3-1 M 38
Dennis, Ralph	DEADMAN'S GAME	Steve Lewis	1-8 MM 6
Dennis, Ralph	DOWN AMONG THE JOCKS	Jeff Meyerson	1 PE 12
Dennis, Robert C.	THE SWEAT OF FEAR	Fred Dueren	10-1 TAD 52
Dennis, Robert C.	THE SWEAT OF FEAR	Don Miller	10 MN R6
Dent, Lester	DOC SAVAGE:THE MAN OF BRONZE (film)	Daryl S.Herrick	1 MB 27
Dent, Lester	DOC SAVAGE:THE MAN OF BRONZE (film)	(not stated)	1 BSA 15
Dent, Lester	HADES & HOCUS POCUS	Michael L. Cook	7 U 31
DePuy, E.Spence	THE LONG KNIFE	Charles Shibuk	9-2 TAD 142
Derby, Mark	SUN IN THE HUNTER'S EYES	Bill Crider	1-6 PP 24
Derleth, August	THE ADVENTURES OF SOLAR PONS	Jon L. Lellenberg	8-2 TAD 144
Derleth, August	THE CHRONICLES OF SOLAR PONS	Allen J. Hubin	7-1 TAD 62
Derleth, August	IN RE: SHERLOCK HOLMES	Douglas G. Greene	12-3 TAD 231
Derleth, August	THE MAN ON ALL FOURS	Richard H.Fawcett	2-2 AD 12
Derleth, August	MR.GEORGE AND OTHER ODD PERSONS	Richard H.Fawcett	1-3 AD 6
Derleth, August	PLACE OF HAWKS	Richard H.Fawcett	2-3/4 AD 13
Derleth, August	THE RETURN OF SOLAR PONS	Arthur C. Scott	2-2 MM 5

Derleth, August	SAC PRAIRIE PEOPLE	Richard H.Fawcett	2-1 AD 5
Derleth, August	SHADOW OF NIGHT	Richard H.Fawcett	2-3/4 AD 13
Derrick, Lionel	DEVINE DEATH	Steve Lewis	2-1 MF 26
Detection Club	THE FLOATING ADMIRAL	Fred Dueren	13-3 TAD 251
Detection Club	THE FLOATING ADMIRAL	Iona Kristopolis	1-3 M 17
Detection Club	THE FLOATING ADMIRAL	Ethel Lindsay	4-5/6 PP 18
Detection Club	THE FLOATING ADMIRAL	Charles Shibuk	13-4 TAD 362
Detzer, Karl	CAR 99 (film)	William K.Everson	9-2 TAD 136
Devine, D.M.	ILLEGAL TENDER	Barzun & Taylor	10-2 TAD 126
Devine, Dominic	SUNK WITHOUT TRACE	Allen J. Hubin	13-3 TAD 200
Devine, Dominic	SUNK WITHOUT TRACE	Steve Lewis	4-2 MF 31
DeWaal, Ronald Burt	THE INTERNATIONAL SHERLOCK HOLMES	Ethel Lindsay	3-5 PP 40
DeWaal, Ronald Burt	WORLD BIBLIOGRAPHY OF SHERLOCK HOLMES AND DR.WATSON	Allen J. Hubin	11-1 TAD 17
DeWaal, Ronald Burt	WORLD BIBLIOGRAPHY OF SHERLOCK HOLMES AND DR.WATSON	Jon L.Lellenberg	8-2 TAD 145
DeWeese, Gene, & Robert Coulson	NOW YOU SEE IT/HIM/THEM...	Don Miller	8 MN 16
DeWeese, Jean	THE DOLL WITH OPAL EYES	Mary A. Grochowski	2-5 PP 34
DeWeese, Jean	NIGHTMARE IN PEWTER	Mary A. Grochowski	2-5 PP 35
Dewey, Thomas B.	PREY FOR ME	Steve Lewis	2 MN 7
Dewey, Thomas B.	THE TAURUS TRIP	Steve Lewis	1A MF 24
Dexter, Colin	LAST BUS TO WOODSTOCK	Barzun & Taylor	11-3 TAD 281
Dexter, Colin	SERVICE OF ALL THE DEAD	Douglas G. Greene	3-6 PP 30
Dexter, Colin	SERVICE OF ALL THE DEAD	Steve Lewis	4-3 MF 35
Dexter, Colin	THE SILENT WORLD OF NICHOLAS QUINN	Allen J. Hubin	11-1 TAD 18
Dexter, Colin	THE SILENT WORLD OF NICHOLAS QUINN	Steve Lewis	2-2 MF 34
Dexter, Ted, & Clifford Makins	TESTKILL	Jon L. Breen	12-1 TAD 77
Diamond, I.A.L., & Billy Wilder	THE PRIVATE LIFE OF SHERLOCK HOLMES (film)	J.Randolph Cox	4-3 TAD 178
Dibdin, Michael	THE LAST SHERLOCK HOLMES STORY	Larry L. French	13-1 TAD 63
Dickie, James, ed.	THE UNDEAD	Fred Dueren	9-4 TAD 334
Dickinson, Peter	THE GREEN GENE	Robert C.S.Adey	4-2 PP 28
Dickinson, Peter	KING & JOKER	Allen J. Hubin	9-4 TAD 310
Dickinson, Peter	THE LIVELY DEAD	Allen J. Hubin	8-4 TAD 308
Dickinson, Peter	ONE FOOT IN THE GRAVE	Allen J. Hubin	13-3 TAD 200
Dickinson, Peter	THE GLASS-SIDED ANTS'-NEST	Don Miller	2-2 MM 5
Dickinson, Peter	THE LIVELY DEAD	Don Miller	2-3 MM 4
Dickinson, Peter	THE LIZARD IN THE CUP	Don Miller	1-10 MM 8
Dickinson, Peter	THE OLD ENGLISH PEEP SHOW	Lianne Carlin	3-4 MR 12
Dickinson, Peter	THE POISON ORACLE	Allen J. Hubin	7-3 TAD 220
Dickinson, Peter	THE SINISTER STONES	John Harwood	4-6 MR 38
Dickinson, Peter	WALKING DEAD	Allen J. Hubin	11-2 TAD 117
Dickinson, Peter	WALKING DEAD	Steve Lewis	2-5 MF 27
Dickson, Carter	BEHIND THE CRIMSON BLIND	James Kingman	9-2 TAD 143
Dickson, Carter	CURSE OF THE BRONZE LAMP	Angelo Panagos	11-2 TAD 127
Dickson, Carter	THE JUDAS WINDOW	Maryell Cleary	2-5 PP 30
Dickson, Carter	THE JUDAS WINDOW	James Sandoe	7-3 TAD 209
Dickson, Carter	MURDER IN THE ZOO	Maryell Cleary	2-5 PP 30
Dickson, Carter	NIGHT AT THE MOCKING WIDOW	Guy M. Townsend	2-2 MM 6
Dickson, Carter	SEEING IS BELIEVING	Mary A. Grochowski	1-3 PP 26
Dickson, Carter	THE THIRD BULLET	Martin M. Wooster	3-3 PP 26
Dickson, Carter, & John Rhode	FATAL DESCENT	Mary A.Grochowski	1-3 PP 26
Dickson, Gordon	THE SPACE SWIMMERS	Gary Zachrich	71 PU 20
Didelot, Francis	DEATH OF THE DEPUTY	Angelo Panagos	14-3 TAD 272
Didelot, Francis	MURDER IN THE BATH	Angelo Panagos	14-3 TAD 272
Diehl, William	SHARKY'S MACHINE	Allen J. Hubin	12-1 TAD 6
Dietrich, Robert	ANGEL EYES	Marvin Lachman	1-4 MF 51
Dietrich, Robert	STEVE BENTLEY'S CALYPSO CAPER	Arthur C. Scott	1-6 MM 10

Dikty, Alan S.	THE AMERICAN BOY'S BOOK SERIES BIBLIOGRAPHY 1895-1935	Robert Jennings	3 BB 3
Dillard, R.H.W.	THE BOOK OF CHANGES	Jon L. Lellenberg	8-1 TAD 59
Diment, Adam	THE GREAT SPY RACE	Robert E. Washer	1-4 QC 20
DiPego, Gerald	WITH A VENGEANCE	Amnon Kabatchnik	9 CL 3
"Diplomat"	MURDER IN THE STATE DEPARTMENT	Allen J. Hubin	1-1 TAD 27
Dirckx, John H.	DR. THORNDYKE'S DILEMMA	Allen J. Hubin	8-1 TAD 67
Disney, Doris Miles	WHO RIDES A TIGER	Marvin Lachman	7-3 TAD 212
Disney, Doris Miles	WINIFRED	Myrtis Broset	1-10 MM 7
Dixon, Franklin W.	THE MASKED DONKEY	Karen Rockow	3-3 BC 328
Dixon, Peter L., & Laird P.Koenig	THE CHILDREN ARE WATCHING	Lianne Carlin	4-2 MR 41
Dobyns, Stephen	SARATOGA LONGSHOT	Steven M. Krauzer	9-4 TAD 303
Doctorow, E.L.	LOON LAKE	Gary Warren Niebuhr	3-6 PP 17
Dodge, Steve	SHANGHAI INCIDENT	Steve Lewis	10 MN R15
Doliner, Roy	ON THE EDGE	Allen J. Hubin	12-2 TAD 112
Dollond, John	A GENTLEMAN HANGS	Barzun & Taylor	14-1 TAD 88
Dolson, Hildegarde	BEAUTY SLEEP	Mary Groff	7 CL 9
Dolson, Hildegarde	BEAUTY SLEEP	Allen J. Hubin	11-1 TAD 19
Dolson, Hildegarde	PLEASE OMIT FUNERAL	Allen J. Hubin	8-4 TAD 308
Dolson, Hildegarde	TO SPITE HER FACE	Terri Krause	2-2 PP 26
Dominic, R.B.	THE ATTENDING PHYSICIAN	Steve Lewis	4-2 MF 39
Dominic, R.B.	THE ATTENDING PHYSICIAN	Richard Moskowitz	8 LR 2
Dominic, R.B.	EPITAPH FOR A LOBBYIST	Allen J. Hubin	7-3 TAD 221
Donald, Miles	BOAST	Allen J. Hubin	14-2 TAD 124
Donaldson, Norman	GOODBYE, DR. THORNDYKE	Stanley Carlin	6-1 MR 48
Donaldson, Norman	GOODBYE, DR. THORNDYKE	Allen J. Hubin	6-2 TAD 114
Donaldson, Norman	IN SEARCH OF DR. THORNDYKE	Stanley Carlin	4-4 MR 38
Donaldson, Norman	IN SEARCH OF DR. THORNDYKE	E.T.Guymon, Jr.	4-4 TAD 237
Donaldson, Norman	IN SEARCH OF DR. THORNDYKE	Robert E. Washer	3-2 QC 18
Doody, Margaret	ARISTOTLE DETECTIVE	Maryell Cleary	4-5/6 PP 77
Doody, Margaret	ARISTOTLE DETECTIVE	Allen J. Hubin	13-3 TAD 200
Doody, Margaret	ARISTOTLE DETECTIVE	Howard Lachtman	13-3 TAD 249
Doody, Margaret	ARISTOTLE DETECTIVE	Patrice K. Loose	14-4 TAD 364
Doody, Margaret	ARISTOTLE DETECTIVE	Gary Warren Niebuhr	4-5/6 PP 77
Doody, Margaret	ARISTOTLE DETECTIVE	Charles Shibuk	14-4 TAD 376
Dooley, Roger	FLASHBACK	Stan Burns	2-2 MM 4
Dooley, Roger	FLASHBACK	Lianne Carlin	4-4 MR 39
Doty, William L.	BUTTON, BUTTON...	Fred Dueren	13-3 TAD 252
Douglas, Malcolm	THE DEADLY DAMES	Steve Lewis	1-3 MF 42
Douglas, Malcolm	PURE SWEET HELL	Steve Lewis	1A MF 29
Douglass, Donald M.	REBECCA'S PRIDE	Amnon Kabatchnik	4-1 MR 36
Downing, Todd	THE CASE OF THE UNCONQUERED SISTERS	Steve Lewis	3-4 MF 40
Downing, Warwick	THE GAMBLER, THE MINSTREL, AND THE DANCE HALL QUEEN	Steve Lewis	1-1 MF 30
Doyle, Adrian Conan, & John Dickson Carr	THE EXPLOITS OF SHERLOCK HOLMES	Douglas G. Greene	12-3 TAD 233
Doyle, Adrian Conan, & John Dickson Carr	THE EXPLOITS OF SHERLOCK HOLMES	Charles Shibuk	9-4 TAD 334
Doyle, Arthur Conan	A STUDY IN SCARLET	Don Miller	8 MN 41
Doyle, Arthur Conan	ADVENTURES OF GERARD	James Sandoe	14-3 TAD 273
Doyle, Arthur Conan	THE HOUND OF THE BASKERVILLES (film)	Thomas Godfrey	14-4 TAD 331
Doyle, Arthur Conan	THE MYSTERY OF CLOOMBER	Howard Lachtman	1-2 C 135
Doyle, Arthur Conan	THE MYSTERY OF CLOOMBER	Howard Lachtman	14-1 TAD 53
Doyle, Arthur Conan	THE SECOND STAIN (television)	Veronica M.Kennedy	2-2 TAD 122
Doyle, Arthur Conan	SHERLOCK HOLMES: A PLAY (stage)	Deryck Harvey	7-2 TAD 140
Doyle, Arthur Conan	THE SIGN OF THE FOUR	Don Miller	8 MN 41
Doyle, Arthur Conan	THE SPECKLED BAND (film)	Thomas Godfrey	14-4 TAD 331
Doyle, Arthur Conan	TALES OF TERROR AND MYSTERY	Amnon Kabatchnik	2-5 MM 8
Doyle, Arthur Conan	TALES OF TERROR AND MYSTERY	Edward Lauterbach	13-2 TAD 147
Doyle, Arthur Conan	TALES OF TERROR AND MYSTERY	Charles Shibuk	12-3 TAD 255
Doyle, Arthur Conan	WHEN THE WORLD SCREAMED	W.Ritchie Benedict	13-1 TAD 61
Doyle, Arthur Conan and others	SHERLOCK HOLMES: THE PUBLISHED APOCRYPHA (Jack Tracy,ed.)	Howard Lachtman	14-1 TAD 56

Draper, Alfred	SWANSONG FOR A RARE BIRD	Robert E. Briney	4-2 MR 36
Draper, Alfred	SWANSONG FOR A RARE BIRD	Robert E. Washer	4-1 TAD 47
Drummond, Ivor	A STENCH OF POPPIES	Allen J. Hubin	12-3 TAD 204
Drummond, Ivor	THE DIAMONDS OF LORETA	Allen J. Hubin	13-4 TAD 295
Drummond, Ivor	THE NECKLACE OF SKULLS	Allen J. Hubin	10-4 TAD 309
Drummond, Ivor	THE NECKLACE OF SKULLS	Steve Lewis	1-6 MF 39
Drummond, Ivor	THE PRIESTS OF THE ABOMINATION	Steve Lewis	11 MN R15
Drummond, June	FAREWELL STORY	Allen J. Hubin	6-4 TAD 266
Drummond, June	SLOWLY THE POISON	Allen J. Hubin	10-2 TAD 113
Drummond, June	SLOWLY THE POISON	Steve Lewis	2-1 MF 29
Drummond, June	WELCOME, PROUD LADY	Allen J. Hubin	1-2 TAD 62
Druxman, Michael B.	BASIL RATHBONE: HIS LIFE AND HIS FILMS	Jon L. Lellenberg	8-3 TAD 225
DuBreuil, Linda	CROOKED LETTER	Fred Dueren	13-1 TAD 65
Duke, Madelaine	DEATH OF A DANDIE DINMONT	Barzun & Taylor	14-4 TAD 328
Duke, Will	FAIR PREY	Bill Crider	1-6 PP 24
Duke, Winifred	BASTARD VERDICT	Mary Groff	2-5 MM 7
Dulack, Tom	THE STIGMATA OF DR.CONSTANTINE	Barbara A. Buhrer	1-9 MM 5
Duncan, Robert L.	DRAGONS AT THE GATE	Barbara A. Buhrer	10 MN R10
Duncan, Robert L.	DRAGONS AT THE GATE	Stan Burns	10 MN R11
Duncan, Robert L.	DRAGONS AT THE GATE	Don Miller	10 MN R11
Duncan, Robert L.	THE FEBRUARY PLAN	Charles Shibuk	12-1 TAD 30
Duncan, Robert L.	FIRE STORM	Allen J. Hubin	12-2 TAD 112
Duncan, Robert L.	TEMPLE DOGS	Jim Huang	11 CL 10
Dunne, John Gregory	TRUE CONFESSIONS	Peter Wolfe	11-4 TAD 404
Dunne, Thomas L.	THE SCOURGE	Allen J. Hubin	12-1 TAD 6
Dunning, -	DEADLINE	William L.DeAndrea	14-3 TAD 265
Dunning, John	TUNE IN YESTERDAY: THE ULTIMATE ENCYCLOPEDIA OF OLD TIME RADIO 1926-1976	David Bates	4-3 PP 27
Duras, Marguerite	MODERATO CANTABILE	James Mark Purcell	4-4 MR 23
Durbridge, Francis	THE TYLER MYSTERY	Deryck Harvey	6-4 TAD 271
Durgnat, Raymond	THE STRANGE CASE OF ALFRED HITCHCOCK: OR, THE PLAIN MAN'S HITCHCOCK	James Mark Purcell	10-1 TAD 67
Dwiggins, Claire V.	BILL'S DIARY	Richard H.Fawcett	2-1 AD 5
Dwyer, K.R.	DRAGONFLY	Robert E. Washer	21 X 54
Dwyer, K.R.	DRAGONFLY	Allen J. Hubin	9-1 TAD 75
Dwyer, K.R.	DRAGONFLY	Don Miller	10 MN R6
Dwyer, K.R.	DRAGONFLY	Charles Shibuk	10-1 TAD 71
Dwyer, K.R.	SHATTERED	Howard Rapp	6-2 MR 47
Dyer, George	THE CATALYST CLUB	Ammon Kabatchnik	6-2 TAD 118
Dyer, George	THE CATALYST CLUB	Angelo Panagos	11-1 TAD 27
Dyer, George	THE CATALYST CLUB	Mary Lou M.Schultz	14-2 TAD 188
Dyer, George	THE CATALYST CLUB	Mary Lou M.Schultz	14-4 TAD 365
Eames, Hugh	SLEUTHS, INC.	Allen J. Hubin	12-2 TAD 117
Eastman, Roy	MYSTERIES OF BLAIR HOUSE	Angelo Panagos	12-1 TAD 80
Easton, Nat	A BOOK FOR BANNING	Steve Lewis	5-4 MF 26
Easton, Robert O.	MAX BRAND, THE BIG "WESTERNER"	William J. Clark	2-1 FC 6
Easton, Robert O.	MAX BRAND, THE BIG "WESTERNER"	William J. Clark	2-2 FC 8
Eberhart, Mignon G.	THE CASES OF SUSAN DARE	Barzun & Taylor	9-3 TAD 209
Eberhart, Mignon G.	THE MYSTERY OF HUNTING'S END	Jim McCahery	2-3 PP 25
Eberhart, Mignon G.	THE PATIENT IN ROOM 18	Jay Jeffries	8 MN 23
Eberhart, Mignon G.	TWO LITTLE RICH GIRLS	Marvin Lachman	5-2 MR 37
Ebersohn, Wessel	A LONELY PLACE TO DIE	Allen J. Hubin	13-2 TAD 95
Ebersohn, Wessel	A LONELY PLACE TO DIE	Guy M. Townsend	4-1 MF 35
Echard, Margaret	I MET MURDER ON THE WAY	Jane S. Bakerman	3-2 PP 27
Edingtons, The	THE STUDIO MURDER MYSTERY	Jim McCahery	2-4 PP 32
Edmondson, Madeleine, & David Rounds	THE SOAPS	Allen J. Hubin	7-3 TAD 192
Edson, J.T.	BUNDUKI	Kirk McConnell	1-1 WA 9
Edward, Edward D.,ed.	BEST DETECTIVE STORIES OF THE YEAR 1979	Allen J. Hubin	13-1 TAD 28
Edwards, Leo	JERRY TODD AND THE ROSE-COLORED CAT	Robert L. Johnson	1-4 TB 4

Edwards, Leo	JERRY TODD AND THE WHISPERING MUMMY	Robert L. Johnson	1-3 TB 12
Edwards, Samuel	THE VIDOCQ DOSSIER	Becky A.Reineke	5-3 MF 36
Effinger, George Alec	FELICIA	Myrtis Broset	3-3 MF 46
Effinger, George Alec	FELICIA	Fred Dueren	11-2 TAD 192
Effinger, George Alec	FELICIA	Steve Lewis	1-2 MF 24
Egan, Lesley	A CHOICE OF CRIMES	Steve Lewis	5-2 MF 15
Egan, Lesley	A DREAM APART	Bonnie Pollard	12 CL 5
Egan, Lesley	THE BLIND SEARCH	Myrtis Broset	1-4 MF 47
Egan, Lesley	THE BLIND SEARCH	Steve Lewis	1-5 MF 31
Egan, Lesley	THE HUNTERS AND THE HUNTED	Bonnie Pollard	16 CD 9
Egan, Lesley	LOOK BACK AT DEATH	Allen J. Hubin	12-1 TAD 7
Egan, Lesley	LOOK BACK AT DEATH	Steve Lewis	3-3 MF 36
Egan, Lesley	MOTIVE IN SHADOW	Steve Lewis	4-2 MF 40
Egan, Lesley	SCENES OF CRIME	Barbara A. Buhrer	2-4 MM 3
Egan, Lesley	SERIOUS INVESTIGATION	Lianne Carlin	3-4 MR 12
Egan, Lesley	RUN TO EVIL	Lianne Carlin	3-6 MR 24
Egan, Lesley	THE WINE OF VIOLENCE	Lianne Carlin	4-4 MR 40
Egan, Lesley	THE WINE OF VIOLENCE	Robert E. Washer	2-1 QC 17
Egan, Robert	THE BOOKSTORE BOOK	Thomas Bonn	2-4 PQ 49
Egleton, Clive	A PIECE OF RESISTANCE	Robert E. Washer	2-1 QC 18
Egleton, Clive	SKIRMISH	Robert E. Washer	17 X 60
Ehrenfeld, David, & Carol K.Mack	THE CHAMELEON VARIANT	Allen J. Hubin	14-3 TAD 218
Ehrlich, Jack	THE CHATHAM KILLING	Bill Crider	2-2 PP 27
Ehrlichman, John	THE COMPANY	Amnon Kabatchnik	10-1 TAD 60
Eisenberg, Hershey	THE REINHARD ACTION	Allen J. Hubin	13-3 TAD 200
Eisenberg, Hershey	THE REINHARD ACTION	Elizabeth Wentworth	1-3 M 19
Eisenhower, Julie,ed.	MYSTERY AND SUSPENSE: GREAT STORIES FROM THE SATURDAY EVENING POST	Howard Lachtman	10-3 TAD 209
Elder, Mark	THE PROMETHEUS OPERATION	Allen J. Hubin	14-2 TAD 124
Elder, Mark	THE PROMETHEUS OPERATION	George Kelley	4-1 PP 38
Elder, Mark	WOLF HUNT	Fred Dueren	10-4 TAD 340
Ellerback, Rosemary	HAMMERSLEIGH	Barbara A. Buhrer	11 MN R3
Ellin, Stanley	THE BIND	Robert E. Washer	3-5 MR 19
Ellin, Stanley	DREADFUL SUMMIT	Charles Shibuk	14-3 TAD 266
Ellin, Stanley	HOUSE OF CARDS	George Fergus	1-5 MM 10
Ellin, Stanley	THE KEY TO NICHOLAS STREET	George Kelley	4-5/6 PP 71
Ellin, Stanley	THE KEY TO NICHOLAS STREET	Charles Shibuk	14-4 TAD 377
Ellin, Stanley	KINDLY DIG YOUR GRAVE AND OTHER WICKED STORIES	F.M.Nevins, Jr.	1-1 MF 35
Ellin, Stanley	THE LUXEMBOURG RUN	Allen J. Hubin	11-1 TAD 19
Ellin, Stanley	THE LUXEMBOURG RUN	Steve Lewis	2-3 MF 44
Ellin, Stanley	THE LUXEMBOURG RUN	F.M.Nevins,Jr.	2-5 MF 36
Ellin, Stanley	THE PANAMA PORTRAIT	George Kelley	4-5/6 PP 72
Ellin, Stanley	THE SPECIALTY OF THE HOUSE AND OTHER STORIES	Allen J. Hubin	13-3 TAD 201
Ellin, Stanley	THE SPECIALTY OF THE HOUSE AND OTHER STORIES	F.M.Nevins, Jr.	4-5 MF 42
Ellin, Stanley	STAR LIGHT, STAR BRIGHT	Marlowe Archer	4 PE 24
Ellin, Stanley	STAR LIGHT, STAR BRIGHT	Allen J. Hubin	12-3 TAD 204
Ellin, Stanley	STAR LIGHT, STAR BRIGHT	Steve Lewis	4-3 MF 38
Ellin, Stanley	STRONGHOLD	Allen J. Hubin	8-2 TAD 149
Ellin, Stanley	THE WINTER AFTER THIS SUMMER	George Kelley	4-5/6 PP 72
Ellington, Richard	STONE COLD DEAD	Steve Lewis	10 MN R14
Ellis, Edward S.	THE FLY BOYS TO THE RESCUE	C.L.Messecar	3-3 BC 352
Ellis, Edward S.	THE FLYING BOYS IN THE SKY	C.L.Messecar	3-3 BC 352
Ellison, Harlan	NO DOORS, NO WINDOWS	Martin M. Wooster	9 MN R11
Elrick, George S.	SCIENCE FICTION HANDBOOK FOR READERS AND WRITERS	W.Paul Ganley	2 FM 16
Elwood, Roger	SIX SCIENCE FICTION PLAYS	Sheldon A. Wiebe	5 SF 38
England, Barry	CONDUCT UNBECOMING (stage)	Amnon Kabatchnik	4-2 TAD 123
Ernst, Paul	THE BRONZE MERMAID	Edward Lauterbach	7-3 TAD 210
Erskine, Margaret	HARRIET FAREWELL	Allen J. Hubin	9-1 TAD 74

Estes, Winston M.	A SIMPLE ACT OF KINDNESS	Myrtis Broset	2-3 MF 56
Estleman, Loren D.	DR. JEKYLL AND MR. HOLMES	Steve Lewis	4-2 MF 34
Estleman, Loren D.	DR. JEKYLL AND MR. HOLMES	Edward Lauterbach	4-2 PP 31
Estleman, Loren D.	DR. JEKYLL AND MR. HOLMES	Charles Shibuk	14-1 TAD 79
Estleman, Loren D.	MOTOR CITY BLUES	Fred Dueren	4-4 MF 46
Estleman, Loren D.	MOTOR CITY BLUES	Allen J. Hubin	14-1 TAD 17
Estleman, Loren D.	MOTOR CITY BLUES	Steve Lewis	5-3 MF 27
Estleman, Loren D.	MOTOR CITY BLUES	Peter Spivak	14-1 TAD 54
Estleman, Loren D.	SHERLOCK HOLMES VS. DRACULA, OR THE ADVENTURE OF THE SANGUINARY COUNT	Bruce R. Beaman	13-1 TAD 64
Estleman, Loren D.	SHERLOCK HOLMES VS. DRACULA, OR THE ADVENTURE OF THE SANGUINARY COUNT	Amnon Kabatchnik	12-1 TAD 94
Estleman, Loren D.	SHERLOCK HOLMES VS. DRACULA, OR THE ADVENTURE OF THE SANGUINARY COUNT	Meghan Kelly	1-1 M 22
Estleman, Loren D.	SHERLOCK HOLMES VS. DRACULA, OR THE ADVENTURE OF THE SANGUINARY COUNT	Charles Shibuk	13-1 TAD 75
Estow, Daniel	THE MOMENT OF FICTION	Fred Dueren	13-1 TAD 65
Estow, Daniel	THE MOMENT OF FICTION	Steve Lewis	3-6 MF 30
Ethan, John B.	MURDER ON WALL STREET	Arthur C. Scott	11 MN R20
Etkin, Anne, ed.	EGLERIO! IN PRAISE OF TOLKIEN	J.Grant Thiessen	14 SF 18
Eulo, Ken	THE BROWNSTONE	Fred Dueren	14-2 TAD 183
Evans, John	HALO FOR SATAN	Steve Lewis	4-3 MF 41
Evans, John	HALO FOR SATAN	James Sandoe	11-1 TAD 85
Evans, John	HALO IN BLOOD	James Sandoe	11-1 TAD 85
Evans, John	HALO IN BRASS	Douglas M.Armato	9-1 TAD 60
Evans, John	HALO IN BRASS	James Sandoe	11-1 TAD 85
Evans, Kenneth L.	A FEAST FOR SPIDERS	Allen J. Hubin	13-1 TAD 27
Evans, Kenneth L.	A RICH WAY TO DIE	Steve Lewis	3-6 MF 40
Evans, Philip	THE BODYGUARD MAN	Deryck Harvey	7-1 TAD 60
Evers, Mrs. A.M.	BIBLIOGRAPHY OF DR. R.H.VAN GULIK	Douglas G. Greene	13-4 TAD 352
Everson, William K.	THE DETECTIVE IN FILM	Marvin Lachman	5-6 MR 37
Everson, William K.	THE DETECTIVE IN FILM	Charles Shibuk	6-2 TAD 108
Fabian, Stephen	THE BOOK OF STEPHEN FABIAN	J.Grant Thiessen	10 SF 39
Fair, A.A.	DOUBLE OR QUITS	Steve Lewis	1-2 MF 23
Fairman, Paul W.	THE FRANKENSTEIN WHEEL	Lianne Carlin	5-4 MR 33
Farjeon, Jefferson	NUMBER 17 (film)	William K.Everson	2-4 TAD 223
Falkirk, Richard	BLACKSTONE	George Fergus	1 MN 9
Falkirk, Richard	BLACKSTONE	Allen J. Hubin	6-3 TAD 192
Falkirk, Richard	BLACKSTONE ON BROADWAY	Jon L. Breen	14-1 TAD 56
Falkirk, Richard	BLACKSTONE'S FANCY	George Fergus	1 MN 9
Falkirk, Richard	BLACKSTONE'S FANCY	Deryck Harvey	6-4 TAD 259
Fantoni, Barry	MIKE DIME	Steve Lewis	5-4 MF 26
Farber, James	BLOOD ISLAND	Bill Crider	4-3 PP 28
Farhi, Moris	THE PLEASURE OF YOUR DEATH	Robert C.S.Adey	4-5/6 PP 72
Farmer, Philip Jose	A FEAST UNKNOWN	Todd Rutt	1-1 WA 9
Farmer, Philip Jose	THE ADVENTURE OF THE PEERLESS PEER	Allen J. Hubin	8-2 TAD 151
Farmer, Philip Jose	THE ADVENTURE OF THE PEERLESS PEER	Arn McConnell	1-1 WA 9
Farmer, Philip Jose	DARK IS THE SUN	J.Grant Thiessen	10 SF 40
Farmer, Philip Jose	DOC SAVAGE: HIS APOCALYPTIC LIFE	(not stated)	1 BSA 23
Farmer, Philip Jose	DOC SAVAGE: HIS APOCALYPTIC LIFE	Mark J. Golden	4 DR 11
Farmer, Philip Jose	DOC SAVAGE: HIS APOCALYPTIC LIFE	Gary Happenstand	2-2 C 156
Farmer, Philip Jose	THE LORD OF THE TREES	Florence Breen	5 DQ 4
Farmer, Philip Jose	THE MAD GOBLIN	John Cosgriff	2/3 DR 10
Farmer, Philip Jose	MOTHER WAS A LOVELY BEAST	Timothy J. Rutt	1-1 WA 10
Farmer, Philip Jose	RIVERWORLD AND OTHER STORIES	R. Jeff Banks	3-3 PP 18
Farmer, Philip Jose	TARZAN ALIVE: A DEFINITE BIOGRAPHY OF LORD GREYSTROKE	Leonard Perrine	5-4 MR 34
Farrar, Stewart	THE SNAKE ON 99	Charles Shibuk	5-4 TAD 233

Farrar, Stewart	THE TWELVE MAIDENS	Veronica M.Kennedy	8-3 TAD 223
Farris, John	SHARP PRACTICE	Allen J. Hubin	8-2 TAD 146
Farris, John	WHEN MICHAEL CALLS	S.A.Carlin	1-3 MR 6
Faulkner, William	KNIGHT'S GAMBIT	Charles Shibuk	12-2 TAD 166
Faust, Ron	THE WOLF IN THE CLOUDS	Allen J. Hubin	10-3 TAD 205
Faust, Ruth	THE LONG COUNT	Phyllis Baxter	1-2 M 20
Feegel, John R.	AUTOPSY	Fred Dueren	9-4 TAD 334
Feiffer, Jules	ACKROYD	Steven Miller	2 MT 28
Feiffer, Jules	THE GREAT COMIC BOOK HEROES	Fred S. Cook	3 BS 19
Feinman, Jeffrey	THE MYSTERIOUS WORLD OF AGATHA CHRISTIE	Amnon Kabatchnik	9-2 TAD 151
Felix, Charles	THE NOTTING HILL MYSTERY	Allen J. Hubin	10-1 TAD 42
Fenady, Andrew J.	THE MAN WITH BOGART'S FACE	R. Jeff Banks	1-3 MF 44
Fenady, Andrew J.	THE MAN WITH BOGART'S FACE	Thomas Godfrey	2-3 M 45
Fenady, Andrew J.	THE MAN WITH BOGART'S FACE	Jim Huang	7 CL 10
Fenady, Andrew J.	THE MAN WITH BOGART'S FACE	Jim Huang	1-2 PP 24
Fenady, Andrew J.	THE MAN WITH BOGART'S FACE	Amnon Kabatchnik	11-2 TAD 124
Fenady, Andrew J.	THE MAN WITH BOGART'S FACE	Steve Lewis	1-3 MF 39
Fenisong, Ruth	JENNY KISSED ME	Maryell Cleary	3-4 PP 30
Ferguson, John	THE GROUSE MOOR MYSTERY	Charles Shibuk	8-1 TAD 54
Ferrars, E.X.	ALIVE AND DEAD	Allen J. Hubin	8-3 TAD 228
Ferrars, E.X.	BLOOD FLIES UPWARDS	Mary Groff	2-5 MM 8
Ferrars, E.X.	FROG IN THE THROAT	Steve Lewis	5-2 MF 23
Ferrars, E.X.	HANGED MAN'S HOUSE	Barzun & Taylor	14-3 TAD 228
Ferrars, E.X.	THE PRETTY PINK SHROUD	Myrtis Broset	2-6 MF 42
Ferrars, E.X.	THE PRETTY PINK SHROUD	Mary Groff	6 CL 4
Ferris, Paul	HIGH PLACES	Allen J. Hubin	10-4 TAD 307
Ferris, Paul	HIGH PLACES	Steve Lewis	1-5 MF 30
Ferris, Paul	TALK TO ME ABOUT ENGLAND	Allen J. Hubin	12-4 TAD 321
Field, Moira	GUNPOWDER, TREASON AND PLOT	Barzun & Taylor	10-3 TAD 224
Fields, Joseph, & Ewart Adamson	THE WALKING DEAD (film)	William K. Everson	1-2 TAD 55
Filgate, Macartney	RUNWAY TO DEATH	Howard Rapp	4-1 PP 33
Fine, Peter Henry	NIGHT TRAINS	Allen J. Hubin	13-2 TAD 95
Fine, Peter Heath	TROUBLED WATERS	William L.DeAndrea	14-3 TAD 265
Finney, Jack	THE NIGHT PEOPLE	Steve Lewis	2-3 MF 41
Fischer, Bruno	THE EVIL DAYS	James Sandoe	14-4 TAD 366
Fischer, Bruno	THE EVIL DAYS	Charles Shibuk	9-3 TAD 208
Fischer, Bruno	THE FLESH WAS COLD	Steve Lewis	1-1 MF 27
Fischer, Bruno	THE GIRL BETWEEN	Steve Lewis	3-2 MF 38
Fischer, Bruno	HOUSE OF FLESH	Steve Lewis	3-6 MF 32
Fischer, Bruno	QUOTH THE RAVEN	Steve Lewis	1-2 MF 25
Fischer, Bruno	THE RESTLESS HANDS	Robert Samoian	3-6 PP 26
Fischer, Erwin	THE BERLIN INDICTMENT	Amnon Kabatchnik	4-6 MR 34
Fish, Robert L.	A GROSS CARRIAGE OF JUSTICE	Mary A. Grochowski	2-6 PP 35
Fish, Robert L.	THE FUGITIVE	Robert E. Washer	3-6 MR 23
Fish, Robert L.	THE GOLD OF TROY	Steve Lewis	5-1 MF 25
Fish, Robert L.	THE GREEN HELL TREASURE	Marvin Lachman	4-4 MR 33
Fish, Robert L.	THE GREEN HELL TREASURE	Robert E. Washer	3-1 QC 19
Fish, Robert L.	KEK HUUYGENS, SMUGGLER	Allen J. Hubin	10-1 TAD 5
Fish, Robert L.	KEK HUUYGENS, SMUGGLER	Martin M. Wooster	2-5 MF 41
Fish, Robert L.	THE MEMOIRS OF SCHLOCK HOMES	Peter G. Ashman	8-1 TAD 62
Fish, Robert L.	PURSUIT	Allen J. Hubin	12-1 TAD 7
Fish, Robert L.	THE TRICKS OF THE TRADE	Joe R. Christopher	5-3 MR 35
Fish, Robert L.	THE WAGER	Allen J. Hubin	7-4 TAD 295
Fish, Robert L., ed.	WITH MALICE TOWARD ALL	Robert E. Washer	1-3 QC 22
Fish, Robert L.	THE XAVIER AFFAIR	Robert E. Washer	3-6 MR 23
Fisher, Dave, & Joey Black	JOEY COLLECTS	Jose Mendez	2-2 M 55
Fisher, David	THE PACK	Charles Shibuk	10-2 TAD 149
Fisher, David E.	CRISIS	Lianne Carlin	5-2 MR 43
Fisher, David E.	VARIATIONS ON A THEME	Steve Lewis	5-6 MF 38
Fisher, Norman	WALK AT A STEADY PACE	Barzun & Taylor	9-2 TAD 93
Fisher, Steve	THE HELL-BLACK NIGHT	William J. Clark	2-1 FC 6
Fisher, Steve	SAXON'S GHOST	Stanley Carlin	3-2 MR 9

Fitt, Mary	MISMAZE	Steve Lewis	5-3 MF 28
Fitzgerald, Nigel	GHOST IN THE MAKING	Barzun & Taylor	14-3 TAD 228
Fitzhugh, Percy K.	ALONG THE MOHAWK TRAIL	C.L.Messecar	3-3 BC 351
Fitzmaurice, Eugene	CIRCUMSTANTIAL EVIDENCE	Fred Dueren	11-4 TAD 396
Fitzsimons,C.	REFLEX ACTION	Allen J. Hubin	13-4 TAD 295
Flanagan, Graeme	ROBERT BLOCH, A BIO-BIBLIOGRAPHY	Michael L. Cook	4 U 20
Flannery, Sean	EAGLES FLY	George Kelley	4-1 PP 38
Flannery, Sean	EAGLES FLY	Charles Chibuk	14-2 TAD 182
Fleegel, John R.	AUTOPSY	Steve Lewis	3-2 MF 37
Fleetwood, Hugh	A PICTURE OF INNOCENCE	Fred Dueren	13-1 TAD 65
Fleetwood, Hugh	THE GIRL WHO PASSED FOR NORMAL	Allen J. Hubin	6-4 TAD 266
Fleischman, A.S.	DANGER IN PARADISE	Steve Lewis	5-4 MF 25
Fleischman, A.S.	SHANGHAI FLAME	Steve Lewis	2-4 MF 30
Fleming, Ian	COLONEL SUN	Robert Osterman	1-5 MR 6
Fleming, Ian	DIAMONDS ARE FOREVER (film)	Richard S. Lochte	5-2 TAD 104
Fleming, Ian	FOR YOUR EYES ONLY	Douglas G. Greene	12-3 TAD 234
Fleming, Ian	GOLDFINGER	Arthur C. Scott	2-3 MM 5
Fleming, Ian	ON HER MAJESTY'S SECRET SERVICE (film)	John Dempsey	3-3 MR 23
Fleming, Joan	ALIAS POOR FATHER	Allen J. Hubin	6-3 TAD 192
Fleming, Joan	BACKYARD	Allen J. Hubin	9-1 TAD 75
Fleming, Joan	EVERY INCH A LADY	Allen J. Hubin	11-3 TAD 231
Fleming, Joan	EVERY INCH A LADY	Steve Lewis	2-6 MF 32
Fleming, Joan	...TO MAKE AN UNDERWORLD	Steve Lewis	1-1 MF 33
Fleming, Joan	YOUNG MAN, I THINK YOU'RE DYING	Robert E. Washer	4-1 MR 34
Fletcher, David	A LOVABLE MAN	Allen J. Hubin	8-3 TAD 226
Fletcher, David	RAFFLES	William A.Karpowicz	3 MT 17
Fletcher, David	RAFFLES	Jon L. Lellenberg	11-2 TAD 122
Fletcher, J.S.	THE DIAMOND MURDERS	James Kingman	7-4 TAD 287
Fletcher, J.S.	THE MARKENMORE MYSTERY	Barzun & Taylor	10-2 TAD 126
Fletcher, J.S.	THE MIDDLE TEMPLE MURDER	Charles Shibuk	14-2 TAD 182
Fletcher, J.S.	THE RANSOM FOR LONDON	Marvin Lachman	2-4 PP 32
Fletcher, Lucille	EIGHTY DOLLARS TO STAMFORD	Barbara A. Buhrer	11 MN R14
Fletcher, Lucille	EIGHTY DOLLARS TO STAMFORD	Allen J. Hubin	9-1 TAD 74
Fletcher, Lucille	EIGHTY DOLLARS TO STAMFORD	Steve Lewis	1A MF 25
Fletcher, Lucille	NIGHT WATCH (stage)	Amnon Kabatchnik	5-4 TAD 229
Flett, Alfred	NEVER SHAKE A SKELETON	Allen J. Hubin	12-3 TAD 204
Flora, Fletcher	LEAVE HER TO HELL!	Bill Crider	3 PE 19
Florescu, Radu, & Raymond McNally	IN SEARCH OF DRACULA: A TRUE HISTORY OF DRACULA AND VAMPIRE LEGENDS	Veronica M.Kennedy	7-2 TAD 138
Flowers, Charles	IT NEVER RAINS IN LOS ANGELES	Mary Jean DeMarr	4-1 MF 30
Flynn, Brian	THE MYSTERY OF THE PEACOCK'S EYE	Charles Shibuk	7-1 TAD 53
Flynn, Brian	THE ORANGE AXE	Charles Shibuk	9-3 TAD 231
Flynn, J.M.	WARLOCK	Fred Dueren	9-4 TAD 277
Foley, Rae	THE BARCLAY PLACE	Barbara A. Buhrer	10 MN R2
Foley, Rae	THE BROWNSTONE HOUSE	Barbara A. Buhrer	10 MN R13
Foley, Rae	THE DARK HILL	Barbara A. Buhrer	11 MN R13
Foley, Rae	OMINOUS STAR	Stanley Carlin	4-6 MR 36
Follett, James	CROWN COURT	Allen J. Hubin	11-3 TAD 233
Follett, James	CROWN COURT	Steve Lewis	2-6 MF 32
Follett, Ken	EYE OF THE NEEDLE	Barbara A. Buhrer	13 MN R2
Follett, Ken	EYE OF THE NEEDLE	Jim Huang	11 CL 10
Follett, Ken	EYE OF THE NEEDLE	Allen J. Hubin	11-4 TAD 331
Follett, Ken	EYE OF THE NEEDLE	Amnon Kabatchnik	1-5 PP 23
Follett, Ken	TRIPLE	Gary Warren Niebuhr	2-5 PP 38
Foote-Smith,Elizabeth	NEVER SAY DIE	Allen J. Hubin	10-3 TAD 205
Foote-Smith,Elizabeth	NEVER SAY DIE	Steve Lewis	2-1 MF 24
Footner, Hulbert	MADAME STOREY	Douglas G. Greene	12-3 TAD 230
Forbes, Colin	AVALANCHE EXPRESS	Allen J. Hubin	11-1 TAD 17
Forbes, Colin	TARGET FIVE	George Fergus	1 MN 9
Forbes, Stanton	IF LAUREL SHOT HARDY THE WORLD WOULD END	Stanley Carlin	3-6 MR 22
Forbes, Stanton	THE SAD, SUDDEN DEATH OF MY FAIR LADY	Stanley Carlin	3-4 MR 35

Forbes, Stanton	THE WILL AND LAST TESTAMENT OF CONSTANCE COBBLE	Steve Lewis	4-3 MF 37
Ford, Alla T.	UFO'S IN OZ	Michael L. Cook	5 U 31
Ford, George	'GATOR	(anonymous)	1-3 MF 45
Ford, John M.	WEB OF ANGELS	Paul Harwitz	8 LR 4
Ford, Leslie	THE PHILADELPHIA MURDER STORY	Jon L. Breen	5-1 MR 36
Ford, Leslie	TRIAL BY AMBUSH	Barzun & Taylor	12-1 TAD 32
Ford, Paul Leicester	THE GREAT K & A TRAIN ROBBERY	Edward Lauterbach	12-1 TAD 79
Ford, Richard	THE ULTIMATE GOOD LUCK	Gary Warren Niebuhr	4-5/6 PP 64
Forester, C.S.	PAYMENT DEFERRED (film)	William K. Everson	2-4 TAD 224
Forrest, Maryann	HERE	Robert E. Washer	2-1 QC 18
Forrest, Richard	A CHILD'S GARDEN OF DEATH	Frank Denton	1-5 MM 10
Forrest, Richard	A CHILD'S GARDEN OF DEATH	Allen J. Hubin	9-2 TAD 152
Forrest, Richard	A CHILD'S GARDEN OF DEATH	Charles Shibuk	10-3 TAD 239
Forrest, Richard	THE DEATH AT YEW CORNER	Robert C.S.Adey	4-5/6 PP 78
Forrest, Richard	DEATH THROUGH THE LOOKING GLASS	Allen J. Hubin	11-3 TAD 232
Forrest, Richard	DEATH THROUGH THE LOOKING GLASS	Charles Shibuk	12-2 TAD 166
Forrest, Richard	THE DEATH AT YEW CORNER	Steve Lewis	5-2 MF 24
Forrest, Richard	THE WIZARD OF DEATH	Allen J. Hubin	10-3 TAD 204
Forrest, Richard	THE WIZARD OF DEATH	Steve Lewis	1-5 MF 29
Forrest, Richard	THE WIZARD OF DEATH	Charles Shibuk	11-4 TAD 379
Forsyte, Charles	THE DECODING OF EDWIN DROOD	Barzun & Taylor	14-1 TAD 88
Forsyth, Frederick	THE ODESSA FILE	Allen J. Hubin	6-2 TAD 113
Fosburgh, Lacey	CLOSING TIME	Jim Huang	8 CL 6
Fosburgh, Lacey	CLOSING TIME	Mary Groff	3-1 PP 33
Fox, George	AMOK	Joe R. Lansdale	3-5 MF 43
Fox, James	CALL CAR 54	Fred Dueren	11-3 TAD 306
Fox, Pete	MANTIS	Allen J. Hubin	14-2 TAD 125
Fox, Sebastian	ODD WOMAN OUT	Barzun & Taylor	9-2 TAD 93
Fox, Terry Curtis	COPS (stage)	Paul Bishop	1-2 M 12
Fox-Davies, A.C.	THE MAULEVERER MURDERS	Peter Christensen	12-1 TAD 80
Foxx, Jack	DEAD RUN	Allen J. Hubin	9-1 TAD 73
Foxx, Jack	DEAD RUN	Steve Lewis	2-4 MF 34
Foxx, Jack	FREEBOOTY	Steve Lewis	1-2 MF 23
Foxx, Jack	WILDFIRE	Steve Lewis	3-3 MF 38
Francis, Dick	BLOOD SPORT	Charles Shibuk	13-1 TAD 75
Francis, Dick	BONECRACK	Joe R. Christopher	5-5 MR 33
Francis, Dick	DEAD CERT	Lianne Carlin	3-3 MR 31
Francis, Dick	ENQUIRY	Stanley Carlin	3-6 MR 22
Francis, Dick	FLYING FINISH	June Moffatt	8 JD 17
Francis, Dick	HIGH STAKES	Myrtis Broset	1-10 MM 7
Francis, Dick	HIGH STAKES	Barbara A. Buhrer	11 MN R12
Francis, Dick	HIGH STAKES	Allen J. Hubin	9-3 TAD 224
Francis, Dick	HIGH STAKES	Amnon Kabatchnik	2-1 MM 4
Francis, Dick	HIGH STAKES	Charles Shibuk	10-4 TAD 360
Francis, Dick	IN THE FRAME	Allen J. Hubin	10-3 TAD 205
Francis, Dick	IN THE FRAME	Charles Shibuk	12-1 TAD 30
Francis, Dick	KNOCKDOWN	Barbara A. Buhrer	1-5 MM 9
Francis, Dick	KNOCKDOWN	Stan Burns	5/6 MN 17
Francis, Dick	KNOCKDOWN	Allen J. Hubin	8-3 TAD 228
Francis, Dick	KNOCKDOWN	Steve Lewis	1-3 MF 40
Francis, Dick	KNOCKDOWN	Charles Shibuk	9-4 TAD 281
Francis, Dick	ODDS AGAINST	Charles Shibuk	13-4 TAD 363
Francis, Dick	RAT RACE	Allen J. Hubin	4-3 TAD 180
Francis, Dick	RAT RACE	Charles Shibuk	12-2 TAD 166
Francis, Dick	REFLEX	Howard Lachtman	14-4 TAD 361
Francis, Dick	RISK	Allen J. Hubin	11-3 TAD 233
Francis, Dick	RISK	Charles Shibuk	12-4 TAD 368
Francis, Dick	SLAYRIDE	Allen J. Hubin	7-3 TAD 220
Francis, Dick	SMOKESCREEN	Allen J. Hubin	6-3 TAD 192
Francis, Dick	THREE TO SHOW	Robert E. Washer	2-1 QC 17
Francis, Dick	TRIAL RUN	Allen J. Hubin	12-3 TAD 204
Francis, Dick	TRIAL RUN	Steve Lewis	3-6 MF 30
Francis, Dick	TRIAL RUN	Charles Shibuk	14-1 TAD 80
Francis, Dick	WHIP HAND	Allen J. Hubin	13-3 TAD 201
Francis, Dick	WHIP HAND	Marvin Lachman	3-3 PP 31

Francis, Dick	WHIP HAND	Steve Lewis	4-4 MF 37
Francis, Dick	WHIP HAND	Charles Shibuk	14-3 TAD 266
Francis, Richard H.	DAGGERMAN	Allen J. Hubin	13-4 TAD 295
Franke, David	THE TORTURE DOCTOR	Barzun & Taylor	12-1 TAD 32
Franke, David	THE TORTURE DOCTOR	Jon L. Lellenberg	9-3 TAD 222
Frankish, H.	DR. CUNLIFFE, INVESTIGATOR	A.F.Germeshausen	1-3 TAD 101
Frankland, Edward	THE MURDERS AT CROSSBY	Jim Finzel	4-1 PP 30
Franklin, Eugene	MURDER TRAPP	Robert E. Briney	5-5 MF 42
Franklin, Eugene	MURDER TRAPP	Robert E. Briney	4-6 MF 35
Franklin, Max	CHARLIE'S ANGELS	Steve Lewis	1-4 MF 39
Franklin, Steve	THE MALCONTENTS	Stan Burns	10 MN R14
Fraser, Antonia	QUIET AS A NUN	Allen J. Hubin	11-1 TAD 19
Fraser, James	A COCK-PIT OF ROSES	Jim McCahery	3-2 PP 29
Fraser, James	THE EVERGREEN DEATH	Jim McCahery	3-2 PP 29
Fraser, James	HEART'S EASE IN DEATH	Martin Rifkin	5 CL 2
Fray, Al	THE DAME'S THE GAME	Steve Lewis	7 MN 10
Frazer, Andrew	FIND EILEEN HARDIN - ALIVE	John Vining	8-4 TAD 297
Frederic, Macdowell	EMERGENCY PROCEDURE	Robert E. Washer	2-1 QC 18
Fredman, Mike	KISSES LEAVE NO FINGERPRINTS	Paul Bishop	2-2 M 58
Fredman, Mike	KISSES LEAVE NO FINGERPRINTS	Steve Lewis	4-5 MF 32
Fredman, Mike	YOU CAN ALWAYS BLAME THE RAIN	Marlowe Archer	5 PE 40
Fredman, Mike	YOU CAN ALWAYS BLAME THE RAIN	Paul Bishop	2-2 M 57
Fredman, Mike	YOU CAN ALWAYS BLAME THE RAIN	Allen J. Hubin	13-3 TAD 201
Fredman, Mike	YOU CAN ALWAYS BLAME THE RAIN	Andy Jaysnovitch	7 PE 14
Fredman, Mike	YOU CAN ALWAYS BLAME THE RAIN	Steve Lewis	4-4 MF 36
Freeborn, Brian	GOOD LUCK MISTER CAIN	Allen J. Hubin	10-3 TAD 204
Freeborn, Brian	GOOD LUCK MISTER CAIN	Steve Lewis	1-4 MF 37
Freeborn, Brian	TEN DAYS, MISTER CAIN	R.Jeff Banks	1-6 PP 26
Freeborn, Brian	TEN DAYS, MISTER CAIN	Steve Lewis	2-6 MF 32
Freeling, Nicolas	A DRESSING OF DIAMOND	Allen J. Hubin	7-4 TAD 296
Freeling, Nicolas	ARLETTE	Allen J. Hubin	14-4 TAD 299
Freeling, Nicolas	AUPRES DE MA BLONDE	Allen J. Hubin	6-1 TAD 44
Freeling, Nicolas	AUPRES DE MA BLONDE	William Ruble	5-5 MR 32
Freeling, Nicolas	BECAUSE OF THE CATS	Arthur C. Scott	9 MN R20
Freeling, Nicolas	THE BUGLES BLOWING	Jane S. Bakerman	11-2 TAD 122
Freeling, Nicolas	THE BUGLES BLOWING	F.M.Nevins, Jr.	1-5 MF 44
Freeling, Nicolas	CASTANG'S CITY	Jane S. Bakerman	4-5 MF 40
Freeling, Nicolas	DOUBLE BARREL	Don Miller	11 MN R17
Freeling, Nicolas	THE LOVELY LADIES	William Ruble	6-1 MR 46
Freeling, Nicolas	SABINE	Allen J. Hubin	11-3 TAD 230
Freeling, Nicolas	SABINE	Steve Lewis	3-2 MF 36
Freeling, Nicolas	TSING-BOOM	Lianne Carlin	3-1 MR 7
Freeling, Nicolas	THE WIDOW	D.E.Ath	
Freeling, Nicolas	THE WIDOW	Allen J. Hubin	13-2 TAD 95
Freeman, Lucy	THE PSYCHIATRIST SAYS MURDER	Don Miller	8 MN 25
Freeman, R. Austin	THE BEST OF DR.THORNDYKE detective stories	Norman Donaldson	6-4 TAD 262
Freeman, R. Austin	FLIGHTY PHYLLIS	Jay Jeffries	1 MN 7
Freeman, R. Austin	FOR THE DEFENSE, DR. THORNDYKE	Angelo Panagos	11-1 TAD 27
Freeman, R. Austin	THE PENROSE MYSTERY	Arthur C. Scott	9 MN R20
Freeman, R. Austin	PONTIFLEX, SON AND THORNDYKE	Jay Jeffries	1 MN 7
Freeman, R. Austin	THE STONEWARE MONKEY	Arthur C. Scott	9 MN R20
Freeman, R. Austin	THE SURPRISING EXPERIENCES OF MR. SHUTTLEBURY COBB	Jim Finzel	3-6 PP 25
Freeman, R. Austin, & John J.Pitcairn	FROM A SURGEON'S DIARY	Allen J. Hubin	8-4 TAD 312
Freemantle, Brian	CHARLIE M	Steve Lewis	2-3 MF 41
Freemantle, Brian	HERE COMES CHARLIE M	Theodore Dukeshire	4-2 MF 50
Freemantle, Brian	HERE COMES CHARLIE M	Steve Lewis	3-4 MF 38
Fremlin, Celia	DON'T GO TO SLEEP IN THE DARK	Lianne Carlin	4-2 MR 39
Fremlin, Celia	THE JEALOUS ONE	Lianne Carlin	3-6 MR 24
Fremlin, Celia	THE SPIDER ORCHID	Thomas F. Godfrey	12-4 TAD 370
Fremlin, Celia	THE SPIDER ORCHID	Steve Lewis	2-6 MF 30
French, Michael	CLUB CARIBE	Fred Dueren	10-4 TAD 341
Friel, Arthur O.	TIGER RIVER	Robert E. Briney	5-1 MR 39

Frome, David	IN AT THE DEATH	Angelo Panagos	11-4 TAD 381
Frome, David	THE STRANGE DEATH OF MARTIN GREEN	Maryell Cleary	2-3 PP 26
Fugate, Francis, & Roberta B.	SECRETS OF THE WORLD'S BEST-SELLING WRITER: THE STORY TELLING TECHNIQUES OF ERLE STANLEY GARDNER	George Kelley	4-3 PP 27
Fugate, Francis, & Roberta B.	SECRETS OF THE WORLD'S BEST-SELLING WRITER: THE STORY TELLING TECHNIQUES OF ERLE STANLEY GARDNER	Jean Lamb	2-3 M 47
Fugate, Francis, & Roberta B.	SECRETS OF THE WORLD'S BEST-SELLING WRITER: THE STORY TELLING TECHNIQUES OF ERLE STANLEY GARDNER	Steve Lewis	5-2 MF 13
Fuller, Samuel	DEAD PIGEON ON BEETHOVEN STREET	Steve Lewis	1A MF 25
Fuller, Timothy	HARVARD HAS A HOMICIDE	Jim McCahery	1-4 PP 26
Fuller, Timothy	REUNION WITH MURDER	David Rose	2-3 PP 29
Fuller, Timothy	THREE THIRDS OF A GHOST	Jim McCahery	2-5 PP 31
Furst, Alan	YOUR DAY IN THE BARREL	Steve Lewis	1A MF 28
Futrelle, Jacques	GREAT CASES OF THE THINKING MACHINE: 13 DETECTIVE STORIES	James Mark Purcell	10-3 TAD 207
Futrelle, Jacques	GREAT CASES OF THE THINKING MACHINE: 13 DETECTIVE STORIES	Charles Shibuk	10-2 TAD 149
Gaboriau, Emile	MONSIEUR LECOQ	M.S.Cappadonna	10-2 TAD 114
Gadney, Reg	THE CAGE	Allen J. Hubin	11-2 TAD 117
Gaffney, Marjorie	THE RAT (film)	William K. Everson	8-1 TAD 51
Gage, Edwin	PHOENIX NO MORE	Allen J. Hubin	12-2 TAD 112
Gage, Edwin	PHOENIX NO MORE	Steve Lewis	3-1 MF 36
Gage, Nicholas	BONES OF CONTENTION	Allen J. Hubin	7-4 TAD 296
Galbreath, Robert	THE OCCULT: STUDIES AND EVALUATIONS	Robert E. Briney	9 R 28
Galewitz, Herb, ed.	THE CELEBRATED CASES OF DICK TRACY 1931-1951	Stanley Carlin	4-2 MR 34
Gallagher, Richard	MURDER BY GEMINI	Hellgate Newlander	5-2 TAD 102
Gallant, Gladys S.	LIVING IMAGE	Steve Lewis	3-1 MF 35
Gardiner, Dorothy	THE TRANS-ATLANTIC GHOST	Steve Lewis	3-5 MF 41
Gardiner, Dorothy, & Katherine Walker, ed.	RAYMOND CHANDLER SPEAKING	Jeff Meyerson	1-6 MF 45
Gardiner, Dorothy, & Katherine Walker, ed.	RAYMOND CHANDLER SPEAKING	Charles Shibuk	10-4 TAD 361
Gardiner, Wayne J.	THE MAN ON THE LEFT	George Kelley	4-1 PP 39
Gardner, Erle Stanley	THE AMAZING ADVENTURES OF LESTER LEITH	Douglas G. Greene	14-3 TAD 268
Gardner, Erle Stanley	THE AMAZING ADVENTURES OF LESTER LEITH	Charles Shibuk	14-3 TAD 266
Gardner, Erle Stanley	THE AMAZING ADVENTURES OF LESTER LEITH	Martin M. Wooster	4-2 PP 30
Gardner, Erle Stanley	THE CASE OF THE AMOROUS AUNT	F.M.Nevins, Jr.	1-3 MF 49
Gardner, Erle Stanley	THE CASE OF THE BEAUTIFUL BEGGAR	Steve Lewis	8 MN 24
Gardner, Erle Stanley	THE CASE OF THE BEAUTIFUL BEGGAR	F.M.Nevins, Jr.	1-4 MF 54
Gardner, Erle Stanley	THE CASE OF THE BIGAMOUS SPOUSE	F.M.Nevins, Jr.	1-1 MF 37
Gardner, Erle Stanley	THE CASE OF THE BLONDE BONANZA	F.M.Nevins, Jr.	1-2 MF 10
Gardner, Erle Stanley	THE CASE OF THE CARELESS CUPID	F.M.Nevins, Jr.	1-5 MF 50
Gardner, Erle Stanley	THE CASE OF THE CURIOUS BRIDE (film)	William K. Everson	10-4 TAD 313
Gardner, Erle Stanley	THE CASE OF THE DARING DIVORCEE	F.M.Nevins, Jr.	1-3 MF 49
Gardner, Erle Stanley	THE CASE OF THE FABULOUS FAKE	Marvin Lachman	3-3 TAD 201
Gardner, Erle Stanley	THE CASE OF THE FABULOUS FAKE	F.M.Nevins, Jr.	1-5 MF 51
Gardner, Erle Stanley	THE CASE OF THE FENCED-IN WOMAN	Hellgate Newlander	6-2 TAD 112
Gardner, Erle Stanley	THE CASE OF THE HORRIFIED HEIRS	F.M.Nevins, Jr.	1-3 MF 50
Gardner, Erle Stanley	THE CASE OF THE ICE-COLD HANDS	F.M.Nevins, Jr.	1-2 MF 45
Gardner, Erle Stanley	THE CASE OF THE LAZY LOVER	Steve Lewis	5-3 MF 33
Gardner, Erle Stanley	THE CASE OF THE MISCHIEVOUS DOLL	F.M.Nevins, Jr.	1-2 MF 45

Gardner, Erle Stanley	THE CASE OF THE MURDERER'S BRIDE AND OTHER STORIES	Marvin Lachman	3-3 TAD 203
Gardner, Erle Stanley	THE CASE OF THE MURDERER'S BRIDE AND OTHER STORIES	Robert E. Washer	2-2 QC 14
Gardner, Erle Stanley	THE CASE OF THE PHANTOM FORTUNE	F.M.Nevins, Jr.	1-3 MF 50
Gardner, Erle Stanley	THE CASE OF THE POSTPONED MURDER	F.M.Nevins, Jr.	7-1 TAD 58
Gardner, Erle Stanley	THE CASE OF THE QUEENLY CONTESTANT	F.M.Nevins, Jr.	1-5 MF 50
Gardner, Erle Stanley	THE CASE OF THE RELUCTANT MODEL	F.M.Nevins, Jr.	1-1 MF 37
Gardner, Erle Stanley	THE CASE OF THE SHAPELY SHADOW	F.M.Nevins, Jr.	1-1 MF 36
Gardner, Erle Stanley	THE CASE OF THE SPURIOUS SPINSTER	F.M.Nevins, Jr.	1-1 MF 36
Gardner, Erle Stanley	THE CASE OF THE STEPDAUGHTER'S SECRET	F.M.Nevins, Jr.	1-2 MF 45
Gardner, Erle Stanley	THE CASE OF THE TROUBLED TRUSTEE	F.M.Nevins, Jr.	1-4 MF 54
Gardner, Erle Stanley	THE CASE OF THE VELVET CLAWS	Marvin Lachman	2-4 TAD 274
Gardner, Erle Stanley	THE CASE OF THE WORRIED WAITRESS	F.M.Nevins, Jr.	1-4 MF 54
Gardner, Erle Stanley	THE HUMAN ZERO: THE SCIENCE FICTION STORIES OF ERLE STANLEY GARDNER	Steve Lewis	5-2 MF 13
Gardner, John	AIR APPARENT	Robert E. Washer	3-1 QC 19
Gardner, John	THE DANCING DODO	Allen J. Hubin	12-1 TAD 7
Gardner, John	THE LAST TRUMP	George Kelley	4-1 PP 37
Gardner, John	THE LAST TRUMP	William M.Vatavuk	2-3 M 48
Gardner, John	LICENSE RENEWED	Allen J. Hubin	14-4 TAD 299
Gardner, John	THE RETURN OF MORIARTY	Jon L. Lellenberg	8-1 TAD 60
Gardner, John	THE RETURN OF MORIARTY	Denis Quane	3/4 MN 20
Gardner, John	THE RETURN OF MORIARTY	Charles Shibuk	9-4 TAD 334
Gardner, John	THE REVENGE OF MORIARTY	Frank Denton	9 MN R5
Gardner, John	THE REVENGE OF MORIARTY	Jon L. Lellenberg	9-3 TAD 221
Gardner, John	THE REVENGE OF MORIARTY	Charles Shibuk	11-3 TAD 298
Gardner, John	TO RUN A LITTLE FASTER	Theodore Dukeshire	2-6 MF 41
Gardner, John	THE WEREWOLF TRACE	Jon L. Lellenberg	11-1 TAD 23
Gardner, Matt	THE CURSE OF QUINTANA ROO	Lianne Carlin	5-4 MR 33
Garfield, Brian	HOPSCOTCH	Stan Burns	1-8 MM 5
Garfield, Brian	HOPSCOTCH (film)	Richard Moskowitz	8 LR 6
Garfield, Brian	THE PALADIN	Allen J. Hubin	14-1 TAD 17
Garfield, Brian	RECOIL	Amnon Kabatchnik	11-1 TAD 23
Garfield, Brian	RECOIL	Steve Lewis	1-5 MF 34
Garfield, Brian	RELENTLESS	Lianne Carlin	5-3 MR 38
Garfield, Brian	TRIPWIRE	Max Collins	6-1 MR 44
Garfield, Brian	WHAT OF TERRY CONNISTON?	Steve Lewis	1-2 MF 25
Garfield, Brian	WILD TIMES	Bill Crider	2-3 PP 31
Garfield, Leon	THE MYSTERY OF EDWIN DROOD	Barzun & Taylor	14-1 TAD 89
Garfield, Leon	THE MYSTERY OF EDWIN DROOD	Fred Dueren	14-4 TAD 364
Garfield, Leon	THE MYSTERY OF EDWIN DROOD	Howard Lachtman	14-3 TAD 270
Garland, Bob	DERFFLINGER	Allen J. Hubin	12-4 TAD 321
Garner, Alan	THE MOON OF GOMRATH	Gary Zachrich	71 PU 22
Garrett, Randall	MURDER AND MAGIC	Joe R. Christopher	13-3 TAD 247
Garrett, Randall	MURDER AND MAGIC	Douglas G. Greene	12-3 TAD 273
Garrett, Randall	TOO MANY MAGICIANS	Jon L. Lellenberg	9-2 TAD 144
Garrett, Randall	TOO MANY MAGICIANS	Charles Shibuk	12-4 TAD 372
Garrett, Randall, & Vicki A.Heydron	THE STEEL OF RAITHSKAR	J.Grant Thiessen	14 SF 18
Garrity, Dave J.	DRAGON HUNT	Steve Lewis	4-2 MF 38
Garve, Andrew	THE CASE OF ROBERT QUARRY	Amnon Kabatchnik	5-4 MR 29
Garve, Andrew	COUNTERSTROKE	Jane S. Bakerman	12-2 TAD 178
Garve, Andrew	COUNTERSTROKE	Edgar James	1-1 M 22
Garve, Andrew	COUNTERSTROKE	Charles Shibuk	13-1 TAD 75
Garve, Andrew	THE CUCKOO LINE AFFAIR	Charles Shibuk	11-4 TAD 379
Garve, Andrew	THE FAR SANDS	Charles Shibuk	12-2 TAD 166
Garve, Andrew	HOME TO ROOST	Charles Shibuk	11-3 TAD 298
Garve, Andrew	THE LESTER AFFAIR	Allen J. Hubin	7-3 TAD 220
Garve, Andrew	THE LESTER AFFAIR	James Sandoe	14-3 TAD 273
Garve, Andrew	THE LONG SHORT CUT	Jane S. Bakerman	2-5 MF 35

Garve, Andrew	MURDER THROUGH THE LOOKING GLASS	Charles Shibuk	11-4 TAD 379
Garve, Andrew	NO TEARS FOR HILDA	Charles Shibuk	12-2 TAD 166
Garve, Andrew	THE RIDDLE OF SAMSON	Charles Shibuk	11-4 TAD 379
Gash, Jonathan	GOLD BY GEMINI	Peter Blazer	1-2 M 20
Gash, Jonathan	GOLD BY GEMINI	Allen J. Hubin	13-1 TAD 28
Gash, Jonathan	THE GRAIL TREE	Allen J. Hubin	13-4 TAD 295
Gash, Jonathan	THE GRAIL TREE	Steve Lewis	4-5 MF 34
Gash, Jonathan	THE JUDAS PAIR	Mary A. Grochowski	2-3 PP 31
Gash, Jonathan	THE JUDAS PAIR	Allen J. Hubin	11-2 TAD 117
Gash, Jonathan	THE JUDAS PAIR	Steve Lewis	2-3 MF 47
Gash, Jonathan	THE JUDAS PAIR	Steven Miller	4 MT 38
Gask, Arthur	THE RED PASTE MURDERS	Charles Shibuk	13-1 TAD 79
Gatenby, Rosemary	DEADLY RELATIONS	Robert E. Washer	3-4 TAD 274
Gatenby, Rosemary	HANGED FOR A SHEEP	Myrtis Broset	2-5 MM 5
Gault, Wm.Campbell	DON'T CRY FOR ME	Marvin Lachman	5-4 MF 19
Gault, Wm.Campbell	VEIN OF VIOLENCE	Bill Crider	2 PE 20
Gaute, J.H.H., & Robin Odell	THE MURDERER'S WHO'S WHO	W.Ritchie Benedict	6 U 39
Geddes, Paul	A NOVEMBER WIND	Bill Crider	2-4 PP 33
Geddes, Paul	HANGMAN	Allen J. Hubin	11-2 TAD 116
Geherin, David	SONS OF SAM SPADE	Ruth Windfeldt	1-1 M 32
Geller, Michael	A CORPSE FOR A CANDIDATE	Steve Lewis	4-3 MF 39
Geller, Michael	DISCO DEATHBEAT	Paul Harwitz	3-2 M 40
George, Theodore	THE DEADLY HOMECOMING	Robert C.S.Adey	4-3 PP 19
George, Theodore	THE DEADLY HOMECOMING	Amnon Kabatchnik	5-6 MR 32
George, Theodore	THE DEADLY HOMECOMING	Charles Shibuk	6-2 TAD 110
George, Theodore	THE MURDERS ON THE SQUARE	Robert C.S.Adey	4-3 PP 19
George, Theodore	THE MURDERS ON THE SQUARE	Lianne Carlin	5-1 MR 34
George, Theodore	THE MURDERS ON THE SQUARE	Charles Shibuk	5-2 TAD 100
Gerard, Francis	DICTATORSHIP OF THE DOVE	Angelo Panagos	13-3 TAD 270
Gerard, Francis	SORCEROR'S SHAFT	Angelo Panagos	12-1 TAD 80
Germeshausen, Anna L.	CATS IN CRIME...AND OTHERS	Stanley Carlin	3-5 MR 6
Gibson, Walter B.	THE SHADOW: A QUARTER OF EIGHT AND THE FREAK SHOW MURDERS	Amnon Kabatchnik	13-1 TAD 64
Gibson, Walter B.	THE SHADOW SCRAPBOOK	Marlowe Archer	4 PE 24
Gibson, Walter B.	THE SHADOW SCRAPBOOK	Gary Happenstand	2-2 C 156
Gibson, Walter B.	THE SHADOW SCRAPBOOK	F.M.Nevins, Jr.	4-2 MF 51
Gibson, Walter B.	THE WEIRD ADVENTURES OF THE SHADOW	Frank P.Eisgruber	66 PU 62
Gielgud, Val	CONDUCT OF A MEMBER	Barzun & Taylor	10-3 TAD 224
Gielgud, Val	FALL OF A SPARROW	Charles Shibuk	8-3 TAD 219
Gielgud, Val	IN SUCH A NIGHT	Jon L. Breen	12-1 TAD 77
Gielgud, Val, & Holt Marvell	LONDON CALLING	Robert Aucott	6-3 TAD 188
Gifford, Thomas	THE CAVANAUGH QUEST	Myrtis Broset	11 MN R12
Gifford, Thomas	THE CAVANAUGH QUEST	Barbara A. Buhrer	11 MN R12
Gifford, Thomas	THE CAVANAUGH QUEST	Allen J. Hubin	9-4 TAD 311
Gifford, Thomas	THE CAVANAUGH QUEST	Steve Lewis	1-3 MF 39
Gifford, Thomas	THE CAVANAUGH QUEST	Jeff Meyerson	1-3 MF 44
Gifford, Thomas	THE CAVANAUGH QUEST	Charles Shibuk	10-4 TAD 361
Gifford, Thomas	THE GLENDOWER LEGACY	Allen J. Hubin	12-1 TAD 7
Gifford, Thomas	THE GLENDOWER LEGACY	Steve Lewis	3-3 MF 34
Gifford, Thomas	THE GLENDOWER LEGACY	Charles Shibuk	13-1 TAD 75
Gifford, Thomas	HOLLYWOOD GOTHIC	Allen J. Hubin	13-2 TAD 95
Gifford, Thomas	THE WIND CHILL FACTOR	Allen J. Hubin	8-2 TAD 147
Gifford, Thomas	THE WIND CHILL FACTOR	Charles Shibuk	9-3 TAD 208
Gilbert, Anthony	DEATH IN THE WRONG ROOM	Steve Lewis	2-4 MM 4
Gilbert, Anthony	MY NAME IS JULIA ROSS	William K.Everson	5-4 TAD 206
Gilbert, Anthony	THE SPINSTER'S SECRET	Jane S. Bakerman	5-2 MF 33
Gilbert, Harriett	GIVEN THE AMMUNITION	Allen J. Hubin	10-2 TAD 113
Gilbert, Harriett	HOTELS WITH EMPTY ROOMS	Allen J. Hubin	6-4 TAD 266
Gilbert, Michael	AMATEUR IN VIOLENCE	Marvin Lachman	6-4 TAD 264
Gilbert, Michael	BLOOD AND JUDGMENT	Charles Shibuk	11-4 TAD 379
Gilbert, Michael	THE BODY OF A GIRL	Stanley Carlin	5-2 MR 40
Gilbert, Michael	THE BODY OF A GIRL	Allen J. Hubin	5-3 TAD 163

Gilbert, Michael	THE BODY OF A GIRL	Paul McCarthy	3-4 MF 48
Gilbert, Michael	THE BODY OF A GIRL	Charles Shibuk	12-2 TAD 166
Gilbert, Michael	CLOSE QUARTERS	James Mark Purcell	11-3 TAD 252
Gilbert, Michael	THE DANGER WITHIN	Charles Shibuk	11-4 TAD 379
Gilbert, Michael	DEATH HAS DEEP ROOTS	Charles Shibuk	11-4 TAD 379
Gilbert, Michael	THE EMPTY HOUSE	Allen J. Hubin	12-3 TAD 205
Gilbert, Michael	THE EMPTY HOUSE	Steve Lewis	3-6 MF 31
Gilbert, Michael	THE EMPTY HOUSE	Charles Shibuk	14-2 TAD 183
Gilbert, Michael	FEAR TO TREAD	Charles Shibuk	12-2 TAD 166
Gilbert, Michael	FLASH POINT	Allen J. Hubin	8-1 TAD 65
Gilbert, Michael	FLASH POINT	Charles Shibuk	10-1 TAD 71
Gilbert, Michael	THE NIGHT OF THE TWELFTH	Charles Shibuk	12-2 TAD 166
Gilbert, Michael	THE NIGHT OF THE TWELFTH	Guy M. Townsend	2-4 MM 7
Gilbert, Michael	THE 92nd TIGER	Allen J. Hubin	7-1 TAD 62
Gilbert, Michael	PETRELLA AT Q	Allen J. Hubin	11-2 TAD 117
Gilbert, Michael	THE KILLING OF KATIE STEELSTOCK	Steve Lewis	4-5 MF 30
Gilbert, Michael	THE KILLING OF KATIE STEELSTOCK	Allen J. Hubin	13-4 TAD 295
Giles, Herbert A.	HISTORIC CHINA AND OTHER SKETCHES	Douglas G. Greene	12-3 TAD 229
Giles, Kenneth	A PROVENANCE OF DEATH	Robert C.S.Adey	2-2 PP 26
Giles, Raymond	SHAMUS	Joe R. Lansdale	2-3 MF 52
Gill, B.M.	DEATH DROP	Robert C.S.Adey	5-4 MF 34
Gill, B.M.	DEATH DROP	Barzun & Taylor	13-4 TAD 308
Gill, B.M.	DEATH DROP	Allen J. Hubin	14-1 TAD 18
Gill, B.M.	DEATH DROP	Neoma Jost	2-1 M 28
Gill, B.M.	VICTIMS	Robert C.S.Adey	4-4 PP 31
Gill, Bartholomew	McGARR AND THE POLITICIAN'S WIFE	Michael Gaglio	4 MT 20
Gill, Bartholomew	McGARR AND THE POLITICIAN'S WIFE	Jon L. Lellenberg	11-1 TAD 24
Gill, Bartholomew	McGARR AND THE SIENESE CONSPIRACY	Allen J. Hubin	11-2 TAD 117
Gill, Bartholomew	McGARR AND THE SIENESE CONSPIRACY	Steve Lewis	3-1 MF 32
Gill, Bartholomew	McGARR AT THE DUBLIN HORSE SHOW	Allen J. Hubin	13-3 TAD 201
Gill, Bartholomew	McGARR ON THE CLIFFS OF MOHER	Allen J. Hubin	12-1 TAD 7
Gill, Bartholomew	McGARR ON THE CLIFFS OF MOHER	Steve Lewis	3-3 MF 39
Gill, Elizabeth	THE CRIME COAST	James Kingman	12-2 TAD 189
Gill, John	KIKI	Bill Crider	3-6 MF 47
Gillespie, Robert B.	THE CROSSWORD MYSTERY	Steve Lewis	5-5 MF 21
Gillette, William	THE ASTOUNDING CRIME ON TORRINGTON ROAD	Charles Shibuk	8-1 TAD 55
Gillette, William	SHERLOCK HOLMES (film)	William K. Everson	10-4 TAD 313
Gilliland, Alexis	THE IRON LAW OF BUREAUCRACY	J.Grant Thiessen	10 SF 39
Gillis, Jackson	THE KILLERS OF STARFISH	Myrtis Broset	1-6 MF 43
Gillis, Jackson	THE KILLERS OF STARFISH	Allen J. Hubin	11-2 TAD 118
Gilman, Dorothy	THE ELUSIVE MRS. POLLIFAX	Jon L. Breen	5-2 MR 39
Gilman, Dorothy	THE CLAIRVOYANT COUNTESS	Barbara A. Buhrer	8 MN 11
Gilman, George G.	THE VIOLENT PEACE	R. Jeff Banks	2-5 PP 13
Giovanni, Paul	THE CRUCIFER OF BLOOD (stage)	Jackie Meyerson	1-6 PP 22
Glazier, Stephen	THE LOST PROVINCES	Charles Shibuk	14-4 TAD 377
Glazner, Joseph Mark	SMART MONEY DOESN'T SING OR DANCE	Fred Dueren	13-3 TAD 252
Godey, John	THE SNAKE	Allen J. Hubin	12-2 TAD 112
Godey, John	THE THREE WORLDS OF JOHNNY HANDSOME	Robert E. Briney	5-5 MF 43
Godey, John	THE THREE WORLDS OF JOHNNY HANDSOME	Robert E. Briney	5-4 MR 28
Gold, Herbert	SLAVE TRADE	Marlowe Archer	5 PE 16
Goldblatt, Burt, & Chris Steinbrunner	CINEMA OF THE FANTASTIC	Marvin Lachman	5-6 MR 38
Goldman, Lawrence	TIGER BY THE TAIL	Steve Lewis	3-5 MF 37
Goldman, Raymond L.	JUDGE ROBINSON MURDERED!	Barzun & Taylor	10-2 TAD 126
Goldman, Raymond L.	JUDGE ROBINSON MURDERED!	Charles Shibuk	12-3 TAD 274
Goldman, Raymond L.	JUDGE ROBINSON MURDERED!	Charles Shibuk	12-4 TAD 372
Goldman, Raymond L.	MURDER WITHOUT MOTIVE	Charles Shibuk	12-1 TAD 78
Goldman, Raymond L.	OUT ON BAIL	Charles Shibuk	13-1 TAD 78

Goldman, William	MAGIC	Paul Flanagan	1 MT 45
Goldman, William	THE PRINCESS BRIDE	J.Grant Thiessen	4 SF 38
Goldstein, Arthur D.	NOBODY'S SORRY HE GOT KILLED	Amnon Kabatchnik	10 MN R5
Goldstein, Arthur D.	YOU'RE NEVER TOO OLD TO DIE	Barzun & Taylor	12-3 TAD 262
Goldstein, Arthur D.	YOU'RE NEVER TOO OLD TO DIE	Allen J. Hubin	8-2 TAD 149
Goldthwaite, Eston K.	THE SIXPENNY DAME	Steve Lewis	2-1 MM 5
Gollin, James	THE PHILOMEL FOUNDATION	Allen J. Hubin	14-2 TAD 125
Goodchild, George	DEATH ON THE CENTER COURT	Angelo Panagos	13-3 TAD 270
Goodchild, George	McLEAN DEDUCES	James Mark Purcell	9-3 TAD 229
Goodchild, George, &			
C.E.Bechofer Roberts	THE DEAR OLD GENTLEMAN	Barzun & Taylor	12-3 TAD 263
Goodman, Jonathan	BLOODY VERSICLES: THE RHYMES OF CRIME	Lianne Carlin	5-2 MR 44
Goodman, Jonathan	THE BURNING OF EVELYN FOSTER	Barzun & Taylor	11-1 TAD 92
Goodman, Jonathan	THE LAST SENTENCE	Allen J. Hubin	14-1 TAD 18
Goodrum, Charles A.	CARNAGE OF THE REALM	M.S.Cappadonna	12-4 TAD 371
Goodrum, Charles A.	CARNAGE OF THE REALM	Douglas G. Greene	13-1 TAD 62
Goodrum, Charles A.	DEWEY DECIMATED	Jane Gottschalk	3-1 PP 35
Goodstone, Tony, ed.	THE PULPS	Lianne Carlin	4-2 MR 38
Goodstone, Tony, ed.	THE PULPS	Robert E. Washer	3-1 QC 20
Goodstone, Tony, ed.	THE PULPS	Ruth Windfeldt	1-1 M 32
Gordon, Alex	THE CYPHER	Steve Lewis	2-4 MF 32
Gordon, Donald	LEAP IN THE DARK	Don Cole	4-4 MR 35
Gordon, Ethel Edison	THE FREEBODY HEIRESS	Barbara A. Buhrer	8 MN 12
Gordon, Neil	THE SILENT MURDERS	Amnon Kabatchnik	6-4 TAD 268
Gordons, The	CATNAPPED!	Allen J. Hubin	8-2 TAD 150
Gore, William	THE MYSTERY OF THE PAINTED NUDE	Barzun & Taylor	9-2 TAD 93
Gorell, Lord	IN THE NIGHT	Amnon Kabatchnik	7-1 TAD 54
Gores, Joe	DEAD SKIP	Lianne Carlin	5-6 MR 34
Gores, Joe	DEAD SKIP	Allen J. Hubin	6-2 TAD 113
Gores, Joe	DEAD SKIP	Dorothy B. Hughes	3-1 M 37
Gores, Joe	DEAD SKIP	Arthur C. Scott	9 MN R10
Gores, Joe	FINAL NOTICE	Allen J. Hubin	7-1 TAD 61
Gores, Joe	FINAL NOTICE	Amnon Kabatchnik	6-2 MR 48
Gores, Joe	GONE, NO FORWARDING	Gary Happenstand	2-2 C 159
Gores, Joe	GONE, NO FORWARDING	Jim Huang	9 CL 8
Gores, Joe	GONE, NO FORWARDING	Allen J. Hubin	11-4 TAD 331
Gores, Joe	GONE, NO FORWARDING	Steve Lewis	2-5 MF 28
Gores, Joe	GONE, NO FORWARDING	F.M.Nevins, Jr.	2-4 MF 39
Gores, Joe	GONE, NO FORWARDING	F.M.Nevins, Jr.	4-2 MF 51
Gores, Joe	HAMMETT	Robert E. Washer	21 X 54
Gores, Joe	HAMMETT	Stan Burns	9 MN R4
Gores, Joe	HAMMETT	Clay Powers	1-2 WA 7
Gores, Joe	HAMMETT	James Mark Purcell	9-1 TAD 67
Gores, Joe	HAMMETT	Arthur C. Scott	5/6 MN 21
Gores, Joe	HAMMETT	Charles Shibuk	10-1 TAD 72
Gores, Joe	INTERFACE	Allen J. Hubin	7-2 TAD 142
Gores, Joe	INTERFACE	Charles Shibuk	9-3 TAD 209
Gores, Joe, &			
Bill Pronzini	TRICKS AND TREATS	Amnon Kabatchnik	10-1 TAD 64
Gorey, Edward	THE AWDREY-GORE LEGACY	Lianne Carlin	5-5 MR 38
Goshgarian, Gary	ATLANTIS FIRE	Allen J. Hubin	14-2 TAD 125
Gotlieb, Annie, &			
Jacques Sandulescu	THE CARPATHIAN CAPER	Allen J. Hubin	9-1 TAD 74
Gottlieb, Nathan	STINGER	Robert J. Randisi	12-3 TAD 272
Goulart, Ron	CHEAP THRILLS	Stanley Carlin	5-5 MR 37
Goulart, Ron	GHOST BREAKER	Fred Blosser	5-1 TAD 38
Goulart, Ron	GHOSTING	William L.DeAndrea	14-4 TAD 378
Goulart, Ron, ed.	THE HARDBOILED DICKS: AN ANTHOLOGY AND STUDY OF PULP DETECTIVE FICTION	Jeff Meyerson	1-2 MF 37
Goulart, Ron, ed.	THE HARDBOILED DICKS: AN ANTHOLOGY AND STUDY OF PULP DETECTIVE FICTION	Martin M. Wooster	8 MN 27
Goulart, Ron	IF DYING WAS ALL	Robert E. Briney	5-1 MR 38

Goulart, Ron	IF DYING WAS ALL	Hellgate Newlander	5-2 TAD 101
Gould, Chester	THE CELEBRATED CASES OF DICK TRACY	Bill Blackbeard	4-4 TAD 238
Gould, Chester	THE CELEBRATED CASES OF DICK TRACY	Robert E. Washer	3-1 QC 18
Gould, Heywood	ONE DEAD DEBUTANTE	Fred Dueren	12-3 TAD 287
Gould, Heywood	ONE DEAD DEBUTANTE	Steve Lewis	1-2 MF 23
Grady, James	SHADOW OF THE CONDOR	Stan Burns	10 MN R3
Grady, James	SHADOW OF THE CONDOR	Allen J. Hubin	9-1 TAD 72
Graeme, Bruce	A CASE FOR SOLOMON	Philip T. Asdell	2-4 PP 32
Graeme, Bruce	DISAPPEARANCE OF ROGER TREMAYNE	Charles Shibuk	1-2 MF 41
Graeme, Bruce	THE IMPERFECT CRIME	Charles Shibuk	8-3 TAD 220
Graeme, Bruce	NOT PROVEN	Charles Shibuk	10-2 TAD 141
Grafton, C.W.	BEYOND A REASONABLE DOUBT	William L.DeAndrea	14-4 TAD 379
Grafton, C.W.	BEYOND A REASONABLE DOUBT	George Kelley	4-3 PP 23
Grafton, C.W.	BEYOND A REASONABLE DOUBT	Charles Shibuk	14-3 TAD 267
Grafton, C.W.	THE RAT BEGAN TO GNAW THE ROPE	Jim McCahery	3-6 PP 25
Graham, Winston	THE ANGRY TIDE: A NOVEL OF CORNWALL	Martin M. Wooster	2-4 PP 36
Graham, Winston	THE BLACK MOON: A NOVEL OF CORNWALL	Martin M. Wooster	2-2 PP 25
Graham, Winston	DEMELZA: A NOVEL OF CORNWALL	Martin M. Wooster	2-1 PP 30
Graham, Winston	THE FOUR SWANS	Martin M. Wooster	2-3 PP 29
Graham, Winston	JEREMY POLDARK: A NOVEL OF CORNWALL	Martin M. Wooster	2-2 PP 25
Graham, Winston	JEREMY POLDARK: A NOVEL OF CORNWALL	Martin M. Wooster	2-1 PP 29
Graham, Winston	TAKE MY LIFE	Charles Shibuk	13-2 TAD 135
Graham, Winston	THE WALKING STICK	Connie Jessen	1-1 TAD 26
Graham, Winston	WARLEGGAN: A NOVEL OF CORNWALL	Martin M. Wooster	2-2 PP 25
Graham, Winston	WOMAN IN THE MIRROR	Barbara A. Buhrer	3/4 MN 19
Granger, Bill	THE NOVEMBER MAN	D.E.Ath	2-4 PP 28
Granger, Bill	PUBLIC MURDERS	Robert C.S.Adey	4-2 PP 20
Granger, Bill	PUBLIC MURDERS	Fred Dueren	13-3 TAD 252
Granger, Bill	PUBLIC MURDERS	Steve Lewis	4-3 MF 35
Granger, Bill	PUBLIC MURDERS	Eve Simpson	13-4 TAD 351
Granger, Bill	SWEEPS	Fred Dueren	14-1 TAD 81
Grant, Charles L.	THE HOUR OF THE OXRUN DEAD	Steve Lewis	2-3 MF 41
Grant, Charles L.	THE SOUND OF MIDNIGHT	Steve Lewis	3-3 MF 37
Grant, Donald M., & Joseph Payne Brennan	ACT OF PROVIDENCE	Edward Lauterbach	12-4 TAD 370
Grant, James	ISLAND OF GOLD	Mary A. Grochowski	2-1 PP 30
Grant, Maxwell	THE CREEPING DEATH	Billy C. Lee	1-1 PQ 37
Grant, Maxwell	THE CRIME ORACLE AND THE TEETH OF THE DRAGON: TWO ADVENTURES OF THE SHADOW	J. Randolph Cox	8-4 TAD 302
Grant, Maxwell	FINGERS OF DEATH	Steve Lewis	2-1 MF 26
Grant, Maxwell	GREEN EYES	Steve Lewis	1-3 MF 42
Grant, Maxwell	THE KINGS OF CRIME	Steve Lewis	2-2 MM 4
Grant, Maxwell	NORGIL: MORE TALES OF PRESTIDIGITECTION	Allen J. Hubin	12-3 TAD 205
Grant, Maxwell	THE REAL MENACE	Fred Dueren	9-1 TAD 51
Grant, Roderick	A PRIVATE VENDETTA	Allen J. Hubin	12-4 TAD 321
Gray, Berkeley	CONQUEST MARCHES ON	J. Randolph Cox	7-1 TAD 57
Gray, Berkeley	CONQUEST TAKES ALL	J. Randolph Cox	10-2 TAD 138
Gray, Berkeley	CONVICT 1066	J. Randolph Cox	11-2 TAD 126
Gray, Berkeley	LEAVE IT TO CONQUEST	J. Randolph Cox	7-2 TAD 131
Gray, Berkeley	MEET THE DON	J. Randolph Cox	10-4 TAD 316
Gray, Berkeley	MISS DYNAMITE	J. Randolph Cox	6-4 TAD 271
Gray, Berkeley	MR. MORTIMER GETS THE JITTERS	J. Randolph Cox	6-3 TAD 187
Gray, Berkeley	SIX TO KILL	J. Randolph Cox	11-2 TAD 126
Gray, Berkeley	THANK YOU, MR. CONQUEST	J. Randolph Cox	11-2 TAD 126
Gray, Berkeley	VULTURES LTD.	J. Randolph Cox	6-3 TAD 187
Grayson, Rupert	THE MURDERS AT IMPASSE LOUVAIN	Allen J. Hubin	13-3 TAD 202
Greatorex, Wilfred	THREE POTATO, FOUR	Allen J. Hubin	10-2 TAD 112

Greatorex, Wilfred	THREE POTATO, FOUR	Charles Shibuk	12-3 TAD 255
Green, Anna Katharine	THE DOCTOR, HIS WIFE AND THE CLOCK	Jay Jeffries	3/4 MN 7
Green, Anna Katharine	THE HOUSE IN THE WHISPERING PINES	Jay Jeffries	3/4 MN 8
Green, Anna Katharine	THE LEAVENWORTH CASE	Allen J. Hubin	8-4 TAD 299
Green, Anna Katharine	THE MYSTERY OF THE HASTY ARROW	Maryell Cleary	1-3 PP 27
Green, Anna Katharine	THE WOMAN IN THE ALCOVE	Maryell Cleary	1-3 PP 26
Green, Edith Pinero	ROTTEN APPLES	Allen J. Hubin	11-2 TAD 118
Green, Roger Lancelyn	A.E.W.MASON	J. Randolph Cox	5-3 TAD 164
Green, Thomas J.	THE FLOWERED BOX	Steve Lewis	5-2 MF 20
Green, Walton	CORSAIR (film)	William K. Everson	2-1 TAD 48
Green, Walton	CORSAIR (film)	William K. Everson	3-4 TAD 244
Green, William M.	AVERY'S FORTUNE	Amnon Kabatchnik	5-5 MR 34
Green, William M.	THE MAN WHO CALLED HIMSELF DEVLIN	Mary A. Grochowski	2-1 PP 30
Green, William M.	THE MAN WHO CALLED HIMSELF DEVLIN	Allen J. Hubin	12-2 TAD 112
Green, William M.	SEE HOW THEY RUN	Allen J. Hubin	9-3 TAD 224
Green, William M.	SPENCER'S BAG	Amnon Kabatchnik	4-5 MR 34
Greenan, Russell H.	THE QUEEN OF AMERICA	Allen J. Hubin	5-3 TAD 167
Greenaway, Peter Van	A MAN CALLED SCAVENER	Robert C.S.Adey	5-4 MF 33
Greenberg, Martin H., & Isaac Asimov, Charles Waugh	THE THIRTEEN CRIMES OF SCIENCE FICTION	Martin M. Wooster	4-3 MF 45
Greenberg, Martin H., & Carol-Lynn Waugh, Isaac Asimov	THE TWELVE CRIMES OF CHRISTMAS	Fred Dueren	4-5/6 PP 100
Greenburg, Dan	LOVE KILLS	Allen J. Hubin	12-1 TAD 7
Greenburg, Dan	LOVE KILLS	Steve Lewis	3-1 MF 31
Greene, Graham	DOCTOR FISCHER OF GENEVA, OR THE BOMB PARTY	Gary Warren Niebuhr	3-6 PP 16
Greene, Graham	THE HUMAN FACTOR	Allen J. Hubin	11-4 TAD 333
Greene, Graham	THE RETURN OF A.J.RAFFLES	Jon L. Lellenberg	9-4 TAD 308
Greene, Graham	THE RETURN OF A.J.RAFFLES (stage)	Veronica M.Kennedy	9-2 TAD 148
Greene, Harris	FSQ-1	Guy M. Townsend	2-5 MM 10
Greene, Hugh, ed.	THE AMERICAN RIVALS OF SHERLOCK HOLMES	Charles Shibuk	12-2 TAD 167
Greene, Hugh, ed.	COSMOPOLITAN CRIMES: FOREIGN RIVALS OF SHERLOCK HOLMES	Stanley Carlin	5-1 MR 40
Greene, Hugh, ed.	THE FURTHER RIVALS OF SHERLOCK HOLMES	Lianne Carlin	6-2 MR 50
Greene, Hugh, ed.	THE RIVALS OF SHERLOCK HOLMES: EARLY DETECTIVE STORIES	William White	4-2 MR 37
Greenleaf, Stephen	DEATH BED	Allen J. Hubin	14-2 TAD 125
Greenleaf, Stephen	DEATH BED	Robert J. Randisi	14-3 TAD 269
Greenleaf, Stephen	GRAVE ERROR	Steve Lewis	5-4 MF 23
Greenwald, Nancy	LADYCAT	Paul Bishop	2-2 M 56
Gribble, Leonard R.	THE GRAND MODENA MURDER	Steve Lewis	3-4 MF 39
Grierson, Edward	THE SECOND MAN	Charles Shibuk	14-3 TAD 267
Grindea, Miron, ed.	ADAM INTERNATIONAL REVIEW	F.M.Nevins, Jr.	3-1 TAD 58
Grinnell-Milne,Duncan	THE KILLING OF WILLIAM RUFUS	Barzun & Taylor	11-2 TAD 203
Gross, Gerald, ed.	MASTERPIECES OF MURDER: A COLLECTION OF KILLINGS FROM THE TRUE CRIME NARRATIVES OF EDMUND LESTER PEARSON	Francis C. Brown	1-3 TAD 102
Gross, Jack, Jr., & Buddy Rushkin	CLAY PIGEON (film)	Richard S. Lochte	5-1 TAD 41
Grossvogel, David I.	MYSTERY AND ITS FICTION: FROM OEDIPUS TO AGATHA CHRISTIE	Earl F.Bargainnier	1-2 C 132
Gruber, Frank	THE FRENCH KEY MYSTERY	Jeff Meyerson	1-5 MF 47
Gruber, Frank	THE SPANISH PRISONER	Stanley A.Carlin	3-3 MR 29
Gruppe, Henry	THE TRUXTON CIPHER	Barzun & Taylor	9-3 TAD 237

Guild, Norman	OLD ACQUAINTANCES	Charles Shibuk	14-1 TAD 80
Gunn, James	THE MAGICIANS	Allen J. Hubin	10-2 TAD 112
Guthrie, A.B., Jr.	THE GENUINE ARTICLE	Amnon Kabatchnik	11-1 TAD 24
Guthrie, A.B., Jr.	NO SECOND WIND	Allen J. Hubin	13-4 TAD 295
Guthrie, A.B., Jr.	NO SECOND WIND	Steve Lewis	4-3 MF 36
Guthrie, A.B., Jr.	WILD PITCH	Barzun & Taylor	11-3 TAD 281
Haas, Charlie, & Tim Hunter	THE SOUL HIT	Allen J. Hubin	11-1 TAD 20
Hackett, Alice Payne	70 YEARS OF BEST SELLERS	Allen J. Hubin	1-3 TAD 99
Haddad, C.A.	BLOODY SEPTEMBER	Stan Burns	2-3 MM 4
Haddad, C.A.	BLOODY SEPTEMBER	Amnon Kabatchnik	10-1 TAD 69
Haddad, C.A.	THE MOROCCAN	Steve Lewis	3-3 MF 33
Haddad, C.A.	OPERATION APRICOT	Allen J. Hubin	11-3 TAD 230
Hagen, Ordean A.	WHO DONE IT? A GUIDE TO DETECTIVE, MYSTERY AND SUSPEBSE FICTION	Lianne Carlin	2-6 MR 2
Hagen, Ordean A.	WHO DONE IT? A GUIDE TO DETECTIVE, MYSTERY AND SUSPENSE FICTION	Charles Shibuk	3-1 TAD 57
Hagen, Ordean A.	WHO DONE IT? A GUIDE TO DETECTIVE, MYSTERY AND SUSPENSE FICTION	Robert E. Washer	2-1 QC 18
Haggard, H. Rider	MR. MEESON'S WILL	Amnon Kabatchnik	7-1 TAD 53
Haggard, William	THE HIGH WIRE	Don D'Ammassa	1-6 MM 9
Haggard, William	THE POISON PEOPLE	Allen J. Hubin	12-4 TAD 321
Haggard, William	THE PROTECTORS	James Mark Purcell	5-6 MR 33
Haggard, William	THE SCORPION'S TALE	Allen J. Hubin	9-1 TAD 74
Haggard, William	SLOW BURNER	Don D'Ammassa	1-7 MM 7
Haggard, William	THE TELEMANN TOUCH	Don D'Ammassa	9 MN R14
Haggard, William	TOO MANY ENEMIES	James Mark Purcell	5-3 MR 37
Haggard, William	VISA TO LIMBO	Allen J. Hubin	13-3 TAD 202
Haggard, William	YESTERDAY'S ENEMY	Allen J. Hubin	10-3 TAD 204
Haggard, William	YESTERDAY'S ENEMY	Steve Lewis	1-4 MF 37
Haiblum, Isidore	NIGHTMARE EXPRES	W. Paul Ganly	5 U 29
Haig, Alec	FLIGHT FROM MONTEGO BAY	Allen J. Hubin	6-2 TAD 113
Haining, Peter, ed.	THE GHOULS	Stanley A. Carlin	4-4 MR 36
Haining, Peter, ed.	GOTHIC TALES OF TERROR, Vol.I: CLASSIC HORROR STORIES FROM GREAT BRITAIN	Veronica M.Kennedy	6-4 TAD 263
Haining, Peter, ed.	GOTHIC TALES OF TERROR, Vol.II: CLASSIC HORROR STORIES FROM EUROPE AND THE UNITED STATES	Veronica M.Kennedy	7-2 TAD 139
Haining, Peter, ed.	THE PENNY DREADFUL, OR, STRANGE, HORRID AND SENSATIONAL TALES	E.F.Bleiler	8-4 TAD 305
Haining, Peter, ed.	THE SHERLOCK HOLMES SCRAPBOOK	Bruce R. Beaman	3-1 TAD 64
Haining, Peter, ed.	TERROR!	Marlowe Archer	4 PE 24
Haldimand, Madeleine, & J.A.Knipe	MURDER NOW AND AGAIN	Fred Dueren	14-2 TAD 184
Hale, Christopher	MIDSUMMER NIGHTMARE	Jay Jeffries	3/4 MN 7
Hale, Christopher	MURDER ON DISPLAY	Steve Lewis	4-3 MF 40
Halifax, Clifford, & L.T.Meade	STORIES FROM THE DIARY OF A DOCTOR, SECOND SERIES	Allen J. Hubin	5-4 TAD 233
Hall, Adam	THE KOBRA MANIFESTO	Stan Burns	2-5 MM 7
Hall, Brian	MONTENEGRIN GOLD	Allen J. Hubin	11-3 TAD 233
Hall, F.H.	THE LAMB WHITE DAYS	Myrtis Broset	2-1 MF 36
Hall, F.H.	THE LAMB WHITE DAYS	Steve Lewis	1A MF 30
Hall, H.W.	SCIENCE FICTION BOOK REVIEW INDEX 1974-1979	J.Grant Thiessen	14 SF 19
Hall, Oakley	A GAME FOR EAGLES	Robert E. Washer	3-1 QC 18
Hall, Robert Lee	EXIT SHERLOCK HOLMES	R. Jeff Banks	2-5 PP 15
Hall, Robert Lee	EXIT SHERLOCK HOLMES	Barzun & Taylor	11-1 TAD 93
Hall, Robert Lee	EXIT SHERLOCK HOLMES	Allen J. Hubin	10-3 TAD 207
Hall, Robert Lee	EXIT SHERLOCK HOLMES	William A.Karpowicz	2 MT 30
Hall, Robert Lee	EXIT SHERLOCK HOLMES	Steve Lewis	1-5 MF 31

Hall, Robert Lee	EXIT SHERLOCK HOLMES	Charles Shibuk	12-3 TAD 255
Hall, Robert Lee	EXIT SHERLOCK HOLMES	Guy M. Townsend	1-5 MF 51
Hall, Robert Lee	THE KIND EDWARD PLOT	Allen J. Hubin	14-2 TAD 125
Hall, Robert Lee	THE KIND EDWARD PLOT	Guy M. Townsend	4-2 MF 46
Hall, Steve	RAPE OF THE NICOLLET MALL MANNEQUIN	Allen J. Hubin	12-1 TAD 94
Hall, Trevor H.	THE LATE MR. SHERLOCK HOLMES AND OTHER LITERARY STUDIES	Stanley A. Carlin	5-1 MR 39
Hall, Trevor H.	SHERLOCK HOLMES AND HIS CREATOR	Barzun & Taylor	11-3 TAD 281
Hall, Trevor H.	SHERLOCK HOLMES AND HIS CREATOR	Edward Lauterbach	2-3 PP 35
Hallahan, William H.	THE DEAD OF WINTER	Steve Lewis	1-11 MM 4
Hallahan, William H.	THE ROSS FORGERY	Edward Lauterbach	8-2 TAD 143
Hallas, Richard	YOU PLAY THE BLACK AND THE RED COMES UP	Gary Warren Niebuhr	3-6 PP 17
Halley, Laurence	SIMULTANEOUS EQUATIONS	Allen J. Hubin	12-2 TAD 113
Halliday, Brett	THE CORPSE THAT NEVER WAS	Arthur C. Scott	2-4 MM 6
Halliday, Brett	DATE WITH A DEAD MAN	Arthur C. Scott	8 MN 27
Halliday, Brett	MICHAEL SHAYNE'S LONG CHANCE	Steve Lewis	2-4 MF 32
Halliday, Brett	THE UNCOMPLAINING CORPSES	Arthur C. Scott	2-4 MM 6
Halliday, Fred	A CASE OF INDELICATE CHAMPAGNE	Fred Dueren	10-4 TAD 341
Halliday, Fred	MURDER IN THE KITCHEN	Mary A. Grochowski	3-2 PP 31
Halpern, Frank M.	DIRECTORY OF DEALERS IN SCIENCE FICTION AND FANTASY	Allen J. Hubin	8-2 TAD 151
Hamill, Pete	THE DEADLY PIECE	Mary A. Grochowski	2-5 PP 37
Hamill, Pete	DIRTY LAUNDRY	Jim Huang	12 CL 7
Hamill, Pete	DIRTY LAUNDRY	Joe R. Lansdale	4 PE 11
Hamill, Pete	DIRTY LAUNDRY	Steve Lewis	3-5 MF 37
Hamilton, Bruce	DEAD RECKONING	Charles Shibuk	6-2 TAD 118
Hamilton, Donald	THE AMBUSHERS	Jeff Meyerson	1-2 MF 38
Hamilton, Donald	THE BETRAYERS	Martin M. Wooster	1-1 PP 21
Hamilton, Donald	THE INTERLOPERS	Martin M. Wooster	1-3 PP 27
Hamilton, Donald	THE INTRIGUERS	Amnon Kabatchnik	6-1 MR 46
Hamilton, Donald	THE INTRIGUERS	Martin M. Wooster	4-3 MF 46
Hamilton, Donald	THE MENACERS	Martin M. Wooster	1-1 PQ 35
Hamilton, Donald	MURDERERS' ROW	Jeff Meyerson	1-5 MF 50
Hamilton, Donald	THE POISONERS	Martin M. Wooster	3-4 PP 32
Hamilton, Donald	THE RAVAGERS	Jeff Meyerson	1-2 MF 38
Hamilton, Donald	THE REMOVERS	Jeff Meyerson	1-4 MF 53
Hamilton, Donald	THE RETALIATORS	Steve Lewis	1-1 MF 30
Hamilton, Donald	THE TERRORIZERS	Guy M. Townsend	1-6 MF 48
Hamilton, Lord Ernest	THE PERILS OF JOSEPHINE	Charles Shibuk	9-4 TAD 313
Hamilton, Mary Agnes	MURDER IN THE HOUSE OF COMMONS	Barzun & Taylor	11-2 TAD 204
Hammett, Dashiell	THE CONTINENTAL OP	Arthur C. Scott	9 MN R19
Hammett, Dashiell	THE DAIN CURSE	James Sandoe	13-4 TAD 293
Hammett, Dashiell	DEAD YELLOW WOMEN	James Sandoe	14-1 TAD 75
Hammett, Dashiell	THE GLASS KEY (film)	William K. Everson	6-4 TAD 254
Hammett, Dashiell	THE MALTESE FALCON (film)	William K. Everson	7-3 TAD 162
Hammett, Dashiell	THE MALTESE FALCON	Steve Lewis	5-3 MF 31
Hammett, Dashiell	THE MALTESE FALCON	Don Miller	1-5 MM 10
Hammett, Dashiell	RED HARVEST	F.M.Nevins, Jr.	1-6 MR 3
Hammett, Dashiell	THE RETURN OF THE CONTINENTAL OP	James Sandoe	14-1 TAD 75
Hammett, Dashiell	THE THIN MAN (film)	William K. Everson	7-2 TAD 108
Hammett, Dashiell	THE THIN MAN	James Sandoe	14-1 TAD 74
Hammett, Dashiell, & Alex Raymond	SECRET AGENT X-9	J.Randolph Cox	12-4 TAD 369
Hancer, Kevin	THE PAPERBACK PRICE GUIDE	Steve Lewis	5-1 MF 28
Handley, Alan	KISS YOUR ELBOW	Steve Lewis	3-6 MF 37
Hannay, Margaret P.	AS HER WHIMSEY TOOK HER: CRITICAL ESSAYS ON DOROTHY L.SAYERS	F.M.Nevins, Jr.	3-5 MF 45
Hansen, Joseph	FADEOUT	Allen J. Hubin	6-3 TAD 191
Hansen, Joseph	FADEOUT	Len Moffatt	4-1 TAD 49
Hansen, Joseph	THE MAN EVERYBODY WAS AFRAID OF	Barzun & Taylor	13-4 TAD 308
Hansen, Joseph	THE MAN EVERYBODY WAS AFRAID OF	Allen J. Hubin	12-1 TAD 8
Hapi	221A BAKER STREET: THE ADAMANTINE SHERLOCK HOLMES	Allen J. Hubin	7-3 TAD 221

Harbottle, Philip	THE MULTI-MAN	Hickman & Zachrich	69 PU 34
Harcourt, Palma	AGENTS OF INFLUENCE	Mary A. Grochowski	2-1 PP 30
Harcourt, Palma	AT HIGH ROCK	Allen J. Hubin	11-3 TAD 233
Hardin, Robert	AMATEUR HOUR	Christine Mitchell	11-4 TAD 403
Hardwick, Michael	PRISONER OF THE DEVIL: SHERLOCK HOLMES AND THE DREYFUS CASE	Horace Harker	2-2 M 40
Hare, Cyril	AN ENGLISH MURDER	Charles Shibuk	12-2 TAD 167
Hare, Cyril	BEST DETECTIVE STORIES OF CYRIL HARE	Douglas G. Greene	12-3 TAD 233
Hare, Cyril	TENANT FOR DEATH	Charles Shibuk	14-4 TAD 377
Hare, Cyril	TRAGEDY AT LAW	Charles Shibuk	14-2 TAD 183
Hare, Cyril	WHEN THE WIND BLOWS	Charles Shibuk	12-2 TAD 167
Hare, Cyril	THE WIND BLOWS DEATH	James Sandoe	13-4 TAD 393
Hare, Cyril	WITH A BARE BODKIN	James Mark Purcell	10-1 TAD 73
Harling, Robert	THE ENDLESS COLONNADE	Charles Shibuk	9-1 TAD 61
Harling, Robert	THE ENORMOUS SHADOW	Martin M. Wooster	4-5/6 PP 71
Harmon, Jim	THE GREAT RADIO HEROES	Martin M. Wooster	3-5 PP 37
Harmon, Jim	THE GREAT RADIO HEROES	Gary Zachrich	70 PU 27
Harmon, Robert B., & Margaret A. Burger	AN ANNOTATED GUIDE TO THE WORKS OF DOROTHY L. SAYERS	Allen J. Hubin	10-3 TAD 206
Harper, David	THE GREEN AIR	Bill Crider	2-5 PP 34
Harper, David	THE HANGED MEN	Myrtis Broset	2-3 MF 54
Harper, David	THE HANGED MEN	Marvin Lachman	2-5 MF 3
Harper, David	THE HANGED MEN	Steve Lewis	1-2 MF 28
Harper, David	THE PATCHWORK MAN	Myrtis Broset	2-5 MF 44
Harper, David	THE PATCHWORK MAN	Fred Dueren	11-3 TAD 306
Harper, Ralph	THE WORLD OF THE THRILLER	Veronica M. Kennedy	8-4 TAD 303
Harrington, Joseph	BLIND SPOT	Jane S. Bakerman	1-5 PP 21
Harrington, Joyce	NO ONE KNOWS MY NAME	Allen J. Hubin	14-2 TAD 125
Harrington, Joyce	NO ONE KNOWS MY NAME	Iona Kristopolis	2-2 M 57
Harrington, R.E.	DEATH OF A PATRIOT	Allen J. Hubin	13-1 TAD 28
Harrington, R.E.	THE SEVEN OF SWORDS	Allen J. Hubin	9-3 TAD 224
Harrington, William	THE JUPITER CRISIS	Stan Burns	11 MN R15
Harrington, William	MISTER TARGET	Stan Burns	10 MN R14
Harrington, William	SCORPIO	Barbara A. Buhrer	5/6 MN 17
Harrington, William	SCORPIO	Stan Burns	9 MN R2
Harrington, William	SCORPIO	Allen J. Hubin	8-3 TAD 226
Harrington, William	WHICH THE JUSTICE, WHICH THE THIEF	Stan Burns	1-9 MM 5
Harris, Alfred	BARONI	Allen J. Hubin	9-3 TAD 224
Harris, Charlaine	SWEET AND DEADLY	Fred Dueren	14-4 TAD 364
Harris, Leonard	DON'T BE MY HERO	Allen J. Hubin	12-1 TAD 8
Harris, Leonard	THE MASADA PLAN	Jim Huang	8 CL 10
Harris, MacDonald	THE TREASURE OF SAINTE FOY	Allen J. Hubin	14-1 TAD 18
Harris, Marilyn	THE CONJURERS	Veronica M. Kennedy	8-3 TAD 223
Harris, Thomas	BLACK SUNDAY	Allen J. Hubin	8-2 TAD 150
Harris, Timothy	GOODNIGHT AND GOOD-BYE	Peter Blazer	1-2 M 20
Harris, Timothy	GOODNIGHT AND GOOD-BYE	Theodore Dukeshire	4-2 MF 50
Harris, Timothy	GOODNIGHT AND GOOD-BYE	Steve Lewis	5-3 MF 31
Harris, Timothy	KYD FOR HIRE	Bill Crider	1 PE 13
Harris, Timothy	KYD FOR HIRE	Fred Dueren	11-3 TAD 306
Harris, Timothy	KYD FOR HIRE	Theodore Dukeshire	2-3 MF 52
Harris, Timothy	KYD FOR HIRE	Larry L. French	13-1 TAD 64
Harrison, Chip	MAKE OUT WITH MURDER	Jon L. Breen	8-1 TAD 56
Harrison, Chip	MAKE OUT WITH MURDER	Arthur C. Scott	1-2 MF 45
Harrison, Chip	THE TOPLESS TULIP CAPER	Fred Dueren	9-1 TAD 50
Harrison, Chip	THE TOPLESS TULIP CAPER	George Fergus	7 MN 9
Harrison, Chip	THE TOPLESS TULIP CAPER	Arthur C. Scott	1-2 MF 45
Harrison, Harry	MONTEZUMA'S REVENGE	George Fergus	3/4 MN 20
Harrison, Michael	I, SHERLOCK HOLMES	Jon L. Lellenberg	10-3 TAD 208
Harrison, Whit	BODY AND PASSION	Bill Crider	2-4 PP 33
Harrison, William	HELL'S FULL	Myrtis Broset	2-6 MF 42
Hart, Douglas C., & Robert W. Pohle, Jr.	SHERLOCK HOLMES ON THE SCREEN	Kenneth Karpowicz	3 MT 15
Hartley, Norman	QUICKSILVER	Allen J. Hubin	13-1 TAD 28

Hartley, Norman	QUICKSILVER	Charles Shibuk	14-3 TAD 267
Hartley, Norman	THE VIKING PROCESS	Ammon Kabatchnik	9-4 TAD 305
Hartman, Harry	THE HOLY QUIRE	Stanley A. Carlin	4-3 MR 36
Hartman, Mary S.	VICTORIAN MURDERESSES	Barzun & Taylor	13-4 TAD 308
Hartmann, Michael	THE HUNTED	Andy Jaysnovitch	2-5 PP 37
Hartshorne, -	THE MEXICAN ASSASSIN	Allen J. Hubin	12-1 TAD 8
Hartshorne, -	THE MEXICAN ASSASSIN	Steve Lewis	2-6 MF 30
Hassler, Jon	THE LOVE HUNTER	Gary Warren Niebuhr	4-5/6 PP 63
Hastings, Macdonald	CORK IN THE DOGHOUSE	Edward Lauterbach	7-2 TAD 128
Hastings, Phyllis	THE HOUSE ON MALADOR STREET	Robert E. Washer	2-1 QC 17
Hatvary, George Egon	THE SUITOR	Jean Lamb	3-2 M 40
Haughey, Thomas Brace	THE CASE OF THE INVISIBLE THIEF	Allen J. Hubin	12-4 TAD 321
Hawkes, Robert	KILL FOR IT	Fred Dueren	9-3 TAD 213
Hawkins, William E.	THE COWLED MENACE	Steve Lewis	2-4 MF 35
Haworth, Peter, ed.	CLASSIC CRIMES IN HISTORY AND FICTION	R.W.Hays	6-4 TAD 268
Haycraft, Howard, ed.	THE ART OF THE MYSTERY STORY	Bruce R. Beaman	7-3 TAD 212
Haycraft, Howard	MURDER FOR PLEASURE	Allen J. Hubin	2-2 TAD 122
Haycraft, Howard	MURDER FOR PLEASURE	Robert E. Washer	1-2 QC 15
Haydock, Ron	DEERSTALKER! HOLMES AND WATSON ON SCREEN	J. Grant Thiessen	14 SF 18
Hayes, Ralph	THE GOLDEN GOD	Bill Crider	9-4 TAD 306
Hayes, Roy	THE HUNGARIAN GAME	Stan Burns	1-10 MM 7
Hayes, Steve, & Karl Alexander	TIME AFTER TIME (film)	Judith Claire	1-1 M 10
Head, Lee	THE CRYSTAL CLEAR CASE	Allen J. Hubin	11-1 TAD 19
Head, Lee	THE CRYSTAL CLEAR CASE	Dave Paton	4 MT 19
Head, Lee	THE CRYSTAL CLEAR CASE	Steve Lewis	2-3 MF 43
Head, Lee	THE TERRANIUM	Fred Dueren	10-4 TAD 341
Head, Matthew	THE DEVIL IN THE BUSH	Douglas Armato	6-1 MR 43
Head, Matthew	MURDER AT THE FLEA CLUB	Charles Shibuk	14-4 TAD 377
Heal, Anthony	MAN IN THE MIDDLE	Allen J. Hubin	14-2 TAD 125
Heald, Tim	JUST DESSERTS	Fred Dueren	13-3 TAD 251
Heald, Tim	JUST DESSERTS	Allen J. Hubin	12-4 TAD 322
Heath, Eric	MURDER OF A MYSTERY WRITER	Steve Lewis	3-2 MF 39
Heatter, Basil	DEVLIN'S TRIANGLE	Fred Dueren	9-3 TAD 212
Hebden, Mark	A PRIDE OF DOLPHINS	Barbara A. Buhrer	7 MN 9
Heberden, M.V.	DEATH ON THE DOOR MAT	Barzun & Taylor	10-3 TAD 225
Heberden, M.V.	ENGAGED TO MURDER	Charles Shibuk	14-3 TAD 267
Hedges, Joseph	RAINBOW COLORED SHROUD	Donald J. Pattow	9-2 TAD 152
Hedman, Iwan	DECKARE OCH THRILLERS PA SVENSKA	Barzun & Taylor	12-3 TAD 262
Hedman, Iwan	DECKARE OCH THRILLERS PA SVENSKA	Allen J. Hubin	7-4 TAD 294
Hedman, Iwan	DETECTIVE STORIES AND THRILLERS IN SWEDISH 1864-1973	E.F.Bleiler	2-5 MF 7
Hedman, Iwan, & Jan Alexandersson	FOUR DECADES WITH DENNIS WHEATLEY	Allen J. Hubin	7-1 TAD 63
Heller, Frank	THE CHINESE COATS	Allen J. Hubin	4-3 TAD 179
Henaghan, Jim	AZOR!	Steve Lewis	2-3 MF 45
Henderson, James	COPPERHEAD	Ammon Kabatchnik	5-4 MR 32
Henderson, Laurence	MAJOR ENQUIRY	Barzun & Taylor	10-2 TAD 126
Henderson, Laurence	MAJOR ENQUIRY	Steve Lewis	1-1 MF 27
Henege, Thomas	DEATH OF A SHIPOWNER	Allen J. Hubin	14-4 TAD 299
Henissart, Paul	THE WINTER SPY	Fred Dueren	11-3 TAD 306
Henkin, Harmon	CRISSCROSS	Stan Burns	10 MN R4
Henn, Henry	DEATH SWITCH	George Kelley	4-1 PP 37
Hensley, Joe L.	A KILLING IN GOLD	Steven Miller	4-2 PP 29
Hensley, Joe L.	DELIVER US TO EVIL	Barzun & Taylor	14-4 TAD 328
Hensley, Joe L.	MINOR MURDERS	Steve Lewis	4-2 MF 36
Hensley, Joe L.	MINOR MURDERS	Jeff Meyerson	2-6 PP 38
Hensley, Joe L.	MINOR MURDERS	F.M.Nevins, Jr.	4-1 MF 32
Hensley, Joe L.	OUTCASTS	Barzun & Taylor	14-4 TAD 328
Hensley, Joe L.	OUTCASTS	F.M.Nevins, Jr.	5-2 MF 26
Hensley, Joe L.	THE POISON SUMMER	Allen J. Hubin	7-3 TAD 220
Herbert, James	THE SPEAR	Fred Dueren	13-4 TAD 362
Herman, Linda, & Beth Stiel	CORPUS DELICTI OF MYSTERY FICTION	Allen J. Hubin	8-2 TAD 150

Hermes, Margaret	THE PHOENIX NEST	George Kelley	4-4 PP 31
Herring, Richard	HUB	Gary Warren Niebuhr	4-5/6 PP 64
Herrmann, Bernard	MUSIC FROM THE GREAT MOVIE THRILLERS: MUSIC COMPOSED BY BERNARD HERRMANN FOR MOTION PICTURES DIRECTED BY ALFRED HITCHCOCK (record)	F.M.Nevins, Jr.	3-3 TAD 178
Herron, Don	DASHIELL HAMMETT TOUR	Allen J. Hubin	13-2 TAD 97
Herron, Don	DASHIELL HAMMETT TOUR	Andy Jaysnovitch	6 PE 32
Herron, Don	ECHOES FROM THE VAULTS OF YOH-VOMBIS	Michael L. Cook	2 U 49
Hershatter, Richard	FALLOUT FOR A SPY	Robert E. Washer	1-4 QC 20
Herzog, Arthur	ARIES RISING	Allen J. Hubin	14-2 TAD 126
Hesky, Olga	THE DIFFERENT NIGHT	Amnon Kabatchnik	4-5 MR 33
Heydron, Vicki Ann, & Randall Garrett	THE STEEL OF RAITHSKAR	J.Grant Thiessen	14 SF 18
Heyer, Georgette	THE BLACK SHEEP	G.M.Carr	13 MN 21
Heyer, Georgette	PISTOLS FOR TWO	G.M.Carr	13 MN 25
Heyer, Georgette	THEY FOUND HIM DEAD	Myrtis Broset	1-6 MF 42
Heyliger, William	THE CAPTAIN OF THE NINE	C.L.Messecar	3-4 BC 371
Hext, Harrington	THE MONSTER	Barzun & Taylor	9-3 TAD 237
Hickey, T.Earl	THE TIME CHARIOT	Lynn Hickman	64 PU 42
Hickman, Hal	THE BACHELOR PARTY	Barzun & Taylor	13-4 TAD 309
Hickman, Hal	THE BACHELOR PARTY	Allen J. Hubin	11-3 TAD 232
Higgins, George V.	THE FRIENDS OF EDDIE COYLE	Amnon Kabatchnik	5-4 MR 28
Higgins, George V.	KENNEDY FOR THE DEFENSE	F.M.Nevins, Jr.	4-5 MF 43
Higgins, George V.	THE RAT ON FIRE	Dorothy B. Hughes	3-1 M 36
Higgins, George V.	THE RAT ON FIRE	F.M.Nevins, Jr.	5-2 MF 26
Higgins, Jack	A PRAYER FOR THE DYING	John Boyles	14-4 TAD 362
Higgins, Jack	A PRAYER FOR THE DYING	Allen J. Hubin	7-3 TAD 220
Higgins, Jack	THE EAGLE HAS LANDED	Barbara A. Buhrer	1-5 MM 9
Higgins, Jack	THE EAGLE HAS LANDED (film)	Paul Flanagan	1 MT 47
Higgins, Jack	THE EAGLE HAS LANDED	Charles Shibuk	10-2 TAD 149
Higgins, Jack	MIDNIGHT NEVER COMES	Steve Lewis	1-10 MM 8
Higgins, Jack	SOLO	Allen J. Hubin	14-2 TAD 126
Higgins, Jack	STORM WARNING	Jeff Meyerson	1-2 MF 40
Higham, Charles	THE ADVENTURES OF CONAN DOYLE	Jon L. Lellenberg	11-1 TAD 24
Higham, Charles	THE ADVENTURES OF CONAN DOYLE	Charles Shibuk	11-2 TAD 189
Highsmith, Patricia	RIPLEY UNDER GROUND	Amnon Kabatchnik	4-1 MR 35
Highsmith, Patricia	RIPLEY'S GAME	Allen J. Hubin	7-4 TAD 296
Hilaire, Frank	TRAFICANTE	Allen J. Hubin	14-2 TAD 126
Hildick, Wallace	BRACKNELL'S LAW	Sheila D'Ammassa	2 MN 6
Hildick, Wallace	BRACKNELL'S LAW	Allen J. Hubin	8-3 TAD 228
Hilldrup, Robert P.	TO DIE FOR A GOLDEN LEAF	George Kelley	4-2 PP 30
Hill, Christopher	JACKDAW	Allen J. Hubin	9-3 TAD 224
Hill, Ernest	PITY ABOUT EARTH	Hickman & Zachrich	69 PU 34
Hill, Headon	THE NARROWING CIRCLE	Charles Shibuk	2-5 MF 38
Hill, Melville C.	PAPERBACKS CHECKLIST FOR COLLECTORS, Vol.I	Bill Crider	2-4 PQ 51
Hill, Melville C.	PAPERBACKS CHECKLIST FOR COLLECTORS, Vol.I	Andy Jaysnovitch	7 PE 13
Hill, Peter	THE ENTHUSIAST	Allen J. Hubin	12-2 TAD 113
Hill, Peter	THE ENTHUSIAST	Steve Lewis	3-6 MF 28
Hill, Peter	THE FANATICS	Allen J. Hubin	12-2 TAD 113
Hill, Peter	THE HUNTERS	Allen J. Hubin	10-2 TAD 113
Hill, Peter	THE HUNTERS	Steve Lewis	1-3 MF 37
Hill, Peter	THE LIARS	Robert C.S.Adey	4-4 PP 28
Hill, R.Lance	THE EVIL THAT MEN DO	Allen J. Hubin	12-2 TAD 113
Hill, Reginald	A FAIRLY DANGEROUS THING	Jay Jeffries	2 MN 5
Hill, Reginald	A KILLING KINDNESS	Allen J. Hubin	14-4 TAD 299
Hill, Reginald	A PINCH OF SNUFF	Allen J. Hubin	12-1 TAD 8
Hill, Reginald	A VERY CLUBBABLE WOMAN	Jay Jeffries	2 MN 5
Hill, Reginald	AN ADVANCEMENT OF LEARNING	Jay Jeffries	2 MN 5
Hill, Reginald	FELL OF DARK	Jay Jeffries	2 MN 5
Hill, Reginald	RULING PASSION	Allen J. Hubin	11-1 TAD 17

Hill, Reginald	RULING PASSION	Steve Lewis	2-3 MF 42
Hill, Reginald	THE SPY'S WIFE	Allen J. Hubin	14-2 TAD 126
Hillerman, Tony	THE BLESSING WAY	Lianne Carlin	3-4 MR 10
Hillerman, Tony	THE BLESSING WAY	Len & June Moffatt	14 JD 20
Hillerman, Tony	DANCE HALL OF THE DEAD	Allen J. Hubin	7-1 TAD 62
Hillerman, Tony	THE FLY ON THE WALL	Barzun & Taylor	10-2 TAD 127
Hillerman, Tony	THE FLY ON THE WALL	Charles Shibuk	12-4 TAD 369
Hillerman, Tony	LISTENING WOMAN	Allen J. Hubin	11-3 TAD 230
Hillerman, Tony	LISTENING WOMAN	Charles Shibuk	12-3 TAD 255
Hillerman, Tony	PEOPLE OF DARKNESS	Joyce L. Dewes	2-3 M 49
Hillerman, Tony	PEOPLE OF DARKNESS	Allen J. Hubin	14-2 TAD 126
Hillerman, Tony	PEOPLE OF DARKNESS	Dorothy B. Hughes	3-2 M 38
Hilton, James	WAS IT MURDER?	Maryell Cleary	2-6 PP 33
Hilton, James	WAS IT MURDER?	Jon L. Lellenberg	11-2 TAD 122
Hilton, James	WAS IT MURDER?	Charles Shibuk	13-3 TAD 250
Hilton, John Buxton	DEAD-NETTLE	Allen J. Hubin	11-2 TAD 116
Hilton, John Buxton	DEAD-NETTLE	Steve Lewis	2-5 MF 26
Hilton, John Buxton	DEAD-NETTLE	Guy M. Townsend	1-2 PP 22
Hilton, John Buxton	GAMEKEEPER'S GALLOWS	Steve Lewis	1-6 MF 38
Hilton, John Buxton	SOME RUN CROOKED	Steve Lewis	3-1 MF 34
Himmel, Richard	I HAVE GLORIA KIRBY	Steve Lewis	2-5 MF 34
Himmel, Richard	THE TWENTY-THIRD WEB	Allen J. Hubin	10-4 TAD 308
Himmel, Richard	THE TWENTY-THIRD WEB	Amnon Kabatchnik	2-4 MF 45
Himmel, Richard	TWO DEATHS MUST DIE	Bill Crider	3 PE 19
Hinkemeyer, Michael	THE FIELDS OF EDEN	Allen J. Hubin	11-2 TAD 116
Hinkemeyer, Michael	THE FIELDS OF EDEN	Steve Lewis	3-1 MF 33
Hinkemeyer, Michael	THE FIELDS OF EDEN	Charles Shibuk	12-2 TAD 167
Hinkle, Vernon	MUSIC TO MURDER BY	Myrtis Broset	2-5 MF 44
Hinkle, Vernon	MUSIC TO MURDER BY	Fred Dueren	11-4 TAD 396
Hintze, Naomi A.	LISTEN, PLEASE, LISTEN	Veronica M.Kennedy	9-3 TAD 223
Hintze, Naomi A.	YOU'LL LIKE MY MOTHER	Lianne Carlin	3-6 MR 24
Hirschberg, Cornelius	FLORENTINE FINISH	Charles Shibuk	11-3 TAD 298
Hitchcock, Alfred,ed.	ALFRED HITCHCOCK PRESENTS STORIES TO STAY AWAKE BY	James Mark Purcell	5-1 MR 33
Hitchcock, Alfred,ed.	MURDERERS' ROW	Steve Lewis	1-1 MF 33
Hitchens, Dolores	THE BAXTER LETTERS	Marvin Lachman	4-6 MR 32
Hitchman, Janet	SUCH A STRANGE LADY: A BIOGRAPHY OF DOROTHY L. SAYERS	Marvin Lachman	9 MN R7
Hitchman, Janet	SUCH A STRANGE LADY: A BIOGRAPHY OF DOROTHY L. SAYERS	Marvin Lachman	13 MN R3
Hitchman, Janet	SUCH A STRANGE LADY: A BIOGRAPHY OF DOROTHY L. SAYERS	Lloyd Rose	9-1 TAD 69
Hitchman, Janet	SUCH A STRANGE LADY: A BIOGRAPHY OF DOROTHY L. SAYERS	Charles Shibuk	10-2 TAD 149
Hjersman, Peter	THE STASH BOOK	George Kelley	3-4 PP 32
Hjort, James William	EBON ROSES, JEWELLED SKULLS	J. Grant Thiessen	10 SF 41
Hjortsberg, William	FALLING ANGEL	Richard Emery	4-2 PP 30
Hjortsberg, William	FALLING ANGEL	Allen J. Hubin	12-1 TAD 8
Hjortsberg, William	FALLING ANGEL	Steven Miller	3-2 PP 31
Hobhouse, Adam	THE HANGOVER MURDERS	Charles Shibuk	7-2 TAD 134
Hobhouse, Adam	REMEMBER LAST LIGHT? (film)	William K. Everson	3-4 TAD 239
Hoch, Edward D.,ed.	ALL BUT IMPOSSIBLE!	Barzun & Taylor	14-4 TAD 328
Hoch, Edward D.,ed.	BEST DETECTIVE STORIES OF THE YEAR 1976	Allen J. Hubin	10-1 TAD 42
Hoch, Edward D.,ed.	BEST DETECTIVE STORIES OF THE YEAR 1976	Allen J. Hubin	11-1 TAD 19
Hoch, Edward D.,ed.	BEST DETECTIVE STORIES OF THE YEAR 1977	Steve Lewis	2-1 MF 21
Hoch, Edward D.,ed.	BEST DETECTIVE STORIES OF THE YEAR 1980	Sam Yamato	2-2 M 55
Hoch, Edward D.	CITY OF BRASS	Douglas G. Greene	4-3 PP 24
Hoch, Edward D.	THE JUDGES OF HADES AND OTHER SIMON ARK STORIES	Joe R. Christopher	5-3 TAD 163
Hoch, Edward D.	THE JUDGES OF HADES AND OTHER SIMON ARK STORIES	Douglas G. Greene	4-3 PP 23

Hoch, Edward D.	THE MONKEY'S CLUE (&) THE STOLEN SAPPHIRE	Douglas G. Greene	12-3 TAD 273
Hoch, Edward D.	THE SHATTERED RAVEN	J.R.Christopher	3-2 TAD 133
Hoch, Edward D.	THE SHATTERED RAVEN	Mary A. Grochowski	1-4 PP 23
Hoch, Edward D.	THE SHATTERED RAVEN	Robert E. Washer	1-4 QC 20
Hoch, Edward D.	THE SPY AND THE THIEF	Marvin Lachman	5-3 TAD 167
Hoch, Edward D.	THE SPY AND THE THIEF	James Mark Purcell	5-2 MR 43
Hoch, Edward D.	THE THEFTS OF NICK VELVET	Allen J. Hubin	12-2 TAD 113
Hoch, Edward D.	THE THEFTS OF NICK VELVET	F.M.Nevins, Jr.	3-1 MF 44
Hoch, Edward D.	THE THEFTS OF NICK VELVET	Martin M. Wooster	2-6 MF 39
Hoch, Edward D.	THE TRANSVECTION MACHINE	Robert E. Briney	5-2 MR 38
Hochstein, Peter	THE FATAL FETISH	Fred Dueren	10-4 TAD 341.
Hocking, Anne	POISON IS A BITTER BREW	Maryell Cleary	4-4 PP 24
Hodel, Michael P., & Sean M. Wright	ENTER THE LION: A POSTHUMOUS MEMOIR OF MYCROFT HOLMES	Paul Bishop	2-1 M 26
Hodel, Michael P., & Sean M. Wright	ENTER THE LION: A POSTHUMOUS MEMOIR OF MYCROFT HOLMES	Edward Lauterbach	4-1 PP 33
Hodel, Michael P., & Sean M. Wright	ENTER THE LION: A POSTHUMOUS MEMOIR OF MYCROFT HOLMES	Charles Shibuk	14-1 TAD 80
Hodgson, William Hope	CARNACKI, THE GHOST FINDER	R.W.Hays	5-2 TAD 99
Hoffer, William, & William W.Pearce	CAUGHT IN THE ACT: THE TRUE ADVENTURES OF A DIVORCE DETECTIVE	Marlowe Archer	4 PE 24
Hoffman, Daniel	POE POE POE POE POE POE POE	Lianne Carlin	5-2 MR 46
Hoffman, Paul, & Ira Pecznick	TO DROP A DIME	Fred Dueren	11-2 TAD 192
Hogstrand, Olle	THE GAMBLER	Allen J. Hubin	7-3 TAD 220
Holding, Elisabeth S.	THE BLANK WALL	Jane S. Bakerman	1-5 MF 46
Holdstock, Robert,ed.	ENCYCLOPEDIA OF SCIENCE FICTION	W.Ritchie Benedict	6 U 38
Holland, Cecelia	FLOATING WORLDS	Sheldon A.Wiebe	4 SF 24
Holland, Isabelle	MONCRIEF	Barbara A.Buhrer	2-2 MM 3
Holles, Robert	SPAWN	Allen J. Hubin	12-1 TAD 8
Holman, Hugh	SLAY THE MURDERER	Steve Lewis	1A MF 24
Holton, Leonard	A CORNER OF PARADISE	Steve Lewis	2-1 MF 22
Holtsmark, Erling B.	TARZAN AND TRADITION	J.Grant Thiessen	14 SF 19
Holzer, Hans	THE CHINDVIT CONSPIRACY	Fred Dueren	10-2 TAD 130
Holzer, Hans	PSYCHIC DETECTIVE: THE UNICORN	Fred Dueren	9-4 TAD 277
Homes, Geoffrey	BUILD MY GALLOWS HIGH	Theodore Dukeshire	3-4 MF 49
Homes, Geoffrey	THE CASE OF THE MEXICAN KNIFE	Theodore Dukeshire	3-4 MF 49
Homes, Geoffrey	FINDERS KEEPERS	Charles Shibuk	8-4 TAD 300
Homes, Geoffrey	THE MAN WHO MURDERED GOLIATH	Theodore Dukeshire	2-5 MF 43
Homes, Geoffrey	THE MAN WHO MURDERED HIMSELF	Theodore Dukeshire	2-5 MF 42
Homes, Geoffrey	SIX SILVER HANDLES	Charles Shibuk	10-4 TAD 316
Hone, Joseph	THE SIXTH DIRECTORATE	Fred Dueren	10-1 TAD 51
Hone, Ralph E.	DOROTHY L. SAYERS: A LITERARY BIOGRAPHY	Allen J. Hubin	12-4 TAD 322
Hone, Ralph E.	DOROTHY L. SAYERS: A LITERARY BIOGRAPHY	F.M.Nevins, Jr.	3-5 MF 45
Hoover, J. Edgar	PAROLE FIXER	William K. Everson	2-4 TAD 258
Horler, Sydney	THE VAMPIRE	Allen J. Hubin	8-3 TAD 230
Hornung, E.W.	RAFFLES (film)	William K. Everson	6-3 TAD 150
Hornung, E.W.	RAFFLES	Charles Shibuk	10-1 TAD 72
House, Brant	CITY OF THE LIVING DEAD	Lynn Hickman	65 PU 27
House, Brant	CURSE OF THE MANDARIN'S FAN	Lynn Hickman	65 PU 27
House, Brant	OCTOPUS OF CRIME	Gary Zachrich	66 PU 54
House, Robert Wallace	THE CROSS OF THUGER	Standley H.Detwiler	63 PU 52
Household, Geoffrey	A ROUGH SHEET	Martin M. Wooster	2-2 MM 6
Household, Geoffrey	A TIME TO KILL	Martin M. Wooster	2-3 MM 5
Household, Geoffrey	AGAINST THE WIND	Theodore Dukeshire	3-2 MF 49
Household, Geoffrey	THE BRIDES OF SOLOMON AND OTHER SHORT STORIES	Martin M. Wooster	1-5 PP 20
Household, Geoffrey	THE COURTESY OF DEATH	Martin M. Wooster	4-3 MF 45
Household, Geoffrey	DANCE OF THE DWARFS	Charles Shibuk	13-1 TAD 75
Household, Geoffrey	HOSTAGE: LONDON	Guy M. Townsend	2-3 MF 50
Household, Geoffrey	THE LAST TWO WEEKS OF GEORGES RIVAC	Allen J. Hubin	12-1 TAD 8

Household, Geoffrey	RED ANGER	Guy M. Townsend	2-2 MF 40
Household, Geoffrey	ROGUE MALE	Guy M. Townsend	2-2 MF 40
Household, Geoffrey	SABRES ON THE SAND AND OTHER STORIES	Martin M. Wooster	2-1 MM 6
Household, Geoffrey	WATCHER IN THE SHADOWS	Guy M. Townsend	2-2 MF 40
Houser, Lionel, & Mary McCall	I PROMISE TO PAY (film)	William K. Everson	11-2 TAD 129
Howard, Clark	THE KILLINGS	Veronica M.Kennedy	7-3 TAD 217
Howard, Colin	KILLING NO MURDER	Allen J. Hubin	14-4 TAD 301
Howard, James	I LIKE IT TOUGH	Steve Lewis	1-7 MM 8
Howard, James A.	MURDER TAKES A WIFE	Fred Dueren	14-1 TAD 81
Howard, Robert E.	THE VULTURES	Michael L. Cook	4 U 20
Howard, Vechel	MURDER WITH LOVE	Steve Lewis	5-6 MF 37
Howes, Royce	THE CASE OF THE COPY-HOOK KILLING	Steve Lewis	4-4 MF 33
Hoyt, Richard	DECOYS	Allen J. Hubin	14-2 TAD 127
Hoyt, Richard	DECOYS	Steve Lewis	5-2 MF 14
Hubbard, P.M.	THE DANCING MAN	Robert E. Briney	5-5 MF 38
Hubbard, P.M.	THE DANCING MAN	Robert E. Briney	4-5 MR 34
Hubbard, P.M.	THE QUIET RIVER	Barzun & Taylor	12-3 TAD 263
Hubbard, P.M.	THE QUIET RIVER	Steve Lewis	3-3 MF 37
Hubbell, Ned	THE ADVENTURES OF CREIGHTON HOLMES	R. Jeff Banks	2-5 PP 13
Hubbell, Ned	THE ADVENTURES OF CREIGHTON HOLMES	Douglas G. Greene	12-3 TAD 273
Hubert, Tord	THE TRAP	Allen J. Hubin	10-4 TAD 308
Hubin, Allen J.	THE BIBLIOGRAPHY OF CRIME FICTION 1749-1975	David H. Doerrer	3-3 MF 48
Hubin, Allen J.	THE BIBLIOGRAPHY OF CRIME FICTION 1749-1975	Charles Shibuk	12-2 TAD 178
Hudson, Christopher	THE FINAL ACT	Allen J. Hubin	14-4 TAD 300
Hudson, Harry K.	A BIBLIOGRAPHY OF HARD-COVER BOYS' BOOKS	Robert Jennings	5 BB 3
Huggins, Roy	THE DOUBLE TAKE	Angelo Panagos	10-2 TAD 140
Huggins, Roy	77 SUNSET STRIP	Angelo Panagos	10-2 TAD 140
Hughes, Dorothy B.	ERLE STANLEY GARDNER: THE CASE OF THE REAL PERRY MASON	Marvin Lachman	1-5 PP 22
Hughes, Dorothy B.	ERLE STANLEY GARDNER: THE CASE OF THE REAL PERRY MASON	F.M.Nevins, Jr.	2-4 MF 37
Hughes, Dorothy B.	THE EXPENDABLE MAN	Mary Jean DeMarr	5-2 MF 31
Hughes, Dorothy B.	THE SCARLET IMPERIAL	Robert M. Williams	9 MN R20
Hughes, Dorothy B.	THE SO-BLUE MARBLE	Jay Jeffries	3/4 MN 8
Hughes, William	SPLIT ON RED	Steve Lewis	5-6 MF 33
Hugo, Richard	DEATH AND THE GOOD LIFE	Steven M. Krauzer	14-3 TAD 271
Hugo, Richard	DEATH AND THE GOOD LIFE	Steve Lewis	5-3 MF 31
Hugo, Richard	DEATH AND THE GOOD LIFE	F.M.Nevins, Jr.	5-2 MF 27
Hull, E. Mayne, & A.E.van Vogt	THE WINGED MAN	Gary Zachrich	75 PU 26
Hull, Richard	A MATTER OF NERVES	Charles Shibuk	2-4 MF 42
Hull, Richard	LAST FIRST	Charles Shibuk	8-2 TAD 140
Hull, Richard	THE MURDER OF MY AUNT	Jay Jeffries	6 MY 10
Hull, Richard	THE MURDER OF MY AUNT	Charles Shibuk	13-3 TAD 250
Hull, Richard	THE MURDERERS OF MONTY	Jay Jeffries	6 MY 10
Hume, Fergus	HAGAR OF THE PAWN SHOP	Douglas G. Greene	12-3 TAD 230
Hunt, E.Howard	THE HARGRAVE DECEPTION	Allen J. Hubin	14-2 TAD 127
Hunt, E.Howard	ONE OF OUR AGENTS IS MISSING	Louis B. Delpino	6-2 MR 48
Hunt, Kyle	A PERIOD OF EVIL	Robert E. Briney	4-6 MR 33
Hunt, Kyle	AS LONELY AS THE DAMNED	John Harwood	5-3 MR 35
Hunt, Kyle	THE MAN WHO WAS NOT HIMSELF	Angelo Panagos	11-4 TAD 381
Hunt, Roy	FU MANCHU AND COMPANY (art folio)	Stanley A. Carlin	3-3 MR 28
Hunt, Roy	FU MANCHU AND COMPANY (art folio)	Allen J. Hubin	3-2 TAD 134
Hunt, Roy	THE SOMETHING HUNT (art folio)	Allen J. Hubin	1-2 TAD 62
Hunter, Alan	GENTLY DOWN THE STREAM	Douglas G. Greene	13-3 TAD 268

Hunter, Alan	GENTLY IN THE HIGHLANDS	Frank Denton	9 MN R15
Hunter, Alan	GENTLY THROUGH THE WOODS	Pearl G. Aldrich	9-4 TAD 300
Hunter, Alan	THE HONFLEUR DECISION	Allen J. Hubin	14-4 TAD 300
Hunter, Alan	THE HONFLEUR DECISION	Gary Warren Niebuhr	4-3 PP 27
Hunter, Alan	LANDED GENTLY	Guy M. Townsend	11 MN R9
Hunter, Harriet	INCLINATION TO MURDER	Steve Lewis	3-6 MF 33
Hunter, Stephen	THE MASTER SNIPER	Rod Kassel	1-3 M 17
Hunter, Tim, &			
Charlie Haas	THE SOUL HIT	Allen J. Hubin	11-1 TAD 20
Hunvald, Henry	THE MASTERPIECE OF NICE MR.BREEN	Charles Shibuk	6-2 TAD 107
Hurwood, Bernhardt J.	THE INVISIBLES	Stanley A. Carlin	4-6 MR 38
Huston, Fran	THE RICH GET IT ALL	Steve Lewis	3-6 MF 36
Hutter, A.D.	THE DEATH MECHANIC	Joyce L. Dewes	2-1 M 27
Hutter, A.D.	THE DEATH MECHANIC	Fred Dueren	14-2 TAD 184
Hutton, J.F.	TOO GOOD TO BE TRUE	Charles Shibuk	2-1 MF 47
Hutton, John	29 HERRIOTT STREET	Allen J. Hubin	13-4 TAD 295
Huxley, Elspeth	THE AFRICAN POISON MURDERS	Charles Shibuk	14-4 TAD 377
Huxley, Elspeth	A MAN FROM NOWHERE	Barzun & Taylor	14-3 TAD 228
Huxley, Elspeth	MURDER AT GOVERNMENT HOUSE	Michael Trombetta	12-1 TAD 78
Huxley, Elspeth	MURDER ON SAFARI	Douglas G. Greene	4-5/6 PP 69
Hyland, Stanley	WHO GOES HANG?	Barzun & Taylor	11-3 TAD 307
Hyland, Stanley	WHO GOES HANG?	Maryell Cleary	3-4 PP 31
Hyland, Stanley	WHO GOES HANG?	Edward Lauterbach	2-1 TAD 60
Iams, Jack	DO NOT MURDER BEFORE CHRISTMAS	Charles Shibuk	8-2 TAD 141
Iannuzzi, John N.	COURTHOUSE	Barbara A. Buhrer	11 MN R13
Iles, Francis	MALICE AFORETHOUGHT	Charles Shibuk	14-3 TAD 267
Inge, M. Thomas, ed.	HANDBOOK OF AMERICAN POPULAR		
	CULTURE	W.Paul Ganley	2 FM 16
Inge, M. Thomas, ed.	HANDBOOK OF AMERICAN POPULAR		
	CULTURE	Andy Jaysnovitch	5 PE 20
Innes, Michael	THE AMPERSAND PAPERS	Allen J. Hubin	12-3 TAD 205
Innes, Michael	THE AMPERSAND PAPERS	Steve Lewis	3-5 MF 39
Innes, Michael	THE AMPERSAND PAPERS	Charles Shibuk	14-2 TAD 183
Innes, Michael	AN AWKWARD LIE	Jay Jeffries	7 MY 7
Innes, Michael	APPLEBY ON ARARAT	Jay Jeffries	7 MY 7
Innes, Michael	APPLEBY'S ANSWER	Douglas Armato	6-1 MR 43
Innes, Michael	APPLEBY'S ANSWER	Allen J. Hubin	6-4 TAD 266
Innes, Michael	APPLEBY'S OTHER STORY	Allen J. Hubin	7-4 TAD 295
Innes, Michael	APPLEBY'S ANSWER	Jay Jeffries	7 MY 8
Innes, Michael	APPLEBY'S OTHER STORY	Jay Jeffries	7 MY 8
Innes, Michael	THE CASE OF SONIA WAYWARD	Steve Lewis	2-6 MF 35
Innes, Michael	THE DAFFODIL AFFAIR	Michael Trombetta	11-3 TAD 248
Innes, Michael	DEATH BY WATER	Allen J. Hubin	1-3 TAD 102
Innes, Michael	DEATH BY WATER	Guy M. Townsend	1A MF 31
Innes, Michael	FROM LONDON FAR	Myrtis Broset	1-4 MF 48
Innes, Michael	FROM LONDON FAR	Marvin Lachman	5-4 MF 18
Innes, Michael	THE GAY PHOENIX	Frank Occhiogrosso	11-2 TAD 119
Innes, Michael	GOING IT ALONE	Allen J. Hubin	13-4 TAD 296
Innes, Michael	HAMLET, REVENGE!	Jane S. Bakerman	1-3 PP 25
Innes, Michael	HONEYBATH'S HAVEN	Steve Lewis	2-5 MF 29
Innes, Michael	LAMENT FOR A MAKER	Jay Jeffries	7 MY 6
Innes, Michael	THE MYSTERIOUS COMMISSION	Jay Jeffries	5/6 MN 18
Innes, Michael	THE NEW SONIA WAYWARD	Jay Jeffries	7 MY 7
Innes, Michael	ONE MAN SHOW	Arthur C. Scott	1-7 MM 8
Innes, Michael	THE OPEN HOUSE	Jay Jeffries	7 MY 7
Innes, Michael	THE OPEN HOUSE	Amnon Kabatchnik	5-4 MR 29
Innes, Michael	SILENCE OBSERVED	Don Miller	1-9 MM 6
Irving, Clifford, &			
Herbert Burkholz	THE DEATH FREAK	Carl Hoffman	13-2 TAD 147
Isaacs, Susan	COMPROMISING POSITIONS	R. Jeff Banks	2-6 PP 13
Isaacs, Susan	COMPROMISING POSITIONS	Mary Jane DeMarr	3-4 MF 43
Isaacs, Susan	COMPROMISING POSITIONS	Allen J. Hubin	11-4 TAD 332
Isely, Kenneth	A STRANGE CODE OF JUSTICE	Allen J. Hubin	8-2 TAD 148
Israel, Peter	THE STIFF UPPER LIP	Theodore Dukeshire	3-2 MF 49

Israel, Peter	THE STIFF UPPER LIP	Allen J. Hubin	12-1 TAD 9
Israel, Peter	THE STIFF UPPER LIP	Steve Lewis	3-4 MF 38
Israel, Peter	THE STIFF UPPER LIP	Jim McCahery	6 PE 21
Ives, John	THE MARCHAND WOMAN	Allen J. Hubin	13-2 TAD 95
Jaccoma, Richard	YELLOW PERIL	R. Jeff Banks	4-3 PP 11
Jacks, Jeff	MURDER ON THE WILD SIDE	Amnon Kabatchnik	5-4 MR 32
Jackson, Clarence	KICKED TO DEATH BY A CAMEL	Allen J. Hubin	7-1 TAD 62
Jackson, Jon A.	THE BLIND PIG	Steven M. Krauzer	12-3 TAD 272
Jackson, Jon A.	THE BLIND PIG	Steve Lewis	3-6 MF 27
Jackson, Jon A.	THE DIEHARD	Fred Dueren	13-4 TAD 361
Jackson, Jon A.	THE DIEHARD	Mary A. Grochowski	1-1 PP 24
Jackson, Jon A.	THE DIEHARD	Jim Huang	2 CL 2
Jackson, Jon A.	THE DIEHARD	Steven M. Krauzer	10-3 TAD 209
Jackson, Jon A.	THE DIEHARD	Steve Lewis	2-1 MF 25
Jackson, O.T.	AFTERMATH	Fred Dueren	12-2 TAD 135
Jackson, Sir Richard	OCCUPIED WITH CRIME	Robert E. Briney	10-4 TAD 314
Jacobson, Dan	THE WONDER-WORKER	Fred Dueren	10-4 TAD 341
Jaffe, Susanne	THE OTHER ANNE FLETCHER	Allen J. Hubin	14-2 TAD 127
Jaffee, Mary & Irving	BEYOND BAKER STREET	Allen J. Hubin	7-1 TAD 63
Jagoda, Robert	A FRIEND IN DEED	Steve Lewis	2-4 MF 33
Jahn, Mike	KILLER ON THE HEIGHTS	Fred Dueren	11-2 TAD 192
Jahn, Mike	THE QUARK MANEUVER	Steve Lewis	1-5 MF 31
James, David	CROC'	(not stated)	1-3 MF 45
James, Leigh	THE CALIPH INTRIGUE	Allen J. Hubin	12-3 TAD 205
James, P.D.	AN UNSUITABLE JOB FOR A WOMAN	Guy M. Townsend	1-10 MM 9
James, P.D.	THE BLACK TOWER	Barbara A. Buhrer	9 MN R1
James, P.D.	THE BLACK TOWER	Frank Denton	9 MN R4
James, P.D.	THE BLACK TOWER	Allen J. Hubin	9-1 TAD 73
James, P.D.	THE BLACK TOWER	Charles Shibuk	10-1 TAD 72
James, P.D.	COVER HER FACE	Myrtis Broset	2-2 MM 3
James, P.D.	COVER HER FACE	Charles Shibuk	10-2 TAD 149
James, P.D.	DEATH OF AN EXPERT WITNESS	Jane S. Bakerman	2-2 MF 36
James, P.D.	DEATH OF AN EXPERT WITNESS	Steve Lewis	2-3 MF 47
James, P.D.	DEATH OF AN EXPERT WITNESS	Charles Shibuk	12-2 TAD 167
James, P.D.	INNOCENT BLOOD	Barzun & Taylor	13-4 TAD 309
James, P.D.	INNOCENT BLOOD	Tiffany Carroll	2-1 M 28
James, P.D.	INNOCENT BLOOD	Allen J. Hubin	13-3 TAD 202
James, P.D.	INNOCENT BLOOD	Marvin Lachman	3-3 PP 31
James, P.D.	INNOCENT BLOOD	Richard Moskowitz	9 LR 17
James, P.D.	SHROUD FOR A NIGHTINGALE	Jay Jeffries	8 MN 23
James, P.D.	SHROUD FOR A NIGHTINGALE	Steve Lewis	1A MF 24
James, P.D.	SHROUD FOR A NIGHTINGALE	Charles Shibuk	9-4 TAD 281
James, Rebecca	THE HOUSE IS DARK	Barbara A. Buhrer	13B MN 9
Janifer, Lawrence M., & S.J.Treibich	TARGET TERRA	Gary Zachrich	71 PU 21
Japrisot, Sebastien	TRAP FOR CINDERELLA	Joanne M.Schneider	1-3 M 20
Jay, Charlotte	THE VOICE OF THE CRAB	Allen J. Hubin	8-1 TAD 66
Jay, Simon	DEATH OF A SKIN DIVER	Robert C.S.Adey	4-4 PP 26
Jeffers, H.Paul	THE ADVENTURE OF THE STALWART COMPANIONS	Allen J. Hubin	12-2 TAD 113
Jeffers, H.Paul	RUBOUT AT THE ONYX	Steve Lewis	5-6 MF 37
Jeffreys, J.G.	THE THIEFTAKER	Fred Dueren	9-1 TAD 50
Jeffries, Roderic	AGAINST TIME	John Vining	10-2 TAD 141
Jeffries, Roderic	DEAD AGAINST THE LAWYERS	Robert C.S.Adey	4-4 PP 26
Jeffries, Roderic	MURDER BEGETS MURDER	Steve Lewis	4-2 MF 32
Jellett, H., & Ngaio Marsh	THE NURSING HOME MURDER	Douglas M. Armato	6-4 TAD 260
Jenkins, Elizabeth	DR. GULLY'S STORY	Barzun & Taylor	9-3 TAD 237
Jenkins, Elizabeth	HARRIET	Mary Groff	3-2 PP 25
Jenkins, Will F.	MURDER OF THE U.S.A.	David Bates	4 PE 12
Jepson, Edgar	THE GIRL'S HEAD	Charles Shibuk	1-3 MF 43
Jepson, Edgar	NO.19	Charles Shibuk	9-3 TAD 226
Jepson, Edgar	THE SPLENDID ADVENTURES OF HANNIBAL TOD	Charles Shibuk	12-4 TAD 374

Jepson, Selwyn	THE ANGRY MILLIONAIRE	Len Moffatt	2-2 TAD 120
Jepson, Selwyn	THE DEATH GONG	Charles Shibuk	7-4 TAD 289
Jevons, Marshall	MURDER AT THE MARGIN	Allen J. Hubin	11-2 TAD 118
Jobson, Hamilton	THE EVIDENCE YOU WILL HEAR	Barzun & Taylor	9-4 TAD 271
Jobson, Hamilton	THE EVIDENCE YOU WILL HEAR	Stan Burns	11 MN R15
Jobson, Hamilton	THE SHADOW THAT CAUGHT FIRE	Stan Burns	11 MN R5
Jobson, Hamilton	WAITING FOR THURSDAY	Allen J. Hubin	11-4 TAD 333
Johnson, Bud, & Pete Knight	THE KING OF ELFLAND'S DAUGHTER	Sheldon A. Wiebe	5 SF 38
Johnson, E.Richard	THE CARDINALLI CONTRACT	Steve Lewis	1-11 MM 4
Johnson, James L.	A HANDFUL OF DOMINOES	Amnon Kabatchnik	4-4 MR 39
Johnson, Stanley	THE DOOMSDAY DEPOSIT	Allen J. Hubin	13-4 TAD 296
Johnson, Tom, & Will Murray	SECRET AGENT X: A HISTORY	Sampson & Carr	14 SF 21
Johnson,W.Bolingbroke	THE WIDENING STAIN	Philip T. Asdell	3-4 TAD 273
Johnson,W.Bolingbroke	THE WIDENING STAIN	Maryell CLeary	2-6 PP 32
Johnson, Wm.Oscar	THE ZERO FACTOR	Gary Warren Niebuhr	3-2 PP 23
Johnson, Wm.Oscar	THE ZERO FACTOR	Charles Shibuk	13-4 TAD 363
Johnston, Velda	THE FRENCHMAN	Barbara A. Buhrer	2-4 MM 3
Jones, Douglas C.	WINDING STAIR	Gary Warren Niebuhr	3-2 PP 24
Jones, Elwyn	BARLOW EXPOSED	Steve Lewis	2-3 MF 42
Jones, Elwyn, & John Lloyd	THE RIPPER FILE	Jon L. Lellenberg	9-3 TAD 222
Jones, Jennifer	MURDER-ON-HUDSON	Robert Williams	3/4 MN 10
Jones, Victor	MONUMENT OF TERROR	Amnon Kabatchnik	6-2 MR 49
Judson, William	KILMAN'S LANDING	Bill Crider	2-5 MF 40
Julian, Joseph	THIS WAS RADIO: A PERSONAL MEMOIR	Steve Lewis	7 MY 11
Kahn, James	DIAGNOSIS: MURDER	Fred Dueren	13-4 TAD 362
Kahn, Joan, ed.	THE EDGE OF THE CHAIR	Len & June Moffatt	8 JD 17
Kahn, Joan, ed.	SOME THINGS FIERCE AND FATAL	Fred Dueren	9-1 TAD 50
Kains, Josephine	DEVIL MASK MYSTERY	Fred Dueren	12-2 TAD 135
Kallen, Lucille	C.B.GREENFIELD: THE TANGLEWOOD MURDER	Fred Dueren	5-5 MF 41
Kallen, Lucille	C.B.GREENFIELD: THE TANGLEWOOD MURDER	Allen J. Hubin	14-1 TAD 18
Kallen, Lucille	C.B.GREENFIELD: THE TANGLEWOOD MURDER	Steve Lewis	5-1 MF 21
Kallen, Lucille	INTRODUCING C.B.GREENFIELD	M.S.Cappadonna	12-3 TAD 272
Kallen, Lucille	INTRODUCING C.B.GREENFIELD	Fred Dueren	5-5 MF 41
Kallen, Lucille	INTRODUCING C.B.GREENFIELD	Gary Warren Niebuhr	2-3 PP 36
Kamin, Nick	EARTHRIM	Gary Zachrich	74 PU 24
Kaminsky, Stuart	BULLET FOR A STAR	Allen J. Hubin	11-1 TAD 18
Kaminsky, Stuart	BULLET FOR A STAR	James Jobst	2-1 MF 44
Kaminsky, Stuart	BULLET FOR A STAR	Steve Lewis	2-1 MF 25
Kaminsky, Stuart	THE HOWARD HUGHES AFFAIR	Steve Lewis	3-6 MF 40
Kaminsky, Stuart	THE HOWARD HUGHES AFFAIR	Allen J. Hubin	13-1 TAD 28
Kaminsky, Stuart	THE HOWARD HUGHES AFFAIR	Andy Jaysnovitch	6 PE 22
Kaminsky, Stuart	THE HOWARD HUGHES AFFAIR	S. Sasaki	1-2 M 22
Kaminsky, Stuart	MURDER ON THE YELLOW BRICK ROAD	Allen J. Hubin	11-4 TAD 333
Kaminsky, Stuart	MURDER ON THE YELLOW BRICK ROAD	Steve Lewis	2-6 MF 32
Kaminsky, Stuart	MURDER ON THE YELLOW BRICK ROAD	Jim McCahery	1-3 PP 28
Kaminsky, Stuart	NEVER CROSS A VAMPIRE	Allen J. Hubin	14-2 TAD 127
Kaminsky, Stuart	NEVER CROSS A VAMPIRE	Steve Lewis	5-1 MF 21
Kaminsky, Stuart	YOU BET YOUR LIFE	Mary A. Grochowski	2-5 PP 29
Kaminsky, Stuart	YOU BET YOUR LIFE	Allen J. Hubin	13-1 TAD 28
Kaminsky, Stuart	YOU BET YOUR LIFE	Andy Jaysnovitch	4 PE 14
Kaminsky, Stuart	YOU BET YOUR LIFE	Steve Lewis	3-6 MF 28
Kaminsky, Stuart	YOU BET YOUR LIFE	Charles Shibuk	14-1 TAD 80
Kamp, Sarah	OVER THE EDGE	Steve Lewis	3-6 MF 37
Kane, Frank	A REAL GONE GUY	Arthur C. Scott	1-6 MM 10
Kane, Frank	KEY WITNESS	Stephen Mertz	12-1 TAD 79
Kane, Henry	DEATH OF A FLACK	Arthur C. Scott	10 MN R19
Kane, Henry	PETER GUNN	Arthur C. Scott	10 MN R19

Kane, Henry	PRIVATE EYEFUL	Arthur C. Scott	10 MN R19
Kane, Henry	TRINITY IN VIOLENCE	Arthur C. Scott	1-7 MM 8
Kane, Henry	THE TRIPOLI DOCUMENTS	Fred Dueren	11-2 TAD 192
Kantor, Hal	THE VEGAS TRAP	Lianne Carlin	4-3 MR 38
Kaplan, Andrew	HOUR OF THE ASSASSINS	Don Miller	13 MN R5
Kaplan, Arthur	A KILLING FOR CHARITY	Allen J. Hubin	9-3 TAD 224
Kaplan, Arthur	A KILLING FOR CHARITY	Steve Lewis	1A MF 27
Kastle, Herbert	SUNSET PEOPLE	Fred Dueren	13-4 TAD 362
Katz, Shirley	ALLIGATOR	(not stated)	1-3 MF 45
Katz, William	DEATH DREAMS	Fred Dueren	13-3 TAD 252
Kavanagh, Paul	SUCH MEN ARE DANGEROUS	Fred Blosser	4-3 TAD 179
Kay, Terry	AFTER ELI	Gary Warren Niebuhr	4-5/6 PP 63
Kaye, Marvin	A LIVELY GAME OF DEATH	Allen J. Hubin	6-2 TAD 113
Kaye, Marvin	BULLETS FOR MACBETH	Bill Crider	10-1 TAD 59
Kaye, Marvin	THE HISTRONIC HOLMES	Allen J. Hubin	5-2 TAD 103
Kaye, Marvin	MY BROTHER, THE DRUGGIST	Bill Crider	3-6 MF 48
Kaye, Marvin	MY SON, THE DRUGGIST	Jim Huang	6 CL 9
Kaye, Marvin	MY SON, THE DRUGGIST	ALlen J. Hubin	11-1 TAD 18
Kaye, William	WRONG TARGET	Steve Lewis	5-6 MF 35
Keane, John	SHERLOCK BONES: TRACER OF MISSING PETS	Marlowe Archer	5 PE 40
Keating, H.R.F., ed.	AGATHA CHRISTIE: FIRST LADY OF CRIME	Amnon Kabatchnik	2-1 MF 32
Keating, H.R.F., ed.	AGATHA CHRISTIE: FIRST LADY OF CRIME	Howard Lachtman	11-2 TAD 119
Keating, H.R.F.	FILMI, FILMI, INSPECTOR GHOTE	Thomas F. Godfrey	12-4 TAD 370
Keating, H.R.F.	GO WEST, INSPECTOR GHOTE	Meera T. Clark	2-2 C 154
Keating, H.R.F.	GO WEST, INSPECTOR GHOTE	Steve Lewis	5-6 MF 33
Keating, H.R.F.	INSPECTOR GHOTE BREAKS AN EGG	David Brownell	8-2 TAD 141
Keating, H.R.F.	INSPECTOR GHOTE BREAKS AN EGG	Amnon Kabatchnik	4-6 MR 34
Keating, H.R.F.	INSPECTOR GHOTE DRAWS A LINE	Barzun & Taylor	14-1 TAD 89
Keating, H.R.F.	MURDER MUST APPETIZE	Philip T.Asdell	2-2 PP 29
Keating, H.R.F.	THE MURDER OF THE MAHARAJAH	Jon L. Breen	3-5 PP 41
Keating, H.R.F.	THE MURDER OF THE MAHARAJAH	Fred Dueren	14-1 TAD 53
Keating, H.R.F.	THE MURDER OF THE MAHARAJAH	Allen J. Hubin	14-2 TAD 127
Keating, H.R.F.	THE MURDER OF THE MAHARAJAH	Steve Lewis	4-4 MF 40
Keating, H.R.F.	SHERLOCK HOLMES: THE MAN AND HIS WORLD	Michael P. Hodel	2-1 M 29
Keating, H.R.F.	SHERLOCK HOLMES: THE MAN AND HIS WORLD	Ruth Windfeldt	1-1 M 32
Keech, Scott	CIPHERED	Allen J. Hubin	13-3 TAD 202
Keegan, William	A REAL KILLING	Allen J. Hubin	11-1 TAD 20
Keeler, Harry Stephen	THE GREEN JADE HAND	Mary A. Grochowski	1-1 PP 22
Keeler, Harry Stephen	THIEVES' NIGHTS: THE CHRONICLES OF DELANCEY, KING OF THIEVES	Douglas G. Greene	12-3 TAD 231
Keene, Day	FRAMED IN GUILT	Steve Lewis	1-6 MM 10
Keene, Day	TAKE A STEP TO MURDER	Steve Lewis	1A MF 26
Keene, Day	WAKE UP TO MURDER	Steve Lewis	1-10 MM 8
Keene, Faraday	PATTERN IN BLACK AND RED	Charles Shibuk	7-2 TAD 135
Keith, Carlton	A TASTE OF SANGRIA	Barzun & Taylor	9-4 TAD 271
Keller, Beverly	THE BAGHDAD DEFECTIONS	Amnon Kabatchnik	6-2 MR 47
Kelly, Anthony Paul	THREE FACES EAST (film)	William K. Everson	3-2 TAD 76
Kelly, Anthony Paul	THREE FACES EAST (film)	William K. Everson	6-1 TAD 6
Kelly, Bill	PEANUT BUTTER AND JELLY IS NOT FOR KIDS	Guy M. Townsend	1-8 MM 7
Kelly, Bill	SANDWICHES ARE NOT MY BUSINESS	Bill Crider	8-4 TAD 306
Kelly, Bill	SANDWICHES ARE NOT MY BUSINESS	George Fergus	2 MN 7
Kelly, Bill	SANDWICHES ARE NOT MY BUSINESS	Guy M. Townsend	1-8 MM 7
Kelly, Bill	TUNA IS NOT FOR EATING	Bill Crider	9-2 TAD 151
Kelly, James	MUSIC FROM ANOTHER ROOM	Fred Dueren	14-1 TAD 81
Kemelman, Harry	FRIDAY THE RABBI SLEPT LATE	James Sandoe	13-4 TAD 292
Kemelman, Harry	MONDAY THE RABBI TOOK OFF	Stanley A. Carlin	5-3 MR 37
Kemelman, Harry	MONDAY THE RABBI TOOK OFF	James Sandoe	14-3 TAD 272
Kemelman, Harry	WEDNESDAY THE RABBI GOT WET	Jeff Meyerson	1-4 MF 43
Kemelman, Harry	THURSDAY THE RABBI WALKED OUT	Allen J. Hubin	12-2 TAD 113

Kemp, Sarah	OVER THE EDGE	Bonnie Pollard	15 CL 7
Kendrick, Baynard	MAKE MINE MacLAIN	Douglas G. Greene	12-3 TAD 232
Kendrick, Baynard	MAKE MINE MacLAIN	Arthur C. Scott	11 MN R20
Kendrick, Tony	THE CHICAGO GIRL	Steve Lewis	1-2 MF 24
Kendrick, Tony	STEALING LILLIAN	James Jobst	2-1 MF 45
Keneally, Thomas	THE PLACE AT WHITTON	Lianne Carlin	4-5 MR 37
Kennedy, Adam	THE DOMINO PRINCIPLE	R. Jeff Banks	1-11 MM 3
Kennedy, Adam	THE DOMINO PRINCIPLE	Paul Flanagan	1 MT 46
Kennedy, Barbara	THE UNINVITED GUEST	William L.DeAndrea	14-4 TAD 379
Kennedy, Milward	DEATH TO THE RESCUE	Amnon Kabatchnik	9-1 TAD 59
Kennington, Alan	THE NIGHT HAS EYES (film)	William K. Everson	1-2 TAD 50
Kenyon, Michael	THE 100,000 WELCOMES	Robert E. Washer	3-1 QC 20
Kenyon, Michael	THE 100,000 WELCOMES	Robert E. Washer	4-1 TAD 48
Key, Sean A.	THE MARK OF CAIN	Thomas Godfrey	3-2 M 39
Kezer, Glenn	THE QUEEN IS DEAD	Robert J. Randisi	12-3 TAD 272
Kiefer, Warren	THE KIDNAPPERS	Allen J. Hubin	11-1 TAD 20
Kienzle, William X.	DEATH WEARS A RED HAT	Jane S. Bakerman	4-2 MF 41
Kienzle, William X.	DEATH WEARS A RED HAT	Jane Gottschalk	3-3 PP 31
Kienzle, William X.	MIND OVER MURDER	Steve Lewis	5-4 MF 22
Kienzle, William X.	THE ROSARY MURDERS	Jane S. Bakerman	4-2 MF 41
Kienzle, William X.	THE ROSARY MURDERS	Barzun & Taylor	13-3 TAD 209
Kienzle, William X.	THE ROSARY MURDERS	Steve Lewis	3-5 MF 40
Kienzle, William X.	THE ROSARY MURDERS	Guy M. Townsend	6/7 LR 21
Kilian, Crawford	ICEQUAKE	J.Grant Thiessen	9 SF 46
Killough, Lee	THE DOPPELGANGER GAMBIT	Fred Dueren	13-2 TAD 136
Killough, Lee	THE MONITOR, THE MINERS AND THE SHREE	Allan Magnus	12 SF 20
Kimura, Jiro	SECOND INTERNATIONAL CONGRESS OF CRIME WRITERS PICTURE BOOK	Michael L. Cook	5 U 31
Kimura, Jiro	SECOND INTERNATIONAL CONGRESS OF CRIME WRITERS PICTURE BOOK	Allen J. Hubin	12-3 TAD 206
Kimura, Jiro	SECOND INTERNATIONAL CONGRESS OF CRIME WRITERS PICTURE BOOK	Andy Jaysnovitch	6 PE 9
Kincaid, Matt	ONCE AN OUTLAW	Gary Zachrich	74 PU 22
Kindon, Thomas	MURDER IN THE MOOR	Amnon Kabatchnik	8-3 TAD 221
King, C.Daly	THE CURIOUS MR. TARRANT	Allen J. Hubin	11-1 TAD 17
King, C.Daly	THE CURIOUS MR. TARRANT	Amnon Kabatchnik	11 CL 7
King, C.Daly	THE CURIOUS MR. TARRANT	Charles Shibuk	11-1 TAD 97
King, Frank	THE CASE OF THE PAINTED GIRL	Steve Lewis	9 MN R16
King, Harold	CLOSING CEREMONIES	D.E.Ath	2-4 PP 28
King, Rufus	HOLIDAY HOMICIDE	Jon L. Breen	9-3 TAD 227
King, Rufus	MUSEUM PIECE NO.13	Angelo Panagos	12-1 TAD 80
King, Rufus, & Charles Beahan	MURDER BY THE CLOCK (film)	William K. Everson	6-3 TAD 171
King, Stephen	DANSE MACABRE	Joyce L. Dewes	3-2 M 40
King, Stephen	DANSE MACABRE	Martin M. Wooster	4-4 PP 30
King, Stephen	FIRESTARTER	Bill Crider	3-5 PP 42
King, Stephen	FIRESTARTER	Richard Moskowitz	9 LR 18
King, Stephen	NIGHT SHIFT	Martin M. Wooster	4-3 MF 45
King, Vincent	ANOTHER END	Gary Zachrich	75 PU 26
Kingsley, Michael J.	BLACK MAN, WHITE MAN	Amnon Kabatchnik	4-6 MR 38
Kinsley, Lawrence	THE RED-LIGHT VICTIM	Steve Lewis	5-5 MF 24
Kirk, Michael	ALL OTHER PERILS	Barbara A. Buhrer	2-2 MM 3
Kirk, Michael	ALL OTHER PERILS	Allen J. Hubin	8-4 TAD 310
Kirk, Russell	THE PRINCESS OF ALL LANDS	Martin M. Wooster	3-3 PP 33
Kirkwood, James	HIT ME WITH A RAINBOW	Gary Warren Niebuhr	3-2 PP 23
Kirst, Hans Helmut	A TIME FOR TRUTH	Allen J. Hubin	8-2 TAD 147
Kirst, Hans Helmut	EVERYTHING HAS ITS PRICE	Allen J. Hubin	9-4 TAD 310
Kitchin, C.H.B.	THE CORNISH FOX	Barzun & Taylor	12-3 TAD 263
Kittredge, William, & Steven M.Krauzer	GREAT ACTION STORIES	Bill Crider	1-1 PQ 35
Kittredge, William, & Steven M.Krauzer	THE GREAT AMERICAN DETECTIVES	Bill Crider	1-4 PQ 49
Kittredge, William, & Steven M.Krauzer	THE GREAT AMERICAN DETECTIVES	Andy Jaysnovitch	3 PE 23

Klainer, Albert & Jo-Ann	THE JUDAS GENE	Allen J. Hubin	13-4 TAD 296
Klein, Dave	BLIND SIDE	Fred Dueren	14-1 TAD 80
Klein, Dave	BLIND SIDE	Charles Shibuk	13-4 TAD 364
Kline, Otis Adelbert	JAN IN INDIA	W.Paul Ganley	6 U 28
Kluge, P.F.	EDDIE AND THE CRUISERS	Allen J. Hubin	14-2 TAD 128
Kluge, P.F.	THE DAY THAT I DIE	Allen J. Hubin	9-3 TAD 224
Knickmeyer, Steve	CRANMER	Allen J. Hubin	12-2 TAD 113
Knickmeyer, Steve	STRAIGHT	Allen J. Hubin	9-3 TAD 223
Knickmeyer, Steve	STRAIGHT	Jeff Meyerson	1-2 MF 16
Knickmeyer, Steve	STRAIGHT	Steve Lewis	1-2 MF 27
Knickmeyer, Steve	STRAIGHT	Charles Shibuk	11-1 TAD 96
Knight, Clifford	THE AFFAIR OF THE BLACK SOMBRERO	Douglas G. Greene	4-5/6 PP 69
Knight, Clifford	THE AFFAIR OF THE CORPSE ESCORT	Steve Lewis	3-6 MF 35
Knight, Clifford	THE AFFAIR OF THE GINGER LEI	Jon L. Breen	9-3 TAD 225
Knight, Clifford	THE AFFAIR OF THE SCARLET CRAB	Jon L. Breen	9-3 TAD 225
Knight, Damon	CREATING SHORT FICTION	J. Grant Thiessen	14 SF 19
Knight, Damon, ed.	NEBULA AWARD STORIES 1965	August Derleth	65 PU 25
Knight, Kathleen M.	TROUBLE AT TURKEY HILL	Steve Lewis	3-4 MF 41
Knight, Pete, & Bud Johnson	THE KING OF ELFLAND'S DAUGHTER	Sheldon A. Wiebe	5 SF 38
Knight, Stephen	ROGANO	D.E.Ath	2-4 PP 28
Knipe, J.A., & Madeleine Haldimand	MURDER NOW AND AGAIN	Fred Dueren	14-2 TAD 184
Knox, Bill	BOMB-SHIP	Charles Jardinier	2-1 M 27
Knox, Bill	DRAW BATONS	Douglas Armato	6-2 MR 47
Knox, Bill	LIVE BAIT	Steve Lewis	3-6 MF 30
Knox, Bill	RALLY TO KILL	Steve Lewis	1-5 MF 36
Knox, Bill, & Edward Boyd	THE VIEW FROM DANIEL PIKE	Robert C.S.Adey	4-5/6 PP 74
Knox, Bill, & Edward Boyd	THE VIEW FROM DANIEL PIKE	Robert W. Hahn	9-2 TAD 150
Knox, Bill, & Edward Boyd	THE VIEW FROM DANIEL PIKE	Barbara A. Buhrer	10 MN R14
Knox, Bill, & Edward Boyd	THE VIEW FROM DANIEL PIKE	Howard Waterhouse	3-1 MF 40
Koehler, Robert P.	THE HOODED VULTURE MURDERS	F.M.Nevins, Jr.	3-3 MF 47
Koenig, Laird	THE NEIGHBOR	Fred Dueren	12-2 TAD 135
Koenig, Laird P., & Peter L. Dixon	THE CHILDREN ARE WATCHING	Lianne Carlin	4-2 MR 41
Koontz, Dean R.	HOW TO WRITE BEST SELLING FICTION	Jon L. Breen	5-6 MF 43
Kotzwinkle, William	FATA MORGANA	George Kelley	1-4 MF 46
Kraft, David A., ed.	THE COMPLEAT OAK LEAVES	Michael L. Cook	5 U 31
Kram, Walter, & Dean Selmier	BOW AWAY	Marlowe Archer	4 PE 24
Krauzer, Steven M., & William Kittredge	GREAT ACTION STORIES	Bill Crider	1-1 PQ 35
Krauzer, Steven M., & William Kittredge	THE GREAT AMERICAN DETECTIVES	Bill Crider	1-4 PQ 49
Krauzer, Steven M., & William Kittredge	THE GREAT AMERICAN DETECTIVES	Andy Jaysnovitch	3 PE 23
Krone, Chester	BLOOD WRATH	Paul Harwitz	3-2 M 39
Kruger, Paul	A BULLET FOR A BLONDE	Steve Lewis	2-2 MM 4
Krumgold, Joseph	THANKS TO MURDER	Charles Shibuk	6-1 TAD 42
Kuppenberg, Paul	CRIME CAMPAIGN	Fred Dueren	13-1 TAD 65
Kurland, Michael	THE INFERNAL DEVICE	Joe R. Lansdale	3-3 MF 45
Kurland, Michael	THE INFERNAL DEVICE	Edward Lauterbach	12-2 TAD 178
Kurnitz, Harry	INVASION OF PRIVACY	Barzun & Taylor	11-3 TAD 307
Kwitny, Jonathan	VICIOUS CIRCLES: THE MAFIA IN THE MARKET PLACE	Marlowe Archer	5 PE 16
Kyle, Duncan	TERROR'S CRADLE	Barbara A. Buhrer	1-7 MM 7
Lacassin, Francis	MYTHOLOGIE DU ROMAN POLICIER	Allen J. Hubin	8-2 TAD 151

Lachman, Marvin, & Otto Penzler, Chris Steinbrunner	ENCYCLOPEDIA OF MYSTERY AND DETECTION	Allen J. Hubin	10-3 TAD 207
laCour, Tage, & Harald Mogensen	THE MURDER BOOK: AN ILLUSTRATED HISTORY	Lianne Carlin	5-2 MR 45
laCour, Tage, & Harald Mogensen	THE MURDER BOOK: AN ILLUSTRATED HISTORY	Marvin Lachman	5-3 TAD 162
Lacy, Ed	THE BEST THAT EVER DID IT	David Rose	4 PE 11
Lacy, Ed	SHAKEDOWN FOR MURDER	Steve Lewis	1A MF 27
Lacy, Ed	ROOM TO SWING	Jon L. Breen	5-2 MR 42
Lafferty, R.A.	SPACE CHANTEY	Hickman & Zachrich	69 PU 34
LaFountaine, George	FLASHPOINT	Stan Burns	2-2 MM 4
Lait, Jack	BAD COMPANY (film)	William K. Everson	8-1 TAD 120
Laker, Rosalind	THE SMUGGLER'S BRIDE	Barbara A. Buhrer	1-11 MM 3
Lakin, Richard W.	THE BODY FELL ON BERLIN	Howard Rapp	10-1 TAD 73
Lamb, Hugh, ed.	THE TASTE OF FEAR	Steve Lewis	2-1 MF 28
Lamb, J.J.	THE CHINESE STRAIGHT	Fred Dueren	10-1 TAD 52
Lamb, J.J.	LOSERS TAKE ALL	Peter Blazer	1-2 M 19
Lamb, J.J.	LOSERS TAKE ALL	Fred Dueren	13-3 TAD 252
Lamb, J.J.	LOSERS TAKE ALL	Andy Jaysnovitch	7 PE 13
Lambert, Gavin	THE DANGEROUS EDGE	James Mark Purcell	9-4 TAD 309
L'Amour, Louis	HANGING WOMAN CREEK	Bill Crider	1-3 PQ 52
L'Amour, Louis	MOJAVE CROSSING	Bill Crider	1-3 PQ 52
Lancaster, Graham	THE NUCLEAR LETTERS	Allen J. Hubin	12-4 TAD 322
Land, Myrick	LAST FLIGHT	Stan Burns	10 MN R4
Landon, Christopher	STONE COLD DEAD IN THE MARKET	Maryell Cleary	3-4 PP 33
Landrum, Larry N., & Pat Browne, Ray B. Browne	DIMENSIONS OF DETECTIVE FICTION	Allen J. Hubin	10-1 TAD 5
Landrum, Larry N., & Pat Browne, Ray B. Browne	DIMENSIONS OF DETECTIVE FICTION	George Kelley	1-4 MF 50
Lang, Brad	CROCKETT ON THE LOOSE	Bill Crider	9-3 TAD 218
Lange, D.	ON THE TRAIL OF THE SIOUX	C.L.Messecar	3-4 BC 373
Lange, D.	THE SILVER ISLAND OF THE CHIPPEWA	C.L.Messecar	3-2 BC 319
Lange, John	SCRATCH ONE	R. Jeff Banks	9 MN R13
Langley, Bob	DEATH STALK	Allen J. Hubin	12-1 TAD 9
Langley, Bob	DEATH STALK	Steve Lewis	3-6 MF 27
Langley, Bob	DEATH STALK	Charles Shibuk	14-2 TAD 183
Langslow, Jane, & Margaret R.Larminie	GORY KNIGHT	Charles Shibuk	7-2 TAD 130
Langton, Jane	DARK NANTUCKET MOON	Mary A. Grochowski	2-4 PP 34
Langton, Jane	DARK NANTUCKET MOON	Allen J. Hubin	8-3 TAD 227
Langton, Jane	THE MEMORIAL HALL MURDER	Jane S. Bakerman	5-2 MF 35
Langton, Jane	THE MEMORIAL HALL MURDER	Allen J. Hubin	11-4 TAD 333
Langton, Jane	THE MEMORIAL HALL MURDER	Steve Lewis	3-1 MF 34
Langton, Jane	THE MEMORIAL HALL MURDER	Jim McCahery	1-4 PP 27
Langton, Jane	THE MEMORIAL HALL MURDER	David McGee	4-1 MF 29
Langton, Jane	THE MINUTEMAN MURDER	Jane S. Bakerman	5-2 MF 36
Langton, Jane	THE MINUTEMAN MURDER	Myrtis Broset	1-2 MF 41
Langton, Jane	THE MINUTEMAN MURDER	Fred Dueren	14-2 TAD 184
Langton, Jane	THE TRANSCENDENTAL MURDER	Marvin Lachman	5-4 MF 19
Lansdale, Joe R.	ACT OF LOVE	Bill Crider	5-3 MF 36
Lansdale, Joe R.	ACT OF LOVE	Robert J. Randisi	4-2 PP 32
Larminie, Margaret R. & Jane Langslow	GORY KNIGHT	Charles Shibuk	7-2 TAD 130
Larmoth, Jeanine	MURDER ON THE MENU	Marvin Lachman	6-2 TAD 107
LaRosa, Linda J., & Barry Tannenbaum	THE RANDOM FACTOR	Allen J. Hubin	12-1 TAD 9
LaRosa, Linda J., & Barry Tannenbaum	THE RANDOM FACTOR	Steve Lewis	3-1 MF 33
LaRose, Linda J., & Barry Tannenbaum	THE RANDOM FACTOR	Ethel Lindsay	3-5 PP 46
Larson, Charles	MATTHEW'S HAND	Allen J. Hubin	8-2 TAD 150

Lathen, Emma	A STITCH IN TIME	R. Jeff Banks	1-6 PP 24
Lathen, Emma	ASHES TO ASHES	Allen J. Hubin	4-3 TAD 179
Lathen, Emma	BY HOOK OR BY CROOK	Douglas M. Armato	9-2 TAD 145
Lathen, Emma	BY HOOK OR BY CROOK	Myrtis Broset	1-6 MF 42
Lathen, Emma	DOUBLE, DOUBLE, OIL AND TROUBLE	Allen J. Hubin	12-1 TAD 9
Lathen, Emma	GOING FOR THE GOLD	Jane S. Bakerman	5-3 MF 34
Lathen, Emma	GOING FOR THE GOLD	Dorothy B. Hughes	3-1 M 36
Lathen, Emma	GOING FOR THE GOLD	Steve Lewis	5-3 MF 32
Lathen, Emma	THE LONGER THE THREAD	Joe R. Christopher	5-3 MR 34
Lathen, Emma	MURDER AGAINST THE GRAIN	Sheila D'Ammassa	3/4 MN 10
Lathen, Emma	MURDER TO GO	Lianne Carlin	3-3 MR 29
Lathen, Emma	MURDER TO GO	Sheila D'Ammassa	5/6 MN 20
Lathen, Emma	MURDER WITHOUT ICING	Joe R. Christopher	5-6 MR 32
Lathen, Emma	PICK UP STICKS	Lianne Carlin	4-2 MR 39
Lathen, Emma	SWEET AND LOW	Robert E. Washer	17 X 60
Lathen, Emma	SWEET AND LOW	Douglas M. Armato	7-4 TAD 292
Latimer, John	BORDER OF DARKNESS	Lianne Carlin	5-6 MR 34
Latimer, Jonathan	THE FIFTH GRAVE	Jim McCahery	4-3 PP 22
Laumer, Keith	DEADFALL	Robert E. Briney	5-5 MF 43
Laumer, Keith	DEADFALL	Robert E. Briney	5-2 MR 38
Laumer, Keith	FAT CHANCE	Myrtis Broset	2-3 MF 55
Laumer, Keith	FAT CHANCE	George Fergus	5/6 MN 18
Laumer, Keith	FAT CHANCE	Joe R. Lansdale	1-5 MF 43
Laumer, Keith	GREYLORN	Hickman & Zachrich	69 PU 34
Laumer, Keith	THE HOUSE IN NOVEMBER	Gary Zachrich	75 PU 25
Laurance, Alice, & Isaac Asimov	WHO DONE IT?	Fred Dueren	13-4 TAD 351
Laurance, Alice, & Isaac Asimov	WHO DONE IT?	F.M.Nevins, Jr.	4-4 MF 48
Lauria, Frank	LADY SATIVA	Fred Dueren	12-3 TAD 287
Lauterbach, Charles	BAKER STREET BALLADS	Stanley A. Carlin	4-4 MR 40
Lauterbach, Charles	MORE BAKER STREET BALLADS	Allen J. Hubin	13-2 TAD 97
LaValley, Albert J.	FOCUS ON HITCHCOCK	F.M.Nevins, Jr.	6-2 TAD 108
Law, Janice	DEATH UNDER PAR	Fred Dueren	5-3 MF 39
Law, Janice	DEATH UNDER PAR	Steve Lewis	5-3 MF 32
Law, Janice	GEMINI TRIP	Steve Lewis	2-1 MF 26
Law, Janice	THE SHADOW OF THE PALMS	Allen J. Hubin	13-4 TAD 296
Law, Janice	UNDER ORION	Janie Filstrup	2-4 PP 36
Lawrence, Hilda	A TIME TO DIE	Lianne Carlin	4-5 MR 37
Lawrence, Hilda	DEATH OF A DOLL	Jay Jeffries	3/4 MN 7
Layman, Richard	THE CELLAR	Fred Dueren	13-3 TAD 252
Layman, Richard	DASHIELL HAMMETT: A DESCRIPTIVE BIBLIOGRAPHY	F.M.Nevins, Jr.	1-2 C 133
Layman, Richard	DASHIELL HAMMETT: A DESCRIPTIVE BIBLIOGRAPHY	F.M.Nevins, Jr.	3-6 MF 49
Layman, Richard	SHADOW MAN: THE LIFE OF DASHIELL HAMMETT	Barzun & Taylor	14-4 TAD 329
Leather, Edwin	THE DUVEEN LETTER	Steve Lewis	4-5 MF 33
Leather, Edwin	THE MOZART SCORE	Ellen Nehr	4-1 MF 34
Leblanc, Maurice	THE EXTRAORDINARY ADVENTURES OF ARSENE LUPIN, GENTLEMAN-BURGLAR	Charles Shibuk	11-1 TAD 97
Leblanc, Maurice	THE MELAMARE MYSTERY	Charles Shibuk	7-3 TAD 208
LeBourdais, Isabel	THE TRIAL OF STEPHEN TRUSCOTT	Barzun & Taylor	10-2 TAD 127
LeCarre, John	THE HONOURABLE SCHOOLBOY	David Paton	3 MT 9
LeCarre, John	THE HONOURABLE SCHOOLBOY	Peter Wolfe	11-2 TAD 123
LeCarre, John	SMILEY'S PEOPLE	Gillian Eaton	1-3 M 19
LeCarre, John	SMILEY'S PEOPLE	Allen J. Hubin	13-2 TAD 96
LeCarre, John	SMILEY'S PEOPLE	Steven Miller	3-3 PP 34
LeCarre, John	TINKER, TAILOR, SOLDIER, SPY (TV)	Donald Carew	2-2 M 47
LeCarre, John	TINKER, TAILOR, SOLDIER, SPY	Allen J. Hubin	8-1 TAD 66
LeCarre, John	TINKER, TAILOR, SOLDIER, SPY	Martin M. Wooster	4-4 PP 27
Lee, Edward	A FISH FOR MURDER	Steve Lewis	1-8 MM 6
Lee, Tanith	DEATH'S MASTER	W.Paul Ganley	5 U 29
Lee, Tanith	NIGHT'S MASTER	W.Paul Ganley	2 FM 18

Lee, Tanith	SABELLA	Fred Dueren	13-4 TAD 361
Lees, Dan	THE RAINBOW CONSPIRACY	Amnon Kabatchnik	5-2 MR 40
Lees, Hannah, & Lawrence Blochman	DEATH IN A DOLL'S HOUSE	Jay Jeffries	8 MN 23
LeFanu, J.S.	UNCLE SILAS: A TALE OF BARTRAM- HAUGH	Donna Balopole	2-1 MF 45
LeFanu, J.S.	UNCLE SILAS (film)	William K. Everson	11-2 TAD 128
LeGuin, Ursula K.	THE LEFT HAND OF DARKNESS	Gary Zachrich	71 PU 23
Lehman, Ernest	NORTH BY NORTHWEST (filmscript)	Lianne Carlin	5-4 MR 36
Lehman, R.C.	THE ADVENTURES OF PICKLOCK HOLES	Allen J. Hubin	8-4 TAD 311
Leiber, Fritz	THE BEST OF FRITZ LEIBER	Ray Ramsay	1 HP 21
Leiber, Fritz	THE BOOK OF FRITZ LEIBER	Ray Ramsay	1 HP 19
Leiber, Fritz	RIME ISLE	Richard H. Fawcett	2-1 AD 5
Leiber, Fritz	SWORDS AND DEVILTRY	Gary Zachrich	75 PU 25
Leiber, Fritz	THE SWORDS OF LANKHMAR	Hickman & Zachrich	69 PU 34
Leiber, Fritz	THE SWORDS OF LANKHMAR	Gary Zachrich	71 PU 21
Lem, Stanislaw	THE CHAIN OF CHANCE	Allen J. Hubin	12-2 TAD 113
Lem, Stanislaw	THE CHAIN OF CHANCE	Steve Lewis	3-5 MF 35
Lem, Stanislaw	THE CHAIN OF CHANCE	James Mark Purcell	13-2 TAD 145
Lem, Stanislaw	THE INVESTIGATION	James Mark Purcell	9-1 TAD 65
Lemarchand, Elizabeth	THE AFFACOMBE AFFAIR	Veronica M.Kennedy	4-1 TAD 49
Lemarchand, Elizabeth	ALIBI FOR A CORPSE	Veronica M.Kennedy	8-2 TAD 146
Lemarchand, Elizabeth	DEATH OF AN OLD GIRL	Veronica M.Kennedy	4-1 TAD 49
Lemarchand, Elizabeth	STEP IN THE DARK	Steve Lewis	2-1 MF 23
Lemarchand, Elizabeth	SUDDENLY WHILE GARDENING	Steve Lewis	3-6 MF 27
Lemarchand, Elizabeth	SUDDENLY WHILE GARDENING	Paul McCarthy	3-4 MF 48
Lenning, Arthur	THE COUNT	Amnon Kabatchnik	9-3 TAD 219
Leonard, Charles	THE SECRET OF THE SPA	Barzun & Taylor	14-2 TAD 142
Leonard, Elmore	CITY PRIMEVAL: HIGH NOON IN DETROIT	Gary Warren Niebuhr	4-1 PP 15
Leonard, Elmore	FIFTY-TWO PICKUP	Fred Dueren	9-1 TAD 50
Leonard, Elmore	THE HUNTED	Myrtis Broset	2-1 MF 35
Leonard, Elmore	THE SWITCH	Steve Lewis	3-3 MF 35
Leonard, Elmore	UNKNOWN MAN NO.89	Peter Wolfe	11-1 TAD 25
Leonard, Frank	BOX 100	Allen J. Hubin	6-1 TAD 44
Leroux, Gaston	THE MYSTERY OF THE YELLOW ROOM	M.S.Cappadonna	10-4 TAD 312
Leroux, Gaston	THE MYSTERY OF THE YELLOW ROOM	Charles Shibuk	11-1 TAD 97
Leroux, Gaston	THE PHANTOM OF THE OPERA (film)	Charles Shibuk	3-1 TAD 27
Lessa, William A.	DRAKE'S ISLAND OF THIEVES: ETHNOLOGICAL SLEUTHING	Douglas G. Greene	3-5 PP 43
Levack, Daniel J.H., & Tim Underwood	FANTASMS: A JACK VANCE BIBLIOGRAPHY	Charlotte Laughlin	1-4 PQ 52
Levin, Ira	A KISS BEFORE DYING	Allan Kleinberg	9 MN R15
Levin, Ira	THE BOYS FROM BRAZIL	Robert Blaskey	9-4 TAD 309
Levin, Ira	DEATHTRAP (stage)	Jim Huang	6 CL 1
Levin, Ira	DEATHTRAP (stage)	Allen J. Hubin	13-1 TAD 29
Levin, Ira	DEATHTRAP (stage)	Jackie Meyerson	1-2 PP 19
Levine, Larry	SNOWBIRD	Fred Dueren	11-2 TAD 192
Levine, Sidney, & Robin Moore	THE BIG PADDLE	Bill Crider	3-6 PP 28
Lewin, Michael Z.	ASK THE RIGHT QUESTION	Charles Shibuk	12-3 TAD 255
Lewin, Michael Z.	THE ENEMIES WITHIN	Allen J. Hubin	8-1 TAD 66
Lewin, Michael Z.	MISSING WOMAN	Steve Lewis	5-6 MF 39
Lewin, Michael Z.	NIGHT COVER	Steve Lewis	4-4 MF 39
Lewin, Michael Z.	OUTSIDE IN	Allen J. Hubin	14-1 TAD 18
Lewin, Michael Z.	OUTSIDE IN	Steve Lewis	4-5 MF 33
Lewin, Michael Z.	THE SILENT SALESMAN	Allen J. Hubin	11-3 TAD 232
Lewin, Michael Z.	THE WAY WE DIE NOW	Amnon Kabatchnik	6-1 MR 42
Lewin, Michael Z.	THE WAY WE DIE NOW	Steve Lewis	3-2 MF 37
Lewin, Michael Z.	THE WAY WE DIE NOW	Charles Shibuk	12-4 TAD 369
Lewin, Nicholas, & Cedric E.Clute,Jr.	SLEIGHT OF CRIME: FIFTEEN CLASSIC TALES OF MURDER, MAYHEM AND MAGIC	Robert E. Briney	11-1 TAD 26
Lewis, Andy & Dave	KLUTE (film)	Richard S. Lochte	5-1 TAD 41

Lewis, Arthur H.	CHILDREN'S PARTY	Lianne Carlin	5-5 MR 35
Lewis, Arthur H.	COPPER BEECHES	Stanley A. Carlin	5-1 MR 39
Lewis, Arthur H.	COPPER BEECHES	Robert W. Hahn	5-1 TAD 40
Lewis, Elliott	THE DIRTY LINEN	Bill Crider	3-5 PP 42
Lewis, Elliott	TWO HEADS ARE BETTER	Morgan Harrison	1-3 M 16
Lewis, Leonard, & Paul Bonner	AGAIN - JACK THE RIPPER (TV)	Veronica M.Kennedy	7-1 TAD 58
Lewis, Richard S.	APPOINTMENT ON THE MOON	Gary Zachrich	74 PU 22
Lewis, Roy Harley	A CRACKING OF SPINES	R.L.Wenstrup	4-5 MF 38
Lewis, Roy	A WOLF BY THE EAR	Amnon Kabatchnik	5-6 MR 32
Lewis, Roy	NOTHING BUT FOXES	Steve Lewis	3-5 MF 38
Lewis, Ted	GET CARTER	Fred Blosser	5-1 TAD 38
Lewis, Ted	JACK CARTER AND THE LAW	Allen J. Hubin	9-1 TAD 73
Lewis, Wyndham, & Charles Bennett	THE MAN WHO KNEW TOO MUCH	William K. Everson	5-4 TAD 225
Leyford, Henry	MURDER MOON	Hal Brodsky	9-4 TAD 313
Liddy, G.Gordon	OUT OF CONTROL	Theodore Dukeshire	3-6 MF 44
Liebman, Dr.Arthur	MS. MYSTERIES	Pearl G. Aldrich	10-1 TAD 62
Liebman, Dr.Arthur	QUICKIE THRILLERS: 25 MINI-MYSTERIES	Stan Burns	8 MN 12
Lieberman, Herbert	THE CLIMATE OF HELL	Allen J. Hubin	12-1 TAD 9
Lieberman, Herbert	CRAWLSPACE	Stanley A. Carlin	5-4 MR 32
Lifson, David S.	HEADLESS VICTORY	Steve Lewis	3-3 MF 38
Lindsay, Cynthia	DEAR BORIS	Amnon Kabatchnik	9-3 TAD 219
Lindsay, John V.	THE EDGE	Amnon Kabatchnik	10-2 TAD 116
Lindsey, Robert	THE FALCON AND THE SNOWMAN	Charles Jardinier	2-2 M 58
Linington, Elizabeth	NO EVIL ANGEL	Mary Jean DeMarr	3-2 MF 44
Linington, Elizabeth	PERCHANCE OF DEATH	Jane M. Filstrup	11-3 TAD 245
Linington, Elizabeth	POLICEMAN'S LOT	Len Moffatt	2-4 MR 15
Linzee, David	DEATH IN CONNECTICUT	Steve Lewis	1-5 MF 33
Linzee, David	DISCRETION	Allen J. Hubin	12-1 TAD 9
Linzee, David	DISCRETION	F.M.Nevins, Jr.	3-3 MF 47
Lippincott, David	THE VOICE OF ARMAGEDDON	Robert Blaskey	10-1 TAD 60
Littell, Robert	THE AMATEUR	Allen J. Hubin	14-4 TAD 300
Littell, Robert	THE DEFECTION OF A.J.LEWINTER	Allen J. Hubin	6-3 TAD 192
Litzinger, Boyd	WATCH IT, DR. ADRIAN	Allen J. Hubin	11-3 TAD 230
Liven, Larry	A GIFT FROM EARTH	Gary Zachrich	70 PU 26
Lloyd, John, & Elwyn Jones	THE RIPPER FILE	Jon L. Lellenberg	9-3 TAD 222
Lockridge, Frances & Richard	DEATH ON THE AISLE	Steve Lewis	8 MN 24
Lockridge, Richard	DEAD RUN	Barbara A. Buhrer	11 MN R4
Lockridge, Richard	DEAD RUN	Steve Lewis	1-1 MF 28
Lockridge, Richard	DEAD RUN	Guy M. Townsend	1A MF 36
Lockridge, Richard	DEATH IN A SUNNY PLACE	Amnon Kabatchnik	5-3 MR 37
Lockridge, Richard	INSPECTOR'S HOLIDAY	Iwan Hedman	4-4 MR 34
Lockridge, Richard	THE OLD DIE YOUNG	Fred Dueren	5-3 MF 39
Lockridge, Richard	THE OLD DIE YOUNG	Steve Lewis	5-1 MF 25
Lockridge, Richard	OR WAS HE PUSHED?	Allen J. Hubin	8-4 TAD 308
Lofts, Norah	HAUNTINGS: IS ANYBODY THERE?	Fred Dueren	11-2 TAD 192
Lofts, W.O.G., & Derek J. Adley	THE SAINT AND LESLIE CHARTERIS	J. Randolph Cox	5-3 MR 34
Lofts, W.O.G., & Derek J. Adley	THE SAINT AND LESLIE CHARTERIS	Marvin Lachman	6-1 TAD 41
Logue, John	FOLLOW THE LEADER	M.S.Cappadonna	12-4 TAD 371
Logue, John	FOLLOW THE LEADER	Richard Moskowitz	15 CL 5
Long, Patrick	EAGLE SIX	Fred Dueren	10-4 TAD 341
Lorac, E.C.R.	DISHONOUR AMONG THIEVES	Maryell Cleary	4-5/6 PP 71
Lorac, E.C.R.	FELL MURDER	Maryell Cleary	4-5/6 PP 70
Lorac, E.C.R.	FIRE IN THE THATCH	Maryell Cleary	4-5/6 PP 70
Lorac, E.C.R.	PLACE FOR A POISONER	Howard Rapp	5-3 MF 37
Lorac, E.C.R.	THE THEFT OF THE IRON DOGS	Maryell Cleary	4-5/6 PP 70
Loraine, Philip	PHOTOGRAPHS HAVE BEEN SENT TO YOUR WIFE	Stanley A. Carlin	4-5 MR 36
Lord, Glenn	THE LAST CELT	Tevis Clyde Smith	1-1 PQ 33

Lore, Phillips	THE LOOKING GLASS MURDERS	Steve Lewis	4-5 MF 29
Lore, Phillips	WHO KILLED THE PIE MAN?	Stan Burns	10 MN R3
Lorin, Will	CRY RAPE	Richard Moskowitz	12 LR 20
Lortz, Richard	CHILDREN OF THE NIGHT	Veronica M.Kennedy	8-3 TAD 225
Lotz, Wolfgang	A HANDBOOK FOR SPIES	Sam Yamato	1-3 M 20
Lovecraft, H.P.	SUPERNATURAL HORROR IN LITERATURE	Allen J. Hubin	7-1 TAD 63
Lovell, Marc	A PRESENCE IN THE HOUSE	Lianne Carlin	5-4 MR 30
Lovell, Marc	ENQUIRY INTO THE EXISTENCE OF VAMPIRES	Veronica M.Kennedy	8-4 TAD 301
Lovesey, Peter	A CASE OF SPIRITS	Frank Eck	9 MN R6
Lovesey, Peter	A CASE OF SPIRITS	Charles Shibuk	9-2 TAD 146
Lovesey, Peter	A CASE OF SPIRITS	Guy M. Townsend	1-6 MF 48
Lovesey, Peter	ABRACADAVER	Charles Shibuk	6-1 TAD 41
Lovesey, Peter	ABRACADAVER	Guy M. Townsend	1-11 MM 5
Lovesey, Peter	THE DETECTIVE WORE SILK DRAWERS	Jon L. Breen	5-2 MR 39
Lovesey, Peter	THE DETECTIVE WORE SILK DRAWERS	Charles Shibuk	5-1 TAD 38
Lovesey, Peter	THE DETECTIVE WORE SILK DRAWERS	Charles Shibuk	14-1 TAD 80
Lovesey, Peter	INVITATION TO A DYNAMITE PARTY	Charles Shibuk	14-4 TAD 377
Lovesey, Peter	MAD HATTER'S HOLIDAY	Charles Shibuk	7-2 TAD 139
Lovesey, Peter	MAD HATTER'S HOLIDAY	Charles Shibuk	14-3 TAD 267
Lovesey, Peter	SWING, SWING TOGETHER	Steve Lewis	1-1 MF 27
Lovesey, Peter	SWING, SWING TOGETHER	Charles Shibuk	9-4 TAD 302
Lovesey, Peter	SWING, SWING TOGETHER	Charles Shibuk	12-1 TAD 30
Lovesey, Peter	THE TICK OF DEATH	Charles Shibuk	8-2 TAD 143
Lovesey, Peter	THE TICK OF DEATH	Charles Shibuk	9-4 TAD 281
Lovesey, Peter	WAXWORK	Allen J. Hubin	11-4 TAD 332
Lovesey, Peter	WAXWORK	Steve Lewis	2-6 MF 32
Lovesey, Peter	WAXWORK	Charles Shibuk	13-3 TAD 250
Lovesey, Peter	WOBBLE TO DEATH	Charles Shibuk	4-1 TAD 48
Lovesey, Peter	WOBBLE TO DEATH	Charles Shibuk	13-4 TAD 364
Low, Ivy	HIS MASTER'S VOICE	Robert C.S.Adey	5-3 MF 40
Ludlum, Robert	THE GEMINI CONTENDERS	Stephen Mertz	3-1 MF 42
Ludlum, Robert	THE HOLCROFT COVENANT	Allen J. Hubin	11-4 TAD 332
Ludlum, Robert	THE MATARESE CIRCLE	Allen J. Hubin	12-3 TAD 206
Ludlum, Robert	THE MATARESE CIRCLE	Donald G. Smoke	1-1 M 20
Ludlum, Robert	THE MATLOCK PAPER	Steve Lewis	5A MY 2
Ludlum, Robert	THE SCARLATTI INHERITANCE	J. Randolph Cox	5-2 TAD 101
Luhrs, Victor	THE LONGBOW MURDER	Charles Shibuk	10-4 TAD 315
Lupoff, Richard A.	THE OVA HAMLET PAPERS	Michael L. Cook	4 U 20
Lustbader, Eric Van	THE NINJA	Charles Barone	3-5 PP 42
Lustgarten, Edgar	ONE MORE UNFORTUNATE	Gary Warren Niebuhr	4-2 PP 25
Lutz, John	BONEGRINDER	Allen J. Hubin	11-1 TAD 18
Lutz, John	BONEGRINDER	Steve Lewis	2-4 MF 36
Lutz, John	BONEGRINDER	Charles Shibuk	14-1 TAD 80
Lutz, John	BUYER BEWARE	Steve Lewis	1-4 MF 37
Lutz, John	BUYER BEWARE	F.M.Nevins, Jr.	1-3 MF 43
Lutz, John	JERICHO MAN	Joyce L. Dewes	2-2 M 58
Lutz, John	JERICHO MAN	F.M.Nevins, Jr.	4-5 MF 37
Lutz, John	LAZARUS MAN	Mary A. Grochowski	2-4 PP 37
Lutz, John	LAZARUS MAN	F.M.Nevins, Jr.	3-5 MF 44
Lutz, John	LAZARUS MAN	Charles Shibuk	14-2 TAD 183
Lutz, John	THE SHADOW MAN	F.M.Nevins, Jr.	5-5 MF 29
Lyall, Gavin	JUDAS COUNTRY	Allen J. Hubin	8-4 TAD 310
Lyall, Gavin	JUDAS COUNTRY	Denis Quane	5/6 MN 19
Lyall, Gavin	THE SECRET SERVANT	Gary Happenstand	2-2 C 158
Lynch, Frances	TWICE TEN THOUSAND MILES	Barbara A. Buhrer	10 MN R13
Lynch, Marilyn	THE WRITERS	Jose Mendez	2-2 M 58
Lynde, Francis	SCIENTIFIC SPRAGUE	Charles Shibuk	7-3 TAD 209
Lyon, Augusta Wallace	MURDER AT PROSPECT KENTUCKY	Allen J. Hubin	11-3 TAD 230
Lyons, Arthur	ALL GOD'S CHILDREN	Stan Burns	1-5 MM 9
Lyons, Arthur	ALL GOD'S CHILDREN	Charles Shibuk	9-4 TAD 281
Lyons, Arthur	CASTLES BURNING	Paul Bishop	2-1 M 26
Lyons, Arthur	CASTLES BURNING	Steve Lewis	5-1 MF 27
Lyons, Arthur	THE DEAD ARE DISCREET	Steve Lewis	1A MF 29

Lyons, Arthur	HARD TRADE	Steve Lewis	5-4 MF 24
Lyons, Arthur	THE KILLING FLOOR	Allen J. Hubin	10-2 TAD 112
Lyons, Nan & Ivan	SOMEONE IS KILLING THE GREAT CHEFS OF EUROPE	Jim Huang	8 CL 10
Maartens, Maarten	THE BLACK BOX	Allen J. Hubin	4-4 TAD 243
Maas, Peter	MADE IN AMERICA	Steven Miller	2-6 PP 36
Maas, Peter	MADE IN AMERICA	Gary Warren Niebuhr	3-2 PP 23
MacAlister, Ian	VALLEU OF THE ASSASSINS	Fred Dueren	9-3 TAD 212
MacApp, C.C.	WORLDS OF THE WALL	Gary Zachrich	73 PU 33
Macardle, Dorothy	THE UNINVITED	Jim McCahery	1-4 PP 23
MacBeth, George	THE SAMURAI	Bill Crider	2-4 PP 34
MacDonald, John D.	THE BRASS CUPCAKE	Marvin Lachman	14 JD 15
MacDonald, John D.	CONDOMINIUM	Charles Shibuk	12-1 TAD 30
MacDonald, John D.	DARKER THAN AMBER	Robert E. Briney	4-1 MR 36
MacDonald, John D.	DARKER THAN AMBER (film)	Dave Stewart	14 JD 11
MacDonald, John D.	DEAD LOW TIDE	Steve Lewis	1-3 MF 40
MacDonald, John D.	DEAD LOW TIDE	Steven Miller	4-1 PP 32
MacDonald, John D.	THE DREADFUL LEMON SKY	Stan Burns	9 MN R14
MacDonald, John D.	THE DREADFUL LEMON SKY	Peter Wolfe	8-3 TAD 222
MacDonald, John D.	THE EMPTY COPPER SEA	Ed Hirshberg	23 JD 10
MacDonald, John D.	THE EMPTY COPPER SEA	Jim Huang	12 CL 6
MacDonald, John D.	THE EMPTY COPPER SEA	Allen J. Hubin	12-1 TAD 10
MacDonald, John D.	THE EMPTY COPPER SEA	Steve Lewis	3-6 MF 38
MacDonald, John D.	THE EMPTY COPPER SEA	Charles Shibuk	12-3 TAD 255
MacDonald, John D.	THE EMPTY COPPER SEA	Charles Willeford	23 JD 7
MacDonald, John D.	FREE FALL IN CRIMSON	Phil Davis	28 JD 17
MacDonald, John D.	FREE FALL IN CRIMSON	Ed Hirshberg	28 JD 18
MacDonald, John D.	FREE FALL IN CRIMSON	F.M.Nevins, Jr.	28 JD 16
MacDonald, John D.	FREE FALL IN CRIMSON	Steve Lewis	5-4 MF 23
MacDonald, John D.	FREE FALL IN CRIMSON	F.M.Nevins, Jr.	5-4 MF 31
MacDonald, John D.	THE GIRL IN THE PLAIN BROWN WRAPPER	Dave Locke	12 JD 9
MacDonald, John D.	THE GIRL IN THE PLAIN BROWN WRAPPER	Robert E. Washer	1-3 QC 22
MacDonald, John D.	THE GIRL, THE GOLD WATCH, AND EVERYTHING	Martin M. Wooster	4-2 PP 27
MacDonald, John D.	THE GREEN RIPPER	Edgar Hirshberg	25 JD 12
MacDonald, John D.	THE GREEN RIPPER	Jim Huang	15 CL 8
MacDonald, John D.	THE GREEN RIPPER	Charles Willeford	25 JD 10
MacDonald, John D.	THE GREEN RIPPER	Peter Wolfe	13-1 TAD 63
MacDonald, John D.	THE HOUSE GUESTS	Ed Cox	6 JD 1
MacDonald, John D.	THE HOUSE GUESTS	Gail Van Achtoven	16 JD 13
MacDonald, John D.	THE LONG LAVENDER LOOK	Robert E. Briney	5-3 MR 36
MacDonald, John D.	NIGHTMARE IN PINK	Jeff Meyerson	1-3 MF 48
MacDonald, John D.	NIGHTMARE IN PINK	Len & June Moffatt	24 JD 27
MacDonald, John D.	ONE FEARFUL YELLOW EYE	Amnon Kabatchnik	2-4 MF 47
MacDonald, John D.	OTHER TIMES, OTHER WORLDS	Len & June Moffatt	24 JD 28
MacDonald, John D.	THE SCARLET RUSE	G.A.Finch	7-3 TAD 218
MacDonald, John D.	THE TRAP OF SOLID GOLD (TV)	Larry Tauber	7 JD 16
MacDonald, Philip	DEATH AND CHICANERY	Theodore Dukeshire	3-4 MF 50
MacDonald, Philip	MURDER GONE MAD	Lianne Carlin	4-2 MR 41
MacDonald, Philip	MYSTERY AT FRIAR'S PARDON	Angelo Panagos	12-1 TAD 80
MacDonald, Philip	THE RASP	M.S.Cappadonna	13-3 TAD 247
MacDonald, Philip	THE RASP	Charles Shibuk	13-3 TAD 250
MacDonald, Philip	THE WHITE CROW	Maryell Cleary	3-3 PP 27
MacDonald, Philip, & A.Boyd Correll	THE DARK WHEEL	Charles Shibuk	12-2 TAD 189
Macdonald, Ross	THE BLUE HAMMER	Amnon Kabatchnik	1-2 MF 38
Macdonald, Ross	THE BLUE HAMMER	Charles Shibuk	10-4 TAD 361
Macdonald, Ross	THE BLUE HAMMER	Guy M. Townsend	10 MN R9
Macdonald, Ross	THE BLUE HAMMER	Peter Wolfe	9-4 TAD 300
Macdonald, Ross	THE DROWNING POOL	Amnon Kabatchnik	4-3 MR 37
Macdonald, Ross	THE GOODBYE LOOK	Charles Shibuk	2-4 TAD 274
Macdonald, Ross	THE GOODBYE LOOK	Robert E. Washer	1-4 QC 20

Macdonald, Ross	LEW ARCHER, PRIVATE INVESTIGATOR	Amnon Kabatchnik	2-4 MF 47
Macdonald, Ross	LEW ARCHER, PRIVATE INVESTIGATOR	Frank Occhiogrosso	11-4 TAD 404
Macdonald, Ross	THE NAME IS ARCHER	Douglas G. Greene	12-3 TAD 233
Macdonald, Ross	SLEEPING BEAUTY	Allen J. Hubin	6-3 TAD 191
Macdonald, Ross	THE UNDERGROUND MAN	Don Miller	1-8 MM 6
Macdonald, Ross	THE UNDERGROUND MAN	James Sandoe	13-4 TAD 292
MacDonell, Herbert L.	FLIGHT CHARACTERISTICS AND STAIN PATTERNS OF HUMAN BLOOD	Tom Balow	6-1 TAD 43
MacDougall, James K.	DEATH AND THE MAIDEN	Mary A. Grochowski	2-3 PP 34
MacDougall, James K.	DEATH AND THE MAIDEN	Allen J. Hubin	12-1 TAD 10
MacDougall, James K.	THE WEASEL HUNT	Mary A. Grochowski	1-1 PP 24
MacDougall, James K.	THE WEASEL HUNT	Allen J. Hubin	11-1 TAD 19
MacInnes, Helen	AGENT IN PLACE	Amnon Kabatchnik	9-4 TAD 306
MacInnes, Helen	PRELUDE TO TERROR	Allen J. Hubin	11-4 TAD 331
Mack, Carol K., & David Ehrenfeld	THE CHAMELEON VARIANT	Allen J. Hubin	14-3 TAD 218
Mackay, Amanda	DEATH IS ACADEMIC	Allen J. Hubin	10-2 TAD 113
Mackay, Amanda	DEATH ON THE ENO	Kathi Maio	4-5/6 PP 81
MacKenzie, Donald	DEATH IS A FRIEND	Steve Lewis	1-5 MF 34
MacKenzie, Donald	NIGHT BOAT FROM PUERTO VEDRA	Robert E. Briney	3-4 MR 9
MacKenzie, Donald	RAVEN AFTER DARK	Fred Dueren	13-1 TAD 61
MacKenzie, Donald	RAVEN AND THE KAMIKAZE	Steve Lewis	2-4 MF 36
MacKenzie, Donald	RAVEN AND THE PAPERHANGERS	Fred Dueren	3-5 PP 41
MacKenzie, Donald	RAVEN AND THE PAPERHANGERS	Morgan Harrison	2-2 M 57
MacKenzie, Donald	RAVEN AND THE PAPERHANGERS	Allen J. Hubin	14-2 TAD 128
MacKenzie, Donald	THE SPREEWALD COLLECTION	Allen J. Hubin	8-3 TAD 225
MacKinnon, Allan	DANGER BY MY SIDE	Theodore Dukeshire	3-4 MF 49
MacKinnon, Allan	HOUSE OF DARKNESS	Charles Shibuk	8-3 TAD 221
MacKinnon, Allan	NINE DAYS' WONDER	Charles Shibuk	8-4 TAD 296
Mackintosh, May	HIGHLAND FLING	Barbara A. Buhrer	10 MN R1
Maclean, A.D., ed.	WINTER'S TALES 26	Paul Harwitz	3-2 M 40
MacLean, Alistair	ATHABASCA	Bill Crider	4-5 MF 40
MacLean, Alistair	BEAR ISLAND	Lianne Carlin	5-2 MR 41
MacLean, Alistair	CARAVAN TO VACCARES	Don Cole	3-4 MR 31
MacLeish, Roderick	THE MAN WHO WASN'T THERE	Allen J. Hubin	9-4 TAD 310
MacLeod, Charlotte	THE FAMILY VAULT	Charles Shibuk	13-3 TAD 250
MacLeod, Charlotte	THE LUCK RUNS OUT	Jane S. Bakerman	4-2 MF 49
MacLeod, Charlotte	THE LUCK RUNS OUT	Robert E. Briney	5-5 MF 37
MacLeod, Charlotte	THE LUCK RUNS OUT	Mary A. Grochowski	3-3 PP 34
MacLeod, Charlotte	THE LUCK RUNS OUT	Ellen Nehr	4-1 MF 34
MacLeod, Charlotte	THE PALACE GUARD	Steve Lewis	5-5 MF 26
MacLeod, Charlotte	REST YOU MERRY	Robert C.S.Adey	4-5/6 PP 77
MacLeod, Charlotte	REST YOU MERRY	Jane S. Bakerman	4-2 MF 48
MacLeod, Charlotte	REST YOU MERRY	Maryell Cleary	4-5/6 PP 77
MacLeod, Charlotte	REST YOU MERRY	Allen J. Hubin	12-1 TAD 10
MacLeod, Charlotte	REST YOU MERRY	Steve Lewis	3-5 MF 36
MacLeod, Charlotte	REST YOU MERRY	Charles Shibuk	13-2 TAD 135
MacLeod, Charlotte	THE WITHDRAWING ROOM	Jane S. Bakerman	4-6 MF 39
MacLeod, Charlotte	THE WITHDRAWING ROOM	Elizabeth Wentworth	2-2 M 56
MacLevy, James	THE CASEBOOK OF A VICTORIAN DETECTIVE	E.F.Bleiler	9-1 TAD 64
MacMahon, Thomas P.	THE HUBSCHMANN EFFECT	Allen J. Hubin	6-3 TAD 191
MacShane, Frank	THE LIFE OF RAYMOND CHANDLER	Barzun & Taylor	9-4 TAD 271
MacShane, Frank	THE LIFE OF RAYMOND CHANDLER	Mary A. Grochowski	1-3 PP 27
MacShane, Frank	THE LIFE OF RAYMOND CHANDLER	Jon L. Lellenberg	9-4 TAD 302
MacShane, Frank	THE LIFE OF RAYMOND CHANDLER	Charles Shibuk	11-3 TAD 298
MacShane, Frank, ed.	SELECTED LETTERS: RAYMOND CHANDLER	Barzun & Taylor	14-3 TAD 228
Madden, David	BROTHERS IN CONFIDENCE	Bill Crider	1-2 PQ 54
Maddock, Larry	THE TIME TRAP GAMBIT	Gary Zachrich	74 PU 24
Madsen, David	BLACK PLUME	Allen J. Hubin	14-3 TAD 218
Maeder, Thomas	THE UNSPEAKABLE CRIMES OF DR. PETIOT	George Kelley	3-4 PP 34
Magnuson, James	THE RUNDOWN	Robert J. Randisi	12-3 TAD 272
Maguire, Michael	SCRATCHPROOF	Allen J. Hubin	11-1 TAD 20

Maguire, Michael	SCRATCHPROOF	Steve Lewis	1-6 MF 38
Mainwaring, Marion	MURDER IN PASTICHE	Maryell Cleary	3-1 PP 33
Makins, Clifford, & Ted Dexter	TESTKILL	Jon L. Breen	12-1 TAD 77
Malcolm-Smith, George	THE TROUBLE WITH FIDELITY	Arthur C. Scott	1-5 MM 10
Maling, Arthur	BENT MAN	Stan Burns	8 MN 12
Maling, Arthur	BENT MAN	Allen J. Hubin	9-1 TAD 74
Maling, Arthur	DECOY	Steven Miller	3-6 PP 27
Maling, Arthur	DINGDONG	Allen J. Hubin	7-4 TAD 296
Maling, Arthur	GO-BETWEEN	Amnon Kabatchnik	4-2 MR 35
Maling, Arthur	THE KOBERG LINK	Allen J. Hubin	13-1 TAD 29
Maling, Arthur	LUCKY DEVIL	Allen J. Hubin	11-4 TAD 331
Maling, Arthur	THE RHEINGOLD ROUTE	Myrtis Broset	3-5 MF 42
Maling, Arthur	THE RHEINGOLD ROUTE	Allen J. Hubin	12-3 TAD 206
Maling, Arthur	RIPOFF	Stan Burns	1-11 MM 4
Maling, Arthur	SCHROEDER'S GAME	Allen J. Hubin	10-4 TAD 307
Maling, Arthur	SCHROEDER'S GAME	Steve Lewis	1-5 MF 29
Maling, Arthur	THUNDER BAY	Allen J. Hubin	14-4 TAD 300
Maling, Arthur, ed.	WHEN LAST SEEN	Robert C.S.Adey	4-4 PP 28
Maling, Arthur, ed.	WHEN LAST SEEN	Amnon Kabatchnik	8 CL 8
Maling, Arthur, ed.	WHEN LAST SEEN	Steve Lewis	2-2 MF 33
Mallet, Jacqueline	THEY CAN'T HANG ME!	James Sandoe	14-2 TAD 189
Mallett, Richard	WATSON'S REVENGE	Allen J. Hubin	7-3 TAD 221
Maltin, Leonard, ed.	TV MOVIES	F.M.Nevins, Jr.	3-4 MR 21
Malzberg, Barry, & Bill Pronzini	ACTS OF MERCY	Mary A. Grochowski	1-2 PP 24
Malzberg, Barry, & Bill Pronzini	ACTS OF MERCY	Allen J. Hubin	11-2 TAD 116
Malzberg, Barry, & Bill Pronzini	ACTS OF MERCY	Amnon Kabatchnik	11 CL 9
Malzberg, Barry, & Bill Pronzini	ACTS OF MERCY	F.M.Nevins, Jr.	2-5 MF 37
Malzberg, Barry, & Bill Pronzini	NIGHT SCREAMS	Mary A. Grochowski	2-6 PP 36
Malzberg, Barry, & Bill Pronzini	NIGHT SCREAMS	Allen J. Hubin	13-1 TAD 29
Malzberg, Barry, & Bill Pronzini	NIGHT SCREAMS	Charles Shibuk	14-3 TAD 267
Malzberg, Barry, & Bill Pronzini	THE RUNNING OF BEASTS	Myrtis Broset	2-3 MM 3
Malzberg, Barry, & Bill Pronzini	THE RUNNING OF BEASTS	Barbara A. Buhrer	10 MN R1
Malzberg, Barry, & Bill Pronzini	THE RUNNING OF BEASTS	Allen J. Hubin	9-3 TAD 223
Malzberg, Barry, & Bill Pronzini	THE RUNNING OF BEASTS	George Kelley	1-2 MF 37
Malzberg, Barry, & Bill Pronzini	THE RUNNING OF BEASTS	F.M.Nevins, Jr.	1-1 MF 17
Malzberg, Barry, & Bill Pronzini	THE RUNNING OF BEASTS	Charles Shibuk	10-3 TAD 239
Mann, Jack	GEES' FIRST CASE	Charles Shibuk	8-4 TAD 299
Mann, Jack	GREY SHAPES	Lianne Carlin	5-1 MR 36
Mann, Jack	GREY SHAPES	Amnon Kabatchnik	8-4 TAD 296
Mann, Jack	NIGHTMARE FARM	Allen J. Hubin	9-3 TAD 224
Mann, Jessica	CAPTIVE AUDIENCE	Jon L. Breen	3-5 PP 39
Mann, Jessica	THE ONLY SECURITY	Jon L. Breen	3-5 PP 39
Mann, Patrick	STEAL BIG	Paul Harwitz	3-1 M 38
Mann, Patrick	STEAL BIG	Allen J. Hubin	14-4 TAD 300
Manners, Alexandra	THE SINGING SWANS	Barbara A. Buhrer	2-1 MM 3
Manning, Bruce, & Gwen Bristow	THE GUTENBERG MURDERS	Jim McCahery	2-6 PP 31
Manning, Bruce, & Gwen Bristow	THE INVISIBLE HOST	Barzun & Taylor	9-2 TAD 93
Manning, Bruce, & Gwen Bristow	THE INVISIBLE HOST	Jim McCahery	2-6 PP 31

Manning, Bruce, &			
Gwen Bristow	THE NINTH QUEST	R.L.Wenstrup	4-1 PP 29
Mannix, Daniel P.	THE SECRET OF THE ELMS	Barbara A. Buhrer	11 MN R13
Mantell, Laurie	A MURDER OR THREE	Allen J. Hubin	14-4 TAD 300
Mantell, Laurie	MURDER IN FANCY DRESS	Kathi Maio	4-5/6 PP 80
Mara, Bernard	THIS GUN FOR GLORIA	Steve Lewis	1A MF 23
Marble, M.S.	DIE BY NIGHT	R. Jeff Banks	5 PE 16
Marcott, James	HARD TO KILL	Steve Lewis	1A MF 26
Marcus, Steven, ed.	THE CONTINENTAL OP (Hammett)	Allen J. Hubin	8-1 TAD 67
Margolin, Phillip M.	THE LAST INNOCENT MAN	Gary Warren Niebuhr	4-5/6 PP 64
Markham, Robert	COLONEL SUN	Len & June Moffatt	10 JD 21
Markham, Virgil	THE DEAD ARE PROWLING	Charles Shibuk	12-1 TAD 78
Markham, Virgil	THE DEADLY JEST	Charles Shibuk	13-1 TAD 79
Markham, Virgil	DEATH IN THE DUSK	Jay Jeffries	1 MN 7
Markham, Virgil	THE DEVIL DRIVES	Charles Shibuk	11-3 TAD 252
Markham, Virgil	INSPECTOR RUSBY'S FINALE	Angelo Panagos	13-3 TAD 270
Marks, Alan	THE ANTENNA SYNDROME	R. Jeff Banks	2-5 PP 13
Marks, Alan	THE ANTENNA SYNDROME	Joe R. Lansdale	7 PE 12
Markstein, George	TRAITOR	Paul Harwitz	3-2 M 40
Marlowe, Dan J.	FLASHPOINT	Don Cole	4-3 MR 36
Marlowe, Edwina	DANGER AT DAHLKARI	Barbara A. Buhrer	10 MN R2
Marlowe, Stephen	THE CAWTHORNE JOURNALS	Allen J. Hubin	8-3 TAD 228
Marlowe, Stephen	THE VALKYRIE ENCOUNTER	Allen J. Hubin	11-3 TAD 231
Marlowe, Stephen, &			
Richard S. Prather	DOUBLE IN TROUBLE	Jeff Meyerson	1 PE 12
Marr, John S., &			
Gwyneth Cravens	THE BLACK DEATH	Patricia M. Koch	3-5 PP 37
Marric, J.J.	GIDEON'S DRIVE	Amnon Kabatchnik	10-2 TAD 116
Marric, J.J.	GIDEON'S DRIVE	Steve Lewis	2-1 MF 28
Marric, J.J.	GIDEON'S FOG	Allen J. Hubin	8-2 TAD 149
Marric, J.J.	GIDEON'S MEN	Allen J. Hubin	6-2 TAD 114
Marric, J.J.	GIDEON'S POWER	Robert E. Washer	2-1 QC 17
Marric, J.J.	GIDEON'S PRESS	Allen J. Hubin	7-2 TAD 143
Marric, J.J.	GIDEON'S RIDE	Denis Quane	7 MN 10
Marric, J.J.	GIDEON'S RIVER	Len Moffatt	2-4 MR 15
Marsh, Ngaio	A MAN LAY DEAD	Douglas M. Armato	6-4 TAD 260
Marsh, Ngaio	A MAN LAY DEAD	Don Miller	8 MN 25
Marsh, Ngaio	A MAN LAY DEAD	Charles Shibuk	12-1 TAD 30
Marsh, Ngaio	A WREATH FOR REIVERA	Charles Shibuk	10-4 TAD 361
Marsh, Ngaio	BLACK AS HE'S PAINTED	Charles Shibuk	9-4 TAD 281
Marsh, Ngaio	BLACK AS HE'S PAINTED	Charles Shibuk	12-1 TAD 30
Marsh, Ngaio	CLUTCH OF CONSTABLES	Don Miller	10 MN R17
Marsh, Ngaio	DEAD WATER	Don Miller	2-4 MM 5
Marsh, Ngaio	DEATH AT THE BAR	Myrtis Broset	2-1 MF 40
Marsh, Ngaio	DEATH AT THE BAR	Charles Shibuk	12-2 TAD 167
Marsh, Ngaio	DEATH AT THE BAR	Charles Chibuk	14-1 TAD 80
Marsh, Ngaio	DEATH IN ECSTASY	Myrtis Broset	2-1 MF 37
Marsh, Ngaio	DEATH IN ECSTASY	Don Miller	1-10 MM 9
Marsh, Ngaio	DEATH IN ECSTASY	Charles Shibuk	11-2 TAD 189
Marsh, Ngaio	DEATH OF A FOOL	Charles Shibuk	11-3 TAD 298
Marsh, Ngaio	ENTER A MURDERER	Myrtis Broset	2-3 MF 54
Marsh, Ngaio	ENTER A MURDERER	Charles Shibuk	11-2 TAD 189
Marsh, Ngaio	FALSE SCENT	Charles Shibuk	12-2 TAD 167
Marsh, Ngaio	FINAL CURTAIN	Myrtis Broset	12 MN R3
Marsh, Ngaio	GRAVE MISTAKE	Allen J. Hubin	12-1 TAD 10
Marsh, Ngaio	GRAVE MISTAKE	Charles Shibuk	13-3 TAD 250
Marsh, Ngaio	LAST DITCH	Jim Huang	8 CL 10
Marsh, Ngaio	LAST DITCH	Frank Occhiogrosso	11-3 TAD 245
Marsh, Ngaio	LAST DITCH	Charles Shibuk	11-4 TAD 379
Marsh, Ngaio	NIGHT AT THE VULCAN	Charles Shibuk	11-2 TAD 189
Marsh, Ngaio	PHOTO FINISH	Barzun & Taylor	14-1 TAD 89
Marsh, Ngaio	PHOTO FINISH	Meera T. Clark	2-1 C 123
Marsh, Ngaio	PHOTO FINISH	Allen J. Hubin	14-3 TAD 218
Marsh, Ngaio	PHOTO FINISH	Steve Lewis	5-1 MF 26
Marsh, Ngaio	SCALES OF JUSTICE	Myrtis Broset	2-1 MF 38

Marsh, Ngaio	SPINSTERS IN JEOPARDY	Charles Shibuk	12-2 TAD 167
Marsh, Ngaio	VINTAGE MURDER	Douglas M. Armato	6-4 TAD 260
Marsh, Ngaio	VINTAGE MURDER	Don Miller	9 MN R18
Marsh, Ngaio	WHEN IN ROME	Barzun & Taylor	9-4 TAD 271
Marsh, Ngaio	WHEN IN ROME	Charles Shibuk	12-1 TAD 30
Marsh, Ngaio, & H. Jellett	THE NURSING HOME MURDER	Douglas M. Armato	6-4 TAD 260
Marsh, Richard	THE BEETLE	Amnon Kabatchnik	8-3 TAD 189
Marsh, Richard	WHO KILLED LADY POYNDER?	Charles Shibuk	12-3 TAD 274
Marsh, Richard	WHO KILLED LADY POYNDER?	Charles Shibuk	12-4 TAD 372
Marshall, Archibald, & Horace A.Vachell	MOTE HOUSE MYSTERY	Charles Shibuk	13-3 TAD 269
Marshall, William	THE HATCHET MAN	Pearl G. Aldrich	11-3 TAD 248
Marshall, William	SKULDUGGERY	Allen J. Hubin	13-4 TAD 296
Marshall, William	YELLOWTHREAD STREET	Pearl G. Aldrich	10-1 TAD 61
Marshall, William	YELLOWTHREAD STREET	Mary A. Grochowski	1-1 PP 24
Marshall, William	YELLOWTHREAD STREET	Allen J. Hubin	9-3 TAD 223
Martin, Hansjorg	SLEEPING GIRLS DON'T LIE	Peter Wolfe	10-1 TAD 67
Martin, Ian Kennedy	REKILL	Allen J. Hubin	11-3 TAD 231
Martin, Robert	SLEEP, MY LOVE	Angelo Panagos	13-3 TAD 270
Marvell, Holt, & Val Gielgud	LONDON CALLING	Robert Aucott	6-3 TAD 188
Maryk, Michael, & Brent Monahan	DEATHBITE	Guy M. Townsend	4-2 MF 43
Masiello, Joseph	FAMILY TROUBLE	Fred Dueren	11-4 TAD 396
Mason, A.E.W.	MURDER AT THE VILLA ROSA	Steve Lewis	4-5 MF 28
Mason, Douglas R.	HORIZON ALPHA	Gary Zachrich	75 PU 25
Mason, Douglas R.	MATRIX	Gary Zachrich	74 PU 26
Mason, Tally	CONSIDER YOUR VERDICT	Charles Shibuk	9-3 TAD 229
Mason, Van Wyck	THE SEVEN SEAS MURDERS	Douglas G. Greene	12-3 TAD 231
Masterman, J.C.	AN OXFORD TRAGEDY	Jeff Meyerson	2-2 MF 38
Masters, Anthony	THE NATURAL HISTORY OF THE VAMPIRE	Stanley A. Carlin	5-4 MR 35
Masterson, Whit	HUNTER OF THE BLOOD	Steve Lewis	1-5 MF 30
Masterson, Whit	HUNTER OF THE BLOOD	Christine Mitchell	13-1 TAD 63
Masterson, Whit	HUNTER OF THE BLOOD	Charles Shibuk	10-3 TAD 208
Masterson, Whit	THE UNDERTAKER WIND	Allen J. Hubin	6-4 TAD 266
Masur, Harold Q., ed.	ALFRED HITCHCOCK PRESENTS: THE MASTER'S CHOICE	Martin M. Wooster	3-5 PP 39
Masur, Harold Q.	MAKE A KILLING	Arthur C. Scott	1-11 MM 5
Matheson, Richard	HELL HOUSE	Lianne Carlin	4-6 MR 37
Mathewson, Joseph	ALICIA'S TRUMP	Steve Lewis	5-2 MF 15
Matthews, Clayton	HAGER'S CASTLE	Stanley A. Carlin	3-4 MR 11
Matthews, Clayton	THE MENDOZA FILE	Stanley A. Carlin	3-4 MR 11
Matthews, Clayton	NYLON NIGHTMARE	Stanley A. Carlin	4-2 MR 40
Maxwell, Richard	THE MINUS MAN	Allen J. Hubin	8-3 TAD 227
Maybury, Anne	THE BRIDES OF BELLENMORE	Ruth Withee	3-2 MR 10
Maybury, Anne	THE JEWELED DAUGHTER	Barbara A. Buhrer	11 MN R4
Mayer, Robert	SUPER-FOLKS	Sheldon A. Wiebe	5 SF 38
McAleer, John J., ed.	JUSTICE ENDS AT HOME AND OTHER STORIES	Allen J. Hubin	10-4 TAD 308
McAleer, John J.	REX STOUT: A BIOGRAPHY	Kenneth Karpowicz	4 MT 35
McAleer, John J., & Guy M. Townsend, Judson C. Sapp, Arrican Schemer	REX STOUT: AN ANNOTATED PRIMARY AND SECONDARY BIBLIOGRAPHY	Linda Toole	5-2 MF 29
McAllister, Pam, & Dick Riley	THE BEDSIDE, BATHTUB & ARMCHAIR COMPANION TO AGATHA CHRISTIE	F.M.Nevins, Jr.	1-2 C 134
McAllister, Pam, & Dick Riley	THE BEDSIDE, BATHTUB & ARMCHAIR COMPANION TO AGATHA CHRISTIE	F.M.Nevins, Jr.	4-1 MF 33
McAllister, Pam, & Dick Riley	THE BEDSIDE, BATHTUB & ARMCHAIR COMPANION TO AGATHA CHRISTIE	Ruth Windfeldt	1-1 M 30
McAuliffe, Frank	THE BAG MAN	Bill Crider	5-5 MF 40
McBain, Ed	BLOOD RELATIVES	Robert E. Washer	21 X 54
McBain, Ed	BREAD	Allen J. Hubin	8-2 TAD 150

McBain, Ed	DEATH OF A NURSE	Jeff Meyerson	1-4 MF 44
McBain, Ed	DOLL	Gary Happenstand	2-2 C 159
McBain, Ed	EVEN THE WICKED	Myrtis Broset	1-5 MF 40
McBain, Ed	EVEN THE WICKED	Jeff Meyerson	1-4 MF 44
McBain, Ed	GHOSTS	Allen J. Hubin	14-2 TAD 128
McBain, Ed	GOLDILOCKS	Allen J. Hubin	12-1 TAD 9
McBain, Ed	GUNS	Allen J. Hubin	10-2 TAD 112
McBain, Ed	HAIL, HAIL, THE GANG'S ALL HERE!	Lianne Carlin	4-5 MR 36
McBain, Ed	HAIL TO THE CHIEF	Allen J. Hubin	7-2 TAD 141
McBain, Ed	LET'S HEAR IT FOR THE DEAF MAN	Max Collins	6-1 MR 42
McBain, Ed	LONG TIME NO SEE	Allen J. Hubin	10-3 TAD 206
McBain, Ed	SO LONG AS YOU BOTH SHALL LIVE	Allen J. Hubin	10-2 TAD 113
McBain, Ed	TEN PLUS ONE	Myrtis Broset	1-4 MF 47
McBain, Ed	WHERE THERES SMOKE	Robert E. Washer	17 X 60
McBain, Ed	WHERE THERES SMOKE	Myrtis Broset	1-5 MF 40
McBain, Ed	WHERE THERES SMOKE	Sheila D'Ammassa	2 MN 6
McBain, Ed	WHERE THERES SMOKE	Allen J. Hubin	8-4 TAD 309
McBain, Ed	WITHOUT APPARENT MOTIVE (film)	Amnon Kabatchnik	5-4 TAD 229
McCall, Mary, Jr., & Lionel Houser	I PROMISE TO PAY (film)	William K. Everson	11-2 TAD 129
McCarry, Charles	THE BETTER ANGELS	Allen J. Hubin	13-1 TAD 29
McCauley, Kirby	NIGHT CHILLS	Martin M. Wooster	4-3 PP 25
McCloy, Helen	A CHANGE OF HEART	Allen J. Hubin	6-2 TAD 114
McCloy, Helen	BURN THIS	Thomas Godfrey	3-1 M 37
McCloy, Helen	BURN THIS	Steve Lewis	4-4 MF 42
McCloy, Helen	THE CHANGELING CONSPIRACY	Steve Lewis	1-6 MF 38
McCloy, Helen	HE NEVER CAME BACK	Barry A. Pike	9-1 TAD 62
McCloy, Helen	THE IMPOSTER	Steve Lewis	2-1 MF 24
McCloy, Helen	THROUGH A GLASS, DARKLY	Jim McCahery	3-3 PP 29
McClure, James	THE BLOOD OF AN ENGLISHMAN	Jane S. Bakerman	5-2 MF 37
McClure, James	THE BLOOD OF AN ENGLISHMAN	Meera T. Clark	2-1 C 123
McClure, James	THE CATERPILLAR COP	Allen J. Hubin	6-4 TAD 265
McClure, James	THE GOOSEBERRY FOOL	Allen J. Hubin	7-4 TAD 295
McClure, James	ROGUE EAGLE	Frank Occhiogrosso	11-1 TAD 25
McClure, James	ROGUE EAGLE	Guy M. Townsend	11 MN R8
McClure, James	SNAKE	Amnon Kabatchnik	1-1 MF 35
McClure, James	THE STEAM PIG	Allen J. Hubin	6-1 TAD 44
McClure, James	THE SUNDAY HANGMAN	Allen J. Hubin	11-3 TAD 232
McComas, J.Francis,ed	CRIMES AND MISFORTUNES: THE ANTHONY BOUCHER MEMORIAL ANTHOLOGY OF MYSTERIES	J.R.Christopher	4-2 TAD 121
McComas, J.Francis,ed	CRIMES AND MISFORTUNES: THE ANTHONY BOUCHER MEMORIAL ANTHOLOGY OF MYSTERIES	Robert E. Washer	3-5 MR 19
McComas, J.Francis,ed	SPECIAL WONDER: THE ANTHONY BOUCHER MEMORIAL ANTHOLOGY OF FANTASY AND SCIENCE FICTION	J.R.Christopher	4-2 TAD 121
McConnell, Malcolm	CLINTON IS ASSIGNED	Fred Dueren	11-4 TAD 396
McConnor, Vincent	THE PROVENCE PUZZLE	Allen J. Hubin	14-2 TAD 128
McCormick, Donald	WHO'S WHO IN SPY FICTION	Theodore Dukeshire	11-2 TAD 123
McCurtin, Peter	MAFIOSO	Stanley A. Carlin	4-1 MR 37
McCurtin, Peter	MINNESOTA STRIP	Fred Dueren	12-2 TAD 135
McDaniel, David	THE RAINBOW AFFAIR	Len Moffatt	1-3 TAD 103
McDonald, Gregory	CONFESS, FLETCH	Fred Dueren	10-2 TAD 130
McDonald, Gregory	CONFESS, FLETCH	Jeff Meyerson	1-5 MF 37
McDonald, Gregory	CONFESS, FLETCH	Charles Shibuk	10-2 TAD 150
McDonald, Gregory	FLETCH	Fred Dueren	10-2 TAD 130
McDonald, Gregory	FLETCH	Allen J. Hubin	8-3 TAD 229
McDonald, Gregory	FLETCH	Steve Lewis	1-3 MF 37
McDonald, Gregory	FLETCH	Jeff Meyerson	1-5 MF 37
McDonald, Gregory	FLETCH AND THE WIDOW BRADLEY	William L.DeAndrea	14-3 TAD 265
McDonald, Gregory	FLETCH'S FORTUNE	Jim Huang	10 CL 9
McDonald, Gregory	FLETCH'S FORTUNE	Charles Shibuk	12-1 TAD 30
McDonald, Gregory	FLYNN	Jim Huang	8 CL 10

McDonald, Gregory	FLYNN	Allen J. Hubin	11-3 TAD 230
McDonald, Gregory	FLYNN	Charles Shibuk	11-1 TAD 96
McDonald, Gregory	WHO TOOK TONY RINALDI?	Allen J. Hubin	13-4 TAD 296
McDonald, Hugh C.	FIVE SIGNS FROM RUBY	Fred Dueren	10-2 TAD 131
McDonald, Hugh, & Robin Moore	THE BLACK SEA CAPER	George Kelley	3-5 PP 43
McDowell, Michael	COLD MOON OVER BABYLON	Fred Dueren	13-3 TAD 251
McDowell, Michael	COLD MOON OVER BABYLON	Larry Rickert	4-1 PP 37
McFarlane, Arthur E.	BEHIND THE BOLTED DOOR	Amnon Kabatchnik	6-1 TAD 42
McFarlane, Arthur E.	GREAT BEAR ISLAND	C.L.Messecar	3-4 BC 373
McGerr, Patricia	DANGEROUS LANDING	Amnon Kabatchnik	8-4 TAD 307
McGerr, Patricia	FOLLOW THE NIGHT	Angelo Panagos	14-3 TAD 272
McGerr, Patricia	FOR RICHER FOR POORER TILL DEATH	Barzun & Taylor	10-3 TAD 225
McGerr, Patricia	PICK YOUR VICTIM	Amnon Kabatchnik	6-2 TAD 117
McGerr, Patricia	THE SEVEN DEADLY SISTERS	Steve Lewis	3-5 MF 38
McGerr, Patricia	THE SEVEN DEADLY SISTERS	Charles Shibuk	2-2 MF 38
McGinley, Patrick	BOGMAIL	D.E.Ath	2-1 PP 10
McGinley, Patrick	BOGMAIL	Steve Lewis	5-5 MF 21
McGinley, Patrick	BOGMAIL	F.M.Nevins, Jr.	5-5 MF 29
McGirr, Edmund	A MURDEROUS JOURNEY	Allen J. Hubin	8-4 TAD 308
McGivern, William P.	HEAVEN RAN LAST	Charles Shibuk	6-3 TAD 188
McGivern, William P.	NIGHT OF THE JUGGLER	Allen J. Hubin	8-3 TAD 226
McGivern, William P.	REPRISAL	Steve Lewis	4-2 MF 34
McGraw, Lee	HATCHETT	Fred Dueren	10-2 TAD 131
McGraw, Lee	HATCHETT	Steve Lewis	1-2 MF 26
McGraw, Lee	HATCHETT	Robert J. Randisi	12-3 TAD 275
McGuire, Paul	A FUNERAL IN EDEN	Charles Shibuk	6-2 TAD 118
McGuire, Paul	THE BLACK ROSE MURDER	Charles Shibuk	8-3 TAD 219
McGuire, Paul	THREEPENCE TO MARBLE ARCH	Robert C.S.Adey	3-2 PP 28
McHale, Tom	FARRAGAN'S RETREAT	F.M.Nevins, Jr.	5-1 TAD 40
McIlvanney, William	LAIDLAW	Allen J. Hubin	10-4 TAD 307
McIlvanney, William	LAIDLAW	Kenneth Karpowicz	4 MT 27
McInerny, Ralph	BISHOP AS PAWN	Steve Lewis	3-5 MF 35
McInerny, Ralph	HER DEATH OF COLD	Guy M. Townsend	11 MN R10
McInerny, Ralph	HER DEATH OF COLD	Guy M. Townsend	13 MN R7
McInerny, Ralph	SECOND VESPERS	Joyce L. Dewes	2-3 M 49
McInerny, Ralph	SECOND VESPERS	Allen J. Hubin	14-1 TAD 18
McInerny, Ralph	THE SEVENTH STATION	Guy M. Townsend	13 MN R7
McIntosh, J.T.	TAKE A PAIR OF PRIVATE EYES	Robert C.S.Adey	4-1 PP 28
McIntyre, John T.	THE YOUNG CONTINENTALS OF TRENTON	C.L.Messecar	3-2 BC 320
McIntyre, John T.	THE YOUNG CONTINENTALS OF TRENTON	C.L.Messecar	3-4 BC 373
McKay, Kenneth R.	SHADOW OF THE KNIFE	Bill Crider	2-3 PP 30
McKay, Randle, & Lassiter Wren	THE MYSTERY PUZZLE BOOK	Arthur C. Scott	2-3 MM 4
McKenna, Marthe	LANCER SPY (film)	William K. Everson	8-1 TAD 14
McLaughlin, Robert T.	..PENDING INVESTIGATION	Fred Dueren	10-4 TAD 340
McLeave, Hugh	DOUBLE EXPOSURE	Elsa Pendleton	1-3 M 21
McLeave, Hugh	NO FACE IN THE MIRROR	George Kelley	3-5 PP 38
McLeish, Dougal	THE VALENTINE VICTIM	Lianne Carlin	3-4 MR 12
McLendon, James	DEATHWORK	Carl Hoffman	12-4 TAD 371
McLendon, James	EDDIE MACON'S RUN	Allen J. Hubin	14-2 TAD 128
McMullen, Mary	A COUNTRY KIND OF DEATH	Jane S. Bakerman	4-2 MF 46
McMullen, Mary	A DANGEROUS FUNERAL	Jane S. Bakerman	4-2 MF 45
McMullen, Mary	THE MAN WITH FIFTY COMPLAINTS	Steve Lewis	3-5 MF 36
McMullen, Mary	THE OTHER SHOE	Kathi Maio	5-4 MF 37
McMahon, Thomas P.	CORNERED AT SIX	Amnon Kabatchnik	6-2 MR 46
McNally, Raymond, & Radu Florescu	IN SEARCH OF DRACULA: A TRUE HISTORY OF DRACULA AND VAMPIRE LEGENDS	Veronica M.Kennedy	7-2 TAD 138
McNaughton, Brian	GUILTY UNTIL PROVEN GUILTY	Richard Moskowitz	5 LR 4
McNeil, Everett	IN TEXAS WITH DAVY CROCKETT	C.L.Messecar	3-4 BC 371
McNeil, Everett	KIT CARSON IN THE ROCKIES	C.L.Messecar	3-4 BC 372
McQuinn, Donald E.	TARGETS	Allen J. Hubin	14-2 TAD 128

McShane, Mark	NIGHT'S EVIL	Amnon Kabatchnik	5-3 MR 39
McShane, Mark	THE SINGULAR CASE OF THE MULTIPLE DEAD	Robert E. Washer	2-1 QC 18
Meade, L.T., & Clifford Halifax	STORIES FROM THE DIARY OF A DOCTOR, SECOND SERIES	Allen J. Hubin	5-4 TAD 233
Mefford, W.H.	THE GAMES OF 80	Fred Dueren	13-4 TAD 361
Meggs, Brown	THE MATTER OF PARADISE	Barbara A. Buhrer	2-4 MM 3
Meggs, Brown	THE MATTER OF PARADISE	Allen J. Hubin	8-4 TAD 310
Meggs, Brown	SATURDAY GAMES	Allen J. Hubin	7-4 TAD 295
Meldrum, James	THE SEMONOV IMPULSE	Allen J. Hubin	10-2 TAD 112
Melville, James	THE WAGES OF ZEN	Greg Goode	5-6 MF 45
Menendez, Albert J.	THE SHERLOCK HOLMES QUIZ BOOK	Jon L. Lellenberg	8-4 TAD 301
Merivale, Bernard, & Arnold Ridley	THE WRECKER (film)	William K. Everson	4-1 TAD 36
Merlin, Christina	THE SPY CONCERTO	Allen J. Hubin	13-4 TAD 297
Meyer, Lawrence	A CAPITOL CRIME	Allen J. Hubin	10-3 TAD 205
Meyer, Lawrence	A CAPITOL CRIME	Charles Shibuk	12-1 TAD 30
Meyer, Lynn	PAPERBACK THRILLER	Allen J. Hubin	9-1 TAD 73
Meyer, Lynn	PAPERBACK THRILLER	Robert E. Washer	21 X 54
Meyer, Lynn	PAPERBACK THRILLER	Stan Burns	10 MN R3
Meyer, Nicholas	THE SEVEN-PER-CENT SOLUTION	Jon L. Lellenberg	7-4 TAD 290
Meyer, Nicholas	THE SEVEN-PER-CENT SOLUTION (film)	Todd Rutt	1-2 WA 7
Meyer, Nicholas	TARGET PRACTICE	Fred Dueren	9-1 TAD 51
Meyer, Nicholas	TARGET PRACTICE	George Fergus	5/6 MN 18
Meyer, Nicholas	THE WEST END HORROR	Stan Burns	11 MN R5
Meyer, Nicholas	THE WEST END HORROR	Jon L. Lellenberg	9-3 TAD 218
Meyer, Nicholas	THE WEST END HORROR	Charles Shibuk	10-4 TAD 361
Meyers, Manny	THE LAST MYSTERY OF EDGAR ALLAN POE	Allen J. Hubin	12-2 TAD 114
Meyers, Martin	SPY AND DIE	Steve Lewis	1-2 MF 24
Meynell, Laurence	THE EVIL HOUR: A CHRONICLE OF OUR DAYS	Charles Shibuk	13-3 TAD 268
Meynell, Laurence	ONE STEP FROM MURDER	Barzun & Taylor	12-3 TAD 263
Michaels, Alan	DIAMONDS	Allen J. Hubin	14-3 TAD 218
Michaels, Bill, & Lewis Orde	THE NIGHT THEY STOLE MANHATTAN	Allen J. Hubin	14-1 TAD 19
Michaels, Norman, & Chris Steinbrunner	THE FILMS OF SHERLOCK HOLMES	Marvin Lachman	3-3 MF 43
Michel, M. Scott	THE BLACK KEY	Jim McCahery	4-4 PP 25
Middlemiss, Robert	THE PARROT MAN	David Doerrer	2-2 MF 39
Middlemiss, Robert	THE PARROT MAN	Fred Dueren	11-2 TAD 192
Mikolowski, Ken	LITTLE MYSTERIES	David A. Christie	14-3 TAD 269
Miles, John	THE BLACKMAILER	Allen J. Hubin	8-1 TAD 65
Miles, John	THE NIGHT HUNTERS	Barzun & Taylor	11-4 TAD 394
Miles, John, & Tom Morris	OPERATION NIGHTFALL	Allen J. Hubin	9-1 TAD 74
Millar, Margaret	ASK FOR ME TOMORROW	Steve Lewis	1-4 MF 37
Millar, Margaret	BEYOND THIS POINT ARE MONSTERS	Barzun & Taylor	14-3 TAD 228
Millar, Margaret	BEYOND THIS POINT ARE MONSTERS	Marvin Lachman	4-1 TAD 50
Millar, Margaret	THE LISTENING WALLS	Jeff Meyerson	1-1 PP 25
Millar, Margaret	THE MURDER OF MIRANDA	Jane S. Bakerman	3-4 MF 46
Millar, Margaret	THE MURDER OF MIRANDA	Allen J. Hubin	12-4 TAD 322
Millar, Margaret	THE MURDER OF MIRANDA	Steve Lewis	3-6 MF 29
Millard, Joseph	MANSION OF EVIL	Edward Lauterbach	7-3 TAD 208
Millard, Oscar	A MISSING PERSON	Stanley A. Carlin	5-4 MR 30
Miller, Geoffrey	THE BLACK GLOVE	Thomas Godfrey	3-2 M 41
Miller, John	MURDER OF A PROFESSOR	Hal Brodsky	8-2 TAD 141
Miller, Kenneth	THE DARK TUNNEL	Amnon Kabatchnik	7-2 TAD 132
Miller, Lewis B.	THE WHITE RIVER RAFT	C.L.Messecar	3-2 BC 320
Miller, Seton I.	G MEN (film)	William K. Everson	4-1 TAD 29
Miller, Victor B.	FERNANDA	R. Jeff Banks	1-2 MF 44
Miller, Wade	GUILTY BYSTANDER	Jeff Meyerson	1-5 MF 49
Millhiser, Marlys	WILLING HOSTAGE	Barbara A. Buhrer	2-5 MM 5
Mills, James	ONE JUST MAN	Stan Burns	1-7 MM 7

Mills, James	THE SEVENTH POWER	Guy M. Townsend	11 MN R8
Mills, Tarpe	MISS FURY	J. Randolph Cox	12-4 TAD 369
Milne, A.A.	THE RED HOUSE MYSTERY	Charles Shibuk	14-2 TAD 183
Milton, David Scott	KABBALAH	Allen J. Hubin	14-3 TAD 218
Mitchell, Gladys	DEATH AT THE OPERA	Mary A. Grochowski	2-5 MF 42
Mitchell, Gladys	FAULT IN THE STRUCTURE	Jon L. Breen	14-1 TAD 55
Mitchell, Gladys	MINGLED WITH VENOM	Jon L. Breen	14-1 TAD 55
Mitchell, Gladys	WATSON'S CHOICE	Fred Dueren	5-3 MF 39
Mitchell, Gladys	WATSON'S CHOICE	Allen J. Hubin	10-2 TAD 113
Mitchell, Gladys	WINKING AT THE BRIM	Fred Dueren	14-4 TAD 364
Mitchell, James	SMEAR JOB	Allen J. Hubin	11-1 TAD 18
Mitchell, James	SMEAR JOB	Steve Lewis	2-3 MF 44
Mitchell, James	SMEAR JOB	Charles Shibuk	12-1 TAD 30
Mitchelson, Austin, & Nicholas Utechin	THE EARTHQUAKE MACHINE	Edward Lauterbach	10-1 TAD 63
Mitchelson, Austin & Nicholas Utechin	THE EARTHQUAKE MACHINE	Timothy J. Rutt	1-1 WA 9
Mitchelson, Austin & Nicholas Utechin	HELLBIRDS	Edward Lauterbach	10-2 TAD 115
Moffatt, Gwen	MISS PINK AT THE EDGE OF THE WORLD	Allen J. Hubin	9-1 TAD 72
Moffatt, Len & June, & William J.Clark	THE JDM MASTER CHECKLIST	Robert E. Washer	1-3 QC 22
Moffett, Martha	THE COMMON GARDEN	Fred Dueren	10-4 TAD 341
Mogensen, Harald, & Tage laCour	THE MURDER BOOK: AN ILLUSTRATED HISTORY	Lianne Carlin	5-2 MR 45
Mogensen, Harald, & Tage laCour	THE MURDER BOOK: AN ILLUSTRATED HISTORY	Marvin Lachman	5-3 TAD 162
Monaco, James	THE NEW WAVE: TRUFFAUT, GODARD, CHABROL, ROHMER, RIVETTE	James Mark Purcell	10-1 TAD 58
Monahan, Brent, & Michael Maryk	DEATHBITE	Guy M. Townsend	4-2 MF 43
Monig, Christopher	ABRA-CADAVER	Arthur C. Scott	12 MN A12
Monig, Christopher	ONCE UPON A CRIME	Steve Lewis	1A MF 23
Monteleone, Thomas F.	THE SECRET SEA	W. Paul Ganley	2 FM 18
Montgomery, Lyna Lee, & Nancy L.Talburt, ed	A MYSTERY READER: STORIES OF DETECTION, ADVENTURE AND HORROR	Allen J. Hubin	8-3 TAD 230
Moorcock, Michael	THE BLACK CORRIDOR	Gary Zachrich	74 PU 21
Moore, H.F.S.	DEATH AT 7:10	Barzun & Taylor	13-3 TAD 209
Moore, Robin	THE FRENCH CONNECTION (film)	Richard S. Lochte	5-2 TAD 104
Moore, Robin	THE TERMINAL CONNECTION	Myrtis Broset	1-5 MF 41
Moore, Roger	ROGER MOORE'S JAMES BOND DIARY	Lianne Carlin	6-1 MR 47
Moore, Robin, & Sidney Levine	THE BIG PADDLE	Bill Crider	3-6 PP 28
Moore, Robin, & Hugh McDonald	THE BLACK SEA CAPER	George Kelley	3-5 PP 43
Morales, Pablo	BIG DEAL IN VERAGUA	Fred Dueren	12-3 TAD 287
Morales, Pablo	VICTIM FOR HIRE	Fred Dueren	12-3 TAD 287
Morgan, Patrick	DEADLY GROUP DOWN UNDER	Lianne Carlin	3-4 MR 12
Morgan, Patrick	HANG DEAD HAWAIIAN STYLE	Lianne Carlin	3-4 MR 12
Morgan, Patrick	TOO MINI MURDERS	Lianne Carlin	3-4 MR 12
Morgenstein, Gary	TAKE ME OUT TO THE BALLGAME	Allen J. Hubin	13-4 TAD 297
Morice, Anne	DEATH AND THE DUTIFUL DAUGHTER	Jay Jeffries	3/4 MN 9
Morice, Anne	DEATH AND THE HEAVENLY TWIN	Jay Jeffries	3/4 MN 9
Morice, Anne	DEATH IN THE ROUND	Jane S. Bakerman	5-5 MF 36
Morice, Anne	KILLING WITH KINDNESS	Jay Jeffries	3/4 MN 10
Morice, Anne	MURDER IN MIMICRY	Allen J. Hubin	10-3 TAD 205
Morice, Anne	SCARED TO DEATH	Steve Lewis	2-4 MF 32
Morley, Christopher	PREFACES WITHOUT BOOKS	Stanley A. Carlin	4-5 MR 38
Morpurgo, J.E.	ALLEN KANE: KING PENGUIN, A BIOGRAPHY	Thomas L. Bonn	3-2 PQ 37
Morrah, Dermot	THE MUMMY CASE	Jon L. Lellenberg	9-4 TAD 308
Morris, Tom, & John Miles	OPERATION NIGHTFALL	Allen J. Hubin	9-1 TAD 74

Morrison, Arthur	BEST MARTIN HEWITT DETECTIVE STORIES	Charles Shibuk	10-2 TAD 150
Morrison, Arthur	BEST MARTIN HEWITT DETECTIVE STORIES	Guy M. Townsend	1-5 MF 38
Morrison, Arthur	MARTIN HEWITT: INVESTIGATOR	Allen J. Hubin	4-4 TAD 241
Morse, L.A.	THE OLD DICK	Steve Lewis	5-6 MF 40
Mortimer, John	RUMPOLE OF THE BAILEY	Martin M. Wooster	3-3 PP 34
Mortimer, John	THE TRIALS OF RUMPOLE	Jeff Meyerson	3-4 PP 35
Morton, Anthony	THE BARON GOES A-BUYING	Amnon Kabatchnik	6-1 MR 44
Morton, Anthony	HIDE THE BARON	Allen J. Hubin	11-3 TAD 233
Morton, William	THE MYSTERY OF THE HUMAN BOOKCASE	Andy Jaysnovitch	1-5 PP 19
Morton, William	THE MYSTERY OF THE HUMAN BOOKCASE	Angelo Panagos	14-3 TAD 272
Moskowitz, Sam, ed.	HORRORS UNKNOWN	Lianne Carlin	4-6 MR 40
Moskowitz, Sam	THE IMMORTAL STORM	Allen J. Hubin	7-4 TAD 294
Moskowitz, Sam, ed.	THE MAN WHO CALLED HIMSELF POE	Stanley A. Carlin	2-6 MR 9
Moyes, Patricia	ANGEL DEATH	Allen J. Hubin	14-3 TAD 218
Moyes, Patricia	BLACK WIDOWER	Steve Lewis	2-4 MF 35
Moyes, Patricia	BLACK WIDOWER	Denis Quane	5/6 MN 19
Moyes, Patricia	BLACK WIDOWER	Charles Shibuk	11-3 TAD 298
Moyes, Patricia	BLACK WIDOWER	Guy M. Townsend	1-6 MF 47
Moyes, Patricia	THE COCONUT KILLINGS	Myrtis Broset	10 MN R12
Moyes, Patricia	THE COCONUT KILLINGS	Charles Shibuk	12-3 TAD 255
Moyes, Patricia	THE COCONUT KILLINGS	Guy M. Townsend	10 MN R12
Moyes, Patricia	THE CURIOUS AFFAIR OF THE THIRD DOG	Douglas M. Armato	6-2 MR 45
Moyes, Patricia	THE CURIOUS AFFAIR OF THE THIRD DOG	Charles Shibuk	9-3 TAD 208
Moyes, Patricia	MANY DEADLY RETURNS	Charles Shibuk	14-4 TAD 377
Muir, Jean	THE SMILING MEDUSA	Lianne Carlin	3-3 MR 29
Muir, Thomas	DEATH IN SOUNDINGS	Barzun & Taylor	14-2 TAD 142
Muir, Thomas	DEATH WITHOUT QUESTION	Barzun & Taylor	14-2 TAD 142
Mulkeen, Thomas	MY KILLER DOESN'T UNDERSTAND ME	Allen J. Hubin	7-2 TAD 142
Muller, Marcia	EDWIN OF THE IRON SHOES	Allen J. Hubin	11-3 TAD 231
Muller, Marcia	EDWIN OF THE IRON SHOES	Steve Lewis	2-3 MF 48
Muller, Marcia	EDWIN OF THE IRON SHOES	Charles Shibuk	12-1 TAD 30
Mundell, E.H.	DASHIELL HAMMETT: A CHECKLIST	Stanley A. Carlin	3-4 MR 10
Mundell, E.H.	ERLE STANLEY GARDNER: A CHECKLIST	Stanley A. Carlin	3-4 MR 10
Mundell, E.H.	ERLE STANLEY GARDNER: A CHECKLIST	Allen J. Hubin	3-3 TAD 161
Mundell, E.H.	ERLE STANLEY GARDNER: A CHECKLIST	Marvin Lachman	3-4 TAD 272
Mundell, Elmore, & G. Jay Rausch	THE DETECTIVE SHORT STORY: A BIBLIOGRAPHY AND INDEX	Allen J. Hubin	8-1 TAD 66
Mundy, Talbot	JIMGRIM	Fred Blosser	6-3 TAD 189
Munro, Hugh	A CLUE FOR CLUTHA	Robert C.S.Adey	4-2 PP 27
Murdoch, Derrick	THE AGATHA CHRISTIE MYSTERY	Allen J. Hubin	10-1 TAD 5
Murdoch, Derrick	THE AGATHA CHRISTIE MYSTERY	Charles Shibuk	1-2 MF 4
Murdoch, Derrick	THE AGATHA CHRISTIE MYSTERY	Martin M. Wooster	1-4 PP 27
Murphy, James F.,Jr.	QUONSETT	Bill Crider	2-1 PP 28
Murphy, John	THE EL GRECO PUZZLE	Charles Shibuk	10-1 TAD 72
Murphy, John	PAY ON THE WAY OUT	Barbara A. Buhrer	1-6 MM 9
Murphy, John	PAY ON THE WAY OUT	Stan Burns	9 MN R4
Murphy, John	PAY ON THE WAY OUT	Allen J. Hubin	8-4 TAD 308
Murphy, John	PAY ON THE WAY OUT	Steve Lewis	1-1 MF 27
Murphy, Michael	STARRETT VS. MACHEN	Jon L. Lellenberg	10-4 TAD 377
Murphy, Tom	BALLET	D.E.Ath	2-2 PP 14
Murphy, Warren B.	CITY IN HEAT	Jeff Meyerson	10 MN R15
Murphy, Warren B.	LEONARDO'S LAW	Fred Dueren	11-4 TAD 396
Murphy, Warren B., & Richard Sapir	BOTTOM LINE	Steve Lewis	3-6 MF 31
Murphy, Warren B., & Richard Sapir	THE HEAD MEN	Steve Lewis	2-4 MF 33

Murphy, Warren B., & Richard Sapir	HOLY TERROR	Jeff Meyerson	1-3 MF 49
Murphy, Warren B., & Richard Sapir	IN ENEMY HANDS	Steve Lewis	1-2 MF 28
Murphy, Warren B., & Richard Sapir	LAST WAR DANCE	Jeff Meyerson	1-3 MF 48
Murphy, Warren B., & Richard Sapir	MAFIA FIX	Jeff Meyerson	1-6 MF 52
Murphy, Warren B., & Richard Sapir	SLAVE SAFARI	Jeff Meyerson	10 MN R15
Murray, Max	THE VOICE OF THE CORPSE	Barzun & Taylor	9-4 TAD 272
Murray, Will	DOC SAVAGE: SUPREME ADVENTURER	Link Hullar	1 PW 4
Murray, Will	THE DUENDE HISTORY OF THE SHADOW MAGAZINE	Link Hullar	10 DS 29
Murray, Will	THE DUENDE HISTORY OF THE SHADOW MAGAZINE	Richard Moskowitz	9 LR 14
Murray, Will, & Tom Johnson	secret agent X: A HISTORY	Sampson & Carr	14 SF 21
Myagkov, Aleksei	INSIDE THE KGB	Gary Happenstand	2-2 C 158
Myers, Robert	THE SLAVE OF FRANKENSTEIN	Mary A. Grochowski	3-2 PP 29
Mykel, A.W.	THE WINDCHIME LEGACY	Allen J. Hubin	14-3 TAD 219
Names, Larry D.	TWICE DEAD	Thomas L.Motsinger	3-1 MF 41
Nash, Jay Robert	A CRIME STORY	Gary Warren Niebuhr	4-3 PP 6
Nash, Simon	UNHALLOWED MURDER	Douglas G. Greene	4-2 PP 26
Naughton, Edmund	THE MAXIMUM GAME	R. Jeff Banks	2-1 MM 3
Nazarian, Barry	BLOOD RITES	Fred Dueren	13-4 TAD 362
Nebel, Frederick	SIX DEADLY DAMES	Gary Happenstand	2-2 C 156
Nebel, Frederick	SIX DEADLY DAMES	Angelo Panagos	12-1 TAD 80
Nebel, Frederick	SIX DEADLY GAMES	Arthur C. Scott	1-10 MM 9
Neely, Richard	A MADNESS OF THE HEART	Bill Crider	3-3 MF 42
Neely, Richard	DIRTY HANDS	Fred Dueren	10-4 TAD 340
Neely, Richard	LIES	Steve Lewis	2-5 MF 29
Neely, Richard	NO CERTAIN LIFE	Fred Dueren	11-4 TAD 396
Neely, Richard	NO CERTAIN LIFE	Jim Huang	9 CL 6
Neely, Richard	NO CERTAIN LIFE	Steve Lewis	2-5 MF 31
Neely, Richard	THE WALTER SYNDROME	Lianne Carlin	4-2 MR 39
Nelson, Walter	THE SIEGE OF BUCKINGHAM PALACE	Fred Dueren	13-4 TAD 351
Nelson, Walter	THE SIEGE OF BUCKINGHAM PALACE	George Kelley	3-5 PP 38
Neuman, Fredric	THE SECLUSION ROOM	Charles Shibuk	13-2 TAD 135
Nevins, Francis M.,Jr	CORRUPT AND ENSNARE	Allen J. Hubin	11-4 TAD 331
Nevins, Francis M.,Jr	CORRUPT AND ENSNARE	Steve Lewis	3-1 MF 31
Nevins, Francis M.,Jr	THE MYSTERY WRITER'S ART	Stanley A. Carlin	4-4 MR 38
Nevins, Francis M.,Jr	THE MYSTERY WRITER'S ART	Robert E. Washer	3-2 QC 18
Nevins, Francis M.,Jr	NIGHTWEBS	Marvin Lachman	4-6 MR 31
Nevins, Francis M.,Jr	PUBLISH AND PERISH	Robert E. Washer	21 X 54
Nevins, Francis M.,Jr	PUBLISH AND PERISH	Barbara A. Buhrer	1-10 MM 7
Nevins, Francis M.,Jr	PUBLISH AND PERISH	Allen J. Hubin	9-2 TAD 152
Nevins, Francis M.,Jr	PUBLISH AND PERISH	Steve Lewis	1-9 MM 6
Nevins, Francis M.,Jr	ROYAL BLOODLINE: ELLERY QUEEN AUTHOR AND DETECTIVE	Allen J. Hubin	7-4 TAD 293
Nevins, Francis M.,Jr	ROYAL BLOODLINE: ELLERY QUEEN AUTHOR AND DETECTIVE	Marvin Lachman	14 X 54
Newman, Frank	THE SECLUSION ROOM	Allen J. Hubin	12-2 TAD 114
Newman, G.F.	THE NICE BASTARD	Robert C.S.Adey	2-2 MF 37
Nicholls, Peter, ed.	THE SCIENCE-FICTION ENCYCLOPEDIA	W.Ritchie Benedict	12 SF 19
Nichols, Leigh	THE EYES OF DARKNESS	Joyce L. Dewes	3-2 M 41
Nielsen, Helen	AFTER MIDNIGHT	Steve Lewis	3-2 MF 38
Nielsen, Helen	SING ME A MURDER	Robert M. Williams	5/6 MM 20
Nielsen, Torben	AN UNSUCCESSFUL MAN	Allen J. Hubin	10-2 TAD 112
Nielsen, Torben	AN UNSUCCESSFUL MAN	Steve Lewis	1-3 MF 38
Nieminski, John	THE SAINT MAGAZINE INDEX	Bill Crider	2-4 PQ 49
Nieminski, John	THE SAINT MAGAZINE INDEX	Allen J. Hubin	13-2 TAD 97
Nieminski, John	THE SAINT MAGAZINE INDEX	Andy Jaysnovitch	7 PE 13
Niven, Larry	THE PATCHWORK GIRL	Allan Magnus	12 SF 28

Niven, Larry	RINGWORLD	Gary Zachrich	75 PU 25
Nolan, Frederick	THE MITTENWALD SYNDICATE	Barbara A. Buhrer	11 MN R2
Nolan, William F.	DASHIELL HAMMETT: A CASEBOOK	Robert E. Washer	2-1 QC 18
Nolan, William F.	DASHIELL HAMMETT: A CASEBOOK	William White	3-5 MR 8
Nolan, William F.	DEATH IS FOR LOSERS	Stanley A. Carlin	1-5 MR 6
Nolan, William F.	THE RAY BRADBURY COMPANION	Allen J. Hubin	8-3 TAD 230
Norman, Frank	THE DEAD BUTLER CAPER	Allen J. Hubin	12-4 TAD 322
Norman, Frank	THE DEAD BUTLER CAPER	Andy Jaysnovitch	6 PE 22
Norman, John	TARNSMAN OF GOR	Gary Zachrich	66 PU 60
Norris, Luther, ed.	THE NON-CANONICAL SHERLOCK HOLMES	Allen J. Hubin	8-4 TAD 311
Norris, Luther	THE SHERLOCKIAN DOYLE	Allen J. Hubin	2-2 TAD 122
Norris, Luther, ed.	VINCENT STARRETT: IN MEMORIAM	Allen J. Hubin	8-1 TAD 67
North, Jessica	MASK OF THE JAGUAR	Jean Lamb	3-2 M 41
North, Sam	209 THRILLER ROAD	Paul Bishop	2-2 M 58
North, Sam	209 THRILLER ROAD	Allen J. Hubin	14-1 TAD 19
Norton, Alden	HORROR TIMES TEN	Gary Zachrich	70 PU 28
Norton, Andre	DARK PIPER	Gary Zachrich	73 PU 33
Norton, Andre	SORCERESS OF THE WITCH WORLD	Gary Zachrich	70 PU 26
Norton, Andre	THE ZERO STONE	Gary Zachrich	74 PU 20
Norton, Charles A.	MELVILLE DAVISSON POST: MAN OF MANY MYSTERIES	Allen J. Hubin	7-3 TAD 221
Norton, Charles A.	MELVILLE DAVISSON POST: MAN OF MANY MYSTERIES	F.M.Nevins, Jr.	8-1 TAD 59
Novak, Robert	THE BIG PAYOFF	Arthur C. Scott	1-5 MM 10
Nowlan, Philip F.	ARMAGEDDON 2419 A.D.	Gary Zachrich	74 PU 22
Nye, Russel	THE UNEMBARRASSED MUSE: THE POPULAR ARTS IN AMERICA	Jon L. Breen	3-4 TAD 270
O'Brien, Geoffrey	HARDBOILED AMERICA	Charlotte Laughlin	4-2 PQ 46
O'Brien, Geoffrey	HARDBOILED AMERICA	F.M.Nevins, Jr.	5-6 MF 42
Obstfeld, Raymond	THE DEAD-END OPTION	Paul Harwitz	2-2 M 56
Obstfeld, Raymond	THE GOULDEN FLEECE	Steve Lewis	3-6 MF 34
Ocork, Shannon	SPORTS FREAK	Allen J. Hubin	13-4 TAD 297
Odell, Robin, & J.H.H.Gaute	THE MURDERER'S WHO'S WHO	W.Ritchie Benedict	6 U 39
Odlum, Jerome	THE MIRABILIS DIAMOND	Theodore Dukeshire	2-5 MF 43
Odlum, Jerome	THE MORGUE IS ALWAYS OPEN	Barzun & Taylor	11-4 TAD 394
O'Donnell, Lillian	AFTERSHOCK	Myrtis Broset	12 MN R3
O'Donnell, Lillian	AFTERSHOCK	David Paton	3 MT 11
O'Donnell, Lillian	THE BABY MERCHANTS	Barbara A. Buhrer	2-3 MM 3
O'Donnell, Lillian	DIAL 577 R-A-P-E	Allen J. Hubin	7-4 TAD 297
O'Donnell, Lillian	NO BUSINESS BEING A COP	Steve Lewis	3-5 MF 36
O'Donnell, Peter	THE IMPOSSIBLE VIRGIN	Martin M. Wooster	1-6 MF 54
O'Higgins, Harvey J.	THE ADVENTURES OF DETECTIVE BARNEY	Charles Shibuk	12-4 TAD 374
O'Higgins, Harvey J.	DETECTIVE DUFF UNRAVELS IT	Charles Shibuk	7-4 TAD 285
O'Higgins, Harvey J.	INSPECTOR DUFF UNRAVELS IT	Jay Jeffries	6 MY 10
Okun, Lawrence	ON THE EIGHTH DAY	Martin M. Wooster	4-5/6 PP 79
Olcott, Anthony	MURDER AT THE RED OCTOBER	Steve Lewis	5-6 MF 41
Olde, Nicholas	THE INCREDIBLE ADVENTURES OF ROWLAND HERN	Douglas G. Greene	12-3 TAD 231
Olde, Nicholas	THE INCREDIBLE ADVENTURES OF ROWLAND HERN	Charles Shibuk	9-1 TAD 60
Olden, Marc	BOOK OF SHADOWS	Joyce L. Dewes	2-1 M 26
Olden, Marc	THEY'VE KILLED ANNA	Fred Dueren	10-4 TAD 340
Olesker, J.Bradford	THE SEIGE OF SUPERPORT	Allen J. Hubin	11-4 TAD 333
Olsen, Jack	MISSING PERSONS	Allen J. Hubin	14-4 TAD 301
Olsen, Jack	NIGHT WATCH	Patricia M. Koch	4-5/6 PP 78
Olson, Donald	IF I DON'T TELL YOU	Allen J. Hubin	10-1 TAD 42
Olson, Donald	IF I DON'T TELL YOU	Steve Lewis	1A MF 27
Olson, Donald	SLEEP BEFORE EVENING	Steve Lewis	4-2 MF 35
Omre, Arthur	FLIGHT	J. Randolph Cox	3-5 PP 35
Oppenheim E.Phillips	THE GREAT IMPERSONATION	Amnon Kabatchnik	11 CL 7
Oppenheim,E.Phillips	THE GREAT IMPERSONATION	Charles Shibuk	11-3 TAD 298

Oppenheim, E.Phillips	THE GREAT IMPERSONATION	Guy M. Townsend	2-3 MF 49
Orczy, Baroness	LADY MOLLY OF SCOTLAND YARD	Allen J. Hubin	10-4 TAD 308
Orczy, Baroness	THE MAN IN THE CORNER	Michael L. Cook	5 U 31
Orczy, Baroness	THE MAN IN THE CORNER	Charles Shibuk	13-3 TAD 250
Orde, Lewis, & Bill Michaels	THE NIGHT THEY STOLE MANHATTAN	Allen J. Hubin	14-1 TAD 19
Oriol, Laurence	SHORT CIRCUIT	Robert E. Briney	5-5 MF 39
Oriol, Laurence	SHORT CIRCUIT	Robert E. Briney	4-6 MR 37
Ornitz, Samuel	CHINATOWN NIGHTS (film)	William K. Everson	7-1 TAD 40
O'Rourke, Frank	THE ABDUCTION OF VIRGINIA LEE	Bill Crider	1-5 PP 21
O'Rourke, Frank	THE ABDUCTION OF VIRGINIA LEE	Fred Dueren	10-4 TAD 340
Orr, Clifford	THE WAILING ROCK MURDERS	Charles Shibuk	6-4 TAD 268
Ørum, Poul	NOTHING BUT THE TRUTH	Barzun & Taylor	10-3 TAD 225
Ørum, Poul	NOTHING BUT THE TRUTH	Allen J. Hubin	10-3 TAD 204
Ørum, Poul	SCAPEGOAT	Susan Harris Smith	9-1 TAD 71
Osborn, John Jay,Jr.	THE MAN WHO OWNED NEW YORK	Richard Moskowitz	12 LR 20
Osmond, Marion	THE CHINESE BUNGALOW (stage)	William K. Everson	9-1 TAD 6
Ostrander, Isabel	THE CLUE IN THE AIR	Amnon Kabatchnik	6-2 TAD 115
Ostrander, Isabel	THE TWENTY-SIX CLUES	Amnon Kabatchnik	6-2 TAD 112
O'Sullivan, -	I DIE POSSESSED	Angelo Panagos	11-4 TAD 381
Otis, James	BUILDING AN AIRSHIP AT SILVER FOX FARM	C.L.Messecar	3-4 BC 372
Otis, James	THE MINUTE BOYS OF NEW YORK	C.L.Messecar	3-4 BC 372
Ottum, Bob	THE TUESDAY BLADE	Bill Crider	2-1 PP 28
Ousby, Ian	BLOODHOUNDS OF HEAVEN	Jon L. Lellenberg	11-1 TAD 24
Ousby, Ian	BLOODHOUNDS OF HEAVEN	F.M.Nevins, Jr.	1-4 MF 49
Overstreet, Bob	THE COMIC BOOK PRICE GUIDE #11	David Bates	4-3 PP 29
Ozaki, Milton K.	THE DUMMY MURDER CASE	Steve Lewis	2-3 MM 4
Pace, Eric	NIGHTINGALE	Allen J. Hubin	12-2 TAD 114
Packard, Frank L.	THE ADVENTURES OF JIMMIE DALE	Douglas G. Greene	12-3 TAD 230
Page, Marco	FAST COMPANY	Maryell Cleary	3-3 PP 29
Page, Marco	FAST COMPANY	Arthur C. Scott	2-4 MM 6
Page, Marco	THE SHADOWY THIRD	Michael Trombetta	11-2 TAD 125
Pain, Barry	THE MEMOIRS OF CONSTANTINE DIX	Douglas G. Greene	12-3 TAD 230
Palmer, Stuart	THE ADVENTURE OF THE MARKED MAN	Allen J. Hubin	7-1 TAD 63
Palmer, Stuart	ONE FRIGHTENED NIGHT (film)	William K. Everson	1-1 TAD 24
Palmer, Stuart	THE PENGUIN POOL MURDER (film)	William K. Everson	11-2 TAD 128
Palmer, Stuart	PUZZLE OF THE BLUE BANDERILLA	Angelo Panagos	11-1 TAD 27
Palmer, Stuart	THE PUZZLE OF THE SILVER PERSIAN	Angelo Panagos	11-4 TAD 381
Palmer, Stuart	THE RIDDLES OF HILDEGARDE WITHERS	Arthur C. Scott	8 MN 26
Palmer, Stuart	ROOK TAKES KNIGHT	Amnon Kabatchnik	4-2 MR 40
Panek, Leroy Lad	WATTEAU'S SHEPHERDS: THE DETECTIVE NOVEL IN BRITAIN 1914-1940	Paul McCarthy	3-4 PP 35
Panek, Leroy Lad	WATTEAU'S SHEPHERDS: THE DETECTIVE NOVEL IN BRITAIN 1914-1940	F.M.Nevins, Jr.	4-3 MF 44
Panel, Leroy Lad	WATTEAU'S SHEPHERDS: THE DETECTIVE NOVEL IN BRITAIN 1914-1940	Charles Shibuk	13-4 TAD 364
Panshin, Alexei	MASQUE WORLD	Gary Zachrich	74 PU 24
Panshin, Alexei	RITE OF PASSAGE	Gary Zachrich	70 PU 7
Panshin, Alexei	STARWELL	Gary Zachrich	70 PU 7
Panshin, Alexei	THE THURB REVOLUTION	Gary Zachrich	70 PU 7
Parish, James Robert & Michael R.Pitts	THE GREAT SCIENCE FICTION PICTURES	J. Grant Thiessen	14 SF 18
Parish, James Robert & Michael R.Pitts	THE GREAT SPY PICTURES	J. Grant Thiessen	14 SF 18
Parker, Percy S.	GOOD GIRLS DON'T GET MURDERED	Doyglas M. Armato	9-2 TAD 150
Parker, Robert B.	A SAVAGE PLACE	Steve Lewis	5-5 MF 25
Parker, Robert B.	EARLY AUTUMN	Paul Bishop	2-3 M 47
Parker, Robert B.	EARLY AUTUMN	Steve Lewis	5-2 MF 25
Parker, Robert B.	EARLY AUTUMN	Richard Moskowitz	12 LR 19

Parker, Robert B.	GOD SAVE THE CHILD	Allen J. Hubin	8-2	TAD 148
Parker, Robert B.	GOD SAVE THE CHILD	Steve Lewis	3-4	MF 39
Parker, Robert B.	GOD SAVE THE CHILD	Arthur C. Scott	1-9	MM 7
Parker, Robert B.	GOD SAVE THE CHILD	Guy M. Townsend	1-1	MF 26
Parker, Robert B.	THE GODWULF MANUSCRIPT	Allen J. Hubin	7-2	TAD 142
Parker, Robert B.	THE GODWULF MANUSCRIPT	Arthur C. Scott	1-9	MM 7
Parker, Robert B.	THE GODWULF MANUSCRIPT	Charles Shibuk	9-3	TAD 208
Parker, Robert B.	THE JUDAS GOAT	Bill Crider	3	PE 19
Parker, Robert B.	THE JUDAS GOAT	Steve Lewis	3-3	MF 37
Parker, Robert B.	THE JUDAS GOAT	Lewis Shiner	4	PE 13
Parker, Robert B.	LOOKING FOR RACHEL WALLACE	Robert C.S.Adey	5-5	MF 36
Parker, Robert B.	LOOKING FOR RACHEL WALLACE	Steve Lewis	4-3	MF 34
Parker, Robert B.	MORTAL STAKES	Barzun & Taylor	11-4	TAD 394
Parker, Robert B.	MORTAL STAKES	Stan Burns	1-8	MM 5
Parker, Robert B.	MORTAL STAKES	Larry L. French	2-1	MF 32
Parker, Robert B.	MORTAL STAKES	Allen J. Hubin	9-2	TAD 152
Parker, Robert B.	MORTAL STAKES	Charles Shibuk	10-4	TAD 361
Parker, Robert B.	PASSPORT TO PERIL	Steve Lewis	1-4	MF 40
Parker, Robert B.	PROMISED LAND	Jane S. Bakerman	5	PE 16
Parker, Robert B.	PROMISED LAND	Stan Burns	2-4	MM 4
Parker, Robert B.	PROMISED LAND	Jim Huang	7	CL 10
Parker, Robert B.	PROMISED LAND	Steve Lewis	1-1	MF 32
Parker, Robert B.	PROMISED LAND	Charles Shibuk	11-2	TAD 189
Parker, Robert B.	WILDERNESS	Steve Lewis	4-2	MF 33
Parrish, Frank	FIRE IN THE BARLEY	Allen J. Hubin	12-4	TAD 323
Parrish, Frank	STING OF THE HONEY BEE	D.E.Ath	2-2	PP 11
Parrish, Frank	STING OF THE HONEY BEE	Allen J. Hubin	13-2	TAD 96
Parrish, Frank	STING OF THE HONEY BEE	Steve Lewis	4-2	MF 31
Parry, James	THE DISCOVERY	Allen J. Hubin	12-1	TAD 10
Parry, Michel, ed.	REIGN OF TERROR	Martin M. Wooster	4-2	PP 29
Parry, Michel, ed.	THE RIVALS OF DRACULA	Mary A. Grochowski	3-1	PP 35
Parry, Michel, ed.	THE RIVALS OF FRANKENSTEIN	Mary A. Grochowski	3-1	PP 36
Parry, Michel, ed.	THE RIVALS OF FRANKENSTEIN	Martin M. Wooster	4-2	PP 29
Partos, Frank	THE STRANGER ON THE THIRD FLOOR (film)	William K. Everson	5-4	TAD 206
Pate, Janet	THE BOOK OF SLEUTHS	Allen J. Hubin	11-1	TAD 20
Patrick, Andrew	BARETTA	Myrtis Broset	2-1	MF 40
Patrick, Andrew	BARETTA: BEYOND THE LAW	Fred Dueren	11-2	TAD 192
Patrick, Q.	DEATH GOES TO SCHOOL	Douglas G. Greene	4-4	PP 24
Patrick, Q.	FILE ON FENTON & FARR	Charles Shibuk	12-4	TAD 374
Patrick, Q.	MURDER AT CAMBRIDGE	Theodore Dukeshire	2-5	MF 44
Patterson, Harry	THE VALHALLA EXCHANGE	Amnon Kabatchnik	9	CL 3
Patterson, Harry	THE VALHALLA EXCHANGE	Jeff Meyerson	1-4	MF 43
Patterson, James	THE JERICHO COMMANDMENT	Fred Dueren	14-4	TAD 364
Patterson, James	THE JERICHO COMMANDMENT	Allen J. Hubin	12-4	TAD 323
Patterson, James	THE SEASON OF THE MACHETE	Steve Lewis	2-4	MF 31
Patterson, James	THE THOMAS BERRYMAN NUMBER	Steve Lewis	1-5	MF 33
Patterson, Richard N.	THE LASKO TANGENT	Jim Huang	15	CL 8
Patterson, Richard N.	THE LASKO TANGENT	Steve Lewis	4-5	MF 31
Patterson, Richard N.	THE OUTSIDE MAN	Allen J. Hubin	14-4	TAD 301
Paul, Charlotte	A CHILD IS MISSING	Fred Dueren	11-4	TAD 396
Paul, Raymond	WHO MURDERED MARY ROGERS?	Fred Jaeger	4-6	MR 39
Pauley, Barbara Ann	VOICES LONG HUSHED	Barbara A. Buhrer	2-5	MM 5
Payn, James	LOST SIR MASSINGBERD	Allen J. Hubin	12-4	TAD 323
Pearce, William W., & William Hoffer	CAUGHT IN THE ACT: THE TRUE ADVENTURES OF A DIVORCE DETECTIVE	Marlowe Archer	4	PE 24
Pearl, Jack	VICTIMS	Amnon Kabatchnik	6-2	MR 45
Pearlman, Gilbert	THE ADVENTURE OF SHERLOCK HOLMES' SMARTER BROTHER	Jon L. Lellenberg	9-2	TAD 149
Pearlman, Gilbert	THE ADVENTURE OF SHERLOCK HOLMES' SMARTER BROTHER	Don Miller	9	MN 10
Pearson, Edmund L.	THE ADVENTURE OF THE LOST MANUSCRIPTS	Allen J. Hubin	8-1	TAD 67
Pearson, Edmund L.	SHERLOCK HOLMES AND THE DROOD MYSTERY	Stanley A. Carlin	6-1	MR 48

Pearson, Edmund L.	SHERLOCK HOLMES AND THE DROOD MYSTERY	Allen J. Hubin	6-3 TAD 191
Pearson, Edmund L.	SHERLOCK HOLMES AND THE DROOD MYSTERY	James Sandoe	14-3 TAD 273
Peck, Andrew Jay	THE DATE BEING?: A COMPENDIUM OF CHRONOLOGICAL DATA	Stanley A. Carlin	4-4 MR 40
Peck, Andrew Jay	THE DATE BEING?: A COMPENDIUM OF CHRONOLOGICAL DATA	Allen J. Hubin	4-3 TAD 180
Pecznick, Ira, & Paul Hoffman	TO DROP A DIME	Fred Dueren	11-2 TAD 192
Peebles, Niles M.	BLOOD BROTHER, BLOOD BROTHER	Steve Lewis	4-2 MF 37
Peeples, Samuel A.	THE MAN WHO DIED TWICE	Steve Lewis	1-3 MF 41
Peis, Gunter	THE MIRROR OF DECEPTION	Rod Kassel	2-2 M 56
Pemberton, Max	JEWEL MYSTERIES I HAVE KNOWN, FROM A DEALER'S NOTEBOOK	Douglas G. Greene	12-3 TAD 229
Pendleton, Don	THE NEW WAR	William L. DeAndrea	14-3 TAD 265
Pendleton, Don	ST. LOUIS SHOWDOWN	Fred Dueren	9-2 TAD 140
Penny, Rupert	POLICEMAN'S EVIDENCE	Barzun & Taylor	14-4 TAD 329
Pentecost, Hugh	A PLAGUE OF VIOLENCE	Lianne Carlin	4-2 MR 39
Pentecost, Hugh	AROUND DARK CORNERS	Angelo Panagos	14-3 TAD 272
Pentecost, Hugh	BEWARE YOUNG LOVERS	Allen J. Hubin	14-1 TAD 19
Pentecost, Hugh	BEWARE YOUNG LOVERS	Steve Lewis	4-3 MF 40
Pentecost, Hugh	DEATH AFTER BREAKFAST	Steve Lewis	5-2 MF 19
Pentecost, Hugh	DIE AFTER DARK	Steve Lewis	1-3 MF 38
Pentecost, Hugh	DON'T DROP DEAD TOMORROW	Robert E. Briney	5-1 MR 31
Pentecost, Hugh	THE EVIL THAT MEN DO	Amnon Kabatchnik	6-1 MR 47
Pentecost, Hugh	THE FOURTEEN DILEMMA	Myrtis Broset	1-10 MM 7
Pentecost, Hugh	THE FOURTEEN DILEMMA	Barbara A. Buhrer	11 MN R3
Pentecost, Hugh	THE HOMICIDAL HORSE	Ariadne Blackfriar	1-2 M 19
Pentecost, Hugh	THE HOMICIDAL HORSE	Allen J. Hubin	13-3 TAD 202
Pentecost, Hugh	HONEYMOON WITH DEATH	Barbara A. Buhrer	1-11 MM 3
Pentecost, Hugh	MURDER IN LUXURY	Mark Denning	3-2 M 39
Pentecost, Hugh	MURDER IN LUXURY	Allen J. Hubin	14-4 TAD 301
Pentecost, Hugh	RANDOM KILLER	Allen J. Hubin	12-3 TAD 206
Pentecost, Hugh	RANDOM KILLER	Steve Lewis	3-6 MF 29
Pentecost, Hugh	THE STEEL PALACE	Steve Lewis	3-1 MF 32
Pentecost, Hugh	TIME OF TERROR	Barbara A. Buhrer	11 MN R3
Pentecost, Hugh	THE 24th HORSE	Steve Lewis	2 MN 7
Pentecost, Hugh	WALKING DEAD MAN	Allen J. Hubin	6-4 TAD 267
Penzler, Otto, ed.	THE GREAT DETECTIVES	Charles Shibuk	13-1 TAD 75
Penzler, Otto	THE PRIVATE LIVES OF PRIVATE EYES, SPIES, CRIMEFIGHTERS AND OTHER GOOD GUYS	Charles Shibuk	11-2 TAD 189
Penzler, Otto, ed.	WHODUNIT? HOUDINI?: THIRTEEN TALES OF MAGIC, MURDER, MYSTERY	Robert E. Briney	11-1 TAD 26
Penzler, Otto, ed.	WHODUNIT? HOUDINI?: THIRTEEN TALES OF MAGIC, MURDER, MYSTERY	Amnon Kabatchnik	9-4 TAD 302
Penzler, Otto, ed.	WHODUNIT? HOUDINI?: THIRTEEN TALES OF MAGIC, MURDER, MYSTERY	Steve Lewis	1A MF 31
Penzler, Otto, & Chris Steinbrunner, Marvin Lachman	ENCYCLOPEDIA OF MYSTERY AND DETECTION	Allen J. Hubin	9-3 TAD 218
Penzler, Otto, & Chris Steinbrunner, Marvin Lachman	ENCYCLOPEDIA OF MYSTERY AND DETECTION	Allen J. Hubin	10-3 TAD 207
Perkins, Kenneth	VOODOO'D	Angelo Panagos	12-1 TAD 80
Perowne, Barry	RAFFLES OF THE ALBANY	Jon L. Lellenberg	9-4 TAD 308
Perowne, Barry	RAFFLES OF THE ALBANY	Martin M. Wooster	4-3 MF 44
Perowne, Barry	RAFFLES OF THE M.C.C.	Allen J. Hubin	12-4 TAD 323
Perowne, Barry	RAFFLES OF THE M.C.C.	Andy Jaysnovitch	2-4 PP 37
Perowne, Barry	RAFFLES REVISITED	Marvin Lachman	8-1 TAD 60
Perowne, Barry	RAFFLES REVISITED	Jon L. Lellenberg	8-1 TAD 60

Perry, Anne	THE CATER STREET HANGMAN	Allen J. Hubin	13-2 TAD 96
Perry, Anne	PARAGON WALK	Meera Clark	2-1 C 123
Perry, Ritchie	BISHOP'S PAWN	Allen J. Hubin	13-2 TAD 96
Perry, Ritchie	GRAND SLAM	Paul Bishop	2-3 M 47
Perry, Ritchie	HOLIDAY WITH A VENGEANCE	Stan Burns	2-3 MM 3
Perry, Ritchie	TICKET TO RIDE	Allen J. Hubin	8-1 TAD 65
Perry, Ritchie	YOUR MONEY AND YOUR WIFE	Gary Happenstand	2-2 C 158
Perry, Robin	WELCOME FOR A HERO	Steve Lewis	1-1 MF 31
Perry, Roland	PROGRAM FOR A PUPPET	M.S.Cappadonna	14-1 TAD 53
Perry, Roland	PROGRAM FOR A PUPPET	Lawrence Norman	2-1 M 27
Perry, Will	THE KREMLIN WATCHER	Allen J. Hubin	12-2 TAD 114
Perry, Will	MURDER AT THE UN	Steve Lewis	1-1 MF 33
Persico, Joseph E.	THE SPIDERWEB	M.S.Cappadonna	13-1 TAD 62
Persico, Joseph E.	THE SPIDERWEB	Allen J. Hubin	13-3 TAD 202
Peters, Elizabeth	LEGEND IN GREEN VELVET	Barbara A. Buhrer	10 MN R1
Peters, Elizabeth	THE LOVE TALKER	Jane S. Bakerman	5-5 MF 32
Peters, Elizabeth	THE MURDERS OF RICHARD III	Veronica M.Kennedy	8-4 TAD 305
Peters, Ellis	A MORBID TASTE FOR BONES	Allen J. Hubin	12-2 TAD 114
Peters, Ellis	A MORBID TASTE FOR BONES	Steve Lewis	4-4 MF 37
Peters, Ellis	THE HOUSE OF GREEN TURF	Robert E. Washer	1-4 QC 19
Peters, Ellis	MONK'S HOOD	Meera T. Clark	2-2 C 154
Peters, Ellis	NEVER PICK UP HITCH-HIKERS!	Barzun & Taylor	11-4 TAD 394
Peters, Ellis	NEVER PICK UP HITCH-HIKERS!	Guy M. Townsend	2-3 MM 5
Peters, Ellis	ONE CORPSE TOO MANY	Morgan Harrison	2-1 M 28
Peters, Ellis	ONE CORPSE TOO MANY	Allen J. Hubin	14-1 TAD 19
Peters, Ellis	ONE CORPSE TOO MANY	Steve Lewis	4-4 MF 34
Peters, Jean, ed.	COLLECTIBLE BOOKS: SOME NEW PATHS	Charlotte Laughlin	3-1 PQ 19
Petievich, Gerald	MONEY MEN	Jeff Meyerson	4-3 PP 29
Petievuch, Gerald	ONE-SHOT DEAL	Jeff Meyerson	4-3 PP 29
Petty, Barbara	THRILL	Robert J. Randisi	12-3 TAD 274
Peyrou, Manuel	THUNDER OF THE ROSES	Allen J. Hubin	6-2 TAD 114
Philips, Judson P.	A MURDER ARRANGED	Steve Lewis	3-3 MF 37
Philips, Judson P.	BACKLASH	Steve Lewis	1A MF 31
Philips, Judson P.	FIVE ROADS TO DEATH	Steve Lewis	2-5 MF 31
Philips, Judson P.	THE HAWK	Allen J. Hubin	13-4 TAD 298
Philips, Judson P.	HOT SUMMER KILLING	Charles Shibuk	2-3 TAD 199
Philips, Judson P.	WHY MURDER?	Allen J. Hubin	13-1 TAD 29
Philips, Judson P.	WHY MURDER?	Steve Lewis	3-6 MF 34
Phillips, David Atlee	THE CARLOS CONTRACT	Theodore Dukeshire	4-2 MF 50
Phillips, David Atlee	THE CARLOS CONTRACT	Allen J. Hubin	12-1 TAD 10
Phillips, James Atlee	PAGODA	Bill Crider	3-1 MF 39
Phillpott, Eden	"FOUND DROWNED"	Maryell Cleary	3-4 PP 30
Phillpott, Eden	LYCANTHROPE, THE MYSTERY OF SIR WILLIAM WOLF	Mary A. Grochowski	3-2 PP 27
Phillpott, Eden	MY ADVENTURE IN THE FLYING SCOTSMAN	Allen J. Hubin	9-4 TAD 311
Picano, Felice	THE LURE	Fred Dueren	4-4 MF 46
Pierce, Noel	MESSENGER FROM MUNICH	Allen J. Hubin	7-1 TAD 61
Pike, Robert L.	DEADLINE: 2 A.M.	Barbara A. Buhrer	2-4 MM 3
Pileggi, Nicholas	BLYE, PRIVATE EYE	Frank Occhiogrosso	10-4 TAD 310
Pirie, David	A HERITAGE OF HORROR: THE ENGLISH GOTHIC CINEMA 1946-1972	Veronica M.Kennedy	7-2 TAD 137
Pirkis, C.L.	THE EXPERIENCES OF LOVEDAY BROOKE - LADY DETECTIVE	Amnon Kabatchnik	6-4 TAD 270
Pitcairn, John J., & R. Austin Freeman	FROM A SURGEON'S DIARY	Allen J. Hubin	8-4 TAD 312
Pitts, Michael R.	FAMOUS MOVIE DETECTIVES	J. Grant Thiessen	14 SF 18
Pitts, Michael R.	HORROR FILM STARS	J. Grant Thiessen	14 SF 18
Pitts, Michael R., & James Robert Parish	THE GREAT SCIENCE FICTION PICTURES	J. Grant Thiessen	14 SF 18
Pitts, Michael R., & James Robert Parish	THE GREAT SPY PICTURES	J. Grant Thiessen	14 SF 18
Platt, Kin	THE BODY BEAUTIFUL MURDER	Allen J. Hubin	10-2 TAD 113

Platt, Kin	DEAD AS THEY COME	Lianne Carlin	5-4 MR 31
Platt, Kin	THE GIANT KILL	Paul Harwitz	2-3 M 49
Platt, Kin	MATCH POINT FOR MURDER	Stan Burns	1-5 MM 9
Platt, Kin	MATCH POINT FOR MURDER	Allen J. Hubin	8-4 TAD 309
Platt, Kin	THE PRINCESS STAKES MURDER	Allen J. Hubin	6-3 TAD 192
Platt, Kin	THE PRINCESS STAKES MURDER	James Sandoe	13-4 TAD 292
Platt, Kin	THE SCREWBALL KING MURDER	Allen J. Hubin	11-4 TAD 332
Platt, Kin	THE SCREWBALL KING MURDER	Steve Lewis	2-6 MF 33
Player, Robert	THE INGENIOUS MR. STONE	R.W.Hays	9-1 TAD 61
Poe, Edgar Allan	THE BLACK CAT (film)	William K. Everson	2-3 TAD 160
Poe, Edgar Allan	MURDERS IN THE RUE MORGUE (film)	William K. Everson	4-3 TAD 153
Pohl, Frederick	SLAVE SHIP	Gary Zachrich	64 PU 42
Pohle, Robert W.,Jr. & Douglas C. Hart	SHERLOCK HOLMES ON THE SCREEN	Kenneth Karpowicz	3 MT 15
Pointer, Michael	THE PUBLIC LIFE OF SHERLOCK HOLMES	Norman Schatell	8-4 TAD 303
Pointer, Michael	THE SHERLOCK HOLMES FILE	Jon L. Lellenberg	10-1 TAD 70
Pollock, Robert	LOOPHOLE, OR HOW TO ROB A BANK	James Jobst	2-1 MF 44
Polsky, Thomas	CURTAINS FOR THE EDITOR	Arthur C. Scott	8 MN 27
Ponder, Patricia	MURDER FOR CHARITY	Myrtis Broset	2-3 MF 55
Ponder, Patricia	MURDER FOR CHARITY	Steve Lewis	2-4 MF 31
Porter, Joyce	A MEDDLER AND HER MURDER	Maryell Cleary	4-4 PP 27
Porter, Joyce	DEAD EASY FOR DOVER	Guy M. Townsend	4-1 MF 31
Porter, Joyce	DOVER STRIKES AGAIN	Don Miller	8 MN 24
Porter, Joyce	RATHER A COMMON SORT OF CRIME	Luther Norris	3-4 MR 32
Portnoy, Howard N.	HOT RAIN	Stan Burns	13A MN 9
Portway, Christopher	ALL EXITS BARRED	Theodore Dukeshire	2-3 MF 52
Post, Melville D.	THE COMPLETE UNCLE ABNER	Charles Shibuk	10-4 TAD 311
Post, Melville D.	THE COMPLETE UNCLE ABNER	Martin M. Wooster	2-5 MF 9
Post, Melville D.	THE METHODS OF UNCLE ABNER	Allen J. Hubin	7-4 TAD 294
Post, Melville D.	THE STRANGE SCHEMES OF RANDOLPH MASON	Allen J. Hubin	6-4 TAD 265
Post, Melville D.	UNCLE ABNER: MASTER OF MYSTERIES	James Mark Purcell	10-1 TAD 58
Post, Melville D.	WALKER OF THE SECRET SERVICE	R.W.Hays	5-2 TAD 100
Post, Mortimer	CANDIDATE FOR MURDER	Hal Brodsky	8-1 TAD 54
Potter, Jeremy	A TRAIL OF BLOOD	R.W.Hays	5-2 TAD 102
Potter, Jerry Allen	A TALENT FOR DYING	Fred Dueren	14-2 TAD 184
Potter, Jerry Allen	A TALENT FOR DYING	George Kelley	3-5 PP 43
Potts, Jean	MY BROTHERS KEEPER	Barbara A. Buhrer	11 MN R13
Powell, Talmage	THE CAGE	R. Jeff Banks	9-1 TAD 62
Powell, Talmage	CORPUS DELECTABLE	Arthur C. Scott	2-1 MM 6
Powers, Thomas	THE MAN WHO KEPT THE SECRETS	Marvin Lachman	4-3 PP 25
Prager, Arthur	RASCALS AT LARGE, OR THE CLUE IN THE OLD NOSTALGIA	Lianne Carlin	5-1 MR 40
Prather, Richard S.	DEAD-BANG	Stanley A. Carlin	4-4 MR 39
Prather, Richard S.	DOUBLE IN TROUBLE	John Vining	8-3 TAD 219
Prather, Richard S.	FIND THIS WOMAN	Stephen Mertz	2-1 MF 47
Prather, Richard S.	HAVE GAT - WILL TRAVEL	Douglas G. Greene	12-3 TAD 233
Prather, Richard S.	SHELL SCOTT'S MURDER MIX	Stanley A. Carlin	3-5 MR 20
Prather, Richard S.	THE SURE THING	Arthur C. Scott	8 MN 17
Prather, Richard S.	WHO DONE IT?	Arthur C. Scott	8 MN 17
Prather, Richard S. & Stephen Marlowe	DOUBLE IN TROUBLE	Jeff Meyerson	1 PE 12
Preiss, Byron	SCHLOMO RAVEN: PUBLIC DETECTIVE	Fred Dueren	9-4 TAD 277
Preskett, S.John	MURDERS AT TURBOT TOWERS	Amnon Kabatchnik	7-3 TAD 213
Presnell, Frank G.	NO MOURNERS PRESENT	Steve Lewis	2-3 MM 4
Price, Anthony	THE '44 VINTAGE	Allen J. Hubin	12-3 TAD 207
Price, Anthony	OCTOBER MEN	Allen J. Hubin	8-1 TAD 66
Price, Anthony	OTHER PATHS TO GLORY	Robert C.S.Adey	4-3 PP 24
Price, Anthony	OTHER PATHS TO GLORY	Allen J. Hubin	8-3 TAD 227
Price, Anthony	OUR MAN IN CAMELOT	Stan Burns	10 MN R4
Price, Anthony	WAR GAME	Jack Gendelman	2 CL 2
Priestley,John B.	THE DOOMSDAY MEN: AN ADVENTURE	James Sandoe	14-4 TAD 366
Priestley,John B.	THE OLD DARK HOUSE (film)	William K. Everson	4-3 TAD 144
Priestley,John B.	SALT IS LEAVING	Robert E. Washer	17 X 70

Priestley, John B.	SALT IS LEAVING	Barzun & Taylor	11-2 TAD 204
Proctor, Maurice	EXERCISE HOODWINK	Amnon Kabatchnik	4-2 MR 40
Proctor, Maurice	HOMICIDE BLONDE	Lianne Carlin	3-5 MR 22
Profumo, Tony	THE MIME	Fred Dueren	11-4 TAD 396
Pronzini, Bill	BLOWBACK	Allen J. Hubin	10-3 TAD 204
Pronzini, Bill	BLOWBACK	Steve Lewis	1-5 MF 32
Pronzini, Bill	BLOWBACK	Peter Pross	2-3 PP 33
Pronzini, Bill, ed.	THE EDGAR WINNERS	Allen J. Hubin	13-3 TAD 203
Pronzini, Bill	GAMES	Steve Lewis	1-2 MF 25
Pronzini, Bill	GAMES	Charles Shibuk	11-3 TAD 298
Pronzini, Bill	HOODWINK	Gary Happenstand	2-2 C 159
Pronzini, Bill	HOODWINK	Allen J. Hubin	14-4 TAD 301
Pronzini, Bill	HOODWINK	Steve Lewis	5-5 MF 27
Pronzini, Bill	LABYRINTH	Paul Harwitz	2-1 M 29
Pronzini, Bill	LABYRINTH	Allen J. Hubin	13-3 TAD 203
Pronzini, Bill	LABYRINTH	Steve Lewis	4-3 MF 38
Pronzini, Bill	LABYRINTH	F.M.Nevins, Jr.	4-3 MF 43
Pronzini, Bill, ed.	MIDNIGHT SPECIALS	Allen J. Hubin	11-1 TAD 17
Pronzini, Bill, ed.	MIDNIGHT SPECIALS	George Kelley	1-6 MF 46
Pronzini, Bill, ed.	MIDNIGHT SPECIALS	Martin M. Wooster	3-2 PP 30
Pronzini, Bill	THE SNATCH	Barzun & Taylor	10-2 TAD 127
Pronzini, Bill	SNOWBOUND	Allen J. Hubin	7-4 TAD 295
Pronzini, Bill	THE STALKER	Lianne Carlin	4-4 MR 37
Pronzini, Bill	THE STALKER	Amnon Kabatchnik	6-1 MR 46
Pronzini, Bill	THE STALKER	Robert E. Washer	3-1 QC 19
Pronzini, Bill	UNDERCURRENT	Allen J. Hubin	6-4 TAD 266
Pronzini, Bill	UNDERCURRENT	Steve Lewis	5A MY 2
Pronzini, Bill	THE VANISHED	Robert C.S.Adey	4-1 PP 30
Pronzini, Bill, ed.	WEREWOLF!	Mary A. Grochowski	3-1 PP 36
Pronzini, Bill, ed.	WEREWOLF!	Martin M. Wooster	2-6 PP 39
Pronzini, Bill, & Joe Gores	TRICKS AND TREATS	Amnon Kabatchnik	10-1 TAD 64
Pronzini, Bill, & Barry Malzberg	ACTS OF MERCY	Mary A. Grochowski	1-2 PP 24
Pronzini, Bill, & Barry Malzberg	ACTS OF MERCY	Allen J. Hubin	11-2 TAD 116
Pronzini, Bill, & Barry Malzberg	ACTS OF MERCY	Amnon Kabatchnik	11 CL 9
Pronzini, Bill, & Barry Malzberg	ACTS OF MERCY	F.M.Nevins, Jr.	2-5 MF 37
Pronzini, Bill, & Barry Malzberg	NIGHT SCREAMS	Mary A. Grochowski	2-6 PP 36
Pronzini, Bill, & Barry Malzberg	NIGHT SCREAMS	Allen J. Hubin	13-1 TAD 29
Pronzini, Bill, & Barry Malzberg	NIGHT SCREAMS	Charles Shibuk	14-3 TAD 267
Pronzini, Bill, & Barry Malzberg	THE RUNNING OF BEASTS	Myrtis Broset	2-3 MM 3
Pronzini, Bill, & Barry Malzberg	THE RUNNING OF BEASTS	Barbara A. Buhrer	10 MN R1
Pronzini, Bill, & Barry Malzberg	THE RUNNING OF BEASTS	Allen J. Hubin	9-3 TAD 223
Pronzini, Bill, & Barry Malzberg	THE RUNNING OF BEASTS	George Kelley	1-2 MF 37
Pronzini, Bill, & Barry Malzberg	THE RUNNING OF BEASTS	F.M.Nevins, Jr.	1-1 MF 17
Pronzini, Bill, & Barry Malzberg	THE RUNNING OF BEASTS	Charles Shibuk	10-3 TAD 239
Pronzini, Bill, & Collin Wilcox	TWOSPOT	Bill Crider	2-6 MF 36
Pronzini, Bill, & Collin Wilcox	TWOSPOT	Mary A. Grochowski	2-6 PP 35
Pronzini, Bill, & Collin Wilcox	TWOSPOT	Allen J. Hubin	12-3 TAD 207
Pronzini, Bill, & Collin Wilcox	TWOSPOT	Steve Lewis	3-1 MF 36

Proud, Franklin M.	THE WALKING WIND	Ralph Diffinetti	5 PE 20
Pullein-Thompson, J.	GIN AND MURDER	Barzun & Taylor	9-3 TAD 237
Punshon, E.R.	DEATH AMONG THE SUNBATHERS	Edward Lauterbach	7-4 TAD 288
Punshon, E.R.	MYSTERY VILLA	Steve Lewis	5-6 MF 34
Purtell, Joseph	THE TIFFANY CAPER	Allen J. Hubin	8-1 TAD 65
Puzo, Mario	INSIDE LAS VEGAS	Amnon Kabatchnik	11-4 TAD 406
Quayle, Eric	THE COLLECTOR'S BOOK OF DETECTIVE FICTION	Amnon Kabatchnik	5-6 MR 39
Quayle, Eric	THE COLLECTOR'S BOOK OF DETECTIVE FICTION	F.M.Nevins, Jr.	6-2 TAD 110
Queen, Ellery	A FINE AND PRIVATE PLACE	F.M.Nevins, Jr.	4-4 TAD 245
Queen, Ellery	A FINE AND PRIVATE PLACE	Robert E. Washer	3-2 QC 18
Queen, Ellery	A STUDY IN TERROR	Jeff Meyerson	2-3 MF 56
Queen, Ellery	A STUDY IN TERROR	James Sandoe	14-3 TAD 272
Queen, Ellery	AND ON THE EIGHTH DAY	Don Miller	9 MN R8
Queen, Ellery	THE BLACK HEARTS MURDER	Robert E. Washer	2-2 QC 14
Queen, Ellery	THE CAMPUS MURDERS	Robert E. Washer	1-4 QC 20
Queen, Ellery	THE CASE OF THE HEADLESS HIGHNESS (jugsaw puzzle)	Edward Lauterbach	7-4 TAD 293
Queen, Ellery	CAT OF MANY TAILS	Don Miller	11 MN R7
Queen, Ellery	COP OUT	Robert E. Washer	1-3 QC 25
Queen, Ellery	THE DETECTIVE SHORT STORY: A BIBLIOGRAPHY	Charles Shibuk	3-1 TAD 37
Queen, Ellery	ELLERY QUEEN (TV)	F.M.Nevins, Jr.	8-3 TAD 224
Queen, Ellery	ELLERY QUEEN, MASTER DETECTIVE	Guy M. Townsend	2-1 MM 6
Queen, Ellery, ed.	ELLERY QUEEN'S ANTHOLOGY (1964)	Martin M. Wooster	3-3 PP 29
Queen, Ellery, ed.	ELLERY QUEEN'S ANTHOLOGY (1965)	Martin M. Wooster	1-4 PQ 49
Queen, Ellery, ed.	ELLERY QUEEN'S ANTHOLOGY (1967 Mid-Year Edition)	Martin M. Wooster	1-4 PQ 50
Queen, Ellery, ed.	ELLERY QUEEN'S ANTHOLOGY (Spring-Summer 1974)	Marvin Lachman	7-3 TAD 216
Queen, Ellery, ed.	ELLERY QUEEN'S GOLDEN 13	Robert E. Washer	3-1 QC 18
Queen, Ellery, ed.	ELLERY QUEEN'S GRAND SLAM	Robert E. Washer	3-1 QC 18
Queen, Ellery, ed.	ELLERY QUEEN'S HEADLINERS: 26th MYSTERY ANNUAL	James Mark Purcell	5-1 MR 34
Queen, Ellery, ed.	ELLERY QUEEN'S HEADLINERS	Robert E. Washer	3-2 QC 18
Queen, Ellery, ed.	ELLERY QUEEN'S MINIMYSTERIES	Robert E. Washer	2-2 QC 14
Queen, Ellery, ed.	ELLERY QUEEN'S MURDERCADE	Allen J. Hubin	8-3 TAD 230
Queen, Ellery, ed.	ELLERY QUEEN'S JAPANESE GOLDEN DOZEN	Barzun & Taylor	12-1 TAD 33
Queen, Ellery, ed.	ELLERY QUEEN'S JAPANESE GOLDEN DOZEN	J. Randolph Cox	11-4 TAD 402
Queen, Ellery	KISS AND KILL	Robert E. Washer	1-4 QC 20
Queen, Ellery	THE LAST WOMAN IN HIS LIFE	Robert E. Washer	2-2 QC 14
Queen, Ellery	THE LAST WOMAN IN HIS LIFE	Robert E. Washer	3-4 TAD 270
Queen, Ellery, ed.	MASTERPIECES OF MYSTERY	Paul McCarthy	2-1 MF 43
Queen, Ellery	THE MISADVENTURES OF SHERLOCK HOLMES	Mary A. Grochowski	3-3 MF 40
Queen, Ellery	MURDER MENU	Robert E. Washer	2-2 QC 14
Queen, Ellery, ed.	101 YEARS' ENTERTAINMENT: THE GREAT DETECTIVE STORIES 1841-1941	Francis C. Brown	2-2 TAD 121
Queen, Ellery	QUEEN'S BUREAU OF INVESTIGATION	Douglas G. Greene	12-3 TAD 233
Queen, Ellery	THE ROMAN HAT MYSTERY	Allen J. Hubin	12-2 TAD 114
Queen, Ellery	THE ROMAN HAT MYSTERY	Marvin Lachman	2-1 QC 13
Queen, Ellery	TEN DAYS WONDER (film)	F.M.Nevins, Jr.	5-4 TAD 228
Queen, Ellery	THE TRAGEDY OF X	Charles Shibuk	11-4 TAD 403
Queen, Ellery	THE TRAGEDY OF X	Martin M. Wooster	2-4 MF 40
Queen, Ellery	THE VANISHING CORPSE	F.M.Nevins, Jr.	1-6 MR 3
Quentin, Patrick	PUZZLE FOR FIENDS	Steve Lewis	4-4 MF 40
Quentin, Patrick	PUZZLE FOR FIENDS	Charles Shibuk	13-1 TAD 75
Quentin, Patrick	A PUZZLE FOR FOOLS	Lianne Carlin	3-3 MR 31
Quentin, Patrick	A PUZZLE FOR FOOLS	Charles Shibuk	13-4 TAD 364
Quentin, Patrick	PUZZLE FOR PILGRIMS	Charles Shibuk	13-2 TAD 135
Quentin, Patrick	PUZZLE FOR PLAYERS	Charles Shibuk	13-3 TAD 250

Quest, Erica	THE OCTOBER CABARET	Mary A. Grochowski	3-3 PP 30
Quest, Erica	THE OCTOBER CABARET	Steve Lewis	3-6 MF 41
Quest, Erica	THE SILVER CASTLE	Steve Lewis	3-3 MF 36
Quin, B.G.	THE MURDER REHEARSAL	Amnon Kabatchnik	9-2 TAD 145
Quinn, Chelsea	MUSIC WHEN SWEET VOICES DIE	Allen J. Hubin	12-2 TAD 117
Quinn, Derry	THE LIMBO CONNECTION	Charles Shibuk	12-3 TAD 255
Quinn, Seabury	THE ADVENTURES OF JULES DE GRANDIN	Martin M. Wooster	1-2 MF 42
Quinn, Seabury	IS THE DEVIL A GENTLEMAN?	Lianne Carlin	4-4 MR 37
Quinn, Seabury	IS THE DEVIL A GENTLEMAN?	J. Randolph Cox	4-6 MR 39
Quinn, Simon	LAST RITES FOR THE VULTURE	Bill Crider	8-4 TAD 306
Quinn, Simon	THE LAST TIME I SAW HELL	Bill Crider	8-4 TAD 306
Quinnel, A.J.	MAN ON FIRE	Allen J. Hubin	14-3 TAD 219
Rabe, Peter	AGREEMENT TO KILL	Steve Lewis	1-2 MF 24
Racina, Thom	SWEET REVENGE	Steve Lewis	2-4 MF 30
Rackham, John	DANGER FROM VEGA	Gary Zachrich	63 PU 52
Rackham, John	THE PROXIMA PROJECT	Gary Zachrich	71 PU 21
Rackham, John	TREASURE OF TAU CETI	Gary Zachrich	73 PU 34
Rackham, John	WE, THE VENUSIANS	Gary Zachrich	62 PU 30
Rackin, Martin	THE ENFORCER (film)	A.J.Wright	9-1 TAD 27
Radcliffe, Elsa J.	GOTHIC NOVELS OF THE TWENTIETH CENTURY: AN ANNOTATED BIBLIOGRAPHY	Allen J. Hubin	13-1 TAD 64
Radley, Sheila	THE CHIEF INSPECTOR'S DAUGHTER	Jane S. Bakerman	5-4 MF 34
Radley, Sheila	THE CHIEF INSPECTOR'S DAUGHTER	Steve Lewis	5-2 MF 22
Radley, Sheila	DEATH IN THE MORNING	Jane S. Bakerman	5-2 MF 31
Radley, Sheila	DEATH IN THE MORNING	Barzun & Taylor	13-3 TAD 209
Radley, Sheila	DEATH IN THE MORNING	Allen J. Hubin	13-1 TAD 29
Radley, Sheila	DEATH IN THE MORNING	Charles Shibuk	14-2 TAD 183
Rae, Hugh C.	THE INTERVIEW	Robert E. Washer	2-1 QC 18
Rae, Hugh C.	THE ROOKERY	Robert W. Hahn	9-2 TAD 147
Rafferty, S.S.	FATAL FLOURISHES	Douglas G. Greene	12-3 TAD 273
Rafferty, S.S.	FATAL FLOURISHES	Steven Miller	3-3 PP 33
Ralston, Gilbert	MURDER'S MONEY	Bill Crider	9-2 TAD 146
Ramsey, Gordon C.	AGATHA CHRISTIE: MISTRESS OF MYSTERY	Charles Shibuk	1-1 TAD 25
Rand, Ayn	NIGHT OF JANUARY 16th	Amnon Kabatchnik	6-4 TAD 260
Randall, Bob	THE FAN	Mary Groff	1-1 PP 23
Randall, Bob	THE FAN	Jim Huang	7 CL 10
Randisi, Robert J.	THE DISAPPEARANCE OF PENNY	Charles Shibuk	14-2 TAD 183
Ransome, Stephen	THE UNSPEAKABLE	Gary Crews	3-3 MF 45
Rath, Virginia	AN EXCELLENT NIGHT FOR A MURDER	Steve Lewis	3-6 MF 36
Rathbone, Julian	THE EURO-KILLERS	Allen J. Hubin	13-4 TAD 297
Rathbone, Julian	KILL CURE	Robert W. Hahn	9-2 TAD 146
Rathbone, Julian	WITH MY KNIVES I KNOW I'M GOOD	Amnon Kabatchnik	3-6 MR 21
Rausch, G.Jay, & Elmore Mundell	THE DETECTIVE SHORT STORY: A BIBLIOGRAPHY AND INDEX	Allen J. Hubin	8-1 TAD 65
Rawson, Clayton	DEATH FROM A TOP HAT	Arthur C. Scott	1-9 MM 7
Rawson, Clayton	THE GREAT MERLINI: THE COMPLETE SHORT STORIES OF THE MAGICIAN DETECTIVE	Douglas G. Greene	3-4 PP 36
Rawson, Clayton	THE GREAT MERLINI: THE COMPLETE SHORT STORIES OF THE MAGICIAN DETECTIVE	Allen J. Hubin	13-1 TAD 29
Ray, Robert	CAGE OF MIRRORS	Allen J. Hubin	14-3 TAD 219
Raymond, Alex, & Dashiell Hammett	SECRET AGENT X-9	J. Randolph Cox	12-4 TAD 369
Raymond, Clifford	THE MEN ON THE DEAD MAN'S CHEST	Steve Lewis	2-5 MF 32
Reade, Bill	THE IBIZA SYNDICATE	Steve Lewis	2-1 MF 29
Reagan, Thomas B.	BLOOD MONEY	Robert E. Washer	3-5 MR 19
Reagan, Thomas B.	THE INSIDE-OUT HEIST	Marvin Lachman	4-4 MR 33
Reasoner, James M.	TEXAS WIND	Bill Crider	4-6 MF 38
Reasoner, James M.	TEXAS WIND	Steve Lewis	5-5 MF 26
Reasoner, James M.	TEXAS WIND	Robert J. Randisi	4-2 PP 32

Reese, John	OMAR, FATS AND TRIXIE	Fred Dueren	10-2 TAD 131
Reeve, Arthur B.	ENTER CRAIG KENNEDY	Angelo Panagos	14-3 TAD 272
Reeve, Arthur B.	THE EXPLOITS OF ELAINE (film)	William K. Everson	3-2 TAD 79
Reeves, John	MURDER BY MICROPHONE	Allen J. Hubin	12-1 TAD 10
Regester, Seeley	THE DEAD LETTER	Allen J. Hubin	7-3 TAD 214
Regester, Seeley	THE DEAD LETTER	Allen J. Hubin	13-1 TAD 30
Reginald, Robert	SCIENCE FICTION AND FANTASY LITERATURE, A CHECKLIST 1700-1974 & CONTEMPORARY SCIENCE FICTION AUTHORS	Michael L. Cook	6 U 40
Reginald, Robert	SCIENCE FICTION AND FANTASY LITERATURE, A CHECKLIST 1700-1974 & CONTEMPORARY SCIENCE FICTION AUTHORS	Bill Crider	2-4 PQ 48
Reginald, Robert	SCIENCE FICTION AND FANTASY LITERATURE, A CHECKLIST 1700-1974 & CONTEMPORARY SCIENCE FICTION AUTHORS	J. Grant Thiessen	9 SF 47
Reginald, Robert, & M.R.Burgess	CUMULATIVE PAPERBACK INDEX 1939-1959	Charlotte Laughlin	4-2 PQ 46
Reginald, Robert, & M.R.Burgess	CUMULATIVE PAPERBACK INDEX 1939-1959	Billy C. Lee	1-1 PQ 39
Reginald, Robert, & M.R.Burgess	CUMULATIVE PAPERBACK INDEX 1939-1959	William Lyles	2-2 PQ 37
Reid, Philip	THE FUN HOUSE	Fred Dueren	9-3 TAD 213
Reid, Philip	THE FUN HOUSE	Allen J. Hubin	7-4 TAD 296
Reid, Philip	HARRIS IN WONDERLAND	Robert C.S.Adey	4-5/6 PP 74
Reilly, John M., ed.	TWENTIETH-CENTURY CRIME AND MYSTERY WRITERS	Barzun & Taylor	14-2 TAD 142
Reilly, John M., ed.	TWENTIETH-CENTURY CRIME AND MYSTERY WRITERS	Allen J. Hubin	14-1 TAD 54
Reilly, John M., ed.	TWENTIETH-CENTURY CRIME AND MYSTERY WRITERS	Steve Lewis	4-5 MF 27
Reisman, John	P.S. YOUR SHRINK IS DEAD	Fred Dueren	13-2 TAD 136
Reiss, Bob	SUMMER FIRES	Allen J. Hubin	14-3 TAD 219
Renauld, Ron	FADE TO BLACK	Morgan Harrison	2-2 M 56
Rendell, Ruth	A DEMON IN MY VIEW	Jane S. Bakerman	10-1 TAD 63
Rendell, Ruth	A DEMON IN MY VIEW	Steve Lewis	1-3 MF 37
Rendell, Ruth	A GUILTY THING SURPRISED	Gerie Frazier	3-4 MF 44
Rendell, Ruth	A JUDGEMENT IN STONE	Gerie Frazier	3-4 MF 44
Rendell, Ruth	A JUDGEMENT IN STONE	Allen J. Hubin	12-2 TAD 115
Rendell, Ruth	A SLEEPING LIFE	Jane S. Bakerman	3-2 MF 45
Rendell, Ruth	A SLEEPING LIFE	Gary Crews	3-2 MF 46
Rendell, Ruth	A SLEEPING LIFE	Allen J. Hubin	12-1 TAD 11
Rendell, Ruth	A SLEEPING LIFE	Steve Lewis	3-3 MF 38
Rendell, Ruth	DEATH NOTES	Meera T. Clark	2-2 C 154
Rendell, Ruth	DEATH NOTES	Steve Lewis	5-6 MF 38
Rendell, Ruth	THE FACE OF TRESPASS	Allen J. Hubin	7-4 TAD 295
Rendell, Ruth	THE FALLEN CURTAIN	Gerie Frazier	3-4 MF 45
Rendell, Ruth	FROM DOON WITH DEATH	Barzun & Taylor	11-2 TAD 204
Rendell, Ruth	FROM DOON WITH DEATH	Jim McCahery	2-3 PP 28
Rendell, Ruth	THE LAKE OF DARKNESS	Allen J. Hubin	14-3 TAD 219
Rendell, Ruth	THE LAKE OF DARKNESS	Steve Lewis	5-1 MF 22
Rendell, Ruth	MAKE DEATH LOVE ME	Jane S. Bakerman	13-1 TAD 61
Rendell, Ruth	MAKE DEATH LOVE ME	Mary Groff	15 CL 4
Rendell, Ruth	MEANS OF EVIL	Douglas G. Greene	4-2 PP 32
Rendell, Ruth	MEANS OF EVIL	Steve Lewis	4-3 MF 34
Rendell, Ruth	SHAKE HANDS FOREVER	Gerie Frazier	3-4 MF 45
Rendell, Ruth	SHAKE HANDS FOREVER	Allen J. Hubin	9-1 TAD 74
Rendell, Ruth	SOME LIE AND SOME DIE	Gerie Frazier	3-4 MF 44
Rendell, Ruth	SOME LIE AND SOME DIE	Allen J. Hubin	7-1 TAD 63
Rendell, Ruth	TO FEAR A PAINTED DEVIL	Gerie Frazier	3-4 MF 45
Rendell, Ruth	WOLF TO THE SLAUGHTER	Gerie Frazier	3-4 MF 45
Renn, Chris	THE VIOLENT AIR	Allen J. Hubin	14-3 TAD 219
Rennert, Maggie	CIRCLE OF DEATH	Allen J. Hubin	8-3 TAD 229
Rennert, Maggie	OPERATION ALCESTIS	Barbara A. Buhrer	1-8 MM 5

Reno, Marie	FINAL PROOF	Pearl G. Aldrich	9-4 TAD 307
Reno, Marie	FINAL PROOF	Barzun & Taylor	11-4 TAD 394
Reybold, Malcolm	THE INSPECTOR'S OPINION	Allen J. Hubin	9-2 TAD 152
Reynolds, G.W.M.	WAGNER, THE WEHR-WOLF	David Brownell	9-1 TAD 71
Rhode, John	THE ALARM	Charles Shibuk	12-4 TAD 373
Rhode, John	THE CLAVERTON MYSTERY	Charles Shibuk	10-2 TAD 139
Rhode, John	DEATH IN HARLEY STREET	Charles Shibuk	7-3 TAD 209
Rhode, John	THE FATAL GARDEN	Barzun & Taylor	14-2 TAD 143
Rhode, John	HENDON'S FIRST CASE	Paul McCarthy	4-4 MF 44
Rhode, John	THREE COUSINS DIE	Steve Lewis	3-2 MF 39
Rhode, John, & Carter Dickson	FATAL DESCENT	Mary A. Grochowski	1-3 PP 26
Rhodes, Russell	THE HEROD CONSPIRACY	Charles Jardinier	2-2 M 58
Rice, Craig	THE LUCKY STIFF	Theodore Dukeshire	2-5 MF 43
Rice, Craig	THE NAME IS MALONE	Arthur C. Scott	2-2 MM 5
Rice, Craig	THE SUNDAY PIGEON MURDERS	Theodore Dukeshire	2-5 MF 43
Rice, Craig	TELEFAIR	Angelo Panagos	11-4 TAD 381
Rice, Jeff	THE NIGHT STALKER	Veronica M.Kennedy	8-4 TAD 301
Rich, A.T.	THE CURATE FINDS A CORPSE	Hal Brodsky	9-3 TAD 231
Richards, Stanley, ed.	BEST MYSTERY AND SUSPENSE PLAYS OF THE MODERN THEATRE	Lianne Carlin	4-4 MR 37
Richards, Stanley, ed	TEN CLASSIC MYSTERY AND SUSPENSE PLAYS OF THE MODERN THEATRE	Marvin Lachman	6-2 MR 49
Richards, Stanley, ed	BEST MYSTERY AND SUSPENSE PLAYS OF THE MODERN THEATRE	Charles Shibuk	4-4 TAD 243
Richards, Stanley, ed	BEST MYSTERY AND SUSPENSE PLAYS OF THE MODERN THEATRE	Charles Shibuk	13-2 TAD 135
Richmond	RICHMOND, OR SCENES IN THE LIFE OF A BOW STREET OFFICER	Douglas G. Greene	12-3 TAD 228
Richmond	RICHMOND: SCENES IN THE LIFE OF A BOW STREET RUNNER	Allen J. Hubin	9-4 TAD 311
Richmond, Walt & Leigh	PHOENIX SHIP	Gary Zachrich	74 PU 24
Ridgeway, Jason	ADAM'S FALL	John Vining	8-4 TAD 297
Ridley, Arnold, & Bernard Merivale	THE WRECKER (film)	William K. Everson	4-1 TAD 36
Riefe, Alan	THE LADY KILLERS	Steve Lewis	8 MN 15
Riefe, Alan	TYGER AT BAY	Steve Lewis	1A MF 26
Riefe, Alan	TYGER BY THE TAIL	Steve Lewis	1A MF 29
Rifkin, Shepard	LADYFINGERS	Jeffrey Meyerson	11-2 TAD 126
Rifkin, Shepard	McQUAID	Allen J. Hubin	7-2 TAD 142
Rifkin, Shepard	McQUAID IN AUGUST	Steve Lewis	3-6 MF 29
Rifkin, Shepard	THE MURDERER VINE	Jon L. Breen	5-2 MR 42
Rigsby, Howard	LUCINDA	Charles Shibuk	8-4 TAD 298

Riley, Dick, &
  Pam McAllister
	THE BEDSIDE, BATHTUB & ARMCHAIR
	  COMPANION TO AGATHA CHRISTIE
		F.M.Nevins, Jr.	1-2 C 134

Riley, Dick, ¢
  Pam McAllister
	THE BEDSIDE, BATHTUB & ARMCHAIR
	  COMPANION TO AGATHA CHRISTIE
		F.M.Nevins, Jr.	4-1 MF 33

Riley, Dick, &
  Pam McAllister
	THE BEDSIDE, BATHTUB & ARMCHAIR
	  COMPANION TO AGATHA CHRISTIE
		Ruth Windfeldt	1-1 M 30

Rilla, Wolf	THE CHINESE CONSORTIUM	Steve Lewis	4-5 MF 34
Rinehart,Mary Roberts	THE BAT	Bruce R. Beaman	8-1 TAD 53
Rinehart,Mary Roberts	THE CIRCULAR STAIRCASE	Charles Shibuk	10-4 TAD 311
Rinehart,Mary Roberts	THE CIRCULAR STAIRCASE	Martin M. Wooster	1-5 MF 39
Rippon, Marion	THE NINTH TENTACLE	Allen J. Hubin	8-2 TAD 150
Ritchie, Jack	A NEW LEAF AND OTHER STORIES	Ray Puechner	5-4 TAD 228
Roberts,C.E.Bechofer & George Goodchild	THE DEAR OLD GENTLEMAN	Barzun & Taylor	12-3 TAD 263
Roberts, Keith	PAVANE	Gary Zachrich	74 PU 37
Roberts, Willo Davis	WHITE JADE	Allen J. Jubin	8-2 TAD 149
Robeson, Kenneth	DEMON ISLAND	Fred Dueren	8-4 TAD 295
Robeson, Kenneth	THE EVIL GNOME	Steve Lewis	1A MF 24
Robeson, Kenneth	THE MAD GOBLIN	Florence Breen	5 DQ 4
Robeson, Laurie	THE PERFECT CORPSE	Fred Dueren	11-2 TAD 192
Robinson, Frank M.	THE POWER	Charles Shibuk	11-1 TAD 96

Robinson, Spider, & Jeanne	STARDANCE	J. Grant Thiessen	9 SF 46
Robinson, Timothy	WHEN SCHOLARS FALL	James Sandoe	14-3 TAD 273
Robyns, Gwen	THE MYSTERY OF AGATHA CHRISTIE	Charles Shibuk	12-4 TAD 369
Roche, Arthur Somers	PENTHOUSE (film)	William K. Everson	9-2 TAD 92
Roffman, Jan	MASK OF WORDS	Ruth Withee	3-2 MR 10
Roffman, Jan	ONE WREATH WITH LOVE	Steve Lewis	3-3 MF 31
Roffman, Jan	WHY SOMEONE HAD TO DIE	Barbara A. Buhrer	2-5 MM 6
Rogers, Alva	A REQUIEM FOR ASTOUNDING	Ed Wood	62 PU 28
Rogers, Barbara	PROJECT WEB	Allen J. Hubin	13-4 TAD 297
Rogers, Joel Townsley	THE RED RIGHT HAND	Mary A. Grochowski	2-5 MF 42
Rohmer, Elizabeth S. & Cay Van Ash	MASTER OF VILLAINY: A BIOGRAPHY OF SAX ROHMER	Lianne Carlin	5-4 MR 34
Rohmer, Elizabeth S. & Cay Van Ash	MASTER OF VILLAINY: A BIOGRAPHY OF SAX ROHMER	J. Randolph Cox	5-4 TAD 230
Rohmer, Sax	THE DREAM DETECTIVE	Charles Shibuk	11-1 TAD 97
Rohmer, Sax	THE FIENDISH PLOT OF DR. FU MANCHU (film)	Thomas Godfrey	2-3 M 46
Rohmer, Sax	THE SECRET OF HOLM PEEL AND OTHER STRANGE STORIES	Robert E. Briney	4-1 MR 36
Rohmer, Sax	THE WRATH OF FU MANCHU	Martin M. Wooster	10 MN R8
Rolls, Anthony	FAMILY MATTERS	Charles Shibuk	8-2 TAD 137
Rolls, Anthony	LOBELIA GROVE	Charles Shibuk	8-2 TAD 138
Rolt-Wheeler, Francis	THE BOY WITH THE UNITED STATES CENSUS	C.L.Messecar	3-3 BC 352
Rolt-Wheeler, Francis	THE BOY WITH THE U.S.FISHERIES	C.L.Messecar	3-2 BC 319
Rolt-Wheeler, Francis	THE BOY WITH THE UNITED STATES FORESTERS	C.L.Messecar	3-2 BC 320
Ronald, James	MURDER FOR CASH	Charles Shibuk	12-4 TAD 373
Ronald, James	MURDER IN THE FAMILY	Charles Shibuk	9-3 TAD 230
Ronald, James	THE WAY OUT	Charles Shibuk	9-4 TAD 313
Ronns, Edward	NO PLACE TO LIVE	Angelo Panagos	11-1 TAD 27
Ronns, Edward	STATE DEPARTMENT MURDERS	Stephen Mertz	2-1 MF 48
Ronns, Edward	THEY ALL RAN AWAY	Richard Moskowitz	5 LR 3
Roos, Kelley	BAD TRIP	Jon L. Breen	5-1 MR 32
Roos, Kelley	MURDER ON MARTHA'S VINEYARD	Steve Lewis	5-5 MF 23
Roos, Kelley	MURDER ON MARTHA'S VINEYARD	Gary Warren Niebuhr	4-5/6 PP 79
Roosevelt, Capt.Wyn	FRONTIER BOYS IN THE SOUTH SEAS	C.L.Messecar	3-2 BC 318
Rooth, Anne Reed, & James P. White	THE NINTH CAR	Allen J. Hubin	12-4 TAD 323
Roper, L.V.	HOOKERS DON'T GO TO HEAVEN	Steve Lewis	1-2 MF 26
Roscoe, Mike	ONE TEAR FOR MY GRAVE	Steve Lewis	2-5 MF 33
Roscoe, Mike	SLICE OF HELL	Angelo Panagos	13-3 TAD 270
Rose, Geoffrey	A CLEAR ROAD TO ARCHANGEL	Allen J. Hubin	10-2 TAD 112
Rosenbaum, Ron	MURDER AT ELAINE'S	Steve Lewis	3-5 MF 39
Rosenberg, Samuel	NAKED IS THE BEST DISGUISE	Harold Hughesdon	7-4 TAD 297
Rosenblatt, Julia C. & F.H.Sonnenschmidt	DINKING WITH SHERLOCK HOLMES	Jon L. Lellenberg	10-1 TAD 70
Rosenblum, Robert	THE GOOD THIEF	Allen J. Hubin	8-1 TAD 65
Rosenblum, Robert	THE MUSHROOM CAVE	Fred Dueren	10-1 TAD 52
Rosenblum, Robert	THE SWETTHEART DEAL	Charles Shibuk	10-3 TAD 239
Ross, Albert	IF I KNEW WHAT I WAS DOING	Allen J. Hubin	8-1 TAD 65
Ross, Angus	THE AMPURIAS EXCHANGE	David Doerrer	4-1 PP 34
Ross, Angus	THE AMPURIAS EXCHANGE	Allen J. Hubin	10-4 TAD 309
Ross, Angus	THE AMPURIAS EXCHANGE	Steve Lewis	2-1 MF 25
Ross, Angus	THE BURGOS CONTRACT	David Doerrer	4-1 PP 35
Ross, Angus	THE HAMBURG SWITCH	David Doerrer	4-1 PP 35
Ross, Angus	THE HAMBURG SWITCH	Fred Dueren	4-4 MF 46
Ross, Angus	THE HAMBURG SWITCH	Charles Jardinier	1-3 M 21
Ross, Barnaby	THE TRAGEDY OF X	Mary A. Grochowski	2-4 PP 30
Ross, Frank	THE 65th TAPE	Allen J. Hubin	13-1 TAD 30
Ross, Hal	THE FLEUR-DE-LIS AFFAIR	Steve Lewis	1-1 MF 30
Ross, James	THEY DON'T DANCE MUCH	Allen J. Hubin	8-3 TAD 229
Ross, Jonathan	THE BURNING OF BILLY TOOBER	Steve Lewis	1A MF 28
Ross, Jonathan	THE DEADLIEST THING YOU EVER SAW	Amnon Kabatchnik	4-2 MR 35

Rossiter, John	THE DEADLY GOLD	Allen J. Hubin	9-1 TAD 74
Rossiter, John	THE MURDER MAKERS	Allen J. Hubin	10-4 TAD 307
Rossiter, John	THE MURDER MAKERS	Steve Lewis	1-6 MF 39
Rossiter, John	THE VILLAINS	Steve Lewis	1-1 MF 28
Rossman, John F.	SHAMBALLAH	Veronica M.Kennedy	9-3 TAD 223
Rostand, Robert	A KILLING IN ROME	Theodore Dukeshire	2-3 MF 51
Rostand, Robert	THE D'ARTAGNAN SIGNATURE	Amnon Kabatchnik	9-3 TAD 221
Rosten, Leo	SILKY: A DETECTIVE STORY	Jim McCahery	5 PE 40
Rotsstein, Aaron N.	JUDGMENT IN ST. PETER'S	Allen J. Hubin	14-1 TAD 19
Roudybush, Alexandra	A CAPITOL CRIME	Gerie Frazier	3-3 MF 3
Roudybush, Alexandra	A GASTRONOMIC MURDER	Gerie Frazier	3-3 MF 3
Roudybush, Alexandra	BEFORE THE BALL WAS OVER	Gerie Frazier	3-3 MF 2
Roudybush, Alexandra	DEATH OF A MORAL PERSON	Gerie Frazier	3-3 MF 2
Roudybush, Alexandra	THE HOUSE OF THE CAT	Gerie Frazier	3-3 MF 3
Roudybush, Alexandra	SUDDENLY, IN PARIS	Gerie Frazier	3-3 MF 4
Roueche, Berton	FAGO	Steve Lewis	2-3 MF 43
Rounds, David, & Madeleine Edmondson	THE SOAPS	Allen J. Hubin	7-3 TAD 192
Routley, Erik	THE PURITAN PLEASURES OF THE DETECTIVE STORY FROM SHERLOCK HOLMES TO VAN DER VALK	Barzun & Taylor	11-1 TAD 93
Routley, Erik	THE PURITAN PLEASURES OF THE DETECTIVE STORY FROM SHERLOCK HOLMES TO VAN DER VALK	Maryell Cleary	2-6 PP 33
Routley, Erik	THE PURITAN PLEASURES OF THE DETECTIVE STORY FROM SHERLOCK HOLMES TO VAN DER VALK	F.M.Nevins, Jr.	6-2 TAD 109
Rovin, Jeff	HOLLYWOOD DETECTIVE: GARRISON	Marvin Lachman	1-1 MF 34
Roy, Archie	DEADLIGHT	Theodore Dukeshire	2-5 MF 42
Royce, Kenneth	BUSTILLO	Steve Lewis	1-3 MF 38
Royce, Kenneth	THE MINIATURE FRAME	Amnon Kabatchnik	5-5 MR 34
Royce, Kenneth	THE XYY MAN	Lianne Carlin	4-1 MR 35
Rubinstein, Jonathan	CITY POLICE	Veronica M.Kennedy	7-1 TAD 60
Ruehlman, William	SAINT WITH A GUN: THE UNLAWFUL AMERICAN PRIVATE EYE	Jim McCahery	2 PE 18
Ruehlman, William	SAINT WITH A GUN: THE UNLAWFUL AMERICAN PRIVATE EYE	F.M.Nevins, Jr.	8-1 TAD 55
Ruhm, Herbert, ed.	THE HARD-BOILED DETECTIVE: STORIES FROM BLACK MASK MAGAZINE	Allen J. Hubin	10-1 TAD 5
Ruhm, Herbert, ed.	THE HARD-BOILED DETECTIVE: STORIES FROM BLACK MASK MAGAZINE	Amnon Kabatchnik	11 MN R5
Ruhm, Herbert, ed.	THE HARD-BOILED DETECTIVE: STORIES FROM BLACK MASK MAGAZINE	Marvin Lachman	1-2 MF 34
Ruhm, Herbert, ed.	THE HARD-BOILED DETECTIVE: STORIES FROM BLACK MASK MAGAZINE	Steve Lewis	1-2 MF 35
Ruhm, Herbert, ed.	THE HARD-BOILED DETECTIVE: STORIES FROM BLACK MASK MAGAZINE	Frank Occhiogrosso	11-1 TAD 21
Ruhm, Herbert, ed.	THE HARD-BOILED DETECTIVE: STORIES FROM BLACK MASK MAGAZINE	Charles Shibuk	10-2 TAD 150
Rumbelow, Donald	THE COMPLETE JACK THE RIPPER	Mary Groff	7 MN 9
Rumbelow, Donald	THE COMPLETE JACK THE RIPPER	Jon L. Lellenberg	8-4 TAD 307
Ruppelt, Edward J.	THE REPORT ON UNIDENTIFIED FLYING OBJECTS	Gary Zachrich	70 PU 27
Ruse, Gary Alan	HOUNDSTOOTH	Allen J. Hubin	8-4 TAD 310
Ruse, Paul	THE ALUMNI MURDERS	Steve Lewis	5-2 MF 23
Rushkin, Buddy, & Jack Gross, Jr.	CLAY PIGEON (film)	Richard S. Lochte	5-1 TAD 41
Russell, A.J.	THE DEVALINO CAPER	Allen J. Hubin	8-3 TAD 230
Russell, A.J.	POUR THE HEMLOCK	Allen J. Hubin	10-2 TAD 112

Russell, A.J.	POUR THE HEMLOCK	Steve Lewis	1-3 MF 37
Russell, Martin	THE MAN WITHOUT A NAME	Allen J. Hubin	11-1 TAD 19
Russell, Martin	THE MAN WITHOUT A NAME	Steve Lewis	2-3 MF 42
Russell, Richard	PAPERBAG	Steve Lewis	4-2 MF 32
Russell, Richard	REUNION	Fred Dueren	13-1 TAD 65
Russo, John	THE MAJORETTES	Fred Dueren	14-2 TAD 184
Rutherford, Douglas	KICK START	Bill Crider	3-3 MF 43
Rutherford, Douglas	KICK START	Charles Shibuk	9-4 TAD 281
Ryck, Francis	SACRIFICAL PAWN	Allen J. Hubin	7-2 TAD 142
Ryck, Francis	SACRIFICAL PAWN	Guy M. Townsend	1A MF 34
Rymer, James Malcolm	VARNEY THE VAMPYRE	Allen J. Hubin	6-1 TAD 45
Saberhagen, Fred	BERSERKER	Gary Zachrich	66 PU 59
Saberhagen, Fred	THE BLACK MOUNTAINS	Gary Zachrich	75 PU 26
Saberhagen, Fred	THE HOLMES-DRACULA FILE	Joe R. Lansdale	2-6 MF 36
Saberhagen, Fred	THE HOLMES-DRACULA FILE	Edward Lauterbach	12-1 TAD 94
Saberhagen, Fred	THORN	Bill Crider	4-4 PP 30
Sabin, Edwin L.	OLD FOUR TOES	C.L.Messecar	3-3 BC 351
Sabin, Edwin L.	PLUCK ON THE LONG TRAIL	C.L.Messecar	3-2 BC 318
Sabin, Edwin L.	TREASURE MOUNTAIN	C.L.Messecar	3-2 BC 319
Sabin, Edwin L.	WITH CARSON AND FREMONT	C.L.Messecar	3-2 BC 319
Sadler, Mark	CIRCLE OF FIRE	Myrtis Broset	1-4 MF 47
Sadler, Mark	CIRCLE OF FIRE	Free Dueren	10-4 TAD 341
Sadler, Mark	CIRCLE OF FIRE	Allen J. Hubin	6-4 TAD 266
Sadler, Mark	CIRCLE OF FIRE	Jeff Meyerson	1-3 MF 47
Sadler, Mark	HERE TO DIE	Robert E. Washer	3-1 QC 19
Safire, William	FULL DISCLOSURE	Jim Huang	11 CL 10
Sagola, Mario J.	THE MANACLE	Allen J. Hubin	12-2 TAD 114
Saikaku, Ihara	TALES OF JAPANESE JUSTICE	John L. Apostolou	13-4 TAD 351
Sakol, Jeannie	HOT 30	William L.DeAndrea	14-3 TAD 265
Sale, Richard	LAZARUS NO.7	Angelo Panagos	11-2 TAD 127
Sale, Richard	PASSING STRANGE	Angelo Panagos	11-2 TAD 127
Salisbury, Carola	DARK INHERITANCE	Barbara A. Buhrer	2-1 MM 3
Salisbury, Carola	THE PRIDE OF THE TREVALLIONS	Barbara A. Buhrer	8 MN 11
Samson, Joan	THE AUCTIONEER	Barbara A. Buhrer	11 MN R4
Sanchez, Thomas	ZOOT-SUIT MURDERS	Steve Lewis	3-5 MF 35
Sanders, Lawrence	THE ANDERSON TAPES (Film)	Richard S. Lochte	5-1 TAD 42
Sanders, Lawrence	THE ANDERSON TAPES	Robert E. Washer	2-1 QC 17
Sanders, Lawrence	THE FIRST DEADLY SIN (film)	Thomas Godfrey	2-2 M 59
Sanders, Lawrence	THE SECOND DEADLY SIN	(not stated)	3-4 MF 44
Sanders, Lawrence	THE SECOND DEADLY SIN	Robert C.S.Adey	5-4 MF 33
Sanders, Lawrence	THE SECOND DEADLY SIN	Allen J. Hubin	11-1 TAD 18
Sanders, Lawrence	THE SECOND DEADLY SIN	Amnon Kabatchnik	1-2 PP 23
Sanders, Lawrence	THE SIXTH COMMANDMENT	Jane S. Bakerman	2-5 PP 36
Sanders, Lawrence	THE TANGENT FACTOR	Steve Lewis	2-5 MF 30
Sanders, Lawrence	THE TANGENT OBJECTIVE	Sheldon A. Wiebe	5 SF 38
Sanders, Lawrence	THE TENTH COMMANDMENT	Paul Bishop	2-3 M 47
Sanders, Lawrence	THE TENTH COMMANDMENT	Bill Crider	4-5 MF 39
Sanders, Lawrence	THE HAMLET ULTIMATUM	Edgar James	1-2 M 22
Sandulescu, Jacques & Annie Gotlieb	THE CARPATHIAN CAPER	Allen J. Hubin	9-1 TAD 74
Santesson, Hans S.,ed	THE LOCKED ROOM READER	Robert E. Washer	1-4 QC 19
Sapinsley, Alvin	SHERLOCK HOLMES IN NEW YORK (TV)	Robert W. Hahn	10-1 TAD 68
Sapir, Richard	BRESSIO	Allen J. Hubin	9-2 TAD 152
Sapir, Richard, & Warren B. Murphy	BOTTOM LINE	Steve Lewis	3-6 MF 31
Sapir, Richard, & Warren B. Murphy	THE HEAD MEN	Steve Lewis	2-4 MF 33
Sapir, Richard, & Warren B. Murphy	HOLY TERROR	Jeff Meyerson	1-3 MF 49
Sapir, Richard, & Warren B. Murphy	IN ENEMY HANDS	Steve Lewis	1-2 MF 28
Sapir, Richard, & Warren B. Murphy	LAST WAR DANCE	Jeff Meyerson	1-3 MF 48
Sapir, Richard, & Warren B. Murphy	MAFIA FIX	Jeff Meyerson	1-6 MF 52

Sapir, Richard, & Warren B. Murphy	SLAVE SAFARI	Jeff Meyerson	10 MN R15
Sapp, Judson C., & Guy M. Townsend, John J. McAleer, Arrican Schemer	REX STOUT: AN ANNOTATED PRIMARY AND SECONDARY BIBLIOGRAPHY	Linda Toole	5-2 MF 29
Sargent, Pamela	THE SUDDEN STAR	W. Paul Ganley	2 FM 16
Saul, John	COMES THE BLIND FURY	Fred Dueren	14-1 TAD 81
Savage, Mildred	A GREAT FALL	Carolann Purcell	5-1 MR 37
Saxon, Alex	A RUN IN DIAMONDS	Steve Lewis	1-6 MF 40
Saxon, Peter	VAMPIRE'S MOON	Lianne Carlin	3-6 MR 23
Saxon, Peter	THE WARRING SKY	Gary Zachrich	75 PU 24
Sayers, Dorothy L.	CLOUDS OF WITNESS (TV)	Amnon Kabatchnik	7-2 TAD 138
Sayers, Dorothy L.	HANGMAN'S HOLIDAY	R.W.Hays	8-4 TAD 298
Sayers, Dorothy L.	LORD PETER	Marvin Lachman	5-2 MR 37
Sayers, Dorothy L.	THE UNPLEASANTNESS AT THE BELLONA CLUB (TV)	Amnon Kabatchnik	7-2 TAD 138
Sayles, Dorothy	THE HAUNTING OF PELHAM ORANGE (jigsaw puzzle)	Edward Lauterbach	12-1 TAD 94
Scaduto, Tony	A TERRIBLE TIME TO DIE	Steve Lewis	3-1 MF 35
Scarborough, Chuck	STRYKER	Allen J. Hubin	12-1 TAD 11
Schaefer, Jack	SHANE	Martin M. Wooster	13C MN 8
Schapp, Dick, & Jimmy Breslin	.44	Joe R. Lansdale	3-5 MF 43
Schemer, Arrican, & Guy M. Townsend, John J. McAleer, Judson C. Sapp	REX STOUT: AN ANNOTATED PRIMARY AND SECONDARY BIBLIOGRAPHY	Linda Toole	5-2 MF 29
Scherf, Margaret	THE BEADED BANANA	Steve Lewis	3-1 MF 31
Scherf, Margaret	THE BEAUTIFUL BIRTHDAY CAKE	Stanley A. Carlin	4-4 MR 36
Scherf, Margaret	DON'T WAKE ME UP WHILE I'M DRIVING	Amnon Kabatchnik	11-3 TAD 246
Scherf, Margaret	IF YOU WANT A MURDER WELL DONE	Steve Lewis	1A MF 26
Schick, Frank L.	THE PAPERBOUND BOOK IN AMERICA	William Lyles	2-2 PQ 37
Schickel, Richard	THE MEN WHO MADE THE MOVIES: ALFRED HITCHCOCK (TV)	James Mark Purcell	12-4 TAD 376
Schier, Norma	THE ANAGRAM DETECTIVES	Greg Doon	3-2 MF 44
Schier, Norma	THE ANAGRAM DETECTIVES	Allen J. Hubin	12-3 TAD 207
Schier, Norma	THE ANAGRAM DETECTIVES	F.M.Nevins, Jr.	4-1 MF 32
Schisgall, Oscar	BARRON IXELL: CRIME BREAKER	Angelo Panagos	12-1 TAD 80
Schmidt, Josef, & Armin Arnold	KRIMINAL ROMAN FUHRER	Allen J. Hubin	12-1 TAD 12
Schmitz, James H.	THE DEMON BREED	Gary Zachrich	71 PU 22
Scholefield, Alan	VENOM	Allen J. Hubin	12-2 TAD 115
Schreuders, Piet	PAPERBACKS, U.S.A.	Bill Crider	3-4 PQ 55
Schreuders, Piet	PAPERBACKS, U.S.A.	Charlotte Laughlin	4-2 PQ 46
Schultz, James W.	WITH THE INDIANS IN THE ROCKIES	C.L.Messecar	3-4 BC 372
Schwartz, Saul	THE DETECTIVE STORY	Allen J. Hubin	9-3 TAD 225
Scott, Gavin	A FLIGHT OF LIES	Allen J. Hubin	14-4 TAD 301
Scott, Jack Denton	THE SEA-FILE	George Kelley	4-1 PP 34
Scott, Jack S.	A CLUTCH OF VIPERS	Steve Lewis	3-6 MF 38
Scott, Jack S.	THE BASTARD'S NAME WAS BRISTOW	Allen J. Hubin	11-1 TAD 19
Scott, Jack S.	THE GOSPEL LAMB	Steve Lewis	5-3 MF 29
Scott, Jack S.	THE SHALLOW GRAVE	Allen J. Hubin	12-1 TAD 11
Scott, Jack S.	THE SHALLOW GRAVE	Allen J. Hubin	13-1 TAD 30
Scott, Jack S.	THE SHALLOW GRAVE	Steve Lewis	3-1 MF 34
Scott, Jack S.	THE SHALLOW GRAVE	Guy M. Townsend	2-4 MF 45
Scott, Jeremy	THE TWO FACES OF ROBERT JUST	Pamela Craig	2-1 M 29
Scott, Justin	THE SHIPKILLER	Allen J. Hubin	12-2 TAD 115
Scott, Justin	THE SHIPKILLER	Charles Shibuk	13-2 TAD 135
Scott, Ronald McNair, & T.H.White	DEAD MR. NIXON	E.F.Bleiler	3-2 MF 43
Scott, Roney	SHAKEDOWN	Bill Crider	6 PE 17
Scott-Giles, C.W.	THE WIMSEY FAMILY	Maryell Cleary	3-4 PP 34
Scott-Giles, C.W.	THE WIMSEY FAMILY	Fred Dueren	13-2 TAD 136

Scott-Heron, Gil	THE VULTURE	Rita & Jon Breen	5-1 MR 36
Seaman, Donald	THE CHAMELEON COURSE	Allen J. Hubin	9-3 TAD 225
Seaman, Donald	THE TERROR SYNDICATE	Allen J. Hubin	10-3 TAD 206
Seaman, Donald	THE TERROR SYNDICATE	Steve Lewis	1-4 MF 38
Sela, Owen	AN EXCHANGE OF EAGLES	Allen J. Hubin	10-4 TAD 309
Sela, Owen	AN EXCHANGE OF EAGLES	Steven Miller	4 MT 18
Sela, Owen	THE BEARER PLOT	Amnon Kabatchnik	6-1 MR 45
Sela, Owen	THE BENGALI INHERITANCE	Frank Eck	8-4 TAD 306
Sela, Owen	THE PORTUGUESE FRAGMENT	Steve Lewis	2-1 MM 5
Selmier, Dean, & Walter Kram	BOW AWAY	Marlowe Archer	4 PE 24
Selwyn, Francis	SERGEANT VERITY AND THE BLOOD ROYAL	Robert C.S.Adey	3-6 MF 48
Senecal, Jacquemard	THE ELEVENTH LITTLE INDIAN	Allen J. Hubin	13-1 TAD 28
Severy, Melvin L.	THE DARROW ENIGMA	Allen J. Hubin	5-3 TAD 164
Sewart, Alan	THE TURN-UP	Robert C.S.Adey	5-2 MF 38
Seymour, Gerald	THE HARRISON AFFAIR	Allen J. Hubin	14-3 TAD 219
Seymour, Gerald	HARRY'S GAME	Barbara A. Buhrer	9 MN R1
Seymour, Gerald	HARRY'S GAME	Allen J. Hubin	9-1 TAD 73
Seymour, Gerald	HARRY'S GAME	James Jobst	2-1 MF 44
Shaffer, Anthony	SLEUTH (stage)	Amnon Kabatchnik	3-4 MR 33
Shaffer, Anthony	SLEUTH (stage)	Amnon Kabatchnik	4-2 TAD 124
Shagan, Steve	CITY OF ANGELS	Allen J. Hubin	8-3 TAD 226
Shah, Diana K.	THE MACKIN COVER	Steve Lewis	2-2 MF 34
Shannon, Dell	COLD TRAIL	Barbara A. Buhrer	13 MN R2
Shannon, Dell	CRIME ON THEIR HANDS	Robert E. Washer	2-1 QC 17
Shannon, Dell	KILL WITH KINDNESS	Stanley A. Carlin	1-6 MR 4
Shannon, Dell	UNEXPECTED DEATH	William Dearnaley	4-1 TAD 51
Shannon, Dell	UNEXPECTED DEATH	Robert E. Washer	3-4 TAD 272
Shapiro, Milton J.	THE HAWK	Bill Crider	9-2 TAD 151
Sharp, Alan	THE LAST RUN (film)	Richard S. Lochte	5-2 TAD 104
Shaw, Joseph T., ed.	THE HARDBOILED OMNIBUS	Al Scott	5/6 MN 24
Shaw, Robin	RUNNING	Allen J. Hubin	6-2 TAD 114
Sheckley, Robert	THE GAME OF X	Fred Dueren	14-2 TAD 184
Sheckley, Robert	THE GAME OF X	Martin M. Wooster	1-8 MM 7
Sheldon, Sidney	BLOODLINE	R. Jeff Banks	2-6 PP 13
Sheldon, Sidney	THE NAKED FACE	Allen J. Hubin	12-1 TAD 11
Sheldon, Sidney	THE NAKED FACE	Jeff Meyerson	1-3 MF 47
Sheldon, Sidney	THE NAKED FACE	Robert E. Washer	4-1 MR 34
Sheldon, Sidney	THE NAKED FACE	Robert E. Washer	3-1 QC 18
Shepard, Leslie, ed.	THE DRACULA BOOK OF GREAT VAMPIRE STORIES	Fred Dueren	11-4 TAD 396
Sheppard, Judith	CRIME AND DETECTIVE FICTION: A HANDBOOK OF DEALERS AND COLLECTORS IN BRITAIN AND AMERICA	D.E.Ath	2-1 PP 10
Sherburne, James	DEATH'S PALE HORSE	Allen J. Hubin	13-4 TAD 297
Sherburne, James	DEATH'S PALE HORSE	Richard Moskowitz	10 LR 10
Sherman, Dan	DYNASTY OF SPIES	Gary Happenstand	2-2 C 158
Sherman, Dan	THE MOLE	Allen J. Hubin	10-3 TAD 206
Sherman, Don	KING JAGUAR	Paul Bishop	2-2 M 58
Sherman, Harold	THE GREEN MAN AND HIS RETURN	Michael L. Cook	7 U 31
Sherry, Sylvia	THE HAVEN-SCREAMERS	Lianne Carlin	3-6 MR 23
Shibuk, Charles	A PRELIMINARY CHECKLIST OF THE DETECTIVE NOVEL AND ITS VARIANTS: SUPPLEMENT ONE	Allen J. Hubin	1-1 TAD 26
Shirreffs, Gordon R.	THE MARAUDERS	Steve Lewis	1-3 MF 41
Sifakis, Carl	A CATALOGUE OF CRIME	Fred Dueren	13-2 TAD 136
Silverberg, Robert	NEEDLE IN A TIME STACK	Gary Zachrich	66 PU 59
Silverberg, Robert	NIGHTWINGS	Gary Zachrich	73 PU 34
Silverberg, Robert	UP THE LINE	Gary Zachrich	74 PU 22
Silverman, Robert	THE CUMBERLAND DECISION	Steve Lewis	2-3 MF 47
Simenon, Georges	MAIGRET AMONG THE RICH	Fred Dueren	12-2 TAD 135
Simenon, Georges	MAIGRET AMONG THE RICH	Charles Shibuk	12-2 TAD 167
Simenon, Georges	MAIGRET AND THE APPARITION	Frank Occhiogrosso	10-4 TAD 310

Simenon, Georges	MAIGRET AND THE BLACK SHEEP	F.M.Nevins, Jr.	1-5 MF 44
Simenon, Georges	MAIGRET AND THE BUM	Don Miller	13 MN R6
Simenon, Georges	MAIGRET AND THE HOTEL MAJESTIC	Amnon Kabatchnik	2-5 MF 40
Simenon, Georges	MAIGRET AND THE TOY VILLAGE	Peter Wolfe	13-1 TAD 63
Simenon, Georges	MAIGRET AND THE WINE MERCHANT	Amnon Kabatchnik	5-5 MR 37
Simenon, Georges	MAIGRET AT THE CORONER'S	Richard Moskowitz	10 LR 11
Simenon, Georges	THE PATIENCE OF MAIGRET	Arthur C. Scott	13 MN R6
Simmel, Johannes M.	THE CAESAR CODE	Fred Dueren	9-3 TAD 212
Simmel, Johannes M.	THE CAESAR CODE	Steve Lewis	1-1 MF 29
Simmel, Johannes M.	THE CAIN CONSPIRACY	Fred Dueren	10-2 TAD 130
Simmons, Diane	LET THE BASTARDS FREEZE IN THE DARK	Allen J. Hubin	14-3 TAD 220
Simmons, Geoffrey I.	THE Z PAPERS	Myrtis Broset	1-6 MF 42
Simon, Leonard	THE IRVING SOLUTION	Allen J. Hubin	10-4 TAD 308
Simon, Leonard	THE IRVING SOLUTION	Amnon Kabatchnik	9 CL 3
Simon, Neil	MURDER BY DEATH (film)	James Mark Purcell	9-4 TAD 301
Simon, Roger L.	THE BIG FIX	Stan Burns	8 MN 22
Simon, Roger L.	THE BIG FIX	Jim Huang	12 CL 7
Simon, Roger L.	PEKING DUCK	Steve Lewis	3-6 MF 32
Simon, Roger L.	PEKING DUCK	Jim McCahery	5 PE 40
Simon, Roger L.	WILD TURKEY	Robert C.S.Adey	4-4 PP 27
Simpson, Dorothy	THE NIGHT SHE DIED	Jane S. Bakerman	5-5 MF 34
Simpson, Dorothy	THE NIGHT SHE DIED	Douglas G. Greene	4-5/6 PP 18
Simpson, Dorothy	THE NIGHT SHE DIED	Steve Lewis	5-5 MF 22
Simpson, George E., & Neal Burger	THIN AIR	David Bates	4-4 PP 29
Simpson, Helen, & Clemence Dane	ENTER SIR JOHN	Paul McCarthy	3-3 PP 28
Simpson, Helen, & Clemence Dane	MURDER (film)	William K. Everson	7-1 TAD 31
Simpson, Helen, & Clemence Dane	MURDER (film)	James Mark Purcell	10-4 TAD 314
Sims, Edward H.	THE GREATEST ACES	Gary Zachrich	75 PU 24
Sims, George	HUNTERS POINT	Fred Dueren	10-4 TAD 340
Sinclair, Andrew	THE FACTS IN THE CASE OF E.A.POE	Allen J. Hubin	14-3 TAD 220
Sinclair, Murray	TOUGH LUCK,L.A.	(not stated)	2-2 M 57
Sinclair, Murray	TOUGH LUCK,L.A.	Steve Lewis	5-2 MF 17
Singer, Norman	DIAMONDSTUD	Fred Dueren	9-3 TAD 212
Singer, Norman	DIAMONDSTUD	Steve Lewis	1-2 MF 28
Singer, Norman	THE SHAKEDOWN KID	Steve Lewis	1-2 MF 27
Sinstadt, Gerald	THE FIDELIO SCORE	Marvin Lachman	9-2 TAD 144
Sjowall, Maj, & Per Wahloo	THE FIRE ENGINE THAT DISAPPEARED	Amnon Kabatchnik	3-4 MR 34
Sjowall, Maj, & Per Wahloo	THE LOCKED ROOM	Allen J. Hubin	7-1 TAD 62
Sjowall, Maj, & Per Wahloo	THE LOCKED ROOM	Don Miller	11 MN R16
Sjowall, Maj, & Per Wahloo	MAN ON A ROOF (film)	Chris & Janie Filstrup	10-3 TAD 210
Sjowall, Maj, & Per Wahloo	THE MAN WHO WENT UP IN SMOKE	Don Miller	9 MN R17
Sjowall, Maj, & Per Wahloo	MURDER AT THE SAVOY	Don Miller	12 MN R6
Sjowall, Maj, & Per Wahloo	THE TERRORISTS	Barzun & Taylor	11-1 TAD 93
Sjowall, Maj, & Per Wahloo	THE TERRORISTS	Frank Occhiogrosso	11-2 TAD 120
Skene-Melvin, David, & Ann	CRIME, DETECTIVE, ESPIONAGE, MYSTERY AND THRILLER FICTION & FILM: A COMPREHENSIVE BIBLIOGRAPHY OF CRITICAL WRITING THROUGH 1979	Michael L. Cook	5-2 MF 30
Skvorecky, Josef	MISS SILVER'S PAST	Allen J. Hubin	9-1 TAD 73
Skvorecky, Josef	THE MOURNFUL DEMEANOR OF LIEUTENANT BORUVKA	Allen J. Hubin	8-2 TAD 147

Sladek, John	BLACK AURA	Theodore Dukeshire	3-4 MF 48
Sladek, John	BLACK AURA	Allen J. Hubin	13-2 TAD 96
Sladek, John	BLACK AURA	Steve Lewis	4-2 MF 37
Sladek, John	BLACK AURA	Jeff Meyerson	2-6 PP 37
Sladek, John	INVISIBLE GREEN	Mary A. Grochowski	2-5 PP 36
Sladek, John	INVISIBLE GREEN	Allen J. Hubin	12-3 TAD 207
Sladek, John	INVISIBLE GREEN	Jeff Meyerson	2-6 PP 37
Slater, Nigel	FALCON	Allen J. Hubin	13-1 TAD 30
Slesar, Henry	THE CASE OF THE SHAKY SHOWMAN	Edward Lauterbach	7-4 TAD 292
Slesar, Henry	THE CASE OF THE SNORING SKINFLINT (game)	Edward Lauterbach	7-2 TAD 138
Slesar, Henry	THE THING AT THE DOOR	Allen J. Hubin	8-2 TAD 150
Slesar, Henry	THE THING AT THE DOOR	Jim McCahery	2-5 PP 34
Slung, Michele B.,ed.	CRIME ON HER MIND	Allen J. Hubin	9-1 TAD 75
Slung, Michele B.,ed.	CRIME ON HER MIND	Charles Shibuk	10-2 TAD 150
Slung, Michele B.,ed.	WOMEN'S WILES	Allen J. Hubin	13-3 TAD 203
Small, Austin J.	THE CRIMSON DEATH	Steve Lewis	3-2 MF 41
Smith, Bevan, & John Ball	THE KILLING IN THE MARKET	Mary Groff	1-3 PP 29
Smith, Bevan, & John Ball	THE KILLING IN THE MARKET	Andrew Stewert	4 MT 36
Smith, Charles M.	REVEREND RANDOLLPH AND THE AVENGING ANGEL	Allen J. Hubin	11-2 TAD 116
Smith, Charles M.	REVEREND RANDOLLPH AND THE AVENGING ANGEL	Steve Lewis	2-6 MF 30
Smith, Charles M.	REVEREND RANDOLLPH AND THE AVENGING ANGEL	Guy M. Townsend	13 MN R8
Smith, Charles M.	REVEREND RANDOLLPH AND THE FALL FROM GRACE, INC.	D.E.Ath	2-1 PP 14
Smith, Charles M.	REVEREND RANDOLLPH AND THE FALL FROM GRACE, INC.	Allen J. Hubin	12-2 TAD 115
Smith, Charles M.	REVEREND RANDOLLPH AND THE FALL FROM GRACE, INC.	Steve Lewis	3-4 MF 38
Smith, Charles M.	REVEREND RANDOLLPH AND THE WAGES OF SIN	Allen J. Hubin	8-2 TAD 148
Smith, Charles M.	REVEREND RANDOLLPH AND THE WAGES OF SIN	Guy M. Townsend	13 MN R7
Smith, Derek	WHISTLE UP THE DEVIL	Douglas G. Greene	13-4 TAD 353
Smith, Dennis	GLITTER AND ASH	Paul Bishop	2-1 M 27
Smith, Dennis	GLITTER AND ASH	Allen J. Hubin	13-4 TAD 298
Smith, Don	CHINA COASTER	Bill Crider	3-4 PP 31
Smith, Edgar	A REASONABLE DOUBT	Robert E. Washer	3-1 QC 20
Smith, Elizabeth F.	GENTLE ALBATROSS	Myrtis Broset	1-2 MF 42
Smith, George H.	KAR KABALA	Gary Zachrich	74 PU 25
Smith, George H.	THE SECOND WAR OF THE WORLDS	Edward Lauterbach	10-1 TAD 69
Smith, Guy N.	NIGHT OF THE CRABS	Bill Crider	4-1 PP 31
Smith, J.C.S.	JACOBY'S FIRST CASE	Allen J. Hubin	13-4 TAD 298
Smith, Joseph B.	PORTRAIT OF A COLD WARRIOR	Gary Happenstand	2-2 C 159
Smith, Kay Nolte	THE WATCHER	Allen J. Hubin	14-3 TAD 220
Smith, Lou	MASTER PLOT	Allen J. Hubin	11-3 TAD 230
Smith, Mark	THE DEATH OF THE DETECTIVE	R. Jeff Banks	3 PE 20
Smith, Martin Cruz	CANTO FOR A GYPSY	Allen J. Hubin	6-2 TAD 113
Smith, Martin Cruz	GORKY PARK	Lawrence Block	2-3 M 47
Smith, Martin Cruz	GORKY PARK	Dorothy B. Hughes	3-2 M 38
Smith, Martin Cruz	GORKY PARK	Howard Lachtman	14-4 TAD 361
Smith, Martin Cruz	GORKY PARK	Gary Warren Niebuhr	4-3 PP 5
Smith, Martin Cruz	NIGHTWING	Fred Dueren	11-4 TAD 396
Smith, Michael	LEGACY OF THE LAKE	Fred Dueren	14-1 TAD 80
Smith, Myron J., Jr.	CLOAK-AND-DAGGER BIBLIOGRAPHY, AN ANNOTATED GUIDE TO SPY FICTION 1937-1975	F.M.Nevins, Jr.	1-4 MF 50
Smith, Myron J., Jr.	CLOAK-AND-DAGGER BIBLIOGRAPHY, AN ANNOTATED GUIDE TO SPY FICTION 1937-1975	Allen J. Hubin	10-2 TAD 116
Smith, Robert Arthur	THE FOX TRAP	Fred Dueren	12-2 TAD 135

Smith, Robert Arthur	THE PREY	Bill Crider	1-1 PQ 37
Snell, David	LIGHTS...CAMERA...MURDER	Allen J. Hubin	13-1 TAD 30
Snell, David	LIGHTS...CAMERA...MURDER	Andy Jaysnovitch	7 PE 11
Snow, C.P.	THE AFFAIR	Jon L. Breen	4-6 MF 36
Snow, Kathleen	NIGHT WALKING	Allen J. Hubin	12-1 TAD 11
Solomon, Brad	THE GONE MAN	Randy Himmel	10 LR 21
Solomon, Brad	THE GONE MAN	Allen J. Hubin	11-3 TAD 231
Solomon, Brad	THE GONE MAN	Steve Lewis	2-2 MF 35
Solomon, Brad	THE GONE MAN	Charles Shibuk	13-4 TAD 364
Solomon, Brad	THE OPEN SHADOW	Randy Himmel	10 LR 21
Solomon, Brad	THE OPEN SHADOW	Steve Lewis	3-6 MF 27
Solomon, Brad	THE OPEN SHADOW	Charles Shibuk	14-1 TAD 80
Solovay, Jacob C.	SHERLOCK HOLMES: TWO SONNET SEQUENCES	Stanley A. Carlin	3-2 MR 26
Sonnenschmidt, F.H., & Julia C.Rosenblatt	DINING WITH SHERLOCK HOLMES	Jon L. Lellenberg	10-1 TAD 70
Southcott, Audley	CROSS THAT PALM WHEN I COME TO IT	Robert C.S.Adey	5-2 MF 38
Spain, John	DEATH IS LIKE THAT	Theodore Dukeshire	6 PE 18
Spain, John	DEATH IS LIKE THAT	Stephen Mertz	2-4 MF 44
Spain, John	DIG ME A GRAVE	Theodore Dukeshire	6 PE 18
Spain, John	THE EVIL STAR	Theodore Dukeshire	6 PE 18
Spain, Nancy	DEATH GOES ON SKIS	Steve Lewis	1-6 MF 40
Sparrow, Gerald	VINTAGE VICTORIAN MURDER	David Brownell	7-1 TAD 61
Speight, T.W.	UNDER LOCK AND KEY	Allen J. Hubin	11-3 TAD 232
Spencer, Ross H.	THE DADA CAPER	Mary A. Grochowski	1-6 PP 26
Spencer, Ross H.	THE DADA CAPER	Mary A. Grochowski	12-2 TAD 178
Spencer, Ross H.	THE DADA CAPER	Jim Huang	8 CL 10
Spencer, Ross H.	THE DADA CAPER	Donald J. Pattow	11-4 TAD 404
Spencer, Ross H.	THE RADISH RIVER CAPER	Paul Harwitz	3-2 M 40
Spencer, Ross H.	THE REGIIS ARMS CAPER	Allen J. Hubin	13-1 TAD 30
Spencer, Ross H.	THE STRANGER CITY CAPER	Allen J. Hubin	13-3 TAD 203
Spewack, Samuel	MURDER IN THE GILDED CAGE	Charles Shibuk	1-5 MF 48
Spiering, Frank	PRINCE JACK	Mary Groff	13/14 CL 11
Spillane, Mickey	THE BODY LOVERS	R. Jeff Banks	10 MN R12
Spillane, Mickey	THE ERECTION SET	Max Collins	5-5 MR 36
Spillane, Mickey	I, THE JURY	Marvin Lachman	3-1 TAD 59
Spillane, Mickey	KISS ME, DEADLY	Charles Shibuk	13-4 TAD 353
Spillane, Mickey	THE LAST COP OUT	Max Collins	6-1 MR 41
Spillane, Mickey	THE MIKE HAMMER STORY (recording)	R. Jeff Banks	5 PE 19
Spillane, Mickey	MY GUN IS QUICK	Steve Lewis	1A MF 28
Spillane, Mickey	MY GUN IS QUICK	Arthur C. Scott	10 MN R19
Spillane, Mickey	THE TWISTED THING	Stephen Mertz	3-1 MF 38
Spore, Keith	DEATH OF A SCAVENGER	Fred Dueren	13-3 TAD 251
Sprigg, Christopher	FATALITY IN FLEET STREET	Charles Shibuk	7-2 TAD 129
Springer, Nancy	THE BOOK OF SUNS	Sheldon A. Wiebe	5 SF 38
St.Clair, Leonard	THE EMERALD TRAP	Allen J. Hubin	7-3 TAD 221
St.George, Judith	HAUNTED	George Kelley	4-2 PP 30
St.James, Bernard	APRIL THIRTIETH	Barzun & Taylor	11-4 TAD 394
St.James, Bernard	APRIL THIRTIETH	Allen J. Hubin	12-2 TAD 115
St.James, Bernard	THE WITCH	Adriadne Blackfriar	1-1 M 24
St.James, Ian	THE BALFOUR CONSPIRACY	Allen J. Hubin	14-4 TAD 301
St.James, Ian	THE MONKEY STONES	Allen J. Hubin	14-1 TAD 19
St.John, David	DIABOLUS	Stanley A. Carlin	4-5 MR 35
St.John, David	ON HAZARDOUS DUTY	Larry Rickert	4-3 PP 6
St.John, David	RETURN FROM VORKUTA	Marvin Lachman	1-4 MF 51
St.John, David	THE TOWERS OF SILENCE	Larry Rickert	4-3 PP 6
St.Martin, Thomas	JILL	D.E.Ath	2-4 PP 28
Stableford, Brian M.	CRADLE OF THE SUN	Gary Zachrich	74 PU 23
Stacpoole, H.deVere	GREEN CORAL	Charles Shibuk	10-2 TAD 138
Stagge, Jonathan	DEATH, MY DARLING DAUGHTERS	Steve Lewis	2-4 MF 32
Stagge, Jonathan	TURN OF THE TABLE	Douglas G. Greene	14-2 TAD 187
Strahan, Kay Cleaver	THE DESERT MOON MYSTERY	Charles Shibuk	7-2 TAD 132
Stang, Joanne	SHADOWS ON THE SCEPTERED ISLE	Allen J. Hubin	14-3 TAD 220

Stanley, John, & Kenn Davis	THE DARK SIDE	Fred Dueren	10-4 TAD 340
Stanley, Ray	THE HIPPY CULT MURDERS	Stanley A. Carlin	4-1 MR 37
Stanwood, Donald A.	THE MEMORY OF EVA RYKER	Mary A. Grochowski	12-1 TAD 95
Stanwood, Donald A.	THE MEMORY OF EVA RYKER	Allen J. Hubin	12-1 TAD 6
Stapledon, Olaf	FAR FUTURE CALLING	Michael L. Cook	7 U 31
Stark, Richard	DEADLY EDGE	Robert E. Washer	3-1 QC 19
Stark, Richard	PLUNDER SQUAD	Robert C.S.Adey	4-4 PP 26
Stark, Richard	THE SOUR LEMON SCORE	Jeff Meyerson	1-6 MF 51
Starr, Jimmy	THREE SHORT BIERS	Angelo Panagos	11-4 TAD 381
Starrett, Vincent	THE CASEBOOK OF JIMMY LAVENDER	Allen J. Hubin	7-3 TAD 220
Starrett, Vincent	THE PRIVATE LIFE OF SHERLOCK HOLMES	Jon L. Lellenberg	9-1 TAD 72
Starrett, Vincent	THE UNIQUE HAMLET	Alida Roochwarg	4-2 MR 31
Stasheff, Christopher	THE WARLOCK IN SPITE OF HIMSELF	Gary Zachrich	73 PU 35
Stedman, Raymond W.	THE SERIALS	Stanley A. Carlin	4-6 MR 40
Stedman, Raymond W.	THE SERIALS	Marvin Lachman	5-3 TAD 164
Steele, Curtis	THE ARMY OF THE DEAD	Lynn Hickman	64 PU 33
Steele, Curtis	HOSTS OF THE FLAMING DEATH	Lynn Hickman	65 PU 27
Steele, Curtis	THE INVISIBLE EMPIRE	Lynn Hickman	64 PU 33
Steele, Curtis	LEGIONS OF THE DEATH MASTER	Lynn Hickman	64 PU 33
Steele, Curtis	MARCH OF THE FLAME MARAUDERS	Gary Zachrich	66 PU 56
Steele, Curtis	MASTER OF BROKEN MEN	Lynn Hickman	65 PU 27
Steiger, Brad	SEX AND SATANISM	Gary Zachrich	74 PU 22
Stein, Aaron Marc	A NOSE FOR IT	Paul Harwitz	2-2 M 56
Stein, Aaron Marc	COFFIN COUNTRY	Steve Lewis	1-6 MF 39
Stein, Aaron Marc	DAYS OF MISFORTUNE	Jane S. Bakerman	1-6 MF 52
Stein, Aaron Marc	DEATH MEETS 400 RABBITS	Steve Lewis	5-1 MF 27
Stein, Aaron Marc	LOCK AND KEY	Steve Lewis	1-9 MM 6
Stein, Aaron Marc	ONE DIP DEAD	Jane S. Bakerman	15 CL 6
Stein, Aaron Marc	ONE DIP DEAD	Steve Lewis	3-6 MF 35
Stein, Aaron Marc	THE ROLLING HEADS	Steve Lewis	3-6 MF 28
Stein, Benjamin, & Herbert	ON THE BRINK	Jim Huang	12 CL 7
Stein, Sol	THE RESORT	Richard Moskowitz	9 LR 16
Steinbrunner, Chris, & Burt Goldblatt	CINEMA OF THE FANTASTIC	Marvin Lachman	5-6 MR 38
Steinbrunner, Chris, & Norman Michaels	THE FILMS OF SHERLOCK HOLMES	Marvin Lachman	3-3 MF 43
Steinbrunner, Chris, & Otto Penzler, Marvin Lachman	THE ENCYCLOPEDIA OF MYSTERY AND DETECTION	Arthur C. Scott	1A MF 13
Steinbrunner, Chris, & Otto Penzler, Marvin Lachman	THE ENCYCLOPEDIA OF MYSTERY AND DETECTION	Allen J. Hubin	9-3 TAD 218
Steinbrunner, Chris, & Otto Penzler, Marvin Lachman	THE ENCYCLOPEDIA OF MYSTERY AND DETECTION	Allen J. Hubin	10-3 TAD 207
Stephan, Leslie	MURDER R.F.D.	Allen J. Hubin	11-4 TAD 332
Stephan, Leslie	MURDER R.F.D.	Steve Lewis	2-5 MF 27
Stephens, Reed	THE MAN WHO KILLED HIS BROTHER	Randy Himmel	10 LR 19
Stephens, Reed	THE MAN WHO KILLED HIS BROTHER	Steve Lewis	5-2 MF 17
Steranko, James	CHANDLER	Fred Dueren	10-2 TAD 130
Sterling, Thomas	THE EVIL OF THE DAY	Charles Shibuk	14-4 TAD 377
Stern, Madeleine, ed.	BEHIND THE MASK: THE UNKNOWN THRILLERS OF LOUISA MAY ALCOTT	Amnon Kabatchnik	9-2 TAD 149
Stern, Madeleine, ed.	PLOTS AND COUNTERPLOTS BY LOUISA MAY ALCOTT	Amnon Kabatchnik	11-4 TAD 405
Stern, Richard Martin	SNOWBOUND SIX	Charles Shibuk	12-2 TAD 167
Stevens, Francis	CLAIMED	Lynn Hickman	65 PU 26
Stevens, Louis	STATE'S ATTORNEY (film)	William K. Everson	11-2 TAD 129
Stevens, Shane	BY REASON OF INSANITY	D.E.Ath	2-2 PP 14
Stevenson, Florence	THE CURSE OF THE CONCULLENS	Robert E. Briney	5-5 MR 36
Stevenson, John	THE MERCHANT OF MENACE	Sam Yamato	2-1 M 29

Stevenson, Robert L.	DR. JEKYLL AND MR. HYDE (film)	William K. Everson	2-4 TAD 254
Stevenson, Robert L.	THE STRANGE CASE OF DR. JEKYLL AND MR. HYDE	Martin M. Wooster	4-1 PP 31
Steward, Barbara, & Dwight	EVERMORE	Allen J. Hubin	12-1 TAD 11
Steward, Barbara, & Dwight	EVERMORE	Amnon Kabatchnik	1-4 PP 28
Stewart. Fred Mustard	THE MEPHISTO WALTZ	Charles Shibuk	11-4 TAD 379
Stewart, R.F.	...AND ALWAYS A DETECTIVE: CHAPTERS ON THE HISTORY OF DETECTIVE FICTION	Barzun & Taylor	13-4 TAD 309
Stewart, R.F.	...AND ALWAYS A DETECTIVE: CHAPTERS ON THE HISTORY OF DETECTIVE FICTION	Allen J. Hubin	13-3 TAD 203
Stewart, R.F.	...AND ALWAYS A DETECTIVE: CHAPTERS ON THE HISTORY OF DETECTIVE FICTION	Ethel Lindsay	4-2 PP 31
Stewart, Ramona	THE NIGHTMARE CANDIDATE	Jean Lamb	3-1 M 39
Stewart, Ramona	THE POSSESSION OF JOEL DELANEY	Stanley A. Carlin	4-2 MR 36
Stiehl, Beth, & Linda Herman	CORPUS DELICTI OF MYSTERY FICTION: A GUIDE TO THE BODY OF THE CASE	Allen J. Hubin	8-2 TAD 150
Stilson, Charles B.	POLARIS AND THE IMMORTALS	Gary Zachrich	70 PU 26
Stilwell, Steven A.	THE ARMCHAIR DETECTIVE INDEX, VOLUMES I-X	Charles Shibuk	13-4 TAD 364
Stockbridge, Grant	THE CITY DESTROYER	David Bates	4-5/6 PP 74
Stockbridge, Grant	DEATH REIGN OF THE VAMPIRE KING	Steve Lewis	8 MN 15
Stockbridge, Grant	HORDES OF THE RED BUTCHER	Scott Owen	1-3 PQ 50
Stone, Scott C.S.	SPIES	Allen J. Hubin	13-4 TAD 298
Storme, Peter	THE THING IN THE BROOK	Charles Shibuk	7-1 TAD 53
Stout, Rex	A FAMILY AFFAIR	Robert E. Washer	21 X 54
Stout, Rex	A FAMILY AFFAIR	Jay Jeffries	5/6 MN 18
Stout, Rex	A FAMILY AFFAIR	Lee Poleske	6 LW 1
Stout, Rex	A FAMILY AFFAIR	Arthur C. Scott	5/6 MN 21
Stout, Rex	A FAMILY AFFAIR	Arthur C. Scott	9 MN A14
Stout, Rex	A FAMILY AFFAIR	Charles Shibuk	10-2 TAD 150
Stout, Rex	DEATH OF A DOXY	Don Miller	9 MN A61
Stout, Rex	DEATH OF A DUDE	James Keddie, Jr.	3-2 TAD 132
Stout, Rex	THE DOORBELL RANG	Don Miller	9 MN A62
Stout, Rex	FER-DE-LANCE	Marvin Lachman	2-2 TAD 119
Stout, Rex	FER-DE-LANCE	Jo Ann Vicarel	9 MN A42
Stout, Rex	IF DEATH EVER SLEPT	Don Miller	9 MN A61
Stout, Rex	JUSTICE ENDS AT HOME	Myrtis Broset	3-5 MF 43
Stout, Rex	THE LEAGUE OF FRIGHTENED MEN (film)	(not stated)	5 LW 2
Stout, Rex	THE LEAGUE OF FRIGHTENED MEN	Jo Ann Vicarel	9 MN A42
Stout, Rex	MEET NERO WOLFE (film)	J.T.M.	4 LW 3
Stout, Rex	THE NERO WOLFE COOK BOOK	Marvin Lachman	7-1 TAD 57
Stout, Rex	PLEASE PASS THE GUILT	Marvin Lachman	7-2 TAD 136
Stout, Rex	PLOT IT YOURSELF	Steve Lewis	1A MF 23
Stout, Rex	THE PRESIDENT VANISHES	Charles Shibuk	11-1 TAD 96
Stout, Rex	THE RED BOX	F.M.Nevins, Jr.	2-3 MR 18
Stout, Rex	THE RED BOX	Charles Shibuk	10-1 TAD 72
Stout, Rex	THE RED BOX	Jo Ann Vicarel	9 MN A42
Stout, Rex	THE RUBBER BAND	Charles Shibuk	9-4 TAD 281
Stout, Rex	THE RUBBER BAND	Jo Ann Vicarel	9 MN A42
Stout, Rex	SOME BURIED CAESAR	Charles Shibuk	10-1 TAD 72
Stout, Rex	TRIPLE ZECK	Bruce R. Beaman	7-4 TAD 291
Stout, Rex	TROUBLE IN TRIPLICATE: A NERO WOLFE THREESOME	Douglas G. Greene	12-3 TAD 233
Stout, Rex	WHERE THERE'S A WILL THERE'S A WAY	John J. McAleer	3-5 MR 21
Stowe, James L.	WINTER STALK	Howard Lachtman	13-2 TAD 145
Stratemeyer, Edward	DAVE PORTER ON CAVE ISLAND	C.L.Messecar	3-2 BC 318
Stratemeyer, Edward	FIRST AT THE NORTH POLE	C.L.Messecar	3-4 BC 372

Stratton, Ted	TOURIST TRAP	Barbara A. Buhrer	11 MN R14
Straub, Peter	GHOST STORY	Fred Dueren	13-4 TAD 361
Stribling, T.S.	BEST DR. POGGIOLI DETECTIVE STORIES	James Mark Purcell	10-1 TAD 59
Stribling, T.S.	CLUES OF THE CARIBBEES	Charles Shibuk	11-1 TAD 97
Striker, Randy	KEY WEST CONNECTION	Steve Lewis	5-3 MF 27
Strong, Michael	DANGER FEEDS MY FEAR	George Kelley	3-5 PP 44
Strong, Michael	THE WOLVES CAME DOWN THE MOUNTAIN	Allen J. Hubin	13-2 TAD 97
Stubbs, Jean	THE GOLDEN CRUCIBLE	Mary A. Grochowski	4 MT 25
Stubbs, Jean	THE PAINTED FACE	Richard Emery	4-2 PP 28
Sue, Eugene	THE MYSTERIES OF PARIS (film)	William K. Everson	8-1 TAD 51
Sugar, Andrew, ed.	BEST STORIES FROM ARGOSY'S 94 YEARS	Robert E. Briney	10-1 TAD 66
Sullivan, Robert	THE DISAPPEARANCE OF DR.PARKMAN	Barzun & Taylor	14-4 TAD 329
Swan, Phyllis	FIND SHERRI!	Steve Lewis	4-3 MF 36
Swan, Phyllis	TRIGGER LADY	Fred Dueren	13-3 TAD 252
Swerdlow, Joel	CODE Z	Allen J. Hubin	12-4 TAD 323
Symons, Julian	A THREE-PIPE PROBLEM	Jon L. Lellenberg	8-3 TAD 223
Symons, Julian	A THREE-PIPE PROBLEM	Jeff Meyerson	1-3 MF 48
Symons, Julian	THE BELTING INHERITANCE	James Sandoe	13-4 TAD 293
Symons, Julian	THE BELTING INHERITANCE	Charles Shibuk	12-3 TAD 255
Symons, Julian	THE BLACKHEATH POISONINGS	D.E.Ath	2-1 PP 14
Symons, Julian	THE BLACKHEATH POISONINGS	Allen J. Hubin	12-1 TAD 11
Symons, Julian	THE BLACKHEATH POISONINGS	Steve Lewis	3-5 MF 37
Symons, Julian	THE BLACKHEATH POISONINGS	Charles Shibuk	13-4 TAD 364
Symons, Julian	THE COLOR OF MURDER	Charles Shibuk	12-2 TAD 167
Symons, Julian	THE MAN WHO LOST HIS WIFE	Paul McCarthy	2-1 MF 43
Symons, Julian	THE MAN WHO LOST HIS WIFE	Luther Norris	3-4 MR 32
Symons, Julian	MORTAL CONSEQUENCES	Marvin Lachman	5-3 MR 40
Symons, Julian	MORTAL CONSEQUENCES	Charles Shibuk	10 MN R18
Symons, Julian	MORTAL CONSEQUENCES	Wendell H. Taylor	5-3 TAD 159
Symons, Julian	MURDER! MURDER!	Douglas G. Greene	12-3 TAD 234
Symons, Julian	THE PLOT AGAINST ROGER RYDER	James Sandoe	14-4 TAD 366
Symons, Julian	THE TELL-TALE HEART: THE LIFE AND WORKS OF EDGAR ALLAN POE	Marvin Lachman	2-3 PP 32
Symons, Julian	THE TELL-TALE HEART: THE LIFE AND WORKS OF EDGAR ALLAN POE	Ethel Lindsay	4-4 PP 28
Symons, Julian	THE THIRTY-FIRST OF FEBRUARY	Charles Shibuk	12-2 TAD 167
Symons, Julian, ed.	VERDICT OF THIRTEEN: A DETECTION CLUB ANTHOLOGY	Barzun & Taylor	12-3 TAD 263
Symons, Julian, ed.	VERDICT OF THIRTEEN: A DETECTION CLUB ANTHOLOGY	Fred Dueren	13-4 TAD 361
Tack, Alfred	INTERVIEWING'S KILLING	Barzun & Taylor	12-1 TAD 33
Takagi, Akimitsu	NO PATENT ON MURDER	Fred Dueren	10-4 TAD 340
Talbot, Hake	RIM OF THE PIT	Don D'Ammassa	8 MN 22
Talbot, Hake	RIM OF THE PIT	Jeff Meyerson	1-5 MF 49
Talburt, Nancy Ellen, & Lyna L. Montgomery	A MYSTERY READER: STORIES OF DETECTION, ADVENTURE AND HORROR	Allen J. Hubin	8-3 TAD 230
Tannen, Jack	HOW TO IDENTIFY AND COLLECT AMERICAN FIRST EDITIONS	Allen J. Hubin	10-2 TAD 114
Tannenbaum, Barry, & Linda J. LaRosa	THE RANDOM FACTOR	Allen J. Hubin	12-1 TAD 9
Tannenbaum, Barry, & Linda J. LaRosa	THE RANDOM FACTOR	Steve Lewis	3-1 MF 33
Tannenbaum, Barry, & Linda J. LaRosa	THE RANDOM FACTOR	Ethel Lindsay	3-5 PP 46
Tarrant, John	THE CLAUBERG TRIGGER	Allen J. Hubin	12-3 TAD 207
Taschjian, Claire	THE PEKING MAN IS MISSING	Mary A. Grochowski	4 MT 27
Taschjian, Claire	THE PEKING MAN IS MISSING	Jim Huang	6 CL 9
Taschjian, Claire	THE PEKING MAN IS MISSING	Steve Lewis	2-2 MF 33
Taylor, Edith	THE SERPENT UNDER IT	Amnon Kabatchnik	5-6 MR 31
Taylor, John Russell	HITCH: THE LIFE AND TIMES OF ALFRED HITCHCOCK	F.M.Nevins, Jr.	4-2 MF 52

Taylor, Mary Ann	RED IS FOR SHROUDS	Steve Lewis	5-4 MF 21
Taylor, Phoebe Atwood	BANBURY BOG	Lianne Carlin	3-4 MR 12
Taylor, Phoebe Atwood	COLD STEEL	Charles Shibuk	14-3 TAD 267
Taylor, Phoebe Atwood	THE CUT DIRECT	Charles Shibuk	12-4 TAD 369
Taylor, Phoebe Atwood	PROOF OF THE PUDDING	Mary A. Grochowski	2-4 PP 31
Taylor, Phoebe Atwood	THREE PLOTS FOR ASEY MAYO	Douglas G. Greene	12-3 TAD 231
Taylor, Sam S.	SO COLD, MY BED	Bill Crider	6 PE 17
Taylor, Wendell H., & Jacques Barzun	A BOOK OF PREFACES TO FIFTY CLASSICS OF CRIME FICTION 1900-1950	Charles Shibuk	11-2 TAD 124
Taylor, Wendell H., & Jacques Barzun	A CATALOGUE OF CRIME	William J. Clark	16 JD 14
Taylor, Wendell H., & Jacques Barzun	A CATALOGUE OF CRIME	Marvin Lachman	4-5 MR 32
Taylor, Wendell H., & Jacques Barzun	A CATALOGUE OF CRIME	Charles Shibuk	4-4 TAD 243
Taylor, Wendell H., & Jacques Barzun	A CATALOGUE OF CRIME	Robert E. Washer	3-2 QC 18
Teilhet, Darwin L.	HERO BY PROXY	Robert C.S.Adey	5-3 MF 40
Teilhet, Darwin L.	MURDER IN THE AIR	Charles Shibuk	8-2 TAD 140
Teresa, Vincent	WISEGUYS	Allen J. Hubin	11-3 TAD 233
Terman, Douglas	FIRST STRIKE	Allen J. Hubin	13-3 TAD 203
Terman, Douglas	FIRST STRIKE	Bill Scanlon	1-3 M 18
Terman, Douglas	FREE FLIGHT	Allen J. Hubin	14-1 TAD 20
Terrall, Robert	SAND DOLLARS	Steve Lewis	3-3 MF 34
Tey, Josephine	A SHILLING FOR CANDLES	Charles Shibuk	14-2 TAD 183
Tey, Josephine	BRAT FARRAR	Charles Shibuk	10-4 TAD 361
Tey, Josephine	THE DAUGHTER OF TIME	Don Miller	5/6 MN 21
Tey, Josephine	THE DAUGHTER OF TIME	Charles Shibuk	10-2 TAD 150
Tey, Josephine	THE FRANCHISE AFFAIR	Charles Shibuk	10-3 TAD 239
Tey, Josephine	TO LOVE AND BE WISE	Don Miller	8 MN 16
Tey, Josephine	YOUNG AND INNOCENT (film)	William K. Everson	3-4 TAD 242
Tey, Josephine	YOUNG AND INNOCENT (film)	James Mark Purcell	12-1 TAD 81
Thayer, Lee	GUILT EDGED	Maryell Cleary	2-5 PP 32
Theroux, Paul	THE FAMILY ARSENAL	Peter Wolfe	10-1 TAD 60
Thevenin, Raymond, and others	MADAME LE JUGE	Barzun & Taylor	11-3 TAD 281
Thierry, James F.	THE ADVENTURE OF THE ELEVEN CUFF BUTTONS	Allen J. Hubin	13-2 TAD 97
Thomas, Craig	WOLFSBANE	Theodore Dukeshire	3-4 MF 49
Thomas, Craig	SNOW FALCON	Allen J. Hubin	14-3 TAD 220
Thomas, Frank	SHERLOCK HOLMES AND THE GOLDEN BIRD	Edward Lauterbach	13-2 TAD 146
Thomas, Frank	SHERLOCK HOLMES AND THE SACRED SWORD	Horace Harker	2-2 M 40
Thomas, Jim	CROSS PURPOSE	Amnon Kabatchnik	2-6 MF 41
Thomas, Ross	CHINAMAN'S CHANCE	Allen J. Hubin	11-4 TAD 332
Thomas, Ross	THE FOOLS IN TOWN ARE ON OUR SIDE	Steve Lewis	8 MN 23
Thomas, Ross	THE MORDIDA MAN	Dorothy B. Hughes	3-1 M 36
Thomas, Ross	THE MORDIDA MAN	Steve Lewis	5-6 MF 34
Thomas, Ross	THE MORDIDA MAN	Gary Warren Niebuhr	4-3 PP 5
Thomas, Ross	YELLOW-DOG CONTRACT	C.A.Finch	12-1 TAD 79
Thomas, Ross	YELLOW-DOG CONTRACT	Guy M. Townsend	11 MN R8
Thompson, Estelle	FIND A CROOKED SIXPENCE	Steve Lewis	2-5 MF 36
Thompson, Estelle	HUNTER IN THE DARK	D.E.Ath	2-1 PP 14
Thompson, Estelle	HUNTER IN THE DARK	Steve Lewis	3-6 MF 28
Thompson, Gene	MURDER MYSTERY	Steve Lewis	5-2 MF 18
Thompson, Gene	MURDER MYSTERY	Sam Yamato	2-2 M 56
Thompson, Jim	THE ALCOHOLICS	Bill Crider	1-3 PQ 51
Thompson, Jim	THE GRIFTERS	Bill Crider	3-4 PP 32
Thompson, Jim	THE KILLER INSIDE ME	Larry Rickert	4-1 PP 29
Thompson, Thomas	SERPENTINE	Steven Miller	3-6 PP 27
Thomson, H.Douglas	MASTERS OF MYSTERY: A STUDY OF THE DETECTIVE STORY	Jane S. Bakerman	13/14 CL 9

Thomson, H.Douglas	MASTERS OF MYSTERY: A STUDY OF THE DETECTIVE STORY	Jon L. Breen	3-3 TAD 200
Thomson, H.Douglas	MASTERS OF MYSTERY: A STUDY OF THE DETECTIVE STORY	M.S.Cappadonna	12-1 TAD 95
Thomson, H.Douglas	MASTERS OF MYSTERY: A STUDY OF THE DETECTIVE STORY	Charles Shibuk	12-1 TAD 30
Thomson, June	A QUESTION OF IDENTITY	Barzun & Talor	12-1 TAD 33
Thomson, June	A QUESTION OF IDENTITY	Mary Groff	8 CL 9
Thomson, June	DEATH CAP	Jim Huang	2 CL 2
Thomson, June	DEATH CAP	Jim Huang	11-1 TAD 21
Thomson, June	DEATH CAP	Steve Lewis	3-1 MF 37
Thomson, June	THE LONG REVENGE	Allen J. Hubin	8-4 TAD 309
Thomson, June	NOT ONE OF US	Amnon Kabatchnik	5-2 MR 39
Thornburg, Newton	CUTTER AND BONE	Jeff Meyerson	1-4 MF 43
Thornburg, Newton	KNOCKOVER	Fred Dueren	8-4 TAD 295
Thorndyke, Russell	DEVIL IN THE BELFRY	Angelo Panagos	13-3 TAD 270
Thornton, Francis J.	THE SNAKE HARVEST	Carl Hoffman	13-3 TAD 268
Thorp, Roderick	NOTHING LASTS FOREVER	F.M.Nevins, Jr.	4-1 MF 33
Thorwald, Jurgen	THE CENTURY OF THE DETECTIVE	R.W.Hays	4-1 TAD 47
Tidyman, Ernest	SHAFT (film)	Richard S. Lochte	5-1 TAD 41
Tilton, Alice	BEGINNING WITH A BASH	Charles Shibuk	7-2 TAD 128
Tilton, Alice	THE IRON CLEW	Maryell Cleary	3-4 PP 31
Tine, Robert	STATE OF GRACE	Allen J. Hubin	14-3 TAD 221
Tippette, Giles	WILSON'S GOLD	Bill Crider	4-3 MF 42
Titus, Eve	BASIL OF BAKER STREET	Stanley A. Carlin	3-6 MR 24
Titus, Eve	BASIL OF BAKER STREET	Donald J. Pattow	8-3 TAD 223
Todd, Peter	THE ADVENTURES OF HERLOCK SHOLMES	Allen J. Hubin	10-1 TAD 5
Todd, Peter	THE ADVENTURES OF HERLOCK SHOLMES	Martin M. Wooster	2-5 MF 41
Toepfer, Ray Grant	ENDPLAY	Steve Lewis	2-1 MF 29
Tomlinson, Everett T.	BOY SAILORS OF 1812	C.L.Messecar	3-2 BC 320
Tomlinson, Everett T.	FOR THE STARS AND STRIPES	C.L.Messecar	3-4 BC 372
Tomlinson, Everett T.	FOUR BOYS IN THE YOSEMITE	C.L.Messecar	3-3 BC 352
Tomlinson, Everett T.	FOUR BOYS ON PIKE'S PEAK	C.L.Messecar	3-4 BC 371
Tomlinson, Everett T.	THE PENNANT	C.L.Messecar	3-2 BC 319
Tomlinson, Everett T.	THE YOUNG MINUTE-MAN OF 1812	C.L.Messecar	3-2 BC 320
Tomlinson, Everett T.	THE YOUNG SHARPSHOOTER	C.L.Messecar	3-2 BC 319
Toole, Wyc	DEATH IN DEEP SHADOWS	Allen J. Hubin	10-4 TAD 307
Torrey, Roger	42 DAYS TO MURDER	Charles Shibuk	9-2 TAD 143
Tourney, Leonard	THE PLAYER'S BOY IS DEAD	Thomas Godfrey	3-2 M 39
Tourteau,Jean-Jacques	D'ARSENE LUPIN A SAN-ANTONIO: LE ROMAN POLICIER FRANCAIS DE 1900 A 1970	Jack Edmund Nolan	5-2 MR 46
Towne, Stuart	DEATH OUT OF THIN AIR	Angelo Panagos	9-3 TAD 230
Townsend, Guy M., & John J. McAleer, Judson C. Sapp, Arrican Schemer	REX STOUT: AN ANNOTATED PRIMARY AND SECONDARY BIBLIOGRAPHY	Linda Toole	5-2 MF 29
Townsley, Joel	THE RED RIGHT HAND	Charles Shibuk	12-2 TAD 179
Toye, Randall	THE AGATHA CHRISTIE WHO'S WHO	Howard Lachtman	14-1 TAD 54
Trachtman, Paula	DISTURB NOT THE DREAM	M.S.Cappadonna	14-3 TAD 270
Tracy, Don	CRISS CROSS (film)	William K. Everson	7-1 TAD 24
Tracy, Don	HIGH, WIDE AND RANSOM	Steve Lewis	1-2 MF 28
Tracy, Jack	THE ENCYCLOPEDIA SHERLOCKIANA	Fred Dueren	13-2 TAD 136
Tracy, Jack	THE ENCYCLOPEDIA SHERLOCKIANA	Jim Huang	5 CL 2
Tracy, Jack	THE ENCYCLOPEDIA SHERLOCKIANA	Charles Shibuk	13-2 TAD 135
Tracy, Jack, ed.	SHERLOCK HOLMES: THE PUBLISHED APOCRYPHA BY SIR ARTHUR CONAN DOYLE & ASSOCIATED HANDS	Horace Harker	2-2 M 40
Tracy, Jack	SHERLOCK HOLMES CALENDAR 1978	Jim Huang	5 CL 2
Travers, Ben	PLUNDER (stage)	Jackie Meyerson	1-5 PP 18
Travis, Gretcher	2 SPRUCE LANE	Barbara A. Buhrer	11 MN R14
Treat, Lawrence	P AS IN POLICE	Robert E. Washer	3-1 QC 18
Treibich, S.J., & Lawrence M. Janifer	TARGET TERRA	Gary Zachrich	71 PU 21

Trevanian	THE LOO SANCTION	George Fergus	9 MN R15
Trevanian	SHIBUMI	Steven Miller	3-4 PP 33
Trevor, Elleston	THE THETA SYNDROME	Amnon Kabatchnik	2-1 MF 34
Trew, Anthony	ZHUKOV BRIEFING	Barbara A. Buhrer	2-4 MM 4
Trott, Nicholas	MONKEY BOAT	Hal Brodsky	8-2 TAD 139
Troy, Simon	NO MORE A-ROVING	Barzun & Taylor	11-4 TAD 394
Truesdale, June	THE MORGUE THE MERRIER	Steve Lewis	3-6 MF 39
Truman, Margaret	MURDER IN THE WHITE HOUSE	Billy Barton	5-5 MF 31
Truman, Margaret	MURDER IN THE WHITE HOUSE	Thomas Godfrey	2-1 M 28
Truman, Margaret	MURDER IN THE WHITE HOUSE	Richard Moskowitz	8 LR 5
Truman, Margaret	MURDER IN THE WHITE HOUSE	F.M.Nevins, Jr.	4-4 MF 47
Truman, Margaret	MURDER ON CAPITOL HILL	F.M.Nevins, Jr.	5-6 MF 47
Tuck, Donald H.	THE ENCYCLOPEDIA OF SCIENCE FICTION AND FANTASY	Allen J. Hubin	7-3 TAD 221
Tucker, Wilson	THE TIME MASTERS	David Bates	2 PE 21
Tucker, Wilson	TO KEEP OR KILL	Steve Lewis	5-3 MF 28
Tucker, Wilson	THE WARLOCK	Lianne Carlin	3-3 MR 30
Turner, Bessie	A WOMAN IN THE CASE: A STORY	Allen J. Hubin	7-2 TAD 134
Turner, J.V.	MURDER - NINE AND OUT	Allen J. Hubin	6-3 TAD 190
Turner, Robert	THE GIRL IN THE COP'S POCKET	Steve Lewis	2-4 MM 5
Turner, Robert	SHROUD 9	Pat Erhardt	3-3 MR 29
Turner, Robert	SOME OF MY BEST FRIENDS ARE WRITERS BUT I WOULDN'T WANT MY DAUGHTER TO MARRY ONE!	Stanley A. Carlin	4-2 MR 18
Turner, Robert	SOME OF MY BEST FRIENDS ARE WRITERS BUT I WOULDN'T WANT MY DAUGHTER TO MARRY ONE!	F.M.Nevins, Jr.	4-2 TAD 122
Turton, Godfrey	THE DEVIL'S CHURCHYARD	Veronica M. Kennedy	9-3 TAD 222
Tuska, Jon	THE DETECTIVE IN HOLLYWOOD	Mary Groff	1-3 PP 30
Tuska, Jon	THE DETECTIVE IN HOLLYWOOD	Amnon Kabatchnik	12 CL 3
Tuska, Jon	THE DETECTIVE IN HOLLYWOOD	F.M.Nevins, Jr.	2-4 MF 38
Tuska, Jon	PHILO VANCE: THE LIFE AND TIMES OF S.S.VAN DINE	Lianne Carlin	5-2 MR 45
Tuska, Jon	PHILO VANCE: THE LIFE AND TIMES OF S.S.VAN DINE	J. Randolph Cox	5-3 TAD 166
Tuska, Jon	PHILO VANCE: THE LIFE AND TIMES OF S.S.VAN DINE	Allen J. Hubin	5-2 TAD 103
Tute, Warren	A MATTER OF DIPLOMACY	Robert E. Washer	2-1 QC 18
Tyler, W.T.	THE MAN WHO LOST THE WAR	Allen J. Hubin	14-3 TAD 221
Tynan, Kathleen	AGATHA	Barbara A. Buhrer	13 MN R1
Tynan, Kathleen	AGATHA	Jim Huang	11 CL 10
Uhnak, Dorothy	THE BAIT	Barzun & Taylor	9-2 TAD 93
Uhnak, Dorothy	THE INVESTIGATION	Jane S. Bakerman	2-1 MF 41
Uhnak, Dorothy	THE INVESTIGATION	Jim Huang	9 CL 6
Uhnak, Dorothy	THE INVESTIGATION	Amnon Kabatchnik	6 CL 3
Uhnak, Dorothy	THE LEDGER	James Sandoe	13-4 TAD 292
Ulsh, Wayne C.	RIP-OFF	R. Jeff Banks	3 PE 21
Underwood, Michael	A TROUT IN THE MILK	Amnon Kabatchnik	5-5 MR 34
Underwood, Michael	CRIME UPON CRIME	Charles Jardinier	2-3 M 48
Underwood, Michael	CROOKED WOOD	Allen J. Hubin	12-2 TAD 116
Underwood, Michael	CROOKED WOOD	Steve Lewis	3-3 MF 36
Underwood, Michael	THE FATAL TRIP	Allen J. Hubin	11-4 TAD 331
Underwood, Michael	MENACES, MENACES	Barzun & Taylor	10-3 TAD 225
Underwood, Michael	VICTIM OF CIRCUMSTANCE	Allen J. Hubin	13-4 TAD 298
Underwood, Peter, ed.	THIRTEEN FAMOUS GHOST STORIES	Fred Dueren	11-2 TAD 192
Underwood, Tim, & Daniel J.H.Levack	FANTASMS: A JACK VANCE BIBLIOGRAPHY	Charlotte Laughlin	1-4 PQ 52
Unekis, Richard	THE CHASE	John Vining	10-2 TAD 141
Upfield, Arthur W.	AN AUTHOR BITES THE DUST	Barzun & Taylor	14-1 TAD 89
Upfield, Arthur W.	AN AUTHOR BITES THE DUST	Guy M. Townsend	1A MF 32
Upfield, Arthur W.	DEATH OF A LAKE	Michael Cropper	3-4 MF 50
Upfield, Arthur W.	THE GREAT MELBOURNE CUP MYSTERY	Philip T. Asdell	4-5/6 PP 66
Upfield, Arthur W.	JOURNEY TO THE HANGMAN	Guy M. Townsend	1A MF 32
Upfield, Arthur W.	MAN OF TWO TRIBES	Michael Cropper	3-4 MF 51

Upfield, Arthur W.	THE MOUNTAINS HAVE A SECRET	Michael Cropper	3-4 MF 51
Upfield, Arthur W.	MURDER MUST WAIT	Michael Cropper	3-4 MF 51
Upfield, Arthur W.	THE NEW SHOE	Don Miller	12 MN R5
Upfield, Arthur W.	THE NEW SHOE	Arthur C. Scott	1-2 MF 33
Upfield, Arthur W.	THE NEW SHOE	Charles Shibuk	10-2 TAD 116
Upfield, Arthur W.	THE NEW SHOE	Martin M. Wooster	1-2 MF 32
Upfield, Arthur W.	THE SANDS OF WINDEE	Don Miller	12 MN R5
Upfield, Arthur W.	WINGS ABOVE THE DIAMANTINA	Michael Cropper	3-4 MF 51
Upton, Robert	A GOLDEN FLEECING	D.G.Smoke	1-3 M 18
Uris, Leon	TOPAZ (film)	F.M.Nevins, Jr.	3-3 MR 22
Urquhart, Macgregor	FRAIL ON NORTH CIRCULAR	Robert C.S.Adey	4-1 PP 29
Utechin, Nicholas, & Austin Mitchelson	THE EARTHQUAKE MACHINE	Edward Lauterbach	10-1 TAD 63
Utechin, Nicholas, & Austin Mitchelson	THE EARTHQUAKE MACHINE	Timothy J. Rutt	1-1 WA 9
Utechin, Nicholas, & Austin Mitchelson	HELLBIRDS	Edward Lauterbach	10-2 TAD 115
Vachell, Horace A., & Archibald Marshall	MOTE HOUSE MYSTERY	Charles Shibuk	13-3 TAD 269
Valin, Jonathan	DEAD LETTER	F.M.Nevins, Jr.	5-6 MF 46
Valin, Jonathan	FINAL NOTICE	F.M.Nevins, Jr.	5-2 MF 29
Valin, Jonathan	THE LIME PIT	Paul Bishop	2-1 M 27
Valin, Jonathan	THE LIME PIT	Allen J. Hubin	13-3 TAD 203
Valin, Jonathan	THE LIME PIT	Steve Lewis	4-4 MF 35
Valin, Jonathan	THE LIME PIT	Charles Shibuk	14-4 TAD 377
Van Ash, Cay, & Elizabeth Sax Rohmer	MASTER OF VILLAINY: A BIOGRAPHY OF SAX ROHMER	Lianne Carlin	5-4 MR 34
Van Ash, Cay, & Elizabeth Sax Rohmer	MASTER OF VILLAINY: A BIOGRAPHY OF SAX ROHMER	J. Randolph Cox	5-4 TAD 230
Van Ash, Cay, & Elizabeth Sax Rohmer	MASTER OF VILLAINY: A BIOGRAPHY OF SAX ROHMER	Marvin Lachman	9 R 27
Vance, Jack	BLUE WORLD	Gary Zachrich	64 PU 42
Vance, Jack	THE DIRDIR	Gary Zachrich	73 PU 34
Vance, Jack	THE LANGUAGES OF PAO	Gary Zachrich	64 PU 43
Vance, John Holbrook	THE FOX VALLEY MURDERS	Lianne Carlin	3-3 MR 30
van de Wetering, Janwillen	THE CORPSE ON THE DIKE	Steve Lewis	1-1 MF 30
van de Wetering, Janwillem	DEATH OF A HAWKER	Allen J. Hubin	10-4 TAD 308
van de Wetering, Janwillem	THE JAPANESE CORPSE	Myrtis Broset	2-6 MF 41
van de Wetering, Janwillem	THE JAPANESE CORPSE	Steve Lewis	2-5 MF 28
van de Wetering, Janwillem	THE MAINE MASSACRE	George N. Dove	3-2 MF 42
van de Wetering, Janwillem	THE MAINE MASSACRE	George N. Dove	12-2 TAD 181
van de Wetering, Janwillem	OUTSIDER IN AMSTERDAM	Frank Denton	8 MN 13
van de Wetering, Janwillem	TUMBLEWEED	Jane S. Bakerman	2-2 PP 28
van de Wetering, Janwillem	TUMBLEWEED	Myrtis Broset	1-2 MF 42
Van Dine, S.S.	THE KENNEL MURDER CASE (film)	William K. Everson	2-2 TAD 85
Van Greenaway, Peter	THE MEDUSA TOUCH	Robert C.S.Adey	4-5/6 PP 73
Van Greenaway, Peter	THE MEDUSA TOUCH	Allen J. Hubin	7-2 TAD 143
Van Gulik, Robert	CELEBRATED CASES OF JUDGE DEE	Barzun & Taylor	12-1 TAD 33
Van Gulik, Robert	CELEBRATED CASES OF JUDGE DEE	M.S.Cappadonna	10-4 TAD 312
Van Gulik, Robert	CELEBRATED CASES OF JUDGE DEE	Charles Shibuk	10-2 TAD 150
Van Gulik, Robert	THE CHINESE BELL MURDERS	Barzun & Taylor	12-1 TAD 33
Van Gulik, Robert	THE CHINESE BELL MURDERS	Charles Shibuk	11-2 TAD 189
Van Gulik, Robert	THE CHINESE GOLD MURDERS	Charles Shibuk	13-3 TAD 251
Van Gulik, Robert	THE CHINESE LAKE MURDERS	Charles Shibuk	13-3 TAD 251
Van Gulik, Robert	THE CHINESE NAIL MURDERS	Barzun & Taylor	12-1 TAD 33

Van Gulik, Robert	THE CHINESE NAIL MURDERS	Charles Shibuk	11-2 TAD 189
Van Gulik, Robert	THE HAUNTED MONASTERY and THE CHINESE MAZE MURDERS	Charles Shibuk	11-1 TAD 97
Van Gulik, Robert	JUDGE DEE AT WORK: EIGHT CHINESE DETECTIVE STORIES	Douglas G. Greene	12-3 TAD 234
Van Gulik, Robert	THE LACQUER SCREEN	Don Miller	2-5 MM 9
Van Gulik, Robert	THE MONKEY AND THE TIGER	Don Miller	8 MN 26
Van Gulik, Robert	THE PHANTOM OF THE TEMPLE	Don Miller	10 MN R17
Van Gulik, Robert	POETS AND MURDER	Don Miller	2-4 MM 6
Van Gulik, Robert	THE WILLOW PATTERN	Gary Happenstand	2-2 C 160
Vann, J.Donn	GRAHAM GREENE: A CHECKLIST OF CRITICISM	Pat Erhardt	4-1 MR 32
Van Sickle, Dirck	MONTANA GOTHIC	J. Grant Thiessen	10 SF 40
Van Scyoc, Sidney	SALT FLOWER	Gary Zachrich	75 PU 26
Van Vogt, A.E.	QUEST FOR THE FUTURE	Gary Zachrich	75 PU 24
Van Vogt, A.E.	REFLECTIONS OF A.E.VAN VOGT	W. Paul Ganley	5 U 29
Van Vogt, A.E., & E.Mayne Hull	THE WINGED MAN	Gary Zachrich	75 PU 26
Veley, Charles	NIGHT WHISPERS	Elizabeth Wentworth	2-1 M 28
Vercors	YOU SHALL KNOW THEM	Michele B. Slung	8-3 TAD 221
Vermandel, Janet G.	LAST SEEN IN SAMARRA	Allen J. Hubin	6-2 TAD 114
Versin, Pierre	ENCYCLOPEDIE DE L'UTOPIE ET DE LA SCIENCE	Bruce Robbins	20 X 39
Vestal, Stanley	THE WINE ROOM MURDER	Hal Brodsky	7-3 TAD 213
Vestal, Stanley	THE WINE ROOM MURDER	Angelo Panagos	11-4 TAD 381
Vickers, Roy	THE DEPARTMENT OF DEAD ENDS: FOURTEEN DETECTIVE STORIES	Joe R. Christopher	14-4 TAD 364
Vickers, Roy	THE DEPARTMENT OF DEAD ENDS: FOURTEEN DETECTIVE STORIES	Charles Shibuk	12-2 TAD 167
Vickers, Roy	THE EXPLOITS OF FIDELITY DOVE	Angelo Panagos	13-3 TAD 270
Vickers, Roy	THE GIRL IN THE NEWS (film)	William K. Everson	5-4 TAD 222
Vidal, Gore	MATTERS OF FACT & FICTION	George Kelley	1-5 MF 39
Viereck, George S.	THE HOUSE OF THE VAMPIRE	Mary A. Grochowski	4 MT 39
Vinge, Joan D.	THE SNOW QUEEN	J. Grant Thiessen	14 SF 19
Vinson, James, ed.	CONTEMPORARY NOVELISTS	Mary Groff	2-3 PP 35
Vipond, Don	NIGHT OF THE SHOOTING STAR	Allen J. Hubin	9-1 TAD 72
Vulliamy, C.E.	CAKES FOR YOUR BIRTHDAY	Jim McCahery	2-5 PP 33
Vulliamy, C.E.	TEA AT THE ABBEY	Charles Shibuk	7-1 TAD 55
Wade, Henry	A DYING FALL	George Kelley	4-4 PP 42
Wade, Jennifer	THE SINGING WIND	Janie Filstrup	1-1 PP 23
Wager, Walter	BLUE LEADER	Marlowe Archer	4 PE 24
Wager, Walter	BLUE LEADER	Paul Bishop	6 PE 20
Wager, Walter	BLUE LEADER	Bill Crider	5-5 MF 40
Wager, Walter	SLEDGEHAMMER	Stan Burns	9 MN R13
Wager, Walter	SLEDGEHAMMER	Charles Shibuk	10-1 TAD 72
Wager, Walter	SWAP	Stan Burns	2-1 MM 4
Wager, Walter	TELEFON	Stan Burns	1-10 MM 8
Wager, Walter	TELEFON	Allen J. Hubin	8-4 TAD 310
Wager, Walter	TIME OF RECKONING	George Kelley	4-5/6 PP 77
Wager, Walter	VIPER THREE	Stan Burns	1-7 MM 7
Wagner, Elaine	A CASE OF BOTTLED MURDER	Allen J. Hubin	7-1 TAD 62
Wagner, Karl Edward	THE YEAR'S BEST HORROR STORIES, SERIES VIII	Fred Dueren	14-1 TAD 81
Wagoner, David	THE HANGING GARDEN	Allen J. Hubin	14-3 TAD 221
Wahloo, Per, & Maj Sjowall	THE FIRE ENGINE THAT DISAPPEARED	Amnon Kabatchnik	3-4 MR 34
Wahloo, Per, & Maj Sjowall	THE LOCKED ROOM	Allen J. Hubin	7-1 TAD 62
Wahloo, Per, & Maj Sjowall	THE LOCKED ROOM	Don Miller	11 MN R16
Wahloo, Per, & Maj Sjowall	MAN ON A ROOF (film)	C. & J. Filstrup	10-3 TAD 210
Wahloo, Per, & Maj Sjowall	THE MAN WHO WENT UP IN SMOKE	Don Miller	9 MN R17

Wahloo, Per, & Maj Sjowall	MURDER AT THE SAVOY	Don Miller	12 MN R6
Wahloo, Per, & Maj Sjowall	THE TERRORISTS	Barzun & Taylor	11-1 TAD 93
Wahloo, Per, & Maj Sjowall	THE TERRORISTS	Frank Occhiogrosso	11-2 TAD 120
Wainwright, John	A NEST OF RATS	Allen J. Hubin	11-3 TAD 232
Wainwright, John	THE BASTARD	Allen J. Hubin	11-1 TAD 20
Wainwright, John	DEATH OF A BIG MAN	Fred Dueren	12-3 TAD 287
Wainwright, John	DEATH OF A BIG MAN	Robert W. Hahn	9-1 TAD 69
Wainwright, John	DEATH OF A BIG MAN	Charles Shibuk	12-3 TAD 255
Wainwright, John	DO NOTHIN' TILL YOU HEAR FROM ME	C.J.Murdoch	4 MT 22
Wainwright, John	DOMINOES	Iona Kristopolis	2-2 M 56
Wainwright, John	THE EVIDENCE I SHALL GIVE	Deryck Harvey	7-3 TAD 217
Wainwright, John	THE HARD HIT	Charles Shibuk	12-4 TAD 369
Wainwright, John	POOL OF TEARS	Steve Lewis	2-3 MF 43
Wainwright, John	SQUARE DANCE	Barbara A. Buhrer	1-8 MM 5
Wainwright, John	WHO GOES NEXT?	Allen J. Hubin	11-1 TAD 20
Walker, Dale L.	JACK LONDON, SHERLOCK HOLMES AND SIR ARTHUR CONAN DOYLE	Allen J. Hubin	7-4 TAD 297
Walker, Irma	THE MAUNALOA CURSE	Mary A. Grochowski	2-2 PP 29
Walker, Katherine S., & Dorothy Gardiner	RAYMOND CHANDLER SPEAKING	Jeff Meyerson	1-6 MF 45
Walker, Katherine S., & Dorothy Gardiner	RAYMOND CHANDLER SPEAKING	Charles Shibuk	10-4 TAD 361
Walker, Mark	CASSIS...RESORT TO VENGEANCE	Steve Lewis	3-6 MF 35
Walker, Martin	THE INFILTRATOR	Allen J. Hubin	12-2 TAD 116
Walker, Peter N.	PANDA ONE INVESTIGATES	Deryck Harvey	7-1 TAD 60
Wallace, Edgar	THE BRIGAND	Steve Lewis	1-7 MM 8
Wallace, Edgar	THE FOUR JUST MEN	William K. Everson	6-2 TAD 77
Wallace, Edgar	THE HAIRY ARM	Robert Williams	2 MN 8
Wallace, Edgar	THE MAN FROM MOROCCO	Amnon Kabatchnik	4-1 MR 34
Wallace, Edgar	THE MISSION THAT FAILED	Stanley A. Carlin	4-3 MR 36
Wallace, Irving	THE PIGEON PROJECT	Martin M. Wooster	3-3 MF 44
Wallace, Irving, & David Wallechinsky	THE PEOPLE'S ALMANAC	Timothy J. Rutt	1-1 WA 9
Wallace, Robert	THE CORPSE PARADE	Gary Zachrich	66 PU 58
Wallechinsky, David, & Irving Wallace	THE PEOPLE'S ALMANAC	Timothy J. Rutt	1-1 WA 9
Walling, R.A.J.	THE CORPSE WITH THE DIRTY FACE	Steve Lewis	3-6 MF 33
Wallmann, Jeffrey M.	JUDAS CROSS	Allen J. Hubin	7-4 TAD 296
Walsh, Paul E.	THE MURDER ROOM	Jim McCahery	4-3 PP 23
Walton, Evangeline	WITCH HOUSE	Veronica M.Kennedy	9-3 TAD 222
Wambaugh, Joseph	THE GLITTER DOME	F.M.Nevins, Jr.	5-5 MF 28
Ward, Edward	THE MAIN CHANCE	Allen J. Hubin	10-3 TAD 206
Warner, Douglas	DEATH OF A NUDE	Barzun & Taylor	14-2 TAD 143
Warner, Harry, Jr.	ALL OUR YESTERDAYS	Allen J. Hubin	2-4 TAD 275
Warner, Mignon	A MEDIUM FOR MURDER	Fred Dueren	14-2 TAD 184
Warner, Mignon	THE TAROT MURDERS	Allen J. Hubin	11-4 TAD 332
Warren, Brooke	THE FACE AT THE WINDOW (film)	William K. Everson	2-3 TAD 175
Warren, George	RUN FOR BLOOD	Paul Harwitz	8 LR 4
Warren, George	RUN FOR BLOOD	Paul Harwitz	2-1 M 26
Warren, George	RUN FOR BLOOD	J. Grant Thiessen	10 SF 40
Washburn, Mark	THE ARMAGEDDON GAME	Steve Lewis	1-5 MF 33
Waters	THE EXPERIENCES OF A FRENCH DETECTIVE OFFICER	Allen J. Hubin	10-1 TAD 42
Waters	RECOLLECTIONS OF A DETECTIVE POLICE-OFFICER	Everett F. Bleiler	6-4 TAD 269
Watson, Clarissa	THE BISHOP IN THE BACK SEAT	Allen J. Hubin	13-3 TAD 204
Watson, Clarissa	THE FOURTH STAGE OF GAINSBOROUGH BROWN	Allen J. Hubin	10-3 TAD 204
Watson, Colin	BROOMSTICKS OVER FLAXBOROUGH	Robert C.S.Adey	4-2 PP 28
Watson, Colin	CHARITY ENDS AT HOME	Steve Lewis	2-6 MF 34
Watson, Colin	CHARITY ENDS AT HOME	Jim McCahery	2-4 PP 31
Watson, Colin	CHARITY ENDS AT HOME	Don Miller	5/6 MN 24

Watson, Colin	THE FLAXBOROUGH CHRONICLE	Jim McCahery	1-3 PP 23
Watson, Colin	THE FLAXBOROUGH CRAB	Jim McCahery	3-1 PP 34
Watson, Colin	HOPJOY WAS HERE	Don Miller	9 MN R17
Watson, Colin	JUST WHAT THE DOCTOR ORDERED	Don Miller	11 MN R17
Watson, Colin	KISSING COVENS	Don Miller	1-11 MM 4
Watson, Colin	KISSING COVENS	Guy M. Townsend	1-9 MM 7
Watson, Colin	LONELYHEART	Jim McCahery	2-4 PP 31
Watson, Colin	SIX NUNS AND A SHOTGUN	Allen J. Hubin	8-2 TAD 149
Watson, Colin	SIX NUNS AND A SHOTGUN	Don Miller	9 MN R9
Watson, Colin	SNOBBERY WITH VIOLENCE	Lianne Carlin	5-2 MR 46
Watson, Colin	SNOBBERY WITH VIOLENCE	Wendell H. Taylor	5-3 TAD 159
Watson, Geoffrey	THE NOORIABAD FILE	Allen J. Hubin	13-3 TAD 204
Watson, Lawrence	IN A DARK TIME	Allen J. Hubin	13-3 TAD 204
Waugh, Charles, & Isaac Asimov, Martin H.Greenberg	THE THIRTEEN CRIMES OF SCIENCE FICTION	Martin M. Wooster	4-3 MF 45
Waugh, Carol-Lynn R., Isaac Asimov, Martin H.Greenberg	THE TWELVE CRIMES OF CHRISTMAS	Fred Dueren	4-5/6 PP 100
Waugh, Hillary	FINISH ME OFF	Barzun & Taylor	10-3 TAD 225
Waugh, Hillary	FINISH ME OFF	Stanley A. Carlin	3-6 MR 22
Waugh, Hillary	THE GLENNA POWERS CASE	William L.DeAndrea	14-4 TAD 378
Waugh, Hillary	LAST SEEN WEARING	Maryell Cleary	3-4 PP 31
Waugh, Hillary	MADMAN AT MY DOOR	Allen J. Hubin	12-1 TAD 12
Waugh, Hillary	MANHATTAN EAST	Stanley A. Carlin	4-3 MR 37
Waugh, Hillary	MURDER ON THE TERRACE	Robert C.S.Adey	2-5 PP 32
Waugh, Hillary	THE SHADOW GUEST	Stanley A. Carlin	4-4 MR 36
Waugh, Hillary	THAT NIGHT IT RAINED	Arthur C. Scott	13A MN 9
Waugh, Hillary	THE YOUNG PREY	Stanley A. Carlin	4-3 MR 37
Way, Peter	DIRTY TRICKS	Allen J. Hubin	11-3 TAD 232
Way, Peter	DIRTY TRICKS	Steve Lewis	2-4 MF 31
Webb, Jack	THE GILDED WITCH	Robert C.S.Adey	4-3 PP 23
Webb, James R.	THE ORGANIZATION (film)	Richard S. Lochte	5-2 TAD 104
Webster, Henry K.	THE GHOST GIRL	Charles Shibuk	11-2 TAD 127
Webster, Henry K.	WHO IS THE NEXT?	Steve Lewis	5-5 MF 20
Webster, Henry K.	WHO IS THE NEXT?	Charles Shibuk	14-4 TAD 377
Webster, Noah	A BURIAL IN PORTUGAL	Allen J. Hubin	7-4 TAD 295
Webster, Noah	A WITCHDANCE IN BAVARIA	Barbara A. Buhrer	2-5 MM 6
Webster, Noah	AN INCIDENT IN ICELAND	Steve Lewis	4-2 MF 32
Weill, Gus	A WOMAN'S EYES	Keith Ekblaw	1-1 MF 11
Weill, Gus	THE BONNET MAN	Allen J. Hubin	12-1 TAD 12
Weill, Gus	THE BONNET MAN	Steve Lewis	3-5 MF 36
Wein, Jacqueline	ROOMMATE	M.S.Cappadonna	12-3 TAD 272
Weinberg, Robert,ed.	THE MAN BEHIND DOC SAVAGE	John Vining	9-4 TAD 307
Weintraub, William	THE UNDERDOGS	J. Grant Thiessen	9 SF 43
Weir, Hugh C.	MISS MADELYN MACK, DETECTIVE	Hal Brodsky	10-1 TAD 73
Weisman, John	EVIDENCE	Allen J. Hubin	14-3 TAD 221
Weisman, John	EVIDENCE	Steve Lewis	5-6 MF 39
Welch, Timothy	THE TENNIS MURDERS	Bill Crider	10-1 TAD 65
Welcome, John, ed.	BEST SMUGGLING STORIES	Frank D.McSherry,Jr	2-3 TAD 198
Welles, Patricia	ANGEL IN THE SNOW	Fred Dueren	13-3 TAD 251
Welles, Patricia	ANGEL IN THE SNOW	Bernard Nichunsky	1-3 M 20
Wellesley, Gordon	NIGHT TRAIN TO MUNICH (film)	William K. Everson	6-1 TAD 11
Wellman, Manley Wade	SHERLOCK HOLME'S WAR OF THE WORLD	Edward Lauterbach	9-2 TAD 148
Wells, Anna Mary	A TALENT FOR MURDER	Charles Shibuk	14-4 TAD 377
Wells, Anna Mary	MURDERER'S CHOICE	Charles Shibuk	14-4 TAD 377
Wells, Charlie	THE LAST KILL	Theodore Dukeshire	4-1 MF 30
Wells, Tobias	HAVE MERCY UPON US	Allen J. Hubin	8-2 TAD 148
Wentworth, Patricia	THE CASE IS CLOSED	Maryell Cleary	1-5 PP 19
Wentworth, Patricia	GREY MASK	Maryell Cleary	1-5 PP 19
West, Eliot	THE KILLING KIND	Steve Lewis	2-4 MF 33
West, John B.	DEATH ON THE ROCKS	Jeff Meyerson	1 PE 12
West, Morris	THE SALAMANDER	Michael Cropper	3-5 MF 44
Westlake, Donald E.	BANK SHOT	Barzun & Taylor	9-2 TAD 94

Author	Title	Reviewer	Reference
Westlake, Donald E.	BROTHERS KEEPERS	Don Miller	10 MN R5
Westlake, Donald E.	BUTCHER'S MOON	Allen J. Hubin	7-4 TAD 294
Westlake, Donald E.	CASTLE IN THE AIR	Allen J. Hubin	13-3 TAD 204
Westlake, Donald E.	DANCING AZTECS	Robert C.S.Adey	4-3 PP 25
Westlake, Donald E.	JIMMY THE KID	Don Miller	9 MN R8
Westlake, Donald E.	KILLING TIME	Charles Shibuk	13-4 TAD 364
Westlake, Donald E.	KILLY	Barzun & Taylor	9-2 TAD 94
Westlake, Donald E.	NOBODY'S PERFECT	Steve Lewis	5-1 MF 22
Westlake, Donald E.	TWO MUCH!	Stan Burns	9 MN R3
Westlake, Donald E.	WHO STOLE SASSI MANOON?	Robert E. Washer	1-4 QC 19
Weston, Carolyn	ROUSE THE DEVIL	Steve Lewis	1-1 MF 29
Weston, Carolyn	SUSANNAH SCREAMING	Allen J. Hubin	9-1 TAD 73
Weverka, Robert	MURDER BY DECREE	Joe R. Lansdale	3-5 MF 43
Whaley, F.J.	THE MYSTERY OF NUMBER FIVE	Charles Shibuk	11-1 TAD 27
Wheeler, Gordon	EASY COME	Stan Burns	2 MN 6
Wheeler, Keith	EPITAPH FOR MISTER WYNN	Robert E. Washer	3-1 QC 19
White, Ethel Lina	FEAR STALKS THE VILLAGE	Marvin Lachman	9-3 TAD 277
White, Ethel Lina	THE SPIRAL STAIRCASE (film)	William K. Everson	7-1 TAD 31
White, James	MAJOR OPERATION	Gary Zachrich	75 PU 25
White, James	THE WATCH BELOW	Gary Zachrich	64 PU 43
White, James P., & Anne Reed Rooth	THE NINTH CAR	Allen J. Hubin	12-4 TAD 323
White, John Manchip	THE GAME OF TROY	Lianne Carlin	4-5 MR 36
White, John Manchip	NIGHT CLIMBER	Gary Zachrich	74 PU 26
White, Lionel	THE MEXICO RUN	George Fergus	2 MN 7
White, Osmar	SILENT REACH	Allen J. Hubin	13-4 TAD 298
White, T.H.	DARKNESS AT PEMBERLEY	Robert C.S.Adey	1-2 PP 20
White, T.H.	DARKNESS AT PEMBERLEY	Marvin Lachman	2-5 MF 3
White, T.H.	DARKNESS AT PEMBERLEY	Charles Shibuk	11-3 TAD 298
White, T.H., & Ronald McNair Scott	DEAD MR. NIXON	E.F.Bleiler	3-2 MF 43
White, Ted	PHOENIX PRIME	Gary Zachrich	63 PU 54
White, Terence deVere	MY NAME IS NORVAL	David McGee	4-1 MF 29
Whitechurch, Victor L.	THE ADVENTURES OF CAPTAIN IVAN KORAVITCH: LATCH OF THE IMPERIAL RUSSIAN ARMY	Charles Shibuk	10-2 TAD 139
Whitechurch, Victor L.	STORY OF THE RAILWAY	Edward Lauterbach	11-4 TAD 402
Whitehouse, Arch	THE YEARS OF THE SKY KINGS	Gary Zachrich	70 PU 28
Whitfield, Raoul	GREEN ICE	Martin M. Wooster	4-5/6 PP 67
Whitfield, Raoul	THE "VIRGIN" KILLS	Steve Lewis	5-5 MF 24
Whitley, Alex	ARMSTRONG	Barzun & Taylor	11-1 TAD 93
Whitney, Phyllis A.	MYSTERY OF THE ANGRY IDOL	Steve Lewis	2-6 MF 34
Whitney, Phyllis A.	THE STONE BULL	Barbara A. Buhrer	13A MN 9
Whitney, Steven	SINGLED OUT	Allen J. Hubin	12-2 TAD 116
Whitney, Steven	SINGLED OUT	Amnon Kabatchnik	3-1 MF 42
Whitney, Steven	SINGLED OUT	Steve Lewis	3-3 MF 32
Whittington, Harry	THE HUMMING BOX	Theodore Dukeshire	3-4 MF 49
Whittington, Harry	ONE DEADLY DAWN	Steve Lewis	9 MN R16
Whittington-Egan, R.	THE RIDDLE OF BIRDHURST RISE	Neville W. Wood	10-1 TAD 65
Whyte-Melville, G.J.	M. OR N.	Allen J. Hubin	10-1 TAD 42
Wilcox, Collin	AFTERSHOCK	Robert E. Washer	17 X 60
Wilcox, Collin	AFTERSHOCK	Stan Burns	5/6 MN 17
Wilcox, Collin	AFTERSHOCK	Allen J. Hubin	8-4 TAD 310
Wilcox, Collin	DEAD AIM	Barzun & Taylor	11-4 TAD 394
Wilcox, Collin	DEAD AIM	Lianne Carlin	5-1 MR 34
Wilcox, Collin	DOCTOR, LAWYER...	R. Jeff Banks	11 MN R11
Wilcox, Collin	DOCTOR, LAWYER...	Steve Lewis	2-1 MF 23
Wilcox, Collin	DOCTOR, LAWYER...	Guy M. Townsend	11 MN R11
Wilcox, Collin	POWER PLAYS	Steve Lewis	3-6 MF 29
Wilcox, Collin	THE THIRD FIGURE	Allen J. Hubin	1-3 TAD 103
Wilcox, Collin	THE WATCHER	Allen J. Hubin	11-3 TAD 233
Wilcox, Collin	THE WATCHER	Steve Lewis	2-5 MF 29
Wilcox, Collin, & Bill Pronzini	TWOSPOT	Bill Crider	2-6 MF 36
Wilcox, Collin, & Bill Pronzini	TWOSPOT	Mary A. Grochowski	2-6 PP 35

Wilcox, Collin, & Bill Pronzini	TWOSPOT	Steve Lewis	3-1 MF 36
Wilden, Theodore	EXCHANGE OF CLOWNS	Martin M. Wooster	4-5/6 PP 81
Wilden, Theodore	TO DIE ELSEWHERE	Steve Lewis	2-1 MF 29
Wilder, Billy, & I.A.L.Diamond	THE PRIVATE LIFE OF SHERLOCK HOLMES (film)	J. Randolph Cox	4-3 TAD 178
Wiles, Domini	DEATH FLIGHT	Steven Miller	3 MT 13
Wilhelm, Kate	CITY OF CAIN	Jim Huang	10 CL 9
Wilkerson, Michael, & Dick	SOMEONE CRY FOR THE CHILDREN	Thomas Godfrey	3-2 M 39
Wilkerson, Michael, & Dick	SOMEONE CRY FOR THE CHILDREN	George Kelley	4-3 PP 28
Williams, Charles	AGROUND AND DEAD CALM	Amnon Kabatchnik	5-2 MR 41
Williams, David	MURDER FOR TREASURE	Iona Kristopolis	2-3 M 47
Williams, David	TREASURE BY DEGREES	Allen J. Hubin	11-2 TAD 118
Williams, David	TREASURE BY DEGREES	Steve Lewis	2-5 MF 26
Williams, David	TREASURE UP IN SMOKE	Ralph Diffinetti	4 PE 15
Williams, David	TREASURE UP IN SMOKE	Allen J. Hubin	12-2 TAD 116
Williams, David	UNHOLY WRIT	Allen J. Hubin	10-4 TAD 307
Williams, David	UNHOLY WRIT	Steve Lewis	2-1 MF 21
Williams, Gordon M.	THE SIEGE OF TRENCHER'S FARM	Robert E. Washer	2-1 QC 17
Williams, Hawley	BATTER UP!	C.L.Messecar	3-4 BC 371
Williams, Hawley	QUARTERBACK RECKLESS	C.L.Messecar	3-3 BC 351
Williams, Sidney	THE DRURY CLUB CASE	James Kingman	12-1 TAD 80
Williamson, Jack	DARKER THAN YOU THINK	Martin M. Wooster	3-5 PP 36
Williamson, Jack	THE HUMANOID TOUCH	J. Grant Thiessen	14 SF 19
Williamson, Sherman	THE GLORY GAME	Steve Lewis	2-4 MF 30
Williamson, Sherman	THE GLORY TRAP	Allen J. Hubin	11-3 TAD 231
Williamson, Tony	THE SAMSON STRIKE	Allen J. Hubin	14-1 TAD 20
Willis, Ted	THE LEFT-HANDED SLEEPER	Allen J. Hubin	9-3 TAD 224
Willis, Ted	WESTMINSTER ONE	Allen J. Hubin	8-3 TAD 228
Willock, Ruth	I, VICTORIA STRANGE	Barbara A. Buhrer	8 MN 11
Wills, Garry	AT BUTTONS	Gary Warren Niebuhr	2-3 PP 36
Wills, Thomas	YOU'LL GET YOURS	Stephen Mertz	4 PE 13
Wilmer, Dale	DEAD FALL	Charles Shibuk	9-2 TAD 142
Wilmot, Robert P.	BLOOD IN YOUR EYE	Steve Lewis	2-1 MF 30
Wilson, Colin	LINGARD	Lianne Carlin	5-6 MR 36
Wilson, Colin	THE PHILOSOPHER'S STONE	W. Paul Ganley	6 U 26
Wilson, Colin	THE SCHOOLGIRL MURDER CASE	Barzun & Taylor	9-4 TAD 272
Wilson, Jacqueline	MAKING HATE	Steve Lewis	2-6 MF 33
Wilson, P.W.	THE OLD MILL	Charles Shibuk	7-4 TAD 290
Wilson, Robert Anton	MASKS OF THE ILLUMINATI	Martin M. Wooster	4-3 PP 29
Wingate, William	SHOTGUN	Allen J. Hubin	14-1 TAD 20
Winks, Robin W., ed.	THE HISTORIAN AS DETECTIVE: ESSAYS ON EVIDENCE	F.M.Nevins, Jr.	3-2 TAD 132
Winn, Dilys	MURDER INK	J. Randolph Cox	11-2 TAD 119
Winn, Dilys	MURDER INK	Jim Huang	6 CL 5
Winn, Dilys	MURDER INK	William A.Karpowicz	3 MT 19
Winn, Dilys	MURDER INK	Charles Shibuk	11-2 TAD 189
Winn, Dilys	MURDERESS INK	W.Ritchie Benedict	8 U 144
Winn, Dilys	MURDERESS INK	Norman D. Hinton	13-2 TAD 145
Winn, Dilys	MURDERESS INK	Ellen Nehr	4-1 MF 34
Winn, Dilys	MURDERESS INK	Charles Shibuk	13-3 TAD 251
Winn, Dilys	MURDERESS INK	Ruth Windfeldt	1-1 M 30
Winslow, Pauline Glen	THE BRANDENBURG HOTEL	Myrtis Broset	1-2 MF 42
Winslow, Pauline Glen	THE BRANDENBURG HOTEL	Steve Lewis	1-1 MF 31
Winslow, Pauline Glen	COPPER GOLD	Allen J. Hubin	12-1 TAD 12
Winslow, Pauline Glen	GALLOWS CHILD	Allen J. Hubin	11-3 TAD 232
Winslow, Pauline Glen	THE WITCH HILL MURDERS	Allen J. Hubin	11-1 TAD 20
Winslow, Pauline Glen	THE WITCH HILL MURDERS	Steve Lewis	2-1 MF 22
Winsor, Roy	ALWAYS LOCK YOUR BEDROOM DOOR	Myrtis Broset	2-1 MM 3
Winsor, Roy	THREE MOTIVES FOR MURDER	Fred Dueren	9-4 TAD 334
Winsor, Roy	THREE MOTIVES FOR MURDER	Steve Lewis	1-2 MF 26
Winterbotham, Russ	THE LORD OF NARDOS	Gary Zachrich	66 PU 60
Wise, Arthur	BLOOD RED ROSE	Bill Crider	4-3 PP 28

Witting, Clifford	CATT OUT OF THE BAG	Jim Finzel	4-2 PP 26
Witting, Clifford	LET X BE THE MURDERER	Charles Shibuk	2-4 MF 43
Wohl, James P.	THE BLIND TRUST KILLS	Mary A. Grochowski	2-3 PP 34
Wohl, James P.	THE BLIND TRUST KILLS	Allen J. Hubin	12-2 TAD 116
Wohl, James P.	THE NIRVANA CONTRACTS	Allen J. Hubin	11-2 TAD 117
Wolf, Leonard	A DREAM OF DRACULA: IN SEARCH OF THE LIVING DEAD	Veronica M.Kennedy	7-2 TAD 138
Wolf, Leonard, ed.	THE ANNOTATED DRACULA	Jon L. Lellenberg	8-4 TAD 307
Wolf, Leonard, ed.	WOLF'S COMPLETE BOOK OF TERROR	M.S.Cappadonna	13-1 TAD 62
Wolfe, Jonathan	KILLER SEE, KILLER DO	Fred Dueren	11-2 TAD 192
Wolfe, Michael	THE CHINESE FIRE DRILL	Amnon Kabatchnik	1-9 MM 6
Wolfe, Michael	THE CHINESE FIRE DRILL	F.M.Nevins, Jr.	1-2 MF 40
Wolfe, Michael	MAN ON A STRING	Allen J. Hubin	7-2 TAD 142
Wolfe, Michael	THE PANAMA PARADOX	Allen J. Hubin	11-1 TAD 18
Wolfe, Peter	BEAMS FALLING: THE ART OF DASHIELL HAMMETT	John Lutz	13-3 TAD 248
Wolfe, Peter	DREAMERS WHO LIVE THEIR DREAMS: THE WORLD OF ROSS MACDONALD'S NOVELS	F.M.Nevins, Jr.	11-3 TAD 246
Wolff, Geoffrey	INKLINGS	Allen J. Hubin	11-2 TAD 116
Wood, Aldace	THE MYSTERY OF THE MUSICAL REQUIEM!	E.S.& K.G.Lauterbach	9-3 TAD 219
Wood, Edward, & Robert E. Briney	SF BIBLIOGRAPHIES	Allen J. Hubin	6-1 TAD 45
Wood, H.F.	THE PASSENGER FROM SCOTLAND YARD: A VICTORIAN DETECTIVE NOVEL	Edward Lauterbach	11-4 TAD 406
Wood, H.F.	THE PASSENGER FROM SCOTLAND YARD: A VICTORIAN DETECTIVE NOVEL	Steve Lewis	2-5 MF 30
Woodhouse, Martin	BLUE BONE	Amnon Kabatchnik	6-1 MR 44
Woodhouse, Martin	PHIL AND ME	Robert E. Washer	4-1 TAD 50
Woods, Katherine	MURDER IN A WALLED TOWN	Charles Shibuk	12-4 TAD 375
Woods, Sara	A THIEF OR TWO	Barzun & Taylor	14-3 TAD 229
Woods, Sara	THE LAW'S DELAY	Myrtis Broset	1-4 MF 48
Woods, Sara	THE LAW'S DELAY	Steve Lewis	1-5 MF 29
Woods, Sara	THE LAW'S DELAY	Guy M. Townsend	2-4 MM 7
Woods, Sara	MY LIFE IS DONE	Barzun & Taylor	10-3 TAD 225
Woods, Sara	MY LIFE IS DONE	Allen J. Hubin	10-2 TAD 113
Woods, Sara	MY LIFE IS DONE	Steve Lewis	1-4 MF 38
Woodthorpe, R.C.	DEATH WEARS A PURPLE SHIRT	Charles Shibuk	8-1 TAD 53
Woodthorpe, R.C.	ROPE FOR A CONVICT	Mary Groff	1-6 PP 23
Woolf, Miles, Jr.	SEASON OF THE OWL	Gary Warren Niebuhr	4-3 PP 6
Woolley, Edward M.	DONALD DIRK: THE MORNING RECORD COPYBOY	C.L.Messecar	3-2 BC 318
Woolley, Edward M.	DONALD DIRK: THE MORNING RECORD COPYBOY	C.L.Messecar	3-2 BC 320
Woolrich, Cornell	ANGELS IN DARKNESS	Allen J. Hubin	12-2 TAD 116
Woolrich, Cornell	THE BRIDE WORE BLACK	Steven Miller	3-1 PP 34
Woolrich, Cornell	DEATH IS MY DANCING PARTNER	Angelo Panagos	12-1 TAD 80
Woolrich, Cornell	MANHATTAN LOVE SONG	Jim McCahery	4-3 PP 21
Worboys, Anne	THE BARRANCOURT DESTINY	Allen J. Hubin	12-1 TAD 12
Wren, Lassiter, & Randle McKay	THE MYSTERY PUZZLE BOOK	Arthur C. Scott	2-3 MM 4
Wren, M.K.	A MULTITUDE OF SINS	Allen J. Hubin	8-4 TAD 311
Wren, M.K.	NOTHING'S CERTAIN BUT DEATH	Bonnie Pollard	9 CL 7
Wren, M.K.	OH, BURY ME NOT	Steve Lewis	2-5 MF 32
Wren, M.K.	SEASONS OF DEATH	Meera T. Clark	2-1 C 123
Wright, Laurie R.	THE PERFECT CORPSE	Myrtis Broset	1-4 MF 47
Wright, Richard B.	FINAL THINGS	Gary Warren Niebuhr	4-1 PP 15
Wright, Sean M.	SHERLOCK HOLMES CALENDAR 1978	Jim Huang	5 CL 2
Wright, Sean M., & Michael P. Hodel	ENTER THE LION	Paul Bishop	2-1 M 26
Wright, Sean M., & Michael P. Hodel	ENTER THE LION	Edward Lauterbach	4-1 PP 33

Wright, Sean M., & Michael P. Hodel	ENTER THE LION	Charles Shibuk	14-1 TAD 80
Wyck, Francis	THE SERN CHARTER	Steve Lewis	1A MF 30
Wylie, Philip	THE MURDERER INVISIBLE	J. Randolph Cox	3-4 TAD 270
Wyllie, John	SKULL STILL BONE	Allen J. Hubin	8-3 TAD 229
Wyndham, John	CHOCKY	Gary Zachrich	70 PU 26
Wynne, Anthony	THE DAGGER	Angelo Panagos	11-2 TAD 127
Wynne, Anthony	DEATH OF A GOLFER	Angelo Panagos	11-2 TAD 127
Wynne-Jones, Tim	ODD'S END	Gary Warren Niebuhr	4-1 PP 15
Xantippe	DEATH CATCHES UP WITH MR. KLUCK	Charles Shibuk	7-2 TAD 131
Yarbro, Chelsea Quinn	OGILVIE, TALLANT & MOON	Steve Lewis	1-4 MF 39
Yarbro, Chelsea Quinn	OGILVIE, TALLANT & MOON	Christine Mitchell	11-1 TAD 21
Yarbro, Chelsea Quinn	THE PALACE	Fred Dueren	13-3 TAD 252
Yarrow, Arnold	"SOFTLY, SOFTLY" CASEBOOK	Arthur C. Scott	11 MN R19
Yates, Brock	DEAD IN THE WATER	Barbara A. Buhrer	9 MN R2
Yates, Donald A.	LATIN BLOOD	Allen J. Hubin	6-2 TAD 114
Yates, Dornford	SHOAL WATER	Charles Shibuk	12-2 TAD 190
Yates, George W.	THE BODY THAT WASN'T UNCLE	Steve Lewis	3-5 MF 39
York, Andrew	THE CAPTIVATOR	Allen J. Hubin	7-3 TAD 220
York, Andrew	THE FASCINATOR	Steve Lewis	1-5 MF 35
York, Andrew	THE INFILTRATOR	Guy M. Townsend	1A MF 16
York, Andrew	TALLANT FOR DISASTER	Jane S. Bakerman	10 CL 8
Yorke, Margaret	CAST FOR DEATH	Thomas F. Godfrey	12-4 TAD 370
Yorke, Margaret	THE COME-ON	D.E.Ath	2-2 PP 14
Yorke, Margaret	THE COME-ON	Steve Lewis	3-6 MF 28
Yorke, Margaret	THE COST OF SILENCE	Jane S. Bakerman	4-5 MF 41
Yorke, Margaret	THE COST OF SILENCE	Allen J. Hubin	11-1 TAD 20
Yorke, Margaret	DEAD IN THE MORNING	Steve Lewis	4-2 MF 40
Yorke, Margaret	THE POINT OF MURDER	Jane S. Bakerman	5-2 MF 33
Yorke, Margaret	THE SCENT OF FEAR	Jane S. Bakerman	5-3 MF 35
Young, Jim	THE FACE OF THE DEEP	Allan Magnus	12 SF 27
Young, John Sacret	CHANDLER (film)	Richard S. Lochte	5-2 TAD 104
Younger, Jack	CURSE OF THE PHARAOHS	Robert E. Briney	17 R 18
Yuill, P.B.	HAZELL AND THE MENACING JESTER	Robert C.S.Adey	2-5 PP 35
Yuill, P.B.	HAZELL AND THE THREE CARD TRICK	Allen J. Hubin	10-1 TAD 42
Zackel, Fred	CINDERELLA AFTER MIDNIGHT	Allen J. Hubin	14-1 TAD 20
Zackel, Fred	CINDERELLA AFTER MIDNIGHT	Steve Lewis	5-1 MF 23
Zackel, Fred	COCAINE AND BLUE EYES	Allen J. Hubin	12-1 TAD 12
Zaroulis, N.L.	THE POE PAPERS: A TALE OF PASSION	Larry L. French	11-1 TAD 22
Zaroulis, N.L.	THE POE PAPERS: A TALE OF PASSION	Michael Gaglio	2 MT 26
Zelazny, Roger	THE CHANGING LAND	J. Grant Thiessen	14 SF 19
Zelazny, Roger	ISLE OF THE DEAD	Gary Zachrich	71 PU 22
Zochert, Donald	ANOTHER WEEPING WOMAN	Steve Lewis	4-5 MF 30
Zochert, Donald	ANOTHER WEEPING WOMAN	Allen J. Hubin	14-3 TAD 221
Zochert, Donald	MURDER IN THE HELLFIRE CLUB	Fred Dueren	14-1 TAD 81
Zochert, Donald	MURDER IN THE HELLFIRE CLUB	Carl Larsen	5-2 MF 30
Zochert, Donald	MURDER IN THE HELLFIRE CLUB	Edward Lauterbach	3-6 PP 28
Zorro	THE GRAY CREATURES	Lynn Hickman	64 PU 33
Zorro	12 MUST DIE	Lynn Hickman	64 PU 33
-	A QUESTION OF GUILT (TV)	Mary Groff	1-2 PP 20
-	A SHRIEK IN THE NIGHT (film)	Thomas Godfrey	14-4 TAD 331
-	THE AFFAIR OF THE LOST COMPRESSION	Allen J. Hubin	9-2 TAD 153
-	AGATHA (stage)	Paul Bishop	2-4 PP 29
-	ALL THROUGH THE NIGHT	Thomas Godfrey	14-4 TAD 331
-	BULLDOG JACK (film)	William K. Everson	2-2 TAD 111
-	THE CAT O' NINE TAILS (film)	Richard S. Lochte	5-1 TAD 42
-	CANNONBALL RUN (film)	Link Hullar	7 DQ 17
-	DEATH ON THE NILE (film)	Donald A. Yates	3-1 MF 45

-	DINNER FOR ADELE, OR NICK CARTER IN PRAGUE (film)	Thomas Godfrey	2-3 M 46
-	DIXON HAWKE'S CASE BOOK NO.19	Douglas G. Greene	14-1 TAD 74
-	EMPIRE OF PASSION (film)	Thomas Godfrey	2-2 M 60
-	ENOS (TV)	Lorin Brennan	3-2 M 51
-	ESCAPE FROM NEW YORK (film)	Link Hullar	7 DQ 17
-	FERRET FANTASY'S CHRISTMAS ANNUAL FOR 1972	Allen J. Hubin	6-4 TAD 265
-	THE FIRESIDE THEATRE'S BIG MYSTERY JOKE BOOK	Allen J. Hubin	8-1 TAD 66
-	THE FORMULA (film)	Thomas Godfrey	2-3 M 45
-	FURY (film)	James Mark Purcell	12-1 TAD 81
-	THE GANGSTER CHRONICLES (TV)	Lorin Brennan	3-1 M 42
-	THE GREEN MAN (film)	Thomas Godfrey	2-3 M 46
-	HART TO HART (TV)	Lorin Brennan	3-1 M 43
-	THE HAUNTING OF JULIA (film)	Thomas Godfrey	14-4 TAD 331
-	HILL STREET BLUES (TV)	Lorin Brennan	3-2 M 50
-	THE JADE PUSSYCAT (film)	Andy Jaysnovitch	1 PE 17
-	MAGNUM, P.I. (TV)	Lorin Brennan	3-1 M 43
-	NERO WOLFE (TV)	Lorin Brennan	3-1 M 42
-	PLAY MISTY FOR ME (film)	Richard S. Lochte	5-2 TAD 103
-	THE REVENGE OF THE PINK PANTHER (film)	Jim Huang	10 CL 10
-	SELECTED WRITINGS OF RHYS W.HAYS	Allen J. Hubin	11-1 TAD 20
-	SEXTON BLAKE AND THE HOODED TERROR (film)	William K. Everson	2-2 TAD 98
-	SEXTON BLAKE: STAR OF UNION JACK AND DETECTIVE WEEKLY	J. Randolph Cox	6-1 TAD 40
-	SINCERELY TONY/FAITHFULLY VINCENT	Allen J. Hubin	9-2 TAD 153
-	SKY DRAGON (film)	Thomas Godfrey	14-4 TAD 331
-	STAR TREK (film)	Bill Laidlaw	1 DQ 3
-	TERROR TRAIN (film)	Thomas Godfrey	2-2 M 60
-	THEATER OF BLOOD (film)	Veronica M.Kennedy	6-4 TAD 261
-	THIEF (film)	Thomas Godfrey	3-2 M 47
-	THE TIMES OF LONDON ANTHOLOGY OF DETECTIVE STORIES	Martin M. Wooster	1-6 PP 25
-	TISHNIKAR: PAINTER OF DEATH	Marlowe Archer	4 PE 24
-	THE VAMPIRE BAT (film)	William K. Everson	4-3 TAD 169
-	VEGAS (TV)	Andy Jaysnovitch	1 PE 18
-	WAIT UNTIL DARK (film)	Stanley A. Carlin	1-3 MR 6
-	WHODUNNIT? (British TV)	Veronica M.Kennedy	8-1 TAD 62
-	YOU CAN'T GET AWAY WITH MURDER (film)	Thomas Godfrey	14-4 TAD 331
(anonymous)	REVELATIONS OF A LADY DETECTIVE	Amnon Kabatchnik	7-2 TAD 131
(anonymous)	THE SMILING CORPSE	Allen J. Hubin	1-1 TAD 27
(various)	GREAT CASES OF SCOTLAND YARD, Vol.1	Barzun & Taylor	13-3 TAD 209

*****

NOTE: Reviewers listed without given names due to space limitations
are more fully identified thus:

Barzun & Taylor   = Jacques Barzun; Wendell Hertig Taylor

Hickman & Zachrich   = Lynn Hickman; Gary Zachrich

Sampson & Carr   = Robert Sampson; Wooda Nicholas Carr